# Mitra's

## Legal & Commercial Dictionary

*Kolkata*

Eastern Law House Private Ltd.
54 Ganesh Chunder Avenue
Kolkata 700 013

*New Delhi*

Eastern Law House Private Ltd.
Govind Bhawan, 3rd Floor, Room No. T-2
4384/4A, Ansari Road, Daryaganj
New Delhi 110 002

# Mitra's
## Legal & Commercial
# Dictionary

SIXTH EDITION

*by*

**Tapash Gan Choudhury**
Advocate, High Court, Calcutta

Kolkata New Delhi
**EASTERN LAW HOUSE**

*Published and processed by*
EASTERN LAW HOUSE PRIVATE LTD.
54 Ganesh Chunder Avenue
Kolkata 700 013
Tel: (033) 4063-2301
Email: mail@elh.co.in
www.elh.co.in

First Edition ........ 1973
Second Edition ........ 1976
Third Edition ........ 1979
Fourth Edition ........ 1985
Fifth Edition ........ 1990
Sixth Edition ........ 2006
Reprint ........ 2026



ISBN 978-81-7177-358-9

Printed at
Dey's Offset, Kolkata

## Preface to the Sixth Edition

My father used to say: "your life depends on your power to master words, specially those words which are judicially defined and/or interpreted". The importance of the utterance was felt when I joined the legal profession in 1975. Words are but the instruments by which meanings or intentions are expressed. Often the same word has in differing contexts to do service to convey different meanings [*L. Schuler A.G.* v *Wickman Machine Tool Sales Ltd.* (1973)2 WLR 683 (HL)]. English being a flexible language, a word is capable of having several meanings. But "that does not mean", so observed Viscount Dilhorne in *Kammins Ballrooms Co. Ltd.* v *Zenith Investments (Torquay) Ltd.* [(1970)30 WLR 287 (IIL)], "that one can disregard the natural and ordinary meaning of the words used unless it is apparent that some other meaning was intended". If language is clear and explicit, the court must give effect to it, "for in that case the words of the statute speak the intention of the Legislature" [*Warburton* v *Loveland* (1832)2 Dow & Cl 480, 489, per Tindal, CJ.]. And in so doing it must bear in mind that its function is *jus dicere*, not *jus dare*: the words of a statute must not be overruled by the judges, but reform of the law must be left in the hands of Parliament [*Cheney* v *Conn* (1968)1 WLR 242]. If the words of an Act are so inflexible that they are incapable in any context of having any but one meaning, the court must apply that meaning, no matter how unreasonable the result is – it cannot insert other words. But such cases are rare because the English language is a flexible instrument [*Kammins Ballrooms Co. Ltd.* v *Zenith Investments (Torquay) Ltd.* (1970)3 WLR 287 (HL), per Lord Reid]. Even in such cases, the court has a responsibility to discharge. The meaning of an ordinary word of English language being not a question of law, if "the context shows that a word is used in an unusual sense, the court will determine in other words what the unusual sense is [*Cozens* v *Brutus* (1973) AC 854, 861 per Lord Reid]. When a word or phrase goes undefined (in a statute), the judges have to work out for themselves the meaning of it, doing the best they can interpret the will of the legislature in regard to it [*Seaford Court Estates* v *Asher* (1949)2 KB 481, 499 per Lord Denning MR]. Lord Reid, however, observed in *B.S. Brown & Son Ltd.* v *Craiks Ltd.* (1970)1 WLR 752, 754 that judicial observations can never be regarded as complete definitions: they must be read in the light of the facts and issues raised in the particular case.

Keeping in mind the judicial pronouncements stated and principles laid down above, I undertook the work of the Sixth Edition of Mitra's *Legal & Commercial Dictionary* in early 2000. It took six years of painstaking efforts to complete the work in line with the judicial pronouncements made and principles stated. The dictionary, as revised, has thus become a comprehensive one.

My endeavour will be fruitful if this edition becomes of real use not only to the members of the Bar and the Bench but also to the students studying law and its other users.

At the end, I express my gratitude to all those who helped me in doing the job. I am particularly indebted to my better half Mrs. Shampa Gan Choudhury and daughter Miss Shinjini Gan Choudhury for providing me necessary support in burning the midnight candle, my son Master Arnab Gan Choudhury for allowing me to concentrate on the work even at the cost of depriving himself of my attention, Mr. Asok De, the man at the healm of affairs, for his immense patience and rendering me co-operation in all respect in completing the work and the staff of Eastern Law House, for rendering valuable assistance to me in the preparation of the work at my beck and call.

Kolkata
5th August 2006 TAPASH GAN CHOUDHURY

# Preface to the First Edition

The Utility of a dictionary of legal and commercial terms is now very well recognized in our country. In legal and commercial world, certain words and phrases have gained peculiar connotation and import, often different from their ordinary meaning. One cannot get at such technical meaning without the help of a dictionary or a book of reference.

The meaning of words, phrases and maxims can be had from four different sources, namely, (1) classical English and Indian dictionaries; (2) interpretation clauses in statutes, rules, by-laws, notifications, etc.; (3) judicial decisions by courts of record in India and abroad; and (4) standard treatises of jurists and great authors. Every attempt has been made, consistent with its bulk, to equip the book with material from the above sources. Cross-references have been given to enhance the utility of the book.

It is designed to lay down and explain the implications of English, Latin and Indian legal and commercial words, phrases and maxims in common use in our country at the present time.

Every attempt has been made to bring out the publication as a handy and useful book of reference for all who are connected with legal, commercial and mercantile world.

I am grateful to many of my friends and acquaintances for the help and assistance rendered by them. Particular mention should be made of Shri Sudhir Kumar Brahmachari, Advocate, in this connection.

Calcutta
26th March 1973

S.D. Mitra

# Selected Table of Abbreviations

| | | |
|---|---|---|
| A & E | ... | Adolphus and Ellis (England) |
| A 2d | ... | Atlantic Reporter, Second Series |
| AC | ... | Law Reports, Appeal Cases (England) |
| ACJ | ... | Allahabad Civil Journal |
| AIR | ... | All India Reporter |
| AIR SCW | ... | All India Reporter Supreme Court Weekly |
| ALJ | ... | Australian Law Journal |
| All Cr C | ... | Allahabad Criminal Cases |
| All ER | ... | All England Law Reports |
| All LJ | ... | Allahabad Law Journal |
| All LR | ... | Allahabad Law Reports |
| All Ren Cas | ... | Allahabad Rent Cases |
| All WC | ... | Allahabad Weekly Cases |
| Alta SC | ... | Alberta Supreme Court |
| Am Rep | ... | American Reports |
| Andh LT | ... | Andhra Law Times |
| Andh WR | ... | Andhra Weekly Reporter |
| APLJ | ... | Andhra Pradesh Law Journal |
| App Cas | ... | Appeal Cases (England) |
| AWR | ... | Allahabad Weekly Reporter |
| B & Ald | ... | Barnewall & Alderson (England) |
| B & C | ... | Barnewall & Cresswell (England) |
| B & P | ... | Bosanquet & Puller (England) |
| B & PNR | ... | Bosanquet & Puller's New Reports (England) |
| B & S | ... | Best & Smith (England) |
| Bea | ... | Beavan's Reports |
| Bih LJ | ... | Bihar Law Journal |
| Bing (NC) | ... | Bingham's New Cases (England) |
| Bl Com | ... | Blackstone's Commentaries |
| Bligh NS | ... | Bligh, New Series (1827-1837) |
| BLJR | ... | Bihar Law Journal Reports |
| BLR | ... | Bengal Law Reporter |
| Bom CR | ... | Bombay Cases Reporter |
| Bom LR | ... | Bombay Law Reporter |
| C & P | ... | Carrington & Payne (England) |
| CA | ... | Court of Appeals |
| CA 2d | ... | California Appellate Reports, Second Series |
| CA 3d | ... | California Appellate Reports, Third Series |
| CA Fla | ... | California Appellate Reports, Florida |
| CA Ind | ... | California Appellate Reports, Indiana |
| CA Pa | ... | California Appellate Reports, Pennsylvania State |
| CA Tex | ... | California Appellate Reports, Texas |
| CA Va | ... | California Appellate Reports, Virginia |

| | | |
|---|---|---|
| Cab & El | ... | Cababe & Ellis (England) |
| Cal App 2d | ... | California Appellate Reports, Second Series |
| Cal 2d | ... | California Reports, Second Series |
| Cal 3d | ... | California Reports, Third Series |
| Cal Reptr | ... | California Reporter |
| Car & Kir | ... | Carrington & Kirwan's English Nisi Prius Reports |
| CB | ... | Common Bench Reports (England) |
| CBNS | ... | Common Bench Reports, New Series (England) |
| CCA | ... | Circuit Court of Appeals (USA) |
| CCA Alaska | ... | Circuit Court of Appeals, Alaska |
| CCA Ariz | ... | Circuit Court of Appeals, Arizona |
| CCA Ark | ... | Circuit Court of Appeals, Arkansas |
| CCA Iowa | ... | Circuit Court of Appeals, Iowa |
| CCA Kan | ... | Circuit Court of Appeals, Kansas |
| CCA Mass | ... | Circuit Court of Appeals, Massachusetts |
| CCA Mich | ... | Circuit Court of Appeals, Michigan |
| CCA NJ | ... | Circuit Court of Appeals, New Jersey Reports |
| CCA NM | ... | Circuit Court of Appeals, New Mexico |
| CCA Or | ... | Circuit Court of Appeals, Oregan |
| CCA Utah | ... | Circuit Court of Appeals, Utah Reports |
| CCR | ... | Common Cases Reserved |
| Ch | ... | Law Reports, Chancery Appeals (England) |
| Ch App | ... | Chancery Appeal Cases, English Law Reports |
| Ch D | ... | Law Reports, Chancery Division (England) |
| Chand LR | ... | Chandigarh Law Reports |
| CHN | ... | Calcutta High Court Notes |
| Civ & Cr | ... | Civil & Criminal Cases |
| Civ LJ | ... | Civil Law Journal |
| Cl & F | ... | Clark & Finnelly |
| CLJ | ... | Calcutta Law Journal |
| CLR | ... | Commonwealth Law Reports (England) |
| Co Litt | ... | Coke on Littleton (England) |
| Comp Cas | ... | Company Cases |
| Comp LJ | ... | Company Law Journal |
| Cowp | ... | Cowper's English King's Bench Reports |
| Cox CC | ... | Cox's Criminal Cases (England) |
| Cox Eq | ... | Cox's Equity |
| CPD | ... | Law Reports Common Pleas Division (England) |
| Cr App R | ... | Criminal Appeal Reports (England) |
| Cr App R (SC) | ... | Criminal Appeal Reports (Supreme Court) |
| Cr LJ | ... | Criminal Law Journal |
| Cr LR | ... | Criminal Law Reporter |
| Cr M & R | ... | Crompton, Meeson & Roscoe (England) |
| Cur Civ Cas | ... | Current Civil Cases |
| Cur Civ LJ | ... | Current Civil Law Journal |
| Cur LJ | ... | Current Law Journal |
| Cut LR | ... | Cuttack Law Reports |
| Cut LT | ... | Cuttack Law Times |
| Cut WR | ... | Cuttack Weekly Reporter |
| CWN | ... | Calcutta Weekly Notes |
| Del LT | ... | Delhi Law Times |
| DGF & J | ... | De Gex, Fisher & Jones (England) |
| DLR | ... | Dominion Law Reports (Canada) |
| DMC | ... | Divorce & Matrimonial Cases |
| Doug | ... | Douglas' English King's Bench Reports |
| Drew & Sm | ... | Drewry & Smale (England) |

E & B ... Ellis & Blackburn (England)
ELT ... Excise Law Times
Em App ... Emergency Court of Appeals (USA)
ER ... English Reports
Ex Cr ... Canada Law Reports, Exchequer
Ex LR ... Exchequer Law Reports
Exch ... Exchequer Reports (England)
F & F ... Foster & Finlason (England)
F 2d ... Federal Reporter, Second Series (USA)
F Supp ... Federal Supplement
Fac LR ... Factory Law Reports
FAJ ... Food Adulteration Journal
FJR ... Factories Journal Reporter
FLR ... Federal Law Reports (Australia)
Gau LR ... Gauhati Law Reports
Gaz LR ... Gazette Law Reports, New Zealand
Guj LR ... Gujarat Law Reports
H & C ... Hurlstone & Coltman (England)
H & N ... Hurlstone & Norman (England)
Hag Con ... Haggard, Consistory Cases
HL ... House of Lords (England)
HL Cas ... House of Lords Cases (England)
IA ... Indian Appeals
IC ... Indian Cases
Ill ... Illinois Reports
ILR ... Indian Law Reporter
Ind App ... Indiana Appellate Court Reports
IR ... Irish Reports
Ir R ... Irish Law Reports for year 1894
ITJ ... Income Tax Journal
ITR ... Income Tax Reports
Jab LJ ... Jabalpur Law Journal
JIC ... Judicial Interpretation of Crimes
John ... Johnson's Reports
JP ... Justice of the Peace (England)
JT ... Judgments Today
Kant LJ ... Karnataka Law Journal
Kash LJ ... Kashmir Law Journal
KB ... Law Reports, King's Bench (England)
Kent Comm ... Kent's Commentaries on American Law
Ker LJ ... Kerala Law Journal
Ker LT ... Kerala Law Times
Ky ... Kentucky Reports
L Ed ... Lawyer's Edition, U.S. Supreme Court Reports
L Ed 2d ... Lawyer's Edition, U.S. Supreme Court Reports, Second Series
La App ... Louisiana Court of Appeals
Lab IC ... Labour & Industrial Cases
Lab LJ ... Labour Law Journal
Leach ... Leach, Crown Cases (1730-1814)
LJ Ch ... Law Journal Chancery, New Series (England)
LJCP ... Law Journal Common Pleas, New Series (England)
LJ Ex ... Law Journal Exchequer, New Series (England)
LJKB ... Law Journal King's Bench, New Series (England)
LJMC ... Law Journal Magistrates' Cases, New Series (England)
LJOSKB ... Law Journal, Old Series, King's Bench (England)

| | | |
|---|---|---|
| LJPC | ... | Law Journal Privy Council, New Series (England) |
| LJQB | ... | Law Journal Queen's Bench, New Series (England) |
| Lloyd's Rep | ... | Lloyd's Reports |
| LR Eq | ... | Law Reports Equity Cases (England) |
| LR Ex | ... | Law Reports, Exchequer (England) |
| LR HL | ... | Law Reports, House of Lords (England) |
| LR Ir | ... | Law Reports, Irish |
| LR QB | ... | Law Reports, Queen's Bench (England) |
| LT | ... | Law Times Reports, New Series (England) |
| M&M | ... | Moody & Malkin (England) |
| M&S | ... | Maule & Selwyn (England) |
| M&W | ... | Meeson & Welsby (England) |
| Mac & G | ... | Macnaghten & Gordon (England) |
| Mah LJ | ... | Maharashtra Law Journal |
| Mah LR | ... | Maharashtra Law Reporter |
| Man & G | ... | Manning & Granger's Reports, Common Pleas |
| MBLJ | ... | Madhya Bharat Law Journal |
| MIA | ... | Moore's Indian Appeals |
| Minn | ... | Minnesota Reports |
| Misc 2d | ... | Miscellaneous Reports, Second Series |
| MLJ | ... | Madras Law Journal |
| MLW | ... | Madras Law Weekly |
| Mo | ... | Missouri Reports (USA) |
| Mo App | ... | Missouri Appeals |
| Mont | ... | Montana Reports |
| Moo PC | ... | Moore's Privy Council Reports |
| Moo PC NS | ... | Moore's Privy Council, New Series (England) |
| Moody | ... | Moody's Chancery Cases |
| MPLJ | ... | Madhya Pradesh Law Journal |
| MPWN | ... | Madhya Pradesh Weekly Notes |
| MPWR | ... | Madhya Pradesh Weekly Reports |
| MWN | ... | Madras Weekly Notes |
| Mys LJ | ... | Mysore Law Journal |
| NBR | ... | National Bankruptcy Register (USA) |
| NE 2d | ... | North Eastern Reporter, Second Series (USA) |
| NH | ... | New Hampshire Reports (USA) |
| NI | ... | Northern Ireland Law Reports |
| NJL | ... | New Jersey Law Reports |
| NSWR | ... | New South Wales Reports (Australia) |
| NW 2d | ... | North Western Reporter, Second Series |
| NYS 2d | ... | New York Supplement, Second Series (USA) |
| NZLR | ... | New Zealand Law Reports |
| Okl | ... | Oklahoma (USA) |
| OLR | ... | Ontario Law Reports |
| OR | ... | Ontario Reports |
| Ori LR | ... | Orissa Law Review |
| P | ... | Pacific Reporter |
| P & CR | ... | Property & Compensation Reports |
| P & D | ... | Perry & Davison (England) |
| P 2d | ... | Pacific Reporter, Second Series |
| P Wms | ... | Peere Williams' Reports, Chancery |
| Pa Supper | ... | Pennsylvania Superior Court Reports |
| Pat LJR | ... | Patna Law Journal Reports |

| | | |
|---|---|---|
| Pat LT | ... | Patna Law Times |
| PTC | ... | Patents & Trade Marks Cases |
| Puerto Rico | ... | Puerto Rico Reports |
| Punj LJ | ... | Punjab Law Journal |
| Punj LR (DS) | ... | Punjab Law Reporter (Delhi Section) |
| QB | ... | Queen's Bench Reports/ Law Reports, Queen's Bench (England) |
| QBD | ... | Law Reports, Queen's Bench Division (England) |
| Qd R | ... | Queensland Reports |
| QLR | ... | Queensland Law Reporter (England) |
| Raj LR | ... | Rajasthan Law Reporter |
| Ren CJ | ... | Rent Control Journal |
| Ren LR | ... | Rent Law Reporter |
| Rep | ... | Coke's Reports (England) |
| Rettie | ... | Session Cases, Scottish, 4th Series (England) |
| Rev LR | ... | Revenue Law Reports |
| RPC | ... | Reports of Patent Cases |
| RR | ... | Revised Reports |
| S Ct | ... | Supreme Court Reporter (USA) |
| SASR | ... | South Australian State Reports |
| Sc LR | ... | Scottish Law Reporter |
| SCA | ... | Supreme Court Appeal |
| SCC | ... | Supreme Court Cases |
| SCC (Cri) | ... | Supreme Court Cases (Criminal) |
| SCC (L&S) | ... | Supreme Court Cases (Labour & Service) |
| SCD | ... | Supreme Court Decisions |
| SCJ | ... | Supreme Court Journal |
| SCR | ... | Supreme Court Reports |
| SCR | ... | Canada Law Reports (Supreme Court) |
| SCWR | ... | Supreme Court Weekly Reporter |
| SE 2d | ... | South Eastern Reporter, Second Series |
| Sim LJ | ... | Simla Law Journal/ Simons Law Journal |
| SLJ | ... | Service Law Journal |
| SLR | ... | Service Law Reporter |
| SLT | ... | Scots Law Times (England) |
| So 2d | ... | Southern Reporter, Second Series |
| Sol J | ... | Solicitors' Journal (England) |
| Sri LJ | ... | Srinagar Law Journal |
| STC | ... | Sales Tax Cases |
| STJ | ... | Sales Tax Journal |
| SW 2d | ... | South Western Reporter, Second Series (USA) |
| Tax LR | ... | Taxation Law Reporter |
| Tex Civ App | ... | Texas Civil Appeals |
| Tex Com App | ... | Texas Commission of Appeals |
| Tex Cr App | ... | Texas Criminal Appeals |
| TLR | ... | Times Law Reports (England) |
| TR | ... | Term Reports (England) |
| UPLBEC | ... | UP Local Bodies & Educational Cases |
| US | ... | United States Supreme Court Reports |
| Ves | ... | Vesey, Junior, English Chancery Reports |
| VLR | ... | Victorian Law Reports (England) |
| W Va | ... | West Virginia |
| Wall | ... | Wallace (USA) |
| WAR | ... | Western Australian Reports |
| Wash 2d | ... | Washington Reports, Second Series |
| Wend | ... | Wendell, NY |
| WLC | ... | Western Law Cases |
| WLR | ... | Weekly Law Reports (England) |
| WN | ... | Weekly Notes (England) |
| WR | ... | Weekly Reporter (England) |
| WWR | ... | Western Weekly Reports (England) |

# Aa

**A.** Denotes "one of several media". [*Gujarat University* v *K.R. Mudholkar* 1963 Supp (1) SCR 112, 129: AIR 1963 SC 703].

The article "A" is not necessarily a singular term. It is often used in the sense of "any" and is then applied to more than one individual object. [*Lewis* v *Spies* 350 NYS 2d 14, 17]. "A" may sometimes be read as some. But it is difficult to read "A" as all. [Stroud's *Judicial Dictionary*, 5th Ed.].

**A fortiorari.** From a stronger reason; all the more; by even greater force of logic.

**A fortiori.** More conclusively; with a stronger reason than a conclusion already accepted; chiefly; for a still stronger reason; in chief; mainly; with greater force.

A term used in logic to denote an argument to the effect that because one ascertained fact exists, therefore another, which is included in it, or analogous to it, and which is less improbable, unusual, or surprising, must also exist. [Black's *Law Dictionary*, 5th Ed.].

**A posteriori.** An argument based on observation or experiment; from the effect to the cause; a method of reasoning from the consequence to the antecedent.

**A priori.** Accordingly; as a result of; deducibly; deductively; derivatively. Proceeding, as an argument, from cause to effect, from antecedent to consequent, or from an assumption to its logical conclusion; opposed to a posteriori; an argument based on analogy or abstract consideration.

**A&M.** Ancient and Modern.

**A1.** Excellent; superior; first-class; first-rate; a first class vessel in Lloyd's Register of Shipping.

**A3.** A standard European size of paper, 420 × 297 mm.

**A4.** A standard European size of paper, 210 × 297 mm.

**A5.** A standard European size of paper, 210 × 148 mm.

**AAC.** *Anno ante Christum*, the year before Lord Christ.

**Aan Santhathi.** Male issue. It does not mean male descendants. [*M.E. D'Cruz* v *Nagiah Naidu* AIR 1929 Mad 64: 55 MLJ 683].

> **NOTE: Unless excluded by the context, an adopted son is included in the expression. [*Balasubramania Pillai* v *Petcha Pillai* AIR 1917 Mad 837].**

**AAR.** The abbreviation stands for "against all risk". It is the most comprehensive type of marine insurance.

**Ab abusu ad usum non valet consequentia.** No valid conclusion as to the use of a thing can be drawn from its abuse. This maxim cannot apply "where an abuse is directly charged and offered to be proved." [*Stockdale* v *Hansard* (1839)9 A&E 1, 116, *per* Lord Denman].

**Ab initio.** From the beginning; from the first act; from the inception.

**Abad.** Land under cultivation. A village or tract which is designated in revenue phrase as Abad is one from which revenue may be levied.

**Abadharita jama.** Fixed rent. [*Kumud* v *Kunja* 62 CLJ 67].

**Abadi.** A house site in a village on which dwellings are erected by tenant.

The part of village lands on which dwellings are erected.

**Abadkari.** Right derived from the first clearing away and occupying land.

**Abandon.** Give up completely or absolutely, or before completion; forsake entirely or desert (a person or a post of responsibility); leave or desert (ship, building etc.); surrender; forsake; cede; relinquish with the intent of never again resuming one's right or interest.

"The word 'abandon' in its ordinary general meaning does not signify merely 'leaving' but 'leaving completely and finally; giving up all concern in'". [*Kallooar* v *R.* (1964)50 WWR 602].

The word 'abandon' has been explained as meaning 'to leave completely and finally; forsake utterly; to relinquish, renounce; to give up all concern in something'. [*G.T. Lad* v *Chemicals and Fibres India Ltd.* AIR 1979 SC 582: (1979)2 SCR 613: (1979)1 SCC 590 referring to *Random House Dictionary*, Unabridged Ed.].

**Abandonment.** The act of leaving a person, thing or place with no intention of returning; the act of giving up an idea or stopping an activity with no intention of returning to it; the act of intentionally relinquishing a known right absolutely and unconditionally and without reference to any particular person or persons.

'Abandonment' means 'relinquishment of an interest or claim'. When used in relation to an office, it means 'voluntary relinquishment'. It must be total and under such circumstances as clearly to indicate an absolute relinquishment. [*G.T. Lad* v *Chemicals and Fibres India Ltd.* AIR 1979 SC 582: (1979)2 SCR 613: (1979)1 SCC 590].

Abandonment is an act whereby a person gives up his ownership without creating proprietary rights in another person. There are two elements of abandonment, namely, the intention to abandon and the act by which effect is given to the intention. [*Kanhiya Shanker* v *Mohabata Sadhu* AIR 1960 Punj 494: 62 Punj LR 494].

Abandonment when used with reference to a person having a derivative interest, *e.g.*, a tenant or a raiyat, essentially means the giving up of his right in the property with the intention that he will no longer have any concern with it and that it is to revert to the person it is ultimately to belong to. The necessary intention to abandon must be there. [*Lala Shri Ram* v *Nund Kishore* ILR (1957)2 All 391: AIR 1958 All 107].

Abandonment is a voluntary positive act. A man must expressly say that he gives up his right. If he remains quiet, it cannot be said that he is forsaking his title to property or his interest. [*Gur Pershad* v *Asharfi Devi* AIR 1956 Punj 143].

NOTE: Abandonment is different from surrender which connotes relinquishment to another.

**Abandonment of child.** Desertion or wilful forsaking of a child; foregoing parental duties in respect of a child.

NOTE: Exposing or leaving a child under the age of 12 years in any place by the father or mother or by any person having the care of such a child with the intention of wholly abandoning such child is punishable under s. 317 of the Indian Penal Code with imprisonment upto seven years or with fine or with both.

**Abandonment of copyright.** It turns on state of mind of copyright proprietor and occurs whenever he engages in some overt action which manifests his purpose to surrender his rights in the work and allow the public to enjoy it.

**Abandonment of easement.** It is the relinquishment by the owner of the dominant heritage of a right to easement which he has actually acquired.

NOTE: To establish abandonment of an easement created by a deed, there must be some conduct on the part of owner of servient estate adverse to and inconsistent with existence of easement and continuing for statutory period, or non-user must be accompanied by unequivocal and decisive acts clearly indicating an intent on part of owner of easement to abandon use of it. Intention and completed act are both essential. A mere occasional or temporary obstruction or use of an easement by the servient owner is not an abandonment.

**Abandonment of goods.** Quitting possession of goods voluntarily without any intention of transferring them to another.

**Abandonment of ship.** In a policy of marine insurance, abandonment is of the essence of a claim for constructive total loss. In "reference to constructive total loss, it is defined to be a cession or transfer of the ship from the owner to the underwriter, and of all his property and interest in it, with all the claims that may arise from the ownership, and all the profits that may arise from it including the freight then being earned". [*Rankin* v *Potter* (1873) LR 6 HL 83, *per* Martin B.].

**Abandonment of voyage.** There is an abandonment of the voyage when a purpose of abandoning the original place of destination for some other place of discharge is definitely formed. As soon as such purpose is definitely formed and manifested, the underwriter is *ipso facto* discharged from liability for all subsequent losses. If the resolution is formed after the commencement of the risk, the voyage is said to be charged.

**Abate.** To become less strong, severe, intense; diminish or take away; quash *e.g.* a writ or action; put an end to *e.g.* a nuisance; abolish; abrogate; annul; cancel; defeat; destroy; discontinue; dissolve; eliminate; exterminate; invalidate; nullify; obliterate; quell; repeal; rescind; revoke; terminate; void.

Abate is a generic term derived from the French word "Abattre" and signifies to quash, to beat down or destroy.

**Abatement.** Abolition; abrogation; annulment; cancellation; discontinuance; dissolution; elimination; extermination; invalidation; nullification; obliteration; revocation, termination, *e.g.*, abatement of a bequest; abatement of a cause of action; abatement of a legacy; abatement of debts, taxes etc.

Alleviation; curtailment; declination; diminution, mitigation; reduction; suppression.

**Abatement of action or suit.** It means an entire overthrow or destruction of the suit so that it is quashed and ended. In civil law, an abatement of a suit is a complete termination of it.

The concept of abatement is known to civil law. If a party to a proceeding either in the trial court or any appeal or revision dies and the right to sue survives or a claim has to be answered, the heirs and legal representatives of the deceased party would have to be substituted and failure to do so would result in abatement of proceedings. [*Mst. Bibi Rahmani Khatoon* v *Harkoo Gope* AIR 1981 SC 1450: 1981(3) SLR 553: (1981)3 SCC 173].

NOTE: Under Or. XXII, r. 1 of the Civil Procedure Code 1908, the death of a plaintiff or defendant shall not cause the suit to abate if the right to sue survives. Under r. 7 of Or. XXII, the marriage of a female plaintiff or defendant shall not cause the suit to abate. Under r. 8 of Or. XXII, the insolvency of a plaintiff in any suit which the assignee or receiver might maintain to the benefit of his creditors, shall not cause the suit to abate.

**Abatement of legacies.** Under certain circumstances, legatees are obliged to part with the whole or portions of their legacies, although the subjects devised to them remained, and were not adeemed at the testator's death. This obligation is termed "abatement of legacies". [Roper on *Legacies*, 4th Ed., p. 356].

An abatement of a legacy is a *pro rata* diminution of general legacies made necessary in order to pay debts and specific legacies.

It is a proportional diminution or reduction of the pecuniary legacies, when the funds or assets out of which such legacies are payable are not sufficient to pay them in full.

NOTE: The legacies abate rateably, in the case of a deficiency, on the principle of the maxim 'equality is equity' or 'equity delighteth in equality'. [*Miller* v *Huddlestone* (1851)3 Mac & G 513].

Sections 175, 327 and 330 of the Indian Succession Act 1925, deal with abatement of legacies under various circumstances. Section 175 lays down that where an annuity is bequeathed, but the assets of the testator are not sufficient to pay all the legacies given by the will, the annuity shall abate in the same proportion as the other pecuniary legacies given by the will. Section 327 provides that of the assets, after payment of debts, necessary expenses and specific legacies, are not sufficient to pay all the general legacies in full, the latter shall abate or be diminished in equal proportions. Section 330 states that if the assets are not sufficient to answer the debts and the specific legacies, an abatement shall be made from the latter rateably in proportion to their respective amounts.

**Abatement of legal proceedings.** Abatement of legal proceedings means end of legal proceedings not because of decision but because of cessation of cause of action.

**Abatement of nuisance.** The removal, stoppage, prostration, or destruction of that which causes a nuisance, whether by breaking or pulling it down, or otherwise removing, destroying, or effacing it.

It means the summary removal or remedy of a nuisance by the party injured without having recourse to legal proceedings. It is not a remedy which the law favours and is not usually advisable.

NOTE: It is a self-remedy allowed in English law to one injured by a nuisance. The abatement must be done peaceably and without causing unnecessary damage. The abatement of a nuisance is the removal or destruction of a nuisance and not its mere prevention.

**Abatement of proceedings.** Abatement of proceedings in criminal law connotes its termination without any decision on the merits and without the assent of the prosecutor.

**Abatement of rent.** An agreement to accept rent less than that comprised in the original deed.

NOTE: The essence of abatement of rent is that it diminishes, if not permanently, at all event for an indeterminate period the rent of holding.

A tenant is entitled to abatement of rent on the ground of diluvion or deficiency in area proved by measurement. [*Bireswar* v *Jogendra* AIR 1929 Cal 413]. Where a part of the land is taken up for railway or other public purposes, the tenant is entitled to abatement. [*Khagendra* v *Sasi* AIR 1928 Cal 406].

**Abatement of taxes.** Diminution or decrease in the amount of tax imposed.

NOTE: Abatement of taxes relieves property of its share of the burdens of taxation after the assessment has been made and the tax levied.

**Abatement, plea in.** A plea in abatement is one which shows some ground for abating or quashing the action and prayer made to that effect.

In common law pleading, it is one which without disputing justice of plaintiff's claim, objects to place, mode, or time of asserting it. It allows plaintiff to renew suit in another place or form, or at another time, and does not assume to answer action on its merits, or deny existence of particular cause of action on which plaintiff relies.

**Abbreviation.** The act of reducing, shortening or contracting. Abbreviations are short conventional expressions employed to refer to statutes, dates, etc., to save space.

NOTE: Abbreviations should not be used in public documents which have the only effect of making them utterly unintelligible. [*Corporation of Calcutta* v *Padma Debi* AIR 1957 Cal 466: 61 CWN 129].

**ABC.** The rudiments of any subject.

**Abdicate.** Give up or renounce (a responsibility, duty, privilege and prerogatives etc.); abandon; abjure; quit; relinquish; surrender; vacate; withdraw.

**Abdication.** Abandonment, abjuration, demission, dethronement, quitting, relinquishment, renunciation, uncrowning, vacating.

Renunciation of the privileges and prerogatives of an office. It is the relinquishment of an office which has devolved by act of law. It is said to be a renunciation, quitting and relinquishing, so as to have nothing further to do with a thing, or the doing of such actions as are inconsistent with the holding of it.

NOTE: *'Abdication' and 'resignation'—distinction.* Abdication is frequently confounded with resignation. It, however, differs from it in that an "abdication" is done purely and simply while "resignation" is given in favour of some person.

**Abduct.** Carry away wrongfully, illegally by force, fraud or deception; kidnap; pirate; subjugate; take surreptitiously.

**Abduction.** Kidnapping; the act of leading someone away by force or fraudulent persuasion.

▸ *Meaning under the Indian Penal Code 1860, s. 362.* It signifies the forcibly compelling or deceitfully inducing any person to go from any place.

NOTE: In most cases in USA, it applies to females under a given age. It signifies the act of the unlawful taking or detention of any female for purposes of marriage, concubinage or prostitution. By statutes in some states, abduction, however, includes the withdrawal of a husband from his wife, as where another woman alienates his affection and entices him away and causes him to abandon his wife. In Indian law, it may be committed in respect of a person of either sex and of any age.

**Abet.** Encourage and support or assist, especially an offender or wrong-doer or an offence or wrong-doing; instigate; countenance; afford aid; cooperate with; endorse; facilitate.

**Abetment.** Act of encouraging, inciting or aiding another.

▸ *Meaning under the Indian Penal Code 1860, s. 107.* Abetment is constituted either by instigation or conspiracy or by aid.

A person abets the doing of a thing when (1) he instigates any person to do that thing or (2) engages with one or more other person or persons in any conspiracy for the doing of that thing ... or (3) intentionally aids, by any act or illegal omission, the doing of that thing. [*Faguna Kanta Nath* v *State of Assam* AIR 1959 SC 673 referring to s. 107, IPC].

NOTE: A person is said to 'instigate' another to an act, when he actively suggests or stimulates him to the act by any means of language, direct or indirect, whether it takes the form of express solicitation, or of hints, insinuation or encouragement.

'Conspiracy' consists in the agreement of two or more persons to do an unlawful act, or to do a lawful act by unlawful means.

A person abets by aiding, when by act done either prior to, or at the time of, the commission of an act, he intends to facilitate, and does in fact facilitate, the commission thereof.

Under the Indian law for an offence of abetment it is not necessary that the offence should have been committed. A man may be guilty as an abettor whether the offence is committed or not. [*Faguna Kanta Nath* v *State of Assam* AIR 1959 SC 673].

**Abettor.** A person who abets; a person who encourages, incites, or sets another on to commit a crime.

▸ *Meaning under the Indian Penal Code 1860, s. 108.* 'Abettor' means the person who abets (1) the commission of an offence, or (2) the commission of an act which would be an offence, if committed by a person capable by law of committing an offence with the same intention or knowledge as that of the abettor.

NOTE: An 'abettor' must be an instigator or a conspirator or an intentional helper.

**Abeyance.** A state of temporary disuse or suspension or inactivity; lapse in succession during which there is no person in whom title is vested.

The word 'abeyance', is equivalent to suspension which means 'temporarily withholding', temporary forced withdrawal. [*Anuradha* v *Santosh Nath* AIR 1976 Del 246].

**ABH.** Actual bodily harm.

**Abhijog.** Plaint; complaint; beginning of a suit.

**Abide by.** To conform to; to acquiesce in; to submit to; to adhere to; to obey, to accept the consequences of.

**Abjure.** Renounce, or abandon by or on oath an opinion, cause, claim etc.; repudiate; abandon.

**Abkari.** Taxes or duties on the manufacture and sale of spirituous liquors, and intoxicating drugs.

It is a revenue term derived from duties levied on the manufacture and sale of inebriating liquors, as tari or toddy, pachwai, arrack, etc., and on intoxicating drugs, whether in substance, infusion, or extract, as opium, bhang, charas etc. [*Namasivaya* v *Subramania* 34 IC 927].

**Abkari darogha.** An officer appointed to superintend distilleries, spirit shops and the like.

**Ablation.** The surgical removal of a tissue or an organ from the body; the disintegration of part of the nose cone on a missile or spacecraft when it enters the atmosphere.

**Abnegate.** Renounce or reject a right or belief; give up or deny to oneself a right or privilege.

**Abnegation.** Denial; the rejection or renunciation of a doctrine; self-denial.

**Abnormal.** Not according to rule; different from the usual or average or expected, especially in a way that is worrying, harmful or not wanted; unnatural, irregular.

The word means a state of mind so different from that of ordinary human beings that reasonable men would term it abnormal. [*R* v *Byrne* (1960)3 All ER 1 (CA): (1960)2 QB 396; *Rose* v *R* (1961) AC 496: (1961)2 WLR 506].

**Abnormality.** A feature or characteristic in a person's body or behaviour that is not usual and may be harmful, worrying or cause illness; irregularity.

**Abnormality of mind.** It means a state of mind so different from that of ordinary human beings that the reasonable man would term it abnormal. It is wide enough to cover the mind's activities in all its aspects, not only the perception of physical acts and matters and the ability to form a rational judgment whether an act is right or wrong, but also the ability to exercise will power to control physical acts in accordance with that rational judgment. [*R* v *Byrne* (1960)3 All ER 1 (CA): (1960)2 QB 396; *Rose* v *R* (1961) AC 496: (1961)2 WLR 506].

> NOTE: Abnormality of mind induced by drugs or alcohol not being due to inherent causes is not abnormality of mind. [*R.* v *Gittens* (1984)3 All ER 252].

**Abode.** One's home; fixed place of residence for the time being; habitual residence; dwelling place; sojourn; fixed residence; habitancy; habitation; homestead; inhabitation; living place; residency.

"A man's residence where he lives with his family and sleeps at night, is always his place of abode in the full sense of that expression". [*R.* v *Hammond* (1852)17 QB 772, *per* Lord Campbell, C.J.].

In ordinary language no one would speak of a place of business as a man's place of abode or residence; but for "the purposes of some statutes the words 'place of abode' might include place of business ..." [*R.* v *Lilley, ex p. Taylor* (1910)104 LT 77, *per* Ridley].

**Abolish.** Annul; cancel; declare null and void; override; overrule; prohibit; quash; repeal; repudiate; rescind; revoke; set aside; abrogate; annihilate; eliminate; eradicate; dissolve; exterminate; negate; to do away with wholly; dispense with.

It has its root in the Latin word "abolere", which means to destroy utterly.

**Aboriginal.** Native to the soil; indigenous; primitive; races and natural phenomena inhabiting or existing in a land from the earliest times.

**Abortion.** The expulsion of a foetus especially by medical induction from the womb before it is able to survive independently, especially in the first 28 weeks of a human pregnancy; the knowing destruction of life of an unborn child from the womb other than for the purpose of producing a live birth or removing a dead foetus; the termination of pregnancy.

**Abortive.** Unsuccessful; fruitless; unfinished; coming to naught; imperfectly developed; brought forth or born prematurely.

**Abortive trial.** A trial where the case has gone off and no verdict has been pronounced without the fault, or contrivance of the parties.

**About.** On the subject of; in connection with; at a time near to; occupied with; approximately; nearly; more or less; almost; all round; in every direction; in rotation or succession.

When used with reference to time, the term is of flexible significance, varying with the circumstances and the connection in which it is employed.

With relation to quantity, it suggests only an estimate of probable amount. [*Norrington* v *Wright* 115 US 188: 29 L ed 366].

In connection with distance or locality, it is of relative significance, varying with the circumstances.

**Above.** Higher; superior; on the upper side; superior in rank or position; more than; in excess of; surpassing in authority, quality, or power; in a previous or an earlier place; beyond the reach or influence of.

When an object is above another, it exceeds it in height. In the figurative sense, 'above' is employed mostly to convey the idea of superiority.

**Above par.** At a price above nominal or face value; at a premium.

**Abrasion.** The scrapping or wearing away (of skin, coin, rock etc.); a damaged area resulting from the scrapping or wearing away.

Abrasions are injuries involving loss of the superficial epithelial layer of the skin, and are produced by a blow, a fall or a slide on a rough surface or being dragged in a vehicular accident, by scratching or grazing with the finger nails, thorns, by teeth bites, or by friction and pressure of strings or ropes tied around neck or other parts of the body.

**Abridge.** Give the substance of in fewer words; condense; epitomize; capsulize; curtail; contract; reduce; summarize; cut down; compress.

It implies preserving the substance, the essence, of a work in language suited to such purpose. To abridge requires the exercise of mind. An abridgement is the condensation of the views of a person.

To abridge, in the legal sense of the word, is to preserve the substance, the essence of the work in language suited to such a purpose, language substantially different from that of the original. To constitute a proper abridgement, the arrangement of the book abridged must be preserved, the ideas must also be taken and expressed in language not copied but condensed. [*Macmillan & Co.* v *Cooper* AIR 1924 PC 75: 51 IA 109].

**Abrogation.** As against agreement, it means officially ending an agreement. When a contract is abrogated by war, it does not involve destruction of the contract so far as already performed. That which is abrogated is the further performance of the contract. [*Schering* v *Stockholms Enskilda Bank* (1946) AC 219]. The outbreak of war may have the effect of abrogating obligations outstanding under a contract by reason of supervening illegality [*Fibrosa* v *Fairbairn* (1943) AC 32] or impossibility.

As against law, it means the destruction or annulling of a former law by an act either of the legislative power or constitutional authority or usage. Abrogation of law may be express or implied. Express abrogation means abrogation by express provision or enactment; the repeal of a law or provision by a subsequent one referring directly to it. Implied abrogation takes place when the new law contains provisions which are positively contrary to former laws, without expressly abrogating such laws.

**Abscond.** To depart suddenly and secretly especially unlawfully or to avoid arrest; to escape and hide oneself; to remove oneself for the sake of not being discovered; decamp; disappear; flee; run away.

> NOTE: Absconding leads to presumption of guilt. Absconding does not necessarily mean absconding from one's residence although usually when a person is hiding from his place of residence he is said to be absconding. A person may hide even in his place of residence or away from it and in either case he will be absconding when he does so. [*State* v

*Umraokhan* ILR (1956)6 Raj 434: AIR 1957 Raj 126: 1957 Cr LJ 477; *K.J.M.S. Abdul Kader* v *Union of India* 1977 Cr LJ 1708].

**Absconder.** One who hides, conceals oneself.

To be an 'absconder' in the eye of law, it is not necessary that a person should have run away from his home, it is sufficient if he hides himself to evade the process of law, even if the hiding place be his own home. [*Kartarey* v *State of U.P.* AIR 1976 SC 76: 1976 Cr LJ 13: 1975 SCC (Cri) 803: 1975 Cr LR (SC) 690: (1976)1 SCC 172].

**Absconding debtor.** One who absconds from his creditors; one who has intentionally concealed himself from his creditors, or withdrawn himself from the reach of their suits with intent to frustrate their just demands.

NOTE: If a debtor absconds, he commits an act of insolvency under s. 61(*d*) of the Provincial Insolvency Act 1920, as well as under s. 9(*d*) of the Presidency Towns Insolvency Act 1909.

**Absconding offender.** A person against whom a warrant has been issued and who has absconded or is concealing himself in order that such warrant cannot be executed.

NOTE: Sections 83 and 85 of the Code of Criminal Procedure 1973 provide for the attachment and sale of the property of a person absconding and against whom a proclamation has been issued.

**Absence.** The fact or state of being away from a place or person; the time or duration of being away; disappearance; non-existence; unavailability, shortage; want; deficiency.

"Absence ...... connotes the opposite of physical presence". [*Wilkinson* v *Wilkinson* (1962)1 All ER 922, 927 (CA), *per* Willmer, L.J.].

In its relation to court proceedings, "it includes inability to attend to the business of the court". [*R.* v *Steeves, Ex p. Cormier* (1909), 39 NBR 435, 437 (Canada), *per* McLeod, J.]. Judicial separation obtained in the "absence" of the respondent meant his or her non-appearance in the suit. [*Phillips* v *Phillips* LR 1 P&D 169].

**Absence beyond seas.** Absence out of the realm or power of the King.

**Absence of mind.** Inattentiveness; lack of attention; mental abstraction.

**Absent.** Not present at or in; not existing; lacking; missing; inattentive.

"Absent" does not connote that the person referred to was ever previously present; its ordinary sense is, to describe a person or persons as not being in a particular place at the time referred to. [*Ashbury* v *Ellis* (1893) AC 339].

**Absoluta sententia expositore non indiget.** Plain words require no explanation.

**Absolute.** Without any incumbrance; unconditional; unlimited; despotic; ruling arbitrarily or with unrestricted power.

The "word 'absolute' ...... when used in a technical sense in connection with the vesting of property may signify at least two different legal concepts. In one sense it may be used to denote the lack of limitation of the extent or duration of an interest in personal property while in another it may mean the freedom of the interest from dependence on other things or persons". [*Halley* v *Minister of National Revenue* (1963) Ex CR 372, 375, *per* Thurlow, J.].

• **Rule absolute** p. 767.

**Absolute assignment.** In English law, an absolute assignment need not necessarily be equivalent to a sale out and out; it may be only an equitable assignment. [*Bence* v *Shearman* 47 WR 350: (1898)2 Ch 582; *Brand* v *London Rubber Co.* (1904)1 KB 387]. A sub-lease for the whole residue of the lessee's term operates as an absolute assignment of the lease. [*Bryant* v *Hancock* (1898)1 QB 716]. A mortgage may be assigned absolutely but only by express terms and not by way of charge only. [*Durham* v *Robertson* (1898)1 QB 765].

In India, absolute assignment means a transfer of the entire interest of the assignor.

**Absolute deed.** A document of conveyance without restriction or defeasance; generally used in contradistinction to mortgage deed.

**Absolute discretion.** When the method of decision, the number and the character of factors to be considered are left to the subjective determination of the person exercising discretion and such a person may decide in whatever way appears best to him and according to any consideration he likes, the holder of the authority is said to yield absolute discretion. [*Penumbra of Natural Justice* by Tapash Gan Choudhury, 2nd Ed. 2001, p. 312].

NOTE: In public regulation there is no such thing as absolute discretion, that is that action can be taken on any ground or for any reason that can be suggested to the mind of the administrator; no legislative Act can, without any express language, be taken to contemplate an unlimited arbitrary power exercisable for any purpose, however capricious or irrelevant, regardless of the nature or purpose of the statute. [*Roncarolli* v *Duplessis* (1959) SCR 121: (1959) DLR 2d 689].

**Absolute liability.** Liability or responsibility without fault or negligence. [*Rylands* v *Fletcher* (1808)3 HL 330; *Clark-Aiken Co.* v *Cromwell-Wright Co., Inc. (Mass)* 323 NE 2d 876].

**Absolute majority.** A majority over all others combined; more than half.

**Absolute owner.** A person capable of disposing of the whole interest in land, although the land or his interest therein is burdened, charged or encumbered.

**Absolute ownership.** Ownership without any condition or encumbrance.

**Absolute privilege.** A privilege that immunizes an actor from suit, no matter how wrongful the action might be, and even though, it is done, with an improper motive. [Black's *Law Dictionary*, 8th Ed.].

NOTE: Certain central questions for judicial consideration should be raised before absolute privilege is made available as a defence. What was the occasion and how the parties were positioned to it? Was the occasion such which, in furtherance of public policy and convenience, should receive judicial protection by reason of necessity to safeguard its free and unaffected identity? If occasions were such that they required total protection, absolute privilege would be available. In case of absolute privilege, notwithstanding malice, the action would not succeed. [*Govind Shantaram Walavalker* v *Pandharinath* 1985 Mah LJ 236: AIR 1985 Bom 224].

Absolute privilege is restricted to certain recognized occasions. It is not generally available. The law with regard to absolute privilege extending to the enumeration of occasions is not covered by any strait-jacket formula, but is ever in the prooess of evolution. By reason of the necessity to protect persons from actions in tort, juridically such occasions have been identified for affording protection. These are classified in several ways, but can be broadly stated to be one concerning judicial proceedings, quasi-judicial proceedings, official communications by one officer of the State to another, proceedings of the legislative bodies, fair and accurate publication of reports of judicial and parliamentary proceedings, communications between persons concerned in judicial proceedings, like client and lawyer or client and solicitor. With regard to the extension of absolute privilege in these matters and upon these occasions, the underlying principle that attracts the privilege is the necessity on the ground of public policy and convenience to keep free the flow of information, and assure and safeguard freedom of expression. [*Govind Shantaram Walavalker* v *Pandharinath* 1985 Mah LJ 236: AIR 1985 Bom 224].

**Absolution.** A formal release from guilt, obligation, or punishment; an ecclesiastical declaration of forgiveness of sins; a remission of penance; forgiveness; acquittal; amnesty; exculpation; exoneration; pardon; purgation.

**Absolve.** Set or pronounce free from blame or obligation or debt or responsibility; acquit; pronounce not guilty; pardon or give absolution for a sin.

**Absorb.** Include or incorporate as part of itself or oneself; take in; engross completely; occupy wholly; swallow up.

**Abstain.** To refrain or forbear from doing something; restrain oneself; keep oneself back.

**Abstention.** The act of withholding or keeping back something or oneself; abstinence from action; avoidance; elusion; holding off.

**Abstract.** That which comprises in itself the essence of a larger thing; synopsis; abridgement; capsule; compendium; a concise statement of a text, esp. of a legal document; a summary.

**Abstract of title.** A concise statement, usually prepared for a mortgagee or purchaser of real property, summarizing the history of a piece of land, including all conveyances, interests, liens and encumbrances that affects title to the property. [Black's *Law Dictionary*, 7th Ed].

It is a summary of the most important parts of the deeds and other instruments composing the evidences of a title to real estate, arranged usually in chronological order. It also contains a statement of all charges, encumbrances, liens and liabilities to which the property may be subjected, and of which it is in any way material for purchasers to be apprised.

The abstract of title is a summary of the documents by which any dispositions of the property have been made during the period for which title has to be shown, and of all the facts, such as births, marriages, deaths, or other matters affecting the devolution of the title during the same period. [Halsbury's *Laws of England*, 3rd Ed., vol. 34, p. 274].

**Abuse.** (*Noun*). Bad treatment; damage; defilement; debasement; dishonour; impairment; molestation; outrage; violation; persecution; physical or mental maltreatment.

(*Verb*). Use improperly or injuriously or for a bad purpose; misuse; hurt by treating wrongly; insult verbally; maltreat; assault; manhandle; molest; degrade; dishonour; employ a thing in a manner contrary to natural or legal rules for its use.

Bramwell, B. observed: "To my mind the word 'abused' conveys no definite meaning; it is not a word of art; in popular language it means calling names—abusing by words ...." [*Re Thompson* (1860)6 H&N 193: 3 LT 409].

Pollock, C.B. observed: "I am not aware that the word 'abuse' applied to a woman is ever used except with reference to sexual intercourse. Certainly in more than one Act of Parliament the word 'abuse' has had that meaning applied to it." [*Re Thompson* (1860)6 H&N 193: 3 LT 409].

In *Corpus Juris Secundum*, 'abuse' as noun is stated thus: "It has been said that the word is not a term of art in the law and that its everyday popular sense is well known; but that its proper signification when employed depends upon the context and subject-matter. In its largest sense, (it means) ill-use or improper treatment of another; misuse. In the plural as used with reference to the authority of governmental commissions to correct 'abuses', the word has been held to mean a disregard of duty imposed by law; any improper use of a right or privilege." [Vol. 1, p. 402].

"'Abuse' means misuse, i.e., using ... position for something for which it is not intended. That abuse may be by corrupt or illegal means or otherwise than those means ........" [*M. Narayanan Nambiar* v *State of Kerala* AIR 1963 SC 1116: (1963)2 Cr LJ 186; Prevention of Corruption Act 1947, s. 5(1)(*d*)].

• **Flagrantly abused position** p. 358.

**Abuse of discretion.** An adjudicator's failure to exercise sound, reasonable and legal decision-making. [Black's *Law Dictionary*, 8th Ed].

Abuse of discretion implies not merely error of judgment, but perversity with passion, prejudice, partiality, or moral delinquency. [*People* v *New York Cent R. Co.* 29 NY 418, 431, *per* Hogeboom, J.].

**Abuse of distress.** It is such use of distrained goods as makes the distrainer liable for wrongful appropriation.

**Abuse of process.** The improper and tortious use of a legitimately issued court process to obtain a result that is either unlawful or beyond the process's scope. [Black's *Law Dictionary*, 8th Ed.].

Abuse of process of the court is a term generally applied to a proceeding, which is wanting in *bona fides* and is frivolous, vexatious, or oppressive. [Halsbury's *Laws of England*, 3rd Ed., vol. 8, p. 16].

It is tort based on damage caused by the improper use of a legal process, for some purpose other than that for which it was designed. [*R.* v *Tepford Justices Ex p. Bdhan* (1991)2 All ER 654].

The term is generally used in connection with action for using some process of the court maliciously to the injury of another person. [*Thathunaik* v *Condu Reddi* 1 IC 221, *per* Abdur Rahim, J.].

**Abut.** To join at a border or boundary; adjoin; attach; be contiguous. "With reference to land to 'abut' means to actually touch". [*Barnett* v *Covell* (1903)68 JP 93 at p. 94, *per* Lord Alverstone, C.J.].

The "language 'with all the houses and grounds abutting on or upon the said road' ...... synonymous with the expression 'bounded by the said road'". [*R.* v *Strand Board of Works* (1863)4 B&S 526, 549, *per* Cockburn, C.J.].

Where two or more properties, with entrances from two or more streets, are occupied for one purpose, they are one entity, in an "improvement area" and "abut" on all the streets. [*The Oxford* v *London County Council* (1898)2 Ch 491].

"Abut" does not always import actual contiguity; thus, where a railway company, in making a statutory bargain with a local authority, agreed that if the company should acquire any land "abutting" on a stated road, they (the company) would widen the road, it was held that the obligation attached as the company acquired land which was only separated from the road by a small stream, the evidence being that the company had induced the authority to believe that the obligation would attach if the company acquired the land which they had in fact acquired [*R.* v *South Eastern Railway* 8 LGR 401] and a residential lot, separated at the rear from a street by a piece of vacant land, has been held to "abut" on to that street. [*Krasey* v *St. Boniface* 58 WWR 219].

**Abutter.** The owner of an adjoining property; one whose property abuts, or joins at a border or boundary, as where no other land, road, or street intervenes.

**Accede.** To agree; abide by; accept; acknowledge; acquiesce; concur; conform; submit; subscribe to.

**Acceleration.** The shortening of the time for the vesting in possession of an expectant interest; the falling into possession of an estate or interest in remainder or expectancy by reason of the particular estate or preceding interest being or becoming void; the advancing of a loan agreement's maturity date so that payment of the entire debt is due immediately.

**Accept.** Take when offered; receive with approval or satisfaction or with intent to retain; consent to receive (a thing offered); give an affirmative answer to (an offer or proposal); receive as adequate, valid or correct (an opinion, explanation etc.); undertake (an office or responsibility); agree to meet (a draft or bill of exchange); acknowledge as valid or received; accede to; acquiesce.

To receive; to agree to; to promise to pay; to receive with favour. [*T. Nanjappa & Sons* v *Assistant Commissioner of Commercial Taxes* (1968)22 STC 281].

**Acceptance.** Acquiescence; assent; concordance; consent; endorsement; ratification; accession; an affirmative answer to an invitation or proposal; consent to receive; any form or act by which one positively or constructively acknowledges the validity or sufficiency of an act done by another; an agreement, either by express act or by implication from conduct, to the terms of an offer so that a binding contract is formed.

An offer is turned into a contract by acceptance. [*Christie, Owen and Davies* v *Stockton* (1953)1 WLR 1353].

**Acceptance of hundi/bill of exchange.** The acceptance of a hundi means signification by the drawee of his assent to the order of the drawer to pay the bill according to the tenor. Thus, the drawee becomes an acceptor when he has signed his assent upon the bill. No particular form for acceptance is prescribed by law. But there cannot be, apart from any mercantile usage, an oral acceptance of the hundi, much less an acceptance by conduct, where at least no question of estoppel arises. [*Seth Jagjivan Mavji Vithlani* v *Ranchhoddas Meghji* (1955)1 SCR 503: AIR 1954 SC 554: 1954 SCJ 626: 1954 SCA 842].

'Acceptance' in regard to a bill of exchange is a technical term. It does not mean 'taking' or 'receiving'. Acceptance of a bill of exchange is the signification by the drawee of his assent to the order of the drawer. It is the act by which the drawee evinces his consent to comply with, and be found by, the request contained in a bill of exchange directed to him, and is the drawee's agreement to pay the bill when it falls due. In commercial parlance acceptance of a bill of exchange is the drawee's signed engagement to honour the draft as presented. [*American Express Bank Ltd.* v *Calcutta Steel Co.* (1993)2 SCC 199: JT 1992 (Supp) SC 606: (1993)76 Comp Cas 768].

**Acceptor.** A person or an entity that accepts a negotiable instrument and agrees to be primarily responsible for its payment or performance; one who has given his acceptance on a cheque or draft or bill.

**Acceptor for honour.** When a bill of exchange has been noted or protested for non-acceptance or for better security and any person accepts it supra protest for honour of the drawer or any one of the indorsers, such person is called an "acceptor for honour". [Negotiable Instruments Act 1881, s. 7].

**Acceptor supra protest.** One who accepts a bill that has been protested, for the honour of the drawer or an indorser.

**Access.** The act, opportunity, or means of approaching; passage; the right or opportunity to reach, use or visit; an opportunity or ability to enter, approach, pass to and from or communicate with.

In the context of matrimonial relationship, 'access' is understood in the sense of sexual intercourse, or the opportunity of communicating together so that sexual intercourse may have taken place. In s. 112 of the Evidence Act 1872, the expressions "access" or "non-access" are used to mean existence or non-existence of opportunities for sexual intercourse; it does not mean actual cohabitation. [*Goutam Kundu* v *State of West Bengal* AIR 1993 SC 2295: (1993)3 SCC 418: 1993 SCC (Cri) 928: 1993 Cr LJ 3233: (1993)3 SCR 917: JT 1993(3) SC 443]. The word "access" in s. 112 of the Evidence Act connotes only existence of opportunity for marital intercourse. [*Karapaya Servai* v *Mayandi* AIR 1934 PC 49: 38 CWN 427: 66 MLJ 288: 36 Bom LR 394; confirmed by the Supreme Court as the law correctly laid down in *Chilukuri Venkateswarlu* v *Chilukuri Venkatanarayana* 1954 SCR 427: AIR 1954 SC 176: 1954 SCJ 84; followed in *Kanti Devi* v *Poshi Ram* AIR 2001 SC 2226: (2001)5 SCC 311: JT 2001 Supp (1) SC 87].

Access to a place for public or public access to a place means "open to all the public in fact, whether by right of permission," and does not necessarily connote that this must be as of right. [*Young* v *Neilson* 20 Rettie 62, *per* Lord Adam].

**Accessio.** An increase or addition to a thing; that which arises as produced from the principal thing.

It is a manner of acquiring property in a thing which becomes united with that which a person already possesses.

It "is the combination of two chattels belonging to different persons into a single article as when a vehicle let on hire-purchase has new accessories fitted to it". [Salmond & Heuston on the *Law of Torts*, 20th Ed., p. 117].

**Accession.** The act of acceding or agreeing; a coming into possession of a right or office; the process by which a nation becomes a party to a treaty that has already been agreed on by other nations; the acquisition of title to personal property by bestowing labour on a raw material to convert it to another thing; a property owner's right to all that is added to the land, naturally or by labour, including land left by floods and improvements made by others; an improvement to existing personal property.

In its broader sense, it may be defined to be the means by which title to the increments, to one's property, movable or immovable, is acquired, whether by natural or artificial means, *e.g.*, accession of a province to a country. In its restricted sense, it applies to the acquisition of title to the increments to one's movable property, brought about by artificial means, such as labour or the addition of material other than the intermixture of goods or things of the same kind.

NOTE: The law of accession may be stated thus: Where any corporeal substance, over which rights of property are exercised, receives an additional increase or improvement either in a natural way, as by the growth of fruits or the pregnancy of animals or in an artificial way as by the erection of houses on land, receding of a river or lake, such addition, increase or improvement falls primarily to the owner of the original substance. [*Encyclopedia of the Laws of England*].

If any corporeal substance receives an accession by natural or artificial means, as by the growth of vegetables, the pregnancy of animals, the embroidery of cloth, the original owner is entitled by his right of possession to the property in its improved state. Similarly, when the goods of one man are affixed to the land or chattel, for example, a ship, of another, they may become part of it and so accrue to the owner of the principal thing. [Halsbury's *Laws of England*, 3rd Ed., vol. 29, p. 378].

An accession to the land would suggest that over a course of years, imperceptible accretion to the land has taken place and it was impossible to distinguish the original land from the accreted land. In such a case, the accreted land may possibly partake of the character of the original land. [*Shrimant Appasaheb Tuljaram Desai* v *Bhalchandra Vithalrao Thube* AIR 1961 SC 589: (1961)1 SCA 735: (1961)2 SCR 163].

**Accessory.** As noun means an additional or extra thing; a small attachment or fitting.

As adjective means additional; contributing or aiding in a minor way.

The word means aiding or contributing in secondary way or assisting in or contributing to as a subordinate. [*Gilfoil* v *Greenspon* La App, 216 So 2d 829, 831].

▸ *General meanings.* An additional or extra thing; a small attachment or fitting; something of secondary or subordinate importance; accompaniment; contributory; an adjunct; appurtenance; supplemental; additional; a person or thing that aids subordinately; aiding the principal design; or assisting subordinately the chief agent, as in the commission of a crime; a person who helps in or knows the details of an act, especially illegal, without taking part in it; abettor; accomplice in crime; advisor; co-conspirator; collaborator.

▸ *Meaning in popular sense.* In its popular sense, it means 'aiding in producing, or contributing to produce, some effect'. [*Gipps* v *Gipps & Hume* (1864)11 HL Cas 1 at p. 29, *per* Lord Chelmsford].

▸ *Meaning in criminal law.* In criminal law, it means 'one who counsels or commands another to commit an offence, or who conceals the offender'. [*Gipps* v *Gipps & Hume* (1864)11 HL Cas 1, 29, *per* Lord Chelmsford].

Accessories are persons 'who aid or abet the principal offender in the commission of the offence, before or after'. [*Stacey* v *Whitehurst* (1865)18 CBNS 344, 355, *per* Willes, J.].

'Persuasion, advice, encouragement, suggestion or words of like import all fall into one important category of acts which will suffice to constitute the actor an accessory'. [*R.* v *Ready & Manning* (1942) VLR 85, 88, *per curiam*].

▸ *Meaning in commercial parlance.* In commercial parlance, it means an object or device that is not essential in itself, but that adds to the beauty, convenience or effectiveness of something else. [*K.B. Dani* v *State of Karnataka* 1979 Kant LJ 286 (DB); *Commissioner of Sales Tax* v *Gulmohar Industries* (1980)46 STC 122 (All); *Commissioner of Sales Tax* v *Kohinoor India Pvt. Ltd.* (1980)45 STC 332 (All)].

It is 'something contributing in subordinate degree to a general result or effect; an adjunct or accompaniment'. [*Indian Mica and Micanite Industries Ltd.* v *Union of India* AIR 1967 Pat 369].

▸ *Meaning as an aid of instrument.* As an aid of instrument, "accessories" are not necessarily confined to particular machines. The same item may be an accessory of more than one kind of instrument. [*Annapurna Carbon Industries Co.* v *State of Andhra Pradesh* AIR 1976 SC 1418: (1976)3 SCR 561: (1976)2 SCC 273: (1976)37 STC 378].

**Accident.** An event that is without apparent cause, or is unexpected; an unfortunate event, especially one causing physical harm or damage, brought about unintentionally; occurrence of things by chance, without any design or known or assignable cause; a contingency, especially any unpleasant or unfortunate occurrence involving injury, loss, suffering or death; unforeseen and injurious occurrence not attributable to mistake, neglect, or misconduct.

The courts have established a long line of cases which identify the essential characteristics of an accident as an event which was neither expected nor intended and which causes hurt or loss. [*Hansey* v *White* (1900)1 QB 481; *Fenton* v *Thorley* (1903) AC 433; *Boyle* v *Wright* (1969) VLR 699].

In ordinary language "accident" covers acts of God. [*Makin* v *London & North Eastern Railway* (1943) KB 467].

"I think the idea of something fortuitous and unexpected is involved in both words, 'peril' or 'accident'". [*Hamilton, Fraser & Co.* v *Pandorf & Co.* (1887)12 App Cas 518, 524, *per* Lord Halsbury, L.C.].

"The word 'accident' is not a technical legal term with a clearly defined meaning. Speaking generally, but with reference to legal liabilities, an accident means any unintended and unexpected occurrence which produces hurt or loss. But it is often used to denote any unintended and unexpected loss or hurt apart from its cause; and if the cause is not known the loss or hurt itself would certainly be called an accident. The word 'accident' is also often used to denote both the cause and the effect, no attempt being made to discriminate between them. The great majority of what are called accidents are occasioned by carelessness, but for legal purposes it is often important to distinguish careless from other unintended and unexpected events". [*Fenton* v *Jhorley & Co. Ltd.* (1903) AC 443, 453, *per* Lord Lindley].

"The word 'accident' is difficult to define, indeed, one judge very many years ago said the word was undefinable. The dictionary definition given in Murray's *Oxford Dictionary* is ......... 'Anything that happens without foresight or expectation, or is an unusual effect of a known cause'. The application of that definition depends almost entirely on the point of need from which the particular matter is approached. If, quite unexpectedly, someone coming up to me, hits me in the face and gives me a black eye, the event, so far as I am concerned, is quite unexpected, yet I would not say that I had got the black eye by an accident; I would say that I got it by an unprovoked assault. Nor would it be an accident so far as the attacker is concerned. Yet, under the Workmen's Compensation Acts ...... an injury by an unprovoked attack has been decided to be an injury by accident for the purposes of those Acts". [*Mills* v *Smith* (1963)2 All ER 1078, 1079, *per* Paull, J.].

Accident is an occurrence or event which is unforeseen and startles one when it takes place but does not startle one when it does not take place. It is the happening of the unexpected, not the happening of the expected, which is called an accident. [*Union of India* v *Sunil Kumar Ghosh* AIR 1984 SC 1737: (1984)4 SCC 246].

The happening of something which is not inherent in the normal course of events, and which is not ordinarily expected to happen or occur, is called a mishap or an accident. [*Union of India* v *Sunil Kumar Ghosh*, supra].

A collision of two trains or derailment of a train or blowing up of a train is something which no one ordinarily expects in the course of a journey. That is why it falls within the parameters of accident. But a jolt to the bogie which is detached from one train and attached to another cannot be termed as an accident. No shunting can take place without such a jerk or an impact at least when it is attached or annexed to a train by a shunting engine. If a passenger trembles inside the compartment or trembles out of it when he is getting inside or stepping out of the compartment, it cannot be said that an accident has occurred to the train or a part of it. It is doubtless an accident to the passenger. [*Union of India* v *Sunil Kumar Ghosh* AIR 1984 SC 1737: (1984)4 SCC 246].

In the work place, the courts sometimes give a wider meaning to accident. Under the Workmen's Compensation Act 1923, accident includes not only such occurrences as collisions, tripping over floor obstructions, fall of roof but also less obvious ones causing injury, e.g., strain which causes rupture, exposure to a draught causing chill, exertion in a stokehold causing apoplexy and shock causing neurasthenia. [*Bai Shakri* v *Naraindas* AIR 1961 Guj 34].

The word 'accident', in accident policies, means an event which takes place without one's foresight or expectation. A result, though unexpected, is not an accident; the means and cause must be accidental. Death resulting from voluntary physical exertions or from intentional acts of the insured is not accidental, nor is disease or death caused by the vicissitudes of climate or atmosphere the result of an accident; but where, in the act which precedes an injury, something unforeseen or unusual occurs which produces the injury, the injury results through accident. [Black's *Law Dictionary*, 7th Ed.].


- **Fatal accident** p. 347.
- **Inevitable accident** p. 455.
- **Railway accident** p. 724.


**Accident arising out of and in course of employment.** Means that the accident must be connected with the employment and must arise with it; there must be a casual connection or association between the employment and the accidental injury. [*Parwatibai* v *Rajkumar Mills* AIR 1959 MP 281].

> NOTE: Accident cannot arise in course of employment if it takes place on a public road in the absence of any circumstance showing that the nature of employment of the workman required him to be there. [*Commissioner* v *Kaniz Fatema* AIR 1961 Cal 310].
>
> Again, injury to a seaman who fell off an access ladder when returning to his ship without leave was held not to be an accident arising out of and in the course of employment. [*Finlayson* v *Hogarth & Sons* 1967 SLT (Sh Ct) 47].

**Accident insurance.** An agreement to indemnify against expense, loss of time, suffering, or death resulting from an accident. It is a contract to pay a fixed sum in case of death resulting from accident, either generally, or limited to accidents of a particular type.

The term is generally applied to insurance against accidents causing bodily harm. This kind of insurance is akin to life insurance.

**Accommodation.** An adjustment or adaptation to suit a special or different purpose; a convenient arrangement; a settlement or compromise; an arrangement made as a favour to another, not upon a consideration received. The word implies no consideration.

The word is regularly used in connection with markets in the sense of space or room. [*Brackenborough* v *Spailding Urban District Council* (1942) AC 310 (HL)].


- **Living accommodation** p. 538.
- **Residential accommodation** p. 754.


**Accommodation address.** An address used on letters to a person who is unable or unwilling to give a permanent address.

**Accommodation bill.** A bill to raise money on credit.

It is one to which the accommodating party, be he the acceptor, drawer or indorser, has put his name, without consideration, for the purpose of benefiting or accommodating some other party who desires to raise money on it, and is to provide for the bill when due.

"An 'accommodation bill' has been defined to be a bill on which the drawer has no right to sue the acceptor" [*King* v *Phillips* 13 LJ Ex 332, *per* Pollock, C.B.] because it is given by the acceptor for the drawer's accommodation.

**Accommodation endorser.** An endorser who acts as surety for another person. He is a third person who endorses a note without any consideration merely for the benefit of the holder thereof.

**Accommodation loan.** A loan for which the lender receives no consideration in return.

**Accommodation works.** Accommodation works are works which a railway is required to make and maintain for the accommodation of the owners and occupiers of lands adjoining the railway, such as gates, bridges, culverts, fences, crossings, tunnels, drains, water sources or other passages, over, under or by the sides of the railway, etc. [The Railways Act 1989, s. 16].

NOTE: Works of accommodation do not comprise matters beneath the surface of the land, *e.g.*, drains. [*R.* v *Fisher* 32 LJMC 12].

**Accompany.** To go with; attend; escort; coexist with.

Things "accompanying" or "to accompany", each other, should, as nearly as possible, be simultaneous. [Stroud's *Judicial Dictionary*, 6th Ed.].

The ordinary meaning of "accompany" is "go with". [*PL. SP. NK. Nagappa Chettiar* v *Commissioner of Income-tax* (1954)26 ITR 741 (Mad): AIR 1955 Mad 162].

**Accomplice.** A partner or helper, especially in a crime or wrongdoing.

One who is in some way concerned or associated in commission of crime; partaker of guilt; one who aids or assists, or is an accessory. [*McLenaon* v *US* 19 F 2d 465, 466].

"The definition given in the Century Dictionary is 'any participator in an offence whether as principal or as accessory,' and in the Encyclopaedia Britannica, 'one who is associated with another or others in the commission of a crime, whether as principal or accessory.' Either of these definitions is ... sufficient". [*R.* v *Webbe & Brown* (1926) SASR 108, 111, 112, *per* Cur].

"A person is an accomplice in the crime charged if he took part in its commission, and was 'privy to the criminal intent of the thing done': *R.* v *Cramp* [(1880)14 Cox C C 390], *i.e.*, if he aided not only in the commission of what he knew to be a criminal act, but in the commission of what he knew to be, or to be likely to involve, the particular criminal act charged, so that what was done was in the course of carrying out a common purpose". [*R.* v *Surridge, R.* v *Harris* (1942) NSWR 278, 282, *per* Jordan, C.J.].

The primary meaning of "accomplice" is any party to the crime charged and someone who aids and abets the commission of crime. [*Sheshanna Bhumanna Yadav* v *State of Maharashtra* AIR 1970 SC 1330: 1970 Cr LJ 1158: 1970 SCC (Cri) 337: (1970)2 SCC 122: (1971)1 SCR 617].

An accomplice is a person who participates in the commission of the actual crime charged against an accused. He is to be a *participes criminis*. [*R.K. Dalmia* v *Delhi Administration* AIR 1962 SC 1821: (1962)2 Cr LJ 805: (1963)1 SCR 253].

The word 'accomplice' is not defined in the Evidence Act. However, it is accepted that the word is used in its ordinary sense which means and signifies a guilty partner or associate in a crime. [*M.O. Shamsudhin* v *State of Kerala* (1995)3 SCC 351: JT 1995(3) SC 367: 1995 SCC (Cri) 509].

It is generally understood that an accomplice means a guilty associate or partner in crime. An accomplice by becoming an approver becomes a prosecution witness. [*Shankar* v *State of*

*T.N.* (1994)4 SCC 478: 1994 SCC (Cri) 1252: 1994 Cr LJ 3071].

There are two cases, however, in which a person has been held to be an accomplice even if he is not a *participes criminis*. Receivers of stolen property are taken to be accomplices of the thieves from whom they receive goods, or a trial for theft. Accomplices in previous similar offences committed by the accused on trial are deemed to be accomplices in the offence for which the accused is on trial, when evidence of the accused having committed crimes of identical type on other occasions be admissible to prove the system and intent of the accused in committing the offence charged. [*R.K. Dalmia* v *The Delhi Administration* AIR 1962 SC 1821: (1962)32 Comp Cas 699: (1962)2 Cr LJ 805].

**Accord and satisfaction.** An agreement to substitute for an existing debt some alternative form of discharging that debt, coupled with the actual discharge of the debt by the substituted performance. The new agreement is called the 'accord', and the discharge is called the 'satisfaction'. [Black's *Law Dictionary*, 8th Ed.].

"'Accord and satisfaction' means an agreement between the parties that something shall be given to, or done for, the person who has the right of action, in satisfaction of the cause of action. There must be not only agreement ('accord') but also consideration ('satisfaction'). Such an arrangement is really one of substituted performance". [E.W. Chance: *Principles of Mercantile Law,* p. 101 (P.W. French ed.), 13th Ed., 1950].

After a breach of contract has taken place the cause of action that arises from the breach may be discharged by accord and satisfaction, that is to say, by an agreement between the parties providing for the acceptance by the promise of something else than the remedy to which he is entitled by law, coupled with performance of the consideration agreed upon. [Halsbury's *Laws of England*, 3rd Ed., vol. 8, p. 206].

"Accord and satisfaction" imply an agreement to take the money in satisfaction of the claim in respect of which it is sent. If accord is a question of agreement, there must be either two minds agreeing or one of the two persons acting in such a way as to induce the other to think that the money is taken in satisfaction of the claim and to cause him to act upon that view. In either case it is a question of fact. [*Day* v *McLea* (1889)22 QBD 610, 613, *per* Lord Justice Bowell].

Accord and satisfaction "is an agreement between two at the least to satisfie an offence that the one hath made to the other, when a man hath done a trespasse, or such like, unto another for the which hee hath agreed with him to satisfie and content him with some recompence, which, if it be executed and performed, then, because that this recompence is a full satisfaction for the offence, it shall be a good barre in the law, if the other, after the accord performed, should sue againe any action for the same trespasse" (Termes de la Ley), "and, generally, in all actions, where damages, only are to be recovered, arbitrament, or accord with satisfaction, is a good plea". [*Blake's* case, 6 Rep 44; *Nathan* v *Ogdens* 22 TLR 57; *Hirachand Punamchand* v *Temple* (1911)2 KB 330].

"Accord and satisfaction is the purchase of a release from an obligation whether arising under contract or by means of any valuable consideration, not being the actual performance of the obligation itself. The accord is the agreement by which the obligation is discharged. The satisfaction is the consideration which makes the agreement operative. Formerly it was necessary that the consideration should be executed: 'I release you from your obligation in consideration of £50 now paid by you to me'. Later it was conceded that the consideration might be executory: 'I release you from your obligation in consideration of your promise to pay me £50, and give me a letter of withdrawal'. The consideration on each side might be an executory promise, the two mutual promises making an agreement enforceable in law, a contract". [*British Russian Gazette and Trade Outlook* v *Associated Newspapers* (1933)2 KB 616, 643, 644, *per* Scrutton, L.J. followed in *Union of India* v *Kishorilal Gupta* AIR 1959 SC 1362].

"'Accord and satisfaction' necessarily involve some contractual modification of the original bargain". [*Gwyther* v *Boslymon Quarries* (1950)1 All ER 384, 392, *per* Roxburgh, J.].

Accord and satisfaction occurs where, following the conclusion of a contract, one party obtains his release from his obligation, by promising or giving consideration other than that which the other party has to accept under the contract. The agreement is the 'accord', the consideration is the 'satisfaction'. [*D&C Builders Ltd.* v *Rees* (1966)2 QB 617; *Budget-rent-a-Car* v *Goodman* (1991)2 NZLR 715].

Accord and satisfaction discharges the cause of action for breaches of contract already committed. When the accord and satisfaction is by substituted agreement, it is a question of construction of that agreement whether it also extinguishes all pre-existing rights and obligations and totally discharges the original contract. [*Union of India* v *Kishorilal Gupta* AIR 1953 Cal 642].

Under s. 63 of the Indian Contract Act 1872 a promisee may accept, instead of the performance of the promise made to him, any satisfaction which he thinks fit. This is a case of accord and satisfaction under the English law of contract. [*Dipchand* v *Abhechand & Co.* AIR 1962 Cal 166].

**According to law.** The phrase refers to overall decision, which must be according to law, which it would not be, if there is a miscarriage of justice, due to mistake of law. [*Hari Shankar* v *Rao Girdhari Lal Chowdhury* 1962 Supp (1) SCR 933: AIR 1963 SC 698].

It is neither desirable nor possible to give an exhaustive definition of the expression 'according to law'. [*Malini Ayyappa Naicker* v *Seth Manghraj* AIR 1969 SC 1344]. To act according to law is to act in conformity with legal formalities.

A decision shall not be according to law if the court which made the order had no jurisdiction or the court has based its decision on evidence which should not have been admitted, or the unsuccessful party has not been given a proper opportunity of being heard, or the burden of proof has been placed on the wrong shoulders. [*Bell & Co. Ltd.* v *Waman Hemraj* 40 Bom LR 125: AIR 1938 Bom 223].

**Accordingly.** As suggested or required by the circumstances; consequently; therefore; in a conformable manner; suitably; consequently; in a similar manner. [*National Insurance Co. Ltd.* v *Life Insurance Corporation of India* AIR 1963 SC 1911: (1963)3 Comp Cas 529: (1964)2 SCR 182].

**Account.** A record or statement of money, goods or services received or expended, with the balance; a statement of the administration of money in trust; a statement in writing of debits and credits, or of receipts and payments; a statement of pecuniary transactions.

It is a detailed statement of the mutual demands in the nature of debit and credit between parties.

It is a detailed statement of the debits and credits between parties to a contract or to a fiduciary relationship; a reckoning of monetary dealings. [Black's *Law Dictionary*, 7th Ed.].

"By 'account', I understand the parties to mean some account contained in some ledger or book ......" [*Allnutt* v *Ashenden* (1843)5 Man & G 392, 397, *per* Tindal, C.J.].

In the context of business transactions, "the word 'accounts' must include invoices, whether sales invoices or purchase invoices, that is to say, invoices for goods supplied to the subject who is liable for purchase tax and invoices made out by him for sales which he makes". [*Customs & Excise Comrs.* v *Ingram* (1948)1 All ER 927, 929, *per* Lord Goddard, C.J.].

In the context of stock exchange activities, account "means the period beginning on the day after an account day and ending on the next following account day ......... Account day is ...... sometimes referred to as settling day or pay day. [Halsbury's *Laws of England*, 3rd Ed., vol. 36, p. 547n].

"In wills and estates, an account is a brief financial statement of the manner in which an executor or administrator has performed the official duties of collecting the estate's assets and paying those who are entitled". [Black's *Law Dictionary*, 8th Ed.].

The word 'account' has been defined in *Words and Phrases*, Permanent Ed., Vol. IA at pp. 336 to 338 to mean: (*i*) a claim or demand by one person against another creating a debtor-creditor relation; (*ii*) a formal statement in detail of transactions between two parties arising out of contracts or some fiduciary relation. At p. 343 of the same book the word has also been defined to mean the preparation of record or statement of transactions or the like; a statement and explanation of one's administration or conduct in money affairs, a statement or record of financial transactions, a reckoning or computation, a registry of pecuniary transactions or a reckoning of money transactions, a written or printed statement of business dealing or debits and credits, or a certain class of them. It is thus seen that while the former definitions give the word 'account' a restrictive meaning the latter give it a comprehensive meaning. Similarly is the above word defined, both restrictively and expansively, in Black's *Law Dictionary* (Sixth Ed.) to mean: A detailed statement of the mutual demands in the nature of debit and credit between parties, arising out of contracts or some fiduciary relation. A statement in writing, of debits and credits, or of receipts and payments; a list of items of debits and credits, with their respective dates. A statement of pecuniary transactions; a record or course of business dealings between parties; a list of statement of monetary transactions, such as payments, losses, sales, debits, credits, accounts payable, accounts receivable etc., in most cases showing a balance or result of comparison between items of an opposite nature. [*CBI* v *V.C. Shukla* AIR 1998 SC 1406: JT 1998(2) SC 172: 1998 Cr LJ 1905: (1998)3 SCC 410: 1998 SCC (Cri) 761].


- **Active account** p. 34.
- **Appropriation account** p. 71.
- **Budget account** p. 113.
- **Joint account** p. 486.
- **Mutual account** p. 596.
- **On account** p. 625.
- **Outstanding accounts** p. 632.
- **Profit and loss account** p. 696.
- **Revenue account** p. 760.
- **Share premium account** p. 794.
- **Suspense account** p. 824.


**Account book.** It is a book kept by a merchant, trader, or other person, in which are entered from time-to-time the transactions of his trade or business.

NOTE: It connotes an intention that it should serve as a permanent record. [*Ambalavan Pillai* v *Gowri Ammal* AIR 1936 Mad 871].

In account books regularly kept in due course of business, usually the pages are interconnected and particularly in daily accounts, the balance of one day or one page is carried over to the next day or page so that interpolation or replacement of page becomes very difficult. [*Hira Meher* v *Birbal Prasad* AIR 1958 Ori 4].

"To account is to reckon ...... A book which contains successive entries of items may be a good memorandum book; but until those entries are totalled or balanced, or both, as the case may be, there is no reckoning and no account. In the making of totals and striking of balances from time to time lies the chief safeguard under which books of account have been distinguished from other private records as capable of containing substantive evidence on which reliance may be placed". [*Mukundram* v *Dayaram* AIR 1914 Nag 44; relied on in *Central Bureau of Investigation* v *V.C. Shukla* AIR 1998 SC 1406: (1998)3 SCC 410: 1998 Cr LJ 1905: JT 1998(2) SC 172].

In order that a document could be relied upon as an account book, it must have the characteristic of, being foolproof. A bundle of sheets detachable and replaceable at a moment's pleasure can hardly be characterised as an account book. [*Zenna Sorabji* v *Mirabelle Hotel Co. (P) Ltd*. AIR 1981 Bom 446].

Ordinarily collection of sheets of papers bound together with the intention that such binding shall be permanent and the papers used collectively in one volume shall be said to be a book of account. Unbound sheets of paper cannot be treated as account book, specially when there are interpolations and overwritings therein. [*Dharam Chand Joshi* v *Satya Narayan Bazaz* AIR 1993 Gau 35].

Spiral notebook recording monetary transactions, entries of receipt of money from certain persons on left side of page and payment to certain persons on right side with entries also totalled and balanced and duly reckoned is a 'book of account' and is not a bundle of loose sheets of papers as contained in files. [*Central Bureau of Investigation* v *V.C. Shukla* AIR 1998 SC 1406: (1998)3 SCC 410: 1998 Cr LJ 1905: JT 1998(2) SC 172].

There is a distinction between faked books and books with irregularities and mistakes. The latter may be used after making necessary correction. [*Sarat Kumar Pal* v *Sudhir Kumar Pal* AIR 1960 Cal 231].

**Account mutual.** See MUTUAL ACCOUNT p. 596.

**Account payee.** The words "account payee" on a cheque are a direction to the collecting banker to place the proceeds to the credit of the actual payee specified in the cheque. [*Morison* v *London County and Westminster Bank, Ltd*. (1914)3 KB 356, 373, 374, *per* Lord Reading, C.J.]. They do not restrict the negotiability of the cheque. [*Universal Guarantee Pty. Ltd*. v *National Bank of Australasia Ltd*. (1965)39 ALJ 11], but they put upon the banker the onus of taking care to see that the customer for whom the banker collects the cheque and whose account is credited, is really the payee named in the cheque. [*Underwood* v *Bank of Liverpool* (1924)1 KB 775, 793, 794].

NOTE: In *Bevan* v *National Bank Ltd., Bevan* v *Capital and Counties Bank Ltd*. [(1906)23 TLR 65, 68], it has been observed that it was direction to the receiving banker that the drawer desired to pay the particular cheque into the bank which kept the account of the payee. To disregard a direction of that kind, if the banker had information which might lead him to think that the account into which he was paying the amount was not the payee's account, would be negligence.

**Account rendered.** An account produced by the creditor and presented for the debtor's examination and acceptance. [Black's *Law Dictionary*, 8th Ed.].

Accounts submitted to the person entitled to accounts. [*Radhikaprasad* v *Nand Kumar* ILR (1944) Nag 63: AIR 1944 Nag 7].

NOTE: In the case of an account rendered, the accounting party must satisfy the court that it was correctly rendered, *i.e.*, he must support it in court. If the account is stated or settled, the other party is bound, unless it can be opened. An account rendered may be turned into an account stated or settled if it is not challenged for such a time that an acceptance will be implied. [*Radhikaprasad* v *Nand Kumar* ILR (1944) Nag 63: AIR 1944 Nag 7].

**Account stated or settled.** The expression has more than one meaning. It sometimes means a claim to payment made by one party and admitted by the other party to be correct. An account may also be stated where the account contains items both of credit and debit, and the figures on both sides are adjusted between the parties and a balance struck. Accounts are settled or stated if they are submitted by one party and accepted as correct by the other. The account submitted need not be in writing and the acceptance may be inferred by conduct. [*Gordon Woodroffe & Co. (Madras) Ltd*. v *Sk. M.A. Majid & Co*. AIR 1967 SC 181: (1967)1 SCA 52: (1967)2 SCJ 387: (1966)2 SCWR 442].

An account stated is "an agreement by both parties that all the articles are true". [*Trueman* v *Hurst* 2 TLR 42, *per* Mansfield, C.J.].

NOTE: The "essence of an account stated is not the character of the items on one side or the other, but the fact that there are cross items of account and that the parties mutually agree the several accounts of each, and by treating the items so agreed on the one side as discharging the items on the other side protanto, go on to agree that the balance only is payable. Such a transaction is in truth bilateral and creates a new debt and a new cause of action. There are mutual promises, the one side agreeing to accept the account of the balance of the debt as true (because there must in such cases be, at least in the end, a creditor to whom the balance is due) and to pay it, the other side agreeing the entire debt as at a certain figure and their agreeing that it has been discharged to such and such an extent, so that there will be complete satisfaction on payment of the agreed balance. Hence, there is mutual consideration to support the promises on either side and to constitute the new cause of action. The account stated is accordingly binding, save that it may be reopened on any ground for instance, fraud or mistake which would justify setting aside any other agreement". [*Bishun Chand* v *Seth Girdhari Lal* AIR 1934 PC 147: 50 TLR 465, *per* Lord Wright].

The essence of an account stated being bilateral promise to pay made by one party is good enough consideration for the promise made by the other party. [*Ethirajulu Naidu* v *K.R.C. Chettiar* AIR 1975 Mad 333].

"An account stated, in the interpretation which is placed on the expression by the law of England, is mere evidence establishing only a *prima facie* liability and not in itself constituting a debt. If by such evidence an admission is shown of money being due, a promise to pay the amount is indeed inferred by the law. But the liability may be rebutted by disputing the debt charged in the account, as for instance by proving mistake among other ordinary defences". [*Camillo Tank Steamship Co.* v *Alexandria Engineering Works* 38 TLR 134, 137, *per* Lord Haldane].

"There are two forms of accounts stated. An account stated may take the form of a mere acknowledgment of a debt, and in those circumstances, though it is quite true it amounts to a promise and an existence of a debt may be inferred that can be rebutted, and it may very well turn out that there is no real debt at all, and in those circumstances there would be no consideration and no binding promise. But, on the other hand, there is an account stated which is a very usual form between merchants in business, in which the account stated is an account which contains entries on both sides, and in which the parties who have stated the account between them have agreed that the items on one side should be set against the items on the other side and the balance only should be paid; the items on the smaller side are set off and deemed to be paid by the items on the larger side, and there is a promise for good consideration to pay the balance, arising from the fact that the items have been so set off and paid in the way described". [*Siqueira* v *Noronha* (1934) AC 332, *per* Lord Atkin].

There can be an account stated between a moneylender and his client notwithstanding that the account is necessarily unilateral. [*Bishun Chand* v *Seth Girdhari Lal* AIR 1934 PC 147: 50 TLR 465].

A sum stated to be due under an agreement which is wholly void cannot form the basis of an account stated. [*Re Home & Colonial Insurance Co.* (1930)1 Ch 102]. This applies also to betting debts. [*Alberg* v *Chandler* 64 TLR 394; *Law* v *Dearnley* (1950)1 KB 400].

"There is a real account stated, called in old law an insimul computassent, that is to say, when several items of claim are brought into account on either side, and, being set against one another, a balance is struck, and the consideration for the payment of the balance is the discharge of the items of each side. It is then the same as if each item was paid and a discharge given for each, and in consideration of that discharge the balance was agreed to be due. It is not necessary, in order to make out a real account stated, that the debts should be debts *in praesenti*, or that they should be legal debts ...... It is to be taken as if the sums had been really paid down on each side; and the balance is recoverable as if money had been really taken in satisfaction; subject to this, that where sum of the items are such that, if they had been actually paid, the party paying then would have been able to recover then back as on a failure of consideration, the account stated would be invalidated. [*Laycock* v *Pickles* (1863)4 B&S 497, *per* Mr. Justice Blackburn].

In account stated there must first be a statement of account between the parties and an admission of balance due from one party to the other. The striking of a balance is an essential ingredient of the term account stated. [*Tarachand* v *Mt. Dhapu* AIR 1957 Raj 110].

An account stated can take the form of a mere acknowledgment. Other elements being present, a document does not cease to be an account stated merely because it does not contain entries on both sides. [*Durga Prasad* v *Fateh Chand* AIR 1968 Cal 292].

**Account suit.** A suit for accounts means a suit by a person who is entitled to accounts from a person who is liable to render accounts either on the basis of a contract or because of fiduciary relationship. [*Pannalal Lodha* v *Omraomal Lodha* AIR 1953 Cal 244].

It is an action brought against the defendant who ought to render an account but does not do so. For example, the manager of a Hindu Undivided Family is liable to account on the footing of what has been spent and what remains. He is liable to account for the family property as it stands at the time of the demand.

A suit is not a suit for an account unless the plaint asks for taking of accounts. A suit cannot be regarded as a suit for accounts merely because accounts have to be examined. [*Jagannath* v *Pandharinath* AIR 1937 Nag 172].

NOTE: A suit for a specific sum of money is not a suit for accounts, although accounts have to be examined for giving a decree. [*Bhourilal Agarwalla* v *Ashutosh Roy* 65 CWN 1067].

**Accountable receipt.** A written acknowledgment of the receipt of money or goods to be accounted for by the receiver. It differs from an ordinary receipt or acquittance, in this that the latter imports merely that money has been paid. [*Clark* v *Newsan* (1847)1 Ex 31].

**Accounting party.** Accounting party is one who is liable to render accounts to any other party.

NOTE: As a general principle of law, it is the agent who is the accounting party to the principal. But where the agent is not in a position to ascertain his dues without going into his principal's accounts, he can sue the principal for accounts. [*Life Insurance* v *Gurdial Singh* AIR 1960 Punj 607; *Narandas Morardas Gaziwala* v *Papammal* AIR 1967 SC 333].

**Accredit.** To give official authorisation or status to; to send (a person) with credentials as an envoy.

**Accredited.** Officially recognized; generally accepted.

**Accredited representative.** An accredited representative is a person who is a designated authority to act on behalf of another person, group, or organization, usually by being granted that authority by law or by the rules of the group or organization. [Black's *Law Dictionary*, 7th Ed.].

**Accretion.** The growing together or cohesion of separate things to form one; growth by organic enlargement; a layer of a substance that is slowly added to the earth; the process of new layers being slowly added to the earth; growth or formation by external additions; an accumulation or external addition; increase, as of land along the seashore or a river, by deposit of alluvium; increase by natural growth or forces.

"The act of accretion, when it is done by alluvial deposit, contemplates the adding to existing land by the process of building up against that land. Accretion can occur in one of several ways: One is where tidal water recedes gradually and imperceptibly from the land; another is where land by alluvial deposit is added to the dry land or foreshore. In the latter case, if it is tidal water the addition must end up situate above the mean high-water mark of ordinary tides. If it is not tidal water, there is no need to worry about the movement of tides, as long as the land has lost the character of lake or river bottom. In either case the act of accretion means an adding to, a fixing on to the existing dry land ...... If there is either a water channel or a strip of land or a ridge or other barrier between the upland, no accretion can be considered. It is not joined to that land, so it cannot become part of it". [*Re Bulman* (1966)56 WWR 225, 230, 231, *per* Ruttan, J.].

NOTE: The principle of accretion recognised in the English law is derived from the civil law which says that where there is an acquisition of land from the sea or a river by gradual, slow, and imperceptible means, there, from the supposed necessity of the case, and the difficulty of having to determine, year by year, to whom an inch, or a foot, or a yard belongs, the accretion by alluvion is held to belong to the owner of the adjoining land. [*Lopes* v *Muddun Mohun Thakoor* (1870)13 MIA 467; *Sri Balusu* v *Collector of Godavari* 26 IA 107].

Accession; the increase of a legacy etc. by the share of a failing co-legatee.

The right of heirs or legatees to unite their shares of the estate with the portion of any co-heirs or legatees who do not accept their portion, fail to comply with a condition, or die before the testator. [Black's *Law Dictionary*, 8th Ed.].

Any increase in trust property other than increases ordinarily considered as income. [Black's *Law Dictionary*, 8th Ed.].

**Accrue.** It is derived from the Latin, 'ad' and 'creso' to grow to.

The dictionary meaning of the word "accrue" is to "to come as an accession, increment, or produce; to fall to one by way of advantage; to fall due." [*Morvi Industries Ltd.* v *Commissioner of Income Tax (Central), Calcutta* AIR 1971 SC 2396: (1972)4 SCC 451: (1972)1 SCR 970].

A title "accrues" when the instrument creating it, or the fact constituting it, first becomes operative. [*Reid* v *Reid* 31 Ch D 402].

A cause of action for a tort "accrues" when it becomes effective, *i.e.*, when the resulting damage manifests itself, *i.e.*, at the time the act complained of was committed.

As regards financial matters, "accrued" suggests that the interest arises by way of an accession to or any advantage bestowed upon some other person. [*Trustees Executors & Agency Co. Ltd.* v *Federal Commissioners of Taxation* (1944)69 CLR 270, 287, *per* Starke, J.].

"Accruing dividend", in a public limited company, is a dividend in process of being earned, but not yet declared. [*Re Lysaght* (1898)1 Ch 115].

"Rent accrues when it becomes due, and at no other time". [*Slack* v *Sharpe* 8 A&E 373, *per* Patterson, J.].

**Accrued income.** "Accrued income" is money earned but not yet received. The income can be said to accrue when it becomes due. [*Morvi Industries Ltd.* v *Commissioner of Income Tax (Central), Calcutta* AIR 1971 SC 2396: (1972)4 SCC 451: (1972)1 SCR 970]. An income accrues or arises when an individual acquires a right to receive the same. [*Commissioner of Income Tax, Madras* v *A. Gajapathi Naidu* AIR 1964 SC 1653: (1964)7 SCR 767: (1964)53 ITR 114: (1964)1 SCJ 478].

**Accumulated income.** Income that is retained in an account; esp., income that a trust has generated, but that has not yet been reinvested or distributed by the trustee.

**Accumulated profit.** Profit that has accrued but not yet been distributed; earned surplus. Accumulated profit is one that relates to the past. The profit that arises *in praesenti* is called current profit. [*C.I.T.* v *Murugappan* ILR (1967)2 Mad 256; *Re Spanish Prospecting Co. Ltd.* AIR 1954 SC 470: (1955)1 SCR 313; *P.K. Badiani* v *C.I.T.* (1976)4 SCC 562; *Tea Estates India Pvt. Ltd.* v *C.I.T., West Bengal* (1976)4 SCC 446: 1977 SCC (Tax) 91].

In taxation law, the expression "accumulated profits" must mean profits which had accumulated prior to the accounting year of which the income, profits and gains were being assessed, while current profits would mean the profits of the accounting year. [*Commissioner of Income Tax, Kerala, Ernakulam* v *V. Damodaran Trivandrum* AIR 1980 SC 478: (1980)1 SCR 944: (1980)1 SCC 173: (1980)121 ITR 572].

**Accumulated surplus.** Earnings in excess of a corporation's capital and liabilities. [Black's *Law Dictionary*, 8th Ed.].

**Accumulation.** An amassing; increase; a collected mass.

**Accusation.** A statement charging a person with an offence or crime; a formal charge of criminal wrongdoing.

'Accusation' meant allegation of misconduct. [*R.* v *Tomlinson* (1895)1 QB 706].

'Accusation' is a charge made to a competent officer against one who has committed a crime with a view to bring him to justice and punishment. [*S.K. Nizamuddin* v *State of Bihar* 1974 Pat LJR 516].

**Accuse.** A statement charging a person with an offence or crime; to charge a person judicially or publicly with an offence; to charge with fault or error; blame; implicate; denounce; indict.

"To accuse, in ordinary parlance, in the form 'to accuse (a person) of', means, to charge with the crime or fault of, etc." [Murray's *Dictionary* as referred to in *R.* v *Kempel* (1900)31 QLR 631 (CA)].

NOTE: *'Accuse' and 'censure'—difference.* There is a difference between accuse and censure. To accuse is only to assert that which is pro-judicial to another; to censure is to take the fault for granted. It is extremely wrong to accuse another without sufficient grounds, but still worse to censure him without the most substantial grounds.

**Accused.** The defendant or defendants in a criminal case; the person or persons charged with a crime.

A person whom someone has blamed for wrongdoing. Specifically, a person who has been subjected to actual restraints on liberty through an arrest or a person against whom a formal indictment or information has been returned. [Black's *Law Dictionary,* 7th Ed.].

As adjective, of or relating to someone or something implicated in wrongdoing. As noun, a person who has been blamed for wrongdoing; esp., a person who has been arrested and brought before a magistrate or who has been formally charged with a crime (as by indictment or information); a person against whom legal proceedings have been initiated. [Black's *Law Dictionary*, 8th Ed.].

The expression 'accused' has to be literally interpreted. [*Ramua* v *State of UP* 1992 Judicial Interpretation of Crimes (JIC) 519 (All)].

▸ *Meaning under the Indian Oaths Act 1873, s. 5.* It means a person actually arraigned, that is, put on a trial. [*Laxmipat Choraria* v *State of Maharashtra* AIR 1968 SC 938: (1968)1 SCA 682: (1968)2 SCR 624].

▸ *Meaning under the Evidence Act 1872, s. 24.* An 'accused person' is the person against whom evidence is sought to be led in a criminal proceeding. [*Abraham Varghese* v *State of Kerala* ILR (1964)2 Ker 312: AIR 1965 Ker 175].

▸ *Meaning under the Criminal Procedure Code 1973.* The word 'accused' in the Cr PC denotes different meanings according to the context in which it is deployed; in that sometimes the said word is employed to denote a person accused, sometimes person against whom there is an accusation, but who is yet not put on trial and sometimes to denote a person on trial and so on. [*Directorate of Enforcement* v *Deepak Mahajan* AIR 1994 SC 1775: JT 1994(1) SC 290: (1994)3 SCC 440: 1994 Cr LJ 2269: 1994 SCC (Cri) 785: (1994)70 ELT 12].

The word is used only in a generic sense in sub-secs. (1) and (2) of s. 167 of the Criminal Procedure Code denoting the person whose liberty is actually restrained on his arrest by a competent authority on well-founded information or formal accusation or indictment. Therefore, the word 'accused' limited to the scope of sub-secs. (1) and (2) of s. 167 includes 'any person arrested'. Thus, a person arrested under the Foreign Exchange Regulation Act (FERA) or the Customs Act 1962, is assimilated with the characteristics of an 'accused' within the range of s. 167(1) and as such is liable to be detained under s. 167(2), Cr. P.C. by a Magistrate when produced before him. [*Directorate of Enforcement* v *Deepak Mahajan* AIR 1994 SC 1775: JT 1994(1) SC 290: (1994)3 SCC 440: 1994 Cr LJ 2269: 1994 SCC (Cri) 785: (1994)70 ELT 12].

NOTE: The term, however, does not apply to a defendant in a civil action.

**Accused of any offence.** Only a person against whom a formal accusation relating to the commission of an offence has been levelled, which in the normal course may result in his prosecution, would fall within the ambit of the phrase 'accused of any offence'. The phrase is to be so meant in the context of Art. 20 of the Constitution of India guaranteeing the benefit against testimonial compulsion. [*Veera Ibrahim* v *State of Maharashtra* AIR 1976 SC 1167: (1976)2 SCC 302: 1976 SCC (Cri) 278: (1976)3 SCR 672: 1976 Cr LJ 860].

The expression "accused of any offence" in s. 25 of the Evidence Act 1872 would cover the case of an accused who has since been put on trial, whether or not at the time when he made the confessional statement, he was under arrest or in custody as an accused in that case or not. [*Bheru Singh* v *State of Rajasthan* (1994)2 SCC 467: 1994 SCC (Cri) 555: JT 1994(1) SC 501].

**Achandrarka Statiyal.** See GENERATION TO GENERATION p. 386.

**Acknowledge.** To own or admit as true; confess; to declare or admit the authority of; to assent to the validity of; to show appreciation of; to report and respond to the receipt or arrival of; confirm the receipt of.

**Acknowledgement.** Admission; affirmation; assertion; authentication; certification; validation; a recognition of something as being factual; the act of making it known that one has received something.

In the context of an instrument, an acknowledgement is a verification of the fact of execution, but is not a verification of the contents of the instrument executed; in other words, an acknowledgement is the method of authenticating an instrument by showing it was the act of the person executing it. [Black's *Law Dictionary*, 7th Ed.].

It is a proceeding whereby a person who has executed an instrument may, by declaring it to be his act and deed, entitle it to be received in evidence without further proof of execution or both.

**Acknowledgement of debt or liability.** An admission that a debt is due or that source claim or liability is still in existence.

NOTE: The words used must relate to a present subsisting debt or liability and indicate the existence of jural relationship between the parties, e.g. that of a debtor and a creditor and the intention to admit such jural relationship. Such an intention need not be in express terms and can be inferred by implication from the nature of admission and the surrounding circumstances. Generally speaking, a liberal construction of the statement in question should be given. [*Lakshmiratan Cotton Mills Co. Ltd.* v *The Allumineum Corporation of India* AIR 1971 SC 1482].

Under s. 18, Limitation Act 1908 one of the essential requirements for a valid acknowledgement is that the writing concerned must contain an admission of a subsisting liability. A mere admission of a past liability is not sufficient to constitute such an 'acknowledgement'. Hence a mere recital in a document as to the existence of a past liability, coupled with a statement of its discharge, does not constitute an 'acknowledgement' within this section. [*Valliama Champaka Pillai* v *Sivathanu Pillai* AIR 1979 SC 1937: (1980)1 SCR 354: (1979)4 SCC 429].

**Acquaintance.** Knowledge of any person or thing. It is less than familiarity or intimacy.

"Acquaintance seems to connote something more than bare recognition but falling short of the intimacy of friendship and still further short of ties of relationship by blood or affinity—a little less than keen and less than kind. [*Salvesen's Trustees* v *Wye* (1954) SLT 299, 303, *per* the Lord President (Cooper)].

In the context of physical relationship, acquaintance springs from occasional intercourse; familiarity from frequent intercourse; and intimacy from frequent intercourse, but unreserved communication.

**Acquaintance rape.** Rape of a girl or woman by a person known to her especially by the victim's social companion. It is also known as date rape.

**Acquiesce.** Agree, consent or concur tacitly; assent.

Give an implied consent to any act; the accrual of a right by one's mere silence, or without express assent or acknowledgement.

**Acquiescence.** Passive consent; quiet submission to an act of which one had knowledge.

It arises where a person knows that he is entitled to impeach a transaction or enforce a right but neglects to do so for such a length of time that under the circumstances of the case, the other party may fairly infer that he has waived or abandoned his right. The word "acquiescence' does not mean simply an active intelligent consent, but will be implied if a person is content not to oppose irregular acts which he knows are being done. [*Evans* v *Smallcombe* LR 3 HL 249, *per* Cairns, C. ].

If a person having a right, and seeing another person about to commit, or in the course of committing, an act infringing upon that right, stands by in such a manner as really to induce the person committing the act, and who might otherwise have abstained from it, to believe that he assents to its being committed, he cannot afterwards be heard to complain of the act. This, as Lord Cottenham said in *Leeds* v *Amherst* [16 LJ Ch 5], is the proper sense of the term "acquiescence".

The term "acquiescence" is used in two senses. In its proper legal sense it implies that a person abstains from interfering while a violation of his legal rights is in progress; in another sense it implies that he refrains from seeking redress when a violation of his rights, of which he did not know at the time, is brought to his notice .... Acquiescence operates by way of estoppel. It is quiescence in such circumstances that assent may reasonably be inferred, and is an instance of estoppel by words or conduct. [Halsbury's *Laws of England,* 3rd Ed., vol. 14, p. 638].

NOTE: There can only be acquiescence where there is knowledge. The court never binds parties by acquiescence where there is no knowledge. [*Weldon* v *Dicks* (1878)10 Ch D 247, 262, *per* Malins, V.C.].

**Acquire.** Obtain; gain possession or control of; buy; take in exchange; take in pawn or otherwise receive.

'Acquire' means come into possession of. [*Indore UM Mills* v *Basantilal S. Kumar* 1968 MPLJ 438].

If the word 'acquire' is assigned its more generic connotation, namely, that it means to receive or to come into possession of, then in the context of transfer or partition, that word can be given its full meaning without any violence to the language used. [*Radhabai* v *State of Maharashtra* AIR 1970 Bom 232, 237 (FB)].

The use of the word 'acquire' necessarily postulates a change of relationship vis-a-vis a thing or property which is said to be acquired and which was not existing before. The notion of ownership of property implies various component rights, *viz*, that of possession, enjoyment, destruction, alienation, exclusion and others incidental to the right of ownership. A person who acquires a thing or property gets this right for the first time from someone else; otherwise the use of the word 'acquire' is unappropriate and will not convey the correct meaning. [*Salubai* v *Chandu* AIR 1966 Bom 194, 210].

The word 'acquire' signifies the obtaining of title as a result of positive act done by the acquirer and will not apply to a case where, on account of death, the right devolves upon the heir of the deceased. [*Narayanan Ainhrenthiri* v *Sinaha* AIR 1953 TC 397 (DB)].

The word 'acquires' in the phrase 'person who acquires goods' means 'acquire title to the goods'. [*John Mackintosh & Sons Ltd.* v *Baker's Stores (Seaford) Ltd.* (1965)3 All ER 412, *per* Browne, J.].

**Acquired.** The connotation of the word is obviously the widest and includes every kind of acquisition. [*Jagannath Guku* v *Gadabai* AIR 1968 Bom 25, 29].

"As used by lawyers the word 'acquired' has long covered transactions of a purely passive nature and means little more than receiving". [*Congreve & Congreve* v *Inland*

*Revenue Commissioners* (1946)2 All ER 170, 183, *per* Wrottesley, J.].

When the hire-purchase and credit sale agreement speaks of the deposit being 'acquired' by an arrangement between specified persons, it means obtained otherwise than by exchange or provision of commensurate value. [*Kingsley* v *Sterling Industrial Securities* (1966)2 WLR 1265].

A property is said to be 'acquired' when prior to the acquisition, the person acquiring it had no interest in the property. [*Salubai* v *Chandu* AIR 1966 Bom 194].

When the Constitution provides that the Parliament may make laws for the government of any territory surrendered or otherwise 'acquired', the word 'acquired' should in that case "receive no narrow meaning. It is not used in a proprietary sense and in a constitution intended to endure and apply to changing conditions .... it may receive a meaning wide enough to include the acquisition of the power of government over the territory contemplated by the mandate and Trusteeship Agreement. [*Fishwick* v *Cleland* (1960)106 CLR 186, 197].

Article 1(3) of the Constitution of India provides: "The territory of India shall comprise—(*a*) the territories of the States; (*b*) the Union territories specified in the First Schedule; and (*c*) such other territories as may be acquired." In the context of Art. 1(3), the expression "acquired" should be taken to be a reference to "acquisition" as understood in Public International Law. If there were any public notification, assertion or declaration by which the Government of the country had declared or treated a territory as part and parcel of the territory of India, the courts would be bound to recognize an "acquisition" as having taken place, with the consequence that the territory would be part of the territory of the Union within Art. 1(3)(*c*). [*N. Masthan Sahib* v *The Chief Commissioner, Pondicherry* AIR 1963 SC 533: (1964)1 SCA 119: 1962 Supp (1) SCR 981].

**Acquisition.** Something acquired; anything gained or won; gaining of possession or control over something.

▸ *Meaning under the Land Acquisition Act 1894, ss. 6 and 16.* Taking possession of the land for a pubic purpose or for a company, thereby vesting absolutely in the Government, free from all encumbrances.

> NOTE: Mere alteration of the outward form of property is not 'acquisition'. [*Re Dunbar* (1905) AC 285].

'Acquisition' means that the entire bundle of rights which vested in the original owner of a property passes on from him to the acquirer and nothing should be left in the owner or holder. [*Charanjit Lal Chowdhury* v *Union of India* AIR 1951 SC 411].

Acquisition is the act by which a person acquires property or a thing. Acquisition means transfer. [*Devi Dass Gopal Krishnan* v *State of Punjab* AIR 1967 SC 1895: (1969)1 SCJ 19]. By acquisition, the ownership or the title of the owner is transferred. [*C.I.T., Punjab* v *(Dr.) Shamlal Narula* AIR 1963 Punj 411: 50 ITR 513].

By 'acquisition' is meant to acquire something from one person and to have it vested in another whether it is ownership or the property rights or other rights. [*Jayantilal* v *State of Gujarat* AIR 1962 Guj 297].

> NOTE: Taking over the management does not amount to 'acquisition'. Thus, the deprivation of the landholder of the right of management and control over the forest without his legal title thereto or beneficial enjoyment thereof being effected does not amount to acquisition of land. [*Guru Datta Sharma* v *State of Bihar* AIR 1961 SC 1684].

The narrow view that 'acquisition' necessarily means acquisition of title in whole or part of the property has not, however, been accepted by the Court in the context of Art. 31(2) of the Constitution of India. The word "acquisition" has quite a wide concept meaning the procuring of property or the taking of it permanently or temporarily. It does not necessarily imply acquisition of legal title by the State in the property taken possession of. The taking by the State for an indefinite period of the exclusive possession of property constitutes an acquisition of property within the meaning of Art. 31(2) of the Constitution. [*Dwarkadas Shrinivas of Bombay* v *Sholapur Spinning & Weaving Co. Ltd* AIR 1954 SC 119: 1954 SCR 674: 1954 SCJ 175].

NOTE: *'Acquisition' and 'requisition'—distinction.* The two concepts of "acquisition" and "requisition" cannot but be ascribed to be totally distinct and independent. Whereas acquisition involves an element of permanency and finality involving a transfer of title, the concept of requisition is merely to take over the domain or control over the property without acquiring the rights of ownership and must be, by its very nature, be of temporary duration. [*Kewal Chand Mimani (D) by Lrs.* v *S.K. Sen* AIR 2001 SC 2569: JT 2001(6) SC 264: (2001)6 SCC 512].

**Acquisition of territory.** It occurs when territory is acquired by a sovereign State for the first time. It may be by conquest or cession following a treaty or by occupation of territory hitherto unoccupied. [*Rajinder Chand* v *Sukhi* AIR 1957 SC 286].

Where change of sovereignty takes place by cessation, the acquisition of territory is complete as soon as the cessation is complete. [*State of Orissa* v *Ratna Prabha* AIR 1961 Ori 161].

Mere physical possession of territory by force of arms does not amount to acquisition within the meaning of Arts. 1(3)(*c*) and 2 of the Constitution of India till the territory is annexed; the territory conquered during the Indo-Pakistan War of December 1971 did not become part of the territory of India. [*S.R. Bhansali* v *Union* AIR 1973 Raj 49].

**Acquit.** Declare not guilty; set free; release or discharge from accusation, burden or obligation; legally certify the innocence of one charged with crime; pay or discharge a debt or claim.

**Acquittal.** The process of freeing or being freed from a charge, especially by a judgment of not guilty; the legal and formal certification of the innocence of a person who has been charged with a crime; one legally acquitted by a judgment rendered otherwise than in pursuance of a verdict as where one is discharged by a magistrate for lack of or insufficiency of evidence; discharge from prosecution after the accused has been properly tried and found not guilty.

The word "acquittal" is *verbum equivocum*, and may in ordinary language be used to express either the verdict of a jury, or the formal judgment of the Court, that the prisoner go thereof without day. [*Burgess* v *Boetefeur* 13 LJMC 126, *per* Tindal, C.J.].

In its application to departmental proceedings, the word 'acquittal' means that the servant concerned has been clearly and fully exonerated of the charges levelled against him. [*Ghulani Nabi Baba* v *State of J&K* AIR 1966 J&K 27].

NOTE: There is no appeal against acquittal unless there is distinct statutory authority. [*R.* v *Keepers of the Peace and Justices of the County of London* 25 QBD 357; *Benson* v *Inland Transport Board* (1942) AC 520].

- **Honourable acquittal.** It is acquittal of an accused after full consideration of evidence because the prosecution witnesses were disbelieved and the prosecution had miserably failed to prove the charges. [*Hafizuddin Inayatullat Kazi* v *J.C. Agarwal* 1980 Bom Cr 984].

**Acquittal on merit.** 'Acquittal on merit' means an acquittal on trial, on a consideration of evidence as distinguished from and in contradistinction to acquittals which occur due to certain technical defects, such as want of sanction. [*Jogendra Carabadu* v *Lingraj Patra* AIR 1970 Ori 91].

**Acquittance.** A discharge in writing of a debt or other duty which ought to be paid or done.

"A document by which one is discharged from a debt or other obligation; a receipt or release indicating payment in full". [Black's *Law Dictionary,* 8th Ed.].

A receipt in full is an acquittance. In legal proceedings, a receipt is regarded as an acquittance. [*State* v *Chelters* 31 Am Rep 679].

**Acquitted on the indictment.** In a recognisance meant acquitted on every count. [*R.* v *Bayard* (1892)2 QB 181].

**Act.** To play the part of; impersonate, as in a drama; behave or conduct oneself, e.g., he knows how to act in a society; perform; serve temporarily or as a substitute, as in some office or capacity.

Accomplishment; achievement; dealing; deed; doing; manipulation; measure; performance; transaction.

An alternative name for statutory law; a written ordinance of parliament or other legislative body.

The word connotes something done by a person pursuant to his volition.

The word denotes a matter or thing done. [*Suresh* v *State of U.P.* (1986)2 Crimes 219].

'Act', used with reference to an offence or a civil wrong shall include a series of acts, and words which refer to acts done, extend also to illegal omissions. [General Clauses Act 1897, s. 3(2); *Public Prosecutor, Madras* v *R. Raju* AIR 1972 SC 2504: (1972)2 SCC 410: 1972 Cr LJ 1699: 1972 SCC (Cri) 738: (1973)1 SCR 812].

The word 'act' does not mean only any particular, specific, instantaneous act of a person, but denotes as well a series of acts. [*Om Prakash* v *State of Punjab* AIR 1961 SC 1782: (1961)2 Cr LJ 848: (1962)2 SCR 254: (1962)1 SCJ 189 referring to Indian Penal Code 1860, s. 33].

The words 'act purporting to be done in official capacity' have been construed to apply to nonfeasance as well as to misfeasance. The word "act" extends to illegal omissions. There can be no distinction between acts done illegally and in bad faith and acts done *bona fide* in official capacity. [*State of Maharashtra* v *Chandrakant* AIR 1977 SC 148: (1977)1 SCC 257: (1977)1 SCR 933].

"The term 'act' is one of ambiguous import, being used in various senses of different degrees of generality. When it is said, however, that an act is one of the essential conditions of liability, we use the term in the widest sense of which it is capable. We mean by it any event which is subject to the control of the human will. Such a definition is, indeed, not ultimate, but it is sufficient for the purpose of the law.' [John Salmond: *Jurisprudence,* (Glanville L. Williams ed.), 10th Ed. 1947, p. 367].


- **Central Act** p. 131.
- **Judicial act** p. 493.
- **Municipal Act** p. 594.
- **Overt act** p. 632.
- **State Act** p. 809.
- **Subversive act** p. 819.
- **Temporary act** p. 833.


**Act of God.** An instance of uncontrollable natural forces in operation; an inevitable event occurring by reason of the operations of nature or an act occasioned exclusively by violence of nature unmixed with human agency or human negligence; an event due to natural causes, like, storms, earthquakes, floods etc. so exceptionally severe that no-one could reasonably be expected to anticipate or guard against it.

"Act of God" means not a mere misfortune, but something overwhelming. [*Oakley* v *Portsmouth Steam Packet Co.* 11 Ex 623, *per* Martin, B], such as storms, lightning, and tempests, which could not happen by the intervention of man [*Forward* v *Pittard* 1 TR 33], and loss which could not have been prevented, or avoided, by any reasonable amount of foresight, pains, or care. [*Nugent* v *Smith* 45 LJPC 697].

"By the 'Act of God', is meant a natural, not merely an inevitable, accident". [*Trent Navigation* v *Wood* 4 Doug. 290, *per* Mansfield, C.J. cited in *Forward* v *Pittard* 1 TR 28].

In the Biblical sense of the term, everything almost is said to be an 'Act of

God'; but in a mercantile sense, it means an extraordinary circumstance which could not be foreseen, and which could not be guarded against. [*Pandorf* v *Hamilton* 17 QBD 675].

It means an accident due to natural causes directly and exclusively, without human intervention, and that it could not have been prevented by any amount of foresight, pains and care reasonably to be expected of the person. [*Province of Madras* v *Machado* AIR 1955 Mad 519; (1955)2 MLJ 240].

**Act of grace.** A privilege or concession that cannot be claimed as a right, like declaring pardon or amnesty to numerous offenders.

**Act of law.** "Act of Law", or as it is sometimes expressed "Act in law", is something done by law, or by force of law, whether the hand that does it is willing or not; *e.g.*, a sale of land by the owner to a body which has statutory compulsive powers to acquire it. [*Co. Litt.* 215A; *Winter's Case* 3 Dyer 308b].

Any act which a man is compelled to do, or does under statutory compulsion, is an "act of law". [*Piggott* v *Middlesex County Council* (1909)1 Ch 134, 142, *per* Eve, J].

**Act of Parliament.** In India, it means a Bill which has passed by both the houses of Parliament and has become law with the approval of the President in accordance with the provisions of the Constitution.

In England, it is law made by the British sovereign, with the advice and consent of the Lords and the Commons in Parliament assembled. Acts of Parliament are the written laws of the Kingdom.

**Act of settlement.** Act (12 & 13 Will. III, C. 2, 1701) limiting the Crown to the members of the House of Hanover, provided they be Protestants. The Act also provided that the sovereign must be a member of the Church of England. One clause of the Act made the tenure of Judges' office for life or good behaviour independent of the Crown's will.

**Act of State.** An act done by the sovereign power of a country, or by its delegate, within the limits of the power vested in it. [Black's *Law Dictionary*, 5th Ed.].

"An act of State is essentially an exercise of sovereign power, and hence cannot be challenged, controlled, or interfered with by municipal Courts. Its sanction is not that of law, but that of sovereign power, and, whatever it be, municipal Courts must accept it, as it is, without question". [*Salaman* v *Secretary of State for India* (1906)1 KB 613, 639 (CA), *per* Fletcher Moulton, L.J.].

An 'act of State' is an act done in relation to a foreigner by the sovereign power of a country or its agent either previously authorised or subsequently ratified. Such an act cannot be questioned or made the subject of legal proceedings in any court of law. [*B.K. Mohapatra* v *State of Orissa* JT 1987(4) SC 170: 1987 (Supp) SCC 553: AIR 1988 SC 24: (1988)1 SCR 650: 1988(1) SLR 88].

NOTE: The essence of an act of State is the exercise of sovereign power and that is done arbitrarily, on principles either outside or paramount to the municipal law. [*State of Saurashtra* v *Menon Haji Ismail* AIR 1959 SC 1383: (1960)1 SCR 537: (1960) SCJ 394].

"Of the propriety or justice of an act of State neither the Court below nor the Judicial Committee have the means of forming, or the right of expressing, if they had formed any opinion. It may have been just or unjust, politic or impolitic, beneficial or injurious, taken as a whole, to those whose interests are affected. These are considerations into which their Lordships cannot enter. It is sufficient to say that, even if a wrong has been done, it is a wrong for which no Municipal Court of Justice can afford a remedy". [*Secretary of State in Council of India* v *K.B. Saheba* 4 WR 42 (PC)].

Where a territory is acquired by a sovereign state for the first time that is an act of State. It matters not how the acquisition has been brought about. It may be by conquest; it may be by cession following on treaty, it may be by occupation of territory hitherto unoccupied by a recognised ruler. In all cases the result is the same. [*Vajesingji Joravasinghji* v *Secretary of State for India in Council*

(1924)51 IA 357: 47 MLJ 574; *Rajinder Chand* v *Sukhi* AIR 1957 SC 286].

In USA it is recognised as a common law principle that prevents U.S. Courts from questioning the validity of a foreign country's sovereign acts within its own territory. As originally formulated by the U.S. Supreme Court in 1897, the doctrine provides that "the courts of one country will not sit in judgment on the act of the government of another done within it own territory." [*Underhill* v *Hernandez* 168 US 250, 252: 18 S Ct 83, 84 (1897)].

In India, 'act of State' does not mean all governmental acts as it does in the French and Continental Systems but only some of them. The expression is used also to designate immunities and prohibitions created by statutes. The term sometimes include certain prerogatives and special immunities enjoyed by the sovereign and its agents in the business of internal government. The term includes such official acts into which the court may not enquire or in respect of which an official declaration is binding on the Courts. [*State of Saurashtra* v *Memon Haji Ismail* AIR 1959 SC 1383: (1960)1 SCR 537: 1960 SCJ 394].

NOTE: As between the sovereign and his subjects, there is no such thing as act of State and it is incumbent on his officers to show that their action is within the authority conferred by law. [*Dalmia Dadric* v *C.I.T.* AIR 1958 SC 816: (1958) SCJ 1041].

**Act of war.** An act of armed aggression by a nation without a formal declaration of war.

**Acting.** Serving temporarily or on behalf of another or others; officiating especially in place of another; standing in the place of; transient.

"A person acting under the authority of the company" has been held to mean a person in fact having the authority of the company and not merely a person who might by a certain delegation of power given to him have been authorised to act but who was not in fact so authorised. [*Premier Industrial Bank Ltd.* v *Carlton Manufacturing Co.* (1909)1 KB 106]. This view, however, was dissented from in *Dey* v *Pullinger Engineering Co.* [(1921)1 KB 77] where it was held that a managing director drawing a bill on behalf of a company was "a person acting under its authority" when the articles of association empowered directors to authorise the managing director to draw bills of exchange although they had not in fact exercised this power.

**Actio personalis moritur cum persona.** A personal right of action dies with the person. The extent and limits of this common law doctrine may be summed up thus: "it was a rule of the common law that if an injury were done either to the person or property of another for which damages only could be recovered in satisfaction, the action died with the person to whom or by whom the wrong was done; but this rule was never extended to such personal actions as were founded upon any obligation, contract, debt, covenant, or any other similar duty to be performed: for there the action survived". [Herbert Broom's: *A Selection of Legal Maxims,* 10th Ed., p. 622].

NOTE: This maxim "is not applied in the old authorities to causes of actions on contracts, but to those in tort, which are founded on malfeasance or misfeasance to the person or property of another: which latter are annexed to the person, and die with the person, except where the remedy is given to (or by) the personal representatives by the statute law". [*Raymond* v *Fitch* 2 Cr M&R 588, 597, *per* Lord Abinger].

The maxim has a limited application. It operates in a limited class of actions *ex delicto* such as actions for damages for defamation, assault or other personal injuries not causing the death of the party and in other actions where after the death of the party the relief granted could not be enjoyed or granting it would be nugatory. [*Girijanandini Devi* v *Bijendra Narain Choudhary* AIR 1967 SC 1124: (1967)1 SCR 93].

The maxim has been applied not only to those cases where a plaintiff dies during the pendency of a suit filed by him for damages for personal injuries sustained by him but also to cases where a plaintiff dies during the pendency of an appeal to the Appellate Court, be it the First Appellate Court or the Second Appellate Court against the dismissal of the suit by the Trial Court and/or First Appellate Court, as the case may be. [*M. Veerappa* v *Evelyn Sequeira* AIR 1988 SC 506].

The maxim has been held inapplicable only in those cases where the injury caused to the deceased person has tangibly affected his estate or has caused an accretion to the estate of the wrong doer. [*Rustomji Dorabji* v *W.H. Nurse* AIR 1921 Mad 1; *Ratanlal* v *Baboolal* AIR 1960 MP 200]. The maxim has also been held inapplicable in those cases where a suit for damages for defamation, assault or other personal injuries sustained by the plaintiff had resulted in a decree in favour of the plaintiff because in such a case the cause of action becomes merged in the decree and the decretal debt forms part of the plaintiff's estate and the appeal from the decree by the defendant becomes a question of benefit or detriment to the estate of the plaintiff which his legal representatives are entitled to uphold and defend. [*Gopal* v *Ramchandra* (1902) ILR 26 Bom 597; *Melepurath Sankunni Ezhuthassan* v *Thekittil Geopalankutty Nair* AIR 1986 SC 411].

A claim for rendition of account is not a personal claim. It is not extinguished because the party who claims an account, the party who is called upon to account dies. [*Girijanandini Devi* v *Bijendra Narain Choudhary* AIR 1967 SC 1124: (1967)1 SCR 93].

**Action.** A legal process; a lawsuit; a formal complaint within the jurisdiction of a court of law for the enforcement or protection of a right, the redress or prevention of a wrong, or the punishment of a public offence.

"The primary sense of 'action' as a term of legal art is the invocation of the jurisdiction of a court by writ ...................." [*Herbert Berry Associates Ltd.* v *Inland Revenue Commissioner* (1999)1 WLR 1437, *per* Lord Simon of Glaisdale].

'Action' is a generic term, and means a litigation in a Civil Court for the recovery of individual right or redress of individual wrong, inclusive, in its proper legal sense, of suits by the Crown. [*A.G.* v *Bradlaugh* 14 QBD 667, *per* Brett, M.R.].

In English law, the term "action" is not used in the sense of an original proceeding only and "according to the legal meaning of the term, is a proceeding by which one party seeks in a court of justice to enforce some right against, or to restrain the commission of some wrong, by another party. More concisely it may be said to be 'the legal demand of a right' or 'the mode of pursuing a right to judgment'. It implies the existence of parties, of an alleged right, of an alleged infringement thereof (either actual or threatened) and a court having power to enforce such right." [Halsbury's *Law of England,* 3rd Ed., vol. 1, p. 2].

In English Limitation Act 1939, s. 31 the term "action" was clearly defined to include "any proceeding in a Court of Law". [*Lougher* v *Donovan* (1948)2 All ER 11; *W.T. Lamb & Sons* v *Rider* (1948)2 KB 331].

The expression "action", though a frequent visitor in the realm of English law and legislation, is probably a stray visitor in Indian legislations. But there should be no reason to think that it has been used in any restricted sense of original action only which ends with a decree or final order. A suit or similar original proceeding may end with the decree or the order; but if further legal actions in the shape of execution proceedings are necessary for the enforcement of such decree and order, those proceedings are also "actions" to enforce the right or claim granted by such decree or order. [*Urmila Bala Dasi* v *Probodh Chandra Ghosh* AIR 1989 Cal 283].

The word "action" is a word of very wide amplitude, much wider than the word "suit". [*Bharat Bank* v *General Insurance Co. Ltd.* AIR 1951 Punj 97].

NOTE: *'Action' and 'proceeding'—distinction.* 'Proceeding' is a word with a larger meaning than 'action'. Every action is a proceeding but it is not possible to say that every proceeding is an action. [*Roberts* v *Metropolitan Borough of Battersea* (1949)110 LT 568].


- **Abatement of action** p. 3.
- **Administrative action** p. 41.
- **Amicable action** p. 60.
- **Cause of action** p. 129.
- **Chose in action** p. 141.
- **Joinder of causes of action** p. 486.
- **Multiplicity of actions** p. 594.
- **Municipal action** p. 594.

- **Personal action** p. 659.
- **Real action** p. 727.
- **Relator action** p. 741.
- **Remedial action** p. 743.
- **Splitting cause of action** p. 807.

**Action in rem.** See under IN REM p. 441.

**Actionable.** Giving cause for legal action; furnishing legal ground for an action; remediable by an action at law; litigable; justiciable; chargeable; liable to prosecution; answerable.

**Actionable claim.** Means "a claim to any debt, other than a debt secured by mortgage of immovable property or by hypothecation or pledge of movable property, or to any beneficial interest in movable property not in the possession, either actual or constructive, of the claimant, which the Civil Court recognize as affording grounds for relief, whether such debt or beneficial interest be existent, accruing, conditional or contingent". [Transfer of Property Act 1882, s. 3].

NOTE: If s. 3 of the Transfer of Property Act is looked at, "an 'actionable claim' means a claim to any debt". [*Abu Mahomed* v *Chunder* (1909-10) ILR 36 Cal 345].

Actionable claim represents par excellence the type of property that a person can have by way of a contractual right. [*L. Bansidhar & Sons* v *C.I.T.* 1980 Tax LR 778].

Core of the definition of an "actionable claim" in s. 3 of the Transfer of Property Act is that a claimant should be entitled to knock at the door of a Court and the Court should recognise the claim for granting relief to him.

An 'actionable claim' can be assigned, but in order that there should be an actionable claim, there must be a debt in the sense of an existing obligation. [*Iron & Hardware Co.* v *Shamlal & Bros.* AIR 1954 Bom 423, *per* Chagla, C.J.].

*Actionable claim—what is and what is not—examples:* Breach of contract does not result in any existing obligation on the part of the person who commits the breach. So, the right to recover damages resulting from breach of contract is not an actionable claim and cannot be assigned. [*Abu Mahamed* v *Chunder* (1909-10) ILR 36 Cal 345; *Iron & Hardware Co,* v *Shamlal & Bros.* AIR 1954 Bom 423; *Baroda Cement & Chemicals Ltd.* v *Commissioner of Income-tax* (1986)158 ITR 636 (Guj): 1986 Tax LR 1261].

While a life insurance policy can be regarded as an 'actionable claim', a personal accident policy in which compensation is payable only if death is caused by accident cannot be regarded as 'actionable claim'. [*L. Bansidhar & Sons* v *C.I.T.* 1980 Tax LR 778].

Copyright is a chose in action in England but in India is a beneficial interest in movable property in the actual or constructive possession of the owner thereof. Although strictly not an actionable claim, but capable of being transferred by assignment evidenced by writing executed by the assignor or by his duly authorised agent, the writing containing such assignment need not be registered. [*Gramophone Company of India Limited* v *Shanti Films Corporation* AIR 1997 Cal 63].

A fixed deposit receipt can be assigned. If there is an assignment in writing and the instrument is handed over to the assignee and a notice of assignment of actionable claim has been given to the debtor, the assignment is complete. [(1978)14 Del LT 254].

**Actionable wrong.** The term "actionable wrong" means an illegal or unauthorised act infringing a legal right of another affording him a ground for action in law. [*W.W. Joshi* v *State of Bombay* AIR 1959 Bom 363: ILR (1959) Bom 1267].

NOTE: It is committed when a responsible person has neglected to use a reasonable degree of care for protection of another person from such injury as under existing circumstances should reasonably have been foreseen as a proximate consequence of that negligence.

A citizen of India is entitled to protections and guarantees enshrined in the Constitution and if these guarantees are infringed, it amounts to illegal and unauthorised act infringing a legal right of citizen. Where the petitioners who are citizens of India are challenging the orders of their dismissal on the ground of infringement of Art. 311(2) of the Constitution, the wrong complained of by the petitioners is an actionable wrong and they would be entitled to protection under Art. 226 of the Constitution.

[*W.W. Joshi* v *State of Bombay* AIR 1959 Bom 363: ILR (1959) Bom 1267].

**Active.** Busy doing things; lively and full of ideas; having or causing a chemical effect; abounding in action; agile; lively; brisk; being in or pertaining to a state of action; assiduous; busily employed; energetic; enterprising.

**Active account.** One against which many cheques are drawn and deposited.

**Active bonds.** Interest bearing bonds; bonds bearing a fixed rate of interest payable in full from the date of issue, and include bonds negotiable on the stock exchange.

**Active duty.** Service or action in the field or at sea in time of war; full military or naval status with pay and allowances.

**Active operations duty.** In Maritime law, it means a shipowner's obligation to provide safe working conditions, in the work areas controlled by the shipowner for the stevedore and longshoremen who are loading or unloading the ship. [Black's *Law Dictionary*, 7th Ed.].

**Active politics.** Means almost whole time in politics. [*Pyare Lal Sharma* v *Managing Director* AIR 1989 SC 1854: (1989)2 SCC 448: (1989)3 SCR 428: JT 1989(3) SC 133: 1989(4) SLR 1: (1989)3 SLJ 1: (1989)3 Comp LJ 70].

**Active service.** In relation to a force means the work of a member of the armed forces, especially during a war. A force shall be deemed to be on active service when engaged in operations against an enemy, when situated in an area in which such operations are taking place. A person shall be deemed to be on active service in or with a force which is on active service.

**Activity for profit.** This preposition has many shades of meaning but when used with the active participle of a verb it means "for the purpose of" and connotes the end with reference to which something is done. It is not therefore enough that as a matter of fact an activity results in profit but it must be carried on with the object of earning profit. Profit-making must be the end to which the activity must be directed or in other words, the predominant object of the activity must be making a profit. [*Additional Commissioner of Income Tax, Gujarat, Ahmedabad* v *Surat Art Silk Cloth Manufacturers' Association, Surat* AIR 1980 SC 387: (1980)2 SCR 77: (1980)2 SCC 31: (1980)121 ITR 1].

**Actual.** Existing in fact; real; accurate; absolute; authentic; *bona fide*; categorical; categorically true; correct; *de facto*; definite; positive; precise; realistic; substantive; tangible; unfallacious; well-founded; something real, in opposition to constructive.

NOTE: The word 'actual' does not, usually, advance the meaning. Speaking generally a thing is not more itself because it is spoken of as 'actual', nor is an act more done or enjoined because it is said or required, to be "actually" done. [*Gladstone* v *Padwick* LR 6 Ex 203].

But where a word has a constructive legal meaning not completely corresponding to the fact it indicates, then the addition of 'actual' will intensify that word, so that it will not be fully satisfied by such legal meaning. [*R.* v *St. Nicholas, Rochester* 3 LJ MC 45]. Thus, where a freeholder must have been in 'actual possession' to qualify for something, that means a possession in fact as distinguished from merely a possession in law. [*Murray* v *Throniley* 2 CB 217].

**Actual cost.** The actual price paid for goods by a party, in the case of real *bona fide* purchase, which may not necessarily be the market value of the goods. It is a general or descriptive term which may have varying meaning according to the circumstances in which it is used.

In the context of acquiring assets, it means what a person had, in fact, expended or laid out for the purpose of acquiring the depreciable assets. [*C.I.T.* v *Polychem Ltd.* (1975)98 ITR 574 (Bom) (DB)]. The expression includes price of the asset, preliminary and incidental expenses in acquisition and installation thereof. [*C.I.T.* v *JK Cotton Spg. & Wvg. Mills* (1975) Tax LR 506: (1975)98 ITR 153].

NOTE: The accepted accountancy rule for determining the cost of fixed assets is to include all expenditure necessary to bring such assets into existence and to put them in working condition. In case money is borrowed by a newly started company which is in the process of constructing and erecting its plant, the interest incurred before the commencement of production on such borrowed money can be capitalised and added to the cost of the fixed assets which have been created as a result of such expenditure. The above rule of accountancy should be adopted for determining the actual cost of the assets in the absence of any statutory definition or other indication to the contrary. [*Challapalli Sugar Ltd.* v *The Commissioner of Income Tax, A.P., Hyderabad* AIR 1975 SC 97: (1975)2 SCR 538: (1975)3 SCC 572: (1975)98 ITR 167]. 'Actual cost' is not the actual cost as originally determined at the time of acquisition of the assets. Actual cost may be subject to subsequent modifications and alterations. [*Saharanpur Electric Supply Co. Ltd.* v *CIT* (1992)2 SCC 736: (1992)194 ITR 294: (1992)1 SCR 117: JT 1992(1) SC 287].

**Actual damages.** Compensation for actual injuries or loss. [*Chappell* v *City of Springfield* Mo., 423 SW 2d 810, 814]. Damages that repay actual losses. It is also called Compensatory damages.

**Actual delivery.** It denotes the giving of real possession to the vendee or his servants or special agents who are identified with him in law and represent him. It is a formal immediate transfer of the property to the vendee. It "means delivery of goods to the purchaser or his agent, and delivery to the common carrier is not 'actual delivery'." [*Bengal Immunity Co. Ltd.* v *State of Bihar* (1955)2 SCR 803: AIR 1955 SC 681, *per* Venkatarama Ayyar, J.].

**Actual occupation.** It "means occupation in fact as distinguished from constructive occupation". [*Brewer* v *Papatoetoe Town Board* (1934) NZLR 774, 777, *per* Fair, J.].

The word 'actual' when used in conjunction with the word 'occupation' is effective to exclude any constructive, legal, or notional occupation which might otherwise arise, and which does not completely correspond to the fact which it indicates. [*Brewer* v *Papatoetoe Town Board,* supra].

**Actual possession.** In respect of a free holder, 'actual possession' means a possession in fact as distinguished from merely a possession in law. [*Murray* v *Throniley* 2 CB 217].

Where two or more are in possession, the 'actual possession' is that of the one who has the title. [*French* v *Gething* (1922)1 KB 236; *Canvey Island Commissioners* v *Preedy* (1922)1 Ch 179].

Actual or physical possession of goods does not require that the goods be grasped by the hand; the idea is satisfied if the goods are so placed that the possessor, or his agent, has the dominion and control over the goods so as to be able to prevent anyone else from removing or interfering with them. [*Charlesworth* v *Mills* (1982) AC 231, *per* Halsbury, C.].

**Actual residence.** The abode where one actually resides, not mere legal residence. It does not mean a temporary abiding place. [*Mohan Singh* v *Lijam Ram* AIR 1956 Punj 188].

**Actual seizure.** It means no more than seizure. [*Gladstone* v *Padwick* LR 6 Ex 2003].

**Actual service.** An act done personally by an individual; actual delivery of the notice or process to the person to whom it is directed. It is also termed 'personal service'.

**Actually delivered.** The expression "actually delivered" can only mean physical delivery of the goods, or such action as puts the goods in the possession of the purchaser, it does not contemplate mere symbolical or notional delivery. [*Shree Bajarang Jute Mills Ltd.* v *State of A.P.* (1964)6 SCR 691: (1964)2 SCJ 540: (1964)15 STC 430: AIR 1966 SC 376; *Bengal Timber Trading Co. Ltd.* v *Commissioner of Sales Tax, M.P.* AIR 1967 SC 1348: (1967)2 SCR 547: (1967)19 STC 366].

**Actually worked under an employer.** The expression "actually worked under the employer" must necessarily comprehend all those days during which the workmen was in the employment of the employer and for which he had been paid wages either under express or implied contract of service or by compulsion of statute, standing orders etc. [*Workmen of American Express International Banking Corporation* v *Management of American Express International Banking Corporation* (1985)4 SCC 71: AIR 1986 SC 458; referring to s. 25B(2)(*a*)(*ii*) of the Industrial Disputes Act 1947].

**Actuary.** An expert in statistics and probability theory, especially one who calculates insurance risks and premiums, mortality rates, and the like.

**Actus curiae neminem gravabit.** An act of the Court shall prejudice no one.

NOTE: This maxim is founded upon justice and good sense and affords a safe and certain guide for the administration of the law. As long as there remains a necessity, in any stage of the proceedings in an action, for an appeal to the authority of the Court, or any occasion to call upon it to exercise its jurisdiction, the court has, even where there has been some express arrangement between the parties, an undoubted right, and is, moreover, bound to interfere, if it perceives that its own process or jurisdiction is about to be used for purposes which are not consistent with justice. [*Wade* v *Simeon* 13 M&W 647].

There is no higher principle for the guidance of the Court than the one that no act of the Court should harm a litigant and it is the bounden duty of court to see that if a person is harmed by mistake of the court, he should be restored to the position he would have occupied but for the mistake. [*Jang Sing* v *Brij Lal* 65 Punj LR 884]. Upon this principle is based s. 144, Code of Civil Procedure 1908 (restitution).

**Actus dei nemini facit injuriam.** The act of God is prejudicial to no one.

NOTE: Duties are either imposed by law or undertaken by contract, and the ordinary rule of law is that when the law creates a duty, and the party is disabled from performing it, without any default of his own, by the act of God, the law excuses him, but when a party by his own contract creates a duty upon himself, he is bound to make it good, notwithstanding any accident by inevitable necessity.

**Actus legis nemini est damnosus.** An act in law shall prejudice no man. The law wrongs no man.

**Actus legis nemini facit injuriam.** The act of law injures no man.

**Actus non facit reum nisi mens sit rea.** The act itself does not constitute guilt unless done with a guilty intent.

NOTE: The maxim is a cardinal doctrine of the criminal law. The legislature, however, can create offences which consist solely in doing an act whatever the state of mind of the actor may be. Such cases should be regarded as exceptions to the general rule that a person cannot be convicted of a crime unless it is committed with a wrongful intention. [*Younghusband* v *Luftig* (1949)2 KB 354].

**Actus reus.** Result forbidden by law.

NOTE: In cases a man is able to show that his conduct whether in the form of action or inaction was involuntary, he is not to be held liable for any harmful result produced by it, it being an *actus reus*, but his defence is that he is not legally responsible for this *actus reus*. [Kenny on *Criminal Law*, 18th Ed., p. 27].

**A.D.** Anno Domini,—in the year of our Lord.

**Ad certum diem.** At a certain day.

**Ad curiam.** At a court.

**Ad hoc.** For a particular or special purpose (an ad hoc appointment).

It is a Latin expression which means 'for this'.

**Ad idem.** A Latin expression which means to the same point or matter; of the same mind.

NOTE: Negotiating parties are *ad idem* when they are quite agreed, so that a binding contract has been made between them. So long as a new term is put forward by one party and not accepted by the other, this cannot be. [Wharton's *Law Lexicon*].

Under s. 13 of the Indian Contract Act 1872 two or more persons are said to consent when they agree upon the same thing in the same sense. In other words, there must be *consensus ad idem*.

**Ad infinitum.** A Latin expression which means without limit; for ever; indefinitely.

**Ad interim.** A Latin expression which means for the intervening time; temporarily. During the intervening period; in the mean time.

**Ad litem.** For the suit; for the purpose of the suit; pending the suit.

NOTE: Order 32, r. 3 of the Code of Civil Procedure 1908, provides for the appointment of a guardian *ad litem* where the defendant is a minor.

• **Guardian ad litem** p. 402.

**Ad nauseam.** To an excessive or disgusting degree.

**Ad promisor.** A surety, guarantor.

**Ad quaestionem facti non respondent judices.** To questions of fact judges do not answer.

**Ad valorem.** According to the value; relates to taxes or duty or fee in proportion to the estimated value of the goods.

**Adalat.** Adalat means a court of justice.

Dewani Adalat means a civil court and Nizamat or Foujdari Adalat means a criminal court under the Company Rule. Sadar Dewani Adalat and Sadar Nizamat Adalat means respectively the High Court of Civil Jurisdiction and Criminal Jurisdiction.

• **Dewany adalat** p. 258.

**Adapt.** Adapt is to make fit (as for a specific or new use or situation) often by modifying; to adjust with some modification.

**Adaptation.** The act of adapting or fitting one thing to another; the state of being suited or fitted; the process of adapting or adjusting to new conditions; the change in the response of an organ of sense due to prolonged or repeated stimulation.

▸ *Meaning under the Copyright Act 1957, s. 2(a).* Adaptation means—(*i*) in relation to a dramatic work, the conversion of the work into a non-dramatic work; (*ii*) in relation to a literary work or an artistic work, the conversion of the work into a dramatic work by way of performance in public or otherwise; (*iii*) in relation to a literary or dramatic work, any abridgement of the work or any version of the work in which the story or action is conveyed wholly or mainly by means of pictures in a form suitable for reproduction in a book, or in a newspaper, magazine or similar periodical; (*iv*) in relation to a musical work, any arrangement or transcription of the work; and (*v*) in relation to any work, any use of such work involving its rearrangement or alteration.

**Adapted for use.** The word "adapted for use" must be construed as "suitable for use". [*Bolani Ores Ltd.* v *State of Orissa* AIR 1975 SC 17: (1975)2 SCR 138: (1974)2 SCC 777].

**Adapting for sale.** The expression points clearly to something being done to the article in question, which, in some way, makes it in itself a little different from what it was before. [*Cockram* v *Topical Preservation Co.* (1951)2 All ER 520].

**Addict.** As noun means a person who habitually uses a substance, esp. a narcotic drug [Black's *Law Dictionary*, 8th Ed.]; one who is habituated to some practice such as using alcohol or drugs.

As verb transitive means to apply or devote oneself persistently or habitually; with to; to cause to pursue or practice continuously; with to.

Addict means a person who habitually is given to a practice. [*Sunder Dumanna* v *Billimoria* AIR 1959 Bom 346: 60 Bom LR 1314].

**Additional.** The term embraces 'the idea of joining or uniting one thing to another, so as thereby to form one aggregate'. [*Ex parte Boddie* 21 SE 2d 4, 8; *Ashok Service Centre* v *State of Orissa* AIR 1983 SC 394: (1983)2 SCC 82: (1983)3 SCR 363: (1983)53 STC 1].

**Additional sales tax.** The additional sales tax is a tax upon sales of goods and not upon the income of a dealer. [*S. Kodar* v *State of Kerala* AIR 1974 SC 2272: (1974)4 SCC 422: (1974)34 STC 73: (1975)1 SCR 121].

The additional sales tax is in the nature of a surcharge over and above what is due and payable by an assessee under the principal Act. [*Ashok Service Centre* v *State of Orissa* AIR 1983 SC 394: (1983)2 SCC 82: (1983)2 SCR 363: (1983)53 STC 1].

**Address.** Generally, a place of business or residence. Place where mail or other communications will reach a person. [*Munson* v *Bay State Dredging & Contracting Co.* 50 NE 2d 633, 636].

• **Accommodation address** p. 15.

**Adduce.** To offer or bring forward for proof or consideration; to put forward for consideration (something) as evidence or authority.

**Ademption.** With respect to wills and estates, it means the destruction or extinction of a testamentary gift by reason of a bequeathed asset's ceasing to be part of the estate at the time of the testator's death; a beneficiary's forfeiture of a legacy or bequest that is no longer operative. [Black's *Law Dictionary*, 8th Ed.].

NOTE: If anything which has been specifically bequeathed does not belong to the testator at the time of his death, or has been converted into property of a different kind, the legacy is adeemed; that is, it cannot take effect, by reason of the subject-matter having been withdrawn from the operation of the will. [Indian Succession Act 1925, s. 152].

The rule of ademption of legacy applies to specific legacies and not to demonstrative legacies. [*Sabeb Mirza* v *Umed Khanum* 19 Cal 444].

**Adequate.** Sufficient for a specific purpose; lawfully and reasonably sufficient.

The *Words and Phrases* (Permanent Edition, Vol. 2) the word "adequate" has been defined at p. 545, thus: 'adequate' means fully equal to requirements or occasions, commensurate but in its primary and more popular significance nothing can be said to be 'adequate' which is not equal to what is required, suitable to the case or occasion, fully sufficient, proportionate, and satisfactory. [*Sonia Bhatia* v *State of U.P.* AIR 1981 SC 1274: (1981)3 SCR 239: (1981)2 SCC 585].

**Adequate consideration.** The word 'consideration' qualified by the word 'adequate' makes consideration stronger so as to make it sufficient and valuable having regard to the facts and circumstances of the case. Adequate consideration must postulate that consideration must be capable of being measured in terms of money value having regard to market price. [*Sonia Bhatia* v *State of U.P.* AIR 1981 SC 1274: (1981)2 SCC 585: (1981)3 SCR 239].

'Adequate consideration' generally is one which is a fair equivalent in value for benefit obtained ...... 'Adequate consideration' required in action for specific performance merely means that contract price must be substantially just and fair valuation under all circumstances. [*Sonia Bhatia* v *State of U.P.*, supra].

In the absence of a definition of the phrase "adequate consideration", the common parlance meaning of the term has to be accepted. The words "adequate consideration" have been held to denote consideration other than mere love and affection. When the law insists that there should be "adequate consideration" and not good consideration, it excludes mere love and affection. [*Tulsidas Kilachand* v *Commissioner of Income Tax, Bombay* AIR 1961 SC 1023: (1961)3 SCR 351: (1961)42 ITR 1: (1962)2 SCJ 500; *Major V.P. Singh* v *State of U.P.* AIR 1991 SC 1502: 1991 Supp (2) SCC 346: JT 1991(3) SC 14: (1993)199 ITR 188].

**Adha and Urdha.** The expression indicates a grant all below the surface as well as all on it or above it. [*Satya Niranjan* v *Ram Lal* 52 IA 109: AIR 1925 PC 42].

**Adhesive.** As noun means a substance that causes adhesion.

As adjective means have the quality of adhering; tending or causing to adhere; sticky; clinging; gummed.

NOTE: An adhesive thing tends to join itself to the surface of any other body with which it is placed in contact.

**Adhi.** A pledge or deposit, which may be of two kinds—*Gopya*, to be preserved entire and perfect, or *Bhogye* to be used or enjoyed. [Wilson's *Glossary*].

**Adhiar.** A cultivator who assists in cultivating land on condition of receiving half the crop. The meaning depends on facts. An adhiar may be a labourer or he may be a tenant. [Wilson's *Glossary; Emperor* v *Asimulla Mondal* AIR 1925 Cal 1068: 26 Cr LJ 651: 85 IC 939]. Very largely an adhiar is a tenant. [*Deb Nath Das Bairagi* v *Ram Sundar Barman* 19 CWN 1205: 31 IC 579].

**Adjacent.** Lying near or adjoining or close to; contiguous; neighbouring.

NOTE: 'Adjacent' is not a word to which a precise and uniform meaning is attached by ordinary usage and it is entirely a question of circumstances what degree of proximity will justify application of the word. In *Wellington* v *Lower Hutt* [(1904) AC 773], two boroughs in New Zealand, six miles apart at their closest, were held to be 'adjacent' for the purpose of making statutory contributions to the cost of building a bridge; but in *Stanward Corpn.* v *Denison Mines Ltd.* [67 DLR (2d) 743], two mining claims 1$^{1}/_{4}$ miles apart were held not to be 'adjacent'.

*'Adjacent' and 'adjoining'—distinction.* Adjacent differs from adjoining. Adjacent implies that the two objects are not widely separated, though they may not actually touch, whereas adjoining means that the two objects are so joined or united to each other that no third object intervenes.

**Adjective law.** Law regulating procedure for the enforcement of a right e.g., the law of evidence, the law regulating limitation of suits, law as to pleadings etc.

**Adjoining.** Touching; contiguous.

Adjoining implies meeting and touching at some point or line. When used in conjunction with the word 'land', the word 'adjoining' in its primary sense means that which lies near so as to touch in some part the land which it is said to adjoin. [*Re Ecclesiastical Commissioner* (1936) Ch 430].

Adjoining conveys that two things may adjoin which are not next to each other. [*Cave* v *Horsell* (1912)9 KB 533].

**Adjourn.** Put off; postpone; break off with the intention of resuming later.

The word 'adjourn' must be construed with reference to the object of the context, and with reference to the object of the enquiry. [*Fitzgerald's* case, LR 5 QB 1, 10, *per* Mellor, J.].

**Adjourn sine die.** An adjournment to a date that is not at the present moment fixed. [*Menaka Bala* v *Hiralal* AIR 1933 Cal 816: 37 CWN 583].

A Latin expression which means 'without date'.

NOTE: A legislative body adjourns *sine die* when it adjourns without appointing a day on which to appear or assemble again. [*State ex rel. Jones* v *Atterbury*, Mo, 300 SW 2d 806, 811].

**Adjournment.** A putting off or postponing of business or of a session until another time or place; the period or interval during which a session is put off.

NOTE: Unless the object of the context or inquiry otherwise warrants, the term 'adjournment' in connection with a meeting should be applied only to the case of a meeting which has already convened and which is thereafter postponed and not to a case where a notice convening a meeting is cancelled and subsequently, a notice for holding the same meeting on a later date is issued. [*Jayant Bhai Manubhai Patel* v *Arun Subodh Bhai Mehta* AIR 1989 SC 1289: (1989)2 SCC 484: JT 1989(3) SC 156: (1989)2 SCR 110].

**Adjudicate.** To rule upon judicially; decide judicially regarding a claim etc.; settle in the exercise of judicial authority.

**Adjudication.** Act of judgment; adjudgment; authoritative decision; determination of issues; judicial decision; reasoned judgment; the formal giving or pronouncing a judgment or decree in a cause.

The word implies a hearing by a court, after notice, of legal evidence on the factual issues involved in a case [*Genzer* v *Fillip* Tex Civ App, 134 SW 2d 730, 732] and contemplates that the claims of all the parties thereto have been considered and set at rest. [*Miller* v *Scobie* 11 So 2d 892, 894].

• **Administrative adjudication** p. 41.

**Adjunct.** Something joined or added to another thing but not forming part of it;

attached in a subordinate or temporary capacity; added as an accompanying object or circumstance.

**Adjust.** To bring to a more satisfactory state, settle, resolve; set off one against the other.

Rearrange, set right, regulate or equalise, so as to restore the balance. [*Re Buckinghamshire County Council* (1952)2 QB 515].

To arrive at a new agreement with a creditor for the payment of a debt.

**Adjustment.** The act, process, means, or result of adjusting; arrangement; settlement; an instrument or means whereby something may be adjusted.

A settlement of a claim or debt in a case in which the amount involved is uncertain or in which full payment is not made.

NOTE: A suit may be adjusted by any lawful compromise or agreement. [Code of Civil Procedure 1908, Or. 23, r. 3].

A decree may be adjusted under Or. 21, r. 2, CP Code by any lawful compromise. Such a contract may be either executed or executory. If the liability remains as before but conditional upon something to be done in future, that is not an adjustment which can be certified under Or. 21, r. 2. The adjustment must extinguish the liability either in full or in part. If the alleged adjustment creates a new decree which has to be executed not as an adjustment of the old decree, then it is not an adjustment within the meaning of Or. 21, r. 2. [*Md. Basir* v *Abdul Fazal* AIR 1965 Cal 209].

When there is a completed contract which immediately extinguishes and takes the place of the decree, such contract is an adjustment within the meaning of Or. 21, r. 2, CPC; where, on the one hand, there is only an agreement to adjust the decree on the fulfilment of a future condition, and the decree is left in existence pending the fulfilment of the conditions, on the other, there is no adjustment within the meaning of Or. 21, r. 2, CPC. [*Banko Das* v *Oddi Arjun* 215 IC 35: AIR 1944 Pat 279].

**Administration.** "Administration" means 'management of the affairs'. [*State of Kerala* v *Very Rev. Mother Provincial* AIR 1970 SC 2079: (1971)1 SCR 734: (1970)2 SCC 417].

The word 'administration' signifies the Government of the day or the governmental machine by which policy is implemented. By policy is meant formation of a general line or course of action—the idea of leadership and the taking of a major decision on a matter of discretion. [Garner's *Administrative Law* (1967)].

Administration in relation to an estate, in law means management and settling of that estate. It is a power to deal with the estate. [*R.B. Jodha Mal Kuthiala* v *Commissioner of Income Tax, Punjab, Jammu Kashmir, Himachal Pradesh, Patiala* AIR 1972 SC 126: (1972)1 SCR 639: (1971)3 SCC 369].

The word 'administration' means letters of administration of the personal estate and effects of a deceased person, whether general or limited, or with the will annexed or otherwise.

NOTE: Administration consists in (1) payment of funeral expenses of the deceased, (2) collection, realisation and preservation of assets, (3) payment of debts and legacies, (4) acts in respect of adverse claims to assets, (5) dealings with creditors and legatees and (6) distribution of assets among heirs and next of kin. [*Amir Bibi* v *Abdul* AIR 1928 Mad 760].

• **Letters of administration** p. 531.

**Administration bond.** A bond given to court under the provisions of s. 291 of the Indian Succession Act 1925.

**Administration durante absentia.** That which subsists during the absence of the executor, and until he has proved the will. [*In re Cassidy* (1932)162 ER 1477].

**Administration durante minori actate.** That which is granted when the executor is a minor. It continues till the minor attains the lawful age to act.

**Administration of justice.** The expression means exercise of judicial power to maintain and uphold rights and punish wrongs. [*Harinager Sugar Mills* v *Shyam Sundar* AIR 1961 SC 1669].

The expression 'administration of justice' may ordinarily, and in the absence of anything indicating any contrary intention, cover and include within its ambit several things as competent parts of it, namely, the constitution, organisation of court, jurisdiction and powers and the laws to be administered by the courts. [*State of Bombay* v *Narottamdas* 1951 SCR 51, 120].

The expression "administration of justice" must necessarily include the power to try suits and proceedings of a civil as well as criminal nature irrespective of who the parties to the suit or proceeding or what its subject-matter may be. This power must necessarily include the power of defining, enlarging, altering, amending and diminishing the jurisdiction of the courts and defining their jurisdiction of territorially and pecuniarily. [*Indu Bhusan De* v *State of West Bengal* AIR 1986 SC 1783: (1986)3 SCR 547: (1986)3 SCC 682: JT 1986 SC 129].

**Administration suit.** Administration suit is in essence one for accounts and application of the estate of the deceased for the satisfaction of the dues of all the creditors. [*Bahadurkhanji* v *Begum Mehrunnissa* AIR 1955 Sau 55].

NOTE: Order 20, r. 13, Code of Civil Procedure 1908, indicates how a decree is to be passed in an administrative suit.

An administration suit by an heir is essentially a suit for division of the assets left by the deceased. [*Kamalam* v *Saradambal* AIR 1953 Mad 576].

**Administrative action.** The term is capable of bearing a wide range of meanings. Generally speaking, the term refers to broad areas of governmental activities in which the repositories of power may exercise every class of statutory function. [*Subramanya* v *Joint Registrar* AIR 1965 AP 69: (1964)2 Andh LT 94].

NOTE: Administrative functions are of three kinds—executive, quasi-legislative, quasi-judicial. An executive act is purely an administrative act performed by an administrative authority or an 'agency' as it is termed in the American Administrative Procedure Act 1946. "The executive power connotes the residue of governmental functions that remain after legislative and judicial functions are taken away". [*Ram Jawaya* v *State of Punjab* (1955)2 SCR 225 (236)]. The quasi-legislative function or administrative legislation is subordinate legislation that makes rules, regulations and the like to fill in the details of legislative enactments. A quasi-judicial function resembles a judicial function; but it has not all the attributes of a judicial function. [*H.S. Mills* v *Shyam Sundar* AIR 1961 SC 1669, 1675].

**Administrative adjudication.** The process used by an administrative agency to issue regulations through an adversary proceeding. [Black's *Law Dictionary*, 8th Ed.].

The expression means the quasi-judicial function exercised by an administrative agency or body. The term 'adjudication' denotes the agency process for the formulation of an order and requires notice and adherence to procedure. The expression is now in common use in Administrative law.

**Administrative discretion.** A public official's or agency's power to exercise judgment in the discharge of its duties; a public official's power or right to act in certain circumstances according to personal judgment and conscience, often in an official or representative capacity. [Black's *Law Dictionary*, 8th Ed.].

This means that a determination may be reached, in part at least, upon the basis of considerations not entirely susceptible of proof or disproof. A statute is said to confer discretion when it refers an official for the use of his power to beliefs, expectations or tendencies instead of facts. These lack the degree of certainty. They involve matter of degree or an appeal to judgment. [Freund's *Administrative Powers over Persons and Property*, p. 71 (1928)].

**Administrative law.** Body of law created by administrative agencies in the form of rules, regulations, orders, and decisions.

'A first approximation to a definition of administrative law is to say that it is the law relating to the control of governmental power ... The governmental power in question is not that of Parliament: Parliament as the legislature is sovereign and beyond legal control. But the powers of all other public authorities are subordinated to the law, just as much in the case of the Crown and ministers as in the case of local authorities and other public bodies.' [*Administrative Law* by H.W.R. Wade, 5th Ed., p. 4].

NOTE: Administrative law is divided into three parts: (1) the statutes endowing agencies with powers and establishing rules of substantive law relating to those powers; (2) the body of agency-made law consisting of administrative rules, regulations, reports, opinions containing findings of fact, and orders; and (3) the legal principles governing the acts of public agents when those acts conflict with private rights. [Black's *Law Dictionary*, 8th Ed.].

**Administrative tribunal.** An administrative agency before which any matter may be heard or tried, as distinguished from a purely executive agency; an administrative agency exercising a judicial function. [Black's *Law Dictionary*, 8th Ed.].

Administrative tribunals stand somewhere between courts and administrative bodies. They are administrative bodies set up with the idea of discharging quasi-judicial duties.

NOTE: Constitutionally, they are recognised in Arts. 32, 136, 226 and 227. The words 'all courts and tribunals' in Art. 227 and the words 'any court or tribunal' in Art. 136 give to the system of administrative tribunals a firm constitutional base. 'They are governmental bodies appertaining to the executive and not to the judicial branch by the State, though in various matters they are armed with judicial powers analogous to those normally carried out by courts of law'. [*Bharat Bank Ltd.* v *Their Employees* AIR 1950 SC 188, 206].

**Administrator.** A person who manages or heads a business, public office, or agency; a person appointed by the court to manage the assets and liabilities of an intestate decedent. [Black's *Law Dictionary*, 8th Ed.].

▸ *Meaning under the Indian Succession Act 1925, s. 2(a).* A person appointed by a competent authority to administer the estate of a deceased person when there is no executor.

**Administratrix.** A woman who administers the estate of an intestate; a woman to whom letters of administration have been granted; a female administrator.

**Admiral.** A naval officer ranking with General in the army.

**Admiralty.** A court that exercises jurisdiction over all maritime contracts, torts, injuries, or offences; the system of jurisprudence that has grown out of the practice of admiralty courts. [Black's *Law Dictionary*, 8th Ed.].

**Admissible evidence.** Evidence that is relevant and is of such a character that the court should receive it. [Black's *Law Dictionary*, 8th Ed.]. Such evidence must not be unfairly prejudicial, based on hearsay, or privileged.

NOTE: Evidence is receivable by the court, only if it is both relevant and admissible. In general, all evidence which is relevant to an issue is admissible; and all that is irrelevant or insufficiently relevant, ought to be excluded. [*Hollington* v *Hewthorn & Co. Ltd.* (1943) KB 587].

**Admission.** Any statement or assertion made by a party to a case and offered against that party; an acknowledgment that facts are true. [Black's *Law Dictionary*, 8th Ed.].

An admission is a statement, oral or documentary, or contained in electronic form which suggests any inference as to any fact in issue or relevant fact, and which is made by any of the persons, and under the circumstances mentioned in ss. 18 to 20 of the Evidence Act. [Indian Evidence Act 1872, s. 17].

Admission is a concession or voluntary acknowledgement made by a party or someone identified with him in legal interest of the existence of certain facts which are in issue or relevant to an issue in the case. [*Ajodhya Prasad* v *Bhawani Shankar* ILR (1956)2 All 399: AIR 1957 All 1 (FB)].

NOTE: Admissions are of two kinds—(*a*) judicial admissions, and (*b*) extra judicial admissions. The former are formal admissions made by a party during the proceedings of the case and are fully binding on the party and can be made the foundation of the rights of the parties. Extra judicial admissions are only partially binding. [*Ajodhya Prasad* v *Bhawani Shankar* ILR (1956)2 All 399: AIR 1957 All 1 (FB)].

Admission by an accused in a criminal proceeding goes by the name of 'confession'. [*Korada Gedha* v *Raghabo Pati* AIR 1963 Ori 121 (DB)].

**Admit.** Admit means to accept as true or valid; to allow entry; to give entrance or access; acknowledge; permit; to allow to join or become associated with; let in.

To allow or let in; concede; acknowledge. [*Hundoji* v *State of A.P.* AIR 1956 AP 100: (1956)57 Cr LJ 577].

**Admitted in evidence.** A document can only be said to be admitted in evidence when it is formally proved and tendered in evidence. [*Gordhansingh* v *Suwalal* AIR 1959 Raj 156].

This expression in s. 36 of the Indian Stamp Act 1899 means the act of letting the document in as part of the evidence, as a result of the judicial determination of the question whether the document is admissible or not for want of stamp. [*Brij Raj* v *Raja Ram* AIR 1957 Hyd 35].

**Adolescent.** Between childhood and adulthood; the age which follows puberty and precedes the age of majority.

**Adoption.** Custody; fosterage; guardianship. It may also mean acknowledgement; admission; approbation; approval; assumption; co-optation; embracement; ratification; sanction.

To take into one's family the child of another and give him or her the rights, privileges, and duties of a child and an heir.

NOTE: The giving and receiving are absolutely necessary to the validity of an adoption (of a child), they are the operative part of the ceremony, being that part of it which transfers the body from one family to another; but the Hindu law does not require that there shall be any particular form so far as giving and acceptance are concerned; for a valid adoption all that the law requires is that the natural father shall be asked by the adoptive parent to give his son in adoption, and that the boy shall be handed over and taken for this purpose. [*L. Debi Prasad (dead) by LRs.* v *Smt. Tribeni Devi* AIR 1970 SC 1286: (1970)1 SCC 677: (1971)1 SCR 101].

Adoption among the Hindus is regulated by the Hindu Adoptions and Maintenance Act 1956. In its application to contracts, it means the process by which a person agrees to assume a contract previously made for that person's benefit.

**Adult.** A person who has reached the legal age of majority.

**Adulterate.** Debase especially foods by adding other or inferior substances.

An article of food is 'adulterated' when any substance, other than that which the article purports to be, is mixed with, or added to, or placed upon it, either to increase the bulk or weight or apparent size of the article, or to give it a deceptive appearance. [*Fitzpatrick* v *Kelly* LR 8 QB 337; *Roberts* v *Egerton* LR 9 QB 494].

▸*Meaning under the Prevention of Food Adulteration Act 1954, s. 2(ia).* An article of food shall be deemed to be adulterated—(*a*) if the article sold by a vendor is not of the nature, substance or quality demanded by the purchaser and is to his prejudice, or is not of the nature, substance or quality which it purports or is represented to be; (*b*) if the article contains any other substance which affects, or if the article is so processed as to affect, injuriously the nature, substance or quality thereof; (*c*) if any inferior or cheaper substance has been substituted wholly or in part for the article so as to affect injuriously the nature, substance or quality thereof; (*d*) if any constituent of the article has been wholly or in part abstracted so as to affect injuriously the nature, substance or quality thereof; (*e*) if the article had been prepared, packed or kept under insanitary conditions whereby it has become contaminated or injurious to health; (*f*) if the article consists wholly or in part of any filthy, putrid rotten, decomposed or diseased animal or vegetable substance or is insect-infested or is otherwise unfit for human consumption; (*g*) if the article is obtained from a diseased animal; (*h*) if the article contains any poisonous or other ingredient which renders it injurious to health; (*i*) if the container of the article is composed, whether wholly or in part, of any poisonous or deleterious substance which renders its contents injurious to health; (*j*) if any colouring matter other than that prescribed in respect thereof is present in the article, or if the amounts of that prescribed colouring matter which is present in the article are not within the prescribed limits of variability; (*k*) if the article contains any prohibited preservative or permitted preservative in excess of the prescribed limits; (*l*) if the quality or purity of the article falls below the prescribed standard or its constituents are present in quantities not within the prescribed limits of variability, which renders it injurious to health; (*m*) if the quality or purity of the article falls below the prescribed standard or its constituents are present in quantities not within the prescribed limits of variability but which does not render it injurious to health:

Provided that, where the quality of purity of the article, being primary food, has fallen below the prescribed standards or its constituents are present in quantities not within the prescribed limits of variability, in either case, solely due to natural causes and beyond the control of human agency, then, such article shall not be deemed to be adulterated within the meaning of this sub-clause.

*Explanation*.—Where two or more articles of primary food are mixed together and the resultant article of food, (*a*) is stored, sold or distributed under a name which denotes the ingredients thereof; and (*b*) is not injurious to health,then, such resultant article shall not be deemed to be adulterated within the meaning of this clause.

Under s. 2(*i*)(*f*) [now renumbered s. 2(*ia*)(*f*)] an article of food shall be deemed to be adulterated if the article consists wholly or in part of any filthy, putrid, disgusting, rotten, decomposed or diseased animal or vegetable substance or is insect-infested or is otherwise unfit for human consumption. The mere fact that any part of an article was insect-infested may not be conclusive proof of its being adulterated under sub-clause (*f*). Further proof that the article was unfit for human consumption is a must. [*Municipal Corporation of Delhi* v *Kacheroo Mal* AIR 1976 SC 394: (1976)2 SCR 1: (1976)1 SCC 412: 1976 Cr LJ 336: 1976 SCC (Cri) 30].

**Adulteration.** It means the infusion of some foreign substance. [*Francis* v *Maas* 3 QBD 341, *per* Cockburn, C.J.].

"When a simple article take tea has foreign ingredients added to it, like gypsum and prussian blue, which are not required for the process of preparing and drying it, but are added for the purpose of making it look green, that is adulteration". [*Roberts* v *Egerton* (1874) LR 9 QB 494, 500, *per* Blackburn, J.]

The ordinary sense of adulteration connotes the mixing of deleterious or other substance with the main and basic article, but the definition in the Calcutta Municipal Act 1923 has been widened to include even those articles where the contents do not include the basic substance either wholly or partly. [*Ballabhdas Agarwal* v *J.C. Chakraborty* AIR 1960 SC 576: (1960)2 SCR 739: 1960 Cr LJ 752: 1960 SCJ 1048].

**Adulterator.** A person who adulterates.

**Adultery.** Voluntary sexual intercourse between a married person and a person of opposite sex, married or not, other than his or her spouse during the subsistence of the marriage.

Adultery is defined as 'the sin of incontinence between two married persons, or it may be when only one of them is married.' [*Babineau* v *Babineau* (1924)4 DLR 951 (CA)].

NOTE: There can be adultery without complete penetration in the full sense of the word. [*C.* v *C.* (1943) NZLR 45, 48, *per* Callan, J.]. An attempt at sexual intercourse without complete penetration may amounts to adultery. [*Rutherford* v *Richardson* (1923) AC 1].

In its present day meaning, it has been held that artificial insemination by a donor does not constitute adultery. [*Maclennan* v *Maclennan* (1958) SLT 12].

- **Incestuous adultery** p. 443.
- **Living in adultery** p. 538.

**Advance.** Pay before it is due; furnish something before an equivalent is received; to supply beforehand.

'Advance' normally means the furnishing of money for some specific purpose. [*Burnes* v *Trade Credits* (1981)2 All ER 122].

The "word 'advances' is ambiguous and may either refer to prepayments of what will become due in future or be a polite euphemism for loans; but when 'advances' are declared to be 'repayable' (though only conditionally) they certainly lean to the side of loans". [*Lincolnshire Sugar Co. Ltd.* v *Smart* (1937) AC 697, *per* Lord Macmillan].

- **Secured advance** p. 782.

**Advantage.** Benefit, gain, especially benefit resulting from some course of action; position or condition of superiority.

**Adventure.** As noun means a hazardous or an unusual and exciting experience; a daring enterprise; a commercial speculation; a commercial undertaking having an element of risk.

As verb means to venture upon; take the chance of; to risk the loss of; imperil; to run risks; to venture upon daring or dangerous undertakings.

An adventure connotes a stray operation. [*Radha Devi* v *Commissioner of Income Tax* 55 CWN 734]. Any speculation is an adventure. [*Alexander* v *Commissioner of Income Tax* AIR 1953 Mad 166].

- **Joint adventure** p. 486.

**Adverse.** Opposing or opposed; antagonistic; hostile; detrimental; having an opposing or contrary interest, concern, or position.

Use of land is "adverse", as against owner, if it is not made in subordination to him, is open and notorious and is not wrongful as to him; "adverse" means that one making use shall not recognize in those as against whom it is claimed to be adverse an authority either to prevent or to permit its continuance, and refers to non-recognition of such authority at time use is made. [*Benson* v *Fekete* Mo, 424 SW 2d 729, 738].

**Adverse possession.** The use or enjoyment of real property with a claim of right when that use or enjoyment is continuous, exclusive, hostile, open and notorious. [Black's *Law Dictionary*, 8th Ed.].

Possession which is inconsistent with the right of a person who claims to be the true owner. Trespass does not constitute adverse possession. There must be real possession accompanied by intent to possess. It must be 'adverse' to the owner and must not be permissive. [*C.C. Bucks* v *Moran* (1989)3 WLR 152].

Means hostile possession which is expressly or impliedly in denial of the title of the true owner. Such possession must be actual and exclusive under a claim of right, adequate in continuity, in publicity and in extent, so as to show that it is adverse to the true owner. Such possession in denial of the title of the true owner must be peaceable, open and continuous. It must be open and hostile enough to be capable of being known to the party interested. [*Bhago* v *Deep Chand* AIR 1964 Punj 187].

NOTE: Ordinarily classical requirement of adverse possession is that it should be *nec vi, nec clan precario.* The possession required must be adequate in continuity, in publicity and in extent to show that it is adverse to competitor. But a co-heir in possession cannot render his possession adverse to the other merely by any secret hostile animus on his own part. [*P. Lakshmi Reddi* v *L. Lakshmi Reddi* AIR 1957 SC 314: 1957 SCR 195: 1957 SCA 197: 1957 SCJ 248: (1957)1 Andh WR 46; *Gazi Reazul* v *Mehbulal* (1980)2 CLJ 548].

Adverse possession or hostile title must be established by consistent course of conduct and it cannot be shown by stray or sporadic act; possession must be open and without any attempt at concealment. [*Kshitish Chandra*

*Bose* v *Commissioner of Ranchi* AIR 1981 SC 707: (1981)2 SCR 764: (1981)2 SCC 103].

To make an adverse possession effective against co-sharer ouster is necessary. Non-participation of profit is no ouster. [*Karbalai Begum* v *Md. Sayeed* AIR 1981 SC 77: 1980 All LJ 902].

The right to property is extinguished by adverse possession under s. 27 of the Limitation Act 1963.

**Adverse witness.** A witness who is biased against the examining party, who is willing to testify, or who is identified with an adverse party. [Black's *Law Dictionary*, 8th Ed.].

A witness whose mind discloses a bias to the party calling him. Under the Common Law Procedure Act 1854, an adverse witness is one who, in the opinion of the presiding Judge, is hostile. [*Rice* v *Howard* 16 QBD 681]. It is also termed hostile witness.

NOTE: Under s. 154 of the Indian Evidence Act 1872 a party calling a witness may cross-examine him as hostile. The adverse witness may be asked leading questions (s. 143); or questions as to his previous statements in writing (s. 145); or any questions under s. 146; or his credit may be impeached (s. 155). And this can be done with the leave of the Judge.

**Advertisement.** A public notice, as in a newspaper or on a radio or television programme; a giving notice, notification, information.

Notice given in a manner designed to attract public attention. [*Edwards* v *Lubbock County* Tex Civ App, 33 SW 2d 482, 484].

Information communicated to the public, or to an individual concerned, as by handbills, newspaper, television, billboards, radio. [*First Nat. Corporation* v *Perrine* 43 P 2d 1073, 1077].

NOTE: Advertisement includes any notice, circular, label, wrapper or other document, and any announcement made orally or by means of producing or transmitting light, sound or smoke. [Drugs and Magic Remedies (Objectionable Advertisement) Act 1954, s. 2(a)].

**Advice.** View; opinion; guidance offered by one person to another.

An opinion expressed as to wisdom of future conduct. [*Hughes* v *Van Bruggen* 105 P 2d 494, 496].

Advice implies real or pretended knowledge or experience, often professional or technical, on the part of the one who advises.

• **Railway advice** p. 724.

**Advice, letter of.** A letter from one merchant or banker to another, giving information of business transactions.

**Advice note.** A document given to a purchaser of goods to inform him that the goods have been despatched to him.

**Advocate.** A person who defends or pleads for another; a professional pleader in a court of justice; a person learned in the law, and duly admitted to practice.

NOTE: A person in order to be termed as an advocate must not only possess a degree in law but must have his name entered in any roll maintained under the Advocates Act, *viz.*, either the roll maintained by the Bar Council of India or the roll maintained by the State Bar Councils termed as State Roll. [*Aparna Mallik* v *Bar Council of India* AIR 1983 Cal 37: 87 CWN 170].

**Advocate General.** An officer appointed by the Governor of a State to advise the State Government upon legal matters and to represent it in court.

NOTE: The Governor of a State can appoint a person fit for the judgeship of a High Court to be Advocate General for the State. It is the duty of the Advocate General to give advice to the State Government upon legal matters and to perform such legal duties as may be assigned to him by the Governor. The Advocate-General has the right to speak in and participate in the proceeding of a State Legislature, but he is not entitled to vote. [Constitution of India, Arts. 165 and 177].

**Aerodrome.** Airfield; airport; a place for landing and departure of aircraft.

▸ *Meaning under the Aircraft Act 1934, s. 2(2).* Aerodrome means any definite or limited ground or water area intended to be used, either wholly or in part, for the landing or departure of aircraft, and includes all buildings, sheds, vessels, piers and other structures thereon or appertaining thereto.

**Affairs of State.** Affairs of State include any matter of public nature with which the State is concerned or the disclosure of which will be prejudicial to the public service. The exclusion is not confined to official communications or documents but extends to all others likely to prejudice the public interest. [*Asiatic Petroleum Co.* v *Anglo-Persian Co.* (1916)1 KB 822].

▸*Meaning under the Indian Evidence Act 1872, s. 123.* In the latter half of the Nineteenth Century affairs of State may have had a comparatively narrow content. Having regard to the notion about governmental functions and duties which then obtained, affairs of State would have meant matters of political or administrative character relating, for instance, to national defence, public peace and security and good neighbourly relations. Thus, if the contents of the documents were such that their disclosure would affect either the national defence or public security or good neighbourly relations they would claim the character of a document relating to the affairs of State. There may be another class of documents which could claim the said privilege. If the proper functioning of the public service would be impaired by the disclosure of any document or class of documents such document or class of documents may also claim the status of documents relating to public affairs. When the Act was passed the concept of governmental functions and their extent was limited and so was the concept of the words "affairs of State" correspondingly limited. With the change in time, the concept of governmental functions has changed. The inevitable consequence of the change in the concept of the functions of the State is that the State in pursuit of its welfare activities undertakes to an increasing extent activities which were formally treated as purely commercial, and documents in relation to such commercial activities undertaken by the State in the pursuit of public policies of social welfare are also apt to claim the privilege of documents relating to the affairs of State. [*State of Punjab* v *Sodhi Sukhdev Singh* AIR 1961 SC 493: (1961)2 SCR 371: (1961)2 SCJ 691: (1961)1 SCA 434].

**Affect.** To produce an effect upon; to produce a material influence upon or alteration in; to make an impression on, influence; to produce a change; prevail upon; act on; bear upon; cause to vary.

The word 'affect' is a word of wide import. In the context of its occurrence, it may be construed to mean 'touch' or 'relate to' or 'concern'. [*Daniraiji Vrajlalji, Junagadh* v *Maharaj Shri Chandraprabha* AIR 1975 SC 784: (1975)3 SCR 32: (1975)1 SCC 612].

**Affidavit.** A written statement confirmed by oath, for use as evidence in court.

A written or printed declaration or statement of facts, made voluntarily, and confirmed by the oath or affirmation of the party making it, taken before a person having authority to administer such oath or affirmation. [*State* v *Knight* 549 P 2d 1397, 1401].

A sworn statement in writing made especially under oath or on affirmation before an authorised Magistrate or officer. [*M. Veerabhadra Rao* v *Tek Chand* 1984 (Supp) SCC 571: AIR 1985 SC 28: (1985)1 SCR 1003].

**Affidavit of service.** An affidavit certifying the service of a writ, notice, summons, or other documents or process.

**Affiliation.** The act or process of affiliating or being affiliated, allied, or associated, with another person, body or organisation; friendly relationship; connection; combination; union.

> NOTE: Affiliation imports less than membership in an organisation, but more than sympathy, and a working alliance to bring to fruition the proscribed programme of a proscribed organisation, as distinguished from mere co-operation with a proscribed organisation in lawful activities, is essential. [*Bridges* v *Wixon Cal*, 326 US 135: 89 L Ed 2103].

**Affinity.** A close agreement; relation; spiritual relation or attraction held to exist between certain persons. [*State ex inf. Norman* v *Ellis* 28 SW 2d 363, 367].

Relation which one spouse because of marriage has to blood relatives of the other. [*State* v *Hooper* 37 P 2d 52].

The connection existing in consequence of marriage, between each of the married persons and the kindred of the other. [*Kest* v *Lewis* 159 NE 2d 449, 450].

> NOTE: Affinity is distinguished into three kinds—(1) Direct, or that subsisting between the husband and wife's relations by blood, or between the wife and the husband's relations by blood, (2) Secondary, or that which subsists between the husband's and his wife's relations by marriage, (3) Collateral, or that which subsists between the husband and the relations of the wife's relations. [Wharton's *Law Lexicon*].

**Affirm.** Make a formal declaration; confirm; ratify; assert strongly; state as a fact.

In the context of appellate courts, to confirm a judgment, decree or order means to declare as valid and correct the judgment, decree or order delivered by the lower court.

**Affirmanti non neganti incumbit probatio.** The burden of proof lies upon him who affirms, not upon him who denies. The reason is not that it is impossible to prove a negative, but that a negative does not admit of the simple and direct proof of which an affirmative is capable. [Taylor on *Evidence*, 12th Ed., vol. I, p. 252].

**Affirmation.** A solemn and formal declaration by a person who conscientiously declines to take an oath; a solemn assertion that an affidavit is true.

**Afforestation.** The act of turning ground into a forest.

**Affray.** The fighting, by mutual consent, of two or more persons in some public place, to the terror of onlookers. [Black's *Law Dictionary*, 8th Ed.].

▸ *Meaning under the Indian Penal Code 1860, s. 159.* When two or more persons, by fighting in a public place, disturb the public peace, they are said to "commit an affray".

> NOTE: To be an affray, the fighting must be mutual. If one person unlawfully attacks another who resorts to self-defence, the first is guilty of assault and battery, but there is no affray.

**Affreightment.** The contracting of a ship to carry goods.

A contract made either by a charterparty or by a bill of lading, by which a shipowner agrees to carry goods in his ship for reward.

**Aforethought.** Premediated; deliberate; *e.g.*, malice aforethought.

**After.** Later; succeeding; subsequent to; inferior in point of time or of priority or preference.

Subsequent in time to [*Cheney* v *National Surety Corporation* 10 NYS 2d 706]; on and after. [*New York Trust Co.* v *Portland Ry. Co.* 189 NYS 346, 348].

> NOTE: Where an act has to be done within so many days after a given event, the day of such event is not to be reckoned and the party to do the act has the whole of the last day of the prescribed time in which to do it. [Stroud's *Judicial Dictionary*, 5th Ed.].

**After sight.** The expression "after sight" means, in a promissory note, after presented for sight, and, in a bill of exchange, after acceptance, or noting for non-acceptance, or protest for non-acceptance. [Negotiable Instruments Act 1881, s. 21].

**Afternoon.** It may mean the whole time from noon to midnight; or it may mean the earlier part of that time, as distinguished from the evening. The meaning must be determined by the context.

**Agachha.** Useless or valueless for fruit bearing or timber purposes [*Nathuni Rai* v *Rameshwar* AIR 1924 Pat 147].

**Age.** The length of time that a person or thing has existed or is likely to exist; a particular point in or part of one's life, often as a qualification, e.g., old age, era, interval of years, stage of life, term of life.

NOTE: In calculating a person's age, the day of his birth must be counted as a whole day and he attains the specified age on the day preceding, the anniversary of his birthday. [*Prabhu Dayal Sesma* v *State of Rajasthan* AIR 1986 SC 1948: (1986)3 SCR 665: (1986)4 SCC 59: JT 1986 SC 256: 1986 SCC (Cri) 411: 1986(3) SLR 48].


- **Lawful age** p. 518.
- **Legal age** p. 524.


**Age of consent.** Age at which persons may marry without parental approval; age at which a girl is legally capable of agreeing to sexual intercourse and before which sexual relations with her, regardless of her consent, constitute statutory rape.

**Agent.** One who transacts business for another; a person who acts for another; one who acts as broker and provides a specified service, *e.g.*, estate agent, travel agent; a means by which something is done; any force or substance having power to effect a material change in bodies.

▸ *Meaning under the Indian Contract Act 1872, s. 182.* 'An "agent" is a person employed to do any act for another or to represent another in dealings with third persons. The person for whom such act is done, or who is so represented, is called the "principal".

NOTE: The essential point about an agent's position is his power of making the principal answerable to third persons. A person does not become an agent on behalf of another merely because he gives him advice in matters of business. [*Mohesh Chandra Bosu* v *Radha Kishore Bhattacharjee* (1908)12 CWN 28, 32]. Nor is a person referred to in a contract as agent an agent if by the terms of the contract the relationship is one of principal and principal. [*Superintendent of Stamps, Bombay* v *Breul & Co.* (1944)46 Bom LR 686].

The law of partnership has often been stated to be a breach of the general law of principal and agent and s. 18 of the Indian Partnership Act 1932 expressly recognises that doctrine when it lays down that 'a partner is the agent of the firm for the purposes of the business of the firm.'

▸ *Meaning under the Limitation Act 1963, Art. 4.* The 'agent' within the meaning of the article is a person employed to do any act for another or to represent another in dealings with third persons. Contract of agency need not be created by a written document. It may be inferred from the circumstances and the conduct of the parties. [*Benaras Hindu University* v *Gokul Das* 1986 All LJ 31, *per* B.D. Aggarwal, J.].

▸ *Meaning under the Representation of the People Act 1951.* An agent is ordinarily a person authorised by a candidate to act on his behalf on a general authority conferred on him by the candidate. Ordinarily, the agent is the understudy of the candidate and has to act under the instructions given to him, being under his control. [*Chandrakanta Goyal* v *Sahan Singh Jodh Singh Kohli* AIR 1996 SC 861: (1996)1 SCC 378: (1996)1 SCJ 284: JT 1995(9) SC 114].

Under the Act 1951, an agent includes not only a person, who has been specifically engaged by the candidate as his election agent to work for him in the election but also a person who does in fact work for him and whose services have been accepted by the candidate. The expression 'agent' as defined in Expl. I to s. 123 of the Act 1951 includes an election agent, a polling agent and any person who is held to have acted as an agent in connection with the election with the consent of the candidate. For the purposes of the Act, the expression agent has a much wider connotation that it is ordinarily understood to have under the law of contract. [*Nani Gopal Swami* v *Abdul Hamid Chaudhury* AIR 1959 Assam 200 (DB); *Hazoora Singh* v *Commissioner of Income Tax* (1986)160 ITR 746].

▸ *Meaning under the Mines Act 1952, s. 2(c).* 'Agent' when used in relation to a mine means any person whether appointed as such or not, who acts as the representative of the owner in respect of the management of the mine or of any part thereof, and as such superior to a manager under this Act.

NOTE: *'Servant' and 'agent'—distinction.* A servant acts under the direct control and supervision of the master, and is bound to conform to all reasonable orders given him in the course of his work ... An agent though bound to exercise his authority in accordance with all lawful instructions which may be given to him from time to time by his principal, is not subject in its exercise to the direct control or supervision of the principal. [*Chandi Prasad Singh* v *State of Uttar Pradesh* AIR 1956 SC 149].

It is permissible for the principal to give detailed instruction to the agent. A delegated authority, however, exercises a substantial measure of freedom and acts according to his own discretion. [*Municipal Council* v *Prabhu Narain* AIR 1968 Raj 297].


- **Commission agent** p. 157.
- **Del credere agent** p. 244.
- **Duly authorised agent** p. 286.
- **Forwarding agent** p. 370.
- **General agent** p. 383.
- **Insurance agent** p. 469.
- **Mercantile agent** at p. 574.
- **Recognized agent** p. 735.
- **Special agent** p. 804.


**Agent of necessity.** Agency of necessity arises in a limited number of cases where, by reason of an emergency (1) the relation of principal and agent is deemed to exist between persons not otherwise in contractual relations or (2) authority to act on behalf of another is implied as between persons already in contractual relations. The authority arises only under necessity; and, if questioned, it will lie upon the party contracting with the agent to show that such was the nature of the circumstances. [Halsbury's *Laws of England*, 4th Ed., vol. 1, para 724, pp. 432-433].

**Agent provocateur.** A spy; a secret agent hired to penetrate an organisation to gather evidence against its members or to incite trouble.

A person who entices another to commit an express breach of law—which breach the other person would not otherwise have committed and who then proceeds to inform against the other person, in respect of such an offence. [*R.* v *Mealey and Sheridan* (1975)60 Cr App R 59].

**Aggrieved.** Having a grievance; injured; damnified; having suffered loss or injury.


- **Party aggrieved** p. 644.
- **Person aggrieved** p. 657.


**Aggrieved person.** A man who has suffered a legal grievance—a man against whom a decision has been pronounced, which has wrongfully deprived him of something or wrongfully refused him something or wrongfully affected his title. [*Re Sidebotham* (1880)24 Ch D 458].

The expression 'aggrieved person' means a person who has got a legal grievance, i.e. a person is wrongfully deprived of anything to which he is legally entitled and not merely a person who suffered some sort of disappointment. [*Gopal Prasad Chourasia* v *Prasanna Kumar Shrivastava* 1999 Jab LJ 478, 487 (MP) (DB)].

A person can be said to be aggrieved, if apart from the general interest of such a person as a member of the public may have, he has particular or special interest in the subject-matter supposed to be wrongly decided. [*Thiruvengadam* v *Muthu Chettiar* AIR 1970 Mad 34, 37].

The expression does not mean a person who suffers from psychological or imaginary injury. A person aggrieved must necessarily be one whose right or interests are affected, or jeopardised. [*Gram Sabha* v *Ram Raj Singh* 1968 AWR (HC) 844].

The expression "aggrieved person" denotes an elastic, and to an extent, an elusive concept. It cannot be confined within the bounds of a rigid, exact and comprehensive definition. At best, its features can be described in a broad tentative manner. Its scope and meaning depends on diverse, variable factors such as the content and intent of the statute of which contravention is alleged, the specific circumstances of the case, the nature and extent of the petitioner's interest, and the nature of the prejudice or injury suffered by him. English courts have sometimes put a restricted and sometimes a wide construction on the expression "aggrieved person". [*Jasbhai Motibhai Desai* v *Roshan Kumar, Haji Bashir Ahmed* AIR

1976 SC 578: (1976)3 SCR 58: (1976)1 SCC 671].

**Agio.** It relates to money-changing. The percentage charged for changing paper money into cash, or an inferior for a more valuable currency; the excess value of one currency over another.

**Agnate.** A relative whose kinship is traceable exclusively through males; a paternal kinsman.

'Agnate' means a person whose relation to the deceased can be traced without the intervention of a female. [*Ahmad Dar* v *Mukhti* AIR 1951 J&K 21].

▸ *Meaning under the Hindu Succession Act 1956, s. 3(a).* One person is said to be an agnate of another if the two are related by blood or adoption wholly through males.

**Agrarian.** Relating to land or to a division or distribution of land; of or relating to fields or lands or their tenure; of or relating to, or characteristic of the farmer or his way of life.

**Agrarian reform.** The expression includes ameliorative measures for agriculturists unrelated to rights in land. [*V.N. Narayanan Nair* v *State of Kerala* AIR 1971 Ker 98].

Agrarian reform includes elimination of concentration of agricultural wealth and means of production in a few private hands, raising of economic standards and bettering rural health and social conditions, distribution of land to the landless, development of rural economy, reservation of land for promotion of agricultural production. Where general scheme of legislation is definitely for any of these purposes, that is to say, for an agrarian reform, and under its provisions something ancillary thereto in the interest of rural economy has to be undertaken to give full effect to the reform, that would also fall under the expression 'agrarian reform'. [*Godavari Sugar Mills* v *Kamble* 77 Bom LR 261, 286, 289].

Agrarian reform, the Supreme Court observed [*Kannan Devan Hills Produce Co. Ltd.* v *State of Kerala* AIR 1972 SC 2301: (1972)2 SCA 455], is wider than land reform. It includes besides land reform something more and that something more is illustrated by the definition of "common purpose" which runs as under:

"'Common purpose' means any purpose in relation to any common need, convenience or benefit of the village and includes the following purposes: (*i*) extension of the village Abadi; (*ii*) providing income for the Panchayat of the village concerned for the benefit of the village community; (*iii*) village roads and paths; village drains; village wells, ponds or tanks; village water courses or water channels; village bus stands and waiting places; manure pits; hada rori; public latrines; cremation and burial grounds; panchayat ghar; jani ghar; grazing grounds; tanning places; mela grounds; public places of religious or charitable nature; and (*iv*) schools and playgrounds, dispensaries, hospitals and institutions of like nature, water-works or tube-wells whether such schools, playgrounds, dispensaries, hospitals, institutions, water-works or tube-wells may be managed and controlled by the State Government or not."

The definition of "common purpose" has been sustained by the Supreme Court in *Ranjit Singh* v *State of Punjab* [AIR 1965 SC 632: (1965)1 SCR 82].

NOTE: 'Agrarian reform' is more humanist than mere land reform and, scientifically viewed, covers not merely abolition of intermediary tenures, Zamindaris and the like but restructuring of village life itself, taking in its broad embrace the socio-economic regeneration of the rural population [*State of Kerala* v *G.R. Silk Mfg. (Wvg.) Co.* AIR 1973 SC 2734: (1973)2 SCC 713] and thus covers creation of economic unit of rural production, establishment of adequate credit system, implementation of modern production in techniques, construction of irrigation systems and adequate drainage, making available fertilizers, fungicides, herbicides and other methods of intensifying and increasing agricultural production, providing readily available means of communication and transportation, to facilitate proper marketing of the village produce, putting up of silos warehouses, etc. to the extent necessary for preserving produce and handling it so as to bring it conveniently within the reach of the consumers when they need it, training of village youth in modern agricultural practices with a view to maximising production and help solve social problems that are found in relation to the life of the agricultural community. [*State of Kerala* v *G.R. Silk Mfg. (Wvg.) Co.*, supra].

**Agree.** To admit, concede; to settle terms by common consent, arrange; to give assent, accede; to come to terms; to be of one mind.

**Agreed rent.** Rent agreed to between the parties, not any unilateral demand to which the tenant has not consented. [*S. Venkataramanaswami Ayyar* v *Abdul Wahab* AIR 1969 Mad 473: (1969)1 MLJ 122].

**Agreement.** An arrangement between parties as to a course of action; mutual understanding; a coming together of minds.

It is a contract between parties who are subjected to certain obligations or to whom the contemplated rights are thereby secured.

By the contraction of two words 'aggregatio' and 'mentium' and by the short pronunciation of them, one word is made, viz., 'aggreamentum', which is no other than an union, collection, copulation, and conjunction of two or more minds in anything done or to be done. [*Foster* v *Wheeler* 36 Ch D 698].

Though 'agreement' signifies primarily a contract, that is, a legally binding arrangement between two or more persons, by which rights are acquired by one or more to acts or forbearances on the part of the other or others [*Re Symon, Public Trustee* v *Symon* (1944) SASR 102, 110, *per* Mayo, J.], it is a broader term and may lack an essential element of a contract.

The term 'agreement' is used in law in two different senses. It may mean either a provisional arrangement or a concluded bargain. Whether it is intended to be the one or the other depends on the contract in which the word occurs and, when there is ambiguity, on the surrounding circumstances as well. [*Shamji Baih* v *Jagoo Hemchand Shah* ILR (1949) Nag 581].


- **Arbitration agreement** p. 73.
- **Hire-purchase agreement** p. 418.
- **International agreement** p. 474.


**Agricultural.** Of or pertaining to agriculture; connected with husbandry or tillage of the ground. [*Meenakshamma* v *Commissioner of Wealth Tax* AIR 1967 AP 189].

**Agricultural land.** Land ordinarily used for the purpose of agriculture or for purposes subservient to or allied to agriculture. [*Meenakshamma* v *Commissioner of Wealth Tax* AIR 1967 AP 189].

Agricultural land must be land which could be said to be either actually used, or ordinarily used, or meant to be used for agricultural purposes. In other words, 'agricultural land' must have a connection with an agricultural use or purpose. [*Commissioner of Wealth Tax, A.P.* v *Court of Wards, Paigah* 1976 Tax LR 952: (1976)3 SCC 864: (1977) SCJ 21: (1977)1 SCR 146].

It means land which is used or is capable of being used for agricultural purposes. Land which was once agricultural but which at the relevant time is being used as an aerodrome for military purposes after requisition by Government cannot be termed as agricultural land. [*Krishna Rao* v *Third Wealth Tax Officer* AIR 1963 Mys 111].

**Agricultural produce.** Agricultural produce includes all produce of agricultural or horticultural and all articles of food or drink wholly or partly manufactured from any such produce and fleeces and skins of animals. [Agricultural Produce (Grading and Marking) Act 1937, s. 2(*a*)].

▸*Meaning under the Warehousing Corporations Act, 1962, s. 2(a).* Agricultural produce means any of the following classes of commodities, namely—(*i*) foodstuffs, including edible oil-seeds; (*ii*) cattle fodder, including oil-cakes and other concentrates; (*iii*) raw cotton, whether ginned or unginned, and cotton-seed; (*iv*) raw jute; and (*v*) vegetable oils.

Agricultural produce as used in C.P. Code is confined to growing crop standing on the land on which it has grown or cut crop lying on the threshing floor or fodder stack. Once the grain is separated from the chaff, it ceases to remain agricultural produce. [*Bhabhoot Singh* v *Ganshyam* AIR 1962 Raj 82 contra *Union Bank of India, Guntur* v *D. Venkataramiah* AIR 1985 AP 375].

Agricultural produce is the produce of the land resulting from the application of human effort to the land in the shape of manuring, tilling, ploughing, planting, sowing, watering, weeding, pruning, harvesting, etc., Forest trees of spontaneous growth cannot be regarded as agricultural or horticultural produce grown on land. [*Ramkrishniah* v *State* AIR 1957 AP 28].

Agricultural produce mean the thing grown on land and would not include an animal, insect or worm fed on the crop raised on the land. Cocoons are reared on mulberry leaves grown on land, but merely because of that it does not mean that cocoons would be agricultural produce. They are not at all agricultural produce. [*State of Karnataka* v *Krishna Gowda* (1982)2 Kant LJ 589 (DB)].

**Agriculture.** The primary sense in which the term agriculture is understood is agar—field and cultra—cultivation, i.e., the cultivation of the field, and if the term is understood only in that sense agriculture would be restricted only to cultivation of the land in the strict sense of the term meaning thereby, tilling of the land, sowing of the seeds, planting and similar operations on the land. They would be the basic operations and would require the expenditure of human skill and labour upon the land itself. There are however other operations which have got to be resorted to by the agriculturist and which are absolutely necessary for the purposes of effectively raising the produce from the land. They are operations to be performed after the produce sprouts from the land, e.g., weeding, digging the soil around the growth, removal of undesirable undergrowths and all operations which foster the growth and preserve the same not only from insects and pests but also from depredation from outside, tending, pruning, cutting, harvesting, and rendering the produce fit for the market. The latter would all be agricultural operations when taken in conjunction with the basic operations above described. It is only if the products are raised from the land by the performance of basic operations that the subsequent operations attach themselves to the products of the land and acquire the characteristic of agricultural operations. The term "agriculture" has got to be understood as connoting this integrated activity of the agriculturist. [*Commissioner of Income Tax* v *Raja Benoy Kumar Sahas Roy* AIR 1957 SC 768: 1957 SCJ 740: (1957)32 ITR 466: 1958 SCR 101].

> NOTE: Horticulture, which denotes the cultivation of garden or orchards, is a species of agriculture in its primary and more general sense. [*Murugesa Chetti* v *Chinnathambi Goundan* (1901) ILR 24 Mad 421].
>
> Horticulture is included in the definition of 'agriculture' for the purpose of Urban Land (Ceiling and Regulation) Act 1976. [*Strichand Jain* v *Competent Authority* AIR 1993 All 19: 1993 All LJ 68].

**Agriculturist.** A person who cultivates the soil and rears animals; a person who performs services on farm; a person who is engaged in farming as the leading pursuit.

▸*Meaning under the Civil Procedure Code 1908, s. 60(i), Proviso cls. (b) and (c).* The provisions of cl. (*b*) in the case of an agriculturist suggest a person who tills the soil in order to maintain himself. The word 'agriculturist' under cl. (*c*) must carry the same meaning as the word 'agriculturist' in cl. (*b*). Even if it is not necessary that a person must till the land with his own hands to come within the meaning of the word agriculturist, he must at least show that he was really dependent for his living on tilling the soil and was unable to maintain himself otherwise. Where a person is an agriculturist in the widest sense of the term, he is not an agriculturist within the meaning of the clauses, if he is not really dependent for his maintenance on tilling the soil and is liable to maintain himself otherwise. [*Shrimant Appasaheb Tuljaram Desai* v *Bhalchandra Vithalrao Thube* AIR 1961 SC 589: (1961)2 SCR 168: (1961)1 SCA 735: (1962)2 SCJ 563, *per* Majority (Imam and Raghutar Dayal, JJ.)].

An agriculturist contemplated by the clauses is any person who occupies himself with agriculture. A person occupying himself with agriculture would be an agriculturist though he does not cultivate with his own hands and carries on agriculture in a very large scale. He would still be an agriculturist though he has other means of livelihood besides agriculture. [*Shrimant Appasaheb Tuljaram Desai* v *Bhalchandra Vithalrao Thube,* supra, *per* Sarkar, J. (contra)].

**Aid.** As noun means assistance; auspices; backing; co-operation; endorsement; espousal; furtherance; guidance; helpfulness; patronage; sponsorship; subsidy; subsistence; support; benefaction; charity.

As verb means assist; be auxiliary to; be of service; collaborate; cooperate with; facilitate; further; promote; render help; support; act in co-operation with; supplement the efforts of others.

The word 'aid' in Arts. 29 and 30 of the Constitution of India covers grant under Art. 337. [*In re Kerala Education Bill 1957* AIR 1958 SC 956: 1959 SCR 995].

**Aid and abet.** To assist or facilitate the commission of a crime, or to promote its accomplishment. [Black's *Law Dictionary*, 8th Ed.].

Aiding and abetting almost inevitably involves a situation in which the secondary party and the main offender are together at some stage discussing the plans which they may be making in respect of the alleged offence, and are in contract so that each knows what is passing through the mind of the other. [*A-G's Reference* (1975)2 All ER 684, 686].

**Air pollution.** Any harmful substance or energy emitted directly or indirectly into the air, esp. if the harm is to the environment or to the public health or welfare [Black's *Law Dictionary*, 8th Ed.]; the contamination of air, especially by industrial waste gases, fuel exhaust, or smoke.

**Air transport service.** A service for the transport by air of persons, mail or any other thing, animate or inanimate, for any kind of remuneration whatsoever, whether such service consists of a single flight or a series of flights. [Air Corporation Act 1953, s. 2(*ii*)].

**Aircraft.** Any form of craft designed for flight through or navigation in the air, as airplanes, dirigibles, balloons, helicopters, kites, and gliders; a machine capable of flight.

▸ *Meaning under the Air Corporations Act 1953, s. 2(i); Aircraft Act 1934, s. 2(1).* Aircraft means any machine which can derive support in the atmosphere from reactions of the aid other than reactions of the air against the earth's surface and includes balloons, whether fixed or free, airships, kites, gliders and flying machines.

NOTE: Aircraft includes aeroplanes, balloons, kite balloons, airships, gliders or other machines for flying. [Air Force Act 1950, s. 4(*ii*)].

**Airport.** A complex of runways and buildings for the take off, landing, and maintenance of civil aircraft, with facilities for passengers. [*Concise Oxford Dictionary*, 9th Ed.].

A field laid out as a base for aircraft, including all structures and appurtenances necessary for operations, housing, storage, repair, and maintenance. [Webster *Comprehensive Dictionary*, International Ed.].

**Airstrip.** An area used or intended to be used for the landing and take-off of aircraft with short take-off and landing characteristics and includes all buildings and structure thereon or appertaining thereto. [International Airports Authority Act 1971, s. 2(*b*)].

**Akar.** Immovable property. [*Hamir Singh* v *Zakir* 1 All 57].

**Al aulad.** *Al aulad* though etymologically means offspring or progeny, it may be interpreted as lineal male descendants having regard to the custom prevalent in the place. [*Perkash* v *Rameshwar Nath* 31 Cal 561].

**Ala malik.** Superior owner is known as *ala malik*. [*Rajinder Chand* v *Sukhi* AIR 1957 SC 286]

**Alcohol.** Pure colourless liquid, which forms part of drinks such as wine and whisky and which is formed by the action of yeast on sugar solutions.

- **Power alcohol** p. 674.

**Alcoholism.** The pathological effect, as distinguished from physiological effect, of excessive indulgence in intoxicating liquors.

**Alderman.** A member of a city council or other local governing body.

In modern times, this title is conferred on the persons associated with and next in order to the mayor in the government of a city or town corporate.

**Aleatory contract.** A contract the effect of which depends on an uncertain event. Under the Indian Contract Act 1872 such contracts are known as contingent contracts. [Indian Contract Act 1872, ss. 31 to 36].

**Alias.** Otherwise called: a second name applied to a person where he has been styled or has styled himself by more names than one. [Wharton's *Law Lexicon*].

**Alibi.** Elsewhere. It is a defence resorted to where the party accused, in order to prove that he could not have committed the crime with which he is charged, offers evidence that he was in a different place at the time the offence was committed. [Wharton's *Law Lexicon*].

*Alibi* postulates physical impossibility of the accused at the scene of offence by reason of his presence at some other place. [*Dudh Nath* v *State of U.P.* AIR 1981 SC 911: 1981 Cr LJ 618; *State* v *N.G. Pimple* AIR 1984 SC 63: 1984 Cr LJ 4: (1984)1 SCC 446].

The Latin word *alibi* means "elsewhere" and that word is used for convenience when an accused takes recourse to a defence line that when the occurrence took place he was so far away from the place of occurrence that it is extremely improbable that he would have participated in the crime. [*Binay Kumar Singh* v *State of Bihar* AIR 1997 SC 322: (1997)1 SCC 283: 1997 SCC (Cri) 333: 1997 Cr LJ 362: JT 1996(10) SC 79].

> NOTE: The relevancy of *alibi* is illustrated by example (*a*) to s. 11 of the Indian Evidence Act 1872. Evidence of *alibi* is admissible to contradict a witness. Illustration (*c*) to s. 153 of the above Act.

**Alien.** Foreign; from a foreign country; a foreigner, especially one who is not a naturalized citizen of the country where he or she is living.

A foreign born person who has not qualified as a citizen of the country; but an alien is a person within the meaning of the due process clause of the US Constitution to the same extent as a citizen. [*Galvan* v *Press* 347 US 522: 98 L Ed 911].

**Alien enemy.** A citizen or subject of a country at war with the country in which the citizen or subject is living or travelling. [Black's *Law Dictionary*, 8th Ed.].

An "alien enemy" is defined as a person who, by reason of owing a permanent or temporary allegiance to a hostile power, becomes, in time of war, impressed with the character of an enemy. [1 Kent. Comm. 74: 2 Kent Comm. 63]. The expression "alien enemy" denotes a status that depends not upon the nationality of the contracting party, but upon his place of business during the war. [*Porter* v *Freudenberg* (1915)1 KB 857].

**Alienate.** Transfer ownership of or title to property to another person, to convey.

**Alienation.** The act or result of alienating; the transfer of property and possession of land, tenements and other things, from one person to another.

It means every mode of passing realty by the act of the party, as distinguished from passing it by operation of law.

Alienation implies a transaction by which property is given to another person. [*Re Gaskell & Walters' Contract* (1906)2 Ch 1, p. 10].

" 'Alienation' denotes the act, or series of acts, of alienating, and takes place whenever the owner of land, or of an interest therein, so acts as to divest himself of his interest or some lesser interest, and to vest the same in another person". [*Lang* v *Castle* (1924) SASR 255].

- **Lawful alienation** p. 518.
- **Restraint on alienation** p. 756.

**Alienee.** One to whom a transfer of property is made.

**Alieni juris.** Under the mastership of another.

**Alimony.** Money payable by a man to his wife or former wife or by a woman to her husband or former husband after they are separated or divorced. In UK, the word is now replaced by maintenance.

It comes from Latin 'alimonia' meaning sustenance. It, therefore, means the sustenance or support of the wife by her divorced husband and stems from the common law right of the wife to support by her husband. It is generally restricted to money unless otherwise authorized by statute.

- **Alimony pendente lite.** It means temporary alimony. An allowance made pending a suit for divorce or separate maintenance including a reasonable allowance for preparation of the suit as well as for support.
- **Permanent alimony** p. 654.
- **Temporary alimony** p. 833.

**Aliquis non debet esse judex in propria causa, quia non potest esse judex et pars.** A person ought not to be judge in his own cause, because he cannot act as judge and party.

**Aliter.** Otherwise.

**Aliunde.** From another source; from elsewhere; in any other way.

**All.** Each and every [*Burnett* v *Scotland Railway* 54 LJ QB 539; *Shyamlal* v *Takhatmal* AIR 1957 MP 98]; the entire substance or extent of; everything that one has; whole being.

But by context it may mean any. [*Jarman* v *Vye* 35 LJ Ch 821].

**All-India service.** All-India service means the service known as the Indian Administrative Service or the service known as the Indian Police Service or any other service specified in s. 2A of the All-India Services Act. [All-India Services Act 1951, s. 2; see Art. 312, Constitution of India 1950].

**Allegans contraria non est audiendus.** He who alleges contradictory things is not to be heard.

> NOTE: A man shall not be permitted to "blow hot and cold" with reference to the same transaction, or insist, at different times, on the truth of each of two conflicting allegations, according to the promptings of his private interest. [*Wood* v *Dwarris* 11 Exch. 493]. The doctrine of estoppel, at any rate by deed and *in pais,* is in great measure a development of the principle expressed in this maxim.

**Allegation.** An assertion, especially an unproved one; an accusation; the assertion, claim, declaration, or statement of a party to an action, made in a pleading setting out what he expects to prove; the act of alleging; that which is alleged.

**Allegiance.** Obligation of fidelity and obedience to government from a citizen in consideration for protection that government gives; the obligation of fidelity in general.

> NOTE: Allegiance is of three kinds—natural; local; acquired. The first is due from all natural-born subjects; the second from all aliens resident within the realm; and the third from inhabitants of conquered territory, formerly ceded by a foreign power.

**Alliance.** Union with another.

**Allot.** Allocate; apportion; assign; demarcate; distribute; divide; earmark; portion out; specify.

The word 'allot' means, distribute by lot, or in such a way that the recipients have no choice; to assign as a lot or apportion to. [*District Council of United Khasi and Jaintia Hills* v *Miss Sitimon Sawian* AIR 1972 SC 787: (1972)1 SCR 398: (1971)3 SCC 708].

In company law, the true meaning of the word 'allot' must be first, the creation of lots of shares and then the division of them into value and classes and, lastly, allocation of them individually or numerously to a particular applicant or applicants. [*Re Calcutta Stock Exchange Association* AIR 1957 Cal 438].

**Allotment.** Allotment means the act of allotting; something that is allotted; a share or portion of something; assignment in severality of a specific portion to each co-sharer on partition.

The word 'allotment' means apportioning; the action of allotting; share allotted to one; small portion of land let out for cultivation. [*District Council of United Khasi and Jaintia Hills* v *Miss Sitimon Sawian* AIR 1972 SC 787: (1972)1 SCR 398: (1971)3 SCC 708].

Allotment is an appropriation to some person or corporation of a certain number of shares, but not necessarily of any specific shares. [Halsbury's *Laws of England*, 4th Ed., vol. 7, para 366, p. 202].

▸ *Meaning under company law.* In company law, allotment of shares means the appropriation, out of the previously unappropriated capital of a company, of a certain number of shares to a person. Till such allotment the shares do not exist as such. It is an allotment in this sense that the shares come into existence. Issue of forfeited shares is not an allotment of them but only a sale. [*Sri Gopal Jalan* v *Calcutta Stock Exchange* AIR 1964 SC 250: 1964 SCD 254: (1964)1 SCA 371: (1963)3 SCJ 505].

In India, allotment of shares by a company is made under ss. 69 to 75 of the Companies Act 1956.

▸ *Meaning under Administration of Evacuee Property Act 1950, s. 2(a).* Allotment means the grant by a person duly authorised in this behalf of a right of use or occupation of any immovable evacuee property to any other person, but does not include a grant by way of lease.


• **Letter of allotment** p. 530.

• **On allotment** p. 625.


**Allow.** To put no obstacle in the way of; permit to occur or do; to admit; accredit; approve; empower; endorse; give authority.

The word has no rigid or precise meaning, its import varying according to circumstances or context in connection with which it is used. It may mean to bestow or assign to any one as his right or due. To approve of, accept as true, admit, concede, adopt, or fix. To grant something as a deduction or an addition; to abate or deduct; as, to allow a sum for leakage. [*Pittsburgh Brewing Co.* v *Commissioner of Internal Revenue* 107 F 2d 155, 156].

The word 'allow' means some positive sanction and not mere permission or sufferance. [*Pundarikaksha Basu* v *Chandra Singh* AIR 1967 Cal 538].

**Allowance.** A deduction, an average payment, a portion assigned or allowed; a difference permitted in excess or abatement; the act of allowing.

Allowance means something given as compensation, rebate or deduction. [*Arunachalla* v *State of Madras* AIR 1956 SC 300].


• **Dearness allowance** p. 229.

• **Make allowance** p. 551.

• **Subsistence allowance** p. 818.


**Alluvion.** Alluvion is land imperceptibly gained from the sea or the river by washing up of sand and soil so as to form *terra firma*. [Wharton's *Law Lexicon*].

Alluvion is an accession to land by gradual addition of matter as by deposit of alluvium.

Alluvion is that increase of the earth on a shore or bank of a stream or the sea, by the force of the water, as by current or waves, which is so gradual that no one can judge how much is added at each moment of time. [*Garnett* v *State* 289 A 2d 542, 545].

NOTE: Where land is formed by alluvion, that is, by the casting up of earth or sand on the shore of the sea, the additional increment belongs to the Crown, where the casting up of the earth or sand takes place suddenly. But where new land is formed by small accretions, and the additions or increments are so gradual as to be inappreciable, these belong to the owner of the adjacent land, whether the accretions are due to natural or to artificial causes, provided in the latter case the user of the land is lawful. [Halsbury's *Laws of England*, 3rd Ed., vol. 7, p. 463]. Section 12, W.B. Land Reforms Act 1955, has deviated from this legal position by enacting that such land would vest in the State.

**Ally.** A State connected with another by treaty.

**Alongside.** Close to or along the side; at the side of; side by side with.

A clause in a charter-party that cargo "shall be brought alongside" for shipment means that the character is to bring the cargo as near to the ship as practicable.

**Alter.** To make a change in; modify; change some of the elements or ingredients or details without substituting an entirely new thing or destroying the identity of the thing affected; change partially.

The word 'alter' means only change or modify or revise but not abolish. [*District Local Board, Jalgaon* v *Krishna Sakharam* AIR 1950 Bom 18].

The word 'alter' cannot include 'reverse'. [*Panu Naik* v *Chinani Malik* AIR 1948 Pat 435: 49 Cr LJ 589].

Alteration in any building includes changes and additions as well, provided it is improvement on the old structure. [*Corporation of Calcutta* v *Raj Kumar* AIR 1954 Cal 20: 57 CWN 925].

**Amalgamate.** Combine or unite to form one structure, organisation etc.; centralise; combine; commingle; consolidate; unify.

**Amalgamation.** The act of combining or uniting; consolidation; merger; union of diverse elements so as to form a homogeneous whole or new body.

In its application to companies, it "contemplates a state of things under which two companies are so joined as to form a third entity, or one company is absorbed into and blended with another company". [Buckley on *Companies Act*, 13th Ed., p. 586].

In its application to land and buildings or premises, the word has to be taken in its general sense, namely, the making or the conversion of plots of land or buildings into one either by erection of one boundary wall or by removal of the marks of separation between them. [*Administrator, Howrah Municipality* v *Calcutta Electric Supply* 62 CWN 293].

**Amalnama.** Authority to manage or administer property; an order for possession; a warrant from a competent public functionary to an individual, authorising his taking possession and management of landed or other property; an order from a zamindar to his cultivators to give possession to a renter.

Where the deed is in such a form that it can neither be called a lease nor an agreement for a lease, but it gives a right to possession it may come within the description of an amalnama. [*Bijoli Prova* v *H.C. Dutta* 71 CWN 681].

**Ambiguity.** Double meaning, either deliberate or caused by inexactness of expression; an expression able to be interpreted in more than one way; uncertainty of meaning of an expression used in a written instrument; want of clearness or definiteness.

NOTE: There be two sorts of ambiguities of words; the one is *ambiguitas patens* and the other *latens*. *Patens* is that which appears to be ambiguous upon the deed or instrument; *latens* is that which seemeth certain and without ambiguity, for anything that appeareth upon the deed or instrument; but there is some collateral matter out of the deed that breedeth the ambiguity. [Bacon's *Law Tracts*, p. 99].

A latent ambiguity must be distinguished from a patent ambiguity, which arises where the description is on the face of it indefinite, and not apt to determine any subject, such as in a gift to 'one of the sons' of a named person who has more than one son. In such cases, no evidence is admissible to resolve the ambiguity. [Halsbury's *Laws of England,* 3rd Ed., vol. 39, p. 971].

• **Latent ambiguity** p. 512.

**Ambulatory.** Able to be altered; amenable; changeable; modifiable; renunciatory; repudiatory; reversible; revocable; variable.

A will is said to be ambulatory till death, that is, changeable or revocable. At death it ambulates no more.

**Amend.** Add to; adjust; alter; correct; revise; improve; mend; refashion; refine; reform; upgrade; remove faults; make change for better.

To make right; to correct or rectify; to change the wording of; to formally alter (a statute, constitution, motion, etc.) by striking out, inserting, or substituting words. [Black's *Law Dictionary*, 8th Ed.].

In relation to any statute the term means to alter by additions, substitutions and omissions. [*Deorajin Debi* v *Satyadhan Ghosal* AIR 1954 Cal 119: 58 CWN 64].

**Amendment.** Adjustment; betterment; change or modify for the better; improvement; modification; refinement; revampment; revision; act of improving or correcting; alteration by modification, deletion, or addition.

A formal revision or addition proposed or made to a statute, constitution, pleading, order, or other instrument; a change made by addition, deletion, or correction. [Black's *Law Dictionary*, 8th Ed.].

In Parliamentary law, it means a 'motion that changes another motion's wording by striking out text, inserting or adding text, or substituting text.' [Black's *Law Dictionary*, 8th Ed.].

A broad definition of the word 'amendment' will include any alteration or change. The word 'amendment' when used in connection with the Constitution may refer to the addition of a provision on a new and independent subject, complete in itself and wholly disconnected from other provisions, or to some particular article or clause, and is then used to indicate an addition to, the striking out, or some change in that particular article or clause. [*Kesavananda Bharati* v *State of Kerala* (1973)4 SCC 225].

Amendment is, in fact, a wider term and it includes abrogation or deletion of a provision in an existing statute. There is no real distinction between repeal and an amendment. [*Bhagatram Sharma* v *Union of India* AIR 1988 SC 740: 1988 (Supp) SCC 30: (1988)1 SCR 1034: JT 1987 SC 476: 1987(5) SLR 713].

**Amenity.** In Latin it is expressed as *amoenitas* which means 'pleasantness'. It is something "tangible or intangible that increases the enjoyment of real property, such as location, view, landscaping, security, or access to recreational facilities". [Black's *Law Dictionary*, 8th Ed.].

"Amenity" appears to mean "pleasant circumstances or features, advantages", e.g. wide streets and plenty of air and room between houses. [*Re Ellis and Ruislip Northwood U.D.C.* (1920)1 KB 343, 370].

An amenity is generally something which enhances the desirability or pleasantness of the property, in the context of its enjoyment. A strict necessity or even a necessity could also be an amenity, depending on the circumstances of the case. [*Subramaniam* v *Rajaram* AIR 1966 Mad 355: (1966)1 MLJ 230].

NOTE: Repairs of an accommodation cannot be said to be amenity. When a tenant is in occupation of an accommodation, it cannot be said that he is in enjoyment of any amenity. Amenities are something which are not let out to him but of which he is allowed the enjoyment, such as the supply of water or electricity or a licence to use a pathway, garage, garden, etc. [*J.N. Verma* v *Anis Begum* 1964 AWR (HC) 702].

The 'standard amenities' in relation to a dwelling mean (*a*) a fixed bath or shower in a bathroom; (*b*) a wash-hand basin; (*c*) a hot and cold water supply at a fixed bath shower; (*d*) a hot and cold water supply at a sink; (*e*) a hot and cold water supply at a washhand basin; (*f*) a water closet; and (*g*) satisfactory facilities for storing food. [Section 43 of the Housing Act 1964 of England].

**Amicable.** Done in a friendly spirit, mutually forbearing; agreed or assented to by parties having conflicting interests or a dispute.

**Amicable action.** An action between friendly parties brought and carried on by mutual consent to obtain judgment of the court on a doubtful question of law.

**Amicus curiae.** An impartial adviser in a court of law; friend of the court.

A person who is not a party to a lawsuit but who petitions the court or is required by the court to file a brief in the action because that person has a strong interest in the subject-matter. [Black's *Law Dictionary*, 8th Ed.].

**Amin.** A revenue surveyor, land measurer, etc.; an officer of a civil court entrusted with the execution of a warrant or order.

**Ammunition.** Any resources for attack or defence; any one of various articles used in the discharge of firearms and ordinance.

NOTE: Ammunition for any firearm includes—(*i*) rockets, bombs, grenades, shells and other missiles; (*ii*) articles designated for torpedo service and submarine mining; (*iii*) other articles containing or designated or adapted to contain explosive, fulminating or fissionable material or noxious liquid, gas or other such thing whether capable of use with firearms or not; (*iv*) charges for firearms and accessories for such charges; (*v*) fuses and friction tubes; (*vi*) parts of and machinery for manufacturing, ammunition, and (*vii*) such ingredients of ammunition as the Central Government may, by notification in the Official Gazette, specify in this behalf. [Arms Act 1959, s. 2(*b*)].

**Amnesty.** A general pardon, especially for political offences; a sovereign act of oblivion for past acts, granted by a government to all persons who have been guilty of crime, generally political offences like sedition, treason, rebellion. It is the abolition and forgetfulness of the offence. [*Knote* v *US* 95 US 149, 152: 24 L Ed 442].

NOTE: Amnesty may be of two types—express amnesty and implied amnesty. Express amnesty is one granted in direct terms. Implied amnesty is one which results when a treaty of peace is made between contending parties.

**Amortisation.** This has the following meaning—(*a*) the gradual reduction of a liability, by paying it off by instalments, usually through the operation of a sinking fund; (*b*) the gradual charging against revenue of expenditure, the benefit from which will be derived over a long period at the end of which the object of expenditure will have no residual value; (*c*) redemption of bonds and shares by means of annual drawings from a sinking fund or the complete extinguishment of a loan by a single payment out of some special fund set aside for that purpose. [Osborn & Grandage's *Concise Commercial Dictionary*].

The act or result of gradually extinguishing a debt, such as a mortgage, usually by contributing payments of principal each time a periodic interest is due; the act or result of apportioning the initial cost of a usually intangible asset, such as a patent, over the asset's usual life. [Black's *Law Dictionary*, 8th Ed.].

**Amotion.** A turning out; as the eviction of a tenant or the removal of a person from office; the common-law procedure available to shareholders to remove a corporate director for cause; the wrongful moving or carrying away of another's property. [Black's *Law Dictionary*, 8th Ed.].

NOTE: A power of amotion is incidental to a corporation, unless it has been taken away by statute. [Halsbury's *Laws of England*, 4th Ed., vol. 9, para 1266, p. 751].

**Amusement.** Something that amuses, especially a pleasant diversion; the feeling of delight or joy; the state of being amused.

Amusement would mean diversion, pastime or enjoyment or a pleasurable occupation of the senses, or that which furnished it. [*M.J. Sivani* v *State of Karnataka* AIR 1995 SC 1770: (1995)6 SCC 289: JT 1995(4) SC 141: (1995)2 SCJ 620].

NOTE: Amusements include theatres, dramatic performances, cinemas, sports and the like.

[*Srinivasamurthy* v *State of Mysore* AIR 1959 SC 894].

**An.** The English indefinite article, equivalent to "one" or "any". "An" is sometimes read in the most absolute sense as meaning "any-whatsoever". [*Ex p. Pratt* 53 LJ Ch 614, *per* Cotton, L.J.]. It is seldom used to denote plurality.

**Analogous.** Akin; alike; coequal; correlative; corresponding; equipollent; equivalent; homologous; matching; parallel; related; resembling; similar.

**Analogy.** Affinity; close relation; close resemblance; common feature equivalence; like quality; logical relation; parallel relation; point in common; point of resemblance; similar relation.

**Anarchy.** Absence of authority; breakdown of administration; chaos; disorder; disorderliness; lawlessness; misgovernment; misrule; mob law; mob rule; political disorder; unruliness; uprising.

**Ancestor.** Ascendant; forefather; predecessor; primogenitor; procreator; one from whom a person lineally descended.

'Ancestor' is derived of the Latin word antecessor. Antecessor is applied to a natural person.

In Hindu law the word signifies a direct ascendant in the paternal or maternal line. [*Karuppai* v *Sankaranarayanan* 27 Mad 300].

**Ancestral property.** According to the Mitakshara school of Hindu law, ancestral property has peculiar meaning and incidents. Property inherited by a male Hindu from his male ancestors in the male line is his ancestral property as regards his male issues and the son acquires an interest in it by birth. [*Muhammad Husain* v *Kishva Nandan* 64 IA 250: AIR 1937 PC 233]. It is also called joint family property or coparcenary property.

The term 'ancestral property' is not confined to such property as the father had derived from the ancestors, but includes 'paternal' property or such as had been acquired by the father by whatever title and was possessed by him at the time of his decease. [*Rajamohun Gossain* v *Gourmohun Gossain* 8 MIA 91].

**Anchorage.** A place where ships anchor; a duty imposed on ships for anchoring in a harbour; a toll for anchoring.

**Ancient.** Having had an existence of many years without interruption; belonging to or having existed from a remote antiquity.

**Ancient light.** An ancient light is a defined aperture in a *building* through which, as of right, there has been actually enjoyed an access and use of light for the full period of 20 years and without interruption. [Stroud's *Judicial Dictionary*, 5th Ed.].

**Ancient monument.** The expression means any structure, erection or monument, or any tumulus or place of interment, or any cave, rocks, sculpture, inscription or monolith, which is of historical, archaeological or artistic interest and which has been in existence for not less than one hundred years, and includes—(*i*) the remains of an ancient monument; (*ii*) the site of an ancient monument; (*iii*) such portion of land adjoining the site of an ancient monument as may be required for fencing or covering in or otherwise preserving such monument, and (*iv*) the means of access to, and convenient inspection of, an ancient monument. [Ancient Monuments and Archaeological Sites and Remains Act 1958, s. 2(*a*); Ancient Monument Preservation Act 1904, s. 2(1)].

**Ancient writings.** These are deeds and other documents which are more than 30 years old. These when put in evidence 'prove themselves'. In other words, they do not ordinarily require proof of their execution when they come from the proper custody. [Indian Evidence Act 1872, s. 90].

**Ancillary.** Aiding; attendant upon; collateral; serving as an adjunct; supplemental; supporting; complementing; dependent; secondary; sequential; subordinate.

"Ancillary" means that which depends on, or is subordinate or subsidiary to some other. [*Rai Ramkrishna* v *State of Bihar* (1964)1 SCR 897].

**And.** Also; added to; as well as.

It is a particle denoting addition, emphasis, or union and used as a connective between words, phrases, clauses, and sentences.

The word 'and' is generally used in cumulative sense, requiring fulfilment of all the conditions that it joins together. It is the antithesis of'or'. [*Iswar Singh* v *State of Uttar Pradesh* AIR 1968 SC 1450: (1969)1 SCJ 105; *M. Satyanarayana* v *State of Karnataka* AIR 1986 SC 1162: 1986(1) SLR 312].

Sometimes, 'and' has to be taken disjunctively, or distributive as equivalent to 'or'. [*Chairman of the Howrah Municipality* v *Khetra Krishna Mitter* 131 IC 702].

**And in any case.** In every case. [*Pershad Singh* v *Rampertab* 22 Cal 77].

**Angary.** The right of a belligerent, subject to compensation for loss, to seize or destroy natural property under military necessity.

> NOTE: "There is a well ascertained right of a belligerent sovereign to take possession of the property of neutrals so found within his territory or territory occupied by his forces for the purpose of warfare. This is the right of angary. It appears to me to be well recognised by the conventions of civilised nations, which constitute the body of international law, and it is equally clear that it is only so recognised on the footing that the sovereign so exercising this right makes full compensation for the property he so seizes". [*Commercial & Estates Co. of Egypt* v *Board of Trade* (1925)1 KB 271, 273 (CA), *per* Atkin, LJ].

**Anglo-Indian.** An Anglo-Indian means a person whose father or any of whose other male progenitors in the male line is or was of European descent but who is domiciled within the territory of India and is or was born within such territory of parents habitually resident therein and not established there for temporary purposes only. [Constitution of India 1950, Art. 366(2)].

**Animal.** Any living creature other than a human being. [Indian Penal Code 1860, s. 47].

In law the term 'animals' includes all creatures not belonging to the human race.

In law animals are divided into two classes: domestic and wild, and this classification affects the rights of property in them and also liability for their behaviour. [Halsbury's *Laws of England*, 4th Ed., vol. 2, para 201, p. 85].

• **Dangerous animal** p. 223.

• **Domestic animals** p. 278.

**Animal mansuetæ naturæ.** Domestic animal, e.g., a dog, a cow, or a horse.

> NOTE: One who keeps a domestic animal is not rendered liable by the mere fact that the animal does damage in following a natural propensity of its kind to do damage in certain circumstances. [*Buckle* v *Holmes* (1926)2 KB 125 (130)]. But if the damage is due to some negligent act of the owner of the animal, he is liable on the ordinary principles of law of negligence. [*Pitcher* v *Martin* (1937)3 All ER 918; *Aldham* v *United Dairies* (1940)1 KB 507: (1939)4 All ER 522].

**Animalia feræ naturæ** Animals of a wild and untameable disposition, *e.g.*, a tiger or a gorilla.

> NOTE: He who keeps a dangerous animal is at his peril. If any harm is done by dangerous animals the keeper is ordinarily liable without any proof of negligence. [*Read* v *Lyons* (1947) AC 156, 171].

**Annex.** Add as a subordinate part with another, larger, or of higher importance. It is derived from the Latin 'annectere', meaning to tie or bind to.

Annex means 'to add to the end, to join or attach; to affix, to append.' Annexure is something which is added, joined or attached, affixed or appended. [*Panna* v *Mukhdiar Singh* AIR 1972 Punj 451].

**Annexation.** The act of attaching, adding, joining, or uniting one thing to another.

The act of attaching; the state of being attached; the point at which a fixture becomes a part of the realty to which it is attached; a formal act by which a nation, state or municipality incorporates land within its domination. [Black's *Law Dictionary*, 8th Ed.].

In its application to sovereign power, annexation occurs where the occupying power acquires and makes the acquired territory as its own. Annexation gives a *de jure* right to administer the territory. Annexation means that there is not only possession but uncontested sovereignty over the territory. As long as hostilities are continuing the annexation is premature or anticipated. When the territory is conquered and subjugated there is true annexation. Article 1(3)(*c*) of the Constitution of India provides for the territories that may be acquired. [*Mons Sebastiao* v *State of Goa* (1970)1 SCR 87: AIR 1970 SC 329: (1970)1 SCA 75].

Annexation means that there is not only possession but uncontested sovereignty over the territory. [*Rev. Mons Sebastio Francisco Xavier Dos Remedios Monteiro* v *State of Goa* (1969)3 SCC 419: AIR 1970 SC 329: (1970)1 SCR 87: 1970 Cr LJ 499].

**Annexed to the land.** Fastened to the land.

NOTE: Where a chattel is so annexed that it cannot be removed without great damage to the land it may be regarded as annexed in perpetuity to the land. Thus looms attached to the floor or seats fastened to the floor of a cinema are part of the land. [*Holland* v *Hodgson* 1872 LR 7 CP 328; *Vaudeville Electric Cinema Ltd.* v *Muriset* (1923)2 Ch 74].

**Annotate.** To write notes on; to comment upon.

**Annoy.** To disturb or irritate, especially by repeated acts; to vex, harass, molest, cause mental disturbance.

**Annoyance.** Discomfort; vexation. It may result from either physical or mental conditions. It includes feeling of imposition and oppression.

An act which is an interference with the pleasurable enjoyment, in reason, is an annoyance.

NOTE: Annoyance is a wider term than nuisance. If one finds a thing which reasonably troubles the mind and pleasure—not of a fanciful person or a skilled person who knows the truth, but of an ordinary sensible person, that seems to be an 'annoyance' although it may not appear to amount to physical detriment to comfort. [*Tod Heatley* v *Benham* (1888)40 Ch D 80; *S.K. Roy Chowdhury* v *Afroj Jehan* 71 CWN 586; *Chandra Kant* v *Gajendra Kumar* (1971)12 Guj LR 551].

What is nuisance or annoyance is essentially a question of fact depending upon the facts and circumstances of each case. [*Gopal Vaman* v *Krishnaji Tatyarao* (1979)1 Kant LJ 319]. Constant abusing or using vulgar language or persisting in creating loud noise by a neighbour may constitute nuisance or annoyance. [*Gopal Vaman* v *Krishnaji Tatyarao*, supra].

**Annual charge.** A charge to secure an annual liability, but does not include any tax in respect of property or income from property imposed by a local authority, or the Central or a State Government. [Income Tax Act 1961, s. 27; *Veerappa Chettiar* v *Commissioner of Income Tax* AIR 1959 Mad 56: (1959)2 MLJ 158].

NOTE: *'Annual charge' and 'capital charge'—distinction.* 'Annual charge' means a charge to secure an annual liability whereas 'capital charge' means a charge created for a capital sum, that is to say, a charge created to secure the discharge of a liability of a capital nature. [*The New Piece Goods Bazaar Co. Ltd., Bombay* v *Commissioner of Income Tax* AIR 1950 SC 165: 1950 SCR 553: 1950 SCJ 437: (1950)18 ITR 516].

**Annual letting value.** Annual letting value is that which a hypothetical tenant may reasonably be expected to pay for the building. [*Lokemanya Mills* v *Borough Municipality* (1962)1 SCR 306].

**Annual value.** Annual value of any property shall be deemed to be the sum for which the property might reasonably be expected to let from year to year. [Income-tax Act 1961, s. 23(1)(*a*)].

"Annual value" to mean the annual rent at which the building may be expected to let. [*D.G. Gouse and Co.* v *State of Kerala* AIR 1980 SC 271: (1980)1 SCR 804: (1980)2 SCC 410].

Annual value is the gross annual rent at which the premises might reasonably be expected to let. In the absence of evidence of reasonable rental, a fair return of capitalised value of the building may in a proper case represent the reasonable annual rent. [*Corporation of Calcutta* v *Union Jute Company* AIR 1957 Cal 230: 60 CWN 153].

**Annuity.** A yearly grant or allowance; an investment of money entitling the investor to a series of equal annual sums over a stated period; a sum payable in respect of a particular year; a right to receive fixed, periodic payments, either for life or for a term of years.

An annuity is a sum which is to be secured by setting apart a portion of the personal property of the estate and has to be paid in the shape of an annual payment. [*Re Dowding* (1904)1 Ch 441, 445, *per* Kekewich, J.; *O'Connor* v *Minister of National Revenue* (1943) Ex LR 168, 182, 185].

An annuity is a certain sum of money payable yearly either as a personal obligation of the grantor or out of property not consisting exclusively of land. [Halsbury's *Laws of England,* 3rd Ed., vol. 32, p. 534].

"An annuity is a right to receive *de anno in annum* a certain sum; that may be given for life, or for a series of years; it may be given during any particular period, or in perpetuity; and there is also this singularity about annuities that although payable out of the personal assets, they are capable of being given, for the purposes of devolution, as real estate. They may be given to a man and his heirs and may go to the heir as real estate". [Jarman on *Wills*, p. 1113].

Ordinarily an annuity is a money payment of a fixed sum annually made and is a charge personally on the grantor. [*Commissioner of Wealth Tax, Gujarat* v *Mrs. Arundhati Balkrishna* AIR 1971 SC 915: (1970)3 SCR 819: (1970)1 SCC 561: (1970)77 ITR 505].

An annuity is a certain sum of money payable yearly either as a personal obligation of the grantor or out of property. [*Late Nawab Sir Mir Osman Ali Khan* v *Commissioner of Wealth Tax, Hyderabad* 1986 (Supp) SCC 700: (1986)3 SCR 1072: (1986)162 ITR 888: AIR 1987 SC 522].

NOTE: In order to constitute an annuity, the payment to be made periodically should be a fixed or predetermined one, and it should not be liable to any variation depending upon or on any ground relating to the general income of the fund or estate which is charged for such payment. [*Commissioner of Wealth Tax, Lucknow* v *P.K. Banerjee (Dead) by LRs.* AIR 1981 SC 401: (1981)1 SCR 657: (1981)1 SCC 63: (1980)125 ITR 641].

Illustrations of annuity given in s. 173 of the Indian Succession Act show that it is a right to receive a specified sum and not an aliquot share in the income arising from any fund or property. [*Commissioner of Wealth Tax, Gujarat* v *Mrs. Arundhati Balkrishna* AIR 1971 SC 915: (1970)3 SCR 819: (1970)1 SCC 561: (1970)77 ITR 505].

• **Deferred annuity** p. 242.
• **Life annuity** p. 535.

**Annul.** Declare invalid; cancel; abolish; annihilate; obliterate; make void or of no effect.

**Anomalous mortgage.** A mortgage which is not a simple mortgage, a mortgage by conditional sale, a usufructuary mortgage, an English mortgage or a mortgage by deposit of title deeds within the meaning of s. 58 of the Transfer of Property Act is called an anomalous mortgage. [Transfer of Property Act 1882, s. 58(*g*)].

**Anonymous.** Of unknown name; of unknown or undeclared source of authorship; featureless, impersonal.

**Answerable.** Liable to be called to account; responsible; liable to answer.

'Answerable' is merely an equivalent for 'liable'. [*River Wear Commissioners* v *Adamson* (1877)2 AC 743].

**Ante.** The word used in a report or text-book refers the reader to a previous part of the book. [Wharton's *Law Lexicon*].

**Antecedent debt.** Means antecedent in fact as well as in time, that is to say, the debt must be truly independent of and not part of the transaction impeached. [*Prasad* v *Govindaswami Mudaliar* AIR 1982 SC 84: (1982)2 SCR 109: (1982)1 SCC 185].

Means with regard to debt 'antecedent to the transaction'. [*Brij Narain* v *Mangla Prasad* 51 IA 129].

NOTE: A borrowing made on the occasion of the grant of a mortgage is not an antecedent debt. The father of a joint Hindu family may sell or mortgage the joint family property including the sons' interest therein to discharge a debt contracted by him for his own personal benefit if the debt was antecedent to the alienation and if it was not tainted with immorality.

**Antedate.** A date assigned to an event or document earlier than the actual date of the event or document.

**Antenatal.** Happening or occurring or existing before birth; relating to the period of pregnancy.

**Antenuptial.** Occurring before marriage.

**Anthrax.** A malignant boil caused in man by infection from animals either directly or through articles manufactured from their hair, skin, etc. [Jowitt's *Dictionary of English Law*, 2nd Ed.].

**Anticipatory bail.** The facility which s. 438 of the Criminal Procedure Code 1973, affords is generally referred to as 'anticipatory bail', an expression which was used by the Law Commission in its 41st Report. Neither the section nor its marginal note so describes it but, the expression 'anticipatory bail' is a convenient mode of conveying that it is possible to apply for bail in anticipation of arrest. It is granted in anticipation of arrest and is effective at the very moment of arrest. An order of anticipatory bail constitutes, so to say, an assurance against police custody following upon arrest for offence or offences in respect of which the order is issued. [*Gurbaksh Singh Sibbia* v *State of Punjab* AIR 1980 SC 1632: (1980)2 SCC 565: (1980)3 SCR 383: 1980 Cr LR (SC) 475: 1980 Cr LJ 1125: 1980 SCC (Cri) 465].

NOTE: *Ordinary order of bail and order of anticipatory bail—distinction.* The distinction between an ordinary order of bail and an order of anticipatory bail is that whereas the former is granted after arrest and therefore means release from the custody of the police, the latter is granted in anticipation of arrest and is therefore effective at the very moment of arrest. [*Gurbaksh Singh Sibbia* v *State of Punjab*, supra].

**Anticipatory breach of contract.** A breach from the moment actual breach becomes inevitable.

NOTE: Under the rule a party is allowed to anticipate an inevitable event and is not obliged to wait till it happens. The breach which he anticipates is of just the same character as the breach which would actually have occurred if he had waited. [*Universal Cargo Carriers Corporation* v *Citati* (1957)2 All ER 70].

The rule shortly indicated by this phrase is that on the promisor's repudiation of the contract, even before the time for performance has arrived, the promisee may at his option treat the repudiation as an immediate breach, putting an end to the contract for the future and giving the promisee a right of action for damages.

Section 39 of the Indian Contract Act 1872 deals with this rule.

**Antiquity.** The state or quality of being ancient; anything belonging to ancient times.

NOTE: Antiquity includes—(*i*) any coin, sculpture, manuscript, epigraph, or other work of art or craftsmanship; (*ii*) any article, object or thing detached from a building or cave; (*iii*) any article, object or thing illustrative of science, art, crafts, literature, religion, customs, morals or politics in bygone ages; (*iv*) any article, object or thing of historical importance, and (*v*) any article, object or thing declared by the Central Government by notification in the Official Gazette, to be an antiquity for the purpose of Ancient Monuments and Archaeological Sites and Remains Act. [Ancient Monuments and Archaeological Sites and Remains Act 1958, s. 2(*b*)].

Antiquities include any movable object which the Central Government, by reason of their historical or archaeological associations, may think it necessary to protect against injury, removal or disperson. [Ancient Monuments Preservation Act 1904, s. 2(2)].

**Anuloma.** The form of marriage with woman of inferior caste, as for example, a Brahmin marrying a Kshatriya wife, a Vaisya wife and a Sudra wife, or a Kshatriya marrying a Vaisya wife and a Sudra wife etc. [*Rama*

*Sami* v *Sundaralingasami* 17 Mad 422, 435; Wilson *Glossary*].

> NOTE: The Hindu Marriage Validity Act 1949, legalised such marriage expressly with effect from April 15, 1949. Even before that *anuloma* marriages were permitted and recognised by texts. [Mulla on *Hindu Law,* 11th Ed. (edited by Dr. Bijan Mukherjea, J.), p. 543].

**Anumatipatra.** A deed expressive of assent or concurrence; especially a deed executed by husband about to die, authorising his widow to adopt a son. [Wilson's *Glossary*].

**Any.** Some; one out of many; an indefinite number.

"Any" does not necessarily mean only one person, but may have reference to more than one or to many. [*Doherty* v *King* Tex Civ App, 183 SW 2d 1004, 1007].

Word "any" has a diversity of meaning and may be employed to indicate "all" or "every" as well as "some" or "one" and its meaning in a given statute depends upon the context and the subject-matter of the statute. [*Donohue* v *Zoning Bd. of Appeals of Town of Norwalk* 235 A 2d 643, 646, 647; *Balaganesan Metals* v *M.N. Shanmugham Chetty* AIR 1987 SC 1668: (1987)2 SCR 1173: (1987)2 SCC 707: JT 1987(2) SC 247; *Lucknow Development Authority* v *M.K. Gupta* AIR 1994 SC 787: (1994)1 SCC 243: (1994)80 Comp Cas 714: (1994)1 SCC 243: JT 1993(6) SC 307].

The word 'any' excludes limitation or qualification. It connotes wide generality. Its use points to distributive construction. [*Veerappa Shiddalingappa* v *State of Mysore* AIR 1965 Mys 227].

'Any' may mean 'one' as contrasted with 'more than one'. [*In re Sundoorji Lalji* AIR 1947 Bom 30].

'Any' means all. [*Chief Inspector of Mines* v *Karam Chand Thapar* (1962)1 SCR 9].

**Any other.** The expression 'any other' cannot be given a narrow meaning so as to exclude some. [*Union of India* v *Indian Sugar Mills* AIR 1968 SC 22: (1968)2 SCJ 591: (1967)3 SCA 397; *Dev Kumar Singhji* v *State of Madhya Pradesh* AIR 1967 MP 268].

The words 'any other' mean analogous to those specified before. [*Moran Mar Basselios* v *Mar Poulose* AIR 1954 SC 526: 1954 SCJ 736: 1955 SCR 520; *Benoy Krishna* v *Surajbali* AIR 1963 Cal 100].

**Apabyabahara.** *Apabyabahara* means abuse of powers. [*Surendra Mohanty* v *Nabakrishna Choudhury* AIR 1958 Ori 168: 1958 Cr LJ 1055].

**Apartment.** A suite of rooms usually furnished and rented.

A building arranged in several suites of connecting rooms, each suite designed for independent housekeeping, but with certain mechanical conveniences, such as heat, light, or elevator services, in common to all families occupying the building. [Black's *Law Dictionary,* 5th Ed.]

▸*Meaning under the W.B. Apartment Ownership Act 1972, s. 3(a).* Part of a property, having a direct exit to a road, street or highway or to a common area leading to such road, street or highway which together with its undivided interest in the common areas and facilities forms an independent residential unit.

**Apology.** Admission of error or discourtesy accompanied by an expression of regret; admission of wrong or mistake with expression of regret.

> NOTE: Under the first proviso to s. 4 of the Contempt of Courts Act 1952, an accused may be discharged or the punishment remitted on apology being made to the satisfaction of the court. Except where courts are scandalised or scurrilous attacks are made on Judges and administration of justice, an unconditional apology made unreservedly at the first opportunity with a view to sincerely purge that contempt is generally accepted. [*State of Hyderabad* v *C. Natarajan* ILR (1954) Hyd 170: AIR 1954 Hyd 180].
>
> An apology is not a weapon of defence to purge the guilty of their offence; nor it is intended to operate as a universal panacea, but is intended to be evidence of real contriteness. [*Shareef* v *Hon'ble Judges* (1955)1 SCR 757: AIR 1955 SC 19: 1955 SCJ 54: 1955 SCA 205].

**Apostasy.** Renunciation of a religious faith; abandonment of a previous loyalty;

defection; desertion of one's faith, religion, party, or principles, abandonment of religious vow without dispensation.

**Apparent.** Readily visible or perceivable; that which is obvious, evident, or manifest; that which appears to the eye or mind; plain, patent.

**Apparent easement.** See under EASEMENT p. 291.

**Apparent error.** An "apparent error" means a patent mistake, an error which one could point out without any elaborate argument. [*Karam Chand Thapar and Bros. (Coal Sales) Limited* v *State of Uttar Pradesh* AIR 1976 SC 2101: (1976)4 SCC 257: (1976)38 STC 593: (1977)1 SCR 25].

**Appeal.** Apply to a higher court for a reconsideration of the decision of a lower court; refer to a higher court to review a case; the referral of a case to higher court; the removal of a cause from an inferior to a superior court for the purpose of testing the soundness of the decision of the inferior court; the removal of a cause or suit from an inferior to a superior Judge or court for re-examination or review; a proceeding taken to rectify an erroneous decision of a court by submitting the question to a higher court or court of appeal.

"The word (appeal) is in fact merely a term of convenient usage, part of a system of linguistic shorthand which accepts the need for a penumbra of uncertainty in order to achieve universal comprehensibility at a very low level of exactitude. Thus, while 'appeal' is a generic term broadly meaningful to all lawyers in describing a feature common to a wide range of legal systems, it would be misleading to impute a precise meaning to the term, or to assume, on the grounds that the word (or its translated equivalent) has international currency, that the concept of an appeal means the same thing in a wide range of systems.

"On any orthodox definition, an appeal includes three basic elements: a decision (usually the judgment of a court or the ruling of an administrative body) from which an appeal is made; a person or persons aggrieved by the decision (who is often, though by no means necessarily party to the original proceedings) and a reviewing body ready and willing to entertain the appeal". [*Final Appeal—A Study of the House of Lords in its Judicial Capacity* by Louis Blom & Cooper QC, Clavedon Press, Oxford, 1972, p. 44].

An appeal is described as "the right of entering a superior Court and invoking its aid and interposition to redress the error of the Court below". [*A.G.* v *H.I. Sillem* (1864) 33 LJ Ex 209: 11 ER 1200: 10 LT 434: 12 WR 641, *per* Lord Westbury, L.C.].

An appeal amounts in essence and pith to a complaint to a higher forum that the decision of subordinate forum is erroneous and therefore liable to be rectified or set right. An appeal strictly so called is the one in which the question is "whether the order of the Court from which the appeal is brought was right on the materials which that Court had before it". [*Ponnamma* v *Arumagam* (1905) AC 383: 92 LT 740, *per* Lord Davey].

The word "appeal" is defined as the judicial examination of a decision by a higher court of a decision of an inferior court. [*Lakshmiratan Engineering Works Ltd.* v *Asstt. Commissioner (Judicial) I, Sales Tax* AIR 1968 SC 488; *V.C. Shukla* v *State Through C.B.I.* AIR 1980 SC 962: 1980 (Supp) SCC 92: (1980)2 SCR 380: 1980 Cr LR 122 (SC): 1980 Cr LJ 690]. The purpose is to rectify any possible error in the order under appeal. [*V.C. Shukla* v *State Through C.B.I.*, supra].

"An appeal in legal parlance is held to mean the removal of a cause from an inferior or subordinate forum in order to test and scrutinise correctness of the impugned decision". [*Cref Finance Ltd.* v *Puri Construction Ltd.* AIR 2001 Del 414].

"There is no definition of appeal in the Code of Civil Procedure but their Lordships have no doubt that any application by a party to an appellate court is an appeal within the ordinary acceptance of the term and that it is no less an appeal because it is irregular or incompetent.

[*Nagendranath Dey* v *Suresh Chandra Dey* AIR 1932 PC 165].

NOTE: An appeal is a rehearing and in a moulding relief to be granted in a case on appeal, the Appellate Court is entitled to take into account even facts and events which have come into existence after the passing of the decree appealed against. [*Amarjit Kaur* v *Pritam Singh* (1975)1 SCR 605: AIR 1974 SC 2068].

Ordinarily the Supreme Court under Art. 136 of the Constitution would be averse to interfere with concurrent findings of facts recorded by the High Court and the Trial Court. But where there are material irregularities affecting the said findings or where the Court feels that justice has failed and the findings are likely to result in unduly excessive hardship, the Supreme Court cannot decline to interfere merely on the ground that findings in question are findings of fact. [*Ganga Bishan* v *Jay Narayan* AIR 1986 SC 441].

*'Appeal' and 'revision'—distinction.* An appeal is a continuation of a suit or proceedings wherein the entire proceedings are again left open for consideration by the appellate authorities which has the power to review the entire evidence subject, of course, to the prescribed statutory limitations. But in the case of revision whatever powers the revisional authority may have, it has no power to reassess and reappreciate the evidence unless the statute expressly confers on it that power. That limitation is implicit in the concept of revision. [*Lachhman Dass* v *Santosh Singh* (1995)4 SCC 201: JT 1995(7) SC 437].

'Appeal' and 'revision' are expression of common usage in Indian statute and the distinction 'appellate jurisdiction' and 'revisional jurisdiction' is well-known though not well defined. Ordinarily, appellate jurisdiction involves a rehearing, as it were, on law as well as fact and is invoked by an aggrieved person. Such jurisdiction may, however, be limited in some way as, for instance has been done in the case of second appeal under the Code of Civil Procedure, and under some Rent Acts in some States. Ordinarily, again, revisional jurisdiction is analogous to a power of superintendence and may sometimes be exercised even without its being invoked by a party. The extent of revisional jurisdiction is defined by the statute conferring such jurisdiction. The conferment of revisional jurisdiction is generally for the purpose of keeping tribunals subordinate to the revision tribunal within the bounds of their authority to make them act according to the procedure established by law and according to well defined principles of justice. Revisional jurisdiction as ordinarily understood with reference to our statute is always included in appellate jurisdiction but not *vice versa*. [*Sri Raja Lakshmi Dyeing Works* v *Rangaswamy Chettiar* AIR 1980 SC 1253: (1980)4 SCC 259].


- **Certificate of fit for appeal** p. 132.
- **Cross appeal** p. 210.
- **Sex appeal** p. 790.


**Appeal court.** A court taking cognizance of appeal. [*In re Madanlal* AIR 1960 AP 622].

**Appear.** Present oneself formally or publicly, especially as the counsel or accused in a law court; be evident.


- **Fails to appear** p. 338.


**Appearance.** It may have different meaning in different context. Its general meanings are: arrival into view; manifestation; complexion; external aspect, face, form; outward look; outward show; personal presence.

In law, it means: entrance in a case; presence in court; response to an action; submission to a court's jurisdiction.

NOTE: A party may be said to have appeared in the suit, if he has filed a plaint or a written statement, but that does not mean that he will be deemed to have been present when the suit is called on for hearing, if he is not actually present in person or by a pleader instructed to answer all material questions about the case as laid down in the Code itself. [*Suraj Prasad* v *Rambaran Singh* AIR 1956 Pat 127]. Order 9 of the Code of Civil Procedure 1908 deals with the appearance of parties and the consequences of non-appearance.

Where the plaintiff, though physically present in court, refuses to take part in the proceedings after the dismissal of his application for adjournment, as represented by his counsel, he cannot be said to have been present there as plaintiff partaking in the proceedings. He must be held not to have appeared at the hearing. [*Seetamma* v *Kameswar Rao* AIR 1967 Ori 152: ILR 1965 Cut 500: 31 Cut LT 1131; *Marothi Suryarao* v *Poluri* AIR 1967 AP 152: (1966)1 Andh LT 349: (1966)1

Andh WR 340; *Thummala V. Suryyamma* v *A.P. State Electricity* AIR 1975 AP 90; *Gopi Halwai* v *Zainab* AIR 1975 Pat 42: 1974 BLJR 393]. Presence of party's lawyer may amount to appearance of party. [*Re Ramineri* AIR 1980 AP 129].

• **Entering appearance** p. 310.

**Appellant.** A person who appeals to a higher court.

**Appellate.** Relating to or taking cognizance of appeals, specifically a superior tribunal having the power under law to sit in judgment over another tribunal.

**Append.** Annex; attach; affix; to add as a supplement, annexure or appendix.

**Appendage.** Appendage is an adjunct to something large or more important; appurtenance; a dependent or subordinate person; a subordinate part.

**Appendant.** A thing of inheritance belonging to another inheritance which is more worthy. It differs from appurtenance in that appendant must ever be by prescription, *i.e.,* a personal usage for a considerable time, while an appurtenance may be created at this day. [Wharton's *Law Lexicon*].

**Appertain.** To belong or to be connected as a rightful part or attribute of something more substantial; belong as a possession or right; be appropriate.

**Appliance.** Accessory; adjunct; apparatus, a device or piece of equipment used for a specific task; facility; mechanism; precision tool.

• **Domestic electrical appliances** p. 278.

**Applicant.** One who requests something; a petitioner; a candidate.

Applicant means a person who has made an application. [*Shaukat Ali* v *State* ILR (1956)2 All 587: AIR 1956 All 523].

▸*Meaning under the Limitation Act 1963, s. 2(a).* Applicant includes—(*i*) a petitioner; (*ii*) any person from or through whom an applicant derives his right to apply; (*iii*) any person whose estate is represented by the applicant as executor, administrator or other representative.

**Application.** A request made orally or in writing to a court; 'a request' motion to a 'court or judge'; the action of making an appeal, request or petition to a person; the request so made.

An application is the making of an appeal, request, or petition; to a person the request so made. [*Prem Raj* v *Ram Charan* AIR 1974 SC 968: (1974)2 SCC 1: (1974)3 SCR 494].

**Apply.** To make a prayer or request orally or in the form of a written application.

**Appoint.** To name or select, as a person for a position, a time and place for an act or meeting, etc.

The plain meaning of this word is to 'ordain or nominate to an office'. [*Keshav Singh Dwarkadas* v *Indian Engineering Co.* AIR 1969 Bom 227].

Appoint means to designate or to nominate. [*Kalyan Singh* v *Baldev Singh* AIR 1961 HP 3].

The *corpus juris* defines the word as 'to designate or nominate'. Choice of a particular person to fill a particular post constitutes the essence of appointment. [*Prosanta Kumar* v *Jagannath Jew* AIR 1971 Ori 246: ILR (1971) Cut 1125: (1971)37 Cut LT 503].

NOTE: The word appointed does not mean necessarily already appointed. It may also mean to be appointed at any future time. [*Assam State* v *Sristi Kar* AIR 1957 SC 414: 1957 SCA 697: 1957 SCR 295].

**Appointee.** One who is benefited by the execution of a power of appointment; also a person selected for a particular purpose. [Jowitt's *Dictionary of English Law,* 2nd Ed].

**Appointment.** An engagement; placing in office; ordination; installation; selection; a power or right to control or designate the disposition of property.

Appointment means direction, designation, the selection of a person for an office. [Wharton's *Law Lexicon*].

Appointment means an actual act of posting a person to a particular office.

[*Basant Lal* v *State of Punjab* ILR (1969)2 Punj 292: AIR 1969 Punj 178].

Appointment obviously refers to appointment to an office. The term appointment therefore implies the conception of tenure; duration, emolument and duties and obligations fixed by law or by some rule having the force of law. [*Sukhandan Thakur* v *State of Bihar* AIR 1967 Pat 617].

Appointment can only mean post, station or office, and not the whole service. [*R.P. Kapur* v *Pratap Singh* (1964)1 SCR 224].

The word 'appointment' in the context of the Companies Act is used in the sense of 'election'. Instances of such usage of the term are found in the provisions relating to the election of auditors in ss. 224 and 255 of the Act. [*M. Ramchandra Bail* v *M.R. Kannaih* 1966 Cr LJ 1276: AIR 1966 Mad 40].

• **Date of appointment** p. 224.
• **Pleasure of appointment** p. 667.

**Apportionment.** The act or an instance of apportioning. A division of the whole into parts (usually unequal) proportioned to the rights of more claimants than one. It is either apportionment in respect of time or apportionment in respect of estate.

'Apportionment' has been defined as a division or distribution of the subject-matter in proportionate shares; the act of distributing or allotting in proper shares, and the division of whole into parts. [*Rajash Sarvagna Kumara Krishna* v *Rajah Navaneetha Krishna* AIR 1957 AP 523].

> NOTE: Section 36 of the Transfer of Property Act 1882, provides for apportionment by time and s. 37 deals with apportionment by estate. Provision for apportionment of compensation on acquisition is made in ss. 29 and 30 of the Land Acquisition Act 1894.

**Apportionment of contract.** A contract is said to be apportionable when the acts to be done under the contract are so distinct that if one is performed without the others, the party performing it has the right to enforce the contract *pro tanto* against the other party. Thus, if *A* enters into a contract to supply machinery to *B* for a certain price and to keep it in repair for a yearly payment, *A* becomes entitled to recover the price of machinery as soon as he delivers it, without waiting for the performance of the rest of the contract. [Jowitt's *Dictionary of English Law*, 2nd Ed.].

**Apposition.** A word is said to be used in apposition to another in contradistinction to being used disjunctively; thus, if two nouns occur with word 'or' between them, and if the word 'or' be taken to mean 'otherwise called' the second noun is used in apposition. But if the two nouns mean two different things, the nouns are said to be used disjunctively. [*Ibid*].

**Appraisers.** Persons appointed to value goods, repairs, labour, etc. An appraiser is appointed by a competent authority to ascertain and state the true value of property submitted to his inspection, and he is usually sworn to perform such duty conscientiously and to the best of his ability. Under the ancient English law, appraisers of goods valuing goods too high were required to take them at the price appraised.

**Apprehend.** Capture; confine; detain by legal process; legally restrain; place under arrest; put in restraint; send to prison; take captive; take into custody; take prisoner.

Its other meanings are: be acquainted with; be apprised of; be aware of; be cognizant of; be conscious of; discover by observation; fathom; have an impression.

**Apprehension.** Arrest; capture; confinement; detention; holding in custody; imprisonment; internment; taking hold; seizure in the name of the law.

Its other meanings are: alarm; anticipation of adversity; anxiety; sense of danger; trepidation, perception; comprehension; belief; understanding.

**Apprentice.** A person who is learning a trade by being employed in it for an agreed period at low wages; a beginner; a novice.

"In legal acceptation, an apprentice is a person bound to another for the purpose of learning his trade, or calling; the contract being of that nature that the master teaches and the other serves the master with the intention of learning". [*Clapham* v *St. Pancras* 29 LJMC 143, 144, *per* Cockburn, C.J.].

▸*Meaning under Apprentices Act 1961, s. 2(a).* Apprentice means a person who is undergoing apprenticeship training in designated trade in pursuance of a contract of apprenticeship.

NOTE: The purpose of the engagement under the particular scheme is only to offer training under certain terms and conditions. Besides, the apprentices are not given wages within the meaning of that term under the Act. If they were regular employees, they would have been entitled to additional remuneration such as daily allowance and other allowances which are available to the regular employees. An apprentice is not an employee. [*The Employees' State Insurance Corporation* v *The Tata Engineering and Locomotive Co. Ltd.* AIR 1976 SC 66: (1976)2 SCR 199: (1975)2 SCC 835].

The apprentices are mere trainees for a particular period for a distinct purpose and the employer is not bound to employ them in their works after the period of training is over. [*The ESI Corporation* v *Tata Engg. & Locomotive Co. Ltd.*, supra].

**Approbate.** To approve; to sanction formally or officially.

NOTE: *Approbate and reprobate.* Take advantage of one portion of a document and reject another portion.

It is a phrase borrowed from Scottish Law, where it is used to express the principle embodied in the English doctrine of election—namely, that no party can accept and reject the same instrument. [*Verschures Creameries Ltd.* v *Hall & Netherlands Steamship Co.* (1921)2 KB 608; *Douglas Menzies* v *Umphelby* (1908) AC 224, 232, *per* Scrutton, L.J.].

The maxim that a person cannot 'approbate and reprobate' is only one application of the doctrine of election, its operation must be confined to reliefs claimed in respect of the same transactions and to the persons who are parties thereto. A party cannot, after taking advantage under an order, be heard to say that it is invalid and asked to set it aside, or to set up to the prejudice of persons who have relied upon it. [*Nagubai* v *Shama Rao* AIR 1956 SC 593].

**Appropriation.** The act of appropriating or setting apart; prescribing the destination of a thing; designating the use or application of a fund. [*McKenzie Const. Co.* v *City of San Antonio* Tex Civ App, 50 SW 2d 349, 352].

In governmental accounting, it means an expenditure authorised for a specified amount, purpose, and time.

**Appropriation account or statement.** An account or statement of a business which shows the profits available for distribution or appropriation and how they are dealt with.

**Appropriation of payments.** The application of a payment to the discharge of a public debt.

**Approval.** Consent; a favourable opinion; act of confirming; ratifying; assenting; sanctioning.

Approval implies knowledge and exercise of discretion after knowledge. [Black's *Law Dictionary*, 5th Ed.].

'Approval' is nothing but sanction on being satisfied of a particular fact which is found to be good and satisfactory. It does not amount to technical audit or investigation or picking the holes. [*Devarakonda* v *All India Council for Technical Education* (1997)3 Andh LT 117].

NOTE: *'Approval' and 'permission'—distinction.* Ordinarily, the difference between approval and permission is that in the first case the action holds good until it is disapproved, while in the other case it does not become effective until permission is obtained. [*U.P. Avas Evam Vikas Parishad* v *Friends Co-op. Housing Society Ltd.* AIR 1996 SC 114: (1995)2 SCJ 225: 1995 Supp (3) SCC 456: 1995 AIR SCW 3800].

**Approval, sale on.** A sale in which completion hinges on the buyer's satisfaction, regardless of whether the goods conform to the contract. Title and risk of loss remain with the seller until the buyer approves. [Black's *Law Dictionary*, 8th Ed.].

NOTE: When goods are delivered to the buyer on approval, the property passes to the buyer when he signifies his approval. If he does not signify his approval to the seller but retains the goods without notice of rejection, then after the expiry of the prescribed time if any or of reasonable time, the property passes to the buyer. [Section 24 of the Sale of Goods Act 1930].

**Approve.** Confirm; sanction; give or have a favourable opinion; commend.

**Approved bill.** A bill to which no reasonable objection can be made, and which ought to be approved; a bill drawn by a solvent, trustworthy party.

**Approved plan.** A plan lawfully approved by a local authority, and not merely one which has in fact been approved.

**Approver.** One who offers proof, especially, a criminal who confesses and testifies against one or more accomplices. [Black's *Law Dictionary*, 8th Ed.].

An approver is an accomplice in crime who accuses others of the same offence, and is admitted as a witness at the discretion of the court to give evidence against his companions in guilt. His testimony must necessarily be of an unsatisfactory nature and is not usually believed unless corroborated in some material particular by independent untainted testimony. [*Re Meunier* (1894)2 QB 415].

NOTE: Section 306 of the Code of Criminal Procedure 1973, provides for the tender of pardon to an accomplice. The motivating fact for an approver to turn is the hope of pardon and not repentance at the evil in which he has participated. The condition for tender of pardon is that the accomplice shall make a full and true disclosure of the whole of the circumstances within his knowledge relative to the concerned offence. Besides, the court is to see that the approver's evidence has been corroborated sufficiently in material particulars. [*State of A.P.* v *C.G. Rao* (1964)3 SCR 297].

Unless an approver is already on bail, he is not entitled to bail till the termination of trial. But then he must be kept in judicial custody, not police custody.

**Approximate.** Very near, closely resembling or fairly correct. [*Om Prakash* v *Maya Ram* AIR 1964 All 430: 1963 All LJ 628].

**Approximate quantity.** The expression "approximate quantity" is meant to convey that the quantity to be supplied must be in the close vicinity of the quantity of the specified. [*State of Kerala* v *Alasserry Mohammed* AIR 1978 SC 933: (1978)2 SCR 820: (1978)2 SCC 386: 1978 Cr LJ 925: 1978 Cr LR (SC) 100: 1978 SCC (Cri) 198].

**Appurtenance.** That which belongs to something else; an adjunct; an appendage; an accessory; something annexed to another thing more worthy as principal, and which passes as incident to it, as a right of way or other easement of land.

An appurtenance has been defined in the *Oxford English Dictionary* as follows: A thing that belongs to another, 'belonging'; a minor property, right, or privileges, belonging to another more important, and passing in possession with it; an appendage. An appurtenance belongs to the building concerned and has no existence of its own. [*D.G. Gouse and Co.* v *State of Kerala* AIR 1980 SC 271: (1980)1 SCR 804: (1980)2 SCC 410].

**Appurtenant.** Belonging to; accessory or incident to; adjunct, appended, or annexed to.

The word appurtenant has diverse meanings depending upon the context in which it is used it. It is a term of variable import, scope and ambit. In its primary sense, it imports nothing more than what is strictly appertaining to the subject-matter of demise or grant, and which would in truth, pass without being specially mentioned. [*Kamalaben* v *Bulchand* (1993)2 Guj LR 1083; Halsbury's *Laws of England*, 4th Ed., vol. 27, p. 103].

A thing is deemed to be incidental or appurtenant to land when it is by right used with the land for its benefit, as in the case of a way, or water-course, or of a passage for light, air, or heat from or across the land of another.

This word means 'pertaining to' or 'belonging to'; it does not mean adjacent to, and so proximity of the appurtenant land is not essential. What is essential is the concept of belonging for more beneficial enjoyment of the parent property. [*Harnam Singh* v *Bhikhimbar Singh* AIR 1980 All 50: 1980 All LR 434].

**Apratibandha.** When the inheritance descends from father to son or grandfather to grandson, it is called *apartibandha* or unobstructed inheritance. [*Bapuji* v *Pandurang* 6 Bom 616; Wilson's *Glossary*].

NOTE: Property in which a person acquires an interest by birth is *apratibandha daya* according to the Mitakshara school of Hindu law.

**Aputra.** A man who has no son, who has never had, or who has lost an only son and may therefore adopt one.

**Aquatic rights.** Rights which individuals have to the use of water of the sea and rivers for the purpose of fishing and navigation and also to the soil in the sea and rivers. Rights exercisable in running or still water.

**Arable land.** Fit for cultivation. [*Abdul Jabbar* v *State of W.B.* 71 CWN 129, 14]. Arable land means not only land capable of cultivation but also actually cultivated. [*Ishwarlal Girdharlal* v *State* (1968)1 SCA 569: (1968)2 SCR 267: AIR 1968 SC 870; Stroud's *Judicial Dictionary*].

NOTE: *'Arable land' and 'waste land'—distinction.* The expression "arable land" must be construed to mean "lands which are mainly used for ploughing and for raising crops and the expression "waste land" would mean "land which is unfit for cultivation or habitation, desolate and barren land with little or no vegetation thereon. [*Raja Anand Brahma Shah* v *State of U.P.* AIR 1967 SC 1081: (1967)1 SCR 373].

**Arbitrage.** The buying and selling of stocks or bills of exchange to take advantage of varying prices in different markets; the simultaneous purchase in one market and sale in another of a security or commodity with the hope of making profit on price differences in different markets.

**Arbitrarily.** Without any reasonable cause. [*Quinion* v *Horne* (1960)1 Ch 596].

**Arbitrary.** Capricious; based on or derived from uninformed opinion or random choice; despotic; without adequate determining principle; non-rational; without fair, solid and substantial cause, *i.e.*, without cause based upon the law.

**Arbitration.** The settlement of a dispute by an arbitrator; the reference of a dispute to an impartial person chosen by the parties to the dispute who agree to abide by the arbitration award to be given after hearing of both the parties.

An arbitration is the reference of a dispute or difference between not less than two parties for determination, after hearing both sides in a judicial manner, by a person or persons other than a court of competent jurisdiction.

▸*Meaning under the Arbitration and Conciliation Act 1996, s. 2(1)(a).* Arbitration means any arbitration whether or not administered by permanent arbitral institution.

• **International arbitration** p. 474.

**Arbitration agreement.** A written agreement to submit present or future differences to arbitration, whether an arbitrator is named therein or not. [Arbitration Act 1940, s. 2(*a*)].

▸*Meaning under the Arbitration and Conciliation Act 1996, s. 7(1).* Arbitration agreement means an agreement by the parties to submit to arbitration all or certain disputes which have arisen or which may arise between them in respect of a defined legal relationship, whether contractual or not.

**Arbitration clause.** A clause in a deed providing for arbitration in case of disputes between the parties. If the contract is void or illegal, the arbitration clause also falls. [*Goolbai Hornmasji* v *Jugalkishore* AIR 1952 Bom 95].

**Arbitrator.** A person appointed to settle a dispute; an arbiter; a disinterested person chosen by the parties for the purpose of settlement of a disputed question.

**Arbitrium est judicium.** The maxim means that the award of an arbitrator is the same thing as a judgment.

**Archaka.** Derived from 'Archa' meaning idol. A priest who alone is allowed personally to attend upon the idol. His duties are those of offering of worship in the temple on behalf of the community. [*Narasimma* v *Anautha* 4 Mad 391; Wilson's *Glossary*].

**Archives.** A chamber or place where ancient records, charters, and evidences are kept; a place where public, historical, or institutional records are systematically preserved; any systematic compilation of materials, especially writings, in physical and electronic form.

**Area.** Arena; confines; bounds; the extent or measure of a surface; a region or tract; a space allocated for a specific purpose; the scope or range of an activity; jurisdiction; limits; range; scope; territory; zone.

- **Defence area** p. 241.
- **Local area** p. 540.

**Argument.** War of words; verbal conflict; oral contention; altercation; course of reasoning; discourse designed to convince, expression of opinion for or against; statement tending to prove a point; submission.

> NOTE: In reasoning Locke observes that men ordinarily use four sorts of arguments. The first is to allege the opinion of men, whose parts and learning, eminence, power or some other cause have gained a name, and settled their reputation in the common esteem with some kind of authority; this may be called *argumentum ad verecundium*. The second is to require the adversary to admit what they allege as a proof or to require a better; this he calls *argumentum an ignorantium*. The third is to press a man with consequences drawn from his own principles, concessions or actions; this is known by the name of *argumentum ad hominem*. The fourth is using proofs drawn from any of the foundation of knowledge or probability; this he calls *argumentum ad judicium*, and he observes that it is the only one of all the four that bring true instruction with it, and advances us in our way to knowledge. [Wharton's *Law Lexicon*].

**Arhatiya.** Purchaser purchasing goods from dealer and selling them in market at a profit. He is a dealer within the meaning of U.P. Sales Tax Act, s. 2(*c*)—distinction between Kachha and Pucca arhatiya pointed out. [*C.S.T.* v *Bishambar Singh* (1981)2 SCC 27: 1981 SCC (Tax) 64: (1981)1 SCR 548: (1981)47 STC 80].

**Arising out of employment.** The words 'arising out of employment' are understood to mean 'during the course of the employment'. The expression "arising out of employment" is again not confined to the mere nature of the employment. The expression applies to employment as such to its nature, its conditions, its obligations and its incidents. [*Mackinnon Mackenzie & Co. (P) Ltd.* v *Ibrahim Mohammed Issak* AIR 1970 SC 1906: (1970)1 SCR 869: (1969)2 SCC 607].

- **Injury arising out of employment.** These words describe an injury directly and naturally resulting in a risk reasonably incident to the employment. [*Thomas* v *Proctor & Gamble Mfg. Co.* 179 P 372, 374].

These words mean injury resulting from some risk incidental to the duties of the service which, unless engaged in the duty owing to the master, it is reasonable to believe the servant would not otherwise have suffered. In other words, there must be a casual relationship between the accident and the employment. If by reason of any of the factors, namely, nature of employment, its conditions, obligations and incidents, the servant is brought within the zone of special danger, the injury would be one which arises out of employment. [*Mackinnon Mackenzie & Co. (P) Ltd.* v *Ibrahim Mohammad Issak* AIR 1970 SC 1906: (1970)1 SCR 869: (1969)2 SCC 607].

**Armed neutrality.** The maintenance by a nation of an armed force held ready to repel any aggression on the part of belligerent nations between which it is neutral.

**Armistice.** A temporary, but for the time being total, suspension of hostilities by arrangement between the Governments of the belligerents, usually for the purpose of considering overtures by one of the parties for the consideration of peace. [Jowitt's *Dictionary of English Law*, 2nd Ed.].

**Arms.** Articles of any description designated or adapted as weapons for offence or defence and includes firearms, sharp-edged and other deadly weapons and parts of and machinery for manufacturing arms, but does not include articles designated solely for domestic or agricultural uses, such as a lathi or an ordinary walking stick and weapons incapable of being used otherwise than as toys or of being converted into serviceable weapons. [Arms Act 1959, s. 2(1)(*c*)].

NOTE: A sword is 'arms' within the meaning of s. 2(1)(*c*) of the Arms Act 1959. [*Neel* alias *Niranjan Majumdar* v *State of West Bengal* AIR 1972 SC 2066: (1972)2 SCC 668: (1973)1 SCR 675: 1973 SCC (Cri) 64].

**Arrangement.** In its application to ordering, it means adaption; arraying; collocation; conformation; method; systematisation.

In its application to plan, it means conception; contrivance; course of action; ground plan; lay out; programme of action.

In its application to understanding, it means abatement of differences; adjustment by agreement; harmonisation; mutual assent or understanding.

**Arrears.** An amount still outstanding; money which is overdue and unpaid.

"'Arrears' presupposes a time fixed for payment of a sum of money and the lapse of time thereafter without payment". [*Paice* v *Ayton* (1941) VLR 63, 68, *per* Mann, C.J.].

"Arrears" mean money unpaid at the due time. [*Dhan Singh Ramkrishna Chaudhuri* v *Laxminarayan Ramkishan* AIR 1974 SC 1613: (1975)1 SCR 94: (1974)2 SCC 393].

**Arrest.** Seize a person and take into custody, especially, by legal authority; deprive a person of his liberty by legal authority; seize a ship by legal authority; stop or check.

The deprivation of liberty by legal authority, in a professionally competent and adept manner amounts to 'arrest'. The act of apprehending a person for the alleged commission of an offence or by the action of an authority is defined as arrest.

Arrest is defined as 'the act of depriving a person of liberty under governmental authority for the purpose of taking that person into detention and charging the person with a criminal offence'. [United Nations, 'Human Rights and Pre-trial Detention', New York 1994, p. 6].

Arrest consists of the actual seizure or touching of a person's body with a view to his detention. The mere pronouncing of words of arrest is not an arrest, unless the person sought to be arrested submits to the process and goes with the arresting officer. An arrest may be made either with or without a warrant. [Halsbury's *Laws of England*, 3rd Ed., vol. 10, p. 342].

The word 'arrest' is derived from the French word 'Arreter' meaning 'to stop or stay' and signifies a restraint of the person. Lexicologically, the meaning of the word 'arrest' is given in various dictionaries depending upon the circumstances in which the said expression is used. [*Directorate of Enforcement* v *Deepak Mahajan* AIR 1994 SC 1775: (1994)3 SCC 440: 1994 SCC (Cri) 785: 1994 Cr LJ 2269: (1994)70 ELT 912: JT 1994(1) SC 290: (1995)82 Comp Cas 103].

The word 'arrest', when used in its ordinary and natural sense, means the apprehension or restraint or the deprivation of one's personal liberty. The question whether the person is under arrest or not, depends not on the legality of the arrest, but on whether he has been deprived of his personal liberty to go where he pleases. When used in the legal sense in the procedure connected with criminal offences, an arrest consists in the taking into custody of another person under the authority empowered by law, for the purpose of holding or detaining him to answer a criminal charge or of preventing the commission of a criminal offence. The essential elements to constitute an arrest in the above sense are that there must be an intent to arrest under the authority, accompanied by a seizure or detention of the person in the manner known to law, which is so understood by the person arrested. [*Roshan Beevi* v *Joint Secretary to Government of Tamil Nadu* 1983 Mad

LW (Cr) 289: 1984 Cr LJ 134 (Mad) (FB): AIR 1984 NOC 103 (Mad)].

NOTE: The words 'arrest' and 'custody' are not synonymous terms. In every arrest, there is custody but not *vice versa*. [*Directorate of Enforcement* v *Deepak Mahajan* AIR 1994 SC 1775: (1994)3 SCC 440: 1994 SCC (Cri) 785: 1994 Cr LJ 2269: (1994)70 ELT 912: JT 1994(1) SC 290: (1995)82 Comp Cas 103].

• **Lawful arrest** p. 518.

**Arrest warrant.** See under WARRANT p. 892.

**Arson.** The act of maliciously setting fire to property.

Arson, *ab ardendo*, is the malicious and wilful burning of the house or outhouses of another man. This is an offence of very great malignity: because, first, it is an offence against the right of habitation which is acquired by the law of nature as well as by the laws of society; next, because of the terror and confusion that necessarily attends it; and, lastly, by burning the very substance of the thing is absolutely destroyed.

**Article.** A particular object or substance; a material thing or class of things; material or tangible object.

NOTE: A machine is a tangible thing which can both be seen and felt and as such it answers the description of an 'article'. A "machine" is a "thing" and is therefore an "article". [*Zaffar Mohammad* v *State of West Bengal* AIR 1976 SC 171: (1976)2 SCR 782: (1976)1 SCC 428: 1976 Cr LJ 190: 1976 SCC (Cri) 46: 1976 Cr LR (SC) 44].

A separate and distinct part of an instrument or writing; one of several things presented as connected or forming a whole.

A literary composition forming an independent part of a publication, *e.g.* an article in a newspaper.

• **Postal article** p. 673.

**Articles.** A connected series of propositions; a system of rules; the subdivisions of a document, code, book, etc.; a specification of distinct matters agreed upon or established by authority or requiring judicial action.

A system of rules established by legal authority; as articles of war, articles of the navy, articles of faith.

A contractual document executed between parties, containing stipulations or terms of agreement; as articles of agreement, articles of partnership.

A naval term meaning employment contract. [*South Chicago Coal & Dock Co.* v *Bassett*, 104 F 2d 522, 526].

**Articles of association.** These are regulations for the management and internal arrangement of a company and the terms and conditions on which the shareholders agree, amongst themselves, as to how the business of the company shall be carried on.

NOTE: Table A of the First Schedule to the Companies Act (s. 28) consists of a specimen set of regulations applicable to a company limited by shares. The Act prevails over the articles.

**Articulated vehicle.** A motor vehicle in which a semi-trailer is attached. [Motor Vehicles Act 1988, s. 2(2)].

**Artificial.** Not real; fake; anything that does not originate naturally but is produced by human art or effort.

As opposed to "natural", it means created or produced by man. [*California Casualty Indemnity Exchange* v *Industrial Accident Commission of California* 13 Cal 2d 529].

**Artificial insemination.** The injection of semen into the vagina or uterus other than by sexual intercourse; method by which a female is impregnated through injection of semen from a donor and other than through sexual intercourse.

**Artificial person.** A corporation or a company which is vested with legal powers and liabilities and subject to rights and duties, so far as possible, as though it were a natural person.

**Artificial silk.** Silk not natural. Artificial silk includes products such as, Terylene, Terene, Decron, Nylon, Nylex etc. [*Kishinchand* v *Joint Commercial Tax Officer* (1969)1 MLJ 229].

**Artisan.** Skilled workman, mechanic and handicraftsman. [*Cachar Cha Sramik* v *Manager, Majhegram Tea Estate* AIR 1960 Assam 123].

The word 'artisan', has to be understood in common parlance in a wider sense as an art or an artist or one employed in any of the industrial arts or one who produces an article of commercial value or utility with manual dexterity, either by manual labour or with the help of tools or machine and brings into existence a product for sale or service. An element of not only creativity would be applied to bring into existence an article or commercial goods with dexterity employing manual or technical labour or with the aid of tools etc. However, it is not exhaustive. Each case must be considered on its own facts and attendant circumstances to find whether the workman is an artisan. [*State of Orissa* v *Adwait Charan Mohanty* 1995 Supp (1) SCC 470: 1995 SCC (L&S) 522: JT 1995(2) SC 6: 1995(1) SLR 723].

NOTE: Ordinarily the driver of a motor car is not an artisan. [*Maniklal Upadhyay* v *Ramesh Chandra* AIR 1955 Cal 290: 59 CWN 466].

**Artistic work.** Artistic work means—(*i*) a painting, a sculpture, a drawing (including a diagram, map, chart or plan), an engraving or a photograph, whether or not any such work possesses artistic quality; (*ii*) a work of architecture; and (*iii*) any other work of artistic craftsmanship. [Copyright Act 1957, s. 2(*c*)].

**Arzi.** A petition, an address, a memorial, a respectful statement or representation, whether oral or written. [Wilson's *Glossary*].

**As.** To the same extent or degree; equally; for instance; in the manner of; in the way that; while; at the same time that; because; considering that; however; though; in the capacity or form; for the reason that.

In the manner prescribed. [*Variavan Saraswathi* v *Eachampi Thevi* 1993 Supp (2) SCC 201].

**As against, as between.** These words contrast the relative position of two persons with a tacit reference to a different relationship between one of them and a third person. For instance, the temporary bailee of a chattel is entitled to it, as between himself and a stranger, or as against a stranger; reference being made by this form of words to the rights of the bailor. [Wharton's *Law Lexicon*].

**As far as may be necessary.** The expression may operate to exclude certain provisions or part thereof. [*S.B. Trading* v *Shyamlal* AIR 1951 Cal 539: ILR (1953)2 Cal 15].

**As far as possible.** The expression means that the principle is to be followed, unless it is not possible to follow it in the particular circumstances of a case. [*Rani* v *Deputy Director* AIR 1959 All 525: 1959 All LJ 438].

**As he deems fit.** The expression 'as he deems fit' does not bestow a power to make any order on considerations *de hors* the statute which the authorities consider best according to their notions of justice. The general terms are used so that different orders under the Act may be passed in consideration of different circumstances. [*Rajaram Mahadev Paranjpe* v *Abu Maruti* AIR 1962 SC 753].

**As if.** The expression 'as if' is used to make one applicable in respect of another. [*Morlays (B'Ham) Ltd.* v *Roshan Lal* AIR 1961 Bom 156; *Akhtari Begum* v *Appellate Authority* AIR 1956 MB 175; *Kuppa Gounder* v *Joint Sub-Registrar* AIR 1960 Mad 401].

The expression 'as if it were land revenue' means that the same in its proper nature is not land revenue at all. But it would be treated for the particular purpose as land revenue, e.g., recovery of any amount due. [*State of Mysore* v *Official Liquidator* AIR 1965 Mys 261].

**As it may judge.** The expression confides in clear and unambiguous terms the authority to judge. [*Karanpura Development* v *Kamakshya Narain* 1956 SCR 325: AIR 1956 SC 446: 1956 SCA 591: 1956 SCJ 511].

**As nearly as may be.** The expression indicates only an approximation. [*Raghunadha Rao* v *State of Orissa* ILR (1955) Ori 510: AIR 1955 Ori 113].

**As of right.** The enjoyment 'as of right' must mean an enjoyment had, not secretly or by stealth or by tacit sufferance or by permission asked from time to time, on each occasion or even of many occasions of using it; but an enjoyment had openly, notoriously, without particular leave at the time, by a person claiming to use it without danger of being treated as trespasser, as a matter of right, whether strictly legal by prescription and adverse user or by deed conferring the right, or though not legal yet lawful to the extent of excusing a trespass as by consent, or agreement in writing. [*Tickle* v *Brown* (1836)4 Ad & El 369].

**As soon as may be.** The expression means within the time which was reasonably convenient or requisite. [*Abdul Jabar* v *State* AIR 1957 SC 281].

**As the case may be.** The expression indicates one out of the various situations indicated and not otherwise. [*Khan Chand Tiloke Ram* v *State of Punjab* AIR 1966 Punj 424].

**Asami.** A cultivator, a tenant, a renter, a non-proprietary cultivator; also a dependant; also a debtor, a culprit, a criminal, a defendant in a civil or criminal action.

**Ascendants.** The progenitors of a family. Those from whom a person is descended.

**Ascertain.** Find out as a definite fact; render certain; estimate and determine; find out by investigation. [*US* v *Carver* 260 US 482].

The word 'ascertain' has two meanings. The strict and proper meaning is to make certain. In a loose and popular sense it means to get to know. [*Bhagwant* v *K.L. Chincholkar* ILR (1956) Nag 38: AIR 1956 Nag 183].

Goods are "ascertained" when these are "identified and appropriate to the contract" under s. 18 of the Sale of Goods Act 1920. [*P.S. etc. Chettiar & Co. Ltd.* v *Express Newspapers Ltd., Bombay* AIR 1968 SC 741, 744].

**Assault.** A violent verbal attack; an act of rape; vigorous start made to a lengthy or difficult task.

An act that threatens physical harm to a person, whether or not actual harm is done. Any intentional display of force as would give the victim reason to fear or expect immediate bodily harm, constitutes an assault. An assault may be committed without actually touching, or striking, or doing bodily harm.

NOTE: Assault may be of various kinds like aggravated assault, simple assault. Aggravated assault is committed with the intention of doing some additional crime; or one attended with circumstances of peculiar outrage or atrocity. This includes assault with a dangerous or deadly weapon. In USA, a person is guilty of aggravated assault if he: (*a*) attempts to cause serious bodily injury to another, or causes such injury purposely, knowingly or recklessly under circumstances manifesting extreme indifference to the value of human life; or (*b*) attempts to cause or purposely or knowingly causes bodily injury. [Model Penal Code, s. 211.1]. Simple assault remains unaccompanied by any circumstances of aggravation. In USA, a person is guilty of simple assault if he: (*a*) attempts to cause or purposely, knowingly or recklessly causes bodily injury to another; or (*b*) negligently caused bodily injury to another with a deadly weapon; or (*c*) attempts by physical menace to put another in fear of imminent serious bodily injury. [Model Penal Code, s. 211.1].

**Assay.** Means in mining, the testing of samples of ore to ascertain how much metal they contain; the testing of coins etc., to ascertain how much gold or silver they contain.

**Assembly.** A company of persons gathered for deliberation and legislation, worship or entertainment; a legislative body, specifically the lower house of a legislature.

• **Unlawful assembly** p. 866.

**Assent.** Consent; express agreement; a declaration of willingness to do something in compliance with a request.

It implies a conscious approval of facts actually known.

NOTE: Assent may be express or implied. Express assent is that which is openly declared. Implied assent is presumed by law and proved by conduct of parties. Assent may also be mutual. It means the meeting of minds of both or all the parties to a contract.

**Assertion.** A declaration or allegation; affirmation; announcement; asseveration; avouchment; disclosure; positive declaration; pronouncement.

- **Implied assertion** p. 432.

**Assess.** Estimate the size or quality of; estimate the value of a property for taxation; fix the amount of a tax etc. and impose it on a person or community.

**Assessee.** Assessee means a person by whom any tax or any other sum of money is payable under the Income Tax Act and includes—(*a*) every person in respect of whom any proceeding under this Act has been taken for the assessment of his income or assessment of fringe benefits or of the income of any other person in respect of which he is assessable, or of the loss sustained by him or by such other person, or of the amount of refund due to him or to such other person; (*b*) every person who is deemed to be an assessee under any provision of this Act; (*c*) every person who is deemed to be an assessee in default under any provision of this Act. [Income Tax Act 1961, s. 2(7)].

▸ *Meaning under the Companies (Profits) Surtax Act 1964, s. 2(1).* Assessee means a person by whom surtax or any other sum of money is payable under the Companies (Profits) Surtax Act 1964, and includes every person in respect of whom any proceedings under that Act has been taken for the assessment of his chargeable profits or of the amount of refund due to him or of the chargeable profits of any other person in respect of which he is assessable or of the amount of refund due to such other person.

▸ *Meaning under the Gift Tax Act 1958, s. 2(iii).* Assessee means a person by whom gift-tax or any other sum of money is payable under this Act and includes—(*a*) every person in respect of whom any proceeding under this Act has been taken for the determination of gift-tax payable by him or any other person or the amount of refund due to him or such other person; (*b*) every person who is deemed to be an assessee under this Act; (*c*) every person who is deemed to be an assessee in default under this Act.

**Assessment.** The term "assessment", is generally used in the country for the actual procedure adopted in fixing the liability to pay a tax on account of particular goods or property or whatever may be the object of the tax in a particular case and determining its amount. [*Assistant Collector of Central Excise, Calcutta* v *National Tobacco Co. of India Ltd.* AIR 1972 SC 2563: (1972)2 SCC 560: (1973)1 SCR 822: 1978 ELT (J) 416].

The word 'assessment' is used as meaning sometimes the computation of income, sometimes the determination of the amount of tax payable and sometimes the whole procedure laid down in the Income Tax Act for imposing liability upon the taxpayer. [*Commissioner of Income Tax* v *Khanchand Ramdas* AIR 1938 PC 175; *Kalawati Devi* v *Commissioner of Income Tax* AIR 1968 SC 162: (1968)2 SCR 674: (1968)2 SCJ 61; *Sales Tax Officer* v *Sudarsanam* AIR 1970 SC 311; *Sales Tax Officer* v *Iyengar & Sons* AIR 1970 SC 511].

In its application to income-tax, "assessment" is one integrated process involving not only the assessment of the total income but also the determination of the tax. [*Kalyan Kumar Ray* v *C.I.T.* (1991)191 ITR 634 (SC)].

"Assessment" is the process of determining the total income of the assessee and the sum payable by the assessee as income-tax, surcharge, super tax, etc. [*The Commissioner of Income Tax, Kanpur* v *J.K. Commercial Corporation Ltd.* AIR 1977 SC 459: (1977)1 SCR 512: (1976)4 SCC 517].

- **Escaped assessment** p. 315.
- **Income escaping assessment** p. 446.

**Assessment year.** Assessment year means the period of twelve months commencing on the 1st day of April every year. [Companies (Profits) Surtax Act 1964, s. 2(3); Income Tax Act 1961, s. 2(9)].

**Assessor.** A person who assesses taxes or estimates the value of property for taxation or insurance purposes; a person called upon to advise a judge, committee of inquiry etc. on technical questions.

**Asset.** A useful or valuable quality; property and possessions, especially regarded as having value in meeting debts, commitments etc.

"Asset" means property in general all that one owns. The word "assets" has been defined in the Twentieth Century Dictionary as follows: Property in general; all that one owns, considered as applicable to the payment of his debts ... As a singular: Any portion of one's property or effect so considered. [*D.G. Gouse and Co.* v *State of Kerala* AIR 1980 SC 271: (1980)1 SCR 804: (1980)2 SCC 410].

'Asset' means items of properties held by a person minus the liabilities to be discharged by him. [*Shri Prithvi Cotton Mills Ltd.* v *Broach Borough Municipality* AIR 1968 Guj 124].

▸*Meaning under the Administrators-General Act 1963, s. 2(a).* 'Asset' means all the property, movable and immovable, of a deceased person, which is chargeable with and applicable to the payment of his debts and legacies, or available for distribution amongst his heirs and next-of-kin.

NOTE: 'Asset' includes property of every description, movable and immovable, but does not include—(*i*) agricultural land and growing crops, grass or standing trees on such land; (*ii*) any building owned or occupied by a cultivator or receiver of rent or revenue out of agricultural land, provided that the building is on or in the immediate vicinity of the land and is a building which the cultivator or the receiver of rent or revenue by reason of his connection with the land requires as a dwelling house or a store-house or an outhouse; (*iii*) animals; (*iv*) a right to any annuity in any case where the terms and conditions relating thereto preclude the commutation of any portion thereof into a lump sum grant; (*v*) any interest in property where the interest is available to an assessee for a period not exceeding six years. [Wealth Tax Act 1957, s. 2(*e*)]. The word 'asset' as defined by s. 2(*e*) of the Wealth Tax Act 1957, includes property of every description. The right to the share of the income would certainly be an asset. [*Ahmed G.H. Ariff* v *Commissioner of Wealth Tax, Calcutta* (1969)2 SCC 471].


- **Capital asset** p. 122.
- **Current asset** p. 212.
- **Distribution of capital assets** p. 273.
- **Fixed asset** p. 357.
- **Intangible asset** at p. 470.
- **Liquid assets** p. 536.
- **Net asset** p. 606.
- **Value of assets** p. 875.
- **Wasting assets** p. 894.


**Assign.** In its application to 'designate', it means appoint; ascribe; attribute; authorise; commit powers to another; delegate, depute; empower; entrust.

In its application to transfer of ownership, it means alienate; consign; convey; make over to another; transfer to another.

Assign means to transfer or formally to make over to another. It denotes generally to transfer property especially personal estate or set over a right to another. In its generic sense, thus, the words 'assign' or 'transfer' include every transfer of property from one to the other. [*Dr. Anand T. Sabnis* v *Vasnat Pratap Pandit* AIR 1980 Bom 69].

A person to whom property or rights are legally transferred.

"The word 'assign' does not mean 'heir'; it means a person substituted for another by an act of some kind or other". [*Doe d. Lewis* v *Lewis* (1842)9 M&W 662, 664, *per* Parke, B.].

**Assignable.** That may be assigned or transferred; transferable; negotiable, as a promissory note.

**Assignee.** A person appointed to act for another; a person to whom property, rights or powers are transferred by another; allottee; grantee; recipient; transferee.

**Assignment.** In its application to 'allotment', it means allocation; apportionment; appropriation; dispensation; distribution.

In its application to 'designation', it means appointment; authorisation;

deputation; nomination; placing in office.

In its application to 'task', it means business; charge; duty; function; mission; responsibility; stint.

In its application to transfer of ownership, it means alienation; conferment; consignment; conveyance; delivery; disposition; mutual transfer; transference.

"Assignment" means the transfer of the claim, right or property to another. [*The Commissioner of Gift Tax, Madras* v *N.S. Getty Chettiar* AIR 1971 SC 2410: (1971)2 SCC 741: (1971)82 ITR 99: (1972)1 SCR 736].

"Assignment" is defined as a transfer or making over to another of the whole of any property, real or personal, in possession or in action, or of any estate or right therein. It is defined as the transfer by a party of all rights to some kind of property usually intangible property such as rights in a lease, mortgage, agreement of sale of partnership. [*Gopal Saran* v *Satyanarayan* AIR 1989 SC 1141: (1989)3 SCC 56: JT 1989 (Supp) SC 21: (1989)1 SCR 767].

"Assignment" is a transfer of interest or title usually expressed in writing whereby contracting parties covenant for themselves and assigns so that upon the happening of certain events the assigns may stand in the shoes of the original covenantees.

• **Absolute assignment** p. 8.

• **Grant and assignment–distinction.** See under GRANT p. 398.

**Assignor.** Assignor is one who transfers or assigns any property to another.

**Associate.** As noun means a business partner or colleague; a friend or companion; a subordinate member of a body, institute, etc.; a thing connected with another.

As adjective means joined in companionship, function, or dignity; allied; in the same group or category; of less than full status, *e.g.*, associate member.

As verb means connect in the mind; join or combine; make oneself a partner; declare oneself in agreement; combine for a common purpose.

'Associate' implies joining with another or others as companion partner, etc. [*Ramashankar Kaushik* v *Election Commission of India* AIR 1974 SC 445: (1974)2 SCR 265: (1974)1 SCC 271].

**Associate director.** He is one who acts as a director but who is not formally appointed a director. He is in effect a consultant of the directors, selected and appointed by the directors and responsible to them.

**Associated.** The expression "associated" means "being connected with" or "in relation to". [*Commissioner, Madras H.R. and C. Endowments* v *Narayana Ayyangar* AIR 1965 SC 1916: (1965)3 SCR 168].

**Associated companies.** 'Associated companies' are companies with common interests or associations which may arise from the following—(1) control of two or more companies by the same individuals; (2) mutual shareholding insufficient to constitute one company a subsidiary of another; (3) mutual trade associations; (4) some directors who are members of two or more boards to enable the companies to pursue common policies. [Osborn & Grandage's *Concise Commercial Dictionary*].

**Association.** A group of people organized for a joint purpose; a society; fellowship, human contact or co-operation; the act of a number of persons in uniting together for some special purpose.

> NOTE: Two vital elements of an association are members and a common purpose for which they associate. [*Ramashankar Kaushik* v *Election Commission of India* AIR 1974 SC 445: (1974)2 SCR 265: (1974)1 SCC 271].

• **Articles of association** p. 76.

• **Trade association** p. 848.

• **Unlawful association** p. 867.

**Association of persons.** 'An association of persons' means an association in which two or more persons voluntarily join in a common purpose or common action. [*M.V. Shanmugam and Co.* v *The Commissioner of Income Tax, Madras* AIR 1970 SC 1707:

(1970)2 SCC 139: (1971)1 SCR 340: (1971)81 ITR 310].

An 'association' of persons must be one in which two or more persons join in a common purpose or common action, and when the words occur in a section which imposes a tax on income, the association must be one the object of which is to produce income, profits or gains. [*Commissioner of Income Tax, Bombay* v *Smt. Indira Balkrishna* AIR 1960 SC 1172: (1960)3 SCR 513: (1961)1 SCJ 153].

NOTE: To constitute as 'association of persons', there must be combination of individuals who are engaged together in some joint enterprise, banded together as if they were co-adventurers, but not constituting a partnership. Such association must be one which produces income, profits or gains. Another test laid down is that as soon as there was election to retain the property and manage it as a joint venture the person so electing became an association of individuals. [*Mohammed Noorulla* v *Commissioner of Income Tax, Madras* AIR 1961 SC 1043: (1961)3 SCR 515: (1961)42 ITR 115: (1961)1 SCJ 607].

**Assurance.** A positive declaration that a thing is true; a solemn promise or guarantee; insurance, especially life insurance; certainty; the deed or instrument by which real property is conveyed.

**Assured.** A person who has been insured by some insurance company against losses or perils mentioned in the policy of insurance; a person in whose favour an insurance policy stands.

**Asthal.** Place of residence or abiding, especially the kind of free monastery in which communities of religious mendicants reside together under a *mahant*, a chief or abbot. [Wilson's *Glossary*].

**Asthan.** An institution of ascetics and *sanyasis* having no worldly connections of wealth or family. [*Rampat* v *Durga Bharti* 60 IC 440].

**Asylum.** Sanctuary; protection, especially for those pursued by the law; any of various kinds of institution offering shelter and support to distressed or destitute individuals, especially the mentally ill; in time of war, a place of refuge in neutral territory for belligerent warships.

"'Asylum', according to its original derivation and in its widest meaning, simply signifies a refuge—a place of retreat and security. In its English acceptation, the word is most commonly used to denote an establishment for the detention and cure of persons suffering from mental disease—and also a place for the reception and upbringing of destitute orphans ..." [*Dilworth* v *Commissioner of Stamps* (1899) AC 107, 108, *per* Lord Watson].

NOTE: The conception of asylum in international law involves two elements; (*a*) shelter, which is more than merely temporary refuge; and (*b*) a degree of active protection on the part of the authorities in control of the territory of asylum.

**At any time.** The expression 'at any time' means only 'at any time the party concerned likes'. [*Central Bank of India* v *H.F. Insurance Co.* AIR 1965 SC 1288: (1965)1 SCJ 498].

NOTE: The expression is of wide amplitude and admits of no limitation. [*National Industrial Corporation* v *Registrar of Companies* AIR 1963 Punj 239; *S.C. Prashar* v *Vasantsen* AIR 1963 SC 1356: (1963)1 SCJ 687; *State of Assam* v *Deva Prasad* AIR 1969 SC 831: (1969)2 SCJ 406].

**At arm's length.** Parties are said to negotiate at arm's length when one is not under the control or influence of the other.

**At call.** Means money deposited with bankers and others the repayment of which may be demanded without notice.

**At discretion.** The expression means the same thing as "during pleasure". [*Delea* v *Cork* 19 WR 471]. Thus instructions may be given by a client to his broker to buy or sell a stock or commodity at the broker's direction as to price.

**At large.** Not limited to any particular place, person, matter or question; free; unrestrained.

**At least.** 'At least' means not less than. [*Anokhamal* v *Chief Panchayat Officer* ILR (1956)6 Raj 1044: AIR 1957 Raj 388].

NOTE: When so many days at least are said, the two terminal days must be excluded. [*Rambharoselal* v *State of Madhya Pradesh* AIR 1955 Nag 35: ILR (1955) Nag 1].

**At once.** 'At once' means within a reasonable time. [*R.* v *Rogers* (1877)3 QB 28].

**At or about the time.** The expression 'at or about the time of marriage' in s. 27 of the Hindu Marriage Act 1955, means at the actual time of marriage or near about the time of marriage. [*Krishnan* v *Padma* AIR 1968 Mys 226: (1967)2 Mys LJ 432].

The expression "at or about the time" occurring in s. 157 of the Indian Evidence Act 1872, means that the statement to which it refers must be made at once or at least shortly after when a reasonable opportunity for making it presents itself. What is a reasonable time is a question of fact in each case. The main test is whether the statement was made as early as could reasonably be expected in the circumstances of the case and before there was an opportunity for tutoring or concoction. [*Rameshwar* v *State of Rajasthan* 1952 SCR 377].

**At or before settlement of issues.** The expression means either before or simultaneously with the settlement of issues. [*Venkatarama Chettiar* v *Munnaiah* AIR 1968 AP 205].

**At present.** Literally 'at present' means the time now passing and refers to the day on which the matter is to take place. The expression has a secondary significance which is not as limited in point of time. [*Model Industries* v *Rambhan* ILR (1946) Nag 73: AIR 1946 Nag 152].

**At sight.** In a promissory note or bill of exchange the expression "at sight" means on demand. [Negotiable Instruments Act 1881, s. 21].

**At the instance of.** The expression means at the motion or solicitation of.

NOTE: The expression excludes independent persons. A complaint by a responsible officer of the company, even though there is no specific authorisation, would be at the instance of the company. [*Public Prosecutor* v *Abdul Wahab* AIR 1969 Mad 280: (1968)1 MLJ 306].

**At the same time.** The expression means during the same period, at the same moment, not before or earlier. [*Gaya Prasad* v *State of Bihar* AIR 1969 Pat 311].

**Atheism.** Disbelieve in God.

**Attach.** Add; add as an accessory; adhere; adjoin; affix; conjoin; fasten together; bind.

Confiscate; expropriate; impound; take or seize under legal authority summarily; garnish.

'Attach' means to take or apprehend by commandment or writ or precept. [*P.P. Appu* v *Executive First Class Magistrate* 1972 Ker LT 32: 1972 Ker LJ 63].

NOTE: *'Attach' and 'arrest'—distinction.* Attach differs from arrest, because it takes not only the body, but sometimes the goods, whereas an arrest is only against the person; besides he who attaches keeps the party attached in order to produce him in court on the day named, but he who arrests lodges the person arrested in the custody of a higher power, to be forthwith disposed of. [Wharton's *Law Lexicon*].

**Attached to the earth.** Attached to the earth means—(*a*) rooted in the earth, as in the case of trees and shrubs; (*b*) imbedded in the earth, as in the case of walls or buildings; or (*c*) attached to what is so imbedded for the permanent beneficial enjoyment of that to which it is attached. [Transfer of Property Act 1882, s. 3].

NOTE: The principle of English law that whatever is annexed to the land becomes a part of the land does not apply to India. [*Jnan Chand* v *Jugal Kishore* AIR 1960 Cal 331].

**Attachment.** A seizure by legal process; the writ or precept commanding such seizure.

NOTE: A decree may be executed in various ways. One of the modes of execution is attachment and sale of any property of the judgment-debtor. [Code of Civil Procedure 1908, s. 60].

Attachment of different kinds of property in execution of decree is made under the provisions of rr. 42 to 54 of Or. 21, Code of Civil Procedure 1908.

**Attained.** The word "attained" means acquired or reached. [*N.C. Dalwadi* v *State of Gujarat* AIR 1987 SC 1933: (1987)3 SCR 640: (1987)3 SCC 558: JT 1987(3) SC 139].

**Attempt.** Aim at; be at work; be in action; employ oneself; endeavour; go all out for; labour for; make a try; make the effort. Attempt, in criminal law, is an endeavour to commit a crime or unlawful act.

Though it is not possible to give a precise or exhaustive definition of attempt, it may be broadly stated that an intentional act which a person does towards the commission of an offence but which fails in its object through circumstances independent of the volition of that person is attempt. [*State of U.P.* v *Ram Chandra* AIR 1962 All 359: 1962 All LJ 13].

NOTE: In every crime there are three stages—intention; preparation; attempt. In the third stage, that is, if attempt is successful, the crime is complete. In case the attempt fails, the crime is not complete but the law punishes the person attempting the criminal act. *Intention* is the direction of conduct towards the object chosen; but the law does not take notice of an intention without an act. *Preparation* consists in devising or arranging the means or measures necessary for the commission of the crime. And *attempt* is the direct movement towards the commission after the preparations are made. The test for determining if the acts constitute attempt or preparation is whether the overt acts already done by the offender are completely harmless or would fructify into commission of an offence. [*In re Tustipada Mandal* AIR 1960 Cut 75].

Depending largely on circumstances it is a mixed question of law and fact and it defies precise and exact definition. A person attempts to commit a particular offence when—(*i*) he intends to commit that particular offence; (*ii*) he having made preparations and with the intention to commit the offence does an act towards its commission; such an act need not be the penultimate act towards the commission of that offence but must be an act during the course of committing that offence. [*State of Maharashtra* v *Md. Yakub* AIR 1980 SC 1111: 1980 Cr LJ 793: 1980 SCC (Cri) 513: (1980)3 SCC 57: (1980)2 SCJ 163: 1980 Cr LR (SC) 251: (1980)2 SCR 1158].

Attempt to commit offences is punishable under s. 511 of the Indian Penal Code. And an attempt to commit suicide is punishable under s. 309 of the Code, though the actual commission cannot be punished.

**Attest.** To bear witness to; to affirm the truth or genuineness of; testify; certify; certify the validity of; be evidence of; bear witness to a fact; affirm to be true or genuine.

Where an instrument is required to be 'attested', the meaning is that a witness shall be present at its execution and shall testify on it that it has been executed by the proper person. [*Freshfield* v *Reed* 11 LJ Ex 193].

To "attest" an instrument is not merely to subscribe one's name to it as having been present at its execution, but includes also, essentially the presence, in fact, at its execution of some disinterested person capable of giving evidence as to what took place. [*Roberts* v *Phillips* 24 LJQB 171; *Seal* v *Claridge* 7 QBD 516; *Sharp* v *Birch* 8 QBD 111; *Ford* v *Kettle* 9 QBD 139].

**Attestation.** By attestation is meant the signing of a document to signify that the attestor is a witness to the execution of the document. [*Beni Chand* v *Smt. Kamla Kunwar* AIR 1977 SC 63: (1977)1 SCR 578: (1976)4 SCC 554].

**Attestation clause.** Attestation clause is the clause at the end of a written instrument signed by the witnesses to its execution, stating that they have witnessed it.

**Attested.** "Attested" in relation to an instrument means and shall be deemed always to have meant attested by two or more witnesses each of whom has seen the executant sign or affix his mark to the instrument, or has seen some other person sign the instrument in the presence and by the direction of the executant, or has received a personal acknowledgment of his signature or mark or of the signature of such other person, and each of whom has signed the instrument in the presence of the executant, but it shall not be necessary that more than one of such witnesses shall have been present at the same time, and no particular form of attestation shall be necessary. [*Kumar Harish Chandra Singh*

*Deo* v *Bansidhar Mohanty* AIR 1965 SC 1738: (1966)1 SCR 153; Transfer of Property Act 1882, s. 3].

**Attested copy.** Attested copy means a copy of a document verified to be true.

**Attesting witness.** He is the person who must see the execution of a document and sign.

In *Burdet* v *Spilsbury* [1842-43]10 CL & F 340, Lord Campbell observed (at p. 417):

"What is the meaning of an attesting witness to a deed? Why, it is, a witness who has seen the deed executed, and who signs it as a witness."

The Lord Chancellor stated: ".........the party who sees the will executed is in fact a witness to it, if he subscribes as a witness, he is then an attesting witness".

An attesting witness is one who signs the document in the presence of the executant after seeing the execution of the document or after receiving a personal acknowledgment from the executant as regards the execution of the document. [*Beni Chand* v *Smt. Kamla Kunwar* AIR 1977 SC 63: (1977)1 SCR 578: (1976)4 SCC 554].

**Attorney.** An agent, or one acting on behalf of another. [*Nardi* v *Poinsatte* DC Ind, 46 F 2d 347, 348]. A person, especially a lawyer, appointed to act for another in business or legal matters; in USA meant as a qualified lawyer, especially one representing a client in a law court.

It is an ancient English word, and signifies one that is set in the turn, stead, or place of another.

The word "attorney" signifies anyone who acts in the turn or place of another and the power to authorise an attorney in the general sense, for example to execute a deed, has existed from a very remote period. [Halsbury's *Laws of England*, 3rd Ed., vol. 36, pp. 4, 5].

• **Warrant of attorney** p. 892.

**Attorney's lien.** The right of an attorney-at-law to hold or retain in his possession the money or property of a client until his proper charges have been adjusted and paid. It requires no equitable proceeding for its establishment.

> NOTE: This right of a High Court attorney has been expressly recognised in s. 171, Indian Contract Act. If a document is meant to be produced in court at the earliest opportunity, the exercise of this right of lien will be excluded by an implied contract to the contrary. [*Lalchand* v *Pyare* AIR 1971 MP 245: 1971 MPLJ 672. For fuller discussion see Saha on *C.P. Code*, 4th Ed., pp. 598-600].

**Attorney-General.** The chief law officer of the Government in India, UK, USA and other countries. In USA, the Attorney-General is a Cabinet officer who heads the Department of Justice.

**Attornment.** Attornment means the acknowledgment of a new lord on the alienation of land, and the assent or agreement of the tenant to attorn, as "I become tenant to the purchaser". [Wharton's *Law Lexicon*].

A person in occupation of property may establish the relation of landlord and tenant between himself and another person by attornment, that is to say, by acknowledging that he is tenant to that other person. [Halsbury's *Laws of England*, 4th Ed., vol. 27, para 3, p. 10].

The word 'attornment' has not been defined in the Transfer of Property Act or any other law. It has been borrowed from English law. It simply means agreement or acknowledgment by a tenant that he holds the tenement of a new person as the landlord. Such an agreement or attornment acts as an estoppel to prevent the tenant attorning from denying title of the one to whom he has attorned. [*Madanlal* v *Manakchand* AIR 1971 Raj 55].

The word 'attornment' by the tenant would mean acceptance of the new owner as landlord and estopping the tenant to dispute the landlord's title thereafter. [*Mohd Ilyas* v *Mohd. Adil* AIR 1994 Del 212].

> NOTE: Once the tenant has agreed to accept the person claiming title from the previous

landlord, that amounts to effective attornment in favour of the landlord and is no more dependent on the future conduct of the tenant by way of payment of rent or otherwise. [*Uppalapati Veera Venkata Satyanarayanaraju* v *Josyula Hanumayamma* AIR 1967 SC 174].

**Auction.** A sale of goods, usually in public, in which articles are sold to the highest bidder by one licensed and authorised for that purpose. An auctioneer is employed by the seller and primarily acts as his agent.

An auction is a manner of selling or letting property by bids, and usually to the highest bidder by public competition. [Halsbury's *Laws of England*, 3rd Ed., vol. 2, p. 69].

**Auction purchaser.** An auction purchaser is one who is declared to be the purchaser at an auction sale.

NOTE: Where immovable property is sold in execution of a decree and such sale has become absolute, the property shall be deemed to have vested in the purchaser from the time when the sale becomes absolute. [Code of Civil Procedure 1908, s. 65].

In private auction sale when the highest bid is accepted and the deposit is received by the auctioneer, the bidder must be deemed to be the purchaser. [*Manjappa* v *Ramiah* AIR 1963 Mys 210].

**Audi alteram partem.** Hear the other side; hear both sides.

Under the rule, a person who is to decide must give the parties an opportunity of being heard before him and fair opportunity to those who are parties in the controversy for contradicting or correcting anything prejudicial to their view. The meaning, in its wider amplitude, has been explained by the Supreme Court in *Union of India* v *Tulsiram Patel* AIR 1985 SC 1416, 1460: (1985)3 SCC 398, 476 thus:

"... *audi alteram partem* rule, in its fullest amplitude means that a person against whom an order to his prejudice may be passed should be informed of the allegations and charges against him, be given an opportunity of submitting his explanation thereto, have the right to know the evidence, both oral or documentary, by which the matter is proposed to be decided against him, and to inspect the documents which are relied upon for the purpose of being used against him, to have the witnesses who are to give evidence against him examined in his presence and have the right to cross-examine them, and to lead his own evidence, both oral and documentary, in his defence..." [For elaborate discussion on the subject see *Penumbra of Natural Justice* by Tapash Gan Choudhury, 2nd Ed., 2001].

**Audit.** An official examination of accounts; a systematic inspection and review of accounting records involving analyses, tests and confirmations.

**Auditor.** A person who conducts an audit; one who checks the accuracy, fairness, and general acceptability of accounting records and statements and then attests to them.

**Aulad.** Children, progeny, descendants. It includes male and female children. [*Chiragh Bibi* v *Sultan Bakshi* AIR 1928 Lah 40; *Bibi Alimunnissa* v *Abdul Aziz* AIR 1936 Pat 527].

Unless a contrary intention appears, the word means legitimate issues. [*Bhaiya Sher Bahadur* v *Bhaiya Ganga* 41 IA 1: 18 CWN 401].

Aulad means 'heirs or direct descendants'. [*State of Bihar* v *Radha Krishna Singh* AIR 1983 SC 684: (1983)3 SCC 118: (1983)2 SCR 808].

**Aurasa.** Uterine, as a son by a wife. A material brother, or son of the same mother. [Wilson's *Glossary*]. The expression *'auras putra pautradik'* are not words of general inheritance but are words of limitation consistent with custom. [*Ekradeswar* v *Jameshwari* 41 IA 275: 42 Cal 582: 18 CWN 1249: 17 Bom LR 18].

**Authentication.** Authentication is attestation made by a proper officer by which he certifies that a record is in due form of law, and that the person who certifies it is the officer appointed so to do. [Wharton's *Law Lexicon*].

NOTE: In order that an agent may present a document for registration before a registering officer, the agent must be duly authorised by power-of-attorney duly executed and authenticated. [Indian Registration Act 1908, ss. 32 and 33].

Orders and other instruments made and executed in the name of the Governor shall be authenticated in such manner as may be specified in rules to be made by the Governor, and the validity of an order or instrument which is so authenticated shall not be called in question on the ground that it is not an order or instrument made or executed by the Governor. [Constitution of India 1950, Art. 166(2)]. Similarly orders and other instruments executed in the name of the President are authenticated in such manner as may be specified in rules made by the President. [Article 77(2) of the Constitution of India]. These rules are called the Rules of Business.

Under s. 54 of the Companies Act 1956, a document or proceeding that requires authentication may be signed by a director, the secretary or other authorised officer of the company.

**Author.** The writer of a literary work (as a book); one that originates or gives existence.

Author means—(*i*) in relation to a literary or dramatic work, the author of the work; (*ii*) in relation to a musical work, the composer; (*iii*) in relation to an artistic work other than a photograph, the artist; (*iv*) in relation to a photograph, the person taking the photograph; (*v*) in relation to a cinematograph film or sound recording the producer (w.e.f. 11.5.1995); and (*vi*) in relation to any literary, dramatic, musical or artistic work which is computer-generated, the person who causes the work to be created (w.e.f. 11.5.1995). [Copyright Act 1957, s. 2(*d*)].

The term involves originating, making, producing as the inventive or master mind the thing which is to be protected, whether it be a drama or a painting or a photograph. But a mere copyright of a written matter is not an author. In a literary work, the person who originates the language is the author and in an artistic work the person who executes the design is the author. A translator of a literary work is the 'author' of his translation. [*Byrne* v *Statistic Co.* (1914)1 KB 622].

**Author of the trust.** A person who creates a trust is called the author of the trust [Indian Trusts Act 1882, s. 3].

**Authorised capital.** The total amount of share capital of all classes, which a company is authorised, by its memorandum of association, to issue. Alternative adjectives to 'authorised' are 'nominal' and 'registered'.

**Authority.** In its application to documentation, it means authoritative example; authoritative rule for future similar cases; judicial precedent; prior instance.

In its application to power, it means authoritativeness; control; dominance; domination; force; governance; influence position of power.

In its application to right, jurisdiction; legal power; prerogative; right to command; right to determine or settle issues.

A legal body invested with some power.

Authority (in Administrative Law) is a body having jurisdiction in certain matters of public nature. The ability conferred upon a person by the law to alter by his own will directed to that end, the rights, duties, liabilities or other legal relations either of himself or of other person, must be present *ab extra* to make a person an authority. [*Ved Prakash* v *State of Haryana* AIR 1981 SC 643: 1981 Cr LJ 161: (1981)1 SCC 449: 1981 SCC (Cri) 182: 1981 Cr LR (SC) 107].

'Authority' in law belongs to the province of power: "Authority (in Administrative Law) is a body having jurisdiction in certain matters of a public nature". [*Som Prakash Rekhi* v *Union of India* AIR 1981 SC 212: (1981)2 SCR 111: (1981)1 SCC 449: 1981(1) SLR 154].

A body of persons who are not recognised by law as a legal entity cannot be considered to be an authority within the meaning of the word in the Constitution of India. [*Badri Prasad* v *President, District Board* AIR 1952 All 681].

- **Judicial authority** p. 494.
- **Lawful authority** p. 518.
- **Local authority** p. 540.
- **Passport authority** p. 646.
- **Public authority** p. 707.
- **Under the authority of** p. 862.


**Authority controlled by State.** Right to exercise powers controlled by the state machinery.

**Authority of law.** The expression 'authority of law' in Art. 31(1) of the Constitution of India means the permission under the State law to do a thing. [*Ahmedali* v *State of Madhya Pradesh* AIR 1960 MP 282].

**Autocracy.** Absolute Government by one person unchecked by constitutional limitations or restrictions, the name of an unlimited monarchial Government.

**Autocrat.** An absolute prince or sovereign; an absolute ruler; a dictatorial person.

**Autograph.** That which is written with one's own hand.

**Automation.** The co-ordinated automatic control of machine systems and the automatic transport, testing and treatment of materials and products throughout a sequence of operations. The term embraces automatic data processing systems used to control machine systems.

**Automatism.** Automatism is an act which is done by the muscles without any control by the mind such as a spasm, a reflex action or a convulsion; or an act done by a person, who is not conscious of what he is doing such as an act done whilst suffering from concussion or whilst sleep-walking ......... Loss of memory afterwards is never a defence in itself so long as he was conscious at the time ......... Nor is an act to be regarded as an involuntary act simply because it is unintentional or its consequences are unforeseen. [Stroud's *Judicial Dictionary*, 5th Ed.].

Automatism is the involuntary unconscious action of a person, in which state, he can perform some acts, not being conscious of what he is doing. Automatism arising from psychomotor epilepsy has been regarded as insane automatism. [Modi on *Medical Jurisprudence*, 21st Ed., p. 465]. In automatism there is a condition in which the epileptic carries out apparently purposive behaviour without conscious control. Research investigations have revealed that automatism is a very rare cause of violent crimes. [Linford Rees on *A New Short Text Book of Psychiatry*, Indian Edition 1988, p. 221].

NOTE: The main instances of automatism are: sleep-walking, concussion, some cases of epilepsy, hypoglycaemia and dissociative states. [Glanville Williams on *Text Book of Criminal Law*, 1978 Ed., p. 609].

Against a criminal charge, automatism is a defence that the act or omission or event with which the accused is charged was involuntary. An act, omission to act or event on the part of the accused is involuntary where it is beyond his control; when it is beyond the control of that person's mind, the situation is known as one of automatism. [Cross & Jones on *Introduction to Criminal Law*, 9th Ed., para 6.21, p. 92].

**Autonomy.** The right of self-government; personal freedom; the political independence of a nation.

**Autopsy.** An examination of a dead body to determine the cause of death, especially in a criminal investigation; post-mortem examination of a human body, especially to determine the cause of death for medical or legal purposes.

**Avarudha-stri.** A continuously kept concubine. [*Bai Nagubai* v *Bai Manghibai* 53 IA 153: AIR 1926 PC 73].

**Aver.** To maintain as true. [Wharton's *Law Lexicon*]. Aver is to verify or prove to be true in pleading a cause; to allege or assert in pleading; to declare positively.

**Average.** According to *Shorter Oxford English Dictionary* the word 'average' means 'arithmetical mean' to estimate by dividing the aggregate of a series by the number of its units'. The same is the connotation of the word 'average' according to the *Random House Dictionary of the English Language* where the total receipt has been stated to mean the total receipt from sales divided by the number of the units sold. [*Harbans Kumari* v *State of Uttar Pradesh* (1979)2 SCC 239: (1979)2 SCR 28: AIR 1980 NOC 4: AIR 1981 SC 1215].

The term 'average' includes certain charges which are to be borne partly by the ship and partly by the cargo, such as the expense of towing or beaconage. These and similar charges were also sometimes known as 'petty average'. The word has many different meanings in shipping world. [Halsbury's *Laws of England*, 4th Ed., vol. 43, para 734, p. 507].

• **General average loss** p. 383.

**Averment.** A positive statement; an affirmation, especially one with an offer of proof; in pleading, to allege or assert positively.

"The word 'averment' has no very definite meaning. It may include both allegations of law and allegations of fact ......" [*Brady* v *Thornton* (1947)75 CLR 140, 146, *per* Starke, J.].

**Avocation.** A minor occupation; a vocation or calling; a diversion; subordinate or occasional employments, or hobbies as distinguished from one's ordinary or principal occupation.

"Avocation" plainly means one's vocation, calling or profession. Dictionary meaning of the word "avocation" is a distraction or diversion from one's regular employment. Fowler in *Modern English Usage* says "avocation originally a calling away, an interruption, a distraction". [*The Management of Express Newspapers Ltd.* v *B. Somayajulu* AIR 1964 SC 279: (1964)3 SCR 100: (1964)2 SCJ 203].

**Avoid.** To keep away from; shun; to prevent the occurrence or effectiveness of; to refrain from.

Avoid does not mean evaded and it has been used in the sense of escapement. [*Mansukhlal* v *Commissioner of Income Tax* AIR 1969 SC 835: (1969)2 SCJ 388].

**Avyavaharika.** The term "Avyavaharika" has been variously translated as being that which is not lawful or what is not just or what is not admissible under the law or under normal conditions. Colebrooke translated it as a debt for a cause repugnant to good morals. There is another track of decision which has translated it as meaning a debt which is not supported as valid by legal arguments. ...... The translation given by Colebrooke is the nearest approach to its true concept. [*S.M. Jakati* v *S.M. Borkar* AIR 1959 SC 282: 1959 SCR 1384].

**Award.** Give or order to be given as a payment, compensation, or prize; grant; assign; the decision or determination rendered by arbitrators upon a controversy submitted to them; the document embodying such decision.

NOTE: Under s. 11 of the Land Acquisition Act 1894, the Collector is to make the award. Order rejecting a claim petition submitted under s. 110A of the Motor Vehicles Act 1939 on the ground that the same is barred by limitation would be an award. [*Krishen Lal* v *J.G. Insurance* AIR 1977 J&K 90].

• **Date of award** p. 224.

**Axiom.** An established or widely accepted principle; a self-evident truth.

**Ayes.** The word means affirmative votes; those who vote in the affirmative.

**Ayma.** Land granted by Mogul Government, either rent-free or subject to a small quit rent to learned and religious persons of the Mohamedan faith or for religious and charitable uses in relation to Mohammedanism. [Wilson's *Glossary*].

# Bb

**Babu.** A Hindu gentleman; a polite form of address; equivalent to Sir or Mr.; in Bengal Regulation VIII of 1795, baboos are defined 'persons of the blood and family of the Raja of Benares. Babu is a synonym of father'.

**Babuana.** It is a grant of property in accordance with the family custom of some Raj Estate generally made to junior male members of the family in lieu of money maintenance. It is a grant for the maintenance of the grantee and his descendants and is inalienable. [*Durgadut* v *Rameswar* ILR 36 Cal 943].

> NOTE: Immovable properties acquired from the income and profits of the babuana properties are to be considered as accretions to the babuana properties. [18 CWN 1249].

**Baby.** A very young child or infant of either sex, especially one not yet able to walk; one who has the appearance, behaviour, or disposition of a young child, especially one with little courage or fortitude; one's own responsibility, invention, concern, achievement, etc., regarded in a personal way.

• **Battered baby** p. 98.

**Bachelor.** An unmarried man. A divorced man should not be described as a "bachelor".

The usual title of the first degree that is conferred on a university graduate.

A young knight serving under another's banner.

**Bachelor girl.** An independent unmarried young woman.

**Back.** The rear surface of the human body from the shoulders to the hips; the keel of a ship; the lining attached to the unexposed side of a thing.

To support, assist or uphold financially or morally; to indorse; to sign so as to show acceptance or approval.

**Back-date.** To put a date earlier than the actual date.

**Back-door.** Underhand; secret; indirect.

**Back-freight.** Freight payable by the owner of goods to the shipowner for the carriage of goods from the port to which the goods had been shipped to some other suitable port when the goods cannot be delivered at the destined port for reasons for which the shipowner is not responsible.

**Back-to-back houses.** Houses built in back-to-back terraces so that each house, other than those at the end, have only one outside wall. Thus, houses built in blocks of four, both back-to-back as well as side-to-side, but each having, two outside walls would not be regarded as "back-to-back". [*Chorley Borough Council* v *Barratt Developments* (1979)3 All ER 634].

**Backlog.** Arrear of uncompleted work; a reserve, reserves.

**Backward.** Slow in growth or development; retarded.

**Backward class.** The expression would include all kinds of backwardness—social, educational or otherwise, and the State is the sole authority to classify communities as backward. [*Kesava* v *State of Mysore* AIR 1956 Mys 20: ILR (1955) Mys 597].

Backwardness under Art. 15(4) of the Constitution of India must be social and political and that social backwardness in the ultimate analysis is the result of poverty to a very large extent. [*Triloki Nath Tiku* v *State of Jammu and Kashmir* AIR 1967 SC 1283: (1967)2 SCR 265: 1967 SLR 192].

In order to qualify for being called a "backward class citizen", he must be a member of socially and educationally backward class. It is social and educational backwardness of class which is material for the purposes of both Arts. 15(4) and 16(4) of the Constitution of India. [*Shri Janki Prasad Parimoo* v *State of Jammu and Kashmir* AIR 1973 SC 930: (1973)3 SCR 236: (1973)1 SCC 420: 1973(1) SLR 719].

**Backwardation.** This is a Stock Exchange term. It is the condition existing when the stock can be bought cheaper as a matter of account.

The percentage paid by a person selling stock for the right of delaying the delivery of it.

**Bad blood.** Hostility; long-standing enmity; strife.

**Bad character.** Bad name; bad reputation; disreputability; a person's predilection toward evil.

In limited circumstances, proof of bad character may be introduced into evidence to discredit a witness.

**Bad cheque (Brit cheque).** A cheque that is not honoured because the account either contains insufficient funds or does not exist. Also termed: valueless cheque, worthless cheque, unmarketable cheque, unserviceable cheque, bogus cheque, false cheque, rubber cheque, nugatory cheque.

**Bad debt.** Irretrievable debt; a debt that is not recoverable; a debt that is uncollectible and that may be deductible for tax purposes.

A debt becomes a bad debt when the creditor has no reasonable expectations of recovering it from the debtor or when there is no ray of hope at all on which the creditor can rely for recovering the amount from his debtor. [*Raja Bahadur Mukundlal Bansilal* v *C.I.T.* (1952)22 ITR 94 (Bom); *Jadavji Narsidas & Co.* v *C.I.T.* (1963)47 ITR 411 (Bom); *C.I.T.* v *Jain Glass Works* (1974) Taxation 36(3)-80 (All)].

A debt becomes bad debt when the creditor has no reasonable chance of recovering it from the debtor. [*Deoniti Prasad* v *Commissioner of Income-tax* AIR 1953 Pat 360].

NOTE: A 'bad debt' is a 'worthless debt'. [*C.I.T.* v *Coats of India Ltd.* (1998)232 ITR 324 (Cal)].

Whether a debt is bad is a factual matter which depends on actual facts relevant thereto and not on the hopes, fears or judgment of the creditor himself. [*T.S.P.L.P. Chidambaram Chettiar* v *C.I.T.* (1967)64 ITR 181 (Mad)]. A debt does not become bad by the mere circumstance that the debtor gets into difficulties. [*Som Chand Maluk Chand* v *C.I.T.* (1936)4 ITR 382 (Lah)]. Mere delay in recovery does not also convert a debt into a bad debt. A statute-barred debt is not necessarily bad; neither is a debt which is not statute-barred, necessarily good. In every case it is a question of fact to be determined after consideration of all the relevant circumstances. [*Commissioner of Income-tax* v *S.M. Chitnavis* AIR 1932 PC 178; *Kantilal* v *Commissioner of Income-tax* AIR 1955 Bom 53].

**Bad faith.** Abscondence; breach of faith; broken faith; dishonesty of belief or purpose; disingenuousness; subterfuge; malversation; unfairness; unfaithfulness.

It means dishonesty, though not necessarily for a financial motive. [*Cannock Chase District Council* v *Kelly* (1977)36 P&CR 219].

The term "bad faith" is not simply bad judgment or negligence, but rather it implies the conscious doing of a wrong because of dishonest purpose or moral obliquity; it is different from the negative idea of negligence in that it contemplates a state of mind affirmatively operating with furtive design or ill-will. [*Stath* v *Williams* Ind App., 367 NE 2d 1120, 1124].

Bad faith, *mala fides* and malice are synonymous terms, though not admitting of precise definition. Bad faith is a shade milder than malice and implies breach of faith or wilful failure to respond to one's known obligation or duty. [*Bhupinder Singh* v *State of Haryana* AIR 1968 Punj 406].

**Bad title.** Defective title; one which conveys no property to the purchaser of the estate; one which is so radically defective that it is not marketable.

Any title which an unwilling purchaser cannot be forced to take is a bad one.

**Badi.** A plaintiff, a complainant, a suitor.

**Bahi.** An account book, a journal, a diary, a ledger. [Wilson's *Glossary*].

**Bai bil wafa.** Deed of conditional sale or an out and out sale with a contract for repurchase. [*Jhanda Singh* v *Wahiduddin* ILR 33 All 585].

**Bail.** *(Noun).* Bond; assurance; guaranty; indemnity; pledge; security; undertaking.

*(Verb).* To procure release of one charged with an offence by insuring his future attendance in court and compelling him to remain within jurisdiction of court. [*Manning* v *State ex rel. Williams* 190 Okl 65: 120 P 2d 980, 981].

The dictionary meaning of the word 'bail' is to set free or liberate a person arrested or imprisoned on taking security for his appearance. [*Kali Dass* v *SHO, Police Station* 1979 Cr LJ 345 (J&K)].

Money etc. required as security against the temporary release of a prisoner pending trial; release or secure the release of a prisoner on payment of bail.

**Bail bandit.** A person who commits a crime while on bail.

**Bail out.** Financial assistance given to a falling business, economy etc. to save it from collapse.

**Bailable offence.** A criminal charge for which a prisoner may be released from custody after providing proper security.

**Bailee.** A person or party to whom goods are committed for a purpose, *e.g.*, custody or repair, without transfer of ownership.

**Bailiff.** A sheriff's officer who executes writs and processes and carries out distraints and arrests; the agent or steward of a landlord; an official in a court of law, who keeps order, looks after prisoner etc.; a court officer who maintains order during court proceedings; a person to whom some authority, care, guardianship, or jurisdiction is delivered, committed, or entrusted; one who is deputed or appointed to take charge of another's affairs; an overseer or superintendent.

"Bailiff" of a court means one who receives his appointment from the judge of the court. [*Tarrant* v *Baker* 14 CB 199].

In another sense, "bailiff" means, a person having the care of property and accountable for the uncertain profits thereof.

**Bailment.** The act of delivering goods etc. for a specified purpose.

A delivery of personal property by one person (*the bailor*) to another (*the bailee*) who holds the property for a certain purpose under an express or implied-in-fact contract. [Black's *Law Dictionary*, 8th Ed.].

"'Bailment' is a delivery of things, whether it be of writings, goods, or stuffe to another—sometimes to be delivered backe to the bailor, i.e. to him that so delivered it—sometimes to the use of the baylee, i.e. of him to whom it is delivered; and sometimes also it is delivered to a third person". [Termes de la Ley].

The term "bailment", according to its ordinary legal sense, "relates to something which is in the hands of a person who is to return it in specie". [*R.* v *Hassall* 30 LJMC 175; *R.* v *Ashwell* 16 QBD 190, *per* Cockburn, C.J.].

▸ *Meaning under the Indian Contract Act 1872, s. 148.* A 'bailment' is the delivery of goods by one person to another for some purpose, upon a contract that they shall, when the purpose is accomplished, be returned or otherwise disposed of according to the directions of the person delivering them.

Bailment is a technical term of the Common law though etymologically it might mean any kind of handing over. It involves change of possession. One who has custody without possession, like a servant, or a guest using his host's goods, is not a bailee. On the whole, a bailment may be described as a delivery on condition, to which the law usually attaches an obligation to redeliver the goods, or otherwise deal with them as directed, when the condition is satisfied; but there may be in particular cases a bailment without an enforceable obligation. [*Anamalai Timber Trust* v *Tripunithura* ILR (1954) TC 208: AIR 1954 Trav-Co 305].

**Bailor.** A person or party that entrusts goods to a bailee.

**Bailsman.** A person who stands bail for another.

**Bainama.** A written agreement to sell a thing accompanied by payment of earnest money.

**Bakasht.** The word is the invention of survey authorities and is used by them to denote the actual cultivating possession either of the proprietor or tenure holders, as the case may be. It is deliberately invented to avoid the responsibility of deciding the character of the possession. [*Durga Prasad Thakur* v *Baswan Pandey* AIR 1928 Pat 209: 9 Pat LT 317].

**Baki.** Remainder, balance, arrears, especially of revenue, in which sense the term is current in most parts in India. Also balance of an account. [Wilson's *Glossary*].

**Balance.** The difference between an amount due and an amount paid; an amount left over; the difference between credits and debits in an account; something left over, remainder; an amount in excess especially on the credit side of an account; the amount required to equalize the two sides of an account.

The term 'balances' means 'the difference', if any, between the debit and credit side of an account. [*Custodian of Evacuee Property* v *Rabia Bibi* (1976)4 SCC 270].

• **Bank balance** p. 94.
• **Cash balance** p. 127.
• **Trial balance** p. 857.

**Balance of payments.** The difference in value between payments into and out of a country; a country's international receipts and payments account.

**Balance of power.** A situation in which States of the world have roughly equal power.

**Balance of trade.** The difference in value between imports and exports into a country.

**Balance sheet.** A statement of financial condition at a given date; a statement of account of the business of traders, merchants, partners or others; a written statement of the balance of assets and liabilities of an organisation at a particular point.

A balance sheet is a statement prepared from records kept on the basis of double entry showing at a given date, the sources from which an enterprise derived its funds (for example, from shareholders, creditors, partners or proprietors) and the various ways in which those funds were invested or applied (for example, in fixed assets, current assets, investments, loans and advances and other claims). It is a statement in a summarised form of the balances of the ledger accounts remaining after all revenue and expense accounts have been closed by transfer to revenue or profit and loss account. [*Leonard Biermans Workers' Union* v *Second Industrial Tribunal* AIR 1962 Cal 375: 65 CWN 1029].

**Bale.** A package of goods wrapped in cloth and marked so as to be identifiable on a bill of lading. [Black's *Law Dictionary*, 8th Ed.].

"Bale", "is an ambiguous word which may mean many things, and therefore it is for a jury to say what it means in a mercantile contract". [*Gorrissen* v *Perrin* 27 LJCP 32, *per* Cresswell, J.].

**Ballast.** A heavy material, e.g., lead, stone, etc., placed in the hold of a ship to keep it steady when not carrying sufficient cargo; broken rocks or stones used as a base for roads and railway lines.

**Ballastage.** A toll payable for the privilege of taking ballast from the bottom of a port or harbour.

**Ballot.** A small ball used in secret voting; a sheet of paper used to cast a secret vote; the action or system of secret voting; the right to vote.

The word has been derived from "ballota" which existed at a time when there was no question voting machine. It does not include a voting machine. [*A.C. Jose* v *Sivani Pillai* (1982)2 SCC 656].

**Ballot box.** A sealed box into which voters put completed ballot papers.

**Ballot paper.** A slip of paper used to register a vote.

**Bandh or bundh.** A dam, a dyke, a causeway, a raised bank or mound of earth constructed to confine the waters of a river or reservoir, or to preserve a roadway across plains inundated in the rainy season; this is sometimes employed, though laxly, to designate the piece of water confined by an embankment.

**Bandhak or bundhuk.** A pledfie, a pawn, a mortgage.

**Bandhu.** *Bandhus* are *Bhinna-gotra sapindas*. They are of three kinds—(1) *Atma-bandhus*; (2) *Pitri-bandhus*; and (3) *Matri-bandhus*. They are all cognates, that is, persons related to the deceased through a female, such as a sister's son, a brother's daughter's son, etc. Under the orthodox Hindu law, the *bandhus* used to succeed after the *sapindas* and *samanodaks*.

**Bandobust.** Agreement; settlement; bargain; adjustment; arrangement; settlement of revenue to be paid by the zamindar; renter or farmer tenancy settlement.

**Banging a market.** Openly offering securities at decreasing prices with a view to lowering the prices.

**Bank.** Commercially, it is a place where money is deposited for the purpose of being let out to interest, returned by exchange, disposed of to profit, or to be drawn out again as the owner shall call for it; a financial establishment which uses money deposited by customers for investment, pays it out when required, makes loan at interest, exchanges currency, etc.; building where this business takes place; an establishment for the custody of money received from, or on behalf of, its customers. Its essential duty is to pay their drafts on it; its profits arise from the use of money left unemployed by them.

> NOTE: "To constitute the business of banking today the banker must also undertake to pay cheques drawn on himself (the banker) by his customers in favour of third parties upto the amount standing to their credit in their 'current accounts' and to collect cheques for his customers and credit the proceeds to their current accounts". [*United Dominions Trust Ltd.* v *Kirkwood* (1966)1 All ER 968, 986 (CA), *per* Diplock, L.J.].

**Bank (Embankment).** The sloping edge of land by a river, water course or channel, the area of ground alongside river; an elevation in the sea or a river bed.

Banks of a canal mean the land on either side of the canal which confines the water. [*Monmouthshire Canal & Ry. Co.* v *Hill* (1859)28 LJ Ex 283, 285, *per* Martin, B.].

▸*Meaning under the (English) Land Drainage Act 1930, s. 81.* Banks mean "banks, walls, or embankments adjoining or confining or constructed for the purposes of or in connection with, any channel or sea front, and includes all land between the bank and low-water mark".

**Bank balance.** The amount of money held in a bank account at a given moment.

**Bank bill.** A bill drawn by one bank on another.

**Bank draft.** A cheque, draft, or other order for payment of money drawn by an authorised officer of a bank upon either his own bank or some other bank in which funds of his bank are deposited. [*Perry* v *West* 110 NH 351: 266 A 2d 849, 852].

**Bank holiday.** A day on which banks are officially closed.

"Bank holiday" includes any public holiday or day of public rejoicing or mourning [(English) Shops Act 1950, s. 74]. In India, it is usually public holiday including Sunday, and any other day declared as a public holiday by the Central Government by a notification issued under the Explanation to s. 25 of the Negotiable Instruments Act 1881.

**Bank machine.** Cash dispenser.

**Bank manager.** A person in charge of a local branch of a bank.

**Bank note.** A banker's promissory note, especially from a central bank, payable to the bearer on demand, and serving as money.

▸ *Meaning under the Forgery Act 1913, s. 18.* In England, the expression "bank note" includes any note or bill of exchange of the Bank of England or Bank of Ireland, or of any other person, body corporate, or company carrying on the business of banking in any part of the world, and includes "bank bill", "bank post bill", "blank bank note", "blank bank bill of exchange", and "blank bank post bill".

▸ *Meaning under the Currency of Bank Notes Act 1954, s. 3.* In England, bank notes means "notes of the Bank of England payable to bearer on demand".

**Bank roll.** A roll of bank notes; funds.

**Bank statement.** A printed statement of transactions and balance issued periodically to the holder of a bank account.

**Banker.** A person who manages or owns a bank or group of banks; a keeper of the bank or dealer in some gambling games; a card game involving gambling; a person who engages in the business of banking.

As of general acceptation, a "banker" is one "who traffics with the money of others for the purpose of making profit ........." If he keeps open shop for the receipt of money from all who choose to deposit it with him, if his business is to trade for profit in money deposited with him for that purpose, he answers the description of a 'banker'. [*Re Shields* (1901)1 Ir R 172, *per* Fitz Gibbon, L.J.].

A banker is one who in the ordinary course of his business honours cheques drawn upon him by persons from and for whom he receives money on current accounts. [*Duraiswami Chettiar* v *Dingigul Urban Co-operative Bank* AIR 1957 Mad 745].

**Banker's order.** An instruction to a bank to pay money or deliver property, signed by the owner or the owner's agent.

**Banking company.** A banking company means "a company which carries on as its principal business the accepting of deposits of money on current account or otherwise, subject to withdrawal by cheque, draft or order". [*Bank of Chettinad Ltd. of Colombo* v *Income Tax Commr., Colombo* (1948) AC 378].

**Banking policy.** Any policy which is specified from time to time by the Reserve Bank in the interest of the banking system or in the interest of monetary stability of sound economic growth, having due regard to the interests of the depositors, the volume of deposits and other resources of the bank and the need for equitable allocation and the efficient use of these deposits and resources. [Banking Regulations Act 1949, s. 5(*ca*)].

**Bankrupt.** Insolvent; declared in law as unable to pay debts; an insolvent person whose estate is administered and disposed for the benefit of the creditors; an insolvent debtor.

**Bankruptcy court.** A court having jurisdiction in bankruptcy; a court that is exclusively concerned with administering bankruptcy proceedings.

**Bankruptcy notice.** A notice which is served by a creditor on a debtor requiring the debtor within a limited time to pay the debt or secure or compound for the same. Non-compliance with the notice constitutes an act of bankruptcy.

**Bar.** A bar is a place "where liquors are sold exclusively or mainly for immediate consumption". [*Iles* v *Waterson* (1927) Gaz LR 33, 34, *per* Stringer, J.].

▸ *Meaning under the (English) Licensing Act 1964, s. 201.* "Bar" includes any place exclusively or mainly used for the sale and consumption of intoxicating liquor.

Every bar counter over which intoxicating liquor is sold direct to customers is a "bar" within the (English) Licensing Act 1964, (c. 26), s. 76(5). [*Carter* v *Bradbeer* (1975)1 WLR 1204].

▸ *Meaning under the The Sale of Liquor Act 1962, s. 2 (New Zealand).* "'Bar' in relation to any licensed premises includes any part of those premises that is used principally or exclusively for the sale, supply or consumption of liquor".

In law, 'bar' means the whole body of lawyers qualified to practice in a given court or jurisdiction; the legal profession, or an organised subset of it. It may also mean the railing in a courtroom that separate the front area, where the judge, court personnel, lawyers, and witnesses conduct court business, from the back area, which provides seats for observers; by extension, a similar railing in a legislative assembly.

The term 'bar' in a court room applied to the area impliedly reserved for the principals of the court, i.e., the judge, the attorneies, the court officers and members of the jury. [*Encyclopaedia Americana*, Vol. 3, p. 214]. In *Corpus Juris Secundum* [Vol. 9, p. 1537], 'bar' is defined as a place which 'counsellors and advocates occupy', in a court room. In Bouvier's *Law Dictionary*, the term 'bar' is defined as a particular part of the court room where lawyers sit. [*P.C. Jose* v *Nandakumar* AIR 1997 Ker 243].

Its other meanings are: ban; barrier; blockage; circumscription; embargo; impediment; limitation; prevention; prohibition; blacklist; circumscribe; debar; limit; prohibit; shut out; spurn.

**Barat.** Assignment. [*Indu Bala Debya* v *Monimala Devi* AIR 1955 Pat 505].

**Bardana.** Bardana, a term of Hindi language, does not mean gunny bags made of jute alone, but it can also mean boxes, wooden packing, etc. and covers all kinds of containers. [*State of Rajasthan* v *Ghasiram Mangilal* 1969(1) SCWR 900: (1969)2 SCJ 710].

**Barga.** An agreement by which the cultivator engages to pay the landlord half the produce, the latter providing half the seed and paying the whole revenue.

**Bargadar.** Any person who under the system generally known as *adhi*, *barga* or *bhag*, cultivates the land of another person on condition of delivering a share of the produce of such land to that person and includes a person who under the system generally known as *kisani* or any other description cultivates the land of another person on condition of receiving a share of the produce of such land from that person. [West Bengal Land Reforms Act 1955, s. 2(2)].

**Bargain.** A mutual undertaking, contract, or agreement; an agreement on the terms of a transaction or sale; something acquired or offered cheaply; an agreement between parties for the exchange of promises or performances.

NOTE: A bargain is not necessarily a contract because the consideration may be insufficient or the transaction may be illegal. [Black's *Law Dictionary*, 7th Ed.].

A bargain is only another name for a contract which may exist upon the slightest valuable consideration. [*Crossman* v *R.* (1886)56 LJQB 241].

• **Unconscionable bargain** p. 861.

**Barge.** A barge is a large flat-bottomed boat used for transporting heavy burdens on canals and rivers but is not generally an ocean-going vessel.

Barges are flat-bottomed boats meant for carrying goods on inland waters and are usually fitted with engines. Barges are bound to be heavy vessels which can take the load. [*V.M. Salgaokar & Bros. P. Ltd.* v *Union of India* AIR 1992 SC 1194: (1992)2 SCC 635: JT 1992(2) SC 277: 1992 AIR SCW 1158].

**Barhi.** Profit, increase, interest.

**Baron.** The fifth and lowest degree of nobility, next to a viscount, and above that of a knight or baronet. It includes a life peer under the Life Peerages Act 1958.

**Barratry.** Fraud or gross negligence of a ship's master or crew at the expense of its owners or users.

"A fraudulent breach of duty by the master, in respect to his owners, or, in other words a breach of duty in respect to his owners, with a criminal intent, or *ex maleficio* is barratry". [*Earle* v *Rowcroft* (1806)8 East 126, 138, 139, *per* Lord Ellenborough, C.J.].

In the Italian dictionary the word 'barratrare' means to cheat, and whatsoever is done by a cheat, a fraud, a cozening, or a trick is barratry in him. [*Vallejo* v *Wheeler* (1774)1 Cowp 143, 154, *per* Lord Mansfield, C.J.].

▸*Meaning under the (English) Marine Insurance Act 1906, Sch. I, para 11.* The term barratry includes every wrongful act wilfully committed by the master or crew to the prejudice of the owner, or, as the case may be, the charterer.

The term "barratry" in the Lloyd's Policy (of Marine Insurance) includes every wrongful act wilfully committed by the master or crew to the prejudice of the owner, or, as the case may be, the charterer, and this is so whether the act of the master is induced by motive of benefit to himself, malice to the owners, or a disregard of those laws which it was his duty to obey, and upon his observance of which his owners relied.

**Barrister.** A person called to the bar by the benches of Inns of Court and entitled to practise as an advocate in the higher courts, in Britain and other Commonwealth countries.

**Basic wage.** A minimum wage earned before possible additional payments such as overtime etc.

The phrase "basic wages" is ordinarily understood to mean that part of the price of labour which the employer must pay to all workmen belonging to all categories. [*Muir Mills Co. Ltd., Kanpur* v *Their Workmen* AIR 1960 SC 985: (1960)3 SCR 488: (1961)1 SCJ 1].

The phrase "basic wages" means all emoluments which are earned by an employee while on duty or on leave or on holidays with wages in either case in accordance with the terms of the contract of employment and which are paid or payable in cash to him, but does not include—(*i*) the cash value of any food concession; (*ii*) any dearness allowance (that is to say, all cash payments by whatever name called paid to any employee on account of a rise in the cost of living), house rent allowance, overtime allowance, bonus, commission or any other similar allowance payable to the employee in respect of his employment or of work done in such employment; (*iii*) any presents made by the employer. [*Ticycles of India, Ambattur* v *M.K. Gurmani* (2001)7 SCC 204: JT 2001(7) SC 73].

> NOTE: Basic wage never includes the additional emoluments which some workmen may earn, on the basis of a system of bonuses related to the production. [*Muir Mills* v *Their Workmen* (1960)3 SCR 488: AIR 1960 SC 985: (1961)1 SCJ 1].

**Bastard.** A person born of parents not married to each other; illegitimate, an unpleasant or despicable person; adulterine; child born before marriage; illegitimate child.

Illegitimate child; a child born to a married woman whose husband could not possibly be the father. [Black's *Law Dictionary*, 7th Ed.].

A child born to a married woman whose husband could not be or is otherwise proved not to be the father. [Black's *Law Dictionary*, 8th Ed.].

Bastards are such children as are not born either in lawful wedlock, or within a competent time after its determination.

**Bastardize.** Declare a person illegitimate; corrupt; debase.

**Bastinado.** Punishment by beating with a stick on the soles of the feet.

**Bastu.** Site or foundation of a house; a dwelling house.

**Batai.** Division of the crop between the cultivator and the landlord or the Government in that capacity.

**Batil.** Void from the beginning.

Under the Mahomedan law, a marriage with a woman prohibited by reason of consanguinity or affinity or fosterage is void or batil.

**Batta.** Discount. In revenue matters, the amount added to or deducted from any payment according to the currency in which it is paid as compared with a fixed standard coin. [Wilson's *Glossary*].

According to its ordinary meaning, 'batta' is an extra payment over and above pay. Though that extra payment may be a common feature, it does not form part of, but is outside and over and above the pay. It is not a part of the basic pay. [*Panchiri Boat Service* v *State of Travancore-Cochin* AIR 1955 TC 97: 1955 Ker LT 668 (DB)].

**Battered baby.** An infant that has suffered repeated violence from adults, especially, its parents.

**Battered wife.** A wife subjected to repeated violence by her husband.

**Battery.** Portable container of a cell or cells carrying an electric charge, as a source of current.

In law, it means an act, including touching, inflicting unlawful personal violence on another person, even if no physical harm is done; the illegal beating or touching of another person; the application of force to another, resulting in harmful or offensive contact.

NOTE: It is not necessary to prove an intention to injure to support an action in battery. Intentional hostile touching is sufficient. [*Wilson* v *Pringle* (1986)3 WLR 1].

**Batwara.** A share or portion; division of crop in shares; the partition of an estate by co-heirs; distribution of the lands of a village in allotments as originally made or agreed upon.

The word is now most generally in use to imply a separation of coparcenary holdings at the desire of some or all of the coparceners, or the detachment of the share of an individual so as to constitute his share an entirely distinct property, made with the sanction of the revenue authorities.

**Bawdy house.** A house resorted to by persons of both sexes for the purposes of prostitution.

**Bay-bill-wuffa.** Mortgage by condition sale.

**Bay mokasa.** An exchange, a barter.

**Bayana.** Earnest money or deposit. [*Mohammad Amir Ali* v *Khaja Jamaluddin* (1964)2 Andh WR 183: (1964)2 Andh LT 180].

**Bazaar.** Bazaar is daily market or market-place; a place of sale of miscellaneous goods for no profits to sellers but for the purpose of raising funds for charitable purpose. [Wharton's *Law Lexicon*]. Bazaar is market, a daily market, a market-place. As opposed to bazaar; a *hat* is held only on certain days.

**B.C.** Before Christ or the Christian era.

**Beacon.** An artificial structure erected for the purpose of being used as a leading mark, e.g., a lighthouse, for the guidance of ships and other vessels.

**Bear.** A speculator who expects prices to fall and sells securities he does not possess, hoping that he will make a profit by subsequently repurchasing at a lower price.

**Bearer.** One who or that which bears, carries, or has in possession; a person to whom a note, cheque, or draft is made payable without naming him; person who presents a cheque or other order to pay money.

One who possesses a negotiable instrument marked "payable to bearer" or indorsed in blank. [Black's *Law Dictionary*, 8th Ed.].

NOTE: A cheque bearing the words "pay cash or order" is not payable to bearer within the meaning of the (English) Bills of Exchange Act 1882 (c. 61), s. 3(1). [*Cole* v *Milsome* (1951)1 All ER 311].

A debenture payable "to bearer" is, in effect, a promissory note, and passes from hand to hand free from any equities which might have attached to it as between the company and the original holder. [*Re, Marseilles Imperial Land Co.* LR 11 Eq 478].

**Bed of the river.** The space between the banks occupied by the river at its fullest flow. [*Ashgar Ali* v *Secretary of State* AIR 1930 Cal 764].

It is that portion of its soil which is alternately covered and left bare, as there may be an increase or diminution in the supply of water, and which is adequate to contain it at its average and mean stage during the entire year, within reference to the extraordinary freshets of the winter and spring or the extreme droughts of the summer or autumn. This, when applied to a tidal river, means without reference to extraordinary tides at any time of year. [*Thames Conservators* v *Smeed* (1897)2 QB 334].

**Begar.** The word 'begar' is not a word of common use in English language. It is a word of Indian origin which like many other words has found its way in the English vocabulary. It is very difficult to formulate a precise definition of the word 'begar'. It is a form of forced labour under which a person is compelled to work without receiving any remuneration. Molesworth describes 'begar' as 'labour or services exacted by a Government or person in power without giving remuneration for it'. Wilson's *Glossary of Judicial and Revenue Terms* gives the following meaning of the word 'begar': "A forced labourer, one pressed to carry burthens for individuals or the public. 'Begar' may be loosely described as labour or service which a person is forced to give without receiving any remuneration for it. 'Begar' is thus clearly a form of forced labour. [*People's Union for Democratic Rights* v *Union of India* AIR 1982 SC 1473: (1982)3 SCC 235: (1982)2 Lab LJ 454: (1983)1 SCR 456].

**Behave.** To act; conduct oneself or itself; to comfort oneself properly.

**Behaviour.** Way of acting; manner of behaving; whether good or bad; conduct; 'manner of having holding, or keeping one's self, carriage of one's self, with respect to morals, and the requirements of law'. [Bouvier's *Law Dictionary*, 3rd Ed., vol. 1, p. 334].

> NOTE: The expression 'behaviour' connotes something more than the way a person talk. Behaviour is not synonymous with talk. [ *K.V. George* v *State of Kerala* 1972 Cr LJ 1095: 1972 Ker LT 267].

• **Security for good behaviour** p. 783.

**Belagan.** The word does not necessarily denote a rent-free grant but may merely mean that rent had not yet been agreed upon or assessed. [*Janakdulari Kuer* v *Meghan Telli* AIR 1942 Pat 310: 23 Pat LT 704].

**Belief.** A person's religion; religious conviction.

Probable knowledge; mental conviction; acceptance of something as true or actual; doctrinal statement; doctrine; dogma, precept, tenet.

A conviction of the truth of a proposition, existing subjectively in the mind, and induced by argument, persuasion, or proof addressed to the judgment. [*Latrobe* v *J.H. Cross Co.* DC Pa, 29 F 2d 210, 212].

'Belief' is an assurance gained by evidence and from other persons. 'Belief' is necessarily based on at least assumed facts. [*Cook* v *Singer Sewing Mach. Co.* 138 Cal App 418: 32 P 2d 430, 431].

> NOTE: A belief is inculcated in the mind of a person by various factors, by evidence of witnesses or by inference from given premises. [*Malla Mahmadoo* v *State* AIR 1952 J&K 49: 54 Cr LJ 150].

**Believe.** Feel sure of the truth of; have faith in the existence of; feel certain about the truth of; accept as true.

• **Reason to believe** p. 728.

**Belligerent.** As a personality trait, refers to one who is overly assertive, hostile or combative. [Black's *Law Dictionary*, 5th Ed.].

In international law, it means engaged in lawful war [Black's *Law Dictionary*, 5th Ed.]; a country involved in a war or other hostile action [Black's *Law Dictionary*, 7th Ed.]; a country involved in a war or other armed international conflict. [Black's *Law Dictionary*, 8th Ed.].

**Belong.** To appertain to; to be the property of; to be a member of; to be appropriate; to own.

To be the property or rightful possession of. [*Commissioner of Wealth Tax, West Bengal* v *Biswanath Chatterjee* AIR 1976 SC 1492: (1976)3 SCR 1096: (1976)3 SCC 385].

**Belonging to.** The expression should be understood not necessarily to mean 'owned by', but as indicative of complete control and dominion over the property in dispute. [*Nirmal Singh* v *Punjab State* ILR (1965)1 Punj 19: 66 Punj LR 959]. The phrase is capable of connoting interest less than absolute title *e.g.*, interest of permanent and heritable lessee. [*Mohammad Amir* v *Municipal Board* AIR 1965 SC 1923: (1966)1 SCJ 484].

**Bemiadi.** Not limited for a fixed period of time (generally used in connection with a lease or tenancy).

> NOTE: The expression would not be taken to negative the permanence of the tenancy, but at the same time the use of the word does not necessarily convey a permanent heritable right to the grantee, yet it may do so. The word itself does not conclude the matter. [*Bara Lal* v *Bhaju Mian* AIR 1955 Pat 499: ILR (1955) Pat 767].

**Benami.** The word '*benami*' is used to denote two classes of transactions which differ from each other in their legal character and incidents. In one sense it signifies a transaction which is real, as for example, when *A* sells properties to *B* but the sale deed mentions *X* as the purchaser. Here the sale itself is genuine, but the real purchaser is *B*, *X* being his *benamdar*. This is the class of transaction which is usually termed as *benami*. *Benami* is mere name lending. His name is simply an *alias* for that of the other person beneficially interested. But the word '*benami*' is also occasionally used, perhaps not quite accurately, to refer to a sham transaction, as for example, when *A* purports, to sell his property to *B* without intending that his title should cease or pass to *B*. [*Sree Meenakashi Mills* v *Commissioner of Income Tax* 1956 SCR 691: 1956 SCA 1139: AIR 1957 SC 49: 1957 SCJ 1; *Bhim Singh* v *Kan Singh* AIR 1980 SC 727].

The genesis of the concept of '*benami*' is that consideration for transfer must flow from one person and the transfer is taken in the name of the other person and the consideration so flowing for the transfer was not intended to be a gift in favour of the person in whose name the transfer is taken. [*Syed Abdul Khader* v *Rami Reddy* AIR 1979 SC 553: (1979)2 SCC 601].

> NOTE: To find out whether a transaction is *benami*, regard must be had to the following facts, namely: (*i*) the source of the purchase money; (*ii*) the possession of the property; (*iii*) the position of the parties and their relation to one another; (*iv*) the circumstances of the alleged transfer; (*v*) the motive of the alleged transfer; (*vi*) the custody and production of the deed; and (*vii*) the previous and subsequent conduct of the parties.

**Benami transaction.** "Benami transaction" means any transaction in which property is transferred to one person for a consideration paid or provided by any other person [Benami Transactions (Prohibition) Act 1988, s. 2(*a*)]. A transaction must be *benami* irrespective of its date or duration. [*Mithilesh Kumari* v *Prem Behari Khare* AIR 1989 SC 1247].

**Bench.** The office of judge; a judge's seat in a law court; a law court; judges collectively.

**Beneficial enjoyment.** The possession and benefit of land or other property, but without legal title. [Black's *Law Dictionary*, 8th Ed.].

No more than enjoyment by a person in his own right and for his own benefit, not as trustee for another. [*A-G* v *Sefton* (1865)11 HL Cas 257].

**Beneficial ownership.** A beneficiary's interest in trust property; a corporate shareholder's power to buy or sell the shares, though the shareholder is not registered on the corporation's books as the owner. [Black's *Law Dictionary*, 8th Ed.].

The expression means such right to enjoyment of property as exists where the legal title is in one person and the right of such beneficial use or interest is in another and where such right is recognized by law and can be enforced by the courts at the suit of such owner or of someone on his behalf.

**Beneficiary.** A person who receives benefits, especially under a trust, will, or life insurance policy; one who is lawfully entitled to the profits and proceeds of an estate or property, the title to which is vested in another, as in a trustee; the person to whom the amount of an insurance policy or annuity is payable.

A person who is designated to benefit from an appointment, disposition, or assignment (as in a will, insurance policy, etc.); one designated to receive something as a result of a legal arrangement or instrument. [Black's *Law Dictionary*, 7th Ed.].

(1) A person for whose benefit property is held in trust; esp. one designated to benefit from an appointment, disposition, or assignment (as in a will, insurance policy, etc.), or to receive something as a result of a legal arrangement or instrument. (2) A person to whom another is in a fiduciary relation, whether the relation is one of agency, guardianship, or trust. (3) A person who is initially entitled to enforce a promise, whether that person is the promisee or a third party. [Black's *Law Dictionary*, 8th Ed.].

A beneficiary is "one who is beneficially entitled to, or interested in, property; i.e. entitled to it for his own benefit, and not merely as trustee, or executor, holding it for others. The word is nearly equivalent to 'cestui que trust', which, on account of its cumbersomeness and inexpressiveness, 'beneficiary' has begun to supersede in modern law". [Stroud's *Judicial Dictionary of Words and Phrases*, 6th Ed.].

▸ *Meaning under the Indian Trusts Act 1882, s. 3.* The person for whose benefit the confidence is reposed and accepted is called the beneficiary.

▸ *Meaning under the Wakfs Act 1954, s. 3(a).* Beneficiary means a person or object for whose benefit a wakf is created and includes religious, pious and charitable objects and any other objects of public utility.

A beneficiary is one who is beneficially entitled to or interested in property. [*Rani Padma Sundari* v *Rani Parbati Debi* ILR 37 Pat 138].

Beneficiaries are persons who have beneficial interest in property but have no title or legal ownership. [*Province of Bihar* v *F.R. Hayes* (1946)14 ITR 326].

**Beneficium invito non datur.** A benefit cannot be conferred upon a person unwilling to accept it.

**Benefit.** Profit; advantage; promotion of welfare or prosperity; helpful result; a favourable or helpful factor or circumstance; assistance; comfort; convenience; gain; relief; return, utility, well-being; fruit; privilege; interest.

The word 'benefit' includes benefits, express or otherwise, in terms of money but requiring computation. [*Proprietor Lenox Photo Manufacturing* v *Presiding Officer, Labour Court* AIR 1965 Mad 450: (1965)2 MLJ 150].

NOTE: For the purposes of s. 4 of the Wealth Tax Act 1957, the word 'benefit' means for the immediate benefit of the individual or his wife or minor child. If a property is transferred to trustees to hold in trust for the life of *A* and then for *B*, the property is not held for benefit of *B* during life time of *A*. [*His Highness Yeshwant Rao Ghorpade* v *Commissioner of Wealth Tax, Bangalore* AIR 1967 SC 135, 137].

A power to trustees to make advances for a person's "benefit" enables them to pay the person's debts. [*Lowther* v *Bentinck* LR 19 Eq 167; *Re Stranger* 64 LT 693, cited whole; but see *Re Price* 34 Ch D 603].

A gift "for the benefit of" a hospital means either a gift for the general purposes of the hospital or a gift to supplement the funds available for carrying on the work of the hospital. [*Re Morgan's Will Trusts* (1950)1 All ER 1097].

**Benefit of doubt.** Doubt which are real, genuine, well founded which a normal man with normal intelligence in a given circumstances would naturally harbour, are doubts which come within the fold of 'reasonable doubt' entitling one to the benefit thereof. It is not a doubt of a vacillating mind that has no moral courage to decide but shelters itself in a vain idle scepticism. [*State* v *Sarangdhar Bhoi* 1972 Cut LT 734].

NOTE: If the facts and circumstances are susceptible of two interpretations, one in favour of the prosecution and the other in support of the defence version, then the rule which applies to circumstantial evidence would prevail, and the benefit of doubt, if any, would have to go to the accused. [*Rishipal* v *State* AIR 1962 All 13; *Shivaji Sahebrao Bobade* v *State of Maharashtra* AIR 1973 SC 2622].

**Benevolent societies.** Societies formed for any benevolent or charitable purposes. They may be registered in England under the Friendly Societies Act 1974, and in India, under the Societies Registration Act 1860.

**Bequeath.** Leave (a personal estate) to a person by a will; to give, a personal property, by a will; hand down to posterity; devolve upon; endow with; give away at death; devise.

'Bequeath' in its ordinary sense signifies the declaration of a man's will concerning the succession to his own property after his death.

To be understood in its ordinary sense, it means "as referring to a gift by will of the testator's own property and nothing else". [*Holyland* v *Lewin* 26 Ch D 266, *per* Selbrone, C.].

"The ordinary accepted meaning and interpretation of the word 'bequeathed' confines it to property derived under a testamentary instrument". [*Re Armstrong, Marescaux* v *Armstrong* (1879)49 LJ Ch 53, *per* Hall, V.-C.].

**Bequest** The act or an instance of bequeathing; the act of giving property, usually personal in nature, by will; property, usually personal property other than money, disposed of in a will.

NOTE: 'The terms "legacy" and "bequest" in their ordinary sense are used of a gift of money or a chattel, but with a proper controlling context are capable of meaning a devise of land'. [Halsbury's *Laws of England*, 3rd Ed., vol. 39, p. 1016].

**Bestiality.** Sexual intercourse between a person and an animal.

NOTE: It is a punishable offence under s. 377 of the Indian Penal Code. Under s. 13(2)(*ii*) of the Hindu Marriage Act 1955, s. 27(1A)(*i*) of the Special Marriage Act 1954 and s. 10(2) of the Divorce Act 1869 the wife can apply for divorce on the ground that the husband has been guilty of bestiality.

**Bet.** Bet is something that is laid, staked, or pledged typically between two parties on the outcome of a contest or any contingent issue; wager; the act of giving such a pledge; something to wager on.

**Betrothal.** It is no more than a promise to marry. It precedes marriage; but unlike marriage it is revocable.

**Better equity.** Where as between rival claimants in a court of equity the court holds that one of them, either on the ground of notice or of priority in time or for some other sufficient reason, is entitled to priority over the other, such claimant is said to have the "better equity".

**Betterment.** An improvement put upon a property which enhances its value more than mere replacement, maintenance, or repairs. Betterment is improvement that adds to the value of a property or facility.

**Betting.** A form of wagering contract under which money or money's worth is made payable on the result of some uncertain event, such, for instance, as a horse race, a football match or a boxing contest.

**Bhag.** A share, a part, a portion; a share in kind; tax, duty, the share of the Government. Share or portion of inheritance.

**Bhag chashi/bargadar.** It means a person who under the system generally known as *adhi*, *barga* or *bhag* cultivates the land of another person on condition of delivering a share of produce of such land to that person and includes a person who under the system generally known as *kisani* or by any other description cultivates the land of another person on condition of receiving a share of the produce of such land from that person. [W.B. Land Reforms Act 1955, s. 2(2)].

**Bhagidar.** A sharer, a partner; an accomplice.

**Bhang.** The leaves and flower-tops of Indian hemp used as a narcotic.

**Bhaoli.** Distribution of the products of the harvest, in previously stipulated proportions between the landlord and tenant. Rent paid in kind, as the value of a share of the produce.

**Bhara.** Hire; wages; rent; recompense. In Bengal, it is especially the hire of any inanimate thing, and therefore does not imply wages.

**Bharatiya.** A tenant; a renter.

**Bhatha land.** The expression "bhatha land" means land which forms part of the bed of a river on which vegetables, melon, cucumber etc., can be grown during the lean period after the rainy season is over, when the level of the water in the river is quite low. [*State of Gujarat* v *V.D. Chaturbhai* (1980)2 SCR 1182: (1980)3 SCC 318].

**Bhedi.** A dyke; an embankment.

**Bhomicharas.** The Bhomicharas are the representatives of Rajput Rulers who conquered the country and established their sovereignty over it in the thirteenth century. [*Thakur Amar Singhji* v *State of Rajasthan* AIR 1955 SC 504: (1955)2 SCR 303: 1955 SCJ 523].

**Biannual.** Occurring, appearing twice a year.

**Bias.** Partiality; partisanism; partisanship; predetermination; predilection; predisposition; prejudgment; prejudication; prejudice; undetachment; undispassionateness.

In law, it means a condition of mind which sways judgment and renders judge unable to exercise his functions impartially in particular case.

"By bias, I understand a real likelihood of an operative prejudice, whether conscious or unconscious". [*Rex* v *Queen's County Justices* (1908)2 IR 285, 294, *per* Lord O'Brien, LCJ.].

A predisposition to decide for and against one party, without proper regard to the true merits of the dispute is bias. [*Secretary to Government, Transport Department, Madras* v *Manuswami Mudaliar* 1988 (Supp) SCC 651: AIR 1988 SC 2232; *Ratan Lal Sharma* v *Managing Committee, Dr. Hari Ram (Co-Education) Higher Secondary School* AIR 1993 SC 2155: (1993)4 SCC 10].

NOTE: For various forms of bias and its various facets—vide Ch. 5, *Penumbra of Natural Justice* by Tapash Gan Choudhury, 2nd Ed., 2001].

**Bibliography.** A list of books referred to in a scholarly work, usually printed as an appendix.

**Bid.** Offer; offer to do work for a stated price; offered price; quoted price.

Bid is a statement of what one will give or take for something; an offer of a price; something offered as a bid; the amount of such bid.

A buyer's offer to pay a specified price for something that may or may not be for sale; a submitted price at which one will perform work or supply goods. [Black's *Law Dictionary*, 8th Ed.].

NOTE: A bid is a mere offer and can be retracted by the bidder at any time before the auctioneer announces the completion of the contract. A person who bids at an auction thereby does not conclude a contract, but states an offer, by which, until he withdraws it himself, he may be liable for the amount of his bid. But on the other hand, like all other offers, it is subject to the ordinary incidents of law, that until it is accepted, is open to the bidder to withdraw it and render it as if it had not been made. [*Jovermull* v *Joygopaldas* 45 Mad 799: AIR 1922 Mad 486]. When a particular bid is accepted the contract is complete. [*Muthu Pillai* v *Secretary of State* AIR 1923 Mad 582].

**Bidding.** The offers at an auction.

**Biennial.** Lasting two years; recurring every two years.

**Bigamy.** The crime of marrying when already married to another person.

When a person contracts a second marriage after coming into force of the

Hindu Marriage Act 1955, while the first marriage is subsisting, he commits the offence of 'bigamy'. [*Gopal Lal* v *State of Rajasthan* AIR 1979 SC 713: (1979)2 SCR 1171: (1979)2 SCC 170: 1979 Cr LJ 652: 1979 SCC (Cri) 401].

NOTE: Bigamy is a felonious offence of a husband or wife marrying again during the life of the first wife or husband.

Bigamy is punishable under ss. 494 and 495 of the Indian Penal Code. A bigamous Hindu marriage is punishable under s. 17 of the Hindu Marriage Act 1955.

**Bigha.** A measure of land, varying in extent in different parts of India. [Wilson's *Glossary*].

**Bilateral.** Of, on, or with two sides.

**Bilateral contract.** A contract in which both the contracting parties are bound to fulfil obligations reciprocally towards each other; as a contract of sale, where one becomes bound to deliver the things sold and the other to pay the price of it.

A contract in which each party promises a performance, so that each party is an obligor on that party's own promise and an obligee on the other's promise; a contract in which the parties obligate themselves reciprocally, so that the obligation of one party is correlative to the obligation of the other. [Black's *Law Dictionary*, 8th Ed.].

**Bill.** A draft or form of an Act, presented to the legislature, but not enacted; a draft of a proposed law; a printed or written statement of charges for goods supplied or services rendered and the amount owed; a poster.


- **Accommodation bill** p. 15.
- **Approved bill** p. 72.
- **Bank bill** p. 94.
- **Documentary bills** p. 278.
- **Foreign bills** p. 364.
- **Money bill** p. 589.
- **Renewal of a negotiable bill** p. 745.
- **Sight bill** p. 797.
- **Sola bill** p. 802.


**Bill broker.** A person engaged in the purchase and sale of bills of exchange.

**Bill of attainder.** A bill declaring a person attained and his property confiscated.

A special legislative act prescribing punishment, without a trial, for a specific person or group. [Black's *Law Dictionary*, 8th Ed.].

**Bill of credit.** An authority in writing from one person to another very common among merchants, bankers and those who travel, empowering a person to receive or take up money of their correspondents abroad. It is more usually termed a letter of credit. [Jowitt's *Dictionary of English Law*, 2nd Ed.].

Legal tender in the form of paper, issued by a State and involving the faith of the State, designed to circulate as money in the ordinary uses of business. [Black's *Law Dictionary*, 8th Ed.].

**Bill of exchange.** A three party instrument in which first party draws an order for the payment of a sum certain on a second party for payment to a third party at a definite future time. [Black's *Law Dictionary*, 5th Ed.].

A 'bill of exchange' is an instrument in writing containing an unconditional order, signed by the maker, directing a certain person to pay a certain sum of money only to, or to the order of, a certain person or to the bearer of the instrument. [Negotiable Instruments Act 1881, s. 5]. A bill of exchange is sometimes called a draft.

NOTE: A 'bill of exchange' includes also a hundi, and any other document entitling or purporting to entitle any person, whether named therein or not, to payment by any other person of, or to draw upon any other person for, any sum of money. [Indian Stamp Act 1899, s. 2(2)].

Bill of exchange includes a hundi and a cheque. [Limitation Act 1963, s. 2(c)].

**Bill of goods.** A consignment of merchandise.

**Bill of health.** A certificate regarding infectious disease on a ship or in a port at the time of sailing.

**Bill of lading.** A shipmaster's detailed list of the ship's cargo.

Bill of lading is a memorandum signed by masters of ships in their capacity of carriers, acknowledging the receipt of merchant's goods, of which there are usually three parts—one part belongs to the consignor, one sent to the consignee and one preserved by the master. It is the evidence of the title, to the goods shipped; and by its endorsement and delivery, the transfer of the property in the goods specified therein is generally effected.

A bill of lading is a writing, signed on behalf of the owner of the ship in which goods are embarked, acknowledging the receipt of the goods, and undertaking to deliver them at the end of the voyage subject to such condition as may be mentioned in the bill of lading. It is well settled in commercial world that a bill of lading represents the goods and the transfer of it operates as a transfer of goods. [*J.V. Gokal and Co. (P.) Ltd.* v *Assistant Collector, Sales Tax* AIR 1960 SC 595: (1960)2 SCR 852: (1960)11 STC 186: 1960 SCJ 671].

NOTE: A bill of lading serves three purposes viz. (1) it is a receipt for the goods shipped containing the terms on which they have been received; (2) it is evidence of the contract for the carriage of goods; (3) it is a document of title for the goods specified therein. [*Ellerman and Bucknull Steamship Co. Ltd.* v *Sha Misrimal Bherajee* AIR 1966 SC 1892: (1966)2 SCA 103].

**Bill of rights.** The English Constitutional Settlement of 1689; the original constitutional amendments in USA of 1791.

One of the four great charters of English liberty (1689), embodying in statutory form all the principles of the other three charters, namely, Magna Carta, the Petition of Right (1628), and the Habeas Corpus Act (1679).

**Bill of sale.** A certificate of transfer of personal property, especially as a security against debt.

An instrument for conveying title to personal property, absolutely or by way of security. [Black's *Law Dictionary*, 8th Ed.].

A bill of sale is a solemn contract whereby a man passes to another the right or interest that he hath in goods and chattels. A bill of sale has been described as an instrument in writing whereby one transfers to another the property he has in goods or chattels, or as a document given with respect to the transfer of goods or chattels, used in cases where possession is not intended to be given. [Halsbury's *Laws of England*, 4th Ed., vol. 4, para 601, p. 237].

**Billhead.** A printed account form.

**Billion.** A thousand million.

**Bilticut.** The price fixed at the time of entering into a contract *bilticut* would include the cost of the goods and all expenses that may be incurred up to the delivery of the goods to the railway. Delivery is made to the railway and as soon as they have been accepted for carriage, the goods are ordinarily, unless a different intention appears, at the risk of the buyer. The seller performs his duty when the goods are put on rail taking reasonable care. [*Suresh Kumar Rajendra Kumar* v *K. Assan Koya & Sons* AIR 1990 Ker 20, 24 (DB)].

It means only a contract for the price having to be paid against the delivery of the railway receipt. [*Moolji Jaitha & Co.* v *Seth Kirodimal* AIR 1961 Ker 21, 22].

**Binary number.** The representation of a number in binary notation, that is, 0 or 1. This representation is widely used in digital computers, its advantage being that numbers can be expressed in terms of only two alternative choices or conditions.

**Bipartite.** Consisting of two parts.

**Biradari.** Brotherhood; the fraternal relation; relationship. [Steingass's *Dictionary*].

One tribe, man belonging to one tribe, brotherhood. [*Urdu-Hindi Dictionary* by Muhammed Mustafa Khan, 1959 Ed.].

Denotes only brotherhood which does not mean merely members of the family of a particular person but the entire brotherhood or caste or tribe in a broader and general sense of a group of persons of which some may or may not constitute the family. [*State of Bihar* v *Radha Krishna Singh* AIR 1983 SC 684: (1983)3 SCC 118: (1983)2 SCR 808].

**Birth certificate.** An official document identifying a person by name, place, date of birth, and parentage.

**Birth right.** A right of possession or privilege one has from birth.

**Bisect.** Divide into two strictly equal parts.

**Bisexual.** Having characteristics of both sexes.

**Bishnottar.** Land held rent-free by Brahmans professing the worship of *Vishnu* or granted in honour of that divinity.

**Bishnprit.** Land held rent-free by Brahmans or religious persons, professing the especial service of the deity *Vishnu*.

**Black and white.** Recorded in writing or print.

**Black ball.** Reject a candidate in a ballot originally by voting with a black ball.

**Black marketing.** Dealing (buying or selling) in goods or services at a price higher than that fixed by regulation, or unauthorised dealing in prohibited or rationed goods.

An illegal marketing for goods that are controlled or prohibited by the government. [Black's *Law Dictionary*, 8th Ed.].

**Blacklist.** A list of persons, firms, companies etc., with whom no dealings are to be had.

To put the name of (a person) on a list of those who are to be boycotted or punished. [Black's *Law Dictionary*, 8th Ed.].

NOTE: Blacklisting any person in respect of business ventures has civil consequence for the future business of the person concerned in any event. Even if, the rules do not express so, it is an elementary principle of natural justice that parties affected by any order should have right of being heard and making representations against the order. [*Raghunath Thakur* v *State of Bihar* AIR 1989 SC 620: (1989)1 SCC 229: JT 1988(4) SC 728: 1988 Supp (3) SCR 867].

**Blackmail.** Originally, rent payable in cattle, labour or produce as distinguished from rent payable in silver or white money. Subsequently it meant the toll levied by freebooters along the Scottish border.

A person is guilty of blackmail if with a view to gain to himself or another or with intent to cause loss to another, he makes any unwarranted demand with menaces.

It is an extortion of payment in return for not disclosing discreditable information, a secret etc.

**Blank acceptance.** An acceptance written on the paper before the bill is made, and delivered by the acceptor.

**Blank endorsement.** Where the name of the endorsee is not mentioned in the instrument, the endorsement is said to be blank. [Negotiable Instruments Act 1881, s. 16].

**Blank transfer.** A transfer of shares which is executed without the name of the transferee being filled in.

**Blasphemy.** Irreverence toward God, religion, a religious icon, or something else considered sacred. [Black's *Law Dictionary*, 8th Ed.].

In English law, blasphemy is the offence of speaking matter relating to God, Jesus Christ, the Bible, or the Book of Common Prayer, intended to wound the feelings of mankind or to excite contempt and hatred against the church by law established, or to promote immorality.

**Blockade.** It is disposition of troops or armed vessels so as to cut off all external communications with an enemy's port, fortress, city, etc.

Action taken against enemy nation so as to isolate, obstruct and prevent communications, commerce, supplies, and persons from entering into or leaving such nation. Such blockades may be by sea, or land, or both. [Black's *Law Dictionary*, 5th Ed.].

In international law, it means a belligerent's prevention of access to or egress from an enemy's ports by stationing ships to intercept vessels trying to enter or leave those ports. [Black's *Law Dictionary*, 8th Ed.].

NOTE: In time of war the Crown may promulgate blockades of ports or any portion of the coast belonging to an enemy. The Crown has also, by right of its prerogative, a *jus angariae*, that is to say a right to appropriate the property of a neutral where necessity requires in time of war. This right is blockades. [Halsbury's *Laws of England*, 4th Ed., vol. 18, para 1903, p. 989].

**Blood.** The relationship arising by descent from a common ancestor [Black's *Law Dictionary*, 7th Ed.]; ancestry; breed; consanguinity; family tie; genealogy; lineage; pedigree.

- **Half blood** p. 404.
- **Uterine blood** p. 871.
- **Whole blood** p. 897.

**Blood brother.** A brother by birth.

**Blood money.** Money paid to the next of kin of a person who has been killed.

**Blue book.** An official or widely recognized book of rules containing economic or commercial information, names of official etc.; a report issued by Parliament or the Privy Council in UK bound in blue.

**Blueprint.** A photographic print of the final stage of engineering or other plans in white on a blue background; a detailed plan, especially in the early stages of a project or idea.

**Board's report.** See DIRECTOR'S REPORT p. 261.

**Boat.** A 'boat' is a small open vessel usually propelled by oars, though sometimes by sail also. [*Panduronga Timbo Industries* v *Union of India* AIR 1992 SC 1194: (1992)2 SCC 635: JT 1992(2) SC 277].

**Body corporate.** The expression 'body corporate' is used in legal parlance to mean 'a public or private corporation'. [*Ashoka Marketing Ltd.* v *Punjab National Bank* (1990)4 SCC 406: AIR 1991 SC 855].

**Body of individuals.** When several individuals are found to have joined together for the purpose of making profit, the group of individuals may be conveniently described as 'a body of individuals'. Even if business is not originally started and it is interested by the individuals and it is continued as a joint business venture, the income of such business is assessed in the status of 'a body of individuals'. [*Meera & Company, Ludhiana* v *CIT, Punjab J&K and Chandigarh, Patiala* (1997)4 SCC 677].

**Body search.** A search, especially one conducted by customs officials or the police, of a person's body for illicit weapons, drugs etc.

**Bolt-hole.** A means of escape; a secret refuge.

**Bona fide.** Truly; actually; without simulation or pretence; innocently; in the attitude of trust and confidence; without notice of fraud, etc.

In or with good faith; honestly, openly, and sincerely; without deceit or fraud. [*Merrill* v *Dept. of Motor Vehicles* 458 P 2d 33].

Real, actual, genuine, and not feigned. [*Bridgeport Mortgage & Realty Corporation* v *Whitlock* 20 A 2d 414, 416].

'Bona fide' means a good faith or genuinely; in other words, it conveys absence of intent to deceive. [*Subhadran Devi* v *Sundar Devi Tek Chand* AIR 1965 Punj 188].

The phrase connotes good faith which is suggestive of honesty of purpose.

NOTE: Content of the phrase is closely related with things and actions which have relation to mind or motive of individual. [*Chandralekha* v *P.K. Suseela Row* (1969)2 MLJ 17].

Nothing is *bona fide* which is not done with due care and attention. [*Sohan Lal* v *Poonam Chand* AIR 1961 Raj 32].

**Bona fide mistake.** Errors or omissions that are patent, correction of which does not involve a decision on any controversial issue. [*Ganges Manufacturing Co.* v *State* 76 CWN 389].

Mistake made unintentionally, inadvertently, in good faith. [*Mirabal* v

*General Motors Acceptance Corp.* CA III, 537 F 2d 871, 878].

**Bona fide requirement.** The expression connotes something more than desire to have something and much less than absolute necessity. [*Bhogilal* v *Subramania Iyer* AIR 1954 Mad 514: (1953)2 MLJ 625].

NOTE: In the matter of occupying an accommodation by the landlord himself, it is not enough that he really means to occupy it himself, it must be necessary for him to occupy it and the necessity must be a *bona fide* or genuine one. [*Girja Debi* v *RC & EO* AIR 1965 All 366].

**Bona vacantia.** Goods without an apparent owner and to which the Crown has right.

Goods without an apparent owner in which no one claims a property, such as lost property, shipwreck, treasure trove, or the personal property of an intestate without next-of-kin.

NOTE: The finder of lost property is *prima facie* entitled to it, but in general, *bona vacantia* belong to the Crown in right of its prerogative.

The property of a dissolved company is deemed *bona vacantia* subject to an order of the court and to the power of the Crown to disclaim.

**Bonanza.** A source of wealth or prosperity; a large output.

**Bond.** A thing that ties another down or together; a certificate issued by a government or a public company promising to repay borrowed money at a fixed rate of interest at a specified time; a debenture; an insurance policy held by a travel agent, tour operator, airline, etc. which protects travellers' holidays and money from the company's bankruptcy; a deed by which a person is bound to make payment to another.

An instrument under seal, usually a deed poll, whereby one person binds himself to another for the payment of a specified sum of money either immediately or at a fixed future date. The person who so binds himself is called the obligor and the person to whom he is bound the obligee; and the instrument itself is sometimes called an obligation. [Halsbury's *Laws of England*, 4th Ed., vol. 12, para 1385, p. 556].

NOTE: Bond includes any instrument whereby a person obliges himself to pay money to another, on condition that the obligation shall be void if a specified act is performed, or is not performed, as the case may be. [Limitation Act 1963, s. 2(*d*)].

Bond includes—(*a*) any instrument whereby a person obliges himself to pay money to another, on condition that the obligation shall be void if a specified act is performed, or is not performed, as the case may be; (*b*) any instrument attested by a witness and not payable to order or bearer, whereby a person obliges himself to pay money to another; and (*c*) any instrument so attested, whereby a person obliges himself to deliver grain or other agricultural produce to another. [Indian Stamp Act 1899, s. 2(5)].


- **Active bonds** p. 34.
- **Administrative bond** p. 40.
- **Bottomry bond** p. 110.
- **Gold bond** p. 389.
- **Joint and several bond** p. 487.
- **Post-obit bond** p. 673.
- **Security bond** p. 783.


**Bondage.** Slavery; sadomasochistic practices, including the use of physical restraints or mental enslavement.

**Bonded debt.** A debt secured by a bond; a business or government debt represented by issued bonds.

**Bonded goods.** Imported goods deposited in a Government warehouse until duty is paid.

**Bonded labour.** See LABOUR p. 508.

**Bonded warehouse.** A customs-controlled warehouse for the retention of imported goods until the duty owed is paid.

A secure place approved by the customs authorities for the deposit of dutiable goods upon which duty has not been paid.

**Bondholder.** A person holding a bond or bonds granted by a private person or a public company.

**Bonus.** An unsought or unexpected extra benefit; seasonal gratuity to employees beyond their normal pay; an extra-dividend or issue paid to the shareholders of a company; distribution of profits to the holders of an insurance policy.

Any extra consideration given for what is received, or something given in addition to what is ordinarily received by, or strictly due to the recipient is a bonus. But when industrial jurisprudence speaks of 'bonus', it enters the area of right and claim to what is due beyond strict wages. [*The Mumbai Kamgar Sabha, Bombay* v *Abdulbhai Faizullabhai* AIR 1976 SC 1455: (1976)3 SCC 832].

Under the Industrial Disputes Act, the term 'bonus' is applied to a cash payment made in addition to wages. It generally represents the cash incentive given conditionally on certain standards of attendance and efficiency being attained. [*Muir Mills Co. Ltd.* v *Suti Mills Mazdoor Union, Kanpur* AIR 1955 SC 170: (1955)1 SCR 991: 1955 SCJ 214].

**Bonus share.** If a company declares a bonus out of undivided capitalised profits and allots to its shareholders in satisfaction of the bonus unissued shares in the company as fully paid up, the shares so allotted are known as bonus shares and they are capital and not income in the hands of the shareholders. [*Inland Revenue Commissioners* v *Blott* (1921)2 AC 171; *C.I.T.* v *Dalmia Investment Co. Ltd.* (1964)52 ITR 567 (577-578) (SC)].

**Book.** It ordinarily means a collection of sheets of paper or other material, blank, written or printed, fastened or bound together so as to form a material whole. Loose sheets or scraps of paper cannot be termed as 'book' for they can be easily detached and replaced. [*Central Bureau of Investigation* v *V.C. Shukla* AIR 1998 SC 1406: (1998)3 SCC 410: 1998 Cr LJ 1905: JT 1998(2) SC 172].

In its ordinary sense it signifies a collection of sheets of paper bound together in a manner which cannot be disturbed or altered except by tearing apart. The binding is of a kind which is not intended to be movable in the sense of being undone and put together again. A collection of papers in portfolio, or a clip, or strung together on a piece of twine which is intended to be untied at will, would not, in ordinary English, be called a book. [*Mukundram* v *Dayaram* AIR 1914 Nag 44].

'Book' means a collection of sheets of paper or other substance, bound together, and protected by covers and having a shape, size and value and must satisfy the physical and functional characteristics. [*Commissioner of Income Tax* v *Elcon Engineering Co. Ltd.* (1974)96 ITR 672: 1976 Tax LR 448: (1974)1 ITJ 314].


- **Blue book** p. 107.
- **Day book** p. 225.
- **Log-book** p. 542.
- **Minute book** p. 583.
- **Paper book** p. 638.
- **Seal book** p. 779.
- **Text book** p. 840.
- **Warehouse book** p. 892.


**Book debts.** Include all such debts, as in the ordinary course of carrying on business, would be entered in books, although not actually entered. [*Shipley* v *Marshall* 32 LJCP 258; *Official Receiver* v *Tailby* 56 LJQB 33].

**Book value.** The value of something as shown on book-keeping records as distinguished from market value; the value of an asset equal to cost less depreciation; the value of a corporation's capital stock equal to its book value less its liabilities (as debt or preferred stock).

**Books of accounts.** Books in which merchants, traders or businessmen generally keep their accounts, *i.e.* statements of debits and credits or receipts and payments. [*Manish Dixit* v *State of Rajasthan* AIR 2001 SC 93: (2001)1 SCC 596: 2001 Cr LJ 133].

NOTE: A register kept at the counter of a hotel need not contain any statement of account. So, until it is shown that such register also pertained to the pecuniary transactions involving the customers of the hotel, the same cannot be treated as a book of accounts. [*Manish Dixit* v *State of Rajasthan*, supra].

**Boomerang.** A plan or scheme that recoils on its originator.

**Bootleg.** Make, distribute or smuggle illicit goods, especially, alcohol; pirate, such as, a musical recording.

**Bootlegger.** "Bootlegger" under s. 2(*b*) of the Bombay Prohibition Act 1949 means a person who distills, manufactures, stores, transports, imports, exports, sells or distributes any liquor, intoxicating drug or other intoxicant in contravention of any provision of the Act and the rules and orders made thereunder, or any other law for the time being in force or who knowingly expends or applies any money or supplies any animal, vehicle, vessel or other conveyance or any receptacle or any other material whatsoever in furtherance or support of the doing of any of the things described alone by or through any other person, or who abets in any other manner the doing of any such things. [*Rashidmiya* alias *Chhava Ahmedmiya Shaik* v *Police Commissioner, Ahmedabad* AIR 1989 SC 1703: (1989)3 SCC 321: JT 1989(2) SC 323: (1989)3 SCR 182].

**Booty.** Plunder gained especially in war or by piracy.

**Borrow.** To receive money with the implied or expressed intention of returning the same usually with interest; take something for temporary use.

'Borrowing' necessarily implies repayment at some time and under some circumstances. [*Re Southern Brazilian Rio* (1905)2 Ch 78].

NOTE: 'Borrow' includes the raising of money by the grant of annuities. [Constitution of India 1950, Art. 366].

**Bottomry bond.** A contract for the loan of money on a ship, usually at extraordinary interest, for maritime risks encountered during a certain period or for a certain voyage. [Black's *Law Dictionary*, 8th Ed.].

▸ *Meaning under the Indian Stamp Act 1899, Art. 16.* Any instrument whereby the master of a sea-going ship borrows money on the security of the ship to enable him to preserve the ship or to prosecute her voyage.

**Bought and sold.** It refers to a transaction resulting in buying on the one hand and selling on the other. [*Sri Krishna Coconut Co.* v *East Godavari Coconut and Tobacco Market Committee* (1967)1 SCR 974: AIR 1967 SC 973].

**Boundary.** A line marking the limits of an area, territory, etc. Something that indicates or fixes a limit or extent.

**Bourgeois.** A conventionally middle-class, selfishly materialistic, upholding the interest of the capitalist class; non-communist.

**Boycotting.** The system under which the life of a man is made unendurable and impossible by an organised refusal to have any dealing with him. Boycotting is theoretically the spontaneous outcome of the feelings of the persons applying it to a particular individual, but in practice it is the effect of a fear that anyone refusing to take part in the boycott will himself be boycotted. The system originated in Ireland in 1880, and the first victim was a land agent named Boycott.

**Brahma.** The creator God in Hinduism.

**Brahma form of marriage.** In this form of marriage the father or other guardian of the bride was to make a gift of the damsel adorned with dress and ornaments to a bachelor versed in the Brahma or Veda, and of good character who was sought out and invited by the guardian to accept the bride.

**Brahman.** A member of the highest Hindu caste, the priesthood caste.

**Brahmottar.** Land granted rent-free to Brahmins for their support and that of their descendants as a reward for their sanctity or learning, or to enable them to devote themselves to religious duties and education.

**Brass.** Brass is but an alloy of copper and zinc and is a complete and finished product by itself. Brass or brass scrap is not used as a raw material in the manufacture of other alloys. [*Khandelwal Metal and Engg.*

*Works* v *Union of India* AIR 1985 SC 1211: (1985)3 SCC 620: 1985 Supp (1) SCR 750: (1985)20 ELT 222].

**Breach.** 'Breach' means infringement or violation of a promise or obligation. [*Skandia Insurance Co. Ltd.* v *Kokilaben Chandravadan* AIR 1987 SC 1184: (1987)2 SCC 654: (1987)2 SCR 752: JT 1987(2) SC 43; *Sohan Lal Passi* v *P. Sesh Reddy* AIR 1996 SC 2627: (1996)5 SCC 21: JT 1996(6) SC 728: 1996 SCC (Cri) 871].

**Breach of contract.** Failure to perform the obligation under the contract.

Violation of a contractual obligation by failing to perform one's own promise, by repudiating it, or by interfering with another party's performance. [Black's *Law Dictionary*, 8th Ed.].

NOTE: Breach of contract occurs where that which is complained of is a breach of duty arising out of the obligations undertaken by the contract. [*Jarvis* v *May, Davis, Smith* (1936)1 KB 399].

**Breach of peace.** An infringement or violation of the public peace by any disturbance or riot etc.

The criminal offence of creating a public disturbance or engaging in disorderly conduct, particularly by making an unnecessary or distracting noise. [Black's *Law Dictionary*, 8th Ed.].

**Breach of privilege.** Breach of the authority or power, e.g., of the Parliament or of the State Legislature.

**Breach of promise.** The breaking of a promise.

**Breach of trust.** A trustee's violation of either the trust's terms or the trustee's general fiduciary obligations; the violation of a duty that equity imposes on a trustee, whether the violation was wilful, fraudulent, negligent, or inadvertent. [Black's *Law Dictionary*, 8th Ed.].

Breach of any duty imposed on a trustee, as such, by any law for the time being in force. [Indian Trusts Act 1882, s. 3].

**Bread.** Usually baked and leavened food made of a mixture whose basic constituent is flour or meal.

NOTE: Bread includes all forms of bread which are prepared by moistening, kneading, baking, frying or roasting meal or flour, with or without the addition of yeast, leaven or any other substance for puffing or lightening the article. Shirmal and tanur-ki-roti are bread. [*Kayani & Co.* v *Commissioner of Sales Tax* AIR 1953 Hyd 252]. *Singaras* and *nimkis* are not bread. [*Delhi Mistanna Bhandar* v *State* AIR 1957 Assam 31].

**Breath test.** When the breath of any person driving a motor vehicle is tested to ascertain whether he has alcohol in his body, it is called a breath test.

**Bribe.** Persuade a person to act illegally or dishonestly in one's favour by a gift of money, services etc.

It may be described as something offered to influence the judgment unduly or corrupt the conduct.

To bribe is to control by means of tangible inducements rather than by persuasion or coercion. [*Encyclopaedia of Social Science*, p. 690].

NOTE: According to 'Biblical' and 'Roman Law', the Judge who takes bribe was said to be "corrupted by the filth". [*Encyclopaedia of Crime and Justice*, p. 120].

**Bribery.** The corrupt payment, receipt, or solicitation of a private favour for official action. [Black's *Law Dictionary*, 8th Ed.].

The offering, giving, receiving, or soliciting of any thing of value to influence action as an official or in discharge of legal or public duty. [*Allen* v *State* 72 P 2d 516, 519].

The corrupt tendering or receiving of a price for official action. [*State* v *London* 78 P 2d 548, 554].

Bribery in its legal sense implies corruption. [*Gardner* v *Robertson* 1921 SC 132, 139, *per* Lord Salvesen].

**Bride and bridegroom.** 'Bride' means a woman who has just been married or is about to be married, and bridegroom means a man who has just been married or is about to be married. [*L.V. Jadhav* v *Shankarrao* 1983 Cr LJ 1501 (SC)].

**Bridge.** A building erected across a river, ditch, valley or other place for crossing by travellers.

> NOTE: Culvert in common parlance would come under the expression 'bridge'. [*Mercantile Express Co.* v *Assistant Collector* AIR 1958 Cal 630: 62 CWN 661].

**Bridging loan.** A loan from a bank etc. to cover the short interval between buying a house etc and selling another.

**Brief.** An abbreviated statement of the pleadings, proofs, and affidavits in any legal proceeding with a concise narrative of the facts and merits of the case for use of the counsel at the trial or hearing.

**Bring-and-buy sale.** A charity sale at which participants bring items for sale and buy what is brought by others.

**Brit cheque.** See BAD CHEQUE p. 91.

**Brit jajmani.** The right to the performance of the domestic ceremonies of a house-holder and the fees payable thereupon.

**Broker.** A mercantile agent who in the ordinary course of his business is employed to make contracts for the purchase or sale of property or goods of which he is not entrusted with the possession or documents of title. [Halsbury's *Laws of England*, 4th Ed., vol. 1, para 712, p. 424].

A broker is an agent whose ordinary course of business is to negotiate and make contracts for the sale and purchase of goods and other property, of which he is not entrusted with possession or control. [*Alapati Ramamurthi* v *Ramanujam* AIR 1961 AP 408].

Word meaning an agent, but used generally in a more special sense for one who buys or sells on behalf of another. He must act according to the instructions given to him and as a general rule his task is finished when he has made the contract between the buyer and the seller ... Types of brokers are: stock brokers, bill brokers, wool brokers, produce brokers and insurance brokers. [*A. Setty & Sons* v *State of Mysore* (1961)12 STC 731; *CST* v *Vijay Kumar* (1968)21 STC 31 (All)].


- **Bill broker** p. 104.
- **Pawn-broker** p. 647.


**Brokerage.** The commission payable to a broker on the price realised.

Where the owner of property employs a broker to find a purchaser and agrees to compensate him therefor, the compensation is known as "brokerage commission".

**Brothel.** An establishment in which prostitutes are available; a common habitation of prostitutes.

> NOTE: Brothel includes any house, room, conveyance or place or any portion of any house, room, conveyance or place, which is used for purposes of sexual exploitation or abuse for the gain of another person or for the mutual gain of two or more prostitutes. [Immoral Traffic (Prevention) Act 1956, s. 2(*a*)].

**Brother.** The term 'brother' in its primary sense means a brother of the whole blood and that in its secondary and extended sense it includes a brother of half-blood also. [*General Manager, Gwalior Sugar Co., Dabra* v *Srilal* AIR 1958 MP 133].


- **Half brother** p. 404.


**Brought into.** The term denotes only a physical act of shifting a thing from one place to another. The term does not *per se* connote any permanent retention. [*Haji Mohammad Usman* v *Commissioner of Income Tax* AIR 1954 Nag 221: ILR (1954) Nag 114].

> NOTE: Brought into city means brought into the municipal limits for purposes of consumption, use or sale. [*Jothi Timber Mart* v *Corporation of Calicut* (1969)2 SCWR 206: (1969)2 SCC 348].

**Bruise.** An injury appearing as an area of discoloured skin on a human or animal body, caused by a blow or impact which ruptures underlying blood vessels; hurt mentally.

**Brutum fulmen.** A judgment void upon its face which is in legal effect no judgment at all, and by which no rights are divested, and from which none can be obtained, and neither binds nor bars any one.

**Bucketing.** Receipt of orders to purchase and sell stocks without intention of actually executing such order.

**Buddhism.** A widespread Asian religion or philosophy, founded by Goutama Buddha in India in 5th C. BC which teaches that elimination of the self and earthly desires is the highest goal.

**Budget.** The amount of money needed or available; annual estimate of national revenue and expenditure; a statement of probable revenue and expenditure and of financial proposals for the ensuing year as presented to or passed upon by a legislative body; a summary of probable income for a given period, as of a family or an individual, with approximate allowances for certain expenditures over that period.

A statement of an organization's estimated revenues and expenses for a specified period, usu. a year; a sum of money allocated to a particular purpose or project. [Black's *Law Dictionary*, 7th Ed.].

**Budget account.** A bank account, or account with a store or public utility, into which one makes regular payments to cover bills.

**Buffer state.** A small state situated between two larger ones potentially hostile to one another and regarded as reducing the likelihood of open hostilities.

**Buffer stock.** A reserve of commodity to offset price fluctuations.

**Buffer zone.** A zone separating potential belligerents.

**Buggery.** Anal intercourse; a carnal copulation against nature.

**Building.** What is a 'building' must always be a question of degree and circumstances; its "ordinary and usual meaning is a block of brick or stone work, covered in by a roof". [*Moir* v *Williams* (1892)1 QB 264, *per* Asher, MR].

The ordinary and natural meaning of the word 'building' includes the fabric and the ground on which it stands. [*Victoria City* v *Bishop of Vancouver Island* (1921) AC 384, 390].

▸ *Meaning under the Cantonments Act 1924, s. 2(iv).* Building means a house, outhouse, stable, latrine, shed, hut or other roofed structure, whether of masonry, brick, wood, mud metal or other material, and any part thereof, and includes a well and a wall (other than a boundary wall) but does not include a tent or other portable and temporary shelter.

▸ *Meaning under the Bengal Municipal Act 1932, s. 3(2).* Building includes a house, outhouse, stable, privy, urinal, shed, hut wall (other than a boundary wall not exceeding ten feet in height) and any other structure, whether of masonary, bricks, wood, mud metal or any other material whatsoever, but does not include a *hogla* or other similar kind or temporary shed erected on ceremonial or festive occasions.

The existence of a roof is not always necessary for a structure to be regarded as a building. Residential buildings ordinarily have roof but an open air stadium or a swimming pool is a building without a roof. [*Ghanshiam Das* v *Debi Prasad* AIR 1966 SC 1998: (1966)2 SCJ 749].

Building means house, shop, hut (*jhopras*), etc. with roof thereon constructed for human habitation or otherwise. [*Century Spinning and Manufacturing* v *District Municipality* (1968)2 SCR 211: AIR 1968 SC 859].

Building does not include land. [*C.I.T., Bombay* v *Alps Theatre* AIR 1967 SC 1552: (1967)2 SCJ 597]. Building is a structure of a nature of a house built where it is to stand and includes "the fabric of which it is composed, the ground upon which its walls stand and the ground embraced within those walls". [*D.G. Gouse and Co. (agents) Pvt. Ltd.* v *State of Kerala* (1980)2 SCC 410: (1980)1 SCR 804: AIR 1980 SC 271].

**Building contract.** A contract for the building of anything—not necessarily a house, but any other physical construction. [*Carlisle Rural Council* v *Carlisle Corporation* (1909)1 KB 471].

**Bull.** Stock Exchange. This is a Stock Exchange term for a speculator who buys securities with a view to a quick resale at a higher price.

**Bull market.** A market with shares rising in price.

**Bulletin.** An official report concerning some public event issued for the information of the public.

**Bullion.** It includes all kinds of gold alloy of all grades of fineness, suitable for the making of gold jewellery. [*Vishwanathan* v *State of Madras* (1963)14 STC 702].

The expression in the popular sense means gold or silver in the mass. It connotes gold or silver regarded as raw material and it may be either in the form of raw gold or silver or ingots or bars of gold or silver. [*Dy. Commissioner of Sales Tax* v *G.S. Pai* AIR 1980 SC 611: (1980)1 SCC 142: (1980)1 SCR 938: (1980)45 STC 58].

NOTE: Manufactured or finished product of gold and silver is not bullion. [*State* v *K. Ipi Peter* 1982 Cr LJ 122: 1982 Mad LJ (Cr) 75].

Ornaments and other articles of gold cannot be regarded as "bullion" because they are not raw or unwrought gold or gold in the mass, but they represent manufactured or finished products of gold. [*Dy. Commissioner of Sales Tax* v *G.S. Pai* AIR 1980 SC 611: (1980)1 SCC 142: (1980)1 SCR 938: (1980)45 STC 58].

**Bum-bailiff.** A bailiff empowered to collect debts or arrest debtors for non-payment.

**Bumpy.** A young male homosexual, especially a prostitute.

**Bunga.** A hostel where pilgrims coming from various parts of India to pay a visit to the Golden Temple stay. [*Shiromani Gurdwara* v *Raja Shiv Rattan* ILR (1955) Punj 1108: AIR 1955 SC 576].

**Burden of proof.** The duty of proving a disputed assertion or charge.

The expression 'burden of proof' really means two different things. It means sometimes that a party is required to prove an allegation before judgment can be given in his favour; it also means that on a contested issue one of the two contending parties has to introduce evidence. The burden of proof is of importance only where by reason of not discharging the burden which was put upon it, a party must eventually fail. Where however the parties have joined issue and have led evidence and the conflicting evidence can be weighed to determine which way the issue can be decided the abstract question of burden of proof becomes academic. [*Narayan Bhagwantrao* v *Gopal Vinayak Gosavri* AIR 1960 SC 100: 1960 SCJ 263: (1960)1 SCR 733: (1960)2 SCA 153].

NOTE: When a person is bound to prove the existence of any fact, it is said that the burden of proof lies on that person. [Indian Evidence Act 1872, s. 101].

There is a difference between the burden of proof on the pleadings and the burden of adducing evidence. The former depends upon the facts asserted or denied and is determined by rules of substantive or statutory law or by presumption of law or fact. Such a burden never shifts. If the entire evidence has been adduced by both the parties and the tribunal feels it can make up its mind as to the truth of the version of either party, then the decision will not turn upon the burden. But where the evidence is conflicting or equally balanced so as to make it difficult to arrive at a definite conclusion, then the burden of proof on the pleadings turns the scale. The question of onus may also be decisive where one or both the parties has not adduced any evidence at all on the particular issue. [*Nigayya Gowdu* v *Chenganna Gowdu* AIR 1957 AP 264].

**Bureaucracy.** Officials of a government regarded as inflexible.

Government by departments, each under a Chief; a word to describe the system used in the invidious sense.

**Bureaucrat.** An inflexible or insensitive administrator.

**Burglar.** A person who commits burglary.

**Burglary.** Entry into a building illegally with intent to commit theft, do bodily harm, or do damage.

**Burial.** The burying of a dead body; a funeral.

**Burial ground.** A cemetery.

**Burka.** A long enveloping garment worn in public by Muslim women.

**Bursar.** A treasurer of a college or university.

**Bus-stand.** A place where bus services commence or terminate. [*Municipal Board, Pushkar* v *State Transport Authority* AIR 1965 SC 458: 1963 Supp (2) SCR 373].

The place where the buses stand for commencing their transport service or where they stand after terminating their service is popularly known as a bus-stand. [*Rajagopala Prabhu* v *Commr. Municipal Corporation* 1980 Ker LT 644 (DB)].

**Bush lawyer.** A person claiming legal knowledge without qualifications for it in Australia and New Zealand.

**Business.** The word 'business' connotes some real, substantial and systematic or organised course of activity or conduct with a set purpose. [*Narain Swadeshi Weaving Mills* v *The Commr. of Excess Profits Tax* (1955)1 SCR 952: AIR 1955 SC 176 (decision of five Judge Bench), followed in *Mazagaon Dock Ltd.* v *The Commr. of Income-tax and Excess Profits Tax* 1959 SCR 848: AIR 1958 SC 861: 1958 SCJ 1261: (1958)34 ITR 368].

The word 'business' is one of wide import and it means an activity carried on continuously and systematically by a person by the application of his labour or skill with a view to earning an income. [*Barendra Prasad Ray* v *ITO* (1981)2 SCC 693: AIR 1981 SC 1047].

To constitute activities as 'business', they are to be carried on continuously in an organised manner, with a set purpose (be it illegal) to augment own resources of persons carrying on the same. [*Central Bureau of Investigation* v *V.C. Shukla* AIR 1998 SC 1406: (1998)3 SCC 410: 1998 Cr LJ 1905: JT 1998(2) SC 172].

It is an activity carried on continuously and systematically by a person by the application of his labour or skill with a view to earning an income. It does not necessarily mean trade or manufacture only and includes within its scope professions, vocations, and callings for a fairly long time. [*Barendra Prosad Roy* v *I.T.O.* AIR 1981 SC 1047: (1981)2 SCC 693: 1981 SCC (Tax) 149: (1981)3 SCR 387: (1981)129 ITR 295: 1981 Tax LR 657].

▸ *Meaning under the Income Tax Act 1961, s. 2(13).* Business includes any trade, commerce or manufacture or any adventure or concern in the nature of trade, commerce or manufacture.

Business means an enterprise which is an occupation as distinguished from pleasure. [*Secretary, Madras Gymkhana* v *Management* AIR 1968 SC 554: (1968)1 SCA 379: (1968)2 SCJ 138].

The expression 'business' is a word of indefinite import. In taxing statutes it is used in the sense of an occupation or profession which occupies the time, attention and labour of a person normally with the object of making profit. [*State of Andhra Pradesh* v *Abdul Bhaki* AIR 1965 SC 531: 1965 SCD 334: (1965)1 SCJ 297; *Hindustan Steel* v *State of Orissa* AIR 1970 SC 253; *P.W.D.* v *Commr. of Workmen Compensation* 1981 Lab IC 493].

The term 'business' is of wide import and each case has to be determined with reference to the particular kind of activity or occupation of the person concerned. Though ordinarily it implies a continuous activity in carrying on a particular trade or avocation, it might also include an activity which might be called "quiescent". [*Commissioner of Income Tax, West Bengal* v *Calcutta National Bank Ltd. (in liquidation)* AIR 1959 SC 928: 1959 Supp (2) SCR 660: (1959)37 ITR 171: 1960 SCJ 980].

A single transaction does not constitute business. The concept of business postulates continuity of transactions. [*Manipur Administration* v *Nila Chandra Singh* AIR 1964 SC 1533; *Ramji Prasad* v *State* AIR 1967 Ori 29].

Business includes even forward contracts. [*Chimanlal Premchand* v *State of Bombay* AIR 1960 SC 96: 1960 SCJ 82: 1960 Cr LJ 168: (1960)1 SCR 164].


- **Capital employed in business** p. 122.
- **Carry on business** p. 125.
- **Discontinuance of business** p. 264.

- **For the purpose of business** p. 362.
- **In the ordinary course of business** p. 443.
- **Marine insurance business** p. 562.
- **Place of business** p. 665.
- **Same business** p. 773.


**But.** Except for the fact; if not; unless; on the contrary. The word indicates an exception or condition.

**Butcher.** One who kills animals or sells the flesh of such animals for human consumption by way of trade.

**Butty gang.** A gang of men contracted to work on a large job and sharing the profits equally.

**Buy-back.** Repurchase of goods, shares etc. often by agreement.

**Buyer.** A person who buys or agrees to buy goods [Sale of Goods Act 1930, s. 2(1)].

Buyer includes a person who has agreed to buy and who has actually bought. [*Surendra Maneklal* v *Bai Narmada* AIR 1963 Guj 239]. Buyer means a person who has actually made the purchase. [*Abdulla Ahmed* v *Animendra Kissen* 1950 SCR 30].

**Buyer's market.** An economic position in which goods are plentiful and cheap and buyers have the advantage.

**By.** The expression 'by' indicates the utmost limit of time, being the end or the expiry of the date or period indicated. The word used with reference to time indicates either 'in course of' or 'on'.

The term 'by' should be construed as 'on or before'. [*Muthu Chettiar* v *Narayanan Chettiar* 51 Mad 672: AIR 1928 Mad 528].

**By an Act.** By a provision directly enacted in the statute in question and which is gatherable from its express language or by necessary implication therefrom.

A power conferred by a bylaw is not one conferred by the Act. [*Indramoni Pyarelal* v *W.R. Natu* (1963)1 SCR 721: AIR 1963 SC 274: (1963)2 SCJ 59].

**Bylaw.** A rule or administrative provision adopted by an organisation for its internal governance and its external dealings. [Black's *Law Dictionary*, 8th Ed.].

A bylaw has been said to be an ordinance affecting the public or some portion of the public, imposed by some authority clothed with statutory powers, ordering something to be done or not to be done, and accompanied by some sanction or penalty for its non-observance. Further, it involves this consequence—that if validly made, it has the force of law within the sphere of its legitimate operation. [Halsbury's *Laws of England*, 4th Ed., vol. 28, para 1323, p. 728].

> NOTE: Bylaws must be *intra vires* the authority who makes it, not repugnant to the law to the contrary, certain in its terms, positive and reasonable. [*Municipal Committee* v *Kaluram Hiralal* AIR 1944 Nag 73; *Commissioners of Calcutta Port* v *Asit Ranjan* AIR 1962 Cal 530].
>
> Bylaws govern the corporate bodies. As between Acts, Rules and bylaws, bylaws are controlled by the Rules and Acts and Rules by the Acts.

**Byproduct.** An incidental or a secondary product made in the manufacture of something else; a secondary result.

**Bystander.** A mere spectator; a person who stands by but does not take part.

Bystanders are persons who are present at the time of occurrence and not the persons who gather on the spot after the occurrence. [*Mahendrapal* v *State* AIR 1955 All 328: 1955 Cr LJ 892].

# Cc

**Cabaret.** A 'cabaret' is a cafe or restaurant where patrons are entertained by performers who dance and sing after the practice of certain French taverns. [*Mohammed* v *State of Kerala* 1984 Ker LT 276].

**Cabinet.** The committee of senior ministers responsible for controlling Government policy; in USA, a body of advisers to the President composed of the heads of the executive departments of the Government.

It is the name for the inner Council of Ministers collectively responsible for the policy of the Government; a group of advisers responsible to the head of the state, who themselves usually head executive departments of Government.

> NOTE: Cabinet is responsible for executive Government policy, and is answerable to Parliament.

**Cable.** The thick rope to which a ship's anchor is fastened; a rope-like line used for submarine telegraphs; a bundle of insulated wires passing through a pipe laid underground; a thick rope of wire or hemp; an encased group of insulated wires for transmitting electricity or electrical signals.

**Cadastral survey.** A survey undertaken in connection with a record-of-rights.

**Cadastre.** A register of survey of lands.

**Cadre.** In service jurisprudence, the expression 'cadre' means the unit of strength of a service or a part of it as determined by the employer [*State of Maharashtra* v *Purushottam* AIR 1996 SC 2228: (1996)9 SCC 266: JT 1996(6) SC 672: (1996)2 SCJ 534: 1996(2) SLR 558]; a basic unit of servicemen, forming a nucleus for expansion when necessary.

It may also mean trained personal essential in the conduct and management of an organisation, enterprise, etc.; a nucleus; skeleton; framework.

Cadre does not mean post but it means the strength of the establishment. [*Nahiria Ram* v *Union of India* AIR 1958 SC 113].

The word 'cadre' is defined to mean the strength of an establishment or service sanctioned as a separate unit. The word does not mean a post. [*Director General of Health Services* v *Bikash Chatterjee* AIR 1969 Cal 525: 73 CWN 249].

> NOTE: Service is a narrower body than the cadre. Cadre post may be permanent or temporary. [*O.P. Singla* v *Union of India* (1984)4 SCC 450].

- **Cadre posts.** All posts in the service, whether permanent or temporary, are generally regarded as cadre posts. [*O.P. Singla* v *Union of India* AIR 1984 SC 1595: (1984)4 SCC 450: 1984(3) SLR 34: (1985)1 SCR 351].
- **Ex cadre post.** An "ex cadre post" means a post outside the cadre of posts comprised in a service. [*O.P. Singla* v *Union of India* AIR 1984 SC 1595: (1984)4 SCC 450: 1984(3) SLR 34: (1985)1 SCR 351].

**Calculated.** Calculated primarily means to compute mathematically, but when applied to a human action it is used in the sense of, to intend, to design to plan or to adopt to achieve a purpose. [*Rattan Singh* v *Moga Transport Co.* AIR 1959 Punj 196: 61 Punj LR 14].

The word 'calculated' means designed, it denotes more than mere likelihood.

[*Sheopal Singh* v *Ram Pratap* AIR 1965 SC 677: (1965)1 SCR 175].

**Calculating machine.** A machine which can complete the basic arithmetical functions of multiplication and division, plus usually, addition and subtraction. The process may be mechanical or electronic.

**Calendar.** A systematic arrangement of subdivisions of time, as years, months, days, weeks, etc.; a system by which the beginning, length, and subdivisions of the year are fixed; a chart or series of pages showing the days, weeks, and months of a particular year, or giving special seasonal information; a timetable or programme of appointments, special events, etc.; a schedule or list of things or events classified or chronologically arranged.

**Calendar month.** Each of usually twelve periods into which a year is subdivided.

Calendar month is a period of time consisting of thirty days in April, June, September and November, or thirty-one days in the remainder of the months, except February, which consists of 28 days, except in leap year, when the intercalary day is added, making twenty-nine days.

- **Bengali calendar month.** The expression 'Bengali calendar month' means the Bengali month as defined in the Bengali calendar which means the whole of a Bengali month beginning from the first day and ending with the last day of the Bengali month. [*Jagat Mohan* v *Basiran Bibi* 61 CWN 127].

**Calendar year.** The period of 365 days (common year) or 366 days (Leap year) from 1st January to 31st December, used for reckoning time in ordinary affairs; a period from the midnight of the 31st December to the midnight of the succeeding 31st December.

▸ *Meaning under the Copyright Act 1957, s. 2(e).* The year commencing on the 1st day of January.

▸ *Meaning under the Factories Act 1948, s. 2(bb).* Calendar year means the period of twelve months beginning with the first day of January in any year.

NOTE: Calendar year should be calculated from the first day of January. The expression should not be construed to mean a period of 365 days calculated from any day within the calendar. [*Kanhayyalal* v *Deputy Commissioner* AIR 1958 MP 211].

**Calendering.** Calendering is a final process in which heat and pressure are applied to a fabric by passing it between heated rollers, imparting a flat, glossy, smooth surface. Calendering is applied to fabrics in which a smooth, flat surface is desirable, such as most cottons, many linen and silks, and various man-made fabrics. Calendering is not usually a permanent process. [*Mafatlal Fine Spinning & Mfg. Co. Ltd.* v *Collector of Central Excise* AIR 1989 SC 784: (1989)2 SCC 446: (1989)40 ELT 28 (SC): JT 1989(1) SC 160].

**Call.** Urge; invite; nominate.

An invitation or summons to appear or be present; an option of buying stock at a fixed price at a given date.

To summon in any way; to insist upon payment of, as by written notice; to communicate by telephone; to ask for a showdown on anything.

A visible natural object or an established point mentioned in the descriptive part of a deed for tracing a line of vision or boundary; payable on demand, or without previous notice, as a loan or deposit.

A request or command to come or assemble; a demand for payment of money.

A "call" on a company's shares is used in two senses: (1) the application to the shareholders to pay; (2) the amount to be paid. [*Newry, etc., Railway* v *Edmunds* 2 Ex 121, *per* Parke, B.]. Instalments by which a share is payable, are not "calls". [*Hubbersty* v *Manchester, Sheffield & Lincolnnshire Railway* 8 B&S 421, *per* Kelly, C.B.].

A call is a demand for payment of the amount or part of the amount which has not been paid or satisfied on a share, made by the company through its governing body upon its members prior to winding up, or by its liquidator when it is in course of winding up. [Halsbury's *Laws of England*, 3rd Ed., vol. 6, p. 225].

The word 'call', in relation to shares, is capable of three meanings. It may either mean the resolution, or its notification, or the time when it becomes payable. [*Ambergate, Nottingham & Boston & Eastern Function Ry. Co.* v *Mitchell* (1849)4 Exch. 540, *per* Parke, B.].

• **In advance of calls** p. 438.

**Call at a port.** To 'call at a port' is a well-known sea-term; it means to call for the purposes of business, generally to take in or unload cargo, or to receive orders; it must mean that the vessel may stop at the port of call for a time, or else the liberty to call would be idle. [*Leduc* v *Ward* (1888)20 QBD 475 (CA), *per* Lord Esher, M.R.].

**Call option.** It is a Stock Exchange term for the right to buy a certain security during a specified period at the price ruling at the time the bargain is struck.

**Call to the bar.** The conferring of the degree of Barrister-at-Law on members of an Inn of Court.

**Calling.** A profession, or occupation or vocation; habitual occupation, vocation or business.

The word 'calling' is of wide connotation. According to its dictionary meaning it means one's usual occupation, vocation, business or trade. [*National Union of Commercial Employees* v *M.R. Meher* ILR (1959) Bom 1130: AIR 1960 Bom 22: 61 Bom LR 642].

The word 'calling' is a wider word than 'trade', and in its natural meaning would certainly include many occupations that would not be included in the word 'trade'. [*Turner* v *Baigent* (1952) NZLR 271, *per* Stanton, J. also reported (1952) GLR 151].

'Calling' is a more general term than 'trade' or 'profession', but when used together with these words, its meaning must be restricted to a sense analogous to 'trade' or 'profession'. [*Hayes* v *Patrick and Womitowy* (1961)36 WWR, Sask (CA) 562, *per* Culliton, J. (Canada)].

The word 'calling' denotes the following of a profession or trade. [*Secretary, Madras Gymkhana Club Employees Union* v *Management of the Gymkhana Club* AIR 1968 SC 554: (1968)1 SCR 742].

NOTE: The expression 'calling' is sufficiently wide to include in it activities not necessarily concerned with the profit motive. [*Province of Bombay* v *Western India Automobile Association* ILR (1949) Bom 591: AIR 1949 Bom 141].

Carrying on a school is a 'calling'. [*Doe d. Bish* v *Keeling* 1 M&S 95; *Kemp* v *Sober* 20 LJ Ch 602].

The profession of teaching is a 'calling'. [*Galwey* v *Barden* (1899)1 Ir R 514, *per* Porter, M.R.].

**Can.** The word 'can' is used to express ability to perform, either mentally or physically.

The word 'can' is defined as "to be able"; to have the power or capacity [*S.R. Bommai* v *Union of India* AIR 1994 SC 1918: (1994)3 SCC 1: JT 1994(2) SC 215]; be potentially capable of.

In informal speech and writing, can is now acceptable in the sense of may, to express permission, especially in questions or negative statements, *e.g.*, can I leave now?

'Can' has other meanings too. It may mean a vessel for holding or carrying liquids; a tin container in which food or drink is hermetically sealed to enable storage over long periods; record on film or tape for future use.

**Cancellation.** Abandoning; abolishing; annulment; cessation; expunction; invalidation; nullification; rescission; revocation; termination.

Any manner of obliteration or defacing. [*Ward* v *Lumley* 29 LJ Ex 322].

In a marine insurance, or charterparty, 'cancel' sometimes means to become void; thus a memorandum on a charterparty provided that the charter should be 'cancelled' on either of certain events happening, and that was held to mean that if either event happened the charter should become void. [*Adamson* v *New Castle Steamship Insurance* 4 QBD 462].

**Cancellation of document.** To "cancel" a document, is to put an end to it by drawing lines over it, or over its signatures, "in the form of lattice work, or *cancelli*; though the phrase is now used, figuratively, for any manner of obliteration or defacing it. [*Ward* v *Lumley* 29 LJ Ex 322].

> NOTE: Cancellation has a well-known meaning, namely, that a person who has executed a document or will otherwise be bound by it, seeks to be relieved of it on the ground of misrepresentation, fraud, undue influence and so on. [*Narayana Moothy* v *Purna Chandra* AIR 1936 Mad 266].

**Candidate.** A nominee or aspirant for any position, office, award or honour.

One who seeks or offers himself, or is put forward by others, for an office, privilege, or honour. [*State ex rel. Ranney* v *Corey* Ohio App, 47 NE 2d 799, 800].

The correct sense of the word 'candidate' is a person offering himself to the suffrages of the people. [*Morris* v *Burdelt* 2 M&S 217, *per* Lord Ellenborough].

▸*Meaning under the (English) Representation of the People Act 1949, s. 103.* 'Candidate' (*a*) in relation to a parliamentary election, means a person who is elected to serve in Parliament at the election or a person who is nominated as a candidate at the election, or is declared by himself or by others to be a candidate on or after the day of the issue of the writ for the election, or after the dissolution or vacancy in consequence of which the writ was issued; (*b*) in relation to an election under the local government Act, means a person elected or having been nominated or having declared himself a candidate for election, to the office to be filled at the election.

'Candidate' means a person who has been or claims to have been duly nominated as a candidate at any election, and any such person shall be deemed to have been a candidate as from the time when, with the election in prospect, he began to hold himself out as a prospective candidate. [Representation of the People Act 1951, s. 79(*b*); *Jyoti Basu* v *Debi Ghosal* AIR 1982 SC 983: (1982)1 SCC 691: (1982)2 SCR 318].

'Candidate' means 'standing for election, being candidate'. [*Sudhir Laxman Hendre* v *Shripat Amrit Dange* AIR 1960 Bom 249: 1959 Bom LR 500; *Sarla Devi* v *Birendra Singh* AIR 1961 MP 127].

'A candidate at the election' is a candidate who is actually at the poll and the other is not. [*Ramnarayan Maluram* v *Vishnu Krishna Rao* 1957 Jab LJ 108: AIR 1957 MP 20; *Vishwa Mitra* v *District Judge* AIR 1956 All 89].

> NOTE: A person becomes a candidate as soon as he clearly and unambiguously declares his intention to stand as a candidate. [*Khader* v *Munnuswami* AIR 1955 SC 775: (1955)2 SCR 469: 1955 SCJ 803].
>
> The expressions 'a candidate at the election' and 'a candidate for the election' denote a candidate at any stage of election starting with the filing of nomination papers and ending with the declaration of the result. [*Ramnarayan Maluram* v *Vishnu Krishna Rao* AIR 1957 MP 20: 1957 Jab LJ 108].


- **Defeated candidate** p. 240.
- **Local candidate** p. 540.


**Candidature.** Standing for election, being candidate.

The term 'candidature' must have reference to a person's qualification for being nominated in fact. [*Sudhir Laxman* v *Shripat Amrit* AIR 1960 Bom 249: 61 Bom LR 500].

Candidature is the bundle of rights and qualifications which entitles a person to stand as a candidate in a particular constituency as well as the factum of his being a candidate. [*Raghunath* v *Kishore* AIR 1958 Ori 260]. Candidature means the state of being a candidate. [*Sarala* v *Birendra* AIR 1961 MP 127].

**Cannot.** The word "cannot" emphatically connotes a situation of impasse. The word "cannot" would mean "not to be able" or "not to have the power or capacity". In Stroud's *Judicial Dictionary*, 5th Ed., the word "cannot" is defined to include a legal inability as well as physical impossibility. [*S.R. Bommai* v *Union of India* AIR 1994 SC 1918: (1994)3 SCC 1: JT 1994(2) SC

215]. The term is often equivalent to "shall not".

**Canon law.** Ecclesiastical law; a body of Roman ecclesiastical law based on the opinions of the ancient Latin fathers, the decrees of general councils, and the decretal epistles and bulls of the Holy.

**Canvasser.** A canvasser is a person who solicits and persuades individual voters, though not necessarily one by one separately, to vote for a candidate. [Halsbury's *Laws of England*, 4th Ed., vol. 15, para 700, p. 376].

A canvasser means any person who solicits or persuades or attempts to persuade any person to vote or to abstain from voting at an election or to vote or to abstain from voting for any candidate at an election.

Onc who goes from house to house in an effort to take orders for goods.

**Canvassing.** It is the system of persuading the electors through the medium of speech, vocal or written. It is the method of inducing the elector to act in a particular manner. By means of canvassing the candidate and his supporters attempt to change the mind of the voter and persuade him to vote for a particular candidate. [*Hari Ram* v *Election Tribunal* AIR 1970 All 146: 1969 All LJ 550].

**Capacity.** The role in which one performs an act; the power to create or enter into a legal relation under the same circumstances in which a normal person would have the power to create or enter into such a relation; the mental ability to understand the nature and effect of one's acts. [Black's *Law Dictionary*, 8th Ed.].

Capacity, is a legally conferred power to affect the rights of oneself and other persons to whom the exercise of the capacity is directed, subject to certain generally and legally defined limits—limits which vary in relation to each particular form of capacity. Capacity in this form is an incident of status. [*Sri Mahalinga Thambiran Swamigal* v *His Holiness Sri La Sri Kasivasi Arulnandi Thambiran Swamigal* AIR 1974 SC 119: (1974)2 SCR 74: (1974)1 SCC 150].

**Capital.** The most important town or city in a country or region, usually its seat of government and administrative centre.

With reference to criminal law, it means punishable by death or of pertaining to the death penalty.

In economics, it means wealth employed in or available for producing more wealth.

In a business or mercantile sense, it means money or assets invested, or available for investment, in a business, especially those that help generate profits.

"Capital is not in truth a technical term. For the purpose of economics capital has been defined as produced wealth as distinguished from land and other natural resources used productively for gain. But in a business or mercantile sense ... it is simply the means with which business is carried on, and it may consist of money or property convertible into money". [*Incorporated Interests Pty., Ltd.* v *Federal Comr. of Taxation* (1943)67 CLR 508, *per* Starke, J. (Canada)].

In commerce and as applied to individuals, it is understood to mean the sum of money which a merchant, banker or trader invests in any undertaking or which he contributes to the common stock of a partnership, or joint activity. Capital is the source of income and income is the fruit of capital. [*Commissioner of Income Tax* v *Shamlal* AIR 1963 Punj 411].

The 'capital' of a joint-stock company, "means the money subscribed pursuant to the memorandum of association, or what is represented by that money". [*per* Lindley, L.J., *Verner* v *General & Commercial Trust* (1894)2 Ch 239; cited by Byrne, J., *Foster* v *New Trinidad Lake Asphalt Co.* (1901)1 Ch 212, and by Romer, J., *Cross* v *Imperial Continental Gas Association* (1923)2 Ch 553].

The word 'capital', both in Acts relating to companies and in common parlance, is often used in different senses, meaning sometimes money already obtained, and sometimes the amount the company is authorised to obtain. [*A.-G.* v *Anglo-Argentine Tramways Co.* (1909)1 KB 677, *per* Channell, J.].

NOTE: "It is impossible to say that 'capital' has a single technical meaning which *prima facie* should be attributed to the word in any statutory provision. The Companies Act distinguishes between nominal, issued, and paid-up capital, and the significance of the word in a particular case depends upon the context in which it is used". [*Incorporated Interests Pty., Ltd.* v *Federal Comr. of Taxation* (1943)67 CLR 508, *per* Latham, CJ. (Australia)].


- **Authorised capital** p. 87.
- **Circulating capital** p. 142.
- **Equity share capital** p. 314.
- **Fixed capital** p. 357.
- **Floating capital** p. 359.
- **Nominal share capital** p. 609.
- **Preference share capital** p. 678.
- **Working capital** p. 903.


**Capital asset.** A long-term asset used in the operation of a business or used to produce goods or services, such as equipment, land, or an industrial plant. [Black's *Law Dictionary*, 8th Ed.]. It is also termed fixed asset.

NOTE: Excluded from the definition are, among other things, stock in trade, inventory, and property held by the taxpayer primarily for sale to customers in the ordinary course of trade or business. [Black's *Law Dictionary*, 7th Ed.].

▸ *Meaning under the Income Tax Act 1961, s. 2(14).* Capital asset means property of any kind held by an assessee, whether or not connected with his business or profession, but does not include—(*i*) any stock-in-trade, consumable stores or raw materials held for the purposes of his business or profession; (*ii*) personal effects, that is to say, movable property (including wearing apparel, jewellery and furniture) held for personal use by the assessee or any member of his family dependent on him; (*iii*) agricultural land in India; (*iv*) $6^1/_2$% Gold Bonds 1977, or 7% Gold Bonds 1980, or National Defence Gold Bonds 1980, issued by the Central Government; (*v*) Special Bearer Bonds 1991, issued by the Central Government; (*vi*) Gold Deposit Bonds issued under the Gold Deposit Scheme 1999 notified by the Central Government.

NOTE: The term 'capital asset' has an all embracing connotation and includes every kind of property as generally understood except those that are expressly excluded from the definition. [*Syndicate Bank Ltd.* v *Additional Commissioner of Income Tax* (1985)155 ITR 681 (Kant); *Krishna Iyer* v *Additional Income Tax Officer* (1966)59 ITR 145; *Commissioner of Income Tax, Bangalore* v *B.C. Srinivasa Setty* AIR 1981 SC 972: (1981)2 SCC 460: (1981)2 SCR 938: (1981)128 ITR 294].

**Capital charge.** A charge created for a capital sum, *i.e.* a charge to secure the discharge of a liability of a capital nature. [*The New Press Goods Bazaar Co. Ltd., Bombay* v *Commissioner of Income Tax, Bombay* AIR 1950 SC 165].

**Capital employed in business.** Funds used to acquire assets for being used in the business. [*Jayaram Mills* v *Commissioner* AIR 1959 Mad 376]. It shall be taken to be the price or value of the assets or the amount of the debts. [*Jayaram Mills* v *Commissioner*, supra].

**Capital expenditure.** Expenditure for permanent additions or improvements to property, as opposed to money spent for repairs; expenditure for long term betterments or additions [Black's *Law Dictionary*, 5th Ed.]; an outlay of funds to acquire or improve a fixed asset. [Black's *Law Dictionary*, 8th Ed.].

"'Capital expenditure' is not expenditure of money taken from capital, but the laying out of money which, upon its being laid out, becomes in itself capital. That is irrespective of the source from which the money comes". [*R.* v *Wraith, Ex p. Kent County Council* (1907)2 KB 756 (DC), *per* Darling, J.].

Where the expenditure is made for the initial outlay or for extension of a business or a substantial replacement of the equipment, it is capital expenditure. [*Assam Bengal Cement Co. Ltd.* v *Commr. of Income Tax, West Bengal* AIR 1955 SC 89].

If the expenditure is made for acquiring or bringing into existence an asset or advantage for the enduring benefit of the business, it is properly attributable to capital and is of the nature of capital expenditure. [*Assam Bengal Cement Co. Ltd.* v *Commr. of Income Tax, West Bengal* AIR 1955 SC 89].

NOTE: It is also termed as capital improvement; capital outlay.

**Capital gains.** A profit from the sale of investments or property; profit from the sale of capital investments, such as stocks, real estate etc.; any profit or gain arising from the transfer of a capital asset; the profit realized when a capital asset is sold or exchanged [Black's *Law Dictionary*, 7th Ed.]; gains actually realised as a result of sale, exchange or transfer. [*Duggan* v *CIT, Bombay City* (1952)21 ITR 458: AIR 1952 Bom 261].

**Capital goods.** Goods (such as equipment and machinery) used for the production of other goods or services. [Black's *Law Dictionary*, 8th Ed.].

'Capital goods' means: (*a*) machines, machinery, plant, equipment, apparatus, tools or appliances used for producing or processing of any goods or for bringing about any change in any substance for the manufacture of final products; (*b*) components, spare parts and accessories of the aforesaid machines, machinery, plant, equipment, apparatus, tools or appliances used for aforesaid purpose; and (*c*) moulds and dies, generating sets and weigh bridges used in the factory of the manufacturer. [*Commissioner of Central Excise, Coimbatore* v *Jawahar Mills Ltd.* AIR 2001 SC 2500: JT 2001(6) SC 65: (2001)132 ELT 3: (2001)6 SCC 274; Central Excise Rules 1944, r. 57-Q, Expl. (1)(*a*)].

**Capital punishment.** The death penalty for a crime; punishment by death for capital crimes.

The penalty of death inflicted in pursuance of judicial sentence being brought to answer. [Hale: *Pleas of the Crown*, Vol. 1, p. 497].

**Capital reserve.** Any reserve which is not free for distribution through the profit and loss account.

**Capitalisation.** The act or process of capitalising or converting something into capital; the amount or sum resulting from this act or process; the total amount of long-term financing used by a business, including stocks, bonds, retained earnings, and other funds; the total par value or stated value of the authorised or outstanding stock of a corporation. [Black's *Law Dictionary*, 8th Ed.].

Conversion of profits or income into capital is capitalisation.

NOTE: The profits of a company can be capitalised in accordance with the articles of association and the law. On the capitalisation of profits they cease to be profits in the hands of the company. The nature of the assets changes although it does not make any difference in the total assets of the company. But profits stand transmuted and transformed into capital. The most common example of capitalisation of profits is by issuance of bonus shares to the shareholders. [*P.K. Badiani* v *CIT, Bombay* (1976)4 SCC 562].

**Capitalised value.** The capital value of an asset based on its current earning power in relation to the expected rate of return from that type of asset.

**Capitulation.** An agreement or set of conditions; a statement of the main divisions of a subject; surrender.

In International Law, this means the drawing up of conditions for the surrender of a fortress, an army or territory to an enemy.

**Capture.** Act of catching or controlling by force, threats or strategy; the seizure of enemy property in war; take prisoner; seize as a prize; obtain by force or trickery; portray in permanent form.

**Carat.** A unit of weight for precious stones, now equivalent to 200 milligrams; a measure of purity of gold, pure gold being 24 carats.

This is a term used in assessing the value of gold and precious stones. In respect of gold, it represents the proportion of gold contained in any gold alloy and for this purpose the metal is divided into 24 parts. Thus, "24 carats" indicates pure gold and any lesser number of carats shows the proportion of gold contained in the alloy, e.g., 9 carats. In weighing precious stones, a carat represents 3.17 tory grains. Carat is used from the time of Elizabeth I onwards as denoting a proportion of fine gold in the manufactured article. [*Westwood* v *Cann* (1952)2 QB 887].

**Carbon paper.** Paper made by coating with a mixture consisting principally of a wax and a pigment. The colour is obtained from the pigment, usually a carbon black of law oil absorption, plus toners, usually like pigments, or oil soluble dyes which are added to increase the blackness. [*Collector of Central Excise, Kanpur* v *Krishna Carbon Paper Co.* AIR 1988 SC 2223: (1989)1 SCC 150: JT 1988(4) SC 762: (1988)37 ELT 480: (1989)72 STC 280: 1988 Supp (3) SCR 12].

NOTE: It is manufactured by coating the tissue paper with a thermosetting ink (made to a liquid consistency) based mainly on wax, non-drying oils, pigments and dyes by means of a suitable coating roller and equalising rod and then passing it through chilled rolls. It is used between two sheets of plain paper in order to reproduce on the lower sheet that which is written or typed on the upper sheet, i.e., making replicas or carbon copies. It cannot be properly described as paper. [*State of Uttar Pradesh* v *M/s. Kores (India) Ltd.* (1976)4 SCC 477: AIR 1977 SC 132: (1977)1 SCR 837: (1977)39 STC 8].

**Care.** Watchful attention; custody; discretion; support; vigilance.

NOTE: There are three degrees of care which are frequently recognised corresponding to the three degrees of negligence, viz. slight care, ordinary care, and great care. This division into three degrees of care does not, however, command universal assent.

- **Reasonable care** p. 729.

**Careless driving.** Driving a motor vehicle on a road without due care in disregard of the safety of other persons using the road.

**Cargo.** The goods or merchandise conveyed in a ship, aeroplane or vehicle; freight.

▶*Meaning under the Dock Workers (Regulation of Employment) Act 1948, s. 2(a).* 'Cargo' includes anything carried or to be carried in a ship or other vessel.

NOTE: A very small quantity of goods in proportion to the carrying capacity of the ship could not be called a cargo. It must, to some extent, approach the carrying capacity. [*Miller* v *Borner* (1900)1 QB 691].

Cargo does not include a passenger's own personal luggage, carried on board by him. [Klein: *Dictionary of Banking*].

**Cargo insurance.** See under INSURANCE p. 468.

**Carnal knowledge.** Sexual intercourse; penetration to the slightest degree by the male organ of generation; coitus; copulation.

'Carnal knowledge' means the penetration such as would be sufficient to constitute sexual intercourse. [*R.* v *Marsden* (1893)2 QB 149].

Carnal knowledge of a child is unlawful sexual intercourse with a female child under the age of consent.

**Carriage.** A wheeled vehicle especially a horse-drawn vehicle designed for private use and comfort; a railway passenger coach; a wheeled vehicle for transport of goods or animals; the act of carrying.

Transport of freight or passengers. [Black's *Law Dictionary*, 8th Ed.].

The term 'carriage' is wide enough to include a motor car. [*Hira Chand* v *Emperor* AIR 1931 Lah 572: 32 Cr LJ 946].


- **Hackney-carriage** p. 404.
- **Stage carriage** p. 807.


**Carriage way.** The part of a road intended for vehicles; a way over which the public have a right of way for the passage of vehicles; it is comprised in a highway.

**Carrier.** An individual or organization engaged in transporting passengers or goods for hire; a bearer, messenger.

Carrier in its general sense means a person who undertakes to transport the goods of other persons from one place to another for hire. It is not, however, every person who undertakes to carry goods for hire that is deemed a common carrier.

▸ *Meaning under the Inland Air Travel Tax Act 1971, s. 2(b).* Carrier means a corporation, company or other person undertaking the carriage of a passenger on an inland journey.

> NOTE: If anyone does the business of carrying goods as a public employment, he would be a carrier and the fact that the Government is doing the business would not make any difference. [*Rahim Sahib* v *Governor-General of India* (1955)1 MLJ 406].

• **Common carrier** p. 158.
• **Public carrier** p. 707.

**Carry on business.** A person carries on a trade or business when he "habitually does and contracts to do a thing capable of producing profit", but it has been said that it is not necessary in order to constitute the carrying on of a trade that the persons engaged in it should make or desire to make a profit by it. [Halsbury's *Laws of England,* 4th Ed., vol. 27, para 540, p. 437].

The phrase 'carries on business' is in itself one of varying import according as it is construed with an implied addition, so as to make it mean the whole business, the principal part of the business, any part of the business or that part of the business which may properly be supposed to have been contemplated. [*P.K. Kesavan Nair* v *C.K. Babu Naidu* AIR 1954 Mad 892].

> NOTE: Whether a person carries on business in a particular commodity must depend upon the volume, frequency, continuity and regularity of transactions of purchase and sale in a class of goods and the transactions must ordinarily be entered into with a profit motive. [*State of Gujarat* v *Raipur Manufacturing Co.* AIR 1967 SC 1066: (1967)1 SCR 618: (1967)19 STC 1].

**Carry on trade.** The expression 'trade' means exchanging of goods for goods or goods for money. It connotes repeated activity in the nature of business carried on with profit motive, the activity being manual or mercantile as distinguished from the liberal arts or learned professions or agriculture. The question whether a trade is carried on by a person depends on a consideration of the nature of the trade, the various steps taken for carrying on the trade and other relevant facts. [*State of Punjab* v *Bajaj Electricals* AIR 1968 SC 739: (1968)2 SCR 536: (1968)2 SCJ 258].

**Carryover.** The process of postponing the completion of a contract for the purchase or sale of stocks or shares to a later date than that originally fixed. The buyer usually pays the seller interest on the capital involved and this interest is known as contango.

An income-tax deduction (especially for a net operating loss) that cannot be taken entirely in a given period but may be taken in a later period (usually the next five years) [Black's *Law Dictionary*, 8th Ed.]. It is also termed carryforward.

**Cart stand.** In the case of a public cart stand, it is the availability of the place for use by the members of the public for keeping their vehicles for a time to let their vehicles stand there, that makes the place a cart stand. Both in the case of a public cart stand and a private cart stand what makes it a cart stand is the willingness of the owner of the place to let the vehicles of other besides himself to use the place, to let vehicles of others to stand there, whether on payment of fees or for other consideration. [*Anamallais Bus Transport* v *Commissioner* ILR (1957) Mad 1032: AIR 1957 Mad 781].

**Carte blanche.** Full discretionary power given to a person. A white sheet of paper given by one man to another containing only the signature of the former, so that the latter may inscribe what conditions he pleases. It implies unlimited authority given by one person to another.

**Cartel.** A collusive international association of independent enterprises formed to monopolize production and distribution of a product or service, control prices etc. [Collins: *English Dictionary*].

An international combination of independent enterprises in the same branch of production, aiming at a monopolistic control of the market by means of weakening or eliminating competition. [Webster's *Comprehensive Dictionary*, International Ed.].

A combination of firms for certain purposes especially to keep up prices and kill competition. [Chambers's *English Dictionary*].

A combination of producers or sellers that join together to control a product's production or price. Also, an association of firms with common interests, seeking to prevent extreme or unfair competition, allocate markets, or share knowledge. [Black's *Law Dictionary*, 8th Ed.].

An association by agreement of companies or sections of companies having common interests, designed to prevent extreme or unfair competition and to allocate markets, and perhaps also to exchange scientific or technical knowledge or patent rights and to standardize products, with competition regulated but not eliminated by substituting competition in quality, efficiency, and service for price-cutting. [*American Jurisprudence* 2d, vol. 54, p. 677].

Cartel has three quite different meanings: (1) an agreement between hostile nations; (2) an anticompetitive combination usually that fixes commercial prices; and (3) a combination of political groups that work toward common goals. [*A Dictionary of Modern Legal Usage*, Bryan A. Garner].

The cartel is an association of producers who by agreement among themselves attempt to control production, sale and prices of the product to obtain a monopoly in any particular industry or commodity. [*Union of India* v *Hindustan Development Corporation* AIR 1994 SC 988: 1994 AIR SCW 943: JT 1993(3) SC 15: (1993)3 SCJ 348: (1993)3 SCC 499].

In international law, 'cartel' means an 'agreement between belligerents about the means of conducting whatever relation they allow during wartime; esp., such an agreement regarding the exchange of prisoners'. [Black's *Law Dictionary*, 8th Ed.].

**Case.** A cause or suit for trial; a statement of the facts in a cause subjudice, drawn up for higher court's consideration; a cause that has been decided and may be cited; an instance of something occurring; a state of affairs, hypothetical or actual.

A set of circumstances or conditions; a situation requiring investigation or action by police or other agency; the object of investigation or consideration; a suit or action in law or equity.

Case means a trial; an action involving some point of law or fact between two or more parties.

The word 'case' in ordinary usage means event, happening, situation, circumstances. The expression 'case' in legal sense means a case, suit or proceeding in court or tribunal. [*J.C. Yadav* v *State of Haryana* AIR 1990 SC 857: (1990)2 SCC 189: JT 1990(1) SC 278: 1990(1) SLR 860].

A case is a formal legal proceeding instituted in a court of law for the enforcement or prosecution of a right of suitor, the enforcement of an obligation binding another in favour of the suitor, the redress or prevention of a wrong or the punishment of a public offence. [*Nirmal Das* v *State Transport (Appellate) Tribunal* AIR 1972 All 200].

In criminal jurisdiction, 'case' means ordinarily a proceeding for the prosecution of a person alleged to have committed an offence. In other contexts, the word may represent other kinds of proceedings. [*Bhimappa Busappa* v *Laxman Shivarayappa* AIR 1970 SC 1153: (1970)1 SCC 665: (1971)1 SCR 1: 1970 Cr LJ 1132: 1970 SCC (Cri) 263].

'Case' in s. 193(2), Criminal Procedure Code includes proceedings which are not necessarily confined to trial of offences. Bail applications and transfer petitions are cases which can be transferred to Additional Sessions Judge for disposal.

[*Virjivan P. Seth* v *Ratanlal* AIR 1964 AP 59: 1963 MLJ (Cri) 323].

NOTE: The word is of comprehensive import and includes civil proceedings other than suits. [*S.S. Khanna* v *F.J. Dillon* (1964)4 SCR 409].

The expression 'case' is not limited in its import to the entirety of the matter in dispute in an action. It includes a civil proceeding, a part of a proceeding. [*Baldevdas Shivlal* v *Filmistan Distributors* AIR 1970 SC 406: (1970)1 SCR 435: (1970)1 SCJ 342: (1969)2 SCC 201; *S.S. Khanna* v *F.J. Dillon* (1964)4 SCR 409: AIR 1964 SC 497].


- **Cognizable case** p. 151.
- **Hard cases** p. 405.
- **Leading case** p. 521.
- **Prima facie case** p. 684.
- **Summons case** p. 821.
- **Transfer of a case** p. 852.
- **Warrant-case** p. 892.


**Case decided.** A case may be said to be decided if the court adjudicates for the purpose of the suit some right or obligation of the parties in controversy; every order in the suit cannot be regarded as a case decided within the meaning of s. 115, Code of Civil Procedure 1908. [*Baldevdas Shivlal* v *Filmistan Distributors* AIR 1970 SC 406: (1970)1 SCR 435: (1970)1 SCJ 342: (1969)2 SCC 201].

**Case instituted.** A case is instituted when a suitor brings it before a court and draws attention of the court to the offence and desires that the court may take cognizance of it. In order to see, therefore, as to how a case has been instituted, one has to look to the manner in which it has been brought before the court by the suitor. [*Badri Prasad* v *Kripa Shankar* AIR 1967 All 468: 1967 Cr LJ 1255].

**Cash.** Ready money; money or its equivalent paid promptly after purchasing; money in coins or notes, as distinct from cheques or orders.

Nowadays the word 'cash' does not mean mere cash in one's pocket; but it includes a chose in action like money on current or deposit account at the bank. [*Re Wellstead's Will Trusts, Wellstead* v *Hanson* 1949 Ch 296].

'Cash' has a narrower meaning than money, and when taken in conjunction with the Government Promissory Notes it means cash in the ordinary meaning of the word and nothing more. [*Sarojini Dassi* v *Ganendra Nath* 23 CLJ 241: 33 IC 102].

**Cash balance.** Excess of credits over debits. [*The Custodian of Evacuee Property* v *Smt. Rabia Bai* AIR 1976 SC 2557: (1977)1 SCR 255: (1976)4 SCC 270].

**Cash discount.** It is discount which is allowed when the purchaser makes payment promptly or within the period of credit allowed. It is a discount granted in consideration of expeditious payment. [*Deputy Commissioner of Sales Tax (Law) Board of Revenue (Taxes)* v *Advani Coorlikon (P) Ltd.* AIR 1980 SC 609: 1980 Tax LR 1601: (1980)1 SCR 931: (1980)1 SCC 360: (1980)45 STC 32. (1981)8 ELT 801].

**Cash on delivery.** A sale upon condition that cash shall be paid on delivery of the goods; a system of paying the carrier for goods when they are delivered.

**Cashier.** A person entrusted with the monetary matters of an individual, a firm or a company, bank, etc.

**Cast iron.** 'Cast iron' is defined in the *Concise Oxford Dictionary* as "a hard alloy of iron, carbon and silicon cast in a mould". According to New Lexicon Webster's *Dictionary of English Language*, the word 'cast iron' means "an iron carbon alloy produced in a blast furnace. It contains up to 4% carbon, and is more brittle, but more easily fused, than steel". According to Van Nostrand's Scientific Encyclopaedia, 'cast iron' is primarily the product of remelting and casting pig iron. 'Cast iron' is different from 'cast iron castings'. [*Bengal Iron Corpn.* v *CTO* AIR 1993 SC 2414: 1994 Supp (1) SCC 310: (1993)90 STC 47: (1993)66 ELT 13: (1993)3 SCR 433: JT 1993(3) SC 134].

**Caste.** A caste is a horizontal segmental division of society spread over a district or a region or the whole State and also sometimes outside it. There are four essential features of the caste system which maintained its homohierarchicus character (*i*) hierarchy, (*ii*) commensality, (*iii*) restrictions on marriage and (*iv*) hereditary occupation. Most of the castes are endogamous groups. [*K.C. Vasanth Kumar* v *State of Karnataka* AIR 1985 SC 1495: 1985 (Supp) SCC 714: 1985 Supp (1) SCR 352].

A caste is a social combination of persons governed by its rules and regulations. If its rules and regulations so provide, it may admit a new member just as it may expel an existing member. The rules and regulations of the caste may not be formalised: they may not exist in black and white: they may consist only of practices and usages. [*C.M. Arumugam* v *S. Rajgopal* AIR 1976 SC 939: (1976)1 SCC 863: (1976)3 SCR 82].

• **Half caste** p. 404.

• **Scheduled castes** p. 777.

**Casting vote.** A deciding vote by a presiding officer, in case of equality of votes cast.

The vote given by the chairman or president of a deliberative assembly when the suffrages of the meeting are equal. [*Nell* v *Longbottom* (1894)1 QB 767].

**Casual.** Subject to, resulting from or occurring by chance; occurring without regularity; occasional; employed for irregular periods.

The word 'casual' actually means subject to or produced by chance or accidental or fortuitous, all of which suggest absence of any previously entertained object or intention. [*Lalithamma* v *R. Kannan* AIR 1966 Mys 178].

Whatever depends upon chance or accident is casual. [*Ramanathan Chettiar* v *Commissioner of Income Tax* ILR (1963) Mad 546: (1963)2 MLJ 438].

According to *Shorter Oxford English Dictionary*, the word 'casual' is defined to mean: (*i*) subject to or produced by chance; accidental; fortuitous; (*ii*) coming at uncertain times; not to be calculated on, unsettled. [*Ramanathan Chettiar* v *Commissioner of Income Tax* AIR 1967 SC 657: (1967)63 ITR 458: (1967)1 ITJ 188].

Anything which is in the area of expectancy and can be foreseen cannot be aptly described as casual. [*Ramanathan Chettiar* v *Commissioner of Income Tax* ILR (1963) Mad 546: (1963)2 MLJ 438]. A receipt of interest which is foreseen and anticipated cannot be regarded as casual even if it is not likely to occur again. [*Ramanathan Chettiar* v *Commissioner of Income Tax* AIR 1967 SC 657: (1967)63 ITR 458: (1967)1 ITJ 188].

**Casual visit.** A 'casual visit' means a visit which cannot be defined as a regular visit, which occurs without any fixed regularity or at certain intervals. Occasional or casual visits mean visits which are not regular, which take place at uncertain intervals and not for specific or certain objects connected with a person's regular plan of life. [*Shamnath Mushran* v *Commissioner of Income Tax* (1950)18 ITR 840: AIR 1950 All 612].

> NOTE: Visit made by an assessee to meet his friends and relations and to get his eye treated were held to be casual or occasional visit. [*Shamnath Mushran* v *Commissioner of Income Tax*, supra].

**Casus belli.** An occurrence giving rise to war.

**Casus omissus.** A situation not provided for by a statute or contract, and therefore governed by case law or new judge-made law. [Black's *Law Dictionary*, 8th Ed.].

**Categorical.** Direct; unqualified; absolute; unconditional; explicit.

**Category.** A series or order of all the predicates or attributes contained under a genus; class; division.

The categories of Aristotle are substance, quantity, quality, relation, place, time, posture, possession, action, passion.

**Cattle.** Domesticated quadrupeds held as property or raised for use; specifically bovine animals kept on a firm or ranch.

'Cattle' mean livestock and also means domesticated, bovine animals collectively, cows, bulls, steers or oxen; the term is not applied to calves and heifers. [*State of Gujarat* v *Bharwad Vaja Dhara* 1972 Guj LR 792].

NOTE: Cattle includes elephants, camels, buffaloes, horses, mares, geldings, ponies, colts, fillies, mules, asses, pigs, rams, ewes, sheep, lambs, goats, and kids. [Cattle Trespass Act 1871, s. 3; Indian Forest Act 1927, s. 2(1)].

**Cattle fair.** A periodical concourse of buyers and sellers in a place generally for sale and purchase of cattle at times or on occasions ordained by custom. [*Municipal Committee, Amritsar* v *State of Punjab* AIR 1969 SC 1100: (1969)2 SCJ 632: (1969)1 SCC 475].

**Cattle fodder**. Anything used for feeding a cattle is cattle fodder. There is no material difference between cattle-feed and cattle fodder. [*Omrao Industrial Corpn.* v *Sales Tax Officer* (1974)33 STC 343].

NOTE: Rice bran is used primarily for feeding cattle and in common parlance it would be classified as a cattle fodder. [*Commissioner of Sales Tax, U.P.* v *Narain Das* (1978)42 STC 470].

**Causa causaus: causa proxima.** The immediate cause.

**Causa mortis.** In respect of death.

**Causa proxima, non remota spectatur.** The immediate and not the remote cause is to be regarded.

**Causa sine qua non.** Some preceding link but for which the causa causans, that is, the immediate cause could not have become operative.

**Cause.** A matter to be settled at law; an individual's case offered at law, for example, plead a cause; the side taken by a party in a dispute; that which gives rise to an action; something that brings about an effect or a result; a ground of legal action, case; a matter or question to be decided. Cause means a suit or action; motive or reason; that which produces an effect.

"Cause" is not a technical word signifying one kind or another, it is *causa jurisdictionis*, any suit, action, matter, or other similar proceeding competently brought before, and litigated in, a court. [*Re Green* 51 LJQB 41, *per* Selborne, C.; sub nom. *Green* v *Penzance* 6 App Cas 657].

NOTE: "Cause" includes any action, suit or other original proceeding between a plaintiff and defendant. [*M.L. Sethi* v *R.P. Kapur* AIR 1972 SC 2379: (1972)2 SCC 427: (1973)1 SCR 697].


- **Just cause** p. 500.
- **Justiciable cause** p. 501.
- **Lawful cause** p. 518.
- **Matrimonial causes** p. 569.
- **Reasonable and probable cause** p. 728.
- **Reasonable cause** p. 729.
- **Show cause** p. 796.
- **Sufficient cause** p. 820.
- **Unavoidable cause** p. 861.


**Cause celebre.** A legal case that excites widespread interest.

**Cause list.** List in which the matters for hearing by a court are set down in succession.

In English practice, a printed roll of actions, to be tried in the order of their entry, with the names of the solicitors for each litigant; a schedule of pending cases.

**Cause of action.** "The term 'cause of action' means all those things necessary to give a right of action, whether they are to be done by the plaintiff or a third person". [*Hernaman* v *Smith* (1855)10 Exch 659, 666, *per* Parke, B.].

"'Cause of action' has been held ... to mean every fact which is material to be proved to entitle the plaintiff to succeed—every fact which the defendant would have a right to traverse". [*Cooke* v *Gill* (1873) LR 8 CP 107, 116, *per* Brett, J.].

'Cause of action' means "rights which can be enforced, or liabilities which can be redressed by legal proceedings ......". [*Sugden* v *Sugden* (1957)1 All ER 300, 302 (CA), *per* Denning, L.J.].

'Cause of action' means the bundle of essential facts which is necessary for the plaintiff to prove before he can succeed in the suit or to put it differently, it refers to the media upon which court arrives at a conclusion in his favour. [*Re*

*Lakshminarayan Chettiar* AIR 1954 Mad 594 (FB)].

The expression "cause of action" has sometimes been employed to convey the restricted idea of facts or circumstances which constitute either the infringement or the basis of a right and no more. In a wider and more comprehensive sense, it has been used to denote the whole bundle of material facts which a plaintiff must prove in order to succeed. [*Gurdit Singh* v *Munsha Singh* AIR 1977 SC 640: (1977)2 SCR 250: (1977)1 SCC 791].

The 'cause of action' means every fact which if traversed, it would be necessary for the plaintiff to prove in order to support his right to a judgment of the court. In other words, it is a bundle of facts which taken with the law applicable to them gives the plaintiff a right to relief against the defendant. [*State of Rajasthan* v *Swaika Properties* AIR 1985 SC 1289: (1985)3 SCC 217: (1985)3 SCR 598].

NOTE: It is bundle of such facts which taken with the law applicable to them gives the plaintiff a right to relief against the defendant. It must include some act done by the defendant since in the absence of such an act no cause of action can possibly accrue. It is not limited to the actual infringement of the right sued on but includes all the material facts on which it is founded. It does not comprise evidence necessary to prove such facts, but every fact necessary for the plaintiff to prove to enable him to obtain a decree. Everything which if not proved would give the defendant a right to immediate judgment must be part of the cause of action. But it has no relation whatever to the defence which may be set up by the defendant nor does it depend upon the character of the relief prayed for by the plaintiff. [*ABC Laminart Pvt. Ltd.* v *A.P. Agencies, Salem* AIR 1989 SC 1239: (1989)2 SCC 163: (1989)2 SCR 1: JT 1989(2) SC 38].

**Caution.** An admonition or warning; a formal warning and reprimand.

Security given to ensure performance of some obligation. [Black's *Law Dictionary*, 8th Ed.].

**Caution money.** A sum deposited as security for good conduct.

**C.A.V.** "Curia advisari vult", which means that the court wishes to consider the matter, will consider the matter.

**Caveat.** A Latin expression which means "let him or her beware".

A warning or proviso or caution; a formal notification to a court or court officer not to take a certain step till the notifier is heard.

A caveat is simply a warning given by a person having or asserting an interest in the estate of the deceased against the court issuing any probate without notice to the caveator. It is not a notice to any particular person. [*In the goods of, Nanda Lal Sett* AIR 1955 Cal 88: 58 CWN 568; ss. 284 and 285 of the Indian Succession Act 1925].

**Caveat actor.** Let the doer, or actor, beware.

**Caveat emptor.** Let the buyer beaware.

The maxim summarises the rule that a purchaser must examine, judge, and test for himself. This maxim is more applicable to judicial sales, auctions, and the like, than to sales of consumer goods where strict liability, warranty, and other consumer protection laws protect the buyer.

The general rule is that each party to a contract may observe silence even in regard to facts which he believes would be operative upon the mind of the other. This is the rule which in contracts for the sale of goods is summed up in the maxim *"caveat emptor"*. The seller is under no duty to disclose defects; the buyer must use his own eyes to discover them. The same rule applies to contracts generally (though other terms may be implied). The rule, however, does not justify misrepresentation. [Sutton and Shannon on *Contracts*, 6th Ed., p. 141].

'Caveat emptor' does not mean in law or Latin that the buyer must take a chance, it means that he must take care. It applies to the purchase of specific things, *e.g.*, to a horse or a picture upon which the buyer can and usually does exercise his own judgment. It applies also whenever the buyer voluntarily chooses what he buys. It applies also whenever by usage or otherwise it is a term of the contract, express or implied, that the buyer shall not rely on the skill or judgment of the seller. [*Wallis* v *Russel* (1902)2 IR 585 (CA), *per* Fitzgibbon, L.J.].

**Caveat viator.** Let the traveller be aware.

This applies where gratuitous permission is given to persons to pass over private land, who must take the risk of accident arising from the negligence of the owner. [Rawson's *Pocket Law Lexicon*].

Caveat viator means that the traveller must use reasonable care for his own safety; but a traveller or passer-by on premises on or over which he has a right to be or to pass is entitled to be protected from the negligence of those who are under some duty to passers-by or users of the premises. The degree of duty varies according to whethor the victim of the accident has a contract involving care of even absolute assurance or warranty on the part of the defendant is regard to the soundness of the premises or otherwise, or whether the plaintiff was a visitor or licensee. [*Indermaur* v *Dames* (1866) LR 1 CP 274; *Latham* v *Johnson* (1913)1 KB 398; *Latham* v *Johnson Western Railway Co.* (1915)1 KB 564].

NOTE: The case of a trespasser is quite different, but even then the owner of the land or person in possession has no right to lay a trap for him or commit any other wilful injury. [*Bird* v *Holbrook* (1928)4 Bing 628]. With that exception, the owner of the premises is not obliged to ensure a trespasser's safety or to warn him of danger [*Great Central Railway Co.* v *Bates* (1921)3 KB 578], but the trespasser does not lose his right as a member of the public if the defendant was guilty of a public nuisance towards the person injured. [*Barnes* v *Ward* (1850)9 CB 392; *Cooke* v *Midland Great Western Railway of Ireland* (1909) AC 229].

**Cease.** To bring to an end, terminate; to come to an end; to bring an activity or action to an end, discontinue.

'Cease' means discontinue or put an end to. There is no scope for importing any notion of suspension into that expression. [*Narayana* v *State of Andhra Pradesh* AIR 1959 AP 471: ILR (1959) Andh 254].

**Cede.** To yield or give up; to transfer.

**Celibacy.** An unmarried or single state of life.

**Cellar.** Any vault or underground room.

**Censor.** An official authorised to examine printed matter, films, news etc. before public release, and to suppress any parts on the grounds of obscenity, a threat to security etc.; an official who examines publications for objectional matter; an official who reads communications and deletes such matters; a person or an authority who regulates or prohibits the publication of any newspaper or the production of any play or cinematograph or any part of the press.

**Census.** The official counting or enumeration of people of a state, nation, district, or other political subdivision. It contains classified information relating to social and economic conditions. [*City of Compton* v *Adams* 203 P 2d 745, 746].

**Central Act.** Central Act shall mean an Act of Parliament, and shall include—(*a*) an Act of the Dominion Legislature or of the Indian Legislature passed before the commencement of the Constitution, and (*b*) an Act made before such commencement by the Governor-General in Council or the Governor-General, acting in a legislative capacity. [General Clauses Act 1897, s. 3(7)].

NOTE: An order of the President under Art. 373 of the Constitution, for the purpose of construction with reference to the General Clauses Act is a Central Act. [*Prahlad Jena* v *State* AIR 1950 Ori 157: 51 Cr LJ 1189].

**Central Government.** Central Government shall—(*a*) in relation to anything done before the commencement of the Constitution, mean the Governor-General or the Governor-General in Council, as the case may be; and shall include—(*i*) in relation to functions entrusted under sub-sec. (1) of s. 124 of the Government of India Act 1935, to the Government of a Province, the Provincial Government acting within the scope of the authority given to it under that sub-section; and (*ii*) in relation to the administration of a Chief Commissioner's

Province, the Chief Commissioner acting within the scope of the authority given to him under sub-sec. (3) of s. 94 of the said Act; and (*b*) in relation to anything done or to be done after the commencement of the Constitution, mean the President; and shall include—(*i*) in relation to functions entrusted under cl. (1) of Art. 258 of the Constitution to the Government of a State, the State Government acting within the scope of the authority given to it under that clause; (*ii*) in relation to the administration of a Part C State before the commencement of the Constitution (Seventh Amendment) Act 1956, the Chief Commissioner or the Lieutenant-Governor or the Government of a neighbouring State or other authority acting within the scope of authority given to him or it under Art. 239 or Art. 243 of the Constitution, as the case may be; and (*iii*) in relation to the administration of a Union Territory, the administrator thereof acting within the scope of the authority given to him under Art. 239 of the Constitution. [General Clauses Act 1897, s. 3(8)].

'Central Government' means the President acting through the Council of Ministers. [*Surajmal* v *State of Madhya Pradesh* AIR 1958 MP 103].

NOTE: The Central Government is not an individual but an organisation. Indian Railways is nothing but a part of the Central Government. [*S.C. Chowla* v *Harbans Lal Khullar* AIR 1994 Del 63].

The word 'Central Government' includes the Chief Commissioner acting within the scope of the authority given to him under Art. 239 of the Constitution of India. [*Satya Dev Busheri* v *Padam Dev* AIR 1955 SC 5 referring to s. 3(8) of the General Clauses Act 1897].

**Cereal.** Relating to grain or to the plants that produce it; made of grain; a prepared foodstuff of grain.

Cereals mean grain used as food, such as wheat, barley etc.

NOTE: Paddy and husked paddy (that is to say rice) both fail within the category of cereals. But the husk when separated from rice does not independently fall within the category of cereals, the reason being husk as husk is neither grain nor seed and is not human food. [*Lakshmi Narayan Rice Mills* v *Assistant Commissioner* 66 CWN 1].

**Certificate.** A formal document attesting a fact; a written declaration or testimonial; a writing signed and legally authenticated; a writing or statement certifying that the one named therein has satisfactorily completed a certain educational course; a document in which a fact is formally attested.

- **Birth certificate** p. 106.
- **Death certificate** p. 230.
- **Share certificate** p. 794.
- **Succession certificate** p. 819.

**Certificate of fit for appeal.** The phrase in Art. 134(1)(*c*) of the Constitution that 'the case is a fit one for appeal' gives a wide discretion to the High Court to grant or refuse to grant the certificate. The phrase means something more than a question of law or a substantial question of law and that the point involved must be of general importance. [*D.L. Airways* v *Union of India* AIR 1956 Punj 1: ILR (1955) Punj 1345].

**Certificate of sale.** It is a certificate granted by the court where a sale of immovable property has become absolute, specifying the property sold and the name of the person who at the time of sale is declared to be the purchaser. Such certificate shall bear date of the day on which the sale becomes absolute. [Code of Civil Procedure 1908, Or. 21, r. 94].

**Certified copy.** A copy of a document, signed and certified as a true copy by the officer having the custody of the original. A certified copy is an authenticated copy. By long usage, the term 'certified copy' has obtained a special meaning in view of the provision in s. 76 of the Evidence Act, namely, a copy obtained under s. 76 on payment of the necessary fee. [*Malayalam Plantation* v *Commissioner of Income Tax* ILR (1959) Ker 30: AIR 1959 Ker 34].

**Certify.** To attest as being true or as represented or as being up to a standard; to inform with certainty.

To authenticate or verify in writing; to attest as being true or as meeting certain criteria. [Black's *Law Dictionary*, 8th Ed.].

The expression 'certify' means to make a declaration in writing under hand and seal; to make attestation in writing as to the truth of the facts or the result of the execution proceedings in the transferee court and the circumstances thereof. [*Shimoga Oil Mills* v *Sri Radhakrishna Oil Mills* AIR 1969 AP 263].

▸ *Meaning under the Constitution of India, Art. 134(1)(c).* The word 'certify' in Art. 134(1)(*c*) has a clear meaning. It requires that when giving the leave to appeal, the High Court must first determine the issue of law which in its opinion is needed to be settled by the Supreme Court and such question must be clearly set out in its order. [*T.B. Thakore* v *State of Maharashtra* (1969)3 SCC 369].

NOTE: The word 'certify' in Art. 134(1)(c) is a strong word postulating the exercise of judicial discretion in determining if the question requiring decision by the Supreme Court involves a matter of principle or a substantial question of law of great general importance. Such certificate is not to be given as a matter of course on the mere ground that the impugned decision is considered to be erroneous. There must be exceptional or special circumstances like infringement of essential principles of justice or some difficult question of law of great public or private importance. It is not to be granted so as to convert Supreme Court into an ordinary court of further appeal. [*State of Bihar* v *Bhagirath Sharma* (1973)2 SCC 257].

**Certiorari.** "Certiorari" is a late Latin word being the passive form of the word "certiorari" meaning 'inform' and occurred in the original Latin words of the writ which translated read "we, being desirous for certain reasons, that the said record should by you be certified to us". Certiorari was essentially a royal demand for information; the King, wishing to be certified of some matter, orders that the necessary information be provided for him. [*Prabodh Verma* v *State of Uttar Pradesh* AIR 1985 SC 167: (1985)1 SCR 216: (1984)4 SCC 251: 1985(2) SLR 714].

It is a writ of common law origin issued by a superior to an inferior court requiring the latter to produce a certified record of a particular case tried therein. The writ is issued in order that the court issuing the writ may inspect the proceedings and determine whether there have been any irregularities.

NOTE: A writ of *certiorari* lies whenever a body of persons having legal authority to determine questions affecting the rights of subjects and having the duty to act judicially act in excess of their legal authority; it does not lie to remove or adjudicate upon the order which is of an administrative or ministerial nature. [*Sadhu Singh* v *Delhi Administration* AIR 1966 SC 91: (1966)1 SCR 243].

A writ of *certiorari* can be issued for (*a*) correcting errors of jurisdiction committed by inferior court or tribunals, where orders are passed by them without jurisdiction, or in excess of jurisdiction, or as a result of failure to exercise jurisdiction; (*b*) correcting errors, where in exercise of jurisdiction the court or tribunals act illegally or improperly, e.g. where it decides a question without giving an opportunity to be heard to the party affected by the order, or where the procedure adopted in dealing with the dispute is opposed to principles of natural justice. [*Syed Yaqub* v *Radhakrishnan* AIR 1964 SC 477; *Hindustan Aeronautic Ltd., Koraput Division* v *Registering Authority and Taxing Officer, Koraput* (1995)1 Ori LR 192].

An error of law which is apparent on the face of the record can be corrected by the writ of *certiorari*, but not an error of fact unless in recording the said finding, the inferior court or tribunal had erroneously refused to admit admissible and material evidence, or had erroneously admitted inadmissible evidence, which has influenced the impugned finding. [*Syed Yaqub* v *Radhakrishnan* AIR 1964 SC 477].

If a finding of fact is based on no evidence, that is an error of law which can be corrected by a writ of *certiorari*. [*Syed Yaqub* v *Radhakrishnan*, supra].

Where the conclusion of law recorded by an inferior court or tribunal is based on an obvious misinterpretation of a relevant statutory provision, or in ignorance of it or in disregard of it, or on reasons which are wrong in law, the said conclusion can be corrected by a writ of certiorari. [*Syed Yaqub* v *Radhakrishnan*, supra].

**Certiorarified mandamus.** The expression means a merger of the two writs, *viz.*, *certiorari* and *mandamus*. *Mandamus* comes in to help *certiorari*. In the Indian context this has been applied in *State of Madhya Pradesh* v *Bhailal Bhai* [AIR 1964 SC 1006], where an officer under a taxing statute had a quasi-judicial function to assess the tax. He did so and collected the tax. In a petition under Art. 226 of the Constitution of India, the act was held to be *ultra vires* and void. Since *certiorari* could only quash the order, a *mandamus* was required to direct refund of the amount collected. *Mandamus* was thus certiorarified and then issued.

**Cess.** A tax in India, Scotland and Ireland; a levy.

The word "cess" is used in Ireland and is still in use in India although the word "rate" has replaced it in England. It means a tax and is generally used when the levy is for special administrative expense which the name (health cess, education cess, road cess, etc.) indicates. [*India Cement Ltd.* v *State of Tamil Nadu* AIR 1990 SC 85: (1990)1 SCC 12: JT 1989(4) SC 190: 1989 Supp (1) SCR 692].

The word 'cess' has a definite legal connotation indicating tax allocated to a particular thing, not forming part of the general fund. Cess is only tax and not a mere fee. [*Shanmugha Oil Mill* v *Coimbatore Market Committee* ILR (1960) Mad 171: AIR 1960 Mad 160].

A 'cess' is a tax levied for a specific purpose often with a prefixed word defining the object. [*Gwalior Sugar Co. Ltd.* v *State of Madhya Bharat* AIR 1954 MB 196, 201].

NOTE: The 'cess' is nothing more than an addition to existing taxes. As it is a percentage of another tax, the determination of the cess is not by an independent assessment. It is an arithmetical calculation based on the result of assessment under other Act or Acts. [*Ahmedabad Mfg. & Calico Printing Co. Ltd.* v *State of Gujarat* AIR 1967 SC 1916].

It is not necessary for the purpose of levy of cess that there should be *quid pro quo* between the service actually rendered and the amount of tax levied. [*Shanmugha Oil Mill* v *Coimbatore Market Committee* ILR (1960) Mad 171: AIR 1960 Mad 160].

**Cessante ratione legis, cessat ipsa lex.** The reason for the law ceasing, the law itself ceases.

NOTE: A law does not cease to be operative because it is out of keeping with the present time. But this principle does not apply where the custom outlines the condition which gave it birth. [*Mirza Raja* v *Pushpavathi Visweswar* (1964)2 SCR 403, 430].

**Cession.** The ceding or giving up of rights, property, and specially of territory by a State; the territory etc. so ceded; surrender; an assignment of property or rights to another or others; the act of relinquishing property rights.

NOTE: It is an important method of acquiring territorial sovereignty. It rests on the principle that the right of transferring its territory is a fundamental attribute of a State.

Cession of a part of Indian territory in favour of a foreign State can be effected only by an amendment of the Constitution. [*In re, Berubari Union* AIR 1960 SC 845, 846].

A settlement of boundary dispute is not cession. [*Maganbhai* v *Union of India* AIR 1969 SC 783, 798].

**Cestui que trust.** *Cestui que* trust is the person (frequently termed beneficiary) who possesses the equitable right to property and receives the rents, issues and profits thereof, the legal estate of which is vested in a trustee.

He who has a right to a beneficial interest in and out of an estate the legal title to which is vested in another.

**Cestui que vie.** The person for whose life lands, tenements, or hereditaments are held; the person whose life measures the duration of a trust, gift, estate, or insurance contract.

**c.f.** Carried forward.

**cf.** Compare.

**C.F.** Cost and freight.

**C.F.I.** Cost, freight and insurance.

**C.F.I. contract.** It means that the price named in the contract includes the expense of the goods, their carriage, and their insurance during the transit to the purchaser. [*Ireland* v *Livingston* (1871) LR 5 HL 406, Blackburn, J.].

NOTE: Under a C.F.I. contract there is an absolute duty on the vendor to procure the shipment of the goods under such a Bill of Lading as will, subject to its exceptions, ensure their delivery at the port of destination. [*Lecky* v *Ogilvy* 3 Com Ca 29].

The essential feature of an ordinary C.F.I. contract for the sale of goods rests on the fact that performance of the bargain is to be fulfilled by delivery of documents and not by actual physical delivery of the goods by the seller. In a C.F.I. contract the seller undertakes—(*a*) to ship at the port of shipment within the time mentioned in the contract goods of the description contained in the contract; (*b*) to procure on shipment a contract of affreightment under which the goods will be delivered at the destination contemplated by the contract; (*c*) to effect an insurance on the goods for the benefit of the buyer; (*d*) to make out an invoice of the goods; and (*e*) to tender these documents to the buyer—the bill of lading, the invoice and the policy of insurance. [*B.R. Harman* v *Pran Ballav* AIR 1960 Cal 524: 64 CWN 798].

In a C.F.I. contract, property in the goods passes to the buyer as soon as the documents are delivered to him. [*India Coffee and Tea* v *State of Madras* AIR 1954 Mad 1030: 67 Mad LW 647].

Such contract is also known as C.I.F. contract.

**Chairman.** A person chosen to preside over meetings, *e.g.*, one who presides over the meetings of the Board of Directors; a name given to a presiding officer of an assembly, public meeting, convention, deliberative or legislative body, board of directors, committee, etc. [*T.N. Seshan, Chief Election Commissioner of India* v *Union of India* (1995)4 SCC 611: JT 1995(5) SC 337: 1995 AIR SCW 3341].

NOTE: *Functions of a Chairman.* The function of the Chairman would be to preside over meetings, preserve order, conduct the business of the day, ensure that precise decisions are taken and correctly recorded and do all that is necessary for smooth transaction of business. The nature and duties of this office may vary depending on the nature of business to be transacted but by and large these would be the functions of a Chairman. [*T.N. Seshan, Chief Election Commissioner of India* v *Union of India* (1995)4 SCC 611: JT 1995(5) SC 337: 1995 AIR SCW 3341].

**Challan.** A document sent with goods, treasure or individuals; an invoice; a voucher; a pass, a passport. A memorandum of money received and invested.

The traditional way of indicating initiation of prosecution *i.e.* a police charge-sheet under s. 190(1)(*b*) of the Cr. P.C. or complaint under s. 190(1)(*a*) of the Cr. P.C. [*Rajesh Laxman Hirodkar* v *State of M.P.* AIR 1995 MP 93: 1994 MPLJ 846].

The expression 'challan' means only panchanama which is prepared at the time of seizure. [*Dharmendra Jhavar* v *State of M.P.* AIR 1995 MP 93].

**Challenge.** Calling into question; protest; a questioning of the right or validity of a vote or voter; to invite into competition; to put into dispute; to render doubtful.

NOTE: Challenge is of two kinds: (1) challenge to the array, and (2) challenge to the polls. The right to challenge may be exercised by any party, which includes the Crown. [Halsbury's *Laws of England*, 4th Ed., vol. 26, para 620, p. 324].

**Chamber.** A hall used by a legislative or a judicial body; room used by a member of the legal profession; a judge's room used for official proceedings not required to be held in open court; a large underground cavity; a cave; a room in which a monarch or other great personage gives audience.

**Champerty.** A transaction or agreement by which a person, not a party in a suit, bargains to aid in or carry on its prosecution or defence in consideration of a share of the subject-matter in suit.

A bargain by a stranger with a party to a suit, by which such third person undertakes to carry on the litigation at his own cost and risk, in consideration of receiving, if successful, a part of the proceeds or subject sought to be recovered. [*Schnabel* v *Taft Broadcasting Co., Inc.* Mo App, 525 SW 2d 819, 823].

Champerty is a species of maintenance, in which the intermeddler renders assistance by bargaining for a share of profits of litigation. [*Varsavaya Venkata* v *Poosapathi* ILR 18 Mad 230: 52 IA 1].

NOTE: Champerty (abolished in England by s. 13 of the Criminal Law Act 1967) was a particular kind of maintenance, namely, maintenance of an action in consideration of a promise to give to the maintainer a share in the subject-matter or proceeds thereof. [Halsbury's *Laws of England*, 4th Ed., vol. 9, para 400, p. 272].

The English law of champerty and maintenance does not apply to India. [*Fischer* v *Kamala Naicker* 8 MIA 170]. Such cases are decided with reference to s. 23 of the Indian Contract Act. [*Kunwar Ram Lal* v *Nil Kanth* 20 IA 112].

Champertous agreements in India are not *per se* void. On the other hand, a fair agreement to supply funds to carry on a suit in consideration of having a share in the property, if recovered, has not been considered opposed to public policy. But such agreements should not be enforced as being opposed to public policy if they fall in one of the categories, namely, (1) if they are extortionate and unconscionable, so as to be inequitable against the party; or (2) if they are made not with the *bona fide* object of assisting a claim believed to be just and obtaining a reasonable recompense therefor, but for improper objects as (*a*) for the purpose of gambling in litigation, or (*b*) of injuring or oppressing others by abetting and encouraging unrighteous suits. [*Suganchand* v *Balchand* ILR (1957)7 Raj 204: AIR 1957 Raj 89; s. 23 of the Indian Contract Act 1872].

**Chance.** Absence of explainable or controllable causation; accident; fortuity; hazard; result or issue of uncertain and unknown conditions or forces; risk.

- **Game of chance.** Game of chance is a game involving the element of wagering; each of the players must have a chance of losing as well as winning.

**Chancellor.** A state or legal official of various kinds; the head of the Government in some European countries *e.g.* Germany; the non-resident honorary head of a university; a bishop's law officer; an officer of an order of knighthood who seals commissions etc.

**Chancellor, Lord.** He is an officer of the greatest weight and power in Great Britain; is superior in point of precedency to every temporal Lord; appoints all Justices of the Peace throughout Great Britain; nominates the judges of the High Court, except the Lord Chief Justice, who is nominated by the Prime Minister; appoints and can remove almost all country court judges. He is responsible for public records.

**Chancellor of the exchequer.** He is a Minister of State in charge of the revenue in Great Britain. The Chancellor of the Exchequer was appointed originally to act as a check on the Lord Treasurer. The office is now a part of the Treasury. He at present is in substance the Finance Minister and is always a member of the Cabinet and is responsible for the management of the financial affairs of the State.

**Chancery.** The Lord Chancellor's court, a division of the High Court of Justice in UK; a court of equity in USA; an office attached to an embassy or consulate; a public record office.

**Chandina land.** *Chandina* or bazar lands are non-agricultural lands. [*Sasi Kant* v *Sandhyamoni* 26 CWN 483].

**Change.** The general meaning of the word 'change' is to make or become different, to transform or convert. [*Forward Construction Co.* v *Prabhat Mandal* AIR 1986 SC 391: 1985 Supp (3) SCR 766: (1986)1 SCC 100].

It has also been instructively defined thus: To cause to turn or pass from one statute another, to vary in form, or essence, to alter or make different, to alter the site or route, to substitute another thing or things for; as, to change clothes, to shift, to give or procure another kind of money for, as, to change a dollar, to give away for a money equivalent of a different kind, to exchange, as, to change places with a person, to place fresh linen on; as, to change a bed or baby. [*Reeta* v *Berhampur University* AIR 1993 Ori 27: (1992)2 Ori LR 341: (1992)74 Cut LT 603].

The word 'change' as intransitive verb has been defined thus: Take another instead of, resign, get red of, for; give or get smaller or foreign coin for; put on different clothes, put fresh clothes or coverings on (exa—a baby, replace a used nappy with clean one); go from one to another; change trains, give and receive, change; make or become different, one's mind, change one's purpose or opinion; up, down (in motor driving change to a higher, lower, gear). [*Reeta* v *Berhampur University* AIR 1993 Ori 27: (1992)2 Ori LR 341: (1992)74 Cut LT 603].

It may also mean: to replace with or exchange for another; to give or receive something in return; to give or receive money in exchange for the equivalent sum in small denomination or different currency; to pass from one phase to the following one; to alight from and board another; a variation, deviation or modification; the substitution of one thing for another; anything that is or may be substituted for something else; a different or fresh set.

**Character.** The collective qualities or characteristics; moral strength; a part played by an actor; an outstanding individual; a testimonial; person; personality; human being; attribute; dominant quality; essential quality of one's nature; marked traits; prime ingredients; temperament.

- **Bad character** p. 91.
- **Good moral character** p. 391.

**Charge.** Accusation; allegation; arraignment; castigation; imputation; incrimination; exhortation.

Command; dictate; direction; injunction; proclamation.

Cost; assessment; disbursement; expenditure; expense; fee; obligation; ask as a price; debit (a person or an account).

Custody; care; control; custodian; guidance; jurisdiction.

Lien; claim on property; encumbrance; hold on property; hypothecation; pecuniary burden; a financial liability or commitment.

Responsibility; accountability; allegiance; burden; commitment; imperative duty.

Empower; authorize; confer power on; delegate authority to; invest with authoritative power.

As noun, the word 'charge' is defined, *inter alia*, thus: a formal accusation of an offence as a preliminary step to prosecution; an instruction or command; an assigned duty or task; a responsibility; an encumbrance, lien, or claim; a person or thing entrusted to another's care; price, cost or expense. [Black's *Law Dictionary*, 8th Ed.].

As verb, the word 'charge' is defined, amongst others, thus: to accuse (a person) of an offence; to instruct or command; to impose a lien or claim; to encumber; to entrust with responsibilities and duties; to demand a fee. [Black's *Law Dictionary*, 8th Ed.].

The term "charge" is a broad one and may mean "any amount which may be demanded as a price for the rendering of some service or as price of some goods". [*Sree Gajanana Motor Transport Co. Ltd.* v *State of Karnataka* AIR 1977 SC 418: (1977)1 SCR 665: (1977)1 SCC 37].

▸ *Meaning in criminal proceeding.* "Charge" is the "solemn act of calling before a magistrate an accused person and stating, in his hearing, in order that he may defend himself, what is the accusation against him". [*R.* v *D'Eyncourt* (1888)21 QBD 109].

The word 'charge' is wider in purport and includes, beside the element of offence, the reference to the person who is alleged to have committed it. [*In re Lachman Nanda* AIR 1966 MP 261: 1966 Cr LJ 1012].

▸*Meaning in property matter.* Where immovable property of one person is by act of parties or operation of law made security for the payment of money to another, and the transaction does not amount to a mortgage, the latter person is said to have a charge on the property. [Transfer of Property Act 1882, s. 100].

> NOTE: *Mortgage and charge—distinction.* Every mortgage is a charge but every charge is not mortgage. [*D.S. Mote* v *A.C. Datar* (1974)2 SCC 799].
>
> The broad distinction between a mortgage and a charge is this: whereas a charge only gives right to payment out of a particular fund or particular property without transferring that fund or property, a mortgage is in essence a transfer of an interest in specific immovable property. [*Shiva Prasad* v *Beni Madhab* (1922)1 Pat 387: AIR 1922 Pat 529].


- **Annual charge** p. 63.
- **Capital charge** p. 122.
- **Criminal charge** p. 206.
- **Deferred charge** p. 242.
- **Floating charge** p. 359.
- **Further charge** p. 379.
- **Joinder of charges** p. 486.
- **Law charges** p. 515.
- **Service charge** p. 788.
- **Terminal charge** p. 836.


**Charge d'affaires.** An ambassador's deputy; an envoy to a minor country; a person who temporarily assumes the command of a diplomatic mission in the absence of the regularly appointed chief; a diplomatic representative of the fourth rank accredited by one foreign minister to another, and not to the Chief of State.

**Charge-sheet.** In criminal jurisprudence, it means a record of cases and charges made at a police station.

A police record showing the names of all persons brought into custody, the nature of the accusations, and the identity of the accusers. [Black's *Law Dictionary*, 8th Ed.].

Charge-sheet is a paper kept at the police station to receive each night the names of the persons brought and taken into custody, the nature of the accusation, and the name of the accuser in each case. It is under the care of the inspector on duty. Unless the accuser is willing to sign the charge-sheet, the accused will generally not be detained.

In Indian context in criminal jurisprudence it means a police report after investigation submitted under s. 173, Cr. P.C. in prescribed form.

In military law, charge-sheet means a four-part charging instrument containing —(1) information about the accused and the witnesses, (2) the charges and specifications, (3) the preferring of charges and their referral to a summary, special, or general court-martial for trial, and (4) for a summary court-martial, the trial record. [Black's *Law Dictionary*, 8th Ed.].

**Charitable purpose.** A purpose must, in order to be charitable, be directed to the benefit of the community or a section of the community. [*Re Compton, Powell* v *Compton* 1945 Ch 123].

▸*Meaning under the Charitable Endowments Act 1890, s. 2.* Charitable purpose includes relief of the poor, education, medical relief and advancement of any other object of general public utility, but does not include a purpose which relates exclusively to religious teaching or worship.

▸*Meaning under the Gift Tax Act 1958, s. 2(va); Income-tax Act 1961, s. 2(15)* Charitable purpose includes relief of the poor, education, medical relief, and advancement of any other object of general public utility not involving the carrying on of any activity for profit.

To serve a charitable purpose it is not necessary that the object should be to benefit the whole of mankind or all persons in a particular country or State. It is sufficient if the intention to benefit a section of the public as distinguished from a specified individual is present. [*Ahmedabad Rana Caste Association* v *The Commissioner of Income Tax, Gujarat* AIR 1972 SC 273: (1972)1 SCR 744: (1971)3 SCC 475: (1971)82 ITR 704].

NOTE: The expression 'charitable purpose' is wide enough to include religious purposes as well. [*Thangaswami Chettiar* v *Commissioner of Income Tax* ILR (1966)1 Mad 243: AIR 1966 Mad 103; *Commissioner of Income Tax, Madras* v *Andhra Chamber of Commerce, Madras* AIR 1965 SC 1281: (1965)55 ITR 722: (1965)1 SCJ 725: (1965)2 SCA 330].

A provision for the family of the wakf or for himself cannot be regarded as charitable purpose. [*Fazlul Rabbi* v *State of West Bengal* AIR 1965 SC 1722: (1965)2 SCA 137: (1965)2 SCJ 833].

**Charity.** Alms-giving; giving voluntarily to those in need; kindness, benevolence; liberality to the poor; a gift of real or personal property for the public benefit; aid given to the poor, the suffering, or the general community for religious, educational, economic, public-safety, or medical purposes.

'Charity' in common parlance is a word denoting a giving to someone in necessitous circumstances and in law a giving for public good. A gift to one's ownself or kith and kin may be meritorious and pious but is not a charity in the legal sense. [*Fazlul Rabbi* v *State of West Bengal* AIR 1965 SC 1722: (1965)2 SCA 137: (1965)2 SCJ 833].

NOTE: Charity may be *dan* or *utsarga*. In former the donor on giving up ownership over a thing makes another owner. In latter the donor gives up ownership for the benefit of all. In either view, the donor retains no control over the thing dedicated. [*C.I.T.* v *F.I.C.C.I.* AIR 1981 SC 1408: (1981)3 SCR 489: 1981 Tax LR 1062; (1981)3 SCC 156: (1982)2 Comp LJ 451].

Charity may be classified under the following four heads—(1) relief of poverty, (2) advancement of education, (3) advancement of religion, and (4) other purposes beneficial to the community, not falling within the preceding heads. [*Income Tax Special Purposes Commissioners* v *Pemsel* (1891) AC 531].

**Charta de non ente non valet.** A deed relating to a thing not in existence is of no avail.

The maxim relates primarily to the subject-matter of any grant or to the person to whom a grant is made of an immediate interest in possession.

**Charter-party contract.** A contract by charter-party is a contract by which an entire ship or some principal part thereof is let to a merchant, who is called the charterer, for the conveyance of goods on a determined voyage to one or more places, or until the expiration of a specified period; in the first case it is called a voyage charter-party, and in the second a time charter-party. [Halsbury's *Laws of England*, 4th Ed., vol. 43, para 402, p. 239; *Union of India* v *Gosalia Shipping (Pvt.) Ltd.* AIR 1978 SC 1196: (1978)3 SCR 943: (1978)3 SCC 23].

**Chartered ship.** It is ship which is hired or freighted.

**Chas.** Cultivation; tillage.

**Chasa.** A cultivator; a ploughman; a husbandman.

**Chastisement.** Punishment, especially with the rod; whip.

In legal sense, refers to the correction of a child by its parent, an apprentice or scholar by his master, or a criminal by an officer.

**Chastity.** Sexual abstinence; virginity; celibacy; purity; continence.

It means the state of purity or abstinence from unlawful sexual connection.

**Chattels.** Any property other than freehold land, including tangible goods and leasehold interests; a personal possession; an article of personal property; a movable or transferable property.

The word "chattels" is one of the widest words known to the law in relation to personal property, and includes deeds and other papers, and chose in action, for instance the shares in a joint stock of company. [Halsbury's *Laws of England*, 4th Ed., vol. 25, para 1007, p. 517].

**Cheat.** As verb means to deceive and defraud; to practice deception.

As noun means swindling; defrauding; the act of fraudulently deceiving.

The words "cheat and defraud" usually mean to induce a person to part with the possession of property by reason of intentionally false representations relied and acted upon by such person to his harm. They include not only the crime of false pretenses, but also all civil frauds, and include all tricks, devices, artifices, or deceptions used to deprive another of property or other right.

▸*Meaning under the Indian Penal Code 1860, s. 415.* Whoever, by deceiving any person, fraudulently or dishonestly induces the person so deceived to deliver any property to any person, or to consent that any person shall retain any property, or intentionally induces the person so deceived to do or omit to do anything which he could not do or omit if he were not so deceived, and which act or omission causes or is likely to cause damage or harm to that person in body, mind, reputation or property, is said to cheat.

**Chela.** A servant, a slave, a pupil, a disciple, especially one brought up by a religious mendicant to become a member of his order.

**Chemical.** The expression "chemical" means, according to the *Collins English Dictionary*, any substance used in or resulting from a reaction involving changes to atoms or molecules or used in chemistry. The *Concise Oxford Dictionary*, 6th Ed., defines "chemical", as made by, or relating to, chemistry. [*Member Secy. A.P. Board for Water Pollution Control* v *Andhra Pradesh Rayons Ltd.* AIR 1989 SC 611: 1988 Supp (3) SCR 380: JT 1988(4) SC 154: (1989)1 SCC 44].

**Chemical industry.** An industry would be known as a chemical industry if it carries on predominantly chemical activities and is involved in chemical endeavours. [*Member Secretary, Andhra Pradesh State Board* v *A.P. Rayons Ltd.* AIR 1989 SC 611].

**Chemist.** A dealer in medicinal drugs, usu. also selling other medical goods and toiletries; an authorized dispenser of medicines; a person practising or trained in chemistry.

**Cheque.** A written order to a bank to pay the stated sum from the drawer's account; the printed form on which a written order to a bank to pay the stated sum from the drawer's account is written.

A bill of exchange drawn on a specified banker and not expressed to be payable otherwise than on demand and includes the electronic image of a truncated cheque and a cheque in the electronic form [Negotiable Instruments (Amendment and Miscellaneous Provisions) Act 2002].

A cheque is defined by the Bills of Exchange Act 1882, s. 73, as a bill of exchange drawn on a banker, payable on demand, and generally the provisions of that Act applicable to bills apply to cheques. [Halsbury's *Laws of England*, 4th Ed., vol. 3, para 38, p. 32].


- **False cheque** p. 341.
- **Holder of a cheque** p. 420.
- **Post-dated cheque** p. 672.
- **Traveller's cheque** p. 854.


**Child.** A young human being below the age of puberty; an unborn or newborn human being; one's son or daughter at any age; a young person of either sex at any age less than maturity, but most commonly one between infancy and youth; a legitimate son or daughter.

▸*Meaning under the Child Marriage Restraint Act 1929, s. 2(a).* Child means a person who, if a male, has not completed twenty-one years of age, and if a female has not completed eighteen years of age.

▸*Meaning under the Children Act 1960, s. 2(e).* Child means a boy who has not attained the age of sixteen years or a girl who has not attained the age of eighteen years.

▸*Meaning under the Children (Pleading of Labour) Act 1933, s. 2.* Child means a person who is under the age of fifteen years.

▸*Meaning under the Factories Act 1948, s. 2(c); Mines Act 1952, s. 2(e).* Child means a person who has not completed his fifteen years of age.

▸*Meaning under the Child Labour (Prohibition and Regulation) Act 1986, s. 2(11).* Child means a person who has not completed the age of 14 years.

The word 'child' has different meanings in different contexts. Where the word is used without reference to parentage, it is generally synonymous with the word 'infant' and means a person who has not attained majority. Where the word is used with reference to parentage, as in s. 125 (old s. 488), Criminal Procedure Code 1973, it means a descendant of the first degree, a son or a daughter, and has no reference to age. In certain context it may include descendants of more remote degree and be equivalent to 'issue'. [*Nanak Chand* v *Chandra Kishore* AIR 1970 SC 446: (1970)1 SCR 565: (1970)1 SCA 144: (1970)1 SCJ 176].

NOTE: In the interpretation of deeds and wills the presumption is that the expression 'child' means a legitimate child, or, if the disposition comes into operation after the date of legitimation, a legitimated person. It will now *prima facie* include an adopted child, where the adoption order was made before the date of the disposition. [Halsbury's *Laws of England*, 3rd Ed., vol. 21, p. 137].


- **Abandonment of child** p. 2.
- **Delinquent child** p. 246.
- **Illegitimate child** p. 428.
- **Posthumous child** p. 673.
- **Surrogate child** p. 824.


**Child marriage.** A marriage to which either of the contracting parties is a child. [Child Marriage Restraint Act 1929, s. 2(*b*)].

**Chit fund organisation.** A chit fund organisation is an organisation of a number of people who join together and subscribe amounts monthly so that that person or the subscriber who is in need of funds may draw the amount less discount. It is an organisation run on a co-operative basis for the benefit of the subscribers, the funds to be utilised by them as and when a particular subscriber needs it. [*Narasimloo* v *Rajanna* ILR (1958) AP 409].

**Chose in action.** The expression 'choses in action' or 'things in action' in the literal sense means things recoverable by action, as contrasted with a chose in possession which is a thing of which a person may have not only ownership but also actual physical possession. [Halsbury's *Laws of England*, 4th Ed., vol. 6, para 1, p. 2].

NOTE: A chose in action is known in India as an actionable claim defined by s. 3 of the Transfer of Property Act 1882. A chose in possession comes under "goods" as defined in s. 2(7) of the Sale of Goods Act 1930.

**Choultry.** It means a shelter or resting place for travellers.

Choultry is an ancient institution and is principally meant for lodging of pilgrims and travellers. In old days such institutions were some humble sheds and other structures to enable the pilgrims to stay for a short while when they came to visit temples and other religious places. The concept of a choultry today may be completely different from that with which one may be familiar a hundred years ago. There must, however, be no idea of profit motive in running or administering a choultry. Besides the expenditure for running a choultry with amenities should not be made with an idea to realise it from the visitors using the same. In other words, the choultry must in truth and reality bear the hall-mark of a charitable institution and should not partake of the character of a hotel run for profit. The choultry cannot be divorced from the other offices, shops and concerns which are mainly located within its precincts in order to render much needed and other necessary services to the pilgrims coming to pay homage to the Holy shrine. [*Municipal Council, Tirupathi* v *Tirumalai Tirupathi Devasthanam* (1974)1 SCC 683].

A 'choultry' or 'satram' is understood as a building ordinarily given free of rent or let on a very moderate rent, and such a building will never be of the character of a 'shopping complex-cum-lodging house'. [*Aliya Arabic College* v *Kasargod Municipality* (1988)2 Ker LT 11].

**C.I.F. contract.** See C.F.I. CONTRACT p. 135.

**Cinema.** A motion picture theatre; motion picture industry; the art or technique of making motion pictures.

Cinema is a building in which photographs or pictures are shown.

The word 'cinema' is an abbreviated form of cinematograph which, in its ordinary signification, includes a film exhibition. In common parlance a cinema is equated to a film exhibiting theatre. [*Nazeena Traders* v *Regional Provident Fund Commissioner* AIR 1965 AP 200].

**Cinematograph.** A camera for producing motion pictures, so constructed that a large number of separate exposures or frames are made in very rapid succession.

▸ *Meaning under the Copyright Act 1957, s. 2(f).* 'Cinematograph' shall be construed as including any work produced by any process analogous to cinematography.

▸ *Meaning under the Cinematograph Act 1952, s. 2.* It includes any apparatus for the representation of moving pictures or series of pictures.

NOTE: The VCR/VCP are within the ambit of the definition of 'cinematograph'. [*Laxmi Video Theatres* v *State of Haryana* AIR 1993 SC 2328: (1993)3 SCC 715].

**Circular.** A communication for general circulation; having the form of a circle; forming or bounded by a circle.

**Circular note.** A request in writing by a bank to one of its correspondents in a foreign country to pay a specified sum to a specified person.

Instruments, similar to "letters of credit" drawn by resident bankers upon their foreign correspondents, in favour of persons travelling abroad.

**Circulating capital.** 'Circulating capital' means capital employed in the trading operations of the business and the dealings with it comprise trading receipts and trading disbursements. [*Sutlej Cotton Mills Limited* v *Commissioner of Income Tax, Calcutta* (1978)4 SCC 358: (1979)1 SCR 976: (1979)116 ITR 1: AIR 1979 SC 5].

**Circumstances.** Attendant or accompanying facts, events or conditions; subordinate or accessory facts.

As used in a statute for an allowance for the wife in a divorce action, having regard to the "circumstances" of the parties, it includes practically everything which has a legitimate bearing on present and prospective matters relating to the lives of both parties.

In the matter of imposition of tax on "circumstances", the word "circumstances" means a man's financial position, his status as a whole depending, among other things, on his income from trade or business. [*Ram Narain* v *State of Uttar Pradesh* AIR 1957 SC 18: 1956 SCA 1114: 1956 SCR 664: 1956 SCJ 725].

• **Change in the circumstances.** The expression "change in the circumstances" ordinarily implies a change in the material circumstances of the party, his property or otherwise, the increase or decrease of his liabilities and so forth.

NOTE: *Meaning under the Criminal Procedure Code 1973, s. 127.* 'Change in the circumstances' means change in the existence of circumstances of the party paying or receiving (maintenance) allowance, which would justify an increase or decrease of the monthly payment (maintenance allowance) originally fixed (under s. 125). [*Meenakshi* v *J. Balakrishnan* 1980 Cr LJ 1200: 1980 MLJ (Cr) 293]. The circumstances contemplated must include financial circumstances, and in that view, the inquiry as to the change of circumstances must extend to a change of financial circumstances of the wife. [*Bhagwan Dutt* v *Kamala Devi* AIR 1975 SC 93: 1975 Cr LJ 40].

**Circumstantial evidence.** Circumstantial evidence is evidence that tends to prove a fact by proving other events or circumstances which afford a basis for a reasonable inference of the occurrence of the fact in issue or otherwise.

NOTE: All judicial evidence is either direct or circumstantial. Evidence is direct when the principal fact is proved directly by witnesses or documents. When it is proved by circumstances, the evidence is indirect and called circumstantial evidence. And the latter may be of two kinds—conclusive and presumptive.

Circumstantial evidence is presumptive proof, when the fact itself is not proved by direct testimony, but is to be inferred from circumstances, which either necessarily or usually attend such facts. It is obvious that a presumption is more or less likely to be true according as it is more or less probable that the circumstances would not have existed unless the fact which is inferred from them had also existed; and that a presumption can only be relied on until the contrary is actually proved. [Wharton's *Law Lexicon*].

The circumstantial evidence should not be consistent with the guilt of the accused but should be inconsistent with the innocence. [*Mangleshwarri Prasad* v *State* AIR 1954 SC 715: 1954 Cr LJ 1797; *Vidyasagar* v *State of U.P.* AIR 1977 SC 1116: 1977 Cr LJ 950].

It is a settled rule of "circumstantial evidence" that where circumstances are susceptible of two equally possible inferences, the courts should accept that inference which favours the accused rather than an inference which goes in favour of the prosecution. [*Ram Das* v *State of Maharashtra* AIR 1977 SC 1164: (1977)2 SCC 124: 1977 Cr LJ 955: 1977 SCC (Cri) 254].

**Citation.** The citing of a book or other source; a mention in an official dispatch; a note accompanying an award, describing the reasons for it; a public commendation for exceptional military conduct or achievement; a judicial summons; a court-issued writ that commands a person to appear at a certain time and place to do something demanded in the writ, or to show cause for not doing so; calling upon a person who is not a party to an action or proceeding to appear before the court; a reference to a legal precedent or authority, such as a case, statute, or treatise, that either substantiates or contradicts a given position.

**Citizen.** A member of a State, either native or naturalized.

Citizen, in relation to a country specified in the First Schedule to the Citizenship Act, means a person who, under the citizenship or nationality law for the time being in force in that country, is a citizen or national of that country. [Citizenship Act 1955, s. 2(*b*)].

Citizens are those persons who have full political rights as distinguished from nationals who may not enjoy full political rights and are still domiciled in that country. [*State Trading Corporation of India Ltd.* v *Commercial Tax Officer* AIR 1963 SC 1811: (1963)2 SCJ 605; (1963)33 Comp Cas 1057].

NOTE: Every person who has his domicile in the territory of India shall be a citizen of India, if he was born in the territory of India or either of whose parents were so born or who has been ordinarily resident in the territory of India for not less than five years immediately preceding the commencement of the Constitution (Art. 5). Secondly, any person who has migrated to the territory of India from the territory included in Pakistan shall be deemed to be a citizen of India, if he satisfied the conditions laid down in Arts. 6(*a*) and 6(*b*)(*i*). Any person who does not come within the purview of Arts. 6(*a*) and 6(*b*)(*i*), but who has migrated to India and has been registered, as laid down in Art. 6(*b*)(*ii*), shall also be deemed to be a citizen of India. Similarly a person of Indian origin, residing outside India shall be deemed to be a citizen of India if he has been registered as such by an accredited diplomatic or consular representative of India in the country where he has been residing (Art. 8). [*State Trading Corporation of India Ltd.* v *Commercial Tax Officer* AIR 1963 SC 1811: (1963)2 SCJ 605: (1963)33 Comp Cas 1057].

Under the Constitution, all citizens are persons but all persons are not citizens. Accordingly, juristic persons are not citizens. [*State Trading Corporation of India Ltd.* v *Commercial Tax Officer*, supra].

**Citizenship.** The status of being a citizen; the quality of an individual's response to membership in a community.

NOTE: *Citizenship and nationality—distinction.* Citizenship and nationality are not interchangeable terms. Nationality has reference to jural relationship which may arise for consideration under international law. On the other hand, citizenship has reference to the jural relationship under municipal law. In other words, nationality determines the civil rights of a person, natural or artificial, particularly with reference to international law, but citizenship is intimately connected with civic rights under municipal law. Accordingly all citizens are nationals of the particular State, but all nationals may not be citizens of the State. [*State Trading Corporation* v *Commercial Tax Officer* AIR 1963 SC 1811: (1963)2 SCJ 605].

**Civil.** Of or relating to citizens (as civil liberties); of or relating to the State or its citizenry; of, relating to, or based on civil law; relating to private rights and to remedies sought by action or suit distinct from criminal proceedings; established by law.

The word 'civil' according to dictionary means relating to the citizen as an individual; 'civil rights'. In Black's *Law Dictionary*, it is defined as "relating to provide rights and remedies sought by civil actions as contrasted with criminal proceedings". In law it is understood as an antonym of criminal. Historically the two broad classifications were civil and criminal, revenue, tax and company etc. were added to it later. But they too pertain to the larger family of 'civil'. [*Most Re V.P.M.A. Metropolitan* v *Moran Mar Marthoma* AIR 1995 SC 2001: 1995 Supp (4) SCC 286: JT 1995(5) SC 1].

NOTE: The word 'civil' is used in a number of senses. It is used in contrast with 'military'. [*State* v *Keshav Sen* AIR 1960 Raj 279].

**Civil commotion.** A riot or similar disturbance; a public uprising by a large number of people who, acting together, cause harm to people or property.

It means an insurrection of the people for general purposes, though not amounting to rebellion, but it is probably not capable of any very precise definition. The elements of turbulence or tumult are essential ...... The term thus expresses a stage intermediate between riot and civil war, although technically it no doubt includes a riot. Once fighting begins, however, matters have got beyond a mere civil commotion. [Halsbury's *Laws of England*, 4th Ed., vol. 25, para 623, p. 323; *Damodardas Nagori* v *Ruby General Insurance* AIR 1965 MP 32].

**Civil contempt.** Civil contempt means wilful disobedience to any judgment, decree, direction, order, writ or other process of a court or wilful breach of an undertaking given to a court. [Contempt of Courts Act 1971, s. 2(*b*)].

NOTE: Contempt may be committed by a person by wilfully disobeying the order or process of court or wilfully committing breach of undertaking given to a court. Mere disobedience or breach, as the case may be, will not be sufficient to find contempt. Wilfulness will have to be found on the facts and circumstances. Once that is found, the court must take serious notice of the contemner's conduct. The order, even erroneous if it is, calls for compliance and there can then be no excuse. The contempt in such a case will be civil contempt. [*Vincent Panikulangara* v *V.R. Krishna Iyer* (1983)2 Crimes 618 (Ker): 1983 Ker LT 829].

**Civil court.** Courts constituted for deciding purely civil question between persons seeking their civil rights should be considered to be civil courts, though they may be constituted by special statutes. [*Sriramarao* v *Suryanarayanamurthi* AIR 1954 Mad 340].

NOTE: A Deputy Commissioner acting as revenue authority is a civil court. [*Arakhita Das* v *Hari Mohapatra* ILR (1963) Cut 628: AIR 1963 Ori 162]. Civil court in a wider sense includes revenue court. [*State of Rajasthan* v *Keshav Sen* AIR 1960 Raj 279].

**Civil death.** The loss of rights—such as the rights to vote, make contracts, inherit, and sue—by a person who has been outlawed or convicted of a serious crime, or who is considered to have left the temporal world for the spiritual by entering a monastery. [Black's *Law Dictionary*, 8th Ed.].

Civil death is the status of a living person equivalent in its legal consequences to natural death, especially extinguishment of civil rights and duties.

NOTE: A person who enters into a religious order renouncing all worldly affairs is regarded as civilly dead.

**Civil defence.** Civil defence includes any measures not amounting to actual combat, for affording protection to any person, property, place or thing in Indian or any part of the territory thereof against any hostile attack, whether from air, land, sea or other places, or for depriving any such attack of the whole or part of its effect, whether such measures are taken before, during, at or after the time of such attack.

[Civil Defence Act 1968, s. 2(*a*); Defence of India Act 1971, s. 2(*a*)].

▸*Meaning under the Defence of India Act 1962, s. 2(a).* Civil defence includes any measures not amounting to actual combat, for affording defence against any form of hostile attack by a foreign power or for depriving any form of hostile attack by a foreign power of its effect either wholly or in part whether such measures are taken before, during or after the time of the attack.

**Civil law.** That body of law which every particular nation has established for itself. It is more properly called "municipal" law, to distinguish it from the "law of nature", and from international law.

Laws concerned with civil or private rights and remedies, as contrasted with criminal laws, are called civil laws.

**Civil liberty.** Freedom of action and speech subject to the law; freedom of the individual citizen from government control or restraint of, or interference with, his property, opinions, or affairs, except as the public good may require; freedom from undue governmental interference or restraint.

Personal, natural rights guaranteed and protected by Constitution; e.g. freedom of speech, press, freedom from discrimination, etc. Body of law dealing with natural liberties, shorn of excesses which invade equal rights of others. Constitutionally, they are restraints on government. [*Sowers* v *Ohio Civil Rights Commission* 252 NE 2d 463, 476].

**Civil list.** It is the annual sum granted by the British Parliament at the commencement of each reign for the expenses of the Royal household and establishment. It is the provision made for the Crown out of the taxes, in lieu of its proper patrimony, and in consideration of the assignment of that patrimony to the public use. The Civil List Act 1972, as amended by SI 1975 No. 133, fixed the Civil List at the annual sum of £1,400,000.

**Civil offence.** Term used to describe violations of statutes making the act a public nuisance. Also describes an offence which is *malum prohibitum* and not considered reprehensible. [Black's *Law Dictionary*, 5th Ed.].

An offence which is triable by a criminal court. [Army Act 1950, s. 3(*ii*); Air Force Act 1950, s. 4(*xii*); Border Security Force Act 1968, s. 2(*d*)].

Every offence of which Magistrates can take cognizance as a trial court or while holding inquiry before commitment to the Court of Session or to the High Court is a civil offence. [*Saliman Bibi* v *Hafiz Mohammad* AIR 1964 All 371: (1964)2 Cr LJ 184].

**Civil post.** A post other than a post connected with defence and a person who is serving under the State in a civil capacity is ordinarily a person who holds a civil post, even if such post is temporary. [*R. Christopher* v *Executive Engineer, Irrigation Workshop, Izatanagar* AIR 1966 All 97: (1966)1 Lab LJ 799].

NOTE: A civil post is distinguished in Art. 310 of the Constitution of India from a post connected with defence; it is a post on the civil as distinguished from the defence side of the administration, an employment in a civil capacity under the Union or a State. [*State of Assam* v *Kanak Chandra Dutta* AIR 1967 SC 884: (1967)1 SCR 679: (1967)2 SCJ 461: (1967)1 SCWR 228].

Civil post in Art. 311 of the Constitution of India, *prima facie* means an appointment or office on the civil side of the administration as distinguished from a post under the Defence Forces. [*Brojo Gopal* v *Commissioner of Police* 59 CWN 628: AIR 1955 Cal 556].

**Civil prison.** Any jail or place used for detention of any criminal prisoner under the Prisons Act 1894, or under any other law for the time being in force. [Air Force Act 1950, s. 4(*xiii*); Army Act 1950, s. 3(*iii*); Border Security Force Act 1968, s. 2(*e*)].

NOTE: A judgment-debtor for the payment of money may be arrested and detained in civil prison under s. 51(*c*) and rr. 37 to 40 of Or. 21, Code of Civil Procedure. In case of disobedience of an order of injunction court has power to detain in civil prison the person guilty of such disobedience. [Code of Civil Procedure 1908, rr. 1 and 2, Or. 39].

**Civil proceeding.** It is a process for the recovery of individual right or redress of individual wrong; inclusive, in its proper legal sense, of suits by the Crown. [Stroud's *Judicial Dictionary*, 5th Ed.].

Civil proceeding includes, at least, all proceedings affecting civil rights which are not criminal. [*Ramesh* v *Gendalal Motilal* AIR 1966 SC 1445: (1966)2 SCA 83: (1966)2 SCJ 762].

Civil proceeding is a proceeding in which some rights to property or other civil rights are involved, no matter whether the jurisdiction of the court is ordinary, special or extraordinary. [*Dhanalakshmi Vilas* v *President, Cashew Industries* ILR (1961)2 Ker 43: AIR 1962 Ker 1].

NOTE: If the proceeding is in aid of establishing a civil right or for disputing one, it would be a civil proceeding. The test should be whether, but for the provisions of any statute, the right claimed or denied could be established in a civil court. Broadly speaking, if the proceedings taken establish or negative a man's office or would affect his right to property of any kind it will be a civil proceeding. [*Guru Gobinda* v *Sankari* AIR 1963 Cal 364].

▸ *Meaning under the Constitution of India, Art. 133.* The words "civil proceedings" cover all proceedings which directly affect civil rights. [*Arbind Kumar Singh* v *Nand Kishore Prasad* AIR 1968 SC 1227: (1968)3 SCR 322].

The expression 'civil proceeding' used in Art. 133(1) is wide enough to cover any proceeding of a civil nature decided by the High Court, whether in its original appellate or revisional jurisdiction. Further, if the proceeding involves the assertion or enforcement of a civil right, it is a civil proceeding. [*Union of India* v *R.D. Gupta* AIR 1970 Tripura 86].

NOTE: There is no ground for restraining the expression 'civil proceeding' only to those proceedings which arise out of civil suits or proceedings which are tried as civil suits, nor is there any rational basis for excluding from its purview proceedings instituted and tried in the High Court in exercise of its jurisdiction under Art. 226, where the aggrieved party seeks relief against infringement of civil rights by authorities purporting to act in exercise of the powers conferred upon them by revenue statutes. [*S.A.L. Narayan Row* v *Ishwarlal Bhagwandas* AIR 1965 SC 1818].

A proceeding under Art. 226 for a writ to bring up a proceeding for consideration must be a civil proceeding, if the original proceeding concerned civil rights. [*Ramesh* v *Gendalal Motilal Patni* AIR 1966 SC 1445: (1966)3 SCR 198].

**Civil remedy.** Remedy available in a court of civil jurisdiction apart from the liability of the offender to be punished under the criminal law.

**Civil rights.** The rights of citizens to political and social freedom and equality.

NOTE: In USA, civil rights mean the individual rights of personal liberty guaranteed by the Bill of Rights and by the 13th, 14th, 15th, and 19th Amendments, as well as by legislation such as the Voting Rights Act. In USA, civil rights include esp. the right to vote, the right of due process, and the right of equal protection under the law.

Civil rights are not limited to common law rights only and would include *inter alia* any right to property, reputation, status and office of a person, though these may be creatures of statutes. [*Guru Gobinda* v *Sankari Prasad* AIR 1963 Cal 364].

**Civil servant.** A member of a civil service.

They are persons who are members of civil service of the Union of India or an All India Service or a civil service of a State or who hold a civil post under the Union or a State, occupy in law a special position. The ordinary law of master and servant does not apply to them. [*Union of India* v *Tulsiram Patel* AIR 1985 SC 1416].

**Civil service.** The permanent professional branches of State administration, excluding military and judicial branches and elected politicians; the administrative branches of a government.

This term includes all servants of the State, other than holders of political or judicial offices, who are employed in a civil capacity and whose remuneration is paid wholly and directly out of monies voted by the legislature. Naval, military and air services do not form part of the civil service.

**Claim.** Demand as one's due or property; submit a request for payment under an insurance policy; a right or title to a thing; a contention or assertion.

A claim is a demand for something due or believed to be due; a right to something, especially a title to a debt, privilege or other thing in the possession of another; an assertion open to challenge; something that is claimed, especially a tract of land staked out.

The aggregate of operative facts giving rise to a right enforceable by a court; the assertion of an existing right, any right to payment or to an equitable remedy, even if contingent or provisional; a demand for money, property or a legal remedy to which one asserts a right. [Black's *Law Dictionary*, 8th Ed.].

The word "claim" means a demand for something as "due" or "to seek or ask for on the ground of right" etc. [*Hameedia Hardware Stores* v *B. Mohon Lal Sowcar* AIR 1988 SC 1060: (1988)2 SCC 513: (1988)3 SCR 384: JT 1988(1) SC 664].

The primary meaning of the word 'claim' is such as to attach it to the object that is claimed, and is not the same thing as the cause of action by which the claim may be supported or as the grounds on which it may be based. [*West Wake* v *Ching* (1956)3 All ER 821].

Ordinarily, the word 'claim' is used to mean the substantive claim and not any costs. Where the latter are also intended to be covered, the expression used is 'claim and cost'. [*Bharat Saw Mill Co. Ltd.* v *Tarapada Sru* ILR (1951)1 Cal 341].


- **Actionable claim** p. 33.
- **Counter-claim** p. 200.
- **Third party claims** p. 842.


**Claim of right.** The expression 'claim of right' does not refer to actual legal right. It means belief in legal right. [*Pappu* v *Damodaran* AIR 1968 Ker 126].

**Class.** A group of people, things, qualities or activities having common features, traits or characteristics.

▶ *Meaning under the Constitution of India, Art. 15(4).* The word 'class' means a homogeneous section of the people grouped together because of certain likeness or common traits and who are identifiable by some common attributes, such as, status, rank, occupation, residence in a locality, race, religion and the like. In determining whether a particular section forms a class, caste cannot be excluded altogether, but the determination solely based upon the caste or community cannot be accepted. [*State of Andhra Pradesh* v *P. Sagar* (1968)3 SCR 595: AIR 1968 SC 1379: 1969 SCD 372: (1969)1 SCA 82: (1968)2 SCJ 778; *Triloki Nath Tiku* v *State of J&K* AIR 1969 SC 1: (1969)1 SCJ 306: (1969)1 SCWR 489].

**Classification.** Arrangement into groups or categories on the basis of established criteria.


- **Reasonable classification** p. 729.


**Clause.** A single statement in a treaty, law, bill or contract; a separate statement or proviso in a legal document; a distinct section or provision of a legal document or instrument.

A clause in a will means some collocation of words in the will which, when removed out of the will, will leave the rest of the will intelligible. There is no rule which says that the clause itself must be capable of being read as a document by itself if taken alone. [*Swinton* v *Bailey* (1878)4 App Cas 70, *per* Lord Cairns].


- **Attestation clause** p. 84.
- **Escalation clause** p. 315.
- **Estate clause** p. 320.
- **Gold clause** p. 389.
- **Habendum clause** p. 403.
- **Inchmaree clause** p. 444.
- **Interpretation clause** p. 476.
- **Saving clause** p. 776.
- **Testimonium clause** p. 839.

**Clear days.** When statute used the expression 'clear days' in respect of notice and appearance, it means exclusive of the days of sending of the notice and the day fixed for appearance. Sundays would be included but fraction of days would not count. [*J.N. Pramanick* v *D.M., Nadia* 81 CWN 986, 990].

**Clearance.** In maritime law, it means a certificate permitting a vessel to sail; the right of a ship to leave port, or the certificate issued by the port collector evidencing the ship's right to leave port.

It is a certificate issued by the customs showing that the vessel named in it has complied with the customs requirements and is authorised to proceed to sea; and the acts which have to be done at the customs to procure such a certificate constitutes the process of clearing the vessel. [*Thalmann Freres & Co.* v *Texas Star Flour Mills* (1899)15 TLR 471].

**Clerical error.** An error made in copying or writing out.

An error resulting from a minor mistake or inadvertence, esp. in writing or copying something on the record, and not from judicial reasoning or determination. [Black's *Law Dictionary*, 8th Ed.].

It means errors, mistakes, or omissions by clerk, writer, counsel, or judge which are not the result of exercise of judicial function. [*Pacific Finance Corporation of California* v *La Monte* 133 P 2d 921; *Wilson* v *City of Fergus Falls* 232 NW 322].

A clerical error is one made in transcribing or otherwise and it must be apparent on the face of the record and therefore capable of being corrected. It is in the nature of an inadvertent omission or mistake. The term 'clerical error' is distinguishable from a judicial error which can be corrected only on review or an appeal. [*Mansha Ram* v *Tej Bhan* ILR (1961)1 Punj 728: AIR 1962 Punj 110].

A clerical error is a mistake in writing or typing and is an error occasioned by an accidental slip or omission of the court. It represents that which the court never intended to say. It is an error apparent on the face of the record and does not depend for its discovery on argument or disputation. [*Smt. Sooraj Devi* v *Pyare Lal* AIR 1981 SC 736: (1981)2 SCR 485: (1981)1 SCC 500: 1981 Cr LJ 296: 1981 SCC (Cri) 188].

**Client.** A person who seeks advice and service of a lawyer; a person who entrusts his case to a lawyer in prosecuting or defending an action in a court of law; a person using the services of an architect or other professional person; a customer.

**Clog on equity of redemption.** Any provision inserted to prevent redemption on payment or performance of the debt or obligation for which the security was given is what is meant by a clog or fetter on the equity of redemption.

A clog is something which is inconsistent with the idea of security; it is in the nature of a repugnant condition. [*Santley* v *Wilde* (1899)2 Ch 474].

NOTE: In India the right of redemption is a statutory right which cannot be fettered by any condition which impedes or prevents redemption. [*Sher Khan* v *Swami Dayal* 49 IA 60: AIR 1922 PC 142; Transfer of Property Act 1882, s. 60].

**Closure.** A proceeding or procedure to stop debate in a deliberative body, especially in a legislative assembly, in order to secure a prompt vote.

A motion employed at a meeting to terminate debate and bring a matter to vote. Its object is to prevent undue obstruction. The closure motion may be moved by a member that the "question be now put". [See r. 244 of the Rules of the Rajya Sabha and r. 362 of the Rules of the Lok Sabha].

It also means a closing or shutting up, e.g., the closure of a factory.

▸ *Meaning under the Industrial Disputes Act 1947, s. 2(cc).* 'Closure' means the permanent closing down of a place of employment or part thereof. [*Hindustan Lever Employee's Union* v *State of Maharashtra* 1998 Mah LR 1365 (Bom)].

NOTE: In the case of a closure under Industrial Disputes Act 1947 the employer does not merely close down the place of business but he closes the business finally and irrevocably. The closure has to be genuine and *bona fide* in the sense that it should be a closure in fact and not a mere pretence of closure. [*Tatanagar Foundry Co. Ltd.* v *Their Workmen* (1969)3 SCC 464].

**Cloth.** 'Cloth' means 'piece of pliable, woven or felted stuff, suitable for wrapping or winding around, spreading or folding over, drying, wiping, or other purpose; a swaddling or winding cloth, wrap, covering, veil, curtain, handkerchief, towel, etc.' [*Oxford English Dictionary*].

The word 'cloth' means something made by weaving, felting, knitting or knotting, using natural or synthetic fibres. [*A. Marimuthu* v *Thiruhuraipundi Town Panchayat* (1992)1 MLW 111 (Summary of Cases)].

Cloth is woven, knitted or felted material which is pliable and is capable of being wrapped, folded or wound around. It need not necessarily be material suitable for making garments because there can be 'cloth' suitable only for industrial purpose; but nevertheless it must possess the basic feature of pliability. Hard and thick material which cannot be wrapped or wound around cannot be regarded as 'cloth'. [*Filterco* v *Commissioner of Sales Tax* (1986)2 SCC 103: (1986)1 SCR 239: AIR 1986 SC 626: (1986)24 ELT 180: (1986)61 STC 318].

- **Ready-made clothing.** The expression 'ready-made clothing' must mean clothing which is ready for immediate use and which is meant for such use. It cannot mean as article which may not be meant for immediate use in form which it is, but just happens to be in the shape of any article of appeal. [*Muralidhar Dalmia* v *State* 1952 All WR (HC) 664: 1953 Cr LJ 612: 1953 All LJ 129: AIR 1953 All 245 (DB)].

**Club.** A heavy stick with a thick end, used as a weapon; an association of persons united by a common interest, or object or for social intercourse.

Except a proprietary club or an investment club, it may be defined as a society of persons associated together, not for the purpose of trade, but for social reasons, the promotion of politics, sport, art, science or literature, or for any other lawful purpose; but trading, activities will not destroy the nature of a club if they are merely incidental to the club's purposes. [Halsbury's *Laws of England*, 4th Ed., vol. 6, para 201, p. 56].

A club is the most anomalous group of human beings that is known to law. It is a union of persons for social intercourse or for the promotion of certain pursuits which are closely allied to social intercourse, and the members usually regulate their conduct to which they subscribe. A club has no existence apart from its members. It differs from a corporation in that respect. [*Feeney* v *MacManus* 1937 IR 23].

**Co-opt.** To add as a member; to assimilate; absorb [Black's *Law Dictionary*, 8th Ed.]; take over; adopt.

Co-opt is to choose or elect as a fellow member or colleague. To bring in a new person as a member.

Co-opt means to elect into a body by the votes of its existing members. [*B.N. Singh* v *State of U.P.* AIR 1960 All 754].

The word is derived from 'opt' which means 'choose', and the choice necessarily involves ascertaining the wishes of the members already elected.

**Co-ordinate.** As verb means to bring (various parts, movements, etc.) into a proper or required relation to ensure harmony or effective operation; to act in harmonious and reciprocal relation; to work or act together effectively; to put in the same rank, class or order.

As adjective means equal in rank and importance; existing together in similar relation. Equal, of the same order, rank, degree or importance; not subordinate. [*Empire Ins. Co. of Texas* v *Cooper* Tex Civ App, 138 SW 2d 159, 164]. Example: Courts of coordinate jurisdiction.

As noun means one who or that which is of the same order, rank, power, etc.

**Co-ordination.** Harmonious or effective working together of different parts; the arrangement of parts etc. into an effective relation; the act of coordinating.

Co-ordination in its normal connotation means harmonizing or bringing into proper relation in which all things co-ordinated participate in a common pattern of action. The power to co-ordinate, therefore, is not merely power to evaluate; it is a power to harmonize or secure relationship for concerned action. [*Gujarat University* v *Shri Krishna Ranganath* AIR 1963 SC 703].

▸ *Meaning under the Constitution of India, Seventh Schedule, Union List, Entry 66.* The expression 'co-ordination' used in Entry 66 of the Union List of the Seventh Schedule to the Constitution does not merely mean evaluation. It means harmonisation with a view to forge a uniform pattern for a concerted action according to a certain design, scheme or plan of development. It, therefore, includes action not only for removal of disparities in standards but also for preventing the occurrence of such disparities. It would, therefore, also include power to do all things which are necessary to prevent what would make 'co-ordination' either impossible or difficult. [*State of Tamil Nadu* v *Adhiyaman Edu Research Institute* (1995)4 SCC 104].

**Co-owners.** Persons owning property jointly or in common.

NOTE: *Co-ownership and partnership—distinction.* One of the principal differences is that co-ownership is not necessarily the result of agreement, whereas partnership is. The second difference is that co-ownership does not necessarily involve community of profit or of loss, but partnership does. A third difference is that one co-owner can, without the consent of the other, transfer his interest, etc. to a stranger. A partner cannot do this. In a partnership each partner acts for all. In a co-ownership one co-owner is not as such the agent, real or implied, of the other. [*Champaran Cane Concern* v *State of Bihar* AIR 1963 SC 1737: (1964)2 SCR 921: (1963)49 ITR (SC) 152: (1962)2 SCJ 499].

**Codicil.** It is a supplement to a will, containing anything which the testator wishes to add or any explanation or revocation of what the will contains.

It is defined as a "supplement or addition to a ill, not necessarily disposing of the entire estate but modifying, explaining, or otherwise qualifying the will in some way". [Black's *Law Dictionary*, 8th Ed.].

▸ *Meaning under the Indian Succession Act 1925, s. 2(b).* "Codicil" means an instrument made in relation to a will, and explaining, altering or adding to its dispositions, and shall be deemed to form part of the will.

NOTE: A codicil is of a similar nature to a will as regards both its purposes and the formalities relating to it, but in general it is supplemental to and considered as annexed to a will previously made, being executed for the purpose of adding to, varying or revoking the provisions of that will. A codicil is nevertheless capable of independent existence, so that the revocation of a will does not necessarily affect the revocation of a codicil thereto. [Halsbury's *Laws of England*, 3rd Ed., vol. 39, p. 482].

When admitted to probate, the codicil becomes a part of the will.

**Codification.** The process of collecting and arranging systematically, usually by subject, the laws of a state or country, or the rules and regulations covering a particular area or subject of law or practice [Black's *Law Dictionary*, 5th Ed.]; the process of compiling, arranging, and systematizing the laws of a given jurisdiction, or of a discrete branch of the law, into an ordered code; and the code that results from this process. [Black's *Law Dictionary*, 8th Ed.].

**Coercion.** Compulsion by physical force or threat of physical force; conduct that constitutes the improper use of economic power to compel another to submit to the wishes of one who wields it. [Black's *Law Dictionary*, 8th Ed.].

"Coercion takes an infinite number of forms, but it may properly be thus defined: the moment that the person who influences the other does so by the threat of taking away from that other something he then possesses, or of preventing him from obtaining an advantage he would otherwise have obtained, then it becomes coercion and it ceases to be persuasion or consideration." [*Ellis* v *Barker* (1871)40 LJ Ch 603, 607, *per* Lord Romilly, M.R.].

▸ *Meaning under the Indian Contract Act 1872.* "Coercion" in s. 15 is the committing, or threatening to commit, any act forbidden by the Indian Penal Code, or the unlawful detaining, or threatening to detain, any property, to the prejudice of any person whatever, with the intention of causing any person to enter into an agreement.

"Coercion" in s. 72 must be understood in the ordinary sense. It includes every kind of compulsion even if it does not measure up to definition under s. 15 of the Contract Act. [*T.G.M. Asad* v *Coffee Board* AIR 1969 Mys 230].

NOTE: Actual violence is not necessary to constitute coercion; imaginary terrors may be sufficient for that purpose. [*Boyse* v *Rossborough* 6 HL Cas 2, 48].

The threat to commit suicide is coercion. [*Purabi Banerjee* v *Basudeb Mukherjee* AIR 1969 Cal 293].

**Cognate.** Related by blood; related on mother's side; related through a female; one who is kin to another.

One person is said to be a cognate of another if the two are related by blood or adoption but not wholly through males. [Hindu Succession Act 1956, s. 3(*c*)].

Word 'cognate' literally means 'akin in nature'. [*Ram Briskh* v *State* 1978 All Cr C 253].

In Roman law, the term means a blood relationship and implies that the kinship derives from a lawful marriage. In Scots and later civil law, the term implies kinship from the mother's side. [Black's *Law Dictionary*, 8th Ed.].

**Cognizable case.** Cognizable case means a case in which, a police officer may, in accordance with the First Schedule of the Code of Criminal Procedure or under any other law for the time being in force, arrest without warrant. [Code of Criminal Procedure 1973, s. 2(*c*)].

**Cognizance.** A court's right and power to try and determine cases; the taking of judicial or authoritative notice; acknowledgment, or admission of an alleged fact. [Black's *Law Dictionary*, 8th Ed.].

Cognizance means jurisdiction or right to try and determine causes, the right to take notice of and determine a cause. [*Bommarasegowda* v *B.T. Gundappa* AIR 1954 Mys 121].

The word 'cognizance' has no esoteric or mystic significance in criminal law or procedure. It merely means 'become aware of' and, when used with reference to a court or judge, to take notice of judicially. [*Ajit Kumar Palit* v *State of W.B.* (1963)1 SCR 955: (1963)1 Cr LJ 797: AIR 1963 SC 765: 1964 MLJ (Cr) 12: (1964)1 SCJ 75].

The word 'cognizance' means to apply mind for the purpose of taking cognizance in respect of the facts constituting the offence. [*Ramlakhan Mahto* v *Rameshwar Mahto* 1974 Pat LJR 476].

The word 'cognizance' indicates the point when a magistrate or a judge first takes judicial notice of an offence. [*State of West Bengal* v *Mohammed Khalid* (1995)1 SCC 684, 696].

It is a word of indefinite import, and is perhaps not always used in exactly the same sense. In its broad and literal sense it means 'taking notice of an offence' and would include the intention of initiating judicial proceedings against the offender in respect of that offence or taking steps to see whether there is any basis for initiating judicial proceedings or for other purposes. At the stage of taking cognizance, the magistrate has simply to be satisfied whether the allegations against the accused *prima facie* make out a case for trial or not and nothing beyond that. [*S.K. Siraj* v *State of Orissa* 1994 Cr LJ 2410, 2415 (Ori)].

NOTE: Taking cognizance does not involve any formal action or indeed action of any kind; it occurs as soon as a magistrate, as such, applies his mind to the suspected commission of the offence. [*Resulbaksh* v *Emperor* ILR (1943) Kant 524; *Dalu Gour* v *Moheshwar Mahato* 48 Cr LJ 347; *J.P. Varma* v *Emperor* ILR (1946) Nag 780].

Section 190 of the Code of Criminal Procedure 1973 empowers a Magistrate of the First and Second classes to take cognizance of an offence in three ways, *viz.*, (*i*) on complaint; (*ii*) on police report; and (*iii*) on information from any person other than a police officer, or upon his own knowledge.

• **Taking cognizance of an offence** p. 827.

**Cohabitation.** The fact or state of living together, especially as partners in life, usually with the suggestion of sexual relations. [Black's *Law Dictionary*, 8th Ed.].

Cohabitation means a dwelling or living together in conjugal relationship and not secret acts of intercourse. [*Maung Maung* v *Ma Sein Kui* AIR 1940 Rang 181].

Cohabitation means living together as husband and wife. Cohabitation consists in the husband acting as a husband towards the wife and the wife acting as a wife towards the husband; the wife rendering housewifely duties to the husband and the husband cherishing and supporting his wife as a husband should. Of course, sexual intercourse usually takes place between parties of moderate age, if they are cohabiting. [*Thomas* v *Thomas* (1948)2 KB 294; *Harvinder Kaur* v *Harmandar Singh* AIR 1984 Del 66, 69].

Cohabitation means the setting up of a matrimonial home together, although sexual intercourse is not a necessary ingredient of it. [Eversley on *Domestic Relations,* 6th Ed., p. 144].

NOTE: "The very word 'cohabitation' involves the conception that it must be bilateral". [*Cook* v *Cook* (1949)1 All ER 384 (DC), *per* Lord Merriman, P.].

"Cohabitation may be of two sorts, one continuous, the other intermittent. The parties may reside together constantly, or there may be only occasional intercourse between them, which may, nevertheless, amount to cohabitation in the legal sense of the term. Such cohabitation may indeed exist together with an agreement to live apart ... The circumstances of life, such as business duties, domestic service, and other things, may separate husband and wife, and yet, notwithstanding, there may be cohabitation." [*Huxtable* v *Huxtable* (1899)68 LJPC 83, 85 (DC), *per* Jeune, P.].

• **Illicit cohabitation** p. 428.
• **Lascivious cohabitation** p. 512.
• **Lewd and lascivious cohabitation** p. 531.

**Coin.** Coin is metal used for the time being as money, and stamped and issued by the authority of some State or Sovereign Power in order to be so used. [Indian Penal Code 1860, s. 230].

• **Indian coin.** Indian coin is metal stamped and issued by the authority of the Government of India in order to be used as money; and metal which has been so stamped and issued shall continue to be Indian coin notwithstanding that it may have ceased to be used as money. [Indian Penal Code 1860, s. 230].

**Coke.** The infusible, cellular, coherent residue obtained when coal is subjected to destructive distillation. It consists mainly of carbon, is hard, porous and grey, and has a submetallic luster. Any similar substance left as a residue when petroleum, shale oil, etc. are distilled to dryness. [*Indian Carbon Limited* v *Superintendent of Taxes, Gauhati* AIR 1972 SC 154: (1972)1 SCR 316: (1971)3 SCC 612: (1971)28 STC 603].

• **Coke oven plant.** "Coke oven plant" means the plant and equipment with which the manufacture of hard coke has been, or is being, carried on, and includes—(*i*) all lands, buildings, works, machinery and equipment, vehicles, railways, tramways and sidings, belonging to, or in the coke oven plant, (*ii*) all workshops belonging to the coke oven plant including buildings, machinery, instruments, store, equipment of such workshops and the lands on which such workshops stand, (*iii*) all coke in stock or under production, and other stores, stocks and instruments, belonging to the coke oven plant, (*iv*) all power stations belonging to the coke oven plant or operated for supplying electricity for the purpose of working the coke oven plant or a number of coke oven plants, (*v*) all lands, buildings and equipment belonging to the coke oven plant where the washing of coal is carried on, (*vi*) all other fixed assets, movable or immovable, and current assets belonging to a coke oven plant, whether within its premises or outside. [*Bharat Coking Coal Ltd.* v *Shri Parmeshwar Kumar Agarwala* (1979)3 SCC 609].

**Collateral.** Supplementary; accompanying, but secondary and subordinate to; not direct in line, but on a parallel or diverging line of descent; of or relating to persons who are related by blood but are neither ancestors nor descendants [Black's *Law Dictionary*, 8th Ed.]; side by side; parallel; additional.

'Collateral' means literally situated at the side, hence parallel or additional and not, if the nature of the transaction does not require it, secondary. [*In re Athill* 16 Ch D 211].

NOTE: A contract of guarantee is collateral to the principal contract between the creditor and the principal debtor.

- **Collateral consanguinity.** The relationship between persons (collateral relations) who are descended from the same ancestor (*e.g.*, brothers, cousins etc.); as opposed to *lineal consanguinity*, which exists between persons of whom one is descended from the other (father and son, grandfather and grandson, etc.). The latter persons are referred to as lineal ancestors or lineal descendants as the case may be.

- **Collateral security.** Security given in addition to the principal security in order to safeguard the interest of the creditor. [*Imperial Bank* v *Bengal National Bank* AIR 1930 Cal 536].

  Collateral security is any property which is assigned or pledged to secure the performance of an obligation and as additional thereto, and which upon the performance of the obligation is to be surrendered or discharged. [*In re Wiggins Ltd.* (1931) OR 337].

**Collection.** The act or process of collecting; things collected.

'Collection' in the context of a taxing statute can mean only recovery of tax already assessed and levied and in respect of which liability to pay has arisen. It is a stage which follows upon and cannot include the process of assessment and quantification of liability. [*Kantilal Popatlal* v *State* AIR 1966 Guj 268: (1966)7 Guj LR 96].

In banking, it means the process through which an item (such as a cheque) passes in a payor bank. [Black's *Law Dictionary*, 8th Ed.].

**Collective bargaining.** Negotiations between an employer and the representatives of organized employees to determine the conditions of employment, such as wages, hours, discipline, and fringe benefits [Black's *Law Dictionary*, 8th Ed.]; intermediation; interposition; mediatorship; negotiation.

**Collector.** One who or that which collects money etc. due (tax collector, rent collector); one who receives taxes, duties etc., or collects debts.

**Colliery.** The word 'colliery' includes or may include all contiguous and connected veins and seams of coal which are worked as one concern, together with the workings and machinery necessary for working the minerals, and the business of selling the coal worked. [Halsbury's *Laws of England*, 4th Ed., vol. 31, para 13, p. 16].

**Collocation.** The arrangement or marshalling of the creditors of an estate in the order in which they are to be paid according to law.

**Collusion.** A deceitful agreement or compact between two or more persons to do some act in order to prejudice a third person or for some improper purpose.

In legal matrix, it means a secret understanding between ostensible opponents in a law suit; a secret agreement between two persons that one should institute a suit against the other, in order to obtain the decision of a judicial tribunal for some sinister purpose [*Nagubai Ammal* v *B. Sharma Rao* AIR 1956 SC 593: 1956 SCR 451: 1956 SCJ 655: 1956 SCA 959: ILR (1956) Mys 152; *Rupchand* v *Raghuvanshi* AIR 1964 SC 1889: (1965)2 SCJ 584]; a secret agreement for illegal purposes or a conspiracy. [*Subhas Chandra* v *Ganga Prasad* AIR 1967 SC 878: (1967)1 SCR 331: (1967)2 SCJ 159].

Collusion is essentially play-acting by two or more persons for one common purpose—a concerted performance of a fabula disguised as a judicium—an unreal and fictitious pretence of a contest by confederates whose game is the same. [Spencer-Bower and Turner on *Res Judicata*, 2nd Ed., 1969, para 378]. Lord Selborne, LC in *Bosewell* v *Coaks* [(1894)6 Rep 167] stated there is no judge; but a person invested with the ensigns of a judicial office is misemployed in listening to a fictitious cause proposed to him, there is no party litigating ... no real interest brought into question and to use the words of a very sensible civilian on this point, *fabula non judicium, hoc est; in scena, non in foro, res agitur*. That is the true meaning of the word 'collusion' as applied to a judicial proceeding. [*Gram Panchayat of Village Naulakha* v *Ujagar Singh* (2000)7 SCC 543: JT 2000 Supp (2) SC 1].

The word 'collusion' means a secret agreement for illegal purposes or a conspiracy. The use of the word 'collusion' suggests that a person knew what he was about and that he did it secretly or fraudulently. Collusion implies that a man does something evil designedly. [*Subhash Chandra Dass Mushib* v *Ganga Prasad Munship* AIR 1967 SC 878: (1967)1 SCWR 271: (1967)2 SCJ 159: (1967)1 SCR 331].

Collusion implies a community of purpose and intention between parties colluding. [*Indo-Allied Industries* v *Punjab National Bank* AIR 1970 All 108]. It implies the existence of two or more parties capable of dealing with each other independently with the object of entering into an arrangement which may serve as a cloak to cover up the real state of affairs. When one party is in the position to dominate the will of the other, it would not be a case of collusion but compulsion. [*V.S. Rahi* v *Ram Chambeli* (1984)1 SCC 612].

**Collusive proceeding.** If in a judicial proceeding the claim made is fictitious and the contest between the parties unreal and the decree passed therein is a mere mask having the similitude of a judicial determination and worn by the parties, the proceeding is collusive. [*Varadammal* v *Ambala* (1971)1 MLJ 65].

NOTE: *Collusive proceeding and fraudulent proceeding—distinction.* There is a fundamental distinction between a collusive and a fraudulent proceeding in that while the former is the result of an understanding between the parties, both the claim and the contest being fictitious and the purpose to confound third parties, in the latter the contest is real, though the claim is untrue, and the purpose is to injure the defendant by a verdict of the court obtained by practising fraud in it. [*Nagubai Ammal* v *B. Shama Rao* AIR 1956 SC 593: 1956 SCR 451: 1956 SCJ 655].

**Colony.** A body of emigrants or their descendants in a remote region under the control of a parent country; any aggregation of individuals in a common group, as of alien residents in a country, or of bees, beavers, etc.

A dependent territorial entity subject to the sovereignty of an independent country, but considered part of that country for purposes of relations with third countries; a group of people who live in a new territory but retain ties with their parent country; the territory inhabited by such a group. [Black's *Law Dictionary*, 8th Ed.].

**Colourable.** The opposite of '*bona fide*'; that which is not what it purports to be; intended to deceive; deceptive; counterfeit, e.g. the court found the conveyance to be a colourable transfer.

'Colourable' is not tainted with bad faith or evil motive, it is not pejorative or crooked. Colourability is conceptually bound up with incompetency. A thing is colourable which is, in appearance only and not in reality, what it purports to be. In Indian terms, it is 'maya'. [*R.S. Joshi, Sales Tax Officer, Gujarat* v *Ajit Mills Ltd.* AIR 1977 SC 2279: 1977 SCC (Tax) 536: (1977)40 STC 497: (1977)4 SCC 98: (1978)1 SCR 338].

**Colourable imitation or variation.** In trademarks, it means any mark, whether or not created with an intent to deceive, whose resemblance to a registered mark is likely to cause confusion or mistake. [Black's *Law Dictionary*, 8th Ed.].

A mark can be said to be a colourable imitation of another mark when it is not really initiation of any other mark but just appears to be so and can pass off as such. [*Kundan Lal* v *State* AIR 1958 All 643: 1958 Cr LJ 1102].

NOTE: No general rule can be laid down as to what is or is not a mere colourable variation from a trade mark. All which can be done is to ascertain in every case, as it occurs, whether there is such a resemblance as to deceive a purchaser using ordinary caution. [*Leather Cloth Co.* v *American Leather Cloth Co.* (1865)11 HL Cas 523].

**Colourable legislation.** When a court says that a particular legislation is a colourable one, it means that the legislature has transgressed its legislative powers in an overt or indirect manner, it adopts a device to outslep the limits of its power. [*P. Vajravelu Mudaliar* v *Special Deputy Collector for Land Acquisition, Madras* (1964)2 SCJ 703: (1964)2 SCA 396: AIR 1965 SC 1017].

The idea conveyed by the expression 'colourable legislation' is that although apparently the legislature in passing the statute purported to act within the limits of its powers, yet in substance and in reality transgressed these powers, the transgression being veiled by what appears on proper examination, to be a pretence or disguise. [*V. Sesha Sharma* v *State of A.P.* AIR 1960 AP 461].

NOTE: The doctrine of colourable legislation does not involve any question of *bona fide* or *mala fide* on the part of the legislative. The whole doctrine resolves itself into the question of competency of a particular legislature to enact a particular law. [*K.C. Gajapathi Narayan Deo* v *State* AIR 1953 SC 375: 1953 SCJ 592: 1954 SCR 1]. The idea conveyed by the expression is that although apparently a legislature in passing a statute purported to act within the limits of its powers, yet in substance and in reality it transgressed these powers, the transgression being veiled by what appears on proper examination, to be a mere pretence or disguise. [*K.C. Gajapathi Narayan Deo* v *State,* supra; *Gullapalli Nageswara Rao* v *Andhra Pradesh State Road Transport Corporation* AIR 1959 SC 308; 1959 Supp (1) SCR 319].

Legislation ostensibly under one or other powers conferred by the Constitution but in truth and fact not falling within the content of that power is merely colourably constitutional, but is really not so. [*State of Bihar* v *Kameshwar* AIR 1952 SC 252].

**Comity of nations.** Comity, as between nations, is the recognition by each of the laws of the others whenever those laws are applicable and this recognition is limited by the paramount regard which each country has for its own laws and its own citizens.

NOTE: The expression is generally used to indicate the practice adopted by the courts of justice in one country of giving effect to the laws of another country and the judgments given by its courts. [Mozley & Whiteley's *Law Dictionary*].

**Commencement.** A beginning; origin.

Commoncement, used with reference to an Act or Regulation, shall mean the day on which the Act or Regulation comes into force. [General Clauses Act, s. 3(13)]. An Act can only commence in a particular area on the date on which that Act comes into force in that area. The mere fact that it was in operation in other areas will not result in the Act having commenced in the area where it had not yet been applied. [*M. Manickchand* v *Elias Saleh Mohamed Sait* (1969)1 SCC 206].

**Commencement of tenancy.** The expression refers to the original or first tenancy under which the tenant or his predecessors-in-title entered into possession of the land as a tenant and since then he or his predecessors-in-title have been in continuous and uninterrupted possession of the land. [*Bahiman* v *Raje Nilkanthrao* AIR 1960 Bom 271].

**Comment.** An explanatory statement made by the drafters of a particular statute, code section, or rule [Black's *Law Dictionary,* 7th Ed.]; annotation; interpretation; remark; word of explanation.

• **Fair Comment** p. 339.

**Commerce.** Financial transactions, especially the buying and selling of merchandise, on a large scale. [*Laxmi Engineering Works* v

*P.S.G. Industrial Institute* AIR 1995 SC 1428: (1995)3 SCC 583: JT 1995(3) SC 433: (1995)84 Comp Cas 121].

The exchange of goods and services, especially on a large scale involving transportation between cities, states, and nations. [Black's *Law Dictionary*, 8th Ed.].

Commerce is "traffick", trade, or merchandize, in buying and selling of goods. [*People* v *Fisher* 14 Wend 15].

'Commerce' involves essentially an exchange or buying and selling of commodities. The element of trade is contained in it. [*Ram Swarup* v *Janki Das Jai Kumar* AIR 1976 Del 219: ILR (1976)1 Del 153].

In a popular or narrower sense 'commerce' is sometimes used to refer to external trade or dealings with other countries. [Tomlin's *Law Dictionary*].

**Commercial.** 'Commercial' denotes 'pertaining to commerce'. It means 'connected with, or engaged in commerce; mercantile; having profit as the main aim'. [*Laxmi Engineering Works* v *P.S.G. Industrial Institute* AIR 1995 SC 1428: (1995)3 SCC 583: JT 1995(3) SC 433: (1995)84 Comp Cas 121].

**Commercial causes.** These are causes (or cases) that arise out of the transactions of merchants and traders, especially those relating to the construction of mercantile documents, export or import of merchandise, affreightment, insurance, banking and mercantile agency and mercantile usages.

**Commercial establishment.** Only those premises can be said to be a commercial establishment where two minds meet to strike a business deal for profit. The purpose of the meeting of the two minds is to be for profit, though the profit may not be the necessary result. [*Ram Chander* v *State* AIR 1963 Punj 148].

NOTE: The establishment of a chartered accountant is not covered by the definition of commercial establishment. [*N.K. Merchant* v *State* AIR 1968 Bom 283: (1968)1 Lab LJ 187: 1968 Cr LJ 1041].

Traditionally, lawyers do not carry on a trade or business nor do they render services to customers. Thus, the office of a lawyer or firm of lawyers cannot be comprehended within the meaning of the expression 'commercial establishment'. [*V. Sashidharan* v *M/s. Peter and Karunakar* AIR 1984 SC 1700: (1984)4 SCC 230: (1985)1 SCR 601].

**Commercial premises.** Nothing more than premises used for purposes of business [*Palghat Electric Corporation* v *Veeraraghava* AIR 1941 Mad 439]. The premises used for commercial purpose means premises used for business which entails the element of profit and loss to a person. If certain premises are used for doing a business the object of which is to make a profit, then the premises is used for commercial purpose. [*Amalgamated Electricity Co.* v *State of Rajasthan* AIR 1983 Raj 154].

**Commission.** A warrant or authority, from the government or a court, that empowers the person named to execute official acts; the authority under which a person transacts business for another; a body of persons acting under lawful authority to perform certain public services; the act of doing or perpetrating; a fee paid to an agent or employee for a particular transaction, usually as a percentage of the money received from the transaction. [Black's *Law Dictionary*, 8th Ed.].

The word 'commission' is one of equivocal meaning. It is used to denote a trust or authority exercised, or the instrument by which the authority is exercised, or the persons by whom the trust or authority is exercised. [*R.* v *Dudman* 4 B&C 854, *per* Abbott, C.J.].

With reference to financial matters, the word commission means allowances made to agents or others for effecting sales or carrying out business transactions.

In matters of insurance, commission is an amount settled before hand which goes to the person who brings the business for the company. [*State of Maharashtra* v *Chandrakant Solanki* 1995 Cr LJ 832 (Bom)].

NOTE: *'Commission' and 'rebate'—distinction.* Commission is an allowance for service or labour in discharging certain duties. Mostly it is a percentage on price or value or upon the amount of money involved in the transaction. Rebate, on the other hand, is a remission or a payment back and is of the nature of deduction from the gross amount. It is a discount and includes a refund of a portion of the price paid by a purchaser. [*Cotton Pressing Factory* v *Commissioner of Income Tax* ILR (1960) Bom 987: 62 Bom LR 675].

**Commission agent.** One who sells or buys goods for another and receives by way of remuneration a commission or percentage upon the amount involved in each transaction.

In matters of agriculture, 'commission agent' means a person who on behalf of his principal trader and in consideration of a commission or percentage upon the amount involved in such transaction buys agricultural produce and makes payment in cash, keeps it in his custody and delivers it to the principal trader in due course or who receives and takes in his custody agricultural produce sent for sale within the market area or from outside the market area, sells the same in the market area and collects payment therefor, from the buyer and remits the sale proceeds to his principal trader. [*State of MP* v *Shrinath* AIR 1994 SC 2538: (1994)4 SCC 707: (1994)95 STC 565: JT 1994(4) SC 471: 1994 AIR SCW 3583].

**Commission del credere.** The commission received by the seller's agent for guaranteeing a buyer's debt. [Black's *Law Dictionary*, 7th Ed.].

The phrase *'del credere'* is borrowed from the Italian language, in which its signification is equivalent to our word 'guarantee' or 'warrantee'.

**Commission merchant.** One who buys and sells goods, either as an agent for a commission, or as a trader or merchant for his own account.

**Commissioner.** A person who is given a mission of work by an order of court; a person who holds a commission to perform certain acts or a specific task; a public official appointed as head of an executive department, usually on a state or municipal level.

A person who directs a commission; a member of a commission; the administrative head of an organization, such as a professional sport. [Black's *Law Dictionary*, 8th Ed.].

▸ *Meaning under the General Clauses Act, s. 3(14).* The chief officer-in-charge of the revenue administration of a division.

A person authorised by letters-patent, Act of Parliament, or other lawful warrant, to examine any matters, or execute any public office, etc. [Wharton's *Law Lexicon*, 14th Ed., p. 217].

**Commit.** Commit means to entrust; to place in a prison or mental hospital; to send one to take his trial in a court of law.

To do; perpetrate; place in trust or custody; devote, pledge.

To perpetrate (a crime); to send (a person) to prison or to a mental health facility, esp. by court order. [Black's *Law Dictionary*, 8th Ed.].

"The meaning of 'commit' ......... is to 'perpetrate'—to do a fault—to be guilty of a crime; and 'perpetrate' is to commit, to act—always in an ill sense". [*Clift* v *Schwabe* 17 LJCP 2, *per* Pollock, C.B.].

**Committee.** A body of persons appointed for a specific function by, and usually out of, a larger body; a person entrusted with the charge of another person or another person's property.

A group of people appointed or elected to consider, determine, or manage a matter. [Black's *Law Dictionary*, 7th Ed.].

A subordinate group to which a deliberative assembly or other organisation refers business for consideration, investigation, oversight, or action. [Black's *Law Dictionary*, 8th Ed.].

'Committee' is he to whom the consideration or ordering of any matter is referred either by some court or consent of the parties to whom it pertains. [*Prakash*

*Kumar Nemichand Parakh* v *Collector of Nashik* AIR 1994 Bom 94].

"The term 'committee' means an individual or a body to which others have committed or delegated a particular duty, or who have taken on themselves to perform it in the expectation of their act being confirmed by the body they profess to represent or act for". [*Reynell* v *Lewis* 16 LJ Ex 30, *per* Pollock, C.B.].

'Committee' simply means a person or persons to whom anything is committed. [*Re Scottish Petroleum Co.* 51 LJ Ch 845, *per* Kay, J.].

It has got other meanings too. It may mean a 'person who is civilly committed, usually to a psychiatric hospital, *e.g.*, the board determined that the committee was dangerous and should not be released.' It may also mean the 'guardian for the person so committed, *e.g.*, the patient's lawyer objected to the appointment of the committee. [Black's *Law Dictionary*, 8th Ed.].

**Committee of inspection.** It is a committee appointed by the court at the time of making an order for winding up a company or any time thereafter to act with the liquidator. The committee has the right to inspect the accounts kept by the official liquidator. No member of the committee can purchase any property of the company, since he is in a fiduciary position. [*Durga Prasad* v *Official Liquidator Banaras Bank* AIR 1963 SC 1322].

It is also defined as a committee consisting of trustee or trustees appointed by the general body of creditors of a bankrupt, for the purpose of superintending the administration of the bankrupt's properties.

**Committing Magistrate.** 'Committing Magistrate' means the Magistrate who commits the case for trial to the Court of Sessions.

The phrase 'Committing Magistrate' is merely a compendious way of referring to the Magistrate who held the preliminary enquiry on which the committal was made.

**Commodum ex injuria sua nemo habere debet.** No one ought to derive benefit from injury perpetrated by himself.

**Common carrier.** An individual or company which, for a fee, provides public transport.

A carrier that is required by law to transport passengers or freight, without refusal, if the approved fare or charge is paid. [Black's *Law Dictionary*, 7th Ed.].

A commercial enterprise that holds itself out to the public as offering to transport freight or passengers for a fee. [Black's *Law Dictionary*, 8th Ed.].

"A common carrier is one who, in the language of Lord Holt in *Coggs* v *Bernard* [(1703)2 Lord Raym 909], exercises a public employment; and the law charges him 'to carry goods against all events, but acts of God, and of the enemies of the King'". [*Crouch* v *London & North Western Ry. Co.* (1854)14 CB 255, 296, *per* Cresswell, J.].

"A common carrier is a person who professes to carry for whosoever is willing to employ him, and is responsible for any damage to the goods in his possession though guilty of no negligence, unless such damage is caused by certain excepted things". [*Tamvaco* v *Timothy & Green* (1882) Cab & El 1, 2, *per* Cave, J.].

▸*Meaning under the Carriers Act 1865, s. 2.* Common carrier denotes a person, other than the Government, engaged in the business of transporting for hire property from place to place, by land or inland navigation, for all persons indiscriminately.

NOTE: To constitute a person a common carrier he must be ready to carry for hire or a business and not as a casual occupation. It is essential that he should hold himself out as being ready to carry goods for any person or to carry any passengers no matter who they may be. If he carries for particular persons or certain passengers only he is not a common carrier, and the relationship between him and the owner of the goods or the passengers is one of special contract. If he retains a right of selection as to whom or what he shall carry he is not a common carrier. [Halsbury's *Laws of England*, 3rd Ed., vol. 4, pp. 130, 131].

To render a person liable as a common carrier he must exercise the business of carrying as a public employment and must undertake to carry goods for all persons indiscriminately and hold himself out, either expressly or by course of conduct, as ready to engage in the transportation of goods for hire as a business and not merely as a casual occupation. [*Ramalinga Nadar* v *Narayana* AIR 1971 Ker 197].

The question in any particular case whether the carrier is a common carrier or a private carrier has to be decided on the ascertainment of what is publicly professed. This profession may be by public notice or by actual indiscriminate carrying of goods. The profession to carry goods indiscriminately may be limited to particular goods or to particular routes or even as to two or more specified points. [*The River Steam Navigation Co. Ltd.* v *Shyam Sunder Tea Co. Ltd.* AIR 1962 SC 1276].

**Common intention.** Common intention denotes action in concert and necessarily postulates a pre-arranged plan, a prior meeting of minds and elements of participation in action. [*Mohan Singh* v *State* 1962 Supp (3) SCR 848: AIR 1963 SC 174].

Common intention within the meaning of s. 34 of the Indian Penal Code 1860 implies a pre-arranged plan. To convict an accused of an offence applying the section, it should be proved that the criminal act was done in concert pursuant to the pre-arranged plan. In most cases the intention is to be inferred from his act or conduct or other relevant circumstances. [*Ramchand Tolaram* v *State* AIR 1956 Bom 287: 1956 Cr LJ 585]. Common intention means a pre-arranged plan. [*Devilal* v *State of Rajasthan* AIR 1971 SC 1444].

**Common law.** Law derived from customs and judicial precedent rather than statutes.

The body of law derived from judicial decisions, rather than from statutes or constitutions; general law common to the country as a whole, as opposed to special law that has only local application; the body of law deriving from law courts as opposed to those sitting in equity; the body of law to which no constitution or statute applies. [Black's *Law Dictionary*, 7th Ed.].

The term 'common law' has been used in different senses. In one sense it signifies the particular portion of the municipal law of England which was formerly administered exclusively by the common law tribunals, and is now administered by them concurrently with, and as modified by, equitable doctrines and in this sense the English common law includes the statute law as well as the unwritten law. Generally, however, when we speak of the English common law we mean the unwritten law as defined by Blackstone—that portion of the law of England which is based, not upon legislative enactment but upon immemorial usage and the general consent of the people.

Chancellor Kent defined the common law as "those principles, usages and rules of action applicable to the Government and security of persons and property, which do not rest for their authority upon any express and positive declarations of the will of the legislature". [1 Kent Comm 469].

NOTE: *English law—sources.* The common law of England was one of the three main historical sources of English law. The other two were legislation and equity. The common law evolved from custom and was the body of law created by and administered by the King's Courts. Equity developed to overcome the occasional rigidity and unfairness of the common law. Originally the King himself granted or denied petitions in equity; later the task fell to the Chancellor, and later still to the Court of Chancery.

**Common purpose.** 'Common purpose' means any purpose in relation to any common need, convenience or benefit. In its application to village, it includes the following purposes—(*i*) extension of the village Abadi; (*ii*) providing income for the Panchayat of the village concerned for the benefit of the village community; (*iii*) village roads and paths; village drains, village wells, ponds or tanks, village water courses or water channels; village bus stands and waiting places; manure pits; hada rori; public latrines; cremation and burial grounds; panchayat ghar; janj ghar, grazing grounds; tanning places; mela grounds; public places of religious or charitable nature; and (*iv*) schools and play-grounds, dispensaries, hospitals and institutions of like nature, water-works or tube-wells whether such schools, play-grounds, dispensaries, hospitals, institutions, water-works or tube-wells may be managed and controlled by the State Government or not. [*The Kannan Devan Hills Produce* v *State of Kerala* AIR 1972 SC 2301: (1973)1 SCR 356: (1972)2 SCC 218].

**Common seal.** The official seal of a corporate body.

**Commotion.** A confused and noisy disturbance or outburst; loud and confusing noise; brawal; clamour; confusion; disorder; embroilment; frances; turbulence.

• **Civil commotion** p. 144.

**Communicate.** Acquaint; apprise; convey; divulge; impart; inform; let know; make known; notify; pronounce; publicize; reveal; speak one's mind; transmit.

The ordinary meaning of the word 'communicate' is to impart, confer or transmit information. [*State of Punjab* v *Khem Ram* AIR 1970 SC 214: (1970)2 SCR 657: (1970)2 SCA 392].

Communication means bringing home effective knowledge of facts. It must be in the language known to the person. [*Harikisan* v *State of Maharashtra* AIR 1962 SC 911: (1962)2 SCA 233: 64 Bom LR 522: (1962)1 Cr LJ 797].

The expression 'communicate' as used in s. 39(2) of the Cr PC 1898 is not synonymous with the expression 'publish' which means 'to make public'. It means 'to bestow, convey, make known, recount to impart as to communicate information to anyone'. [*Gurbachan Singh* v *Sagira* AIR 1956 Punj 254: 1956 Cr LJ 1430].

The word 'communicate' as used in Prevention Detention Act is a strong word. It requires that sufficient knowledge of the basic facts constituting the grounds should be imparted effectively and fully to the detenu in writing in a language which he understands so as to enable him to make a purposeful and effective representation. [*Kubic Darusz* v *Union of India* AIR 1990 SC 605: (1990)1 SCC 568: (1990)1 SCR 98: JT 1990(1) SC 38: 1990 Cr LJ 796: 1990 SCC (Cri) 227: (1990)48 ELT 171]. Communication to the detenu of that awareness in the mind of the detaining authority suitably exhibited in the order of detention, appears to be the *sine qua non*, which alone would make the representation purposeful and effective. [*M. Marimutu* v *Joint Secretary to the Government of India* 1999 Mad LJ (Cr) 458, 463 (Mad)].

In preventive detention, it means that sufficient knowledge of the basic facts constituting the "grounds" should be imparted effectively and fully to the detenu in writing in a language which he understands. [*Lallubhai Jogibhai Patel* v *Union of India* AIR 1981 SC 728: (1981)2 SCR 352: (1981)2 SCC 427: 1981 Cr LJ 286: 1981 SCC (Cri) 463].

• **To be communicated.** The expression "to be communicated" means to be delivered at the address of the person to whom the communication is directed. [*Words and Phrases Legally Defined*, 2nd Ed., vol. 1, p. 287, Edited by John B. Saunders].

**Communication.** The sharing of knowledge by one with another; intercourse; connection; act of or system of transmitting information.

• **Wireless communication** p. 900.

**Communis error facit jus.** Common error makes law. This maxim has to be applied with great caution. It is sometimes said, *communis error facis jus*; but *communis opinion* is evidence of what the law is—not where it is an opinion merely speculative and theoretical, floating in the minds of persons; but where it has been made the groundwork and substratum of practice. [*Isherwood* v *Oldknow* 16 RR 305, *per* Lord Ellenborough].

**Commutable.** Convertible into money; exchangeable.

**Commutation.** An exchange or replacement.

In criminal law, the word means "a reduction or change of penalty" [Webster's *Comprehensive Dictionary*, International Edition]; "the executive's substitution in a particular case of a less severe punishment for a more severe one that has already been judicially imposed on the defendant". [Black's *Law Dictionary*, 8th Ed.].

In commercial and civil law, the word means "the substitution of one form of payment for the other" [Black's *Law Dictionary*, 8th Ed.]; a "substitution of one kind of payment or service for another" [Webster's *Comprehensive Dictionary*, International Edition]; "to substitute one liability for another". [*Trimmer* v *Walsh* 32 LJQB 364].

**Company.** As noun means aggregation; assembly; caucus; coalition; conclave; congregation; convocation; crowd; association; body corporate; commercial enterprise; corporate body; corporation; guild; joint concern.

"'Company' denotes ...... a legal entity, the validity of which and the effect of which depends on the law of the country in which it is established". [*Colquhoun* v *Heddon* (1890)6 TLR 153, 154, *per* Pollock, B.].

"The word 'company' has no strictly technical meaning. It involves, I think, two ideas—namely, first that the association is of persons so numerous as not to be aptly described as a firm; and, secondly, that the consent of all the other members is not required to the transfer of a member's interest". [*Re Stanley, Tennant* v *Stanley* (1906)1 Ch 131, 134, *per* Buckley, J.].

The word 'company' imports an association of a number of individuals formed for some common purpose. Such an association may be incorporated (that is, a body corporate with perpetual succession and a common seal) or it may be unincorporated. An incorporated company is a legal person separate and distinct from the individual members of the company, whereas an unincorporated company has no such separable existence and is not in law distinguishable from its members. [Halsbury's *Laws of England*, 4th Ed., vol. 7, para 1, p. 11].

A company necessarily implies a voluntary association of persons who under certain agreement or articles of association bind together to form a body or assemblage of persons for the purpose of carrying on any trade or business and are as such recognized and registered as company or incorporated as such under some statute. [*Kanwar Chandra Singh* v *State of Rajasthan* ILR (1961)11 Raj 486].

A company is an association of persons for some common object or objects. A company has a legal personality. It is an artificial person as opposed to a natural person. It comes into existence on its registration in accordance with law. The Memorandum of Association and the articles of association of a company which are filed at the time of its registration are considered as the constitutional documents which contain the fundamental terms which govern it. [*National Textile Workers' Union* v *P.R. Ramakrishnan* (1983)1 SCC 228: AIR 1983 SC 75: (1983)1 SCR 922: (1983)1 Comp LJ 1].

The word 'company' under s. 3(*i*) of the Companies Act 1956 means a company formed and registered under the Companies Act 1956, or an existing company (*i.e.* formed and registered under the previous companies laws). A company is, in some respects, an institution like a state functioning under its basic constitution consisting of the Companies Act and the Memorandum of Association. [*Life Insurance Corporation of India* v *Escorts Ltd.* AIR 1986 SC 1370: (1986)1 SCC 264: 1985 Supp (3) SCR 909: (1986)1 Comp LJ 91].

A company for the purposes of s. 23-C of the Customs Act is defined to mean any corporate body and includes a firm or other association of individuals. [*Agrawal Trading Corporation* v *The Collector of Customs* (1972)1 SCC 553].


- **Banking company** p. 95.
- **Defunct company** p. 243.
- **General meeting of company** p. 385.
- **Government company** p. 396.
- **Holding company** p. 420.

- **Indian company** p. 449.
- **Insurance company** p. 469.
- **Investment company** p. 479.
- **Joint stock company** p. 487.
- **Limited company** p. 536.

- **Open company.** A company would be deemed to be open in which the public are substantially interested where more than half the voting power is vested in the public. [*Commissioner of Income Tax, Madras* v *The Amrutanjan Ltd.* AIR 1964 SC 1804: (1964)8 SCR 9: (1964)53 ITR 218: (1964)2 SCJ 513].

- **Private company** p. 686.
- **Public company** p. 707.
- **Register of members of a company** p. 739.
- **Shell company** p. 794.
- **Subsidiary company** p. 817.
- **Unlimited company** p. 867.


**Compensation.** Equivalent given for injury; equivalent given for loss sustained; financial remuneration; indemnification; reclamation; recoupment; reward for service.

Remuneration and other benefits received in return for services rendered; esp., salary or wages; payment of damages, or any other act that a court orders to be done by a person who has caused injury to another and must therefore make the other whole. [Black's *Law Dictionary*, 8th Ed.].

It means "just equivalent" of what has been deprived of [*N.B. Jeejeebhoy* v *Assistant Collector, Thana* AIR 1965 SC 1096: (1965)1 SCR 636]; anything given to make things equal in value; anything given as an equivalent, to make amends for loss or damage. [*Rustom Cavasjee Cooper* v *Union of India* AIR 1970 SC 564: (1970)3 SCR 531: (1970)1 SCC 248].

In ordinary parlance the word 'compensation' means anything given to make things equivalent; a thing given to or to make amends for loss, recompense, remuneration or pay; it need not therefore necessarily be in terms of money. [*State of Gujarat* v *Shantilal Mangaldas* AIR 1969 SC 634: (1969)1 SCA 461: (1969)2 SCJ 322: (1969)1 SCC 509]. Although compensation connotes equivalency, it may under a statute indicate what the Legislature treats as equivalent. [*Commissioner of Income Tax* v *Sham Lal* AIR 1963 Punj 411].

Compensation denotes a sum of money payable to a person on account of the loss or damage caused to him by the breach of contract. [*Dhapai* v *Dalla* AIR 1970 All 206: 1969 All LJ 718].

According to dictionary, it means 'compensation or being compensated; thing given as recompense'. In legal sense it may constitute actual loss or expected loss and may extend to physical, mental or even emotional suffering, insult or injury or loss. [*Lucknow Development Authority* v *M.K. Gupta* AIR 1994 SC 787: (1994)1 SCJ 103: (1994)1 Comp LJ 1].

'Compensation' when directed to be paid by the employer to a workman who is injured by an accident arising out of and in the course of his employment has its natural meaning—that is to say, "something that is to be paid which makes up for the loss that the man has sustained". [*Great Western Ry. Co.* v *Helps* (1918) AC 141, 144, 145, *per* Lord Dunedin].

Compensation is a very well understood expression. Its meaning has been developed in relation to the compulsory acquisition of land. "Compensation *prima facie* means recompense for loss, and when an owner is to receive compensation for being deprived of real or personal property his pecuniary loss must be ascertained by determining the value to him of the property taken from him. [*Nelungaloo Pty. Ltd.* v *Commonwealth* (1948)75 CLR 495, 571, *per* Dixon, J.].


- **Just compensation** p. 500.
- **Legal compensation** p. 525.


**Complainant.** Accuser; aggrieved party; charger; complaining party; denouncer; one instigating an action; petitioner for legal redress; preferror of charges; prosecutor; suitor.

One who enters a legal complaint against another; one who makes a complaint; a prosecutor. [*Natabar Samal* v *Bidulata Dei* (1974)40 Cut LT 1187].

One who complains, especially, one who enters a formal complaint before a Magistrate or other authority is a complainant.

One who makes an allegation, accusation or a charge, in order to prosecute a person, is a complainant. [*Municipal Council, Jaipur* v *Prabhu Narain* AIR 1968 Raj 297: 1968 Cr LJ 1449].

Complainant is a person presenting a complaint to a criminal court. But the person moving public servant to file a complaint under s. 188, IPC is not a complainant of the case. [*Natabar Samal* v *Bidulata Dei* (1974)40 Cut LT 1187; *Associated Cement Co. Ltd.* v *Keshavanand* 1998 Cr LR (SC) 176].

Complainant is defined as the party who brings a legal complaint against another, especially, the plaintiff in a civil suit; a person who, under oath, signs a statement (called a 'complaint') establishing reasonable grounds to believe that some named person has committed a crime. [Black's *Law Dictionary*, 8th Ed.].

**Complaint.** Allegation; accusation; bill of indictment; accusal; case for the prosecution; charge; first pleading; formal allegation; petition; plaint; plaintiff's initiatory pleading; pleading in a civil action; a grievance; a statement of wrong, grievance, or injury; the first paper setting forth the plaintiff's cause of action.

In civil law, the word 'complaint' means the 'initial pleading that starts a civil action and states the basis for the court's jurisdiction, the basis for the plaintiff's claim, and the demand for relief'. In criminal law, the word 'complaint' means a 'formal charge accusing a person of an offence'. [Black's *Law Dictionary*, 8th Ed.].

"Complaint" is one that initiates the prosecutions on the basis of which the accused, if found guilty, is punishable with imprisonment. [*Bholanath Amritlal Purohit* v *State of Gujarat* AIR 1971 SC 194: (1971)1 SCR 817: (1970)2 SCC 414: 1971 Cr LJ 258: 1977 SCC (Cri) 469 referring to Post Office Act 1898, s. 57]. It is a formal document indicating an officer of the postal department for a criminal offence. [*Bholanath Amritlal Purohit* v *State of Gujarat*, supra, referring to Post Office Act 1898, s. 73].

▸*Meaning under the Code of Criminal Procedure 1973, s. 2(d).* "Complaint" means any allegation made orally or in writing to a Magistrate, with a view to his taking action under the Criminal Procedure Code that some person, whether known or unknown, has committed an offence, but does not include a police report.

NOTE: Under s. 190(1)(a) of the Code of Criminal Procedure 1973, a Magistrate may take cognizance of any offence upon receiving a complaint of facts which constitute such offence. The word 'complaint' has a wide meaning since it includes even an oral allegation. It may, therefore, be assumed that no form is prescribed which the complaint must take. It may only be said that there must be an allegation which *prima facie* discloses the commission of an offence with the necessary facts for the Magistrate to taken action. Section 190(1)(a), Cr PC makes it necessary that the alleged facts must disclose the commission of an offence. [*Bhimappa Basappa Bhu Sannavar* v *Laxman Shivarayappa Samagouda* (1970)1 SCC 665: AIR 1970 SC 1153: (1971)1 SCR 1: 1970 SCC (Cri) 263].

A report by a police officer sent, after *suo motu* enquiry in a non-cognizable offence, to chief judicial magistrate does not amount to a complaint. [*Gaya Kahar* v *State of Bihar* (1997)2 BLJ 58 (Pat)].

**Compos mentis.** Master of one's mind; of sound mind; having use of and control over of one's own mental faculties.

**Composition.** In legal parlance, it means a compromise, especially a legal agreement to pay a sum in lieu of a larger sum or other obligation.

An agreement between a debtor and two or more creditors for the adjustment or discharge of an obligation for some lesser amount; an agreement among the debtor and two or more creditors that the debtor will pay the creditors less than their full claims in full satisfaction of their claims. [Black's *Law Dictionary*, 8th Ed.].

A composition is an agreement between the compounding debtor and all or some of his creditors by which the compounding creditors agree with the debtor and (expressly or impliedly) with each other to accept from the debtor payment of less than the amounts due to them in full satisfaction of the whole of their claims. [Halsbury's *Laws of England*, 4th Ed., vol. 3, para 999, p. 547].

**Composition deed.** A deed reflecting the terms of an agreement between a debtor and a creditor to discharge or adjust a debt. [Black's *Law Dictionary*, 8th Ed.].

▸ *Meaning under the Indian Stamp Act 1899, Art. 22.* Composition deed is an instrument executed by a debtor whereby he conveys his property for the benefit of his creditors, or whereby payment of a composition or dividend on their debts is secured to the creditors, or whereby provision is made for the continuance of the debtor's business, under the supervision of inspectors or under letters of licence, for the benefit of his creditors.

**Compound.** As adjective, it means: aggregated; amalgamated; assimilated; blended; entangled; hybridized; incorporated; interlaced; merged; mingled; united; variegated.

As verb, it means: accrue; add to; annex; append; enhance; enlarge; enrich; exaggerate; grow larger; intensity; make larger; multiply; sub-join; supplement.

'Compound' means the walled or fenced enclosure of a residence, cantonment, or factory; also, any similar enclosed place.

- **Compound a crime.** It means: to cover up or condone a crime for a consideration; forbear from prosecuting from private motives; 'to agree for consideration not to prosecute (a crime)' [Black's *Law Dictionary*, 8th Ed.]; 'an agreement not to prosecute a felon in consideration of the return of the goods or other reward'. [Blackstone's *Commentaries*, p. 133; *R.* v *Burgess* (1885)16 QBD 141].
- **Compound a debt.** It means: to compromise, settle for less than the sum due; condone a liability in exchange for money etc.; to 'settle a debt by a money payment, in lieu of other liability; to adjust by agreement' [Black's *Law Dictionary*, 8th Ed.]; 'arranging with creditors to their satisfaction'. [*Pennell* v *Rhodes* (1846)15 LJQB 352, 355, *per* Patterson, J.].

  *"To 'compound'* a debt or claim, is to accept, in satisfaction of it, something less than, or something different from, that which may be claimed as of right—generally by way of compromise or agreement". [*Irish Land Commission* v *Grant* (1884)10 App Cas 14, 30, 31, *per* Lord Selborne, L.C.].

**Compound interest.** Interest upon interest, i.e., when the interest of a sum of money is added to the principal and then bears interest, which, thus, becomes a sort of secondary principal. [*Wringley* v *Gill* (1906)1 Ch 165].

**Compromise.** The settlement of a dispute by mutual concession; an adjustment of a controversy by mutual consent in order to prevent or settle a lawsuit; an 'agreement between two or more persons to settle matters in dispute between them'. [Black's *Law Dictionary*, 8th Ed.].

"I understand 'compromise' to mean an agreement to settle an action or threatened action". [*Marshall (W.F.), Ltd.* v *Barnes and Fitzpatrick* (1953)1 All ER 970, 977, *per* Pearson, J.].

'The word "compromise" denotes an agreement between parties to a dispute to settle it out of court. The dictionary meaning of the word is a settlement of differences by mutual concession. Thus, it is the mutual act of the parties to the suit to settle the dispute between them concerned in the suit by agreement'. [*R.N. Bannad and Sons* v *State Bank of India* AIR 1989 Kant 28].

A compromise is always bilateral and means a mutual adjustment. [*Kunjilal* v *Nathmal* 1956 MBLJ 1240: AIR 1957 MB 14 (DB)].

One of the meanings of compromise is arbitration. According to some authorities that was its original meaning and it is still primary meaning. [*Jiwanbai* v *Ramkumar* AIR 1947 Nag 17 (FB)].

With reference to debt, it means a 'debtor's partial payment coupled with the creditor's promise not to claim the rest of the amount due or claimed'. [Black's *Law Dictionary*, 8th Ed.].

**Compulsory deposit.** Deposit made under compulsion; deposit required by law or other rule; enforced deposit; binding deposit; forced deposit.

In its application to Provident Funds Act, compulsory deposit means a subscription to, or deposit in a Provident Fund which, under the rules of the Fund, is not, until the happening of some specified contingency, repayable on demand otherwise than for the purpose of the payment of premium in respect of a policy of life insurance (or for the payment of subscription, or premium in respect of a family pension fund) and includes any contribution and any interest or increment which has accrued under the rules of the Fund on any such subscription, deposit, contribution, and also any such subscription, deposit, contribution, interest or increment remaining to the credit of the subscriber or depositor after the happening of any such contingency. [Provident Funds Act 1925, s. 2(*a*); *Union of India* v *Hira Devi* AIR 1952 SC 227: 1952 SCR 765: 1952 SCJ 326].

Moneys standing to the credit of an undischarged insolvent in the Government Provident Fund are compulsory deposits and the Official Assignee is not entitled to call upon him to place the money at his disposal for the benefit of the creditors. [*In the matter of Walter Edward Shead* AIR 1913 Rang 148].

▸ *Meaning under the Code of Civil Procedure 1908, s. 60(1)(k).* Compulsory deposits are not liable to attachment if they are so declared by the Provident Funds Act.

**Compute.** To estimate numerically; calculate; reckon.

**Computed.** The word 'computed' is not to be understood only as involving a complex process of arithmetic or calculation. It simply means calculation, whether simple or otherwise. [*Proprietor, Lenox Photo* v *Presidency Officer* AIR 1965 Mad 450: (1965)2 MLJ 150].

In the context of s. 80-J(1) of the Income Tax Act 1961, the word 'computed' has been held to have been used by the legislature as involving not only inclusion but also exclusion of items which may otherwise be regarded as falling within the expression 'capital employed'. [*Lohia Machines Ltd.* v *Union of India* (1985)2 SCC 197, 235].

**Conceal.** To hide; keep from sight, discovery, or knowledge; camouflage; cover up; keep out of sight; keep secret; keep to oneself; keep underground; render; suppress.

To conceal is to keep away a person or a thing from being either noticed or apprehended. [*Premkumar* v *State of Karnataka* 1994 Cr LJ 3641, 3645 (Kant)].

**Concealment.** The act of refraining from disclosure; an act by which one prevents or hinders the discovery of something; the act of removing from sight or notice; hiding; a cover up.

Concealment is an affirmative act intended or known to be likely to keep another from learning of a fact of which he would otherwise have learned.

"If a man purposely avoids answering a question, and thereby does not state a fact which it is his duty to communicate, that is concealment. Concealment properly so called means non-disclosure of a fact which it is a man's duty to disclose ......" [*London Assurance* v *Mansel* (1879) Ch D 363, 370, *per* Jessel, M.R.].

This must amount to the suppression or nondisclosure of facts, which one, under the circumstances, is bound, both legally and equitably, to disclose to another, the latter having an undoubted right to be put in possession of such facts, as in the case of contracts of insurance. [*Lonides* v *Pender* (1874) LR 9 QB 531].

**Concern.** The word "concern" is not a term of art, having a precise, fixed meaning. It has several nuances, and is used to convey diverse shades of meaning over a wide spectrum. It may mean "to have a relation to, or bearing on, be of interest, or, importance" or "to have an anxiety worry". [*R. Dalmia* v *The Commissioner of Income*

*Tax, New Delhi* AIR 1977 SC 988: (1977)2 SCR 654: (1977)2 SCC 467: (1977)106 ITR 895].

• **Industrial concern** p. 452.

**Concerned.** Involved; interested; having interest or involvement.

The dictionary meaning of the word 'concerned' is interested, solicitous, interestedly engaged, etc. [*Food Inspector, Palghat Municipality* v *Tharam Rice & Oil Mills* 1974 Ker LT 685 (FB)].

Some of the many meanings of the word 'concerned' are: 'to be in a relation of practical connexion with', 'to have to do with', 'to have a part in', 'to be implicated or involved in' and 'to have to do with something, especially something culpable'. [*Ashbury* v *Reid* (1961) WAR 49].

"Concerned" as an adjective may mean "interested", "involved". [*R. Dalmia* v *The Commissioner of Income Tax, New Delhi* AIR 1977 SC 988: (1977)2 SCR 654: (1977)2 SCC 467: (1977)106 ITR 895].

• **Person concerned in the management of the business.** The expression 'person concerned in the management of the business' may take in not only a person who directly participates or engages in the management of the business but also one who indirectly controls its management through the managerial staff, from behind the scenes. [*R. Dalmia* v *The Commissioner of Income Tax, New Delhi* AIR 1977 SC 988: (1977)2 SCR 654: (1977)2 SCC 467: (1977)106 ITR 895].

**Concerned in.** The words 'concerned in' mean 'interested in, involved in, mixed up with'. [*Sachidananda Banerjee, Asstt. Collector of Customs* v *Sitaram Agarwala* AIR 1966 SC 955: 1966 Cr LJ 712: (1966)2 SCR 1].

> NOTE: When a person enters into some kind of transaction or attempts to enter with respect to prohibited goods and it is clear that the act is done with some kind of prior arrangement or agreement, it must be held that such a person is concerned in dealing with prohibited goods. [*Sachidananda Banerjee, Asstt. Collector of Customs* v *Sitaram Agarwalla* AIR 1966 SC 955: (1966)2 SCJ 111: (1966)1 SCA 640: 1966 Cr LJ 712].

**Concerning.** The word 'concerning' means 'about', 'regarding', 'pertaining to'. [*Pradeep Kumar Tripathi* v *Telecom District Manager* AIR 1994 All 325, 328 (DB)].

**Concession.** Allowance; rebate; abatement; authority; authorization; conferment; grant; impartment; permission; privilege; sanction; a government grant for specific privileges; the voluntary yielding to a demand for the sake of settlement.

In international law, it means a 'contract in which a country transfers some rights to a foreign enterprise, which then engages in an activity (such as mining) contingent on state approval and subject to the terms of the contract'. [Black's *Law Dictionary*, 8th Ed.].

**Conciliation.** The act of bringing into agreement; the settlement or attempt to settle a dispute by the proposal of measures acceptable to the disputants.

A settlement of a dispute in an agreeable manner; a process in which a neutral person meets with the parties to a dispute and explores how the dispute might be resolved; a relatively unstructured method of dispute resolution in which a third party facilitates communication between parties in an attempt to help them settle their differences. [Black's *Law Dictionary*, 8th Ed.].

The term "conciliation" has both a broad and a narrow meaning. In its more general sense, it covers the great variety of methods whereby a dispute is amicably settled with the aid of other States or of impartial bodies of inquiry or advisory committees. In the narrow sense, "conciliation" signifies the reference of a dispute to a commission or committee to make a report with proposals to the parties for settlement, such proposals not being of a binding character. [*Words and Phrases Legally Defined*, Edited by John B. Saunders, 2nd Ed.].

Conciliation is a process of formulating proposals of settlement after an investigation of the facts and an effort to reconcile opposing contentions, the parties to the dispute being left free to accept or reject the proposals formulated.

NOTE: The fact that the parties are perfectly free to decide whether or not to adopt the proposed terms of settlement distinguishes conciliation from arbitration. [Starke's *International Law*, 6th Ed., p. 405].

**Conclusive.** Decisive; final; leading to a conclusion; complete; finished; ultimate; beyond dispute; authoritative; convincing.

**Conclusive evidence.** Evidence so strong as to overbear any other evidence to the contrary [Black's *Law Dictionary*, 8th Ed.]; evidence that, though not irrebuttable, so preponderates as to oblige a fact-finder to come to a certain conclusion. [Black's *Law Dictionary*, 7th Ed.].

It is also termed conclusive proof.

NOTE: When the law says that a particular kind of evidence would be conclusive as to the existence of a particular fact, it implies that that fact can be proved either by that evidence or some other evidence which the court permits or requires to be adduced. In the former, the court has no option, but in the latter, the court is to consider whether the evidence adduced is sufficient. The aim of the expressions 'conclusive evidence' and 'conclusive proof' is to give finality to the establishment of the existence of a fact from the proof of another. [*Somawanti* v *State of Punjab* (1963)3 SCR 774: AIR 1963 SC 151: (1963)1 SCA 548: (1963)2 SCJ 35].

*Interpretation of Evidence Act 1872, s. 4 read with Drugs and Cosmetics Act 1940, s. 25(3) vis-a-vis the Constitution of India, Art. 21.* Section 4 of the Evidence Act says that when one fact is declared by the said Act to be conclusive proof of another, "the court shall, on proof of the one fact, regard the other as proved, and shall not allow evidence to be given for the purpose of disproving it." The expression "conclusive evidence" employed in s. 25(3) of the Drugs and Cosmetics Act cannot have a different implication as the legislative intention cannot be different. However, any legal provision which snarls at an indicted person without affording any remedy to him to disprove an item of evidence which could nail him down cannot be approved as consistent with the philosophy enshrined in Art. 21 of the Constitution. The first effort which courts should embark upon in such a situation is to use the power of interpretation to dilute it to make the provision amenable to Art. 21. [*Amery Pharmaceuticals* v *State of Rajasthan* AIR 2001 SC 1303: JT 2001(3) SC 497: (2001)2 SCJ 400: 2001 Cr LJ 1686: (2001)4 SCC 382].

**Conclusive proof.** 'Conclusive proof' means that no contrary evidence shall be effective to displace it unless the so-called conclusive evidence is inaccurate on its face, or fraud can be shown. [Halsbury's *Laws of England*, 4th Ed., vol. 17, p. 22, para 28 quoted in *Chettiah Vettil Ammal* v *Taluk Land Board* (1980)1 SCC 499, 520].

NOTE: When the legislature chose to employ the expression that a certain fact "shall be conclusive proof" of another fact, normally, the parties are disabled from disrupting such proof. This can be discerned from the definition of the expression "conclusive proof" in s. 4 of the Evidence Act 1872 which provides: "when one fact is declared by this Act to be conclusive proof of another, the court shall, on proof of the one fact, regard the other as proved, and shall not allow evidence to be given for the purpose of disproving it". [*Kamti Devi* v *Poshi Ram* AIR 2001 SC 2226: JT 2001 Supp (1) SC 87: (2001)5 SCC 311]. An artificial probative effect is thus given by law to certain facts and no evidence is allowed to be produced with a view to combating that effect. [*Din Dayal* v *State* AIR 1956 All 520: 1956 Cr LJ 1031].

*"Conclusive evidence" and "conclusive proof"—no difference.* There is no difference between the effect of the expression "conclusive evidence" from that of "conclusive proof" the aim of both being to give finality to the establishment of the existence of a fact from the proof of another. [*Somawanti* v *State of Punjab* AIR 1963 SC 151: (1963)3 SCR 774: (1963)1 SCA 548: (1963)2 SCJ 35].

**Concubine.** Mistress; a woman who cohabits with a man not being his wife; (among polygamous people) secondary wife.

When a woman consents to cohabit with a man generally as though the marriage relationship exists between them, and actually commences cohabitation with him in pursuance of that understanding, she becomes his concubine or his kept mistress. [*Subbaramaiah* v *Venkata Subbamma* AIR 1957 AP 914].

NOTE: Concubines have a recognized status below that of wife and above that of harlot. Almost a wife according to ancient authorities, the distinction of a concubine from a harlot was due to a modified chastity, in that she was attached to one man only although in an irregular union. [*Bai Nagubai* v *Bai Monghibai* AIR 1926 PC 73].

The word 'concubine' is defined as a woman who goes with a man outside lawful wedlock. A single act of adultery committed by a wife, would not make her the concubine of another man and entitle her husband to obtain dissolution of his marriage under the Act. [*Alla Krishnaveni* v *Alla Brahma Reddi* AIR 1954 Mad 762].

**Concurrent jurisdiction.** The jurisdiction of several courts both authorised to deal with the subject-matter at the choice of the suitor.

Jurisdiction exercised simultaneously by more than one court over the same subject-matter and within the same territory, with the litigant having the right to choose the court in which to file the action. [Black's *Law Dictionary*, 7th Ed.].

In the context of s. 3(1) of the Provincial Insolvency Act, the expression 'concurrent jurisdiction' was held to mean that even though a court subordinate to a District Court may be invested with jurisdiction under the Act, the District Court would still continue to possess jurisdiction under the Act. [*Bhagwanji Haridas* v *Premjee Parashotam* ILR (1958) Bom 1115: AIR 1959 Bom 47].

The words 'concurrent jurisdiction' also mean jurisdiction shared by two or more States, especially over the physical boundaries (such as rivers or other bodies of water) between them. [Black's *Law Dictionary*, 7th Ed.].

**Conditio praecedens adimpleri debet priusquam sequatur effectus.** A condition precedent must be fulfilled before the effect can follow. In case of a conditional contract the condition precedent must happen before either party becomes bound by the contract.

**Condition.** The state or mode in which a person or thing exists; a stipulation; an event, fact, or the like that is necessary to the occurrence of some other, though not its cause; something upon the fulfilment of which something else depends; clause; stated term.

A future and uncertain event on which the existence or extent of an obligation or liability depends; an uncertain act or event that triggers or negates a duty to render a promised performance. [Black's *Law Dictionary*, 8th Ed.].

"'Condition', is a restraint or bridle annexed and joined to a thing, so that by the not performance or not doing thereof the partie to the condition shall receive prejudice and losse, and, by the performance and doing of the same, commoditie and advantage". [*Termes de la Ley*].

The dictionary meaning of the word 'condition' is a provision or stipulation. [*Bagalkot Cement Co.* v *R.K. Pathan* AIR 1963 SC 439: (1963)2 SCJ 355].

▸ *Meaning under the Sale of Goods Act 1930, s. 12(2).* A condition is a stipulation essential to the main purpose of the contract, the breach of which gives rise to a right to treat the contract as repudiated.

A condition is a term of the contract which goes so directly to the root of the contract, or, in other words, is so essential to its very nature, that if the circumstances are, or become, inconsistent with the condition, all executory obligations under the contract may be treated as discharged by a party who is not in default. [Sutton and Shannon on *Contracts*, 6th Ed., pp. 86, 294].

NOTE: A condition is different from warranty which is a stipulation collateral to the main purpose of the contract, the breach of which gives rise to a claim for damages but not a right to reject the goods and treat the contract as repudiated.

Conditions may be either (1) promissory, *i.e.*, something which one party, expressly or impliedly, promises to do or not to do, or promises is true; or (2) contingent, *i.e.*, something as to which no such promise is made on which the obligations of the parties, or some of them, depend. [Sutton and Shannon on *Contracts*, 6th Ed., pp. 86, 294].

A condition may also be either precedent or subsequent. A condition precedent is a condition, express or implied, that the contract shall not bind one or both of the parties until or unless some event has happened. A condition subsequent is a condition, express or implied, that, upon the happening of some event after the contract has become binding, it shall cease to be binding, or that one party or both parties shall have the right to avoid it. [Sutton and Shannon on *Contracts*, 6th Ed., pp. 86, 294].

**Conditional.** Subject to or dependent on a condition.

**Conditional discharge.** An order made by a criminal court whereby an offender will not be sentenced for an offence unless a further offence is committed within a stipulated period.

**Conditional legacy.** A bequest the existence of which depends upon the happening or not happening of some uncertain event by which it is either to take effect or to be defeated.

**Conditional legislation.** A legislature legislates conditionally when it enacts that a legislation shall come into operation at all or in some particular area only upon an executive declaration or upon the happening of a particular event. [*Hodge* v *Queen* (1883)9 App Cas 117; *Edward Mills* v *State of Ajmere* AIR 1955 SC 25; *Hamdard Dawakhana* v *Union of India* (1960)2 SCR 671; *Bangalore Wollen Mills* v *Corpn. of Bangalore* AIR 1962 SC 1263].

When the delegate's power is that for determining when a legislatively declared rule shall be effective it is called the conditional legislation. [*Edward Mills Co. Ltd.* v *State of Ajmere* AIR 1955 SC 25: 1955 SCJ 42: (1955)1 SCR 735; *Hamdard Dawakhana* v *Union of India* (1960)2 SCR 671; *Bangalore Woollen Mills* v *Corporation of Bangalore* AIR 1962 SC 1263].

NOTE: In conditional legislation "law is full and complete when it leaves the legislative chamber, but the operation of law is made dependent upon the fulfilment of a condition and what is delegated to an outside body is the authority to determine, by the exercise of its own judgment, whether or not, the condition has been fulfilled". [*per* Mukherjee, J. in *Delhi Laws Act* case 1951 SCR 737].

Conditional legislation is a species of delegated legislation and narrower in scope than the latter.

**Conditional limitation.** A conditional limitation divests an estate which has vested and vests it in another person. A provision that if a particular event shall happen the interest shall pass to another person is a conditional limitation. The provisions of s. 28 of the Transfer of Property Act and s. 131 of the Indian Succession Act are instances of conditional limitation.

**Conditions of sale.** Conditions of sale are the terms set forth in writing, upon which an estate or interest is to be sold by public auction.

**Conditions of service.** The expression 'conditions of service' means all those conditions which regulate the holding of a post by a person right from the time of his appointment till his retirement and even beyond it. [*I.N. Subba Reddy* v *Andhra University* AIR 1976 SC 2049: (1976)3 SCR 1013: (1977)1 SCC 554; *State of Madhya Pradesh* v *Shardul Singh* (1970)3 SCR 302: (1970)1 SCC 108: 1970 SLR 101].

NOTE: Dismissal from service is a matter which falls within the conditions of service. [*Mysore State Road Transport Corpn.* v *Mirja Khasim Ali Beg* AIR 1977 SC 747: 1977 SCWR 25: (1977)2 SCR 282].

Conditions of service would take in the termination of services and incidentally, the conditions subject to which such termination could be brought about. [*Associated Cement Companies Ltd.* v *P.N. Sharma* AIR 1965 SC 1595, 1606, 1607].

The expression 'conditions of service' would take in its fold fixation of the age of superannuation. [*State of Andhra Pradesh* v *S.K. Mahinuddin* AIR 1994 SC 1474: 1994 AIR SCW 922].

The expression includes transfer of employees [*General Officer Commanding-in-Chief* v *Subhash Chandra Yadav* AIR 1988 SC 876: (1988)2 SCC 351: JT 1988(1) SC 458: 1988(1) SLR 759: (1988)3 SLJ 91]; and the power to take disciplinary action. [*Lilly Kurian* v *Sr.*

*Lewina* AIR 1979 SC 52: (1979)1 SCR 820: (1979)2 SCC 124: 1979(1) SLR 26].

**Condominium.** Ownership in common with others; a single real-estate unit in a multi-unit development in which a person has both separate ownership of a unit and a common interest, along with the development other owners, in the common areas; joint sovereignty by two or more nations; a politically dependent territory under the joint sovereignty of two or more nations. [Black's *Law Dictionary*, 8th Ed.].

**Condonation.** Absolution; clemency; disposition to pardon; exoneration; extrication; forgiveness; mercy; pardon; reprieve; willingness to forgive.

A victim's express or implied forgiveness of an offence by treating the offender as if there had been no offence. [Black's *Law Dictionary*, 8th Ed.].

To constitute condonation there must be two things: forgiveness and restoration. [*Dr. N.G. Dastane* v *Mrs. S. Dastane* AIR 1975 SC 1534: (1975)3 SCR 967: (1975)2 SCC 326].

**Condonation of matrimonial offences.** Condonation of matrimonial offences means the conditional forgiveness of all such offences as are known to, or believed by, the offended spouse, so as to restore as between the spouses the *status quo ante*. [Halsbury's *Laws of England*, 3rd Ed., vol. 12, pp. 302, 303].

Condonation means forgiveness of the matrimonial offence and the restoration of offending spouse to the same position as he or she occupied before the offence was committed. [Saha: *Marriage & Divorce*, 6th Ed., p. 382].

**Condone.** To forgive or overlook an offence or wrongdoing; treat an offence or wrongdoing as forgiven; approve or sanction, usually reluctantly; voluntarily pardon.

**Conduct.** Personal behaviour, whether by action or inaction; the manner in which a person behaves [Black's *Law Dictionary*, 7th Ed.]; behaviour pattern; code; dealings; established practice; propriety; way of acting.


- **Infamous conduct** p. 456.
- **Malicious conduct** p. 553.
- **Safe conduct** p. 768.
- **Wrongful conduct** p. 907.


**Conducting the prosecution.** It means taking charge of the entire proceedings free from any guidance and control by anyone else. [*Roop K. Shorey* v *State* AIR 1967 Punj 42: 1967 Cr LJ 251].

**Confect.** The word 'confect' is defined 'to make up, compound, or prepare from ingredients or materials [*Sadanand Khanchand* v *State of Maharashtra* 1977 Cr LJ 1341]; make by putting together ingredients.

**Confection.** The word 'confection' is defined as 'the process of compounding, preparing, or making something' and also 'a sweet preparation of fruit or the like as a preserve or candy'. [*Sadanand Khanchand* v *State of Maharashtra* 1977 Cr LJ 1341].

**Confectionary.** A room or shop where confections are prepared; a sweetmeat made of sugar, syrup or honey or the like. [*Parry & Co. Ltd.* v *Parry & Co.* AIR 1963 Mad 460].

NOTE: An article of confectionary comes into being only as a result of a process of preparation in which several ingredients are used. [*Sadanand Khanchand* v *State of Maharashtra* 1977 Cr LJ 1341].

**Confederation.** A union or alliance of States with some political power belonging to a central authority. It originates from the Latin word *confoederatus*.

**Confession.** Acknowledgment of a fault, wrongdoing, guilt; disclosure of fault; a voluntary declaration or acknowledgment by a party against whom some misdeed or default is alleged in respect of such allegation; admission; self-acquisition.

A criminal suspect's oral or written acknowledgment of guilt, often including details about the crime. [Black's *Law Dictionary*, 8th Ed.].

The confession is a form of admission consisting of direct acknowledgment of guilt in criminal charge. It must be in express words by the accused in a criminal case of the truth of the guilt fact charged or some essential part of it. [*Shanker* v *State of T.N.* (1994)4 SCC 478: 1994 SCC (Cri) 1252: 1994 Cr LJ 307: JT 1994(3) SC 54].

A statement in order to amount to a "confession" must either admit in terms the offence, or at any rate substantially all the facts which constitute the offence. [*Veera Ibrahim* v *State of Maharashtra* AIR 1976 SC 1167: (1976)3 SCR 672: (1976)2 SCC 302: 1976 Cr LJ 860: 1976 SCC (Cri) 278].

NOTE: A statement which contains an exculpatory assertion of some fact, which if true, would negative the offence alleged cannot amount to a confession. [*Veera Ibrahim* v *State of Maharashtra* AIR 1976 SC 1167: (1976)3 SCR 672: (1976)2 SCC 302: 1976 Cr LJ 860: 1976 SCC (Cri) 278]. A statement that contains a self exculpatory matter cannot amount to a confession. [*Shanker* v *State of T.N.* (1994)4 SCC 478: 1994 SCC (Cri) 1252: 1994 Cr LJ 307].

*'Judicial confession' and 'extra-judicial confession'—difference.* The fact that a confession is extra-judicial and not judicial does not really make any difference. The only material difference between a judicial and an extra-judicial confession is that whereas the former is recorded by a Magistrate with all the formalities provided by s. 164 of the Criminal Procedure Code in order to facilitate ascertainment of the confession having been given voluntarily, the aid of these formalities and the evidence of the Magistrate are not available in the case of extra-judicial confession. All the same, if it could otherwise be ascertained that the extra-judicial confession has been made voluntarily and it was true, its probative value would be the same as that of a judicial confession. [*Om Prakash* v *State* AIR 1957 All 388: 1957 Cr LJ 695].

Usually and as a matter of caution, courts require some material corroboration to an extra-judicial confessional statement—corroboration which connects the accused person with the crime in question. [*Ratan Gond* v *State* 1959 SCR 1336: AIR 1959 SC 18: 1959 SCJ 222: 1959 Cr LJ 108].

• **Voluntary confession** p. 885.

**Confession and avoidance.** A plea in which a defendant admits allegation but pleads additional facts that deprive the admitted facts of an adverse legal effect. [Black's *Law Dictionary*, 7th Ed.]. Thus, if statement of claim alleges a breach of contract, the defendant may confess and avoid by admitting the breach and alleging that the plaintiff has waived it. A plea of contributory negligence is also an example of confession and avoidance.

**Confidence.** Assured expectation; firm trust; faith; reliance on another's discretion; a relation of trust; a communication made in trust and not intended for public disclosure [Black's *Law Dictionary,* 7th Ed.]; affiance; firm belief; assurance of secrecy; privacy; secrecy.

• **Official confidence** p. 622.

**Confidential.** Secret; auricular; imparted in secret; not for publication; not to be spoken of; private; spoken in confidence.

**Confidential report.** A 'confidential report' is intended to be a general assessment of work performed by a Government servant subordinate to the reporting authority, that such reports are maintained for the purpose of serving as data of comparative merit when questions of promotion, confirmation etc. arise. They also show that such reports are not ordinarily to contain specific incidents upon which assessments are made except in cases where as a result of any specific incident a censure or a warning is issued and when such warning is by an order to be kept in the personal file of the Government servant. [*R.L. Butail* v *Union of India* (1970)2 SCC 876: (1971)2 SCR 55: 1970 SCR 926].

**Confirm.** It originates from the Latin word 'confirmare'. The word 'confirm' has many and varied meanings, like, authenticate; approve; assent; concede; concur; corroborate; acknowledge; guarantee; ratify; uphold; verify; make certain; sanction; state with assurance that something is true.

Sometimes 'confirm' "means merely 'verify'; it is commonly used in that sense at the meetings of public bodies who 'confirm' the minutes of their last meeting, not meaning thereby that they give them force, but merely that they declare them accurate". [*R.* v *York* 1 E & B 594, *per* Campbell, C.J.; *Shabbir Fatima* v *The Chancellor, University of Allahabad* AIR 1966 All 45].

**Confirmare nemo potest priusquam jus ei acciderit.** No person can confirm a right before the right shall come to him.

**Confirmee.** One to which anything is confirmed; one who is confirmed.

**Confirmor.** The person who confirms anything to a confirmee.

**Confiscate.** It originates from the Latin word *confiscare* which means 'put in a chest'.

It means: take or seize by authority of law; appropriate to the public treasury usually by way of a penalty; compulsorily acquire; take summarily.

The word 'confiscate' can mean either that the property is appropriated to the State by way of penalty or that ownership therein passes to the State because of want of proved private title. [*State of Himachal Pradesh* v *Singla Brothers, Salan* 1976 Cr LT 475 (HP)].

**Confiscation.** Seizure of property for the public treasury; seizure of property by actual or supposed authority. [Black's *Law Dictionary*, 7th Ed.].

Confiscation in the Roman law meant seizing or taking into the hands of the Emperor, and transfer to the imperial fiscus or treasury. It applied equally to land and goods.

"Confiscation must be an act done in some way on the part of the Government of the country where it takes place, and in some way beneficial to that Government; though the proceeds may not, strictly speaking, be brought into its treasury". [*Levin* v *Allnutt* 15 East 269, *per* Ellenborough, C.J.].

The word 'confiscation' does not necessarily import that the appropriation is to be made as penalty for a crime nor when used in that sense does it necessarily imply that the forfeiture has accrued upon conviction, but it may also be properly used applicable to appropriation of property by government as an act of State. [*Rajah Salig Ram* v *Secretary of State for India* 12 BLR 167].

Confiscation is not synonymous with forfeiture. Confiscation is not a part of the sentence for an offence, but is only one of the modes by which courts can dispose of property which comes before it in criminal trials. Forfeiture unlike confiscation is not a mode of disposal of property coming before courts in criminal trials, but is an established form of punishment; it is recognized as such in s. 53, Indian Penal Code. [*State of Kerala* v *Mathai* ILR (1961)1 Ker 374: 1961 Ker LJ 15: (1961)1 Ker LR 223: 1961 Ker LT 169].

**Conflict.** A serious disagreement or argument; a prolonged armed struggle; a clash between different aims, interests, ideas, etc.

**Conflict of laws.** A difference between the laws of different States or countries in a case in which a transaction or occurrence central to the case has a connection to two or more jurisdictions. [Black's *Law Dictionary*, 8th Ed.].

A short title to describe that branch of the private law of nations which deals with cases in which differing laws of different communities come into collision. [Dicey: *Conflict of Laws*; Holland: *Jurisprudence*].

The branch of English law known as the conflict of laws, or private international law, in contradistinction to the ordinary local or domestic law of England, is concerned with cases having a foreign element. By a "foreign element" is meant a contract with some system of law other than English law. [Halsbury's *Laws of England*, 4th Ed., vol. 8, para 401, p. 307].

**Confusion.** The word has a technical meaning in its application to property matters. "Confusion is the intermingling of two or more pieces of personal property so that the property rights in each can no longer be distinguished. Thereafter, no specific identification or separation of the formerly separate chattel is possible. Such an intermingling occurs most often with fungible goods like gas, oil, grain, mineral ore, or unmarked timber". [Barlow Burke: *Personal Property in a Nutshell* (2d ed. 1993), p. 379].

**Confusion of goods.** Intermixture of goods owned by different persons so that the property of each can no longer be distinguished. As for instance a mixture of liquids, as wine and wine, or wine and honey, or melted silver and gold.

The mixture of things of the same nature but belonging to different owners so that the identification of the things is no longer possible. [Black's *Law Dictionary*, 8th Ed.].

> NOTE: If the mixture of things occurs by common consent of the owners, they are owners in common, but if the mixture is done wilfully by one person alone, that person loses all right in the property unless—(1) the goods can be distinguished and separated among owners, or (2) the mixing person's goods are equal in value to the goods with which they were intermingled. [Black's *Law Dictionary*, 8th Ed.].

**Conjugal.** Of or relating to the married state, often with an implied emphasis on sexual relations between spouses. [Black's *Law Dictionary*, 8th Ed.].

'Conjugal' means 'of or pertaining to marriage or to husband and wife in their relations to each other'. [*Saroj Rani* v *Sudarshan Kumar* AIR 1984 SC 1562: (1984)4 SCC 90: (1985)1 SCR 303, referring to *Shorter Oxford English Dictionary*, 3rd Ed. vol. 1, p. 371].

**Conjugal rights.** The rights and privileges arising from the marriage relationship, including the mutual rights of companionship, support, and sexual relations. [Black's *Law Dictionary*, 8th Ed.].

The right which husband and wife have to each other's society and marital intercourse. [*Saroj Rani* v *Sudarshan Kumar* AIR 1984 SC 1562: (1984)4 SCC 90: (1985)1 SCR 303, referring to *Dictionary of English Law*, 1959 ed., p. 453 by Earl Jowitt].

**Connivance.** It originates from the Latin word 'conniventia' and means tacit permission or silent or indirect assent, especially to wrongdoing; a guilty assent to or knowledge of a wrongful or criminal act during its occurrence; act of maneuvering; act of scheming; complicity; contrivance; corrupt consent; corrupt cooperation; implied assent; secret approval; underhanded complicity.

It may also mean the ignoring of a wrongdoer's illegal conduct, especially, a secret or indirect condonation of another's unlawful act [Black's *Law Dictionary*, 7th Ed.]; the act of indulging or ignoring another's wrongdoing, especially when action should be taken to prevent it. [Black's *Law Dictionary*, 8th Ed.].

> NOTE: In a divorce action, the plea of connivance is taken as a defence that points to the plaintiff's corrupt consent, implied or express, to the action being complained of.

**Consanguinity.** The relationship of persons of the same blood or origin. [Black's *Law Dictionary*, 8th Ed.].

▸ *Meaning under the Indian Succession Act 1925, ss. 25 and 26.* Consanguinity is the connection or relation of persons descended from the same stock or common ancestor. There are two kinds of consanguinity, lineal and collateral. Lineal consanguinity is that which subsists between two persons, one of whom is descended in a direct male line from the other. Collateral consanguinity is that which subsists between two persons who are descended from the same stock or ancestor but neither of whom is descended in a direct line from the other.


- **Collateral consanguinity** p. 153.
- **Lineal consanguinity** p. 536.


**Conscience.** 'The moral sense or right or wrong, especially, a moral sense applied to one's own judgment and actions'. 'In law', it means 'the moral rule that requires justice and honest dealings between people'. [Black's *Law Dictionary*, 8th Ed.].

The word 'conscience' is described in the *Students English Dictionary* as follows: 'ordinary knowledge or judgment of right and wrong, the moral sense or sense of right and wrong; good or clear; bad or guilty; consciousness that one's actions are right or wrong'. [*Raghava Menon* v *Health Inspector, Koduvayur* 1972 Ker LJ 817: 1972 MLJ (Cr) 772].

**Conscription.** Compulsory enrolment of men for military service.

**Consensus ad idem.** The common consent necessary for the formation of a valid contract. Two or more persons are said to consent when they agree upon the same thing in the same sense. [Indian Contract Act 1872, s. 13].

A Latin expression which means 'an agreement of parties to the same thing; a meeting of minds'. [Black's *Law Dictionary*, 8th Ed.].

**Consensus facit legem.** Consent makes law.

**Consensus non concubitus facit matrimonium.** Consent, and not coition, constitutes marriage. The principle behind the maxim is this: *Concubitus* may take place for the mere gratification of present appetite, but *marriage* requires an agreement of the parties looking to the *consortium vitae*. [*Dalrymple* v *Dalrymple* 2 Hagg Consist 54].

**Consensus tollit errorem.** Consent takes away error. The acquiescence of a party who might take advantage of an error obviates its effect. On this maxim depends the doctrine of waiver.

**Consent.** Express willingness; give permission; agree; to yield or accede, as to a proposal or request, when one has the right, power, or wish not to do so; to give assent; a rational and voluntary concurrence in an act or contract; accord; acquiescence; affirmance; approval; assent; concordance; concurrence; ratification.

'Consent' implies the exercise of a free and untrammeled right to forbid or without what is being consented to it always involves a voluntary act and conscious acceptance of what is proposed to be done by another and concurred in by the former. [*Rabinarayana Das* v *State* 1992 Cr LJ 269: (1992)1 Crimes 462].

▸ *Meaning under the Indian Contract Act 1872, s. 13.* In the law of contract, two or more persons are said to consent when they agree upon the same thing in the same sense.

In its application to law of contract, total lack of consent makes a contract void; a tainted consent makes it voidable. [*Deo Nandan* v *Chhote* AIR 1983 All 9].

▸ *Meaning under the Sale of Goods Act 1930, s. 30(2).* The word 'consent' means agreeing on the same thing in the same sense as defined in s. 13 of the Indian Contract Act and does not mean free consent as defined in s. 14 of the Indian Contract Act. [*Central National Bank Ltd.* v *United Industrial Bank Ltd.* AIR 1954 SC 181: 1954 SCR 391: 1954 SCJ 54].

The term 'consent' is a much stronger word than knowledge because it implies conscious assent. [*Haji C.H. Mohammed Koya* v *T.K.S.M.A. Muthukoya* AIR 1979 SC 154: (1979)1 SCR 664: (1979)2 SCC 8].

NOTE: *'Consent' and 'connivance'—distinction.* Consent implies that parties are *ad idem* but connivance does not necessarily imply that parties are of one mind. They may or may not be, depending upon the facts of situation. [*Charan Lal Sahu* v *Giani Zail Singh* AIR 1984 SC 309: (1984)2 SCR 6: (1984)1 SCC 390].


- **Age of consent** p. 49.
- **Free consent** p. 373.


**Consequential relief.** Some relief which follows directly from the main relief (declaration), the valuation of which is not capable of being definitely ascertained and which is not specifically provided for and cannot be claimed independently of the declaration as a substantial relief. [*Balaram Mondal* v *Sahebjan* AIR 1950 Cal 85; *Sri Krishna* v *Shyam Behari* AIR 1955 All 177; *Purushottam Dass* v *Har Narayan* AIR 1978 Del 114 (FB)].

**Consider.** 'Consider' means to apply mind with a view to form opinion. [*Tapan Baruah* v *Laxmi Kanta Das* 1988 Cr LJ (NOC) 31 (Gau)].

The word 'consider' postulates careful thinking or due application of the mind.

[*The Barium Chemicals Ltd.* v *Sh. A.J. Rana* (1972)1 SCC 240].

In service jurisprudence, the word 'consider' merely connotes that there should be active application of the mind by the disciplinary authority after considering the entire circumstances of the case in order to decide the nature and extent of the penalty to be imposed on the delinquent employee. This matter can be objectively determined only if the delinquent employee is heard and is given a chance to satisfy the authority regarding the final order that may be passed by the said authority. In other words, the term 'consider' postulates consideration of all the aspects, the pros and cons of the matter after hearing the aggrieved person. [*The Divisional Personnel Officer, Southern Railway* v *T.R. Challappan* AIR 1975 SC 2216: (1976)3 SCC 190: (1976)1 SCR 783: 1975(2) SLR 587: 1976 SLJ 8].

**Consideration.** Careful thought; a fact taken into account when making a decision; perusal with a purpose followed by a decision [*Somi Angkang* v *Union of India* (1985)2 Gau LR 1]; compensation; a payment or reward.

Something (such as an act, a forbearance, or a return promise) bargained for and received by a promisor from a promisee; that which motivates a person to do something; esp. to engage in a legal act. [Black's *Law Dictionary*, 8th Ed.].

*Corpus Juris Secundum* defines 'consideration' thus: "a benefit to the party promising, or a loss or detriment to the party to whom the promise is made". [Vol. 17, pp. 420-421, 425].

▸ *Meaning under the Indian Contract Act 1872, s. 2(d).* The word 'consideration' has been defined thus: "When, at the desire of the promisor, the promisee or any other person had done or abstained from doing, or does or abstains from doing, or promises to do or to abstain from doing, something, such act or abstinence or promise is called a consideration for the promise".

In its application to contractual matter, it has a technical meaning and it means an act or promise by which some right, interest, profit or benefit accrues to one party or by which some forbearance, detriment, loss, or responsibility is given, suffered or undertaken by the other, and in return for which the party who receives of the benefit, or for whom the detriment is suffered, promises or conveys something to the other [Jowitt's *Dictionary of English Law*, 2nd Ed.]; a reasonable equivalent or other valuable benefit passed on by the promisor to the promisee or by the transferor to transferee. [*Sonia Bhatia* v *State of U.P.* AIR 1981 SC 1274: (1981)3 SCR 239: (1981)2 SCC 585].

▸ *Meaning under the Transfer of Property Act 1872.* The word 'consideration' has not been defined in the Transfer of Property Act, but it has been used in that Act in the same sense as in the Indian Contract Act and excludes natural love and affection. [*Smt. Shakuntala* v *State of Haryana* AIR 1979 SC 843: (1979)3 SCC 226: (1979)3 SCR 232].

• **Adequate consideration** p. 38.
• **Good consideration** p. 390.
• **Valuable consideration** p. 874.

**Consign.** The term 'consign' is of wide connotation and its meaning should be restricted by the context it is used. [*Faiyaz Ahmad* v *State of U.P.* 1994 JIC (Judicial Interpretation on Crime) 457].

In common parlance, it means to hand over; to deliver to a person's possession or trust; to assign; to entrust or commit to the care of another; to transfer to another's custody or charge; to make over or relegate.

In its commercial usage, the word 'consign' means to forward or deliver, as merchandise, for sale or disposal; to give (goods) to a carrier for delivery to a designated recipient [Black's *Law Dictionary*, 8th Ed.]; to give (merchandise or the like) to another to sell, usu. with the understanding that the seller will pay the owner for the goods from the proceeds. [Black's *Law Dictionary*, 8th Ed.].

To "consign" ordinarily (in commercial transactions) means to send or transmit goods to a merchant, or factor for sale. [*Gillespie* v *Winberg* 4 Daly Com Pl 320].

**Consignee.** A person to whom property has been consigned; one to whom goods are consigned.

**Consignee of cargo.** A consignee of cargo, "is a person residing at the port of delivery to whom the goods are to be delivered when they arrive there". [*Wolff* v *Horncastle* 1 B & P 322, *per* Buller, J.].

**Consignee of goods.** "The consignee of the goods ... means some person other than the consignor to whom the consignor parts with the real control of the goods". [*The Urna* (1920) AC 899, 903 (PC), *per cur*.].

**Consignment.** The sending of property to a person for keeping, sale or shipment; the act of consigning goods for custody or sale.

> NOTE: "It is frequently used where goods are delivered 'on approval' or 'on sale or return' where a sale *to* and not *by* the consignee is contemplated". [*Universal Guarantee Pty. Ltd.* v *Metters Ltd.* (1966) WAR 74, 79, *per* Jackson, J.].

It may also mean a written instrument by which something is consigned. "A 'consignment' is a species of mercantile conveyance operating upon the particular effects consigned, which, though it may be defeasible, may operate in the meantime and enable the consignee by his acts to bind the consignor". [*Lucena* v *Craufurd* 2 B & PNR 299, *per* Chambre, J.].

**Consolidated fund.** In England, it is a public fund into which the main part of the revenue is paid and out of which are paid interest on the national debt and other charges. 'The effect of the Bill of Rights (1688) is that there can be no taxation without authority of Parliament expressed in formal enactment. The bulk of the revenue is therefore raised under specific enactment, but all revenue from whatever source is paid into the Exchequer, that is to say, into an account with the Bank of England called "the Account of Her Majesty's Exchequer". The moneys so credited form one fund, known as the "Consolidated Fund", from which issues are made on legislative authority'. [Halsbury's *Laws of England*, 3rd Ed., vol. 33, pp. 11, 12].

In India, the consolidated fund is composed of all revenues received in the case of the Government of India by such Government and in the case of the Government of a State by such State Government, all loans raised by that Government by the issue of treasury bills, loans or ways and means advances and all moneys received by that Government in repayment of loans. No moneys out of such fund can be appropriated except in accordance with law and for the purposes and in the manner provided in the Constitution of India. Article 266 of the Constitution of India deals with the Consolidated Fund of India and of the States.

**Consolidation.** Aggregation; amalgamation; assemblage; fusion; integration; unification; the act or process of uniting; the state of being united.

In its application to corporations, it means the unification of two or more corporations by dissolving the existing ones and creating a single new corporation [Black's *Law Dictionary*, 7th Ed.]; a union of the stock, property, or franchises of two or more companies whereby the conduct of their affairs is permanently or for a long period put under one management, whether the agreement between them is by lease, sale, or other form of contract, and whether the effect is the dissolution of one, both, or neither of the companies. [Black's *Law Dictionary*, 7th Ed.].

In its application to civil law, it means the court-ordered unification of two or more actions, involving the same parties and issues, into a single action resulting in a single judgment or, sometimes, in separate judgments. [Black's *Law Dictionary*, 8th Ed.].

▸ *Meaning under the West Bengal Land Reforms Act 1955, s. 2(5).* In its application to land matters, "consolidation" includes rearrangement of parcels of land comprised in a holding or in different holdings for the purpose of rendering such holding or holdings more compact.

Two or more pieces of land which are contiguous to one another and owned by the same person may be consolidated or made one. [*Uttam Chindhaji* v *Tulsi Ram* AIR 1962 Bom 197: 63 Bom LR 116].

**Consolidation Act.** A consolidation Act is one which puts together a number of enactments which had previously been scattered over various earlier Acts repealed by it. The Code of Civil Procedure 1908, is an Act to consolidate and amend the laws relating to the procedure of the courts of civil judicature.

**Consortium.** In business usage, it means partnership or association; cartel; confederacy; combination of financial institutions; an association, especially, of several business companies.

In conjugal relationship, consortium involves "a sharing of two lives, a sharing of the joys and sorrows of each party, of their successes and disappointments". In its fullest sense it implies a companionship between each of them, entertainment of mutual friends, sexual intercourse—all those elements which, when combined, justify the old common law dictum that a man and his wife are one person". [*Crabtree* v *Crabtree* (No. 2) (196 ') ALR 820, 821, *per* Selby, J.; *Harvinder Kaur* v *Harmander Singh* AIR 1984 Del 66, 69-70]. "Companionship, love, affection, comfort, mutual services, sexual intercourse—all belong to the married state. Taken together, the make up the consortium." [*Best* v *Samuel Fox & Co. Ltd.* (1951)2 KB 639, 665 (CA), *per* Birkett, L.J., affd. (1952)2 All ER 394 (HL)]. The companionship, fellowship or togetherness of the husband and wife alone is indicative of consortium. [*Minor Farooque* v *Municipal Corporation, Ahmedabad* AIR 1985 Guj 114]. It means conjugal fellowship of husband and wife, and the right of each to the company, society, co-operation, affection, and aid of the other in every conjugal relation. [*Roseberry* v *Starkovich* 387 P 2d 321, 322].

**Conspiracy.** An agreement by two or more persons to commit an unlawful act; a combination for an unlawful purpose. [Black's *Law Dictionary*, 7th Ed.].

"*Conspiracie* (*conspiratio*) though both in Latin and French it be used for an agreement of men, to do anything either good or bad: yet in our lawyers books, it is always taken in the evil part". [John Cowell: *The Interpreter* (1607)].

Conspiracy consists in the agreement of two or more persons to do an unlawful act, or to do a lawful act by unlawful means. It is an indictable offence at common law. The essence of the offence of conspiracy is the fact of combination by agreement. The agreement may be express or implied, or in part express and in part implied. [Halsbury's *Laws of England*, 4th Ed., vol. 11, para 58, p. 44].

Conspiracy is a combination of agreement between several persons to carry into effect a purpose harmful to some individual or to particular classes of people or to the public at large.

NOTE: Conspiracy is both a crime and a tort. The agreement of two or more persons to do any unlawful act or to do a lawful act by unlawful means is a crime. The unlawful act which the conspirators agree to do may be either crime or civil wrong. The gist of the offence is the fact of such agreement or combination; it is not necessary that some overt act should have been done in furtherance of the agreement. The tort of conspiracy, on the other hand, is constituted only if the agreed combination is carried into effect and damage to the plaintiff is caused. [*Crofter* v *Veitch* (1942) AC 435].

In order to constitute a single general conspiracy there must be common design and a common intention of all the work in furtherance of the common design. ... A general conspiracy must be distinguished from a number of separate conspiracies having a similar general purpose. [*Mohd. Hussain Umar Kochra* v *K.S. Dalipsinghji* AIR 1970 SC 45: (1970)1 SCR 130: (1969)3 SCC 429: 1970 Cr LJ 9: 1970 SCC (Cri) 99].

Conspiracy is always hatched in the stealth of darkness. Direct evidence of conspiracy is rare. It is to be inferred from circumstances. [*Suraj Parkash* v *State (Delhi Administration)* (1986)2 Crimes 556 (Del)].

If conspiracy is not established, association of a co-accused with main accused is rendered unbelievable. [*Abdul Sattar* v *Union Territory, Chandigarh* AIR 1986 SC 1438: 1986 Cr LJ 1072 (SC): (1986)1 Supreme 214: 1985 SCC (Cri) 505: 1985 (Supp) SCC 599: 1985 Cr LR (SC) 485: 1985 All Cr C 427: 1985 All Cr R 522].

• **Criminal conspiracy** p. 207.

**Constituency.** Body of members; collective members; electorate; electors; voters; a body of voters in a specified area who elect a representative member to a legislative body; the residents of an electoral district; a territorial area for election to the legislature and for local election.

**Constituent.** Component; component part; element; factor; ingredient; particle; section; segment.

It may have a technical meaning as having the power to frame or modify a constitution, *e.g.*, a constituent assembly.

▸ *Other meanings.* A voter; one represented politically or in business; a person who gives another the authority to act as a representative; a principal who appoints an agent.

**Constitute.** Be a feature; be inherent; belong intrinsically; consist; bring about; bring about by legislation; create; give legal form to; make legal; put in force; set up.

The word 'constitute' conveys the meaning 'to establish'. [*Bhabani Shankar Tripathy* v *Secretary Government* (1992)73 Cut LT 567, 578 (Ori)].

The word 'constitute' is said to mean, *inter alia*, 'to set up, establish, found (an institution, etc.)'. [*R.C. Mitter & Sons, Calcutta* v *Commissioner of Income Tax* AIR 1959 SC 863: (1959)36 ITR 194 (SC): 1959 SCJ 1011].

NOTE: "The term 'constituted' (as applied to a company) is not equivalent to 'incorporated'; it is of wider import. It seems to be equivalent to 'established'." [*Re East & West India Dock Co.* (1888)38 Ch D 576, 582, *per* Chitty, J.].

**Constitution.** The form in which a State is organised; the system or body of fundamental principles and rules in accordance with which a State is governed.

The fundamental and organic law of a nation or state that establishes the institutions and apparatus of government, defines the scope of governmental sovereign powers, and guarantees individual civil rights and civil liberties; the written instrument embodying this fundamental law, together with any formal amendments. [Black's *Law Dictionary*, 8th Ed.].

Jowitt's *Dictionary of English Law* defines the term 'constitution' as any regular form or system of Government. [*Umaji Keshao Meshram* v *Radhika Bai* AIR 1986 SC 1292: 1986 (Supp) SCC 401: (1986)1 SCR 731].

The Constitution is the fundamental or basic law to which all other laws must conform. It is superior to the will of the legislature, the validity of whose Acts is to be determined by its provisions; and it is the sole charter by which the rights of the union as well as the State Governments are to be determined. It antedates all other laws and all of them must whether by adaptation or modification be brought into line with and be placed on a footing as if the laws made under the Constitution. [*Prahlad Jena* v *State* ILR (1950) Cut 222].

NOTE: Constitution is permanent; it is an organic statute; it grows by its own inherent force. [*Golak Nath* v *State of Punjab* AIR 1967 SC 1643: (1967)2 SCJ 486].

Kelsen considers the Constitution as the Ground Norm from which the Statutes are derived. And the relationship between the two is one of higher-lower norms. [Kelsen's *Pure Theory of Law* (1967), Art. 35].

A constitutional instrument being *sui generis* its interpretation cannot always run on the same lines as the interpretation of statutes made in exercise of the power conferred by it. The Constitution must receive generous interpretation so as to give all the citizens the full measure of justice so proclaimed instead of the "austerity of tabulated legalism". The expositors of the Constitution are to concern themselves not with words or mere words only, but as much, with the philosophy or the "spirit and the senses" of the Constitution. [*Akhil Bharatiya Soshit Karmachari Sangh* v *Union of India* AIR 1981 SC 298: (1981)2 SCR 185: (1981)1 Lab LJ 209].

Constitution is the mechanism under which the laws are to be made and not merely an Act which declares what the law is to be. A Constitution must not be construed in any narrow or pedantic sense; construction most beneficial to the widest possible amplitude of its powers, must be adopted. [*India Cement Ltd.* v *State of T.N.* JT 1989(4) SC 190: 1989 Supp (1) SCR 692: AIR 1990 SC 85: (1990)1 SCC 12: (1991)188 ITR 690].

A Constitution may be (1) unwritten, resting mainly on custom and convention, or (2) written, drawn up in legal form.

• **Interpretation of Constitution** p. 476.

**Constitutional law.** Constitutional law is that part of English law which relates to the system of Government of the country. Nevertheless the boundaries of constitutional law have never been satisfactorily defined, partly because there is no constitutional document possessing an extraordinary sanctity, partly because the constitutional rules are susceptible of change, and partly because there is no fundamental difference between public law and private law and it is not possible to assign exclusive provinces to each. [Halsbury's *Laws of England*, 4th Ed., vol. 8, para 801, p. 521].

Constitutional law is the fundamental or basic law to which all other laws conform. It is superior to the will of the legislature, the validity of whose Acts is determined by its provisions.

Jowitt's *Dictionary of English Law* defines the term 'constitutional law' as all rules which directly or indirectly effect the distribution or exercise of the sovereign power, the law relating to the legislature, the executive and the judiciary. [*Umaji Keshao Meshram* v *Radhika Bai* AIR 1986 SC 1272: 1986 (Supp) SCC 401: (1986)1 SCR 731].

Constitutional law is the body of those legal rules which determine the constitution of the state. The structure of the supreme legislature and the methods of its action pertain to constitutional law. Constitutional law is the body of those legal principles which determine the constitution of a state, that is, the essential and fundamental portions of the state's organisation. [*Prahlad Jena* v *State* ILR (1950) Cut 222].

**Construction.** As applied to building, 'construction' means the act or mode of constructing; that which is constructed; the act of building by combining or arranging parts or elements [Black's *Law Dictionary*, 7th Ed.]; the thing so built. [Black's *Law Dictionary*, 7th Ed.].

In relation to building, 'construction' and 'reconstruction' are interchangeable terms and the only difference is that 'construction' will be used where a new building is put up where none existed before, but 'reconstruction' will apply to a building which is rebuilt in place of an existing building. [*Sadhu Singh* v *District Board* AIR 1962 Punj 204: ILR (1962)1 Punj 407].

The word 'construction' has a different meaning too. It means the 'act or process of interpreting or explaining the sense or intention of a writing (usu. a statute, opinion, or instrument)' [Black's *Law Dictionary*, 7th Ed.]; the act of construing, or the interpretation thereby arrived at.

The expression 'construction' as applied to a document, at all events, as used by English lawyers includes two things: (1) the meaning of the words; and (2) their legal effect or the effect which is to be given to them. The effect of the words in a question of law. [*Delhi Iron Syndicate* v *Sidha Nath* 1956 AWR 211 (HC); *M.L. Das and Sons* v *Sampatmull* AIR 1954 Cal 103: 57 CWN 894].

• **Harmonious construction** p. 406.

**Constructive.** Legally imputed; having an effect in law though not necessarily in fact; that which is established by the mind of law in its act of construing facts, conduct, circumstances, or instruments.

**Constructive notice.** Constructive notice is information or knowledge of fact imputed by law to a person, although he may not have actual notice of facts by which he is sought to be affected, because the person concerned could have discovered the fact by proper diligence, and his situation was such as to cast upon him the duty of inquiring into it. [*Penumbra of Natural Justice* by Tapash Gan Choudhury, 2nd Ed., p. 121].

Constructive notice is the knowledge which the courts impute to a person (upon a presumption so strong of the existence of the knowledge that it cannot be allowed to be rebutted) either from his knowing something which ought to have put him to further inquiry, or from his wilfully abstaining from inquiry to avoid notice. [*Hunt* v *Luck* (1901)1 Ch 45, 52].

**Constructive possession.** Control or dominion over a property without actual possession or custody of it [Black's *Law Dictionary*, 8th Ed.], e.g. possession through a tenant or any agent; being in a position to exercise dominion or control over a thing. [*U.S.* v *DiNovo* CA Ind, 523 F 2d 197, 201].

A person has constructive possession of property if he has power to control and intent to control such item. [*Com.* v *Stephens* 331 A 2d 719, 723].

Constructive possession means possession in law though not in fact, that is to say, though a party may not be in possession of the property, the law attributes to him the advantages and results of possession fictitiously by applying the legal fiction that possession follows title. The expression is also used with reference to possession of the whole inferred from actual possession of a part. [*Kamta Prasad* v *State* AIR 1961 All 438].

NOTE: If a person is owner of a property but does not use it for some time, it cannot be said that he is in constructive possession of it. He is in actual possession so long as he has the power to bring it into use whenever he likes. [*Mahendra Nath* v *Tarak Chandra* AIR 1932 Cal 504].

**Constructive res judicata.** The rule of constructive *res judicata* is embodied in Explanation IV to s. 11 of the Code of Civil Procedure 1908 which provides that any matter which might and ought to have been made ground of defence or attack in a former suit shall be deemed to have been a matter directly and substantially in issue in such suit.

The principle implies that where the parties have had an opportunity of controverting a matter, that should be taken to be the same thing as if the matter had been actually controverted and decided. [*Beharilal* v *Ram Swarup* AIR 1949 All 144].

NOTE: Where a matter has been actually in issue, it is necessary to constitute the matter *res judicata* that it should have been heard and decided. But where a matter has been *constructively* in issue, it will be *deemed* to have been heard and decided against the party omitting to allege it except when an admission by the defendant obviates a decision. [*Government of Bombay* v *P.A. Wadia* (1949)76 IA 85].

**Constructive total loss.** In insurance law, a total loss is either (1) actual or (2) constructive. "Actual"—when the subject-matter of insurance is either wholly destroyed or so damaged that it would be impracticable to repair the injury; "constructive" when the subject-matter, although still in existence, is either actually lost "to the owners", or beneficially lost to them and notice of abandonment has been given to the underwriters.

A constructive total loss in insurance law is that which entitles the insured to claim the whole amount of the insurance, on giving the notice of abandonment. The notice of abandonment is an offer made by the shipowner to the underwriter to vest the property in the ship in the underwriter, so that he may deal with it as his own.

"A constructive total loss is a device intended to subserve the purpose of indemnity by enabling the assured, when, by insured perils, the postulated danger of loss or deprivation is caused, to disentangle himself, subject to definite limits and conditions, from the danger and throw the burden on the underwriters. If the assured elects to avail himself of this option, he must do so by giving notice of abandonment within a reasonable time after the receipt of sufficient information. He is not allowed to await events to see how things turn out, or to decide what may best suit his interests. If he duly elects to abandon on good grounds, the risk is ended, because the assured can recover as for a total loss and the salvage vests in the underwriter." [*Rickards* v *Forestal Land, Timber & Rys. Co., Ltd.*, *Robertson* v *Middows, Ltd.*, *Kahn* v *Howard (W.H.) Brothers & Co., Ltd.* (1942) AC 50, 83, 84, 86, 87, *per* Lord Wright].

NOTE: "... The question what facts will constitute constructive total loss under a hull policy where the vessel is damaged by a peril of the sea appears to be fundamentally different from the question what facts will discharge the contract contained in the charterparty when the vessel has been damaged by a peril of the sea. In each case the amount of expenditure required to repair the vessel (if she is repairable) is a vital consideration." [*Carras* v *London & Scottish Assurance Corpn., Ltd.* (1936)1 KB 291, 313, 314 (CA), *per* Greene, L.J.].

**Constructive trust.** Constructive trust arises from equitable operation; thus when an estate is subject to a trust or equitable interest or lien, and a person purchases it for value with either actual or constructive notice of it, the estate will be subject to the trust or equitable interest in the hands of such a purchaser. The doctrine of constructive trust also arises upon the renewal of a lease by trustee or executor *de son tort* or person having a limited interest in his own name or by one of the several partners or by agent, mortgagor, mortgagee or person jointly interested with an infant. [Wharton's *Law Lexicon*]. Sections 80 to 83 of the Indian Trusts Act 1882, deal with the various cases of constructive trusts.

**Consuetudo est altera lex.** A custom has the force of law.

**Consul.** Consul is an official appointed by a Government to reside in a foreign country to facilitate the commercial interests of citizens of the appointing country.

Consuls are agents of a State in a foreign country, but not diplomatic agents. Their primary duty in such capacity is to protect the commercial interests of their appointing State, but commonly a great variety of other duties are performed by them for the subjects of their State; for example, the execution of notarial acts, the granting of passports, the solemnisation of marriages, and the exercise of a disciplinary jurisdiction over the crews of vessels belonging to the State appointing them. [Starke's *International Law*, 6th Ed., p. 331].

**Consult.** Ask advice; ask an opinion; ask for recommendations; ask for suggestions; deliberate; interchange views; seek counsel; seek the opinion; search for an answer; seek facts from.

'Consult' means to seek opinion or advice of another; to take counsel; to deliberate together; to confer; to deliberate on; to discuss to take counsel to bring about devise; contrive; to ask advice of; to seek the information of; to apply for information or instruction to; refer to. [*Union of India* v *Sankalchand Himatlal Sheth* AIR 1977 SC 2328: (1978)1 SCR 423: 1978(1) SLR 186: (1977)4 SCC 193].

The word 'consult' implies a conference of two or more persons or the impact of two or more minds in respect of a topic in order to enable them to evolve a correct or at least a satisfactory solution. Such consultation may take place at a conference table or through correspondence. The form is not material, but the substance is important. [*R. Pushpam* v *State of Madras* AIR 1953 Mad 392: (1953)1 MLJ 88].

**Consultation.** Consultation is a process which requires meeting of minds between the parties involved in the process of consultation on the material facts and points involved to evolve a correct or at least satisfactory solution. There should be meeting of minds between the proposer and the persons to be consulted on the subject of consultation. There must be definite facts which constitute the foundation and source for final decision. The object of the consultation is to render consultation meaningful to serve the intended purpose.

Prior consultation in that behalf is mandatory. [*Indian Administrative Service (S.C.S.) Assn.* v *Union of India* 1993 Supp (1) SCC 730: 1993(1) SLR 69: JT 1992 (Supp) 83].

Consultation means that, on the one side, the proper must supply sufficient information to the person to be consulted to enable him to tender advice, and, on the other hand, a sufficient opportunity must be given to the person consulted to tender advice. [*Rollo* v *Minister of Town and Country Planning* (1948)1 All ER 13 (CA); *Fletcher* v *Minister of Town and Country Planning* (1947)2 All ER 946].

NOTE: The essence of consultation is the communication of a genuine invitation to give advice, and the mere sending of a letter which is not received is not sufficient. [*Agricultural, Horticultural and Forestry Industry Training Board* v *Aylesbury Mushrooms* (1972)1 WLR 190].

Consultation or deliberation is not complete or effective before the parties thereto make their respective points of view known to the other or others and discuss and examine the relative merits of their views. If one party makes a proposal to the other who has a counter proposal in his mind which is not communicated to the proposer, the direction to give effect to the counter proposal, without anything more, cannot be said to have been issued after consultation. [*Chandra Mouleshwar Prosad* v *Patna High Court* AIR 1970 SC 370; *M.M. Gupta* v *State of Jammu & Kashmir* AIR 1982 SC 1579: (1982)3 SCC 412: (1983)1 SCR 593; *Akhil Bharatiya Grahak Panchayat* v *State of Maharashtra* AIR 1985 Bom 14].

Provision for consultation may be mandatory or directory. Consultation, even if it be held to be mandatory, cannot be construed to mean concurrence. [*L. Hirway* v *M.B. State* AIR 1958 MP 135].

▸ *Meaning under the Constitution of India, Arts. 217(1) and 222(1).* 'Consultation' in Art. 217(1) has the same meaning as under Art. 222(1) to mean full and effective consultation after placing full and material particulars before the functionaries mentioned in the said Article. It does not mean concurrence. [*S.P. Gupta* v *President of India* AIR 1982 SC 149: 1981 (Supp) SCC 87: (1982)2 SCR 365].

**Consume.** Eat or drink; completely destroy; burn up; disappear; exhaust; spend; swallow; reduce to nothing or tiny particulars; engage the full attention of; engross; dominate.

'Consume' means to destroy, or use up, to eat or drink up. In its economic sense consumption may mean just the use which a purchaser chooses to make of the goods purchased for his own purpose. He does not destroy them nor does he have to diminish their value or utility.

The use of the word 'consume' contemplates the complete exhaustion of the goods purchased in the process of manufacture or other goods, losing their identity completely. [*Deccom Limeshell & Co.* v *State of Tamil Nadu* (1992)87 STC 29, 30 (Mad)].

The word 'consume' is to be construed in its natural and ordinary sense. It is not necessary to torture the expression into meaning something artificial if its natural meaning is not repugnant to reason. [*Caldwell* v *Fones* (1923)2 KB 309, 312 (DC), *per* Lord Hewart, C.J.].

**Consumer.** A person who buys goods or services for personal, family, or household use, with no intention of resale; a natural person who uses products for personal rather than business purposes. [Black's *Law Dictionary*, 8th Ed.].

A purchaser of goods or services; one who consumes; individuals who purchase, use, maintain and dispose of products and services. [*Lucknow Development Authority* v *M.K. Gupta* AIR 1994 SC 787: (1994)1 SCC 243: (1994)80 Comp Cas 714: JT 1993(6) SC 307].

▸ *Meaning under the Consumer Protection Act 1986, s. 2(d)(i).* Any person who buys any goods for consideration which has been paid or promised or partly paid and partly promised, or under any system of deferred payment and includes any user of such goods other than the person who buys such goods for consideration paid or promised or partly paid and partly promised, or under any system of deferred payment when such use is made with the approval of such person.

**Consummation.** Consummation means (1) the completion of a thing; (2) the completion of a marriage between spouses by cohabitation, or sexual intercourse.

In matrimonial jurisprudence, it means an act by which the spouses perfected their marriage and had a sex-relation. In legal parlance, it means full and complete penetration; a partial penetration or committing an abortive attempt to intercourse (an incomplete act of coitus) would not constitute consummation. [*Amarendra Chowdhury* v *Nalini Chowdhury* (1975)77 Punj LR (D) 100; *Indu Kumari Pathak* v *S.K. Pathak* (1983)2 DMC 64]. The practice of coitus interruptus prevents any real intercourse and so consummation. [*Rice* v *Raynold-Spring Rice* (1948) LJR 675]. However, it has since been held that erection and penetration is sufficient to consummate a marriage even though there has been no emission. [*R.* v *R. (otherwise F.)* (1952) WN 236].

**Consumption.** The act or process of consuming; the utilization of economic goods in the satisfaction of wants or in the process of production resulting chiefly in their destruction, deterioration or transformation, using up, waste, gradual destruction.

The word 'consumption' has wider meaning. It means also 'use up', 'spend', etc. [*Jiyajee Rao Cotton Mills Ltd.* v *State of M.P.* (1962)2 SCJ 145: 1962 Supp (1) SCR 282: AIR 1963 SC 414; *Union of India* v *V.M. Salgaoncar and Bros. Pvt. Ltd.* AIR 1998 SC 1367: (1998)4 SCC 263].

Consumption in its primary sense means the act of consuming and in ordinary parlance means the use of an article in a way which destroys, wastes or uses up that article. But in legal contexts, the word consumption has a wider meaning. It is not necessary that by the act of consumption the commodity must be destroyed or used up. [*Burmah-Shell Oil Storage* v *Belgaum Borough Municipality* AIR 1963 SC 906: (1963)2 SCA 221: 1963 Supp (2) SCR 216; *Kathiawar Industries Ltd.* v *Jaffrabad Municipality* AIR 1979 SC 1721: (1979)4 SCC 56: (1980)1 SCR 243].

The conversion of a commodity into a different commercial commodity by subjecting it to some processing is consumption with the meaning of the Explanation (now omitted) to Art. 286 of the Constitution of India, no less than the final act of user when no distinct commodity is being brought into existence, but what was brought into existence is being used up. [*Anwarkhan Mahboob* v *State of Bombay* AIR 1961 SC 213: (1961)1 SCR 709].

Consumption denotes the taking in of something to convert that something into another. [*Dy. CST* v *A.B. Ismail* (1986)2 SCR 522: JT 1986 SC 427: (1986)2 SCC 567: 1986 (Supp) SCC 218: AIR 1987 SC 1885].

In its economic sense it does not mean only use of goods in the production of consumers' goods or final utilisation of consumers' goods. A manufacturer consumes commodities which are ordinarily called raw materials when he produces semi-finished goods which have to undergo further process of production before they can be transformed into consumers' goods. At every such intermediate stage of production, some utility or value is added to goods which are used as raw materials and at every such stage the raw materials are consumed. [*State of Karnataka* v *B.R. Shetty* AIR 1981 SC 1206: (1981)2 SCC 564: 1981 SCC (Tax) 134: (1981)47 STC 369: 1981 Tax LR 2977: (1981)3 SCR 280].

NOTE: Consumption consists in the act of taking such advantage of the commodities and services produced as constitute the 'utilisation' thereof. For each commodity, there is ordinarily what is generally considered to be the final act of consumption. For some commodities, there may be even more than one kind of final consumption. Thus grapes may be 'finally consumed' be eating them as fruits; they may also be consumed by drinking the wine prepared from 'grapes'. Again, the final act of consumption may, in some cases, be spread over a considerable period of time. Books, articles of furniture, paintings, etc. may be mentioned as examples. In the absence of any word to limit the connotation of the word 'consumption' to the final act of consumption, it will be proper to think that the word connotes any kind of user which is ordinarily spoken of as consumption of the particular commodity. [*Anwar Khan Mahboob Khan* v *State of Bombay* (1960)11 STC 693: AIR 1961 SC 213: (1961)1 SCR 709].

A dealer who purchases live-stock, viz. sheep and goats, slaughters them and secures mutton, hides and skins, consumes the former to produce the latter.

The use of tobacco for the production of commercially different articles like bidis must be regarded as consumption. [*Anwar Khan Mahboob Khan* v *State of Bombay* (1960)11 STC 693: AIR 1961 SC 213: (1961)1 SCR 709].

Milling of paddy is 'consumption' when the millers convert paddy into rice, which is commercially a different commodity. [*State of Karnataka* v *B. Raghurama Shetty* (1981)1 Kant LJ 467 (SC)].

Conversion of paddy into rice is consumption of paddy. [*State of Karnataka* v *B. Raghurama Shetty* (1981)2 SCC 564].

**Contango.** A market in which long-term futures or options contracts sell at a premium over short-term contracts; the premium so paid. [Black's *Law Dictionary*, 8th Ed.].

In the law of the Stock Exchange this means a percentage paid by a buyer of stock, of which delivery is to be taken on a certain date, for being allowed to delay taking delivery until some other date. [Jowitt's *Dictionary of English Law*, 2nd Ed.].

A term used in the stock exchange to denote the process of postponing the completion of a contract, either for the purchase or sale of stocks or shares, to a later date than that originally fixed. When this happens the buyer usually pays the seller interest on the capital involved, the seller retaining the stocks or shares till the transaction is ultimately completed. This interest is called a 'contango'. If, on the other hand, the buyer is anxious to pay for and take up the stocks or shares but the seller is unable to deliver, the buyer would not pay interest to the seller, but on the contrary exacts a payment from him, as consideration for postponing the completion of the contract. This payment is called a 'backwardation', or shortly a 'back'. [Wharton's *Law Lexicon*, 14th Ed., p, 164].

**Contemporanea expositio est optima et fortissima in lege.** A contemporaneous exposition is the best and most powerful in law. The maxim as laid down by Coke was applied to construction of ancient statutes but not to interpretation of Acts which are comparatively modern. [*Senior Electric Inspector* v *Laxmi Narain* AIR 1962 SC 159]. This principle applies only to the construction of ambiguous language in old statutes. *Contemporanea expositio* could have no application to a modern Act. [*Dyopack Systems* v *Union of India* AIR 1988 SC 782 (801-802)]. In constructing a statute it is legitimate to take into account existing laws and the manner in which they were acted upon and enforced. This rule is even more appropriate in the case of the Constitution because the Constitution continues in force all laws consistent with itself. [*State of Bombay* v *United Motors* AIR 1953 SC 252].

**Contempt.** The act or state of despising; the condition of being despised; conduct that defies the authority or dignity of a court or legislature [Black's *Law Dictionary*, 7th Ed.]; defiance or disregard of orders; wilful disregard.


- **Civil contempt** p. 144.
- **Criminal contempt** p. 207.


**Contempt of court.** Disobedience to or disrespect for a court of law and its officers.

Conduct that defies the authority or dignity of a court. [Black's *Law Dictionary*, 8th Ed.].

▸ *Meaning under the Contempt of Courts Act 1971, s. 2(a)*. Contempt of court means civil contempt and criminal contempt.

Contempt of court is a disobedience to the rules, orders, process, or dignity of a court, which has power to punish for such offence by attachment. Contempts are either *direct*, which only insult or resist the powers of the court, or the persons of the judges who preside there; or *consequential*, which without such gross insolence or direct opposition, plainly tend to create a universal disregard of their authority. Contempts may be divided into acts of contempt committed in the court itself and out of court. [Wharton's *Law Lexicon*].

Contempt of court is disobedience to the court, by acting in opposition to the authority, justice and dignity thereof. It signifies a wilful disregard or disobedience of the court's order; it also signifies such conduct as tends to bring the authority of the court, and the administration of law into dispute. [*Shri Baradakanta Mishra, Ex-Commissioner of Endowments* v *Shri Bhimsen Dixit* AIR 1972 SC 2466: (1973)2 SCR 495: (1973)1 SCC 446: 1973 Cr LJ 19: 1973 SCC (Cri) 360: 1973 Cr LR (SC) 415].

NOTE: Contempt of court may be classified either as (1) criminal contempt, consisting of words or acts obstructing, or tending to obstruct or interfere with, the administration of justice or (2) contempt in procedure, otherwise known as civil contempt, consisting of disobedience to the judgments, orders or other process of the court, and involving a private injury. [Halsbury's *Laws of England*, 4th Ed., vol. 9, para 2, p. 3].

The overriding question in all cases of contempt of court must, however, be whether the action or remark of the alleged contemner is or is not calculated to interfere with, interrupt or thwart the course of justice. Unless the question can be answered in the affirmative, there can be no case of contempt of court. There are two kinds of this offence; one direct and another indirect. If a person makes any remark derogatory to the dignity of the Judge, and if that remark is calculated either to put the Judge in an embarrassing position so that free administration of justice is jeopardised or to make the litigant public lose confidence in him, he thwarts justice indirectly and commits contempt of court of the kind which has been called scandalising a court or a Judge. No action can, however, be taken if the criticism is reasonable and is offered for the public good. Action can be taken for contempt if the criticism is made against the Judge in his judicial functions. [*State* v *Tribhuvan Nath* AIR 1959 Pat 262: ILR 37 Pat 1130].

**Contempt of Parliament.** Any act or omission which obstructs or impedes either House of Parliament in the performance of the functions or which obstructs or impedes any member or officer of such House in the discharge of his duty or which has a tendency, directly or indirectly, to produce such results may be treated as contempt, even though there is no precedent of the offence. [May's *Parliamentary Practice*, 15th Ed., p. 109]. Each House of Indian Parliament has power to punish for contempt under Art. 105(3) of the Constitution of India. [*Raj Narain* v *Atmaram* AIR 1954 All 319].

**Contend.** To debate earnestly; maintain or assert in argument, argue; bicker; carry on an argument; challenge; contest; contradict; have words with; make an issue; oppose; *adfirmare*; affirm; asseverate.

**Continental shelf.** It is the submerged bed of the sea, contiguous to a continental land mass and formed in such a manner as to be really an extension of or appurtenant to this land mass but not situated in general at a greater depth beneath the sea level than 200 metres. Some jurists assert that a new principle of customary international law has emerged, entitling the coastal State to exclusive rights for the purpose of exploring or exploiting the resources of the sea bed and the sub-soil of the Continental Shelf. Article 2 of the Convention on the Continental Shelf, signed at Geneva in 1958 grants to the coastal State "sovereign rights" of an exclusive nature for the purpose of exploring and exploiting the natural resources of the shelf.

**Contingency fund.** A fund to cover incidental or unforeseen expenses. It is in the nature of an imprest and moneys are paid into this fund from time to time.

NOTE: Article 267 of the Constitution of India provides for the creation of a Contingency Fund for India and also for the States. This Fund is placed at the disposal of the President or the Governor who shall make advances for meeting unforeseen expenditure pending its authorisation by Parliament under Art. 115 or Art. 116 or by the State Legislatures under Art. 205 or Art. 206.

**Contingency staff.** Staff not in regular employment. Their employment is conditional upon (*a*) the funds being available for the contingency for which the casual employment is created or (*b*) the duration of the work for such casual employment or (*c*) the employee actually doing the work or job and not being entitled to pay or wages for the period he does no work or job. [*Kartar Singh* v *State* AIR 1955 Pepsu 25: ILR (1954) Pepsu 687].

**Contingent contract.** A 'contingent contract' is a contract to do or not to do something, if some event, collateral to such contract, does or does not happen. [Indian Contract Act 1872, s. 31].

NOTE: Contingent contracts to do or not to do anything if an uncertain future event happens, cannot be enforced by law, unless and until that event has happened. If the event becomes impossible, such contracts become void. [Indian Contract Act 1872, s. 32].

Contingent contracts to do or not to do anything if an uncertain future event does not happen, can be enforced when the happening of that event becomes impossible, and not before. [Indian Contract Act 1872, s. 33].

**Contingent debt.** A debt that is not presently fixed but that may become fixed in the future with the occurrence of some event. [Black's *Law Dictionary*, 8th Ed.].

NOTE: A contingent debt, strictly speaking, is not a debt at all. A contingent debt has no present existence because it is payable only when the contingency happens, and *ex hypothesi* that may or may not happen. [*Shanti Prasad* v *Director of Enforcement* AIR 1952 SC 1764].

**Contingent interest.** An interest that the holder may enjoy only upon the occurrence of a condition precedent. [Black's *Law Dictionary*, 8th Ed.].

Where, on a transfer of property an interest therein is created in favour of a person to take effect only on the happening of a specified uncertain event, or if a specified uncertain event shall not happen, such person thereby acquires a contingent interest in the property. Such interest becomes a vested interest on the happening of the event. [*Rajes Kanta* v *Shanti Debi* AIR 1957 SC 255].

An interest is said to be contingent if the right of enjoyment is made dependent upon some event or condition which may or may not happen. On the happening of the event or condition, a contingent interest becomes a vested interest. [*Usha Subbarab* v *B.E. Vishveswariah* AIR 1996 SC 2260: (1996)5 SCC 201: JT 1996(6) SC 607].

**Contingent legacy.** A contingent legacy is one bequeathed on a contingency, *e.g.*, if the legatee attains a certain age.

A legacy that depends on an uncertain event and thus has not vested. [Black's *Law Dictionary*, 8th Ed.].

NOTE: Sections 124 and 125 of the Indian Succession Act 1925, deal with contingent bequests.

**Contingent liability.** A liability that will occur only if a specific event happens; a liability that depends on the occurrence of a future and uncertain event. [Black's *Law Dictionary*, 8th Ed.].

It is a liability which by reason of something done by the person bound will necessarily arise or come into being if one or more certain events occur or do not occur. [*Winter* v *Inland Revenue Comrs.* (1961)3 All ER 855 (HL), *per* Lord Reid].

**Contingent remainder.** One which is either limited to a person not in being or not certain or ascertained, or so limited to a certain person that his right to the estate depends upon some contingent event in the future. [*Maryland Nat. Bank* v *Comptroller of Treasury* 287 A 2d 291, 294].

Contingent remainder is an executory remainder limited so as to depend on an event or condition which may never happen or be performed, or which may not happen or be performed till after the determination of the preceding estate. [Wharton's *Law Lexicon*].

> NOTE: Sections 21 to 24 of the Transfer of Property Act 1882 provide for this.

**Continuing.** To continue is to maintain without interruption a condition, course or action; to maintain in existence, endure; to remain in a place or condition, stay; to carry on or keep up, maintain.

Uninterrupted; persisting; not requiring renewal; enduring. [Black's *Law Dictionary*, 8th Ed.].

> NOTE: The conception underlying the word 'continuing' is the same whether it is concerned in relation to breaches of contracts or wrongs independent of contracts or offences. The conception is that so far as breaches and wrongs are concerned, they give rise to a fresh cause of action *de die in diem* so long as the wrongful state of affairs subsists, and so far as offences are concerned they give rise to a fresh offence *de die in diem*, so long as the omission which has been made penal by the statute is not rectified. [*State* v *Umashankar Laxminarayan* AIR 1962 MP 311: (1962)2 Cr LJ 485].

**Continuing guarantee.** A guarantee that governs a course of dealing for an indefinite time or by a succession of credits. [Black's *Law Dictionary*, 8th Ed.].

▸ *Meaning under the Indian Contract Act 1872, s. 129.* A guarantee which extends to a series of transactions is called a continuing guarantee.

> NOTE: A continuing guarantee may at any time be revoked by the surety, as to future transactions, by notice to the creditor. [Indian Contract Act 1872, s. 130].

**Continuing offence.** A crime (such as a conspiracy) that is committed over a period of time, so that the last act of the crime controls when the statute of limitation begins to run. [Black's *Law Dictionary*, 8th Ed.].

A continuing offence is one which continues and a non-continuing offence is one which is committed once and for all. [*Bhagirath Kanoria* v *State of M.P.* AIR 1984 SC 1688: (1984)4 SCC 222: (1984)3 Comp LJ 49: 1984 SCC (Cri) 590: (1985)1 SCR 626].

A "continuing offence" is one which is susceptible of continuance and is distinguishable from the one which is committed once and for all. The distinction between the two kinds of offences is between an act or omission which constitutes an offence once and for all and an act or omission which continues, and, therefore, constitutes a fresh offence every time or occasion on which it continues. [*State of Bihar* v *Deokaran Nenshi* (1972)2 SCC 890: AIR 1973 SC 908: (1973)1 SCR 1004: 1973 Cr LJ 347: 1973 SCC (Cri) 114]. The question whether a particular offence is a continuing offence or not must necessarily depend upon the language of the statute which creates that offence, the nature of the offence and the purpose intended to be achieved by constituting the particular act as an offence. [*Bhagirath Kanoria* v *State of M.P.* AIR 1984 SC 1688: (1984)4 SCC 222: (1984)3 Comp LJ 49: 1984 SCC (Cri) 590: (1985)1 SCR 626; *G. Patel Vokari Ltd.* v *Dundayya Gurushiddaiah Hiremath* (1991)2 SCC 141].

The expression 'continuing offence', though not a very happy expression, has acquired a well-recognised meaning in criminal law. Normally and in the ordinary course an offence is committed only once. But there may be offences which can be committed from day-to-day and it is offences falling under the latter category that these are described as continuing offences. [*State* v *Bhiwandiwalla* AIR 1955 Bom 161 (DB): 1955 Cr LJ 666].

> NOTE: *Continuing offence—examples of.* The offence of non-payment of the employer's contribution to the provident fund before the due date is a continuing offence. [*Bhagirath Kanoria* v *State of M.P.* AIR 1984 SC 1688: (1984)4 SCC 222: (1984)3 Comp LJ 49: 1984 SCC (Cri) 590: (1985)1 SCR 626]. As long as the default continues, the offence is deemed to repeat and, therefore, it is taken as a continuing offence. The offence commences from the date of default and continues until compliance is

made and the default comes to an end. [*Maya Rani Punj* v *Commissioner of Income Tax* (1986)1 SCC 445: AIR 1986 SC 293: (1986)157 ITR 330: (1987)65 STC 416].

The offence under s. 630 of the Companies Act 1956 is not one time but a continuing offence. Thus, wrongful withholding, or wrongfully obtaining possession and wrongful application of the company's property, that is, for purposes other than those expressed or directed in the articles of the company and authorised by the Companies Act cannot be said to be terminated by a single act or fact but would subsist for the period until the property in the offender's possession is delivered up or refunded. Considered from another angle, it consists of a continuous series of acts which endures after the period of consummation on refusal to deliver up or refund the property. It is not an instantaneous offence and limitation begins with the cessation of the criminal act, i.e., with the delivering up or refund of the property. It will be a recurring or continuing offence until the wrongfully possession, wrongful withholding or wrongful application is vacated or put an end to. The offence continues until the property wrongfully obtained or wrongfully withheld or knowingly misapplied is delivered up or refunded to the company. [*G. Patel Volkart Ltd.* v *Dundayya Gurushiddaiah Miremath* (1991)2 SCC 141].

*Continuing offence—what is not—example.* Omission to pay motor vehicles tax for a particular quarter is a complete offence by itself and it is not a continuing offence. [*Channabasappa* v *State* (1979)1 Kant LJ 120].

**Continuing wrong.** If a duty continues from day-to-day, the non-performance of that duty from day-to-day is a continuing wrong. [*Maya Rani Punj* v *Commissioner of Income Tax* AIR 1986 SC 293: (1986)1 SCC 445: (1986)157 ITR 330: (1987)65 STC 416].

NOTE: It is the very essence of a continuing wrong that it is an act which creates a continuing source of injury and renders the doer of the act responsible and liable for the continuance of the said injury. If the wrongful act causes an injury which is complete, there is no continuing wrong even though the damage resulting from the act may continue. If, however, a wrongful act is of such a character that the injury caused by itself continues, then the act constitutes a continuing wrong. [*Commr. of Wealth Tax, Amritsar* v *Suresh Seth* (1982)2 SCJ 170].

**Continuous employment.** It means working with reasonable regularity and work does not cease to be 'continuous' because of interruption in occupation due to periods of temporary illness, such as are incident to people of normal health. Continuously does not denote absolute continuity. [*Banaras Hindu University* v *Indra Pratap Singh* AIR 1992 SC 780: (1992)2 SCC 2: 1992 AIR SCW 572: JT 1992(1) SC 495].

**Continuous service.** It means uninterrupted service, and includes service which may be interrupted merely on account of sickness or authorised leave or an accident or a strike which is not illegal or a lock-out or a cessation of work which is not due to any fault on the part of the employee concerned. [*Sur Enamel and Stamping Works (P) Ltd.* v *The Workmen* AIR 1963 SC 1914: (1964)3 SCR 616; *Lalappa Lingappa* v *Laxmi Vishnu Textile Mills Ltd.* AIR 1981 SC 852: (1981)2 SCC 238: (1981)2 SCR 796].

**Continuous voyage.** Where the citizens in a neutral State adjacent to enemy territory purchase contraband for resale to the enemy in order to avoid interception at sea, the doctrine of continuous voyage becomes applicable. This consists in treating an adventure which involves the carriage of goods in the first instance to a neutral port and then to some ulterior and hostile destination as being for certain purposes one transportation only to an enemy destination with all the consequences that would attach were the neutral port not imposed. Accordingly, if these goods are contraband, they are liable to seizure. The doctrine was expanded in classical terms by Lord Stowell in the Maria.

**Continuously.** The word 'continuously' has one definite meaning only to convey uninterruptedness in time sequence or essence and on the other hand the very word would also mean "recurring at repeated intervals so as to be of repeated occurrence". That apart, used as an adjective it draws colour from the context too. [*Raymond Ltd.* v *M.P. Electricity Board* AIR 2001 SC 238: (2001)1 SCC 534: JT 2000 Supp (3) SC 39].

**Contra bonos mores.** Against good morals.

**Contraband.** Banned goods; bootlegged goods; bootlegged trade; bootlegged traffic; captured goods; confiscated goods; confiscated property; prohibited articles; restricted goods; smuggled commerce; smuggled goods; smuggled trade.

Contraband is the designation for such goods as the belligerents consider objectionable because they may assist their enemy in the conduct of war.

> NOTE: *Absolute contraband and relative contraband—distinction.* A distinction is drawn between *absolute* and *relative* contraband. Articles clearly of a war like or military character are considered to be absolute contraband; for example, arms of all kinds, military clothing, camp equipment, machinery for the manufacture of munitions, and gun-mountings. Articles useful for purposes of peace as well as war are considered to be relative contraband, for example, food, fuel, field-glasses, railway rolling stock, and if intercepted on their way to the enemy government or to the enemy forces are treated as absolute contraband and are liable to seizure by a hostile belligerent. It is doubtful if the distinction is now of any practical value. [Starke's *International Law*, 6th Ed., p. 472].

**Contract.** Accord; agreement; arrangement; avouchment; binding agreement; collective agreement; commitment; deal; instrument evidencing an agreement; legal document; mutual pledge; mutual promise; undertaking; pledged word; ratified agreement; written terms.

It is defined, *inter alia*, as an agreement between two or more parties creating obligations that are enforceable or otherwise recognizable at law; the writing that sets forth such an agreement; a promise or set of promises by a party to a transaction, enforceable or otherwise recognizable at law; the writing expressing that promise or set of promises; loosely, an enforceable agreement between two or more parties to do or not to do a thing or set a things; a compact. [Black's *Law Dictionary*, 8th Ed.].

"A contract is a deliberate engagement between competent parties, upon a legal consideration, to do or to abstain from doing some act". [*Wilson* v *Bury* 5 QBD 518, Brett, L.J.].

▸ *Meaning under the Indian Contract Act 1872, s. 2(h).* An agreement enforceable by law is a contract.

Whilst it is probably impossible to give one absolute and universally correct definition of a contract, the most commonly accepted definition is "a promise or set of promises which the law will enforce". The expression "contract" may, however, be used to describe any or all of the following: (1) that series of promises or acts themselves constituting the contract; (2) the document or documents constituting or evidencing that series or promises or acts, or their performance; (3) the legal relations resulting from that series. [Halsbury's *Laws of England*, 4th Ed., vol. 9, para 201, p. 80].

> NOTE: Contracts have been divided, according to the mode of their formation, into three classes: (1) contracts of record; (2) contracts under seal; and (3) simple contracts. Contracts of record, however, are not contracts in the sense in which that term is here employed but are judgments and recognisances which are enrolled in the record of the proceedings of a court of record, and in law imply a debt though the obligation arises from the entry on the record and not from any agreement between the parties. Leaving aside contracts of record, all contracts may be divided into contracts under seal and simple contracts. [Halsbury's *Laws of England*, 4th Ed., vol. 9, para 209, p. 86].


- **Aleatory contract** p. 55.
- **Apportionment of contract** p. 70.
- **Bilateral contract** p. 104.
- **Breach of contract** p. 111.
- **Building contract** p. 113.
- **C.F.I. contract** p. 135.
- **Charter-party contract** p. 139.
- **CIF contract** p. 141.
- **Contingent contract** p. 186.
- **Dissolution of contract** p. 271.
- **Divisible contract** p. 275.
- **Essence of the contract** p. 316.

**Contract carriage.** A motor vehicle which carries a passenger or passengers for hire or reward and is engaged under a contract, whether expressed or implied, for the use of such vehicle as a whole for the carriage of passengers mentioned therein and entered into by a person with a holder of a permit in relation to such vehicle or any person authorised by him in this behalf on a fixed or an agreed rate or sum—(*a*) on a time basis, whether or not with reference to any route or distance; or (*b*) from one point to another; and in either case, without stopping to pick up or set down passengers not included in the contract anywhere during the journey, and includes—(*i*) a maxi-cab; and (*ii*) a motor-cab notwithstanding that separate fares are charged for its passengers. [Motor Vehicles Act 1988, s. 2(7)].

NOTE: A contract carriage is required to be hired as a whole for a fixed or agreed sum under a prior contract express or implied whether by a single person or a party with the owner of the vehicle. [*Pandit Ramchandra Harihar* v *State of Karnataka* (1995)3 Kant LJ 333, 358].

**Contract for sale.** Agreement under which seller agrees to convey title to property upon payment by buyer under terms of contract.

A contract for the present transfer of property for a price. [Black's *Law Dictionary*, 8th Ed.].

A contract of sale is a contract whose main object is the transfer of the property in, and the delivery of the possession of, a chattel as a chattel to the buyer. [*T.V. Sundaram Iyengar & Sons* v *State of Madras* AIR 1974 SC 2309: (1975)2 SCR 372: (1975)3 SCC 424: (1975)35 STC 24].

▸*Meaning under the Transfer of Property Act 1882, s. 54.* A contract for sale of immovable property is a contract that a sale of such property shall take place on terms settled between the parties.

NOTE: In the case of a contract for sale, the thing produced as a whole has individual existence as the sole property of the party who produced it, at sometime before delivery, and the property therein passes only under the contract relating thereto. To constitute a sale, there must be an agreement, express or implied, relating to the sale of goods and completion of the agreement by passing off title in the very goods contracted to be sold. [*Commissioner of Sales Tax, M.P.* v *Premji* (1970)2 SCC 287].

**Contract labour.** A workman shall be deemed to be employed as 'contract labour' in or in connection with the work of an establishment when he is hired in or in connection with such work by or through a contractor, with or without the knowledge of the principal employer [Contract Labour (Regulation and Abolition) Act 1970, s. 2(*b*)].

**Contract of employment.** If an agreement is for the personal labour of the person engaged, the contract is one of employment, whether the work is time-work or piece-work or whether the employee did the whole of the work himself or whether he obtained the assistance of other persons also for the work. [*Harish*

*Chandra* v *Triloki Singh* 1957 SCR 370: AIR 1957 SC 444: 1957 SCA 616: 1957 SCJ 297].

**Contract of guarantee.** A 'contract of guarantee' is a contract to perform the promise, or discharge the liability, of a third person in case of his default. The person who gives the guarantee is called the 'surety'; the person in respect of whose default the guarantee is given is called the 'principal debtor', and the person to whom the guarantee is given is called the 'creditor'. A guarantee may be either oral or written. [Indian Contract Act 1872, s. 126].

A contract of guarantee is a tripartite agreement which contemplates the principal debtor, the creditor and the surety. [*Mahabir Shum Sher* v *Lloyds Bank* AIR 1968 Cal 371: 72 CWN 91]. First of all there is a contract between the principal debtor and the creditor. Then there must be a contract between the surety and the creditor by which the former guarantees the debt to the latter. There must be a further contract by which the principal debtor asks the surety to act as such, though such a request need not always be express and may be implied. [*Janwatraj* v *Jethmal* AIR 1958 Raj 343: ILR (1958)8 Raj 975].

▸*Meaning under the Hire-purchase Act 1972, s. 2(a).* A contract of guarantee in relation to any hire-purchase agreement means a contract whereby a person referred to as the surety guarantees the performance of all or any of the hirer's obligations under the hire-purchase agreement.

**Contract of indemnity.** A 'contract of indemnity' is a contract by which one party promises to save the other from loss caused to him by the conduct of the promisor himself, or by the conduct of any other person. [*Lala Shanti Swarup* v *Munshi Singh* AIR 1967 SC 1315: (1967)1 SCWR 172, referring to Indian Contract Act 1872, s. 124].

NOTE: The expression 'contract of indemnity' in the Contract Act has been used in a narrow sense and the general law about the contract of indemnity is much wider than the definition in the Act. A contract of fire insurance or marine insurance is always a contract of indemnity, though under the Contract Act it would more properly come under s. 31 of the Act defining contingent contracts. [*Tropical Insurance* v *Zenith Life* AIR 1941 Lah 68].

**Contract of sale of goods.** A contract of sale of goods is a contract whereby the seller transfers or agrees to transfer the property in goods to the buyer for a price [Sale of Goods Act 1930, s. 4].

NOTE: In a contract of sale of goods there is a transfer of property in the goods from the seller to the buyer, but there is none in an agreement to sell. [*Sales Tax Officer* v *Budh Prakash* AIR 1954 SC 459: 1954 SCJ 573].

**Contracting out.** Persons for whose benefit a statute has been passed may contract with others so as to deprive themselves of the benefit of the statute. This is known as 'contracting out'. Certain Acts, however, prohibit contracting out; for example, s. 17 of the Workmen's Compensation Act 1923, provides that any contract whereby a workman relinquishes any right of compensation shall be null and void. [See also s. 3A of the Employer's Liability Act 1938; s. 25 of the Minimum Wages Act 1948 and s. 23 of the Payment of Wages Act 1936].

NOTE: When the consideration or object of an agreement is of such a nature that, if permitted, it would defeat the provisions of any law, such an agreement is void under s. 23 of the Indian Contract Act 1872.

**Contractor.** One who contracts to do work or provide supplies for another. [Black's *Law Dictionary*, 8th Ed.].

A person who undertakes a contract to provide materials and labour for a job; one who contracts to do work or provides supplies for another.

Every "person who makes an agreement with another for the doing of work is a contractor, in a general sense". [*M'Gregor* v *Dansken* 36 SLR 393].

A "contractor" is a person who, in the pursuit of an independent business, undertakes to do specific jobs of work for other persons, without submitting himself to their control in respect to the details of the work. [*Iron Co.* v *Dodson* 7 Lea 373; *Chintaman Rai* v *State of MP* 1958 SCR 1340: 1958 Cr LJ 803(2): 1958 SCJ 753: AIR 1958 SC 388].

A contractor is a person who, in the pursuit of any independent business, undertakes to do a specific piece of work for other persons, using his own means and methods without submitting himself to their control in respect to all its details, and who renders service in the course of an independent occupation representing the will of his employer only as to the result of his work and not as to the means by which it is accomplished. [*Setzer* v *Whitehurst* Ky, 339 SW 2d 454, 456].

- **Independent contractor** p. 448.
- **Managing contractor** p. 556.

**Contradict.** Assert the contrary; assert the opposite; controvert; deny; disagree; disprove; give denial to; go counter to; go in opposition to; oppose; rebut; refute; traverse.

Contradict means to affirm to the contrary. [*Tashildar Singh* v *State of Uttar Pradesh* 1959 Supp (2) SCR 896].

**Contribution.** In its application to donation, it means alms; assistance; bounty; dispensation; endowment; gift; grant of a share; largesse. The word 'contribution' has been defined, *inter alia*, as giving money or other aid for a specified object. A contribution is an aid or payment without any consideration. [*Graphite India Ltd.* v *Dalpat Rai Mehta* (1978)82 CWN 903, 904].

In its application to indemnification, it means compensation; indemnity; offsetting; paying back; payment; reimbursement; reparation; repayment.

In its application to participation, it means abetment; alliance; collaboration; collusion; complicity; league.

**Contributory.** Casually sharing in some act; aiding; assisting; auxiliary; instrumental; lending assistance; one who contributes or who has a duty to contribute.

A person who, as a result of being or representing a past or present member of a corporation, is liable to contribute to the corporation's debts upon its winding up. [Black's *Law Dictionary*, 7th Ed.].

The term "contributory" means every person liable to contribute to the assets of a company in the event of its being wound up. [*Re Aidall Ltd.* (1933) Ch 323 (CA), *per* Maugham, J.].

Section 428 of the Companies Act 1956, defines 'contributory' as every person liable to contribute to the assets of a company in the event of its being wound up, and includes the holder of any shares which are fully paid up; and for the purposes of all proceedings for determining, and all proceedings prior to the final determination of, the persons who are to be deemed contributories, includes any person alleged to be a contributory.

**Contributory negligence.** Negligence on the part of the injured party through failure to take precautions against an accident.

The act or omission amounting to want of ordinary care on part of complaining party, which, concurring with defendant's negligence, is proximate cause of injury. [*Honaker* v *Crutchfield* 57 SW 2d 502].

Conduct by a plaintiff which is below the standard to which he is legally required to conform for his own protection and which is a contributing cause which cooperates with the negligence of the defendant in causing the plaintiff's harm. [*Li* v *Yellow Cab Co. of California* 13 Cal 3d 804].

Contributory negligence consists of the absence of that ordinary care which a sentient being ought reasonably to have taken for his own safety, and which had it been exercised would have enabled him to avoid the injury of which he complains, or the doing of some act which he ought not to have done and but for which the calamity would not have occurred. [*Wakelin* v

*London & South Western Ry. Co.* (1886)12 AC 41]. Thus a passenger in a taxi cab when puts his arm outside the window and is suddenly hit by a lorry coming from opposite direction resulting his arm being chopped, the passenger is guilty of contributory negligence. [*Foo Kok Food* v *Yap Hai Chwee* 1972 ACJ 385].

NOTE: It is the act or default of the plaintiff which under English law may serve to reduce or extinguish his damages. 'The contributory negligence of the plaintiff is no bar to his claim but will reduce the damages to which he is entitled. Where any person suffers damage as the result partly of his own fault and partly of the fault of any other person or persons, a claim in respect of the damage is not defeated by reason of the fault of the person suffering the damage, but the damages recoverable in respect of it will be reduced to such extent as the court thinks just and equitable having regard to the claimant's in the responsibility for the damage'. [Halsbury's *Laws of England*, 4th Ed., vol. 12, para 1212, p. 499].

The theory of contributory negligence comes into play only when the person who suffers injury or dies in an accident is found to have contributed to the occurrence. [*New India Assurance Co. Ltd.* v *Ramanand* (1992)2 WLC 344, 351 (Raj)].

**Control.** To exercise a directing, restraining, or governing influence over; the power of directing; commanding; the power of restraining; a means of restraint; a check.

The term 'control' is of a very wide connotation and amplitude and includes a large authority of powers which are incidental or consequential to achieve the powers vested in an authority. [*Corporation of the State of Nagpur, Civil Lines, Nagpur* v *Ramchandra G. Modak* AIR 1981 SC 626: (1981)3 SCR 22: (1981)2 SCC 714].

The expression 'control' commands power to issue directions regarding how they may be done by a superior authority to an inferior authority. [*K.S. Ramamurthy Reddiar* v *The Chief Commissioner, Pondicherry* AIR 1963 SC 1464: (1964)1 SCR 656].

The word 'control' is synonymous with superintendence, management or authority to direct, restrict or regulate. [*Shamrao Vithal Co-operative Bank Ltd.* v *Kasargod Panduranga Mallya* AIR 1972 SC 1248: (1972)4 SCC 600: (1972)2 SCR 162].

The word 'control' suggests check, restraint or influence. Control is entitled to regulate and hold in check and restraint from action. [*State of Mysore* v *Allum Karibasappa* AIR 1974 SC 1863: (1974)2 SCC 498: (1975)1 SCR 601].

▸ *Meaning under Art. 235 of the Constitution.* The word 'control' as used in Art. 235 includes disciplinary control or jurisdiction over District Judge. It is not merely the power to arrange the day to day working of the court but contemplates disciplinary jurisdiction as well over the presiding Judges. [*G.S. Nagmoti* v *State of Mysore* (1969)3 SCC 325: 1970 SLR 911].

The word 'control' as used in Art. 235 includes disciplinary control over District Judges and Judges inferior to the post of District Judge. This control is vested in the High Court to effectuate the purpose of securing independence of the subordinate judiciary. [*Baradakanta Mishra* v *High Court of Orissa* AIR 1976 SC 1899: (1976)3 SCC 327: 1976 (Supp) SCR 561].

The word 'control' in Art. 235 must have a different content. It includes something in addition to mere superintendence. It is a control over the conduct and discipline of the Judges. [*State of West Bengal* v *Nripendra Nath Bagchi* AIR 1966 SC 447: (1966)1 SCR 771].

▸ *Meaning under the Arms Act.* The word 'control' under the Arms Act means power over the weapon so that direction as to its custody, production, use or disposal may be given. [*In re K. Thimma Reddi* AIR 1957 AP 758].

• **Effective control** p. 294.

• **Exchange control** p. 327.

**Controlling interest.** In common parlance, a person is said to have 'controlling interest' in a company when such a person acquires, by purchase or otherwise, the majority of the vote carrying shares in that company for the control of the company resides in the voting powers of its shareholders. [*Commissioner of Income Tax, West Bengal* v *Jeewanlal Ltd.* AIR 1953 SC 473: (1953)24 ITR 475: 1953 SCJ 643: 1954 SCR 189].

'Controlling interest' does not refer to the Director's beneficial interest in the company, but to the power of controlling by votes the decisions binding on the company in the shape of resolution passed on general meeting. [*Inland Revenue Commissioners* v *G. Bibby* (1945)1 All ER 667].

**Convention.** A formal or stated meeting of delegates or representatives, especially for legislative, political, religious, or professional purposes; an assembly or meeting of members belonging to an organisation or having a common objective; a generally accepted rule or practice; usage or custom; precedent; an agreement or compact, especially one among nations; a multilateral treaty; an agreement or model engagement between persons.

▸ *Meaning in parliamentary practice.* In USA it means an assembly of the delegates of a political party to select candidates for office.

In UK it means an assembly of the House of Lords and Commons without summons from the Crown.

▸ *Meaning in constitutional law.* In the field of constitutional law, the word 'convention' refers to rules of political practice which are regarded as binding on the sovereign and statesmen, but which are not enforceable in a court of law.

**Conversion.** The act of changing from one form to another; the process of being exchanged. [Black's *Law Dictionary*, 8th Ed.].

It may also mean the wrongful possession or disposition of another's property as if it were one's own. [Black's *Law Dictionary*, 8th Ed.]. The tort of conversion consists in an act of wilful interference without lawful justification with any chattel in a manner inconsistent with the right of another whereby that other is deprived of the use and possession of it. [*Dhan Singh* v *Union of India* AIR 1958 SC 274].

The term also denotes a change from one religion to another. It is judicially upheld that a conversion does not necessarily result in extinguishment of casts and notwithstanding conversion, a convert may enjoy the privileges, social and political, by virtue of his being a member of the community with its acceptance. [*C.M. Arumugam* v *S. Rajgopal* AIR 1976 SC 929: (1976)2 SCC 859].

**Conversion of goods.** Wrongful appropriation to one's own use of the goods of another; an unauthorised assumption and exercise of the right of ownership over goods or personal chattels belonging to another, to the alteration of their condition or the exclusion of the owner's rights; any unauthorised act which deprives an owner of his property permanently or for an indefinite time; unauthorised and wrongful exercise of dominion and control over another's personal property, to exclusion of or inconsistent with rights of owner [*Catania* v *Garage De Le Paix, Inc.* Tex Civ App, 542 SW 2d 239, 241]; an intentional dealing with a chattel which is seriously inconsistent with the possession or right to immediate possession of another person. [Street on *Torts*, 4th Ed., p. 35].

> NOTE: To constitute conversion there must be a positive wrongful act of dealing with the goods in a manner inconsistent with the owner's rights, and an intention in so doing to deny the owner's rights or to assert a right inconsistent with them. This inconsistency is the gist of the action. [Halsbury's *Laws of England*, 3rd Ed., vol. 38, pp. 775, 776].

**Conveyance.** Transfer of property from one owner to another; a means of transport; a vehicle.

In its most common usage, it means transfer of title to land from one person, or class of persons, to another by deed. The term may also include assignment, lease, mortgage or encumbrance of land. It means an instrument by which some estate or interest in lands is transferred from one person to another.

'Conveyance' means transfer of ownership. [*Commissioner of Gift Tax, Madras* v *N.S. Getty Chettiar* (1971)82 ITR 599: AIR 1971 SC 2410: (1972)1 SCR 736: (1971)2 SCC 741].

**Convict.** A person found guilty of a crime and serving a sentence of confinement for that crime; accused; condemned person; condemned prisoner; fugitive; guilty person.

**Conviction.** In a general sense, it means the result of a criminal trial which ends in a judgment or sentence that the accused is guilty as charged; the act or process of judicially finding someone guilty of a crime; the final consummation of the prosecution including the judgment or sentence, or as is frequently the case, the judgment or sentence itself. [*Ex parte White* 75 Okl Cr 204].

A conviction is an act of a court of competent jurisdiction adjudging a person to be guilty of a punishable offence. [*R.* v *London County Quar Sessions, Ex p. Metropolitan Police Comr.* (1948)1 KB 670, 679, *per* Atkinson, J.].

The primary meaning of the word 'conviction' is judicial determination of a case and it involves two matters, a finding of guilt or the acceptance of a plea of guilt followed by sentence. The word is also used in a secondary sense, that is, to express a verdict of guilt or acceptance of a plea of guilt before the adjudication which is only completed by sentence. [*S. (an Infant)* v *Manchester City Recorder* (1969)3 All ER 1230].

'Conviction' means final conviction and not by trial court merely. [*Dhanaji Ram* v *Union of India* AIR 1965 Punj 153].

It's other meaning is a strong belief or opinion.

**Coparcenary.** Coparcenary is a form of co-tenancy where property descended to two or more persons on the death of the owner.

NOTE: A Hindu coparcenary is a much narrower body than the Hindu joint family; it includes only those persons who acquire by birth an interest in the joint or coparcenary property, these being sons, grandsons and great-grandsons of the holder of the joint property for the time being. [*Narendranath* v *Commissioner of Wealth Tax* AIR 1970 SC 14: (1969)2 SCJ 727].

A Hindu coparcenary is a narrower body than the joint family, only males who acquire by birth an interest in the joint or coparcenary property can be members of the coparcenary or coparceners. A male member of a joint family and his sons, grandsons and great-grandsons constitute a coparcenary. [*State of Maharashtra* v *Narayan Rao Sham Rao Deshmukh* AIR 1985 SC 716: (1985)2 SCC 321: (1987)163 ITR 31: (1985)3 SCR 358].

• **Hindu coparcenary** p. 416.

**Coparcenary property.** Property owned by a joint Hindu family is coparcenary property or joint family property. Coparcenary property means the property which consists of ancestral property or of joint acquisitions or of property thrown into common stock and accretion thereto. [*Kapur Kaur* v *Kishan Singh* AIR 1970 Punj 270].

**Coparceners.** When two or more persons together form an heir, they are called in law coparceners, or more shortly, parceners. [William's *Real Property*, 24th Ed., p. 392].

**Copy.** An imitation or reproduction of an original. [Black's *Law Dictionary*, 8th Ed.].

Copy means nothing more than a true reproduction of the original. [*Rosamma* v *Balakrishnan* AIR 1958 Ker 154: 1958 Ker LJ 261].

▸ *Meaning under copyright law.* A copy is that which comes so near to original as to give every person seeing it the idea created by original and must be such that ordinary observation would cause it to be recognized as having been taken from the work of another. [*Turner* v *Century House Pub. Co.* 290 NYS 2d 637, 642].

▸ *Meaning under the Arbitration Act 1940 (since repealed), s. 14(2).* What the word 'copy' in s. 14(2) requires is that it must be a full reproduction of the original and that it should be accurate or true. [*Hindustan*

*Construction Company Ltd.* v *Union of India* AIR 1967 SC 526: (1967)1 SCR 843: (1967)2 SCJ 219].

A copy means a document prepared from the original which is an accurate or true copy of the original. In Webster's *New World Dictionary*, the word "copy" means "a thing made just like another, full reproduction or transcription". [*Hindustan Construction Co. Ltd.* v *Union of India* AIR 1967 SC 526: (1967)1 SCR 843: (1967)2 SCJ 219].

▸ *Meaning under the Representation of the People Act 1951, s. 31(3).* The word 'copy' does not mean an absolutely exact copy, but means that the copy shall be so true that nobody can by any possibility misunderstand it. The test whether the copy is a true one is whether any variation from the original is calculated to mislead an ordinary person. [*Murarka Radhey Shyam Raj Kumar* v *Roop Singh Rathore* AIR 1964 SC 1545: (1964)1 SCA 688: (1964)3 SCR 573: (1965)1 SCJ 153].

▸ *Meaning under the Code of Civil Procedure 1908, Or. 41, r. 1.* Copy within the meaning of Or. 41, r. 1 means a certified copy. [*State of U.P.* v *C. Tobit* AIR 1958 SC 414: 1958 SCR 1275: 1958 Cr LJ 809: 1958 SCJ 735; *Union of India* v *M.M. Anand* AIR 1988 Del 271].

▸ *Meaning under the Code of Criminal Procedure 1898, s. 419 (new Cr. P.C. 1973, s. 382).* The word 'copy' occurring in the section means a certified copy and a petition of appeal filed under that section must be accompanied by a certified copy of the judgment order appealed against. [*State of U.P.* v *C. Tobit* AIR 1958 SC 414: 1958 SCR 1275: 1958 Cr LJ 809: 1958 SCJ 735].

- **Attested copy** p. 85.
- **Cerfified copy** p. 132.
- **True copy** p. 858.

**Copyright.** A property right in an original work of authorship (such as a literary, musical, artistic, photographic or film work) fixed in any tangible medium of expression, giving the whole the exclusive right to reproduce, adapt, distribute, perform, and display the work. [Black's *Law Dictionary*, 7th Ed.].

The right to copy; a property right in an original work of authorship (including literary, musical, dramatic, choreographic, pictorial, graphic, sculptural, and architectural work; motion pictures and other audiovisual works; and sound recordings) fixed in any tangible medium of expression, giving the holder the exclusive right to produce, adapt, distribute, perform, and display the work; the body of law relating to such works. [Black's *Law Dictionary*, 8th Ed.].

- **Abandonment of copyright** p. 2.
- **Common law copyright.** "Common law copyright" is that right which an author has in his unpublished literary creations, a kind of property right whose extent is to give him control over first publication of his work or to prevent its publication. [*Hemingway's Estate* v *Random House, Inc.* 279 NYS 2d 51, 54].

**Coram.** In presence of; before.

**Coram non-judice.** Outside the presence of a judge; before a judge or court that is not the proper one or that cannot take legal cognizance of the matter. [Black's *Law Dictionary*, 7th Ed.].

When a suit is brought and determined in a court which has no jurisdiction in the matter, then it is said to be coram non-judice, and the judgment is void. [Black's *Law Dictionary*, 5th Ed.].

**Corporation.** An entity (usually a business) having authority under law to act as a single person distinct from the shareholders who own it and having rights to issue stock and exist indefinitely; a group or succession of persons established in accordance with legal rules into a legal or juristic person that has legal personality distinct from the natural persons who make it up, exists indefinitely apart from them, and has the legal powers that its constitution gives it. [Black's *Law Dictionary*, 8th Ed.].

A corporation may be defined as a body of persons (in the case of a corporation aggregate) or an office (in the case of a corporation sole) which is recognised by the law as having a personality which is distinct from the separate personalities of the members of the body or the personality of the individual holder for the time being of the office, in question. [Halsbury's *Laws of England*, 4th Ed., vol. 9, para 1201].

Corporation, in its widest sense, may mean any association of individuals entitled to act as an individual. Corporation established by or under an Act of legislature can only mean a body corporate which owes its existence, and not merely its corporate status, to the Act. For example, a Municipality, a Zilla Parishad or a Gram Panchayat owes its existence and status to an Act of Legislature. On the other hand, an association of persons constituting themselves into a company under the Companies Act or a society under the Societies Registration Act owes its existence not to an Act of Legislature but to acts of parties though it may owe its status as a body corporate to an Act of Legislature. A company incorporated under the Companies Act is created by the Companies Act but comes into existence in accordance with the provisions of the Act. [*S.S. Dhanoa* v *Municipal Corporation, Delhi* AIR 1981 SC 1395: (1981)3 SCC 431: (1981)3 SCR 864; *Sabhajit Tewary* v *Union of India* AIR 1975 SC 1329: (1975)1 SCC 485: (1975)3 SCR 616; *Sukhdev Singh* v *Bhagatram Sardar Singh Raghuvanshi* AIR 1975 SC 1331: (1975)1 SCC 421: (1975)3 SCR 619].

▸ *Meaning under the Code of Civil Procedure 1908.* The Code uses the expression 'corporation' as meaning a legal person which includes a company registered under the Companies Act. Order XXIX of the Code of Civil Procedure deals with suits by or against a corporation and there is nothing in the Code of Civil Procedure that a corporation referred to under s. 20 means only a statutory corporation and not a company registered under the Companies Act. [*Hakam Singh* v *Gammon (India) Ltd.* AIR 1971 SC 740: (1971)1 SCC 286: (1971)3 SCR 314].

▸ *Meaning under the Payment of Bonus Act 1965.* The definition of the term 'corporation' under s. 2(11) takes in bodies corporate established by law as well as bodies corporate established under any law. [*Shri Ambika Mills Ltd. No. 1* v *Textile Labour Association, Ahmedabad* AIR 1973 SC 1081: (1973)3 SCR 313: (1973)3 SCC 787].

NOTE: The essential elements in the legal concept of a corporation are: (1) a continuous identity, *i.e.*, the original member or members or his or their successors are one; (2) the persons to be incorporated; (3) the name by which the persons are incorporated; (4) a place, and (5) words sufficient in law to show incorporation. In law the individual incorporators are members of which it is composed or something wholly different from the corporation itself, for a corporation is a legal person just as much as an individual. A corporation aggregate can express its will by deed under a common seal. [*S.P. Mittal* v *Union of India* AIR 1983 SC 1: (1983)1 SCC 51: (1983)3 SCR 729].

• **Foreign corporation** p. 364.
• **Statutory corporation** p. 811.

**Corporation tax.** Any tax on income, so far as that tax is payable by companies and is a tax in the case of which the following conditions are fulfilled—(*a*) that it is not chargeable in respect of agricultural income; (*b*) that no deduction in respect of the tax paid by companies is, by any enactment which may apply to the tax, authorised to be made from dividends payable by the companies to individuals; (*c*) that no provision exists for taking the tax so paid into account in computing for the purposes of Indian income-tax the total income of individuals receiving such dividends, or in computing the Indian income-tax payable by, or refundable to, such individuals. [Constitution of India 1950, Art. 366(6)].

**Corporeal.** Having consisting of or relating to a physical material body; not spiritual; not immaterial or intangible, substantial; perceivable by the bodily senses.

NOTE: Hereditaments are of two kinds, corporeal and incorporeal. Corporeal consists of such as affect the senses; such as may be seen and handled by the body; incorporeal are not the object of sensation, can neither be seen nor handled, are creatures of the mind, and exist only in contemplation. Corporeal hereditaments consist wholly of substantial and permanent objects, all of which may be comprehended under the general denomination of land only. [Cheshire's *Modern Real Property*, 9th Ed., p. 100].

**Corps.** A body of troops with special duties, such as, intelligence corps, medical corps; a main subdivision of an army in the field, consisting of two or more divisions; a body of persons engaged in a special activity, *e.g.*, diplomatic corps; a number of persons acting together.

▸ *Meaning under the Army Rules 1954, r. 40.* The expression 'corps' in r. 40 is not used in the same sense which the expression 'army corps' is used. The expression 'corps' in r. 40 must be given the same meaning as set out in sub-rule (3) of r. 187 and it would mean that every battalion in the infantry and every regiment in the cavalry would be itself be a corps. Corps from a tiny small part of what is called army corps. [*Lt. Col. Prithi Pal Singh Bedi* v *Union of India* AIR 1982 SC 1413: (1982)3 SCC 140: 1982 SCC (Cri) 642: (1983)1 SCR 393].

• **Diplomatic corps** p. 259.

**Corpse.** A dead body of a human being.

**Corpus delicti.** A Latin expression which means the existence of essential fact or facts which prove the commission of a crime; the facts and circumstances constituting a breach of a law.

NOTE: The *corpus delicti* in murder has two components—death as the result, and criminal agency of another as the means. Where there is direct proof of the one, the other may be established by circumstantial evidence. Dead body itself is not *corpus delicti*. The expression means that a crime has been committed, that is to say, a man is dead and that his death has been caused by a crime. [*Surchand* v *State* 1972 MLJ (Cr) 196].

**Correspond.** In the *Shorter Oxford English Dictionary*, 3rd Ed., vol. I, the word 'correspond' is said to mean "(1) to answer to something else in the way of fitness; to agree with; be conformable to; be congruous or in harmony with. (2) To answer to in character or function; to be similar to". In Butterworths: *Words and Phrases—Legally Defined*, 2nd Ed., vol. I, it is said "to correspond", does not usually, or properly, mean to be identical with, but 'to harmonize with', or, 'to be suitable to ...' [*Jagir Singh* v *Ranbir Singh* AIR 1979 SC 381: (1979)2 SCR 282: (1979)1 SCC 560: 1979 Cr LJ 318: 1979 Cr LR (SC) 29: 1979 SCC (Cri) 348].

**Corroboration.** Confirmation or support by additional evidence or authority; formal confirmation or ratification. [Black's *Law Dictionary*, 8th Ed.].

Corroboration is some testimony supporting a material point in the testimony to be corroborated; it may be supplied by the evidence of some other person or by some attendant circumstances or by some facts established aliunde. [Halsbury's *Laws of England*, 3rd Ed., vol. 18, p. 371].

Corroboration does not mean merely evidence which supports evidence of a complainant. It must also support that evidence in a material particular, and must be evidence which itself implicates the accused—that is, shows or tends to show guilt of the offence charged. [*R.* v *Witham* (1962) Qd R 49, 53, *per* Hanger, J.].

**Corroborative evidence.** Corroborative evidence is evidence which shows or tends to show that the story of the accomplice that the accused committed the crime is true, not merely that the crime has been committed, but that it was committed by the accused. [*R.* v *Baskerville* (1916)2 KB 658 (CCA)].

**Corrupt.** Spoiled; tainted; vitiated; depraved; debased; morally degenerate. As used as a verb, to change ones morals and principles from good to bad.

In a larger sense, it denotes conduct which is morally unsound or debased.

[*Dr. S. Dutt* v *State of U.P.* AIR 1966 SC 523: (1966)1 SCR 493: 1966 Cr LJ 459].

**Corrupt practice.** A practice which is morally unsound or debased. Corrupt practices are for the most part aimed at abuses of influence. In corrupt practices, a corrupt intent is an essential ingredient.

▸ *Meaning in election law.* In an election, if in the course of canvassing any attempt is made to incline, persuade or influence the will of an elector so as to notice him to give vote in favour of any candidate on the ground of sect, caste or sub-caste, it becomes a corrupt practice. [*Hari Ram* v *Election Tribunal* AIR 1970 All 146].

The word 'practice' does not import habitual repetition of an action. A single act of the nature given in s. 123 of the Representation of the People Act 1951 would be corrupt practice. [*Sheokumar* v *M.A. Khan* AIR 1960 MP 37].

Carrying the voters to booth is corrupt practice. [*Dharmesh Prasad* v *Faiyazal Azam* AIR 1984 SC 1516].

NOTE: *Corrupt practice and illegal practice—distinction.* In corrupt practices a corrupt intent is an essential ingredient whereas in illegal practices all that has to be ascertained is whether the act is forbidden by law. The distinction between a corrupt and an illegal practice depends not on the characteristics of the offence but on the consequence flowing from the offence. [Halsbury's *Laws of England*, 3rd Ed., vol. 14, p. 163].

**Corruption.** An act done with an intent to give some advantage inconsistent with official duty and the rights of others; the act of an official or fiduciary person who unlawfully and wrongfully uses his station or character to procure some benefits for himself or for any other person, contrary to duty and the rights of others.

Corruption is impairment of integrity, virtue or moral principle, depravity; inducement to wrong by bribery or other unlawful or improper means; a departure from honesty, integrity or fair dealing.

NOTE: A public servant is said to commit an offence of criminal misconduct in the discharge of his duty if he, by corrupt or illegal means or by otherwise abusing his position as a public servant, obtains for himself or for any other person any valuable thing or pecuniary advantage. Such act is corruption. [*Bishamber Lal* v *State of Punjab* AIR 1966 Punj 175]. Asking for a bribe which was not paid is no offence. [*State of Madras* v *Rajagopala Ayyar* AIR 1956 Mad 613: 57 Cr LJ 1330].

**Corruptly.** In a corrupt or a depraved manner; by means of corruption or bribery; a thing done with an evil mind, done with an evil intention.

NOTE: Except there be an evil mind or an evil intention accompanying the act, it is not corruptly done.

When the word corruptly is used, it means an act done by a man knowing that he is doing what is wrong, and doing so with evil feelings and evil intentions. [*Bradeford Election Petition No. 2* (1869)19 LT 723].

**Cost.** Expense; price; the sum or equivalent expended, paid or charged for something.

The word 'cost' has a definite connotation, and is used generally in contradistinction of the expression 'value'. [*Hindustan Polymers* v *Collector of Central Excise* AIR 1990 SC 1676: (1989)4 SCC 323: (1989)43 ELT 165: JT 1989(3) SC 674: (1989)3 SCR 974: (1983)3 Comp LJ 165].

In legal parlance, the word 'cost' means expenses awarded by court to prevailing party.

"Costs" signify the sum of money which the court orders one party to pay to another party in respect of the expense of litigation incurred. Except where especially provided by statute or by rule of court, the costs of proceedings are in the court's discretion. [Halsbury's *Laws of England*, 4th Ed., vol. 12, para 1108, p. 414].

• **Actual cost** p. 34.
• **Landed cost** p. 511.
• **Security for costs** p. 783.

**Costs shall abide the event.** The expression means that the successful party must get the costs. Where the order is that the costs shall abide the result, the whole matter is in the discretion of the court not only to allow or disallow the general costs of the action but also to allow or disallow costs of interlocutory applications or appeal from a preliminary question. [*Hardawari Ram* v *Vidya Sagar* AIR 1955 Pepsu 193].

**Costs shall follow the event.** The expression means that the costs are to be distributed according to the results of the several issues, while the party who is successful on the whole gets the general costs. [*Raid* v *Joseph* (1918) AC 717].

**Counsel.** Advice and assistance given by one person to another in regard to a legal matter, propose line of conduct, claim, or contention; a lawyer engaged in the trial or management of a case in court; a lawyer appointed to advise and represent in legal matters an individual client or a corporate and especially a public body.

• **Leading counsel** p. 521.

**Counter-claim.** A claim presented by a defendant in opposition to or deduction from the claim of the plaintiff. [Black's *Law Dictionary*, 5th Ed.].

A claim for relief asserted against 'an opposing party after an original claim has been made; esp., a defendant's claim in opposition to or as a setoff against the plaintiff's claim. [Black's *Law Dictionary*, 8th Ed.].

> NOTE: Counter-claim is a weapon of offence and enables the defendant to enforce a claim against the plaintiff as effectively as in an independant action. Counter-claim is allowed to be raised to avoid multiplicity of proceedings between the parties. [*Ghulam* v *Ghulam Ahmed* AIR 1956 J&K 38].

**Counterfeit.** To forge, copy or imitate (something) without a right to do so and with the purpose of deceiving or defrauding; esp., to manufacture fake money (or other security) that might be used in place of the genuine article. [Black's *Law Dictionary*, 7th Ed.].

To unlawfully forge, copy, or imitate an item, esp. money or a negotiable instrument (such as a security or promissory note) or other officially issued item of value (such as a postage stamp or food stamp), or to possess such an item without authorization and with the intent to deceive or defraud by presenting the item as genuine. [Black's *Law Dictionary*, 8th Ed.].

Counterfeit in common parlance signifies fabrication or false image or representation. In its broadest sense, counterfeit means making of copy without authority or right and with a view to deceive or defraud by passing copy as original or genuine. [*Smith* v *State* 256 A 2d 357].

▸ *Meaning under the Indian Penal Code 1860, s. 28.* A person is said to "counterfeit" who causes one thing to resemble another thing, intending by means of that resemblance to practise deception, or knowing it to be likely that deception will thereby be practised.

The word 'counterfeit' does not connote exact reproduction of the original counterfeit and the difference between the counterfeit and the original is not limited to a difference existing only by reason of faulty reproduction. [*Local Government* v *Seth Motilal Jain* AIR 1937 Nag 341].

Ordinarily "counterfeit" implies the idea of an exact imitation. But for the purpose of the Indian Penal Code there can be counterfeiting even though the imitation is not exact and there are differences in detail between the original and the imitation so long as the resemblance is so close that deception may thereby be practised. [*State of U.P.* v *Hafiz Mohammad Ismail* AIR 1960 SC 669: (1960)2 SCR 911: 1960 Cr LJ 1017: (1961)1 SCJ 166].

**Countermand.** An action that has the effect of voiding something previously ordered; a revocation. [Black's *Law Dictionary*, 7th Ed.].

> NOTE: It may be either express or implied. It becomes express where the order or instruction already given is explicitly annulled or recalled. It becomes implied where the party's conduct is incompatible with the further continuance of the order or instruction, as where a new order is given inconsistent with the former order.

**Counterpart.** In conveyancing, a corresponding part of an instrument; one of two or more copies or duplicates of a legal instrument [Black's *Law Dictionary*, 8th Ed.].

**Countersign.** To write one's own name next to someone else's to verify the other signer's identity. [Black's *Law Dictionary*, 8th Ed.].

To 'countersign' means to sign opposite to, alongside of or in addition to another signature or to add one's signature to a document already signed by another for authentication or confirmation. [*M. Duraiswamy* v *Shri Murugan Bus Service* 1986 (Supp) SCC 1: AIR 1986 SC 1980: (1986)2 SCR 68: JT 1986 SC 518].

Countersign signifies signing in addition to the signature of another in order to attest the authenticity of the signature. By this process the authenticity of the signature on the writing is attested by the person countersigning. [*M. Ramaswamy* v *Manju Bakhru* AIR 1963 Punj 419].

**Course.** The word "course" etymologically denotes movement from one point to another. [*State of Travancore-Cochin* v *Shanmugha Vilas Cashew Nut Factory* AIR 1953 SC 333: 1954 SCR 53: 1953 SCJ 471: (1953)4 STC 205].

'Course' ordinarily convey the meaning of continuous progress from one point to the next in time or space and conveys the idea of a period of time, duration, and not a fixed point of time. [*Commissioner of Income Tax, New Delhi* v *East West Import and Export (P) Ltd*. AIR 1989 SC 836: (1989)1 SCC 760: JT 1989(1) SC 226: (1989)176 ITR 155: (1989)1 SCR 570: (1989)1 Comp LJ 280].

**Course of employment.** Events that occur or circumstances that exist as a part of one's employment; esp., the time during which an employee furthers an employer's goals through employer-mandated directives. [Black's *Law Dictionary*, 7th Ed.].

The expression means while engaged in the service of the employer, while engaged generally in the employer's work, as distinguished from acts done when the employee steps outside of his employment to do an act for himself, not connected with his employer's business.

'In the course of employment' must mean in the course of the work which a man is employed to do, and what is incident to do—in other words, in the course of his service. [*Davidson (Charles R.) & Co.* v *M'Robb or Officer* (1918) AC 304].

NOTE: The course of employment does not necessarily cease with the conclusion of the day's work. The course of employment continues while the workman is lawfully upon the employer's premises. [*Sparey* v *Bath Rural District Council* (1931)146 LT 285].

The 'course of employment' of a workman does not begin until he has reached the place of employment and does not continue when he has left the place of employment, the journey to and from the place of employment being excluded. [*Saurashtra Salt Manufacturing* v *Bai Velu Raja* AIR 1958 SC 881].

When a man is going to or coming from work, along a public road, as a passenger in a vehicle provided by his employer, he is not then in the course of employment—unless he is obliged by the terms of his employment to travel in that vehicle. It is not enough that he should have the right to travel in the vehicle or be permitted to travel in it. He must have an obligation to travel in it. [*Vandyke* v *Fender* (1970)2 All ER 335].

**Court.** An organ of the Government, belonging to the judicial department, whose function is the application of the laws to controversies brought before it and the public administration of justice; a body in the Government to which the administration of justice is delegated; a body organised to administer justice; an incorporeal, political being, composed of one or more judges, who sit at fixed times and places, attended by proper officers, pursuant to lawful authority, for the administration of justice; an organised body with defined powers, meeting at certain times and places for the hearing and decisions of causes and other matters brought before it, and aided in this, its proper business, by its proper officers, viz., attorneys and counsel to present and manage the business, clerks to record and attest its acts and decision, and ministerial officers to execute its commands, and secure due order in its proceedings.

A 'court' is an agency created by the sovereign for the purpose of administering justice. It is a place where justice is judicially administered. It is a legal entity. It is a Tribunal presided over by one or more Judges on whom are conferred certain judicial powers for administering justice in accordance with law. When a Judge takes his seat in court, the court is said to have assembled for administering justice. [*Supreme Court Legal Aid Committee* v *Union of India* (1994)6 SCC 731: 1995 SCC (Cri) 39: JT 1996(6) SC 544: (1995)2 SCJ 36].

The expression also means the 'building where the judge or judges convene to adjudicate disputes and administer justice'. [Black's *Law Dictionary*, 7th Ed.]. 'Court' includes not only the building in which the court is held but also the judges and officials who preside there. [*Mohammad Ghouse* v *State of A.P.* AIR 1959 AP 497].

The word 'court' is used compendiously to denote not only the court proper but also the presiding judge. [*State of West Bengal* v *Nripendra Nath Bagchi* AIR 1966 SC 447].

In order to constitute a court in the strict sense of the term, an essential condition is that the court should have, apart from having some of the trappings of a judicial tribunal, power to give a decision or a definitive judgment which has finality and authoritativeness which are the essential tests of a judicial pronouncement. [*Brajnandan Sinha* v *Jyoti Narain* AIR 1956 SC 66: 1956 Cr LJ 156: 1956 SCJ 155: 1956 SCA 52: (1955)2 SCR 665].

▸*Meaning under the Contempt of Courts Act 1971.* The term 'court' has not been defined in the Act. The term 'court' is used in s. 2 of the Act in a wide sense, as including a tribunal legally authorised to deal with a particular matter judicially. It is enough if the tribunal is entrusted with certain judicial functions which include the function of deciding litigated questions according to law, deciding them not arbitrarily, but according to certain rules and procedures which ensure that the person called upon to decide them acts with fairness and impartially. [*Satdev Pandey* v *Baba Raghav Das* 1953 Cr LJ 943: AIR 1953 All 419].

▸*Meaning under the Criminal Procedure Code.* There is no definition of 'court' in the Criminal Procedure Code. But a 'court' is ordinarily understood as a place where justice is judicially administered. For the sake of brevity, the Code uses the term 'court' and 'magistrate' generally, if not always, as convertible terms. [*Re Ramnath Bholgothra* AIR 1953 Mad 953].

▸*Meaning under the Evidence Act 1872.* Broadly speaking, court is a place where justice is administered. The term 'court' is defined in s. 3 of the Evidence Act as including all judges and magistrates and all persons, except arbitrators, legally authorised to take evidence. This definition is by no means exhaustive and it is an inclusive definition framed for the purpose of the Evidence Act.

NOTE: *Court, what is—example.* A Commissioner under the Workmen's Compensation Act 1923, is a court and a court subordinate to the High Court. [*Mohanlal* v *Fine Knitting* AIR 1960 Bom 387].

A Sales Tax Officer is a court within the meaning of s. 195 of the Criminal Procedure Code. [*State* v *Kantilal* AIR 1956 Bom 230].

The Registrar under the Co-operative Societies Act, to all intents and purposes, is a court discharging the same functions and duties in the same manner as a court of law is expected to do. [*Kisen Sahakari Sheetgarh Evamvary Factory Limited* v *R.C. Gupta* 1995 MPLJ 616].

The tribunal which is to exercise the jurisdiction for executing the decree is a 'court' within the meaning of s. 45-C of the Banking Companies Act 1949, whatever may be its status when it passed the decree as a tribunal. [*Shri Ram Narain* v *The Simla Banking and Industrial Company Ltd.* AIR 1956 SC 614: 1956 SCR 603: 1956 SCJ 579].

*Court, what is not—example.* Employees' Insurance Court is not a court for the purposes of Art. 137 of the Limitation Act 1963. [*Popular Process Studio* v *Employees' State Insurance Corporation* AIR 1970 Bom 13: (1970)2 Lab LJ 336].

An arbitrator under the Co-operative Societies Act to whom a reference is made under the act is not a court. [*Chempazhanthi Service Co-operative Ltd.* v *Co-operative Tribunal* 1979 Ker LT 629].

Compensation officer under H.P. Abolition of Big Landed Estates and Land Reforms Act 1954, is not a court. [*Daya Ram* v *Smt. Rashmu* AIR 1966 HP 36].


- **Appeal court** p. 68.
- **Bankruptcy court** p. 95.
- **Civil court** p. 144.
- **Contempt of court** p. 184.
- **Criminal court** p. 207.
- **Full court** p. 377.
- **High court** p. 413.
- **Inferior court** p. 456.
- **Inns of court** p. 461.
- **International Court of Justice** p. 474.
- **International criminal court** p. 475.
- **Leave of court** p. 523.
- **Open court** p. 625.
- **Prize court** p. 690.
- **Probate court** p. 691.
- **Scandalising the court** p. 777.
- **Supreme Court** p. 822.
- **Ward of court** p. 891.


**Court immediately below.** The expression means the court from whose decision the appeal has been filed. [*Durga Prasad* v *Banaras Bank* AIR 1963 SC 1322: (1963)1 SCJ 519; *Ladli Prasad* v *Karnal Distillery Co. Ltd.* AIR 1963 SC 1279: (1964)1 SCR 270: (1964)2 SCJ 12].

**Court-martial.** An *ad hoc* military court, convened under military authority, to try and punish those who violate the uniform code of military justice, particularly members of the armed forces. [Black's *Law Dictionary*, 7th Ed.].

A court convened by or under the authority of the Crown to try an offence against naval, military or air force discipline, or against the ordinary law, committed by a member of the armed forces or the women's services. Courts-martial proceed according to the Acts regulating the discipline of the particular service. [Jowitt's *Dictionary of English Law*, 2nd Ed.].

▸ *Meaning under the Army Act 1950, s. 3(vii).* Court-martial means a court-martial held under the Army Act.

**Court of inquiry.** A court of inquiry functions to enquire into any matter appearing to be connected with an industrial dispute. It only investigates into facts. It has nothing to do with mediation, or with the settlement of an industrial dispute. It is in the nature of a fact-finding body and is constituted as occasion arises. Section 6 of the Industrial Disputes Act 1947 deals with courts of inquiry.

**Court of Justice.** The words "Court of Justice" denote a Judge who is empowered by law to act judicially alone, or a body of Judges which is empowered by law to act judicially as a body, when such Judge or body of Judges is acting judicially. [Indian Penal Code 1860, s. 20].

**Court of record.** A court of record is defined as a 'court whereof the acts and judicial proceedings are enrolled for a perpetual memorial and testimony, and which has power to fine and imprison for contempt of its authority'. [Jowitt's *Dictionary of English Law*].

"Court of record is a court where acts and judicial proceedings are enrolled in parchment for a perpetual memorial and testimony, which rolls are called the 'record' of the court, and are of such high and super eminent authority that their truth is not to be questioned". [*Words & Phrases*, Permanent Ed., vol. 10, p. 429].

A court that is required to keep a record of its proceedings; a court that may fine and imprison people for contempt. [Black's *Law Dictionary*, 8th Ed.].

NOTE: Courts are either of record where their acts and judicial proceedings are enrolled for a perpetual memorial and testimony and they have power to fine and imprison; or not of record being courts of inferior dignity, and in less proper sense the King's Courts—and these are not entrusted by law with any power to fine or imprison the subject of the realm, unless by the express provision of some Act of

Parliament. These proceedings are not enrolled or recorded. [Wharton's *Law Lexicon*].

Certain courts are expressly declared by statute to be courts of record. In the case of courts not expressly declared to be courts of records, the answer to the question whether a court is a court of record seems to depend in general upon whether it has power to fine or imprison, by statute or otherwise, for contempt of itself or other substantive offences; if it has such power, it seems that it is a court of record. The proceedings of a court of record preserved in its archives are called records, and are conclusive evidence of that which is recorded therein. [*Delhi Judicial Service Association* v *State of Gujarat* AIR 1991 SC 2176: (1991)4 SCC 406: 1991 AIR SCW 2419: JT 1991(3) SC 617].

Under Art. 129 of the Constitution of India, the Supreme Court is a court of record and has all the powers of such a court including the power to punish for contempt of itself. Under Art. 215 of the Constitution every High Court is a court of record and has all the powers of such a court including the power to punish for contempt of itself.

**Court of Session.** The expression in s. 408 of the Criminal Procedure Code 1898, refers to the Court of Session presided over by the Sessions Judge. [*Kamleshwar Singh* v *Dharamdeo Singh* AIR 1957 Pat 375: 58 Cr LJ 879].

**Court of Small Causes.** Court of Small Causes in s. 24 of the Code of Civil Procedure 1908, includes both Court of Small Causes constituted under the Provincial Small Cause Courts Act and court invested with jurisdiction of a Court of Small Causes. [*Pitambar Shivlal* v *Patel Hargovanbai* AIR 1972 Guj 119].

**Court which passed a decree.** Court which passed a decree, or words to that effect, shall, in relation to the execution of decrees, unless there is anything repugnant in the subject or context, be deemed to include—(*a*) where the decree to be executed has been passed in the exercise of appellate jurisdiction, the court of first instance, and (*b*) where the court of first instance has ceased to exist or to have jurisdiction to execute it, the court which, if the suit wherein the decree was passed was instituted at the time of making the application for execution of the decree, would have jurisdiction to try such suit. [Code of Civil Procedure 1908, s. 37].

**Covenant.** A formal agreement or promise, usually in a contract. [Black's *Law Dictionary*, 7th Ed.].

A covenant is an agreement under seal whereby the parties, or some or one of them, are or is bound to do or not to do a specified thing, as covenants in a lease under seal to pay rent or not to carry on certain trades; or whereby they undertake that a certain state of affairs exists, as a covenant in a conveyance that the grantor is entitled or that he has not incumbered. [Halsbury's *Laws of England*, 4th Ed., vol. 12, para 1539, p. 661].

A covenant is an agreement, convention or promise of two or more parties, by deed in writing, signed, sealed and delivered, by which either of the parties pledged himself to the other that something is either done or shall be done, or stipulates for the truth of certain facts. He who thus promises is called the covenantor and he to whom it is made is called the covenantee. [Wharton's *Law Lexicon*].

NOTE: A covenant may be express or implied. An express covenant is an agreement which is framed in express terms, or is inferred on the construction of the entire instrument. An implied covenant, or covenant in law, is one which the law implies either from the nature of the transaction or from the use of certain technical words. [Halsbury's *Laws of England*, 3rd Ed., vol. 23, pp. 598, 599].


- **Negative covenant** p. 602.
- **Personal covenant** p. 659.
- **Positive covenant** p. 670.
- **Usual covenants** p. 871.


**Covenants running with the land.** A covenant runs with the land where it is annexed to the land and which is an exception to the general rule that all covenants are personal. A covenant runs with the land when the benefit or burden of it, whether at law or in equity, passes to the successors in title of the covenantee or the covenantor, as the case may be. [Law of Property Act 1925, s. 80].

NOTE: Covenants for title implied in sales under s. 55(2) and implied covenants in mortgages under s. 65 and implied covenants for quiet enjoyment under s. 108(c) and restrictive covenants referred to in the first paragraph of s. 40 of the Transfer of Property Act 1882, are instances of covenants running with the land. While s. 40 contemplates negative covenants, s. 11 contemplates both positive and negative covenants.

**Cover.** Means (1) any form of security given to cover a liability, *e.g.*, security or cash lodged by a client with his broker when the client buys securities without making payment in full; and (2) the relationship, in the case of dividend of a company, between the earning of a company and the amount distributed by way of dividend out of those earnings. Distribution in full means that the dividend is covered once. The term is also used of assets, cover for a loan or debenture stock.

**Coverture.** Covering; shelter; the position of a married woman, considered to be under her husband's protection.

"Coverture" is by-law applied to the state and condition of a married woman, who is *sub potestati viri* (under the power of her husband) and therefore unable to contract with any to the damage of herself or husband, without his consent and privity, or his allowance and confirmation thereof. When a woman is married, she is called a Femme Couvert, and whatever is done concerning her during marriage is said to be done during coverture. [*The Pocket Lawyer and Family Conveyancer*, 3rd Ed. 1833, p. 96].

Coverture is a French word signifying anything that covereth, as apparel, a coverlet.

**Cowle.** A lease for a long period. The word ordinarily denotes a lease and not a mortgage. [*T.K. Lakshmana Iyer* v *State of Madras* AIR 1968 SC 1489: (1968)3 SCR 542: (1969)1 SCA 1, referring to Wilson's *Glossary*].

**Credit.** It has got different meaning in different context. It may mean belief, trust. It may also mean one's ability to borrow money; the faith in one's ability to pay debts; the ability of a customer to obtain goods or services before payment. It may further mean the time that a seller gives the buyer to make the payment that is due; an entry in an account recording a sum received.

• **Bill of credit** p. 104.
• **Letter of credit** p. 530.
• **Trader's credit** p. 850.

**Credit transfer.** This is a method of payment through banks without cheques. The creditor having agreed, the debtor prepares a standard form of credit voucher showing the amount due, the name of the creditor and his branch bank. The debtor hands the voucher to his bank who charges his account with the payment. Alternatively, a debtor may hand the prepared credit voucher to any bank with cash to cover the payment. The vouchers are cleared through to the creditor's bank and credited to his account. [Osborn & Grandage's *Concise Commercial Dictionary*].

**Creditor.** A person to whom a debt is owing by any person who is the "debtor" [*Rooney* v *Inheritance Tax Commission of Kansas* 53 P 2d 500, 501]; one who has a right to require the fulfilment of an obligation or contract [*Murphy* v *Jos Hollander, Inc.* 34 A 2d 780, 783]; one to whom money is due, and, in ordinary acceptation, has reference to financial or business transactions. [*Erickson* v *Grande Ronde Lumber Co.* 92 P 2d 170, 177].

In law of bankruptcy, a creditor is a person or entity having a claim against the debtor predating the order for relief concerning the debtor. [Black's *Law Dictionary*, 7th Ed.]. The word 'creditor' is used in the sense of a person having a claim which can be proved under the bankruptcy, whether it is strictly a debt or not. [*Wood* v *DeMattos* (1865) LR 1 Exch 91]. 'Creditor' means any person who, at the date of payment to him, would have had to come in and prove and rank with the other creditors in the bankruptcy. A surety would be such a person. [*Re Black Pool* v *Black Pool* (1901)1 Ch 77].

Section 126 of the Indian Contract Act 1872 defines a creditor as a person to whom a guarantee is given.

In its broad sense the word 'creditor' means one who has any legal liability upon a contract, express or implied, or in tort; in its narrow sense, the term is limited to one who holds a demand which is certain and liquidated.

> NOTE: To become a creditor there should be a debt legal or equitable owing or accruing. It must be an actual debt which means a definite ascertained sum of money which is now payable or will become payable in future by reason of present obligation. It should not be a conditional or contingent one. [*C. Krishnaiah* v *M.A. Muthiah* AIR 1958 AP 342: ILR (1958) AP 42].


- **Displaced creditor** p. 268.
- **Judgment creditor** p. 492.
- **Secured creditor** p. 781.


**Crime.** A crime is an unlawful act or default which is an offence against the public, and renders the person guilty of the act or default liable to legal punishment. While a crime is often also an injury to a private person, who has a remedy in a civil action, it is an act or default contrary to the order, peace, and well-being of society that a crime is punishable by the State. [Halsbury's *Laws of England*, 3rd Ed., vol. 10, p. 271].

A crime "is an offence for which the law awards punishment". [*Mann* v *Owen* (1829)9 B&C 595, 602, *per* Littledale, J.].

A crime or misdemesnor is an act committed, or omitted, in violation of a public law either forbidding or commanding it. This general definition comprehends both crimes and misdemesnors which, properly speaking, are more synonymous terms: though, in common usage, the word "crime" is made to denote such offences as are of a deeper and more atrocious dye; while a smaller fault and omission of less consequence are comprised under the gentler names of 'misdemesnors' only. [*R.* v *Tyler* (1891)2 QB 594, *per* Bowen, L.J.].

A crime is an act committed or omitted in violation of a law forbidding or commanding it, and to which is annexed, upon conviction, either, or a combination, of the following punishments: (1) death; (2) imprisonment; (3) fine; (4) removal from office; or (5) disqualification to hold and enjoy any office of honour, trust, or profit.

> NOTE: A crime is an act deemed by law to be harmful to society in general, even though its immediate victim is an individual. The notion of crime as a threat to the whole community is a material counterpart of the formal rule that the State alone is master of a criminal prosecution. No private person has a direct interest in a criminal proceeding, although exception may be made by the statute in certain cases. It is common knowledge that a criminal prosecution is not intended for the private satisfaction of a personal vendetta or revenge. [*P.A.R. Sadhanantham* v *Arunchalam* AIR 1980 SC 856:1980 SCC (Cri) 649: (1980)2 SCC 141].


- **Compound a crime** p. 164.
- **White-collar crime** p. 897.


**Criminal.** One who has committed a criminal offence; one convicted of a crime; gangster; hardened offender; underworld character.


- **Fugitive criminal** p. 376.
- **Habitual criminal** p. 404.


**Criminal breach of trust.** Whoever, being in any manner entrusted with property, or with any dominion over property, dishonestly misappropriates or converts to his own use that property, or dishonestly uses or disposes of that property in violation of any direction of law prescribing the mode in which such trust is to be discharged, or of any legal contract, express or implied, which he has made touching the discharge of such trust, or wilfully suffers any other person so to do, commits "criminal breach of trust". [Indian Penal Code 1860, s. 405].

**Criminal charge.** To accuse a person of criminal conduct. [Black's *Law Dictionary*, 7th Ed.]. 'Criminal charge' connotes nothing more nor less than a criminal accusation. It has no reference whether a charge is to be framed or not [*In re Nagabhushanam* AIR 1966 AP 72]. Any offence which is created by any statute and is punishable by any penalty imposed thereby would be included within the concept of a criminal charge. [*Sunil Kr. Ghose* v *State of West Bengal* AIR 1970 Cal 384].

**Criminal conspiracy.** When two or more persons agree to do or cause to be done, (1) an illegal act, or (2) an act which is not illegal by illegal means, such an agreement is designated a criminal conspiracy: Provided that no agreement except an agreement to commit an offence shall amount to a criminal conspiracy unless some act besides the agreement is done by one or more parties to such agreement in pursuance thereof. [Indian Penal Code 1860, s. 120A].

Criminal conspiracy is an agreement by two or more persons to commit an unlawful act; a combination for an unlawful purpose. [Black's *Law Dictionary*, 7th Ed.].

**Criminal contempt.** It is an "act that obstructs justice or attacks the integrity of the court". [Black's *Law Dictionary*, 7th Ed.].

Section 2(*c*) of the Contempt of Courts Act 1971 defines "criminal contempt" to mean publication of any matter, or the doing of any other act which (*i*) scandalises or tends to scandalise, or lowers or tends to lower the authority of, any court; or (*ii*) prejudices, or interferes or tends to interfere with, the due course of any judicial proceeding; or (*iii*) interferes or tends to interfere with, or obstructs or tends to obstruct, the administration of justice in any other manner.

NOTE: Clause (*c*) of s. 2 of the Contempt of Courts Act 1971 merely codifies the definition of "criminal contempt" which had previously been crystallized by judicial decisions. [*S. Abdul Karim* v *M.K. Prakash* AIR 1976 SC 859: (1976)1 SCC 975: (1976)3 SCR 276: 1976 Cr LJ 641: 1976 SCC (Cri) 217].

In the categorisation of contempt in the three sub-cls. (*i*) to (*iii*), only category (*ii*) refers to "judicial proceeding". Scandalising of court in its administrative capacity will be covered by sub-cls. (*i*) and (*iii*).

The phrase "administration of justice" in sub-cl. (*iii*) is far wider in scope than a "course of any judicial proceeding". The last words "in any other manner" of sub-cl. (*iii*) further extend its ambit and give it a residuary character. Although sub-cls. (*i*) to (*iii*) describe three distinct species of "criminal contempt", they are not always mutually exclusive. Interference or tendency to interfere with any judicial proceeding or administration of justice is a common element of sub-cls. (*ii*) and (*iii*). This element is not required to be established for a criminal contempt of any of the kind falling under sub-cl. (*i*). [*Rachapudi Subba Rao* v *Advocate General, A.P.* AIR 1981 SC 755: (1981)2 SCC 577: 1981 SCC (Cri) 566: 1981 Cr LJ 315].

A publication which contains highly objectionable and scandalizing remarks about the courts is clear case of court's criminal contempt as defined under s. 2(*c*) of the Contempt of Courts Act 1971. [*Jitendra Maheshwari* v *Govind Ray* 1995 Cr LJ 1514 (MP)].

Filing of successive miscellaneous applications suppressing dismissal of earlier ones amounts to criminal contempt of court by interfering with due course of justice. [*Re A.K. Prakash* 1995 Cr LJ 1663 (Ker)].

A criminal contempt proceeding is punitive in nature.

**Criminal court.** Court trying criminal cases.

NOTE: Section 6 of the Criminal Procedure Code 1973 states that besides the High Courts and the courts constituted under any law other than Criminal Procedure Code for the time being in force there should be four classes of Criminal Courts in India, namely, (*i*) Courts of Session; (*ii*) Judicial Magistrate of the first class and, in any metropolitan area, Metropolitan Magistrate; (*iii*) Judicial Magistrate of the second class; and (*iv*) Executive Magistrates.

A Municipal Magistrate appointed to deal with offences against the Calcutta Municipal Act 1951 is a court constituted under a law other than the Cr. P.C. for the time being in force and comes within this section. [*Ramgopal* ILR 52 Cal 962, 969].

**Criminal force.** Whoever intentionally uses force to any person, without that person's consent, in order to the committing of any offence, or intending by the use of such force to cause, or knowing it to be likely that by the use of such force he will cause injury, fear or annoyance to the person to whom the force is used, is said to use criminal force to that other. [Indian Penal Code 1860, s. 350].

NOTE: The following are the ingredients of criminal force: (*i*) the intentional use of force to any person; (*ii*) such force must have been used without the person's consent; (*iii*) the force must have been used—(*a*) in order to the committing of an offence; or (*b*) with the intention to cause, or knowing it to be likely that he will cause, injury, fear or annoyance to the person to whom it is used.

**Criminal intimidation.** Whoever threatens another with any injury to his person, reputation or property, or to the person or reputation of any one in whom that person is interested, with intent to cause alarm to that person, or to cause that person to do any act which he is not legally bound to do, or to omit to do any act which that person is legally entitled to do, as the means of avoiding the execution of such threat, commits criminal intimidation. [Indian Penal Code 1860, s. 503].

NOTE: The following are the ingredients of criminal intimidation: (1) Threatening a person with any injury—(*i*) to his person, reputation or property; or (*ii*) to the person, or reputation of any one in whom that person is interested. (2) The threat must be with intent—(*i*) to cause alarm to that person; or (*ii*) to cause that person to do any act which he is not legally bound to do as the means of avoiding the execution of such threat; or (*iii*) to cause that person to omit to do any act which that person is legally entitled to do as the means of avoiding the execution of such threat.

**Criminal law.** The body of law defining offences against the community at large, regulating how suspects are investigated, charged, and tried, and establishing punishments for convicted offenders [Black's *Law Dictionary*, 7th Ed.]; that body of law, whether dealing with *mala prohibita* or *mala in se*, the infraction of which is a crime or an offence punishable by a criminal proceeding. [Stroud's *Judicial Dictionary*, 3rd Ed.].

**Criminal misconduct.** A transgression of some established and definite rule of action inviting criminal action; a forbidden act inviting criminal action when done; unlawful behaviour inviting criminal action; a public officer's corrupt violation of assigned duties by malfeasance, misfeasance, or nonfeasance inviting criminal action.

▸*Meaning under the Prevention of Corruption Act 1988.* The expression is to be understood in the context of what is said in s. 13(1) which runs thus: "A public servant is said to commit the offence of criminal misconduct—(*a*) if he habitually accepts or obtains or agrees to accept or attempts to obtain from any person for himself or for any other person any gratification other than legal remuneration as a motive or reward such as is mentioned in s. 7; or (*b*) if he habitually accepts or obtains or agrees to accept or attempts to obtain for himsel f or for any other person, any valuable thing without consideration or for a consideration which he knows to be inadequate from any person whom he knows to have been, or to be, or to be likely to be concerned in any proceeding or business transacted or about to be transacted by him, or having any connection with the official functions of himself or of any public servant to whom he is subordinate, or from any person whom he knows to be interested in or related to the person so concerned; or (*c*) if he dishonestly or fraudulently misappropriates or otherwise converts for his own use any property entrusted to him or under his control as a public servant or allows any other person so to do; or (*d*) if he—(*i*) by corrupt or illegal means, obtains for himself or for any other person any valuable thing or pecuniary advantage; or (*ii*) by abusing his position as a public servant, obtains for himself or for any other person any valuable thing or pecuniary advantage or (*iii*) while holding office as a public servant, obtains for any person any valuable thing or pecuniary advantage without any public interest; or (*e*) if he or any person on his behalf, is in possession or has, at any time during the period of his office, been in possession for which the public servant cannot satisfactorily account, of pecuniary resources or property disproportionate to his known sources of income".

NOTE: Accepting or obtaining or attempting to obtain illegal gratification would be a criminal misconduct. [*State of U.P.* v *Surinder Pal Singh* AIR 1989 SC 811: (1989)2 SCC 470: 1989 SCC (Cri) 402: JT 1989(1) SC 169: 1989 Cr LJ 998: (1989)1 SCR 347: 1989(1) SLR 561].

A public servant is said to commit an offence of criminal misconduct in the discharge of his duty if he, by corrupt or illegal means or by otherwise abusing his position as a public servant, obtains for himself or for any other persons any valuable thing or pecuniary advantage. [*Bishambar Lal* v *State of Punjab* AIR 1966 Punj 175: ILR (1965)1 Punj 651].

**Criminal negligence.** Gross negligence so extreme that it is punishable as a crime. [Black's *Law Dictionary*, 7th Ed.].

Gross or culpable neglect or failure to exercise that reasonable and proper care and precaution to guard against injury either to the public generally or to an individual in particular, which having regard to all the circumstances, it was the imperative duty of the accused person to have adopted. [*H.B. Spiers* v *Johiuddin* AIR 1932 Cal 461].

A criminal negligence or culpable negligence is acting without the consciousness that the illegal or mischievous act will follow, but in circumstances which saw that the actor or author has not exercised the caution incumbent upon him and if he had he would have the consciousness. [*Balchandra Woman* v *State of Maharashtra* 1968 SCD 198; *S.N. Hussein* v *State of A.P.* AIR 1972 SC 685: 1972 Cr LJ 496; *Krishna* v *State of Assam* 1979 Cr LJ 1258].

NOTE: *Example of criminal negligence.* Involuntary man-slaughter or other negligent homicide can be based on criminal negligence, as when an extremely careless automobile driver kills someone.

**Criminal proceeding.** A proceeding instituted to determine a person's guilt or innocence or to set a convicted person's punishment; a criminal hearing or trial.

The expression 'criminal proceeding' means a proceeding which lies under the law of procedure in a criminal court and which is in accordance with some requirement of, or is performed under some power conferred by the relevant procedural provisions.

When a man sets the criminal law in motion against a person by giving information to the police that a person has committed a cognizable offence, he institutes a criminal proceeding against that person within the meaning of s. 211 of the Indian Penal Code 1860. [*Karim Buksh* v *Queen Empress* ILR 17 Cal 574; *Queen Empress* v *Najunda Rau* ILR 20 Mad 79].

NOTE: A criminal proceeding is instituted by giving information to the police that a person has committed cognizable offence. [*Albert* v *State of Kerala* AIR 1966 Ker 11: 66 Cr LJ 26].

Proceedings under ss. 125 and 126 of the Criminal Procedure Code are criminal proceedings. [*Harbhajan Kaur* v *Sant Singh* AIR 1969 Del 298: 1969 Cr LJ 1243].

**Criminal trespass.** The offence committed by one who, without licence or privilege to do so enters or surreptitiously remains upon or in any land, building or occupied structure.

▸ *Meaning under the Indian Penal Code 1860, s. 441.* Whoever enters into or upon any property in the possession of another with intent to commit an offence or to intimidate, insult or annoy any person in possession of such property, or, having lawfully entered into or upon such property, unlawfully remains there with intent thereby to intimidate, insult or annoy any such person, or with intent to commit an offence, is said to commit criminal trespass.

NOTE: The offence of criminal trespass is committed when a person without effective consent enters or remains on property or in building of another knowingly or intentionally or recklessly when he had notice that entry was forbidden or received notice to depart but failed to do so. [*Day* v *State* Tex Cr App, 532 SW 2d 302, 306].

**Crop(s).** The produce of cultivated plants, esp. cereals; cultivated plants or grains collectively; the season's total yield of this.

The meaning to be ascribed to the word 'crop' is that it connotes in its larger signification, products of the soil that are grown and raised yearly and are gathered during a single season. In this sense the term includes *fructus industriales* and having regard to the etymology of the word "crop", it has been held to mean only products after they have been severed from the soil. [*Rev. Fr. K.C. Alexandar* v *State of Kerala* AIR 1973 SC 2498: (1974)1 SCR 399: (1973)2 SCC 737].

• **Growing crops** p. 401.

**Crop insurance.** See under INSURANCE p. 468.

**Cross appeal.** An appeal by the appellee, usually heard at the same time as the appellant's appeal. [Black's *Law Dictionary*, 8th Ed.].

NOTE: If *A* files an appeal against *B*, the latter too may file a cross appeal against *A* if both are dissatisfied with the decree. Instead of filing a cross appeal *B* may file a cross objection to the decree on the self-same grounds on which he could have filed a cross appeal. The procedure is laid down in Or. 41, r. 22 of the Code of Civil Procedure 1908.

**Cross-examination.** The questioning of a witness at a trial or hearing by the party opposed to the party who called the witness to testify. [Black's *Law Dictionary*, 8th Ed.].

Cross-examination is examination of a witness on one side by the other, generally after examination in chief, *i.e.*, examination by the party calling.

▸ *Meaning under the Indian Evidence Act 1872, s. 137.* The examination of a witness by the adverse party shall be called his cross-examination.

NOTE: Questions lawful in cross-examination are dealt with in s. 146. The purpose of cross-examination is to discredit a witness before the fact-finder in any of several ways, as by bringing out contradictions and improbabilities in earlier testimony, by suggesting doubts to the witness, and by trapping the witness into admissions that weaken the testimony. The cross-examiner is typically allowed to ask leading questions but is traditionally limited to matters covered on direct examination and to credibility issues.

**Crossed cheque.** A cheque usually crossed by putting two parallel traverse lines across the face of the cheque.

NOTE: A cheque may be crossed generally or specially. Section 123 of the Negotiable Instruments Act 1881, deals with cheques crossed generally and s. 124 deals with cheques crossed specially.

Section 123 provides that where a cheque bears across its face an addition of the words "and company" or any abbreviation thereof, between two parallel traverse lines or of two parallel traverse lines simply either with or without the words "not negotiable" that addition shall be deemed a crossing and the cheque shall be deemed to be crossed generally.

Section 124 provides that where a cheque bears across its face an addition of the name of a banker either with or without the words "not negotiable" that addition shall be deemed a crossing and the cheque shall be deemed to be crossed specially, and to be crossed to that banker.

Where a cheque is crossed generally the banker on whom it is drawn shall pay only to a banker; and where a cheque is crossed specially "the banker on whom it is drawn shall pay only to the banker to whom it is crossed or his agent for collection.

**Cruelty.** The intentional and malicious infliction of mental or physical suffering on a living creature, especially a human; abusive treatment; outrage. [Black's *Law Dictionary*, 8th Ed.].

The legal conception of cruelty, which is not defined by statute, is generally described as conduct of such a character as to have caused danger to life, limb, or health (bodily or mental), or as to give rise to a reasonable apprehension of such danger. [Halsbury's *Laws of England*, 3rd Ed., vol. 12, p. 269].

▸ *Meaning under the Indian Penal Code 1860, s. 498A.* In s. 498A cruelty has been defined as (*i*) any wilful conduct which is of such a nature as is likely to drive the woman to commit suicide or to cause grave injury or danger to life, limb or health of the woman; or (*ii*) harassment of the woman where such harassment is with a view to coercing her or any person related to her to meet any unlawful demand for any property or valuable security or is on account of failure by her or any person related to her to meet such demand. [*Dilbag Singh* v *State of H.P.* (1995)4 SLJ 3086].

NOTE: The term 'cruelty' in s. 498A has to be given an extended meaning. If the woman continues to suffer the mental agony or torture as a result of the acts done to her by the husband or his relatives forcing her to leave the matrimonial home, it must be said that the cruelty is continuing. [*Bhaskar Mitra* v *State of Bihar* (1997)2 BLJ 182].

The word 'cruelty' in common English acceptation denotes a state of conduct which is painful and distressing to another. The legislative intent is clear enough to indicate that in the event of there being a state of conduct by the husband to the wife or by any relative of the husband which can be attributed to be painful or distressing, the same would be within the meaning of s. 498A. [*Arvind Singh* v *State of Bihar* AIR 2001 SC 2124: 2001 Cr LJ 2556: JT 2001(5) SC 127: (2001)6 SCC 407].

▸ *Meaning under the Hindu Marriage Act 1955.* Cruelty is one of the grounds for judicial separation and divorce under the Hindu Marriage Act 1955. The word 'cruelty' has not been defined in the Hindu Marriage Act. [*Sova Rani* v *Madhukar Reddi* AIR 1988 SC 121: (1988)1 SCC 105: (1988)1 SCR 1010]. So far as the Hindu Marriage Act is concerned, it is not necessary, as under the English law, that the cruelty must be of such a character as to cause danger to life, limb or health or as to give rise to a reasonable apprehension of such a danger. Clearly, danger to life, limb or health or a reasonable apprehension of it is a higher requirement than a reasonable apprehension that it is harmful or injurious for one spouse to live with the other. [*Dr. N.G. Dastane* v *S. Dastane* AIR 1975 SC 1534: (1975)2 SCC 326: (1975)3 SCR 967].

NOTE: Cruelty is a question of fact. Where the conduct of the respondent spouse is so bad that the other should not be called on to endure it, cruelty is established; it is immaterial whether the respondent's conduct was aimed at the other spouse or due to unwarranted indifference, attributable, perhaps, to selfishness or laziness. [*Trambak Narayan* v *Kumudini* AIR 1967 Bom 80].

Cruelty is not confined to physical cruelty. It includes mental cruelty as well. [*Kalpana Srivastava* v *Surendra* AIR 1985 All 253].

Cruelty is a ground for judicial separation and divorce under the Divorce Act 1869 and the Special Marriage Act 1954.

- **Legal cruelty** p. 525.
- **Matrimonial cruelty** Lopes and Lindley, LJJ. in *Russell* v *Russell* [(1895) P 315 affirmed in HL (1897) AC 395] defined matrimonial cruelty thus: "There must be danger to life, limb, or health, bodily or mental, or a reasonable apprehension of it, to constitute legal cruelty". There must be misconduct of a grave and weighty nature and it must be proved that there is a real injury to health or a reasonable apprehension of such injury [*Le Brocq* v *Le Brocq* (1964)1 WLR 1085; *Noble* v *Noble and Ellis (No. 2)* (1964)1 All ER 577, affirmed in (1964)1 All ER 769; *Mulhouse* v *Mulhouse* (1964)2 All ER 50], and the conduct must be capable of appearing the description of cruelty in the generally accepted use of that word. [*Mulhouse* v *Mulhouse* (1964)2 All ER 50].

NOTE: *Examples of matrimonial cruelty*

- Duress, or threats, or habitual insult and studied unkindness, tending to injury to health. [*Kelly* v *Kelly* LR 2 P&D 59].
- Terrifying a wife into immorality. [*Coleman* v *Coleman* 35 LJ P&M 37].
- Publicly outraging a wife's feelings by insulting language and assaulting her, even though no personal injury be inflicted. [*Milner* v *Milner* 31 LJ P&M 159].
- Knowingly or recklessly imparting a venereal disease. [*Boardman* v *Boardman* LR 1 P&D 233].
- The practice of coitus interruptus. [*Trice* v *Cackett* (1950)1 All ER 677].
- Demand for dowry. [*Shobha Rani* v *Madhukar Reddi* AIR 1988 SC 121: (1988)1 SCC 105: (1988)1 SCR 1010].

- Husband disowning paternity of children and putting charge of chastity of wife. [*Khadijabibi Umar Aliya* v *Husan Yusuf Umar Aliya* (1993)1 Guj LR 437].

**Culpa lata.** Gross negligence.

**Culpa levis.** Slight negligence.

**Culpable homicide.** Whoever causes death by doing an act with the intention of causing death, or with the intention of causing such bodily injury as is likely to cause death, or with the knowledge that he is likely by such act to cause death, commits the offence of culpable homicide. [Indian Penal Code 1860, s. 299].

NOTE: 'Culpable homicide' is not murder when the case is brought within the five exceptions to s. 300, I.P.C. [*Kishore Singh* v *State of M.P.* AIR 1977 SC 2267: (1977)4 SCC 524: (1978)1 SCR 635: 1977 Cr LJ 1937].

**Culpae paena par esto.** Let punishment be in proportion to the crime.

**Cultivable land.** Land which can be brought under cultivation is cultivable land, unless some provision of law provides for holding it otherwise in certain circumstances. [*Athmanathaswami* v *K. Gopalaswami* AIR 1965 SC 338: (1964)3 SCR 763: (1964)1 SCJ 105: 1964 SCD 549].

**Cultivate.** Prepare and use soil etc. for crops or gardening; raise or produce crops. [*The Concise Oxford Dictionary*, 9th Ed.].

To work by stirring, fertilizing, sowing and reaping; raise crops from; to bestow labour and care upon for the purpose of aiding and improving growth. [Webster's *Comprehensive Dictionary*, International Ed.].

The word 'cultivate' means to prepare (land) for crops, till or to raise (crops) by farming or gardening etc. [*Manjee* v *State of Rajasthan* 1996 JIC 823 (Raj)].

**Cultivator.** Cultivator includes not only the person who actually toils on the land on his own account but also the owner of the land who gets it cultivated through his farm servant or daily labourer. [*Nallakaruppan Chettiar* v *Subbiah* AIR 1960 Mad 331].

**Culvert.** An underground channel carrying water across a road, etc.

'Culvert' in common parlance would come under the expression 'bridge'. [*Mercantile E. Co.* v *Assistant Customs Collector* AIR 1958 Cal 630].

**Curfew.** A regulation restricting or forbidding the public circulation of people, especially requiring people to remain indoors between specified hours, usually at night. [*The Concise Oxford Dictionary*, 9th Ed.].

A regulation that forbids people (or certain classes of them) from being outdoors between certain hours. [Black's *Law Dictionary*, 7th Ed.].

**Currency.** Coined money and such bank notes or other paper money as are authorised by law and do in fact circulate from hand to hand as a medium of exchange. [Black's *Law Dictionary*, 5th Ed.].

An item (such as a coin, Government note, or bank note) that circulates as a medium of exchange. [Black's *Law Dictionary*, 8th Ed.].

NOTE: Currency includes all coins, currency notes, bank notes, postal notes, postal orders, money orders, cheques, drafts, travellers' cheques, letters or credit, bills of exchange and promissory notes. [Foreign Exchange Regulation Act 1947, s. 2(*b*)].


- **Foreign currency** p. 364.
- **Hard currency** p. 406.
- **Indian currency** p. 450.
- **National currency** p. 598.


**Current asset.** Any property convertible into cash in the normal operation of business at any early date, usually within one year.

An asset that is readily convertible into cash, such as a marketable security, a note, or an account receivable. [Black's *Law Dictionary*, 8th Ed.].

▸ *Meaning under the Industries (Development and Regulation) Act 1951, s. 3(aa).* Bank balances and cash, and includes such other assets or reserves as are expected to be realised in cash or sold or consumed within a period of not more than twelve months in the ordinary course of business, such as, stock-in-trade, amounts due from sundry debtors for sale of goods and for services rendered, advance tax payments and bills receivable, but does not include sums credited to a provident fund, a pension fund, a gratuity fund or any other fund for the welfare of the employees, maintained by a company owning an industrial undertaking.

It is also termed as liquid asset; quick asset; short-term asset.

**Current liability.** A liability payable in the normal operation of a business at an early date, usually within one year, normally by expending current assets.

Collectively, all debts and other liabilities that are payable within one year. [Black's *Law Dictionary*, 7th Ed.].

A business liability that will be paid or otherwise discharged with current assets or by creating other current liabilities within the next year (or operating cycle). [Black's *Law Dictionary*, 8th Ed.].

▸ *Meaning under the Industries (Development and Regulation) Act 1951, s. 3(ab).* Liabilities which must be met on demand or within a period of twelve months from the date they are incurred, and includes any current liability which is suspended under s. 18FB.

The phrase "current liability" carries with it the idea of a liability that is presently enforceable. [*Warren Co.* v *Commissioner of Internal Revenue* CCA Ga, 135 F 2d 679, 684, 685].

It is also known as short-term debt.

**Custody.** The care and control of a thing or person; keeping, guarding, care, watch, inspection, preservation or security of a thing, carrying with it the idea of the thing being within the immediate personal care and control of the person to whose custody it is subjected; immediate charge and control and not the final, absolute control of ownership, implying responsibility for the protection and preservation of the thing in custody; also the detainer of a man's person by virtue of lawful process or authority. [Black's *Law Dictionary*, 5th Ed.].

The term is very elastic and may mean actual imprisonment or physical detention or mere power, legal or physical, of imprisoning or of taking manual possession. [Black's *Law Dictionary*, 5th Ed.].

Custody, in criminal law is the same thing as detention in civil law, and is synonymous with 'imprisonment'. [*Words and Phrases*, Permanent Ed., p. 722]. 'Imprisonment' is the detention of a person contrary to his will. [*Words and Phrases*, Permanent Ed., p. 722].

'Custody' means physical imprisonment as distinct from being on bail. Even if the accused is in prison after his arrest in a criminal case without an order or warrant of remand by a competent court, he is in custody as distinct from being on bail. The word 'custody', therefore, embraces both legal imprisonment as well as illegal imprisonment. [*Surjeet Singh* v *State of U.P.* 1984 All LR 98: 1984 All LJ 375].

▸ *Meaning under the Criminal Procedure Code 1973.* Under s. 439 "custody" includes physical surrender by the accused before the court coupled with submission to the jurisdiction and orders of the court. He who is under the control of the court or is in the physical hold of an officer with coercive power is in custody for purpose of s. 439. This word is of elastic semantics but its core meaning is that the law has taken control of the person. [*Niranjan Singh* v *Prabhakar Rajaram Kharote* AIR 1980 SC 785: (1980)2 SCC 559: (1980)3 SCR 15].

▸ *Meaning under the Guardians and Wards Act 1890.* 'Custody' in s. 25 means any form of custody, actual or constructive or in other words physical or legal. [*Sarada Nayar* v *Vayankara* AIR 1957 Ker 158; *Geeta* v *Ratan* AIR 1966 MP 221].

• **Legal custody** p. 525.

**Custom.** A tariff or duty assessed by law, levied upon goods imported or exported; the official department that administers this.

In another sense, custom means the habitual practice of a community or people; an old and general usage that has obtained the force of law; general rules and practices that have become generally adopted through unvarying habit and common use.

The word 'custom' means usual practice, establish usage, business patronage or support. [*Re Sulaiman* 1971 LW (Cr) 267].

A custom is a particular rule which has existed either actually or presumptively from time immemorial, and has obtained the force of law in a particular locality, although contrary to or not consistent with the general common law of the realm. A custom to be valid must have four essential attributes. First, it must be immemorial; secondly, it must be reasonable; thirdly, it must have continued without interruption since its immemorial origin; and, fourthly, it must be certain in respect of its nature generally as well as in respect of the locality where it is alleged to obtain and the persons whom it is alleged to affect. [Halsbury's *Laws of England*, 4th Ed., vol. 12, para 401, p. 2 and para 406, p. 5].

▸ *Meaning under the Hindu Succession Act 1956, s. 3(d); Hindu Marriage Act 1955, s. 3(a).* Custom signifies any rule which, having been continuously and uniformly observed for a long time, has obtained the force of law among Hindus in any local area, tribe, community, group or family: Provided that the rule is certain and not unreasonable or opposed to public policy; and provided further that in the case of a rule applicable only to a family, it has not been discontinued by the family.

NOTE: *Custom and usage—distinction.* The terms "custom" and "usage" are often used interchangeably. Strictly speaking, there is a technical distinction between the two. Usage represents the twilight stage of custom. Custom begins where usage ends.

Usage is an international habit of action that has not yet received full legal attestation. Usages may be conflicting, custom must be unified and self-consistent.

A custom, in the intendment of law, is such a usage as hath obtained the force of a law. [Starke's *International Law*, 6th Ed., p. 34].

The term "custom" has more or less been identified as relating to practices going back to ancient times. The term "usage" seems more appropriate as describing a course of conduct which is recognised as being normal in various types of occupations and contractual relationships. In other words, usage is a question of fact and does not necessarily involve time immemorial. [*Re Gainers, Ltd. & Local 319 United Packinghouse Workers of America* (1964)47 WWR 544, 552 (Alta SC), *per* Riley, J.].

*Custom and prescription—distinction.* Custom is long practice operating as a source of law. Prescription is long practice operating as a source of rights. Both must, however, be reasonable and consistent with statute law.

*Custom—binding nature in India.* A "custom" in order to be binding, must derive its force from the fact that by long usage it has obtained the force of law, but the English rule that "a custom in order that it may be legal and binding, must have been used so long that the memory of man runneth not to the contrary" should not be strictly applied to Indian conditions. [*Thakur Gokalchand* v *Parvin Kumari* AIR 1952 SC 231: 1952 SCR 825].

In India what is necessary to be proved is that the usage has been acted upon in practice for such a long period and with such invariability as to show that it has by common consent been submitted to as the established governing rule. [*Subhani* v *Nawab* AIR 1941 PC 21].


• **Family custom** p. 345.

• **General custom** p. 383.


**Customary easement.** An easement may be acquired by virtue of a local custom. Such easements are called customary easements. [Indian Easements Act 1882, s. 18].

**Customary rites and ceremonies.** The expression means such sastric ceremonies which the caste or community to which the party belongs are customarily followed. [*Rabindra Nath* v *State* AIR 1969 Cal 55: 1969 Cr LJ 164].

**Customer.** One who regularly or repeatedly makes purchases of, or has business dealings with, a tradesman or business [*Aiken Mills* v *United States* DCSC 53 F Supp 524, 526]; ordinarily, one who has had repeated business dealings with another; a buyer, purchaser, consumer or patron.

In banking, ordinarily a person who keeps an account at the bank is its customer. All individuals or companies with whom they do business may properly be called customers. [*Importers Co.* v *Westminster Bank* (1927)2 KB 297].

Broadly speaking, a customer is a person who has the habit of resorting to the same place or person to do business. A person whose money has been accepted by the bank on the footing that the banker will honour up to the amount standing to his credit is a customer of the bank. [*Central Bank* v *Gopinathan* AIR 1970 Ker 74: ILR (1969)1 Ker 167].

**Customs duties.** Duties of customs, or customs, or customs duties, in the strict sense are pecuniary charges or tolls payable upon goods exported from or imported into the country, as contrasted with excise duties which are payable upon goods produced and consumed within the country. [Halsbury's *Laws of England*, 4th Ed., vol. 12, para 501, p. 65].

Customs duties are duties charged upon commodities on their importation into or exportation out of a country. [Wharton's *Law Lexicon*].

Taxes on the importation and exportation of commodities; the tariff or tax assessed upon merchandise imported from, or exported to a foreign country.

**Cy-pres.** Means 'near to it'. Where a clear charitable intention is expressed, it will not be permitted to fail because the mode, if specified, cannot be executed, but the law will substitute another mode *cy-pres*, that is, as near as possible to the mode specified by the donor. [Halsbury's *Laws of England*, 4th Ed., vol. 5, para 696, p. 430].

It is one of the cardinal rules governing execution of charitable trusts that the intention of the donor must be observed and the *cy-pres* principle has been evolved as an auxiliary to this rule and is never allowed to defeat it. [*Ajab Singh* v *Harnam Kaur* AIR 1954 Punj 150]. The principle on which the doctrine of *cy-pres* rests is that the court treats charity in the abstract as the substance of the gift and the particular disposition as the mode, so that in the eye of the court the gift notwithstanding that the particular disposition may not be capable of execution subsists as a legacy which never fails and cannot lapse. [(1876)3 IA 32]. If the intention cannot be executed literally, another mode may be adopted consistent with the general intention of the author. [*Ratilal* v *State of Bombay* AIR 1954 SC 388, 394].

# Dd

**Dacoity.** When five or more persons conjointly commit or attempt to commit a robbery, or where the whole number of persons conjointly committing or attempting to commit a robbery, and persons present and aiding, such commission or attempt, amount to five or more, every person so committing, attempting or aiding, is said to commit "dacoity". [Indian Penal Code 1860, s. 391].

Dacoity is a robbery committed by five or more persons, otherwise there is no difference between the dacoity and robbery. The gravity of the offence consists in the terror it causes by the presence of a number of offenders.

> NOTE: Dacoity is perhaps the only offence which the legislature has made punishable at four stages. When five or more persons assemble for the purpose of committing a dacoity, each of them is punishable under s. 402 of the I.P.C. merely on the ground of joining the assembly. Another stage is that of preparation and if any one makes preparation to commit a dacoity, he is punishable under s. 399. The definition of 'dacoity' in s. 391 of the I.P.C. shows that the other two stages, namely, the stage of attempting to commit and the stage of actual commission of robbery, have been treated alike, and come within the definition. [*State* v *Dhanpat Chamara* AIR 1960 Pat 582]. In other words, attempting to commit dacoity is also dacoity.

**Dag.** A lot or portion of an estate which has been measured and of which the measurement is recorded in the order of time at which it was made. [Wilson's *Glossary*].

**Daily.** Occurring, appearing, or pertaining to everyday; constant; regular; routine; common.

The *prima facie* meaning of daily is "everyday" inclusive of Sunday. [*London County Council* v *South Metropolitan Gas Co.* (1903)2 Ch 532, *per* Joyce, J.].

"'Daily' is an adjective, the precise meaning of which is to be ascertained from the context in which it is used and particularly the substantive which it qualifies. The dictionaries show that 'daily' may mean every week day and Sunday or every week day ..." [*Foster* v *Howard* (1949) VLR 311: (1949) ALR 779, *per* Barry, J.].

**Daily labourer.** It "means a man who, by the terms of his engagement or the course of his labour, is not only a labourer, but one who works every week day and day by day ......" [*McDonald* v *Brown* (1918)87 LJKB 1119 (DC), *per* Darling, J.].

A "daily labourer is one who goes out to his work everyday". [*McDonald* v *Brown,* supra].

**Daily newspaper.** It is one published day by day, rather than periodically.

"When a journal is spoken of as a 'daily newspaper' the phrase is used to describe a publication which is published day by day, rather than periodically, for example, at intervals of a week or a month". [*Foster* v *Howard* (1949) VLR 311: (1949) ALR 779, *per* Barry, J.].

**Daimi kaimi.** The expression indicates permanent tenancy. [*Surendra Kumar* v *Bipin Chandra* AIR 1934 Cal 681: 38 CWN 1001].

**Dairy.** A place, building or establishment where milk is kept and butter or cheese is made; the place of farming or of a farm that is concerned with the production of milk, butter, cheese etc.; a farm devoted to such production; an establishment for the sale or distribution chiefly of milk and milk products.

▸ *Meaning under the Cantonments Act 1924, s. 2(x).* Dairy includes any farm, cattle-shed, milk-store, milk-shop or other place from which milk is supplied or in which milk is kept for purposes of sale or is manufactured for sale into butter, ghee, cheese or curds, and, in relation to a dairyman who does not occupy any premises for the sale of milk, includes any place in which he keeps the vessels used by him for the storage or sale of milk.

**Dairyman.** Dairyman includes any cow-keeper, purveyor of milk or occupier of a dairy. [*Umfereville* v *London County Council* 75 LT 550].

**Daiva form of marriage.** A form of marriage in which the damsel was given to a person who officiated as priest in a sacrifice performed by the father in lieu of *dakshina* or *fee*.

NOTE: This form of marriage was prevalent under the indigenous Hindu Law.

**Dakhal or quabza.** Taking possession, occupancy, engaging or meddling in an affair of another.

The words 'dakhal' or 'quabza' cannot refer to cultivator possession as tenant; the words in a sale deed must in the context refer to possession as a usufructuary mortgagee. [*Jagmohan Ahir* v *Ram Kishen* AIR 1936 Oudh 322].

**Dakhalnama.** A deed of possession or occupancy; a document giving right of occupancy. [*Diwan Manwar* v *Annoda Persad* ILR 5 Cal 644, 647 (FB)]. Acknowledgment of the delivery of possession. [*Prag Chaubey* v *Bhajan* ILR 4 All 291, 292 (FB); Wilson's *Glossary*].

**Dakhila.** A receipt for money or goods, payment of revenue or rent. [Wilson's *Glossary*].

**Dakhilkar.** The word is commonly used in the upper part of India as meaning a tenant with occupancy rights. [*Doma Singh* v *Jaigovind* AIR 1931 Pat 361].

**Dalal.** An agent between buyer and seller, a broker, a salesman. [Wilson's *Glossary*].

**Dalali.** Brokerage, agency, commission. A tax upon brokers. [Wilson's *Glossary*].

NOTE: Dalali, which the assessees get from persons to whom goods are sold, are for income tax purposes certainly payments which have to be included in the income of the firm from which profits are to be determined. [*Daya Chand Hardial* v *Commissioner of Income Tax* AIR 1954 Punj 52].

**Dam.** A dam is a portion of the flowing water of a river which has been temporarily arrested [*White* v *White* 42 SLR 333, *per* Kincairney, L.O.]; a barrier constructed to hold back water and raise its level, forming a reservoir for preventing flooding; a barrier constructed in a stream by a beaver.

**Damage.** Loss, injury, or deterioration caused by the negligence, design, or accident of one person to another, in respect of the latter's person or property.

By damage is understood every loss or diminution of what is a man's own, occasioned by the fault of another; the harm, detriment, or loss sustained by reason of an injury.

'Damage' means the harm or loss suffered or presumed to be suffered by a person as a result of some wrongful act, and a sum of money given to compensate act. A sum of money given to compensate the damage is called 'damage'. [*Amiya Kumar* v *Krishna Singh* 1994 MPLJ 218].

NOTE: Neither in common parlance nor in legal phraseology is the word 'damage' used as applicable to injuries done to the person, but solely as applicable to mischief done to property. [*Smith* v *Brown* (1871) LR 6 QB 729].

▸ *Meaning under the Merchant Shipping Act 1958, s. 443.* The expression 'damage' is not necessarily confined to physical damage. Ordinarily damage is caused by physical contact of the ship, such as in collision. But damage can also be caused to property by breach of contract or acts of commission or omission on the part of the carrier or his agents or servants by reason of the negligent operation and management of the vessel, as, for example, when cargo is damaged by exposure to weather or by negligent stoware; or, by the misconduct of those in charge of the ship, like when cargo is disposed of contrary to the instructions of the owner or by reason of theft and other misdeeds. In all these cases, damage arises by reason of loss caused by what is done by the ship or by the breach, negligence or misdeeds of those in charge of the ship. It must however be noticed that the expression 'damage done by any ship' has been construed by the English Courts as not to apply to claims against the carrying ship for damage done to cargo. [*M.V. Elisabeth* v *Harwan Investment and Trading (P) Ltd.* AIR 1993 SC 1014: 1993 Supp (2) SCC 433: (1992)1 SCR 1003].

NOTE: *'Damage' and 'damages'—distinction.* The word 'damage' is to be distinguished from its plural 'damages' which means a compensation in money for a loss or damage.

The words 'damages' and 'damage' in law have more than one meaning, and great care has to be exercised in examining the context in which they severally appear. 'Damage' may mean injury; 'damage', and 'damages' especially, may mean sums paid under the order of the court for compensation for a breach of contract or a wrong. [*Swansea Corpn.* v *Harpur* (1912)3 KB 493 (CA), *per* Fletcher Moul Ton, LJ.].

The word 'damage' and 'damages' form more than one meaning. It may mean injury; the words may mean sums paid under order of the court for compensation for a breach of contract. Damage means any loss whether actionable as an injury or not. It may be defined as pecuniary compensation which the law awards to a person for the injury he has sustained by reason of the act or default of another whether that act or default is a breach of contract or a tort; damages are the recompense given by process of law to a person for the wrong that another has done to him. [*Benoy Bhusan* v *Sabitri* AIR 1977 Cal 199: (1977)1 CLJ 175].

*Damage and injury—distinction.* The words 'damage' and 'injury' are given as synonyms for each other. The first is generally used in respect to property and the second in relation to persons. 'Damage' has a more restrictive meaning than 'injury' as the latter word may mean a wrong which 'damage' never does. The word 'damage' includes 'injury' when the latter word is used to denote physical harm to persons. [*Provintial Secretary-Treasurer* v *York* (1957)16 DLR (2d) 198, *per* Bridges, J.].

'Injury' is limited to actionable wrong, while 'damage' means loss or harm occurring in fact, whether actionable as an injury or not. [*Crofter Hand Woven Harris Tweed Co. Ltd.* v *Veitch* (1942) AC 435 (HL), *per* Lord Simon, LC.].

**Damages.** A pecuniary compensation or indemnity, which may be recovered in the courts by any person who has suffered loss, detriment, or injury, whether to his person, property, or rights, through the unlawful act or omission or negligence of another [Black's *Law Dictionary*, 5th Ed.]; a sum of money awarded to a person injured by the tort of another [Black's *Law Dictionary*, 5th Ed.]; money claimed by, or ordered to be paid to, a person as compensation for loss or injury. [Black's *Law Dictionary*, 8th Ed.].

"Damages are the sum of money which a person wronged is entitled to receive from the wrongdoer as compensation for the wrong". [Frank Gahan: *The Law of Damages*, p. 1 (1936)].

Damages may be defined as the pecuniary compensation which the law awards to a person for the injury he has sustained by reason of the act or default of another, where that act or default is a breach of contract or a tort; or, put more shortly, damages are the recompense given by process of law to a person for the wrong that another has done him. [Halsbury's *Laws of England*, 3rd Ed., vol. 11, p. 216].

Damages are given to a man as a compensation and satisfaction for some injury sustained; as for a battery, for imprisonment, for slander, or for trespass. [2 Bl Com 438].

"'Damages' to an English lawyer imports this idea, that the sums payable by way of damages are sums which fall to be paid by reason of some breach of duty or obligation, whether that duty or obligation is imposed by contract, by the general law, or legislation". [*Hall Brothers S.S. Co. Ltd.* v *Young* (1939)1 KB 748, 756 (CA), *per* Greene, M.R.].

The word 'damages' has different shades of meaning. It must take its colour and content from its context and it cannot be read in isolation nor can be read out of context when used in a section of a statute. [*Organo Chemical Industries* v *Union of India* AIR 1979 SC 1803: (1979)4 SCC 573].

- **Actual damages** p. 35.
- **Compensatory damages.** Such damages are awarded as compensation for and are merged by the material loss suffered by the plaintiffs. [*Whitfield* v *De Lauret & Co. Ltd.* (1920)29 CLR 71, *per* Knox, CJ.].

"Damages are, in their fundamental character, compensatory, whether the matter complained of be a breach of contract or a tort, the primary theoretical notion is to place the plaintiff in as good a position, so far as money can do it, as if the matter complained of had not occurred ...... this primary notion is controlled and limited by various considerations, but the central idea is compensation, or, as Blackstone (Vol. 2, p. 438 in his commentary) says—'compensation and satisfaction'." [*Whitfield* v *De Lauret & Co. Ltd.* (1920)29 CLR 71, *per* Isaacs, J.].

Compensatory damages are such as will compensate the injured party for the injury sustained, and nothing more; such as will simply make good or replace the loss caused by the wrong or injury. [Black's *Law Dictionary*, 5th Ed.].

Compensatory damages are damages awarded to a person as compensation, indemnity, or restitution for harm sustained by him. [*Northwestern Nat. Cas. Co.* v *McNulty* CA Fla, 307 F 2d 432, 434].

Compensatory damages are damages sufficient in amount to indemnify the injured person for the loss suffered. [Black's *Law Dictionary*, 8th Ed.].

- **Exemplary damages.** Exemplary damages are damages on an increased scale, awarded to the plaintiff over and above what will barely compensate him for his property loss, where the wrong done to him was aggravated by circumstances of violence, oppression, malice, fraud, or wanton and wicked conduct on the part of the defendant, and are intended to solace the plaintiff for mental anguish, laceration of his feelings, shame, degradation, or other aggravations of the original wrong, or else to punish the defendant for his evil behaviour or to make an example of him, for which reason they are also called "punitive" or "punitory" damages or "vindictive" damages.

NOTE: Exemplary damages are damages which may be awarded against a person to punish him for outrageous conduct. [*Wetherbee* v *United Insurance Co. of America* 18 CA 3d 266].

Exemplary damages are based upon an entirely different public policy consideration—that of punishing the defendant or of setting an example for similar wrongdoers in cases in which it is proved that a defendant has acted wilfully, maliciously, or fraudulently.

Exemplary damages are given only in cases of conscious wrong doing in contumelious disregard of another's rights. [*Whitfield* v *De Lauret & Co. Ltd.* (1920)29 CLR 71, 77, *per* Knox, CJ.].

There are two categories of cases in which exemplary damages are awarded, viz., (*i*) where there has been oppressive, arbitrary, or unconstitutional action by the servants of the Government, and (*ii*) where the defendant's conduct has been calculated by him to make a profit which may well exceed the compensation payable to the plaintiff. [*Rookes* v *Barnard* (1964)1 All ER 367, 410, 411 (HL), *per* Lord Devlin].

- **General damages.** General damages are compensation for general damage. General damage is the kind of damage which the law presumes, when a contract is broken or a tort is committed, to flow from the wrong complained of and to be its natural or probable consequence. Thus, general damages are those which the law implies in every breach of contract and in every violation of a legal right. [Halsbury's *Laws of England*, 3rd Ed., vol. 11, p. 217].

General damages are such as the law will presume to be the direct natural or probable consequence of the act complained of. [*Stroms Bruks Akt* v *Hutchison* (1905) AC 515 (HL), *per* Lord Macnaghten].

General damages are such as the law itself implies or presumes to have accrued from the wrong complained of, for the reason that they are its immediate, direct, and proximate result, or such as necessarily result from the injury, or such as did in fact result from the wrong, directly and proximately, and without reference to the special character, condition, or circumstances of the plaintiff. [*Myers* v *Stephens* 233 CA 2d 104].

- **Lawful damages** p. 518.
- **Liquidated damages.** An amount contractually stipulated as a reasonable estimation of actual

damages to be recovered by one party if the other party breaches. [Black's *Law Dictionary*, 8th Ed.].

Liquidated damages is the sum which a party to contract agrees to pay if he breaks some promise and, which having been arrived at by good faith effort to estimate actual damage that will probably ensue from breach, is recoverable as agreed damages if breach occurs. [*In re Plywood Co. of Pa.* CA Pa, 425 F 2d 151, 154].

By the term "liquidated damages" is meant, in the first place, a sum assessed by the parties to a contract and agreed upon by them to be paid as damages by the party who is in default. The term is also applied to sums expressly made recoverable as liquidated damages under a statute. [Halsbury's *Laws of England*, 3rd Ed., vol. 11, pp. 219, 220].

The term "liquidated damages" is applicable when the amount of the damages has been ascertained by the judgment in the action, or when a specific sum of money has been expressly stipulated by the parties to a bond or other contract as the amount of damages to be recovered by either party for a breach of the agreement by the other. [*Stein* v *Bruce* 366 SW 2d 732, 735].

NOTE: *Liquidated damages and penalty—distinction.* The purpose of a penalty is to secure performance, while the purpose of liquidated damages is to fix the amount to be paid in lieu of performance. [Black's *Law Dictionary*, 5th Ed.].

The essence of a penalty is a payment of money stipulated as *in terrorem* of the offending party; the essence of liquidated damages is a genuine covenanted pre-estimate of damage. [*Clydebank Engineering & Shipbuilding Co.* v *Don Fose Ramos Yzquierdo Y Castaneda* (1905) AC 6].

Though the parties to a contract who use the words 'penalty' or 'liquidated damages' may *prima facie* be supposed to mean what they say, yet the expression used is not conclusive. The court must find out whether the payment stipulated is in truth a penalty or liquidated damages. [*Dunlop Pneumatic Tyre Co. Ltd.* v *New Garage & Motor Co. Ltd.* (1915) AC 79, *per* Lord Dunedin].

The question where a sum stipulated is penalty or liquidated damages is a question of construction to be decided upon the terms, and inherent circumstances of each particular contract, judged of as at the time of the making of the contract, not as at the time of the breach. [*Public Works Comr.* v *Hills* (1906) AC 368 (PC)].

The distinction between a penalty and genuine liquidated damages, as they are called, is not always easy to apply, but the courts have made the task simpler by laying down certain guiding principles. In the first place, if the sum payable is so large as to be far in excess of the probable damage on breach, it is almost certainly a penalty. Secondly, if the same sum is expressed to be payable on any one of a number of different breaches of varying importance, it is again probably a penalty, because it is extremely unlikely that the same damage would be caused by these varying breaches. Thirdly, where a sum is expressed to be payable on a certain date, and a further sum in the event of default being made, this latter sum is *prima facie* a penalty, because mere delay in payment is unlikely to cause damage. Finally, it is to be noted that the mere use of the words 'liquidated damages' is not decisive, for it is the task of the court and not of the parties to decide the true nature of the sum payable. [P.S. Atiyah: *An Introduction to the Law of Contract*, 3rd Ed. 1981; pp. 316-17].

• **Nominal damages.** Nominal damages are awarded for the vindication of a right where no real loss or injury can be proved.

"Nominal damages are damages awarded for the infraction of a legal right, where the extent of the loss is not shown, or where the right is one not depending upon loss or damage, as in the case of rights of bodily immunity or rights to have one's material property undisturbed by direct invasion. The award of nominal damages is made as a judicial declaration that the plaintiff's right has been violated". [Charles T. McCormick: *Handbook on the Law of Damages*, p. 85 (1935)].

Where (1) a plaintiff whose rights have been infringed has not in fact sustained any actual damage therefrom or fails to prove that he has; or (2) although the plaintiff has sustained actual damage, the damage arises not from the defendant's wrongful act, but from the conduct of the plaintiff himself; or (3) the plaintiff is not concerned to raise the question of actual loss, but brings his action simply with the view of establishing his right, the damages which he is entitled to receive are called nominal.

[Halsbury's *Laws of England*, 3rd Ed., vol. 11, p. 220].

"Nominal damages" is a technical phrase which means that you have negatived anything like real damage, but that you are affirming by your nominal damages that there is an infraction of a legal right which, though it gives you no right to any real damages at all, yet gives you a right to the verdict or judgment because your legal right has been infringed. But the term 'nominal damages' does not mean small damages. The extent to which a person has a right to recover what is called by the compendious phrase damages, but may be also represented as compensation for the use of something that belongs to him, depends upon a variety of circumstances, and it certainly does not in the smallest degree suggest that because they are small they are necessarily nominal damages". [*Mediana (Owners)* v *Comet (Owners, etc.), The Mediana* (1900) AC 113, 116, *per* Lord Halsbury, L.C.].

Nominal damage is a technical phrase which means that the court has negatived like real damage, but is affirming that there is an infraction of a legal right. [*Indian Hume Pipe Co.* v *Venkanna* AIR 1963 AP 58].

- **Pecuniary damages.** Damages that can be estimated and monetarily compensated. [Black's *Law Dictionary*, 8th Ed.].

NOTE: In estimating such damages not merely the loss of money or saleable property or rights but also all such loss, deprivation, or injury as can be made the subject of calculation and of recompense in money are also taken into consideration. This phrase is now widely considered a redundancy in view of the fact that damages are always technical.

- **Prospective damages.** Future damages that, based on the facts pleaded and proved by the plaintiff, can reasonably be expected to occur. [Black's *Law Dictionary*, 8th Ed.].

The term "prospective damages" is applied to the damages which are awarded to a plaintiff, not as compensation for the ascertained loss which he has sustained at the time of commencing his action, but in respect of loss which it may reasonably be anticipated he will suffer thereafter in consequence of the defendant's act or omission. In some cases such damages are considered too remote. [Halsbury's *Laws of England*, 3rd Ed., vol. 11, pp. 222-223].

- **Remote damages** p. 744.

- **Special damages.** Damages that are alleged to have been sustained in the circumstances of a particular wrong [Black's *Law Dictionary*, 8th Ed.]; those which are the actual, but not the necessary, result of the injury complained of, and which in fact follow it as a natural and proximate consequence in the particular case, that is, by reason of special circumstances or conditions. [*Twin Coach Co.* v *Chance Vought Aircraft, Inc.* 163 A 2d 278, 286].

Special damages are compensation for special damage which is not presumed by law to be the natural and probable or direct consequence of the act or omission complained of but which does in fact result in the circumstances of the particular case and of the injured party's claim to be compensated. In contrast to general damages special damages must be claimed specifically and proved strictly, and are recoverable only where they can be included in the appropriate measure of damages and are not too remote. [Halsbury's *Laws of England*, 3rd Ed., vol. 11, p. 218].

Special damages are given in respect of any consequences reasonably or probably arising from the breach complained of. [*Prehn* v *Royal Bank of Liverpool* (1870) LR 5 Exch 92, *per* Martin, B.].

'Special damages' are such as the law will not infer from the nature of the act. They do not follow in ordinary course. They are exceptional in their character, and therefore, they must be claimed especially and proved strictly. In cases of contract, special or exceptional damages cannot be claimed unless such damages were within the contemplation of both parties at the time of the contract. [*Stroms Bruks Akt., Bolag* v *Hutchison* (1905) AC 515, 525, 526, *per* Lord Macnaghten].

- **Statutory damages.** Damages provided by statute (such as a wrongful death and survival statute), as distinguished from damages provided under the common law [Black's *Law Dictionary*, 8th Ed.]; damages resulting from statutorily created causes of actions, as opposed to actions at common law. [Black's *Law Dictionary*, 5th Ed.].

The term "statutory damages" is one of common usage but has, it seems, no precise accepted meaning. Thus, it is used loosely in reference to damages for breach of a duty imposed by statute, and in these sense the most common example is the action for damages for personal injuries due to a breach of statutory duty, which is an action in tort. [*Words & Phrases Legally Defined* by John. B. Saunders, 2nd Ed.].

NOTE: The term "statutory damages" is more appropriate in cases where the right to claim damages is conferred by statute, or where the damages are regulated or limited by statute. [Halsbury's *Laws of England*, 3rd Ed., vol. 11, p. 221].

- **Unliquidated damages.** Damages that have been established by a verdict or award but cannot be determined by a fixed formula, so they are left to the discretion of the judge. [Black's *Law Dictionary*, 7th Ed.].

Damages are termed unliquidated when they have not been assessed beforehand by the parties or some statute, in which case the jury are at liberty, subject to the rules governing the measure of damages, to award such damages as they think appropriate to the injury which the plaintiff has sustained. [Halsbury's *Laws of England*, 3rd Ed., vol. 11, p. 220].

**Damdupat.** The rule of Damdupat is a branch of Hindu law. It applies to Bombay Presidency, Berar and the town of Calcutta. According to this rule the amount of interest on a loan or debt recoverable at any one time cannot exceed the principal. [*Hariram* v *Madan Gopal* AIR 1920 PC 77: 33 CWN 493].

NOTE: The rule of Damdupat as recognised by Hindu law, in the absence of any statute, is no longer of binding force and cannot be given effect to as it clearly hits Art. 15(1) of the Constitution of India and as such would be void under Art. 13(1). [*Sheokaran Singh* v *Daulatram* AIR 1955 Raj 201].

**Damnosa hæreditas.** An unprofitable inheritance; a losing inheritance.

**Damnum sine injuria.** Damage without wrongful act; damage or injury inflicted without any act of injustice; loss or harm for which there is no legal remedy. It is also termed *damnum absque injuria*.

"There are cases in which the law will suffer a man knowingly and wilfully to inflict harm upon another, and will not hold him accountable for it. Harm of this description—mischief that is not wrongful because it does not fulfil even the material conditions of responsibility—is called *damnum sine injuria*, the term *injuria* being here used in its true sense of an act contrary to law (*in jus*), not in its modern and corrupt sense of harm." [John Salmond: *Jurisprudence*, pp. 372-73 (Glanville L. Williams Ed., 10th Ed. 1947)].

"There are many forms of harm of which the law takes no account. Damage so done and suffered is called *damnum sine injuria*, and the reasons for its permission by the law are various and not capable of exhaustive statement. For example, the harm done may be caused by some person who is merely exercising his own rights; as in the case of the loss inflicted on individual traders by competition in trade, or where the damage is done by a man acting under necessity to prevent a greater evil". [R.F.V. Heuston, Salmond on the *Law of Torts*, p. 13 (17th Ed. 1977)].

NOTE: Where there is no infringement of a legal right, the mere fact of harm or loss resulting from an act or omission is not wrongful, even though the loss is substantial. Thus, where a schoolmaster sets up a rival school next door to the defendant's and boys from the plaintiff's school flocked to the defendant's, no suit could be maintained for damage caused by a rival in the exercise of the right to employ himself. [*Gloucester Grammar School* case (1401)11 Hen IV].

**Damosh.** A beel or inland pool of shallow water being part of the deserted bed of a river. Hence the words *damosh koha* cannot include the bed of a large flowing navigable river. [*Midnapur Zamindary Co. Ltd.* v *Bijoy Singh* AIR 1941 Cal 1].

**Dan.** Gift; present.

**Danapatra.** A deed of gift.

**Danga.** Highland, upland, ascent; also used laxly for in general or any particular spot, as *kalai-danga*, inferior land; *gochar-danga*, pasture land or grazing ground.

**Danger.** Peril, risk, hazard, exposure to injury from pain or other evil, and can vary in degree according as the apprehended injury is expected to occur at once or at some future time. [*Lalbhai Tikamlal* v *Municipal Commissioner* 33 Bom 334].

**Danger alternative.** The principle of alternative danger implies that where a person is suddenly put in a position of imminent danger by the wrongful act or default of another, then what he does in the agony of the moment cannot be regarded as negligence. [*British School of Motoring* v *Simons* (1971)1 All ER 317].

**Dangerous.** Perilous; hazardous; unsafe; attended with risk; likely to cause serious bodily harm; exposing to or involving danger; able or likely to inflict injury.

NOTE: "Anything, in a manner of speaking, is dangerous if, either owing to negligence or owing to the fact that it is impossible for everybody on every occasion, however carefully thoy may conduct themselves, to avoid some mischance of hand or eye, injury may be caused. ... Almost everything is dangerous from one point of view, but one has to see whether danger should be reasonably anticipated from the use of things without protection". [*Kinder* v *Camberwell Borough Council* (1944)2 All ER 315, *per* Lord Caldecote, C.J.].

**Dangerous animal.** An animal having mischievous propensities.

NOTE: A person who keeps a dangerous animal, e.g., a tiger does so at his peril. Whoever keeps an animal accustomed to attack and bite mankind, with the knowledge that it is so accustomed, is *prima facie* liable at the suit of any person attacked and injured by the animal, without any averment of negligence or default in the securing or taking care of it. [*May* v *Burdett* (1846)9 QB 101].

**Dangerous driving.** Driving perilously; driving in a manner able or likely to inflict injury.

NOTE: Careless driving may well be dangerous though all careless driving is not necessarily dangerous driving. [*R.* v *Scammell* (1967)2 All ER 97]. The manner in which a man is driving depends on all the circumstances existing at the time, and the space, the condition of the road and the presence of members of the public are all matters to be taken into consideration when deciding whether the manner of driving was dangerous to the public. [*Beresford* v *Richardson* (1921)1 KB 243]. The driving may be dangerous without actual danger. [*Kingman* v *Seager* (1938)1 KB 397].

**Dangerous drug.** A drug that has potential for abuse or injury, usually requiring a label warning that it cannot be dispensed without a prescription. [Black's *Law Dictionary*, 7th Ed.].

NOTE: Dangerous drug includes cocoa leaf, hemp and opium and all manufactured drugs. [Dangerous Drugs Act 1930, s. 2(*h*)].

**Dangerous machinery.** A part of the machinery is dangerous if it is a reasonably foreseeable cause of injury to anybody acting in a way in which a human being may be expected to act in circumstances which may reasonably be expected to occur. [*Eaves* v *Morris Motors Ltd.* (1961)3 AWR 233].

A machinery or part thereof is dangerous if in the ordinary course of its working danger may reasonably be anticipated from it when working without protection, taking into account the various factors incidental to its working, including the carelessness of the workman. [*J.B. Mangharam* v *ESI Corporation* AIR 1969 MP 110].

NOTE: In a literal sense the cutting or grinding parts of all machines designed to perform the operations of cutting or grinding may be said to be dangerous. [*Lauder* v *Barr* (1927) SC (J) 21].

The question whether a part of a machine is a dangerous part is one of fact in each case; but the question must also be decided according to the right principle of law, and in law a part of a machine is dangerous if it is a possible cause of injury to anybody acting in a way a human being may be reasonably expected to act in circumstances which may be reasonably expected to occur, taking into account the possibility of inadvertent or indolent conduct. [Halsbury's *Laws of England*, 3rd Ed., vol. 17, pp. 74, 75].

**Dangerous person.** A person who either by himself or as a member of or leader of a gang, habitually commits or attempts to commit or abets the commission of offences, punishable under Chapter XVI or Chapter

XVII of the Indian Penal Code 1860 or any of the offences punishable under Chapter V of the Arms Act 1959. [*Rashidmiya* alias *Chhava Ahmedmiya* v *Police Commissioner, Ahmedabad* AIR 1989 SC 1703: (1989)3 SCC 321: 1989 SCC (Cri)) 559].

**Dangerous petroleum.** Dangerous petroleum means petroleum having its flashing point below seventy-six degrees Farenheit. [Petroleum Act 1934, s. 2(*b*)].

**Dangerous structure.** Any structure which according to the opinion of a surveyor is in a ruinous or dangerous state.

**Dar-bast.** Entire, whole. The whole of a district or estate, as opposed to a portion of it.

**Dar-ijara.** A sub-lease of farm.

**Dar-o-bast-hakuk.** All right and title whatever.

**Dargah.** A place of worship of Mohamadans where a great person is buried; usually a Mohamadan shrine or the tomb of the reputed holy Mohamadan.

**Darkhast.** A contract; a tender; a representation; an application; a petition.

**Darputni.** The word 'darputni' appears to have acquired the meaning of permanent tenure with fixity of rent. [*Kumud Nath* v *Kunjabala* 62 CLJ 67].

**Darshani hundi.** A hundi payable at sight.

**Dasi.** In Hindu law the word does not mean a female slave, but a woman who lives as dependent in the family. [*Bai Monghi* v *Bai Nagu* AIR 1923 Bom 130]. *Dasi* includes a woman kept as a constant concubine. [*Kripal Narain* v *Sukurmoni* ILR 19 Cal 91].

**Dasi-putra.** An illegitimate son by a dasi. This son is himself brought up as a member of the family. [*Chaturbhuj Patnaik* v *Krishna* 17 CWN 442].

**Data.** Facts from which a conclusion is to be drawn; known facts or things used as a basis for inference or reckoning; quantities or characters operated on by a computer.

**Date.** The time at which an event occurs: a statement of the time of execution or making; the period of time in which something belongs; a day of the month, especially specified by a number.

Another meaning of the word is an appointment of social engagement, especially with a person of the opposite sex.

NOTE: When time begins to run from a particular date, the time begins to run from the day following. [*Williams* v *Nash* (1859)28 LJ Ch 886]. Law does not, as a rule, take account of fractions of the day. [*Trow* v *Ind Coope* (1967)2 All ER 900]. 'Date' is the whole period of twenty-four hours and 'time' is the moment during that period which is critical. [*Ibid*].

**Date of appointment.** It means the date of assuming duties and not date of appointment order.

NOTE: An order of appointment may be of three kinds. It may appoint a person with effect from the date he assumes charge of the post or it may appoint him with immediate effect or it may appoint him simpliciter without saying as to when the appointment shall take effect. [*Dr. Amarjit Singh Ahluwalia* v *State of Punjab* AIR 1975 SC 984: (1975)3 SCR 82: (1975)3 SCC 503].

**Date of award.** Date of award means the date when the award is either communicated to the party or is known to him whether actually or constructively. [*Raja Harish Chandra Raj Singh* v *The Deputy Land Acquisition Officer* AIR 1961 SC 1500: (1962)1 SCR 676: (1962)1 SCJ 696; *Devasahayam Nadar* v *Poothatham* (1966)2 MLJ 258; *Japagnanam* v *P.N. Samuel* ILR (1967)1 Mad 104: (1967)2 MLJ 243].

**Date of deed.** Date of deed means the date on which document is made.

NOTE: If the deed bears a date, there is a general, though not a conclusive, presumption that the document was made on the day of the date it bears. [*Mina Kumari* v *Vijoy Singh* 44 Cal 662: 44 IA 72: 21 CWN 585].

If the deed bears no date or bears an impossible date, *e.g.*, the 30th day of February, oral evidence is admissible in a court of law to prove the date, and the validity of the deed will not be affected by the omission of date or erroneous date. [*Esberger & Son* v *Capital and Counties Bank Ltd.* (1913)2 Ch 366].

**Date of election.** It means the date on which a candidate in an election is declared by the Returning Officer to be elected. [*Bhakti Bhusan Mandal* v *Khagendra Kumar Bondoyapadhyay* AIR 1968 Cal 69; Representation of People Act 1951].

**Date of hearing.** It means the date on which the action comes for hearing.

**Date of order.** Date on which the order is passed. It may also mean the date when the order is pronounced.

▸ *Meaning under the Cr. P.C., s. 144.* Where the proceeding under s. 144, Cr. P.C. is the forerunner of the subsequent proceeding under s. 145, the date of the order for the purpose of proviso should be taken to be the date on which the proceeding under s. 144 was started. [*Gangadhar Singh* v *Shyam Sundar* AIR 1958 Ori 153: 1958 Cr LJ 919].

▸ *Meaning under the taxation law.* The date of the order is the date on which it was passed. [*Mahabir Prasad* v *Commissioner of Income Tax* (1955)27 ITR 268; *Haji Ghulam Hussain* v *Commissioner of Income Tax* , *U.P.* (1957)31 ITR 231].

The date of the order does not mean the date when the officer passed the order but the date when such order was either communicated to the party or the date when it was pronounced or published in such a manner that the party may be deemed to have had notice of it on the date of such pronouncement or publication. Limitation should not be computed from a date earlier than that on which the party aggrieved actually knew of the order or had an opportunity of knowing the order. [*A.M. Muthiah Chettiar* v *Commissioner of Income Tax* (1951)19 ITR 402].

> NOTE: *Starting point for limitation where an order is passed in the absence of a party.* Where a court passes an order in the absence of a party without having previously informed that party of the date on which it was going to pass the order, the date of passing order cannot validly be made the starting point for limitation. [*Sewa Ram* v *Massu* AIR 1927 Lah 839; *Haji Ghulam* v *Commissioner of Income Tax, UP* (1957)31 ITR 231, 239].

**Datta.** A gift without any consideration.

**Dattaka homam.** Sacrifice by fire, the essential ceremony performed during the adoption of a son among the Dwija classes.

**Dattaka putra.** An adopted son; a son given in adoption.

**Dattam and samarpimpabidina.** The word appearing in the sale deed connotes an absolute gift. [*Kalicherla Seshacharlu* v *Vidwan* AIR 1937 Mad 789].

**Dauhitra.** A daughter's son.

> NOTE: In the absence of other male lineal heir, he succeeds to the property of the maternal grandfather.

**Day.** The time of sunshine between one night and the next; the period of the earth's rotation of its axis; the mean solar day of 24 hours beginning at midnight.

Daytime runs from the beginning of the last hour before sunrise to the expiration of the first hour after sunset. [Halsbury's *Laws of England*, 4th Ed., vol. 2, para 268, p. 114].

Day begins from one midnight and ends with the next. [*Prabhunath Singh* v *Superintendent, Central Jail* ILR (1961)1 All 427].

The word 'day' as per English calender begins at midnight and covers a period of 24 hours thereafter. [*Ramkishan Onkarmal Agarwal* v *State of Maharashtra* AIR 1994 Bom 87].

'Days' include every day including Sundays and holidays. 'Working days' are distinguished from 'days'. [*Nielsen* v *Wait* (1885)16 QBD 67].

Day means a period of twenty-four hours beginning at midnight. [Factories Act 1948, s. 2(*e*); Mines Act 1952, s. 2(*f*); Plantations Labour Act 1951, s. 2(*d*)].

The word 'day' in s. 256, Cr. P.C. 1973 means only the time when the case is called for hearing. [*P. Thimmayya* v *P.C. Chinna Thimmappa* AIR 1969 AP 222: 1969 Cr LJ 852].

**Day book.** Diary, journal; a book formerly used in accounting for recording the transactions of the day. A diary kept by men in profession or trade.

A tradesman's journal; a book in which all transactions of the day are set down.

**Daya.** Inheritance, heritage, property. According to Mitakshara, there are two classes of *daya*—(1) *Apratibandho* or unobstructed heritage, *i.e.* property in which a person acquires an interest by birth, and (2) *Sapratibandha* or obstructed heritage, *i.e.* property, the right to which accrues not by birth but on the death of the last owner without leaving male issue.

**Dayabhaga.** An ancient digest of Hindu law of supreme authority in Bengal. It was compiled by Jimuta Vahana, who is said to have flourished between the 13th and the 15th Century A.D.

**Dayada.** An heir, whether direct, collateral or contingent; a claimant. In popular language it is one who takes a deceased's estate by obstructed succession. [*Bai Parson* v *Bai Somali* ILR 36 Bom 424, 433; Wilson's *Glossary*].

**Days of grace.** Time allowed for the payment of a bill after it has become legally due. Time of indulgence granted to an acceptor for the payment of his bill of exchange. A number of days allowed, as a matter of favour or grace, to a person who has to perform some act, or make some payment, after the time originally limited for the purpose has elapsed.

The days of grace are clearly days before the expiry of which there is no right of action for the party giving the days of grace. [*Ramabrahman* v *Rammi Reddi* AIR 1928 Mad 250].

**De bene esse.** The expression is used when anything is allowed to be done at the present time with a view to its being examined at a future time, and then standing or falling according to the merit of the thing in its own nature. In modern times it is chiefly used in reference to an examination, out of court and before trial, of witnesses who are old, dangerously ill or about to leave the country, on the terms that if the witnesses continue ill or absent, their evidence be read at the trial, but if they recover or return, the evidence be taken in the usual manner. [Wharton's *Law Lexicon*].

NOTE: Where a witness is about to leave the jurisdiction of the court, or other sufficient cause is shown to the satisfaction of the court why his evidence should be taken immediately, the court may, upon the application of any party or of the witness, at any time after the institution of the suit, take the evidence of such witness. [Code of Civil Procedure 1908, Or. 18, r. 16].

**De bonis non or administration de bonis non.** Latin "of the goods not administered". An administration granted for the purpose of settling the remainder of an estate that was not administered by the former executor or administrator. [Black's *Law Dictionary,* 7th Ed.].

**De die in diem.** From day to day; continuously; daily.

**De facto.** A Latin expression which means "in point of fact"; existing in fact; actual.

**De facto guardian.** A *de facto* guardian is one who is not a legal guardian in the sense that he is neither a natural guardian nor a testamentary guardian nor a guardian appointed by court, but who being interested in the minor through stranger takes charge of the management of the minor's property. [*Palani Goundam* v *Vanjiakkal* AIR 1956 Mad 476].

**De hors.** Outside or beyond the scope of; foreign to; irrelevant.

**De jure.** As a matter of law; existing by right or according to law. [Black's *Law Dictionary*, 8th Ed.].

Descriptive of a condition in which there has been total compliance with all requirements of law; legitimate; lawful; by right and just title. [Black's *Law Dictionary*, 5th Ed.].

**De minimis non cura lex.** The law does not concern itself with trifles.

**De novo trial.** A trial from the beginning; a new or fresh trial.

**De son tort.** A French term which means "by his own wrongdoing"; wrongful.

- **Executor de son tort.** An executor *de son tort* is an executor of his own wrong. A person who assumes to act as executor of an estate without any lawful warrant or authority, but who, by his intermeddling, makes himself liable as an executor to a certain extent, is called an executor *de son tort*. If a stranger takes upon him to act as executor without any just authority, he is called in law an "executor of his own wrong", *de son tort*. [Black's *Law Dictionary,* 5th Ed.].

**Dead body**. A corpse; the body of a human being deprived of life.

**Dead freight.** Freight payable by a charterer in respect of cargo not shipped; the amount paid by a charterer for that part of the vessel's capacity which he does not occupy although he has contracted for it.

The term 'dead freight' denotes an agreed sum to be paid in respect of space not filled according to charter, or damages provided for by a charter, in the event of the freighter not loading a full cargo. [*Pearson* v *Goschen* 33 LJCP 265; *Gray* v *Carr* LR 6 QB 522; *Clink* v *Radford* (1891)1 QB 625; *Kish* v *Taylor* (1911)1 KB 625].

**Dead letter.** Law that has absolute by long disuse; a piece of mail that is undeliverable by the postal service because of insufficient or incorrect address and absence of return address.

**Dead loans.** Loans unpaid at the specified date for which no date of repayment has been stipulated.

**Dead reckoning.** The position of a ship reckoned with regard to course and speed only from a previous position fixed by reference to celestial or terrestrial objects not allowing for effect of current or wind.

**Dead rent.** In connection with the mining lease, it means a rent payable in addition to a royalty. It is so called because it is payable whether the mine is being worked or not.

**Dead stock.** Goods that remain in inventory because there is no market for them. [Black's *Law Dictionary,* 8th Ed.].

**Dead time.** Time that does not count for a particular purpose, such as time not included in calculating an employee's wages or time not credited towards a prisoner's sentence. [Black's *Law Dictionary,* 7th Ed.].

**Dead wall.** Where a wall is without any house or building behind it and is merely intended to fence off or separate the road from the space of ground by the side of it having no windows and doors, that is a dead wall. [*Arnell* v *London & North Western Railway* 12 CB 718].

**Dead weight.** "Dead weight" is a guarantee by a shipowner of a ship's carrying capacity with reference to the contemplated voyage, and the description of the cargo proposed to be shipped. [*Mackill* v *Wright* 12 App Cas 120; *Carnegie* v *Conner* 24 QBD 45].

**Deal.** An arrangement to attain a desired result by a combination of interested parties, the prime object being usually the purchase, sale, or exchange of property for a profit; an act of buying and selling; a bargain to purchase at a favourable price. [Black's *Law Dictionary,* 5th Ed.].

To distribute (something); to transact business with (a person or entity); to conspire with (a person or entity). [Black's *Law Dictionary,* 8th Ed.].

**Deal with.** The words 'deal with' mean "to have something to do with, to concern oneself, to treat, to make arrangement, to negotiate with respect to something". [*Assistant Collector of Customs* v *Sitaram Agarwala* AIR 1966 SC 955: (1966)2 SCR 1].

**Dealer.** A person or business dealing in (esp. retail) goods.

One who buys to sell, not one who buys to keep, or makes to sell; one who purchases goods for resale to final customer. [Black's *Law Dictionary,* 5th Ed.].

A person who purchases goods or property for sale to others; a retailer; a person or firm that buys and sells securities for its own account as a principal, and then sells to a customer. [Black's *Law Dictionary,* 8th Ed.].

Dealer means one who sells articles in the same condition in which he bought that. [*Ratanlal Rastogi* v *Corporation for Calcutta* 76 CWN 288; *Ramanatha Agencies* v *Food Inspector, Badagara Municipality* 1973 Ker LT 295].

A dealer means a trader or a person who buys goods and sells that without processing them. [*Varjivandas Hirji* v *D.T. Ghatpande* AIR 1969 Bom 95].

A person is a dealer who keeps on selling although he does not buy. [*In re K.T. Pappanna* AIR 1954 Mad 96].

NOTE: An agriculturalist who merely sells his agricultural produce is not a dealer. [*Deputy Commissioner of Agricultural Income Tax* v *Travancore Rubber* AIR 1965 Ker 71].

▸ *Meaning under Bombay Sales Tax Act 1953.* Dealer means any person who carries on the business of selling goods in the State of Bombay, whether for commission, remuneration or otherwise. [*State of Bombay* v *Ratilal Vadilal & Bros.* AIR 1961 SC 1106: (1961)12 STC 18: (1962)2 SCR 367].

▸ *Meaning under Central Sales Tax Act 1956, s. 2(b).* Any person who carries on (whether regularly or otherwise) the business of buying, selling, supplying or distributing goods, directly or indirectly, for cash, or for deferred payment, or for commission, remuneration or other valuable consideration, and includes—(*i*) a local authority, a body corporate, a company, any co-operative society or other society, club, firm, Hindu undivided family or other association of persons which carries on such business; (*ii*) a factor, broker, commission agent, *del credere* agent or any other mercantile agent, by whatever name called, and whether of the same description as hereinbefore mentioned or not, who carries on the business of buying, selling, supplying or distributing goods belonging to any principal whether disclosed or not; and (*iii*) an auctioneer who carries on the business of selling or auctioning goods belonging to any principal, whether disclosed or not and whether the offer of the intending purchaser is accepted by him or by the principal or a nominee of the principal.

Every person who acts as an agent, in any State, of a dealer residing outside that State and buys, sells, supplies, or distributes goods in the State or acts on behalf of such dealer as (*i*) a mercantile agent as defined in the Sale of Goods Act 1930, or (*ii*) an agent for handling of goods or documents of title relating to goods, or (*iii*) an agent for the collection or the payment of the sale price of goods or as a guarantor for such collection or payment, and every local branch or office in a State of a firm registered outside that State or a company or other body corporate, the principal office or headquarters whereof is outside that State, shall be deemed to be a dealer for the purposes of the Act under Explanation 1 to s. 2(*b*).

A Government which, whether or not in the course of business, buys, sells, supplies or distributes goods, directly or otherwise, for cash or for deferred payment, or for commission, remuneration or other valuable consideration, usually, except in relation to any sale, supply or distribution of surplus, unserviceable or old stores or materials or waste products or obsolete or discarded machinery or parts or accessories thereof, be deemed to be a dealer for the purposes of this Act under Explanation 2 to s. 2(*b*).

The definition of "dealer" in s. 2(*b*) of the Central Act includes the Government in express terms. Hence, the Central Government is squarely covered by the definition. [*The Joint Director of Food, Vishakapatnam* v *State of Andhra Pradesh* AIR 1976 SC 2322: (1976)38 STC 329: (1976)3 SCC 598: (1977)1 SCR 59].

NOTE: The restricted definition of the term 'dealer' in the Central Act is not wide enough to cover all kinds of agents, such as brokers or a commission agent simpliciter but would include a *del credere* agent or a mercantile agent who carries on the business of buying or selling goods not as an agent simpliciter on behalf of the disclosed principal but as a principal *vis-a-vis* its customers. [*Bagal Kot Cement Co.* v *State of Mysore* AIR 1976 SC 357: (1976)2 SCR 852: (1976)1 SCC 336].

▸ *Meaning under Drugs (Control) Act 1950, s. 2(a).* Dealer means a person carrying on either personally or through any other person, the business of selling any drugs, whether wholesale or retail.

▸ *Meaning under Hyderabad General Sales Tax Act, 1950.* Any person, local authority, company, firm, Hindu undivided family or any association or associations of persons engaged in the business of buying, selling or supplying goods in the Hyderabad State whether for a commission, remuneration or otherwise and includes a State Government which carries on such business and any society, club or association which, buys or sells or supplies goods to its members. [*State of Andhra Pradesh* v *H. Abdul Bakhi & Bros.* AIR 1965 SC 531: (1964)15 STC 644: (1964)7 SCR 664].

▸ *Meaning under Kerala General Sales Tax Act, 1963.* In order to fall within the definition of "dealer", a person must sell goods produced by him, by manufacture, agriculture, horticulture or otherwise. [*The Deputy Commissioner of Agricultural Income Tax* v *Palampadam Plantations Ltd., Kottayam* AIR 1969 SC 930: (1969)24 STC 231: (1969)1 SCC 662].

▸ *Meaning under Orissa Sales Tax Act, s. 2(c).* Before a person can be a dealer, he must be carrying on the business of purchasing or selling or supplying goods. [*State of Orissa* v *Titaghur Paper Mills* AIR 1985 SC 1293].

▸ *Meaning under Rajasthan General Sales Tax Act, 1954, s. 2(f).* 'Dealer' is defined as meaning any person who carries on the business of buying, selling, supplying or distributing goods, directly or otherwise, whether for cash, or for deferred payment, or for commission, remuneration, or other valuable consideration. [*Shri Gopal Industries Ltd.* v *State of Rajasthan* AIR 1971 SC 2054: (1971)28 STC 327: (1971)2 SCC 532].

▸ *Meaning under West Bengal Sales Tax Act, 1994, s. 2(10).* Any person who carries on the business of selling or purchasing goods in West Bengal or any person making sales under s. 15 and includes—(*a*) an occupier of a jute-mill or shipper of jute; (*b*) Government, a local authority, a statutory body, a trust or other body corporate which, or a liquidator or a receiver appointed by a Court in respect of a person, being a dealer as defined in this clause, who, whether or not in the course of business, sells, supplies or distributes directly or otherwise goods for cash or for deferred payment or for commission, remuneration or other valuable consideration.

NOTE: A co-operative society or a club or any association which sells goods to its members is a dealer under Explanation 1 to s. 2(10).

A factor, a broker, a commission agent, a *del credere* agent, an auctioneer, an agent for handling or transporting of goods or handling of documents of title to goods or any other mercantile agent, by whatever name called, and whether of the same description as hereinbefore mentioned or not, who carries on the business of selling goods and who has, in the customary course of business, authority to sell goods belonging to the principals, is a dealer within the meaning of Explanation 2 to s. 2(10).

A "firm" has not been included in the definition of the word "dealer" in the said section. A firm cannot be treated as a separate unit for purposes of assessment of Sales Tax under the Act 1994, treating it as a dealer. [*Pulak Ch. Pal* v *CTO* (1978)42 STC 209 (Cal); *Bengal Steel Centre* v *A.C.C.T., Howrah Circle* (2001)37 STA 31 (West Bengal Appellate and Revisional Board)].

• **Wholesale dealer** p. 897.

**Dear money.** This happens when the available supply of credit is small, and borrowing can only be made at high rates of interest.

**Dearness allowance.** "Dearness allowance" is an attempt to compensate loss in real wages on account of price rise considered as a passing phenomenon by compensation. [*Workmen Employed by Indian Oxygen Ltd.* v *Indian Oxygen Ltd.* 1985 SCR 111: (1985)3 SCC 177: AIR 1986 SC 125].

NOTE: The whole purpose of dearness allowance being to neutralise a portion of the increase in the cost of living, it should ordinarily be on a sliding scale and increase with the rise and decrease with the fall in the cost of living. [*Hindustan Times Ltd.* v *Their Workmen* AIR 1963 SC 1332: (1963)1 Lab LJ 108].

In the matter of grant of dearness allowance, except to the very lowest class of manual labourers whose income is just sufficient to keep body and soul together, it is impolitic and unwise to neutralise the entire rise in the cost of living by dearness allowance. [*Clerks and Depot Cashiers* v *Calcutta Tramways Co.* AIR 1957 SC 78].

**Death.** The ending of life; the cessation of all vital functions and signs. [Black's *Law Dictionary*, 8th Ed.].

The word 'death' denotes the death of a human being, unless the contrary appears from the context. [Indian Penal Code 1860, s. 46].

Where "death" is mentioned in a statute, the word generally refers to the ceasing to live of a natural person; it will require a strong context to make the word include the dissolution of an artificial entity, *e.g.*, a partnership or a company. [*Stewart* v *Brown* 35 SLR 828].

- **Accidental death.** A death resulting from an unusual event; a death that was not voluntary, intended, expected, or foreseeable.
- **Brain death.** The bodily condition of showing no response to external stimuli, no spontaneous movements, no breathing, no reflexes, and a flat reading on a machine that measures the brain's electrical activity. [Black's *Law Dictionary*, 8th Ed.].

NOTE: The conference of Royal Medical Colleges and their faculties in the U.K. in 1976 has laid down the conditions and physical signs which constitute brain death. The criteria are as follows: the patient is in a deep coma. The doctors should make sure that this state of affairs is not due to depressant drugs. Primarily hypothermia and metabolic disturbances which can contribute to coma should be excluded. The patient is maintained on a ventilator because spontaneous respiration has previously been inadequate or had ceased altogether. There should be no doubt that the patient's condition is due to irremediable structural brain damage.

- **Civil death** p. 144.
- **Presumption of death** p. 682.

**Death certificate.** An official document issued by a public registry verifying that a person has died, with information such as the date, time and cause of death, and the signature and the registration number of the attending or examining physician.

**Death duty.** Means and includes estate duty, succession duty, legacy duty, and every duty payable on death.

**Death sentence.** A sentence that imposes the death penalty.

**Debasement.** Lowering in character, purity, or value; the process by which the standard of fineness of the coinage of a country is reduced; the act of reducing the value, quality, or purity of something, especially the act of lowering the value of coins by either reducing the weight of gold and silver in the coins or increasing the coins' alloy amounts; degradation; the state of being degraded.

**Debenture.** A promissory note or bond backed by the general credit of a corporation and shall not be secured by a mortgage or lien on any specific property: certificate issued by customs to an importer for the deduction or refund of duties on merchandize imported and then exported by such importer. [Black's *Law Dictionary*, 5th Ed.].

A debt secured only by the debtor's earning power, not by a lien on any specific asset; an instrument acknowledging such a debt; a bond that is backed only by the general credit and financial reputation of the corporate issuer, not by a lien on corporate assets. [Black's *Law Dictionary*, 8th Ed.].

No precise definition of the word 'debenture' can be found, but various forms of instruments are called debentures. A debenture is a document which either creates or acknowledges a debt. A document may be a debenture although under its terms the debt is only to be repaid out of a part of the profits. The term 'debenture' is usually associated with a company of some kind, and most debentures are securities given by companies, but they are often granted by clubs and occasionally by individuals. [Halsbury's *Laws of England,* 4th Ed., vol. 7, para 813, p. 482].

The word seems to have originated from "debentur mihi", with which various old forms of acknowledgments commenced. [*Levy* v *Abercorris Co.* 37 Ch D 260, *per* Chitty, J.].

A debenture is a written obligation or acknowledgment in an impersonal form, and with conditions more elaborate than those of a promissory note, given by or for a corporation or a company to secure a sum of money. [*British India Steam Navigation Co.* v *Inland Revenue* 7 QBD 165].

A debenture is included under one or other of the three descriptions laid down by Bowen, L.J. as: (1) a simple acknowledgment under seal of the debt; (2) an instrument acknowledging the debt and charging the property of the company with repayment; (3) an instrument acknowledging the debt, charging the property of the company with repayment, and further restricting the company from giving any prior charge. [*English & Scottish Trust* v *Brunton* (1892)2 QB 700].

It is not possible to give an exhaustive definition of debenture. But there are certain characteristics of debenture, e.g., an acknowledgment of indebtedness. [*Lemon* v *Austin Fraiars Investment Trust Ltd.* (1926) Ch 1].

NOTE: Debenture includes debenture stock, bonds and any other securities of a company, whether constituting a charge on the assets of the company or not. [Companies Act 1956, s. 2(12)].

**Debenture stock.** Under the English law, a type of bond representing money borrowed by a company using its property or other fixed assets as security. [Black's *Law Dictionary,* 7th Ed.].

Stock that is issued under a contract providing for periodic, fixed payments. [Black's *Law Dictionary,* 8th Ed.].

NOTE: Debenture stock is generally constituted and secured by a trust deed containing a charge upon the property of the company. A stock certificate is issued to each person, being an allottee or transferee to the stock, stating, *inter alia,* in the case of a registered stock, that the person named therein is the registered proprietor, or, in the case of bearer stock, that the bearer thereof is the proprietor of the amount of stock therein mentioned, and having printed therein the conditions on which the stock is issued and held. [Halsbury's *Laws of England,* 4th Ed., vol. 7, para 823, p. 489].

The position of a debenture stockholder is that of a creditor. [*Dillon* v *Arkins* (1885)17 LR Ir 636].

**Debit.** A sum charged as due or owing; in book-keeping, an entry made on the left side of a ledger or account, noting an increase in assets or a decrease in liabilities; an account balance showing that something remains due to the holder of the account. [Black's *Law Dictionary,* 8th Ed.].

A record of an indebtedness, specifically an entry on the left-hand side of an account constituting an addition to an expenses or asset account or a deduction from a revenue, net worth, or liability account; the sum of the items so entered; a charge against a bank deposit account.

**Debit note.** A note stating that the account of the person to whom it is sent is to be debited in respect of some transaction, *e.g.,* a claim for goods received short, goods damaged in transit etc. [Jowitt's *Dictionary of English Law,* 2nd Ed.].

**Debita sequuntur personam debitoris.** Debts follow the person of the debtor.

**Debt.** Something that is owed, esp. money; a state of obligation to pay something owed; amount due; amount owing; indebtedness; liability; money due; money owed.

Liability on a claim; a specific sum of money due by agreement or otherwise; the aggregate of all existing claims against a person, entity, or state; a non-monetary thing that one person owes another, such as goods or services; a common-law writ by which a court adjudicates claims involving fixed sums of money. [Black's *Law Dictionary*, 8th Ed.].

A sum of money due by certain and express agreement. A specified sum of money owing to one person from another, including not only obligation of debtor to pay but right of creditor to receive and enforce payment. [*State* v *Ducey* 266 NE 2d 233, 235].

A "debt is a sum of money which is now payable or will become payable in the future by reason of a present obligation". [*Webb* v *Stenton* (1883)11 QBD 518 (CA), *per* Lindley, LJ].

A "debt" is a sum payable in respect of a liquidated money demand, recoverable by action. [*Rawley* v *Rawley* 1 QBD 460; *Seldon* v *Wilde* (1910)2 KB 9].

The legal acceptation of debt is, a sum of money due by certain and express agreement. [3 Bl Com 153].

'Debt' is defined as meaning any pecuniary liability. [*Rajkumari Kaushalya Devi* v *Bawa Pritam Singh* AIR 1960 SC 1030].

"The word 'debts' ... means something recoverable by an action for debt, and nothing can be recovered in an action for debt except what is ascertained or can be ascertained. A claim for an amount which is uncertain, and cannot be adjusted in an account, cannot ... be justly called a 'debt'." [*Ogdens, Ltd.* v *Weinberg* (1906)95 LT 567 (HL), *per* Lord Davey].

A debt is a liability to pay in present or in future an ascertainable sum of money. [*P.S.L. Ramanathan Chettiar* v *O.R.M.P.R.M. Ramanathan Chettiar* AIR 1968 SC 1047].

NOTE: When the liability to pay income tax is there, and the assessee has set apart certain amount thought to be necessary for discharging the tax liability, the same has been ascertained and it cannot be said that the amount is not a debt. [*C.W.T.* v *Ahmed Tea Company* AIR 1967 Assam 63: (1963)48 ITR 943].

The word 'debt' is applicable to a sum of money which has been promised at a future day as to a sum now due and payable. [*Union of India* v *Raman Iron Foundry* AIR 1974 SC 1265: (1974)2 SCC 231: (1974)3 SCR 556].

*Essential requisites of debt.* The essential requisites of a debt are (1) an ascertained or ascertainable, (2) an absolute liability, present or future, and (3) an obligation which has already accrued and is subsisting. [*Commissioner of Wealth-tax* v *G.D. Naidu* AIR 1966 Mad 74]. In order to constitute a debt, two conditions must be fulfilled, namely: (1) that there must be a present obligation to pay on the part of the debtor; and (2) that this obligation must be in respect of a liquidated claim or demand against him. [*Jabed Sheikh* v *Taher Malik* 45 CWN 519: AIR 1941 Cal 639].

*Debt—what is—example:*

- Money payable under an order of the Court was held a debt. [*Lees* v *Newton* LR 1 CP 658].
- A dividend declared by a Company is, after its due date, a debt from the company to the shareholder. [*Re Severn, ETC, Railway* (1896)1 Ch 559].
- Debt includes a judgment-debt under s. 2(1)(*a*) of the Provincial Insolvency Act 1920 and under s. 2(*b*) of the Presidency-Towns Insolvency Act 1909. Debt includes a judgment debt and also liability created by preliminary decree. [*Branch Manager, State Bank of India* v *Satyaban Pathal* AIR 1989 Ori 236].

*Debt—what is not—example:*

- A call on shares is not a debt until actually made. [*Re Kershew* 45 Ch D 320].
- Interest which could only be given by way of damages was not a debt. [*Ex p. Charman* (1887) WN 184].
- The word 'debt' can but seldom be construed to include damages for breach of covenant. [*Wilson* v *Knubley* 7 East 128; *Varlo* v *Faden* 1 DGF & J 211]. A debt does not include a claim for damages. [*Md. Hasan Khan* v *Ahmed Hafiz* AIR 1957 Nag 97].
- A garnishee order does not make the garnishior a "creditor" of the garnishee and therefore the amount garnished is not a "debt" due to the garnishor which, in his hands, may be garnished. [*Cooper* v *Lawson* 6 TLR 34].
- Chit liability is not a debt. Participation in chit transactions does not create on the part of organisers and the prized subscribers, the relationship of debtors and creditors.

[*Navjeevan Enterprises (Mys) Pvt. Ltd.* v *T.N. Ramalingaiah* (1982)2 Kant LJ 88].

- The claim for breach of contract relating to forward business is not a debt within the meaning of s. 9(1)(*b*) of the Provincial Insolvency Act because a claim for damages does not amount to a debt unless the damages are ascertained by a court. [*Modi Fulchand Narsidas* v *Navanitlal Ranchhoddas* AIR 1962 Guj 295].
- Amount due by the auction-purchaser of a chit is not a 'debt'. [*M. Gopal* v *Vetrivel Chit Funds Pvt. Ltd.* (1997)1 LW 830].
- Article placed with bank is not debt. Successor of pledgor needs no succession certificate. [*Branch Manager, State Bank of India, Puri* v *Satyaban Pathal* AIR 1989 Ori 236].

A "debt" is a chose-in-action and is heritable and assignable and it is treated as property in India under the Transfer of Property Act which calls it an "actionable claim". [*The Delhi Cloth and General Mills Ltd.* v *Harnam Singh* AIR 1955 SC 590: (1955)2 SCR 402: 1955 SCJ 645].

All debts are liabilities but all liabilities are not debts. [*Commissioner of Wealth Tax* v *Pierce Leslie* AIR 1963 Mad 356; *Commissioner of Wealth Tax* v *Harrison* AIR 1965 Ker 209]. Likewise, every loan is a debt but every debt is not necessarily a loan. [*Sujan Singh* v *Ramchandra Rai* AIR 1949 Nag 104].

- **Accruing debt.** An accruing debt is a debt no yet actually payable, but a debt which is represented by an existing obligation. [*Webb* v *Stenton* (1883)11 QBD 518 (CA)].


- **Acknowledgement of debt** p. 25.
- **Bad debt** p. 91.
- **Bonded debt** p. 108.
- **Compound a debt** p. 164.
- **Contingent debt** p. 186.
- **Family debt** p. 346.
- **Funded debt** p. 378.
- **National debt** p. 598.
- **Secured debt** p. 782.
- **Time-barred debt** p. 843.


**Debt due.** When the obligation is to pay a sum of money *in praesenti*, it is a debt due. A sum due would, therefore, mean a sum for which there is an existing obligation to pay *in praesenti*, or in other words, which is presently payable. [*Union of India* v *Raman Iron Foundry* AIR 1974 SC 1265].

**Debt owing.** When there is an obligation to pay a sum of money at a future debt, it is a debt owing. [*Union of India* v *Raman Iron Foundry* AIR 1974 SC 1265].

**Debtor.** One who is in debt; one who is under obligation to another, as for money or goods or for service, benefit, or help.

One who owes a debt; he who may be compelled to pay a claim or demand; anyone liable on a claim, whether due or to become due. [*First Nat. Bank & Trust Co. in Macon* v *Kunes* 197 SE 2d 446, 449].

In the absence of any definition of the word 'debtor' one has to refer to the dictionary meaning of that word which is 'one who owes a debt'. The purchaser of the equity of redemption surely owes a debt to the mortgagee and is a debtor. The expression 'debtor' includes also a transferee from a debtor. [*Balchand Mahto* v *Munshi Lal* AIR 1955 Pat 494].


- **Absconding debtor** p. 8.
- **Displaced debtor** p. 268.
- **Judgment debtor** p. 492.
- **Principal debtor** p. 685.


**Debutter.** *Debutter* means literally 'belonging to a deity'. Property dedicated to religious uses is called *debutter* property in Hindu law.

NOTE: Religious endowment or *debutter* are of two kinds—public and private. In a public endowment, the dedication is for the use or benefit of the public. But when property is set apart for the worship of a family God in which the public are not interested, the endowment is a private one. Where the founder has divested himself of the interest in the property and transferred it to the temple and the images therein, the protection of the endowment will vest in the Crown and it will be a public endowment. One important test for determination whether an endowment is a public or a private one is to consider whether the founder divested the income of the property absolutely or not. [*Ram Das Gupta* v *Ram Kishan* AIR 1932 Pat 177].

**Deceit.** A fraudulent and deceptive misrepresentation, artifice, or device, used by one or more persons to deceive and trick another, who is ignorant of the true facts, to the prejudice and damage of the party imposed upon. To constitute "deceit", the statement must be untrue, made with knowledge of its falsity or with reckless and conscious ignorance thereof, especially if parties are not on equal terms, made with intent that plaintiff act thereon or in a manner apparently fitted to induce him to act thereon, and plaintiff must act in reliance on the statement in the manner contemplated, or manifestly probable, to his injury. [Black's *Law Dictionary,* 5th Ed.].

The act of intentionally giving a false impression; a tort arising from a false representation made knowingly or recklessly with the intent that another person should detrimentally rely on it. [Black's *Law Dictionary,* 7th Ed.].

It is a false and fraudulent representation as to a matter of fact, made in order to induce a person to act thereon. [Halsbury's *Laws of England,* 4th Ed., vol. 7, para 248, p. 150].

Deceit is a false statement of a fact made by a person knowingly or recklessly with the intent that it shall be acted upon by another, who does act upon it and thereby suffers damage. [Winfield's *Law of Tort,* 5th Ed., p. 379].

**Deceive.** To deceive conveys an element of deceit which induces a state of mind, without the element of fraud, which induces a course of action or inaction. [*Welham* v *Director of Public Prosecutions* (1960)1 All ER 805].

To deceive is to induce a man to believe that a thing is true which is false and which the person practising the deceit knows or believes to be false. [*Re London & Globe Finance Corporation Ltd.* (1903)1 Ch 728].

The word 'deceive' indicates inculcating of one so that he takes the false as true, the unreal as existent, the spurious as genuine. [*P.M. Natarajan* v *Krishna Chandra Gupta* 1975 Cr LJ 899 (All)].

**Deceptively similar.** A mark shall be deemed to be deceptively similar to another mark if it so nearly resembles that other mark as to be likely to deceive or cause confusion. [Trade Marks Act 1999, s. 2(*h*)].

NOTE: Even if the similarities are not identical or akin still their deceptive nature which can be perceived either through sound or look, that is 'visually' or 'phonetically' can lead to the inference that underlying intention or object of the infringer is to encash upon the reputation and goodwill of the prior user of the trade mark as the element of confusion involves the state of mind of the customer who on seeing the mark comes to the conclusion that it differs from the mark of the goods which he had been purchasing for long. . [*Micronix India* v *J.R. Kapoor* 2003(26) PTC 593 (Del)].

**Decide.** To arrive at a solution; to bring to an end any dispute, difference or contest; to settle any question or dispute; to give judgment on any matter or action before any tribunal.

To decide means settle by giving victory to one side. [*Nirmal Ben* v *Indersingh Bagi* AIR 1977 Ori 210].

To decide means 'settle question, issues, disputes, by giving victory to one side; give judgment (between or in favour of, against); come to a resolution'. [*Ramkrishna Gangaram Rathi* v *Kishan Zingraji Madke* AIR 1971 Bom 305].

**Decision.** An act of deciding a dispute; conclusion; determination; giving judgment or order.

A determination arrived at after consideration of facts, and, in legal context, law; a determination of a judicial or quasi-judicial nature; a judgment or decree pronounced by a court in statement of a controversy submitted to it and by way of authoritative answer to the questions raised before it. [Black's *Law Dictionary*, 5th Ed.].

A judicial or agency determination after consideration of the facts and the law; especially, a ruling, order, or judgment pronounced by a court when considering or disposing of a case. [Black's *Law Dictionary*, 8th Ed.].

'Decision' means 'settlement (of question, etc.); conclusion; formal judgment; making up one's mind; resolve; resoluteness; decided character'. [*Ramkrishna Gangaram Rathi* v *Kishan Zingraji Madke* AIR 1971 Bom 305].

The word 'decision' in common parlance is more or less a neutral expression and it can be used with reference to purely executive acts as well as judicial orders. [*Province of Bombay* v *Khushaldass S. Advani* AIR 1950 SC 222: 1950 SCR 621, *per* Fazal Ali, J. referred to in *P.L. Lakhanpal* v *Union of India* AIR 1967 SC 908: (1967)2 SCJ 287: (1967)1 SCR 433].

The expression 'decision' has a wide connotation. Whenever a question is determined, or a judgment is rendered, or a conclusion is arrived at, after weighing the reasons for and against the proposition, it is a decision. In the civil law generally, it means the determination of the question, the final order which disposes of a suit or cause; also, that portion of a statute which orders or directs the performance of duty. Under some circumstances, 'decision' has been held equivalent to or synonymous with 'ascertainment'. [*Gangadhar Lalliram* v *Niravachan Adhikari, Marketing Society, Vijaypur* AIR 1971 MP 16 (DB)].

A decision means not merely a view but an objective determination based upon facts and circumstances of each case after examining the material on record and if possible, after hearing the persons who are going to be aggrieved by that. [*Devarakonda* v *All India Council for Technical Education* (1997)3 Andh LT 117].


- **Final decision** p. 353.
- **Judicial decision** p. 494.


**Declaration.** A formal statement, proclamation, or announcement, esp. one embodied in an instrument. [Black's *Law Dictionary*, 7th Ed.].

The dictionary meaning of the word 'declaration' is the action of making clear; the setting forth of a topic; the action of setting forth or announcing openly, explicitly, or formally; positive statement or assertion. [*Indravijay Singhji Monubhai Rama* v *State of Gujarat* 1977 Cr LR (Guj) 326 referring to *Shorter Oxford English Dictionary*, 3rd Ed.].


- **Dying declaration** p. 288.


**Declaration of dividend.** A company's setting aside of a portion of its earnings or profits for distribution to its shareholders. [Black's *Law Dictionary*, 8th Ed.].

The act of a corporation in setting aside a portion of its net or surplus income for distribution among the stockholders according to their respective interests. [*First Nat. Bank & Trust Co.* v *Glenn* DC Ky, 36 F Supp 552, 554].

**Declaration of trust.** The act by which the person who holds the legal title to property or an estate acknowledges and declares that he holds the same in trust to the use of another person or for certain specified purposes. [Black's *Law Dictionary*, 5th and 7th Eds.].

The name is also used to designate the deed or other writing embodying such a declaration. It is termed as trust instrument; trust deed; trust agreement.

> NOTE: A declaration of trust respecting any land or any interest therein must be manifested and proved by some writing signed by some person who is able to declare such trust or by his will. [Law of Property Act 1925 (c. 20), s. 53(10)(*b*) as quoted in Stroud's *Judicial Dictionary*, 6th Ed.].

**Declare.** Advance; affirm; announce; assert; aver; come out; contend; disclose; divulge; herald; make known; predicate; proclaim; pronounce; put forward; reveal; set forth; state.

**Decree.** "Decree" means a formal expression of an adjudication by which the court conclusively and finally determines the rights of the parties with regard to all or any of the matters in controversy in the suit. [*Deep Chand* v *Land Acquisition Officer* AIR 1994 SC 1901: (1994)4 SCC 99: JT 1994(3) SC 319].

▸ *Meaning under the Code of Civil Procedure 1908, s. 2(2).* Decree means the formal expression of an adjudication which, so far as regards the court expressing it, conclusively determines the rights of the parties with regard to all or any of the matters in controversy in the suit and may be either preliminary or final.

NOTE: The term 'decree' is defined under sub-sec. (2) of s. 2 to mean a formal expression of an adjudication which, so far as regards the court expressing it concerns, covers all or any of the matters in controversy in a suit and may be either preliminary or final. To constitute a decree, one of the conditions, therefore, is that the decision must be arrived at in a suit. [*Ashok Asandas Baherwani* v *Iswarprakash Chopra* (1988)3 Bom CR 47].

*Decree—what is—example:*

- Award under Land Acquisition Act is deemed a decree of a court. [*State of M.P.* v *Seth Gowardhandas* AIR 1993 MP 70 (FB)].
- Order refusing a matrimonial relief is a decree. [*Modiram Kalaramji Jain* v *Lakshmi Modilal Jain* AIR 1991 Bom 440].

*Decree—what is not—example:*

- Rejection of an application for condonation of delay will not amount to a decree. If the application under s. 5 of the Limitation Act was rejected, the resultant order cannot be a decree. [*Mamuda Khateen* v *Deniyan Bibi* AIR 1976 Cal 415: (1976)2 CLJ 357 (FB); *Rattansingh* v *Vijaysingh* AIR 2001 SC 279: JT 2000 Supp (3) SC 499: (2001)1 SCC 469].
- Dismissal of an appeal as time-barred is not a decree. The order rejecting the memorandum of appeal on the ground of it being time-barred is merely an incidental order. [*Mamuda Khateen* v *Deniyan Bibi* AIR 1976 Cal 415: (1976)2 CLJ 357 (FB); *Rattansingh* v *Vijaysingh* AIR 2001 SC 279: JT 2000 Supp (3) SC 499: (2001)1 SCC 469].
- The decision in contempt proceedings cannot be termed as a decree within the meaning of the word 'decree' as defined in the Code of Civil Procedure. [*Ashok Asandas Baherwani* v *Iswarprakash Chopra* (1988)3 Bom CR 47].


- **Court which passed a decree** p. 204.
- **Execution of decree** p. 328.
- **Final decree** p. 353.
- **Preliminary decree** p. 679.


**Decree-holder.** Any person in whose favour a decree has been passed or an order capable of execution has been made. [Code of Civil Procedure 1908, s. 2(3)].

**Decree nisi.** A provisional decree which, on the proper steps being taken, will be made absolute or final unless cause is shown to the contrary.

**Dedication.** An act or ceremony of dedicating to a divine being or to a sacred use; a setting aside for a particular purpose, transfer for the benefit of a deity.

Dedication necessarily presupposes an intention to dedicate; and such intention may be expressed in words or writing or may be inferred from circumstances.

NOTE: In every act of dedication there are two essential parts; one of which is called *Sankalpa* or the formula of resolve, and the other *Utsarga* or renunciation. The ceremonies, as Mandik points out, always begin with a *Sankalpa*, which after reciting the time of gift with reference to age, year, season, month etc. states what, object the founder has in making the gift. *Utsarga*, on the other hand, completes a gift by renouncing the ownership of the founder in the thing given.

In Muslim law, if a property is set apart for a definite purpose, such property would become "dedicated" for a purpose. It cannot be said that it is only in cases when an individual divests himself of the property and after declaration of trust it is binding on the settlor with the object for which the property thereafter to be held. [*U.P. Sunni Central Board of Wakf* v *Mazhar Hassan* (2001)6 SCC 289: JT 2001(6) SC 365].

*Dedication to a temple and a mutt—distinction:* The distinction between 'dedication to a temple and a mutt' is that in the former case it is to be a particular deity, while in the latter, it is to a superior or *mahant*. [*The Bihar State Board of Religious Trust, Patna* v *Mahanth Sri Biseshwar Das* AIR 1971 SC 2057: (1971)1 SCC 574: (1971)3 SCR 680].

**Deducing the title.** The strict meaning of the words 'deducing the title' is stating from what source or whom the party draws forth his title. Ordinarily, the vendor deduces his title by the delivery of the abstract or the showing of his deeds; but that is not strictly expression. [*Oakden* v *Pike* (1965)34 LJ Ch 620].

**Deduction.** That which is deducted; abatement; the process or act of subtracting or taking away.

NOTE: Reducing a worker's wages because he has been disrated for misconduct is not a "deduction".

**Deed.** A deed is an instrument which complies with the following requirements. First, it must be written on parchment or paper. Secondly, it must be executed in the manner specified by some person or corporation named in the instrument. Thirdly, as to subject-matter, it must express that the person or corporation so named makes, confirms, concurs in or consents to some assurance (otherwise than by way of testamentary disposition) of some interest in property or of some legal or equitable right, title, or claim, or undertakes or enters into some obligation, duty or agreement enforceable at law or in equity, or does or concurs in some other act affecting the legal relations or position of a party to the instrument or of some other person or corporation. [Halsbury's *Laws of England*, 4th Ed., vol. 12, para 1301, p. 505].

A conveyance of realty; a writing signed by grantor, whereby title to realty is transferred from one to another. [*National Fire Insurance Co.* v *Patterson* 41 P 2d 645, 647].

A written instrument, signed, and delivered, by which one person conveys land, tenements or hereditaments to another. [Black's *Law Dictionary*, 5th Ed.].

Something that is done or carried out; an act or action; a written instrument by which land is conveyed; at common law, any written instrument that is signed, sealed, and delivered and that conveys some interest in property. [Black's *Law Dictionary*, 8th Ed.].


- **Absolute deed** p. 8.
- **Composition deed** p. 164.
- **Date of deed** p. 224.
- **Delivery of deed** p. 246.
- **Estoppel by deed** p. 321.
- **Mortgage by deposit of title deeds** p. 592.
- **Mortgage deed** p. 592.


**Deed poll.** A deed poll is a deed made by one party only expressing the voluntary intention of the said party though more persons than one may join in expressing by a deed poll the same common intention. A deed poll is so called because the parchment required for such deeds had usually been polled or cut even at the top. A power of attorney is a deed poll.

A deed made by and binding on only one party, or on two or more parties having similar interests is called a deed poll. It is so called because, traditionally, the parchment was "polled" (that is, shaved) so that it would be even at the top (unlike and indenture).

NOTE: Deeds are divided into two kinds—deeds poll and indentures, a deed poll being made by one party only, and an indenture being made between two or more parties. [Williams & Eastwood on *Real Property*, p. 432].

**Deemed.** The word 'deemed' is used a great deal in modern legislation. Sometimes it is used to impose for the purposes of a statute an artificial construction of a word or phrase that would not otherwise prevail. Sometimes it is used to put beyond doubt a particular construction that might otherwise be uncertain. Sometimes it is used to give a comprehensive description that includes what is obvious, what is uncertain and what is, in the ordinary sense, impossible. [*St. Aubyn* v *A.-G.* (1951)2 All ER 473].

When a thing is to be deemed something else, it is to be treated as that something else with the attendant consequences, but it is not that something else. [*R.* v *Norfolk County Council* (1891)60 LJQB 379].

When a person is 'deemed to be' something, the only meaning possible is that whereas he is not in reality that something, the Act requires him to be treated as if he were. [*Chipping and Painting* v *A.T. Zambre* AIR 1969 Bom 274: 70 Bom LR 506; *K. Kamaraja Nadar* v *Kunju Thevar* AIR 1958 SC 687; *Narain Bux Singh* v *State of U.P.* 1981 All LJ 649; *Tirath Raj* v *Director General of Police,*

*Lucknow* 1988 Lab IC 275; *Ram Singasan* v *K.P. Sinha* AIR 1989 Pat 39].

When a statute enacts that something shall be deemed to have been done, which in fact and truth was not done, the court is entitled and bound to ascertain for what purposes and between what persons the statutory fiction is to be resorted to and full effect must be given to the statutory fiction and it should be carried to its logical conclusion. [*State of Bombay* v *Pandurang* AIR 1953 SC 244; *Industrial Supplies (P) Ltd.* v *Union of India* AIR 1980 SC 1858].

Legal fiction cannot be carried beyond the purpose for which it was created. [*K.S. Dharmadatan* v *Central Government* AIR 1979 SC 1495: 1979 Cr LR (SC) 627: 1979 UJ (SC) 800].

In s. 4 of the Indian Income-tax Act 1922, the word 'deemed' brings within the net of chargeability income not actually accruing but which is supposed notionally to have accrued. It involves a number of concepts. By statutory fiction income which can in no sense be said to accrue at all may be considered as so accruing. Similarly the fiction may relate to the place, the person or be in respect of the year of taxability. [*Commissioner of Income Tax* v *Bhogilal Laharchand* AIR 1954 SC 155].

In modern statutes the expression 'deemed' is used a great deal and for many purposes. It is at times used to indicate artificial conceptions which are intended to go beyond legal principles or to give an artificial construction to a word or phrase. [*New Shorrock Spinning and Manufacturing Co. Ltd.* v *N.U. Raval* AIR 1959 Bom 477: 61 Bom LR 618].

It is not that a deeming provision is every time made for the purpose of creating a fiction. A deeming provision might be made to include what is obvious or what is uncertain or to impose for the purpose of a statute an artificial construction of a word or phrase that would not otherwise prevail, but in such cases the motive of the legislature would be relevant. [*Consolidated Coffee* v *Coffee Board* AIR 1980 SC 1468: (1980)46 STC 163].

**Deface.** To mar or destroy the face (that is, the physical appearance of written or inscribed characters as expressive of a definite meaning) of a written instrument, signature, inscription, etc., by obliteration, erasure, cancellation, or super inscription, so as to render it illegible or unrecognizable.

To mar, injure or spoil. [*State* v *Kasnett* 283 NE 2d 636, 638].

Also used in respect of injury to monument, buildings and other structures. So, to deface the flag carries the meaning of dishonour, which imputes a lively sense of shaming or an equivalent acquiescent callousness. [*State* v *Schlueter* 23 A 2d 249, 251].

▸*Meaning under the Indian Coinage Act 1906, s. 2(a).* 'Deface' with its grammatical variations and cognate expressions includes clipping, filing, stamping or such other alteration of the surface or shape of a coin as is readily distinguishable from the effect of reasonable wear.

**Defamation.** Holding up of a person to ridicule, scorn or contempt in a respectable and considerable part of the community. It may be criminal as well as civil. [Black's *Law Dictionary*, 5th Ed.].

The act of harming the reputation of another by making a false statement to a third person; a false written or oral statement that damages another's reputation. [Black's *Law Dictionary*, 8th Ed.].

Defamation is the wrong done by a person to another's reputation by words, signs or visible representations. [*Surendra Nath* v *Bageshwari* AIR 1961 Pat 164].

▸*Meaning under the Indian Penal Code 1860, s. 499.* Whoever by words, either spoken or intended to be read, or by signs or by visible representations, makes or publishes any imputation, concerning any person intending to harm, or knowing or having reason to believe that such imputation will harm, the reputation of such person, is said to defame that person.

NOTE: It is also a civil wrong. Publication is the essence of defamation.

The test of defamation is—would the words tend to lower the plaintiff in the estimation of right-thinking members of society generally. [*Sim* v *Stretch* (1986)2 All ER 1237].

**Defamatory statement.** A defamatory statement is a statement which tends to lower a person in the estimation of right thinking members of society generally or to cause him to be shunned or avoided or to expose him to hatred, contempt or ridicule, or to convey an imputation on him disparaging or injurious to him in his office, profession, calling, trade or business. [Halsbury's *Laws of England*, 4th Ed., vol. 28, para 10, p. 7].

A statement that tends to injure the reputation of a person referred to in it; a statement that is likely to lower a person in the estimation of reasonable people and in particular to cause that person to be regarded with feelings of hatred, contempt, ridicule, fear, or dislike. [Black's *Law Dictionary*, 8th Ed.].

A defamatory statement is one which has a tendency to injure the reputation of the person to whom it refers; which tends, that is to say, to lower him in the estimation of right-thinking members of the society generally and in particular to cause him to be shunned or avoided or regarded with feelings of hatred, contempt, ridicule, fear, dislike or disesteem, or to convey an imputation on him disparaging or injurious to him in his office, profession, calling, trade or business. [*Surendra Nath* v *Bageshwari* AIR 1961 Pat 164].

**Default.** Not doing something required by duty or law; neglect; a failure to pay financial debts; failure to appear at the required time in legal proceeding.

To fail to fulfil a contract or agreement, accept a responsibility; to fail to meet a financial obligation. [*S. Sundaram Pillai* v *V.R. Pattabiraman* AIR 1985 SC 582: (1985)1 SCC 591: (1985)2 SCR 643, referring to Webster's *Third New International Dictionary*].

Failure in performance or failure to act. [*Organo Chemical Industries* v *Union of India* AIR 1979 SC 1803: (1979)4 SCC 573: (1980)1 SCR 61].

Default means nothing more, nothing less, than not doing what is reasonable under the circumstances—not doing something which you ought to do, having regard to the relations which you occupy towards the other persons interested in the transaction. [*Re Young and Haston's Contract* (1885)31 Ch D 168].

'Default' in s. 2(2)(*b*), Civil Procedure Code, is not confined to a default in appearance only; it includes default of all kinds. [*Tafazul* v *Shah Mahammad* AIR 1949 All 261].

NOTE: Non-prosecution of the case, such as by not pressing it amounts to default. Default may include non-appearance, non-payment of fees, failure to produce necessary documents or failure to do other things for successful prosecution. [*Md. Goffar Baig* v *Md. Abdul Khaleek* AIR 1957 AP 991].

'Default' would seem to embrace further failure by the defendant to perform his contract unless prevented by superior force over which he had no control, such as stress of weather. It does not necessarily imply any moral obliquity or any breach of contractual obligation. It simply means non-payment, failure or omission to pay. [*Jalum Singh Katary* v *Secretary of State for India* 8 CWN 725 (PC)].

• **Wilful default** p. 898.

**Defaulter.** One who has failed or neglected to do his duty; one from whom any money or other thing is due, and has failed to pay.

**Defeasance.** Rendering null or void; the termination or annulment of interest in accordance with stipulated conditions (as in a deed); an instrument stating such conditions of limitation. A condition of annulment of the estate granted.

A defeasance is something which defeats the operation of a deed or document. If it is contained in the same deed, it is called a condition. The word 'defeasance' comes from the French word 'defaire', that is to defeat or undo. [*Kadiyala Venkatasubbiah* v *Sarupur Narayanamma* AIR 1972 AP 341].

A provision for defeasance of the security, within the meaning of the statutory provision, is one which defeats or limits the operation of the bill or stipulates for its discharge in stated events. A stipulation is not a defeasance for the purpose of the Bills of Sale Acts unless it is a term which is part and parcel of the agreement under which the bill is given. A subsequent agreement varying or determining a bill of sale is not a defeasance within the Acts, though it may itself be registrable as a bill of sale. Similarly, a mortgage granted prior to the bill is not a defeasance of the bill. [Halsbury's *Laws of England*, 4th Ed., vol. 4, para 704, p. 303].

NOTE: Conditions of defeasance are provided in s. 28 of the Transfer of Property Act 1882 and s. 131 of the Indian Succession Act 1925.

**Defeasible.** Defeasible means that which may be annulled, abrogated, cancelled or made void; capable of defeating, destroying or impairing. [*Kadiyala Venkatasubbiah* v *Sarupur Narayanamma* AIR 1972 AP 341].

**Defeasible title.** Title that is capable of being annulled or made void—not one that is already void or is an absolute nullity. [*Kadiyala Venkatasubbiah* v *Sarupur Narayanamma* AIR 1972 AP 341].

**Defeated candidate.** Defeat involves that there should be contest and one or more of the contestants should lose or be overthrown. Hence, a candidate cannot be said to have been defeated if he had no opportunity to enter into a contest with others and to solicit votes of the electors and then lose on account of not securing sufficient number of votes. [*Anandilal* v *Chief Panchayat Officer* AIR 1957 Raj 163].

**Defect.** An imperfection or shortcoming, especially in a part that is essential to the operation or safety of a product. [Black's *Law Dictionary*, 8th Ed.].

The want or absence of some legal requisite; deficiency; imperfection; insufficiency. [*Galloway* v *City of Winchester* 184 SW 2d 890, 892, 893].

'Defect' means a lack or absence of something essential to completeness. [*Tate* v *Latham & Son* (1897)1 QB 502, *per* Bruce, J.].

The word 'defect', according to its ordinary connotation, covers only omissions, irregularities or deficiencies but not also a fraudulent suppression or distortion of facts. [*Manmatha Nath* v *Sachindra Kumar* AIR 1956 Cal 59].

NOTE: The omission to state the age of a candidate for election in the nomination paper is a 'defect' within the meaning of s. 36(4) of the Representation of the People Act 1951. Having regard to the context, the word 'defect' in s. 36(4) cannot exclude all cases of omission to specify the details prescribed by statute in the nomination paper. [*Brijendralal Gupta* v *Jwalaprasad* AIR 1960 SC 1049: (1960)3 SCR 650].

The existence of a defect in the subject matter of the contract is in certain cases, apart from any question of fraud or misrepresentation, a ground for refusing specific performance. A defect cannot be relied on if there is a provision in the contract excluding reliance on defects, as when the sale is "with all faults", or if the contract is so framed as in terms to leave uncertain the matter complained of; nor, as a rule, can a defect be relied on in reply to a claim for specific performance if, at the date of the contract its existence was unknown to the plaintiff as well as to the defendant. [Halsbury's *Laws of England*, 3rd Ed., vol. 36, pp. 308, 309].

- **Latent defect.** Latent defect are such as would not be revealed by any inquiry, not be apparent by reasonable observation.

A product imperfection that is not discoverable by reasonable inspection and for which a seller or lessor is generally liable if the flow causes harm. [Black's *Law Dictionary*, 8th Ed.].

Latent defect is such as the greatest attention would not enable a person to discover the existence of defects.

A "latent" defect is not simply any defect not discoverable through ordinary use and maintenance, but a defect or a flow, generally in the metal or material itself, which could not be discovered by any known and customary test. [*Parente (Robert A.)* v *Bayville Marine Inc. and General Insurance Co. of America* (1975)1 Lloyd's Rep 333].

A hidden or concealed defect. One which could not be discovered by reasonable and customary inspection; one not apparent on face of goods, product, document, etc.

Defect of which owner has no knowledge, or which, in exercise of reasonable care, he should have had no knowledge. [*Bichi* v *Poinier* 71 Wash 2d 492: 429 P 2d 228, 231].

- **Patent defect.** Patent defects are such as may be discovered by ordinary vigilance.

A patent defect must be a defect which arises either to the eye or by necessary implication from something which is visible to the eye. [*Yandle & Sons* v *Sutton, Young* v *Sutton* (1922)2 Ch 199, *per* Sargant, J.].

A patent defect is not latent where there is none to observe it. The natural meaning of the word 'patent' is objective, not subjective. It means 'observable', not 'observed'. A patent defect must be apparent on inspection, but it is not dependent on the eye of the observer; it can 'blush unseen'. [*Sanderson* v *National Coal Board* (1961)2 All ER 796 (CA): (1961)2 QB 244, *per* Holroyd Pearce, L.J.].

**Defect in machinery.** Defect in machinery is absence of some part of the machinery or a crack or anything of that kind. A defect in the condition of the way or works or machinery or plant means such a state of things that the power and quality of the subject to which the word 'condition' is applied are for the time being altered in such a manner as to interfere with their use. [*McGiffin* v *Palmer's Shipbuilding & Iron Co. Ltd.* (1882)10 QBD 5].

Defect in machinery means a defect of material, in respect either of its original composition or in respect of its original or its after-acquired condition. [*Jackson* v *Mumford* (1902)51 WR 91].

**Defect of jurisdiction.** Where the judge or court has no jurisdiction over the subject-matter of the proceeding or action in which an order is made or a judgment is rendered, so that the order or judgment is wholly void. It must be distinguished from irregular exercise of jurisdiction.

NOTE: Where the expression as a whole reads "from defect of jurisdiction or other cause of a like nature, is unable to entertain it", the expression "cause of a like nature" will have to be read *ejusdem generis* with the expression "defect of jurisdiction". So construed the expression "other cause of a like nature" must be so interpreted as to convey something analogous to the preceding words "from defect of jurisdiction". [*Zafar Khan* v *Board of Revenue, U.P.* AIR 1985 SC 39: (1985)1 SCR 287: 1984 (Supp) SCC 505].

**Defective title.** Any fact calculated to prevent the purchaser obtaining such a title to the property as he was led to expect constitutes a defect of title. [Halsbury's *Laws of England*, 3rd Ed., vol. 34, pp. 219, 220].

A title that cannot legally convey the property to which it applies, usually because of some conflicting claim to that property. [Black's *Law Dictionary*, 7th Ed.].

**Defence.** The act of defending; a defendant's reply, or answer to plaintiff's claim.

Defence means something which a man does in order to defend himself from the legal consequences of the proceedings instituted against him. [*R.* v *Denton (Inhabitants)* (1864)5 B&S 821, *per* Cockburn, C.J.].

"'Defence' commeth of the word defendo" (Co. Litt. 127b); and as applied to a pleading it does not mean "justification", which is the ordinary signification, but a "denial". [3 Bl Com 296; *R.* v *Rhodes* (1899)1 QB 97].

- **Civil defence** p. 144.
- **Self-defence** p. 785.

**Defence area.** That part of the high seas from which a belligerent claims the right of excluding neutral ships.

**Defendant.** A person sued in a civil proceeding or accused in a criminal proceeding. [Black's *Law Dictionary*, 8th Ed.].

A person required to make answer in a legal action or suit; opposite of plaintiff.

NOTE: The word 'defendant' does not include a person merely brought in as third-party. [*Eden* v *Weardale Co.* 28 Ch D 333; *Street* v *Gover* 2 QBD 498]. But when the third-party has been treated as an "opposite party" and has been ordered, at plaintiff's instance, to answer interrogatories, he becomes a defendant and entitled to an order to interrogate the plaintiff. [*Eden* v *Weardale Co.* 35 Ch D 287].

Defendant includes—(*i*) any person from or through whom a defendant derives his liability to be sued; (*ii*) any person whose estate is represented by the defendant as executor, administrator or other representative. [Limitation Act 1963, s. 2(*e*)].

**Deferred annuity.** An annuity that begins making payments on a specified date if the annuitant is alive at that time. [Black's *Law Dictionary*, 8th Ed.].

This is an annuity payable after lapse of a specified time. Should death occur in the meantime, the purchase money is not necessarily returnable.

**Deferred charge.** An expense not currently recognised on an income statement but carried forward on the balance sheet as an asset to be written off in the future. [Black's *Law Dictionary*, 8th Ed.]; expense not chargeable currently on the profit and loss statement and which is carried on the balance sheet; expenditure not recognised as an expense of the period when made but carried forward as an asset to be written off in future periods, such as for advance rent payments or insurance premiums.

**Deferred income.** Money received at a time later than when it was earned, such as a cheque received in January for commissions earned in November. [Black's *Law Dictionary*, 8th Ed.].

**Deferred sentence.** A sentence, the pronouncement of which has been postponed. It does not operate as a suspension of sentence. [Black's *Law Dictionary*, 5th Ed.].

A sentence that will not be carried out if the defendant meets certain requirements, such as complying with conditions of probation. [Black's *Law Dictionary*, 8th Ed.].

**Deferred shares.** They are shares with the right to take the whole or a proportion of profits after a fixed dividend has been paid on the ordinary shares.

**Deficiency.** A lack, shortage, or insufficiency.

NOTE: 'Deficiency of men' in a charter-party has been held to mean the equivalent of lack of men and not "deficiency of willingness in men". [*Royal Greek Government* v *Minister of Transport, The Illissos* (1949)1 KB 525].

**Deficiency of profits.** 'Deficiency of profits' means—(*i*) where the profits have been made in any chargeable accounting period, the amount by which such profits fall short of the abatement in respect of that period; (*ii*) where a loss has been made in any chargeable accounting period, the amount of the loss added to the abatement in respect of that period. [Business Profits Tax Act 1947, s. 2(7)].

**Deficit.** A deficiency or disadvantage; a deficiency in the amount or quality of something; loss in operation of business.

In its popular meaning, it signifies deficiency from any cause. In accounting, it means opposite of surplus on balance sheet.

- **Trade deficit.** In economics, it means the excess of merchandise imports over its exports during a specific period.

**Definite information.** The phrase "definite information" cannot be construed in a universal sense and its meaning must depend on and vary with the circumstances of each case. There is no doubt, however, that the information must be definite, that is, more than mere guess, gossip or rumour. There must be a casual connection between the information and the discovery. [*A.N. Lakshman Shenoy* v *Income-tax Officer* AIR 1958 SC 795: 1958 SCJ 1023].

**Definite portions.** The expression 'definite portions' means that the properties are physically divided if they admit of such division, otherwise in such division as they admit of. [*Udayan Chinubhai* v *CIT, Gujarat* AIR 1967 SC 762: (1967)63 ITR 416].

**Definition.** A description of a thing by its properties; an explanation of the meaning of a word or term; the process of stating the exact meaning of a word by means of other words. [Black's *Law Dictionary*, 5th Ed.].

The meaning of a term as explicitly stated in a drafted document such as a contract, a corporate by-law, an ordinance, or a statute. [Black's *Law Dictionary*, 8th Ed.].

A "definition" is an explicit statement of the full connotation of a term. [*Punjab Land and Reclamation Corporation Ltd.* v *Presiding Officer, Labour Court* (1990)3 SCC 682: (1990)3 SCR 111: JT 1990(2) SC 490].

**Deflation.** This is a check to inflation following contraction of credit and reduction in purchasing power.

A general decline in the price of goods and services. [Black's *Law Dictionary*, 7th Ed.].

**Defraud.** To deprive one of something by practice of deception or fraud.

To make a misrepresentation of an existing material fact, knowing it to be false or making it recklessly without regard to whether it is true or false, intending one to rely and under circumstances in which such person does rely to his damage; to practise fraud; to cheat or trick; to deprive a person of property or any interest, estate or right by fraud, deceit, or artifice. [Black's *Law Dictionary*, 5th Ed.].

To cause injury or loss to (a person) by deceit. [Black's *Law Dictionary*, 7th Ed.].

There are one or two things that can be said with confidence guide as to the limits of what is meant by 'to defraud'. It may mean to cheat, that is, defrauding involves doing something to someone. Although in the nature of things it is almost invariably associated with the obtaining of an advantage for the person who commits the fraud, it is the effect on the person who is the object of fraud that ultimately determines its meaning. Secondly, popular speech does not give any sure guide as to the limits of what is meant by 'to defraud'. It may mean to cheat someone. It may mean to practise a fraud on someone. It may mean to deprive someone by deceit of something which is regarded as belonging to him or, though not belonging to him, as due to him or his right. [*Welham* v *Director of Public Prosecutions* (1960)1 All ER 805].

NOTE: The expression 'defraud' involves two elements, namely, deceit and injury to the person deceived. Injury is something other than economic loss, that is, deprivation of property, whether movable or immovable, or of money, and it will include any harm whatever caused to any person in body, mind, reputation or such others. In short, it is a non-economic or non-pecuniary loss. [*Dr. Vimla* v *Delhi Administration* AIR 1963 SC 1572].

• **With intent to defraud** p. 900.

**Defunct.** Dead; extinct; devoid of life; gone out of existence; inoperative; lifeless; no longer living; no more; not endowed with life; not existing; not in action; not in force.

**Defunct company.** A defunct company is one which is not carrying on business or in operation.

NOTE: Section 560 of the Companies Act 1956 deals with defunct company. The Registrar of Companies may strike the name of a defunct company off the register according to the procedure laid down in s. 560 of the Companies Act 1956. After the name has been struck off, a notice to that effect will be published in the Official Gazette, whereupon the company shall stand dissolved.

**Degrees of prohibited relationship.** Two persons are said to be within the degrees of prohibited relationship—(*i*) if one is a lineal ascendant of the other; or (*ii*) if one was the wife or husband of a lineal ascendant or descendant of the other; or (*iii*) if one was the wife of the brother or of the father's or mother's brother or of the grandfather's or grandmother's brother of the other; or (*iv*) if the two are brother and sister, uncle and niece, aunt and nephew, or children of brother and sister or of two brothers or of two sisters. [Hindu Marriage Act 1955, s. 3(*g*)].

NOTE: A marriage within prohibited degrees is void. [Hindu Marriage Act 1955, s. 11].

In Mahomedan law a man is prohibited from marrying one on the ground of consanguinity or affinity or fosterage. A marriage within prohibited degrees is void.

A man and any of the persons mentioned in Part I of the First Schedule, and a woman and any of the persons mentioned in Part II of the said Schedule are within the degrees of prohibited relationship. [Special Marriage Act 1954, s. 2(*b*)].

The expression shall have the same meaning as in the Special Marriage Act 1954. [Foreign Marriage Act 1969, s. 2(*a*)].

**Deity.** A God, Goddess, or divine person.

NOTE: "Neither God nor any supernatural being could be a person in law. But so far as the deity stands as the representation and symbol of the particular purpose which is indicated by the donor, it can figure as a legal person. In that capacity alone, the dedicated property can vest in it. Hindu idol is a juristic entity capable of holding property and of being taxed and to defend such property in a court of law. A deity falls within the meaning of the word 'individual'. [*Jogendra Nath* v *CIT* AIR 1969 SC 1089: (1969)3 SCR 234].

**Del credere agent.** An agent who guarantees the solvency of the third party with whom the agent makes a contract for the principal. [Black's *Law Dictionary*, 8th Ed.].

A *del credere* agent is one who, usually for extra remuneration, undertakes to indemnify his employer against loss arising from the failure of persons with whom he contracts to carry out their contracts. [Halsbury's *Laws of England*, 4th Ed.,vol. 1, para 713, p. 425].

*Del credere* is an agreement by which a factor, when he sells goods on credit for an additional commission (called *del credere* commission) guarantees the solvency of the purchaser and his performance of the contract. Such a factor is called *del credere* agent. He is a mere surety, liable only to his principal in case the purchaser makes default. [Wharton's *Law Lexicon*].

NOTE: A *del credere* agent receives possession of the principal's goods for purposes of sale and guarantees that anyone to whom the agent sells the goods on credit will pay promptly for them. For this guaranty, the agent receives a higher commission for sales. The promise of such an agent is almost universally held not to be within the statute of frauds. [Black's *Law Dictionary*, 7th Ed.].

The liability of the *del credere* agent is a contingent pecuniary liability, not a liability to perform the contract; it is a pecuniary liability to make good in the event of the default of the buyer in respect of a pecuniary liability. It does not extend to other obligations of the contract. [*Gabriel* v *Churchill* (1914)3 KB 1272].

**Delay.** As noun means the act of postponing or slowing; an instance at which something is postponed or slowed; the period during which something is postponed or slowed.

As verb means to put off; postpone; defer; procrastinate; hinder.

**Delayed wages.** The expression 'delayed wages' can only mean wages which are admittedly due but the payment of which has been postponed on some excuse or other. [*Arumugham* v *Jawahar Mills* AIR 1956 Mad 79, with reference to s. 15(3) of the Payment of Wages Act 1936].

The expression includes 'refused wages'. [*Jiwanjirao Sugar Co.* v *J.M. Banerji* AIR 1962 MP 310].

**Delegated legislation.** An item of delegated legislation is an instrument made by a person or body under legislative powers conferred by Act. The delegation of legislative power by means of an enabling Act is an aspect of the grant of executive power. The position is thus summed up by Erskine May: "It has been recognized that the greater number of details of an essential subsidiary or procedural character which can be withdrawn from the floors of both Houses, the more time will be available for the discussion of major matters of public concern. Consequently, legislative power is often conferred upon the executive by statute, and various arrangements are made for parliamentary scrutiny of its exercise". [Erskine May: *Parliamentary Practice*, 20th Ed. 1983, p. 609].

Delegated legislation consists of orders, rules, regulations, directions, bye-laws etc. made by a person or body other than the legislative authority by virtue of powers conferred by statute. It is also called subordinate legislation or administrative legislation.

NOTE: The delegate is usually a functionary of the executive, whether formally or *de facto*. An exception arises where the judiciary are given statutory power to make rules of court.

Delegated or subordinate legislation, in order to take effect, must be published or promulgated in some suitable manner, whether such publication or promulgation is prescribed by the parent statute or not. [*Penumbra of Natural Justice* by Tapash Gan Choudhury, 2nd Ed., p. 49].

In India a delegated or subordinate legislation becomes law and binding only when it is actually published in the Official Gazette. [*Harla* v *State of Rajasthan* AIR 1951 SC 467: 1952 SCR 110; *Asia Tobacco Company Ltd.* v *Union of India* 1984(18) ELT 152 (Mad); *Collector of Central Exercise* v *New Tobacco Co.* 1998(97) ELT 388 (SC): (1998)8 SCC 250: AIR 1998 SC 668].

With the passing of the Information Technology Act 2000, promulgation or publication of delegated or subordinate legislation can now be made in Electronic Gazette. [*Penumbra of Natural Justice* by Tapash Gan Choudhury, 2nd Ed., p. 50].

**Delegation.** Authorisation; deputation; deputization; devolution; entrusting; investing with authority; the act of entrusting another with authority or empowering another to act as an agent or representative.

The transfer of authority by one person to another; the assignment of a date to another; entrusting another with a general power to act for the good of those who depute him.

By delegation is meant the devolution from an agent upon another person of a power or duty entrusted to the agent by his principal. [*Words and Phrases Legally Defined* by John B. Saunders, 2nd Ed.].

"Delegation, as the word is generally used, does not imply a parting with powers by the person who grants the delegation, but points rather to a conferring of an authority to do things which otherwise the person would have to do himself". [*Huth* v *Clarke* (1890)25 QBD 391, 395, *per* Wills, J.].

NOTE: There is a distinction between employing someone else to carry on one's business and engaging someone else to perform something which is his business. A master delegates to his own servants the work of carrying on his own business; he may be said to delegate when he employs some outside person to act as his representative. [*Riverstone Meat Co.* v *Lancashire Shipping Co.* (1960)1 All ER 193].

Generally speaking, where there is personal confidence reposed or skill required there can be no delegation, however general the nature of the duties, unless urgent necessity compels the handing over of the responsibility to someone else. [Halsbury's *Laws of England*, 3rd Ed., vol. 1, pp. 169, 170].

**Delegatus non-potest delegare.** The maxim "envisages that when a power has been conferred on a person indicating that the trust is being placed in his individual judgment and discretion, he must exercise that power personally unless expressly empowered to delegate it to another. In other words, when a statute prescribes a particular body to exercise a power, it must be exercised by that body only. It cannot be exercised by others unless it is delegated. Any contrary indication found in the language, scope or object of the statute may negative the intention as expressed by the maxim". [*Penumbra of Natural Justice* by Tapash Gan Choudhury, 2nd Ed., p. 319].

Halsbury's *Laws of England* summarized the principle thus: "In accordance with the maxim *delegatus non-potest delegare*, a statutory power must be exercised only by the body or officer in whom it has been confided, unless sub-delegation of the power is authorised by express words or necessary implication. There is a strong presumption against construing a grant of legislative, judicial or disciplinary power as impliedly authorising sub-delegation; and the same may be said of any power to the exercise of which the designated body should address its own mind". [4th Ed., vol. 1, para 32].

**Delimit.** Allot; circumscribe; confine; define; demarcate; determine; draw the line; encircle; encompass; lay out a boundary; mark limits; mark out.

In its natural sense the word means to mark out as a boundary, to bound, to mark or determine the limits of, to define as a limit or boundary. It is used in the sense of adjusting or demarcating the boundaries between two entities belonging to two different persons or countries or bodies. [*Ram Chandra Reddy* v *State of Andhra Pradesh* AIR 1965 AP 40].

**Delinquent.** At fault; accusable; censurable; condemnable; dishonest; evil-minded; guilty; incorrigible; law breaking; offending; unscrupulous.

He who has been guilty of some crime, offence, or failure of duty or obligation. [Black's *Law Dictionary*, 5th Ed.].

**Delinquent child.** An infant of not more than specified age who has violated criminal laws or engages in disobedient, indecent or immoral conduct, and is in need of treatment, rehabilitation, or supervision. [Black's *Law Dictionary*, 5th Ed.].

A child who has committed an offence that would be a crime if committed by an adult. [Black's *Law Dictionary*, 8th Ed.].

Delinquent child means a child who has been found to have committed an offence. [*Raghubir* v *State of Haryana* AIR 1981 SC 2037: (1981)4 SCC 210: (1982)1 SCR 686].

**Deliverable state.** Goods are said to be in a 'deliverable state' when they are in such state that the buyer would under the contract be bound to take delivery of them. [Sale of Goods Act 1930, s. 2(3)].

NOTE: A deliverable state does not depend upon the mere completeness of the subject-matter in all its parts. It depends on the actual state of the goods at the date of the contract and the state in which they are to be delivered by the terms of the contract. [*Underwood Ltd.* v *Burgh Castle Brick* (1922)1 KB 343].

**Delivery.** The formal act of transferring (or conveying) something, such as a deed; the giving or yielding possession or control of something to another; the thing so transferred or conveyed. [Black's *Law Dictionary*, 8th Ed.]..

The act by which the res or substance thereof is placed within the actual or constructive possession or control of another. [*Poor* v *American Locomotive Co.* CCA III, 67 F 2d 626, 630].

"Delivery" means voluntary transfer of possession from one person to another. [Sale of Goods Act 1930, s. 2(2)].

Delivery means voluntary transfer of possession from one person to another. The term includes symbolical delivery and is not restricted to the physical transfer of the goods themselves, but covers also transfers of possession of documents of title to goods. Where the buyer takes possession pursuant to the leave of the seller, whether concurrent or antecedent, that is a voluntary transfer of possession. [Halsbury's *Laws of England,* 4th Ed., vol. 41, para 757, p. 685].

NOTE: The delivery of a postal article of any description to a postman or other person authorised to receive postal articles of that description for the post shall be deemed to be a delivery to a post office; and the delivery of a postal article at the house or office of the addressee, or to the addressee or his servant or agent or other person considered to be authorised to receive the article according to the usual manner of delivering postal articles to the addressee, shall be deemed to be delivery to the addressee. [Indian Post Office Act 1898, s. 3].

What constitutes delivery depends largely on the intent of the parties. It is not necessary that delivery should be by manual transfer. [*Jones* v *Young* Tex Civ App, 539 SW 2d 901, 904].


- **Actual delivery** p. 35.
- **Cash on delivery** p. 127.


**Delivery of deed.** The placing of a deed in the grantee's hands or within the grantee's control. [Black's *Law Dictionary*, 8th Ed.].

The final and absolute transfer of a deed, properly executed, to the grantee, or to some person for his use, in such manner that it cannot be recalled by the grantor. [Black's *Law Dictionary*, 5th Ed.].

NOTE: In England a deed has no operation until delivery. The delivery may be effected either by acts or by words, *i.e.*, by doing something and saying nothing, as merely handing it to the grantee or his agent; or by doing nothing and saying something as 'I deliver this writing as my act and deed', or language of a similar import; or by doing and saying something.

Delivery is of two kinds—(*a*) absolute when the execution perfects the deed and nothing is left to be done; (*b*) conditional, which is the handing of the writing to some third person, to be delivered by him as the act and deed of the grantor, when certain specified conditions shall be performed. Until the conditions are performed the instrument is called an escrow, scrowl, or writing.

In India, delivery of the deed is not essential to the validity of the transaction. The mere retention of the conveyance by the vendor does not affect the title of the purchasers.

**Delivery of possession.** Delivery of possession is a bilateral act and requires one side to give up possession and the other side to receive or accept it. [*State* v *Sharadkumar Virchand* AIR 1969 Bom 348. 90 Bom LR 710; *Shyam Sunder* v *Bhanwarlal* AIR 1986 MP 161: 1986 MPLJ 63: (1986)1 Ren LR 394].

**Delivery order.** A written order to deliver goods, directed to a warehouseman, carrier, or other person who ordinarily issues warehouse receipts or bills or lading. [Black's *Law Dictionary,* 8th Ed.].

A delivery order is an order by the owner of goods directing the warehouseman, carrier, or other person to hold them on his behalf to deliver them to the person named in the order. A "delivery order" is a document of title according to the definition in s. 2(4) of the Sale of Goods Act. [*Jugeeilal Kamlapat* v *Pratapmal Rameshwar* AIR 1978 SC 389: (1978)2 SCR 219: (1978)1 SCC 69].

**Delusion.** A false belief or impression; the belief of things as realities, which exist only in the imagination; false, unshakable belief which is (*a*) contrary to fact, (*b*) inappropriate to the person's education, intelligence or culture, and (*c*) adhered to in spite of tangible evidence that it is false.

**Demand.** As noun, it means asking for what is due; assertion of legal right; authoritative request; emphatic enquiry; notice of claim; legal claim; request to perform; ultimatum.

As verb, it means ask for with authority; assert a right to; call for; claim; claim as one's due; command; give notice; order; press; request; require; urge; seek relief summon; call into court.

The word 'demand' ordinarily means something more than what is due; it means something which has been demanded, called for or asked for. But the meaning of the word must take colour from the context. It may mean arrears or dues. [*Mangoo Singh* v *Election Tribunal* AIR 1957 SC 871: 1958 SCJ 136: 1958 SCA 422: 1958 SCR 418].


- **Inelastic demand** p. 455.
- **On demand** p. 625.
- **Payable on demand** p. 648.


**Demand draft.** A draft that is payable on the bearer's demand or on proper presentment to the drawer. [Black's *Law Dictionary,* 7th Ed.]. It is also called sight draft.

A bill of exchange payable at sight or on demand. No acceptance is required in the case of such a draft.

**Demand letter.** A letter by which one party explains its legal position in a dispute and requests that the recipient take some action, or else risk being sued. [Black's *Law Dictionary,* 8th Ed.].

**Demand liabilities.** Liabilities which must be met on demand. [Banking Registration Act 1949, s. 5(*f*)].

**Demand note.** An instrument payable on demand, at sight, or on presentation, as opposed to an instrument that is payable at a set future date. [Black's *Law Dictionary,* 7th Ed]. It is also called demand instrument.

A note which expressly states that it is payable on demand on presentation or at sight; a note in which no time for payment is expressed. [*Cassity* v *Cassity* 76 P 2d 862, 866; *Tarlton* v *Johnson* Mo App, 138 SW 2d 49, 52].

**Demeanour.** Outward appearance or behaviour, such as facial expressions, tone of voice, gestures, and the hesitation or readiness to answer questions. [Black's *Law Dictionary,* 8th Ed.].

As respects a witness or other person, relates to physical appearance; outward bearing or behaviour. [*Faircloth* v *State* 208 So 2d 66, 70].

NOTE: The court may record such remarks as it thinks material respecting the demeanour of any witness while under examination. [Code of Civil Procedure 1908, Or. 18, r. 12].

**Demise.** As noun means alienation; bequeathal, cession; conveyancing; testamentary disposition; transfer; transmission; transmittal; it also means cessation of life; decease; departure; end of life; extinction; extinguishment; loss of life.

As verb, it means bequeath; bestow by will; confer by will; convey; devolve upon; endow; grant by will; make testamentary disposition; transfer of ownership; transmit.

The conveyance of an estate by will or lease; the instrument by which such a conveyance is accomplished; the passing of property by descent or bequeath; the death of a person or of a thing. [Black's *Law Dictionary,* 7th Ed.].

The operative word 'demise' in a lease implies an absolute covenant on the part of the lessor or person leasing, for the lessee's quiet enjoyment during the term, which, however, may be, and usually is, qualified by the more limited express covenant. [Wharton's *Law Lexicon*].

The word demise (in a lease) does imply a covenant for title, but only when there is no express covenant inconsistent with such a construction. [*Line* v *Stephenson* (1838)5 Bing NC 183, 186, *per* Lord Denman, C.J.].

**Demolish.** To tear down; raze; destroy utterly; ruin, lay waste to; pull down; completely destroy or break; over throw; refute.

The usual meaning of the word 'demolish' is to destroy (particularly in relation to a building) by violent disintegration of its fabric; to pull or throw down; pull into pieces, reduce to ruins. [*Nelson* v *Healy* (1948) VLR 415, 417, *per* O'Bryan, J. (Australia)].

**Demolition.** The act or result of demolishing; destruction.

**Demonstration.** An outward expression or display; a public display of group feelings for or against a person or cause or any matter of public interest.

NOTE: A demonstration is a visible manifestation of the feelings or sentiments of an individual or a group. It is thus a communication of one's ideas to others to whom it is intended to be conveyed. It is in effect, therefore, a form of speech or of expression, because speech need not be vocal, since signs made by a dumb person would also be a form of speech. A demonstration may take various forms; it may be noisy and disorderly, for instance stone-throwing by a crowd. It may be equally peaceful and ordinary, such as wearing a badge by the members of the group. [*Kameshwar Prasad* v *State of Bihar* AIR 1962 SC 1166: (1962)2 SCA 240].

**Demonstrative legacy.** A legacy paid from a particular source if that source has enough money. [Black's *Law Dictionary,* 7th Ed.]. If it does not, the amount of the legacy not paid from that source is taken from the estate's general assets. [Black's *Law Dictionary,* 7th Ed.].

▸ *Meaning under the Indian Succession Act 1925, s. 150.* Where a testator bequeaths a certain sum of money, or a certain quantity of any other commodity, and refers to a particular fund or stock so as to constitute the same the primary fund or stock out of which payment is to be made, the legacy is said to be demonstrative.

NOTE: *Specific legacy and demonstrative legacy—distinction.* The distinction between a specific legacy and a demonstrative legacy consists in this, that—where specified property is given to the legatee, the legacy is specific; where the legacy is directed to be paid out of specified property, it is demonstrative. [Indian Succession Act 1925, Explanation to s. 150].

**Demurrage.** In Maritime law, "demurrage" has been defined as a liquidated penalty owed by a charterer to a shipowner for the charterer's failure to load or unload cargo by a certain time. [Black's *Law Dictionary,* 7th Ed.]. The strict meaning of "demurrage" is the agreed amount to be paid by the charterer of a ship for each day taken in loading or discharging beyond the respective times fixed for those operations. The word 'demurrage' appears to be more applicable to delay in time after expiration of a fixed time than to delay after the expiration of a reasonable time. [*Dunlop & Sons* v *Balfour, Williamson & Co.* (1892)1 QB 507].

Demurrage is a charge levied for the detention of any rolling stock after the expiry of free time, if any, allowed for such detention. [Railways Act 1989, s. 2(11)].

Demurrage is a charge levied on the goods not unloaded from the wagons within the free time. [*Rai Chand Amulakh Shah* v *Union of India* AIR 1964 SC 1268: (1964)5 SCR 148]. "Demurrage" is usually applied to a stationary detention, but in a Railway Act giving traders "a reasonable sum by way of demurrage for any detention of trucks beyond a reasonable period". "Demurrage" includes detention during transit. [*Charrington* v *London & North Western Railway* (1905)2 KB 437]. "Demurrage", in this connection, means a "charge for damage directly occasioned by reason of a truck lying idle and unemployed". [*R.* v *Marylebone County Court Judge* 75 LJKB 906, *per* Darling, J.].

**Demurrer.** "The word 'demurrer', derived from the Latin *demorari*, or the French demorrer, meaning to 'wait or stay', imports that the party demurring waits or stays in his proceedings in the action until the judgment of the court is given whether he is bound to answer to so insufficient a pleading. Each party may demur to what he deems an insufficient pleading of the other. The demurrer was general when it was to matter of substance; it was special when it was made to matter of form, and must specifically point out the defect". [Edwin E. Bryant: *The Law of Pleading under the Codes of Civil Procedure,* p. 15 (2d Ed. 1899)].

It has been defined as a pleading stating that although the facts alleged in a complaint may be true, they are insufficient for the plaintiff to state a claim for relief and for the defendant to frame an answer. [Black's *Law Dictionary,* 7th Ed.].

Demurrer is an objection to the form or substance of the indictment, apparent on the face of the indictment, and is not to be decided by examination of the depositions. [*R.* v *Deputy Chairman* (1969)3 All ER 1537].

• **General demurrer** p. 383.

**Denomination.** An act of naming; a collective designation, esp. of a religious sect. [Black's *Law Dictionary,* 8th Ed.].

The word 'denomination' means a collection of individuals classed together under the same name, a religious sect or body having a common faith and organization and designated by a distinctive name. [*The Commissioner, Hindu Religious Endowments, Madras* v *Sri Lakshmindru Thirtha Swamiar of Sri Shirur Mutt* AIR 1954 SC 282: 1954 SCR 1005: 1954 SCJ 335, referring to *Oxford Dictionary*, Constitution of India and Madras Hindu Religious and Charitable Endowments Act 1951].

The meaning of "denomination" is "a religious group of a community of believers called by the same name". [*State of Rajasthan* v *Shri Sajjanlal Panjawat* AIR 1975 SC 706: (1974)1 SCC 500: (1974)2 SCR 741, referring to Webster's *Third New International Dictionary*].

• **Religious denomination** p. 742.

**Denote.** Be a sign of; indicate; stand as a name for; signify; be an indication of; convey a meaning; depict; express; mean; portray; referred to; stand for; suggest; symbolize; tell the meaning of.

**Department.** Area; branch; bureau; chapter; division; part; realm; section; zone.

A division of a greater whole; a subdivision; a principal branch or division of government. [Black's *Law Dictionary,* 8th Ed.].

A department is a unit or branch of the Government, either Union or State, under the political control of a Minister or Secretary of State or President of the

Board. Individual officers serving under a department do not constitute a department. The department has an entity distinct and separate from the officers serving under it. [*Ram Chandra* v *District Magistrate* AIR 1952 All 520: ILR (1952)2 All 752].

• **Head of department** p. 408.

**Departure.** A deviation or divergence from a standard rule, regulation, measurement, or course of conduct; a variance between a pleading and a later pleading or proof; a party's desertion of the ground (either legal or factual) taken in the immediately preceding pleading and resort to another ground. [Black's *Law Dictionary,* 8th Ed.].

'Departure' with its grammatical variations and cognate expressions means departure from India by water, land or air. [Passports Act 1967, s. 2(*a*)].

**Dependant.** Regulated by; needing outside support; reliant; subject to; subordinate; unable to exist without; a person who relies on another esp. for financial support.

▸*Meaning in general legal parlance.* The word 'dependant' cannot be construed as meaning nothing but wholly dependent in the sense of not earning anything at all and being entirely dependent on the father for boarding, lodging and food. The term must be construed as meaning somebody not wholly independant or self supporting and in a position to set up separate residence. [*C.I. Davar* v *Amar Nath Kapur* (1962)64 Punj LR 521, *per* Falshaw, CJ.].

NOTE: Dependence may not, in all circumstances, be entirely a matter of finance and this would particularly be so in the case of an unmarried daughter who may be employed but in whose case, for various reasons, it would not be desirable for her to attempt to live away from her parents and on her own. [*Govind Das* v *Kuldip Singh* AIR 1971 Del 151].

▸*Meaning under the Employees' State Insurance Act 1948, s. 2(6A) and Workmen's Compensation Act 1923, s. 2(d).* Any of the following relatives of a deceased insured person, namely—(*i*) a widow, a minor legitimate or adopted son, an unmarried legitimate or adopted daughter, or (*ia*) a widowed mother; and (*ii*) if wholly dependant on the earnings of the insured person at the time of his death, a legitimate or adopted son or daughter who has attained the age of eighteen years and who is infirm; (*iii*) if wholly or in part dependant on the earnings of the insured person at the time of his death—(*a*) a parent other than a widowed mother, (*b*) a minor illegitimate son, an unmarried illegitimate daughter or a daughter legitimate or adopted or illegitimate if married and a minor or if widowed and a minor, (*c*) a minor brother or an unmarried sister or a widowed sister if a minor, (*d*) a widowed daughter-in-law, (*e*) a minor child of a pre-deceased son, (*f*) a minor child of a pre-deceased daughter, where no parent of the child is alive, or (*g*) a paternal grandparent, if no parent of the insured person is alive.

▸*Meaning under the Expenditure-Tax Act 1957, s. 2(g).* 'Dependant' means—(*i*) where the assessee is an individual, his or her spouse or minor child and includes any person wholly or mainly dependant on the assessee for support and maintenance; (*ii*) where the assessee is a Hindu undivided family—(*a*) every coparcener other than the Karta; and (*b*) any other member of the family who under any law or order or decree of a court is entitled to maintenance from the joint family property.

▸*Meaning under the Indian Emigration Act 1922, s. 2(a).* 'Dependant' means any woman or child who is related to an emigrant and any aged or incapacitated relative of an emigrant.

▸*Meaning under the Provident Fund Act 1925, s. 2(c).* Dependant means any of the following relatives of a deceased subscriber to, or a depositor in, a Provident Fund, namely, a wife, husband, parent, child, minor brother, unmarried sister and a deceased son's widow and child, and, where no parent of the subscriber or depositor is alive, a paternal grandparent.

▸*Meaning under the Workmen's Compensation Act 1923, s. 2(d).* Dependant means dependants at the time of death of deceased workmen. [*Charubala Saha* v *Eastern Rly. Administration* AIR 1988 Cal 327].

**Dependent relative revocation.** Revocation of a will may be relative to another disposition which has already been made or is intended to be made, and so dependent thereon that revocation is not intended unless that other disposition takes effect. Such a revocation is known as a dependent relative revocation, and, if from any cause the other disposition fails to take effect, the will remains operative as it was before the revocation. [Halsbury's *Laws of England*, 4th Ed., vol. 50, para 298, p. 155].

NOTE: The effect of cancelling the first will depends upon the validity of the second will and the two ought to be taken as one act done at the same time so that if the later will is not valid tho cancelling of the first, being dependent thereon, ought to be looked upon as null and inoperative and the first will must stand. [*Gobinda Ramanuj* v *Ram Charan* AIR 1925 Cal 1107].

The doctrine of dependent relative revocation, is based on the principle that all acts by which a testator may physically destroy or mutilate a testamentary instrument are, in their nature equivocal. They may be the result of accident, or, if intentional, of various intentions. It is therefore necessary in each case to study the act done by the light of the circumstances under which it occurred and the declarations of the testator with which it may have been accompanied; for unless it is done *animo revocandi* it is no revocation. [*Powell* v *Powell* LR 1 P&D 209; *Garnet Botfield* v *Garnet Botfield* (1901) P 335; *Re Litter* (1950) P 130].

It is a common law doctrine that operates to undo as otherwise sufficient revocation of a will when there is evidence that the testator's revocation was conditional rather than absolute. Typically, the doctrine applies when a testator has physically revoked the will and believes that a new will is valid, although this belief is mistaken. The doctrine undoes only the revocation; it does not always accomplish the testator's intent or validate an otherwise invalid will. [Black's *Law Dictionary*, 8th Ed.].

**Deponent.** Affiant; communicant; communicator; enlightener; one who makes an affidavit; one who testifies under oath; swearer; testifier witness who gives testimony.

One who testifies by deposition; a witness who gives written testimony for later use in court. [Black's *Law Dictionary*, 8th Ed.].

**Deportation.** Sending away; elimination; extrusion; banishment; extradition; expulsion; expatriation; casting out; dismissal.

The act or an instance of removing a person to another country; esp., the expulsion or transfer of an alien from a country. [Black's *Law Dictionary*, 8th Ed.].

**Deposit.** Accumulation; down payment; earnest pledge; dump; instal; lodge; place in a receptacle; slash; store; enter into an account; keep an account; lay by; present money for safe keeping.

The act of giving money or other property to another who promises to preserve it or to use it and return it in kind; esp., the act of placing money in a bank for safety and convenience; the money or property so given. [Black's *Law Dictionary*, 8th Ed.].

▸*Meaning under the Deposit Insurance Corporation Act 1961, s. 2(g).* 'Deposit' means the aggregate of unpaid balances due to a depositor (other than a foreign Government, the Central Government, a State Government or a banking company) in respect of all his accounts, by whatever name called, with a banking company and includes credit balance in any cash credit account but does not include—(*i*) where a banking company at the commencement of this Act is working under a scheme of compromise or arrangement or of reconstruction sanctioned by any competent authority providing for any acceptance of fresh deposits, any amount due to the depositor in respect of his deposit before the date of the coming into force of the scheme to the extent it is not credited after the said date under the provisions of that scheme; or (*ii*) any amount due on account of any deposit received outside India.

NOTE: *Deposit and loan—distinction.* In a sense, a deposit is also a loan with this difference that it is a loan with something more. Both are debts repayable. But when the repayment is to be made is the real point of distinction between the two. A loan is repayable the moment it is incurred. But in the case of a deposit, it is payable according to the terms of the agreement. [*Abdul Hamid* v *Rahamat Bi* AIR 1965 Mad 427: (1965)2 MLJ 368].

Whether a transaction is a loan or deposit does not depend merely on the terms of the document, but has got to be judged from the intention of the parties and all the circumstances of the case. [*Annamalai* v *Veerappa* AIR 1956 SC 12].


- **Compulsory deposit** p. 165.
- **Security deposit** p. 783.


**Deposition.** Declaration under oath; oral statement under oath; solemn declaration; statement on oath; sworn evidence; testification; written declaration under oath.

A witness's out-of-court testimony that is reduced to writing (usually by a court reporter) for later use in court or for discovery purposes; the session at which such testimony is recorded. [Black's *Law Dictionary,* 8th Ed.].

**Depreciation.** A decline in an asset's value because of use, wear, or obsolescence. [Black's *Law Dictionary,* 8th Ed.].

A decline in value of property caused by wear or obsolescence and is usually measured by a set formula which reflects these elements over a given period of useful life of property. [*State Highway Commission* v *Tubles* 411 P 2d 739, 744].

'Depreciation' means 'a decrease in value of property through wear, deterioration, or obsolescence, the allowance made for this in book keeping, accounting, etc.' [*Commissioner of Income Tax* v *Alps Theatre* (1967)65 ITR 377: AIR 1967 SC 1437, referring to Webster's *New World Dictionary*].

'Depreciation' represents the diminution in value of a capital asset, when applied to the purpose of making profit or gain. [*Workmen, N.G. Bank* v *N.G. Bank* AIR 1967 SC 611].

NOTE: 'Depreciation' in its commercial sense applies only to wasting fixed assets, such as plant, machinery and equipment, which inevitably diminish in value when applied to the purpose of seeking profits, or advantages. [*National Petroleum Corpn. Ltd.* v *National Revenue Minister* (1942) Ex CR 102, *per* Maclean, J.].

Land cannot depreciate. [*Commissioner of Income Tax* v *Alps Theatre* (1967)65 ITR 377: AIR 1967 SC 1437].

**Depression.** A period of economic stress that persists over an extended period, accompanied by poor business conditions and high unemployment. [*McCuiston* v *Haggard* 109 SW 2d 413]. In economic parlance, a "depression" is more severe than a "recession".

It may also mean a mental syndrome manifested by sense of inadequacy, self-depreciation, melancholy, and guilt feelings.

**Deprivation.** A taking away or confiscation; e.g., the deprivation of a constitutional right or the taking of property under eminent domain without due process of law.

An act of taking away; a withholding of something; the state of being without something; wanting; a removal or degradation from office. [Black's *Law Dictionary*, 8th Ed.].

**Deputy.** A substitute; a person duly authorised by an officer to exercise some or all of the functions pertaining to the office, in the place and stead of the latter; one appointed to substitute for another with power to act for him in his name or behalf; a substitute for another empowered to act for himself in his name and behalf in all matters in which the principal may act. [*Williams* v *Ferrentino* 199 So 2d 504, 511].

A person appointed or delegated to act as a substitute for another, esp. for an official. [Black's *Law Dictionary,* 8th Ed.].

**Derelict.** As adjective means forsaken; abandoned; cast away; lacking a sense of duty; in breach of a legal or moral obligation.

As noun means personal property abandoned or thrown away by the owner with an intent to no longer claim it; land uncovered by receding water from its former bed; a street person or vagrant; a hobo.

NOTE: All things found derelict on the sea, including flotsam, jetsam or lagan which have not touched the ground and which are brought within the United Kingdom, are *prima facie* droits of Admiralty but do not become actual droits unless there is no claim to ownership, and until then are only derelict. [Halsbury's *Laws of England,* 4th Ed., vol. 1, para 333, p. 231].

**Derivativa potestas non potest esse major primitiva.** The power derived cannot be greater than that from which it is derived.

**Derive.** Conclude; construe; draw a conclusion; draw an inference; extract; make a deduction; acquire; come into possession; procure; secure.

To receive from a specified source or origin. [*Crews* v *Commissioner of Internal Revenue* CCA 10: 89 F 2d 412, 416].

**Derived.** Obtained or received or taken from a definite source; arising or accruing.

- **Income derived from property.** That income which has arisen directly and substantially from the property. It is not sufficient that the property should be indirectly responsible for the income. [*J.K. Trust* v *Commissioner of Income Tax* AIR 1953 Bom 232: (1952)55 Bom LR 135].

**Derogate.** Abase; asperse; belittle; besmirch; bring down; bring into discredit; blacken; bring shame upon; cast a slur upon; cast aspersions; debase; decry; demean; defame; denigrate; detract; dishonour; disparage; lesson the reputation of; make ashamed; malign; pull down; tarnish.

**Descend.** To pass by succession [Black's *Law Dictionary,* 5th Ed]; come down by transmission; come down lineally; pass by devise; pass by inheritance; pass by operation of law.

By the word 'descend' is understood the passing of property to the heir or heirs without disposition by will or by alienation in the form of gift, sale etc. It is transmission by inheritance from an ancestor to the next heir. [*Shiv Singh* v *Jivan Dass* AIR 1958 Punj 164].

**Descendant.** One who follows in lineage, such as a child or grandchild—but not a collateral relative. [Black's *Law Dictionary,* 7th Ed.].

At the present day "descendants" means lineal descendants only and does not include collateral relations [*Riddick* v *Mennard* (1972)1 Ch 379].

- **Lineal descendant** p. 536.

**Descent.** The acquisition of real property by law, as by inheritance; the passing of intestate real property to heirs. [Black's *Law Dictionary,* 7th Ed.].

It is mode of acquisition of title by inheritance by reason of consanguinity, as well as where heir shall be an ancestor or collateral relation.

The strict legal sense of the word 'descent' means taking an estate by inheritance; that is as heir of the former holder, but in common parlance the word is not properly, nor indeed commonly, confined to that meaning, but means succession merely. [*Bickley* v *Bickley* (1967) LR 4 Eq 216].

**Description.** Account; characterization; definition; delineation; depiction; explanation; formulation; outline; portrayal; sketch; specification.

'Description' means: A delineation or account of a particular subject by the recital of its characteristic antecedents and qualities. [*Subhas Chandra* v *State of U.P.* AIR 1980 SC 800: (1980)2 SCR 1024: (1980)2 SCC 324].

Description of a person includes a description of the profession, trade or occupation of the person or if he has no profession, trade or occupation, his style. [*Sims* v *Trollope & Sons* (1897)1 QB 24].

**Desert.** Abandon; give up; leave.

To quit with an intention to cause a permanent separation. It is essentially wilful in nature.

To 'desert' together with its grammatical variations and cognate expressions means to desert the other party to a marriage without reasonable cause and without the consent, or against the will, of such party. [Parsi Marriage and Divorce Act 1936, s. 2(3)].

**Deserter.** In family law, a deserter is a person who wilfully, without reasonable cause and without the consent deserts the other party to a marriage with the intention to bring cohabitation permanently to an end.

In maritime law, a deserter is a man who leaves his ship and does not return to it with no purpose other than to break his agreement. [*Ibrahim* v *State of West Bengal* AIR 1968 SC 731: (1968)2 SCJ 264: 1968 Cr LJ 878].

In military law, a deserter is a person who absents himself with the intent either to quit the service altogether or to avoid some particular duty for which he would be required. [*Virendra Kumar* v *The Chief of Army Staff, New Delhi* AIR 1986 SC 1060: (1986)2 SCC 217].

**Desertion.** The wilful and unjustified abandonment of a person's duties or obligations, especially to military service or to a spouse or family. [Black's *Law Dictionary,* 8th Ed].

▸ *Meaning under the Family Law.* 'Desertion' is the separation of one's spouse from the other, with an intention on the part of the deserting spouse of bringing cohabitation permanently to an end without reasonable cause and without the consent of the other spouse, but the physical act of departure of one spouse does not necessarily make that spouse the deserting party. [Rayden on *Divorce*, 6th Ed., p. 128 as referred to in *Bipin Chandra Jai Singh Bai Shah* v *Prabhavati* AIR 1957 SC 176: 1956 SCR 838: 1957 SCJ 144].

'Desertion' means the intentional permanent forsaking and abandonment of one spouse by the other without that other's consent, and without reasonable cause. It is a total repudiation of the obligations of marriage. For the act of desertion to exist, there must be both the *factum* or physical separation and the *animus deserendi* or the intention to desert. [Halsbury's *Laws of England,* 4th Ed., vol. 13, para 576, p. 284 and para 582, p. 287].

NOTE: Desertion is not the withdrawal from a place but from a state of things, for what the law seeks to enforce is the recognition and discharge of the common obligations of the married state; the state of things may usually be termed, for short, "home". There can be desertion without previous cohabitation by the parties, or without the marriage having been consummated. [Halsbury's *Laws of England,* 4th Ed., vol. 13, para 576, p. 284].

'Desertion' implies an abandonment against the wish of the person charging it. [Divorce Act 1869, s. 3(9)].

Desertion implies two conditions, namely: (*i*) factum of separation, and (*ii*) intention to bring cohabitation permanently to an end. [*Sunil Kumar* v *Satirani* AIR 1969 Cal 573: 73 CWN 721].

▸ *Meaning under the Hindu Marriage Act 1955.* Two ingredients must be established to prove desertion. It should be established that the separate residence of the deserting spouse was without reasonable cause. It should next be established that such separate residence was without the consent of or against the wish of the deserted spouse. The third category of desertion constitutes wilful neglect of the deserted spouse by the deserting spouse. [*K. Siddegowda* v *Parvathamma* AIR 1965 Mys 299].

NOTE: *Spousal desertion elements.* The five elements of spousal desertion are–(1) a cessation of cohabitation, (2) the lapse of a statutory period, (3) an intention to abandon, (4) a lack of consent from the abandoned spouse, and (5) a lack of spousal misconduct that might justify the abandonment. [Black's *Law Dictionary,* 7th Ed.].

To constitute just cause for one spouse leaving apart from the other spouse, there must be grave and weighty matter, i.e., conduct of such kind as, in effect, makes the continuance of married life together impossible. Small and trivial matters, if they fall within the ordinary wear and tear of married life, have no legal significance. On the other hand, matters such as are of a sufficiently grave and weighty character as to amount to just cause, would make it impossible to allege desertion at all. [*Postlethwaite* v *Postlethwaite* (1957)1 All ER 909].

▸*Meaning under the maritime law.* By desertion, in the maritime law, is meant, not a mere unauthorised absence from the ship without leave, but an unauthorised absence from the ship, with an intention not to return to her service, or, as it is often expressed, *animo non revertendi;* that is, with an intention to desert. [*The Cripple Creek* DC Pa, 52 F Supp 710, 712].

NOTE: The gist of desertion, is the existence of an *animus* not to return to the ship, or not other words, to go against the agreement under which the employment of seamen for sea voyages generally taken place. [*Ibrahim* v *State of West Bengal* AIR 1968 SC 731: (1968)2 SCJ 264: 1968 Cr LJ 878].

▸*Meaning under the military law.* Any member of the armed forces who—(1) without authority goes or remains absent from his unit, organization, or place of duty with intent to remain away therefrom permanently; (2) quits his unit, organization, or place of duty with intent to avoid hazardous duty or to shirk important service; or (3) without being regularly separated from one of the armed forces enlists or accepts an appointment in the same or another one of the armed forces without fully disclosing the fact that he has not been regularly separated, or enters any foreign armed service except when authorised is guilty of desertion. [*Virendra Kumar* v *The Chief of Army Staff, New Delhi* AIR 1986 SC 1060: (1986)2 SCC 217].

A person who absents himself with the intent either to quit the service altogether or to avoid some particular duty for which he would be required, is guilty of desertion. [Artillery Records Instructions 1981, para 418 as referred to in *Virendra Kumar* v *The Chief of Army Staff, New Delhi* AIR 1986 SC 1060: (1986)2 SCC 217].

Desertion does not simply mean leaving the posting or mere departure from the post without permission. It means something more, i.e., with the intention never to return to the post or to go away with the idea of avoiding hazardous duty, or shirking any important service. [*State* v *Rawatsingh* AIR 1957 Raj 26].

**Deserve.** Show conduct of qualities worthy of reward, punishment, etc.; to be entitled to or worthy of, by either merit or demerit.

To have a rightful claim or a just claim. [*Hameedia Hardware Stores* v *B. Mohan Lal Sowear* AIR 1988 SC 1060, 1068].

**Design.** A preliminary plan, sketch, or concept, for the making or production of something; a scheme of lines or shapes forming a pattern or decoration; a plan, purpose or intention.

To make, draw or prepare preliminary plans or sketches of; to make drawings or plans.

A plan or scheme; the pattern or configuration of elements in something, such as a work or art. [Black's *Law Dictionary,* 7th Ed.].

In patent law, it means the drawing or the depiction of an original plan for a novel pattern, model, shape, or configuration that is chiefly decorative or ornamental. [Black's *Law Dictionary,* 8th Ed.]. Design involves certain elements. There must be features of shape, configuration, pattern or ornament, and these must be applied to any article by way of industrial means or process. [*King Features* v *Kleeman* (1941) AC 417].

▸*Meaning under the Designs Act 2000, s. 2(d).* "Design" means only a features of shape, configuration, pattern, ornament or composition of lines or colours applied to any article whether in two dimensional or three dimensional or in both forms, by any industrial process or means, whether manual, mechanical or chemical, separate or combined, which in the finished article appeal to and are judged solely by the eye; but does not include any mode or principle of construction or anything which is in substance a mere mechanical device, and does not include any trade mark as defined in cl. (*v*) of sub-sec. (1) of s. 2 of the Trade and Merchandise Marks Act 1958 or property mark as defined in s. 479 of the Indian Penal Code or any artistic work as defined in cl. (*c*) of s. 2 of the Copyright Act 1957.

**Desirable tenant.** A desirable tenant implies that nothing has occurred in the relations between the landlord and the tenant which can be considered to make the tenant an unsatisfactory one. A tenant who had paid his last quarter's rent by driblets under pressure must be regarded as an undesirable tenant. [*Smith* v *Land and House* (1884)28 Ch D 7].

**Despatch.** To send off, especially on official business or for special purposes; transact with promptness; finish quickly; perform promptly; finish off; execute; kill summarily.

Goods moving from one part of an establishment to another for domestic appropriation cannot be said to be despatched. Coal taken from the colliery to its power house about a furlong away for use there in the generation of electricity cannot be said to be despatched. [*Aluminium Corporation of India* v *Coal Board* AIR 1959 Cal 222].

**Despot.** An absolute monarch; autocrat; a hard master; tyrant; an absolute ruler; oppressor; one who governs with unlimited authority.

**Destruction.** Ruination; decimation; annihilation; abolition; collapse; demolition; devastation; extirpation; demolition; obliteration.

Destruction is a change in the nature and utility of the article which is complete and which is accompanied by the leaving of traces that are altogether useless. [*Central India Chemicals* v *Union of India* AIR 1962 MP 301].

**Detain.** Apprehend; confine; hold in check; hold in preventive custody; hold captive; keep in custody; keep within bounds; put under restraint hold or keep back; to restrain from going or proceeding; stop; withholding adversely.

> NOTE: It is implicit in the word 'detain' that the person detained wanted to proceed further but was not allowed to do so. [*Shobha Bhatnagar* v *State* AIR 1959 MP 367].

According to the ordinary meaning the word 'detain' means to keep back. If the wife leaving the house of the husband came to stay with the husband and he allowed her to stay with him, it cannot be said that he has detained her within the meaning of s. 498, Indian Penal Code. [*Alamgir* v *State of Bihar* AIR 1959 SC 436: (1959)2 SCA 116: 1959 SCJ 457: 1959 (Supp) (1) SCR 464: 1959 Cr LJ 527].

**Deterioration.** Abasement; abrasion; corrosion; debasement; decay; decomposition; demission; erosion; gradual impairment.

With respect to a commodity, it means a constitutional hurt or impairment, involving some degeneration in the substance of the thing, such as that arising from decay, corrosion, or disintegration. With respect to values or prices, it means a decline.

The word 'deterioration' imports becoming reduced either in quality or in value. It is wide enough to cover a falling off in the value of goods due to their not having been delivered in time. [*Madras Railway Co.* v *Govindha Rau* 21 Mad 172].

**Determinable.** In its use as 'ascertainable', it means amenable to measurement; appraisable; capable of decision; gaugeable; deducible; subject to measurement; surviable; verifiable.

In its use as 'liable to be terminated', it means coming to an end; drawing to a close; liable to be completed; liable to be discontinued; liable to be ended; liable to come to an end; liable to expire; subject to discontinuance; subject to termination; terminable.

**Determination.** Adjudgment; adjudication; appraisal; appraisement; authoritative opinion; conclusion; considered opinion; court decision; final assessment; judgment.

It means the decision of a court or administrative agency. It implies an ending or finality of a controversy or suit. [*Piccone* v *U.S.* 407 F 2d 866, 873].

It means a final decision by a court or administrative agency; the ending or expiration of an estate or interest in property, or of a right, power, or authority. [Black's *Law Dictionary,* 7th Ed.].

Determination by a competent court connotes the idea of final determination and not a mere opinion or finding. [*Ram Shankar* v *Hubraji* AIR 1969 All 407].

▸ *Meaning under the Constitution of India, Art. 136.* The expression 'determination' signifies an effective expression of opinion which ends a controversy or a dispute by some authority to whom it is submitted under a valid law for disposal. Determination must be judicial or quasi-judicial; purely administrative or executive direction is not contemplated to be made the subject-matter of appeal to this court. [*Jawanta Sugar Mills* v *Lakhmichand* AIR 1963 SC 677].

▸ *Meaning under the Industrial Disputes Act.* The word 'determination' in the definition of award implies adjudication upon relevant materials by the Labour Court or Tribunal. [*Sital Sukhiram* v *Central Government Industrial* AIR 1969 MP 200].

**Detinue.** A form of action which lies for the recovery, in specie, of personal chattels from one who acquired possession of them lawfully, but retains it without right, together with damages for the detention. [Black's *Law Dictionary,* 5th Ed.].

Possessory action for recovery of personal chattels unjustly detained. [*Durst* v *Durst* 193 A 2d 26].

**Devastavit.** A Latin word which means 'He has wasted'. It is a breach of trust or misappropriation of assets held in a fiduciary character; any violation or neglect of duty by an executor or administrator, involving loss to decedent's estate which makes him personally responsible to heirs, creditors, or legatees. [Black's *Law Dictionary,* 5th Ed].

A personal representative in accepting the office accepts the duties of the office, and becomes a trustee in the sense that he is personally liable in equity for all the breaches of the ordinary trusts, which in courts of equity are considered to arise from his office. The violation of his duties of administration is termed a *devastavit:* the term *devastavit* is applicable not only a misuse by the representative of the effects of the deceased, as by spending or converting them to his own use, but also to acts of maladministration or negligence. [Halsbury's *Laws of England,* 4th Ed., vol. 17, para 1542, p. 786].

**Devasthanam.** Temple or abode of a deity.

**Deviation.** Alteration; breach of practice; change of direction; change of position; departure from usage; diversion; variation.

Departure from established or usual conduct or ideology; a change made in the progress of a work from the original terms or design or method agreed upon [*Ward* v *City of Monrovia* 16 Cal 2d 815]; a wondering from the way, variation from the common way, from an established rule, standard, or position. [*S.J. Groves & Sons Co.* v *West Varginia Turnpike Commission* DC W Va, 164 F Supp 816, 821].

In the law of marine, subject to any express term of a charterparty, the shipowner impliedly agrees to proceed from the loading port to the port of discharge by the usual route and without unreasonable delay. A voluntary departure from this route or an unreasonable delay, at any rate if wilful, constitutes a deviation. [Halsbury's *Laws of England,* 4th Ed., vol. 43, para 431, p. 262].

In the context of a railroad carrier, it means a voluntary departure, without necessity or reasonable cause, from the regular or usual route or from a stipulated or customary mode of carriage. [*Ward* v *Gulf, M. & N.R. Co.* 134 SW 2d 917, 924].

**Devise.** Assign; bequeath; endow; convey; give and bequeath; give by will; leave by will; make a bequest; make testamentary dispositions; transmit by will.

A testamentary disposition of land or reality; a gift of real property by the last will and testament of the donor.

When used as a noun, it means a testamentary disposition of real or personal property and when used as a verb, it means to dispose of real or personal property by will.

**Devisee.** The person to whom lands or other real property are devised or given by will.

**Devisor.** A giver of lands or real estate by will; the maker of a will of lands; a testator.

**Devolution.** The transfer or transition from one person to another of a right, liability, title, estate, or office; transference of property from one person to another. [*Hermann* v *Crossen* Ohio App, 160 NE 2d 404, 408].

The act or an instance of transferring one's rights, duties, or powers to another; the passing of such rights, duties, or powers by transfer or succession. [Black's *Law Dictionary,* 8th Ed.].

Devolution is the passing of property from a person dying to a person living. [Halsbury's *Laws of England,* 4th Ed., vol. 17, para 1073, p. 559].

The word devolution implies the passing of property to another on the death of a person and can have no application to transfers *inter vivos, e.g.,* gift. [*M.T. Joseph* v *Gift Tax Officer* AIR 1962 Ker 97].

NOTE: In a wide sense devolution covers partition in a Hindu joint family. [*Santhamma* v *Neelamma* AIR 1956 Mad 642].

**Devolve.** To pass or be transferred from one person to another; to fall on, or accrue to, one person as the successor of another.

To transfer rights, duties, or powers to another; to pass rights, duties or powers by transmission or succession. [Black's *Law Dictionary,* 8th Ed.].

The word 'devolve' means of passing from a person dying to a person living. [*M.K. Balakrishna Menon* v *The Assistant Controller of Estate Duty-cum-Income Tax Officer, Ernakulam* AIR 1971 SC 2392: (1971)2 SCC 909: (1972)83 ITR 162].

**Dewany adalat.** A court trying revenue and other civil cases.

NOTE: By Regulation II of the C.P. Code of 1793, *Mal adalats* or revenue courts were abolished. The trial of these suits were transferred to the Mofussil Dewany Adalats. The Collectors were entrusted only with collection of revenue.

**Dharam (Dharma).** Law, virtue, legal or moral duty. [*Ranchordas* v *Parvatibhai* 26 IA 71: 23 Bom 275; *The Commissioner of Income Tax (Central) Delhi* v *Bijli Cotton Mills (P) Ltd., Hathras, Aligarh* AIR 1979 SC 346: (1979)2 SCR 241: (1979)1 SCC 496: (1979)116 ITR 60].

**Dharamakarta (Dharmakarta).** A *dharmakarta* of a Hindu endowment is no more than a manager or trustee. He is not a shebait or head of the math.

**Dharmakhater.** A Marathe expression which means the head of accounts under which pious or charitable gifts are entered. [*The Commissioner of Income Tax (Central) Delhi* v *Bijli Cotton Mills (P) Ltd., Hathras, Aligarh* AIR 1979 SC 346: (1979)2 SCR 241: (1979)1 SCC 496: (1979)116 ITR 60].

**Dharmarth.** A Sanskrit expression which means anything given for charitable or pious purposes. [*The Commissioner of Income Tax (Central) Delhi* v *Bijli Cotton Mills (P) Ltd., Hathras, Aligarh* AIR 1979 SC 346: (1979)2 SCR 241: (1979)1 SCC 496: (1979)116 ITR 60].

**Dharmashala.** Primarily a place of rest and has subsidiary meaning which connotes a Hindu or a Sikh place of worship. [*Gobind Mal* v *Labh Singh* AIR 1932 Lah 268: 13 Lah 6]

**Dharmila.** The term '*Dharmila*' is not a term of art, but a convenient expression to describe those *inams* which are post-settlement as distinguished from those that are pre-settlement. [*Needunuri Kameshwaramma* v *Subba Rao* AIR 1963 SC 884: (1963)2 SCR 208: (1963)2 SCJ 113].

**Dhatu.** *Dhatu* includes minerals, *e.g.* coal. [*E.C. Agabeg* v *Hargobind* AIR 1929 Pat 190].

**Dialectics.** That branch of logic which teaches the rules and modes of reasoning; art of investigating the truth of opinions; testing of truth by discussion; logical disputation.

**Diara.** Alluvium, an island formed in the bed of a river; land gained by recession of a river. [Wilson's *Glossary*].

**Dictionary.** A book which gives the meaning of words arranged alphabetically.

NOTE: Judges in finding out the meaning of words in Constitution and statutes frequently make use of the layman's cruch—the Dictionary. Yet the value of a dictionary must be considered limited by the fact that in English, as in any other language, the meanings of words are in steady process of change. The aid from the dictionary might in some cases be useful, but as the meaning of words undergoes constant changes, the dictionary cannot be considered as definite guidance in all cases. [*Aswathanarayana* v *Deputy Commercial Tax Officer* (1965)1 STC 795].

Dictionaries give variegated meanings to words. It depends upon the context as to what meaning is to be adopted. [*Tulsiram* v *State of M.P.* (1984)4 SCC 487].

**Dictum.** A statement, remark, or observation. The word is generally used as an abbreviated form of *obiter dictum*, "a remark by the way"; that is, an observation or remark made by a judge in pronouncing an opinion upon a cause, concerning some rule, principle or application of law, or the solution of a question suggested by the case at bar, but not necessarily involved in the case or essential to its determination.

NOTE: Statements which are not necessary to the decision, which go beyond the occasion and lay down a rule that is unnecessary for the purpose in hand (usually termed dicta) have no binding authority on another court, though they may have some merely persuasive efficacy. [Halsbury's *Laws of England*, 4th Ed., vol. 26, para 574, p. 294].

**Difference.** Asymmetry; conflict of opinion; contradiction; disagreement; discongruity; disharmony; divergence; failure to agree; inconsistency; misunderstanding; inconformity.

As respect contract specifications or material described therein, it means a state of being unlike.

**Digest.** A collection or compilation, embodying the chief matter of numerous books, articles, court decisions, etc. in one, disposed under proper heads or titles, and usually by an alphabetical arrangement, for facility in reference; an index to reported cases, providing brief statements of court holdings or facts of cases, which is arranged by subject and subdivided by jurisdiction and courts. [Black's *Law Dictionary*, 5th Ed.].

An index of legal propositions showing which cases support each proposition; a collection of summaries of reported cases, arranged by subject and subdivided by jurisdiction and court. [Black's *Law Dictionary*, 8th Ed.].

**Diligence.** A continual effort to accomplish something; care; caution; the attention and care required from a person in a given situation. [Black's *Law Dictionary*, 7th Ed.].

NOTE: Care of which there are infinite shades, from the slightest momentary thought to the most vigilant anxiety; but the law recognizes only three degrees of diligence—(1) common or ordinary, which men in general exert in respect of their own concerns; the standard is necessarily variable with respect to the facts, although it may be uniform with respect to the principle, (2) high or great, which is extraordinary diligence, or that which very prudent persons take of their own concerns, (3) low or slight, which is that which persons of less than common prudence, or indeed of no prudence at all, take of their own concerns. [Wharton's *Law Lexicon*].

**Diplomatic corps.** The ambassador and other diplomatic personnel assigned by their Government to a foreign capital.

**Diplomatic immunity.** The general exemption of diplomatic ministers from the operation of local law, the exception being that a minister who is plotting against the security of the nation to which he or she is accredited may be arrested and sent out of the country. [Black's *Law Dictionary*, 7th Ed.].

NOTE: A minister's family shares in diplomatic immunity to a great, though ill-defined, degree.

**Diplomatic protection.** Protection given by one country's representatives to a person, usually an individual, against another country's violation of international law. [Black's *Law Dictionary*, 7th Ed.].

**Direct.** As verb, it means to point to; guide; order; command; instruct; advise; suggest; request.

As adjective, it means immediate, proximate; by the shortest course; without circuity; operating by an immediate connection or relation, instead of operating through a medium; straight; free from extraneous influence.

'Direct' implies 'obey' and therefore disobedience of the direction which is a part of the order is disobedience of the order. [*Dudderidge* v *Rawlings* (1912)108 LT 802].

▸*Meaning under the Criminal Procedure Code, s. 159*. The word 'direct' means 'command' which would only signify that something which was not being done should be done. The word therefore would be meaningless in relation to the investigation by the police which is already in progress. The occasion to 'direct an investigation' would therefore arise where the investigation is not done by the police, as in a case covered by the proviso (*b*) to s. 157, Criminal Procedure Code. [*State* v *Balaram Singh* AIR 1970 Ori 107]. It is only in cases where the police decide not to investigate the case that the Magistrate can intervene and either 'direct' an investigation, or in the alternative, himself proceed or depute a Magistrate subordinate to him to proceed to enquire into the case. [*S.N. Sharma* v *B.K. Tiwari* (1970)1 SCC 653].

**Direct evidence.** Evidence that is based on personal knowledge or observation and that, if true, proves a fact without inference or presumption. It is also termed positive evidence. [Black's *Law Dictionary,* 7th Ed.].

> NOTE: Section 60 of the Indian Evidence Act, 1872, provides that oral evidence must always be direct. The word 'direct' is opposed to 'mediate' or 'hearsay'.

**Direct examination.** The first questioning of a witness in a trial or other proceeding, conducted by the party who called the witness to testify. It is also termed examination-in-chief. [Black's *Law Dictionary,* 7th Ed.].

**Direct tax.** A tax that is imposed on property, as distinguished from a tax on a right or privilege. [Black's *Law Dictionary*, 8th Ed.].

> NOTE: A direct tax is presumed to be borne by the person upon whom it is assessed, and not 'passed on' to some other person. [Black's *Law Dictionary*, 8th Ed.].

▸*Meaning under the Central Boards of Revenue Act 1963, s. 2(c)*. 'Direct tax' means—(1) any duty leviable or tax chargeable under—(*i*) the Estate Duty Act 1953, (*ii*) the Wealth-tax Act 1957, (*iii*) the Expenditure-tax Act 1957, (*iv*) the Gift-tax Act 1958, (*v*) the Income-tax Act 1961, (*vi*) the Super Profits Tax Act 1963; and (2) any other duty or tax which, having regard to its nature or incidence, may be declared by the Central Government, by notification in the Official Gazette, to be a direct tax.

▸*Meaning under the Payment of Bonus Act 1965, s. 2(12)*. 'Direct tax' means—(*a*) any tax chargeable under—(*i*) the Income-tax Act 1961; (*ii*) the Super Profits Tax Act 1963; (*iii*) the Companies (Profits) Surtax Act 1964; (*iv*) the agricultural income-tax law; and (*b*) any other tax which, having regard to its nature or incidence, may be declared by the Central Government, by notification in the Official Gazette, to be a direct tax for the purposes of this Act.

**Direction.** The course taken in relation to the point toward which something is moving; a point to or from which a person or thing moves; the course on which something is aimed; an act of guidance; an order; an instruction on how to proceed. [Black's *Law Dictionary,* 7th Ed.].

A 'direction' is said to be 'an order to be carried out', and 'order', for example, so far as the Supreme Court is concerned, is said to be 'a direction other than final judgment'.

Direction means guidance or command. [*V.P.S. Gill* v *Air India* AIR 1988 Bom 416].

> NOTE: *'Direction' and 'finding'—distinction.* 'Direction' means a direction which the appellate or revisional authority, as the case may be, gives to the lower tribunal under the law. A 'finding', on the other hand, means a

finding by the original or appellate authority which is necessary for passing the final order or giving the final decision in the appeal. [*Bhanji Bhagandas* v *Commissioner of Income Tax* AIR 1968 SC 139: (1968)1 SCJ 135: (1968)1 SCR 17; *Income Tax Officer* v *Murlidhar Bhagwan Das* AIR 1965 SC 342: (1964)1 SCJ 583: (1964)6 SCR 411].

**Directly.** In a straight forward manner; in a straight line or course; immediately. [Black's *Law Dictionary,* 7th Ed.].

The word 'directly' means in a direct way, without a person or thing coming between; immediately as directly responsible. [*Shri Shri Tarakeshwar Sio Thakur Jiu* v *Bar Dass Dey & Co.* AIR 1979 SC 1669: (1979)3 SCC 106: ((1979)3 SCR 18].

**Director.** One who manages, guides, or orders; a chief administrator; a person appointed or elected to sit on a board that manages the affairs of a corporation or company by electing and exercising control over its officers. [Black's *Law Dictionary,* 7th Ed].

▸ *Meaning under the Business Profits Tax Act 1947, s. 2(8); Excess Profits Tax Act 1940, s. 2(10).* 'Director' includes any person occupying the position of a director by whatever name called and includes any person who—(*i*) is a manager of the company or concerned in the management of the business, and (*ii*) is remunerated out of the funds of the business, and (*iii*) is the beneficial owner of not less than 20 per cent, of the ordinary share capital of the company.

▸ *Meaning under the Companies Act 1956, s. 2(13).* 'Director' includes any person occupying the position of director, by whatever name called.

• **Managing director** p. 557.

**Director's remuneration.** 'Director's remuneration' includes all remuneration payable by a company to a director thereof in respect of any services rendered to or employment with the company in any capacity whatever. [Business Profits Tax Act 1947, s. 2(8A)].

**Director's report.** It is the report attached to every balance-sheet laid before the company in the general meeting. The report deals with the state of the company's affairs, and the amounts, if any, recommended to be paid by way of dividend or carried to reserve. It is now known as the Board's report. [Companies Act 1956, s. 217].

**Directory provisions.** Statutes are either mandatory or directory; if mandatory, they prescribe, in addition to requiring the doing of things specified, the result that will follow if they are not done, whereas, if directory, their terms are limited to what is required to be done. One of the important tests that must always be employed in order to determine whether a provision is mandatory or directory in character is to consider whether the non-compliance of a particular provision causes inconvenience or injustice and if it does then the court would say that that provision must be complied with and that it is obligatory in its character. [*A.D. Karegaonkar* v *State of Bombay* AIR 1958 Bom 167: 59 Bom LR 22]. It has always been held that where no public policy is involved, the provisions of a statute should be held to be directory only and not mandatory. [*Satyanarayana* v *Venkata Subbiah* AIR 1957 AP 172].

NOTE: The test of determining whether a statutory provision is directory also applies to Constitutions. For Constitutions are deemed statutes for certain purposes of interpretation. Articles 77(1) and 166(1) of the Constitution of India provide for the conduct of business of the Government of India or of a State. It has been held that this provision is 'directory' and a substantial compliance with the requirement will be sufficient. [*State of Bombay* v *Purshottam* AIR 1952 Bom 317].

**Disability.** The inability to perform some function; an objectively measurable condition of impairment, physical or mental. [Black's *Law Dictionary,* 7th Ed.].

In its application to legal disqualification, it means disablement; invalidity; legal incapacity; want of legal capacity; want of legal qualification. The term is generally used to indicate an incapacity for the full enjoyment of ordinary legal rights. Thus, persons under age, insane persons, and convicts are said to be under disability.

In its application to physical inability, it means ailment; debilitation; frailty; handicap; impairment; impotence; incapability; infirmity; unfitness; unsoundness; weakness.

NOTE: Disability is of two classes—(1) absolute, which while it continues, wholly disables the person, such as out-lawry, excommunication, attainder, (2) partial, as minority, lunacy and drunkenness. Minority, insanity or idiocy constitute 'legal disability'. Time does not run against it so long as this disability continues. Sections 6 to 8 of the Limitation Act 1963 provide for this.

- **Legal disability** p. 525.
- **Permanent disability** p. 654.

**Disaffection.** Discontent; disloyalty; estrangement.

In the context of Explanation 1 to s. 124A of the Indian Penal Code 1860, the expression "disaffection" includes disloyalty and all feelings of enmity towards the Government established by law.

Disaffection signifies political alienation or discontent, that is to say, a feeling of disloyalty to the existing Government, which tends to a disposition not to obey, but to resist and subvert the Government. [*In the matter of Saptaha* AIR 1950 Cal 444: 54 CWN 334].

**Disappearance of evidence.** Disappearance of the evidence will be caused if the evidence ceases to be visible or to be traceable. [*Harbans Lal* v *State* AIR 1967 HP 10].

NOTE: Causing disappearance of evidence is made a punishable offence under s. 201 of the Indian Penal Code, when the intention is to screen the offender.

**Disbursement.** The act of paying out money, commonly from a fund or in settlement of a debt or account payable. [Black's *Law Dictionary,* 8th Ed.].

"Disbursements" in a marine policy frequently means outfit. [*Roddick* v *Indemnity Insurance* (1895)2 QB 380]. "Disbursements" is well understood at Lloyd's to be a compendious term used to describe any interest which is outside the ordinary and well-known interests of 'hull', 'machinery', 'cargo' and 'freight'. [*Buchanan* v *Faber* 4 Com Cas 226, 227, *per* Bigham, J.].

NOTE: There are many things which must be paid by the solicitor for his client, and which are obviously disbursements made by him in his character of solicitor. There are frequently large amounts, such as court fees and counsel's fees, which it is duty of the solicitor, and not of the client, to pay, and which are also disbursements of the solicitor in his professional character; and there are also items such as stamps, fees on the registration of deeds etc., which are properly called disbursements. But where payment is made by the solicitor purely as an agent, it is in no sense a disbursement by the solicitor in his professional character. [*Re Lamb* (1889)2 QBD 5].

**Discharge.** To release; liberate; annul; unburden; disincumber; dismiss; extinguish an obligation; terminate employment of person; release as from prison, confinement or military service. [Black's *Law Dictionary,* 5th Ed.].

The payment of a debt or satisfaction of some other obligation; the release of a debtor from monetary obligations upon adjudication of bankruptcy; the dismissal of a case; the cancelling or vacating of a court order; the release of a prisoner from confinement; the relieving of a witness, juror, a jury from further responsibilities in a case; the firing of an employee. [Black's *Law Dictionary,* 7th Ed.].

Any method by which a legal duty is extinguished, especially the payment of a debt or satisfaction of some other obligation. [Black's *Law Dictionary,* 8th Ed.].

"Discharge" means to free from liability. The liability may be in respect of monetary claims like debts, it may be in respect of possession of property, it may be in respect of taking some order as regards property, it may be in respect of many other matters. [*Sarda Prasad* v *Lala Jumna Prasad* AIR 1961 SC 1074: (1961)3 SCR 875: (1962)2 SCJ 631].

As applied to demands, claims, rights of action, incumbrances, etc., to discharge the debt or claim is to extinguish it, to annul its obligatory force, to satisfy it.

The word 'discharge' is ordinarily used only in the context of exonerating a person from liability or relieving him of his obligations, and is not used in the sense of giving up of rights. [*Leela Dhundiraj Divekar* v *E.C. Shinde* AIR 1970 Bom 109].

In its application to contract, it means to cancel the obligation of a contract; to make an agreement or contract null and inoperative.

In its application to criminal law, it means the act by which a person in confinement, held on an accusation of some crime or misdemeanour, is set at liberty.

NOTE: An order of discharge under s. 245 of the Criminal Procedure Code 1973, involves consideration of the merits of the case by the Magistrate. Where the discharge is made without consideration of merits, a fresh complaint reagitating the matter can be made before the same Magistrate. [*Sushil Kumar* v *Banka Mahto* AIR 1957 Cal 393: 1957 Cr LJ 720].

In its application to service matter, it means to relieve of a charge or office; to dismiss from office. Sometimes the word is used in the sense of discharge from service which is dismissal from service. Sometimes it is also used in the sense of pure termination of the contract of employment. [*Calcutta Chemical Co. Ltd.* v *D.K. Barman* AIR 1969 Pat 371].

NOTE: The word "discharge" means discharge of a person in a running or continuing business. It will not be regarded as the discharge of a person when the industry itself ceased to exist on a *bona fide* closure of business. [*Banaras Ice Factory Ltd.* v *It's Workmen* AIR 1957 SC 168: 1957 SCR 143: 1957 SCJ 139].

In its application to military and maritime law, it means the release or dismissal of a soldier, sailor, or marine, from further military or naval service, either at the expiration of his term of enlistment, or previous thereto on special application therefor, or as a punishment.

- **Conditional discharge** p. 169.

- **Discharged from liability.** The words "discharged from liability" means a total extinction of the liability following upon the extinction of the right. [*East & West Steamship Co.* v *S.K. Ramalingam Chettiar* AIR 1960 SC 1058: (1960)3 SCR 820: (1960)2 SCA 544].

**Disciplinary proceeding.** An action brought to reprimand, suspend, or expel a licensed professional or other person from a profession or other group because of unprofessional, unethical, improper, or illegal conduct. [Black's *Law Dictionary,* 7th Ed.].

**Discipline.** Conduct or control gained by enforcing obedience or other; orderly or prescribed conduct or orderly behaviour; self-control; a rule or system of rules of good conduct and orderly behaviour.

The term 'discipline' necessarily involves a state of mind in the person subject to it, which unquestioningly admits superiority to himself for certain limited purposes of another human being. [*Laxmikant Sripat* v *G.R. Gerrad* AIR 1947 Bom 193].

'Discipline' involves more than mere obedience to lawful orders. [*Henry* v *Ryan* (1963) Tas SR 90, *per* Burbury, C.J.].

**Disclaimer.** The repudiation or renunciation of a claim or power vested in a person or which he had formerly alleged to be his; the refusal, or rejection of an estate or right offered to a person; the disavowal, denial, or renunciation of an interest, right, or property imputed to a person or alleged to be his; the rejection, refusal, or renunciation of a claim, power, or property. [Black's *Law Dictionary,* 5th Ed.].

A renunciation of one's legal right or claim; a repudiation of another's legal right or claim; a writing that contains such a renunciation or repudiation. [Black's *Law Dictionary,* 8th Ed.].

The words 'disclaim' and 'disclaimer' connote a renunciation of, or refusal to claim, rights or property which would automatically devolve on or accrue to the person making the disclaimer. [*Re Lister, Ex p. Bradford Overseers & Bradford Corpn.* 1926 Ch 149 (CA)].

'Disclaime, disclamare ... signifieth utterly to renounce ...' [Co Litt 102a].

**Disclose.** Bring into the open; bring into view; bring out; bring to light; divulge; expose; lay bare; make known; make public; reveal; speak out; bring into view by uncovering.

NOTE: *Interpretation in statute.* "The word 'disclose' may admit of two interpretations, the discovery of what was not before known, and a statement of that which was before known; and we are only to look in each Act of Parliament to see in which sense it is used by the Legislature, knowing that in one set of statutes it is used in one sense and in another sense in other statutes." [*R.* v *Skeen* (1859) Bell, CC 97, CCR, *per* Lord Campbell, C.J.].

**Disclose a defence upon the merits.** 'Disclose a defence upon the merits' meant not merely to say there is a defence, but to show what the nature of it was. [*Whiley* v *Wiley* 27 LJCP 305; *Warrington* v *Leake* 11 Ex 304].

**Disclose an offence.** To 'disclose' an offence is not to state it or confess to it; but to make the offence known for the first time. [*R.* v *Skeen* 28 LJMC 91; *R.* v *Gunnell* 55 LT 786].

**Disclosure.** Act of disclosing; revelation; the impartation of that which is secret or not fully understood.

The act or process of making known something that was previously unknown; a revelation of facts. [Black's *Law Dictionary,* 8th Ed.].

- **Compulsory disclosure.** A mandatory disclosure of information, as of matters within the scope of the discovery rules. [Black's *Law Dictionary,* 7th Ed.].

**Discontinuance.** Ending; causing to cease; ceasing to use; giving up; leaving off.

In its application as an art of discontinuing, it means abolishment; breaking off; cessation; discontinuation; dismissal; disuse; invalidation; nullification; postponement; termination.

In its application as interruption of a legal action, it means cessation; discontinuation; moratorium; withdrawal; termination of a lawsuit by the plaintiff; a voluntary dismissal or nonsuit.

**Discontinuance of business.** It means a complete cessation of business. [*Commissioner of Income Tax* v *P.E. Polson* AIR 1945 PC 137].

**Discontinuance of possession.** Connotes abandonment of possession by the owner followed by the taking of possession by another [*Hashim* v *Hamidi* AIR 1942 Cal 180: 46 CWN 561]; a voluntary act of abandonment of possession followed by the actual possession of another. [*Quadir Bux* v *Ramchand* AIR 1970 All 289].

**Discount.** Discount means a deduction from an original price or debt, allowed for paying promptly or in cash [*Benner Tea Co.* v *Iowa State Tax Commission* 109 NW 2d 39, 40]; an allowance or deduction made from a gross sum on any account whatsoever [Black's *Law Dictionary,* 5th Ed.]; a reduction from the full amount or value of something, esp. a price; an advance deduction of interest when a person lends money on a note, bill of exchange, or other commercial paper, resulting in its present value; the amount by which a security's market value is below its face value. [Black's *Law Dictionary*, 7th Ed.].

Discounting by a bank means lending money upon a note, and deducting the interest or premium in advance. [*Russell* v *Lumbermen's Mortg. Co.* 273 NE 2d 803, 804].

The word 'discount' is defined, in its primary meaning, as an abatement or deduction from the amount or from the gross reckoning or value of anything, and as used in commerce (1) is defined to mean a deduction (usually at a certain rate per cent) made for payment before it is due of a bill or account; or any deduction or abatement from the nominal value or price; (2) the deduction made from the amount of a bill of exchange or promissory note by one who gives value for it before it is due. [*Brown* (*Surveyor of Taxes*) v *National Provident Institution* (1921)2 AC 222, 251].

- **Cash discount** p. 127.
- **Trade discount** p. 849.

**Discover.** Ascertain; bring to light; chance upon; come to know; come upon; detect; find out; get a glimpse of.

Discover means to uncover that which was hidden, concealed, or unknown from everyone; to get first sight or knowledge of; to get knowledge of what has existed but has not theretofore been known to the discoverer. [*Shellmar Products Co.* v *Allen-Qualley Co.* CCA III, 87 F 2d 104, 108].

In its primary and abstract sense, the word 'discover' indicates detection as a result of uncovering, revealing or laying open to view what was hidden, concealed or unknown. But the word does not always retain its abstract or primary definition and its meaning varies in accordance with the contextual use. [*Commissioner of Income Tax* v *Jagan Nath* AIR 1957 Punj 226: ILR (1957) Punj 1253].

▸ *Meaning under the Excess Profits Tax Act 1940*. The word 'discovers" in s. 15 is not limited to facts discovered, which existed during the relevant chargeable accounting period for which assessment is reopened under the section but also includes facts so discovered which came into existence subsequent to such accounting period. [*India United Mills* v *Commissioner of Excess Profits Tax, Bombay* AIR 1955 SC 79: (1955)1 SCR 810: 1955 SCJ 36: (1955)27 ITR 20].

**Discovery of documents.** Bring to light on oath the documents which are or have been in possession or power of any party to a suit relating to any matter in question therein.

NOTE: Any party may, without filing any affidavit, apply to the court for an order directing any other party to any suit to make discovery on oath of the documents which are or have been in his possession or power, relating to any matter in question therein. On the hearing of such application the court may either refuse or adjourn the same, if satisfied that such discovery is not necessary, or not necessary at that stage of the suit, or make such order, either generally or limited to certain classes of documents, as may, in its discretion, be thought fit: Provided that discovery shall not be ordered when and so far as the court shall be of opinion that it is not necessary either for disposing fairly of the suit or for saving costs. [Code of Civil Procedure 1908, Or. 11, r. 12].

**Discredit.** To disbelieve; injure the credit or reputation of; dishonour; show to be unworthy of belief or confidence; destroy or impair the credibility of a person, piece of evidence, or a theory; lessen the degree of credit to be accorded to a witness or document, as by impugning the veracity of the one or the genuineness of the other; disparage or weaken the reliance upon the testimony of a witness, or upon documentary evidence, by any means whatever.

NOTE: When a witness is cross-examined, he may be asked questions which tend to shake his credit by injuring his character. In other words, he is cross-examined for the purpose of discrediting him. [Indian Evidence Act 1872, s. 146(3)].

**Discretion.** Discretion means power to make a choice between alternative courses of action. As noun, it means power of choice, liberty of judgment, power of choosing, self-determination. [*Penumbra of Natural Justice,* Tapash Gan Choudhury, 2nd Ed. 2001, p. 291].

When applied to public functionaries, discretion means a power or right conferred upon them by law and acting officially in certain circumstances, according to the dictates of their own judgment and conscience, uncontrolled by the judgment or conscience of others. [*Application of Blackburn* 134 NYS 2d 138, 142].

As applied to public officers, discretion means power to act in an official capacity in a manner which appears to be just and proper under the circumstances. [*Application of Blackburn* 134 NYS 2d 138, 144].

In criminal law and the law of torts, discretion means the capacity to distinguish between what is right or wrong, lawful or unlawful, wise or foolish, sufficiently to render one amenable and responsible for his acts.

When applied to court of justice, it means sound discretion guided by law. It must be governed by rule, not by humour;

it must not be arbitrary, vague, and fanciful, but legal and regular. [*Ramji Dayawala* v *Invest Import* AIR 1981 SC 2085: (1981)1 SCR 899: (1981)1 SCC 80].

NOTE: When it is said that something is to be done within the discretion of the authorities that something is to be done according to the rules of reason and justice, not according to private opinion, according to law and not humour. It is to be not arbitrary, vague and fanciful, but legal and regular. And it must be exercised within the limit to which an honest man competent to the discharge of his office ought to confine himself. [*Sharp* v *Wakefield* (1891) AC 173].

Discretion when conferred upon executive authorities, must be confined within clearly defined limits. It means sound discretion guided by law. It must be governed by rule, not by humour; it must not be arbitrary, vague and fanciful. [*S.G. Jaisinghani* v *Union of India* AIR 1967 SC 1427].

NOTE: A discretionary power is not necessarily a discriminatory power and abuse of power is not to be easily assumed where the discretion is vested in the Government and not a minor official. [*Matajog Dobey* v *H.C. Bharat* AIR 1956 SC 44: 1956 SCA 22: 1956 SCJ 110: (1955)2 SCR 925].

For details about discretion and discretionary power vide *Penumbra of Natural Justice*, Tapash Gan Choudhury, 2nd Ed. 2001.


- **Absolute discretion** p. 9.
- **Abuse of discretion** p. 10.
- **Administrative discretion** p. 41.
- **Judicial discretion** p. 494.


**Discretionary trusts.** Discretionary trusts are such trusts as are not marked out on fixed lines, but allow a certain amount of discretion in their exercise; those which cannot be duly administered without the application of a certain degree of prudence and judgment; trusts where the trustee or another party has the right to accumulate (rather than pay out) the income for each year.

NOTE: Where several persons or objects are designated, a discretion may be given to the trustees as to which are to be benefited and in what proportions. Property may be settled so as to give a person a determinable life interest. This is now generally done by directing that the trustees are to hold the income on "protective trusts" for the benefit of the person during his life; in such a case a discretionary trust arises on the termination of that person's interest during his life. [Halsbury's *Laws of England*, 4th Ed., vol. 48, para 555, p. 303].

**Discrimination.** The effect of a law or established practice that confers privileges on a certain class or that denies privileges to a certain class because of race, age, sex, nationality, religion or handicap [Black's *Law Dictionary*, 7th Ed.]; unfair treatment or denial of normal privileges to persons because of their race, age, nationality or religion [Black's *Law Dictionary*, 5th Ed.]; a failure to treat all persons equally where no reasonable distinction can be found between those favoured and those not favoured. [*Baker* v *California Land Title Co.* DC Cal, 349 F Supp 235, 238, 239].

Discrimination involves differences in the treatment of two or more persons or subjects. [*Lord Mayor, Councillors and Citizens of the City of Melbourne* v *Commonwealth* (1947)74 CLR 31, 61].

The expression indicates an unjust, unfair or unreasonable bias in favour of one against another. [*Bishnu Charan Panda* v *State of Orissa* (1982)54 Cut LT 337 (DB)].


- **Gender discrimination** p. 383.


**Discrimination with reasons.** It means rational classification for differential treatment having nexus to the constitutionally permissible object. [*State of Kerala* v *N.M. Thomas* AIR 1976 SC 490: (1976)1 SCR 906: (1976)2 SCC 310].

**Disease.** Illness (of people or animal or plants) where the body cannot function normally; a deviation from the healthy and normal functioning of the body; any disorder; any depraved condition.


- **Contagious disease.** See INFECTIOUS DISEASE p. 456.
- **Endemic disease** p. 306.
- **Industrial disease** p. 452.
- **Infectious disease** p. 456.
- **Occupational disease** p. 619.
- **Sexually transmitted disease** p. 791.

**Disfigure.** To mar or destroy the figure or beauty of; render unsightly; deform.

A change in the outer shape and figure in such a manner that its appearance becomes worse than before. The appearance in rendered less beautiful. [*Mooli* v *5th A.D.J., Mathura* 1989 All LJ 1249].

**Disfigurement.** That which impairs or injures the beauty, symmetry, or appearance of a person or thing; that which renders unsightly, misshapen or imperfect, or deforms in some manner. [Black's *Law Dictionary,* 5th Ed.].

An impairment or injury to the appearance of a person or thing. [Black's *Law Dictionary*, 8th Ed.].

Disfigurement in the most commonly use sense means a change in the outer shape and figure in such a manner that its appearance becomes worse than before. The appearance, therefore, must result in something which is less beautiful or less pleasing than it was earlier. [*Mooli* v *5th Additional District Judge, Mathura* (1989) All LJ 1249, 1251].

**Dishonestly.** In a manner lacking in honesty; in a manner which is untrustworthy; in a manner characterized by dishonesty; in a fraudulent manner.

▸*Meaning under the Indian Penal Code, s. 24.* A person who does anything with the intention of causing wrongful gain to one person or wrongful loss to another person, is said to do that thing, "dishonestly". [*Dr. S. Dutt* v *State of U.P.* AIR 1966 SC 523: (1966)1 SCR 493: 1966 Cr LJ 459].

> NOTE: The term "dishonestly" is not used in the Code in its popular significance. Unless there is wrongful gain to one person, or wrongful loss to another, an act would not be "dishonest". Wrongful gain includes wrongful retention of and wrongful loss includes being kept out of the property as well as being wrongfully deprived of property. [*Krishan Kumar* v *Union of India* 1959 Cr LJ 1508 (SC): AIR 1959 SC 1390].

**Dishonour.** A state of shame or disgrace; discredit; treat without honour or respect; deprive of honour; violate the chastity of; seduce; refuse to accept or pay, *e.g.* a cheque or a bill of exchange; to decline or fail to pay.

An instrument is dishonoured when a necessary or optional presentment is duly made and due acceptance or payment is refused, or cannot be obtained within the prescribed time, or in case of bank collections, presentment is excused and the instrument is not duly accepted or paid.

**Dismissal.** Used as noun in the sense of discharge, it means discharge from employment; disemployment; dislodgment; displacement; release from employment; removal from office.

Used as noun in the sense of termination of a proceeding, it means conclusion of a proceeding; conclusion of an action; discontinuance; ending of a proceeding; ending of an action; removal of a cause out of court; termination of an action.

In legal parlance, it means an order or judgment finally disposing of an action, suit, motion, etc., without trial of the issues involved [Black's *Law Dictionary,* 5th Ed.]; termination of an action or claim without further hearing, esp. before the trial of the issues involved. [Black's *Law Dictionary*, 8th Ed.].

'Dismissed' has a definite connotation implying a final disposal by the tribunal, rejecting the case of the suitor. [*M.R.M. Periannan Chettiar* v *Commissioner of Income Tax* 39 ITR 159].

In service matter, 'dismissal' is a word of very ambiguous meaning. It has to be understood in the context in which it occurs. One can dismiss a servant, or a contractor. Dismissal is merely a convenient expression for the termination of an employment, whatever its nature may be, and does not necessary import the relationship of master and servant. [*Graham* v *Minister for Industry* (1933) IR 156; workers employed in *Hirakud Dam* v *State of Orissa* AIR 1971 SC 2242: (1971)3 SCR 646: (1971)1 SCC 583: (1971)2 SCR 219].

> NOTE: *'Dismissal' and 'discharge'—difference.* There is a vital difference between dismissal and discharge. Discharge is the termination of

a contract by notice or payment of wages in lieu of notice, whereas the dismissal implies not merely a termination without notice or payment, but essentially indicates a measure of punishment. [*Minerva Mills Ltd.* v *Arbitration Tribunal* (1949)4 DLR (Mys) 37].

*'Dismissal' and 'removal'—difference.* The word 'dismiss' or 'remove' as used in Art. 311 of the Constitution of India comprehends every termination of the services of a Government servant. [*Moti Ram* v *N.E. Frontier Railway* AIR 1964 SC 600: (1964)2 SCA 372].

There is, however, a basic difference between dismissal and removal. Dismissal from service disqualifies a civil servant from future employment, but removal from service ordinarily does not. [*Khem Chand* v *Union of India* AIR 1958 SC 300: 1958 SCR 1080].

**Disorder.** A lack of proper arrangement; an irregularity; a disturbance in mental or physical health; ailment; chaos; derangement; disharmony; fracas; pandemonium.

• **Mental disorder** p. 574.

**Dispauper.** When a person is admitted to sue *in forma pauperis* and afterwards, before the suit is ended, loses the right to sue *in forma pauperis*, he is said to be dispaupered.

When a person, by reason of his poverty, is admitted to sue *in forma pauperis*, and afterwards, before the suit be ended, acquires any lands, or personal estate, or is guilty of anything whereby he is liable to have this privilege taken from him then he loses the right to sue *in forma pauperis*, and is said to be dispaupered. [Black's *Law Dictionary,* 5th Ed.].

As verb, it means to disqualify from being a pauper; to deprive a person of the ability to sue *in forma pauperis*. [Black's *Law Dictionary,* 7th Ed.].

NOTE: The court may, on the application of the defendant or of the Government Pleader, of which seven days' clear notice in writing has been given to the plaintiff, order that the permission granted to the plaintiff to sue as an indigent person be withdrawn—(*a*) if he is guilty of vexatious or improper conduct in the course of the suit; (*b*) if it appears that his means are such that he ought not to continue to sue as an indigent persons; or (*c*) if he has entered into any agreement with reference to the subject-matter of the suit under which any other person has obtained an interest in such subject-matter. [Code of Civil Procedure 1908, Or. 33, r. 9].

**Displaced creditor.** A displaced person to whom a debt is due from any other person, whether a displaced person or not. [Displaced Persons (Debts Adjustment) Act 1951, s. 2(8)].

**Displaced debtor.** A displaced person from whom a debt is due or is being claimed. [Displaced Persons (Debts Adjustment) Act 1951, s. 2(9); *Sukh Lal* v *State Bank of India* AIR 1967 SC 543: (1967)1 SCR 317].

**Displaced person.** Any person who has been displaced from his place or residence.

Any person who, on account of the setting up of the Dominions of India and Pakistan, or on account of civil disturbances or for fear of such disturbances in any area now forming part of West Pakistan, has after the first day of March 1947, left or been displaced from his place or residence in such area and who has been subsequently residing in India, and includes any person who is resident in any place now forming part of India and who for that reason is unable or has been rendered unable to manage, supervise or control any movable property belonging to him in West Pakistan, and also includes the successors-in-interest of any such person. [Displaced Persons (Compensation and Rehabilitation) Act 1954, s. 2(*b*)].

NOTE: A firm may be a displaced person under s. 2(10) of the Displaced Persons (Debts Adjustment) Act. [*Punjab National Bank* v *Punjab Property Development Co.* AIR 1958 Punj 57].

**Dispone.** To convey legally. [*Lima Letiao & Co. Ltd.* v *Union of India* AIR 1968 Goa 29].

**Disponee.** The person to whom anything is disponed. [*Lima Letiao & Co. Ltd.* v *Union of India* AIR 1968 Goa 29].

**Dispose.** The expression "dispose" means to transfer or alienate. [*Dy. Commissioner of*

*Sales Tax* v *Thomas Stephen & Co.* AIR 1988 SC 997: (1988)2 SCC 264: (1988)3 SCR 248: JT 1988(1) SC 631: (1988)69 STC 320: (1988)34 ELT 412].

**Dispose of.** Deal with; get rid of; finish; kill; sell; consume; relinquish; part with.

It is also used to mean the determination of suits.

**Disposition.** The act of transferring something to another's care or possession, especially by deed or will; the relinquishing of property; a final settlement or determination. [Black's *Law Dictionary*, 8th Ed.].

'Disposition' is not a term of law. Further, it has no precise meaning. Its meaning has to be gathered from the context in which it is used. In England, the word has been defined differently in various statutes. [*Goli Eswariah* v *Commissioner of Gift Tax* AIR 1970 SC 1722: (1970)2 SCC 390: (1970)76 ITR 675].

▸*Meaning under the Estate Duty Act 1953 (since repealed).* Disposition may be by transfer, delivery, declaration of trust, settlement upon a person in succession, or otherwise. Thus, settlement is not interchangeable with disposition and *vice versa*. 'Disposition' includes a settlement but settlement is not the only way to dispose. Therefore, a sale is comprehended in the expression 'disposition'. [*T.S. Rajan* v *Collector of Estates Duty, Madras* (1968)69 ITR 342 (Mad) (DB)].

The word 'disposition', in the context, means giving away or giving up by a person of something which was his own. In this sense, a partition in a Hindu undivided family cannot be considered as a disposition. [*The Controller of Estates Duty, A.P., Hyderabad* v *Kancharla Kesava Rao* AIR 1973 SC 2484: (1973)2 SCC 384: (1973)3 SCR 897: (1973)89 ITR 261].

'Disposition' enjoys an extended meaning. The framers of the Act desired by a deeming provision regarding 'disposition' to cover extinguishments of debts and all other rights at the expense of and made by the deceased in favour of the beneficiary. The substantive definition of 'property' in s. 2(15) is not exhaustive but only inclusive and the supplementary operation of Explanation 2 takes in what is not conventionally regarded as 'disposition'. Indeed, 'disposition', even according to Law Dictionaries, embraces 'the parting with, alienation of, or giving up property'. [*The Controller of Estate Duty, Gujarat* v *Shri Kantilal Trikamlal* AIR 1976 SC 1935: (1976)4 SCC 643: (1976)105 ITR 92: (1977)1 SCR 9].

▸*Meaning under the Gift Tax Act 1958, s. 2(xxiv).* The word 'disposition' is used along with the word 'conveyance, assignment' etc. It is clear from the context that the word 'disposition' therein refers to a bilateral or multi-lateral act. [*Goli Eswariah* v *Commissioner of Gift Tax* AIR 1970 SC 1722: (1970)2 SCC 390: (1970)76 ITR 675]

'Disposition' means giving away or giving up by a person of something which was his own. [*The Commissioner of Gift Tax, Madras* v *N.A. Getty Chettiar* AIR 1971 SC 2410: (1971)2 SCC 741: (1971)82 ITR 599: (1972)1 SCR 736].

▸*Meaning under the Maharashtra Agricultural Lands (Ceiling on Holdings) Act 1961.* Though ordinarily the word "disposition" in relation to property would mean disposition made by a deed or will, the qualifying phrase, namely, "including any transfer in exaction of a decree or order of a court, tribunal or authority" used in s. 21(2) extends the meaning of that term to include any disposition made by or under a decree or order of a court. [*Sanjay Dinkar Asarkar* v *State of Maharashtra* AIR 1986 SC 414: (1986)1 SCC 83].

▸*Meaning under the Stamp Act 1899.* The term 'disposition' has been defined as a devise "intended to comprehend a mode by which property can pass, whether by act of parties or by an act of the law" and "includes transfer and charges of property". [*The Madras Refinaries Ltd.* v *The Chief Controlling Revenue Authority, Board of Revenue, Madras* AIR 1977 SC 500: (1977)2 SCR 565: (1977)2 SCC 308].

**Dispossess.** To oust from land by legal process; to eject, to exclude from realty. [*Dhondiram Tatoba Kadam* v *Ramchandra Balwantrao Dubal* (1994)3 SCC 366].

**Dispossession.** Deprivation of, or eviction from, possession of property; ouster. [Black's *Law Dictionary,* 7th Ed.].

Deprivation of, or eviction from, rightful possession of property; the wrongful taking or withholding of possession of land from the person lawfully entitled to it. [Black's *Law Dictionary,* 8th Ed.].

The term 'dispossession' applies when a person comes in and drives out others from possession. It imports ouster; a driving out of possession against the will of the person in actual possession. This driving out cannot be said to have occurred when according to the case of the plaintiff the transfer of possession was voluntary, that is to say, not against the will of the person in possession but in accordance with his wishes and active consent. [*Qadir Bux* v *Ramchand* AIR 1970 All 289].

NOTE: Dispossession should be either by legal process or by physical act of exclusion. It would not include leaving possession voluntarily or by surrender. Thus, a tenant surrendering the land either in accordance with the provisions of law or leaving possession voluntarily would not be covered in the expression 'dispossessed'. [*Dhondiram Tatoba Kadam* v *Ramchandra Balwantrao Dubal* (1994)3 SCC 366].

'Dispossession' implies the coming in of a person and the driving out of another person from possession. It also implies some active element in ousting or dislodging or dispossessing a person against his will or consent. [*Mohini Mohan* v *Srish Chandra* AIR 1978 Cal 434].

Unless the possession of a person prior to his alleged dispossession is proved, he cannot be said to have been dispossessed. [*Rudra Pratap* v *Jagdish* AIR 1956 Pat 116].

**Disprove.** To refute; to prove to be false or erroneous [Black's *Law Dictionary,* 5th and 7th Eds.]; belie; deny; dispel; find unfounded; prove false; prove to be wrong; show to be false.

▸ *Meaning under the Indian Evidence Act 1872, s. 3.* A fact is said to be disproved when, after considering the matters before it, the court either believes that it does not exist, or considers its non-existence so probable that a prudent man ought, under the circumstances of the particular case, to act upon the supposition that it does not exist.

**Dispute.** A conflict or controversy; a conflict of claims or rights; an assertion of a right, claim, or demand on one side, made by contrary claims or allegations on the other; the subject of litigation; the matter for which a suit is brought and upon which issue is joined, and in relation to which jurors are called and witnesses examined. [Black's *Law Dictionary,* 5th Ed.].

A conflict or controversy, esp. one that has given rise to a particular lawsuit. [Black's *Law Dictionary,* 8th Ed.].

Dispute implies some kind of disagreement between the parties concerned, some reference to a legal claim or liability. [*Dinkar Wasudeo* v *Registrar of Co-operative Societies* ILR (1946) Bom 444: AIR 1946 Bom 346].

The meaning of the word "dispute" is "a controversy having both positive and negative aspects. It postulates the assertion of a claim by one party and its denial by the other". [*Canara Bank* v *National Thermal Power Corpn.* JT 2000 Supp (3) SC 491: (2001)1 SCC 43].

▸ *Meaning under the Arbitration Act.* If one party asserts a right and the other repudiates the same, there is a dispute within the meaning of the Arbitration Act. [*Jammu Forest Co.* v *State of J&K* AIR 1968 J&K 86].

NOTE: An Arbitration agreement is to be construed according to its language and in the light of the circumstances in which it is made to determine if the dispute is covered by it. [*Punjab State* v *Moji Ram* AIR 1957 Punj 223].

▸ *Meaning pertaining to an agreement.* A dispute touching or pertaining to the agreement means a dispute as to the term of that agreement, that is to say, as to what is the agreement. [*Co-operative Development and Marketing Union Ltd.* v *Ganesh Sugar Mills Ltd.* AIR 1956 All 601].

▸ *Meaning relating to a contract.* The words 'dispute relating to the contract' are sufficiently wide enough to cover dispute as to whether a contract has or has not been frustrated. [*Chandhan Mul Jhaerta* v *Clive Mills Ltd.* 52 CWN 521: AIR 1948 Cal 257].

▸ *Meaning under the Criminal Procedure Code, s. 145.* Dispute is to mean a reasonable dispute, *bona fide* dispute, a dispute between parties who have some semblances of right or supposed right. [*Maung Hla Pe* v *Manika* AIR 1940 Rang 141].


- **Incidental to a dispute** p. 445.
- **Industrial dispute** p. 452.
- **Trade dispute** p. 849.


**Disqualification.** Something that makes one ineligible; esp., a bias or conflict of interest that prevents a Judge or Juror from impartially hearing a case, or that prevents a lawyer from representing a party. [Black's *Law Dictionary,* 8th Ed.].

The act of making ineligible; the fact or condition of being ineligible. [Black's *Law Dictionary,* 8th Ed.].

NOTE: There is a vital distinction between a disqualification attaching to a conviction and the taking of proceedings consequent upon such conviction. If the petitioner is dismissed from the service because he has been found guilty of an offence involving moral turpitude, it cannot be said that he is suffering from a disqualification attaching to a conviction. [*R. Kumaraswami Aiyar* v *Commissioner, Tiruvannamalai Municipality* (1956)2 MLJ 562].

**Disqualification by or under a law.** A disqualification would be imposed by a law made by Parliament when the Parliamentary statute directly enacts the disqualification or imposes a prohibition upon certain persons to stand for election. The words 'under a law' would signify those cases where the disqualification is not to be found in the Parliamentary statute itself, but is imposed by virtue of powers enabling this to be done. [*G. Narayanaswami Naidu* v *C. Krishnamurthy* AIR 1958 Mad 343].

**Disqualify.** To divest or deprive of qualifications; to incapacitate; to render ineligible or unfit. [Black's *Law Dictionary,* 5th Ed.].

NOTE: To disqualify a person for some purpose means to deprive him of the qualifications required for the purpose. The action of disqualifying is one imposing a legal incapacity on the person. The expression disqualify the candidate from passing the examination connotes the imposition of personal disqualification or ineligibility for passing the examination. [*Pyarelal* v *University of Sagar* AIR 1961 MP 356].

**Disruptive.** "Disruptive" means producing or resulting from or attending disruption. [*State of Punjab* v *Sukhpal Singh* AIR 1990 SC 231: (1990)1 SCC 35: 1990 Cr LJ 584].

**Dissolution.** Act or process of dissolving; termination; winding up; breaking up; abolition; abrogation; annihilation; annulment; dismissal; discontinuance; end; liquidation.

**Dissolution of contract.** Cancellation or abrogation of a contract by the parties themselves, with the effect of annulling the binding force of the agreement, and restoring each party to his original rights.

**Dissolution of marriage.** The act of terminating a marriage; divorce. The term, however, does not include annulment. [*Delhi* v *Jones* 94 SW 2d 47, 48].

'Dissolution' relates to the marriage bond itself whereas the word 'divorce' relates to the parties to the marriage bond. [*Deacock* v *Deacock* (1958)2 All ER 633].

**Dissolution of Parliament.** A civil death of Parliament. [*Purushothaman Nambudiri* v *State of Kerala* AIR 1962 SC 694: 1962 Supp (1) SCR 753: (1962)1 SCJ 477].

NOTE: The House of the People stands dissolved at the expiry of five years; it may, however, be sooner dissolved. But the Council of States is not subject to dissolution. [Article 83 of the Constitution of India].

Dissolution of Parliament kills all bills which have not yet passed. [*Purushothaman Nambudiri* v *State of Kerala,* ibid].

**Dissolution of partnership.** The termination of an existing partnership upon the occurrence of an event specified in the partnership agreement, such as a partner's withdrawal from the partnership, or as specified by law.

NOTE: *'Dissolution' and 'reconstruction' of partnership—distinction.* 'Dissolution' and 'reconstruction' are two distinct legal concepts, for, a dissolution brings the partnership to an end while a reconstruction means the constitution of the partnership under altered circumstances. [*Commissioner of Income Tax, West Bengal-III* v *Pigot Champan & Company* AIR 1982 SC 1085: (1982)2 SCC 330: (1982)135 ITR 620].

**Distant kindred.** In Mahomedan law, distant kindred means all those relations by blood who are neither sharers nor residuaries.

**Distinct.** Clear to the senses or mind; plain; unmistakeable; clearly standing apart, as space or thought, from other objects; evidently not identical; observably or decidedly different; standing apart by itself; disjoined; unconnected. [Webster's *Comprehensive Dictionary,* International Edition].

Not identical; separate; individual; different in kind of quality; clearly perceptible; clearly understandable; definite; unmistakeable. [*Concise Oxford Dictionary*, 9th Ed.].

Distinguished by nature or station; not the same; different in the place or the like; separate; individual; that which is capable of being distinguished; actually divided or apart from other things. [*Gavin* v *Webb* Tex Civ App, 99 SW 2d 372, 379].

**Distinct matters.** Something different from distinct categories.

NOTE: Two transactions might be of the same description, but all the same they might be distinct. [*Member, Board of Revenue* v *Arthur Paul Benthai* AIR 1956 SC 35: 1956 SCJ 56: (1955)2 SCR 842: 1956 SCA 512].

**Distinct subjects.** Subjects as are independent of each other and do not arise out of or relate to the same set of facts or circumstances. [*D.M. Kaushik* v *Graduate Gas Service* AIR 1978 P&H 213].

▸*Meaning under the Court Fees Act 1870, s. 17.* The words 'distinct subjects' mean distinct causes of action in respect of which separate suits should be filed but for the enabling provisions allowing them to be joined together in one suit. [*In re Lakshminarayana Chettiar* AIR 1954 Mad 594: ILR (1954) Mad 289].

The words 'distinct subjects' mean distinct causes of action or distinct kinds of relief. [*Sitabai* v *Shib Sahay* AIR 1944 Pat 387].

'Distinct subject' must arise out of different causes of action. [*D.M. Kaushik* v *Graduate Gas Service* AIR 1978 P&H 213].

**Distinctive.** Characteristic; conspicuous; contrast; diacritical; different; differentiating; indicating difference; peculiar; noticeable; salient; singular; special; uncommon; unique; unworthy.

**Distinctly.** Directly; indubitably; strictly; unmistakeably. [*Mohmed Inayatullah* v *State of Maharashtra* AIR 1976 SC 483: (1976)1 SCC 828: 1976 Cr LJ 481].

**Distinguish.** Classify; contradistinguish; differentiate; draw a distinction; make distinctions; note differences; point out an essential difference; recognize as different.

In legal parlance, "distinguishing" is a mode of differing from the *ratio decidendi*. It may be restrictive or non-restrictive. The process of cutting down the expressed *ratio decidendi* is equally restrictive distinguishing. Restrictive distinguishing cuts down the expressed *ratio decidendi* of the earlier case by treating as material to the earlier decision some fact, present in the earlier case, which the earlier court regard as immaterial. Non-restrictive distinguishing occurs where a court accepts the expressed *ratio decidendi* of the earlier case, and does not seek to curtail it, but finds that the case before it does not fall within this *ratio decidendi* because of some material difference of fact.

**Distress.** A common law right of landlord, now regulated by statute, to seize a tenant's goods and chattels in a non-judicial proceeding to satisfy an arrears of rent. [*Van Ness Industries, Inc.* v *Claremont Painting and Decorating Co.* 324 A 2d 102, 104].

The term 'distress' primarily connotes a summary remedy by which a person is entitled without legal process to take into his possession the personal chattels of another person, to be held as a pledge to compel the performance of a duty, or the satisfaction of a debt or demand. By almost universal sanction the term "distress" is now used to designate both the process of taking; and the chattels taken, though originally it applied only to the taking. [Halsbury's *Laws of England,* 4th Ed., vol. 13, para 201, p. 107].

NOTE: A distress is one of the most ancient and effectual remedies for the recovery of rent. Sections 53 to 59 of the Presidency Small Causes Courts Act 1882, deal with distress for recovery of rent. Any person claiming to be entitled to arrears of rent may apply for distress warrant. The bailiff directed to make the distress may force upon any stable, outhouse or other building. The bailiff is required to seize the movable property found in the premises mentioned in the warrant and belonging to the person from whom the rent is claimed. The bailiff may impound the property so seized. The distrained property is sold on notice to the debtor. The bailiffs shall, on realising the proceeds, pay over the amount to the Registrar; and such amount shall be applied first in payment of the costs of the distress and then in satisfaction of the debt; and the surplus, if any, shall be returned to the debtor.

• **Abuse of distress** p. 10.

**Distribute.** To divide and deal out in shares; apportion; allot; divide and classify; categorise; scatter or spread out, as in area or over a surface; divide and arrange into distinctive parts or functions; allocate; assign; assort; decentralise; disseminate; portion out.

The ordinary and general meaning of the word 'distribute' is sufficient to convey spreading of the goods somewhere by whatever means that may be employed. [*State* v *Nathumal Damumal* AIR 1962 Bom 21].

NOTE: 'Distribute' does not imply an absence of beneficial interest in the property; nor is there any solid distinction in law or fact between 'distribute' and 'dispose of'. [*O'Brien* v *Condon* (1905)1 IR 51].

**Distribution.** Allocation; allotment; appropriation; assignment; dealing out; dispensation; disposal; dissemination; division; handing out; parceling out; partition; assemblage; categorisation; collocation; disposition; gradation; grouping marshaling; ordering; regimentation; systematisation.

To give full and comprehensive effect to the intent of a statute, the word 'distribution' must be broadly construed. It should not be construed in a purely literal sense so as to mean only division of a particular kind or to particular persons. The words apportionment, allotment, allocation, classification clearly fall within the broad sweep of the word 'distribution'. So construed, the word "distribution" will include various facets, aspects, methods and terminology of a broad based concept of distribution. [*State of Tamil Nadu* v *L. Abu Kavur Bai* AIR 1984 SC 326: (1984)1 SCR 725: (1984)1 SCC 515].

Distribution involves the idea of division between several persons which is the same as payment to several persons. [*Punjab Distilling Industries Ltd.* v *Commissioner of Income Tax* AIR 1965 SC 1862: (1965)57 ITR 1].

• **Equitable distribution** p. 314.

**Distribution main.** A "distribution main" is defined (in an Electricity Act) to mean the portion of any main with which a service line is or is intended to be immediately connected. [*State of U.P.* v *Hindustan Aluminium Corpn.* AIR 1979 SC 1459: (1979)3 SCR 709: (1979)3 SCC 229, defined in the context of U.P. Electricity (Regulation of Supply, Distribution, Consumption and Use) Order 1977 and Electricity Act 1910, s. 2(*e*)].

**Distribution of capital assets.** The expression means distribution *in specie* and not distribution of sale proceeds. [*James Anderson* v *Commissioner of Income Tax*

AIR 1960 SC 751: (1960)3 SCR 167: 1960 SCJ 665].

**District.** One of the territorial areas into which an entire state or country, county, municipality or other political sub-division is divided, for judicial, political, electoral, or administrative purposes. [*State ex rel. Schur* v *Payne* 63 P 2d 921, 925].

▸ *Meaning under the Code of Civil Procedure 1908, s. 2(4).* 'District' means the local limits of the jurisdiction of a principal civil court of original jurisdiction called a District Court, and includes the local limits of the ordinary original civil jurisdiction of a High Court.

**District Court.** 'District Court' means the principal civil court of original jurisdiction. [Code of Civil Procedure 1908, s 2(4)].

▸ *Meaning under the Companies Act 1956, s. 2(14).* The principal civil court of original jurisdiction in a district, but does not include a High Court in the exercise of its ordinary original civil jurisdiction.

▸ *Meaning under the Mental Health Act, s. 2(b).* 'District Court' means, in any area for which there is a city civil court, that court, and in any other area the principal civil court of original jurisdiction, and includes any other civil court which the State Government may, by notification, specify as the court competent to deal with all or any of the matters specified in this Act.

▸ *Meaning under the Guardians and Wards Act 1890, s. 4(4).* 'District Court' has the meaning assigned to that expression in the Code of Civil Procedure, and includes a High Court in the exercise of its ordinary original civil jurisdiction.

▸ *Meaning under the Divorce Act 1869, s. 3(3).* 'District Court' means, in the case of any petition under the Divorce Act, the court of the District Judge within the local limits of whose ordinary jurisdiction, or of whose jurisdiction under the Divorce Act, the marriage was solemnized or, the husband and wife reside or last resided together.

'District Court' means, in any area for which there is a city civil court, that court, and in any other area the principal civil court of original jurisdiction and includes any other civil court which may be specified by the State Government, by notification in the Official Gazette, as having jurisdiction in respect of the matters dealt with in Hindu Marriage Act 1955 [s. 3(*b*)].

▸ *Meaning under the Registration Act 1908, s. 2(4).* 'District Court' includes the High Court in its ordinary original civil jurisdiction.

**District Judge.** The Judge of a principal civil court of original jurisdiction, but shall not include a High Court in the exercise of its ordinary or extraordinary original civil jurisdiction. [General Clauses Act 1897, s. 3(17)].

In Chapter VI, Part VI of the Constitution of India 'District Judge' includes judge of a city civil court, additional district judge, joint district judge, assistant district judge, chief judge of a small cause court, chief presidency magistrate, additional chief presidency magistrate, sessions judge, additional sessions judge and assistant sessions Judge. [Constitution of India 1950, Art. 236(*a*)]. The words "District Judge" is defined in Art. 236(*a*) and it includes, among other, an additional district judge. [*State of West Bengal* v *Nripendranath Bagchi* AIR 1966 SC 447: (1966)1 SCR 771].

'District Judge' means a Judge of a principal civil court of original jurisdiction however designated. [Divorce Act 1869, s. 3(2); Indian Succession Act 1925, s. 2(*bb*)].

**Disturbance.** Any act causing annoyance, disquiet, agitation, or derangement to another, or interrupting his peace, or interfering with him in the pursuit of a lawful and appropriate occupation or contrary to the usages of a sort of meeting and class of persons assembled that interferes with its due progress or irritates the assembly in whole or in part. [Black's *Law Dictionary,* 5th Ed.].

At common law, a wrong done to an incorporeal hereditament by hindering or disquieting the owner in the enjoyment of it. Blackstone enumerated five types of such disturbances: disturbances of franchises, common, tenure, ways, and patronage. [3 Bl Comm 235].

Disturbance implies that something is taking place against the will of the person disturbed. [*Horn* v *Sunderland Corporation* (1941)1 All ER 480].

**Divest.** Confiscate; deprive; dispossess; displace; dislodge; disentitle; disendow; disrobe; drive out; evict; expel; expropriate; forbid; laybare; remove; relieve; strip; take away; unseat.

**Dividend.** The ordinary meaning of the term 'dividend' is share of profits, whether at a fixed rate or otherwise, allocated to the holders of shares in a company. The term is generally used with reference to trading or other companies, and to payments made to members of a company as such and not by way of remuneration for services. Although it usually implies a share of profits periodically payable, it may also refer to such shares of profits as are divided only occasionally and are usually called "bonuses" or "bonus dividends". The terms "preference dividend", "preferential dividend", and "cumulative preferential dividend" refer to shares having preferential rights. An "interim dividend" is a dividend payable at some date between the ordinary general meetings. [Halsbury's *Laws of England,* 4th Ed., vol. 7, para 596, p. 349].

"The word 'dividend' is not a word of technical import. Primarily it appears to mean part of anything which is subject to be divided and it is, of course, also sometimes used to describe a share which one person receives along with others equally entitled. It is commonly used in reference to the profits of a joint stock company distributed among the shareholders, but in no way .... is it limited to this last meaning". [*Re McEwen* (1963)40 DLR (2d) 273, 277, *per* Wells, J.].

Dividend in its ordinary meaning is a distributive share of the profits or income of a company given to its shareholders. [*Kantilal Manilal* v *Commissioner of Income Tax, Bombay* AIR 1961 SC 1038: (1961)2 SCR 584: (1961)41 ITR 275: (1961)1 SCJ 506].



"Dividend" in its ordinary connotation means the sum paid to or received by a shareholder proportionate to his shareholding in a company out of the total sum distributed. [*The Commissioner of Income Tax, Calcutta* v *Nalin Behari Lal Singha* AIR 1970 SC 388: (1970)1 SCR 665: (1969)2 SCC 310: (1969)74 ITR 849].

Distribution which is attributable to the accumulated profits of the company immediately before its liquidation is deemed to be 'dividend'. [*Tea Estate India (P) Ltd.* v *Commissioner of Income Tax, W.B. III* AIR 1976 SC 1790: 1976 (Supp) SCR 145: (1976)4 SCC 446: (1976)103 ITR 785].

• **Scrip dividend** p. 779.
• **Tax-free dividend** p. 831.

**Dividend warrant.** A written order to a banker authorising the payment of dividend and is negotiable; a cheque (invariably to order) issued to a shareholder as payment of a dividend.

> NOTE: Every dividend warrant must show the gross amount of dividend, the tax deducted therefrom and the amount of the net payment. Where double taxation relief is obtained the company's net effective rate of tax must also be shown. [Osborn & Grandage's *Concise Commercial Dictionary*].

**Divisible contract.** One which is in its nature and purposes susceptible of division and apportionment, having two or more parts in respect to matters and things contemplated and embraced by it, not necessarily dependent on each other nor intended by the parties so to be. [Black's *Law Dictionary,* 5th Ed.].

A divisible contract is a contract that includes too or more promises each of which can be enforced separately, so that failure to perform one of the promises does not necessarily put the promisor in breach of the entire contract. [Black's *Law Dictionary,* 7th Ed.].

Where a contract consists of a number of considerations for a number of acts, the contract is said to be divisible. Neither party to the contract is discharged from the performance of the whole of his particular part by reason of the fact that the other party has failed to do his part in relation to someone or other of the matters into which the contract is divided. Thus, where *A* agrees to erect 10 houses on a plot belonging to *B*, and *B* agrees to give *A* a lease of each house when completed, *B* cannot refuse to give a lease of each house which is completed if only, say, five are built by *A*, the contract being divisible and the remedy of *B* for *A*'s failure to build the other five being a suit for damages. [Jowitt's *Dictionary of English Law,* 2nd Ed.].

It is also termed as severable contract.

NOTE: Where the contract is partly illegal and partly legal and the illegal part cannot be severed from the legal, the contract is altogether void; but where they can be severed the bad part may be rejected retaining the good part.

**Divorce.** It is derived from the Latin word 'divortium' which means to turn aside and is defined as the legal separation of man and wife, effected by the judgment or decree of a court, and either totally dissolving the marriage relation, or suspending its effects so far as concerns the cohabitation of the parties; legal dissolution of a marriage by a court.

Webster's *Third New International Dictionary* states 'divorce' to mean amongst other things: (*a*) legal dissolution in whole or in part of a marriage relation usually by a court or other body having competent authority; (*b*) an absolute dissolution of a valid marriage made by decree of court for lawful cause arising after the marriage; (*c*) a formal separation of man and wife by the act of one party or by consent according to established custom. As ordinarily understood, therefore, divorce is nothing more nor less than another name for dissolution of marriage, whether the same results from act of parties or is a consequence of proceedings at law, and it would be wrong to record the two terms as not being synonymous with each other, unless the legislature makes a direction to the contrary. [*Mst. Zohara Khatoon* v *Mohd. Ibrahim* AIR 1981 SC 1243: (1981)2 SCC 509: (1981)2 SCR 910: 1981 Cr LJ 754: 1981 SCC (Cri)) 517].

• **Foreign divorce** p. 364.

**Diwany.** It was a term used for fiscal administration and it meant the collection of revenues and customs and administration of justice in civil cases. In 1765 Shah Alam who still claimed sovereignty transferred the Diwany of Bengal, Bihar and Orissa to the East India Company in lieu of Rupees Twenty Six lacs annually.

**Dock.** It has different meanings. It may mean "a structure that encloses water, often between two piers, in which ships are received for loading, unloading, safekeeping, or repair". [Black's *Law Dictionary,* 8th Ed.].

It may also mean the "part of a warehouse or other building (usu. elevated with oversized doors) at which trucks are received for loading and unloading". [Black's *Law Dictionary,* 7th Ed.].

In legal parlance, it means an enclosed space for prisoners on trial in a criminal court.

**Dock warrant.** A document issued by dock authorities certifying that goods enumerated therein are held in a dock warehouse on behalf of the person in whose favour the warrant is drawn.

**Dock worker.** A person employed or to be employed in, or in the vicinity of, any port on work in connection with the loading, unloading, movement or storage of cargoes, or work in connection with the preparation of ships or other vessels for the receipt or discharge of cargoes of leaving port. [Dock Workers (Regulation of Employment) Act 1948, s. 2(*b*)].

**Document.** An original piece of written or printed matter conveying authoritative information or evidence; one of the several papers affixed to a documentary bill and testifying to or effecting the transfer of goods, as a bill of lading, certificate of insurance, etc. [Webster's *Comprehensive Dictionary,* International Edition].

Something tangiable on which words, symbols, or marks are recorded. [Black's *Law Dictionary*, 8th Ed.].

As plural, it means the deeds, agreements, title papers, letters, receipts, and other written instruments used to prove a fact.

Any decipherable information which is set down in a lasting form would be a document. [*Public Prosecutor* v *T. Amrath Rao* AIR 1960 AP 176: 1960 Cr LJ 452].

▸ *Meaning under the Companies Act 1956, s. 2(15).* "Document" includes summons, notice, requisition, order, other legal process, and registers, whether issued, sent or kept in pursuance of this or any other Act, or otherwise.

NOTE: In interpretation of document, substance and not form is material. [*Tarakeshwar Sio Thakur Jiu* v *Bar Dass Dey & Co.* AIR 1979 SC 1669: (1979)3 SCC 106].

The meaning of the word "document" or of a particular part of it is to be sought for in the document itself. Document means the document read as a whole and not piecemeal. [*Delhi Development Authority* v *Durga Chand Kaushish* AIR 1973 SC 2609: (1973)2 SCC 825: (1974)1 SCR 535].

▸ *Meaning under the Indian Evidence Act 1872, s. 3.* "Document" means any matter expressed or described upon any substance by means of letters, figures or marks or by more than one of those means, intended to be used, or which may be used, for the purpose of recording that matter.

NOTE: A writing is a document; words printed, lithographed or photographed are documents; a map or plan is a document; an inscription on a metal plate or stone is a document; a caricature is a document.

Tape-records of speeches are "documents" and stand on no different footing than photographs. [*Ziyauddin Burhanuddin Bukhari* v *Brijmohan Ramdass Mehra* AIR 1975 SC 1788: 1975 (Supp) SCR 281: (1976)2 SCC 17].

▸ *Meaning under the General Clauses Act 1897, s. 3(18).* "Document" usually includes any matter written, expressed or described upon any substance by means of letters, figures, or marks, or by more than one of those means which is intended to be used, or which may be used, for the purpose of recording that matter.

▸ *Meaning under the Indian Penal Code 1860, s. 29.* The word "document" denotes any matter expressed or described upon any substance by means of letters, figures, or marks, or by more than one of those means, intended to be used, or which may be used, as evidence of that matter.

NOTE: It is immaterial by what means or upon what substance the letters, figures or marks are formed, or whether evidence is intended for, or may be used in, a Court of Justice, or not. Thus, a writing expressing the terms of a contract, which may be used as evidence of the contract, is a document. A cheque upon a banker is a document, a power-of-attorney is a document. A map or plan which is intended to be used or which may be used, as evidence is a document. A writing containing directions or instructions is a document.

It is pertaining to note that whatever is expressed by means of letters, figures or marks as explained by mercantile or other usage, shall be deemed to be expressed by such letters, figures or marks within the meaning of this section, although the same may not be actually expressed. Thus, if *A* writes his name on the back of a bill of exchange payable to his order, the meaning of the endorsement, as explained by mercantile usage, is that the bill is to be paid to the holder. The endorsement is a document, and must be construed in the same manner as if the words "pay to the holder" or words to that effect had been written over the signature.


- **Cancellation of document** p. 119.
- **Discovery of document** p. 265.
- **Execution of document** p. 328.
- **Forged document** p. 368.
- **Private documents** p. 686.
- **Privileged document** p. 688.
- **Public document** p. 707.
- **Shipping documents** p. 795.


**Document of title to goods.** A written description, identification, or declaration of goods authorizing the holder (usu. a bailee) to receive, hold, and dispose of the document and the goods it covers. [Black's *Law Dictionary*, 8th Ed.].

▸ *Meaning under the Sale of Goods Act 1930, s. 2(4).* 'Document of title to goods' include a bill of lading, dock-warrant, warehouse-keeper's certificate, wharfinger's certificate, railway receipt, multimodal transport document, warrant or order for the delivery of goods and any other document used in the ordinary course of business as proof to the possession or control of goods or authorising or purporting to authorise, either by endorsement or by delivery, the possessor of the document to transfer or receive goods thereby represented.

**Documentary bills.** Bills of exchange accompanied by bills of lading, invoice and insurance papers. It is necessary to accept the bill of exchange in order to obtain possession of the bill of lading.

**Does not appear.** The expression 'does not appear' or 'absent' applies only where the complainant is in a position to take some decision and either wilfully or due to negligence does not exerçise his volition in favour of attending the court. It does not apply to a person who is dead. [*Ali Dar* v *Mohammad Sharif* AIR 1966 J&K 60: 1960 Cr LJ 412].

**Doffer.** A doffer is a specialised worker, who is engaged to do a particular kind of work and if he is asked to do another kind of work also, though within the fixed working hours, he is entitled to get some compensation for it. [*State of U.P.* v *Muir Mills Co. Ltd.* AIR 1967 All 284: ILR (1966)1 All 250: 1967 Lab LJ 598].

**Domestic.** Belonging to the house or household; concerning or relating to the human or family; of the home, household, or family affairs; pertaining, belonging, or relating to a home; of or pertaining to one's homestead or country; of one's own country, in foreign or international; produced at home; home made; home grown.

**Domestic animals.** Such as are habituated to live in or about the habitations of men or such as contribute to a support, of a family. Example: tamed animals, e.g. horses, sheep, dogs. [Black's *Law Dictionary,* 5th Ed.].

An animal that is customarily devoted to the service of humankind at the time and in the place where it is helped; any animal that is statutorily so designated. [Black's *Law Dictionary,* 8th Ed.].

**Domestic electrical appliances.** Only articles, such as electric stoves, irons, refrigerators, but not such things as lifts. [*Eastern Engineers* v *State of Bombay* (1956)7 STC 229]. Electric fans are domestic electric appliances. [*Viswa & Co.* v *State of Gujarat* AIR 1967 Guj 19: (1966)17 STC 581].

**Domestic jurisdiction.** The area within which a sovereign State enjoys freedom of action.

**Domestic purposes.** Purposes of or relating to the family or the household.

• **Water supply for domestic purposes.** Water supplied for domestic purposes would mean water supplied to satisfy or help to satisfy the needs, or perform or help in performing the services, which, according to the ordinary habits of civilised life, are commonly satisfied and performed in people's homes as distinguished from those needs and services which are satisfied or performed outside those homes, and are not connected with, nor incident to, the occupation of them. [*Metropolitan Water Board* v *Avery* (1914) AC 118].

NOTE: The test is not whether the water is consumed or used in the course of a trade or business, but whether its user is in its nature domestic. [*Nani Lal Ray* v *Satyendra Nath Ray* 54 CWN 42].

**Domestic servant.** Domestic servants are those employees who, forming part of the employer's residential establishment, are engaged upon work of such a character that it brings them into the close personal proximity of the employer and is mainly concerned with the household. [Halsbury's *Laws of England,* 4th Ed., vol. 16, para 508, p. 318].

NOTE: A chauffeur who not only drives but also attends to the mechanism of his employer's car, a stoker and general handyman about a hospital are domestic servants. [*Cameron* v *Royal London Ophthalmic Hospital* (1941)1 KB 350].

**Domestic tribunal.** A domestic tribunal is in general a tribunal composed of laymen. It has no power to administer an oath and no party has the power to compel the attendance of witnesses. It is not bound by the rules of evidence. As long as the tribunal does not exceed its jurisdiction and acts honestly and in good faith, the court cannot intervene in its functioning. [*L.A.P. O'Relliy* v *C.C. Gittens* AIR 1949 PC 313].

Domestic tribunals may include the committees or the councils, or the members of trade unions, of members' clubs, and of professional bodies established by statute while acting in a quasi-judicial capacity.

The phrase "domestic tribunal" is used to refer to committees of associations like trade unions, social clubs, professional bodies who have right to adjudicate upon the rights of or disputes between their members. Sometimes such tribunals are also set up by a statute, *i.e.*, the medical council, bar council or the like. When created by statute or under statutory authority, they should strictly be called 'statutory tribunals' rather than 'domestic tribunals'. In the case of a 'statutory tribunal', the jurisdiction of the tribunal rests on the statute or the rules framed thereunder. [*Imphal Sporting Club* v *All Manipur Sports Association* AIR 1969 Mani 41].

**Domicile.** A settled place of abode, home, house, or dwelling; the place where a person has his legal abode; that place where a man has his true, fixed and permanent home and principal establishment, and to which whenever he is absent, he has the intention of returning. [*Smith* v *Smith* 206 Pa Supper 310].

Domicile is the legal relationship between an individual and a territory with distinctive legal system which invokes that system as his personal law. A person is domiciled in that country in which he either has or is deemed by law to have his permanent home. Every individual is regarded as belonging, at every stage in his life, to some community consisting of all persons domiciled in a particular country. [Halsbury's *Laws of England,* 4th Ed., vol. 8, para 421, p. 318].

The word "domicile" is to identify the personal law by which an individual is governed in respect of various matters such as the essential validity of a marriage, the effect of a marriage on the proprietary rights of husband and wife, jurisdiction in divorce and nullity of marriage, illegitimacy, legitimation and adoption and testamentary and intestate succession to movables. Domicile is the legal relationship between an individual and a territory with a distinctive legal system which invokes that system as his personal law. [*Pradeep Jain* v *Union of India* AIR 1984 SC 1420].

NOTE: The law attributes to every person at birth a domicil which is called a domicil of origin. This domicil may be changed, and a new domicil, which is called a domicil of choice, acquired; but the two kinds of domicil differ in the following respects: (1) the domicil of origin is received by operation of law at birth; the domicil of choice is acquired later by the actual removal of an individual to another country intending to remain there indefinitely; (2) the domicil of origin is retained until the acquisition of a domicil of choice; it cannot be divested, although it remains in abeyance during the continuance of a domicil of choice; the domicil of choice is lost by abandonment whereupon the domicil of origin will revive unless some other domicil is acquired; the domicil of choice is destroyed when it is once lost, but may be acquired a new by fulfilling the same conditions as are required in the first instance. [Halsbury's *Laws of England,* 4th Ed., vol. 8, para 425, p. 320].

A married woman acquires the domicile of her husband, if she has not the same domicile before marriage. The wife's domicile follows that of her husband. [*Attaullah* v *Attaulah* AIR 1953 Cal 530 (SB)].

Nationality and domicil are two entirely different concepts in private international law. A man may have one nationality and different domicils. He may owe allegiance to one country and he may have a domicil in another country. [*Michael Anthony* v *State of Bombay* AIR 1956 Bom 729].

**Dominant heritage or tenement.** The land for the beneficial enjoyment of which the easement right exists is called the dominant heritage, and the owner or occupier thereof the dominant owner. [Indian Easements Act 1882, s. 4].

**Dominant undertaking.** Dominant undertaking means an undertaking which either by itself or along with inter-connected undertakings—(*i*) produces, supplies, distributes or otherwise controls not less than one third of the total goods of any description that are produced or distributed in India or any substantial part thereof, or (*ii*) provides or otherwise controls not less than one-third of any services that are rendered in India or any substantial part thereof. [Monopolies and Restrictive Trade Practices Act 1969, s. 2(*d*). The Act is repealed and replaced by the Competition Act 2002. No such term is defined under the new Act].

**Dominion.** Control; possession; sovereignty. [Black's *Law Dictionary,* 8th Ed.].

The generally accepted definition of "dominion" is perfect control in right of ownership. The word implies both title and possession and appears to require a complete retention of control over disposition. [*Eastex Aviation, Inc.* v *Sperry & Hutchinson Co.* CA Tex, 522 F 2d 1299, 1307].

**Dominus litis.** The controller of a suit or litigation; an advocate who, after the death of his client, prosecuted a suit to sentence for the executor's use. [Wharton's *Law Lexicon*].

**Donatio mortis causa.** A gift made in contemplation of death.

A *donatio mortis causa* is a gift *inter vivos* by which the donee is to have the absolute title to the subject of the gift, not at once, but if the donor dies. The donee's title becomes absolute at the moment of the donor's death, so that the property given never vests in the donor's personal representative, who is obliged, if necessary, to lend his name or give his endorsement to assist the donee in completing his title. [Halsbury's *Laws of England,* 4th Ed., vol. 17, para 1075, p. 560].

**Donation.** A gift; grant; offering; alms; benefaction; bounty; charity; contribution; endowment; philanthropy; largesse.

A gift; a method of acquiring a benefice by a deed of gift alone, without presentation, institution, or induction. [Black's *Law Dictionary,* 8th Ed.].

When a person gives money to another without any material return, he donates that sum. An act by which the owner of a thing voluntarily transfers the title and possession of the same from himself to another, without any consideration is a 'donation'. A gift or gratuitous payment is, in simple English, a donation. The hope of spiritual benefit or political goodwill, the spontaneous affection that benefaction brings, the popularisation of a good cause or the prestige that publicised bounty fetches these and other myriad consequences or feelings may not mar a donation to make it a grant for a *quid pro quo*. Wholly motiveless donation is rare, but material return alone negates a gift or donation. [*The Commissioner of Expenditure Tax, Andhra Pradesh* v *Shri P.V.G. Raju, Rajah of Vizianagaram* AIR 1976 SC 140: (1976)1 SCR 1017: (1976)1 SCC 241: (1975)101 ITR 465].

**Donee.** One to whom a gift is made; the recipient of a gift; the person in whose favour a power of appointment is created or reserved. [Black's *Law Dictionary,* 8th Ed.].

▸ *Meaning under the Gift Tax Act 1958, s. 2(viii), since repealed.* Any person who acquires any property under a gift, and where a gift is made to a trustee for the benefit of another person, it includes both the trustee and the beneficiary.

▸ *Meaning under the Transfer of Property Act 1882, s. 122.* Donee is the person to whom the gift is made and who accepts the gift.

**Donor.** One who gives something without receiving consideration for the transfer; settlor. [Black's *Law Dictionary,* 8th Ed.].

▸ *Meaning under the Gift Tax Act 1958, s. 2(ix), since repealed.* Any person who makes a gift.

▸ *Meaning under the Transfer of Property Act 1882, s. 122.* Donor is the person who can transfer voluntarily and wihtout consideration certain existing movable or immovable property in favour of another.

**Dormant partner.** A partner who shares in the profits but who has no active voice in management of the firm and whose existence is often not publicly disclosed. [Black's *Law Dictionary,* 8th Ed.]. He is also called a silent partner.

**Dormiunt aliquando leges, nunquam moriuntur.** The laws sometimes sleep, never die.

**Double insurance.** Insurance coverage by more than one insurer for the same interest and for the same insured. [Black's *Law Dictionary,* 8th Ed.].

NOTE: The insured is entitled to only a single indemnity from a loss, and to recover this, the insured may either—(1) sue each insurer for its share of the loss, or (2) sue one or more of the insurers for the entire amount, leaving any paying insurers to recover from the others their respective shares of the loss. [Black's *Law Dictionary*, 7th Ed.].

**Double jeopardy.** The fact of being prosecuted or sentenced twice for substantially the same offence. [Black's *Law Dictionary*, 8th Ed.].

NOTE: Double jeopardy is prohibited by the 5th amendment of the American Constitution.

The rules against "double jeopardy" is incorporated in Art. 20(2) of the Constitution of India. This is based on the principle, *nemo debet bis vexari* (no one should be twice vexed). Article 20(2) provides that "no person shall be prosecuted and punished for the same offence more than once." Two conditions are necessary for its application. First, a person should be prosecuted. Secondly, he should be punished. The use of "and" is conjunctive here. [*Venkataraman* v *Union of India* 1954 SCR 1150].

**Double taxation.** The imposition of two taxes on the same property during the same period and for the same taxing purpose; the imposition of two taxes on one corporate profit; imposition of comparable taxes in two or more states on the same taxpayer for the same subject matter or identical goods. [Black's *Law Dictionary*, 8th Ed.].

The expression 'double taxation' is often used in different senses, namely, in its strict legal sense of direct double taxation and in its popular sense of indirect double taxation. Double taxation in the strict legal sense means taxing the same property or subject matter twice, for the same purposes, for the same period and in the same territory. To constitute double taxation, the two or more taxes must have been (1) levied on the same property or subject matter, (2) by the same Government or authority, (3) during the same taxing period, and (4) for the same purpose. [*Sri Krishna Das* v *Town Area Committee, Chirgaon* (1990)3 SCC 645: JT 1990(2) SC 68: (1990)183 ITR 401: (1990)2 SCR 13: (1990)77 STC 395: AIR 1991 SC 2096].

NOTE: There is nothing in the Constitution of India which prevents double taxation being levied. Instances are not wanting in this country in which taxes are levied twice upon the same thing, once for the benefit of the Provincial Government and in the second instance for the benefit of the Local Self-Government bodies, for example, the District Board or the Municipality. [*Cantonment Board* v *Western India Theatres* AIR 1954 Bom 261].

**Doubt.** A feeling of uncertainty; an uncertain state of things; an inclination to disbelieve; ambiguity; apprehension; faltering; hesitancy; inability to decide; indeterminateness; lack of conviction; want of faith.

- **Benefit of doubt** p. 101.
- **Reasonable doubt** p. 729.

**Doul kabuliyat.** An engagement setting forth particulars of the arrangements made for the payment of revenue in respect of specified lands by fixed instalments. [*Tarakeshwar* v *Satis Kanta* AIR 1930 Cal 411; Wilson's *Glossary*].

**Dower.** In Mahomedan law, dower is a sum of money or other property which the wife is entitled to receive from the husband in consideration of the marriage. There are three kinds of dower—(1) prompt, *i.e.*, which is payable on demand, (2) deferred, *i.e.*, which is payable on dissolution of marriage, and (3) partly prompt and partly deferred.

"Dower, under the Muhammadan Law, is the sum of money or other property promised by the husband to be paid or delivered to the wife in consideration of the marriage, and even where no dower is expressly fixed or mentioned at the marriage ceremony, the law confers the right of dower upon the wife as a necessary effect of marriage. To use the language of the Hedaya, 'the payment of dower is enjoined by the law merely as a token of respect for its subject (the woman), wherefore the mention of it is not absolutely essential to the validity of a marriage; and, for the same reason, a marriage is also valid, although the man were to engage in the contract on the special condition that there should be no dower' .... (Hamilton's *Hedaya* by Grady, p. 44). Even after the marriage the dower may be increased by the husband during coverture .... In this sense and in no other can dower under the Muhammadan Law be regarded as the consideration for the connubial intercourse, and if the authors of the Arabic Text-books of Muhammadan Law have compared it to price in the contract of sale, it is simply because marriage is a civil contract under that law .... Such being the nature of the dower, the rules which regulate its payment are necessarily affected by the position of a married woman under the Muhammadan Law. Under that law marriage does not make her property the property of the husband, nor does coverture impose any disability upon her as to freedom of contract. The marriage contract is easily dissoluble, and the freedom of divorce and the rule of polygamy place a power in the hands of the husband which the law-giver intended to restrain by rendering the rules as to payments of dower stringent upon the husband. No limit as to the amount of dower has been imposed, and it may either be prompt, that is, immediately payable upon demand, or deferred, that is payable upon the dissolution of marriage, whether by death or divorce. The dower may also be partly prompt and partly deferred; but when at the time of the marriage ceremony no specification in this respect is made, the whole dower is presumed to be prompt and due on demand". [*Abdul Kadir* v *Salima* (1886) ILR 8 All 149, 157, *per* Justice Syed Mahmood].

"Dower is not the exchange or consideration given by the man to the woman for entering into the contract; but an effect of the contract, imposed by the law on the husband as a token in respect, for its respect, the woman ... Dower being ...... opposed to the usufruct of the woman's person, the right to either is not completed without the other. Hence, on the one hand, dower is said to be confirmed and made binding on the husband by consummation, or by its substitute, a valid retirement, or by death, which by terminating the marriage, puts an end to all the contingencies to which it is exposed; and on the other hand the woman becomes entitled to it as soon as she has surrendered her person". [*Digest of Mohammaden Law* by Baillie as quoted in *Fuzlunbi* v *K. Khader Vali* AIR 1980 SC 1730].

**Down payment.** The portion of a purchase price paid in cash or its equivalent at the time the sale agreement is executed. [Black's *Law Dictionary,* 8th Ed.].

A deposit against the total purchase price in a hire-purchase transaction.

> NOTE: The minimum percentage of the purchase price which must be paid as a down payment is controlled by the Government and is varied as an instrument of monetary policy. [Osborn & Grandage's *Concise Commercial Dictionary*].

**Dowry.** The money, goods or property that a woman brings to her husband in marriage. [Black's *Law Dictionary,* 8th Ed.].

▸ *Meaning under the Dowry Prohibition Act 1961, s. 2.* Any property or valuable security given or agreed to be given either directly or indirectly—(*a*) by one party to a marriage to the other party to the marriage; or (*b*) by the parents of either party to a marriage or by any other person, to either party to the marriage or to any other person; at or before or any time after the marriage in connection with the marriage of the said parties, but does not include dower or mahr in the case of persons to whom the Muslim Personal Law (Shariat) applies.

Giving or agreeing to give any property or valuable security before the marriage, at the time of marriage, and at any time after marriage falls within the definition of 'dowry'. There can be many other instances for payment of money or giving property as between the spouses. For example, some customary payments in connection with birth of a child or other ceremonies are prevalent in different societies. Such payments are not enveloped within the ambit of 'dowry'. [*Satvir Singh* v *State of Punjab* AIR 2001 SC 2828: JT 2001(8) SC 208: (2001)8 SCC 633].

**Dowry death.** Where the death of a woman is caused by any burns or bodily injury or occurs otherwise than under normal circumstances within seven years of her marriage and it is shown that soon before her death she was subjected to cruelty or harassment by her husband or any relative of her husband for, or inconnection with, any demand of dowry, such death shall be called 'dowry death'. [Indian Penal Code 1860, s. 304B].

**Draft.** In one sense it means an unconditional written order signed by one person (the drawer) directing another person (drawee or payer) to pay a certain sum of money on demand or at a definite time to a third person (the payee) or to bearer. [Black's *Law Dictionary,* 8th Ed.]. A cheque is a most common example of a draft.

In another sense it means a plan; outline; sketch; a writing or articles or propositions as framed or drawn up, but not adopted or enacted; to write or compose.

In yet another sense it may mean to recruit or select (someone) e.g. to draft someone into the armed services. [Black's *Law Dictionary,* 8th Ed.].

• **Demand draft** p. 247.
• **Sight draft** p. 797.

**Draftsman.** One who draws or prepares plans, designs, deeds, conveyances, etc. (Webster's *Comprehensive Dictionary*, International Edition); a person who draws or frames a legal document, such as a will, contract, or legislative bill. [Black's *Law Dictionary,* 7th Ed.]. It is also called drafter.

**Dramatic work.** 'Dramatic work' includes any piece of recitation, choreographic work or entertainment in dumb show, the scenic arrangement or acting, form of which is fixed in writing or otherwise but does not include a cinematograph film. [Copyright Act 1957, s. 2(*h*)].

**Drawback.** A Government allowance or refund on import duties when the importer reexports imported products rather than selling them domestically. [Black's *Law Dictionary,* 8th Ed.].

Drawback means the repayment of duties or taxes previously charged on commodities, from which they are relieved on exportation. For example, in the custom's laws of some countries an allowance is made by the Government upon the duties due on imported merchandise when the importer, instead of selling it within the country, re-exports it, and then the difference of the duty is refunded, if already paid. [*State of U.P.* v *Delhi Cloth Mills* (1991)1 SCC 454].

**Drawee.** The person or entity that a draft is directed to and that is requested to pay the amount stated on it. [Black's *Law Dictionary,* 8th Ed.].

▸ *Meaning under the Negotiable Instruments Act 1881, s. 7.* In a bill of exchange or cheque, the person directed to pay is called the drawee.

**Drawee in case of need.** When in the bill or in any endorsement thereon the name of any person is given in addition to the drawee to be resorted to in case of need, such person is called a "drawee in case of need". [Negotiable Instruments Act 1881, s. 7].

**Drawer.** One who directs a person or entity to pay a sum of money stated in an instrument, for example, a person who writes a cheque; the maker of a note or draft.

▸ *Meaning under the Negotiable Instruments Act 1881, s. 7.* The maker of a bill of exchange or cheque is called the drawer.

**Driver.** A person who steers or propels a vehicle; a person who herds animals. [Black's *Law Dictionary,* 8th Ed.].

▸ *Meaning under the Motor Vehicles Act 1988, s. 2(9).* 'Driver' includes, in relation to a motor vehicle which is drawn by another motor vehicle, the person who acts as a steersman of the drawn vehicle.

**Driving.** The act of directing the course of something, such as automobile or a herd of animals. [Black's *Law Dictionary,* 7th Ed.].

> NOTE: A person in the driving seat preparing to drive by switching on is driving. It is not necessary that the vehicle should be in motion. A person is obviously driving although he may be in traffic block or waiting at level crossing or at traffic lights or if he merely fills up with petrol. But if the driver leaves his seat, removes the ignition key and locks up the car for the night, he is quite clearly no longer driving or intending to drive the vehicle. [*Pinner* v *Everett* (1969)3 All ER 257].
>
> The Motor Vehicles Act makes a distinction between the user of a motor vehicle and the

driving of such vehicle. Driving a vehicle is nothing more than physical or manual act of propelling it. [*In re T.V. Moidu* AIR 1960 Mad 265].

- **Dangerous driving** p. 223.

**Driving licence.** 'Driving licence' means the licence issued by a competent authority authorising the person specified therein to drive, otherwise than as a learner, a motor vehicle or a motor vehicle of any specified class or description. [Motor Vehicles Act 1988, s. 2(10)].

**Droit administratif.** It is the law applied by the administrative courts of France which examine the acts of officials done in their official capacity.

**Drug.** A substance intended for use in the diagnosis, cure, treatment or prevention of disease; a natural or synthetic substance that alters one's perception or consciousness. [Black's *Law Dictionary,* 8th Ed.].

'Drug' includes "all medicines for internal or external use of human beings or animals and all substances intended to be used for or in the diagnosis, treatment, mitigation or prevention of disease in human beings or animals". [*Sk. Amir* v *The State of Maharashtra* AIR 1974 SC 469: (1974)3 SCR 89: (1974)4 SCC 210: 1974 SCC (Cri)) 379].

▸ *Meaning under the Drug and Cosmetics Act 1940, s. 3(b).* 'Drug' includes—(*i*) all medicines for internal or external use of human beings or animals and all substances intended to be used for or in the diagnosis, treatment, mitigation or prevention of any disease or disorder in human beings or animals, including preparations applied on human body for the purpose of repelling insects like mosquitoes; and (*ii*) such substances (other than food) intended to affect the structure or any function of the human body or intended to be used for the destruction of vermins or insects which cause disease in human beings or animals, as may be specified from time to time by the Central Government by notification in the Official Gazette; (*iii*) all substances intended for use as components of a drug including empty gelatin capsules; and (*iv*) such devices intended for internal or external use in the diagnosis, treatment, mitigation or prevention of disease or disorder in human beings or animals, as may be specified from time to time by the Central Government by notification in the Official Gazette, after consultation with the Board.

▸ *Meaning under the Drugs and Magic Remedies (Objectionable Advertisements) Act 1954, s. 2(b).* 'Drug' includes—(*i*) a medicine for the internal or external use of human beings or animals; (*ii*) any substance intended to be used for or in the diagnosis, cure, mitigation, treatment or prevention of disease in human beings or animals; (*iii*) any article, other than food, intended to affect or influence in any way the structure or any organic function of the body of human beings or animals; (*iv*) any article intended for use as a component of any medicine, substance or article, referred to in sub-cls. (*i*), (*ii*) and (*iii*).

NOTE: A person taking insulin is taking what, in ordinary parlance, would be called a drug in the sense of a medicine [*Armstrong* v *Clark* (1957)1 All ER 433].

Blood was held to be a drug within the meaning of s. 3(*b*) of the Drugs and Cosmetics Act 1940. [*Subodh S. Shah* v *Director, Food & Drugs* AIR 1997 Guj 83].

- **Dangerous drug** p. 223.
- **Narcotic drug** p. 598.

**Drunkenness.** A state of intoxication; inebriation; the condition resulting from a person's ingestion of excessive amounts of intoxicating liquors sufficient to affect the person's normal capacity for rational thought and conduct; a habitual state of intoxication. [Black's *Law Dictionary*, 8th Ed.].

NOTE: A sane man, who is delirious from fever, or who is so drunk that he cannot understand the terms of a contract, or form a rational judgment as to its effect on his interests cannot contract while drunkenness lasts. He is to be considered a person of unsound mind while drunkenness lasts; and a person who is usually of sound mind, but occasionally of unsound mind, cannot make a contract when he is of unsound mind. [Indian Contract Act 1872, s. 12].

Nothing is an offence which is done by a person who, at the time of doing it, is, by reason of intoxication, incapable of knowing the nature of the act, or that he is doing what is either wrong, or contrary to law, provided that the thing which intoxicated him was administered to him without his knowledge or against his will. [Indian Penal Code 1860, s. 85].

**Due.** The word 'due' has different meaning, and that meaning has to be put on it which fits in with the context. [*Rullia Ram Hakim Rai* v *S. Fateh Singh S. Shamsher Singh* AIR 1962 Punj 256 (FB)].

As adjective, it means owing and demandable; justly claimable; a debt or obligation; collectable; in arrears; outstanding; unpaid; unsettled; according to law; befitting; lawful.

As noun, it means accounts collectable; accounts outstanding; balance to pay; lawful claim; liability; obligation; outstanding debt; overdue payment.

A debt or other obligation is due when it is legally enforceable, that is, when the creditor has a right to demand payment and to enforce collection. [*Custodian General* v *Harnam Singh* AIR 1957 Punj 58].

▸ *Meaning under the Telegraph Act 1885, s. 7B.* The demand raised under the bills against a subscriber is not due from the subscriber if a protest is raised against the same by him and the dues have not been finally determined by arbitrator. "Due" means in this context, 'owing a debt', which has in itself the underlying concept of the debt having been rightly and properly determined by an arbitrator appointed under the Act. [*Orissa Vegetable Oil* v *Union of India* AIR 1990 Ori 51].

**Due and payable.** 'Due' and 'payable' are not convertible terms. A debt is said to be due as soon as it has existence as a debt, though it may be payable at a future date. [*Munsif Jahan* v *Rajendra Prasad* AIR 1946 Oudh 226].

**Due course of law.** The regular and customary administration of law through the legal system; due process. [Black's *Law Dictionary*, 7th Ed.].

The conduct of legal proceedings according to established rules and principles for the protection and enforcement of private rights, including notice and the right to a fair hearing before a tribunal with the power to decide the case. [Black's *Law Dictionary*, 8th Ed.].

To read the words 'due course of law' as merely equivalent to the word 'legally' is to deprive them of the force and significance they carry. 'Due course of law' means the regular, normal process and effect of the law operating on a matter which has been placed before it for adjudication. That is the primary and natural meaning of the phrase, though it may be applied in a secondary sense to the other proceedings held under the direct authority of law, *e.g.*, revenue or taxes collected in due course of law. [*Rudrappa Bin Sankappa* v *Narasing Rao* ILR 29 Bom 213].

**Due diligence.** The diligence reasonably expected from, and ordinarily exercised by; a person who seeks to satisfy a legal requirement or to discharge an obligation [Black's *Law Dictionary*, 7th Ed.].

NOTE: An obligation to exercise due diligence is indistinguishable from an obligation to exercise reasonable care. [*Riverstone Meat Co.* v *Lancashire Shipping Co. Ltd.* (1960)1 All ER 193].

**Due inquiry.** 'Due inquiry' involves giving to the accused party a fair opportunity of meeting the accusation. The tribunal should permit the accused to call evidence in support of his contention. [*General Medical Council* v *Spackman* (1943)2 All ER 337].

**Due process of law.** 'Due' means what is just and proper according to the circumstances of each particular case. The best description of the expression 'due process of law' would be to say that it means in each particular case such an exercise of the powers of Government as the settled maxims of law permit and sanction and under such safeguards for the protection of individual rights as those maxims prescribed for the class of cases to which one in question belongs. [*Gopalan* v *State of Madras* AIR 1950 SC 27: 1950 SCR 88].

**Dues.** Owing or payable as debts; what one owes; an obligatory payment.

• **Harbour dues** p. 405.

**Duly.** Properly, regularly or in due manner, according to law. [*L.I.C. of India* v *D.J. Bahadur* (1981)1 SCC 315: 1981 SCC (L&S) 111: (1981)1 SCR 1083: 1981 Lab LJ 1: (1981)58 FJR 51].

'Duly' in s. 510, Cr. P.C. means properly. [*State of Orissa* v *Kaushalya* AIR 1965 Ori 38].

According to *Concise Oxford Dictionary*, the word 'duly' means rightly, properly, fitly, and according to the Stroud's *Judicial Dictionary* means "done in due course and according to law". The word 'duly' is very significant and excludes any arbitrary exercise of power. [*H.L. Trehan* v *Union of India* AIR 1989 SC 568: (1989)1 SCC 764: (1989)1 Comp LJ 191].

**Duly appointed.** Appointed in accordance with the provisions of the act or with the rules or regulations made thereunder. [Employees' State Insurance Act 1948, s. 2(7)].

**Duly authorised agent.** Agent having not only expressed but implied authorisation also.

▸ *Meaning under the Motor Vehicles Act 1939, s. 110A(1)(c) [now s. 166(1)(d) of the Motor Vehicles Act 1988].* The expression means person not only expressly authorised but also a person having implied authority. [*New India Assurance Co.* v *Punjab Roadways* AIR 1964 Punj 235: 1963 Cr LJ 572].

▸ *Meaning under the Limitation Act 1908, s. 19, Expl. II [now s. 19 of the Limitation Act 1963].* 'Duly authorised' would include duly authorised either by the action of the party indebted or by force of law or order of the court. [*Sahebzada Mohammad Kamgarh Shah* v *Jagdish Chandra Deo Dhalal Deb* (1960)3 SCR 604: AIR 1960 SC 953].

> NOTE: The authority of an agent making an acknowledgment need not always be express; it may be implied and where it is so, it is capable of being presumed from the attendant circumstances. [*Chandanbai* v *Jagjiwanlal* AIR 1958 Raj 110].
>
> The authority of an agent may be express or implied. [Indian Contract Act 1872, s. 186]. An authority is said to be express when it is given by words spoken or written. An authority is said to be implied when it is so inferred from the circumstances of the case; and things spoken or written, or the ordinary course of dealing, may be accounted circumstances of the case. [*Ibid*, s. 187].

**Duly stamped.** An instrument can be said to be 'duly stamped' only if it bears stamps of the amount and description in accordance with the law of the State concerned. The law includes not only the Act but also the rules framed under the Act. [*New Central Jute Mills Co. Ltd.* v *State of West Bengal* AIR 1963 SC 1307: (1964)1 SCR 535: (1964)1 SCJ 195].

▸ *Meaning under the Indian Stamp Act 1899, s. 2(11).* Duly stamped, as applied to an instrument, means that the instrument bears an adhesive or impressed stamp of not less than the proper amount and that such stamp has been affixed or used in accordance with the law for time being in force in India.

> NOTE: If a document bears a stamp of improper description, then it is not duly stamped.

**Dumping.** Placing goods on the market in large quantities at unprofitable prices or prices lower than those charged elsewhere.

> NOTE: Anti-dumping duties are imposed to limit or discourage the importation and sale of goods in unfair competition with home-produced goods.

**Dunnage.** Materials used in the stowage of cargo to prevent shifting or damage or to build up or separate the cargo.

**Duopoly.** In economics, this means the situation in which two independent firms are selling an identical product in the same market.

**Duplicate.** A copy of the original; a counterpart; one of two originals of the same tenor; a document essentially the same as some other document, having precisely the like operation and effect.

**Duplicate originals.** When the counterparts of a document are made and delivered by each party to the other, they are usually spoken of as "duplicate originals".

**Durante minore aetate.** During minority.

**Duress.** Any intimidation or restraint on action or anything tending to restrain free and voluntary action. Generally speaking, duress may be said to exist whenever one, by the unlawful act of another, is induced to make a contract or to perform some other act under circumstances which deprive him of the exercise of free will.

By duress is meant the compulsion under which a person acts through fear of personal suffering, as from injury to body or from confinement, actual or threatened. [Halsbury's *Laws of England,* 4th Ed., vol. 9, para 297, p. 172].

> NOTE: An Act done under duress has not in general the legal effect which it would otherwise have. A deed or contract executed under duress may be avoided afterwards.
>
> Duress is akin to coercion within the meaning of s. 15 of the Indian Contract Act 1872.
>
> Duress must be a question of degree, and may begin from a gentle form of pressure to physical violence, accompanied by threats of death. [*Griffiths* v *Griffiths* 1944 IR 35].

**Durgah.** Grave of a Mahomedan saint; graveyard of Mahomedans.

▸ *Meaning under the Durgah Khawaja Saheb Act 1955, s. 2(c).* Durgah means the institution known as Durgah Khawaja Saheb, Ajmer, and includes the premises called the Durgah Sharif with all buildings connected therewith, together with all additions thereto or all alterations thereof which may hereafter be made from time to time.

**During.** The word 'during' is nothing more than the Latin *durante;*'during coverture' means after the commencement and before the termination of the coverture. [*Archer* v *Kelly* (1860)1 Drew & Sm 300].

**Dutiable goods.** Any goods which are chargeable to duty and on which duty has not been paid. [Customs Act 1962, s. 2(14)].

▸ *Meaning under the Medicinal and Toilet Preparations (Excise Duties) Act 1955.* 'Dutiable goods' means the medicinal and toilet preparations specified in the Schedule as being subject to the duties of excise levied under this Act.

▸ *Meaning under the Land Customs Act 1924, s. 2(d).* 'Dutiable goods' means any article on which duty of land customs is leviable by virtue of a notification issued under s. 5 of the Indian Tariff Act 1894.

**Duty.** In its application to obligation, it means accountability; allegiance; commitment; dictate of conscience; indebtedness; moral necessity; moral obligation; obedience; responsibility.

Duty connotes obligation. It denotes that one cannot refuse to perform the act but is bound to do it. The word is not appropriate in the context of a discretion to do a particular thing. [*Narayana Chetty* v *Venkata Reddi* AIR 1963 AP 452].

> NOTE: According to Stroud's *Judicial Dictionary,* 5th Ed., if by a statute a duty is laid on any person, every member of the public has the right to have that duty performed, and anyone damaged by its non-performance is entitled to maintain a civil action for damages against the person on whom the duty is cast. The word 'duty' excludes any arbitrary exercise of power. [*H.L. Trehan* v *Union of India* AIR 1989 SC 568].

In its application as tax, it means assessment; exaction; excise; imposition; impost; revenue; tariff; taxation; toll; levy.


- **Active duty** p. 34.
- **Active operations duty** p. 34.
- **Customs duties** p. 215.
- **Death duty** p. 230.
- **Estate duty** p. 320.
- **Excise duty** p. 327.
- **Fails to resume duty** p. 338.
- **Legal duty** p. 525.
- **Probate duty** p. 691.
- **Special duty** p. 804.
- **Under colour of duty** p. 862.


**Dwell.** 'To dwell', 'dwelling' are expressions nearly, but not quite, equivalent to 'reside', 'residence'; for to dwell connotes more definitely than 'reside', a place where a person lives and sleeps. [*A-G* v *McLearn* 1 H&C 761].

> NOTE: A person may dwell in two or more places. [*Butler* v *Ablewhite* 28 LJCP 292].
>
> A person having no permanent place of abode dwells at the place where he may temporarily be. [*Alexander* v *Jones* 35 LJ Ex 78].

A corporation can dwell only where it carries on business. [*Taylor* v *Crowland Gas Co.* 24 LJ Ex 233].

**Dwelling house.** The house or other structure in which a person lives; a residence or abode; the house and all buildings attach to or connected with the house; a building, a part of building, a tent, a mobile home, or any enclosed space, that is, used or intended for use as a human habitation. [Black's *Law Dictionary,* 8th Ed.].

"Dwelling house" includes any building or part of it which is used as a dwelling, and the fact that part of the premises comprised in a dwelling house is used as a shop or office or for business, trade or professional purposes does not prevent it from being a dwelling house. [Halsbury's *Laws of England,* 4th Ed., vol. 10, para 83, p. 53].

The term includes not only the structure or building but also adjacent buildings, curtilages, garden, courtyard, orchard and all that is necessary for the convenient occupation of the house, but not that which is only for the personal use and convenience of the occupier. [*Kalipada* v *Tulsidas* AIR 1960 Cal 467]. It includes the accommodation for servants, officers and guests of the family. [*Kalipada* v *Tulsidas* supra].

NOTE: In determining whether a house is a dwelling house, it has to be found out whether the house in question was used by the members of the family for residential purpose. The dwelling house would include not merely the structure where the members of the family actually reside or used to reside, but it would include all appurtenances, that means, if there is a courtyard which was used by the members, such a courtyard, if there is another structure, as for example, a kitchen or cowshed or a shed for garage, if those were or are used by the members of the family as parts of their residential house, all such parts would also be included within the word 'dwelling house.' [*Manik Lal Singh* v *Gouri Shankar* AIR 1968 Cal 245].

**Dying declaration.** A statement of a person who dies. The "dying declaration" is a statement by a person as to the cause of his death or as to any of the circumstances of the transaction which resulted in his death. [*Tapinder Singh* v *State of Punjab* AIR 1970 SC 1566: (1970)2 SCC 113: 1970 SCC (Cri)) 328: (1971)1 SCR 599].

NOTE: They are constantly admitted in evidence. The principle of this exception to the general rule is founded partly on the lawful situation of the dying person, which is considered to be as powerful over his conscience as the obligation of an oath, and partly on a supposed absence of interest in a person on the verge of the next world, which dispenses with the necessity of cross-examination. But before such declarations can be admitted in evidence against a prisoner, it must be satisfactorily proved that the deceased, at the time of making them, was conscious of the danger, and had given up all hopes of recovery.

Contained in s. 32(1), Evidence Act it is an exception to hearsay rule and makes admissible the statement of a person who dies, whether the death is homicidal or suicidal, provided the statement relates to, cause of death, or exhibits circumstances leading to death. [*Sharad Birdhichand Sarda* v *State of Maharashtra* AIR 1984 SC 1622].

A dying declaration made to a police officer during the course of investigation is taken out of the limitation imposed by sub-sec. (2) of s. 162 of the Criminal Procedure Code. It is not possible to sustain any general proposition of law that a dying declaration as a piece of evidence as compared with other pieces of evidence has any inherent weakness in contradistinction with other pieces of evidence, and indeed it is to be appraised on the same principle on which other evidence is weighed and sifted. [*Kishan Singh* v *State* AIR 1963 Punj 170].

**Dying intestate.** The words 'dying intestate' merely mean dying in a state of intestacy. It merely refers to the status of the deceased. [*Duni Chand* v *Anarkali* AIR 1946 PC 173].

"Dying intestate" covers both situations of dying either without having made any will or having made an invalid will. [*Manshan* v *Tej Ram* AIR 1980 SC 558: 1980 SCC (Supp) 367].

NOTE: The words 'dying intestate' in s. 8 of the Hindu Succession Act 1956, are a mere description of the status of the deceased and have no reference, and are not intended to have any reference, to the time of the death of a Hindu male. [*Hiralal Roy* v *Kumud Behari Roy* AIR 1957 Cal 571].

# Ee

**E. & O. insurance.** Errors-and-omissions insurance. It is an agreement to indemnify for loss sustained because of a mistake or oversight by the insured—though not for loss due to the insured's intentional wrongdoing. While this insurance does not cover the insured's intentional wrongdoing, it may cover an employee's intentional, but unauthorised, wrongdoing. [Black's *Law Dictionary*, 8th Ed.].

**E. & O.E.** Errors and omissions excepted. [*Vernon Metal & Produce Co.* v *Joseph & Bros. Co.* 209 NYS 6, 11]. When written at the foot of the invoices or accounts, it indicates that they are open to correction in case of detection of any mistake therein.

**Each and every.** In Collins *Dictionary of the English Language*, the meaning of 'each' is given as "every (one) of two or more considered individually"; and 'every' means "each one (of the class specified), without exception". In Stroud's *Judicial Dictionary of Words and Phrases* the true meaning of 'every' is "each one of all". [*Rishyashringa Jewellery Ltd.* v *Stock Exchange* (1995)6 SCC 714: JT 1995(7) SC 602: AIR 1996 SC 480: (1996)85 Comp Cas 479].

**Earn.** To acquire by labour, service or performance; do something that entitles one to a reward or result, whether it is received or not; achieve by continued effort; get by effort; succeed in reaching.

**Earned income.** Money derived from one's own labour or active participation; earnings from services. [Black's *Law Dictionary*, 8th Ed.].

Income (*e.g.* wages, salaries, or fees) derived from labour, professional service, or entrepreneurship as opposed to income derived from invested capital (*e.g.* rents, dividends, interest). [Black's *Law Dictionary*, 5th Ed.].

In its application to taxation, the term "earned income" conveys the concept of income accruing to the assessee. [*E.D. Sassoon and Co. Ltd.* v *The Commissioner of Income Tax, Bombay* AIR 1954 SC 470: (1955)1 SCR 313: 1954 SCJ 771: (1954)26 ITR 27].

NOTE: The test as to whether a taxpayor's income under a settlement is "earned income is whether in the hands of the recipient it is income earned as a reward for services. [*White* v *Franklin* (1965)1 WLR 492]. It includes remuneration of a trustee out of the trust funds [*Dale* v *I.R.C.* (1954) AC 11] and shares issued on a restricted basis by a company to its employees as an incentive. [*Recknell* v *I.R.C.* (1952) WN 267].

**Earned leave.** Leave earned by a person by virtue of the time spent by him on actual service. [*Union of India* v *Gurman Singh* AIR 1982 SC 1265: (1982)2 SCC 314: (1982)2 SCR 700].

**Earnest.** A nominal payment or token act that serves as a pledge or a sign of good faith; something of value given by a buyer to a seller to bind a bargain; a token of what is to come; pledge.

NOTE: It is somewhat difficult to give a precise definition of the word 'earnest'. Certain characteristics, however, seem to be clear. An earnest must be a tangible thing and that thing must be given at the moment at which the contract is concluded, because it is something given to bind the contract. The thing must be given in token of good faith and as a guarantee that he will fulfil his contract and subject to the terms that if, owing to his default, the contract goes off, it will be forfeited. If, on the other hand, the contract is fulfilled, the earnest may serve a further purpose and operate as part payment. [*Farr, Smith & Co.* v *Messers Ltd*. (1928)1 KB 297; *Kumar Chiranjit* v *Har Swarup* AIR 1926 PC 1].

The object of giving earnest is to make the contract binding; and in its essential nature, it is not a contribution made in the course of the performance of the contract as that is the purpose of part payment. If the property is resold for less than the price for which the vendee had undertaken to purchase it, then the vendor must give credit for the amount of the deposit received from the vendee. [*Puran Chand* v *Official Liquidator* AIR 1960 Punj 51].

Giving earnest or earnings money is a mode of signifying assent to a contract of sale or the like, by giving to the vendor a nominal as a token that the parties are in earnest or have made up their minds. [*Maula Bux* v *Union of India* (1970)1 SCR 928: (1970)2 SCJ 249: AIR 1970 SC 1955 referring to Earl Jowitt in *Dictionary of English Law*].

The following principles emerge regarding "earnest": (1) it must be given at the moment at which the contract is concluded; (2) it represents a guarantee that the contract will be fulfilled or, in other words, "earnest" is given to bind the contract; (3) it is part of the purchase price when the transaction is carried out; (4) it is forfeited when the transaction falls through by reason of the default or failure of the purchaser; (5) unless there is anything to the contrary in the terms of contract, on default committed by the buyer, the seller is entitled to forfeit the earnest. [*Shri Hanuman Cotton Mills* v *Tata Air Craft Ltd*. AIR 1970 SC 1986: (1970)3 SCR 127: (1969)3 SCC 522].

**Earnest money.** A deposit paid by a prospective buyer to show a good faith intention to complete the transaction, and ordinarily forfeited if the buyer defaults. [Black's *Law Dictionary*, 7th Ed.].

NOTE: Earnest money is not the same as deposit of a portion of the price, but has a two-fold character. It is part payment of the price, if the transaction is completed. But it is also an earnest or guarantee that the contract shall be performed. The right of the vendee to the refund of the sum deposited as part of the purchase price does not necessarily extend to a right to the refund of the earnest money also. [*T. Ranganayakamma* v *S.R. Subudhi* AIR 1955 Ori 20].

Giving earnest money is a mode of signifying assent to a contract of sale or the like, by giving to the vendor a nominal as a token that the parties are in earnest or have made up their minds. [*Maula Bux* v *Union of India* (1970)1 SCR 928: (1970)2 SCJ 249: AIR 1970 SC 1955].

The "earnest money" is a part of the purchase price when the transaction gets through and the same is forfeited when the transaction fails through by reason of default or failure on the part of the vendee. [*H.U.D.A.* v *Kewal Krishan Goel* AIR 1996 SC 1981: (1996)4 SCC 249: JT 1996(6) SC 62].

**Earnings.** That which is earned; the price of services performed; the fruit or reward of labour or the price received for personal services, whether in money or chattels; the gains of a person derived from his services or labour.

Revenue gained from labour or services, from the investment of capital, or from assets. [Black's *Law Dictionary*, 8th Ed.].

The full sum for which the man is engaged to work. [*Abram Coal Co.* v *Southern* (1903) AC 306].

"Earnings" in respect of employees means the amount of money received during a period for labour services. In respect of a company, it refers to profits after deduction of direct taxation of profits.

"Earnings" meant money or money's worth, *e.g.* rent, food and clothes. [*Noel* v *Redruth Foundry Co.* (1896)1 QB 453]. A workman allowed to occupy a house belonging to his employer and the use of uniforms given by the employer must be considered as an additional emolument to be taken into account in estimating his earnings. [*Great Northern Ry. Co.* v *Dawson* (1905)1 KB 331].

**Easement.** An easement is a right annexed to land, to utilise other land of different ownership in a particular manner (not involving the taking of any part of the natural produce of that land or any part of its soil) or to prevent the owner of the other land from utilising his land in a particular manner. [Halsbury's *Laws of England*, 4th Ed., vol. 14, para 1, p. 14].

An easement is a privilege without profit which the owner of a neighbouring tenant hath of another existing in respect of their several tenements. [Gale on *Easement*, 16th Ed., para 1-01].

An easement is a right which the owner or occupier of certain land possesses, as such, for the beneficial enjoyment of that land, to do and continue to do something, or to prevent and continue to prevent something being done, in or upon, or in respect of, certain other land not his own. [*Dukhi Mullah* v *Halway* ILR 23 Cal 55].

An easement is a burden upon the proprietary right of the owner in fee. It may consist, either in restraining, for the benefit of the dominant tenement, certain uses which its owner might otherwise make of the servient land, or, in compelling him to submit to uses of that land by others, which are not incompatible with his retaining the right of property. [*Hawkins* v *Rutter* (1892)1 QB 668].

NOTE: Easement postulates the existence of a dominant tenement and a servient tenement. This right must be exercised for the beneficial enjoyment of the dominant heritage. Where the parties are claiming not the rights for the beneficial enjoyment of any dominant heritage but purely personal rights, there can be no right of easement. [*Ram Nandan Singh* v *Ram Kishan* AIR 1958 Pat 571].

Easement includes a right not arising from contract, by which one person is entitled to remove and appropriate for his own profit any part of the soil belonging to another or anything growing in, or attached to, or subsisting upon, the land of another. [Limitation Act 1963, s. 2(*f*)].

*Essential characteristics.* There are four essential characteristics of an easement. They are—(1) there must be a dominant and a servient tenement, (2) easement must accommodate the dominant tenement, (3) dominant and servient owners must be different persons, and (4) a right over land cannot amount to an easement unless it is capable of forming the subject-matter of a grant. As regards the second condition, there must exist the required connection between the two. [*Powell* v *Maddison* (1955)3 All ER 667].

- **Abandonment of easement** p. 2.
- **Apparent easement.** An apparent easement is one the existence of which is shown by some permanent sign which, upon careful inspection by a competent person, would be visible to him. [Indian Easements Act 1882, s. 5].
- **Continuous easement.** A continuous easement is one whose enjoyment is, or may be, continual without the act of man. [Indian Easements Act 1882, s. 5].
- **Customary easement** p. 214.
- **Discontinuous easement.** Discontinuous easement is one that needs the act of a man for its enjoyment. [Indian Easements Act 1882, s. 5].
- **Equitable easements.** Any easement, liberty, or privilege over or affecting land and being merely an equitable interest. [Law of Property Act 1925, s. 2].

  An implied easement created by equity when adjacent lands have been created out of a larger tract. [Black's *Law Dictionary*, 8th Ed.].
- **Implied easement** p. 433.
- **Negative easement.** A negative easement is one, such as a right of light, which gives the owner of land a right to stop his neighbour doing something on the neighbour's own land. [*Phipps* v *Pears* (1964)2 All ER 35].
- **Non-apparent easement.** An easement may be either apparent or non-apparent. An apparent easement is one the existence of which is shown by some permanent sign which, upon careful inspection by a competent person, would be visible to him. A non-apparent easement is one that has no such sign. [Indian Easements Act 1882, s. 5].
- **Positive easement.** Positive easement is one, such as a right of way, which gives the owner of land a right upon himself to do something on or to his neighbour's land. [*Phipps* v *Pears* (1964)2 All ER 35].
- **Quasi-easements.** An easement like right occurring when both tracts of land are owned by the same person; an obligation or license that relates to land but that is not a true easement. [Black's *Law Dictionary*, 8th Ed.].

Right in the nature of easement but not possessing all the essential qualities, is sometimes called as quasi easement.

The term 'quasi-easements' has been applied to those easements which, not being easements of absolute necessity, come into existence for the first time by presumed grant or operation of law on a severance of two or more tenements formerly united in the sole or joint possession or ownership of one or more persons. The law relating to quasi-easements arising on a division of property is based on the same principle, which governs the conveyance of a part of the tenement held by a single owner or possessor. The principle is that on the grant by the owner of an entire property or a part of that property there will pass to the grantee all those continuous and apparent easements, termed quasi-easements which have been and are at the time of the grant in use for the benefit of the part granted. [*Bhola Nath* v *Radha Nath* AIR 1924 Cal 844: 51 Cal 789].

**Easement of light.** An easement of light is a right which a person may acquire, as the owner or occupier of a building with windows and apertures, to prevent the owner or occupier of an adjoining piece of land from building or placing upon the latter's land anything which has the effect of 'illegally' obstructing or obscuring the light coming to the building of the owner of the easement. [Halsbury's *Laws of England*, 4th Ed., vol. 14, para 211, p. 100; *Colls* v *Home & Colonial Stores Ltd.* (1904) AC 179].

NOTE: There is a rule that a person should have at least 45° from the zenith, that the angular height of the obstructing building should be less than 45°, or that the angle of incidence of light over the obstructing building to the 'centre' part of his window should not be less than 45° from the perpendicular above the point of incidence. But this is not a positive rule of law, but a circumstance which the court may take into consideration. And this is specially valuable when the proof of the obstruction is not definite or satisfactory. Under *ordinary* circumstances, the fact that forty-five degrees of sky are left unobstructed by a building *opposite* to the light is *prima facie* evidence that there is not likely to be *material* injury. If the building is not higher than the distance between the window and the building, that is, if the angle of incidence of light over the building to the centre of the window is not more than 45°, the court will not interfere by injunction, unless it is proved that the building is likely to cause material injury to the plaintiff. [*City of London Brewery Co.* v *Tenant* LR 9 Ch App 212, 220].

**Easement of necessity.** An easement of necessity is an easement without which the property retained cannot be used at all, and not one merely necessary to the reasonable enjoyment of the property. [*Union Lighterage Co.* v *London Graving* (1902)2 Ch 557].

NOTE: Easements of necessity or quasi-easements, as they are called, are founded on an implied grant or reservation. Such easements arise out of disposition made by an owner of several heritages, *viz.*, cases of transfer, partition etc. The right does not arise in every case in which the property becomes useless without an easement being raised in favour of the party claiming it. The right is implied only in cases of severance of tenements. In order to filed a claim to an easement of necessity, unity of ownership of the dominant and servient tenement at some time or other is essential. [*Nani Gopal* v *Kshitish Chandra* AIR 1952 Cal 108: ILR (1950)1 Cal 618].

**Eating house.** House in which meals are supplied; restaurant.

'Eating house' means a restaurant where meals or food taken at one time may be had by the customers, and such an 'eating house' is distinguishable from a place where food is manufactured, sold, stocked, distributed or exhibited for sale. [*Sen Mahasay* v *Corporation of Calcutta* AIR 1966 Cal 203: 69 CWN 517: 1966 Cr LJ 525].

**Eaves.** The edge of a roof projecting over the walls of a house; the underside of a projecting roof. They prevent the rain water from running down the wall while coming to the ground.

**Ecclesiastical law.** That part of the law which regulates the administration and the rights and obligations of the Church of England.

**Ecology.** A branch of biology dealing with living organism's habits, modes of life and relations to their surroundings.

**E-Commerce.** The practice of buying and selling goods and services through online consumer services on the Internet. The 'e' as used before 'commerce' is a shortened form of 'electronic'.

**Econometrics.** The systematic analysis of economic data with the aid of a computer, or by mathematical or statistical methods.

**Economic growth.** Expansion in the national income or total volume of production of goods and services of a country.

**Economic planning.** It refers to the State planning to secure the optimum allocation of a country's resources in order to achieve economic objectives at which the Government and the people of the country are aiming.

NOTE: There is a Planning Commission in India set up in 1950 to look after this. They have prepared six plans since 1952. Entry No. 20 in the Concurrent List of the Seventh Schedule to the Constitution of India reads as "Social and Economic Planning"; but the Planning Commission was set up not under this.

**Economic sanction.** Measures for the enforcement of international obligations by means of economic and financial pressure.

**Edible.** Fit to be eaten as food [*Chandausi Oil Mills* v *Sales Tax Commissioner* 1960 All LJ 491]; fit or suitable to be eaten.

**Edible oilseed.** An oilseed which is edible; cotton seed is not edible oilseed. [*Girdharmal Kapur Chand* v *Dev Raj* AIR 1963 SC 1587].

NOTE: A sale of two or more edible oils mixed together is sale of an adulterated article. [*Nathoo Lal* v *State* 1981 FAJ 487 (488) All].

**Edict.** A proclamation, prohibition or command; an order proclaimed by authority. A law promulgated.

**Edition.** The putting forth of the work at successive periods, and whether that is done by movable type or by stereotype does not make any substantial difference. [*Reade* v *Bentley* 27 LJ Ch 254, *per* WOOD, V.C.].

One of the particular forms in which a text is published; a copy of a book in a particular form; a whole number of copies of a book, newspaper, etc., issued at one time.

**Editor.** One who edits; one who directs the content and writing of a newspaper or a particular section of one; the head of a department of a publishing house.

▸ *Meaning under the Press and Registration of Books Act 1867, s. 1(1).* The term 'editor' is defined to mean a person who controls the selection of the matter that is published in a newspaper. The name of that person has to be printed on the copy of the newspaper. [*State of Maharashtra* v *Dr. R.B. Chowdhary* AIR 1968 SC 110: (1967)3 SCR 708: 1968 Cr LJ 95; *Haji C.H. Mohammad Koya* v *T.K.S.M.A. Muthukoya* AIR 1979 SC 154: (1979)1 SCR 664: (1979)2 SCC 8].

**Educated unemployed youth.** It has a definite legal connotation. It denotes a class of citizens who after completing their education are faced with unemployment. A person who is still pursuing his studies in a university is not an educated unemployed youth. [*Bishnu Ram Borah* v *Parag Saikia* AIR 1984 SC 898: (1984)2 SCC 488: (1984)1 SCR 825].

**Education.** The action or process of educating or of being educated; a stage of such process; the knowledge and development resulting from an educational process; the field of study that deals mainly with methods of teaching and learning in schools.

In one sense the word 'education' may be used to describe any form of training, any manner by which physical or mental aptitude, which man may desire to have for the purpose of his work, may be acquired. [*Chartered Insurance Institute* v *London Corporation* (1957)2 All ER 638].

Education means teaching or training up the persons in general learning other than teaching or training up for a business or profession. [*Ramchand* v *Malkapur Municipality* AIR 1970 Bom 154].

▸ *Meaning under the Bombay Rents, Hotel and Lodging House Rates Control Act 1947, s. 6(1).* The term 'education' does not refer to cultural activities or recreational activities relating to fraternising among the members of a club by playing indoor or outdoor games or otherwise as amounting to education. Such activities cannot lead to the conclusion that the premises were let for the purpose of education. [*Haji Ismail Vali Mohmad* v *Sports Club in the name of Union Sports Club* AIR 1992 SC 1855: (1992)1 SCC 315: 1992 AIR SCW 2095: JT 1991(4) SC 410].

▸ *Meaning under the Income Tax Act 1961, s. 2(15).* The sense in which the word 'education' has been used is the systematic instruction, schooling or training given to the young in preparation for the work of life. [*Sole Trustee, Loka Shikshana Trust* v *CIT* (1975)101 ITR 234 (SC): AIR 1976 SC 10: (1976)1 SCC 254: 1976 Tax LR 1: 1976 SCC (Tax) 14].

It involves the process of training which helps develop knowledge, skill, mind and character of students by normal schooling [*Sole Trustee, Loka Shikshana Trust* v *CIT* (supra)] in keeping with the sole aim of education which is to create a well-educated, healthy, young generation imbued with a rational progressive outlook on life. [*The University of Delhi* v *Ram Nath* AIR 1963 SC 1873, *per* P.B. Gajendragadkar, J.].

NOTE: The word 'education' has a restricted meaning for the purpose of the Act.

**Educational institution.** The words are of very wide import and would include a university also. There is a good deal in common between educational institutions which are not universities and those which are universities. Both teach students and both have teachers for the purpose. But a university grants degrees, while other educational institutions cannot. [*Azeez Basha* v *Union of India* AIR 1968 SC 662: (1968)1 SCA 357: (1968)2 SCJ 299].

**Effective control.** The control of the manner of doing the particular act from which the particular tort resulted. [*National Shipping Co.* v *Haripada* AIR 1958 Cal 597].

**Effective representation.** The words 'effective representation' mean a real and meaningful opportunity to an aggrieved person to explain his case before the authority seized with his matter.

The words 'effective representation' appearing in Art. 22(5) of the Constitution of India must be construed so as to provide a real and meaningful opportunity to the detenue to explain his case to the detaining authority in his representation. [*Kamla Kanhaiyalal Khushalani* v *State of Maharashtra* AIR 1981 SC 814: (1981)2 SCR 459: (1981)1 SCC 748: 1981 Cr LJ 353: 1981 SCC (Cri) 287].

**Effects.** Assets; belongings; estate, holdings; legal estate; movable property; personal property; goods and chattels; a person's property; the entire personal estate of a testator unless restrained by the context within narrower limits.

▸ *Meaning under the Merchant Shipping Act 1958, s. 3(10).* 'Effects', in relation to a seaman, includes clothes and documents.

**Egalite de droit.** Formal or legal equality. [*K.C. Vasanth Kumar* v *State of Karnataka* AIR 1986 SC 1495, 1527].

**Egalite de fait.** Practical or factual equality. [*K.C. Vasanth Kumar* v *State of Karnataka* AIR 1986 SC 1495, 1527].

**Ei incumbit probatio qui dicit, non qui negat.** The proof lies upon him who affirms, not upon him who denies.

**Either.** One or other. [*Re Pickworth* 68 LJ Ch 328].

One of the two and not both. [*Re Pickworth* (1899)1 Ch 642].

'Either in the preceding sub-sections' in s. 17(3) of the Land Acquisition Act 1894, means each of the two preceding sub-sections. [*Sadruddin Suleman* v *J.H. Patwardhan* AIR 1965 Bom 224].

**Either ...... or.** The words 'either ...... or' indicate two separate sets of circumstances. [*Govindram Ramprasad* v *Assessing Sales Tax Authority* AIR 1958 MP 16].

**Ejectment.** Dispossession; an action for the recovery of possession of real property and damages and costs.

Ejectment is the mixed action at Common Law to recover the possession of land (which is real), and damages and costs for the wrongful withholding of the land (which are personal).

NOTE: Mere temporary non-occupation does not amount to ejectment. [*Mohammad Amir Ahmed* v *Deoki* 1963 All LJ 338].

**Ejusdem generis.** The full Latin maxim is: *clausula generalis de residue non ea complecitur, quae non ejusdem sint generis cum, iis qua speciatim dicta fuerint*. When particular words forming part of the same class or same category are followed by general words then the general words must be construed in the context of the particular words. This is called *ejusdem generis* rule. [Maxwell on *Interpretation of Statutes*, 12th Ed., p. 229; *Sureswar Dutta* v *State of W.B.* (1979)1 CLJ 565, 567; *D. Mallaiah* v *Government of A.P.* (1986)1 Andh LT 253].

NOTE: Where particular things named (in a document) have same common characteristic which constitutes them a genus and the general words (following an enumeration of specific things or classes of things) can be properly regarded as in the nature of a sweeping clause designed to guard against accidental omissions, then the rule of *ejusdem generis* will apply, and the general words will be restricted to things of the same nature as those which have been already mentioned; but the absence of a common genus between the enumerated words will not necessarily prevent a restricted construction of the general words if justified by the context. The *ejusdem generis* construction will be assisted if the general scope or language of the deed, or the particular clause, indicates that the general words should receive a limited construction will produce some unforeseen loss to the grantor. [Halsbury's *Laws of England*, 4th Ed., vol. 12, para 1526, p. 651].

The rule of *ejusdem generis* is a rule of construction and not a rule of substantive law and is hardly applicable where the intention is clear. If a general word is added to specific words, the general word would take its colour from the specific words, and obviously when there are no specific words in the clause the rule of *ejusdem generis* will not apply. [*Printer's House Private Ltd.* v *Misri Lal* AIR 1970 Punj 1].

Example: Section 2(*a*) Gujarat Tax on Luxurious (Hotel and Lodging Houses) Act 1977 defines charges for lodging to include "charges for air conditioning, telephone, television, radio, music, extra-beds *and the like*". The expression *"and the like"* must be construed *ejusdem generis*. The genus or the class of items envisaged by the preceding words not having been exhaustive of the genus or the class, the words "and the like" have been used so as to bring any other item of the same class or genus within the scope of the words "charges for lodging". [*Express Hotels* v *State of Gujarat* AIR 1989 SC 1949].

**Election.** An act or process of electing; the fact of being elected; the right, power or privilege of making a choice; the act of selecting one or more from a greater number for an office; the exercise of his choice by a man left to his own free will to take or to do one thing or another.

The exercise of a choice, esp., the act of choosing from several possible rights or remedies in a way that precludes the use of other rights or remedies; the doctrine by which a person is compelled to choose between accepting a benefit under a legal instrument and retaining some property right to which the person is already entitled; an obligation imposed on a party to choose between alternative rights or claims, so that the party is entitled to enjoy only one; the process of selecting a person to occupy an office (usually a public office), membership, award, or other title or status. [Black's *Law Dictionary*, 8th Ed.].

▸ *Meaning under the Constitution of India.* The word 'election' in Art. 71(1) must be given wide meaning as comprising the entire election process culminating in a candidate being declared elected. [*Narayan Bhaskar Khare* v *Election Commission of India* AIR 1957 SC 694: 1957 SCJ 663: 1957 SCA 953: 1957 SCR 1081].

The word 'election' has by long usage in connection with the process of selection of proper representatives in democratic institutions acquired both a wide and a narrow meaning. In the narrow sense it is used to mean the final selection of a candidate which may embrace the result of the poll when there is polling, or a particular candidate being returned unopposed when there is no poll. In the wide sense, the word is used to connote the entire process culminating in a candidate being declared elected and it is in this wide sense that the word is used in Part XV of the Constitution in which Art. 329(*b*) occurs. [*N.P. Ponnuswami* v *Returning Officer, Namakhal Constituency* AIR 1952 SC 64: 1952 SCR 218: 1952 SCJ 100; *Election Commissioner of India* v *Shivaji* AIR 1988 SC 61: (1988)1 SCC 277: (1988)1 SCJ 348].

NOTE: The word 'election' in Art. 329(*b*) of the Constitution of India connotes the entire electoral process. The words 'Notwithstanding anything in this Constitution' are quite apt to exclude the jurisdiction of the High Court to deal with any matter which may arise while the elections are in progress. The Article is a complete bar to the High Courts entertaining a writ petition which would interfere with the electoral process and the High Court has no power to issue any writ, order or direction which would have the consequence of interfering with the election while it is in progress. [*Chandra Bhan Shah* v *Returning Officer* AIR 1957 MP 142].

▸ *Meaning under the Representation of the People Act 1951.* 'Election' means not the general election or the entirety of the elections held in the State, but one election held in one constituency. [*P.R. Francis* v *A.V. Aryian* AIR 1968 Ker 252; drawing reference to ss. 80 and 81].

▸ *Meaning under the Representation of the People Act 1951, s. 2(d).* 'Election' means an election to fill a seat or seats in either House of Parliament or in the House or either House of the Legislature of a State, other than the State of Jammu and Kashmir.

NOTE: *Steps in election.* In the case of election there are certain steps to be taken until the poll is taken. In the first place, there is an announcement about the holding of an election. This is followed by nomination of candidates. A scrutiny of nomination is then held. Thereafter, a list of validly nominated candidates is prepared. Then there is a stage of withdrawal by the candidate. After the withdrawal, if any, a candidate may retire from contest, and finally there is poll. Indeed an election is one continuous process involving these steps. [*Yeshwantrao Balwantrao Chavan* v *K.T. Mangalmurti* AIR 1958 Bom 397: ILR (1958) Bom 732].

• **Date of election** p. 225.

• **General election** p. 384.

**Election Commission.** The Commission appointed by the appropriate authority of the government under the constitution of a country to conduct elections of the States and the cadre in case of a federal government and in case of a unitary government to conduct election of a country.

NOTE: The Election Commission in India is appointed by the President under Art. 324 of the Constitution of India.

**Election petition.** Under the Representation of the People Act 1951 it means a petition challenging the validity of an election on one of the grounds mentioned in s. 100. The contents of an election petition are laid down in s. 83 of the Act.

**Elector.** 'Elector' in relation to a constituency means a person whose name is entered in the electoral roll of that constituency for the time being in force and who is not subject to any of the disqualifications mentioned in s. 16 of the Representation of the People Act 1950. [*Hari Prasad Mulshankar Trivedi* v *V.B. Raju* AIR 1973 SC 2602: (1974)3 SCC 415].

▸ *Meaning under the Presidential and Vice-Presidential Elections Act 1952, s. 2(d).* 'Elector' in relation to a Presidential election means a member of the electoral college referred to in Art. 54, and in relation to a Vice-Presidential election means a member of either House of Parliament.

**Electoral right.** 'Electoral right' means the right of a person to stand or not to stand as, or to withdraw from being, a candidate, or to vote or refrain from voting at any election. [Representation of the People Act 1951, s. 79(*d*); Indian Penal Code 1860, s. 171A(*b*)].

**Electoral roll.** The "electoral roll" referred to under the Representation of the People Act 1951, s. 62(1) must be understood to be electoral roll that was in force on the last day for making the nominations for the election. [*Baidyanath Panjira* v *Sitaram Mahto* (1969)2 SCC 447: AIR 1970 SC 314: (1970)1 SCR 839].

> NOTE: It is of the essence of elections that proper electoral rolls should be maintained and in order that proper electoral roll should be maintained it is necessary that after the preparation of electoral roll opportunity should be given to the parties concerned to scrutinize whether the persons enrolled as electors possessed the requisite qualifications. Opportunity should also be given for the revision of the electoral roll and for the adjudication of claims to be enrolled therein and entertaining objections to such enrolment. Unless this is done, the entire obligation cast upon the authorities holding the elections is not discharged and elections are liable to be challenged. [*Chief Commissioner* v *Radhey Sham* AIR 1957 SC 304].

**Electrical goods.** Only such articles the use of which cannot be had except with the application of electrical energy can be termed electrical goods or appliances and the article sold has to be sold as a unit in determining if it comes within the description of electrical goods and cannot be split upon. [*William Jacks* v *State of Madras* (1956)2 MLJ 199: 1956 STC 327].

> NOTE: It is neither possible nor desirable to set forth an exhaustive list of what would constitute 'electrical goods'. It is rather difficult to hold that a lathe by itself, even though driven by electrical energy or designated primarily for use with electrical energy, will be regarded as electrical goods. [*William Jacks* v *Deputy Commercial Tax Officer* (1960)2 MLJ 155: (1960)2 STC 340].

**Eleemosynary corporation.** It is a body corporate constituted for the perpetual distribution of free alms or bounty of its founder. All hospitals and colleges founded for the promotion of piety and learning are corporations of this kind.

**Eligible.** The word 'eligible' must mean and can only mean legally qualified. [*Faramus* v *Film Artistes' Association* (1964)1 All ER 25].

The word may mean either 'legally qualified' or 'fit to be chosen'. [*Baker* v *Lee* (1860)8 HL Cas 495].

**Elopement.** Abandonment of husband by the wife who leaves his home and goes to live with an adulterer.

**Elsewhere.** In another place.

The expression, by the alternative description 'or elsewhere' means anywhere in the world. [*Re Coolgardie Consolidated Gold Mines Ltd.* (1897)76 LT 269].

**Emanation.** The primary meaning of the word is that which issues or proceeds from some source and it is commonly used to describe the physical properties of substances (*e.g.*, radium) which gives out emanations of recognizable character. The word is hardly applicable to a person or a body having a corporate capacity. [*International Railway Co.* v *Niagara Parks Commission* AIR 1941 PC 114].

**Embankment.** A protecting or supporting bank; the process of strengthening by a bank; an earth or stone bank for keeping back water.

▸ *Meaning under the Bengal Embankment Act 1882, s. 3.* 'Embankment' includes—every bank, dam, wall and dyke made or used for, excluding water from, or for retaining water upon, any land; every sluice, spur, groyne, training-wall, berm or other work annexed to, or portion of any such embankment; every bank, dam, dyke, wall, groyne or spur made or erected for the protection of any such embankment or of any land from erosion or overflow by or of rivers, tides, waves or waters; and also all buildings intended for the purposes of inspection and supervision.

**Embargo.** Authoritative stoppage of trade; control of trade; governmental order of prohibition; legal restraint, ban, bar; a prohibition to pass; a stop, arrest or detention of ships; a prohibition imposed in time of war by a belligerent State upon merchant ships against their leaving port a time specified.

**Embassy.** The function or position of an ambassador; a mission abroad undertaken officially especially by an ambassador; a body of diplomatic representatives, specifically one headed by an ambassador; the official residence and offices of an ambassador.

The message or commission given by a sovereign or State to a minister, called an ambassador, empowered to treat or communicate with another sovereign or State; also the establishment of an ambassador.

**Embezzlement.** Fraudulent appropriation of money; theft of money entrusted to one's care; theft of money entrusted to one's management; wrongful appropriation; cheating; defalcation; fraudulent appropriation; appropriation by a servant or clerk of money or goods received by him for and on behalf of his master or employer.

Embezzlement means nothing more nor less than a fraudulent misappropriation, and although it is called embezzlement where it is committed by a clerk or servant, because it is only in that case that it is made punishable under that name, yet the thing actually exists in other cases than those of a clerk and servant, and is made punishable in the case of a banker, merchant, factor or agent. [*Re Bellencontre* (1891)2 QB 122].

**Emblements.** Crops sown by a tenant legally belonging to the tenant.

NOTE: At common law a tenant holding for an uncertain interest, whose interest determines otherwise than by or in consequence of his own act, has the right, under the name of emblements, to enter upon the land after determination to cut and carry away those crops that normally repay within the year the labour by which they are produced. [Halsbury's *Laws of England*, 4th Ed., vol. 1, para 1077, p. 593].

When a lease of uncertain duration determines by any means except the fault of the lessee, he or his legal representative is entitled to all the crops planted or sown by the lessee and growing upon the property when the lease determines and to free ingress and egress to gather and carry them. [Transfer of Property Act 1882, s. 108(*i*)].

**Emergency.** Critical point; crucial period; pressing necessity; pressing need; sudden peril; unexpected happening; unforeseen occurrence; unforeseen condition; urgency; sudden or unexpected occurrence of a state of things.

'Emergency' can be used to describe a state of things which is not the result of a sudden occurrence. A condition of things causing a reasonable apprehension of the near approach of danger would constitute an emergency. [*Larchbank (Owners)* v *British Petrol (Owners), The Larchbank* (1943) AC 299 (HL), *per* Lord Atkin].

NOTE: An 'emergency' may result from an unforeseen combination of circumstances. This combination may not take place all at once, but gradually, and immediate action may be rendered necessary when the culminating point is reached. [*Desh Raj* v *Emperor* AIR 1930 Lah 781].

*Urgency and emergency—difference.* Urgency relates to a situation requiring prompt action. Emergency indicates a situation suddenly arising and demanding prompt action and is a stronger word. [*S. Arjun Singh* v *State of Punjab* AIR 1959 Punj 538: ILR (1958) Punj 1451].

**Emigrant.** Moving from one place or country for the purpose of settling in another; a person who leaves one country or section of a country, to settle in another.

One who leaves his or her country for any reason with the intent to establish a permanent residence elsewhere. [Black's *Law Dictionary*, 8th Ed.].

▸ *Meaning under the Emigration Act 1983, s. 2(d).* Any citizen of India who intends to emigrate, or emigrates, or has emigrated but does not include—(*i*) a dependent of an emigrant, whether such dependent accompanies that emigrant, or deports subsequently for the purpose of joining that emigrant in the country to which that emigrant has lawfully emigrated; (*ii*) any person who has resided outside India at any time after attaining the age of eighteen years, for not less than three years or the spouse or child of such person.

**Emigrate.** Leave one's own country to settle permanently in another.

▸ *Meaning under the Emigration Act 1983, s. 2(f).* 'Emigrate' and 'emigration' mean the departure out of India of any person with a view to taking up any employment (whether or not under an agreement or other arrangements to take up such employment and whether with or without the assistance of a recruiting agent or employer) in any country or place outside India.

**Emigration.** The act of leaving a country with the intent not to return and to reside elsewhere. [Black's *Law Dictionary*, 8th Ed.].

"Emigration is usually defined as the voluntary removal of an individual from his home State with the intention of residing abroad. However, not all emigration is voluntary; there sometimes exists forced emigration, even mass emigration. Emigration may also be due to flight for political reasons or expulsion. One then speaks of refugees or exiles". [Paul Weis, *"Emigration", in 2 Encyclopaedia of Public International Law,* p. 76 (1995)].

**Eminent domain.** The inherent power of a governmental entity to take privately owned property, especially land, and convert it to public use, subject to reasonable compensation for the taking. [Black's *Law Dictionary*, 8th Ed.].

The superior or the permanent dominion of the State or the power of the State over all properties in the State and refers to the power of the State to take for public purposes any property in the State on payment of compensation. In other words, the power of compulsory acquisition of property which, according to every system of jurisprudence the State possesses, is known as the power of "Eminent Domain" on the continent of Europe and under the American Constitution. Article 31(2) of the Constitution of India which has since been repealed represented the principle of eminent domain.

NOTE: In the exercise of its eminent domain power, the State may take any property from the owner and may appropriate it for public purposes. [*Deputy Commissioner and Collector, Kamrup v Durganath Sarma* AIR 1968 SC 394: (1968)1 SCR 561: (1968)1 SCA 64: (1968)2 SCJ 401].

*Eminent domain and taxation—distinction.* "Eminent domain" differs from taxation in that taxation is a contribution levied on people, although both involve the taking of property.

*Eminent domain and police power—distinction.* Eminent domain differs from police power in that the police power is not a taking of any right whether of property or a person from people, but a limitation on the exercise of such rights by people, although the police power may result also in making people lose their property. [H.E. Willis' *Constitutional Law of the United States* 1936, pp. 224-225].

Under the police power, many restrictions may be imposed and the property may even be destroyed without compensation being given, whereas under the power of eminent domain, the property may be appropriated to public use on payment of compensation only. [*Deputy Commissioner and Collector, Kamrup* v *Durganath Sarma* AIR 1968 SC 394: (1968)1 SCR 561: (1968)1 SCA 64: (1968)2 SCJ 401].

NOTE: The nature of the legal power of the State to acquire private land for public purposes by law, considered as the power of eminent domain differs fundamentally from the other two powers viz., the power of taxation and the police power. The difference consists exclusively in the nature of selective fall-out of the exercise of the power of eminent domain. The incidence of the exercise of the State power in the case of taxation and the police power is uniform and equal between the subjects whereas the exercise of the power of eminent domain takes away from a particular individual, subjected to the exercise of that power, something more than his due from him as his lawful support for the State. The exercise of the power of eminent domain is inherently unjust and disturbs the balance of equal distribution of burdens. [*K. Yadaih* v *Government of A.P.* AIR 1984 NOC 5 (AP) (FB)].

**Emolument.** The compensation, salary, fees, perquisites, advantage, gain, or property arising from an office or employment; general advantage; gain; property.

Any advantage, profit, or gain received as a result of one's employment or one's holding of office. [Black's *Law Dictionary*, 8th Ed.].

The advantage or benefit which the employee is entitled to by virtue of his office or employment in addition to his salary. [*Kiddie* v *Port of London Authority* (1929)93 JP 203].

'Emoluments' include all fees, poundage, and other payments, made to any officer or servant, as such, for his own use; also the money value of any apartments, rations or other allowances in kind appertaining to his office or employment. [Stroud's *Judicial Dictionary* quoting Poor Law Officers' Superannuation Act 1896].

- **Annual emolument.** It means the annual profit or advantage which a person has derived from his office. [*R.* v *Postmaster General* (1876)1 QBD 658].

**Empire.** The territory over which the authority of an emperor extends. The word "Empire" carries with it the idea of a State that is vast and composed of many different types of people. One part of an empire is sometimes governed by fundamental laws, very different from those by which another part of the same empire is governed.

**Employ.** To make use of; to hire; to occupy (as time) advantageously; to use or engage the services of; to provide with a job that pays wages or a salary; to devote to or direct toward a particular activity or person.

NOTE: The word 'employ' does not necessarily mean employed in actual work; but may be fulfilled by keeping a person in the service. [*Emmens* v *Elderton* (1852)4 HL Cas 624].

**Employed.** The word 'employed' has two meanings. One has got the sense of being engaged, the other has the sense of a contract of service being established between the workers and the employer. [*State* v *Mohammad Sattar* AIR 1959 All 404: 1959 Cr LJ 793].

The word 'employed' in connection with the affairs of the Union or of a State carries the sense of being engaged or occupied in connection with the affairs of the Union or of a State. [*Pukhraj* v *Ummaidram* AIR 1964 Raj 174: (1964)2 Cr LJ 339].

Employed means engaged or occupied. A person who at a postmaster's request gratuitously assisted him in sorting letters is a person employed under the Post Office. [*R.* v *Reason* 23 LJMC 13].

▸ *Meaning under the Industrial Disputes Act 1947, s. 2(s).* The expression 'employed' has at least two known connotations, but as used in the definition of workmen in the Act, the context would indicate that it is used in the sense of relationship brought about by express or implied contract of service in which the employee renders service for which he is engaged by the employer and the later agrees to pay him in cash or kind as agreed between them or statutorily prescribed. [*Workmen of the Food Corporation of India* v *Food Corporation of India* AIR 1985 SC 670].

▸ *Meaning under the Motor Transport Workers' Act 1961, s. 2(h).* The word "employed" in the definition of the Act is not used in the sense of using the services of a person but rather in the sense of keeping a person in one's service. [*Ghatge and Patil Concerns' Employees' Union* v *Ghatge and Patil (Transports) Private Ltd.* AIR 1968 SC 503: (1968)1 SCR 300]. The definition is made wide to take in all persons working in a professional capacity in an undertaking for running its affairs in any capacity and not only persons employed on wages. [*Ghatge and Patil Concerns' Employees' Union* v *Ghatge and Patil (Transports) Private Ltd.*, supra].

▸ *Meaning under the Prevention of Corruption Act 1947, s. 6(a) and (b).* The word 'employed' must mean 'permanently employed'. This would not include the *ad hoc* or temporary employment of an officer whose services have been loaned by one Government to the other. [*R.R. Chari* v *State of U.P.* AIR 1962 SC 1573: (1962)2 Cr LJ 510].

**Employee.** One who works for another in return for a salary, wages, or other consideration; hired hand; salaried worker; wage earner; staff person; job holder.

A person who works in the service of another person (the employer) under an express or implied contract of hire, under which the employer has the right to control the details of work performance. [Black's *Law Dictionary*, 8th Ed.].

The "employee" is one who works for other for hire. [*Central Board of Direct Taxes* v *Aditya V. Birla* AIR 1988 SC 420: (1988)2 SCR 115: JT 1987(4) SC 653: (1988)170 ITR 137: 1988 (Supp) SCC 120].

▸*Meaning under the Coal Mines Provident Fund and Bonus Schemes Act 1948, s. 2(d).* 'Employee' means any person who is employed in any kind of work, manual or otherwise, in or in connection with a coal mine and who gets his wages directly or indirectly from the employer.

▸*Meaning under the Companies Act 1956, s. 419.* 'Employee' means an employee as such and not an ex-employee or past employee or a person whose contract of service has been put an end to. [*State* v *Girdharilal Bajaj* AIR 1962 Bom 130: ILR (1961) Bom 902].

▸*Meaning under the Employees' Provident Funds and Miscellaneous Provisions Act 1952, s. 2(f).* Any person who is employed for wages in any kind of work, manual or otherwise, in or in connection with the work of an establishment, and who gets his wages directly or indirectly from the employer, and includes any person (*i*) employed by or through a contractor in or in connection with the work of the establishment; (*ii*) engaged as an apprentice, not being an apprentice engaged under the Apprentices Act 1961, or under the standing orders of the establishment.

NOTE: The term "employee" include not only persons employed directly by the employer but also persons employed through a contractor. Moreover, they include not only persons employed in the factory but also persons employed in connection with the work of the factory. Thus, home worker rolling beedies at home is an employee. [*P.M. Patel & Sons* v *Union of India* AIR 1987 SC 447: 1985 Supp (3) SCR 55: (1986)1 SCC 32].

▸*Meaning under the Employees' State Insurance Act 1948, s. 2(9).* 'Employee' means any person employed for wages in or in connection with the work of a factory or establishment to which the Employees' State Insurance Act applies and—(*i*) who is directly employed by the principal employer on any work of, or incidental or preliminary to or connected with the work of, the factory or establishment whether such work is done by the employee in the factory or establishment or elsewhere; or (*ii*) who is employed by or through an immediate employer on the premises of the factory or establishment or under the supervision of the principal employer or his agent on work which is ordinarily part of the work of the factory or establishment or which is preliminary to the work carried on in or incidental to the purpose of the factory or establishment; or (*iii*) whose services are temporarily lent or let on hire to the principal employer by the person with whom the person whose services are so lent or let on hire has entered into a contract of service and includes any person employed for wages on any work connected with the administration of the factory or establishment or any part, department or branch thereof or with the purchase of raw materials for, or the distribution or sale of the products of, the factory or establishment or any person engaged as apprentice, not being an apprentice engaged under the Apprentices Act 1961, or under the standing orders of the establishment; but does not include—(*a*) any member of the Indian naval, military or air forces; or (*b*) any person so employed whose wages (excluding remuneration for overtime work) exceed (such wages as may be prescribed by the

Central Government) a month: Provided that an employee whose wages (excluding remuneration for overtime work) exceed such wages as may be prescribed by the Central Government a month at any time after (and not before) the beginning of the contribution period, shall continue to be an employee until the end of that period.

NOTE: The word "employee" would include not only persons employed in the factory but also persons connected with the work of the factory. The employee may be working within the factory or outside it, or may be employed for administrative purposes and all such employees are included within the definition of "employee". [*Hyderabad Asbestos Cement Products Ltd.* v *Employees Insurance Court* AIR 1978 SC 356: (1978)2 SCR 345: (1978)1 SCC 194].

The expression 'employee' means any person employed for wages in a factory or any person employed for wages in connection with the work of a factory. It also means any person employed for wages in or in connection with the work of an establishment to which the Act applies. [*Shri Narakesari Prakashan Ltd.* v *Employees' State Insurance Corporation* AIR 1984 SC 1916: (1985)1 SCR 962: (1984)4 SCC 627].

▸*Meaning under the Factories Act 1948.* "Employee" means any person employed for wages in or in connection with the work of a factory or establishment to which this Act applies and (1) who is directly employed by the principal employer on any work of, or incidental or preliminary to or connected with the work of the factory or establishment, whether such work is done by the employee in the factory or establishment or elsewhere; or (2) who is employed by or through an immediate employer on the premises of the factory or establishment or under supervision of the principal employer or his agent or work which is ordinarily part of the work of the factory or establishment or which is preliminary to the work carried on in or incidental to the purpose of the factory or establishment. [*B.M. Lakshmanamurthy* v *The Employees' State Insurance Corporation, Bangalore* AIR 1974 SC 759: (1974)3 SCR 142: (1974)4 SCC 365].

▸*Meaning under the Payment of Bonus Act 1965, s. 2(13).* 'Employee' means any person (other than an apprentice) employed on a salary or wage not exceeding three thousand and five hundred rupees per mensem in any industry to do any skilled or unskilled manual, supervisory, managerial, administrative, technical or clerical work for hire or reward, whether the terms of employment be express or implied.

▸*Meaning under the Payment of Gratuity Act 1972, s. 2(e).* 'Employee' means any person (other than an apprentice) employed on wages, in any establishment, factory, mine, oilfield, plantation, port, railway company or shop, to do any skilled, semi-skilled or unskilled, manual, supervisory, technical or clerical work, whether the terms of such employment are express or implied, and whether or not such person is employed in a managerial or administrative capacity, but does not include any such person who holds a post under the Central Government or a State Government and is governed by any other Act or by any rules providing for payment of gratuity.

• **Regular employees** p. 739.

**Employer.** One who employs; a person or business firm that employs workmen, servants, etc., for wages; masters; proprietor; owner; chief; controller.

An "employer" is one who employs, one who engages or keeps men in service, one who uses or enjoys the service of other persons for pay or salary. [*Central Board of Direct Taxes* v *Aditya V. Birla* AIR 1988 SC 420: (1988)2 SCR 115: JT 1987(4) SC 653: (1988)170 ITR 137: 1988 (Supp) SCC 120].

▸*Meaning under the Coal Mines Provident Fund and Bonus Schemes Act 1948, s. 2(e).* 'Employer' means the owner of a coal mine as defined in cl. (*g*) of s. 3 of the Indian Mines Act 1923.

▸*Meaning under the Dock Workers' (Regulation of Employment) Act 1948, s. 2(c)*. 'Employer' in relation to a dock worker means the person by whom he is employed or to be employed as aforesaid.

▸ *Meaning under the Employees' Provident Funds and Miscellaneous Provisions Act 1952, s. 2(e) and Payment of Bonus Act 1965, s. 2(14)*. 'Employer' means—(*i*) in relation to an establishment which is a factory, the owner or occupier of the factory, including the agent of such owner or occupier, the legal representatives of a deceased owner or occupier and, where a person has been named as a manager of the factory under s. 7(1)(*f*) of the Factories Act 1948, the person so named; and (*ii*) in relation to any other establishment, the person who, or the authority which, has the ultimate control over the affairs of the establishment, and where the said affairs are entrusted to a manager, managing director or managing agent, such manager, managing director or managing agent.

▸ *Meaning under the Industrial Disputes Act 1947, s. 2(g)*. 'Employer' means—(*i*) in relation to any industry carried on by or under the authority of any department of the Central Government or a State Government, the authority prescribed in this behalf or where no authority is prescribed, the head of the department; (*ii*) in relation to an industry carried on by or on behalf of a local authority, the chief executive officer of that authority.

The word "employer" occurring in ss. 33 and 33A of the Act meant the identical employer concerned with the industrial dispute, which was the subject-matter of the adjudication and could not include an employer who merely happened to discharge or punish or alter the conditions of service of workmen unless such employer could be shown to be mere nominee or benamidar of the former or fell within the category of his heirs, successors or assigns within the meaning of s. 18(3)(*c*) of the Act. [*S.K.G. Sugar Ltd.* v *Sri Ali Hassan, Chairman, Industrial Tribunal, Bihar* AIR 1959 SC 230: 1959 Supp (1) SCR 254].

▸ *Meaning under the National Service Act 1972, s. 2(a)*. 'Employer' means any person who employs any qualified person for doing any work in any establishment and includes any person interested with the supervision and control of qualified persons in such establishment.

▸ *Meaning under the Payment of Gratuity Act 1972, s. 2(f)*. 'Employer' means in relation to any establishment, factory, mine, oilfield, plantation, port, railway company or shop—(*i*) belonging to or under the control of the Central Government or a State Government, a person or authority appointed by the appropriate Government for the supervision and control of employees or where no person or authority has been so appointed, the head of the Ministry or the Department concerned, (*ii*) belonging to or under the control of any local authority, the person appointed by such authority for the supervision and control of employees or where no person has been so appointed, the chief executive officer of the local authority, (*iii*) in any other case, the person who or the authority which has the ultimate control over the affairs of the establishment, factory, mine, oilfield, plantation, port, railway company or shop, and where the said affairs are entrusted to any other person, whether called a manager, managing director or by any other name, such person.

**NOTE:** The directors of a private limited company are the employers and are liable to pay wages to the workers under the Payment of Wages Act 1936. [*Bhalgora Coal Co.* v *Indrajit Singh* AIR 1964 Pat 292: (1964)9 Fac LR 213].

▸ *Meaning under the Payment of Wages Act 1936, s. 2(ia)*. 'Employer' includes the legal representative of a deceased employer.

▸ *Meaning under the Plantations Labour Act 1951, s. 2(e)*. 'Employer' when used in relation to a plantation means the person who has the ultimate control over the affairs of the plantation, and where the affairs of any plantation are entrusted to any other person (whether called a managing agent, manager, superintendent or by any other name) such other person shall be deemed to be employer in relation to that plantation.

▸*Meaning under the Workmen's Compensation Act 1923, s. 2(e) and Personal Injuries (Compensation Insurance) Act 1963, s. 2(a).* 'Employer' includes any body of persons whether incorporated or not and any managing agent of an employer and the legal representative of a deceased employer, and, when the services of a workman are temporarily lent or let on hire to another person by the person with whom the workman has entered into a contract of service or apprenticeship, means such other person while the workman is working with him.

- **Actually worked under an employer** p. 35.
- **Immediate employer** p. 429.
- **Principal employer** p. 685.

**Employment.** The word 'employment' is one of very wide significance [*Westall Richardson Ltd.* v *Roulson* (1954)2 All ER 448] and has different meanings in different context. It may mean the act of employing; the state of being employed; work for which one has been hired and is being paid by an employer. [Black's *Law Dictionary*, 8th Ed.]. When the word 'employment' is used in connection with a profession or vocation, it means the way in which a man employs himself. [*Davies* v *Braithwaite* (1931)2 KB 628, *per* Rowlatt, J.]. 'Employment' does not mean only where one man is set to work by others to earn money; a man may employ himself so as to earn profits in many ways. [*Partridge* v *Mallandaine* (1886)18 QBD 276 (DC)].

"Employment" means occupation or act of employing or state of being employed. [*S.K. Das Gupta* v *Oil and Natural Gas Commission* AIR 1970 Guj 149].

"Employment" is the contract of service between the employer and the employee whereunder the employee agrees to serve the employer subject to his control and supervision. [*Chintaman Rao* v *State of Madhya Pradesh* AIR 1958 SC 388: 1958 SCR 1340: 1958 SCJ 753: 1958 Cr LJ 803].

▸*Meaning under the Employees' Provident Funds and Miscellaneous Provisions Act 1952, s. 1(3)(b).* The word "employment" must be construed as employment in the regular course of business of the establishment; such employment obviously would not include employment of a few persons for short period on account of some passing necessity or some temporary emergency beyond the control of the company. This must necessarily require determination of the question in each case on its own peculiar facts. [*Provident Fund Inspector, Guntur* v *T.S. Hariharan* AIR 1971 SC 1519: (1971)2 SCC 68: (1971)2 SCA 186].

▸*Meaning under the Income-tax Act 1961.* "Employment" means an act of employing. [*Central Board of Direct Taxes* v *Aditya V. Birla* JT 1987(4) SC 653: AIR 1988 SC 420: (1988)2 SCR 115: (1988)170 ITR 137: 1988 (Supp) SCC 120].

NOTE: *Ingredients and test of employment.* The concept of employment involves three ingredients—(*i*) employer, (*ii*) employee and (*iii*) the contract of employment. The employer is one who employs, that is, one who engages the services of other persons. The employee is one who works for another for hire. The employment is the contract of service between the employer and the employee. [*Chintaman Rao* v *State of M.P.* AIR 1958 SC 388: 1958 SCR 1340: 1958 SCJ 753: 1958 Cr LJ 803].

The real test for deciding whether the contract is one of employment is to find out whether the agreement is for the personal labour of the person engaged, and that if that is so, the contact is one of employment, whether the work is time work or piece work or whether the employee does the whole of the work himself or whether he obtains the assistance of other persons also for the work. [*Dharangadhara Chemcial Works* v *State of Saurashtra* AIR 1957 SC 264: 1957 SCJ 208].

The word "employment" must take its colour and content from its context and cannot be read in isolation. The word "employment" denotes the relationship of master and servant. The test is whether the employer possessed the right not only to control what work the employee was to do, but also the manner in which the work was to be done. [*Har Govind Pant* v *Chancellor, University of Rajasthan* AIR 1978 Raj 72 (FB), *per* A.P. Sen, J.].

*Employment—what is not.* A contract for supply of goods is not a contract of employment in the sense in which that word has been used in Art. 16. [*C.K. Achutan* v *State of Kerala* AIR 1959 SC 490: 1959 Supp (1) SCR 787: (1960)1 SCA 33].

If the word "employment" is construed to mean the relationship of employer and employee, the office of Governor would certainly not be an employment within the meaning of cl. (*d*) of Article 319 because the Governor is the head of the State and holds a high constitutional office which carries with it important constitutional functions and duties. It is true that the Governor is appointed by the President which means in effect and substance the Government of India, but that is only a mode of appointment and does not make the Governor an employee or servant of the Government of India. Every person appointed by the President is not necessarily an employee of the Government of India. [*Hargovind Pant* v *Dr. Raghukul Tilak* (1979)3 SCC 458: (1979)3 SCR 972].


- **Contract of employment** p. 190.
- **Course of employment** p. 201.
- **Gainful employment** p. 380.
- **Hazardous employment** p. 408.
- **In the course of employment** p. 442.

- **Termination of employment.** Termination of employment is the cessation of the relationship between the employer and the employee. [*S.K. Das Gupta* v *O.N.G. Commission* AIR 1970 Guj 149].

**Employment injury.** 'Employment injury' means a personal injury to an employee caused by accident or an occupational disease arising out of and in the course of his employment.

NOTE: A heart failure may be an accident in course of employment; for example, if in the course of employment there is any sudden noise or a sudden shock, or some such event of such intensity that it leads to heart failure which would not otherwise have happened, then it may be said that there is an accident in course of the employment. But where an employee while going into the factory suffered a collapse on account of failure of the heart's function, it was neither an accident as usually understood nor was it the result of occupational disease. [*Ajudhee Bai* v *Employees' State Insurance Corporation* AIR 1959 MP 338].

**Emporium.** A place for wholesale trade for commodities carried over the seas; a store carrying general merchandise; a large retail store selling a wide variety of goods; a centre of commerce; a market.

**En ventre sa mere.** In its mother's womb.

NOTE: A child in the womb of the mother is for most purposes regarded in English law as being already born. In Hindu law a child in his mother's womb is equal in many respects to a child actually in existence. Thus, a son or a daughter in the mother's womb is entitled to inheritance if born alive. The child is also entitled to a share on partition. A child who was in the womb at the time of the death of an intestate and who is subsequently born alive shall have the same right to inherit to the intestate as if he or she had been born before the death of the intestate, and the inheritance shall be deemed to vest in such a case with effect from the date of the death of the intestate.

**Enabling statute.** A statute enabling persons or corporations to do that which, before it was passed, they could not do, as opposed to a prohibiting statute, under which acts are forbidden. [Mozley & Whiteley's *Law Dictionary*, 10th Ed].

A law that permits what was previously prohibited or that creates new powers, especially a congressional statute conferring powers on an executive agency to carry out various delegated tasks. [Black's *Law Dictionary*, 8th Ed.].

**Enactments.** The action or process of making into law; a statute. [Black's *Law Dictionary*, 8th Ed.].

An Act of Parliament or statute or any part thereof. [Jowitt's *Dictionary of English Law*, 2nd Ed].

'Act' means the whole Act, whereas a section or part of a section in an Act may be an enactment. [*Wakefield & District Light Railways Co.* v *Wakefield Corporation* (1906)2 KB 140; *Abdul Aziz* v *State of U.P.* AIR 1958 All 109; *Prabodh Verma* v *State of U.P.* (1984)4 SCC 251: AIR 1985 SC 167: (1985)1 SCR 216].

▸ *Meaning under the General Clauses Act 1897, s. 3(19).* 'Enactment' shall include a regulation and shall also include any provision contained in any Act or in any such regulation as aforesaid.

**Encroachment.** Unlawful gaining upon the possession of a neighbour; taking possession of other's property; entrance upon the rights or domain of another, especially, gradual intrusion; that which is gained or seized by encroaching.

An infringement of another's rights or intrusion on another's property. [Black's *Law Dictionary*, 7th Ed.].

**Encumber.** "Encumber" means burden of legal liability on property. When a land is encumber, it constitutes a burden on the title which diminishes the value of the land. [*State of Himachal Pradesh* v *Tarsem Singh* (2001)8 SCC 104: JT 2001(7) SC 460].

**Encumbrance.** A claim, lien or liability attached to property. It is a burden imposed upon land or interest in land by the owner of the land. Examples are charge, mortgage etc.

It is defined as a "claim or liability that is attached to property or some other right and that may lessen its value, such as a lien or mortgage; any property right that is not an ownership interest". [Black's *Law Dictionary*, 7th Ed.].

The word "encumbrance" means a burden or charge upon property. [*Brij Narain Singh* v *Jumuna Prasad* AIR 1958 Pat 589].

The word "encumbrance" means a burden or charge upon property or a claim or lien upon an estate or on the land. When there is encumbrance on a land, it constitutes a burden on the title which diminishes the value of land. [*State of Himachal Pradesh* v *Tarsem Singh* (2001)8 SCC 104: JT 2001(7) SC 460].

▸ *Meaning under the Land Acquisition Act 1894, s. 16.* The word 'encumbrance' means interests in respect of which a compensation can be claimed. [*Collector of Bombay* v *Nusserwanji* AIR 1955 SC 298: 1955 SCA 692: 1955 SCJ 339].

▸ *Meaning with reference to tenancy.* The term "encumbrance" used with reference to a tenancy means any lien, sub-tenancy, easement or other right or interest created by the tenant on his tenure or holding or in limitation of his own interest therein. [*Bhola Mian* v *S.M. Islam* AIR 1958 Pat 48].

NOTE: The word 'encumbrance' does not include the right of easement. [*M. Ratanchand Chordia* v *Kasim Khaleeli* AIR 1964 Mad 209: ILR (1964)1 Mad 409].

• **Covenant against encumbrances.** A covenant against encumbrances is a covenant to indemnity against all encumbrances, claims and demands upon the property. But the covenant is not broken as soon as an encumbrance is discovered, unless it prevents entry or enjoyment. [*Eastern Mortgage* v *Fazlul* 52 Cal 914: AIR 1926 Cal 385].

**Encyclopaedia.** Book giving information on all branches of knowledge or of one subject, usually arranged alphabetically. It contains a series of articles by many contributors.

**End product.** Means the completed product so far as a particular firm is concerned. Other firms may alter or add to the product before delivering their own end product.

**Endemic disease.** A disease regularly found among specified people or in a specified country.

**Endorse.** Endorse is to write on the back of, especially to sign one's name as payee on the back of (a cheque) in order to obtain the cash or credit represented on the face; to inscribe (one's signature) on a cheque, bill or note; to inscribe (as an official document) with a title or memorandum; to make over to another (the value represented in a cheque, bill or note) by inscribing one's name on the document; to acknowledge receipt of (a sum specified) by one's signature on a document; to express approval of publicly and definitely. 'Endorse' is equivalent to sign. [*Kamala Bala* v *State of West Bengal* AIR 1962 Cal 269].

**Endorsement.** Endorsement is the act or process of endorsing; something that is written in the process of endorsing; a provision added to an insurance contract altering its scope or application; sanction, approval.

- **Blank endorsement** p. 106.
- **Restrictive indorsement** p. 757.
- **Special endorsement** p. 805.

**Endorsement in blank.** If the endorser signs his name only, the endorsement is said to be in blank and if he adds a direction to pay the amount mentioned in the instrument to, or to the order of a specified person, the endorsement is said to be in full and the person so specified is called the endorsee of the instrument. [Negotiable Instruments Act 1881, s. 16].

Endorsement in blank means writing one's name merely on the back of the receipt without specifying any restrictions as to payee, manner of payment, etc., which details may be filled in by the holder thereof. [*State of Bihar* v *Union of India* AIR 1959 Pat 438].

**Endow.** To give money or property to, especially as a source of continuing or permanent income; to give a dower; to bestow upon; to make pecuniary provision for.

**Endowment.** Endowment is the act or process of endowing; something that is endowed, specifically the part of an institution's income derived from donations.

The words 'endowing' or 'endowment' are not limited to the provision out of capital expenditure for the actual amenity bed. 'Endowment' or 'endow' may also mean providing a capital sum out of which income will be produced which will pay for the services which it is desired and will be provided in respect of the endowment in question. [*Adams, Gee* v *Barnet Group Hospital* (1963)3 All ER 285].

NOTE: An endowment can validly be created in favour of an idol or temple without the performance of any ceremony, provided the settlor has clearly and unambiguously expressed his intention in that behalf. Where it is proved that ceremonies were performed that would be valuable evidence of endowment, but absence of such proof would not be conclusive against it. The ceremonies relating to dedication are *Sankalpa*, *Utsarga* and *Pratistha*. *Sankalpa* is really a formal declaration by the settlor of his intention to dedicate the property. *Utsarga* is the formal renunciation by the founder of his ownership in the property, the result whereof is that it becomes impressed with the trust for which he dedicates it. If therefore *utsarga* is proved to have been performed, the dedication must be held to have been done. *Pratistha* takes the place of *utsarga* in dedication of temples. [*Deoki Nandan* v *Murlidhar* 1956 SCR 756: 1957 SCA 85: AIR 1957 SC 133: 1957 SCJ 75].

**Endowment policy.** Endowment policy means a policy of assurance, insuring money to be paid on the survival for a specified period of the person assured, either with or without provision for the payment of money in the event of the death of that person before the expiration of that period.

Insurance policy under which insurer agrees to pay insured a stated sum at end of definite period, or, if insured dies before end of such period, to pay amount to person designated as beneficiary. [*Spellacy* v *American Life Ins. Ass'n*. 131 A 2d 834, 838].

**Ends of justice.** The words 'end of justice', wide as they are, do not mean vague and indeterminate notions of justice, but justice according to the statutes and laws of the land. They cannot mean that express provisions of the statute can be overridden at the dictates of what one might by private emotion or arbitrary preference call or conceive to be justice between the parties. The words 'ends of justice' do not therefore permit the court to take a step or procedure which defeats a statutory provision of the law of the land. [*Debendra Nath* v *Satyabala Dassi* AIR 1950 Cal 217: 54 CWN 110; *A. Venkateswara Rao* v *K. Sibaiah* AIR 1978 AP 403; *Bajrang Bai* v *Ismail* AIR 1978 Pat 339 (FB); *Sundar* v *Mulakharaj* AIR 1981 Del 45].

By "ends of justice" is meant not only justice to the parties but also to witnesses and others who may be inconvenienced. [*Sangram Singh* v *Election Tribunal, Kotah* AIR 1955 SC 425: (1955)2 SCR 1: 1955 SCJ 431].

**Enemy.** Adversary; an antagonist; an opposing military force; a state with which another state is at war.

▸ *Meaning under the Army Act 1950, s. 3(x).* 'Enemy' includes all armed mutineers, armed rebels, armed rioters, pirates and any person in arms against whom it is the duty of any person subject to military law to act.

▸ *Meaning under the Border Security Force Act 1968, s. 2(j).* 'Enemy' includes all armed mutineers, armed rebels, armed rioters, pirates and any person in arms against whom it is the duty of any person subject to the Border Security Force Act to take action.

▸ *Meaning under the Defence of India Act 1962, s. 2(c); Defence of India Act 1971, s. 2(b); Personal Injuries (Emergency Provisions) Act 1962, s. 2(3).* 'Enemy' means—(*i*) any person or country committing external aggression against India; (*ii*) any person belonging to a country committing such aggression; (*iii*) such other country as may be declared by the Central Government to be assisting the country committing such aggression; (*iv*) any person belonging to such other country.

▸ *Meaning under the Enemy Property Act 1968, s. 2(b).* 'Enemy' or 'enemy subject' or 'enemy firm' means a person or country who or which was an enemy, an enemy subject or an enemy firm, as the case may be, under the Defence of India Act 1962 and the Defence of India Rules 1962, but does not include a citizen of India.

• **Alien enemy** p. 55.

**Enemy property.** Enemy property means any property for the time being belonging to or held or managed on behalf of an enemy, an enemy subject or an enemy firm: Provided that where an individual enemy subject dies in the territories to which the Act extends, any property which immediately before his death belonged to or was held by him or was managed on his behalf may, notwithstanding his death, continue to be regarded as enemy property. [Enemy Property Act 1968, s. 2(*c*)].

**Energy.** The power by which anything acts effectively to move or change other things or accomplish any result; habitual tendency to and readiness for effective action; power in active exercise; force in operation; the capacity of doing work and of overcoming inertia, as by heat, light, radiation or mechanical and chemical forces. [Webster's *Comprehensive Dictionary,* International Edition].

▸ *Meaning under the Electricity Act 1910, s. 2(g).* "Energy" means electrical energy—(*i*) generated, transmitted or supplied for any purpose, or (*ii*) used for any purpose except the transmission of a message. [*State of U.P.* v *Hindustan Aluminium Corpn.* AIR 1979 SC 1459: (1979)3 SCR 709: (1979)3 SCC 229].

**Enforce.** Administer; bring to pass; carry into effect; carry into execution; carry out; carry through; compel obedience; execute; implement; make effective; put in action; put in force; put in operation; put into effect; put into execution.

To give force or effect to (a law etc.); to compel obedience to. [Black's *Law Dictionary*, 7th Ed.].

▸ *Meaning under the Companies Act 1956, s. 295(3).* The word 'enforce' means the taking of such action on the part of the creditor which compels the debtor to effect repayment of the loan, such as the institution of a suit, attachment or sale of the latter's properties etc. [*Totalal* v *State* AIR 1963 Raj 6: (1963)1 Cr LJ 61; *Ram Krishna* v *Ratan Chand* AIR 1956 All 32].

**Enforce any right.** The words 'enforce any right' imply some active step being taken to give effect to the right. [*Mercantile Credit Co.* v *Cross* (1965)1 All ER 577].

**Enforcement.** Carrying into effect; carrying out; compulsory execution; effectuation; implementation; imposition.

The act or process of compelling compliance with a law, mandate, or command. [Black's *Law Dictionary*, 7th Ed.].

"Enforcement" means to impose or compel obedience to law or to compel observance of law. [*S.M.D. Kiran Pasha* v *Government of A.P.* JT 1989(4) SC 366: 1990 SCC (Cri) 110: 1989 Supp (2) SCR 105: (1990)1 SCC 328].

**Enfranchise.** To grant voting rights or other rights of citizenship to a person or class; to set free. [Black's *Law Dictionary*, 8th Ed.].

**Engaged.** The word 'engaged' is deplorably ambiguous. An employer 'engages' a servant when he makes an agreement with him for his services. A workman is 'engaged' on work when he is actually carrying it out. In fact, 'engage' of a master has an entirely different meaning to 'engaged in' of a workman. [*Benninga* v *Bijstra* (1946) KB 58].

**English mortgage.** Where the mortgagor binds himself to repay the mortgage-money on a certain date, and transfers the mortgaged property absolutely to the mortgagee, but subject to a proviso that he will retransfer it to the mortgagor upon payment of the mortgage-money as agreed, the transaction is called an English mortgage. [Transfer of Property Act 1882, s. 58(*e*)].

**Engraving.** A print made from an engraved plate, block, or other surface; the process or art of cutting a design, etc. on a hard surface, plate.

> NOTE: Engravings include etchings, lithographs, wood-cuts, prints and other similar works, not being photographs. [Copyright Act 1957, s. 2(*i*)].

**Engross.** To occupy completely; absorb. To copy legibly; to make a formal transcript of; to handwrite a document, especially a deed, in a style characterised by large letters; to prepare a copy of a legal document for execution. To buy large quantities of a stock or commodity in an effort to corner the market and control the price; to monopolise.

**Enjoin.** Command; give orders; impose with authority; disallow; disapprove; ban; block; bring to a standstill; cause to halt; forestall; frustrate; hold in check; forbid by law; lay under embargo; make unlawful; place under interdiction; prohibit by legal injunction; put under an injunction; put under embargo.

**Enjoy.** To experience joy or pleasure in; receive pleasure from the possession or use of; to have the use or benefit of.

**Enjoyed.** 'Enjoyed' means having had the amenity or advantage of using. [*Merstham Manor Ltd.* v *Coulsdon* (1936)2 All ER 422].

**Enlarge.** Add to; aggrandize; amplify; develop; escalate; fatten; inflate; lengthen; magnify; make greater; make larger.

To increase in size or extend in scope or duration; to free from custody or imprisonment. [Black's *Law Dictionary*, 7th Ed.].

**Enquiry.** The act or an instance of asking or seeking information; the act of enquiring; investigation; research; search for knowledge; a query; examination; interrogation; scrutiny; study.

"Enquiry" implies investigation of a matter from various sources in order to find the truth. [*Dr. K.C. Malhotra* v *The Chancellor, H.P. University, Shimla* AIR 1995 HP 156].

Enquiry covers the hearing of the case, *i.e.*, recording evidence, admitting documents and generally completing the record upon which a finding would be based. It is only after all the material has been placed on record by both the sides that the stage of reporting a finding would arise. [*Dr. M.N. Dasanna* v *State of A.P.* (1973)2 SCC 378: (1973)1 SCWR 932].

> NOTE: *Enquiry and trial—distinction.* An enquiry is something different from a trial, and that enquiry stops when trial begins. [*Kingam Savaranna* v *State* AIR 1957 AP 472: 1957 Andh LT 418].

• **Further inquiry** p. 379.

**Enter upon the reference.** An arbitrator enters upon a reference when, after having accepted the reference, he applies his mind and does something in furtherance and execution of the work of arbitration. [*Soneyal Thakur* v *Lachminarayan Thakur* AIR 1957 Pat 395: ILR 36 Pat 773].

An arbitrator enters upon reference not when he accepts the office or takes upon himself the duty, but when he actually enters upon the matter of reference, when the parties are before him or under some peremptory order compelling him to conclude the hearing *ex parte*. [*Industrial*

*Gases Ltd.* v *Ganesh Flour Mills* 1971 All LJ 160].

**Entering appearance.** As regards the defendant in an action, appearance is entered by his delivering to the proper officer of the court a memorandum importing either that he appears to defend the action in person or that some solicitor, whose name is given, appears on his behalf.

**Enterprise.** Business; business commercial establishment; company; corporate body; corporation; firm.

An undertaking, especially a bold or difficult one. A venture or undertaking, especially one involving financial commitment. [*Sizemore* v *Hall* 80 P 2d 1092, 1095].

It may also mean activity; adventure; attempt; campaign; cause; endeavour; engagement; plan; programme; project; scheme; venture.

• **Free enterprise** p. 373.

**Entertain.** To receive and take into consideration. [*Nepram Kali Singh* v *Mutum Chana Singh* AIR 1955 Manipur 39].

The dictionary meaning of the word 'entertain', in legal parlance, is to deal with or admit to consideration. The expression 'entertain' does not mean the same thing as the filing of the application or admission of the application by the court. It entertains when it proceeds to consider on merits or adjudicates upon. [*Lakshmiratam Engineering Works Ltd.* v *Assistant Commissioner, Sales Tax* AIR 1968 SC 488: (1968)2 SCJ 1: (1968)1 SCR 505; *Hindusthan Commercial Bank Ltd.* v *Punnu Sahu (Dead) Through LRs.* AIR 1970 SC 1384: (1971)3 SCC 124]. It would not mean only "to receive and determine" but also "adjudicate upon" or "proceed to consider on merits". [*Jadeja Shivubhai* v *Gujarat State Road Transport* (1977)18 Guj LR 656].

The word "entertain" means the first time a court applies its mind to any matter. [*Premier Insurance Co.* v *Vidyawati* AIR 1978 All 264].

The word 'entertain' means 'proceed to consider on merits or adjudicate upon'. The word 'entertain' should not be meant as 'receive' or 'accept'. [*Re Public Prosecutor* (1974)2 APLJ 150].

The word 'entertain' used in respect of suit means 'to receive and take into consideration'. [*N.K. Singh* v *M.C. Singh* AIR 1955 Monipur 39].

The word 'entertain' may, in certain cases, mean merely to receive or accept, and not to a later stage subsequent to such reception, but whether the word 'entertain' means one or the other would depend on the entire scheme of a statute in which that expression occurs and the legislative purpose underlying that scheme. In the context, the expression 'to entertain any suit' may mean not only to file but also to deal with the suit till its final determination. [*Sankar Kumar Bhattar* v *Tehsildar-cum-Revenue Officer, Basta* AIR 1976 Ori 103].

The word "entertain" has other meanings too. It may as verb transitive mean amuse; occupy agreeably.

**Entertainment.** A performance or a show intended to give pleasure; the act or an instance of entertaining; the process of being entertained; diversions or amusements for guests, etc.

In *Geeta Enterprises* v *State of U.P.* [AIR 1983 SC 1098: (1983)4 SCC 202: (1983)3 SCR 812] the word "entertainment" was defined by referring to different dictionaries thus:

Entertainment is something connected with the enjoyment of refreshment rooms, tables, and the like. It is something beyond refreshment: it is the accommodation provided, whether that includes a musical or other amusement or not. [*Words and Phrases, Judicially Defined*, Vol. 2, pp. 206-207].

An entertainment is a source or means of amusement; a diverting performance, especially a public performance, as a concert, drama, or the like. "Entertainment" denotes that which serves for amusement. [*Words and Phrases,* Permanent Ed., vol. 14A, p. 353].

"Entertainment" means amusement, diversion, distraction, recreation, fun, play, good time, past time, novelty, pleasure, enjoyment, satisfaction. [Reader's *Digest Family Word Finder*, p. 264].

"Entertainment" means the act of diverting, amusing or causing someone's time to pass agreeably. Something that diverts, amuses, or occupies the attention agreeably. A public performance designed to divert or amuse. [Webster's *Third New International Dictionary*, p. 757].

"Entertainment" means the art of entertaining, amusing or diverting, the pleasure afforded to the mind by anything interesting, amusement, other performance intended to amuse. [*Concise English Dictionary* by Hayward and Sparkes].

An entertainment is the gathering together of a number of people to carry out some activity or to be present at some activity presumably with a view to enjoying themselves. [*Bow* v *Heatly* 1960 SLT 311].

The natural meaning of 'entertainment' is amusement and gratification of some sort. The term connotes something in the nature of an organised entertainment. An entertainment must be some exhibition, performance, amusement, game or sport for the purpose of entertainment, that is, for affording some sort of amusement and gratification to those who see or hear it. [*Calico Mills Ltd.* v *State of Madhya Pradesh* AIR 1961 MP 257].

The word 'entertainment' is neither a scientific nor a technical term but is used in a very wide and popular sense or as understood in common parlance so as to include within its ambit entertainment of any kind including one which may be purely educative. [*Geeta Enterprises* v *State of U.P.* AIR 1983 SC 1098: (1983)4 SCC 202: 1983 SCC (Tax) 307: (1983)3 SCR 812].

NOTE: Entertainment may be through exhibition, performance, amusement, game, or sport. The word includes all varieties of entertainments and there is no warrant for confining it to entertainments or amusements other than cinema shows. [*Aswathanarayana* v *State of Andhra Pradesh* AIR 1959 AP 461].

Exhibition of motion pictures by means of V.C.R. and T.V. sets in restaurants etc. is entertainment. [*Deep Snack Bar* v *State of Haryana* AIR 1984 Punj 377: 1984 Cur LJ (Civ & Cr) 277].

**Entice.** To take away by arousing desire; to tempt; to lead on or attract by arousing hope of pleasure, profit etc.; allure.

To wrongfully solicit, persuade, procure, allure, attract; draw by blandishment; coax or seduce. To lure, induce, tempt, incite, or persuade a person to do a thing. [*Berger* v *Levy* 43 P 2d 610, 611].

**Entire.** Complete in all its parts; undivided; whole; something which is not severable; free from admixture; unalloyed; pure.

**Entitled.** Authorised; eligible; empowered; permitted; qualified; qualified for; furnished with proper grounds for seeking or claiming.

**Entitled to possession.** The expression 'entitled to possession' means that where the property is found to be stolen property and found to have been purchased by another person in good faith for value, the person entitled to possession of the same is the person who originally lost possession of the property in consequence of theft or misappropriation. [*Roshan Lal* v *State of Punjab* AIR 1957 Punj 297: 1957 Cr LJ 1448 with reference to Criminal Procedure Code 1973, ss. 452, 453].

**Entitled to receive.** The expression 'entitled to receive' does not mean recoverable at law. It means an existing debt or liability. [*Ramkrishna Ramnath* v *Labour Court* AIR 1963 Bom 201].

**Entity.** Corpus; creature; embodiment; matter; living thing; module; tangible object; unit.

• **Legal entity** p. 525.

**Entrepot trade.** Trade consisting of the importing of goods for the specific purpose of export.

**Entrepreneur.** An "entrepreneur" is one who undertakes on his own account the risk element of an industrial or commercial enterprise.

One who initiates and assumes the financial risks of a new enterprise and who usually undertakes its management. [Black's *Law Dictionary*, 8th Ed.].

**Entrustment.** Assignment responsibility for a thing to a person in whom one has confidence.

The expression 'entrustment' carries with it the implication that the person handing over any property or on whose behalf that property is handed over to another continues to be its owner. Further the person handing over the property must have confidence in the person taking the property so as to create a fiduciary relationship between them. A mere transaction of sale cannot amount to an entrustment. An entrustment need not conform to all the technicalities of the law of trust. [*State of Gujarat* v *Jaswantlal Nathalal* AIR 1968 SC 700: (1968)2 SCJ 334: (1968)2 SCR 408: 1968 Cr LJ 803].

Entrustment is not necessarily a term of law. It may have different implications in different contexts. In its most general significance, all its imports is handing over the possession for some purpose which may not imply the conferment of any proprietary right therein. The ownership or beneficial interest in the property must be in some person other than the person entrusted with the property and the later must hold it on account of some person or in some way for his benefit. [*Rashmi Kumar* v *Mahesh Kumar Bhada* (1997)2 SCC 397: 1997 SCC (Cri) 415: JT 1996(11) SC 175].

**Entry.** When used as 'entrance', it means access; admission; entrance; immigration; ingress; ingression; passage.

When used as 'record', it means account; deposition; information preserved in writing; written record; statement recorded in a book; inscription; note; recorded item; memorandum.

▸ *Meaning in relation to Passports Act 1920, ss. 2 and 3.* 'Entry' in s. 2 means entry by water, land or air.

The word 'Entry' in s. 3 can by no stretch of imagination mean continuance of stay. [*Chhanga Khan* v *State* AIR 1956 All 69; *Sambasivame* v *Pondicherry State* ILR (1964)2 Mad 702: (1964)2 MLJ 301].

▸ *Meaning under the Customs Act 1962, s. 2(16).* 'Entry' in relation to goods means an entry made in a bill of entry, shipping bill or bill of export and includes in the case of goods imported or to be imported by post, the entry referred to in s. 82 or the entry made under the regulations made under s. 84.


- **False entry** p. 341.
- **Fictitious entry** p. 351.
- **Forcible entry** p. 364.


**Envoy.** A diplomatic agent deputed by one State to another. He ranks below Ambassador and above *Charge d' Affaires.*

**Equal justice.** Justice uniform in application or effect. "Equal justice" is an aspect of social justice, the salvation of the very weak and downtrodden, and the methodology for levelling them up to a real, not formal, equality being the accent. [*State of Kerala* v *N.M. Thomas* AIR 1976 SC 490: (1976)1 SCR 906: (1976)2 SCC 310].

**Equal pay for equal work.** If two classes of persons do same work under the same employer, with similar responsibility, under similar working conditions, the doctrine of "equal pay for equal work" would apply. [*Jaipal* v *State of Haryana* AIR 1988 SC 1504; *Bharat Process & Mechanical Engineers Limited Asstts. Apprentice* v *Bharat Process & Mechanical Engineers Ltd.* (1987)1 CLJ 157].

Equal pay for equal work for both men and women means equal pay for equal work for everyone and as between the sexes. [*Randhir Singh* v *Union of India* AIR 1982 SC 879: (1982)3 SCR 298: (1982)1 SCC 618].

NOTE: Article 39(*d*) contained in Part IV of the Constitution of India ordains the State to direct its policy towards securing equal pay for equal work for both men and women. The State is under a constitutional obligation to ensure that equal pay is paid for equal work. The doctrine for equal pay for equal work cannot be disregarded on the ground of one employment being temporary and the other being permanent in nature. A temporary or casual employee performing the same duties and functions is entitled to the same pay as paid to a permanent employee. So also, the difference in mode of selection will not affect the application of the doctrine if both the classes of persons performed similar functions and duties under the same employer. [*Jaipal* v *State of Haryana* AIR 1988 SC 1504].

**Equal protection of the laws.** The doctrine is a positive one. It postulates an equal protection of all alike in the same situation and under like circumstances. [*State of U.P.* v *Deoman* AIR 1960 SC 1125, *per* Subba Rao, J.].

The expression is used also in the Fourteenth Amendment of the Constitution of the United States of America. Willis in his *Constitutional Law of the United States* defines the doctrine thus: "The guarantee of the equal protection of the laws means the protection of equal laws. It forbids class legislation, but does not forbid classification, which rests upon reasonable grounds of distinction".

The doctrine as defined by Willis in his *Constitutional Law of the United States* finds its expression in India in *Charanjit Lal Chowdhury* v *Union of India* [AIR 1951 SC 41: 1950 SCR 869: 1951 SCJ 29]. The word 'laws' as used here denotes specific laws in force. [*Sri Srinivasa Theatre* v *Government of Tamil Nadu* AIR 1992 SC 999: (1992)2 SCC 643: JT 1992(2) SC 312].

NOTE: The doctrine finds its expression in Art. 14 of the Constitution of India which lays down that the State shall not deny to any person the equal protection of the laws within the territory of India.

**Equality.** The state of being equal; uniformity.

NOTE: Equality is a dynamic concept with many aspects and dimensions and it cannot be 'cribbed, cabined and confined' within traditional and doctrinaire limit. From a positivistic point of view, equality is antithetic to arbitrariness.

In fact, equality and arbitrariness are sworn enemies; one belongs to the rule of law in a republic while the other, to the whim and caprice of an absolute monarch. [*E.P. Royappa* v *State of Tamil Nadu* (1974)2 SCR 348: AIR 1974 SC 555; *Maneka Gandhi* v *Union of India* AIR 1978 SC 597: (1978)1 SCC 248; *Union of India* v *Tulsiram Patel* AIR 1985 SC 1416: (1985)3 SCC 398].

**Equality before the law.** This doctrine follows from the concept of the English 'rule of law'. "Equality before the law means that among equals the law should be equal and should be equally administered, that like should be treated alike. [*Law and the Constitution* by Jennings, 3rd Ed., p. 49].

Equality before the law is a negative concept. It declares (*i*) that everyone is equal before the law, (*ii*) that none can claim special privileges, (*iii*) that all classes are equally subjected to the ordinary law of the land. [*State of U.P.* v *Deoman* AIR 1960 SC 1125, *per* Subba Rao, J.].

Equality before the law is a dynamic concept having many facets. One facet—the most commonly acknowledged—is that there shall be no privileged person or class and that none shall be above law. [*Sri Srinivasa Theatre* v *Government of Tamil Nadu* AIR 1992 SC 999: (1992)2 SCC 643: JT 1992(2) SC 312].

NOTE: Article 14 of the Constitution of India confirms this doctrine in laying down that the State shall not deny to any person equality before the law within the territory of India. The word 'law' is used in the said Article in a generic sense—a philosophical sense. [*Sri Srinivasa Theatre* v *Government of Tamil Nadu* AIR 1992 SC 999: (1992)2 SCC 643: JT 1992(2) SC 312].

**Equipment.** Furnishings, or outfit for the required purposes; whatever is needed in equipping; the articles comprised in an outfit. [*Department of Treasury, Gross Income-tax Division* v *Ranger-Cook, Inc.* 49 NE 2d 548, 550; *Farm and Home Saving and Loan Ass'n. of Missouri* v *Empire Furniture Co.* Tex Civ App, 87 SW 2d 1111, 1112].

▸*Meaning under the Merchant Shipping Act 1958, s. 3(11).* 'Equipment', in relation to a ship, includes boats, tackle, pumps, apparel, furniture, life-saving appliances of every description, spars, masts, rigging and sails, fog signals, lights, shapes and signals of distress, medicines and medical and surgical stores and appliances, charts, radio installations, appliances for preventing, detecting or extinguishing fires, buckets, compasses, axes, lanterns, loading and discharging gears and appliances of all kinds and all other stores or articles belonging to or to be used in connection with or necessary for the navigation and safety of the ship.

**Equitable.** That which is fair; that which arises from a liberal construction of a legal rule, untrammelled by technical niceties of the law.

That which is done "fairly, justly and impartially". [*State of U.P.* v *Hindustan Aluminium Corporation* AIR 1979 SC 1459: (1979)3 SCR 709: (1979)3 SCC 229].

**Equitable distribution.** Only that distribution can be said to be "equitable" which is "just and right under all circumstances of the particular case". [*State of U.P.* v *Hindustan Aluminium Corporation* AIR 1979 SC 1459: (1979)3 SCR 709: (1979)3 SCC 229].

**Equitable estate.** In English law in a trust estate the interest of the trustee is called the legal estate and the interest of the beneficiary is called the equitable estate. The law in India knows nothing of the distinction between legal and equitable estates.

**Equity.** Equity is the system of law which, prior to the fusion of law and equity effected by the Supreme Court of Judicature Acts 1873 (of England) and 1875, was administered by the Court of Chancery. These Acts emphasised, rather than diminished, the importance of the principles which made up the former system of equity jurisprudence, and it will be necessary, for the purpose of understanding these principles, to make frequent reference to the practice of the Court of Chancery and from time to time to make some mention of the history of the system. [Halsbury's *Laws of England*, 4th Ed., vol. 16, para 1201, p. 807].

NOTE: Every Court in India is a Court of Equity as well as of law. It possesses as inherent in its constitution all such powers as are necessary to do the right and to undo the wrong. [*Hunoomanpersaud* v *Mst. Babooee Munraj* 6 MIA 393 (410-411)]. Inherent powers are saved by s. 151 of the Code of Civil Procedure 1908.

When the equities are equal, the law should prevail (in *aequali jure melior est conditio possidentis*). [*Sailen Krishna Mazumdar* v *Malik Labhu Masih* AIR 1989 SC 1596].


• **Better equity** p. 102.

• **Clog on equity of redemption** p. 148.


**Equity of redemption.** Incident to every mortgage is the right of the mortgagor to redeem, a right which is called his equity of redemption, and which continues notwithstanding that he fails to pay the debt in accordance with the proviso for redemption. [Halsbury's *Laws of England*, 4th Ed., vol. 32, para 407, p. 190].

NOTE: In India the right of the mortgagor to redeem is provided in s. 60 of the Transfer of Property Act 1882.

**Equity share capital.** Equity share capital means, with reference to any such company, all share capital which is not preference share capital. [Companies Act 1956, s. 85(2)].

**Ergonomics.** It is a study of the efficiency of workers, of which Time and Motion study is a part.

**Error.** Mistake; fault; miscount; miscomputation; inaccuracy; aberrance; aberration; incorrect belief; false conception.

It has been defined as a 'psychological state that does not conform to objective reality; a belief that what is false is true or that what is true is false'. [Black's *Law Dictionary*, 7th Ed.].

It is also defined as a 'mistake of law or of fact in a court's judgment, opinion, or order'. [Black's *Law Dictionary*, 7th Ed.].

The term 'error' when used with reference to the purchase of real estate has been construed to mean a misstatement or misdescription erroneously and not wilfully introduced. The word 'error' is construed in this case to mean any unintentional misdescription. [*Taylor* v *Bullen* (1850)5 Exch 799].

• **Apparent error** p. 67.

• **Clerical error** p. 148.

**Error apparent on the face of the record.** Plain, fundamental error that goes to the foundation of the action irrespective of the evidence; an obvious misapprehension of the applicable law. [*Parks* v *Parks* 98 F 2d 235, 236].

> NOTE: What is an error apparent on the face of the record cannot be described precisely or exhaustively, there being an element of indefiniteness inherent in its very nature and it must be left to be determined judicially on the facts of each case. [*Maula Bux* v *State of Vindhya Pradesh* AIR 1956 Vin Pra 1]. No error can be said to be apparent on the face of the record if it is not self evident, and if it requires an examination or argument to establish it. But there may be cases where this test may break down, for judicial opinions differ. What is self evident to one judge may not be so to another. [*Hari Vishnu* v *Ahmed Ishaq* AIR 1955 SC 233: 1955 SCA 105: (1955)1 SCR 1104].
>
> Error justifying a review under Or. 47, r. 1, C.P. Code may be one of fact or of law. [*Ramaswami Padayachi* v *Shanmugha Padayachi* (1959)2 MLJ 201].

**Error of fact.** Error of fact occurs when, by reason of some fact which is unknown to the court and not apparent on the record (e.g., infancy or death of one of the parties); it renders a judgment void or voidable. [*Schwartz* v *Kominski* 324 NE 2d 91, 93].

**Error of judgment.** The expression 'error of judgment' is not a term of art. It is, in fact, one of the vaguest possible description. It can, colloquially, be used to describe either negligent act or one which, though mistaken, is not negligent. [*Simpson* v *Peat* (1952)1 All ER 447].

**Error of law apparent on the face of record.** An error of the court in applying the law to the case on trial.

> NOTE: The error of law should be so patent that a bare perusal of the judgment and the record would show that there was error. [*Rajinder Parshad* v *Punjab State* AIR 1966 Punj 185: ILR (1966)2 Punj 38]. If on a question two views are possible and the court adopts one, there is no error apparent on the face of the record. [*Rekharani* v *Kamakhya Prosad* AIR 1985 NOC 47 (Gau)].

**Error of law on the face of award.** 'An error of law on the face of the award' means that you can find in the award or a document actually incorporated therein, as for instance a note appended by the arbitrator stating the reasons for his judgment, some legal proposition which is the basis of the award and which you can then say is erroneous. [*Champsey Bhara* v *Jivraj Balloo* (1923) AC 480].

> NOTE: An amount awarded by the arbitrator on an erroneous assumption of law is an error of law on the face of the award. In such case the court can interfere. [*Union of India* v *Rallia Ram* AIR 1963 SC 1685].

**Error qui non resistur, approbatur.** An error which is not resisted is approved.

**Escalation clause.** An 'escalation clause' according to its accepted legal connotation means a clause which takes care of the rise and fall of prices in the market. [*D.C.G. Mills Co. Ltd.* v *Raj. State Electricity Board* AIR 1986 SC 1126: (1986)2 SCC 431: (1986)1 SCR 633].

**Escaped assessment.** When a person is not assessed to tax though he is liable to be taxed, he escapes assessment. [*Tax Officer-cum-Regional Transport Officer* v *Durg Transport Company (Pvt.) Ltd., Durg* (1972)4 SCC 43: 1971 (Supp) SCR 1988: (1972)85 ITR 156].

> NOTE: The term "escaped assessment" includes both non-assessment as well as under-assessment. [*Tax Officer-cum-Regional Transport Officer* v *Durg Transport Company (Pvt.) Ltd., Durg*, supra].

**Escheat.** Reversion of property, especially real property, to the state upon the death of an owner who has neither a will nor any legal heirs. [Black's *Law Dictionary*, 8th Ed.].

Escheat was the right whereby land of which there was no longer any tenant returned, by reason of tenure, to the lord by whom or by whose predecessors in title, the tenure was created. Escheat was an incident of feudal tenure, and was based on the want of a tenant to perform the feudal services. [Halsbury's *Laws of England*, 4th Ed., vol. 17, para 1435, p. 744]. The right of escheat has been abolished.

NOTE: If a Hindu dies intestate leaving no heir, his property devolves on the Government subject to all the obligations and liabilities of an heir. [Hindu Succession Act 1956, s. 29]. The estate of a deceased Mahomedan also escheats to the State on failure of all the heirs.

**Escrow.** The general arrangement under which a legal document or property is delivered to a third person until the occurrence of a condition; the holder of such a document, property. [Black's *Law Dictionary*, 8th Ed.].

An intended deed may, after sealing and any signature required for execution as a deed, be delivered as an escrow (or scroll), that is as a simple writing which is not to become the deed of the party expressed to be bound by it until some condition has been performed. [Halsbury's *Laws of England*, 4th Ed., vol. 12, para 1332, p. 525].

Occasionally a deed is delivered to a third person not a party to it, to be delivered up to the other party or parties, upon the performance of a condition, as the payment of money or the like. It is then said to be delivered as an escrow or mere writing (*scriptum*); for it is not a perfect deed until delivered up on the performance of the condition; but when so delivered up, it operates from the time of its execution. [Williams & Eastwood's *Real Property*, p. 430].

**Espionage.** Intelligence; obtaining of classified information; practice of spying on others; secret watching; spying; subversive activity; surveillance; undercover work.

Espionage, or spying, has reference to the crime of "gathering, transmitting or losing" information respecting the national defence with intent or reason to believe that the information is to be used to the injury of the country concerned, or to the advantage of any foreign nation. [*Rosenberg* v *United States* 97 L Ed 1609].

• **Industrial espionage** p. 453.

**Esquire.** An Esquire was originally one who attended a knight in time of war. At present it is the title appended to the name of one regarded as a gentleman by birth, position, or education, especially in an address of a letter. A Barrister-at-Law is an Esquire by virtue of his office. Similarly Doctors in the several faculties and Justices of the Peace are also Esquires.

**Essence.** That which is indispensable; the gist or substance of any act; the vital constituent of a thing; that without which a thing cannot be itself. [*Norman* v *Department of Labour and Industries* 116 P 2d 360, 362].

"Essence" is a flavouring material and its function is to add flavour to the food, *i.e.*, to make it more palatable. It appeals to the tongue or to the palate. [*Commissioner of Sales Tax, U.P.* v *S.N. Brothers, Kanpur* AIR 1973 SC 78: (1973)2 SCR 852: (1973)3 SCC 496: (1973)31 STC 302].

**Essence of the contract.** An essential stipulation in a contract without which the contract would not have been entered into.

NOTE: When a party to a contract promises to do a certain thing at or before a specified time, and fails to do that thing at or before the specified time, the contract becomes voidable at the option of the promisee, if the intention of the parties was that time should be of the essence of the contract. [Indian Contract Act 1872, s. 55].

Unless a different intention appears from the terms of the contract, stipulations as to time of payment are not deemed to be of the essence of a contract of sale. Whether any other stipulation as to time is of the essence of the contract or not depends on the terms of the contract. [Sale of Goods Act 1930, s. 11].

**Essential commodities.** Commodities essential for survival.

▸ *Meaning under the Essential Commodities Act 1955, s. 2(a).* 'Essential commodities' means any of the following commodities— (*i*) cattle fodder, including oilcakes and other commodities; (*ii*) coal including coke and other derivatives; (*iii*) component parts and other accessories of automobiles; (*iv*) cotton and woollen textiles; (*v*) foodstuffs including edible oilseeds and oils; (*vi*) iron and steel, including manufactured products of iron and steel; (*vii*) paper including newsprint, paper board and straw board; (*viii*) petroleum and petroleum products; (*ix*) raw cotton, whether ginned or unginned and cotton seed; (*x*) raw jute; (*xi*) any other class of commodity which the Central Government may, by notified order, declare to be an essential commodity for the purposes of the Essential Commodities Act, being a commodity with respect to which Parliament has power to make laws by virtue of Entry 33 in List III in the Seventh Schedule to the Constitution.

▸ *Meaning under the West Bengal Maintenance of Public Order Act 1972, s. 2(a).* 'Essential commodity' means food, water, fuel, light or power and it includes such other things as may be declared by the State Government, by notification, to be essential for the life of the community.

**Essential service.** Service essential for survival and existence.

▸ *Meaning under the Essential Services Maintenance Act 1968, s. 2(a).* 'Essential service' means— (*i*) any postal, telegraph or telephone service; (*ii*) any railway service or any other transport service for the carriage of passengers or goods by land, water or air with respect to which Parliament has power to make laws; (*iii*) any service connected with the operation or maintenance of aerodromes, or with the operation, repair or maintenance of aircraft; (*iv*) any service connected with the loading, unloading, movement or storage of goods in any port; (*v*) any service connected with the clearance of goods or passengers through the Customs or with the prevention of smuggling; (*vi*) any service in any mint or security press; (*vii*) any service in any defence establishment of the Government of India; (*viii*) any service in connection with the affairs of the Union, not being a service specified in any of the foregoing sub-clauses; (*ix*) any other service connected with matters with respect to which Parliament has power to make laws and which the Central Government being of opinion that strikes therein would prejudicially affect the maintenance of any public utility service, the public safety or the maintenance of supplies and service necessary for the life of the community or would result in the infliction of grave hardship on the community, may, by notification in the Official Gazette, declare to be an essential service for the purposes of the Essential Services Maintenance Act.

▸ *Meaning under the West Bengal Maintenance of Public Order Act 1972, s. 2(b).* 'Essential service' means any service connected with—(*i*) public conservancy or sanitation, (*ii*) hospitals and dispensaries, (*iii*) tramways or transport, whether provided by the State or by any other authority or individual, or (*iv*) gas works, and includes such other services connected with the matters with respect to which the State Legislature has powers to make laws and which the State Government, being of opinion that the maintenance of such service is necessary for the prevention of grave hardship to the community, may, by notification, declare to be essential service.

**Establish.** To settle, make, or fix firmly; to enact permanently; to make or form; to bring about or into existence; to prove; to convince. [Black's *Law Dictionary*, 8th Ed.].

To make secure or permanent in a certain place, condition, job etc.; to create or set up (an organisation etc.) as on a permanent basis; to settle or fix firmly; make stable or permanent; to set up; found, as an institution or business; to set up, install (oneself or some one else) in business, a position etc. [*Shiromani*

*Gurdwara Prabandhak Committee* v *Mihan Singh* (1993)3 SCC 650: JT 1993(4) SC 202].

For the purpose of Art. 30(1) of the Constitution of India, the word 'establish' means to bring into existence and by the Article the right is given to the minority to bring into existence an educational institution, and if they do so to administer it. [*Azeez Basha* v *Union of India* AIR 1968 SC 662: (1968)1 SCA 357: (1968)2 SCJ 299].

> NOTE: *'Factory'—when said to be established.* A factory cannot be said to be established until a manufacturing process is carried on in any part of the factory, even though the factory may have been registered earlier. [*Great Eastern Electroplaters Ltd.* v *Regional Provident Fund Commissioner* AIR 1956 All 495: (1957)2 Lab LJ 225].
>
> Where a factory starts its work on a trial basis, the trial period should not be excluded in determining the date on which the factory was established. [*Regional Provident Fund Commissioner* v *Great Eastern Electroplaters Ltd.* AIR 1959 All 133: (1958)2 Lab LJ 676].

**Establishment.** The place where one is permanently fixed for residence or business; residence including grounds, furniture, equipage, retinue etc., with which one is fitted out; also an institution or place of business with its fixtures and organised staff, as a large establishment, a manufacturing establishment; organised body of men maintained for a purpose.

▸*Meaning under the Apprentices Act 1961, s. 2(g).* 'Establishment' includes any place where any industry is carried on.

▸*Meaning under the Beedi and Cigar Workers (Conditions of Employment) Act 1966, s. 2(h).* 'Establishment' means any place or premises including the precincts thereof in which or in any part of which any manufacturing process connected with the making of beedi or cigar or both is being or is ordinarily carried on and includes an industrial premises.

▸*Meaning under the Contract Labour (Regulation and Abolition) Act 1970, s. 2(e).* 'Establishment' means—(*i*) any office or department of the Government or a local authority, or (*ii*) any place where any industry, trade, business, manufacture or occupation is carried on.

▸*Meaning under the Employment Exchanges (Compulsory Notification of Vacancies) Act 1959, s. 2(e).* 'Establishment' means—(*a*) any office, or (*b*) any place where any industry, trade, business or occupation is carried on.

▸*Meaning under the National Service Act 1972, s. 2(b).* 'Establishment' means—(*i*) any office, or (*ii*) any place where any industry, trade, business or occupation is carried on and includes any technical institution or training centre.

▸*Meaning under the Weekly Holidays Act 1942, s. 2(a).* 'Establishment' means a shop, restaurant or theatre.

'Establishment' is not the same thing as 'employer' or 'employee', but different from them. [*R.L. Sahni* v *Union of India* AIR 1966 Mad 416: (1966)2 Lab LJ 230].

An 'establishment' is an organization which employs persons between whom and the establishment the relationship of employee and employer exists. [*V. Transports (Private) Ltd.* v *Regional Provident Fund Commissioner* AIR 1965 Mad 466].

• **Commercial establishment** p. 156.

• **Work-charged establishment** p. 902.

**Establishment in private sector.** An establishment not in public sector.

▸*Meaning under the Apprentices Act 1961, s. 2(h); Payment of Bonus Act 1965, s. 2(15).* An establishment which is not an establishment in public sector.

▸*Meaning under the Employment Exchanges (Compulsory Notification of Vacancies) Act 1959, s. 2(g).* 'Establishment in private sector' means an establishment which is not an establishment in public sector and where ordinarily twenty-five or more persons are employed to work for remuneration.

**Establishment in public sector.** An establishment not in private sector.

▸*Meaning under the Apprentices Act 1961, s. 2(i); Employment Exchanges (Compulsory Notification of Vacancies) Act 1959, s. 2(f).* An establishment owned, controlled or managed by—(1) the Government or a department of the Government; (2) a Government company as defined in s. 617 of the Companies Act 1956 (1 of 1956); (3) a corporation (including a co-operative society) established by or under a Central, Provincial or State Act, which is owned, controlled or managed by the Central, Provincial or State Government; (4) a local authority. [*Union of India* v *N. Hargopal* AIR 1987 SC 1227: (1987)2 SCR 910: (1987)3 SCC 308: JT 1987(2) SC 182].

▸*Meaning under the Payment of Bonus Act 1965, s. 2(16).* 'Establishment in public sector' means an establishment owned, controlled or managed by—(*a*) a Government company as defined in s. 617 of the Companies Act 1956 (1 of 1956); (*b*) a corporation in which not less than forty per cent of its capital is held (whether singly or taken together) by—(*i*) the Government; or (*ii*) the Reserve Bank of India; or (*iii*) a corporation owned by the Government or the Reserve Bank of India.

**Estate.** The word is used to describe, first, the nature of a man's interest in land; and then the extent of such interest. The word 'estate' has also a third meaning. It is used to denote the whole of any person's valuable interest in land or goods. [Williams & Eastwood on *Real Property*, p. 5].

"Estate" describes the tenant's relation to the land by indicating the extent of his proprietary interest. Common law first detaches ownership from the land and then attaches it to an imaginary thing called an estate in the land. The tenant does not own the land, but he owns an estate in the land. His interest will vary in size according to the time for which it is to continue in existence. Duration governs quantum. [G.C. Cheshire's *Modern Law of Real Property*].

▸*Meaning under Bengal Land Registration Act 1876.* Under the Bengal Land Registration Act 1876, land can be included in the Register prepared and maintained under that Act only if such land is an "estate" as defined in that Act. The relevant part of that definition is: "estate" includes any land subject to the land revenue, either immediately or prospectively, for the discharge of which a separate engagement has been entered into with Government. [*Sailendra Narayan Bhanja Deo* v *State of Orissa* AIR 1956 SC 346: 1956 SCR 72: 1956 SCJ 449].

▸*Meaning under the Bengal Tenancy Act 1885, s. 3(4).* It means land included under one entry in any of the general registers of revenue-paying lands and revenue-free lands, prepared and maintained under the law for the time being in force by the Collector of a District, and includes Government *khas mahals* and revenue-free lands not entered in any register.

▸*Meaning under the Constitution of India 1950, Art. 31A(2).* The expression 'estate' shall, in relation to any local area, have the same meaning as that expression or its local equivalent has in the existing law relating to land tenures in force in that area, and shall also include—(*i*) any *jagir*, *inam* or *muafi* or other similar grant and in the States of Madras and Kerala, any *Janmam* right; (*ii*) any land held under *ryotwari* settlement; (*iii*) any land held or let for purposes of agriculture or for the purposes ancillary thereto, including waste land, forest land, land for pasture or sites of buildings and other structures occupied by cultivators of land, agricultural labourers and village artisans. [*The Kannan Devan Hills Produce* v *State of Kerala* AIR 1972 SC 2301: (1973)1 SCR 356: (1972)2 SCC 218].

The word 'estate' has undoubtedly in law a diversity of meaning and a variety of signification. It may mean the property of a living person or that of a deceased person which passes to his administrator. Generally speaking, the word means property of every character, but ordinarily it is applied to the property of a deceased person or a ward or a lunatic or a banking etc., according to which meaning it conveys an idea of property which is administered by administrators or executors or courts. [*Jal Kaur* v *Pala Singh* AIR 1961 Punj 391].

NOTE: The basic concept of the word 'estate' is that the person holding the estate should be proprietor of the soil and should be in indirect relationship with the State paying land revenue to it, except where it is remitted in whole or in part. [*Purushothaman Nambudri* v *State of Kerala* AIR 1962 SC 694: (1962)1 SCJ 477; *Gullabhai* v *Union of India* AIR 1967 SC 1110, 1115].


- **Equitable estate** p. 314.
- **Future estate** p. 379.
- **Joint estate** p. 487.
- **Life estate** p. 535.
- **Limited estate** p. 536.
- **Surrender of demised estate** p. 824.


**Estate clause.** An express clause in conveyance, passing all the estate etc. in the property conveyed; usually added after the description of parcels, *i.e.*, the property transferred.

**Estate duty.** A duty levied upon the principal value of all property, real or personal, settled or not settled, which passed or was deemed to pass on death of the owner thereof.

NOTE: In India, Estate Duty was imposed by the Estate Duty Act 1953 which has since been repealed.

**Estate in expectancy.** See EXPECTANCY, ESTATE IN p. 330.

**Estate of inheritance.** It is one which is subject to the owner's power of alienation. It is capable of devolving after the death of the owner upon his heirs.

**Estimate.** Evaluate; appraise; gauge; give an approximate value; put an approximate price on; a valuing or rating by the mind, without actually measuring, weighing, or the like.

A rough or approximate calculation only. [*United States* v *Foster* CCA Iowa, 131 F 2d 3, 7].

**Estimation.** A quantity qualified by the expression 'by estimation' means more or less.

**Estoppel.** A bar that prevents one from asserting a claim or right that contradicts what one has said or done before or what has been legally established as true; a bar that prevents the relitigation of issues; an affirmative defence alleging good-faith reliance on a misleading representation and an injury or detrimental change in position resulting from that reliance. [Black's *Law Dictionary*, 8th Ed.].

There is said to be an estoppel where a party is not allowed to say that certain statement of fact is untrue, whether in reality it is true or not. Estoppel, or 'conclusion' as it is frequently called by older authorities, may, therefore, be defined as a disability whereby a party is precluded from alleging or proving in legal proceedings that a fact is otherwise than it has been made to appear by the matter giving rise to that disability. Estoppel is often described as a rule of evidence, but the whole concept is more correctly viewed as a substantive rule of law. [Halsbury's *Laws of England*, 4th Ed., vol. 16, para 1501, p. 1008].

"Estoppel" means that a party is prevented by his own acts from claiming a right to the detriment of the other party who was entitled to rely on such conduct and has acted accordingly. [*Graham* v *Asbury* 540 P 2d 656, 658].

An estoppel arises when one is concluded and forbidden by law to speak against his own act or deed. [*Gural* v *Engle* 25 A 2d 257, 261].

Estoppel is a rule of equity which forbids truth being pleaded or representation, on which faith another has acted to his detriment, being retracted. [*Commissioner of Income Tax (Central)* v *B.N. Bhattacharjee* AIR 1979 SC 1725: (1979)3 SCR 1133: (1979)4 SCC 121].

NOTE: Estoppel is a rule of evidence and the general rule is enacted in s. 115 of the Evidence Act. The section lays down estoppel by conduct as distinguished from an estoppel by record which constitutes the bar of *res judicata*. [*Sunderbai* v *Devaji* AIR 1954 SC 82]. The basis of estoppel is that it would be unfair or unjust to allow a party to depart from a particular state of affairs which another has taken to be correct. [*Central Newbury Car Auctions Ltd.* v *Unity Finance Ltd.* (1956)3 All ER 904].

The soul of estoppel is equity, not facility for inequity. Estoppel against statute is not permissible because public policy animating a statutory provision may then become the casualty. [*Commissioner of Income Tax (Central)* v *B.N. Bhattacharjee* AIR 1979 SC 1725: (1979)3 SCR 1133: (1979)4 SCC 121].

Estoppel is of four kinds—(1) *By record*, which imports such absolute and incontrovertible variety that no person against whom it is producible shall be permitted to aver against it, *e.g.*, a decision of a court. This is dealt with in ss. 40 to 44 of the Indian Evidence Act 1872; (2) *By deed*, no person can be allowed to dispute his solemn deed, which is, therefore, conclusive against him and those claiming under him, even as to the facts recited in it; (3) *In pais*, *i.e.*, by conduct or representation, as that a tenant cannot dispute his landlord's title. [Wharton's *Law Lexicon*]. Section 116 of the Indian Evidence Act deals with this; and (4) *By conduct*, where a person has, by his declaration, act or omission, permitted another to believe a thing to be true and to act upon such belief, neither he nor his representative shall be allowed to deny its truth. Section 115 of the Evidence Act deals with this.

*'Estoppel' and 'waiver'—distinction.* Waiver is distinct from estoppel in that in waiver the essential element is actual intent to abandon or surrender right, while in estoppel such intent is immaterial. [*Provash Chandra Dalui* v *Biswanath Banerjee* AIR 1989 SC 1834: 1989 Supp (1) SCC 487: (1989)2 SCR 401: JT 1989 (Supp) SC 92].

- **Feeding the estoppel** p. 349.
- **Issue estoppel.** The phrase "issue estoppel" is comparatively new. But it has long been recognised as a form of estoppel *per rem judicatam*. As opposed to "action estoppel", *issue estoppel* arises where some issue between the same parties was incidental to a decision in a former action. The requirements are three—(*i*) that the same question has been decided; (*ii*) that the judicial decision which is said to create the estoppel is final; and (*iii*) that the parties to the judicial decision or their privies were the same persons as the parties to the proceedings in which the estoppel is raised or their privies. [*Carl-zeiss-Stflung* v *Rayner and Keeler Ltd.* (No. 2), (1966)2 All ER 535]. Issue estoppel is not a rule of evidence.

NOTE: The Indian Supreme Court has applied "issue estoppel" in criminal cases. [*Manipur Administration* v *Bira Singh* AIR 1965 SC 87; *Ravinder Singh* v *State of Haryana* AIR 1975 SC 856: 1975 Cr LJ 765: (1975)3 SCC 742].

- **Promissory estoppel** p. 697.

**Estoppel by deed.** Where there is a statement of fact in a deed made between parties and verified by their seals, an estoppel results, and is called "estoppel by deed". If upon the true construction of the deed the statement is that of both or all the parties, the estoppel is binding on each party; if otherwise, it is only binding on the party making it. It seems that an estoppel also arises upon a deed poll, the mode of its execution being equally solemn with that of a deed made *inter partes.* [Halsbury's *Laws of England*, 4th Ed., vol. 16, para 1594, p. 1009].

**Estoppel by silence.** An estoppel which arises where a person who by force of circumstances is under a duty to another to speak, refrains from doing so and thereby leads the other to believe in the existence of a state of facts in reliance upon which he acts to his prejudice. [Ballentine's *Law Dictionary*].

**Estoppel of record.** Estoppel of record or quasi of record also known as estoppel per *rem judicatam* arises (1) where an issue of fact has been judicially determined in a final manner between the parties by a tribunal having jurisdiction, concurrent of exclusive, in the matter, and the same issue comes directly in question in subsequent proceedings between the same parties; (2) where the first determination was by a court having exclusive jurisdiction and the same issue comes incidentally in question in subsequent proceedings between same parties; (3) in some cases where an issue of fact affecting the status of a person or thing has been necessarily determined in a final manner as a substantive part of a judgment *in rem* of a tribunal having jurisdiction to determine that status, and the same issue comes directly in question in subsequent civil or criminal proceedings between any parties whatever. Where the earlier decision is that of a court of record, the resulting estoppel is said to be 'of record'; where it is that of any other tribunal, whether constituted by agreement of the parties or otherwise, the estoppel is said to be 'quasi of record'. [Halsbury's *Laws of England*, 4th Ed., vol. 16, para 1503, p. 1009].

**Etc., et cetera.** When a list of things is given and the list concludes with the general words like 'et cetera', the meaning of the general words is restricted to things of the same class as those which are contained in the list. [*Milne's Trustees* v *Davidson* (1956) SLT 34]. *Et cetera* does not share the characteristics of an inclusive definition and cannot enlarge the scope of the expression preceding it. [*K.V. Mathew* v *District Manager, Telephones* AIR 1984 Ker 40].

**Etiquette.** Etiquette is the usual term for the conduct or procedure required by good breeding or prescribed by authority to be observed in social or official life.

**Evacuee.** A person evacuated from a place of danger; one who has been removed from or has abandoned his home.

▸*Meaning under the Administration of Evacuee Property Act 1950, s. 2(d).* 'Evacuee' means any person—(*i*) who, on account of the setting up of the Dominions of India and Pakistan or on account of civil disturbances or the fear of such disturbances, leaves or has, on or after the 1st day of March 1947, left, any place in a State for any place outside the territories now forming part of India, or (*ii*) who is resident in any place now forming part of Pakistan and who for that reason is unable to occupy, supervise or manage in person his property in part of the said territories to which that Act extends, or whose property in any part of the said territories has ceased to be occupied, supervised or managed by any person or is being occupied, supervised or managed by an unauthorised person, or (*iii*) who has, after the 14th day of August 1947, obtained, otherwise than by way of purchase or exchange, any right to, interest in or benefit from any property which is treated as evacuee or abandoned property under any law for the time being in force in Pakistan, or (*iv*) who has, after the 18th day of October 1949, transferred to Pakistan, without the previous approval of the Custodian, his assets or any part of his assets situated in any part of the territories to which this Act extends, or (*v*) who has, after the 18th day of October 1949, acquired and if the action has been made in person, by way of purchase or exchange, or if the acquisition has been made by or through a member of his family, in any manner whatsoever, any right to, interest in, or benefit from, any property which is treated as evacuee or abandoned property under any law for the time being in force in Pakistan.

▸*Meaning under the Transfer of Evacuee Deposits Act 1954, s. 2(d).* 'Evacuee' means any person who, on account of the setting up of the Dominions of India and Pakistan or on account of civil disturbances or the fear of such disturbances, has on or after the first day of March 1947, left any place in the territories to which this Act extends and who is now residing in any place forming part of Pakistan.

**Evacuee property.** Property of a person evacuated from a place of danger.

▸*Meaning under the Administration of Evacuee Property Act 1950, s. 2(f).* Any property of an evacuee (whether held by him as owner or as a trustee or as a beneficiary or as a tenant or in any other capacity), and includes any property which has been obtained by any person from an evacuee after the 14th day of August 1947, by any mode of transfer which is not effective by reason of the provisions contained in s. 40 of the Administration of Evacuee Property Act 1950, but does not include—(*i*) any ornament and any wearing apparel, cooking vessels or other household effects in the immediate possession of an evacuee; (*ii*) any property belonging to a joint stock company, the registered office of which was situated before the 15th day of August 1947 in any place now forming part of Pakistan and continues to be so situated after the said date.

**Evasion.** An act of eluding, dodging, or avoiding, or avoidance by artifice [*City of Wink* v *Griffith Amusement Co.* 100 SW 2d 695, 701]; a subtle endeavouring to set aside truth or to escape the punishment of the law.

- **Tax evasion** p. 831.

**Eviction.** Act of driving out; act of throwing out; deprivation of possession; ejection; forceable expulsion from property; recovery of property from another's possession.

The act or process of legally dispossessing a person of land or rental property. [Black's *Law Dictionary*, 8th Ed.].

Any wrongful act of a permanent character done by the landlord or his agent with the intention of depriving the tenant of the enjoyment of the demised premises or any part of them will operate as an eviction. [Halsbury's *Laws of England*, 4th Ed., vol. 27, para 236, p. 187].

Eviction of tenant now means, not a mere trespass and nothing more, but something of a more permanent character done by the landlord with the intention of depriving the tenant of the enjoyment of the whole or part of the demised premises. [*Upton* v *Townsend* (1955)17 CB 30].

> NOTE: 'Eviction' is not confined to the act of expulsion, but may extend to the whole process by which recovery of property is obtained at law; in that sense an eviction may be said to commence when the landlord files his suit. [*Ram Labhaya* v *Dhani Ram* AIR 1947 Lah 296].
>
> The words 'eviction' and 'vacation' do not mean mere physical removal of the occupant from the land. The words mean that on eviction the land has to be restored to the original position so as to be used for the purposes for which it was given to the occupant. [*State of Bombay* v *Fakir Kumar* AIR 1961 SC 722].

**Evidence.** Something (including testimony, documents and tangible objects) that tends to prove or disprove the existence of an alleged fact; the collective mass of things, especially testimony and exhibits, presented before a tribunal in a given dispute; the body of law regulating the admissibility of what is offered as proof into the record of a legal proceeding. [Black's *Law Dictionary*, 8th Ed.].

> NOTE: Evidence is the usual means of proving or disproving a fact or matter in issue. The law of evidence indicates what may properly be introduced by a party (that is, what is admissible), and also what standard of proof is necessary (that is, the quality or quantity of evidence necessary in any particular case). In short, the law of evidence governs the means and manner in which a party may substantiate his own case, or refute that of his opponent. [Halsbury's *Laws of England*, 4th Ed., vol. 17, para 1, p. 4].

Evidence, as used in judicial proceedings, has several meanings. The two main senses of the word are: first, the means, apart from argument and inference, whereby the court is informed as to the issues of fact as ascertained by the pleadings; secondly, the subject-matter of such means. The word is also used to denote that some fact may be admitted as proof and also in some cases that some fact has relevance to the issues of fact. In a real sense evidence is that which may be placed before the court in order that it may decide the issues of fact. [Phipson on *Evidence,* 13th Ed., p. 2].

▸ *Meaning under the Indian Evidence Act 1872, s. 3.* 'Evidence' means and includes—(1) all statements which the court permits or requires to be made before it by witnesses, in relation to matters of fact under inquiry; such statements are called oral evidence; (2) all documents including electronic records produced for the inspection of the court; such documents are called documentary evidence.

The word "evidence" means and includes all documents produced for inspection of the court. [*Parry's Confectionary* v *Food Inspector* (1989)1 Crimes 88].

The expression "evidence" as defined in s. 3 means and includes all statements which the court permits or requires to be made before it by witnesses and all documents produced for the inspection of the court. [*Ramnarayan Mor* v *State of Maharashtra* AIR 1964 SC 949: (1964)5 SCR 1064: (1964)2 Cr LJ 44].

▸*Meaning under the Criminal Procedure Code 1973, s. 319(1).* The word "evidence" occurring in sub-sec. (1) is used in a comprehensive and broad sense which would also include the material collected by the investigating officer and the material or evidence which comes before the court and from which the court can *prima facie* conclude that the person not arraigned before it is involved in the commission of the crime. [*Rakesh* v *State of Haryana* AIR 2001 SC 2521: JT 2001(5) SC 639: (2001)6 SCC 248].

NOTE: *Types of evidence.* Evidence may be: (1) Oral—statements made by witnesses in court under oath; (2) Documentary—documents produced for the inspection of the Judge; (3) Direct—evidence of a fact actually seen by a witness with his own eyes; (4) Circumstantial—indirect evidence which is relevant, inasmuch as it establishes facts from which presumptions or conclusions may be drawn; (5) Real—evidence supplied by material objects produced for the inspection of the court; and (6) Hearsay—evidence of a fact not actually seen or heard by a witness himself, but told to him by another person. [Osborn & Grandage's *Concise Commercial Dictionary*].

Direct evidence is limited to cases where the principal fact, or *factum probandum*, is attested directly by witnesses, things or documents. Indirect evidence also known as circumstantial evidence is either conclusive or presumptive: conclusive when the connection between the principal and evidentiary facts—the *factum probandum* and *factum probans*—is a necessary consequence of the law of Nature: presumptive, where it rests on a greater or lesser degree of probability. In one sense, direct evidence too is only presumptive as it rests on a presumption of the accuracy and veracity of witnesses or documents.

*'Evidence' and 'proof'—distinction.* There is a distinction between 'evidence' and 'proof'. As soon as the document is produced for inspection of the court, it becomes evidence. It can be acted upon when it is proved. [*Parry's Confectionery* v *Food Inspector* (1989)1 Crimes 88].


- **Admissible evidence** p. 42.
- **Admitted in evidence** p. 43.
- **Circumstantial evidence** p. 142.
- **Conclusive evidence** p. 167.
- **Corroborative evidence** p. 198.
- **Direct evidence** p. 260.
- **Disappearance of evidence** p. 262.
- **Fabricate false evidence** p. 335.
- **Fabricated evidence** p. 335.
- **Hearsay evidence** p. 410.
- **Indirect evidence** p. 451.
- **Primary evidence** p. 684.
- **Rebutting evidence** p. 732.
- **Secondary evidence** p. 780.


**Evidentiary fact.** A fact furnishing evidence of the existence or non-existence of some other fact.

**Ex cathedra.** From the chair. With official authority. By virtue of one's high office or position.

**Ex concessis.** From the things already conceded; admittedly.

**Ex contractu.** Actions *ex contractu* are actions arising out of breaches of contract, express or implied.

**Ex curia.** Out of court.

**Ex debito justitiae.** As a matter of right as opposed to a matter for the favour or discretion of the court.

A term opposite to *ex gratia*, it means in accordance with the requirement of justice.

**Ex defectu sanguinis.** From failure of blood; for want of issue.

**Ex delicto.** From or arising out of an offence; from the crime.

**Ex dolo malo non oritur actio.** No right of action can arise out of fraud.

**Ex facto jus oritur.** The law arises out of the facts.

**Ex gratia.** As a matter of favour or grace.

**Ex jure naturae.** By the law of nature.

**Ex justa causa.** By a just cause.

**Ex mero motu.** Of his own accord.

**Ex necessitate.** By necessity.

**Ex nihilo nihil fit.** Out of nothing comes nothing.

**Ex nudo pacto non aritur actio.** From a bare contract—*i.e.*, a contract without consideration—an action does not arise.

A consideration of some sort or another is so necessary to the formation of a contract that a *undum pactum*, or agreement to do or to pay something on one side, without any compensation on the other, will not at law support an action. And a man cannot be compelled to perform it.

**Ex officio.** By virtue of an office. Any prerogative or jurisdiction which a person in office has, by virtue of that office, he is said to exercise *ex officio*.

**Ex parte.** Done or made at the instance and for the benefit of one party only, and without notice to, or argument by, any person adversely interested. [Black's *Law Dictionary*, 7th Ed.].

On one side only; by or for one party; done for, in behalf of, or on the application of, one party only. [Black's *Law Dictionary*, 5th Ed.].

The expression does carry with it the connotation that a Court or a Judge or a Tribunal has proceeded in the absence of the other party when it could have had the other party before it or when it was not prevented by law from having the other party before it. [*P.N. Film Ltd.* v *Overseas Films* AIR 1958 Bom 10: ILR (1957) Bom 520].

**Ex post facto.** By a matter happening afterwards; from a later act or event.

**Ex post facto law.** An Act or statute changing the law as to previous events or contracts.

NOTE: In Criminal jurisprudence, the operation of *ex post facto* law is controlled by Art. 20(1), Constitution of India. Even if a criminal law is enacted by any legislature retrospectively its retrospective operation will be regulated by Art. 20(1). A law in force at the time postulates factual existence of the law at the relevant time and that excludes the retrospective application of any subsequent law. [*W.R.E.D. Co.* v *State of Madras* AIR 1962 SC 1753]. No person shall be convicted of any offence except for violation of a law in force at the time of the commission of the act charged as an offence nor shall be subjected to a penalty greater than that which might have been inflicted under the law in force at the time of commission of the offence. [*T. Barai* v *Henry Ah Hoe* AIR 1983 SC 150: 1983 Cr LJ 164: 1983 Cr App R (SC) 30: 1983 Cr LR (SC) 32: 1983 SC Cr R 180: 1983 UJ (SC) 132(2)].

**Ex proprio motu.** Of his own accord.

**Ex proprio vigore.** Of its own force.

**Ex quasi contractu.** Arising as if from a contract. From quasi-contract.

**Ex turpi causa non oritur actio.** An action does not arise from a base cause. The maxim may occasionally defeat a plaintiff in an action in tort; but the mere fact that the plaintiff is wrong-doer is, in general, no defence. Thus, an action by a woman against her paramour for communicating venereal disease failed, as the case fell within the maxim. [*Hegarty* v *Shine* (1878)14 Cox CC 124, 145].

**Ex vi termini.** From the force or meaning of the expression.

**Exaction.** The act of demanding more money than is due; extortion; a fee, reward, or other compensation arbitrarily or wrongfully demanded. [Black's *Law Dictionary*, 8th Ed].

NOTE: An officer of the law is guilty of exaction when he takes any fee or reward where none is due, or takes more than what is due, or takes it before it is due.

**Examination.** The act of eliciting by questions a person's knowledge of facts or scene; the questioning of a witness under oath.

NOTE: A witness undergoes three examinations: (1) Examination-in-chief, which is made by the party calling him; (2) Cross-examination by the opposite party; and (3) Re-examination by the party who called the witness, which is confined to matters arising out of the cross-examination.

Examination of witness includes examination-in-chief as also cross-examination. Examination is not complete when cross-examination is refused. [*Banwarilal* v *State of U.P.* AIR 1956 All 385].

Examination in relation to any goods includes measurement and weighment thereof. [Customs Act 1962, s. 2(17)].

**Examination-in-chief.** The examination of a witness by the party who calls him is called examination-in-chief. [Indian Evidence Act 1872, s. 137].

NOTE: The object of examination-in-chief is to elicit from the witness all the facts he can prove in support of such party's case. These may embrace facts in issue; facts relevant to the issue; in certain cases hearsay and opinions, as to such facts; and any such facts which affect the admissibility or weight of the evidence tendered.

**Excapitalisation.** This is an indication against a stock exchange quotation for a share that the share is being dealt in without benefit of a recent bonus issue or capital distribution.

**Excavate.** To make a hole or cavity in; hollow or dig out; to form or make by hollowing, digging out or scooping; to remove by digging or scooping out, as soil; to uncover by digging as ruins. [Webster's *Comprehensive Dictionary,* International Edition].

Digging land to make bore with a view to fetching water answers excavation. [*Kwality Pulp and Paper Mills, Vapi* v *Gujarat Industrial Development Corporation, Vapi* (1988)1 Guj LR 160].

**Exceptional hardship or depravity.** Exceptional hardship indicates hardship out of the ordinary course. It is impossible to define the quantum of hardship which would constitute exceptional hardship. But the adjective indicates that the Judge must be satisfied that the petitioner has suffered hardship greater than that ordinarily associated with those cases in which petitioners successfully establish their claims. [*Martin* v *Martin* (1941) NI 1].

NOTE: Section 14, Hindu Marriage Act and s. 29, Special Marriage Act provide that it is not permissible to present a petition for divorce before expiration of one year from the date of marriage without the leave of the court. This leave is granted in case of exceptional hardship on the part of the petitioner and exceptional depravity on the part of the respondent. In granting leave each case has to be approached subjectively and the cases should be considered from the point of view of both parties. [*Brewer* v *Brewer* (1964)1 All ER 539, 541: (1964)1 WLR 403, 410]. In deciding whether or not to grant leave, the court would act on *prima facie* evidence contained in the leave application. Court cannot try the case in advance. [*Meghnath* v *Sushila* AIR 1957 Mad 423].

**Exceptis excipiendis.** With all necessary exceptions.

**Excess of privilege.** More extensive than the privilege requires and justifies.

**Excessive interest.** The expression 'excessive' is really a relative term, and whether a particular rate of interest is excessive or not must be determined with reference to current laws prevalent at the time of determination. [*Balchand Mahto* v *Munshi Lal* AIR 1955 Pat 494].

**Exchange.** The act of transferring interests, each in consideration for the other; money or negotiable instruments presented as payment; the interchange or conversion of money; the payment of a debt using a bill of exchange or credit rather than money; an organization that brings together buyers and sellers of securities, commodities, and the like to promote uniformity in the customs and usages of merchants, to facilitate the speedy adjustment of business disputes, together and disseminate valuable commercial and economic information, and to secure to its members the benefits of cooperation in the furtherance of their legitimate pursuits; the building or hall where members of an exchange meet every business day to buy and sell for themselves, or as brokers for their customers, for present and future delivery. [Black's *Law Dictionary*, 8th Ed.].

"Exchange" has the narrow and limited meaning given to it, *i.e.*, "the exchange of any real or heritable property for any other real or heritable property". [*I.R.C.* v *Littlewoods Mail Order Stores*; *Littlewood Mail Order Stores* v *I.R.C.* (1962)2 WLR 1228 (HL)].

▸ *Meaning under the Transfer of Property Act 1882, s. 118.* When two persons mutually transfer the ownership of one thing for the ownership of another, neither thing or both things being money only, the transaction is called an "exchange".

An exchange involves the transfer of property by one person to another and reciprocally the transfer of property by that other to the first person. There must be a mutual transfer of ownership of one thing for the ownership of another. [*CIT* v *Rasiklal Maneklal* AIR 1989 SC 1333: (1989)2 SCC 454: (1989)2 SCR 179: JT 1989(2) SC 16: (1989)177 ITR 198: (1989)2 Comp LJ 341].

> NOTE: The definition of exchange as given in the Transfer of Property Act 1882 (s. 118) is not limited to immovable property but extends also to butter of movable property. [*Commissioner of Income-tax, A.P.* v *Motors & General Stores (P) Ltd.* AIR 1968 SC 200: (1967)3 SCR 876].

• **First of exchange** p. 356.
• **Foreign exchange** p. 365.
• **Stock exchange** p. 813.

**Exchange control.** Exchange control is the system of Government control exercised through the banks over financial transactions between residents of India and those of other countries to prevent loss of capital and valuables.

**Exchequer.** The term "exchequer" is connected with the revenues of the State; department of public service charged with receipt and custody of State revenues.

> NOTE: A Minister of State having special care of the revenue is called the Chancellor of the Exchequer.

• **Chancellor of the exchequer** p. 136.

**Excise duty.** The word 'excise' is usually (though by no means always) employed to indicate a duty imposed on home-manufactured articles in the course of manufacture before they reach the consumer. So regarded, an excise duty is plainly indirect. [*Atlantic Smoke Shops Ltd.* v *Conlon* (1943) AC 550].

The term 'excise duty' has not been precisely nor authoritatively defined anywhere. It is generally used in contradistinction to the term 'customs duty'. Customs duties or duties of custom are levied on goods abroad or imported from abroad; while duties of excise are levied on home-made goods or goods made in the taxing country. Its primary and fundamental meaning in English is still that of a tax on articles produced or manu-factured in the taxing country and intended for home consumption. [*Mewar Textile Mills* v *Union of India* AIR 1955 Raj 114].

Excise duty is a duty on the manufacture of goods and not on sale. Manufacture is complete as soon as by the application of one or more process, the raw material undergoes some change. If a new substance is brought into existence or if a new or different article having a distinct name, character or use results from particular process or processes, such process or activity would amount to manufacture. And the new product is chargeable to excise duty. [*Aditya Mills* v *Union of India* AIR 1988 SC 2237].

**Exclusive licence.** Licence given to a person to the exclusion of others with rights conferred therein.

▸ *Meaning under the Copyright Act 1957, s. 2(j).* 'Exclusive licence' means a licence which confers on the licensee or persons authorised by him to the exclusion of all other persons (including the owner of the copyright) any right comprised in the copyright in a work, and "exclusive licence" shall be construed accordingly.

▸ *Meaning under the Patents Act 1970, s. 2(f).* "Exclusive licence" means a licence from a patentee which confers on the licensee, or on the licensee and persons authorised by him, to the exclusion of all other persons (including the patentee), and right in respect of the patented invention, and "exclusive licensee" shall be construed accordingly.

**Excuse.** Alibi; defence; exculpation; explanation for some delinquency; justification; ostensible reason; a reason alleged for doing or not doing a thing; pretext; pretense.

• **Lawful excuse** p. 518.

**Executed.** 'Executed' and 'execution' used with reference to instruments mean 'signed' and 'signature'. [Indian Stamp Act 1899, s. 2(12)].

**Executed contract.** Where nothing remains to be done by either party, and where the transaction is completed at the moment that the agreement is made, the contract is said to be executed.

**Executio juris non habet injuriam.** The execution of the process of the law does no injury. If an action be brought in a court having jurisdiction on insufficient grounds or against the wrong party, no injury is thereby done for which an action can be maintained. And he is not to be esteemed a wrong-doer who merely avails himself of his legal rights. On the other hand, if an individual, under colour of the law, does an illegal act, or if he abuses the process of the court to make it an instrument of oppression or extortion, this is a fraud upon the law, by the commission of which liability will be incurred.

**Execution.** Carrying out some act or course of conduct to its completion. [*Northwest Steel Rolling Mills* v *Commissioner of Internal Revenue* CCA Wash, 110 F 2d 286, 290].

Execution is a process in action to carry into effect the directions in a decree or judgment. [*Foust* v *Foust* 47 Cal 2d 121].

The word "execution" in its widest sense signifies the enforcement of or giving effect to the judgments or orders of courts of justice. In a narrower sense, it means the enforcement of those judgments or orders by a public officer under the writs of *fieri facias*, attachment, possession, delivery, sequestration, *fieri facias de bonis ecclesiasticis*, etc. [Halsbury's *Laws of England*, 4th Ed., vol. 17, para 401, p. 232].

NOTE: If a decree passed by a court is not complied with, it is to be executed through the executing court. All questions relating to the execution, discharge or satisfaction of the decree are determined by the court executing the decree and not by a separate suit. There is a time-limit for the execution of a decree. The court may order execution—(*a*) by delivery of property specifically decreed; (*b*) by sale or by attachment and sale; (*c*) by detention in prison; (*d*) by appointing a receiver; or (*e*) in such other manner as the relief may require. [Code of Civil Procedure 1908, ss. 36 to 74 and Or. 21].

Execution of instrument means signature [Indian Stamp Act 1899, s. 2(12)]. The word 'execution' is hardly apt when used in regard to a letter and is only appropriate in regard to a deed or instrument, as in such a case certain formalities are insisted upon by law and they are to be followed by the executant in order to make the document effective in law. [*Sivaramakrishnayya* v *Kasiviswandham* AIR 1957 AP 584].

• **Step in aid of execution** p. 812.

**Execution of contract.** Execution of contract includes performance of all acts necessary to render it complete as an instrument and imports idea that nothing remains to be done to make complete and effective contract. [*Travelers Ins. Co.* v *Chicago Bridge & Iron Co.* Tex Civ App, 442 SW 2d 888, 895].

**Execution of decree.** The 'execution of a decree' means enforcement of the decree by process of execution. It embraces all the appropriate means by which a decree is enforced and includes all processes and proceedings in aid of, or supplemental to, execution. [*Anadilal* v *Ram Narain* AIR 1984 SC 1383: (1984)3 SCR 806: (1984)3 SC 561].

**Execution of document.** Execution of a document means something more than mere signing by the party. It must certainly include delivery and it also includes signing in presence of witnesses, where witnesses are necessary. [*Arjun Chandra* v *Kailas* AIR 1923 Cal 149]. It does not merely mean the mechanical act of signing the document or getting it signed without appreciating the contents of the document. [*Keshwar* v *Rajeswari* AIR 1935 Pat 497].

**Executive**. The term 'executive' or 'administrative' is capable of bearing a wide range of meaning. Broadly speaking, the term refers to broad areas of Governmental activities in which repositories of power may exercise every class of statutory function. [*Subrahmanyam* v *J.R. of Co-operative Societies* AIR 1965 AP 69]. The State has three organs—Executive; Legislative; Judiciary.

The branch of government responsible for effecting and enforcing laws; the persons who constitute this branch. [Black's *Law Dictionary*, 8th Ed.].

▸ *Meaning under the Industrial Disputes Act 1947, s. 2(gg).* Executive in relation to a trade union means the body, by whatever name called, to which the management of the affairs of the trade union is entrusted.

The term 'executive' is used in the broader sense as including both a decision as to action and the carrying out of the decision. [*State of Bihar* v *Rani Sonabati Kumari* AIR 1961 SC 221: (1961)1 SCR 728].

**Executor.** One who performs or carries out some act; a person named by a testator to carry out the provisions in the testator's will. [Black's *Law Dictionary*, 8th Ed.].

Executor means a person appointed by a testator to carry out the directions and requests in his will, and to dispose of the property according to his testamentary provisions after his death. [Wharton's *Law Lexicon*, 14th Ed.].

▸ *Meaning under the Indian Succession Act 1925, s. 2(c).* A person to whom the execution of the last will of a deceased person is, by the testator's appointment, confided.

▸ *Meaning under the Estate Duty Act 1953, s. 2(8) (since repealed).* 'Executor' means the executor or administrator of a deceased person.

**Executor of his own wrong.** (*Executor de son tort*). A person who intermeddles with the estate of the deceased, or does any other act which belongs to the office of the executor, while there is no rightful executor or administrator in existence, thereby makes himself an executor of his own wrong. [Indian Succession Act 1925, ss. 303 and 304].

**Executory contract.** A contract in which something is to be done after the contract is concluded.

**Exempla illustrant, non restringunt, legem.** Examples make the law clearer, do not restrict it.

**Exempli gratia.** For the purpose of example. (Abbreviated as *e.g.*).

**Exhibit.** When a party proves a document through a witness he tenders that document after such proof and then the court marks it as an exhibit. Exhibit means a document exhibited for the purpose of being taken into consideration in deciding some question or other in respect of the proceeding in which it is filed. [*Rakhaldas* v *Shantilata* AIR 1956 Cal 619].

**Exhibition.** A public display of works of art, industrial products, etc.; the act or an instance of exhibiting; the state of being exhibited.

• **Indecent exhibition** p. 448.

**Existing law.** Any law, ordinance, order, bye-law, rule or regulation passed or made before the commencement of the Constitution by any Legislature, authority or person having power to make such a law, ordinance, order, bye-law, rule or regulation. [Constitution of India 1950, Art. 366(10)].

NOTE: To have the status of an existing law, the law should have been made by a Legislature having the power to make such law. [*Jeejeebhoy* v *Assistant Collector* AIR 1965 SC 1096: (1965)2 SCA 457].

The expression 'law in force' in Explanation I in Art. 372 of the Constitution and the words 'existing law' in Art. 366(10) both cover the same ground. [*Gannon Dunkerley & Co.* v *Sales Tax Officer* AIR 1957 Ker 146: ILR (1957) Ker 462].

**Exonerate.** To release a person from blame or a duty imposed upon him.

**Expectancy.** That which is expected or hoped for.

In its application to property, it means an 'estate with a reversion, a remainder, or an executory interest'. [Black's *Law Dictionary*, 7th Ed.].

With reference to wills & estates, it means the 'possibility that an heir apparent, an heir presumptive, or a presumptive next-of-kin will acquire property by devolution on intestacy, or the possibility that a presumptive legatee or devisee will acquire property by will'. [Black's *Law Dictionary*, 7th Ed.].

With reference to insurance, it means the 'probable number of years in one's life'. [Black's *Law Dictionary*, 7th Ed.].

Expectancy is the hope of inheritance entertained by the heir. [*Johnson, Moore* v *Johnson* (1891)3 Ch 43].

**Expectancy, estate in.** An estate in expectancy is a present estate the use and enjoyment of which are future. Such an estate, as distinguished from an estate in possession, is an estate the right to the possession of which will only arise at a future date, *e.g.*, on the determination of a prior life estate.

An estate in expectancy may be either a remainder or a reversion. A remainder is created by act of parties and a reversion is created by operation of law.

**Expectant heir.** Every person who is entitled, either absolutely or contingently, to any reversion or remainder in a property or a portion or who has the hope of succession to the property of an ancestor or relative either by reason of his being the heir-apparent or presumptive or by reason merely of any supposed or presumed affection on the part of his ancestor or relative is an expectant heir. [*Beynon* v *Cook* 10 Ch 391].

**Expedit rei publicae ut sit finis litium.** It is for the public good that there should be an end to litigation.

**Expedit reipulicae ne sua requis male utatur.** It is for the public good that no one uses his property badly.

**Expenditure.** 'Expenditure' is equal to 'expense' and expense is money laid out by calculation and intention though in many uses of the word this element may not be present, as when one speaks of a joke at another's expense. But the idea of spending in the sense of 'paying out or away' money is the primary meaning. Expenditure is thus what is paid out or away and is something which is gone irretrievably. [*Indian Molasses Co. (P) Ltd.* v *Commissioner of Income Tax* AIR 1959 SC 1049: 1959 Supp (2) SCR 964: (1959)37 ITR 66: (1960)1 SCA 75].

In its normal meaning the expression "expenditure" denotes spending or paying out or away, that is, something that goes out of the coffers. A mere liability to satisfy an obligation is undoubtedly not expenditure. [*Commissioner of Income Tax, U.P.* v *National Bank Ltd.* AIR 1967 SC 453: (1967)1 SCR 348: (1966)62 ITR 638].

Expenditure means the amount expended and expended means to pay away, lay out or spend. It really represents money out of pocket, a going out. [*Vidya Sagar* v *Surinder Nath* AIR 1969 SC 288: (1969)1 SCJ 388: (1969)1 SCA 75].

'Expenditure' is not necessarily confined to the money which has been actually paid out. It covers a liability which has accrued or which has been incurred although it may have to be discharged at a future debt. [*Madras Industrial Investment Corporation Ltd.* v *CIT* AIR 1997 SC 2063: (1997)4 SCC 666: JT 1997(4) SC 463: (1997)225 ITR 802].

• **Capital expenditure** p. 122.

**Expense.** That which is expended, laid out or consumed; an outlay; charge; cost; price.

An expenditure of money, time, labour or resources to accomplish a result. [Black's *Law Dictionary*, 8th Ed.].

Actual disbursements, not allowances for loss of time. [*Jones* v *Carmarthen* 10 LJ Ex 401].

**Expenses of management.** 'Expenses of management' means all charges, wherever incurred whether directly or indirectly, including commission payments of all kinds and in the case of an insurer having his principal place of business outside India, a proper share of head office expenses which shall not be less than such percentage as may be prescribed, of his gross premium income (that is to say, the premium income without taking into account premiums on reinsurance ceded or accepted) written direct in India during the year. [Insurance Act 1938, s. 40C(2)(*b*)].

**Experientiia docet.** Experience teaches.

**Expert witness.** An expert witness is one who made the subject upon which he speaks a matter of particular study, practice or observation; and he must have a particular and special knowledge of the subject. [*Dole* v *Johnson* 50 N Hamp 454].

▸ *Meaning under the Indian Evidence Act 1872, s. 45.* When the court has to form an opinion upon a point of foreign law, or of science or art, or as to the identity of handwriting or finger impressions, the opinions upon that point of persons specially skilled in such foreign law, science or art or in questions of identity of handwriting or finger impressions are relevant facts. Such persons are called experts.

NOTE: The opinion of an expert engaged by a party suffers from the defect that it is given by a remunerated witness. He knows beforehand why he has been called and what the party calling him wishes to be proved. It is not improbable that he has an unconscious bias in favour of the party. These circumstances to a great extent detract from the weight to be attached to such opinion. [*Abhayanand Mishra* v *State of Bihar* AIR 1959 Pat 328: 1959 Cr LJ 893].

There cannot be any more unsatisfactory evidence than that of an interested party called an expert. [*Judah* v *Isolyne* AIR 1945 PC 174].

The expert's evidence as to handwriting is opinion evidence and it can rarely, if ever, take the place of substantive evidence. Before acting on such evidence it is usual to see if it is corroborated either by clear direct evidence or by circumstantial evidence. [*Sashi Kumar Banerjee* v *Subodh Kumar Banerjee* AIR 1964 SC 529]. Handwriting expert's evidence can never be conclusive. [*Ishwari Prasad* v *Mohammad Isa* AIR 1963 SC 1729: (1963)3 SCR 722].

Though the witness did not possess any technical qualifications inasmuch as he had neither obtained a degree nor a diploma in photography, his experience for over 25 years in photography was held sufficient enough to call him an expert. [*Govinda Reddy, in re* AIR 1958 Mys 150: ILR (1957) Mys 177: 1958 Cr LJ 1489].

**Expire.** The word "expire" means to come to an end or to put an end to, or to terminate or to become void, or to become extinct. [*Pradip Kumar Das* v *State of West Bengal* AIR 1974 SC 2151: 1974 Cr LJ 1476: 1974 SCC (Cri) 943: (1975)1 SCR 327: (1975)3 SCC 335].

**Explain.** It means to account for. It is not the same thing as is usually understood by the expression 'to show cause'.

NOTE: Opportunity of explaining does not contemplate an opportunity to cross-examine witness or to adduce his evidence. [*Gaya Prasad* v *Commissioner, Faizabad Division* AIR 1958 All 466].

**Exploit.** To turn to economic account (as a mine); to take advantage of; utilise.

'Exploitatio' does not mean merely extraction of the ore, but includes turning of the ore to industrial account. [*Metal Corporation of India* v *Union of India* AIR 1970 Cal 15].

**Exploitation.** The act of successfully applying industry to any job, as the working of mines, etc.; the act of using for selfish purposes. [*Timblo Exmaos Ltd., Margo* v *Jorge Anibal Matos Sequeira* AIR 1977 SC 734: (1977)2 SCR 451: (1977)3 SCC 474].

**Explosive.** Pertaining to explosion; liable to explode or to cause explosion; any substance or mixture of substances which, on impact or by ignition, reacts by a violent rearrangement of its molecules accompanied by the sudden expansion of gases and the liberation of relatively large amounts of thermal energy. [Webster's *Comprehensive Dictionary,* International Edition].

▸ *Meaning under the Explosives Act 1884, s. 4(d).* "Explosive" means gunpowder, nitroglycerine, nitroglycol, guncotton, di-nitro-toluene, tri-nitro-toluene, picric acid, di-nitro-phenol, tri-nitro-resorcinol (styphnic acid), cyclo-trimethylene-tri-nitramine, penta-erythritol-tetranitrate, tetryl, nitro-guanidine, lead azide, lead styphynate, fulminate of mercury or any other metal, diazo-di-nitro-phenol, coloured fires or any other substance whether a single chemical compound or a mixture of substances, whether solid or liquid or gaseous used or manufactured with a view to produce a practical effect by explosion or pyrotechnic effect; and includes fog-signals, fireworks, fuses, rockets, percussion-caps, detonators, cartridges, ammunition of all descriptions and every adaptation or preparation of an explosive as defined.

NOTE: The term 'explosive substance' is more comprehensive than explosive. [*Md. Usman* v *State of Maharashtra* AIR 1981 SC 1062: (1981)2 SCC 443: (1981)3 SCR 68: 1981 SCC (Cri) 477: 1981 Cr LJ 588].

**Export.** The word 'export' has reference to taking out of goods which had become part and parcel of the mass of property of the local area and will not apply to goods in transit, *i.e.*, brought into the area for the purpose of being transported out of it. [*Empress Mills* v *Municipal Committee* AIR 1958 SC 341: 1958 SCJ 604].

The word 'export' may conceivably be used in more senses than one. In one sense, export may mean sending or taking out of the country, but in another sense, it may mean sending goods from one country to another. Often, the latter involves a commercial transaction but not necessarily. [*Burmah Shell Oil Storage and Distributing Co. of India Ltd.* v *Commercial Tax Officer* AIR 1961 SC 315: (1961)1 SCR 902: (1960)11 STC 764: (1962)2 SCJ 251].

▸ *Meaning under the Coir Industry Act 1953, s. 3(f).* 'Export' with its grammatical variations and cognate expressions means to take out of the territories to which the Act extends by land, sea or air to any place outside India other than a country or territory notified in this behalf by the Central Government by notification in the Official Gazette.

▸ *Meaning under the Iron Ore Mines Labour Welfare Cess Act 1961, s. 1A(a); Seeds Act 1966, s. 2(6).* 'Export' means taking out of India to a place outside India.

▸ *Meaning under the Tea Act 1953, s. 3(f).* 'Export' means to take out of India by land, sea or air to any place outside India other than a country or territory notified in this behalf by the Central Government by notification in the Official Gazette.

▸ *Meaning under the Customs Act 1962, s. 2(18); Export (Quality Control and Inspection) Act 1963, s. 2(b); Taxes on Entry of Goods into Calcutta Metropolitan Area Act 1970, s. 2(d).* 'Export', with its grammatical variations and cognate expressions, means taking out of India to a place outside India.

• **Illegal export** p. 427.
• **Sale in the course of export** p. 771.

**Export goods.** Any goods which are to be taken out of India to a place outside India. [Customs Act 1962, s. 2(19)].

**Exporter.** 'Exporter' in relation to any goods at any time between their entry for export and the time when they are exported includes any owner or any person holding himself out to be the exporter. [Customs Act 1962, s. 2(20)].

**Exposure.** The act or state of exposing or being exposed. It may also mean the "amount of liability or other risk to which a person is subject". [Black's *Law Dictionary*, 8th Ed.].

• **Indecent exposure** p. 448.

**Express.** Clear; definite; explicit; plain; direct; unmistakable; not dubious or ambiguous; declared in terms; set forth in words; directly and distinctly stated; made known distinctly and explicitly, and not left to inference.

The word 'expressly' is used in antithesis to the word 'impliedly' and only means clearly. [*State of Madras* v *K. Ramaswami* AIR 1958 Mad 585: ILR (1958) Mad 964].

**Express contract.** The reciprocal promises contained in the words of the contract or resulting from a true construction of them and excludes stipulations which may arise out of any usage or custom or which may be inferred from the conduct or course of dealings between the parties. [*Alepaty Ramamoorthy* v *Polisetti Satyanarayana* AIR 1958 AP 550].

**Express trust.** The words 'express trust' are used by way of opposition to trusts arising from implication, trusts resulting or trusts by operation of law. [*Re Barker* (1892)2 Ch 491].

Trusts are either express or arising by operation of law. An express trust as regards land is a trust expressly declared by a deed, will or other written instrument; as to personality (other than leaseholds) the trust can be expressly created orally. To constitute an express trust three matters must be defined: the property subject to the trust, the persons to be benefited, and the interests which they are to take. It is not necessary to use the word "trust", and the trust is express even if it has to be made out from all the terms of the instrument, although the courts are less ready now than formerly to construe words of recommendation as creating a precatory trust. [Halsbury's *Laws of England*, 4th Ed., vol. 16, para 1452, p. 977].

NOTE: An express trust is expressed either by words in writing or by words of mouth; it does not include a trust which arises from the acts of the parties or to a resulting trust or to an implied trust or to a constructive trust. [*Sands* v *Thompson* (1883)48 LT 210].

**Expressio unius est exclusis alterius.** The express mention of one person or thing is the exclusion of another. Where the statutory language is plain and the meaning clear, there is no scope for applying the rule. [*P.T. Cooperative Society* v *R.T. Authority* AIR 1960 SC 801].

**Extempore.** Without preparation.

**Extend.** To extend means to enlarge, expand, lengthen, prolong, to carry out further than its original limit. [*Pravash Chandra Dalui* v *Biswanath Banerjee* AIR 1989 SC 1834: 1989 Supp (1) SCC 487: (1989)2 SCR 401: JT 1989 (Supp) SC 92].

**Extension.** An increase in length of time.

The word "extension" ordinarily implies the existence of something to be extended. [*State* v *Graves* 182 SW 2d 46, 51].

Extension is a term properly used for the purpose of enlarging or giving further duration to any existing right, but does not import the revesting of an expired right; that would not be an extension but a re-creation. [*Brooke* v *Clarke* 1 B&Ald 396].

The word 'extension' imports continuance of an existing thing and effect must be given to the word where it occurs. [*National Industrial Corporation Ltd.* v *Registrar of Companicc* AIR 1963 Punj 239; *Abdul Gaffar* v *State of U.P.* 1974 AWR 127].

The word 'extension' when used in its proper and usual sense in connection with a lease means a prolongation of the lease. [*Pravash Chandra Dalui* v *Biswanath Banerjee* AIR 1989 SC 1834: 1989 Supp (1) SCC 487: (1989)2 SCR 401: JT 1989 (Supp) SC 92].

**Extenuate.** To diminish the gravity of a thing by partial excuse; to diminish the conception of guilt on the plea of attending circumstances.

**External.** The word 'external' is antithesis to internal. Any cause which is not internal must be external. [*Rajani Bai* v *New India Assurance Co.* AIR 1956 Bom 633].

**Extinguishment of right.** Extinguishment of right indicates a total annihilation of right, whether it be in respect of the entire estate or part of it; modification covers a case where a right in the estate is abridged or impaired short of extinguishment to the prejudice of the person in whom the right resides. [*Sant Singh* v *State of Jammu and Kashmir* AIR 1959 J&K 35].

NOTE: Under s. 27 of the Limitation Act 1963, at the determination of the period limited to any person for instituting a suit for possession of any property, his right to such property shall be extinguished.

**Extort.** To demand more than a legal fee by colour of office; to obtain possession or knowledge by force or compulsion. This term necessarily implies the adoption of illegal means.

**Extortion.** Whoever intentionally puts any person in fear of any injury to that person, or to any other, and thereby dishonestly induces the person so put in fear to deliver to any person any property or valuable security or anything signed or sealed which may be converted into a valuable security, commits extortion. [Indian Penal Code 1860, s. 383].

Extortion is defined to be in a large sense any oppression under colour of right. In a strict sense, extortion is the taking of money by any officer by colour of his office, either where none at all is due, or not so much is due, or where it is not yet due. [*Shoppee* v *Nathan* (1892)1 QB 245].

**Extra-judicial.** Any act done or word spoken by a judge, outside the authority and jurisdiction which for the time being he is exercising is called extra-judicial.

**Extra legem positus est civiliter mortuus.** He who is placed out of the law is civilly dead.

**Extra-territoriality (exterritoriality).** A term used in international law to denote the condition of persons who are considered to be outside the territory of the State in which they reside and so are not amenable to its laws, e.g. an ambassador and the persons belonging to his suite, whose residence is extra-territorial and protected by diplomatic privilege.

NOTE: Section 86 of the Code of Civil Procedure 1908 recognises, to a limited extent, the doctrine of "extraterritoriality". No Ruler, Ambassador or Envoy of a foreign State can be sued except with the consent of the Central Government. No decree can be executed against the property of any such Ruler, Ambassador or Envoy.

**Extradition.** Extradition denotes the process, whereby under treaty or upon a basis of reciprocity one State surrenders to another State at its request a person accused or convicted of a criminal offence committed against the laws of the requesting State, such requesting State being competent to try the alleged offender. [Starke's *International Law*, 10th Ed., p. 352].

Extradition is the surrender by one State to another of a person desired to be dealt with for crimes of which he has been accused or convicted and which are justiciable in the courts of the other State. [*State of West Bengal* v *Jugal Kishore More* AIR 1969 SC 1171: (1969)3 SCR 320: 1969 Cr LJ 1559: (1969)1 SCC 440].

The term 'extradition' denotes the process whereby under a concluded treaty one State surrenders to any other State at its request, a person accused or convicted of a criminal offence committed against the laws of the requesting State, such requesting State being competent to try the alleged offender. [*Rosiline George* v *Union of India* (1994)2 SCC 80: 1994 SCC (Cri) 304: JT 1993(6) SC 51].

**Extradition offence.** 'Extradition offence' means—(*i*) in relation to a foreign State, being a treaty State, an offence provided for in the extradition treaty with that State; (*ii*) in relation to a foreign State other than a treaty State or in relation to a Commonwealth country, an offence which is specified in, or which may be specified by notification under the Second Schedule. [Extradition Act 1962, s. 2(*c*)].

**Extradition treaty.** Extradition treaty means a treaty or agreement made by India with a foreign State relating to the extradition of fugitive criminals, and includes any treaty or agreement relating to the extradition of fugitive criminals made before the 15th day of August 1947, which extends to, and is binding on, India. [Extradition Act 1962, s. 2(*d*)].

# Ff

**Fabric.** "Fabric" is defined as a term which covers all textiles no matter how constructed, how manufactured, or the nature of the material from which made [*Delhi Cloth and General Mills Co. Ltd.* v *State of Rajasthan* AIR 1980 SC 1552: (1980)3 SCR 1109: (1980)4 SCC 71, referring to *Mercury Dictionary of Textile Terms*]; a collective term applied to cloth no matter how constructed or manufactured and regardless of the kind of fibre from which made [*Delhi Cloth and General Mills Co. Ltd.* v *State of Rajasthan* AIR 1980 SC 1552: (1980)3 SCR 1109: (1980)4 SCC 71, referring to the *Man-made Textile Encyclopedia* (1959)]; a cloth that is woven or knit, braided, petted, with any textile fibre. [*Delhi Cloth and General Mills Co. Ltd.* v *State of Rajasthan* AIR 1980 SC 1552: (1980)3 SCR 1109: (1980)4 SCC 71, referring to the Fairchild's *Dictionary of Textiles* (1959)].

"Fabric" means woven material. [*Union of India* v *Gujarat Woollen Felt Mills* AIR 1977 SC 1548: (1977)3 SCR 472: (1977)2 SCC 870: 1977 ELT (J 24)].

**Fabricate false evidence.** Whoever causes any circumstance to exist or makes any false entry in any book or record, or makes any document containing a false statement, intending that such circumstance, false entry or false statement may appear in evidence in a judicial proceeding, or in a proceeding taken by law before a public servant as such, or before an arbitrator, and that such circumstance, false entry or false statement, so appearing in evidence, may cause any person who in such proceeding is to form an opinion upon the evidence, to entertain an erroneous opinion touching any point material to the result of such proceeding is said to fabricate false evidence. [*Dr. S. Dutt* v *State of U.P.* AIR 1966 SC 523: (1966)1 SCR 493: 1966 Cr LJ 459; Indian Penal Code 1860, s. 192].

NOTE: *Illustrations of fabricated false evidence.* (*a*) *A* puts jewels into a box belonging to *Z*, with the intention that they may be found in that box, and that this circumstance may cause *Z* to be convicted of theft. *A* has fabricated false evidence. (*b*) *A* makes a false entry in his shop-book for the purpose of using it as corroborative evidence in a Court of Justice. *A* has fabricated false evidence. (*c*) *A*, with the intention of causing *Z* to be convicted of a criminal conspiracy, writes a letter in imitation of *Z*'s handwriting, purporting to be addressed to an accomplish in such criminal conspiracy, and puts the letter in a place which he knows that the officers of the police are likely to search. *A* has fabricated false evidence.

If the evidence fabricated is intended to be used in a judicial proceeding, the offence is committed as soon as the fabrication is complete; it is immaterial that the judicial proceeding has not been commenced, or that no actual use has been made of the evidence fabricated. The mere fabrication is punishable under s. 193 of the Indian Penal Code while the use of fabricated evidence is punishable under s. 196.

**Fabricated evidence.** Evidence manufactured or arranged after the fact, and either wholly false or else warped and discoloured by artifice and contrivance with a deceitful intent. [Black's *Law Dictionary,* 5th Ed.].

False or deceitful evidence that is unlawfully created, usually after the relevant event, in an attempt to achieve or avoid liability or conviction. [Black's *Law Dictionary,* 8th Ed.].

**Face value.** The nominal value written or printed on the face of bonds, notes, share certificates, debentures, and other documents, indicating their par value; the value stated on the face of a security or insurance policy. [Black's *Law Dictionary*, 5th Ed.].

**Facsimile.** Make it like. An exact copy, preserving all the marks of the original.

**Fact.** Absolute certainty; absolute reality; actual occurrence; authenticated incident; documented event; established phenomenon; indisputable event; perceived happening; substantiated incident; verifiable happening.

A thing done; an action performed or an incident transpiring; that which has taken place [*City of South Euclid* v *Clapacs* 213 NE 2d 828, 832]; something that actually exists.

> NOTE: A fact is either a state of things, that is, an existence, or a motion, that is, an event. Fact is an event and it is actual.

▸*Meaning under the Evidence Act 1872, s. 3.* 'Fact' means and includes—(1) any thing, state of things or relation of things, capable of being perceived by the senses; (2) any mental condition of which any person is conscious.


- **Evidentiary fact** p. 324.
- **Jurisdictional fact** p. 498.
- **Malice in fact** p. 553.
- **Material facts** p. 568.
- **Matter of fact** p. 570.
- **Mistake of fact** p. 587.
- **Presumptions of fact** p. 682.
- **Question of fact** p. 721.
- **Simulated fact** p. 799.


**Fact discovered.** The expression "fact discovered" includes not only the physical object produced, but also the place from which it is produced and the knowledge of the accused as to this. [*Mohmed Inayatullah* v *State of Maharashtra* AIR 1976 SC 483: (1976)1 SCR 715: (1976)1 SCC 828: 1976 Cr LJ 481: 1976 SCC (Cri) 199].

The 'fact discovered' referred to in s. 27 of the Evidence Act 1872 cannot be treated as equivalent to the object produced. The fact discovered embraces the place from which the object is produced and the knowledge of the accused as to this and the information given must relate distinctly to this fact. [*Bakshi Mukinda Neo Budha* v *State of Bombay* AIR 1960 Bom 263: 1960 Cr LJ 807].

**Facta sunt potentiora verbis.** Deeds are more powerful than words.

**Factor.** A factor is a mercantile agent who in ordinary course of business is entrusted with the possession of goods to sell them. He has a lien on the goods. [Contract Act 1872, s. 171].

"A factor by the rules of common law and of mercantile usage is an agent to whom goods are consigned for the purpose of sale, and he has possession of the goods, power to sell them in his own name, and a general discretion as to their sale. He may sell them on the usual terms of credit, may receive the price, and give a good discharge to the buyer". [*Principles of the Law of Contract* by William R. Anson (Arthur L. Corbin ed., 3d Am. ed. 1919), p. 523].

"A factor is an agent entrusted with the possession of goods for the purpose of selling them for his principal". [*Stevens* v *Biller* 25 Ch D 31, *per* Cotton, L.J.].

"There are two extensive classes of mercantile agents; namely: factors, who are entrusted with the possession as well as the disposal of property; and brokers, who are employed to contract about it without being put in possession". [*Mercantile Law* by Smith, 9th Ed., p. 106, cited with approval by Brett, L.J., *Ex p. Dixon* 4 Ch D 133, and by Chitty, J., *Stevens* v *Biller* 25 Ch D 31].

**Factory.** A place where a number of traders reside in a foreign country for the convenience of trade; also a building in which goods are manufactured. [Wharton's *Law Lexicon*].

▸*Meaning under the Central Excise and Salt Act 1944, s. 2(e).* 'Factory' means any premises including the precincts thereof whereon or in any part of which excisable goods other than salt are manufactured, or wherein or in any part of which any manufacturing process connected with the production of these goods is being carried on or is ordinarily carried on.

▸ *Meaning under the Employees' Provident Funds and Miscellaneous Provisions Act 1952, s. 2(g).* 'Factory' means any premises, including the precincts thereof, in any part of which a manufacturing process is being carried on or is ordinarily so carried on, whether with the aid of power or without the aid of power.

▸ *Meaning under the Employees' State Insurance Act 1948, s. 2(12).* 'Factory' means any premises including the precincts thereof—(*a*) whereon ten or more persons are employed or were employed for wages on any day of the preceding twelve months, and in any part of which a manufacturing process is being carried on with the aid of power or is ordinarily so carried on, or (*b*) whereon twenty or more persons are employed or were employed for wages on any day of the preceding twelve months, and in any part of which a manufacturing process is being carried on without the aid of power or is ordinarily so carried on, but does not include a mine subject to the operation of the Mines Act 1952, or a railway running shed.

▸ *Meaning under the Factories Act 1948, s. 2(m); Payment of Wages Act 1936, s. 2(ib); Iron Ore Mines Labour Welfare Cess Act 1961, s. 1A(b); Maternity Benefit Act 1961, s. 3(f).* 'Factory' means any premises including the precincts thereof—(*i*) whereon ten or more workers are working, or were working on any day of the preceding twelve months, and in any part of which a manufacturing process is being carried on with the aid of power, or is ordinarily so carried on, or (*ii*) whereon twenty or more workers are working or were working on any day of the preceding twelve months, and in any part of which a manufacturing process is being carried on without the aid of power, or is ordinarily so carried on, but does not include a mine subject to the operation of the Mines Act 1952, or a mobile unit belonging to the armed forces of the union, a railway running shed or a hotel, restaurant or eating place.

The place where a manufacturing process is carried on with the aid of power by less than ten workers is not a factory as defined in s. 2(*m*) of the Factories Act, but if there is a notification under s. 85(1) such a place will be deemed to be a factory, provided the manufacturing process is not being carried on by the owner with the aid of his family. [*Ramchandra Prasad* v *State of Bihar* AIR 1957 Pat 247]. Electric sub-station not generating electricity, only transforming and transmitting the same is not a factory. [*M.P. Electricity Board* v *State of M.P.* 1981 Lab IC 1678].

Factory must be a premises where a manufacturing process is carried on. [*Workmen of Delhi Electric Supply Undertaking* v *The Management of Delhi Electric Supply Undertaking* AIR 1973 SC 365: (1974)3 SCC 108].

▸ *Meaning under the Industries (Development and Regulation) Act 1951, s. 3(c).* 'Factory' means any premises including the precincts thereof, in any part of which a manufacturing process is being carried on or is ordinarily so carried on—(*i*) with the aid of power, provided that fifty or more workers are working or were working thereon on any day of the preceding twelve months; or (*ii*) without the aid of power, provided that one hundred or more workers are working or were working thereon on any day of the preceding twelve months and provided further that in no part of such premises any manufacturing process is being carried on with the aid of power.

• **Textile factory** p. 840.

**Factory prices.** The prices at which goods may be bought at factories, as distinguished from the prices of goods bought from the shopkeepers in the market.

**Facts in issue.** The expression 'facts in issue' means and includes any fact from which either by itself or in connection with other facts, the existence, non-existence, nature or extent of any right, liability or disability, asserted or denied in any suit or proceeding, necessarily follows. [Evidence Act 1872, s. 3].

**Factum probandum.** The fact to be proved; the fact in issue.

**Factum valet quod fieri non debuit.** Where a fact is accomplished or where the act is done and completed, though in contravention of directory provisions, the fact will stand and the act shall be deemed to be legal and binding. But where the provisions are mandatory, the principle does not apply.

**Fails to appear.** The expressions 'does not appear' in Or. 9, CP Code and 'fails to appear' in Or. 17 mean the same thing. [*Motilal Surajmal Joshi* v *Mohammad Safi* AIR 1956 Nag 179: ILR (1956) Nag 132].

NOTE: Where counsel for the defendant applies for an adjournment and on refusal by the court of the same reports 'no instruction', then there is no appearance of the defendant. [*Motilal Surajmal Joshi* v *Mohammad Safi* AIR 1956 Nag 179: ILR (1956) Nag 132].

Where the prayer made by a lawyer is refused and he does not take any further step in the proceedings of an active character, it cannot be said that he does not appear or that having appeared, disappears. [*Tulsiram Bhagwandas* v *Sitaram Srigopal* AIR 1959 Cal 389].

**Fails to resume duty.** The expression applies only to a person who by a voluntary and deliberate act or omission stays away from duty and fails to report, and not to a person who has been prevented by a cause beyond his control from resuming duty. [*Balwant Raj* v *Union of India* AIR 1968 All 14: 1967 All LJ 399].

**Failure.** Lack of success; failing; non-performance of duty or obligation; lapse; deficiency.

Failure and default are synonymous terms. 'Failure', in the dictionary sense, means 'a falling short', 'deficiency', or 'lack'. [*Dhan Singh Ramkrishna Chaudhuri* v *Laxminarayan Ramkishan* AIR 1974 SC 1613: (1974)2 SCC 293: (1975)1 SCR 94].

'Failure' connotes that there is an obligation which has not been performed. Thus, if there is no obligation upon the assessee to make a return, then it would not be a failure on his part to carry out the obligation. The expression 'omission' does not connote any obligation, as the expression 'failure' does. [*Pannalal Nandlal Bhandari* v *Commissioner of Income Tax* AIR 1956 Bom 557: 58 Bom LR 134].

**Failure of consideration.** It means that sufficient consideration was contemplated by the parties at time contract was entered into, but either on account of some innate defect in the thing to be given or non-performance in whole or in part of that which the promisee agreed to do or forbear nothing of value can be or is received by the promisee. [*Holcomb* v *Long Beach Inv. Co.* 129 Cal App 285].

**Failure of justice.** Miscarriage of justice. It occurs when the result of a trial is so palpably wrong as to shock the moral sense.

**Failure of proof.** A "failure of proof" consists in failure to prove the cause of action or defence in its entire scope and meaning. [*Breslin-Griffitt Carpet Co.* v *Asadorian* Mo App, 145 SW 2d 494, 496].

**Fair.** A periodical gathering of buyers and sellers in a place and at a time ordained by Charter or statute or by ancient custom.

The word 'fair' is a term of art and connotes a concourse of buyers and sellers for the purchase and sale of commodities pursuant to a franchise (*i.e.*, a privilege granted under the Crown's prerogative) with an optional addition of provision of amusement. [*Wyld* v *Silver* (1961)3 All ER 1014].

NOTE: Every fair is a market, but every market is not a fair. The two franchises of fair and market are separate and distinct and of equal dignity, and may co-exist in the same place on the same day. [*Mohinder Singh Sahney* v *State of Punjab* AIR 1968 Punj 391].

In legal parlance, it means having the quality of impartiality and honesty; free from prejudice, favouritism, and self-interest; just; equitable; even-handed.

• **Cattle fair** p. 129.

**Fair comment.** Comment made in good faith; a substantially true, honest, careful and reasonable way of the comment.

Comment, in order to be fair, must be based upon facts, and if a defendant cannot show that his comments contain no misstatements of fact, he cannot prove a defence of fair comment. [*Digby* v *Financial News Ltd.* (1907)1 KB 502, *per* Lord Collins, M.R.].

NOTE: The defence of fair comment may be raised in answer to a criminal prosecution for libel. It seems that if the defence is to be raised it must be raised by formal plea and must presumably state the matter of public interest and the facts and matters relied on to support the comment, as in civil actions. [Halsbury's *Laws of England*, 4th Ed., vol. 28, para 285, p. 141].

Comment, on a matter of public interest, is not "fair" if actuated by malice. [*Thomas* v *Bradbury, Agnew & Co.* (1906)2 KB 627]. "Every person has a right to comment on the acts of a public man, which concern him as a subject of the realm, if he do not make his comments the vehicle of malice or slander". [*Turnball* v *Bird* (1861)2 F & F 508, *per* Erle, C.J.].

**Fair price.** In ordinary colloquial language 'price' does not always mean money, and 'fair price' does not always mean 'coin of the realm'. When he say that a man got something and 'paid a fair price' for it, it means only that he paid a fair equivalent for what he got. [*London & Yorkshire Bank* v *Belton* (1885)15 QBD 457: 54 LJQB 538, *per* Lord Cderidge, C.J.].

'Fair price' means a price which is neither more nor less but one which is just and appropriate. [*Banwari Lal Duli Chand* v *State of UP* 1964 All LJ 884].

▸*Meaning under the Essential Supplies Act 1946, s. 3(1).* 'Fair price' has reference to the securing of equitable distribution and availability amongst the general public at reasonable prices. It has no reference to producers or manufacturers of commodities or dealers of such commodities. [*Abhimanya Adak* v *State of West Bengal* AIR 1952 Cal 118: 55 CWN 693].

**Fair rent.** 'Fair rent' has been defined in s. 2(*c*) of the West Bengal Premises Tenancy Act 1956 as rent considered reasonable in relation to the particular circumstances.

The expression 'fair' is used in contradiction with the expression 'unfair' or 'unreasonable'. [*Abbobakar* v *Mahalaxmi Trading Co.* (1998)1 Rent CJ 484 (SC)].

**Fair report.** Report which is substantially accurate giving a just impression of what took place.

'A fair report is a substantially accurate summary of the proceedings, neither more nor less'. [*Thom* v *Associated Newspapers Ltd.* (1964-65) NSWR 396].

**Fair sale.** A sale under a power conferred by a mortgage deed is said to be fair when the sale is conducted with fairness as respects the rights and interests of the parties affected by it.

**Fair trial.** A fair trial is one which is held in accordance with the procedure laid down by law.

One where an accused's legal rights are safeguarded and respected. [*Raney* v *Commonwealth* 153 SW 2d 935, 937, 938].

Fair trial demands that there must not only be fair and impartial and upright judge, but there should be atmosphere of calm in which witnesses can deliver their testimony without fear and intimidation, in which attorneys can assert accused's rights freely and fully, and in which the truth may be received and given credence without fear of violence. [*Raney* v *Commonwealth*, supra].

**Fair wage.** It means between the living wage and the minimum wage. [*Express Newspapers Ltd.* v *Union of India* AIR 1958 SC 578].

NOTE: The principle of fair wages is that wages must be fair, that is to say, sufficiently high to provide a standard family with food, shelter, clothing, medical care and education of children appropriate to the workman but not at a rate exceeding his wage-earning capacity in the class of establishments to which he belongs. A fair wage is thus related to the earning capacity and the work-load. Fair wage is not a living wage, by which is meant a wage which is sufficient to provide not only the essentials above-mentioned but a fair measure of frugal comfort with an ability to provide for old age and evil days. Fair wage lies between the minimum wage, which must be paid in any event and the living wage, which is the goal. [*Kammani Metals* v *Workmen* AIR 1967 SC 1175: (1967)1 SCWR 730: (1967)2 SCR 463].

**Fair wear and tear.** The normal amount of depreciation to cover the use over a period of time of some form of property or other capital asset. "Fair" and "reasonable" in this context mean the same thing. [*Taylor* v *Webb* (1937)2 KB 283].

**Fait accompli.** Thing done and no longer worth arguing against.

**Faith.** Confidence; reliance; belief without evidence; a doctrine or system of doctrines, propositions, etc., held to be true; allegiance or loyal adherence to something.


- **Bad faith** p. 91.
- **Good faith** p. 390.
- **In good faith** p. 440.


**Fakir.** 'Fakir' does not mean a beggar, but a religious man, who devotes his life to meditation and spiritual exercises. [*Ali Muhammad* v *Anjuman-i-islamia* 12 Lah 590: AIR 1931 Lah 379].

**Falling through.** It implies the failure of a contract of sale through the refusal of the buyer to pay the price.

**Falsa demonstratio non nocet.** An erroneous description of a person or a thing in a written instrument. The above rule respecting it signifies that where the description is made up of more than one part, and one part is true, but the other false, there, the part which is true describes the subject with sufficient legal certainty and the untrue part will be rejected and will not vitiate the devise. [Broom's *Legal Maxims*, 10th Ed., p. 426].

NOTE: The rule is that where any property in a will is sufficiently ascertained by the description, it passes by the devise, although all the particulars stated in the will with reference to it may not be true. [*Doe d. Dunning* v *Cranstoun* (1840)7 M&M 1].

**Falsa demonstratione legatum non perimitur.** A legacy will not fail from a false description. Section 78 of the Indian Succession Act 1925 is based on this maxim. If the thing bequeathed by the testator can be sufficiently identified from the description in the will, but some parts of the description do not apply, these parts will be rejected and the bequest shall take effect.

**False.** Untrue; contrary to truth; not true [*State* v *Arnett* 92 SW 2d 897, 900]; intentionally untrue [*In re Venturella* DC Conn, 25 F Supp 332, 333]; not according with fact; contrary to fact; illusory; spurious; hypocritical; sham; feigned; erroneous; incorrect [*State* v *Arnett* 92 SW 2d 897, 900]; not genuine or real [*North American Accident Ins. Co.* v *Tebbs* CCA Utah, 107 F 2d 853, 855]; uttering falsehood, unveracious, dishonest [*Wilensky* v *Goodyear Tire & Rubber Co.* CCA Mass, 67 F 2d 389, 390]; wilfully and intentionally untrue [*In re Brown* DC NY, 37 F Supp 526, 527]; deceitful, deliberately and knowingly false [*People* v *Mangan* 252 NYS 44, 52]; not genuine; illegal; fictitious; faithless; perfidious; roguish; concocted; delusive; devoid of truth; erroneous; incorrect; mendacious; unveracious; artificial; bogus; counterfeit; pseudo; unreal.

The word 'false' may be used in a wider or a narrower sense. In the wider sense it will include all types of falsehood, whether they be intentional or innocent, but in the narrower sense it will cover only such falsehoods which are intentional. The question whether in a particular enactment the word 'false' is used in a restricted sense or in a wider sense would depend on the context in which it is used.

[*Commissioner of Sales Tax* v *Bombay General Stores* AIR 1969 MP 213].

**False answer.** A sham answer in a pleading; one which is false in the sense of being a mere pretence set up in bad faith and without colour of fact.

**False cheque.** A cheque that is not honoured because the amount either contains insufficient funds or does not exist. It is also termed as bad cheque; rubber cheque; bounced cheque; bogus cheque; cold cheque; dry cheque.

**False entry.** An entry which is either deliberately or partially fictitious; an untrue statement of items of account by written words, figures, or marks.

NOTE: One making an original false entry makes a false entry in every book which is made up in regular course from the entry or entries from the original book of entry. [Black's *Law Dictionary*, 5th Ed.].

**False imprisonment.** Restraining personal liberty without lawful authority, for which offence the law has not only decreed a punishment as a public crime, but has also given a private reparation to the party as well by removing the actual confinement for the present by *habeas corpus*, as by subjecting the wrong-doer to an action of trespass etc., usually called an action of false imprisonment, on account of the damage sustained by the loss of time and liberty. [Wharton's *Law Lexicon*].

False imprisonment is illegal arrest; actual detention and complete loss of freedom. [*Mahamad Yusuf-ud-din* v *Secretary of State* 30 IA 154: 30 Cal 872].

False imprisonment is a restraint of a person in a bounded area without justification or consent. [Black's *Law Dictionary*, 8th Ed.].

False imprisonment is wrongful confinement within the meaning of s. 340 of the Indian Penal Code and punishable under s. 342 of the Code.

**False news.** The misdemeanour of spreading false information that causes discord between the State and the people or between important people in the State.

**False personation.** The offence of personating another for the purpose of fraud. This is misdemeanour at common law, and has been made highly penal in many cases under various statutes. [Mozley & Whiteley's *Law Dictionary*, 10th Ed.].

The crime of falsely representing oneself as another person, usually a law enforcement officer, for the purpose of deceiving someone. [Black's *Law Dictionary*, 7th Ed.].

NOTE: If a person wears a soldier's garb to make others believe that he is a soldier, he is punishable under s. 140 of the Indian Penal Code. False personation at an election within the meaning of s. 171D of the Indian Penal Code is made punishable under s. 171F of the Code.

It is also termed as false impersonation.

**False pretences.** The crime of knowingly obtaining title to another's personal property by misrepresenting a fact with the intent to defraud. [Black's *Law Dictionary*, 8th Ed.].

It is also termed as fraudulent pretences.

NOTE: It is well established that a false pretence can be made by conduct. Ordinarily it consists of a false statement as to some existing fact; the statement must be made with the intention of obtaining money, property or valuable security; the thing must be of some value, and the person must have parted with the property, relying on the false pretence. [*R.* v *Seagrave* (1910)4 Cr App Rep 156].

**False return.** A process server's or other court official's recorded misrepresentation that process was served, that some other action was taken, or that something is true. [Black's *Law Dictionary*, 8th Ed.].

A tax return on which taxable income, in case of income tax, and taxable turn over, in case of sales tax or turn over tax, is incorrectly reported or the tax is incorrectly computed.

NOTE: A tax return cannot be said to be 'false' unless there is an element of deliberateness in it. It is possible that even where the incorrectness of the return is claimed to be due to want of care on the part of the assessee and there is no reasonable explanation forthcoming from the assessee for such want of care, the court may, in a given case, infer deliberations and the return may be liable to be branded as a false return. But where the assessee does not include a particular item in the taxable turn over under a *bona fide* belief that he is not liable so to include it, it would not be right to condemn the return as a false return. [*Cement Marketing Company of India Ltd.* v *Assistant Commissioner of Sales Tax, Indore* AIR 1980 SC 346: (1980)1 SCR 1098: (1980)1 SCC 71: (1980)6 ELT 295: (1980)45 STC 197: (1980)124 ITR 15].

**False swearing.** Swearing to what the deponent knows to be untrue.

The act or an instance of a person's deliberately making material false or misleading statements while under oath. [Black's *Law Dictionary*, 8th Ed.].

It is also termed as false oath; perjury.

**False trade description.** 'False trade description' means—(I) a trade description which is untrue or misleading in a material respect as regards the goods or services to which it is applied; or (II) any alteration of a trade description as regards the goods or services to which it is applied, whether by way of addition, effacement or otherwise, where that alteration makes the description untrue or misleading in a material respect; or (III) any trade description which denotes or implies that there are contained, as regards the goods to which it is applied, more yards or metres than there are contained therein standard yards or standard metres; or (IV) any marks or arrangement or combination thereof when applied—(*a*) to goods in such a manner as to be likely to lead persons to believe that the goods are the manufacture or merchandise of some person other than the person whose merchandise or manufacture they really are; (*b*) in relation to services in such a manner as to be likely to lead persons to believe that the services are provided or rendered by some person other than the person whose services they really are; or (V) any false name or initials of a person applied to goods or services in such manner as if such name or initials were a trade description in any case where the name or initials—(*a*) is or are not a trade mark or part of a trade mark; and (*b*) is or are identical with or deceptively similar to the name or initials of a person carrying on business in connection with goods or services of the same description or both and who has not authorised the use of such name or initials; and (*c*) is or are either the name or initials of a fictitious person or some person not *bona fide* carrying on business in connection with such goods or services; and the fact that a trade description is a trade mark or part of a trade mark shall not prevent such trade description being a false trade description. [The Trade Marks Act 1999, s. 2(1)(*i*)].

**Falsus in uno, falsus in omnibus.** False in one thing, false in all. The maxim may be applied to those cases only where a witness speaks of a fact with reference to which he cannot be presumed liable to mistake. The doctrine merely involves the question of weight of evidence which a court may apply in a given set of circumstances but it is not what may be called "a mandatory rule of evidence". [*Nisar Ali* v *State of UP* AIR 1957 SC 366].

**Family.** A group consisting of parents and their children; a group of persons connected by blood, by affinity, or by law; a group of persons usually relatives, who live together. [Black's *Law Dictionary*, 7th Ed.].

The term family embraces a collective body of persons in the house or within the cartilage. [*Khirode* v *Sarada* 12 CLJ 525].

The word 'family' has various meanings. In one sense it means the whole household including servants and perhaps lodgers. In another sense it means everybody descended from a common stock, that is to say, all blood relations; and it may perhaps include the husbands and wives of such persons. In a third sense the word includes children only; thus when a man speaks of his wife and family, he means his wife and children. [*Pigg* v *Clarke* (1876)3 Ch D 672]. Where the word means children, it means legitimate children unless the context indicates the contrary. [*Re Makein (decd.)*

*Makein* v *Makein* (1955)1 All ER 57]. The word 'family' in its popular sense means children. [*Deoki Nandan* v *Murlidhar* AIR 1957 SC 133: 1956 SCR 756: 1957 SCA 85: 1957 SCJ 75].

▸*Meaning under the Central Civil Services (Pension) Rules 1972, r. 54(14)(b).* 'Family' in relation to a Government servant means—(*i*) wife in the case of a male Government servant, or husband in the case of a female Government servant, provided the marriage took place before retirement of the Government servant; (*ii*) son who has not attained the age of twenty-one years and unmarried daughter who has not attained the age of thirty years, including such son and daughter adopted legally before retirement but shall not include son or daughter born after retirement.

NOTE: This definition so far as it seeks to exclude a post-retirement married spouse and post-retirement born child is *ultra vires*. Such wife and child are entitled to pension. [*Bhagwanti* v *Union of India* AIR 1989 SC 2088].

▸*Meaning under the City of Nagpur Corporation Act 1948, s. 114.* The expression 'family' must take colour from the context. The expression in the Act means no more than a person or a group of persons. [*Corporation of the City of Nagpur* v *Nagpur Handloom Cloth Market Co.* AIR 1963 SC 1192: 1963 Supp (2) SCR 796: (1964)2 SCJ 595].

▸*Meaning under the Employees' State Insurance Act 1948, s. 2(11).* 'Family' means all or any of the following relatives of an insured person, namely—(*i*) a spouse; (*ii*) a minor legitimate or adopted child dependant upon the insured person; (*iii*) a child who is wholly dependant on the earnings of the insured person and who is—(*a*) receiving education, till he or she attains the age of twenty-one years, (*b*) an unmarried daughter; (*iv*) a child who is infirm by reason of any physical or mental abnormality or injury and is wholly dependant on the earnings of the insured person, so long as the infirmity continues; (*v*) dependant parents.

▸*Meaning under the Income-tax Act 1961, s. 2(31).* "Family" connotes a group of people related by blood or marriage. According to *Shorter Oxford English Dictionary*, 3rd Edition the word "family" means the group consisting of parents and their children, whether living together or not; in wider sense, all those who are nearly connected by blood or affinity; a person's children regarded collectively; those descended or claiming descent from a common ancestor; a house, kindred; lineage, a race; a people or group of peoples. According to Aristottel (Politics I), it is the characteristic of man that he alone has any sense of good and evil, or just and unjust, and the association of living beings who have this sense make a family and a State. It would follow from the above that the word "family" always signifies a group. Plurality of persons is an essential attribute of a family. A single person, male or female, does not constitute a family. He or she would remain, what is inherent in the very nature of things, an individual, a lonely wayfarer till perchance he or she finds a mate. A family consisting of a single individual is a contradiction in terms. [*C. Krishna Prasad* v *Commissioner of Income-Tax, Bangalore* AIR 1975 SC 498: (1975)2 SCR 709: (1975)1 SCC 160: (1974)97 ITR 493].

▸*Meaning under the Kerala Buildings (Lease and Rent Control) Act 1965.* The expression 'family' which is undefined by the Act is elastic and its ambit has to be determined in all the circumstances of the case, having regard to the habits, ideas and socio-economic milieu of the parties. Going even by its primary meaning the word 'family' includes the son. [*Muhammad* v *Sinnamalu Amma* AIR 1978 Ker 21].

▸*Meaning under the Mussalman Wakf Validating Act.* Technically, the word 'family' may be taken to mean the collective body of persons who live in one house and under one head or manager, and includes within its fold a household consisting of parents, children and servants as the case may be, lodgers or boarders. Under the Mussalman Wakf

Validating Act, it is intended to be used in a broad and popular sense. The term popularly indicates persons descended from one common progenitor and having a common lineage. It will include both agnates and cognates and relations by blood or marriage. [*Asha Bibi* v *Nabissa Sahib* AIR 1957 Mad 583].

▸*Meaning under the Partition Act 1893, s. 4.* The word 'family' ought to be given a liberal and comprehensive meaning and it includes a group of persons related in blood who live in one house under one head or management and that it is not restricted to a body of persons, who can trace their descent from a common ancestor. [*Aley Hasan* v *Toorab* AIR 1958 Pat 232; *Bibuni* v *Padmanav* AIR 1956 Ori 105].

▸*Meaning under the Payment of Gratuity Act 1972, s. 2(h).* 'Family' in relation to an employee shall be deemed to consist of—(*i*) in the case of a male employee, himself, his wife, his children, whether married or unmarried, his dependent parents and the dependent parents of his wife and the widow and children of his predeceased son, if any; (*ii*) in the case of a female employee, herself, her husband, her children, whether married or unmarried, her dependent parents and the dependent parents of her husband and the widow and children of her predeceased son, if any.

▸*Meaning under the Plantations Labour Act 1951, s. 2(ee).* 'Family' when used in relation to a worker means—(*i*) his or her spouse, and (*ii*) the legitimate and adopted children of the worker dependent upon him or her who have not completed their eighteenth year, and includes, where the worker is a male, his parents dependent upon him.

▸*Meaning under the Pondicherry Land Reforms (Fixation of Ceiling of Land) Act, s. 2(10).* "Family" in relation to a person, means the person, the wife or husband, as the case may be, of such person and his or her minor sons and unmarried daughters.

It is not correct that the expression family referred to in s. 2(10) of Pondicherry Act must conform to the concept of joint family. The stress is only on the existence of the relationship mentioned in the section and unity of title or jointness of holding in relation to property are not essential elements for attracting the applicability of the definition. [*Vengadasalam Pillai* v *Union Territory of Pondicherry* AIR 1985 SC 571: (1985)2 SCC 91].

▸*Meaning under the Rent Control Legislation.* In the context of Rent Control Legislation, the expression 'family' often comes on the surface for interpretation. The expression has not been precisely defined in any Rent Control Legislation. The term is not capable of concise definition because what constitutes a family in a given set of circumstances or in a particular society depends upon the habits and ideas of persons constituting that society and the religious or socio-religious customs of the community to which such persons may belong. [*Govind Das* v *Kuldip Singh* AIR 1971 Del 151; *Angamuthammal* v *K.V. Muthu* AIR 1984 Mad 179].

NOTE: A remote relation may in a given set of circumstances be treated as a member of the family, whereas in another set of circumstances the same relation may not be legitimately called a member of the family. [*Abdul Hamid* v *Nur Muhammad* AIR 1976 Del 328 relying on *Govind Das* v *Kuldip Singh* AIR 1971 Del 151]. In that case the expression 'family' was held to include brothers, their wives and children; the discussion was in the context of the Delhi Rent Control Act of 1958.

A foster-son can also be a member of landlord's family. [*Angamuthammal* v *K.V. Muthu* AIR 1984 Mad 179].

▸*Meaning under the West Bengal Land Reforms Act, s. 14K(c).* 'Family' in relation to a raiyat, shall be deemed to consist of—(*i*) himself and his wife, minor sons, unmarried daughters, if any, (*ii*) his unmarried adult son, if any, who does not hold any land as a raiyat, (*iii*) his married adult son, if any, where neither such adult son nor the wife nor any minor son or unmarried daughter of such adult son holds any land as a raiyat, (*iv*) widow of his predeceased son, if any, where neither such widow nor any minor son or unmarried daughter of such widow holds any land as a raiyat, (*v*) minor son or unmarried daughter, if any, of his predeceased son, where the widow of such predeceased son is dead and any minor son or unmarried daughter of such predeceased son does not hold any land as raiyat, but shall not include any other person.

NOTE: The definition of 'family' as contained in s. 14K(c) of the Act is more realistic than the definition of this term in similar laws for imposition of ceiling on agricultural holdings enacted in other States. The definition is much wider, and far more generous and humane because it takes into consideration the existence of a widowed and divorced daughter, which is absent in other Acts. [*Sasanka Sekhar Maity* v *Union of India* AIR 1981 SC 522: (1980)3 SCR 1209: (1980)4 SCC 716].


- **Head of family** p. 408.
- **Hindu joint (undivided) family** p. 416.
- **Undivided family** p. 864.


**Family arrangement/settlement.** An informal agreement among family members, usually to distribute property in a manner other than what the law provides for. [Black's *Law Dictionary*, 8th Ed.].

A family arrangement is an agreement between members of the same family, intended to be generally and reasonably for the benefit of the family, either by compromising doubtful or disputed rights or by preserving the family property or the peace and security of the family by avoiding litigation or by saving its honour. [Halsbury's *Laws of England*, 4th Ed., vol. 18, para 301, p. 135].

Family arrangement is an "informal agreement among family members, usually to distribute property in a manner other than what the law provides for". [Black's *Law Dictionary*, 7th Ed.]. It is also termed family settlement.

If the dispute which is settled is one between near relations then the settlement of such a dispute can be considered as a family arrangement. [*S. Shanmugam Pillai* v *K. Shanmugam Pillai* AIR 1972 SC 2069: (1973)1 SCR 570: (1973)2 SCC 312].

NOTE: To constitute a valid family arrangement—(1) The transaction should be one which is for the benefit of the family generally. (2) The consideration for the arrangement may be preservation of the family property, preservation of the peace and honour of the family or the avoidance of legislation. (3) It is not essential that there should be a doubtful claim or a disputed right to be compromised. If there is one, the settlement may be upheld if it is founded on a reciprocal 'give and take' and there is mutuality between the parties, in the one surrendering one's right and in the other forbearing to sue. In such cases, the court will not too nicely scrutinise the adequacy of the consideration moving from one party to the other. (4) In any case, if such an arrangement has been acted upon, the courts will give effect to it on the ground of estoppel or limitation or the like. (5) A family arrangement may also be upheld if the consideration moves from a third party. (6) If it appears to the court that one party has taken undue advantage of the helplessness of the other and there is no sacrifice of right or interest the agreement is unilateral and is devoid of consideration. (7) The consent of the parties should be freely given to the arrangement and gross inadequacy of consideration may be a determining factor in judging whether the consent was freely given. (8) If the agreement involves or implies an injury to the person or property of one of the parties, the courts retain an inherent power to prevent injustice being done. [*Sundar Sahu Gountia* v *Chamra Sahu Gountia* AIR 1954 Ori 80: ILR (1953) Cut 591].

A family arrangement is entitled to bring about the harmony in the family and the courts should lean strongly in favour of such family arrangement. [*Krishna Behari Lal* v *Gulabchand* AIR 1971 SC 1041: 1971 (Supp) SCR 27: (1971)1 SCC 837].

**Family custom.** The usage of a family transmitted successively from father to son according to law. Unlike *desachar*, which binds all persons within the local limits in which it prevails, a family custom, (*kulachar*) governs the members of a particular family only.

NOTE: Family usages must be certain, invariable, and continuous. Well-established discontinuance must be held to destroy family usages.

**Family debt.** A family debt under Hindu law is a debt which is binding on the family. A debt is not binding on the family unless it is borrowed by the managing member for legal necessity or for the benefit of the estate or for any obligatory religious purposes.

**Family law.** The body of law dealing with marriage, divorce, adoption, child custody and support, child abuse and neglect, paternity, juvenile delinquency and other domestic-relations issues. [Black's *Law Dictionary*, 8th Ed.].

**Family pedigree.** A history of family succession; ancestry or lineage.

NOTE: A family pedigree may be one kept by a member of the family or by some other person on his behalf. Such a pedigree would be admissible in evidence of relationship and it is not necessary for the purpose of admitting the same in evidence to show who made the statements in the pedigree. [*Sitaji* v *B.N. Choudhary* AIR 1951 Pat 358: 28 Pat 447].

A family pedigree kept in the ordinary course of business by a family chronicler and prepared by him from time to time from the information supplied by the members of the family is admissible under s. 32(2) and also under s. 32(6) of the Evidence Act as having been kept by a person engaged by the members of the family to keep a record of the family events before them. [*Mohansing* v *Dalpatsing* 46 Bom 753].

For a family pedigree table to be admissible the following are relevant—

- the genealogy must fall within the four corners of s. 32(5) or s. 13, Evidence Act;
- the genealogy must not be hit by *post litem motam*;
- it cannot be proved by recitals, depositions or facts narrated in judgments held inadmissible in a long course of decisions;
- the genealogy when is proved by oral evidence must show that special means of knowledge disclosing the exact source, time and circumstances under which the knowledge is acquired and this must be clearly and conclusively proved. [*State of Bihar* v *Radha Krishna Singh* AIR 1983 SC 684].

Statements of relationship from pedigrees are admissible under s. 32(5) and (6) only if they are made before the question in dispute is raised. But such pedigrees are not admissible under s. 65(*g*), Evidence Act when the original has not been produced from which the pedigrees were prepared. [*Kishanlal* v *Sohanlal* 1955 Raj LW 338].

**Family physician.** Signifies the physician who usually attends and is consulted by the members of a family in the capacity of a physician. [*Price* v *Ins. Co.* 17 Minn 519].

**Fancy price.** Price in proportion to the buyer's desire to possess, and not in accordance with the market value.

**Faraiz.** The legal knowledge of dividing inheritance according to the Mahomedan law.

**Fare.** Charge for carriage of passengers; charge for conveyance of a person; cost of communication; cost of conveyance; cost of transportation; money paid for passage; payment for the right of carriage; transportation fee; money paid for passage by land, air or by water.

▸*Meaning under the Inland Air Travel Tax Act 1971, s. 2(c).* 'Fare' means the total amount of all charges of whatever nature (including charges, if any, for the provision of food or accommodation) payable to the carrier by or on behalf of a passenger in respect of his inland journey.

▸*Meaning under the Railway Passengers Fares Act 1971, s. 2(a).* 'Fare' means the total amount of all charges of whatever nature payable by a passenger or a group of passengers in respect of his or their carriage and includes—(*i*) haulage charges for supply of carriages of particular type; (*ii*) empty haulage charges on tourist cars and saloons; (*iii*) charges for pilot engines; and (*iv*) charges for dining cars attached to special trains, but does not include—(*i*) tax payable under this Act; (*ii*) terminal taxes, pilgrim taxes and tolls on bridges; (*iii*) reservation charges (including reservation charges for sleeping accommodation); and (*iv*) hire, detention and stabling charges in respect of passenger-traffic booked in reserved carriages and special trains.

**Farm.** As noun, it means a tract of land devoted to agriculture, pasturage, stock raising, or some allied industry. It includes dairy, stock and poultry farms.

As verb, it means to lease or let; to demise or grant for a limited term and at a stated rental; to carry on business or occupation of farming; to cultivate land.

**Farm house.** Dwelling place on a farm.

**Farman.** A mandate, an order, a command, a patent.

**Farmer.** A farmer is a person who holds a farm, or is a tenant or lessee thereof. He is engaged in the tillage of the soil.

**Farming.** Carrying on of the activities appropriate to the land recognisable as farm land. It must at least include the raising of beasts, the cultivation of land and the growing of crops. A farmer does not cause to farm merely because he arranges for others to reap instead of himself. [*Lowe* v *Ashmore* (1971)1 All ER 1057].

**Fasid.** Irregular.

> NOTE: A Muslim marriage contracted without witnesses is fasid, that is, irregular. Similarly, if a Mahomedan marries a fifth wife when he has already four, the marriage is not void, but merely irregular.

**Fasli.** Relating to a harvest; the Mahomedan official era. An agricultural lease containing the term 'fasli' ordinarily means a lease for the agricultural year.

**Fatal accident.** An accident which causes death is a fatal accident.

**Fatawa-i-alamgiri.** It is a work of great authority in Mahomedan law. It was compiled by the order of the Emperor Aurungzeb Alamgir. It contains a bare recital of law cases without any argument.

**Fatawa-i-serajiah.** The highest authority on the law of inheritance amongst the Sunnis of India. It was composed by Siraj-ud-Din Muhammad.

**Father.** A male parent; he by whom a child is begotten; natural father; procreator of a child.

As used in law, this term may, according to the context and the nature of instrument, include a putative as well as a legal father, also a stepfather, an adoptive father, or a grandfather, but is not as wide as the word "parent", and cannot be so construed as to include a female. [Black's *Law Dictionary*, 5th Ed.].

> NOTE: Father in the case of anyone whose personal law permits adoption shall include an adoptive father. [General Clauses Act 1897, s. 3(20)].

▸ *Meaning under the Limitation Act 1963, Art. 109.* The expression "father" as used in the Article in an appropriate case includes grandfather and great grandfather or a paternal uncle or granduncle. [*Sudarshan Prosad* v *Radha Kishun Ram* AIR 1982 All 218].

**Fathom.** As noun it means, a measure of length, six feet, or 1.829 meters. The word is used principally in marine and mining measurements. [Webster's *Comprehensive Dictionary*, International Edition].

A nautical measure of six feet in length. Occasionally the word is used as a superficial measure of land and in mining, and in that case it means a square fathom or thirty-six square feet. [Black's *Law Dictionary*, 5th Ed.].

As verb, it means to find the depth of; sound; to get to the bottom of; understand; interpret; grasp or comprehend.

**Fault.** As noun in its application to mistake, it means aberration; blunder; bungling; erratum; miscalculation; misjudgment; misunderstanding; an error or defect of judgment or of conduct.

As noun in its application to responsibility, it means accountability; answerability; culpability; dereliction; malefaction; misfeasance; negligence; any deviation from prudence, duty, or rectitude; any shortcoming, or neglect of care or performance resulting from inattention, incapacity, or perversity; a wrong tendency, course, or act; bad faith, or mismanagement.

As noun in its application as weakness, it means debility; defect; deficiency;

delicacy; impairment; impotence; infirmity; lack of strength; powerlessness; shortcoming.

As verb it means accuse; admonish; attack; bring into discredit; cast a slur upon; cast blame upon; castigate; censure; denigrate; denounce; hold to blame; impeach; reprehend; reprimand; scold; take to task.

**Faux pas.** False step; blunder; a social blunder.

**Fax.** A method of transmitting over telephone lines an exact copy of a printing; a machine used for such transmission; the communication sent or received by such a machine.

**F.C.S.** The abbreviation stands for "free of capture and seizure" in a policy of marine insurance. They denote that the insurer is not liable for loss of or damage to the goods or ship as a result of capture and seizure by an enemy, by mutinous passengers, by pirates or by the assured's own Government in anticipation of war with the country to which the insurer belongs.

**Fealty.** The obligation of fidelity which the tenant owed to his lord under feudal law.

**Federation.** This is a form of polity, in which there is union of constituent units without unity. The Government is organised at two levels—Union and State. The Union has a general Government while the federating units regional Governments. There is thus a division of powers between these two Governments, which are of co-ordinate authority.

NOTE: A Federation may be formed with units that were previously independent, as for example, the United States of America; again, it may consist of units that were formerly administrative areas as in India.

A Federation is characterised by three features, *viz.* (1) the supremacy of the Constitution; (2) the division of powers between two co-ordinate Governments—general and regional; and (3) an independent authority to interpret the Constitution.

If the word "federation" can be used at all in the context of the Constitution of India, it is a federation of various States which were designated under the Constitution for the purpose of efficient administration of the country. [*M. Karunanidhi* v *Union of India* AIR 1977 Mad 1920].

**Fee.** A charge for labour and services, especially professional services; a heritable interest in land, especially a fee simple absolute. [Black's *Law Dictionary*, 8th Ed.].

A fee is meant to compensate the Government for expenses incurred in rendering service of a special nature to the persons from whom the fee is collected. [*Muthuswamy Raja* v *Kadayanallur Panchayat Union* ILR (1965)2 Mad 501: AIR 1965 Mad 289].

A fee is a charge for special service rendered to individuals by some Government agency. [*The Commissioner, Hindu Religious Endowments, Madras* v *Sri Lakshmindra Thirtha Swamiar of Sri Shirur Mutt* AIR 1954 SC 282: 1954 SCR 1005: 1954 SCJ 335].

A fee is generally defined to be a charge for a special service rendered to individuals by the Government or some other agency like a local authority or statutory corporation. The amount of fee levied is supposed to be based on the expenses incurred by the Government or the agency in rendering the service though in many cases the costs are arbitrarily assessed. In the case of a fee, no account is taken of the varying abilities of different recipients of the service to pay. [*State of Maharashtra* v *The Salvation Army, Western India Territory* AIR 1975 SC 846: (1975)3 SCR 475: (1975)1 SCC 509].

A fee is levied essentially for services rendered and as such there is an element of *quid pro quo* between the person who pays the fee and the public authority which imposes it. [*Kewal Krishan Puri* v *State of Punjab* AIR 1980 SC 1008: (1979)3 SCR 1217: (1980)1 SCC 416].

NOTE: *Conditions of fee.* A fee in order to be a legal fee must satisfy two conditions: (*a*) there must be an element of *quid pro quo*, that is to say the authority levying fee must render some service for the fee levied, however remote the service may be; (*b*) the fee realised must be spent for the purposes of imposition and should not form part of the general revenue of the State. [*Chief Commissioner, Delhi* v *Delhi Cloth & General Mills* AIR 1978 SC 1181: (1978)2 SCJ 142: 48 Comp Cas 588].

*Tax and fee—distinction.* The distinction between a tax and a fee lies primarily in the fact that a tax is levied as a part of a common burden while a fee is a payment for a special benefit or privilege. [*The Commissioner, Hindu Religious Endowments, Madras* v *Sri Lakshmindra Thirtha Swamiar of Sri Shirur Mutt* AIR 1954 SC 282: 1954 SCJ 335: 1954 SCA 415: 1954 SCR 1005].

While a fee is correlated to particular service rendered, a tax is not so correlated. A tax is intended to meet the expenses of the Government. [*Muthuswami Raja* v *Kadayanallur Panchayat Union* ILR (1965)2 Mad 501: AIR 1965 Mad 289].

The chief purpose of a tax is to raise funds for the support of the Government or for a public purpose, while a fee may be charged for the privilege or benefit conferred, or service rendered or to meet the expenses connected therewith. Thus, fees are nothing but payment for some special privilege granted on service rendered. [*Southern Pharmaceuticals and Chemicals, Trichur* v *State of Kerala* AIR 1981 SC 1863: (1982)1 SCR 519: (1981)4 SCC 391].

**Fee simple.** The word 'fee' denotes inheritability, and the word 'simple' indicates that it is inheritable by the general heirs of the owner for the time being whether they are ascendants, descendants or collateral. The fee simple is the largest estate in point of duration, for, being one that is granted to a man *and his heirs*, it will last as long as the person entitled to it for the time being dies leaving an heir, and, therefore, it may last forever in the sense that it may never pass to the Crown for want of an heir. [Cheshire's *Modern Real Property*, 10th Ed., p. 33].

In England, it was originally an estate which endured for as long as the original tenant or any of his heirs survived. "Heirs" comprised any blood relations, although originally ancestors were excluded; not until the Inheritance Act 1833 could a person be the heir to one of his descendants. Thus, when the basic feudal estate first became heritable, it would terminate if the original tenant died without leaving any descendants or collateral blood relations (such as brothers or cousins), even if before his death the land had been conveyed to another tenant who was still alive something which at that stage required the permission of the feudal land. But by 1306 it was settled that where a tenant in fee simple alienated the land, which by then did not require the permission of anyone, the fee simple would continue as long as there were heirs of the new tenant and so on, irrespective of any failure of the original tenant's heirs. Thenceforward a fee simple was virtually eternal. [Robert E. Megarry & M.P. Thompson: *A Manual of the Law of Real Property*, 8th Ed., p. 32].

**Fee tail.** An estate limited to a man and the heirs of his body, generally called an estate tail. [Mozley & Whiteley's *Law Dictionary*, 10th Ed.].

NOTE: If the original tenant died leaving no relatives except a brother, a fee simple would continue, but a fee tail would come to an end. [Robert E. Megarry & M.P. Thompson: *A Manual of the Law of Real Property*, 8th Ed., p. 32].

**Feeding the estoppel.** The doctrine of 'feeding the estoppel' applies only where alienor, vendor or mortgagor makes a fraudulent or erroneous representation that he was authorised to transfer interest in the property by virtue of an absolute title possessed by him. It is only in such a case that the subsequent enlargement of the interest of the alienor or transferor will benefit the transferee; in such a case, certainly an heir or person claiming under the alienor may be equally estopped. [*Kanthimathinatha Pillai* v *Vayyapuri Mudaliar* AIR 1963 Mad 37].

NOTE: Section 43 of the Transfer of Property Act 1882 provides that where a person fraudulently or erroneously represents that he is authorised to transfer certain immovable property and professes to transfer such property for consideration, such transfer shall, at the option of the transferee, operate on any interest which the transferor may acquire in such property at any time during which the contract of transfer subsists.

**Feme covert.** A married woman.

**Feme sole.** An unmarried woman.

**Fence.** A fence is an enclosing structure intended to prevent intrusion. It may consist of a hedge, a ditch, a wall or deep water course. It may be composed of any material capable of offering sufficient obstruction. A barbed wire is a proper material for a fence. A fence separates adjoining lands.

NOTE: Although fences are frequently used to mark the situation of boundaries, none the less they are primarily guards against intrusion, and therefore in this sense the term includes not only hedges, banks, and walls, but also ditches. [Halsbury's *Laws of England*, 3rd Ed., vol. 3, p. 367].

**Ferae naturae.** Of a wild nature, *e.g.*, animals not commonly tamed.

**Ferry.** A boat or vessel used to carry persons or property across water, usually with fixed terminals and short distances; the commercial transportation of persons or property across water; the place where a ferry passes across water, including the continuation of the highway on both sides of the water; the right, usually exclusive given by government franchise, to carry persons or property across water for a fee. [Black's *Law Dictionary*, 8th Ed.].

A continuation of the highway from one side of the water over which it passes to the other, for transportation of passengers or of travellers with their vehicles and such other property as they may carry or have with them. [*U.S.* v *Puget Sound Nav. Co.* DC Wash, 24 F Supp 431, 432].

A liberty to have a boat on a stream, river, arm of the sea, lake, or other body of water for the transportation of passengers and vehicles with their contents, for a reasonable toll. Sometimes limited to the landing place. [*State Highway Commission* v *Smith* 62 SW 2d 1044].

NOTE: A ferry is a franchise that no one can erect without a licence from the Crown. It is in the nature of a highway and is the exclusive right to carry passengers across a river or stream or arm of the sea. It is *publici juris* and when a ferry is erected, another cannot be erected without an *ad quod damnum*. [*Purnendu Bikash* v *District Board* AIR 1963 Cal 74].

'Ferry' includes a bridge of boats, pontoons or rafts, a swing bridge, a fly-bridge and a temporary bridge and the approaches to, and landing places of, a ferry. [Railways Act 1989, s. 2(15)].

**Fetish.** Worship of inanimate objects by savages in the belief that they are inhabited by spirits.

**Feudal system.** A political and social system which prevailed throughout Europe during the Middle Ages. The peculiarity of the feudal system was the division of the ownership of land. The nominal ownership was in one person, while the occupation was in another known as the tenant or feudal inferior. The tenant rendered his lord certain services principally of a military nature. The relation between the landowner and the tenant was a mutually protective one.

**F.G.A.** It is abbreviation for "free from general average" in a policy of marine insurance. They denote that the underwriter is not liable to make good general average losses suffered by the subject of insurance or the general average contributions due from it to other interests engaged in the voyage.

**Fiat.** A short order of a judge commanding something to be done; authoritative order; command; decree having the force of law; direction; directive; judgment; prescription; pronouncement.

**Fictio cedit veritati: fictio juris non est ubi veritas.** Fiction yields to truth: where there is truth, fiction of law does not exist.

**Fictio legis neminem laedit.** A legal fiction must injure no one. Fictions are only to be made for necessity, and to avoid mischief.

**Fiction.** Concoction; fabrication; falsification; false statement; fantasy; feigned story; prevarication; product of imagination; untruthful report.

• **Legal fiction** p. 525.

**Fiction of law.** A supposition of law that a thing is true, without inquiring whether it is so or not, so that it may have the effect of truth so far as is consistent with justice. There are many instances of fictions used in English law. [Mozley & Whiteley's *Law Dictionary*, 10th Ed.].

NOTE: Before the advent of legislation, law was harmonised with society in two ways, namely, by legal fiction and by equity. Legal fiction consists in concealing that a rule of law has changed by retaining the letter of the law intact, although modifying its operation. The reality is the change of law, but the fiction is the concealment. Fiction is thus one of the juristic devices by means of which men fit new legal norms into old principles so as to reorient conduct without the need to junk long-standing postulates. This is illustrated by the universal practice of adoption, whereby outsiders are identified as if they are actually kinsmen.

**Fictitious.** Concocted; counterfeit; delusive; fabricated; fake; false; fancied; fanciful; feigned; forged; founded on fiction; illusory; mythical; sham; unfounded; unreal; untrue; spurious; imaginary.

Imaginary; not real; forged. [*Dharam Deo* v *State* AIR 1958 All 865: 1958 Cr LJ 1453].

NOTE: A fictitious document is not binding on either party or, in other words, it is of no legal consequence. The effect of such a document would be the same both for the transferor and the transferee. [*Shib Das* v *Ghauri Lal* AIR 1965 J&K 11].

**Fictitious entry.** A "fictitious entry" is one which is not genuine. It is an unreal entry. An incorrect or fabricated entry can be said to be fictitious. An entry which is incorrectly introduced into the records by a reason of ill-will or hostility is not only shorn of authenticity but also becomes utterly useless without any lawful basis. [*Bachan* v *Kankar* AIR 1972 SC 2157: (1973)1 SCR 727: (1972)2 SCC 555].

**Fidelity guarantee.** This is a contract by which a person undertakes to make good losses due to fraud or negligence on the part of another person occupying a position of trust. Banks and business houses frequently require a guarantee of this kind on behalf of such of their employees as handle large sums of money, and many insurance offices, in return for an annual premium, enter into guarantees of this kind. [Harmsworth's *Universal Encyclopaedia*].

**Fides servanda.** Good faith must be observed.

**Fiduciary.** A person who is required to act for the benefit of another person on all matters within the scope of their relationship; one who owes to another the duties of good faith, trust, confidence, and candour; one who must exercise a high standard of care in managing another's money or property. [Black's *Law Dictionary*, 8th Ed.].

Derived from Roman law, the word 'fiduciary' as a noun, presupposes a person holding the character of a trustee or a character analogous to that of a trustee, in respect of the trust and confidence involved in it and the scrupulous good faith and candour which it requires. [*V. Velayudhan* v *State Bank of India* AIR 1989 Ker 38].

As adjective it means of the nature of a trust; having the characteristics of a trust; analogous to a trust; relating to or founded upon a trust or confidence.

A person is said to stand in fiduciary relating to another when he has rights and powers which he is bound to exercise for the benefit to that other. Hence he is not allowed to derive any profit or advantage from the relation between them, except with the knowledge and consent of the other person. [Jowitt on *Dictionary of English Law*, 2nd Ed.].

NOTE: A guarantor stands in a fiduciary capacity to creditor. [*V. Velayudhan* v *State Bank of India* AIR 1989 Ker 38].

**Fiduciary contract.** An agreement by which a person delivers a thing to another on the condition that the latter will restore it to the former; a contract based on mutual trust and confidence.

**Fiduciary note issue.** An issue of notes without any bullion reserve to meet them.

**Fiduciary relation.** Relating to or involving a confidence or trust.

NOTE: The fiduciary relation, as it is called, does not depend upon any particular circumstances. It exists in almost every shape. It exists, of course, notoriously in the case of trustee and *cestui que trust*; it exists in the case of guardian and ward of parent and child, of solicitor and client. [*Plowright* v *Lambart* (1885)52 LT 646].

A person is deemed to be in a position to dominate the will of another where he stands in a fiduciary relation to the other. [Indian Contract Act 1872, s. 16(2)(*a*)].

The words "fiduciary capacity" also occur in s. 4(3)(*b*), Benami Transactions (Prohibition) Act 1988. Bar to sue or to take defence as contemplated in s. 4(1) or s. 4(2) does not apply when the person in whose name the property is held is a trustee or other person standing in a fiduciary capacity and the property is held for the benefit of another person for whom he is a trustee or towards whom he stands in such capacity.

**Fieri facias.** A writ of *fieri facias* (commonly called *fi. fa.*) is a writ of execution on a judgment commanding the sheriff that out of the goods and chattels of the defendant he "cause to be made" the amount recovered by the judgment and (usually) costs. Under this writ the sheriff or his officer seizes the goods of the defendant, sells them by auction, and pays the proceeds into court. But the wearing apparel of the debtor and things in actual use cannot be seized. [Code of Civil Procedure 1908, s. 60].

NOTE: The most usual method of execution is by writ of *fieri facias* (commonly called *fi. fa.*). This lies when a sum of money or any costs are payable to any person under a judgment or order, and under the writ the goods and chattels of the debtor are seized and sold for the satisfaction of the judgment or order. The writ is addressed to the sheriff required to execute it, and commands him to seize and sell the judgment debtor's goods. ... Under the writ of *fieri facias* it is his (the sheriff's) duty to seize and sell any goods which he has the power to seize, to an amount reasonably sufficient, but not more than sufficient, to satisfy the debt and his own expenses, and, after sale thereof and such satisfaction, to pay over any residue to the judgment debtor. [Halsbury's *Laws of England*, 3rd Ed., vol. 16, p. 40].

**Fieri non debuit, sed factum valet.** It ought not to have been done, but when done, it is binding.

**F.I.F.O.** "First in, first out"—a term used to indicate a basis for charging out materials for production purposes or for valuing stock on hand at a given date, under which it is assumed that the goods are used or sold in the order in which they were acquired.

**Fihrist.** A list, a catalogue, an inventory.

**File.** As noun it means catalogue; classified index; dossier; folder; orderly arrangement of papers; record; recorded information; registry; report.

Used as verb it means align; array; categorize; bring into order; classify; codify; line up; make orderly; marshal; place in order; put in array; put in order; reduce to order; set in order.

Used as verb it may also mean deliver an instrument; deposit among records of the court; place an instrument in a place of deposit; place on record; put on record; store in the archives.

NOTE: *Filing a petition and presenting a petition—distinction.* Filing a petition means putting upon the file or among the records of the court, while presenting a petition means placing it before the presiding officer of the court for his orders. [*Gopalkrishna Iyer* v *Padmanabhan* AIR 1972 Ker 96].

'Filed' implies that the plaint or memorandum of appeal has been admitted and put on the files of the court. [*Amjad Ali* v *Mohammad Ismail* ILR 20 All 11].

Directing 'file' means a direction to assign it to the record room. [*Delhi Land and Finance* v *Income-tax Officer* AIR 1967 Punj 399].

**Filius nullius.** The son of no one; an illegitimate son.

**Filius populi.** A son of the people; natural child.

**Final.** Conclusive; not liable to be altered or set aside; a concluded adjudication by a court or tribunal; decisive; definitive; ultimate; unappealable.

NOTE: The word 'final' prohibits an appeal and not an application for revision. [*Arumugham* v *Jawahar Mills* AIR 1956 Mad 79].

**Final and conclusive.** Nothing more than that it would not be open to challenge by an appeal or other proceeding.

**Final decision.** A decision is said to be final when so far as the court rendering it is concerned, it is unalterable except by resort to such provisions of law as permit its reversal, modification or amendment. A final decision would operate as *res judicata* if it is not modified or reversed as permitted by law. [*Venkata Reddy* v *Pethi Reddy* AIR 1963 SC 992: 1963 Supp (2) SCR 616].

**Final decree.** A decree is final when the adjudication in the suit completely disposes of the suit.

NOTE: Final decree may be said to become final in two ways: (*i*) when the time for appeal has expired without any appeal being filed against the preliminary decree or the matter has been decided by the highest court; (*ii*) when as regards the court passing the decree, the same stands completely disposed of. It is in the latter sense that the word 'decree' is used in section 2(2) of the Civil Procedure Code. [*Shankar Balwant Lokhande* v *Chandrakant Shankar Lokhande* AIR 1995 SC 1211: (1995)3 SCC 413: JT 1995(3) SC 186].

**Final judgment.** One which puts an end to an action at law by declaring that the plaintiff either has or has not entitled himself to recover the remedy he sues for; a judgment which disposes of the subject-matter of the controversy or determines the litigation as to all parties on its merits; a court's last action that settles the rights of the parties and disposes of all issues in controversy except for the award of costs and enforcement of the judgment.

A court's last action that settles the rights of the parties and disposes of all issues in controversy, except for the award of costs and enforcement of the judgment. [Black's *Law Dictionary*, 7th Ed.].

One which finally disposes of rights of the parties, either upon entire controversy or upon some definite and separate branch thereof. [*Casati* v *Aero Marine Management Co., Inc.* 356 NE 2d 826, 833].

A judgment is considered "final" only if it determines the rights of the parties and disposes of all the issues involved so that no future action by the court will be necessary in order to settle and determine the entire controversy. [*Howard Gault and Son, Inc.* v *First Nat. Bank of Hereford* Tex Civ App, 523 SW 2d 496, 498].

NOTE: No order, judgment or other proceeding can be final which does not at once affect the status of the parties for whichever side the decision may be given. [*Salaman* v *Warner* (1891)1 QB 734].

Where any further step is necessary to prefect an order or judgment, it is not final but interlocutory. [*Collins* v *Paddington* 5 QBD 370].

**Final order.** One which terminates the litigation between the parties and the merits of the case and leaves nothing to be done but to enforce by execution what has been determined. [*Richerson* v *Jones* CA Pa, 551 F 2d 918, 921].

An order is final when it finally disposes of the rights of the parties. [*Bozson* v *Altrincham Urban District Council* (1903)1 KB 547].

NOTE: Where a statute says that 'the order shall be final', it means not only that the matter cannot be brought in question again but also that no appeal lies therefrom. [ *Wills & Sons* v *McSherry* (1914)1 KB 616].

An order is final if it amounts to a final decision relating to the rights of the parties in dispute in the civil proceeding. If after the order, the civil proceeding still remains to be tried and the rights in dispute between the parties have to be determined, the order is not final order within the meaning of Art. 133 of the Constitution of India. [*Jethanand* v *State of UP* (1962)3 SCR 754: AIR 1961 SC 791].

NOTE: A procedural step which does not decide the rights of parties is not a final order. [*State of UP* v *Sujan Singh* AIR 1964 SC 1897: (1965)1 Cr LJ 94].

An order in writ petition determining the rights of the parties about the maintainability of the writ petition and the entitlement of the parties to the relief claimed in the writ petition is a final order. [*Bahadur* v *Gramophone Co.* AIR 1984 Cal 69, 81].

**Financial year.** A period of twelve months in respect of which any profit and loss account in case of an organisation carrying on any business for profit or income and expenditure account in case of a non-profit making organisation is made up.

▸ *Meaning under the General Clauses Act 1897, s. 3(21).* The year commencing on the first day of April.

▸ *Meaning under the Companies Act 1956, s. 2(17).* 'Financial year' means, in relation to a body corporate, the period in respect of which any profit and loss account of the body corporate laid before it in annual general meeting is made up, whether that period is a year or not.

**Finder of goods.** A finder of goods is in the position of a bailee. He has no right to sue the owner for compensation for the trouble and expenses incurred by him to preserve the goods and find out the owner. But he may retain the goods until he receives the compensation. Under certain circumstances, he may sell the goods found. [Indian Contract Act 1872, ss. 168 and 169].

**Finding.** The word 'finding' is a popular rather than technical or legal word. According to its dictionary meaning "finding" means a 'decision' upon a question of fact reached as the result of a judicial examination or investigation by a court, etc. [*Mahabir Kanoo* v *Kedareshwar Bakshi* (1987)1 Cur Civ Cas 638 (Gau)].

NOTE: The word 'finding' covers only the material questions which arise in a particular case for decision by the authority hearing the case or the appeal which, being necessary for passing the final order or giving the final decision in the appeal, has been the subject of controversy between the interested parties or on which the parties concerned have been given a hearing. [*Income Tax Officer, A Ward, Sitapur* v *Murlidhar Bhagwandas* AIR 1965 SC 342: (1964)6 SCR 411: (1964)52 ITR 335: (1964)1 SCJ 583].

A finding can be only that which is necessary for the disposal of an appeal. [*Daffadar Bhagat Singh* v *Income-tax Officer* AIR 1969 SC 340: (1969)1 SCJ 499; *Bhanji Bhagwandas* v *Income-tax Commissioner* AIR 1968 SC 139].

NOTE: The words 'finding' and 'direction' in tax laws mean respectively a finding necessary for giving relief in respect of the assessment for the year in question and a direction which the appellate or revisional authority, as the case may be, is empowered to give. [*Bhanji Bhagwandas* v *Income-tax Commissioner* AIR 1968 SC 139].

**Finding of fact.** The meaning of the expression 'finding of fact' is determination or conclusion by way of reasonable inference from the evidence of a case, either by court or an administrative agency, concerning facts averred by one party, and denied by another. [*Mahabir Kanoo* v *Kedareshwar Bakshi* (1987)1 Cur Civ Cas 638 (Gau)].

A finding of fact means a conclusion on a question of fact by a judge or jury. [*Mahabir Singh* v *Emperor* AIR 1944 Cal 17: 48 CWN 113].

**Finding of law.** A finding on law can only mean a conclusion on a question of law by a judge. [*Mahabir Singh* v *Emperor* AIR 1944 Cal 17: 48 CWN 113].

It is a term that applies to rulings of law made by court in connection with finding of facts.

**Fine.** A sum imposed as punishment for an offence; a forfeiture or penalty paid to an injured party in a civil action; a sum of money paid by a tenant as his entrance into his land; or for the renewal of a lease.

▸ *Meaning under the Indian Penal Code 1860, s. 53.* Fine is a form of punishment to which offenders are liable.

**Fire insurance.** A contract of indemnity, in consideration of the payment of an annual premium, against loss by fire. The common forms are—(1) *Specific policies*, where particular property is specifically insured for a certain sum, *e.g.*, a dwelling-house; (2) *General policies*, where different classes of property, *e.g.*, stock and machinery, are grouped and insured for one fixed amount;

(3) *Concurrent policies*, where two policies have been taken out in respect of the same property in different companies and one of the policies covers additional matter; (4) *Floating policies*, where property is covered in different places; and (5) *Declaration policies*, where the amount of stock varies to a great degree in quantity and value during the period covered by the policy. [Osborn & Grandage's *Concise Commercial Dictionary*].

A contract of insurance by which the underwriter, in consideration of the premium, undertakes to indemnify the insured against all losses in his houses, buildings, furniture, ships in port, or merchandise, by means of accidental fire happening within a prescribed period.

An agreement to indemnify against property damage caused by fire, wind, rain, or other similar disaster. [Black's *Law Dictionary*, 8th Ed.].

**Firearms.** Instruments used in the propulsion of shot, shell or bullets by the action of gunpowder exploded within it; weapons which act by force of gunpowder.

▸ *Meaning under the Arms Act 1959, s. 2(e).* Arms of any description designated or adopted to discharge a projectile or projectiles of any kind by the action of any explosive or other forms of energy, and includes: (*i*) artillery, hand-grenades, riot-pistols or weapons of any kind designated or adopted for the discharge of any noxious liquid, gas or other such things, (*ii*) accessories for any such firearms designated or adopted to diminish the noise or flash caused by the firing thereof, (*iii*) parts of, and machinery for manufacturing firearms, and (*iv*) carriages, platforms and appliances for mounting, transporting and serving artillery.

**Firm.** Persons who have entered into partnership with one another are called collectively a firm. [*Dulichand Laxminarayan* v *Commissioner of Income Tax, Nagpur* AIR 1956 SC 354: 1956 SCR 154: 1956 SCJ 317: (1956)29 ITR 535].

NOTE: 'Firm' is a collective noun, a compendious expression to designate an entity, not a person. In income-tax law a firm is a unit of assessment by special provisions but is not a full person. [*Commissioner of Income Tax, Madras* v *R.M. Chidambaram Pillai* AIR 1977 SC 489: (1977)2 SCR 111: (1977)1 SCC 431: (1977)106 ITR 292].

Partnership is the relation which subsists between persons carrying on a business in common with a view of profit. The word "firm" denotes the persons who constitute the partners. Under English law, a partnership or firm is not a "person" or legal entity although the firm may sue in the firm name. [Halsbury's *Laws of England*, 4th Ed., vol. 35, para 1, p. 4].

• **Unregistered firm** p. 868.

**Firm name.** The name under which the business of partners is carried on is called the "firm name". [*Dulichand Laxminarayan* v *Commissioner of Income Tax, Nagpur* AIR 1956 SC 354: 1956 SCR 154: 1956 SCJ 317: (1956)29 ITR 535].

NOTE: A firm is not a legal entity, although Or. 30, Code of Civil Procedure 1908, provides that the partners of the firm may sue or be sued in the name of the firm. [*Bharat Sarvodaya Mills* v *Malhotra Bros.* AIR 1969 Guj 178].

A firm is not a person and cannot enter into any partnership with an individual. Such person can, however, be admitted into partnership. [*Income Tax Commissioner* v *Jadavji* AIR 1963 SC 1497].

A firm is a creature of contract and its rights and liabilities depend on the terms thereof. For certain purposes, as for instance, suing and being sued, the firm is recognized as an entity. But the essence of the concept of firm is that it is a convenient name or description of individuals entering into combination upon a joint venture. [*Marthavanam* v *Balasubramanian* AIR 1963 Mad 292].

The firm or the firm name is merely a compendious description of all the partners collectively. So where a suit is filed in the name of the firm, it is still a suit by all the partners, unless it is proved that all the partners had not authorised the suit. A firm may not be a legal entity, as a corporation or company, but is still an existing concern, where business is done by a number of persons in partnership. [*Purshottam & Co.* v *Manilal & Sons* AIR 1961 SC 325].

**First hearing.** The day on which the court goes into the pleadings in order to understand the contention of the parties and in suits in which issues have to be framed, the first hearing would be the day on which such issues are framed. [*Hasmukhrai* v *Mavji* AIR 1963 Sau 106].

The expression means the day when the defendant appears in answer to the summons and the court takes up the case in accordance with Or. 9, r. 1 of the Code of Civil Procedure. [*Hiralal* v *Gain Singh* AIR 1951 Punj 441].

**First impression.** A case of first impression is a case for which there is no precedent applicable in all respects. [Mozley & Whiteley's *Law Dictionary,* 10th Ed].

A case is said to be of first impression when there is no authority to guide the court in coming to a decision; the court, therefore, decides according to what it thinks just and reasonable.

**First information report.** An information given under sub-sec. (1) of s. 154, Cr PC is commonly known as First Information Report (FIR) though this term is not used in the Code. It is a very important document. Its nickname suggests it is the earliest and the first information of a cognizable offence recorded by an officer-in-charge of a police station. [*T.T. Antony* v *State of Kerala* AIR 2001 SC 2637: JT 2001(5) SC 440: 2001 Cr LJ 3329: (2001)6 SCC 181].

NOTE: Section 154 of the Code of Criminal Procedure 1973 provides for this. To fall within the scope of the section, a statement must be an "information" and secondly, it must relate to a cognizable offence on the face of it and not merely in the light of subsequent events. [*Vallan Cochal* v *State* ILR (1956) TC 311].

**First of exchange.** The first of a set of foreign bills of exchange usually drawn in triplicate for safety in their delivery. If the first be paid, the others become valueless.

**First offender.** One who has never before been convicted of a crime and, hence, one generally given special consideration in the disposition of his case. For example, first offenders of less serious crimes often receive suspended sentences or are placed on probation. [Black's *Law Dictionary,* 5th Ed.].

A first offender is a 'person who authorities believe has committed a crime but who has never before been convicted of a crime.' Such a person is often treated leniently at sentencing or in plea negotiations. [Black's *Law Dictionary*, 7th Ed.].

**Fiscal statute.** Statute that relates to financial matters, that is money, taxes, public revenues etc., e.g. Income-tax Act, Customs Act, Excise Act, Stamp Act, the Court Fees Act etc.

NOTE: In construing a fiscal statute and in determining the liability to taxation, regard must be had to the strict letter of the law and not merely to the spirit of the statute or the substance of the law. The subject can be taxed only when the case falls strictly within the provisions of the statute. On the other hand, if the case does not come within the provision of the statute, no tax can be imposed by inference or by analogy or by trying to probe into the intention of the legislature or by considering the substance of the matter. [*Fernandez* v *State of Kerala* AIR 1957 SC 657: 1957 SCJ 689: 1957 SCA 983].

In the matter of interpretation of fiscal statute it is not the spirit of the law but the letter of the law that has to be adhered to. Nothing can be imported into the language used by the legislature to enlarge the scope of the provision nor anything could be taken out to curb its application. [*D.N. Mukherjee* v *State of W.B.* 89 CWN 247, 250].

There is no question of equity in regard to a taxing statute. Either the subject is within the words of the enactment or the rules made thereunder or beyond the provisions of the statute. [*Gopalan* v *State of Andhra Pradesh* (1964)2 SCR 888: (1964)1 SCJ 67].

In construing a taxing statute, if two interpretations are possible, effect should be given to the one that favours the subject and not to the one that imposes a burden on him. [*Central India Spinning* v *Municipal Committee* 1958 SCR 1102: AIR 1958 SC 341: 1958 SCJ 604].

Where no definition is provided in the statute itself, for ascertaining the correct meaning of a fiscal entry, reference to a dictionary is not always safe. The correct guide in such a case, is the context and the trade meaning. [*Collector of Central Excise* v *Krishna Carbon Paper Co.* AIR 1988 SC 2223].

**Fiscal year.** A period of twelve consecutive months chosen by a business as the accounting period for annual reports.

**Fish.** A vertebrate cold-blooded animal with gills and fins living wholly in water; an invertebrate animal living wholly in water, e.g. cuttlefish, shellfish, jellyfish; the flesh of fish as food.

NOTE: A fish after cleaning, cutting of head and tail or deshelling remains fish. [*Regional Executive, Kerala Fisherman's Welfare Fund Board* v *Fancy Food* (1995)4 SCC 341: (1995)2 SCJ 216: JT 1995(4) SC 394].

**Fishery.** Business or process of catching, processing, or selling fish; a hatchery or place for catching fish; a right or liberty of taking fish at a particular place or waters; a fishing establishment.

NOTE: The grant of a right to catch fish in specific portions of a lake by the lake-owner is a *profit a prendre*, which is regarded in India as immovable property. [*Ananda Behara* v *State of Orissa* AIR 1956 SC 17].

A fishery does not come within the scope of the Land Acquisition Act. [*Pasupati Roy* v *State of West Bengal* 77 CWN 157].

*Types of fishery.* Fisheries are either free, common or several. A free fishery is the exclusive right of fishing in a public river and is a royal franchise. Common of fishery or common of piscary is the right of fishing in another man's water. No right can exist in the public to fish in an island non-tidal lake. A several fishery is the exclusive right of fishing. The term 'fishery' is also applied to fishing grounds or parts of the sea where at certain seasons numbers of fish are taken. [Wharton's *Law Lexicon*].

**Fishing vessel.** Fishing vessel means a ship fitted with mechanical means of propulsion, which is exclusively engaged in sea fishing for profit. [Merchant Shipping Act 1958, s. 3(12)].

**Fixed assets.** 'Fixed assets' in general comprise those assets which are held for the purpose of conducting a business, in contradistinction to those assets which are held for the purpose of converting into cash, and they include real estate, building, machinery, etc. [*Union of India* v *United Collieries Ltd.* AIR 1985 SC 192: (1985)1 SCC 305: (1985)2 SCR 209].

**Fixed capital.** It is the amount of money which is permanently invested in the business. It may also refer to capital invested in fixed assets like land, buildings, machinery, etc. It may also mean cost of total plant and general equipment. [*Lindheimer* v *Illinois Bell Telephone Co.* III, 292 US 151: 54 S Ct 658: 78 L Ed 1182].

'Fixed capital' is what the owner turns to profit by keeping it in his own possession. [*Sutlej Cotton Mills Ltd.* v *Commissioner of Income-tax, West Bengal* AIR 1979 SC 5: (1979)116 ITR 1: (1979)1 SCR 976: (1978)4 SCC 358].

NOTE: In deciding whether a particular sum is part of a fixed capital of an assessee or his circulating capital, the crucial test is to find out the purpose to which the assessee has appropriated that amount. No doubt, the initial character of the amount at the time of its receipt would be relevant in determining the issue. In the absence of any evidence to the contrary, the amount shall continue to bear the same character, but the subsequent course of dealing may change the character of the amount. [*Tata Locomotive* v *Commissioner of Income-tax* AIR 1963 Bom 62].

**Fixture.** Personal property that is attached to land or a building and that is regarded as an irremovable part of the real property, such as a fireplace built into a home. [Black's *Law Dictionary*, 7th Ed.].

An article in the nature of personal property which has been so annexed to the realty that it is regarded as a part of the land. [*Leawood Nat. Bank of Kansas City* v *City Nat. Bank & Trust Co. of Kansas City* Mo App, 474 SW 2d 641, 644].

The primary meaning from a historical point of view of 'fixtures' is chattels, which are so affixed to land or to a building on land as to become in fact part thereof. Chattels so fixed lose the character of chattels and pass with the ownership of the land. [Cheshire's *Modern Real Property*, 10th Ed., p. 104].

NOTE: In deciding whether or not an object has become a fixture, there are two elements to be considered, namely—(*i*) the degree of annexation, and (*ii*) the purpose of annexation. [Robert E. Megarry & M.P. Thompson: *A Manual of the Law of Real Property*, 8th Ed., p. 20].

Whether a chattel has been so fixed to the land or buildings as to become a fixture depends on the object and the purpose of the annexation, and if the chattel can be removed without doing irreparable damage to the premises, neither the method nor the degree of annexation, nor the quantum of damage that would be done to the chattel or to the premises by the removal, affects the question, save in so far as they throw a light upon the object and purpose of the annexation. If the object and purpose was for the permanent and substantial improvement of the land or building, the article will be deemed to be a fixture, but if it was attached to the premises merely for a temporary purpose or for the more complete enjoyment and use of it as a chattel, then it will not lose its chattel character and it does not become part of the realty. [*Billing* v *Pill* (1963)2 All ER 1061].

The general maxim of the law is that what is annexed to the land becomes part of the land; but it is very difficult, if not impossible, to say with precision what constitutes an annexation sufficient for this purpose. It is a question which must depend on the circumstances of each case. [*Holland* v *Hodgson* (1872) LR 7 CP 328].

In India, the rule of English Common Law as applied to fixture either as between landlord and tenant or as between mortgagor and mortgagee has no application after the enactment of the Transfer of Property Act and other statutes. It should be noted that even in England, the old rule that whatever is annexed to the land becomes part of the land has been considerably relaxed. [*Jnan Chand* v *Jugal Kishore* AIR 1960 Cal 331].

Things attached to the earth are included in immovable property under s. 3(26) of the General Clauses Act 1897. They are known as fixtures and include—(1) things rooted in the earth, e.g., trees, (2) things embedded in the earth, e.g., buildings, and (3) things attached to what is so embedded, e.g., doors and windows. Section 8 of the Transfer of Property Act 1882, provides that if a house is transferred, locks, keys, bars, doors, windows and all other things attached to the house are also transferred. When any land is transferred, building erected on it being embedded in the earth also pass by necessary implication. [*Asgar* v *Mahomed Medhi* 30 IA 71].

**Flagrante delicto.** In the very act of committing the crime.

**Flagrantly.** The expression "flagrantly" means glaringly, notoriously, scandalously. [*Bhagat Ram Patanga* v *State of Punjab* AIR 1972 SC 1571: (1973)1 SCR 92: (1972)2 SCC 170].

• **Flagrantly abused position.** The expression 'flagrantly abused position' as a member of the committee means that the member in disregard of his duty did any act or acts which shocked a reasonable mind. It does not imply that the abuse of position must have occurred for a long period of time and in connection with repeated acts. [*Joginder Singh* v *State of Punjab* AIR 1963 Punj 280].

The expression 'flagrantly abused' requires that even if there is no sinister or oblique motive there must be something to show that in committing the acts complained of, the member concerned was using his position for a wrong purpose or that he was taking some advantage of his position which he ought not to have taken and that he was doing so in a glaring and scandalous manner. [*State of U.P.* v *Mewa Lal* 1961 All LJ 120].

**Flags of convenience.** Ships registered in countries other than those to which they really belong, in order to avoid taxation, are said to be flying flags of convenience. Liberia and Panama are examples of countries which provide shipowners with flags of convenience.

**Flashpoint.** The lowest temperature at which the vapours of petroleum or other combustible liquids will give a flash or slight explosion on exposure to a flame; the temperature at which vapour from oil etc. will ignite in air; the point at which anger, indignation, etc. becomes uncontrollable.

**Flat.** A set of rooms on one floor, for the occupancy of a family; apartment; a floor or separate division of a floor, fitted for housekeeping and designed to be occupied by a single family; an apartment on one floor.

A flat is, in ordinary language, 'a suite of rooms on one floor forming a complete residence'. The term is itself derived from an old English word, meaning 'floor'. [*Boyle* v *Fitz-simons* 1926 IR 378 referring to *Oxford Dictionary*].

In finance, it means without an allowance or charge for accrued interest. [Black's *Law Dictionary*, 7th Ed.].

**Floating capital.** It is capital retained for the purpose of meeting current expenditure; the capital which is consumed at each operation of production and reappears transformed into new products; capital in the form of current, as opposed to fixed, assets. It is also known as circulating capital.

**Floating charge.** A charge, that is, expended to cover any additional property obtained by the debtor while the debt is outstanding; a charge that continues to exist even when the collateral changes in character, classification, or location. It is also termed as floating lien.

A floating charge is a continuing charge on the assets of the company creating it, but permitting the company to deal freely with the property in the usual course of business until the security holder shall intervene to enforce his claim. [*Pennsylvania Co. for Insurance on Lives and Granting Annuities* v *United Railways of Havana & Regla Warehouses* DC Me, 26 F Supp 379, 387, 388].

NOTE: A floating charge moves with the property which it is intended to affect until some event occurs or some act is done which causes it to settle and fasten on the subject of the charge within its reach and grasp. It is of the essence of a floating charge that it remains dormant until the undertaking charged ceases to be a going concern or until the person in whose favour the charge is created intervenes. [Halsbury's *Laws of England*, 4th Ed., vol. 7, para 824, p. 489; *Commissioner of Agricultural Income-tax* v *Nilambar Rubber Co. Ltd.* AIR 1969 Ker 238].

The term 'floating charge' is opposed to what is called a 'fixed charge'. The governing idea in the case of a floating charge is to allow a going concern to carry on its business in ordinary course, the effect of which would be to make the assets liable to constant fluctuation. A floating security is not a future security. It is ambulatory and shifting in its nature, hovering over and so to speak floating with the property which it is intended to affect until some event occurs or some act is done which causes it to settle and fasten on the subject of the charge within its reach and grasp. [*Law & Company* v *Pulinbeharilal* AIR 1933 Cal 154].

**Flotsam.** A name for the goods lost by shipwreck or cast overboard, which remain afloat.

NOTE: If unclaimed, they belong to the State. The finder is entitled to a reward proportionate to the value of the goods.

**F.O.B.** The abbreviation stands for "free on board". This is a contract for the sale of goods to be delivered free on board a ship. The buyer must name a ship upon which they are to be delivered and the seller must put them safety on board, pay the charge of doing so and for the buyer's protection give possession of them to the ship only upon the terms of a reasonable and ordinary bill of lading. The goods are then at the risk of the buyer, he is responsible for the freight, and subject to the seller reserving the right of disposal, the property passes to the buyer.

NOTE: Free on board some location (for example, F.O.B. shipping point; F.O.B. destination): the invoice price includes delivery at seller's expense to that location. Title to goods generally passes from seller to buyer at the F.O.B. location.

The presumption in F.O.B. contracts is that it is the duty of buyers to obtain export licence, though in the circumstances of a particular case, this duty may fall on the sellers. [*B.K. Wadeyar* v *Daulatram Rameshwarlal* AIR 1961 SC 311].

**Fodder.** Dried hay or straw etc. for cattle, horses, etc.

- **Cattle fodder** p. 129.

**Foetus.** The developing young in the uterus, from about the second month of pregnancy to birth; an unborn or unhatched offspring of a mammal, especially an unborn human more than eight weeks after conception.

**Folio.** Leaf of paper etc., numbered only on front; in book-keeping, two opposite pages of ledger, etc., used concurrently; page of ledger, etc., used for both sides of account; page number of printed book; number of words, 72 or 90, taken as a unit in reckoning length of document; and sheet of paper folded once, and so a book of that size. [Osborn & Grandage's *Concise Commercial Dictionary*].

A leaf of a paper or parchment, numbered only on the front; a certain number of words in a legal document, used as a method of measurement; a page number on a printed book; a large book the pages of which are formed by folding a sheet of paper only once in the binding to form two leaves, making available four pages (both sides of each leaf). [Black's *Law Dictionary*, 8th Ed.].

**Food**. Nutritive material absorbed or taken into the body of an organism which serves for purposes of growth, and for the maintenance of the vital process.

That which is eaten or drunk or absorbed for the growth and repair of organisms and the maintenance of life, nourishment, nutriment; nourishment taken in solid as opposed to liquid form. [Webster's *Comprehensive Dictionary*, International Ed.].

What one takes into system to maintain life and growth or what is taken into the body of an organism in order to sustain growth is food.

The expression 'food' has generally been understood to mean nutritive material absorbed or taken into body of an organism which serves for purposes of growth, work or repair and for the maintenance of the vital process. What human beings consume is styled as food and what animals consume is described as animal feed. [*Welcome Hotel* v *State of Andhra Pradesh* AIR 1983 SC 1015: (1983)3 SCR 674: 1983 SCC (Cri) 872: (1983)4 SCC 575].

*The Shorter Oxford English Dictionary* (Third Edition) says that 'food' is "what one takes into the system to maintain life and growth". According to Webster's *Third New International Dictionary*, 'food' means "material consisting of carbohydrates, fats, protein and supplementary substances that is taken or absorbed into the body of an organism in order to sustain growth, repair, and all vital processes and to furnish energy for all activity of the organism; something that nourishes or develops or sustains". This dictionary meaning of the word "food" is not restricted to what is eaten by human beings for nourishment and substance. According to them, what one takes into the system to maintain life and growth or what is taken into the body of an organism in order to sustain growth is food. [*Satpal Gupta* v *State of Haryana* AIR 1982 SC 798: (1982)3 SCR 196: 1982 SCC (Cri) 327: (1982)1 SCC 610].

Food means an article which normally a man eats or drinks to nourish his body and also an article which normally is not considered food but which normally enters into or is used in the composition or preparation of human food. [*Khedar Lal* v *State of U.P.* 1981 FAJ 192, 195 (All)].

'Food' means any article used as food and includes any article which ordinarily enters into or is used in composition or preparation of human food. [*Badrinarayan Sadhu* v *State of Orissa* 1992 Cr LJ 3418 (Ori)].

The word 'food' is a very general term and applies to all that is eaten by human beings for nourishment and takes in subsidiaries. Therefore, supari is a food. [*Pyarili K. Tejani* v *Mahadeo Ramchandra Dange* AIR 1974 SC 224: (1974)1 SCC 167: 1974 Cr LJ 313: 1974 SCC (Cri) 87].

▸ *Meaning under the Patents Act 1970, s. 2(g) (since omitted)*. 'Food' means any article of nourishment and includes any substance intended for the use of babies, invalids and convalescents as an article of food or drink.

▸ *Meaning under the Prevention of Food Adulteration Act 1954, s. 2(v)*. 'Food' means any article used as food or drink for human consumption other than drugs and water and includes—(*a*) any article which ordinarily enters into, or is used in the composition or preparation of human food, and (*b*) any flavouring matter or condiments.

NOTE: According to the definition in the Act 1954, any article used as food or drink for human consumption and any article which ordinarily enters into or is used in the composition or preparation of human food is 'food'. It is not necessary that it is intended for human consumption or for preparation of human food. It is also irrelevant that it is described or exhibited as intended for some other use. It is enough if the article is generally or commonly used for human consumption or in the preparation of human food. [*State of Tamil Nadu* v *R. Krishnamurthy* 1980 SCC (Cri) 200: (1980)1 SCC 167].

'Food' means, under the Prevention of Food Adulteration Rules 1955, the composite preparations which normally go to constitute a meal. [*Collector of Central Excise, Bombay* v *Parle Exports (P) Ltd.* JT 1988(4) SC 454: (1988)38 ELT 741: AIR 1989 SC 644: (1989)75 STC 105: (1989)1 SCC 345: (1990)183 ITR 624].

**Foodstuff.** Any stuff commonly used as food by the generality of living beings is foodstuff. Its meaning cannot be restricted to things which are used as food by human beings. Cattle feed and poultry feed are food to the cattle and poultry, and therefore, they are foodstuffs. [*Satpal Gupta* v *State of Haryana* AIR 1982 SC 798: (1982)3 SCR 196: 1982 SCC (Cri) 327: (1982)1 SCC 610].

The term "foodstuff" is ambiguous. In one sense, it has a narrow meaning and is limited to articles which are eaten as food for purposes of nutrition and nourishment and so would exclude condiments and spices such as yeast, salt, pepper, baking powder and turmeric. In a wider sense, it includes everything that goes into the preparation of food proper (as understood in the narrow sense) to make it more palatable and digestible. Whether the term is used in a particular statute in its wider or narrower sense cannot be answered in the abstract but must be answered with due regard to the background and context. [*State of Bombay* v *Virkumar Gulabchand Shah* AIR 1952 SC 335: 1952 SCR 877: 1952 Cr LJ 1406: 1952 SCJ 496].

▸ *Meaning under the Essential Commodities Act 1955.* The expression 'foodstuffs' is made of two expressions, 'food' plus 'stuff'. In other words, the stuff which is used as food would be foodstuff. Therefore, foodstuff is that which is taken into system to maintain life and growth and to supply waste of tissue. If the raw foodstuff with a view to making it consumable by human beings undergoes a change of its conditions by the process of cooking the derivative is nonetheless foodstuff. [*Welcome Hotel* v *State of Andhra Pradesh* AIR 1983 SC 1015: (1983)3 SCR 674: 1983 SCC (Cri) 872: (1983)4 SCC 575].

▸ *Meaning under the Prevention of Food Adulteration Rules 1955.* Foodstuff has no special meaning of its own. It merely carries in back to the definition of 'food' because foodstuff is anything which is used as food. [*Collector of Central Excise, Bombay* v *Parle Exports (P) Ltd.* JT 1988(4) SC 454: (1988)38 ELT 741: AIR 1989 SC 644: (1989)75 STC 105: (1989)1 SCC 345: (1990)183 ITR 624].

'Foodstuff' need not necessarily mean only the final food product which is consumed. It also includes raw food articles which may after processing be used as food by human beings. Raw cashew nut is a foodstuff. [*K. Janardhan Pillai* v *Union of India* AIR 1981 SC 1485: (1981)2 SCC 45: (1981)2 SCR 676].

NOTE: *Turmeric—whether a foodstuff.* The question whether turmeric is a foodstuff cannot be answered in the abstract and must be viewed in relation to the background and context. [*State of Bombay* v *Virkumar Gulabchand Shah* AIR 1952 SC 335: 1952 SCR 877: 1952 Cr LJ 1406: 1952 SCJ 496].

**F.O.R.** The words stand for 'Free on Railway', which means that the seller is to put the goods into the wagons free of all costs, that is to say, the buyer is not to be made liable to pay any portion of those costs. In India, the F.O.R. contracts do not imply an undertaking on behalf of the seller to procure wagons. [*National Coal Co. Ltd.* v *G.P. Paul* 86 CLJ 220].

**For.** The word is used as a functional word to indicate a purpose or an intended destination or the object toward which one's desire or activity is directed or an actual or implied enumeration or selection or appropriateness or belonging in place of; in exchange as the equivalent of; on behalf of; in spite of. 'For' used with the active participle of a verb means 'for the purpose of'. 'For' has many shades of meaning. It connotes the end with reference to which anything is done. It also bears the sense of 'appropriate' or 'adapted to'; 'suitable to purpose'. [*Indian Chamber of Commerce* v *CIT, West Bengal II, Calcutta* AIR 1976 SC 348: (1976)1 SCR 830: (1976)1 SCC 324].

**For any other sufficient reason.** The expression means a reason sufficient on grounds at least analogous to those specified immediately preceding. [*Benoy Krishna* v *Surajbali* AIR 1963 Cal 100; *Moran Mar Basselios* v *Mar Poulose* (1955)1 SCR 520: AIR 1954 SC 526: 1954 SCJ 736 referring to Code of Civil Procedure 1908, r. 1, Or. 47].

**For the purpose of business.** The expression may include measures for the preservation of the business and for the protection of its assets and property from expropriation, coercive process or assertion of hostile title; it may also include payment of statutory dues and taxes imposed as a precondition to commence or for carrying on a business; it may comprehend many other acts incidental to the carrying on of a business. [*Commissioner of Income-tax* v *Standard Vacuum Oil Co.* AIR 1967 Cal 68].

**For the time being.** The words 'for the time being' are capable of different interpretations according to the context; for example, they might be used with a context showing clearly that they were intended to point on a single period of time. It might be, according to the context, that the same words would apply to a succession of periods. [*Ellison* v *Thomas* (1862)31 LJ Ch 867].

The expression refers to indefinite state of facts, which will arise in future and which may vary from time to time. [*D. Kasturchandji* v *State* AIR 1967 MP 268].

The expression may refer either to a particular point of time or to several periods of time according to the context in which it is used. [*East India Film Studios* v *P.K. Mukherjee* AIR 1954 Cal 41].

**For value received.** These words used in a promissory note mean that consideration has passed.

**Forbear.** Desist from; hold in abeyance; hold off; refrain or abstain from action; avoid voluntarily; be tolerant; be temperate; be patient; withhold action; treat with indulgence; hold back.

**Force.** Used as noun in its application to 'compulsion', it means arbitrary power; authority; coercion; constraining power; duress; enforcement; pressure; subjection; subjugation.

Used as noun in its application to 'legal efficacy', it means authorised might; lawful power; lawful vigour; rightful strength; sanctioned potency; statutory cogency; valid potentiality.

Used as noun in its application to 'strength', it means ability; ableness; authoritativeness; capability; competence; effectiveness; efficacy; firmness; impetus; omnipotence; potency; physical power; stamina; supremacy.

Used as verb in its application to 'break', it means batter; disjoint; fissure; rupture; smash.

Used as verb in its application to 'coerce', it means apply pressure; cause to yield; compel; enforce; enforce obedience; enslave; impose; make obligatory; use violence.

'Force' means 'strength exerted on an object, power, impetus'. [*Ibrahimkutty* v *State of Kerala* 1984 Ker LT 700].

'Force' means 'strength, power, energy, efficacy, validity, influence'. [*N. Abdul Hadi* v *Maju Bi* (1973)1 MLJ 13: 1973 Cr LJ 725].

› *Meaning under the Army Act 1950, s. 4(1).* The word "force" is not defined anywhere in the Act 1950. There is a definition of the expression "the Forces" in s. 3(*xi*) but it does not help, because the expression is "Force" which is different from "the Forces". There is, however, an indication to be found in sub-sec. (2) of s. 4 which throws some light on the sense in which the word "Force" is used in sub-sec. (1) of s. 4. Section 4, sub-sec. (2) clearly contemplates that the "Force" referred to in sub-sec. (1) of s. 4 must be a Force organised on similar lines as the Army with rank structure. So far as the General Reserve Engineering Force (GREF) is concerned, there can be no doubt that it is a Force organised on Army pattern with units and sub-units and rank structure. [*R. Viswan* v *Union of India* AIR 1983 SC 658: (1983)3 SCC 401: (1983)3 SCR 60].

▸ *Meaning under the Indian Penal Code 1860, s. 349.* A person is said to use 'force' to another if he causes motion, change of motion, or cessation of motion to that other, or if he causes to any substance such motion, or change of motion, or cessation of motion as to bring that substance into contact with any part of that other's body, or with anything which that other is wearing or carrying, or with anything so situated that such contact affects that other's sense of feeling:

Provided that the person causing the motion, or change of motion, or cessation of motion, causes that motion, change of motion, or cessation of motion in one of the three ways hereinafter described: First—By his own bodily power. Secondly—By disposing any substance in such a manner that the motion or change or cessation of motion takes place without any further act on his part, or on the part of any other person. Thirdly—By inducing any animal to move, to change its motion, or to cease to move.

- **Application of criminal force.** It means application of power or strength for a purpose which is criminal in character, regardless of the fact whether it is used against a person or a thing. According to the *Shorter Oxford English Dictionary* on 'historical principles', 'application of criminal force' means application of physical power exerted upon an object; especially, violence of physical coercion. [*N. Abdul Hadi* v *Maju Bi* (1973)1 MLJ 13: 1973 Cr LJ 725].

**Force majeure.** The expression means some physical or material restraint, and does not include a reasonable fear or apprehension of such a restraint. [*Hackney Borough Council* v *Dore* (1922)1 KB 431].

The expression bears more extensive meaning than 'act of God' or 'vis major'. As to delay due to breakdown of machinery, it comes within the words 'force majeure', which certainly cover accidents to machinery. The term cannot, however, be extended to cover bad weather, football matches or a funeral. [*Matsoukis* v *Priestman & Co.* (1915)1 KB 681].

The expression "force majeure" is not a mere French version of Latin expression "vis major". It is undoubtedly a term of wider import. Difficulties have arisen in the past as to what could legitimately be included in force majeures. Judges have agreed that strikes, breakdown of machinery, which, though normally not included in "vis major" are included in "force majeure". An analysis of rulings on the subject shows that where reference is made to "force majeure", the intention is to save the performing party from the consequences of anything over which he has no control. This is the widest meaning that can be given to "force majeure". [*Dhanrajamal Gobindram* v *Shamji Kalidas & Co.* AIR 1961 SC 1285: (1961)3 SCR 1020].

**Forced labour.** Labour or service that one is compelled to give with or without remuneration.

▸ *Meaning under the Constitution of India, Art. 23.* Where a person provides labour or service to another for remuneration which is less than the minimum wages, the labour or services provided by him clearly falls within the meaning of the words 'forced labour' and attracts the provision of Art. 23 of the Constitution. [*Sanjit Roy* v *State of Rajasthan* AIR 1983 SC 328: (1983)1 SCC 525: (1983)2 SCR 271].

NOTE: The expression forced labour in Art. 23 of the Constitution is of widest amplitude and in its interpretation covers every possible form of forced labour, begar or otherwise, and it makes no difference whether the person forced to give his labour or service to another is remunerated or not. [*Sanjit Roy* v *State of Rajasthan*, supra].

**Forced sale.** A sale under a process of law, and not by mutual agreement.

**Forcible entry.** Forcible entry takes place when a person enters upon any lands or tenements forcibly without due warrant of law.

NOTE: A person commits an offence both at common law and by statute who enters forcibly upon any lands or tenements without due warrant of law. The offence is punishable with imprisonment and fine. It is not a forcible entry where entry is obtained through an unclosed window or by opening a door with a key, or by means of threats to damage chattels, or by enticing the owner out of possession or excluding him when he is out. A person is not guilty of forcible entry who, although pretending title to land, merely passes over it, with or without attendants armed or unarmed, on his way to church, or to market, or for such like purpose, provided he does no act which either expressly or impliedly amounts to a claim to the lands. There can be no forcible entry upon an easement, such as a right of way. [Halsbury's *Laws of England*, 4th Ed., vol. 11, para 863, p. 508].

**Foreclosure.** To shut out, to bar, to destroy an equity of redemption [*Anderson* v *Barr* 178 Okl 508]; a termination of all rights of the mortgagor or his legatee in the property covered by the mortgage; procedure by which mortgaged property is sold on default of mortgagor in satisfaction of mortgage debt.

Foreclosure is a legal term which implies that the relief given by equity against forfeiture of the security is withdrawn. [*Carter* v *Wake* (1877)4 Ch D 605].

NOTE: The effect of foreclosure is that the conditional conveyance in a mortgage becomes absolute and the property mortgaged vests absolutely in the mortgagee. [*Williams* v *Morgan* (1906)1 Ch 804].

- **Suit for foreclosure.** A suit to obtain a decree that a mortgagor shall be absolutely debarred of his right to redeem the mortgaged property is called a suit for foreclosure. [Transfer of Property Act 1882, s. 67]. No mortgagee, other than a mortgagee by conditional sale or a mortgagee under an anomalous mortgage by the terms of which he is entitled to foreclose can institute a suit for foreclosure.

**Foreign bill.** A bill of exchange not drawn in India and not made payable in, or drawn upon any person resident in India is a foreign bill of exchange. [Negotiable Instruments Act 1881, ss. 11 and 12].

**Foreign corporation.** A corporation created by or under the laws of a foreign country.

**Foreign court.** A court situated outside India and not established or continued by the authority of the Central Government. [Code of Civil Procedure 1908, s. 2(5)].

'Foreign court' means a court situate beyond the limits of the states which has no authority in states and is not established or continued by the Central Government. Thus, on 18th November 1948, the court at Gwalior was a foreign court, and a judgment passed by it was a foreign judgment. [*Raj Rajendra Sardar Moloji Nar Singh Rao Shitole* v *Shankar Saran* AIR 1962 SC 1737].

**Foreign currency.** Any currency other than Indian currency. [Foreign Exchange Management Act 1999, s. 2(*m*)].

**Foreign divorce.** A divorce obtained in the court of a foreign country.

The divorce jurisdiction of a foreign court depends solely upon domicil. Just as the English courts refuse to entertain a suit for the dissolution of marriage unless the parties are domiciled in England, so do they assert that nothing short of domicil enables a foreign court to pronounce a decree for divorce that will be recognised in England.

**Foreign enterprise.** A foreign enterprise is an enterprise situated in a foreign country having been created or registered in accordance with the law of such country. Foreign enterprise will include within it also a foreign company. [*Petron Engineering Construction Pvt. Ltd.* v *Central Board of Direct Taxes* 1988 Supp (3) SCR 1058: JT 1988(4) SC 666: AIR 1989 SC 501: 1989 Supp (2) SCC 7: (1989)1 Comp LJ 43: (1989)175 ITR 523].

**Foreign exchange.** Conversion of money of one country into its equal of another country; process by which money of one country is used to pay balances due in another country. [Black's *Law Dictionary*, 5th Ed.].

The process of making international monetary transactions, specially, the conversion of one currency to that of a different country; foreign currency or negotiable instruments payable in foreign currency, such as travellers' cheques. [Black's *Law Dictionary*, 7th Ed.].

▸ *Meaning under the Foreign Exchange Management Act 1999, s. 2(n).* Foreign exchange means foreign currency and includes—(*i*) deposits, credits and balances payable in any foreign currency, (*ii*) drafts, travellers cheques, letters of credit or bills of exchange, expressed or drawn in Indian currency but payable in any foreign currency, (*iii*) drafts, travellers cheques, letters of credit or bills of exchange drawn by banks, institutions or persons outside India, but payable in Indian currency.

**Foreign frontier.** The frontier separating any foreign territory from any part of India.

**Foreign instrument.** A promissory note, bill of exchange or cheque not drawn or made in India or made payable in or drawn upon any person resident in India shall be deemed to be a foreign instrument. [Negotiable Instruments Act 1881, s. 12].

**Foreign judgment.** One rendered by the courts of a state or country politically and judicially distinct from that where the judgment or its effect is brought in question; one pronounced by a tribunal of a foreign country, or of a sister state. [*Grover & B. Sewing Mach. Co.* v *Radcliffe* 137 US 287].

▸ *Meaning under the Code of Civil Procedure 1908, s. 13.* Notwithstanding the definition of 'judgment' in s. 2 of the Civil Procedure Code, the expression 'foreign judgment' in s. 13 must be understood to mean an adjudication by a foreign court upon the matter before it. [*Brijlal Ramjidas* v *Govindram Gordhandas Seksaria* AIR 1947 PC 192].

NOTE: It is now a well established proposition in private international law that unless a foreign court has jurisdiction in the international sense, a judgment delivered by that court would not be recognised or enforceable in India. [*Sankaran Govindan* v *Lakshmi Bharathi* AIR 1974 SC 1764: (1975)1 SCR 57: (1975)3 SCC 351].

**Foreign jurisdiction.** Any jurisdiction foreign to that of another country; the exercise by a state or nation of jurisdiction beyond its own territory.

▸ *Meaning under the Foreign Jurisdiction Act 1947, s. 2(a).* Any jurisdiction which by treaty, agreement, grant, usage, sufferance or other lawful means the Central Government has for the time being in or in relation to any area outside India.

**Foreign port.** One exclusively within the jurisdiction of another country or state; a port other than a home port. [Black's *Law Dictionary*, 8th Ed.].

Any place not within the territory of India. [Sea Customs Act 1878, s. 3(*e*)].

**Foreign power.** The expression 'foreign power' must be construed in the ordinary way giving the words their ordinary meaning. On a correct interpretation of the words "the relations of India with foreign powers" in s. 3, Pakistan must be regarded as a foreign power, although that country may be a party of the Commonwealth as India is. [*Jagan Nath Sathu* v *The Union of India* AIR 1960 SC 625: (1960)2 SCR 784: 1960 Cr LJ 764: 1960 SCJ 975 referring to Preventive Detention Act 1950, s. 3].

**Foreign security.** Any security, in the form of shares, stocks, bonds, debentures or any other instrument denominated or expressed in foreign currency and includes security expressed in foreign currency, but where redemption or any form of return such as interest or dividends is payable in Indian currency. [Foreign Exchange Management Act 1999, s. 2(*o*)].

**Foreign service.** Foreign service is service in which foreign servant receives his pay with the sanction of Government from any source other than Consolidated Fund of India or Union Territory. [Fundamental Rules, r. 9(7)].

NOTE: The definition covers not only service in India but also the Government servant receiving pay with sanction of Government from any other fund than mentioned which may include foreign employer with sanction of Government of India. If a person enters into a contract with foreign employer and gets salary from it without sanction of Indian Government, he cannot be treated in 'foreign service' within the meaning of Fundamental Rules and his status as such may cease. [*K.V. Mahadeva Rao* v *Union of India* (1992)1 All India Services Law Journal 496 (Bom); *Union of India* v *H.A. Shakur* AIR 1960 Pat 533].

**Foreign State.** A foreign country.

▸ *Meaning under the Code of Civil Procedure 1908, s. 87A(a).* 'Foreign State' means any State outside India, which has been recognised by the Central Government.

▸ *Meaning under the Extradition Act 1962, s. 2(e).* Any State outside India other than a Commonwealth country, and includes every constituent party, colony or dependency of such State.

**Foreign system of law.** For the purposes of private international law, the expression 'foreign system of law' means any system prevailing in a geographical area outside the sphere of operation of the *lex fori*. It, therefore, includes not merely the law existing in a State under a foreign political sovereignty but also the law prevailing in a sub-division of the political State of which the *forum* is part. [Cheshire's *Private International Law*, 11th Ed., p. 8].

**Foreign territory.** Any territory which has been declared under s. 5 of the Indian Tariff Act 1894, to be foreign territory. [Land Customs Act 1924, s. 2(*f*)].

**Foreign trade.** It is that part of the trade of a country which consists of goods imported from and exported to a foreign country.

Commercial interchange of commodities between different countries; export and import trade. [*Standard Oil Co. of New Jersey* v *United States* 120 F 2d 340, 342].

**Foreign vessel.** A ship owned by a resident in a foreign country or a ship sailing under foreign flag.

**Foreigner.** A person who is not a citizen or subject of the state or country of which mention is made, or any one owing allegiance to a foreign state or sovereign; person belonging to or under citizenship of another country.

▸ *Meaning under the Foreigner's Act 1946, s. 2(a).* A person who is not a citizen of India. A citizen of Pakistan is a foreigner within the meaning of the Foreigner's Act. [*Abdul Ghani Hamid* v *State* AIR 1957 AP 143: 1957 Cr LJ 703].

**Foreman.** An employee who supervises the work of other workmen in a factory; a person designated by employer-management to direct work of employees; superintendent; overseer.

**Forensic medicine.** The science which deals with the principles and practice of the different branches of medicine to the elucidation of doubtful questions in a court of justice.

The science of medical jurisprudence, comprising those matters which may be considered as common ground to both medical and legal practitioners, e.g., inquiries relating to suspected murder or doubtful sanity. [Mozley & Whiteley's *Law Dictionary*, 10th Ed.].

That science which teaches the application of every branch of medical knowledge to the purposes of the law; hence its limits are, on the one hand, the requirements of the law, and, on the other, the whole range of medicine. Anatomy, physiology, medicine, surgery, chemistry, physics, and botany lend their aid as necessity arises; and in some cases all these branches of science are required to enable a court of law to arrive at a proper conclusion on a contested question affecting life or property. [Black's *Law Dictionary*, 5th Ed.].

**Forensic science.** The word "forensic" is derived from the Latin word 'forum' which literally means "place of trial". Forensic science in its broadest definition means application of science to law. But it may better be said to be a science where scientific principles and methods are utilised in investigation of crimes.

> NOTE: Entire forensic science owes for its recent development to Edmond Locard, Director of the Institute of Forensic Medicine in Lyons, France whose Exchange principles is the pivot of modern forensic science. According to this principle when any two objects come into contact, there is always a transference of material from each object to the other. Any contact between the criminal and the crime will leave a trace, presence of such an evidence proves that the two objects have been in contact although the two objects may be miles apart when found.

**Foreshore.** The strip of land that lies between the high and low water marks and that is alternately wet and dry according to the flow of the tide; according to the medium line between the greatest and the least range of tide (spring tides and neap tides). [Black's *Law Dictionary*, 5th Ed.].

The seashore up to the point of high water of medium tides, between spring and neap tides, is called the foreshore, and is ordinarily and *prima facie* vested in the Crown, subject to the rights of the Queen's subjects for fishing and navigation only, not only in the sea, but in all tidal navigable rivers, and of passing over the foreshore itself; but it may belong to a subject, either by itself, or as part of a manor. [Stroud's *Judicial Dictionary*, 5th Ed.].

▸ *Meaning under the Major Port Trusts Act 1963, s. 2(g).* 'Foreshore' in relation to a port means the area between the high-water mark and the low-water mark relating to that port.

**Forest.** A large tract of land covered with a natural growth of trees and underbrush [Webster's *Comprehensive Dictionary*, International Edition]; a large area covered chiefly with trees and undergrowth. [*Concise Oxford Dictionary*, 9th Ed.].

The word 'forest' means an extensive tract of land covered with trees and undergrowth, sometimes intermingled with pasture. [*Rum Charitra Das* v *State of Bihar* (1996)2 Pat LJR 69].

A large tract of uncultivated land covered with trees and underwood. [*Itarsi Timber Merchants Association* v *State of Madhya Pradesh* AIR 1997 MP 57].

▸ *Meaning under the Forest Conservation Act 1980.* For the purpose of the Act, the word 'forest' must be understood according to its dictionary meaning. This description covers all statutorily recognised forests whether designated as reserved, protected or otherwise. It will include any area recorded as forest in the government record irrespective of the ownership. [*T.N. Godavarman* v *Union of India* AIR 1997 SC 1228: (1997)2 SCC 267].

**Forest land.** "Forest land", without evidence to show that it had been cleared and prepared or earmarked for agricultural purposes, must be treated as *prima facie* non-agricultural land. [*Controller of Estate Duty, Kerala* v *V. Venugopala Varma Rajah* AIR 1977 SC 121: (1977)1 SCR 346: (1976)105 ITR 593: (1976)4 SCC 3].

**Forest produce.** Produce whether found in, or brought from a forest.

▸ *Meaning under the Indian Forest Act 1927, s. 2(4).* 'Forest produce' includes—(*a*) the following whether found in, or brought from, a forest or not, that is to say,—timber, charcoal, caout-chous, catechu, woodoil, resin, natural varnish, bark, lac, mahua flowers, mahua seeds, kuth and myrabolams, and (*b*) the following when found in or brought from a forest, that is to say—(*i*) trees and leaves, flowers and fruits, and all other parts or produce not hereinbefore mentioned, of trees, (*ii*) plants not being trees (including grass, creepers, reeds and moss), and all parts or produce of such plants, (*iii*) wild animals and skins, tusks, horns, silk cocoons, honey and wax, and all other parts or produce of animals, and (*iv*) peat, surface soil, rock, and minerals (including limestone, laterite, mineral oils and all products of mines or quarries.

The definition of 'forest produce' under s. 2(4) is inclusive and the legislature could not exhaustively enlist all those items which could be a forest produce or could partake a colour or a character of the forest produce. Besides the produce of forest which has a natural growth, the legislature has also included within the definition such product of a forest which is produced with the aid of human skill. Bamboo is included within the meaning of 'tree' under the Act, while timber includes trees when they have fallen or have been felled as also any item fashioned out of timber. Thus, bamboo matting, a man-made product prepared out of forest produce, comes well within the scope and ambit of definition of 'forest produce' as given in s. 2(4). [*State of Maharashtra* v *Suresh Rameshwardas Lohiya* 1993 Mah LJ 108; *State of Orissa* v *P.P. Agarwala* AIR 1998 Ori 54].

▸ *Meaning under the Maharashtra Private Forest (Acquisition) Act 1975.* The expression 'forest' includes all that goes with it, such as trees with fruits on them, shrubs, bushes, woody vegetation, undergrowth, pastures, honeycombs attached to trees, juices dried on trees, things embedded in the earth like mines and quarries with their produce locked up in the land, wild and stray animals (excluding domestic animals like cows, buffaloes, goats, sheep etc.) living in the forest. Fallen trees felled by force of nature cease to be trees due to loss of connection with land that provide them with nourishment but fallen trees if they continue to remain in the same condition form part of the forest; similarly shrubs, bushes and even fruits and honeycombs if they continue to remain in the same position would continue to be forest produce. [*Junn Chand Washmare* v *State of Maharashtra* 1977 Bom LR 499].

**Forfeiture.** Something to which the right is lost by the commission of a crime or fault or the losing of something by way of penalty. [*Ridgeway* v *City of Akron* Ohio App, 42 NE 2d 724, 726].

A punishment annexed by law to some illegal act or negligence in the owner of land, tenements, or hereditaments whereby he loses all interest therein. [*Hammond* v *Johnson* 66 P 2d 894, 900].

In regard to property 'forfeiture' is a loss of the right to possess; and it includes cesser, or determination on bankruptcy, alienation, remarriage or any other event. [*Re Sumner's Settled Estates* (1911)1 Ch 315].

NOTE: According to the dictionary meaning of the word 'forfeiture', the loss or the deprivation of goods has got to be in consequence of a crime, offence or breach of engagement or has to be by way of penalty of the transgression or punishment for an offence. Unless the loss or deprivation of goods is by way of penalty or punishment for a crime, offence or breach of engagement, it would not come within the definition of forfeiture. [*Chairman of the Bankura Municipality* v *Lalji Raja* AIR 1953 SC 248: 1953 SCR 767: 1953 SCA 298: 1953 SCJ 321: 54 Cr LJ 1101; *R.S. Josi* v *Ajit Mills* AIR 1977 SC 2279].

▸ *Meaning under the Transfer of Property Act 1882, s. 114.* The word 'forfeiture' used in s. 114 has a technical meaning, which must be ascertained by reference to s. 111(*g*) of the said Act. Forfeiture in this technical sense is incurred in case the lessee breaks an express condition which provides that on breach thereof the lessor may re-enter, and even in such a case the lessor has to give notice in writing to the lessee of his intention to determine the lease. [*Tippayya Kuppayyavidya* v *Rama Narayana* AIR 1961 Mys 131].

**Forged document or electronic record.** A false document or electronic record made wholly or in part by forgery is designated 'a forged document or electronic record'. [Indian Penal Code 1860, s. 470].

**Forgery.** The false making of an instrument, which purports on the face of it to be good and valid for purposes for which it was created, with a design to defraud any person or persons [*State* v *Goranson* 408 P 2d 7]; the fraudulent making of a false writing having apparent legal significance. [*Nelson* v *State* 167 A 2d 871, 873].

▸ *Meaning under the Indian Penal Code 1860, s. 463.* Whoever makes any false documents or false electronic record or part of a document or electronic record, with intent to cause damage or injury, to the public or to any person, or to support any claim or title, or to cause any person to part with property, or to enter into any express or implied contract, or with intent to commit fraud or that fraud may be committed, commits forgery.

**Form.** Used as noun in its application to 'arrangement', it means classification, custom, design, established practice, format, formula, kind, manner, method, mode, model, order, outline, pattern, plan, shape.

Used as noun in its application to 'document', it means copy, data sheet, instrument, muniments, record, written document, standard letter.

Used as verb, it means arrange, assemble, compose, construct, contrive, create, design, embody, establish, fabricate, formulate, give shape to.

A model or skeleton of an instrument to be used in a judicial proceeding or legal transaction, containing the principal necessary matters, the proper technical terms or phrases and whatever else is necessary to make it formally correct, arranged in proper and methodical order, and capable of being adapted to the circumstances of the specific case. [Black's *Law Dictionary*, 5th Ed.].

The outer shape or structure of something, as distinguished from its substance or matter; established behaviour or procedure, usually according to custom or rule; a model; a sample; the customary method of drafting legal documents, usually with fixed words, phrase and sentences; a legal document with blank spaces to be filled in by the drafter. [Black's *Law Dictionary*, 8th Ed.].

The word 'form' connotes a visible aspect, such as shape or mode in which a thing exists or manifests itself, species, kind or variety. Rice in all forms would mean all kinds or varieties of rice or species of rice, such as broken rice, kichidi rice, pichodi rice or rice flour etc. [*Kayani & Co.* v *Commissioner of Sales Tax* AIR 1953 Hyd 252: ILR (1953) Hyd 363].

**Forma non observata infertur adnullatio actus.** Form not being observed, a nullity of the acts is inferred.

**Forma pauperis.** A privilege given to an indigent person to prosecute without payment of fees and costs incident to such prosecution. When suing, a poor person is generally entitled to proceed *in forma pauperis*.

> NOTE: A suit may be instituted by a pauper under Or. 33 of the Code of Civil Procedure 1908. Explanation to rule defines a pauper as a person when he is not possessed of sufficient means to pay the prescribed court fee for the plaint. The procedure for filing an appeal as a pauper is laid down in Or. 44 of the Code.

**Formal defect.** A formal defect is a defect of form which is prescribed by the rules of procedure, such as misjoinder of parties, or causes of action, non-payment of proper court-fee, failure to disclose cause of action and so forth. [*Atul Krishna* v *Raukishore* AIR 1956 Ori 77: ILR (1956) Cut 1].

**Formal parties.** Parties having no interest in the contest between the actual litigants. But they are added as parties because they have an interest in the subject-matter, which may conveniently be decided in the suit to prevent further litigation.

**Former suit.** The expression 'former suit' means a previously decided suit. [*Prabha Singh* v *Sanka Narasimha Rao* AIR 1957 AP 992 referring to Code of Civil Procedure 1908, s. 11].

**Forthwith.** Immediately; without delay; directly; within a reasonable time under the circumstances of the case; promptly and with reasonable dispatch. [*U.S. ex rel. Carter* v *Jennings* DC Pa, 333 F Supp 1392, 1397].

To do a thing 'forthwith' is to do it as soon as is reasonably convenient. [*Hudson* v *Hill* (1874)43 LJCP 273].

'Forthwith' means 'reasonably soon in the circumstances'. [*Brown* v *Bonnyrig Magistrates* (1936) SC 258].

An act which is to be done 'forthwith' must be held to have been so done when it is done with all reasonable despatch and without avoidable delay. [*Keshav Nilkanth Joglekar* v *The Commissioner of Police, Greater Bombay* AIR 1957 SC 28: 1956 SCR 653: 1957 Cr LJ 10: 1956 SCJ 715; *Gora* v *State of West Bengal* AIR 1975 SC 473: (1975)2 SCR 996: (1975)2 SCC 14: 1975 Cr LJ 429: 1975 SCC (Cri) 391].

The expression 'forthwith' would mean 'as soon as may be', that the action should be performed by the authority with reasonable speed and expedition with a sense of urgency without any unavoidable delay. No hard and fast rule could be laid nor a particular period is prescribed. It depends on the facts and circumstances of each case. [*Navalshankar Ishwarlal Dave* v *State of Gujarat* AIR 1994 SC 1496: JT 1993(3) SC 421: 1994 Cr LJ 2170: 1993 Supp (3) SCC 754: 1993 SCC (Cri) 1126].

The word "forthwith" has been interpreted to mean "as soon as possible; without any delay". If there is some delay which is reasonably explained, then there is no violation of the mandatory requirement of the law. [*Gopal Mondal* v *State of West Bengal* AIR 1975 SC 1807: (1975)2 SCC 590: 1975 Cr LJ 1554: 1975 SCC (Cri) 698].

▸*Meaning under the Representation of the People Act 1951, s. 53(2).* The word 'forthwith' means immediately after the expiry of the time fixed for withdrawal of nomination papers. [*Khaja Khanavar Khadskhan* v *Siddvanhalli* AIR 1968 Mys 18].

**Fortuitous event.** It is an event which is unforeseen caused by irresistible superior force.

**Forum.** A court.

**Forum actus.** The forum of the place where the thing was done.

**Forum originis.** The court of a person's domicil by birth.

**Forward contract.** An agreement to buy or sell a particular non-standardized asset (usually currencies) at a fixed price on a future date. [Black's *Law Dictionary*, 8th Ed.].

A forward contract is a contract for the sale or purchase of goods, which postpones the delivery of goods and the payment of price therefor for a period exceeding eleven days. [*Raymon & Co.* v *Waverley Jute Mills* AIR 1959 Cal 89].

▸*Meaning under the Forward Contracts (Regulation) Act 1952, s. 2(c).* A contract for the delivery of goods and it is not a ready delivery contract.

**Forwarding agent.** An agent who sends goods from the country on behalf of foreign merchants. His contractual rights and liabilities are governed by the ordinary law of agency.

A company or individual whose business it is to receive and ship merchandise for others. [Black's *Law Dictionary*, 7th Ed.].

**Foujdari adalat.** See ADALAT p. 37.

**Found.** The word "found" has different meanings. It may be used as past tense and past participle of 'find'.

It may mean to by the foundation of; establish; give origin to; to cast by melting and pouring into a mold.

▸*Meaning under the Code of Criminal Procedure 1973, s. 188.* The word 'found' means found by the court at the time when the matter comes up for trial, that is to say, any court which is otherwise competent to try the offence can take seisin the moment the accused appears in his presence. [*Sahetrao Bajirao* v *Suryabhan* AIR 1948 Nag 251].

**Founders' shares.** Founders' shares are generally few in number and of small nominal value. They are generally created for and appropriated to the remuneration of the promoters of the company for the services rendered by them in promoting the company. The founders' shares are ordinarily deferred shares receiving no dividend until the preference and ordinary shares have been paid a fair dividend. They are usually issued as fully paid-up shares and sometimes they carry special profits and privileges.

**Foundling.** A deserted or abandoned infant; a child found without a parent or guardian, its relatives being unknown.

**F.O.W.** The words stand for "First Open Water". And the phrase is used in charter-parties with reference to ports in the Baltic, to mean "immediately after the ice breaks up".

**Fractionem diei non receipt lex.** The law does not regard a fraction of a day. As a necessary corollary to this dictum when statute directs that intervening period between the issue of notice for the meeting and the holding of the meeting shall be "so many clear days", then in calculating the days the date of issue of notice and the date of holding the meeting are to be excluded. [*J.N. Pramanik* v *D.M., Nadia* AIR 1978 Cal 324, 332: 81 CWN 986, 990].

**Franchise.** A right to vote; a special privilege conferred by government on individual or corporation, and which does not belong to citizens of country generally of common right [*Artesian Water Co.* v *State Dept. of Highways and Transp.* Deal Super, 330 A 2d 432, 439]; a privilege granted or sold, such as to use a name or to sell products or services; the right given by a manufacturer or supplier to a retailer to use his products and name on terms and conditions mutually agreed upon.

In its simplest terms, a franchise is a license from owner of a trade mark or trade name permitting another to sell a product or service under that name or mark. More broadly stated, a "franchise" has evolved into an elaborate agreement under which the franchisee undertakes to conduct a business or sell a product or service in accordance with methods and procedures prescribed by the franchisor, and the franchisor undertakes to assist the franchisee through advertising, promotion and other advisory services. [*H&R Block, Inc.* v *Lovelace* 493 P 2d 205, 211].

The right to vote at the election for Parliament or for the Indian Legislative Assembly or for the various Provincial Legislative Councils is certainly a franchise, but the word does not include the power to vote on matters coming before a legislative body. The word is also said to be synonymous with the term 'liberty' though the latter is applied usually to the class of franchises conferring immunity of jurisdiction. The term 'franchise' in its electoral sense denotes a right of voting at elections and the qualifications upon which the right is based. [*In re J.M. Sen Gupta* AIR 1925 Cal 48: 51 Cal 874].

**Fraud.** Criminal deception; the use of false representations to gain an unjust advantage; a dishonest artifice or trick; a person or thing not fulfilling what is claimed or expected of him, her, or it. [*Concise Oxford Dictionary*, 9th Ed.].

Deception in order to gain by another's loss; craft; trickery; guile; one who acts fraudulently; a cheat; a deceptive or spurious thing; any artifice or deception practised to cheat, deceive, or circumvent another to his injury. [Webster's *Comprehensive Dictionary*, International Edition].

An intentional perversion of truth for the purpose of inducing another in reliance upon it to part with some valuable thing belonging to him or to surrender a legal right; a false representation of a matter of fact, whether by words or by conduct, by false or misleading allegations, or by concealment of that which should have been disclosed, which deceives and is intended to deceive another so that he shall act upon it to his legal injury. [Black's *Law Dictionary*, 5th Ed.].

Any kind of artifice employed by one person to deceive another. [*Goldstein* v *Equitable Life Assurance Society of U.S.* 289 NYS 1064, 1067].

A knowing misrepresentation of the truth or concealment of a material fact to induce another to act to his or her detriment; a misrepresentation made recklessly without belief in its truth to induce another person to act; a tort arising from a knowing misrepresentation, concealment of material fact, or reckless misrepresentation made to induce another to act to his or her detriment; unconscionable dealing; in contract law, the unconscientious use of the power arising out of the parties' relative positions and resulting in an unconscionable bargain. [Black's *Law Dictionary*, 7th Ed.].

A "fraud" is an act of deliberate deception with the design of securing something by taking unfair advantage of another. It is a deception in order to gain by another's loss. It is a cheating intended to get an advantage. [*S.P. Chengalvaraya Naidu* v *Jagannath* JT 1993(6) SC 331: AIR 1994 SC 853: (1994)1 SCC 1].

'Fraud' arises out of deliberate active role of representator about a fact which he knows to be untrue yet he succeeds in misleading the representee by making him belief it to be true. The representation to become fraudulent must be of fact with knowledge that it was false. [*Shrisht Dhawan* v *Shaw Bros*. JT 1991(5) SC 378: AIR 1992 SC 1555: (1992)1 SCC 534].

'Fraud' is false representation by one who is aware that it was untrue with an intention to mislead the other who may act upon it to his prejudice and to the advantage of the representator. [*State of Maharashtra* v *Buddhikota Subharao (Dr.)* AIR 1989 SC 2292: JT 1989(4) SC 1: 1989 Supp (2) SCC 605: 1989 Supp (1) SCR 315: 1989 Cr LJ 2317: 1990 SCC (Cri) 126].

▸ *Meaning under the Indian Contract Act 1872, s. 17*. 'Fraud' means and includes any of the following acts committed by a party to a contract, or with his connivance, or by his agent, with intent to deceive another party thereto or his agent, or to induce him to enter into the contract—(1) the suggestion, as a fact, of that which is not true, by one who does not believe it to be true; (2) the active concealment of a fact by one who having knowledge or belief of the fact; (3) a promise made without any intention of performing it; (4) any other act fitted to deceive; (5) any such act or omission as the law specially declares to be fraudulent.

NOTE: *Effect of fraud.* Effect of fraud on any proceeding or transaction is that it becomes a nullity. Even the most solemn proceedings stand vitiated if they are actuated by fraud. Such being the nature and consequence of it, the law requires not only strict pleading of it but strict proof as well. [*State of Maharashtra* v *Buddhikota Subharao (Dr.)* AIR 1989 SC 2292: JT 1989(4) SC 1: 1989 Cr LJ 2317: 1989 Supp (2) SCC 605: 1989 Supp (1) SCR 315: 1990 SCC (Cri) 126].

*Fraud—proved when.* 'Fraud' is proved when it is shown that a false representation has been made—(*i*) knowingly, or (*ii*) without belief in its truth, or (*iii*) recklessly, careless whether it be true or false. [*Derry* v *Peek* (1889)14 AC 337: 5 TLR 625].

• **Legal fraud** p. 526.

**Fraudulent.** Based on fraud; proceeding from or characterized by fraud; tainted by fraud; done, made, or effected with a purpose or design to carry out a fraud.

A statement, or claim, or document, is "fraudulent" if it was falsely made, or caused to be made, with the intent to deceive.

**Fraudulent preference.** Every conveyance or transfer of property or charge thereon made, every payment made, every obligation incurred and every judicial proceeding taken or suffered by any person unable to pay his debts as they became due from his own moneys, in favour of any creditor, with a view to giving such creditor a preference over other creditors, is fraudulent and void as against the trustee in bankruptcy if the debtor becomes bankrupt within three months. [Bankruptcy Act (English)].

NOTE: To ascertain whether there has been a fraudulent preference, it is necessary to consider what the dominant or real motive of the person making the preference was, whether it was to defraud some creditors by preferring others or for some other motive. [*Drage* v *Knight* (1926)134 LT 765].

Whether a particular payment to a particular creditor in preference to other creditors amounts to fraudulent preference or not is essentially a question of fact. No single circumstance by itself will generally be conclusive on the question. It is the cumulative effect of several circumstances that will determine the question. [*V.V. Iyer* v *Official Assignee* (1955)2 MLJ 380].

▸*Meaning under the Provincial Insolvency Act 1920, s. 54 and Presidency-Towns Insolvency Act 1909, s. 56.* Every transfer of property, every payment made, every obligation incurred and every judicial proceeding taken or suffered by any person unable to pay his debts as they become due from his own money in favour of any creditor, with a view to giving that creditor a preference over other creditors shall, if such person is adjudged insolvent on a petition presented within three months after the date thereof, be deemed fraudulent and void as against the receiver and shall be annulled by the court.

**Fraudulently.** Doing of a thing with the intent to defraud.

▸*Meaning under the Indian Penal Code 1860, s. 25.* A person is said to do a thing fraudulently if he does that thing with intent to defraud but not otherwise.

A person is said to do a thing fraudulently within the meaning as defined in s. 25, IPC if he does that thing with intent to defraud but not otherwise. The last three words "but not otherwise" clearly indicate that the intent must be an intent to defraud. [*Dr. S. Dutt* v *State of U.P.* AIR 1966 SC 523: (1966)1 SCR 493: 1966 Cr LJ 459].

A person does a thing fraudulently if he does it with an intent to defraud. Two elements are necessary to constitute fraud; deceit that is to say that someone is deceived, and injury or loss to the same person. [*Biswambar* v *Nilamber* AIR 1930 Cal 263].

NOTE: A conclusive test of the fraudulent character of a deception for criminal purposes is this: Did the author of the deceit derive any advantage from it, which could not have been had if the truth had been known. If so, it is hardly possible that the advantage should not have had an equivalent in loss or risk of loss to someone else, and if so, there is fraud. [*Dr. Vimla* v *Delhi Administration* AIR 1963 SC 1572].

**Fraus est celare fraudem.** It is fraud to conceal fraud.

**Fraus et jus nunquam cohabitant.** Fraud and justice never dwell together.

**Free alongside ship (F.A.S.).** Includes all charges (including wharfage and porterage) up to, but not, including hoisting on board.

**Free and open market.** A market such as the Stock Exchange where all may trade and transactions are made publicly.

**Free consent.** Consent is said to be free when it is not caused by—(1) coercion, or (2) undue influence, or (3) fraud, or (4) misrepresentation, or (5) mistake. [Indian Contract Act 1872, s. 14]

NOTE: When consent to an agreement is caused by coercion, fraud or misrepresentation, the agreement is a contract voidable at the option of the party whose consent was so caused. [Indian Contract Act 1872, s. 19].

When consent to an agreement is caused by undue influence, the agreement is a contract voidable at the option of the party whose consent was so caused. [Indian Contract Act 1872, s. 19A].

Where both parties to an agreement are under a mistake as to a matter of fact essential to the agreement, the agreement is void. [Indian Contract Act 1872, s. 20].

**Free enterprise.** An economic system, also called capitalism, adopted by a country in which individuals are free to own capital and undertake economic activity within the laws of the country.

The right to conduct a legitimate business for profit. [*Lafayette Dramatic Productions* v *Ferentz* 9 NW 2d 57, 62].

**Free fishery.** A franchise in the hands of a subject, existing by grant or prescription, distinct from an ownership in the soil. It is an exclusive right, and applies to a public navigable river, without any right in the soil. [Black's *Law Dictionary*, 5th Ed.].

An exclusive right of fishery, existing by grant or prescription from the monarch, to take fish in public water such as a river or an arm of the sea. [Black's *Law Dictionary*, 8th Ed.].

An exclusive right of fishing in a public river, or an arm of the sea. A free fishery differs from a several fishery, because the person having the right of several fishery must be the owner of the soil, but such ownership is not required in the case of a free fishery.

**Freedom of the press.** The right to publish without any previous licence or censorship. [*Virendra* v *Punjab State* AIR 1957 Punj 1: 1957 Cr LJ 88].

The expression 'freedom of the press' means freedom from interference from authority which would have the effect of interference with the content and circulation of newspapers. There cannot be any interference with that freedom in the name of public interest by publishing facts and opinions without which a democratic electorate cannot make responsible judgments. Freedom of the press is the heart of social and political intercourse. [*Indian Express Newspapers (Bombay) Pvt. Ltd.* v *Union of India* AIR 1986 SC 515: (1985)1 SCC 641: (1985)2 SCR 287: (1986)159 ITR 856: (1985)1 Comp LJ 115].

NOTE: The freedom of speech comprehends the freedom of press and the freedom of speech and press are fundamental personal rights of the citizens. Freedom of press involves freedom from restriction in respect of employment in the editorial force. The necessary corollary thereof is that no measure can be enacted which would have the effect of imposing a pre-censorship, curtailing the circulation, of restricting the choice of employment or unemployment in the editorial force. [*Express Newspapers* v *Union of India* AIR 1958 SC 578: 1958 SCJ 1113: 1958 SCA 952: 1959 SCR 12].

**Freehold.** An estate in land held in fee simple, in fee tail, or for term of life; the tenure by which such an estate is held. It is also termed freehold estate; freehold interest.

NOTE: An estate to be a freehold must possess two qualities—(1) immobility, that is, the property must be either land or some interest issuing out of or annexed to land; and (2) indeterminate duration; for if the utmost period of time to which an estate can endure be fixed and determined, it cannot be freehold.

**Freight.** The price or compensation paid for the transportation of goods by a carrier.

'Freight' in the ordinary mercantile sense means the reward payable to a carrier for the carriage of the goods. [*Lime Leitao* v *Union of India* AIR 1968 Goa 29].

▸ *Meaning under the Marine Insurance Act 1963, s. 2(b).* 'Freight' includes the profit derivable by shipowner from the employment of his ship to carry his own goods or other movables, as well as freight payable by a third party, but does not include passage money.

It signifies the earnings or profits derived by the shipowner or hirer of the ship from the use of it himself or by letting it to others to be used or for carrying goods for others. [*Allison* v *Bristol Marine Insurnace Co.* (1876)1 App Cas 209].


- **Back-freight** p. 90.
- **Dead freight** p. 227.


**Freight note.** Statement giving particulars of freight charges.

**Friend.** An intimate and trustworthy companion; one who regards a thing with favour; an adherent. One favourably disposed. [*Ned* v *Robinson* 74 P 2d 1156].

▸ *Meaning under the Preventive Detention Act.* The word 'friend' is obviously not intended to carry the meaning of the term in common parlance. One of the meanings of the word 'friend', according to *Collins English Dictionary* is 'any ally in a fight or cause; supporter'. The term 'friend' used is more in this sense than meaning 'a person known well to another and regarded with liking, affection and loyalty'. [*Johney D'Couto* v *State of Tamil Nadu* JT 1987(4) SC 248: (1987)32 ELT 225: (1988)1 SCC 116: AIR 1988 SC 109: (1988)1 SCR 787: 1988 SCC (Cri) 70: 1988 Cr LJ 178].

**Friendly suit.** A suit brought not in a hostile manner, the object being to settle some points of law or do some act which cannot safely be done except with the sanction of a court of justice. [Mozley & Whiteley's *Law Dictionary*, 10th Ed.].

**Frivolous.** Of little weight or importance; lacking in seriousness; marked by unbecoming levity; meaningless; insignificant; unworthy of serious notice; flippant; trifling; trumpery; lacking seriousness; silly; void of significance or reason; lacking legal basis or legal merit; not reasonably purposeful; of little weight or importance.

A pleading is "frivolous" when it is clearly insufficient on its face, and does not controvert the material points of the opposite pleading, and is presumably interposed for mere purposes of delay or to embarrass the opponent.

NOTE: There is an inherent power in every court to stay and dismiss actions or applications which are frivolous and vexatious and abusive of the process of the court. In order to bring a case within the description, it is not sufficient merely to show that the plaintiff has no cause of action. It must be shown that the alleged cause of action is one which, on the face of it, no reasonable person could treat as *bona fide* and contend that he had a grievance which he was entitled to bring before the court. [*Norman* v *Mathews* (1916)85 LJKB 857].

**From.** As used as a function word, implies a starting point, whether it be of time, place, or condition; and meaning having a starting point of motion, noting the point of departure, origin, withdrawal, etc., as he travelled "from" New York to Chicago. [*Silva* v *MacAuley* 26 P 2d 887].

One meaning of "from" is "out of".

Word "from" or "after" an event or day does not have an absolute and invariable meaning, but each should receive an inclusion or exclusion construction according to intention with which such word is used. [*Acme Life Insurance Co.* v *White* Tex Civ App, 99 SW 2d 1059, 1060].

Words "from" and "to", used in contract, may be given meaning to which reason and sense entitles them, under circumstances of case. [*Woodruff* v *Adams* 25 P 2d 529].

The word 'from' includes the date from which the time is to be reckoned. Although on some occasions the view has been expressed that the question as to whether the stated date should or should not be excluded depends upon the context in which the word 'from' occurs. [*Srinivasa Silk Mills* v *State of Mysore* AIR 1962 Mys 117].

Generally excludes the day from which the time is to be reckoned. [Mozley & Whiteley's *Law Dictionary*, 10th Ed.]

**From generation to generation.** The words 'from generation to generation' cannot be called technical words. Most of the deeds of conveyances in the Indian languages will have the expression which when translated would be: 'as long as the sun and the moon live', while the sun and the moon endure from *'vamsam to vamsamni'* order (*vamsa parampariyai*). These do not import their ordinary verbal signification but convey the sense of 'absolutely' and 'for ever'. [*Radhakishan* v *Balambhat* AIR 1937 Nag 248].

The expression 'generation to generation' shows that a heritable estate is given. [*Giri Bala Dasi* v *Kedar Nath* 56 Cal 180: AIR 1929 Cal 454].

The expression conveys a grant of an absolute right. [*Radha Kisan* v *Balambhat* AIR 1947 Nag 248].

**From time to time.** The expression means 'as the occasion should arise'. [*Holliday* v *Wakefield Corporation* (1887)57 LT 559].

The expression means 'as and when it is appropriate so to do'. [*Re Von Dembrinska* (1954)2 All ER 46].

Occasionally, at intervals, now and then. [Black's *Law Dictionary*, 5th Ed.].

**Frontage.** Extent of front; the way a thing faces; outlook; the fact or action of facing in a certain direction; exposure.

A land abutting on a street or on water. [*Concise Oxford Dictionary*, 9th Ed.].

Frontage denotes line of property on street. [*Jagendorf* v *City of Memphis* Tenn, 520 SW 2d 333, 335].

Extent of front along road or street. [*Tzeses* v *Barbahenn* 17 A 2d 539, 540].

The part of land abutting a street or highway or lying between a building's front and a street or highway. [Black's *Law Dictionary*, 8th Ed.].

**Frustration (of contract).** Frustration may be defined as the premature determination of an agreement between parties, lawfully entered into and in course of operation at the time of its premature determination, owing to the occurrence of an intervening event or change of circumstances so fundamental as to be regarded by the law both as striking at the root of the agreement, and as entirely beyond what was contemplated by the parties when they entered into the agreement. If, therefore, the intervening circumstance is one which the law would not regard as so fundamental as to destroy the basis of the agreement, there is no frustration. Equally if the terms of the agreement showed that the parties contemplated the possibility of such an intervening circumstance arising, frustration does not occur. Neither, of course, does it arise where one of the parties has deliberately brought about the supervening event by his own choice. But where it does arise, frustration operates to bring the agreement to an end as regards both parties forthwith and quite apart from their volition. [*Cricklewood Property* v *Leighton's Investment Trust* (1945) AC 221].

NOTE: The law as to the frustration of a contract is contained in ss. 32 and 56 of the Indian Contract Act 1872. The doctrine of frustration is really an aspect or part of the law of discharge of contract by reason of supervening impossibility or illegality of the act agreed to be done and hence comes within the purview of s. 56 of the Indian Contract Act. It would be incorrect to say that s. 56 applies only to cases of physical impossibility and that where this section is not applicable recourse can be had to the principles of English law on the subject of frustration. So far as the Indian Contract Act deals with a particular subject it is exhaustive, and principles of English law cannot be imported. [*Satyabrata Ghosh* v *Mugneeram* AIR 1954 SC 44: 1954 SCJ 1: 1954 SCR 310: 1954 SCA 187].

The doctrine of frustration is applied not on the ground that the parties themselves agreed to an implied term which operated to release them from the performance of the contract. The relief is given by the court on the ground of subsequent impossibility when it finds that the whole purpose or basis of a contract was frustrated by the intrusion or occurrence of an unexpected event or change of circumstances which was beyond what was contemplated by the parties at the time when they entered into the agreement. [*Mugneeram Bangur* v *Gurbachan Singh* AIR 1959 Cal 576: 63 CWN 549].

A contract is not frustrated merely because the circumstances in which the contract was made are altered. The parties to an executory contract are often faced, in the course of carrying it out, with a turn of events which they did not at all anticipate—a wholly abnormal rise or fall in prices, a sudden depreciation of currency, an unexpected obstacle to execution or the like. Yet this does not in itself affect the bargain they have made. [*Alopi Parshad* v *Union of India* AIR 1960 SC 588: (1960)2 SCR 793: (1960)2 SCA 45: 1960 SCJ 763].

**Fugitive.** A person who flees or escapes; a criminal suspect who flees, evades, or escapes arrest, prosecution, or imprisonment, especially by fleeing the jurisdiction or by hiding. [Black's *Law Dictionary*, 7th Ed.].

**Fugitive criminal.** An individual who is accused or convicted of an extradition offence committed within the jurisdiction of a foreign State or a Commonwealth country and is, or is suspected to be, in some part of India. [Extradition Act 1962, s. 2(*f*)].

**Full blood.** The relationship existing between persons having the same two parents; unmixed ancestry. [Black's *Law Dictionary*, 7th Ed.].

It is also termed whole blood; entire blood.

▸ *Meaning under the Hindu Marriage Act 1955, s. 3(c); Special Marriage Act 1954, s. 2(b).* Two persons are said to be related to each other by full blood when they are descended from a common ancestor by the same wife.

**Full court.** A court composed of all the judges of that court.

**Full faith and credit.** The expression "full faith and credit" denotes such faith and credit as the public acts, records and judicial proceedings have by law or usage in the particular State to which they belong.

NOTE: No greater effect will be given to a judgment or a statute of another State than is given in such State. This is provided for in Art. IV, s. 1 of the American Constitution, s. 118 of the Commonwealth of Australia Constitution Act and Art. 261 of the Constitution of India.

**Full time.** The amount of time considered the normal or standard amount for working during a given period, as a day, week or month. [*Sankar Balaji* v *State of Maharashtra* AIR 1962 SC 517: (1962)1 Cr LJ 497].

'Full time' as the basis for determination of average weekly wages of injured employee means time during which the employee is offered employment, excluding time during which he has no opportunity to work.

**Full time earnings.** 'Full time earnings' means the earnings made by an employee in a day by working full time on that day, the full time to be in accordance with the period of time given in the notice displayed in the factory for a particular day. Payment for overtime or for bonus is not included in computing the total full-time earnings. [*Sankar Balaji* v *State of Maharashtra* AIR 1962 SC 517: (1962)1 Cr LJ 497].

**Fully paid up shares.** 'Fully paid up shares' means that their full face value has been given in money, or money's worth; the phrase is not, ordinarily, to be confined to meaning that the company itself will make no further claim in respect of them. [*Bloomenthan* v *Ford* (1897) AC 156; Stroud's *Judicial Dictionary*, 5h Ed.].

**Functus officio.** A person who has performed his duty or whose office or authority has come to an end is said to be *functus officio*.

The expression *'functus officio'* means having fulfilled the function, having discharged the duty of office, or having accomplished the purpose and therefore of no further force or authority. [*Ram Singh* v *State* AIR 1966 MP 20].

**Fund.** It is a generic term and all-embracing as compared with the term "money", etc., which is specific. A sum of money or other liquid assets set apart for a specific purpose, or available for the payment of debts or claims.

In the plural, this word has a variety of slightly different meanings, as follows: moneys and much more, such as notes, bills, cheques, drafts, stocks and bonds, and in broader meaning may include property of every kind. [*State* v *Finney* 40 P 2d 411, 421].

A sum of money or other liquid assets established for a specific purpose. [Black's *Law Dictionary*, 8th Ed.].

The word 'fund' may mean actual cash resources of particular kind (e.g., money in a drawer or a bank) or it may be a mere accountancy expression used to describe a particular category which a person uses in making up his accounts. [*R.K. Dalmia* v *Delhi Administration* AIR 1962 SC 1821: (1962)2 Cr LJ 805: (1963)1 SCR 253].

The words 'payment out of' when used in connection with the word 'fund' in its first meaning connote actual payment, *e.g.*, by taking the money out of the drawer or drawing a cheque on the bank. When used in connection with the word 'fund' in its secondary meaning they connote that for the purpose of the account in which the fund finds a place, the payment is debited to that fund. [*R.K. Dalmia* v *Delhi Administration* AIR 1962 SC 1821: (1962)2 Cr LJ 805: (1963)1 SCR 253].


- **Chit fund organisation** p. 141.
- **Consolidated fund** p. 176.
- **Contingency fund** p. 185.
- **General fund** p. 384.
- **International Monetary Fund** p. 475.
- **Local fund** p. 540.
- **Provident fund** p. 705.
- **Sinking fund** p. 799.
- **Working funds** p. 903.

**Fundamental disequilibrium.** This occurs when a country's official rate of exchange is out of line with its real value in relation to other countries. The result of such disequilibrium appears in the country's balance of payment and the remedy is to make an adjustment to the country's official rate of exchange. [Osborn & Grandage's *Concise Commercial Dictionary*].

**Fundamental rights.** Those which have their origin in the express terms of the Constitution or which are necessarily to be implied from those terms. [*Sidle* v *Majors* 341 NE 2d 763, 769].

'Fundamental rights' are the modern name for what have been traditionally known as 'natural rights'. They are the primordial rights necessary for the development of human personality. They are the rights which enable a man to chalk out his own life in the manner he likes best. [*L.C. Golak Nath* v *State of Punjab* AIR 1967 SC 1643].

They are the rights of the people preserved by the Constitution and are given a transcendental position under the Constitution of India and are kept beyond the reach of Parliament. [*L.C. Golak Nath* v *State of Punjab* AIR 1967 SC 1643].

NOTE: In India, fundamental rights are laid down in Part III of the Constitution of India 1950. The rights which are guaranteed in Part III of the Constitution are not merely natural rights recognised by the Constitution, but are rights conferred by the Constitution. [*State of Bihar* v *Kameshwar Singh* AIR 1952 SC 252].

The fundamental rights guaranteed to the citizens have nothing to do with the rights of individual citizens *inter se.* [*Datta Mal Chiranji Lal* v *Ladli Prasad* AIR 1960 All 632].

The fundamental rights are binding as directly valid law and no legislation and no administrative edict or governmental rescript which is in violation of them can have legal force or validity. [*Pandurang Kashinath More* v *Union of India* AIR 1959 Bom 134: ILR (1958) Bom 1266].

**Funded debt.** Public debt for the payment of which money has been appropriated. When money is not so appropriated the debt is called floating debt.

**Funding operation.** Generally speaking, it is the replacement of floating, revolving or short-term debt with a fixed loan debt over a definite period.

**Furlough.** A leave of absence from military or other employment duty; a brief release from prison. [Black's *Law Dictionary*, 8th Ed.].

It is a conditional release of a prisoner sentenced to long-term imprisonment. Release on furlough is not granted when it is hazardous to public interest. Period of furlough counts as sentence undergone. [*Charanjitlal* v *State (Delhi)* (1985)28 Del LT 92, 97].

**Furniture.** The movable equipment of a house, room etc., e.g. tables, chairs, and beds; that with which anything is furnished or supplied; equipment or outfit, specifically, movable household articles, such as chairs, tables, bureaus; ornamental appendages or external adjuncts that serve to complete anything.

The term 'furniture' includes that which furnishes, or with which anything is furnished or supplied; whatever must be supplied to a house, a room, place of business, or public building or the like, to make it habitable, convenient, or agreeable; goods, vessels, utensils, and other appendages necessary or convenient for housekeeping; whatever is added to the interior of a house or apartment, for use or convenience. [Black's *Law Dictionary*, 5th Ed.].

According to dictionaries, the expression 'furniture' has a wide connotation and includes all those articles which are used in a dwelling house or a place of business and commerce or a public building to furnish the establishment. [*New Chelur Manufacturers (P) Ltd.* v *C.C.E.* (1997)94 ELT 467: (1998)9 SCC 140: JT 1998(7) SC 592].

NOTE: Not only furniture manufactured out of wood can be regarded as furniture, but furniture manufactured out of metal should also be regarded as furniture. Brass cradle would be furniture. [*Ramakrishna Rao* v *State of Karnataka* (1982)1 Kant LJ 264 (DB)].

A movable article like trestles which is used in either armouries, shop or some homes for convenient stacking or storing of guns is certainly an article of furniture. [*Commissioner of Sales-tax* v *Dhingra & Co.* (1979)43 STC 268; *State of Gujarat* v *Lax Tools Manufacturers* (1980)46 STC 115].

*Furniture and fixtures—distinction.* Furniture as opposed to fixtures consists of the purely movable articles in a house, which are not complementary to any portion of the house, or to any fixture annexed or belonging thereto. For example, chairs are furniture but window-blinds are fixtures. Furniture does not cease to be so merely because it is affixed to earth. [*Public Prosecutor* v *Thangavelu Pillai* (1968)2 MLJ 233].

**Further advance or charge.** A subsequent loan of money to a mortgagor by a mortgagee, either upon the same security as the original loan was advanced or on additional security.

**Further assurance.** One of the usual agreements entered into by a vendor for the protection of the vendee's interest in the subject of purchase, to the effect that the vendor will, at the request and cost of the vendee, execute further conveyances etc. for more perfectly assuring the subject-matter of the conveyance.

NOTE: In India, a covenant of further assurance is usually incorporated in every conveyance for value.

**Further inquiry.** Further inquiry is not limited to inquiry upon further material or further additional evidence. It may involve reconsideration of the evidence already on the record. [*In re Harishchandra Reddy* AIR 1938 Mad 742].

It means further consideration of evidence. For directing further enquiry, it is not necessary that there should be further evidence or material. [*Govind Moti & Co.* v *Sindh Resettlement Corporation Ltd.* AIR 1954 Kutch 33: 1954 Cr LJ 1086].

The expression 'further inquiry' has come to have a technical meaning and that it simply means reconsideration of the matter. [*Udit Narayan Patwari* v *Emperor* AIR 1938 Pat 369; *Shyamlal Ruia* v *State* AIR 1954 Pat 441 (DB): 54 Cr LJ 1451].

**Further relief.** The expression 'further relief' in proviso to s. 42 of the Specific Relief Act 1877 (now s. 34 of the Specific Relief Act 1963) means not any and every kind of relief but one which would complete the claim of the plaintiff and not lead to a multiplicity of suits. That further relief must flow necessarily from the relief of declaration. But if the relief is remote and is not connected with the cause of action, then the plaintiff need not claim it. [*Lala Laxminarayan* v *Rukhmabai* ILR (1950) Nag 834].

The 'further relief' does not refer to a relief which is not at all necessary in view of the declaratory relief which may be granted to him and which alone will serve his purpose quite well. [*Indra Narain* v *Ganga Ram* AIR 1955 All 683].

**Future estate.** An estate to take effect in possession at a future time, e.g., contingent remainders, executory interests.

**Future goods.** Goods to be manufactured or produced or acquired by the seller after the making of the contract of sale. [*Chhotabhai Jethabhai Patel & Co.* v *State of Madhya Pradesh* AIR 1953 SC 108: 1953 SCR 476 referring to Sale of Goods Act 1930, s. 2(6)].

# Gg

**Gaddi.** The word *'gaddi'* is used very loosely in different senses; one use of the word *'gaddi'* appears to be a necessary part of the dignity of a religious ascetic of the highest class. [*Panna Lal* v *Puj Harsh Rishi* AIR 1952 Punj 361].

**Gahan.** A pawn; a pledge or thing in pawn; a mortgage; land held by mortgage tenure.

**Gahan lagan.** *Gahan lagan* is the term generally applied in Bombay to contracts which are mortgages, but which contain a clause of conditional sale if the mortgage debt is not paid within a given time. [*Bapuji* v *Lenavaraji* ILR 2 Bom 231, 238].

**Gain.** Profits; winnings; increment of value; difference between receipts and expenditures; difference between cost and sale price; appreciation in value or worth of securities or property; excess of revenues over expenses from a specific transaction.

An increase in amount, degree, or value; excess of receipts over expenditures or of sale price over cost. [Black's *Law Dictionary*, 8th Ed.].

"'Gain' is 'that which is acquired or comes as a benefit, profit, or advantage', and it may be derived indirectly as well as directly". [*R.* v *Fames* (1903)6 OLR 35, 38, *per* Osler, J.A. (Canada)].

> NOTE: Gain is not limited to pecuniary gain or confined to commercial profits only, and a company is formed for the acquisition of gain which is formed to acquire something, as distinguished from a company formed for spending something. [Halsbury's *Laws of England*, 4th Ed., vol. 7, para 20, p. 21].

- **Capital gains** p. 123.
- **Gains of a trade.** Gains of a trade are those which are gained by the trading, for whatever purpose they are used—whether they are gained for the benefit of a community or for the benefit of individuals. Whether the benefit is to be obtained by dividends or whether it is to be obtained by lightening and diminishing public burdens, it is all the same. [*Mersey Docks* v *Lucas* 53 LJKB 7].
- **Pecuniary gain** p. 649.
- **Wrongful gain** p. 907.

**Gain wrongfully.** A person is said to gain wrongfully when such person retains wrongfully, as well as when such person acquires wrongfully, property to which the person gaining is not legally entitled. [Indian Penal Code 1860, s. 23].

**Gainful employment/occupation.** Any calling, occupation, profession or work which one may profitably pursue. [*Mutual Life Insurance Company of New York* v *Barron* 30 SE 2d 879, 882].

**Gainfully occupied person.** 'Gainfully occupied person' means a person who is engaged in any trade, business, profession, office, employment or vocation and is wholly or substantially dependent thereon for a livelihood, or a person who, though temporarily unemployed, is normally so engaged and dependent. [Personal Injuries (Emergency Provisions) Act 1962, s. 2(4); Personal Injuries (Compensation Insurance) Act 1963, s. 2(*c*)].

**Gains of learning.** 'Gains of learning' means all acquisitions of property made substantially by means of learning, and whether such acquisitions be the ordinary or extraordinary result of such learning. [Hindu Gains of Learning Act 1930, s. 2(*b*)].

**Gamastha.** An agent, a steward, a confidential factor, a representative; an officer employed by zamindars to collect their rents, by bankers to receive money etc., by merchants to carry on their affairs in other places than where they reside and the like. [Wilson's *Glossary*].

**Gambler.** One who follows or practices games of chance or skill, with the expectation and purpose of thereby winning money or other property.

**Gambling.** The dealing, operating, carrying on, conducting, maintaining or exposing for pay of any game; making a bet; to plan, or game, for money or other stake. [Black's *Law Dictionary*, 5th Ed.].

The act of risking something of value, especially money, for a chance to win a prize. [Black's *Law Dictionary*, 8th Ed.].

NOTE: Gambling consists of a consideration, an element of chance, and a reward. [*In re Gaming Devices Seized at American Legion Post No. 109* 176 A 2d 115, 122].

The elements of gambling are payment of a price for a chance to win a prize. [*Boies* v *Bartell* 310 P 2d 834, 837].

Gambling or gaming includes wagering or betting except wagering or betting upon a horse race, when such wagering or betting takes place in the manner stated, but does not include a lottery. Prize competitions which do not require substantial skill ought to be considered as gambling transactions. [*J.N. Gupta* v *State* AIR 1959 Cal 141].

Prize competitions being of a gambling nature cannot be regarded as trade or commerce. [*State of Bombay* v *R.M.D. Chamarbaugwala* AIR 1957 SC 699].

**Gaming.** "Gaming" is the act or practice of gambling on a game of chance. It is staking on chance where chance is the controlling factor. [*K.R. Lakshmanan (Dr.)* v *State of Tamil Nadu* AIR 1996 SC 1153: (1996)2 SCC 226: (1996)86 Comp Cas 66: JT 1996(1) SC 173].

**Gaming house.** It means any house in which cards, dice, tables or other instruments of gaming are kept for the profit of the person occupying such house.

"Gaming house" is defined to mean any house, room, tent, enclosure, space, vehicle, vessel or any place whatsoever in which gaming takes place or in which instruments of gaming are kept or used for gaming. [*Krishnachandra* v *State of Madhya Pradesh* (1964)1 SCR 765: AIR 1965 SC 307: (1965)1 Cr LJ 347].

NOTE: A large number of persons are invited in the house for the purpose of gaming. Such a gaming house is necessarily a nuisance under s. 268 of the Indian Penal Code 1860. In England, gaming houses are now regulated under the Gaming Act 1968, which allows commercial gaming to take place under control by licence, registration and permit.

**Gandharva marriage.** Marriage by mutual consent. One of the unapproved forms of Hindu marriage formerly prevalent among Kshatriyas. It was a union of man and woman through their mutual passion and infatuation.

NOTE: It is noted in Mulla's *Hindu Law*, 12th Ed., that the "Gandharva marriage" is the voluntary union of a youth and a damsel which springs from desire and sensual inclination. It has at times been erroneously described as an euphemism for concubinage. This view is based on a total misconception of the leading texts of the Smritis. It may be noted that the essential marriage ceremonies are as much a requisite part of this form of marriage as of any other unless it is shown that some modification of those ceremonies has been introduced by custom in any particular community or caste. [*Bhaurao Shankar Laokande* v *State of Maharashtra* AIR 1965 SC 1564: (1965)2 SCR 837: (1965)2 Cr LJ 544].

**Gang.** Any company of persons who go about together or act in concert, in modern use, mainly for criminal purposes. [Black's *Law Dictionary*, 5th Ed.].

A group of persons who go about together or act in concert, esp. for antisocial or criminal purposes. [Black's *Law Dictionary*, 8th Ed.].

The word 'gang' means any band or company of persons who go about together or act in concert. The essence of the word is that the persons should act in concert and therefore two or more persons can constitute a gang. [*Sharaf Shah Khan* v *State of Andhra Pradesh* AIR 1963 AP 314: (1963)2 Cr LJ 121].

NOTE: The term 'gang' is well-known and when we talk of certain person's gang, it is understood that it means the gang organised by the person and constituting that person and others. [*Ralla Singh* v *State* ILR (1952) Pepsu 445: 54 Cr LJ 1519: AIR 1953 Pepsu 145].

**Ganti.** A hereditary undertenure at a fixed rent. [*Priya Nath Das* v *Ramtaran* ILR 30 Cal 811 (PC)].

**Garage.** A building in which motor vehicles are stored and cared for. [Webster's *Comprehensive Dictionary*, International Ed.].

A building or shed for using a motor vehicle or vehicles; an establishment which sells petrol etc., or repairs and sells motor vehicles, or does both. [*Concise Oxford Dictionary*, 9th Ed.].

A building for the storage or refitting of motor vehicles. [*Shorter Oxford Dictionary* as referred to in *Barnett & Block* v *National Parcels Insurance Co. Ltd.* (1942)1 All ER 221].

A building for sheltering, cleaning or repairing motor vehicles. [*New Century Dictionary* as referred to in *Barnett & Block* v *National Parcels Insurance Co. Ltd.* (1942)1 All ER 221].

A building for stabling or storing of motor vehicles of all kinds. [*New Standard Dictionary* as referred to in *Barnett & Block* v *National Parcels Insurance Co. Ltd.* (1942)1 All ER 221].

A storehouse for motor vehicles [Nuttal's *Standard Dictionary* as referred to in *Barnett & Block* v *National Parcels Insurance Co. Ltd.* (1942)1 All ER 221].

Garage is a place where one can get reasonable protection and shelter for a car. There cannot be reasonable protection or shelter if there is no roof. [*Barnett & Block* v *National Parcels Insurance Co. Ltd.* (1942)1 All ER 221].

**Garbling.** The process of garbling consists of washing, drying and winnowing with a view to cleaning it by removing all dust and dirt. [*V.M. Patel* v *Inspector of Factories* AIR 1958 Ker 237: 1958 Cr LJ 1026: 1958 Ker LT 161].

**Garden.** A small piece of land, appropriated to the cultivation of herbs, fruits, flowers, or vegetables. [Black's *Law Dictionary*, 5th Ed.].

A plot of ground on which fruit, vegetables and flowers are grown for food or pleasure. [*Cooper* v *Pearse* (1896)1 QB 562, *per* Collins, J.].

The word 'garden' is an ordinary word, to be understood as in ordinary popular usage. The dictionary definitions of 'garden' include the idea of its being an enclosed space. Thus, for instance, in the *Oxford Dictionary*, 'garden' is defined as: 'An enclosed piece of ground devoted to the cultivation of flowers, fruit, or vegetables; often preceded by some defining word, as flower, fruit, kitchen, market, strawberry, garden, etc.' [*Bomford* v *Osborne* (1941)2 All ER 426 (HL), *per* Lord Wright].

**Garment.** An article of clothing; an article of dress; clothes; the outward and visible covering of anything.

The primary meaning of 'garment' is any articles of clothing, whether visible to another or not. It is used generally to cover human body. [*Pareek Hosiery Products* v *Deputy Commissioner of Sales Tax* (1962)13 STC 722].

**Garnishee.** A person who is garnished or warned. The word is especially applied in law to a debtor who is warned by the order of a court to pay his debts, not to his immediate creditor, but to a person who has obtained a final judgment against such creditor. [Mozley & Whiteley's *Law Dictionary*, 10th Ed.].

A person or institution (such as a bank) that is indebted to or is bailee for another whose property has been subjected to garnishment. [Black's *Law Dictionary*, 8th Ed.].

**Gas.** Any air-like substance which moves freely to fill any space available, irrespective of its quantity; a substance (especially found naturally or extracted from coal) used as a domestic or industrial fuel; an explosive mixture of firedamp with air. [*Concise Oxford Dictionary*, 9th Ed.].

In Physics it means that fluid form of matter which is compressible within limits, and which, owing to the relatively free movement of its molecules, diffuses readily and is capable of indefinite expansion in all directions; any gaseous or vaporous mixture other than air; a single jet of flame supplied by illuminating gas. [Webster's *Comprehensive Dictionary*, International Ed.].

NOTE: "Gas" includes fume or vapour. [*Words & Phrases Legally Defined*, 2nd Ed., edited by John B. Saunders].

Though steam and vapour and substances of that description which find their way into the atmosphere, strictly speaking, are gas, they do not pass in ordinary parlance by the name of gas.

**Gas mask.** Mask of flannel soaked in chemicals against poison gas.

**Gazette.** It is a publication of an official character which contains Government notifications, lists of public appointments and honours, legal notices, etc., which are presumed to be genuine.

The official publication of news of all kinds the government desire to make known to the public. [General Clauses Act, s. 3(39)].

**Gazetteer.** A dictionary which contains a historical account, or the general description of any place, district or province; a dictionary of geographical names.

**Gender.** Corresponds to sex or lack of sex. Animate beings are either masculine or feminine. Inanimate objects are neuter.

**Gender discrimination.** Discrimination based on gender, especially against women. It is also known as sex discrimination.

**Genealogical tree.** A genealogical tree is a table showing the descent of a family or animals species in the shape of a tree with branches.

**Genealogy.** An account of descent from an ancestor by enumeration of intermediate persons; a record of descent from some ancestor; a line of descent traced continuously from an ancestor; a list of ancestors and their descendents; descent in a direct line; pedigree.

The summary history or table of a family, showing how the persons there named are connected together. [Black's *Law Dictionary*, 5th Ed.].

**General agent.** One authorised to transact all the business of his principal, or all his business of a particular class.

**General average loss.** A general average loss is a loss caused by or directly consequential on a general average act. It includes a general average expenditure as well as a general average sacrifice. There is a general average act where any extraordinary sacrifice or expenditure is voluntarily and reasonably made or incurred in time of peril for the purpose of preserving the property imperilled in the common adventure. Where there is a general average loss, the party on whom it falls is entitled, subject to the conditions imposed by maritime law, to a rateable contribution from the other parties interested, and such a contribution is called a general average contribution. [Halsbury's *Laws of England*, 4th Ed., vol. 25, para 249, p. 142].

**General crossing.** It means a general cheque crossing where no bank is named. It can be compared with special cheque crossing where within the crossing a bank is named. A cheque so crossed can be paid only into the bank named. Other types of special crossing include "Account payee only", "not negotiable".

**General custom.** A custom that prevails throughout a country and constitutes one of the sources of law of the land; a custom that businesses recognize and follow.

A custom which has been repeatedly recognized by courts and has become entitled to judicial notice. [*Ujagar Singh* v *Jeo* 1959 Supp (2) SCR 781: AIR 1959 SC 1041: 1960 SCJ 16].

**General demurrer.** A demurrer not setting forth any special cause of demurrer. It is framed in general terms without showing specifically the nature of the objection.

An objection pointing out a substantive defect in an opponent's pleading, such as the insufficiency of the claim or the court's lack of subject-matter jurisdiction; an objection to a pleading for want of substance.

**General election.** An election that occurs at a regular interval of time; an election for all seats, as contrasted with a by-election.

NOTE: An election in all the wards of the Municipality in which all the voters are given an opportunity of exercising their franchise is a general election. [*Provat Chandra* v *R.C. Sen* AIR 1955 Cal 83].

**General exceptions.** Exceptions general in nature.

▸ *Meaning under the Indian Penal Code 1860.* Exceptions which are common to all the penal clauses of the Indian Penal Code, or to a great variety of clauses dispersed over many chapters are known as general exceptions. They have been placed in a separate chapter, *viz.*, Chapter IV of the Indian Penal Code spread over ss. 76 to 106. This chapter has been framed in order to obviate the necessity of repeating in every penal clause a considerable number of limitations.

**General fund.** A government's primary operating fund; a state's assets furnishing the means for the support of government and for defraying the legislature's discretionary appropriations; a non-profit entity's assets that are not earmarked for a specific purpose. [Black's *Law Dictionary*, 7th Ed.].

**General law.** Law that is neither local nor confined in application to particular persons; a statute that relates to a subject of a broad nature.

NOTE: In deciding whether a statute is general or special the focus must be on the principal subject-matter and the particular perspective. For certain purpose law may be general and for certain other purpose it may be special. [*L.I.C. of India* v *D.J. Bahadur* (1981)1 SCR 1083: (1981)2 SCJ 209: 1981 Ker LT 251].

**General ledger.** A book or series of books used for recording financial transactions in the form of debits and credits.

**General legacy.** A gift of personal property that the testator intends to come from the estate's general assets, payable in money or items indistinguishable from each other, such as shares of publicly traded stock. [Black's *Law Dictionary*, 8th Ed.].

A pecuniary legacy payable out of the general assets of a testator.

NOTE: A general legacy may or may not be a part of the testator's property. It is a gift of something which, in the event of the testator leaving sufficient assets, must be raised by his executor out of his general estate. In case of general legacies if the assets of the testator after payment of debts, necessary expenses and specific legacies are not sufficient to pay all the general legacies in full, they abate proportionately. [Indian Succession Act 1925, s. 327].

**General lien.** A general lien is a right to detain a chattel, etc., until payment be made, not only of any debt due in respect of the particular chattel, but of any balance that may be due on general account in the same line of business. [Black's *Law Dictionary*, 5th Ed.].

A general lien is a possessory lien by which the lienholder may retain any of the debtor's goods in the lienholder's possession until any debt due from the debtor, whether in connection with the retained goods or otherwise, has been paid. [Black's *Law Dictionary*, 8th Ed.].

"A general lien is the right to retain the property of another for a general balance of accounts; but a particular lien is a right to retain it only for a charge on account of labour employed or expenses bestowed upon the identical property detained." [Kent, Comm. II. 634].

NOTE: Factors, insurance brokers, packers, stockbrokers, and bankers have a general lien over the property of their clients or customers.

Under s. 171 of the Indian Contract Act 1872, bankers, factors, wharfingers, attorneys of a High Court and policy-brokers may, in the absence of a contract to the contrary, retain, as a security for a general balance of account, any goods bailed to them; but no other persons have a right to retain, as a security for such balance, goods bailed to them, unless there is an express contract to that effect.

**General manager.** A manager who has overall control of a business, office, or other organization, including authority over other managers. [Black's *Law Dictionary*, 7th Ed.].

One having general direction and control of a corporation's affairs, and who may do everything which corporation could do in transaction of its business. [*Continental Supply Co.* v *Forrest E. Gilmore Co. of Texas* Tex Civ App, 55 SW 2d 622].

**General meeting of company.** The expression in the Companies Act 1956, includes all kinds of general meetings, annual, extraordinary or statutory. [*Traco Enterprises Ltd.* v *Alexander* AIR 1964 Ker 273: 1964 Ker LJ 846].

**General power.** Power that can be exercised in any one's favour, including the agent, to affect another's interest in property; a power that authorizes the alienation of a fee to any alienee. [Black's *Law Dictionary*, 7th Ed.].

**General public.** The expression 'general public' ordinarily means all members of the public. The expression 'general public' in Art. 19(6) of the Constitution of India 1950, cannot, however, always be construed to mean all members of the public. The interest of a section of the public is included in the above term. [*Jugal Kishore* v *Labour Commissioner* AIR 1958 Pat 442: (1958)2 Lab LJ 234].

**General publication.** A distribution of copies not limited to a selected group, whether or not restrictions are placed on the use of the work. [Black's *Law Dictionary*, 8th Ed.].

**General rule.** A rule applicable to a class of cases or circumstances. [Black's *Law Dictionary*, 8th Ed.].

**General strike.** A total withdrawal of labour in a country by organised or general labour. Such a strike completely dislocates the economic life of an industrial society.

A strike organized to affect an entire industry. [Black's *Law Dictionary*, 7th Ed.].

**General usage.** A usage that prevails throughout a country or particular trade or profession; a usage that is not restricted to a local area. [Black's *Law Dictionary*, 7th Ed.].

**General warranty.** A covenant whereby the grantor agrees to defend the title to the premises transferred against all persons whatsoever as distinguished from a special warranty against persons claiming under the grantor.

A warranty against the claims of all persons. [Black's *Law Dictionary*, 8th Ed.].

**General welfare.** It connotes the public's health, peace, morals, and safety [Black's *Law Dictionary*, 7th Ed.].

**General words.** Such words of a descriptive character as are used in conveyances in order to convey, not only the specific property described but also all kinds of easements, privileges, and appurtenances which may possibly belong to the property conveyed. [Black's *Law Dictionary*, 5th Ed.].

Languages used in deeds to convey not only the specific property described in the conveyance but also all easements, privileges, and appurtenances that may belong to the property. [Black's *Law Dictionary*, 7th Ed.].

**Generalia specialibus non derogant.** General things do not derogate from special. Special Acts are not repealed by general Acts unless there be some express reference to the previous legislation or a necessary inconsistency in the two Acts standing together, which prevents the maxim from being applied. [*Harlow* v *Minister of Transport* (1951)2 KB 98].

The general maxim is, *generalia specialibus non derogant* i.e. general provisions will not abrogate special provisions. [*Gloucester (Bishop)* v *Cunnington* (1943) KB 101; *Wiltshire County Valuation Committee* v *Boyce* (1984)2 KB 125, 586]. "When the legislature has given its attention to a separate subject and made provision for it, the presumption is that a subsequent general enactment is not intended to interfere with the special provision unless it manifests that intention very clearly. Each enactment must be construed in that respect according to its own subject matter and its own terms. [*Barker* v *Edger* (1898) AC 748, 754 (PC); *Biharilal* v *Tamizul Haque* AIR 1988 Gau 1 (6-7)].

NOTE: This legal maxim is attracted ordinarily when there is a conflict between a special and a general statute and an argument of implied repeal is argued. The general rule to be followed in the case of conflict between two statutes is that the latter abrogates the earlier (*leges poseriores priores contratrias abrogant*). This principle carves out an exception out of that rule. A later general law will override a prior special law if the two enactments are so repugnant to each other that they cannot coexist even though no express provision in that behalf is found in the general law. It is only in the absence of an express provision to the contrary and of a clear inconsistency that a special law will remain wholly unaffected by a later general law. [*L.I.C. of India* v *D.J. Bahadur* (1981)1 SCR 1083]. When there is a conflict between a specific provision and the general provision, specific provision prevails over the general provision. The general provisions apply to only such cases which are not governed by the special provisions. The rule applies to resolve conflicts between different statutes as also in the same statute. [*J.K. Cotton Mills* v *State of U.P.* AIR 1961 SC 1170: (1961)3 SCR 185; *Damji Valij Shah* v *L.I.C.* AIR 1966 SC 135; *Union of India* v *India Fisheries* AIR 1966 SC 35; *Iswar Devi* v *Union of India* AIR 1969 Del 183].

The general rule to be followed in case of conflict between two statutes is that the later abrogates the earlier one. In other words, a prior special law would yield to a later general law if either of the two following conditions is satisfied: (*a*) the two laws are inconsistent with each other, (*b*) there is an express reference in the later to the earlier enactment. [*Ajoy Kumar* v *Union of India* AIR 1984 SC 1130: 1984 Lab IC 691: (1984)1 Lab LJ 368].

**Generation.** In one sense, it means a single degree or stage in the succession of persons in natural descent; the average time span between the birth of parents and the birth of their children; group of people born and living contemporaneously; all the people born at a particular time; a body of persons existing at the same time or period.

In another sense, it means the process, act or function of begetting or procreating; reproduction; production or origination by any process; a procreation; production by natural or artificial process.

**Generation to generation.** The phrase is usually used in sale deeds denoting absolutely and for ever.

NOTE: 'Putra-pautradi' conveys also the same meaning.

'Achandrarka Statiyal' is also another term meaning so long as the Sun and the Moon last, that is, for ever. [*Krishnendra Nath* v *Kusum Kamani* AIR 1923 Cal 351].

**Genuine.** Accurate; actual; authentic; original; not sham; pure-bred; real, true; unadulterated; unalloyed; uncoloured; uncounterfeited; undistorted; unimpeachable; unimitated.

The word 'genuine' means not spurious or counterfeit, or belonging to, derived from or descended from the original source of stock; authentic, typical, pure. [*Beharilal* v *Jagarnath Prasad* AIR 1959 Pat 490].

As applied to notes, bonds, and other written instruments, this term means that they are truly what they purport to be, and that they are not false, forged, fictitious, simulated, spurious, or counterfeit.

**Genus.** A general class comprising several species. In logic, it connotes a quality which is common to a whole class, all the members of which are differentiated by that quality from any other class.

In the civil law, It means a general class or division, comprising several species; a man's lineage, or direct descendants.

**Gestation.** The time during which a woman carries a foetus in her womb, from conception to birth. But, as used in medical authorities, this phrase does not mean the actual number of days from conception to birth. [*Dazey* v *Dazey* 122 P 2d 308, 309].

**Gestio pro haerede.** Behaviour as heir. Conduct by which the heir renders himself liable for his ancestor's debts, as by taking possession of title deeds, receiving rents etc. [Rawson's *Pocket Law Lexicon*].

**Ghat.** The word 'ghat' ordinarily means a flight of steps made of wood, brick, stone, iron, etc., for the access to the water of the tank or river. It also means the bank of the river or tank where people ordinarily bathe or where boats are moored for the purpose of a ferry or for loading or unloading goods. The word does not include a tract of land used as a burning ground. [*Chairman of the Howrah Municipality* v *Khetra Krishna* ILR 33 Cal 1290: 10 CWN 1044].

**Ghatwal.** A ferry-man; a person in charge of a landing place or mountain pass.

> NOTE: Lands were granted either rent-free or at a low rate of rent to these people by Mahomedan Government and the tenures were known as ghatawali tenures.

**Ghatwali tenure.** These tenures were created by Mahomedan Government, so that the tenant may provide police and military force to guard the mountain passes from the invasions of lawless tribes. Grants were made either at low rent or at no rent at all. In Santhal Parganas there were three classes of Ghatwali tenures—(*a*) Government ghatwalis, *i.e.*, created by the ruling power, (*b*) Government ghatwalis included in a zamindari estate, and (*c*) zamindari ghatwalis, *i.e.*, created by a zamindar. [*Thakur Rudreshwari Prasad* v *Rani Prabhabati* 1952 SCR 64: AIR 1952 SC 1].

**Gherao.** Coercion of employers, by which their workers prevent them from leaving the premises until certain demands are met. [*Concise Oxford Dictionary*, 9th Ed.].

Primarily the word means an encirclement in the sense of blockade. It may be a complete encirclement or a partial encirclement intended to blockade the egress or ingress from or to a particular office, workshop, factory or even residence. The second kind of *gherao* is an encirclement in depth, that is to say, a virtual occupation of the target to be *gheraoed* resulting in the prevention of ingress by the management or its staff. Between the two meanings there are a number of shades. The blockade is invariably accompanied by wrongful restraint and/or wrongful confinement and occasionally assault, criminal trespass, mischief to person and property, unlawful assembly and various other criminal offences. [*Jay Engineering Works Ltd.* v *State of West Bengal* AIR 1968 Cal 407: 72 CWN 441].

**Gift.** A voluntary transfer of property to another made gratuitously and without consideration. [*Bradley* v *Bradley* Tex Civ App, 540 SW 2d 504, 511].

A gift is commonly defined as a voluntary transfer of property by one to another, without any consideration or compensation therefor. Any piece of property which is voluntarily transferred by one person to another without compensation or consideration. A gift is a gratuity, and an act of generosity, and not only does not require a consideration, but there can be none; if there is a consideration for the transaction it is not a gift. [*Km. Sonia Bhatia* v *State of U.P.* AIR 1981 SC 1274: (1981)2 SCC 585: (1981)3 SCR 239].

> NOTE: The concept of gift is diametrically opposed to the presence of any consideration or compensation. A gift has aptly been described as a gratuity and an act of generosity and stress has been laid on the fact that if there is any consideration then the transaction ceases to be a gift. [*Km. Sonia Bhatia* v *State of U.P.* AIR 1981 SC 1274: (1981)2 SCC 585: (1981)3 SCR 239].

▸*Meaning under the Gift Tax Act 1958, s. 2(xii) (since repealed).* Gift means the transfer by one person to another of any existing movable or immovable property made voluntarily and without consideration in money or money's worth, and includes the transfer of any property deemed to be a gift.

In tax law, a payment is a gift if it is made without conditions, from detached and disinterested generosity, out of affection, respect, charity or like impulses, and not from the constraining force of any moral or legal duty or from the incentive of anticipated benefits of an economic nature.

▸ *Meaning under the Transfer of Property Act 1882, s. 122.* A gift is a transfer of certain existing movable or immovable property made voluntarily and without consideration, by one person, called the donor to another, called the donee, and accepted by or on behalf of the donee.

NOTE: *Requisites of gift.* Essential requisites of "gift" are capacity of donor, intention of donor to make gift, completed delivery to or for donee, and acceptance of gift by donee.

**Gift causa mortis.** A gift of personal property made in expectation of donor's death and on condition that the donor dies as anticipated. [*Antos* v *Bocek* 452 P 2d 533, 534].

NOTE: *Conditions of gift causa mortis.* A "gift *causa mortis*" is effected only if the following conditions are met:

The donor must be stricken with some disorder which makes death imminent, death of donor must ensue as a result of the disorder existing at time the gift was made without any intervening perfect recovery; gift must have been made to take effect only in the event of donor's death by his existing disorder, and there must have been an actual delivery of the subject of the donation to the donee. [*In re Vardalos' Estate* 320 NE 2d 568, 571].

**Gift in contemplation of death.** A gift by a donor immediately before his death while he has knowledge of his impending death.

▸ *Meaning under the Indian Succession Act 1925, s. 191.* A gift is said to be made in contemplation of death where a man, who is ill and expects to die shortly of his illness, delivers to another the possession of any movable property to keep as a gift in case the donor shall die of that illness. Such a gift may be resumed by the giver, and shall not take effect if he recovers from the illness during which it was made, nor if he survives the person to whom it was made.

**Gift inter vivos.** Gifts between the living, which are perfected and become absolute during life time of donor and donee [*Neal* v *Neal* 106 SW 2d 595, 600]; an immediate voluntary, and gratuitous transfer of personalty by one to another. [*Tilton* v *Mullen* 137 NE 2d 125, 128, 130].

NOTE: *Essentials of inter vivos gift.* The essentials of an *inter vivos* gift are: (*i*) donative intention; (*ii*) delivery to donee; in the case of a chose in action not capable of delivery, the donor must during his lifetime strip himself of all dominion over the thing taken; (*iii*) acceptance by donee. [*In re Posey's Estate* 214 A 2d 713, 719].

**Gift testamentary.** Testamentary gift is voluntary transfer of property to take effect upon the death of donor.

**Gilt-edged securities.** These are investments usually carrying a fixed rate of interest, which are considered to have a very low risk of non-payment of interest or redemption moneys when due, *e.g.*, Government Stocks. [Osborn & Grandage's *Concise Commercial Dictionary*].

**Girl.** A female child or youth; a young unmarried woman.

▸ *Meaning under the Suppression of Immoral Traffic in Woman and Girls Act 1956, s. 2(b) (since repealed).* Girl means a female who has not completed the age of twenty-one. [*State of U.P.* v *Kaushailiya* AIR 1964 SC 416: (1964)4 SCR 1002: (1964)1 Cr LJ 304].

• **Bachelor girl** p. 90.

**Glassware.** The dictionary meaning of the expression "glassware" is "articles made of glass". [*Indo International Industries* v *Commissioner of Sales Tax, Uttar Pradesh* AIR 1981 SC 1079: (1981)2 SCC 528: (1981)3 SCR 294: (1981)47 STC 359: (1981)8 ELT 325].

Ware or articles of merchandise or those manufactured or made of glass. Lenses and object glasses used in manufacture of theodolites are glassware. [*P. Orr & Sons* v *Collector of Customs* AIR 1965 Mad 312: (1965)1 MLJ 279].

NOTE: *Glassware—which is not.* In commercial sense, glassware would never comprise articles like clinical syringes, thermometers, lactometers and the like which have specialised significance and utility. [*Indo International Industries* v *Commissioner of Sales Tax, Uttar Pradesh* AIR 1981 SC 1079: (1981)2 SCC 528: (1981)3 SCR 294: (1981)2 SCJ 135: (1981)47 STC 359: 1981 Tax LR 2693: (1981)8 ELT 325].

**Glossary.** Explanations of technical or obsolete terms; a partial dictionary.

**Gnati.** *Gnati* includes *sagotra sapinda* relation and not material relations. [*Chandrappa* v *Gyanamma* AIR 1953 Hyd 275].

**Go slow tactics.** 'Go slow' is a picturesque description of deliberate delaying of production by workmen pretending to be engaged in the factory and is a pernicious practice sometimes adopted by discontented workmen. It is considered as a serious type of misconduct. [*Bharat Sugar Mills* v *Jai Singh* AIR 1961 SC 1183: (1962)3 SCR 684].

**Going concern.** Means a business in actual operation and working order, in which the transfer of ownership would affect no interruption of business.

**Gold.** A yellow metal, the chemical element of atomic number 79, used in jewellery and decoration and as a monetary medium.

▸*Meaning under the Foreign Exchange Regulation Act 1947, s. 2(f) (since repealed).* 'Gold' includes gold in the form of coin, whether legal tender or not, or in the form of bullion or ingot, whether refined or not and jewellery or articles made wholly or mainly of gold.

▸*Meaning under the Gold (Control) Act 1968, s. 2(j).* 'Gold' means gold, including its alloy (whether virgin, melted or remelted, wrought or unwrought), in any shape or form, of a purity of not less than nine carats and includes primary gold, article and ornament.

▸*Meaning under the Gold Control Rules 1963.* The word "gold" is defined in cl. (*c*) of the Explanation to r. 126A to mean gold, including its alloy, whether virgin, melted, remelted, wrought or unwrought, in any shape or form, of a purity of not less than nine carats and includes any gold coin (whether legal tender or not), any ornament and any other article of gold. This definition does not restrict the meaning of the word 'gold' to legal or non-smuggled gold. It is wide enough to include any kind of gold, whether smuggled or non-smuggled. [*Triveni Prasad Ramkaran Verma* v *State of Maharashtra* AIR 1976 SC 2156: 1976 Cr LJ 1707: (1977)1 SCC 114: (1977)1 SCR 519: 1977 SCC (Cri) 38].

**Gold bond.** One payable in gold coin or its equivalent, which means any money acceptable to the government in payment of debts due to it.

**Gold clause.** This is a provision in an international contract, relating to payment, inserted with the object of rendering the contract immune from any currency regulations or depreciation which may affect the contract while it is in force.

A provision calling for payment in gold. [Black's *Law Dictionary*, 8th Ed.].

Provision formerly found in contracts, bonds and mortgages calling for payment in gold. [*Norman* v *Baltimore & Ohio R. Co.* 294 US 240].

**Gold reserves.** That part of a country's total reserves for its currency which is represented by holdings of gold.

**Gold standard.** A monetary system in which every form of currency is convertible on demand into its legal equivalent in gold or gold coin. [Black's *Law Dictionary*, 5th Ed.].

A country is said to be on the gold standard when—(*i*) its Central Bank buys and sells gold at fixed prices; (*ii*) movement of gold into and out of the country is unrestricted; and (*iii*) the unit of currency is based on a given weight of gold of a given fineness.

**Golden handsake.** An employee-dismissal that includes generous compensation. [Black's *Law Dictionary*, 7th Ed.].

**Golden rule.** The cardinal rule applied by the Judges is that the intent of the legislature is to be sought in the actual words used and they are to be understood in their ordinary and natural meaning. And this is known as the "grammatical interpretation" or the "literal rule". But sometimes it leads to absurdity and the "golden rule" comes in to remove it. This rule is a departure from the literal meaning. As observed by Lord Reid in *Luke* v *Inland Revenue Commissioners* (1963) AC 557, 577: "To achieve the obvious intention and to produce a reasonable result, we must do some violence to the words". "The 'golden' rule ...... allows for a departure from the literal rule when the application of the statutory words in the ordinary sense would be repugnant to or inconsistent with some other provision in the statute or even when it would lead to what the court considers to be an absurdity. The usual consequence of applying the golden rule is that words which are in the statute are ignored or words which are not there are read in. The scope of the golden rule is debatable, particularly so far as the meaning of an 'absurdity' is concerned". [Rupert Gross: *Statutory Interpretation*, p. 14 (1976)].

**Good consideration.** A consideration founded on relationship or natural love and affection. It is not a valuable consideration, and will not 'sustain a promise', i.e. whereas in certain cases a consideration is necessary to give legal validity to a promise, so that an action may be brought for breach of the same, a merely 'good' consideration will not be sufficient for this purpose. [Mozley & Whiteley's *Law Dictionary*, 10th Ed.].

Consideration based on natural love or affection or on moral duty; loosely, valuable consideration; consideration that is adequate to support the bargained-for exchange between the parties. [Black's *Law Dictionary*, 8th Ed.].

"A good consideration is that of blood, or the natural love and affection which a person has to his children, or any of his relatives ...... A good consideration is not of itself sufficient to support a promise, any more than the moral obligation which arises from a man's passing his word; neither will the two together make a binding contract; thus a promise by a father to make a gift to his child will not be enforced against him. The consideration of natural love and affection is indeed good for so little in law, that it is not easy to see why it should be called a good consideration ......" [Joshua Williams: *Principles of the Law of Personal Property*, pp. 95-96 (11th Ed. 1881)].

"Stated simply, good or meritorious consideration is nothing more than motive or moral obligation". [Richard A. Lord, Williston on *Contracts*, pp. 325-26 (4th Ed. 1992)].

**Good faith.** A state of mind consisting in—(1) honesty in belief or purpose, (2) faithfulness to one's duty or obligation, (3) observance of reasonable commercial standards of fair dealing in a given trade or business, or (4) absence of intent to defraud or to seek unconscionable advantage. [Black's *Law Dictionary*, 8th Ed.].

Good faith is an intangible and abstract quality with no technical meaning or statutory definition, and it encompasses, among other things, an honest belief, the absence of malice and the absence of design to defraud or to seek an unconscionable advantage, and an individual's personal good faith is concept of his own mind and inner spirit and, therefore, may not conclusively be determined by his protestations alone. [*Doyle* v *Gordon* 158 NYS 2d 248, 259, 260].

Good faith imports the exercise of due care and attention. A person can be excused for having committed an error of judgment only if he exercised due care and attention, and his conduct makes it clear that there was no negligence according to reasonable standards. [*Kedarnath* v *State* AIR 1965 All 233].

Good faith contemplates an honest effort to ascertain the truth of the facts. [*Chandrasekhar Pillai* v *Karthikeyam* AIR 1964 Ker 277].

Honest intention free from taint of fraud or fraudulent resign is a constant element of the connotation of good faith. [*Brijendra Singh* v *State of U.P.* AIR 1981 SC 636: (1981)1 SCC 597: (1981)2 SCR 287: (1981)2 SCJ 170].

▸ *Meaning under the Limitation Act 1963, s. 2(h).* Nothing shall be deemed to be done in good faith which is not done with due care and attention.

NOTE: Section 14, Limitation Act provides for exclusion of time of proceeding *bona fide* in court without jurisdiction. In computing the period of limitation for any suit the time during which the plaintiff has been prosecuting with due diligence another civil proceedings against the defendant shall be excluded where the proceeding relates to the same matter in issue and is prosecuted in a good faith in a court which from a defect of jurisdiction is unable to entertain it. The expression "good faith" qualifies prosecuting the proceeding in the court which ultimately is found to have no jurisdiction. Failure to pay the requisite court fee found deficient on a contention being raised or the error of judgment in valuing a suit filed before a court which was ultimately found to have no jurisdiction has absolutely nothing to do with the question of good faith. [*Vijay Kumar Rampal* v *Diwan Devi* AIR 1985 SC 1669].

▸ *Meaning under the General Clauses Act 1897, s. 3(22).* A thing shall be deemed to be done in "good faith" where it is in fact done honestly, whether it is done negligently or not.

▸ *Meaning under the Indian Penal Code 1860, s. 52.* Nothing is said to be done or believed in good faith which is done or believed without due care and attention.

NOTE: 'Good faith' is defined in a negative fashion by s. 52, Indian Penal Code. The insistence is upon the exercise of due care and attention. Recklessness and negligence are ruled out by the very nature of the definition. The standard of care and attention must depend on the circumstances of the individual case, the nature of the imputation, the need and the opportunity for verification, the situation and context in which the imputation was made, the position of the person making the imputation and a variety of other factors. Good faith, therefore, is a matter for evidence. It is a question of fact to be decided on the particular facts and circumstances of each case. [*Sewakram Sobhani* v *R.K. Karanjia, Chief Editor, Weekly Blitz* AIR 1981 SC 1514: (1981)3 SCR 627: 1981 Cr LR (SC) 397: 1981 Cr LJ 894: 1981 SCC (Cri) 698: (1981)3 SCC 208].

The definition of the term in the General Clauses Act lays stress on the one aspect of honesty only irrespective of negligence, but in the Indian Penal Code stress is laid on two aspects, *viz.*, honesty of intention along with due care and attention. Both the definitions retain the real essence of good faith, which is honesty. Good faith precludes pretence, deceit or lack of fairness and uprightness as also wanton or wilful negligence. [*Kailas Sizing Works* v *Municipality of Bhivandi and Nizampur* AIR 1969 Bom 127].

**Good health.** A state of reasonable healthiness; a state of health free from serious disease. [Black's *Law Dictionary*, 8th Ed.].

**Good moral character.** Good moral character is a pattern of behaviour that is consistent with the community's current ethical standards and that shows an absence of deceit or morally reprehensible conduct.

**Good title.** Good title means nothing but a title free from reasonable doubt.

One free from reasonable doubt, that is, not only a valid title in fact, but one that can again be sold to a reasonable purchaser or mortgaged to a person of reasonable prudence. [*MacGowan* v *Gaines* 253 A 2d 121, 123].

A title that is legally valid or effective. [Black's *Law Dictionary*, 8th Ed.].

**Goods.** Articles of commerce; chattels; commodities; consumer durables; materials; produce; products; staples; things for sale.

A term of variable content and meaning. It may include every species of personal property or it may be given a very restricted meaning. [Black's *Law Dictionary*, 5th Ed.].

Tangible or movable personal property other than money; esp., articles of trade or items of merchandise; things that have value, whether tangible or not. [Black's *Law Dictionary*, 8th Ed.].

▸ *Meaning under the Banking Regulation Act 1949, s. 8, Explanation.* 'Goods' means every kind of movable property other than actionable claims, stocks, shares, money, bullion and specie and all instruments referred to in clause (*a*) of sub-section (1) of section 6.

▸ *Meaning under the Central Excise and Salt Act 1944.* To become "goods" an article must be something which can ordinarily come to the market to be bought or sold. [*Union of India* v *Delhi Cloth and General Mills Co. Ltd.* AIR 1963 SC 791: 1963 Supp (1) SCR 586: 1977 ELT (J 199)].

▸ *Meaning under the Central Sales Tax Act 1956, s 2(d).* 'Goods' includes all materials, articles, commodities and all other kinds of movable property, but does not include newspapers, actionable claims, stocks, shares and securities.

▸ *Meaning under the Customs Act 1962, s. 2(22).* 'Goods' includes—(*a*) vessels, aircrafts and vehicles; (*b*) stores; (*c*) baggage; (*d*) currency and negotiable instruments; and (*e*) any other kind of movable property.

The definition of "goods" in s. 2(22) includes a vessel, aircraft or vehicle. [*Chowgule and Co. Pvt. Ltd.* v *Union of India* AIR 1987 SC 1176: (1987)1 SCC 730: (1987)2 SCR 351: JT 1987(1) SC 496: (1987)28 ELT 39].

▸ *Meaning under the Emergency Risks (Goods) Insurance Act 1971, s. 2(d).* 'Goods' means any materials, commodities or articles and includes materials, commodities or articles used in or for the construction or repair of any ship up to the time at which the ship after completion of construction or repair is launched.

▸ *Meaning under the Forward Contracts (Regulation) Act 1952, s. 2(d).* 'Goods' means every kind of movable property other than actionable claims, money and securities.

▸ *Meaning under the Railways Act 1989, s. 2(19).* 'Goods' includes—(*i*) containers, pallets or similar articles of transport used to consolidate goods; and (*ii*) animals.

▸ *Meaning under the M.P. General Sales Tax Act 1958.* "Goods" means all kinds of movable property other than actionable claims, newspapers, stock, shares, securities or Government stamps and includes all materials, articles and commodities whether or not to be used in the construction, fitting out, improvement or repair of movable or immovable property; and also includes all growing crops, grass, trees, plants and things attached to or forming part of the land which are agreed to be severed before sale or under the contract of sale. [*State of Madhya Pradesh* v *Orient Paper Mills Ltd.* AIR 1977 SC 687: (1977)2 SCR 149: (1977)2 SCC 77: (1977)40 STC 603].

▸ *Meaning under the Major Port Trusts Act 1963, s. 2(h).* 'Goods' includes livestock and every kind of movable property.

▸ *Meaning under the Competition Act 2002, s. 2(i).* 'Goods' means goods as defined in the Sale of Goods Act 1930 and includes: (*a*) products manufactured, processed or mined; (*b*) debentures, stocks and shares after allotment; (*c*) in relation to goods supplied, distributed or controlled in India, goods imported into India.

▸ *Meaning under the Naval and Aircraft Prize Act 1971, s. 2(d).* 'Goods' includes all such things as may be subject to adjudication as prize, but in the case of a naval prize does not include any aircraft or boat, unless the aircraft or boat is a part of the cargo of a ship.

▸ *Meaning under the Orissa Sales Tax Act and the Sale of Goods Act.* Under both the definitions in s. 2(*d*) of the Orissa Sales Tax Act and s. 2(7) of the Sale of Goods Act, the term "goods" means all kinds of movable property (except those specifically excluded) and includes growing crops, grass and things attached to or forming part of the land which are agreed to be severed before sale or under the contract of sale. [*State of Orissa* v *Titaghur Paper*

*Mills Company Limited* AIR 1985 SC 1293: (1985)3 SCR 26: 1985 (Supp) SCC 280: (1985)60 STC 213].

- *Meaning under the Sale of Goods Act 1930, s. 2(7)*. 'Goods' means every kind of movable property other than actionable claims and money, and includes stock and shares, growing crops, grass and things attached to or forming part of the land which are agreed to be severed before sale or under the contract of sale.

- *Meaning under the State Bank of India Act 1955, s. 2(c)*. 'Goods' includes bullion, wares and merchandise.

- *Meaning under the Supply and Prices of Goods Act 1950, s. 2(b)*. 'Goods' means goods to which this Act applies.

- *Meaning under the Trade Marks Act 1999, s. 2(j)*. 'Goods' means anything which is the subject of trade or manufacture.

NOTE: *Examples of goods*:

- Computer programmes are the product of an intellectual process, but once implanted in a medium those are widely distributed to computer owners. Once in the form of a floppy disc or other medium, the programmes may be tailored for specific purpose and it takes status in "goods". [*Associated Cement Companies Ltd*. v *Commissioner of Customs* AIR 2001 SC 862: (2001)4 SCC 593: JT 2001(2) SC 141: (2001)128 ELT 21].
- The music is produced by the artistry of musicians and is itself not "goods", but when transferred to a later-readable disc becomes a readily merchantable commodity. [*Associated Cement Companies Ltd*. v *Commissioner of Customs* AIR 2001 SC 862: (2001)4 SCC 593: JT 2001(2) SC 141: (2001)128 ELT 21].
- Electric energy is "goods" within the meaning of C.P. Berar Sales Tax Act 1947 and Madhya Pradesh General Sales Tax Act 1959. It can be transmitted, transferred, delivered, stored, possessed in the same way as any other movable property. If there can be sale and purchase of electric energy, then it is intended to be covered by the definition of "goods" in the two Acts. [*Commissioner of Sales Tax, Indore, Madhya Pradesh* v *Madhya Pradesh Electricity Board, Jabalpur* (1969)2 SCR 939: (1969)1 SCC 200: AIR 1970 SC 732: (1970)25 STC 188].
- Timber is "goods" within the meaning of s. 2(7) of the Sale of Goods Act and the expression "sale of goods" in the Constitution of India, in Entry 54, List II, having the same meaning as that expression has in the Sale of Goods Act, sale of timber agreed to be severed under the terms of the contract may be regarded as sale of goods. [*State of Maharashtra* v *Champalal Kishanlal Mohota* AIR 1971 SC 908: (1970)1 SCC 611: (1971)1 SCR 46: (1971)27 STC 116].
- When a professor delivers a lecture, it is not goods but, when transcribed as a book, it becomes goods. [*Associated Cement Companies Ltd*. v *Commissioner of Customs* AIR 2001 SC 862: (2001)4 SCC 593: JT 2001(2) SC 141: (2001)128 ELT 21].


- **Abandonment of goods** p. 3.
- **Bill of goods** p. 104.
- **Bonded goods** p. 108.
- **Capital goods** p. 123.
- **Confusion of goods** p. 173.
- **Contract of sale of goods** p. 191.
- **Conversion of goods** p. 194.
- **Document of title to goods** p. 277.
- **Dutiable goods** p. 287.
- **Electrical goods** p. 297.
- **Export goods** p. 332.
- **Finder of goods** p. 354.
- **Future goods** p. 379.
- **Heavy goods vehicle** p. 410.
- **Hosiery goods** p. 421.
- **Imported goods** p. 434.
- **Industrial goods** p. 453.
- **Perishable goods** p. 654.
- **Prohibited goods** p. 696.
- **Sale of goods** p. 771.
- **Slander of goods** p. 800.
- **Smuggled goods** p. 801
- **Specific goods** p. 805.
- **Warehoused goods** p. 892.


**Goodwill.** A business's reputation, patronage, and other intangible assets that are considered when appraising the business, especially for purchase; the ability to earn income in excess of the income that would be expected from the business viewed as a mere collection of assets. [Black's *Law Dictionary*, 8th Ed.].

The advantage or benefit which is acquired by a business, beyond the mere value of the capital, stock, funds or property employed therein, in consequence of the general public patronage and encouragement which it receives from consent or habitual customers. [Wharton's *Law Lexicon*].

The goodwill of a business is an intangible asset being the whole advantage of the reputation and connection formed with the customers together with the circumstances which make the connections durable. It is that competent of the total value of the undertaking which is attributable to the ability of the concern to earn profits over a course of years because of its reputation, location and other features. [*Khushlal Khengar Shah* v *Khorshedbanu* AIR 1970 SC 1147].

In its legal sense, the word 'goodwill' means every affirmative advantage as contrasted with negative advantage that has been acquired in carrying on the business, whether connected with the premises or its name or style and everything connected with or carrying with it, the benefit of the business. It includes the whole advantage of the reputation and connections of the firm or the owner which may have been built up by years of hard work, or gained by lavish expenditure, beyond the mere value of the capital stock and property embarked in the business, in consequence of the general public patronage and encouragement, which is received from species of connections in trade. [*State of Rajasthan* v *Bundi Electric Supply Co.* AIR 1970 Raj 36; *Daulaldas* v *Ganeshdas* AIR 1957 Cal 280].

"Goodwill" denotes the benefit arising from connection and reputation. The original definition by Lord Eldon in *Cruttwell* v *Lye* [(1810)17 Ves 335] that goodwill was nothing more than "the probability that the old customers would resort to the old places" was expanded by Wood, V.C. in *Churton* v *Douglas* [(1859) John 174] to encompass every positive advantage "that has been acquired by the old firm in carrying on its business, whether connected with the premises in which the business was previously carried on or with the name of the firm, or with any other matter carrying with it the benefit of the business". In *Trego* v *Hunt* [(1896) AC 7], Lord Herschell described goodwill as a connection which tended to become permanent because of habit or otherwise. The benefit to the business varies with the nature of the business and also from one business to another. No business commenced for the first time possesses goodwill from the start. It is generated as the business is carried on and may be augmented with the passage of time. Lawson in his *Introduction to the Law of the Property* describes it as property of a highly peculiar kind. In *C.I.T., West Bengal (III)* v *Chunilal Prabhudas & Co.* [AIR 1971 Cal 70: (1970)76 ITR 566], the Calcutta High Court reviewed different approaches to the concept. It has been horticulturally and botanically viewed as "a seed sprouting" or an "acorn growing into the mighty oak of goodwill". It has been geographically described by locality. It has been historically explained as growing and crystallising traditions in the business. It has been described in terms of a magnet as the "attracting force". In terms of comparative dynamics, goodwill has been described as the "differential return of profit". Philosophically it has been held to be intangible. Though immaterial, it is materially valued. Physically and psychologically, it is a "habit" and sociologically it is a "custom". Biologically, it has been described by Lord Macnaghten in *Trego* v *Hunt* [(1896) AC 7] as the "sap and life" of the business. Architecturally, it has been described as the "cement" binding together the business and its assets as a whole and a going and developing concern. A variety of elements goes to its making, and its composition varies in different trades and in different business in the same trade, and while one element may preponderate in one business, another may dominate in another business. And yet because of its intangible nature, it remains insubstantial in form and nebulous in character. [*C.I.T., Bangalore* v *B.C. Srinivasa Setty* AIR 1981 SC 972: (1981)2 SCR 938: (1981)128 ITR 294: (1981)2 SCC 460].

**Goonda.** A dangerous and desperate person. [*Ravinder Kumar* v *District Magistrate* AIR 1960 Punj 332: 1963 Cr LJ 981].

**Gotra.** Family lineage, relationship by descent from a common ancestor of the same name. [*Puddo Kumaree* v *Juggat Kishore* ILR 5 Cal 615].

**Gotraja sapinda.** *Gotraja sapinda* is a *sapinda* belonging to the same *gotra*.

**Government.** The structure of principles and rules determining how a state or organization is regulated; the sovereign power in a nation or state; an organization through which a body of people exercise political authority; the machinery by which sovereign power is expressed. [Black's *Law Dictionary*, 7th Ed.].

From the legal point of view, government may be described as the exercise of certain powers and the performance of certain duties by public authorities or officers, together with certain private persons or corporations exercising public functions. The structure of the machinery of government, and the regulation of the powers and duties which belong to different parts of this structure, are defined by the law, which also prescribes, to some extent, the mode in which these powers are to be exercised or those duties are to be performed. Government generally connotes three estates, namely, the Legislature, the Executive and the Judiciary. In a narrow sense it connotes executive only. [Halsbury's *Laws of England*, 3rd Ed., vol. 7, p. 187; *State of U.P.* v *Nemchandra Jain* (1984)2 SCC 405].

▸*Meaning under the Administrator-General's Act 1913, s. 2(3); Official Trustees Act 1913, s. 3(1).* 'Government' or 'the Government' means in relation to any State, the State Government and in relation to any Union territory, the Central Government.

▸*Meaning under the Code of Civil Procedure 1908, Or. 27, r. 8B.* Government means—(*a*) in relation to any suit by or against the Central Government or against a pubic officer in the service of that Government, the Central Government, and (*b*) in relation to any suit by or against a State Government or against a public officer in the service of a State, the State Government.

▸*Meaning under the Constitution of India.* "Government" includes Legislative, Executive and Judiciary. [*Pashupati Nath Sukul* v *Nem Chandra Jain* AIR 1984 SC 399: (1984)2 SCC 404: (1984)1 SCR 939].

▸*Meaning under the Dock Workers (Regulation of Employment) Act 1948, s. 2(d).* 'Government' means in relation to any major port, the Central Government and in relation to any other port, the State Government.

▸*Meaning under the General Clauses Act 1897, s. 3(23).* 'Government' or 'the Government' shall include both the Central Government and any State Government.

▸*Meaning under the Indian Penal Code 1860, s. 17.* 'Government' denotes the Central Government or the Government of a State.

▸*Meaning under the Indian Ports Act 1908, s. 3(9).* 'Government' as respects major ports, for all purposes, and as respects other ports for the purposes of making rules under cl. (*p*) of s. 6(1) and of the appointment and control of port health officers under s. 17, means the Central Government, and save as aforesaid, means the State Government.

▸*Meaning under the Indian Securities Act 1920, s. 2(c).* The 'Government' or 'Government' in relation to any loan or security means the Government raising the loan or issuing the security.

▸*Meaning under the National Human Rights Commission Chairperson and Members (Salaries, Allowances and Other Condition of Service) Rules 1993.* The expression "Government" used in proviso to r. 3(*b*) has to be construed in the wider sense and the services rendered by a Judge or Chief Justice of a High Court must be held to be a service in connection with the affairs of the Union and as such the proviso to r. 3(*b*) to the Rules would govern the case of such retired Judge or Chief Justice. [*V.S. Mallimath* v *Union of India* AIR 2001 SC 1455: JT 2001(4) SC 1: 2001(3) SLT 130].

▸*Meaning under the Prevention of Corruption Act 1947.* The expression 'Government' in s. 21(12)(*a*) clearly denotes the Executive and not the Legislature. [*R.S. Nayak* v *A.R. Antulay* AIR 1984 SC 684: (1984)2 SCR 495: (1984)2 SCC 183: 1984 Cr LJ 613: 1984 SCC (Cri) 172: 1984(1) SLR 619].

▸*Meaning under the Public Debt Act 1944, s. 2(1A).* 'Government' in relation to any Government security means the Central or State Government issuing the security.


- **Central Government** p. 131.
- **Industry carried on under the authority of the Central Government** p. 455.
- **Local Government** p. 540.
- **Military Government** p. 578.
- **Servant of Government** p. 787.


**Government company.** 'Government company' means any company in which not less than fifty-one per cent of the paid-up share capital is held by the Central Government, or by any State Government or Governments, or partly by the Central Government and partly by one or more State Governments and includes a company which is a subsidiary of a Government company as thus defined. [Companies Act 1956, s. 617].

**Government Pleader.** Any Pleader appointed by the Government to represent it in court in matters connected to any suit by or against the Government.

▸*Meaning under the Code of Civil Procedure 1908, s. 2(7).* 'Government Pleader' includes any officer appointed by the State Government to perform all or any of the functions expressly imposed by the Code of Civil Procedure on the Government Pleader and also any Pleader acting under the directions of the Government Pleader.

▸*Meaning under the Code of Civil Procedure 1908, Or. 27, r. 8B.* 'Government Pleader' means—(*a*) in relation to any suit by or against the Central Government or against a public officer in the service of that Government, such pleader as that Government may appoint either generally or specially for the purpose of Or. 27, C.P. Code; (*b*) in relation to any suit by or against the State Government or against a public officer in the service of a State, the Government Pleader as defined in cl. (7) of s. 2 of the C.P. Code or such other pleader as the State Government may appoint, whether generally or specially, for the purpose of Or. 27, C.P. Code.

**Government premises.** Any premises belonging to, or taken on lease or requisitioned by, the Central Government. [Government Premises (Eviction) Act 1950, s. 2(*b*)].

**Government Provident Fund.** A provident fund, other than a Railway Provident Fund, constituted by the authority of the Secretary of State, the Central Government, the Crown Representative or any State Government for any class or classes of persons in the service of the Government or of persons employed in educational institutions, or employed by bodies existing solely for educational purposes. [Provident Funds Act 1925, s. 2(*d*)].

**Government security.** A security issued by a government, a government agency, or a government corporation. [Black's *Law Dictionary*, 7th Ed.].

Any security issued or guaranteed as to principal or interest by the government or by a person controlled or supervised by and acting as an instrumentality of the government pursuant to authority granted by the government.

▸*Meaning under the General Clauses Act 1897, s. 3(24).* Securities of the Central Government or of any State Government, but in any Act or Regulation made before the commencement of the Constitution shall not include securities of the Government of any Part B State.

▸ *Meaning under the Indian Securities Act 1920, s. 2(a).* 'Government security' means promissory notes (including treasury bills), stock-certificates, bearer bonds and all other securities issued by the Central Government at any time or by the Government of any Part A State before 1st November 1956, or by a State Government on or after that date in respect of any loan contracted either before or after the passing of this Act, but does not include a currency note.

▸ *Meaning under the Public Debt Act 1944, s. 2(2); Forward Contracts (Regulation) Act 1952, s. 2(e); Insurance Act 1938, s. 2(7).* 'Government security' means—(*a*) a security created and issued by the Government for the purpose of raising a public loan and having one of the following forms, namely:—(*i*) stock transferable by registration in the books of the Bank; or (*ii*) a promissory note payable to order; or (*iii*) a bearer bond payable to bearers; or (*iv*) a form prescribed in this behalf; (*b*) any other security created and issued by the Government in such form and for such of the purposes as may be prescribed.

▸ *Meaning under the Securities Contracts (Regulation) Act 1956, s. 2(b).* 'Government security' means a security created and issued, whether before or after the commencement of this Act by the Central Government or a State Government for the purpose of raising a public loan and having one of the forms specified in cl. (2) of s. 2 of the Public Debt Act 1944.

**Government servant.** The words 'servant of Government' denote any officer or servant continued, appointed or employed in India by or under the authority of Government. [Indian Penal Code 1860, s. 14].

NOTE: A person does not cease to be a Government servant simply because he is sent to other body or institution to be paid by them. [*State of Gujarat* v *Ramanlal Keshavlal* (1983)2 SCC 33, 52: 1983 Lab IC 391: 1983 SCC (L&S) 231].

So far the Government servants or the employees of those concerns which are instrumentalities under the state answering Art. 12 of the Constitution of India are concerned their position cannot be equated to that of an employee of a private employer. The relationship is not contractual. Nor they are governed by ordinary master and servant relationship. Once appointed to his post or office the Government servant acquires a status. His rights and obligations are no longer determined by consent of both parties, but by statute or Statutory Rules which may be framed or altered unilaterally by the Government. The legal position of a Government servant is more of a status than a contract. [*Roshanlal* v *Union of India* AIR 1967 SC 1889, 1894].

A Government servant whose appointment though originates in contract, acquires a status and is governed by his Service Rules and not by the terms of contract. [*Union of India* v *Arun Kumar Roy* AIR 1986 SC 737].

Staff artistes of Doordarshan are Government servants just like staff artistes of All India Radio, although initially their appointments were made on contract. [*V.K. Mehta* v *Union of India* AIR 1988 SC 1970].

**Government undertaking.** 'Government undertaking' means any industrial undertaking carried on—(*i*) by a department of the Government, or (*ii*) by a corporation established by a Central, Provincial or State Act, which is owned or controlled by the Government, or (*iii*) by a Government company as defined in section 617 of the Companies Act 1956, or (*iv*) by an institution wholly or substantially financed by the Government. [Patents Act 1970, s. 2(*h*)].

**Government work.** 'Government work' means a work which is made or published by or under the direction or control of—(*i*) the Government or any department of the Government; (*ii*) any Legislature in India; (*iii*) any Court, tribunal or other judicial authority in India. [Copyright Act 1957, s. 2(*k*)].

**Governor.** The chief executive official of a State.

NOTE: The executive power of the State shall be vested in the Governor and shall be exercised by him either directly or through officers subordinate to him in accordance with the Constitution. [Constitution of India, Art. 154].

**Grace.** A favour or indulgence as distinguished from a right; an attractive feature.

- **Days of grace** p. 226.

**Grade.** Rank, position in scale, a scale, a class or position in a class according to value. [*Hari Nandan Sharan Bhatnagar* v *S.N. Dikshit* AIR 1970 SC 40: (1970)1 SCR 421: (1969)2 SCC 245].

**Grammatica falsa non vitiat chartam.** False grammar does not vitiate a deed.

**Grant.** To bestow; to confer upon some one other than the person or entity which makes the grant. [*Porto Rico Ry., Light & Power Co.* v *Colom* CCA Puerto Rico, 106 F 2d 345, 354].

To bestow or confer, with or without compensation, a gift or bestowal by one having control or authority over it, as of land or money. [*Palmer* v *U.S. Civil Service Commission* DC III, 191 F Supp 495, 537].

A conveyance, that is, transfer of title by deed or other instrument. [*Dearing* v *Brush Creek Coal Co.* 186 SW 2d 329, 331].

Transfer of property, real or personal, by deed or writing. [*Commissioner of Internal Revenue* v *Plestcheeff* 100 F 2d 62, 64, 65].

A generic term applicable to all transfers of real property, including transfers by operation of law as well as voluntary transfers. [*White* v *Rosenthal* 35 P 2d 154, 155].

In the widest sense, 'grant' may comprehend everything that is granted or passed from one to another by deed. But commonly, the term is applied to rights created or transferred by the Crown, e.g., grants of pensions, patents, charters, franchise. [*Mohsin Ali* v *State of Madhya Pradesh* AIR 1975 SC 1518: 1975 (Supp) SCR 240: (1975)2 SCC 122].

> NOTE: *Grant and assignment—distinction.* Grant is an agreement of some sort which creates rights in the grantee and an agreement which transfers rights may be termed as an assignment. [*H. Anraj* v *Government of Tamil Nadu* AIR 1986 SC 63: (1986)1 SCC 414: 1985 Supp (3) SCR 342: (1986)61 STC 165].

- **Lost grant** p. 543.

**Gratification.** Gratifying or state of being gratified; a reward; a recompense; gratuity; a source of satisfaction or pleasure; expression of gratification as in congratulations.

▸ *Meaning under the Prevention of Corruption Act 1947, s. 4(1).* The word 'gratification' has to be given its literal dictionary meaning of satisfaction of appetite or desire; it could not be construed only to mean money paid by way of a bribe. [*Sailendra Nath* v *State of Bihar* AIR 1968 SC 1292; *C.I. Emden* v *State of U.P.* AIR 1960 SC 548: (1960)2 SCR 592; *Dhanvatrai* v *State* AIR 1964 SC 575; *State of Assam* v *Krishna Rao* AIR 1973 SC 28].

> NOTE: The word 'gratification' is not restricted to pecuniary gratification or to gratifications estimated in money. Therefore, voluntary acceptance of an amount of money or a valuable thing by a public servant will amount to acceptance of gratification. [*State* v *Pundlick* AIR 1959 Bom 543: 60 Cr LJ 1421; *Iqbal Singh* v *Gurdas Singh* AIR 1976 SC 27: (1976)3 SCC 284: (1976)1 SCR 884].
>
> *Gratification—which is not—as understood under the Representation of the People Act 1951.* The withdrawal of his candidature by a candidate to induce another candidate to stand at an election would not be gratification. [*S.B. Adityan* v *S. Kandaswami* 1959 SCR 868: AIR 1958 SC 857: 1958 SCJ 1072].

**Gratuitous.** Given unearned or without recompense; costing nothing; free; not involving a return benefit, compensation or consideration; uncalled for; unwarranted; chargeless; complimentary; costless; expenseless; free of cost; not subject to a payment; voluntary; dispensable; extraneous; irrelative; irrelevant; non-pertinent; superfluous; undesirable; unprovoked; unjustified; without basis; without foundation.

**Gratuity.** A gratuity is something given freely or without recompense and it cannot be demanded as of right, as it does not involve a return of consideration. Gratuity is voluntarily given by way of favour and is an act of grace. If a person undertakes to perform for another service or labour for a given sum, any amount paid in excess of that sum not having been based upon a fresh consideration is a mere gratuity. [*Harinder Singh* v *S. Bhag Singh* AIR 1961 Punj 443].

Gratuity is a reward for good, efficient and faithful service rendered for a considerable period. [*D.T.C. Retired Employees' Association* v *Delhi Transport Corpn.* AIR 2001 SC 1997: (2001)6 SCC 61: JT 2001 Supp (1) SC 144].

Gratuity is a kind of retirement benefit like the provident fund or pension. Gratuity paid to workmen is intended to help them after retirement whether the retirement is the result of the rules of superannuation or of physical disability. [*Indian Hume Pipe Co. Ltd.* v *The Workmen* AIR 1960 SC 251: (1960)2 SCR 32: 1960 SCJ 550].

NOTE: The fundamental principle in allowing gratuity is that it is a retirement benefit for long services, a provision for old age. [*Workmen* v *Ahmedabad Municipal Corpn.* 1955 LAC 155].

The gratuity, like pension, is a retirement benefit for long and continuous services as a provision for old age. It is earned as a matter of right on fulfilling the conditions subject to which it is earned. It is not a gratuitous payment depending upon the discretion or sweet will or fancy of the employer. Like pension, it can also be recovered through civil suit. [*Sudhir Chandra Sarkar* v *Tata Iron Steel Co. Ltd.* AIR 1984 SC 1064: (1984)3 SCR 325: (1984)3 SCC 369].

Gratuity is not paid to the employee gratuitously or merely as a matter of boon. It is paid to him for the service rendered by him to the employer and when it is once earned it cannot be denied, whatever may be the nature of misconduct on the part of the employee. [*Garment Cleaning Works* v *Workmen* AIR 1962 SC 673].

Where the employee is dismissed for misconduct which has resulted in financial loss to the employer, the amount lost should be deducted from the amount of gratuity. [*Hindustan Times Ltd.* v *Their Workmen* AIR 1963 SC 1332].

Gratuity is wide enough to cover any money gratuitously granted or paid, whether it is paid in one sum or in instalments. [*Holloway* v *Poplar Corporation* (1940)1 KB 173].

**Grave and sudden provocation.** Provocation so sudden that it forces a man to lose his self-control.

NOTE: The test of grave and sudden provocation is whether a reasonable man, belonging to the same class of society as the accused, placed in the situation in which the accused was placed would be so provoked as to lose his self-control. In India, words and gestures may also under certain circumstances cause grave and sudden provocation to an accused so as to bring his act within the first exception to s. 300 of the Indian Penal Code. [*K.M. Nanavati* v *State* AIR 1962 SC 605: (1962)2 SCJ 347; *Boya Marena* v *State of A.P.* (1967)2 Andh WR 395: 1967 MLJ (Cr) 828].

**Grave misconduct.** Conduct that is serious or very serious in nature.

The word 'grave' denotes that the character of conduct is serious or very serious. The term 'gravest acts of misconduct' is incapable of definition. [*Bhagwat Prasad* v *Inspector-General of Police* AIR 1970 Punj 81].

**Green vegetable.** The expression denotes a class of vegetables which are grown in a kitchen garden or in a farm and are used for the table. [*Pan Merchants Association* v *State of Madhya Pradesh* AIR 1956 Nag 54].

**Gresham's law.** This was enunciated by Sir Thomas Gresham (1519-1579) who stated that bad money will always drive out good money, but never the reverse. In a bimetallic system the standard coin possessing the lower market value will remain in circulation while the stronger coin will be retained as bullion where a monometallic system is in use; the lighter coins will circulate while the heavier will be retained.

**Grievous hurt.** Injury or pain of serious nature; physical pain or injury very severe.

▸ *Meaning under the Indian Penal Code 1860, s. 320.* The following kinds of hurt only are designated as grievous—*First*—Emasculation. *Secondly*—Permanent privation of the sight of either eye. *Thirdly*—Permanent privation of the hearing of either ear. *Fourthly*—Privation of any member or joint. *Fifthly*—Destruction or permanent impairing of the powers of any member or joint. *Sixthly*—Permanent disfiguration of the head or face. *Seventhly*—Fracture or dislocation of a bone or tooth. *Eighthly*—Any hurt which endangers life or which causes the sufferer to be during the space of twenty days in severe bodily pain, or unable to follow his ordinary pursuits.

▸ *Meaning under the Parsi Marriage and Divorce Act 1936, s. 2(4).* 'Grievous hurt' means—(*a*) emasculation; (*b*) permanent privation of the sight of either eye; (*c*) permanent privation of the hearing of either ear; (*d*) privation of any member or joint; (*e*) destruction or permanent impairing of the powers of any member or joint; (*f*) permanent disfiguration of the head or face; or (*g*) any hurt which endangers life.

**Gross negligence.** The intentional failure to perform a manifest duty in reckless disregard of the consequences as affecting the life or property of another.

Gross negligence consists of conscious and voluntary act or omission which is likely to result in grave injury when in face of clear and present danger of which alleged tortfeasor is aware. [*Glaab* v *Caudill* Fla App, 236 So 2d 180, 182, 183, 185].

Gross negligence is that entire want of care which would raise the belief that act or omission complained of was result of conscious indifference to rights and welfare of persons affected by it. [*Claunch* v *Bennett* Tex Civ App, 395 SW 2d 719, 724].

Greater negligence than the absence of ordinary care is gross negligence. It is such a degree of negligence as excludes the loosest degree of care, and is said to amount to *dolus.* [*Cashill* v *Wright* (1856)6 E&B 891].

Gross negligence is the intentional failure to perform a manifest duty in reckless disregard of the consequences as affecting the life or property of another; such gross want of care and regard for the rights of others as to justify the presumption of wilfulness and wantonness. [*Nanhelal* v *Assistant Registrar* AIR 1970 MP 39].

In regard to professional negligence, the phrase 'gross negligence' only indicates so marked a departure from the normal standard of conduct of a professional man as to infer a lack of that ordinary care which a man of ordinary skill would display. [*Hunter* v *Hanley* 1955 SLT 213]. In relation to criminal responsibility flowing from negligence, the words 'gross negligence' are not uncommonly used to denote the very high standard of negligence or recklessness required to establish criminal responsibility. [*Ibid*].

**Gross profit.** The difference between sales and the cost of goods sold before allowance for operating expenses and income taxes. [Black's *Law Dictionary*, 5th Ed.].

Total sales revenue less the cost of the goods sold, no adjustment being made for additional expenses and taxes. [Black's *Law Dictionary*, 8th Ed.].

According to authoritative definition of 'gross profit' current among accountants, the expression means the excess of the sales (less returns) over the cost of the goods sold including the expenses directly attributable to putting the goods in a saleable condition. The expenses which can be deducted do not include selling commission. [*S. Ganesan* v *A.K. Joscelyne* AIR 1957 Cal 33].

**Gross rental.** The rent which a landlord may be expected to get in the open market. [*Kalipada Dawan* v *Commissioners of Vishnupur Municipality* AIR 1962 SC 151].

**Gross sales.** Total of all sales at invoice prices, not reduced by discounts, allowances, returns, or other adjustments.

**Ground.** To provide basis for; a foundation or basis; points relied on; soil; earth; earth's surface appropriated to private use and under cultivation or susceptible of cultivation.

• **Insufficient grounds** p. 467.

**Ground rent.** The rent payable for land let to a tenant.

Rent paid to owner of land for use of property; a perpetual rent reserved to himself and his heirs, by the grantor of land in fee-simple, out of the land conveyed. [Black's *Law Dictionary*, 5th Ed.].

Rent paid by a tenant under a long-term lease for the use of undeveloped land, usually for the construction of a commercial building; an inheritable interest, in rental income from land, reserved by a grantor who conveys the land in fee-simple. [Black's *Law Dictionary*, 7th Ed.].

**Grove.** A grove is a cluster of trees sufficient in number specifically planted by human agency to prevent its use for any other purpose, but not large enough to constitute a forest. [*Radhika Prasad* v *State* AIR 1972 MP 124].

The word 'grove' conveys compactness or at any rate substantial compactness as to be recognized as a unit by itself, which must consist of a group of trees in sufficient number to preclude the land on which they stand from being primarily used for a purpose, such as cultivation, other than a grove. [*Chandrojirao* v *State* (1968)1 SCR 961: AIR 1968 SC 494].

**Growing crops.** Crops in the process of growth.

The ordinary meaning of the expression is 'growing plants and cereals' and a plant means a living organism capable of living wholly on inorganic substances and having neither power of locomotion nor special organs of sensation or digestion. Seeds which have even just sprouted would come within the aforesaid definition. [*Chhatradharilal* v *Shyama Bai* AIR 1966 MP 67].

NOTE: Decisions differ as to whether such must be above the surface of the soil, and as to whether matured crops are "growing" crops. The cases as well differ as to whether pasturage grass is a growing crop. Growing crops are personal property. [*Estate of Ruwe* v *Ruwe* 211 NW 2d 610, 613].

Growing crop is movable property. [Code of Civil Procedure 1908, s. 2(13); Transfer of Property Act 1882, s. 3; Indian Registration Act 1908, s. 2(6)].

**Guarantee.** As noun means a formal promise or assurance that an obligation will be fulfilled or that something is of a specified quality and durability; a written or other undertaking to answer for the payment of a debt or for the performance of an obligation by another person liable in the first instance.

As verb transitive means answer for the due fulfilment of (a contract etc.) or the genuineness of (an article); secure the possession of (a thing) for a person; make (a person) secure against a risk or in possession of a thing.

The assurance that a contract or legal act will be duly carried out; something given or existing as security, such as to fulfill a future engagement or a condition subsequent; one to whom a guaranty is made. [Black's *Law Dictionary*, 8th Ed.].

A guarantee is an accessory contract, by which the promisor undertakes to be answerable to the promisee for the debt, default or miscarriage of another person, whose primary liability to the promisee must exist or be contemplated. [Halsbury's *Laws of England*, 4th Ed., vol. 20, para 101, p. 49]. The surety or guarantor, is a person who engages with the creditor of a third party to be answerable, in the second degree, for some debt, default or miscarriage. [*Ibid*, para 104, p. 52].

• **Continuing guarantee** p. 187.
• **Contract of guarantee** p. 191.
• **Fidelity guarantee** p. 351.

**Guarantee insurance.** It is a guarantee against loss in case a person named shall make a designated default or be guilty of specified conduct.

**Guaranty.** See GUARANTEE.

**Guardian.** One who has the legal authority and duty to care for another's person or property, especially because of the other's infancy, incapacity, or disability. [Black's *Law Dictionary*, 8th Ed.].

▸*Meaning under the Children Act 1960, s. 2(k).* 'Guardian' in relation to a child includes any person who, in the opinion of the competent authority having cognizance of any proceeding in relation to a child, has, for the time being, the actual charge of, or control over, that child.

▸*Meaning under the Children (Pledging of Labour) Act 1933, s. 2.* 'Guardian' includes any person having legal custody of or control over a child.

▸*Meaning under the Guardians and Wards Act 1890, s. 4(2).* 'Guardian' means a person having the care of the person of a minor or of his property, or of both his person and property.

Guardian under the Guardians and Wards Act includes guardians appointed or declared under the Act as also testamentary guardians, natural guardians or even *de facto* guardians. [*Nashirwan* v *Sharoshbanu* AIR 1934 Bom 311].

▸*Meaning under the Hindu Minority and Guardianship Act 1956, s. 4(b).* 'Guardian' means a person having the care of the person of a minor or his property or of both his person and property, and includes—(*i*) a natural guardian, (*ii*) a guardian appointed by the will of the minor's father or mother, (*iii*) a guardian appointed or declared by a court, and (*iv*) a person empowered to act as such by or under any enactment relating to any court of wards.

NOTE: Under Mahomedan law, the mother is entitled to the custody of her male child up to seven years and of her female child until puberty. After her comes the father. As to the guardianship of property, the father has the first claim.


- **De facto guardian** p. 226.
- **Lawful guardian** p. 518.
- **Natural guardian** p. 599.
- **Testamentary guardian** p. 839.


**Guardian ad litem.** A special guardian appointed by the court to prosecute or defend, on behalf of an infant or incompetent, a suit to which he is a party, and such guardian is considered an officer of the court to represent the interests of the infant or incompetent in the litigation. [*Kossar* v *State* 179 NYS 2d 71, 73, 76, 79].

NOTE: An infant may not defend, counter-claim or intervene in any proceedings, or appear in any proceedings under a judgment or order notice of which has been served on him, except by his guardian *ad litem*. Further, subject to the provisions of the rules of court, anything which in the ordinary conduct of any proceedings is required or authorised by a provision of the rules to be done by a party to the proceedings can or may, if the party is an infant, be done by his guardian *ad litem*, although the guardian is not himself a party. The purpose of the guardian *ad litem* is to supplement the infant's want of capacity and judgment; like a next friend he is the officer of the court to take all measures for the benefit of the infant in the proceedings in which he appears. [Halsbury's *Laws of England*, 4th Ed., vol. 24, p. 482].

Where the defendant is a minor, the court on being satisfied by the fact of his minority, shall appoint a proper person to be guardian for the suit for such minor. [Code of Civil Procedure 1908, Or. 32, r. 3(1)].

**Guillotine.** It is a more drastic method than closure, to limit the debate in connection with legislative and non-legislative motions. Time is fixed for debate upon a question, irrespective of the nature of course of the eventual debate. The Speaker is given comprehensive powers to apply guillotine in "financial business". [Lok Sabha Rules 221 and 363].

**Gun-cotton.** Cotton steeped in nitric or sulphuric acid, used for blasting.

**Guru.** A Hindu spiritual preceptor.

**Gypsy.** The gypsies are a population of a nomadic character dwelling in tents or caravans. They are scattered over England, the continent of Europe, Northern Asia and America.

▸*Meaning under the Caravan Sites Act 1968, s. 16.* "Gypsies" means persons of nomadic habit of life, whatever their race or origin, but does not include members of an organised group of travelling showmen, or of persons engaged in travelling circuses.

# Hh

**Habeas corpus.** A writ employed to bring a person before a court, most frequently to ensure that the party's imprisonment or detention is not illegal. [Black's *Law Dictionary*, 8th Ed.].

The writ of *habeas corpus* is a writ directed to the person detaining another commanding him to produce the body of the prisoner at a designated time and place, with the day and cause of his caption and detention, to do, submit to, and receive whatsoever the court or judge awarding the writ shall consider in that behalf. [*Ghulam Sarwar* v *Union of India* AIR 1967 SC 1335, 1337].

The Latin term *"habeas corpus"* means 'you must have the body' and a writ for securing the liberty of the person was called *habeas corpus ad subjiciendum*. The writ affords an effective means of immediate release from an unlawful or unjustifiable detention, whether in prison or in private custody. [*Additional District Magistrate, Jabalpur* v *Shivakant Shukla* AIR 1976 SC 1207: 1976 (Supp) SCR 172: (1976)2 SCC 521: 1976 Cr LJ 945].

The full name of the writ is *habeas corpus ad subjiciendum* (you have the body to submit or answer). It is applicable as a remedy in all cases of wrongful deprivation of personal liberty, where there is no legal justification for the detention. [*Greene* v *Home Secretary* (1941)3 All ER 388].

NOTE: The right to an instant determination as to lawfulness of an existing imprisonment is the substantial right made available by this writ. [Lord Halsbury, L.C. in *Cox* v *Hates* (1890)15 AC 506].

The writ of *habeas corpus*, by which the legal authority under which a person may be detained can be challenged is of immemorial antiquity. After a checkered career in which it was involved in the struggles between the common-law courts and the Courts of Chancery and the Star Chamber, as well as in the conflicts between Parliament and the Crown, the protection of the writ was firmly written into English law by the Habeas Corpus Act of 1679. Today it is said to be 'perhaps the most important writ known to the constitutional law of England'. [*Secretary of State for Home Affairs* v *O'Brien* (1923) AC 603, 609].

In India, the Supreme Court and the High Courts have jurisdiction to issue writ of *habeas corpus* under Arts. 32 and 226 respectively of the Constitution of India. A writ of *habeas corpus* is a prerogative writ of highest constitutional importance. It is designed to afford immediate relief from illegal confinement or restraint and issued for the vindication of the right to personal liberty by scrutinising the legality of the restraint. [*Kidar Nath* v *State of Punjab* AIR 1960 Punj 122: 1960 Cr LJ 390].

**Habendum clause.** The part of a deed that defines the extent of the interest being granted and any conditions affecting the grant. The introductory words to the clause are ordinarily *to have and to hold*. It is also termed *to-have-and-to-hold clause*. [Black's *Law Dictionary*, 7th Ed.].

Portion of deed beginning with the words *"to have and to hold"*. [*Bannin* v *Peck* 41 NYS 2d 668, 670].

The clause usually following the granting part of the premises of a deed, which defines the extent of the ownership in the thing granted to be held and enjoyed by the grantee. [*New York Indians* v *U.S.* 42 L Ed 927].

**Habit.** Acquired mode of behaviour; attitude; characteristic behaviour; characteristically repeated action; common practice; customary action; customary conduct; frequently repeated act.

The word 'habit' has a clear, well-understood meaning, being nearly the same as custom and cannot be applied to a single act. When we speak of the habits of a person we refer to his customary conduct, to pursue which he has acquired a tendency from frequent repetitions. [*B.N. Singh* v *State of U.P.* AIR 1960 All 754].

'Habit' implies a tendency or capacity resulting from frequent repetition of the same or similar acts. It indicates depravity of or criminality in character, evidenced by frequent commissions of offences. 'Habit' has to be established by aggregate of facts. [*Gopalan Achari* v *State of Kerala* 1981 Ker LT 448].

Repeated, persistent and similar, but not isolated, individual and dissimilar acts are necessary to justify an inference of habit. [*Vijay Narain Singh* v *State of Bihar* AIR 1984 SC 1334: (1984)3 SCR 435: (1984)3 SCC 14: 1984 Cr LJ 909: 1984 SCC (Cri) 361].

**Habitual.** According to habit; accustomed; continual; customary; ingrained; recurring; regular; repeated; routine; usual.

"Habitual" means repeated several times. [*Management of Monghyr Factory of I.T.C. Ltd., Monghyr, Bihar* v *Presiding Officer, Labour Court, Patna, Bihar* AIR 1978 SC 1428: (1978)3 SCR 1044: (1978)3 SCC 504].

**Habitual criminal.** A person who by force or habit or inward disposition inherent or latent in him has grown accustomed to lead a life of crime. [*Vijay Narain Singh* v *State of Bihar* AIR 1984 SC 1334: 1984 Cr LJ 909: (1984)1 Crimes 914 (*per* A.P. Sen, J.)].

NOTE: The expression "habitual criminal" is the same thing as the "habitual offender" within the meaning of s. 110 of the Code of Criminal Procedure 1973.

**Habitually.** The word 'habitually' means 'repeatedly' or 'persistently'. It implies a thread of continuity stringing together similar respective acts. [*Vijay Narain Singh* v *State of Bihar* AIR 1984 SC 1334: (1984)3 SCR 435: (1984)3 SCC 14: 1984 Cr LJ 909: 1984 SCC (Cri) 361].

The word 'habitually' means 'usually', 'generally', or 'according to custom'. It does not refer to the frequency of occasions but rather to the invariability of practice and the habit has to be proved by totality of facts. [*Smt. Mustakmiya Jabbarmiya Shaikh* v *M.M. Mehta* (1995)3 SCC 237: 1995 SCC (Cri) 454: JT 1995(4) SC 215].

**Hackney-carriage.** Any wheeled vehicle drawn by animals and used for the conveyance of passengers which is kept, or offered, or plies, for hire. [Hackney-Carriage Act 1879, s. 2].

**Haereditas jacens.** An inheritance not taken up.

**Haeres est nomen juris, fillus est nomen naturae.** Heir is a name of law, son is a name of nature.

**Haeres factus.** Heir appointed by will.

**Haeres natus.** Heir by descent.

**Haja.** Destruction of crops by floods or heavy rain [Wilson's *Glossary*].

**Hajat.** Confinement of one charged with commission of offence.

**Hakk.** True; a just or legal right or claim.

**Hakkiyat.** Rights and interests.

**Half blood.** The relationship existing between persons having the same father or mother, but not both parents in common. [Black's *Law Dictionary*, 8th Ed.].

Two persons are said to be related to each other by half blood when they are descended from a common ancestor, but by different wives. [Hindu Marriage Act 1955, s. 3(*c*); Special Marriage Act 1954, s. 2(*b*); Hindu Succession Act 1956, s. 3(*d*)].

**Half brother.** A male sibling with whom one shares the same father or the same mother, but not both; a brother by one parent only. [Black's *Law Dictionary*, 8th Ed.].

**Half caste.** A child of European father and Indian mother.

**Half mast high.** When a flag is lowered to half height of mast as a mark of respect to an illustrious dead person, it is said to be half mast high.

**Half nephew.** The son of one's half brother or half sister.

**Half niece.** The daughter of one's half brother or half sister.

**Half sister.** A female sibling with whom one shares the same father or the same mother, but not both; a sister by one parent only. [Black's *Law Dictionary*, 7th Ed.].

**Hanafi Mussalman.** A follower of the Mussalman faith who conforms to the tenets and doctrines of the Hanafi School of Mussalman law. [Mussalman Wakf Validating Act 1913, s. 2(2)].

NOTE: Mahomedans are divided into two sects, namely, Sunnis and Shias. Sunnis are subdivided into four sects, namely, Hanafis, Malikis, Shafeis and Hanbalis.

**Handcuff.** A pair of lockable linked metal rings for securing a prisoner's wrists. [*Concise Oxford Dictionary*, 9th Ed.].

One of two manacles connected by a chain, and designed to be locked around the wrists. [Webster's *Comprehensive Dictionary*, International Edition].

**Handicap.** Barrier; burden; disability; disadvantage; drawback; hindrance; impairment; impediment; inconvenience; limitation; obstacle; obstruction; shortcoming; stumbling block.

**Handicraft.** Any manual labour exercised by way of trade or for purposes of gain in or incidental to the making of any article or part of an article, or in or incidental to the altering, repairing, ornamenting, finishing or otherwise adapting for sale any article. [*Beadon* v *Parrott* LR 6 QB 718].

NOTE: Agarbatis when manufactured with the aid of power are not handicrafts. [*Padmini Products* v *Collector, Central Excise* AIR 1989 SC 2278: (1989)4 SCC 275: (1989)3 SCR 873: JT 1989(3) SC 404: (1989)43 ELT 195 : (1990)76 STC 411: (1990)185 ITR 440].

**Hank.** The word 'hank' without the aid of any explanation whatsoever means in the cotton trade a coil of a definite length of 840 yards. [*Cannanore Spinning and Weaving Mills* v *Collector of Customs* AIR 1967 Ker 62].

Any coil of cotton yarn less than 768 metres in length. [*The Cannanore Spinning & Weaving Mills Ltd.* v *Collector of Customs and Central Excise, Cochin* AIR 1970 SC 950: (1970)2 SCR 830: (1969)3 SCC 112].

**Hansard.** The official reports of debates in the British Parliament. The name derives from Luke Hansard, Printer of the Journal of the House of Commons from 1774 to 1828. The name has varied at different times. Since 1943 the name Hansard has been added to Official Report. It is termed Hansard Official Report; Hansard's Debates.

**Harbour.** As noun it means a place of shelter for ships; a shelter; a place of refuge or protection; a sheltered place, natural or artificial, on the coast of a sea, lake, or other body of water; a place of security and comfort.

Harbour is a place to shelter ships from the winds and sea, and where ships come for commercial purposes to load and unload goods. [*R.* v *Hannam* (1886)34 WR 355].

As verb it means give shelter to; to afford lodging to; to give a refuge to.

**Harbour dues.** These are amounts paid by shipowners for merchandise being loaded or unloaded, for the purpose of maintenance of the installation in a harbour. These are variously described as tonnage rates, berthing charges, inward and outward harbour rates, buoyage rates etc.

**Hard cases.** A phrase used to indicate judicial decisions which, to meet a case of hardship to a party, are not entirely consonant with the true principle of the law. It is said of such: "Hard cases make bad law". [Black's *Law Dictionary*, 5th Ed.].

A lawsuit involving equities that tempt a judge to stretch or even disregard a principle of law at issue—hence the expression, "Hard cases make bad law". [Black's *Law Dictionary*, 7th Ed.].

**Hard currency.** A strong currency, that is, one for which there is a strong demand in relation to the available supply.

Currency backed by reserves, especially gold and silver reserves. [Black's *Law Dictionary*, 7th Ed.].

NOTE: The exchange rate for a hard currency will tend to stand above parity.

**Hard labour.** A punishment, additional to mere imprisonment, sometimes imposed upon convicts sentenced to a penitentiary for serious crimes or for misconduct while in prison. [Black's *Law Dictionary*, 5th Ed.].

Work imposed on prisoners as additional punishment, usually for misconduct while in prison. [Black's *Law Dictionary*, 7th Ed.].

NOTE: The Indian Penal Code prescribes five kinds of punishment including imprisonment (s. 53 of the Code). Imprisonment may be either rigorous, that is, with hard labour or simple. In case of the former, the prisoner is put to hard labour such as grinding corn, digging earth and the like.

**Hardship.** In general, privation, suffering, adversity; something hard to endure.

• **Undue hardship** p. 864.

**Hardware.** Tools and household articles of metal; manufactured articles of metal; heavy machinery or armaments; weapons; mechanical and electronic components of a computer; any of the machinery that makes up a computer installation; mechanical, electronic, or other devices or materials, as distinguished from people, planning, operational procedures, etc.

NOTE: Hardware includes pots, pans and domestic appliances of that sort and simple articles made of metal. It cannot include complicated machinery like electric motors and articles of that type or electric fan. [*Municipal Board* v *Krishna & Co.* AIR 1934 All 550].

**Harijan.** The word applies to untouchables. [*State* v *Puranchand* AIR 1958 MP 352: 1958 Cr LJ 1398].

**Harm.** The existence of loss or detriment in fact of any kind to a person resulting from any cause; injury, loss, or detriment.

The expression "harm" includes injury to mind, body or property. [*Devendrappa* v *State of Mysore* 1970 Cr LJ 1188].

▸*Meaning under the Indian Penal Code 1860, ss. 81, 88, 89, 91, 92, 93, 95, 100, 104, 106, 415, 469 and 499.* The word "harm" connotes hurt, injury, damage, impairment, moral wrong or evil. It means physical injury—an injurious mental reaction. [*Mrs. Veeda Manezes* v *Yusaf Khan Haji Ibrahim Khan* AIR 1966 SC 1773: (1966)2 SCWR 149: (1966)2 SCJ 720: 1966 Cr LJ 1489].

NOTE: In s. 95, the word "harm" is wide enough to include physical injury as also injurious mental reaction. [*Mrs. Rupan Deol Bajaj* v *Kanwar Pal Singh Gill* JT 1995(7) SC 299].

**Harmful.** Baneful; calamitous; catastrophic; corrosive; crippling; damaging; destructive; detrimental; hurtful; injurious; insalubrious; insidious; mischievous; unhealthy; wounding.

As used in connection with errors committed at trial, it means that rights were seriously affected.

As used in connection with foods, it means noxious, hurtful, pernicious, likely to cause illness or damage.

**Harmful publication.** 'Harmful publication' means any book, magazine, pamphlet, leaflet, newspaper or other like publication which consists of stories told with the aid of pictures or without the aid of pictures or wholly in pictures, being stories portraying wholly or mainly—(*i*) the commission of offences; or (*ii*) acts of violence or cruelty; or (*iii*) incidents of a repulsive or horrible nature; in such a way that the publication as a whole would tend to corrupt a young person into whose hands it might fall, whether by inciting or encouraging him to commit offences or acts of violence or cruelty or in any other manner whatsoever. [Young Persons (Harmful Publications) Act 1956, s. 2(*a*)].

**Harmonious construction.** It is a rule of construction that when there are in any statute two provisions which are in conflict with each other, they should, if possible, be so construed that effect can be given to both and that a construction which renders either of them inoperative and useless should not be adopted, except in the last resort. This is the rule of harmonious construction. [*Bengal Immunity Co.* v *State of Bihar* AIR 1955 SC 661: (1955)2 SCR 603: 1955 SCJ 672: 1955 SCA 1140; *Needle Industries (India) Ltd.* v *Needle Industries Newey (India) Ltd.* AIR 1981 SC 1298: (1981)3 SCR 698; *Raghbir Singh* v *State of Haryana* AIR 1981 SC 2037: 1981 Cr LJ 1497].

> NOTE: It is a recognized rule of construction of statutes that expressions used in a statute should ordinarily be understood in a sense in which they best harmonise with the object of the statute and which effectuate the object of legislature. If an expression is susceptible of more than one meaning, that should be adopted as would carry out the object of the legislature. [*New India Sugar Mills* v *Commissioner of Sales Tax* AIR 1963 SC 1207].
>
> It is the duty of the court to provide a harmonious construction where possible so that the legislative intention may be given effect to. [*Vysyaraju Vadreenarayana* v *Epari Venugopalan* AIR 1980 Ori 63: (1980)49 Cut LT 227].

**Harsh and unconscionable.** The expression means unreasonable and not in accordance with the ordinary rules of fair dealing. There may be an inequality so strong, gross, and manifest that it must be impossible to state it to a man of common sense without producing an exclamation at the inequality of it. [*Samuel* v *Newbold* (1906) AC 461].

**Has.** The present perfect tense of the word 'has' does not have a rigid and fixed connotation. It takes its meaning from the context. It reflects the legislative intent to indicate a complete event connected in some way with the present time. It does not necessarily denote the extent of retrospectivity. [*Mangilal* v *Addl. D.J.* 1980 All Ren Cas 53 (FB)].

**Has been.** The expression means 'is' or 'at one time was'. [*Mubarak Mazdoor* v *K.K. Banerji* AIR 1958 All 323].

The expression 'has been' when occurs in a provision of statute whether it denotes transaction prior to the enactment of the statute in question or a transaction after the coming into force of the statute depends upon the intention of the legislature to be gathered from the provision in which the said provision occurs or from other provisions of the statute. [*Secretary R.T.A., Bangalore* v *D.P. Sharma* AIR 1989 SC 509].

**Hasil.** Produce, profit, especially as a revenue term, the amount derived from the Government share of the produce of the soil and from any other source of taxation or import, revenue, tax, duty. [Wilson's *Glossary*].

**Hastabood.** It is an abstract of each raiyat's account specifying his tenure, the amount of rent payable by him, the quantity of land in or out of cultivation, and the amount of rent realised or in arrear.

**Hat.** A market, a movable market, one held only on certain days in a week, a fair.

A *hat* in its legal meaning and conception is the right to hold a concourse of buyers and sellers and the owner of the *hat* is the person who has this right. The right to hold a *hat* is initially an incident of the ownership of the land. The ownership entitles the owner of the land to hold a *hat* on his land. [*Province of Bengal* v *Hingul Kumari* AIR 1946 Cal 217: 50 CWN 184].

**Have and hold.** This is a common phrase used in conveyancing. The purpose of the phrase "to have and to hold" is to name again the transferee and to define the estate and the amount of interest taken by him. In modern deeds the words "to have and" are omitted as useless.

**Have regard to.** The expression in a statutory provision does not imply that there must be very strict compliance with the statutory provision, but that the provision should be taken for guidance only. [*Mohammad Sagiruddin* v *District Mechanical Engineer* AIR 1966 Pat 184].

The expression "have regard to" has no more definite and technical meaning than that of ordinary usage and only requires that those provisions must be taken into considerations. [*Mysore State Electricity* v *Bangalore Woolen* AIR 1963 SC 1128; *Ashit Mukherjee* v *Sushmita Mukherjee* 90 CWN 1060].

The meaning of the expression 'have regard to' is well-settled. It means that the factors specially enumerated shall be taken into account while performing the exercise. [*Hindustan Zinc Ltd.* v *Andhra Pradesh State Electricity Board* AIR 1991 SC 1473: (1991)3 SCC 299].

**Hawker.** An itinerant or travelling salesman who carries goods about in order to sell them, and who actually sells them to purchasers, in contradistinction to a trader who has goods for sale and sells them in a fixed place of business. A hawker or peddler usually sells his goods in the public streets, or from door-to-door, and commonly is required to have a licence. [Black's *Law Dictionary*, 5th Ed.].

An itinerant or travelling salesperson who sells goods in a public street, especially one who, in a loud voice, cries out the benefits of the items offered for sale; a peddler. [Black's *Law Dictionary*, 7th Ed.].

One who carries goods from place to place for sale. [*Sodan Singh* v *New Delhi Municipal Committee* AIR 1989 SC 1988].

NOTE: Canvassers of books or publications on the street, or from house to house, taking orders for future delivery, are not hawkers. Right to hawk on streets subject to regulations is a fundamental right. [*Sodan Singh* v *New Delhi Municipal Committee* AIR 1989 SC 1988].

**Hazard.** Cause for alarm; dangerous course; dangerous situation; menace; peril; pitfall; precariousness; source of risk; threat, uncertainty; unsafe object.

A danger or risk lurking in a situation which by chance or fortuity develops into an active agency of harm [*Hough* v *Contributory Retirement Appeal Board* 36 NE 2d 415, 417, 418]; exposure to the chance of loss or injury [*Caminetti* v *Guaranty Union Life Ins. Co.* 52 Cal App 2d 330]; a game of chance or wagering.

**Hazardous employment.** High-risk and extra perilous work; high-risk work; work involving extra peril.

**Hazardous insurance.** Insurance effected on property which is unusual or peculiar to danger of destruction by fire, or on the life of a man whose occupation exposes him to special or unusual perils.

**He.** Properly a pronoun of the masculine gender, but usually used and construed in status to include both sexes as well as corporations. [*Buono* v *Yankee Maid Dress Corporation* CCA NY, 77 F 2d 274, 278].

**Head of department.** The expression 'head of department' has two distinct meanings. It may be limited to heads of various departments of the Secretariat, namely, the secretaries of the departments or else it may also include heads of departments of attached offices either under the Union Government or under the State Government. [*Union of India* v *Sudhir Kumar Roy* AIR 1963 Ori 111].

Head of Department for Financial Code and for service rules are not terms of co-extensive connotation and they have different meaning in different context. [*V.S. Murty* v *Deputy Chief Accounts Officer* AIR 1983 SC 403: (1983)2 SCR 404: (1983)2 SCC 115].

**Head of family (or household).** An individual who actually supports and maintains in one household one or more individuals who are closely connected with him by blood relationship, relationship by marriage, or by adoption, and whose right to exercise family control and provide for the dependant individuals is based upon some moral or legal obligation. [*Miller* v *Glenn* DC Ky, 47 F Supp 794, 796, 797].

**Headings.** The headings prefixed to a section or sets of sections in modern statutes are regarded as preamble to those sections. They cannot control the plain words of the statute, but they may explain ambiguous words. [Maxwell on *Interpretation of*

*Statutes*, 12th Ed., p. 11]. If there is any doubt in the interpretation of the words in the section, the heading certainly helps the court to resolve the doubt. [*Bhinka* v *Charan Singh* AIR 1959 SC 960: 1960 SCJ 892].

> NOTE: The description of age at the heading of deposition is not an authentic statement of age and cannot be relied on. [*Jata Swain* v *Natabar Das* AIR 1984 Ori 26, 28].

**Health.** State of being hale, sound, or whole in body, mind or soul, well being; freedom from pain or sickness.

The term "health" implies more than an absence of sickness. Health is a state of complete physical, mental and social well being and not merely the absence of disease or infirmity. [*C.E.S.C. Ltd.* v *Subhash Chandra Bose* JT 1991(6) SC 373: AIR 1992 SC 573: (1992)1 SCC 441: 1992(3) SLR 16].

- **Ill health** p. 427.

**Health insurance.** It is a scheme under which the insurer undertakes to indemnify the policyholder for expenses and loss of time occasioned by disease.

**Hear.** Adjudicate; examine judicially; give a judicial hearing; investigate judicially; try the cause; give audience; listen; become aware of; become conscious of; discern something audible; perceive something audible; take cognizance of.

To "hear" a cause or matter means to hear and determine it. [*Re Green* 51 LJQB 44, *per* Lord Blackburn].

Sometimes however to "hear" is not quite the same as to "hear and determine". [*R.* v *Warwickshire Justices* 4 LJMC 62, *per* Denman, CJ].

▸ *Meaning under the Code of Criminal Procedure 1898, s. 208(1).* The word 'hear' used in relation to the complainant does not mean examining the complainant but means granting audience to the complainant, that is, he has to detail the facts which constitute the offence and to state by what evidence he is going to prove those facts. [*Mohammad Afzal Bag* v *State* AIR 1959 J&K 77].

**Hear the parties.** The phrase 'hear the parties' only means that argument should be heard and does not include oral examination of the parties and their witnesses. The compulsion to hear the parties means compulsion to hear their argument; there can be no compulsion to record statements of the parties and their witnesses in the absence of anything else to show that the person hearing is bound to examine them orally. If the law contemplates that the person hearing is only to receive affidavits of the persons on whom the parties rely, that is, of the parties and their witnesses, the phrase 'hear the parties' cannot include examining them and their witnesses orally. [*Bhagwat Singh* v *State* AIR 1959 All 763: 1959 Cr LJ 1384].

**Heard and finally decided.** It means matter on which the court has exercised its judicial mind and has after argument and consideration come to a decision on a contested matter. [*Pandurang Ramchandra Mandlik* v *Shantabai Ramchandra Ghatge* AIR 1989 SC 2240: 1989 Supp (2) SCR 1: 1989 Supp (2) SCC 627: JT 1989(3) SC 647].

> NOTE: The proceeding either civil or criminal shall be deemed to continue to be pending until it is heard and finally decided, that is to say, in a case where an appeal or revision is heard and finally decided or, where no appeal or revision is preferred, until the period of limitation prescribed for such appeal or revision has expired. [*Rama Dayal Markarha* v *State of Madhya Pradesh* AIR 1978 SC 921: (1978)3 SCR 497: (1978)2 SCC 630: 1978 Cr LJ 917].

**Hearing.** A judicial session, usually open to the public, held for the purpose of deciding issues of fact or of law, sometimes with witnesses testifying; any setting in which an affected person presents arguments to an agency decision-maker; in legislative practice, any proceeding in which legislators or their designees receive testimony about legislation that might be enacted; a trial. [Black's *Law Dictionary*, 7th Ed.].

The word 'hearing' in a broad sense covers the entire stage of trial and not in the restricted sense of only a particular stage beginning with the examination of parties and ending with the argument in the case. [*Bhusan Saran* v *Onkar Singh* AIR 1956 All 715 (DB)].

The expression 'hearing' is used to describe whatsoever takes place before a tribunal clothed with judicial function at any stage of the proceedings subsequent to its inception. [*Mukh Ram* v *Sri Ram* ILR (1959) Punj 2102].

NOTE: The word 'hearing' can admit of a very wide and liberal interpretation. It may include recording of evidence, consideration of arguments on some aspects of suit, examination of various questions relating to suit and so on. The essential prerequisite is whether the judge is applying his mind to some aspects of the case. If he is conducting some routine work or passing interlocutory order, he cannot be said to be hearing the suit. [*Sham Lal* v *Rajinder Kumar Modi* AIR 1993 J&K 50].

The word "hearing" includes "hearings", that is, adjourned as well as original hearings. [*R.* v *London (County) Quarter Sessions Appeals Committee, ex p. Rossi* (1956)1 QB 682].


- **Date of hearing** p. 225.
- **First hearing** p. 355.


**Hearsay.** Traditionally, testimony that is given by a witness who relates not what he or she knows personally, but what others have said, and that is therefore dependent on the credibility of someone other than the witness. [Black's *Law Dictionary*, 8th Ed.].

The word "hearsay" is used in various senses. Sometimes it means whatever a person is heard to say; sometimes it means whatever a person declares on information given by some one else. [*J.D. Jain* v *Management of State Bank of India* AIR 1982 SC 673: (1982)2 SCR 227: 1982 SCC (Cri) 122: 1982 SCC 143].

**Hearsay evidence.** One of the divisions of evidence is that it is either original or unoriginal. By original evidence is meant evidence, either *ab intra* or *ab extra*, which has an independent probative force of its own; unoriginal, also called derivative, transmitted or second-hand evidence, is that which derives its force from, through or some other. And of this derivative evidence there are five forms—the first is when the supposed oral evidence is delivered through oral; this is hearsay evidence. [Best on *Evidence*, Art. 29, p. 17].

Hearsay evidence in its legal sense is evidence given by a testifying witness of a statement made on some other occasion, when it is intended as evidence of the truth of what was asserted. It is essential to appreciate that evidence is only hearsay when tendered to prove the truth of the facts asserted, not when tendered simply to show that the statement was made. Hearsay may be first hand, when a witness says what he heard someone else say, or second-hand (or even more distant) when he relates what he was told that someone else said. It may be oral or documentary, of fact or of opinion. [Halsbury's *Laws of England*, 4th Ed., vol. 17, para 53, p. 39].

NOTE: Section 60 of the Indian Evidence Act 1872, rejects hearsay evidence. But there are exceptions to this rule and they are to be found in ss. 17 to 39 of the Act.

**Heavy goods vehicle.** Any goods carriage the gross vehicle weight of which, or a tractor or a road-roller the unladen weight of either of which, exceeds 12,000 kilograms. [Motor Vehicles Act 1988, s. 2(16)].

**Heavy package.** 'Heavy package' means a package or other object weighing not less than one metric ton which is equal to one thousand kilogrammes or 1204.6 standard pounds or 26.8 standard maunds. [Marking of Heavy Packages Act 1951, s. 2(*a*)].

**Heir.** A person who, under the laws of intestacy, is entitled to receive an intestate decedent's property, especially real property. It is also termed legal heir; heir at law; lawful heir; heir general. [Black's *Law Dictionary*, 8th Ed.].

The term 'heir' cannot normally be limited to issue only. It must mean all persons who are entitled to the property of another under the law of inheritance. [*Angurbala Mullick* v *Debabrata Mullick* AIR 1951 SC 293: 1951 SCR 1125: 1951 SCJ 394; *N. Krishnammal* v *R.*

*Ekambaram* AIR 1979 SC 1298: (1979)3 SCC 273].

The word 'heir' must be construed in a broad and general sense so as to include all those on whom the estate of the deceased devolves whether on intestacy or by means of a testamentary instrument like a will. [*Gulzara Singh* v *Smt. Taj Kaur* AIR 1961 Punj 288].

▸ *Meaning under the Hindu Succession Act 1956, s. 3(f)*. 'Heir' means any person, male or female, who is entitled to succeed to the property of an intestate.

- **Expectant heir** p. 330.
- **Lawful heirs** p. 518.
- **Presumptive heir** p. 682.

**Heir-apparent.** Heir-apparent is he who if he survives his ancestor must succeed.

An heir-apparent is a person who would be the heir if he survived the propositus and if the propositus died intestate.

**Heir at law.** He who, after his father's or ancestor's death, has a right to inherit all his lands, tenements and hereditaments. [Wharton's *Law Lexicon*].

**Heir presumptive.** See PRESUMPTIVE HEIR p. 682.

**Heirloom.** An item of personal property that by local custom, contrary to the usual legal rule, descends to the heir along with the inheritance, instead of passing to the executor or administrator of the last owner; traditional examples are an ancestor's coat of armour, family portraits, title deeds and keys. Popularly, a valued possession of great sentimental value passed down through generations within a family. [Black's *Law Dictionary*, 7th Ed.].

The popular and familiar sense of the word "heirlooms" is things directed to descend by way of inheritance. [*Byng* v *Byng* 10 HL Cas 183, *per* Westbury, C.].

Heirlooms are such goods and personal chattels as shall go, by special custom, to the heir along with the inheritance, and not to the executor or administrator of the last proprietor. The termination 'loom' is of Saxon origin, in which language it signifies a limb or member; so that heirloom is nothing else but a limb or member of the inheritance. [Stroud's *Judicial Dictionary*, 5th Ed.].

**Heirs, executors, administrators and assigns.** These words mean all persons claiming under the person to whom these words refer whether by deed, will or otherwise.

**Held.** The word held means "lawfully held". [*Budhan Singh* v *Nabi Bux* (1969)2 SCC 481: AIR 1970 SC 1880: (1970)2 SCR 10; *Kailash Rai* v *Jai Jai Ram* AIR 1973 SC 893: (1973)3 SCR 411: (1973)1 SCC 527].

The word "held" is technically understood to mean to possess by legal title. [*Budhan Singh* v *Nabi Bux* (1969)2 SCC 481: AIR 1970 SC 1880: (1970)2 SCR 10].

The word "held" means possession by legal title. [*State of U.P.* v *Smt. Sarjoo Devi* AIR 1977 SC 2196: (1977)4 SCC 2: (1978)1 SCR 181].

The word "held" connotes both ownership as well as possession. [*State of Andhra Pradesh* v *Mohd. Ashrafuddin* AIR 1982 SC 913: (1982)3 SCR 482: (1982)2 SCC 1].

**Heliport.** 'Heliport' means an area, either at ground level or elevated on a structure, used or intended to be used for the landing and take-off of helicopters and includes an area for parking helicopters and all buildings and structures thereon or appertaining thereto. [International Airports Authority Act 1971, s. 2(*c*)].

**Hemp.** 'Hemp' means—(*i*) the leaves, small stalks and flowering and fruiting tops of the Indian hemp plant (*Cannabis sativa L.*) including all forms known as *bhang*, *siddi*, or *ganja*; (*ii*) *charas*, that is, resin obtained from the Indian hemp plant, which has not been submitted to any manipulation other than those necessary for packing and transport; and (*iii*) any mixture, with or without neutral materials, any of the above forms of hemp or any drink prepared therefrom. [Dangerous Drugs Act 1930, s. 2(*c*)].

**Hereditament.** 'Hereditament' is defined in the textbooks of authority to signify all such things, whether corporeal or incorporeal, which a man may have to him and his heirs by way of inheritance, and which, if they be not otherwise bequeathed, come to him who is next of blood, and not to executors or administrators as chattels do. [*Lloyd* v *Jones* 17 LJCP 206, *per* Wilde, C.J.].

The most comprehensive words of description applicable to real estate are tenements and hereditaments; as they include every species of realty, as well corporeal as incorporeal. [2 Jarm (8th Ed.) 1270].

"Hereditaments" mean, respectively, whatever can be the subject of tenure, and whatever is capable of devolving upon death, whether as real property or as personal property, to personal representatives; but they are used in a general sense to include both the corporeal things, such as houses and land, and the rights which arise out of them. Where these rights extend to the exclusive possession of the thing which is the subject of property, they are called corporeal hereditaments, a term which is used to denote both the thing itself and the right of property in the thing; where they fall short of this, as for example in the case of *profits a prendre*, they are called incorporeal hereditaments. [Halsbury's *Laws of England*, 4th Ed., vol. 27, para 131, p. 104].

NOTE: Hereditaments are of two kinds—corporeal and incorporeal. Corporeal ones consist of such as affect the senses; such as may be seen and handled by the body; incorporeal ones are not the object of sensation, can neither be seen nor handled, are creatures of the mind and exist only in contemplation. [Cheshire's *Modern Real Property*, 9th Ed., p. 100].

**Hereditary.** Ancestorial; ancestral; genealogical; genetic; hereditable; traditional; transmissible.

That which is the subject of inheritance; that which is genetically transmitted or transmittable from parent to offspring.

**Hereditary interest.** It means an interest acquired by inheritance and not by purchase or other modes of acquisition.

**Hereditary office.** Every office held hereditarily for the performance of duties connected with administration or collection of the public revenue or with the village police, or with the settlement of boundaries or other matters of civil administration.

**Heresy.** Opinion contrary to the orthodox doctrine of the Church, or religion; opinion contrary to the generally accepted doctrine on any subject.

**Heretic.** One who holds an unorthodox opinion in matters of religion; apostate; dissenter; infidel; unbeliever; sectarian.

**Heritage.** An inheritance; an inheritable estate; legacy; lineage; ancestry.

• **Obstructed and unobstructed heritage** p. 616.

**Hessian.** Hessian is a fabric woven in a particular manner, namely, plain weave single yarn, and sacking is a fabric woven with double wrapped yarn. [*Hoare Miller* v *Union of India* 65 CWN 1206].

**Hiba.** It is a gift under Mahomedan Law which takes place by transfer of property made immediately and without any exchange by one person to another and accepted by or on behalf of the latter. It is essential to the validity of a 'hiba' that there should be within (*i*) a declaration of the gift by the donor, (*ii*) acceptance of the gift expressed or implied by or on behalf of the donee, and (*iii*) delivery of possession of the subject-matter of gift by the donor to the donee. [*Imbichimoideenkutty* v *Pathummuni Amma* (1988)1 Ker LT 409].

**Hiba-ba-shart-ul-iwaz.** It is a gift with a stipulation for return.

**Hiba-bil-iwaz.** Hiba-bil-iwaz or gift with exchange is a gift for consideration. It is in reality a sale and has all incidents of a contract sale. In hiba-bil-iwaz there must be actual payment of consideration (iwaz) on the part of the donee and *bona fide* intention on the part of the donor to divest himself *in praesenti* of the property and to confer it upon the donee. [*Imbichimoideenkutty* v *Pathummuni Amma* (1988)1 Ker LT 409].

**H.I.F.O.** Stands for "Highest in, first out". This provides a basis for charging out materials for production purposes or for valuing stock on hand at a given date, under which it is assumed that the goods are used or sold in the order of highness of cost. In short, the dearest goods are disposed of first.

**High Court.** Highest Court of a State.

▸*Meaning under the Advocates Act 1961, s. 2(g).* 'High Court', except in sub-sec. (1) and sub-sec. (1A) of s. 34 and in ss. 42 and 43, does not include a court of the Judicial Commissioner, and in relation to a State Bar Council means—(*i*) in the case of a Bar Council constituted for a State or for a State and one or more Union territories, the High Court for the State; (*ii*) in the case of the Bar Council constituted for Delhi, the High Court of Delhi.

▸*Meaning under the Code of Civil Procedure 1908, s. 2(7A).* 'High Court', in relation to the Andaman and Nicobar Islands, means the High Court in Calcutta.

▸*Meaning under the Code of Criminal Procedure 1898, s. 4(1)(i) (since repealed).* 'High Court', in relation to the Andaman and Nicobar Islands, means the High Court in Calcutta and in relation to any other local area, means the highest court of criminal appeal for that area (other than the Supreme Court) or where no such Court is established under any law for the time being in force, such officer as the State Government may appoint in this behalf.

▸*Meaning under the Contempt of Courts Act 1971, s. 2(d).* 'High Court' means the High Court for a State or a Union territory, and includes the Court of the Judicial Commissioner in any Union territory.

▸*Meaning under the Designs Act 1911, s. 2(7).* High Court shall have the same meaning as assigned to it in cl. (*i*) of s. 2 of the Patents Act 1970; vide *infra*.

▸*Meaning under the General Clauses Act 1897, s. 3(25).* 'High Court', used with reference to civil proceedings, shall mean the highest civil court of appeal (not including the Supreme Court) in the part of India in which the Act or Regulation containing the expression operates.

▸*Meaning under the High Court Judges (Conditions of Service) Act 1954, s. 2(f).* 'High Court' means a High Court for a State and includes a High Court which was exercising jurisdiction in a Part A State or in the corresponding Province before the commencement of the Constitution.

▸*Meaning under the Indian Trade Unions Act 1926, s. 11(1).* The words 'High Court' in s. 11(1) of the Indian Trade Unions Act 1926, mean High Court in the Original Jurisdiction as well as Appellate Jurisdiction. [*Mihir Kumar Gooha* v *Registrar of Trade Unions* AIR 1961 Cal 165].

▸*Meaning under the Industries (Development and Regulation) Act 1951, s. 3(cc).* 'High Court' means the High Court having jurisdiction in relation to the place at which the registered office of a company is situate.

▸*Meaning under the Merchant Shipping Act 1958, s. 3(15).* 'High Court', in relation to a vessel, means the High Court within the limits of whose appellate jurisdiction—(*a*) the port of registry of the vessel is situate; or (*b*) the vessel is for the time being; or (*c*) the cause of action wholly or in part arises.

▸*Meaning under the Patents Act 1970, s. 2(i).* 'High Court' means—(*i*) in relation to the Union territory of Delhi and the Union territory of Himachal Pradesh, the High Court of Delhi; (*ii*) in relation to the Union territory of Arunachal Pradesh and the Union territory of Mizoram, the Gauhati High Court (the High Court of Assam, Nagaland, Meghalaya, Manipur and Tripura); (*iii*) in relation to the Union territory of the Andaman and Nicobar Islands, the High Court at Calcutta; (*iv*) in relation to the Union territory of the Lakshadweep, the High Court of Kerala; (*v*) in relation to the Union territory of Goa, Daman and Diu and the Union territory of Dadra and Nagar Haveli, the High Court at Bombay; (*vi*) in relation to the Union territory of Pondicherry, the High Court at Madras; (*vii*) in relation to the Union territory of Chandigarh, the High Court of Punjab and Haryana; and (*viii*) in relation to any other State, the High Court for that State.

▸ *Meaning under the Trade and Merchandise Marks Act 1958, s. 2(h) (since repealed).* 'High Court' means the High Court having jurisdiction under s. 3.

**High public or political office.** The term 'high public or political office' contemplates only a special class of officers or politicians who may be categorised as follows: (1) official wielding extraordinary powers entitling them to take major policy decisions and holding positions of trust and answerable and accountable for their wrongs; (2) persons responsible for giving to the State a clean, stable and honest administration; (3) persons occupying a very elevated status in whose hands lies the destiny of the nation. High public or political office is an office which forms part of a political department of the government or the political executive. This includes Cabinet Ministers, Ministers, Deputy Ministers and Parliamentary Secretaries who are running the Department formulating policies and are responsible to the Parliament. [*State (Delhi Administration)* v *V.C. Shukla* AIR 1980 SC 1382: (1980)3 SCR 500: 1980 (Supp) SCC 249: (1980)2 SCC 665: 1980 SCC (Cri) 561, 849].

**High seas.** "High seas" denote all parts of the seas not included in the territorial sea and internal waters of any state. The high seas are *res communis* and are open to all nations, so that no State may validly purport to subject any part of them to its sovereignty. Freedom of the high seas comprises, *inter alia*, both for coastal and non-coastal States, freedom of navigation, freedom of fishing, freedom to lay submarine cables and pipelines, and freedom to fly over the high seas. [Halsbury's *Laws of England*, 4th Ed., vol. 18, para 1478, p. 758].

'High seas' mean the seas or oceans beyond the jurisdiction of any country. [Black's *Law Dictionary*, 8th Ed.].

NOTE: Under international law, the high seas traditionally began three miles from the coast, but under the 1982 U.N. Convention on the Law of the Sea, coastal shores now have a 200-mile exclusive economic zone. It is also termed open seas.

Outside territorial waters the law of no one country applies, since the high seas are free. [R.H. Graveson: *Conflict of Laws*, 7th Ed. 1974, p. 584].

**High second class marks.** Means where the marks fall a little short of first class marks. [*Dr. J.P. Kulshreshtha* v *Chancellor, Allahabad University* AIR 1980 SC 2141: (1980)3 SCC 902: (1980)3 SCC 418].

**High treason.** Everyone commits high treason who forms and displays by any overt act, or by publishing any printing or writing, an intention to kill or destroy the Queen, or to do her any bodily harm, tending to death or destruction, maiming or wounding, imprisonment or restrain. [Stephen's *Digest of the Criminal Law*].

**High-water mark.** 'High-water mark' in relation to a port means a line drawn through the highest points reached by ordinary springtides at any season of the year at the port. [Major Port Trusts Act 1963, s. 2(*i*)].

That part of the seashore which the waters usually reach when the tide is highest. [Mozley & Whiteley's *Law Dictionary*, 10th Ed.].

**Highest bidder.** The highest bidder in a sale of property by auction is the person who makes the highest bid in good faith. If the highest bidder is unable to pay, the auctioneer is authorised to make an offer to the next highest.

**Highway.** Broadly, any main route on land, on water or in the air; a free and public roadway or street that every person may use; the main public road connecting towns or cities; the entire width between boundaries of every publicly maintained way when part is open to public use for purposes of vehicular traffic. [Black's *Law Dictionary*, 7th Ed.].

A "highway" is the physical track along which an omnibus runs. [*K.V. Motor Transit Co. Ltd.* v *C.R. Omnibus Co. Ltd.* AIR 1946 PC 137].

The common definition of 'highway' is that it is a way leading from one marked town or inhabited place to another inhabited place, and which is common to all the subjects of the sovereign. Public bridges are highways so far as the right of passage is concerned. [*K.K. Wadhwani* v *State of Rajasthan* AIR 1958 Raj 138].

The highway is a passage over which members of the public are entitled to pass and repass. The essential characteristic of a highway is that every person should have the right to use it for the appropriate kind of traffic. The road or part over which only a particular class of people or a few individuals are allowed to pass and repass cannot be a highway. [*K. Sudarsan* v *Commissioner, Corporation of Madras* AIR 1984 Mad 292].

'Highway' means public road, King's way, or main route by land or water. [*Anurag Mishra* v *State of Madhya Pradesh* 1992 Jab LJ 480].

NOTE: *'Highway' and 'route'—distinction.* A 'highway' is the physical track along which an omnibus runs while a 'route' is an abstract conception of a line of travel between one terminus and another and is distinct from the highway traversed. [*K.V. Motor Transit Co. Ltd.* v *C.R. Omnibus Co. Ltd.* AIR 1946 PC 137].

**Highway man.** One who robs on the highway.

**Hijra.** Flight of Mohammed from Mecca to Medina. This event took place on the night of the 15th of July, A.D. 622. This marks the commencement of the Mohammadan era, which is reckoned from the dawn of the 16th of July, 622.

**Hindu.** The historical and etymological genesis of the word "Hindu" has given rise to a controversy among indologists; but the view generally accepted by scholars appears to be that the word "Hindu" is derived from the river Sindhu otherwise known as Indus which flows from the Punjab. "That part of the great Aryan race", says Monier Williams, "which immigrated from Central Asia, through the mountain passes into India, settled first in the districts near the river Sindhu (now called the Indus). The Persians pronounced this word Hindu and named their Aryan brethren Hindus. The Greeks, who probably gained their first ideas of India from the Persians, dropped the hard aspirate and called the Hindus "INDOI". [*Shastri Yagnapurushdasji* v *Muldas Bhundardas Vaishya* AIR 1966 SC 1119: (1966)3 SCR 242].

NOTE: Hinduism embraces within itself so many diverse forms of beliefs, faiths, practices and worship that it is difficult to define the term "Hindu" with precision. Under the codifying Acts, namely, the Hindu Marriage Act 1955, the Hindu Succession Act 1956, the Hindu Minority and Guardianship Act 1956 and the Hindu Adoptions and Maintenance Act 1956, the orthodox concept of the term 'Hindu' has undergone a radical change and it has been given an extended meaning. The aforesaid codifying Acts not only apply to Hindus by birth or religion, i.e., to converts to Hinduism, but also to a large number of other persons. According to Explanation (*b*) to s. 2(1) of the Hindu Succession Act 1956, Hindu Adoptions and Maintenance Act 1956 and Hindu Marriage Act 1955 as also according to Explanation (*ii*) to s. 3(1) of the Hindu Minority and Guardianship Act 1956, any child, legitimate or illegitimate, one of whose parents is a Hindu by religion and who is brought up as a Hindu is a Hindu. [*Commissioner of Wealth Tax, Madras* v *Late R. Sridharan by L.Rs.* (1976)4 SCC 489: 1976 (Supp) SCR 478: (1976)104 ITR 436].

The word 'Hindu' has had a fairly wide connotation. In origin, it indicated people living in the Indus region. It is only by subsequent usage and extension of meaning that the word acquired a religious and, therefore, in this sense, a more limited significance. But, in some contexts, the term "Hindu", even today, stands for Indians in general. In foreign countries, all Indians are sometimes described as "Hindus". Even as a term used for Indians professing a particular type of beliefs, which are presumed to have an indigenous origin, it is wide enough to include Jains and Sikhs. Hence, this is the meaning given to the term Hindu in the Hindu Succession Act. In a statute dealing with religious endowments, the term, even though not defined, may be presumed to stand for people of this country with certain religious beliefs held or forms of religious worship practised by people of this country originally. [*The Commissioner, Hindu Religious and Charitable Endowments, Mysore* v *Sri Ratnavarma Heggade (Deceased) by his L.Rs.* AIR 1977 SC 1848: (1977)1 SCR 889: (1977)1 SCC 525].

The Buddhists, the Jains, the Sikhs are classical examples of persons ceasing to be Hindu for the purpose of religion, but remaining Hindu for the purpose of administration of law. [A.M. Bhattacharjee: *Hindu Law and the Constitution*, 2nd Ed., p. 139].

**Hindu coparcenary.** A Hindu coparcenary is a narrower body than the Hindu joint family; it includes only those persons who acquire by birth an interest in the joint or coparcenary property, these being sons, grandsons and great-grandsons of the holder of the joint property for the time being. [*Gowli Buddanna* v *CIT, Mysore* AIR 1966 SC 1523: (1966)1 SCJ 686: (1966)60 ITR 293; *Narendranath* v *Commissioner of Wealth-tax* AIR 1970 SC 14: (1969)2 SCJ 727].

**Hindu joint (undivided) family.** A Hindu joint family consists of all persons lineally descended from a common ancestor and includes their wives and unmarried daughters. The common mess, the common worship, the common residence, coupled with the ties of blood and introductions into the family by marriage and adoption make them members of a joint family. [*Nibaran* v *Lalit* AIR 1939 Cal 187: ILR (1938)2 Cal 368].

A Hindu joint family consists of all persons lineally descended from a common ancestor and includes their wives and unmarried daughters. [*Gowli Buddanna* v *CIT, Mysore* (1966)1 SCJ 686: (1966)60 ITR 293: AIR 1966 SC 1523; *Surjit Lal Chhabda* v *CIT, Bombay* (1976)3 SCC 142].

The joint Hindu family is a larger body consisting of a group of persons who are united by the tie of sapindaship arising by birth, marriage or adoption. The joint Hindu family, with all its incidents, is a creature of law and cannot be created by act of parties, except to the extent to which a stranger may be affiliated to the family by adoption. [*Surjit Lal Chhabda* v *CIT, Bombay* (1976)3 SCC 142].

NOTE: Joint family and undivided family are synonymous terms.

A Hindu undivided family is a fleeting body. Its composition changes by births, deaths, marriages and divorces. [*Agarwal and Co.* v *CIT, U.P.* AIR 1970 SC 1343: (1971)1 SCR 237: (1970)2 SCC 48: (1970)77 ITR 10].

There may be a joint Hindu family consisting of a single male member and widows of the deceased coparceners. [*Gowli Buddanna* v *C.I.T., Mysore* AIR 1966 SC 1523: (1966)1 SCJ 686: (1966)60 ITR 293].

▸*Meaning under the Income-tax Act.* The expression "Hindu undivided family" is used in the sense in which a Hindu joint family is understood under the various schools of Hindu Law. [*Attorney-General of Ceylon* v *Arunachalam Chettiar* (1958)34 ITR (Supp) 42; *Gowli Buddanna* v *CIT, Mysore* AIR 1966 SC 1523: (1966)1 SCJ 686: (1966)60 ITR 293].

NOTE: The assessment in the status of a Hindu undivided family can be made only when there are two or more members of the Hindu undivided family. [*C. Krishna Prasad* v *CIT, Bangalore* AIR 1975 SC 498: (1975)2 SCR 709: (1975)1 SCC 160: (1974)97 ITR 493].

**Hinduism.** *The Encyclopaedia of Religion and Ethics*, vol. VI, has described Hinduism as the title applied to that form of religion which prevails among the vast majority of the present population of the Indian Empire. [*Shastri Yagnapurushdasji* v *Muldas Bhundardas Vaishya* AIR 1966 SC 1119: (1966)3 SCR 242].

"Hinduism" has been defined as meaning a complex body of social, cultural, and religious beliefs and practices evolved in and largely confined to the Indian subcontinent and marked by a caste system, an outlook tending to view all forms and theories as aspects of one eternal being and truth, a belief in ahimsa, karma, dharma, samskara, and moksha, and the practice of the way of works, the way of knowledge or the way of devotion as the means of release from the round of rebirths; the way of life and form of thought of a Hindu. In *Encyclopaedia Britannica* (15th Ed.), the term, "Hinduism" has been defined as meaning the civilization of Hindus (originally the inhabitants of the land of the Indus river). It properly denotes the Indian civilization of approximately the last 2,000 years which gradually evolved from Vedism, the religion of the ancient Indo-European peoples who settled in India in the last centuries of the 2nd millennium B.C. [*Commissioner of Wealth Tax, Madras* v *Late R. Sridharan by L.Rs.* (1976)4 SCC 489: 1976 (Supp) SCR 478: (1976)104 ITR 436].

**Hire.** Payment for the temporary use of something or for labour or personal services; wages.

A bailment for a reward or compensation. It is divisible into four sorts—(1) The hiring of a thing for use. (2) The hiring of work and labour. (3) The hiring of care and services to be performed or bestowed on the thing delivered. (4) The hiring of the carriage of goods from one place to another. The three last are but sub-divisions of the general head of hire of labour and services. [Wharton's *Law Lexicon*].

To engage the labour or services of another for wages or other payment; to procure the temporary use of property, usually at a set price. [Black's *Law Dictionary*, 7th Ed.].

▸ *Meaning under the Hire-purchase Act 1972, s. 2(b)*. 'Hire' means the sum payable periodically by the hirer under a hire-purchase agreement.

NOTE: *'Hire' and 'reward'—distinction.* A distinction falls to be drawn between the word 'hire' and the word 'reward'. The first word necessarily imports an obligation to pay but reward imports no obligation to pay. [*Bonham* v *Zurich General Accident & Liability Insurance Co. Ltd.* (1945) KB 292 (CA), *per* Uthwatt, J.].

**Hire and fire.** Hire means to engage the personal services of a servant for a set sum and fire means in the context of the word hire, to dismiss the servant at master's will.

NOTE: In the forensic area exclusively governed by master and servant relationship, the doctrine of hire and fire is still in vogue. But where the servant has acquired a status, the doctrine has been given a go by since long. Thus, a government servant or an employee of the Instrumentality of State are such person whose service cannot be terminated at the sweet will on interpreting *ex post facto* a conduct as misconduct. [*A.L. Kalra* v *Project Equipment Corpn.* AIR 1984 SC 1361; *Central Inland Water Transport* v *Broja Nath Ganguly* AIR 1986 SC 1571]. Law will have to move two centuries backward to accept the contention that some misconduct neither defined nor enumerated and which may be believed by the employer to be misconduct *ex post facto* would expose the workman to a penalty, and one is to return to the days of hire and fire which reverse movement is not possible. [*Glaxo Laboratory* v *Presiding Officer, Meerut* AIR 1984 SC 505, 514; *Rasiklal Vaghajibhai Patel* v *Ahmedabad Municipal Corporation* AIR 1985 SC 505].

**Hire-purchase.** A system whereby the owner of goods lets them on hire for periodic payments by the hirer upon an agreement that when a certain number of payments have been completed, the absolute property in the goods will pass to the hirer, but so that the hirer may return the goods at any time without any obligation to pay any balance of rent accruing after return; until the conditions have been fulfilled, the property remains in the owner. [Jowitt's *Dictionary of English Law*, 2nd Ed.].

A system of letting of goods under a contract, in whatsoever terms it may be expressed and whether it be truly one of sale or hire, whereby goods are taken on hire by one person from another person in consideration of periodical payments to be made by the first mentioned person to the other person, with an option to the first mentioned person to become the buyer of the goods.

**Hire-purchase agreement.** An agreement under which goods are let on hire and under which the hirer has an option to purchase them in accordance with the terms of the agreement and includes an agreement under which—(*i*) possession of goods is delivered by the owner thereof to a person on condition that such person pays the agreed amount in periodical instalments, and (*ii*) the property in the goods is to pass to such person on the payment of the last of such instalments, and (*iii*) such person has a right to terminate the agreement at any time before the property so passes. [Hire-purchase Act 1972, s. 2(*c*)].

Hire-purchase agreements are executory contracts under which the goods are let on hire and the hirer has an option to purchase in accordance with the terms of the agreement. These types of agreements were originally entered into between the dealer and the customer and the dealer used to extend credit to the customer. But as hire-purchase scheme gained in popularity and in size, the dealers who were not endowed with liberal amount of working capital found it difficult to extend the scheme to many customers. Then the financiers came into the picture. The finance company would buy the goods from the dealer and let them to the customer under hire-purchase agreement. The dealer would deliver the goods to the customer who would then drop out of the transaction leaving the finance company to collect instalments directly from the customer.

NOTE: Under hire-purchase agreement, the hirer is simply paying for the use of the goods and for the option to purchase them. The finance charge, representing the difference between the cash price and the hire-purchase price, is not interest but represents a sum which the hirer has to pay for the privilege of being allowed to discharge the purchase price of goods by instalments. [*Charanjit Singh Chadha* v *Sudhir Mehra* (2001)7 SCC 417: JT 2001(2) SC 226].

**Hire-purchase price.** The total sum payable by the hirer under hire-purchase agreement in order to complete the purchase of, or the acquisition of property in, the goods to which the agreement relates and includes any sum so payable by the hirer under the hire-purchase agreement by way of deposit or other initial payment or credited or to be credited to him under such agreement on account of any such deposit or payment, whether that sum is to be or has been paid to the owner or to any other person or is to be or has been discharged by payment of money or by transfer or delivery of goods or by any other means, but does not include any sum payable as a penalty or as compensation or damages for a breach of the agreement. [Hire-purchase Act 1972, s. 2(*d*)].

**Hirer.** The person who obtains or has obtained possession of goods from an owner under a hire-purchase agreement and includes a person to whom the hirer's rights or liabilities under the agreement have passed by assignment or by operation of law. [Hire-purchase Act 1972, s. 2(*e*)].

**Hissa.** A share, a part, a lot, a portion; a share of revenue or rent. [Wilson's *Glossary*].

**History sheet.** History sheet is a technical term used in relation to the composition of a 'book' which under the Police Regulations the Police are enjoined to make. History sheets were to be opened for such citizens only who are or were likely to become habitual criminals or abettors of such criminals. [Police Regulations; *Rameshwar Prasad* v *Superintendent of Police* AIR 1963 All 408].

▸ *Meaning under the Rules of Motor Vehicles Act.* History sheet referred to in the Rules framed under the Motor Vehicles Act relates to an applicant and not to a vehicle or categories of vehicles. It is a continuous methodical record of public events or whole trend of events connected with a person or a thing. It would also refer to aggregate of past events or course of human affairs. [*Nagabhushanam* v *Ankam Ankaiah* AIR 1968 AP 74].

**Hitherto.** In legal use, this term always restricts the matter in connection with which it is employed to a period of time already passed.

**Hoard.** The word "hoard" means to amass and deposit in secret. [*Kamla Prasad* v *The District Magistrate, Saran* AIR 1975 SC 726: (1975)1 SCC 314: 1975 Cr LJ 605: 1975 SCC (Cri) 141].

To acquire and hold (goods) beyond one's reasonable needs, usually because of an actual or anticipated shortage or price increase. [Black's *Law Dictionary*, 8th Ed.].

**Hoarding.** A large structure used to carry advertisements, displaying posters etc.; a billboard; treasure laid by; savings.

Act of holding and acquiring goods in their supply beyond the reasonable needs of the person so holding. [Black's *Law Dictionary*, 5th Ed.].

**Hold.** To possess by a lawful title; to adjudge or decide; to direct and bring about officially; to conduct according to law; to keep in custody or under an obligation; to take or have an estate from another; to conduct or preside at; to convoke, open, and direct the operations of; to possess or occupy; to be in possession and administration of. [Black's *Law Dictionary*, 7th Ed.].

The word 'hold' has several meaning. It connotes both "ownership" as well as "possession". [*State of A.P.* v *Md. Ashrafuddin* AIR 1982 SC 913].

The word does not connote a title of a trespasser, but that it refers to a title that had a legal origin. [*Buddhan Singh* v *Nabi Bux* AIR 1962 All 43].

The word 'hold' includes a two-fold idea of the actual possession of a thing, as also of being invested with legal title. [*K.K. Handique* v *Member, Board of Agricultural Income-tax* AIR 1966 SC 1191].

The word "hold" means own. [*The State of West Bengal* v *Subodh Gopal Bose* AIR 1954 SC 92: 1954 SCR 587: 1954 SCJ 127; *Government of A.P.* v *H.E.H. The Nizam, Hyderabad* AIR 1996 SC 3142: (1996)3 SCC 282: JT 1996(3) SC 629].

The expression 'hold' connotes two concepts, that is, physical possession or legal title. [*Government of A.P.* v *H.E.H. The Nizam, Hyderabad* AIR 1996 SC 3142: (1996)3 SCC 282: JT 1996(3) SC 629].

The word 'hold' means to hold the ownership or use; to keep as one's own; to possess by legal title. [*State of U.P.* v *Sarjo Devi* 1977 UJ (SC) 572; *Manohar Ramkrishna* v *G.G. Desai* AIR 1951 Nag 33].

**Holder.** A person who has legal possession of a negotiable instrument and is entitled to receive payment on it; a person with legal possession of a document of title or an investment security; a person who possesses or uses property.

**Holder in due course.** A person who in good faith has given value for a negotiable instrument that is complete and regular on its face, is not overdue, and, to the possessor's knowledge, has not been dishonoured.

▸ *Meaning under the Negotiable Instruments Act 1881, s. 9.* Any person who for consideration became the possessor of a promissory note, bill of exchange or cheque if payable to bearer, or the payee or endorsee thereof if payable to order, before the amount mentioned in it became payable, and without having sufficient cause to believe that any defect existed in the title of the person from whom he derived his title.

> NOTE: The definition in s. 9 makes it clear that to be a 'holder in due course' a person must be a holder for consideration and the instrument must have been transferred to him before it becomes overdue and he must be a transferee in good faith and another important condition is that the transferee namely the person who for consideration became the possessor of the cheque should not have any reason to believe that there was any defect in the title of the transferor. Though the failure to prove *bona fide* or absence of negligence would not negative the claim of the holder to be a holder in due course, yet in the circumstances of a given case, if there is the patent gross negligence on his part which by itself indicates lack of due diligence, it can negative his claim, for he cannot negligently disregard a 'red flag' which arouses suspicion regarding the title. [*U. Ponnappa Moothan Sons, Palghat* v *Catholic Syrian Bank Ltd.* (1991)1 SCC 113].

**Holder of a promissory note/bill of exchange/cheque.** Holder of a promissory note, bill of exchange or cheque means any person entitled in his own name to the possession thereof and to receive or recover the amount due thereon from the parties thereto. [Negotiable Instruments Act 1881, s. 8].

NOTE: The term 'holder' would not include a person who, though in possession of the instrument, has no right to recover the amount due thereon from the parties thereto, such as a finder of a lost instrument payable to bearer or a thief or even the payee himself who is prohibited by court from receiving the amount. [*Anjanaiah* v *Nagappa* AIR 1967 AP 61].

**Holding.** A court's determination of a matter of law pivotal to its decision; a principle drawn from such a decision; a ruling on evidence or other questions presented at trial; legally owned property, especially land or securities. [Black's *Law Dictionary*, 7th Ed.].

Holding means the land or lands held by a raiyat. [West Bengal Land Reforms Act 1955, s. 2(6) as amended by the West Bengal Land Holding Revenue Act 1979].

**Holding company.** A company shall be deemed to be the holding company of another if, but only if, that other is its subsidiary. [Companies Act 1956, s. 4(4)].

It is generally a company that confines its activity to owning stock in, and supervising management of, other companies. It usually owns a controlling interest in (more than 50% of the voting stock) the companies whose stock it holds. Personal holding company is one formed usually for tax reasons by an individual or small group of individuals for the purpose of holding investments and receiving the income therefrom.

**Holiday.** A day of exemption from labour; a day upon which the usual operations of business are suspended and the courts closed, and, generally, no legal process is served.

**Holograph.** A document in the handwriting of the executant.

A will which is written by the testator with his own hand is a holograph will. The law makes a great presumption of genuineness in favour of a holograph will. [*Ajit Chandra* v *Akhil Chandra* AIR 1969 Cal 551].

NOTE: In some continental country a holograph will need not be attested or witnessed. Some states of U.S.A. as also India, however, refuse to recognise any will, whatsoever, not conforming to the formal statutory requirements relating to attestation clause, witnesses etc.

**Homa.** Burnt offering, oblations of clarified butter poured on fire; other articles may also be offered. [Wilson's *Glossary*].

**Home.** Abode; dwelling place; fixed residence; lodging place; permanent local address; place of abode; place of dwelling; place of existence; place of refuge; place of residence; place of rest; place to live in; residence.

One's own dwelling place; the house in which one lives, especially the house in which one lives with his family; the habitual abode of one's family; a dwelling house. [*Mann* v *Haines* 73 P 2d 1066, 1072].

**Homestead.** The house, outbuildings, an adjoining land owned and occupied by a person or family as a residence. [Black's *Law Dictionary*, 8th Ed.].

'Homestead' means a dwelling house together with any courtyard, compound, garden, outhouse, place of worship, family graveyard, library, office, guest house, tanks, wells, privies, latrines, drains and boundary walls annexed to or appertaining to such dwelling house. [*Abdulla Kabir* v *M.D. Nasiruddin* (1989)2 SCC 361].

**Homicide.** The legal term for killing a man, whether lawfully or unlawfully, is 'homicide'. [Glanville Williams: *Textbook of Criminal Law*, p. 204 (1978)].

Homicide is the killing of a human being by a human being. [Stroud's *Judicial Dictionary*, 5th Ed.].

The killing of one human being by the act, procurement, or omission of another is homicide. [Black's *Law Dictionary*, 8th Ed.].

- **Criminal homicide.** Homicide prohibited and punishable by law, such as murder or manslaughter; the act of purposely, knowingly, recklessly, or negligently causing the death of another human being.
- **Justifiable homicide.** The killing of another in self-defence when faced with the danger of death or serious bodily injury; a killing mandated or permitted by the law, such as execution for a capital crime or killing to prevent a crime or a criminal's escape. It is also termed as excusable homicide.
- **Negligent homicide.** Homicide resulting from the careless performance of a legal or illegal act in which the danger of death is apparent.

**Honest.** Above board; clean; fair; free from fraud; genuine; impeccable; incapable of deceit; principled; stainless; unfaked; well-principled.

**Honorarium.** A payment of money or anything of value made to a person for services rendered for which fees cannot legally be or are not traditionally paid; a voluntary reward for that for which no remuneration could be collected by law; a voluntary donation in consideration of services that admit of no compensation in money; a gratuitous payment, esp. for professional services, as distinguished from compensation for physical labour. [Black's *Law Dictionary*, 8th Ed.].

Honorarium is honorary reward, a fee for professional service rendered. [*Karbhari Bhimaji Rahamare* v *Shanker Rao* AIR 1975 SC 575: (1975)1 SCC 252; *Ganesa* v *Laxmi Co-operative Banking Society* AIR 1937 Mad 379].

**Honour.** As noun means high regard; respectability; sense of responsibility; admiration; adulation; commendation; glorification; righteousness; trustworthiness.

As verb means acclaim; accredit; commemorate; applaud; eulogize; glorify; pay tribute; praise.

It is a courtesy title given to judges and certain other public officials.

- **Acceptor for honour** p. 12.

**Hope.** Desire accompanied by expectation; desire with expectation of fulfilment; expectation and desire combined.

> NOTE: *"Hope" and "believe"—distinction.* The word "hope" suggests a lingering doubt that what is desired and expected may not turn out to be true whereas the word "believe" has logical confidence or rational conviction as its essential element. [*Chandran* v *State of Madras* AIR 1978 SC 1574: (1978)4 SCC 90: 1978 Cr LJ 1693: (1979)1 SCR 176].

**Horse power.** A unit of power capable of lifting 33,000 pounds a foot a minute.

**Horticulture.** The science and art of growing fruits, vegetables, flowers, or ornamental plants; that department of the science of agriculture which relates to the cultivation of gardens or orchards, including the growing of vegetables, fruits, flowers and ornamental shrubs, and trees.

> NOTE: Agriculture includes horticulture. [*Srinath Jagatguru Sringeri* v *Duraiswami Naidu* AIR 1931 Mad 659: 54 Mad 900].

**Hosiery goods.** The dictionary meaning of the word 'hosiery' is knitted or woven underclothing; knitted goods; socks and stockings. Hosiery goods are no doubt means for wearing, but they are knitted goods. They are not displayed when worn. [*Commissioner of Sales Tax* v *Mahajan Brother* (1963)14 STC 808].

**Hospital.** An institution for the treatment and care of sick, wounded, infirm, or aged persons; the building used for such purpose.

> NOTE: Hospital is built, staffed and equipped mainly for diagnosis of disease, treatment of the sick and injured, cure of mental abnormality, prevention of health and physical well-being. [*Social S.G. of Assisi Sisters* v *K.S.E.B.* (1988)1 Ker LT 727].
>
> *"Hospital", "clinic" or "dispensary"—distinction.* Hospital is a place where sick and injured persons receive medical care of such nature that some patients are required to utilise a bed during part or all of their stay while dispensary and clinic are for ambulatory patients who return to their homes after each visit. Generally, hospital is the genus of which clinic and dispensaries are only species and the purpose of all is generally treatment of the sick. [*Employees' Provident Fund Inspector* v *Poly Clinic Pvt. Ltd.* (1988)2 Ker LT 41].

**Hostel.** A house of residence or lodging for students, nurses, etc.; a lodging house; a supervised shelter for the use of young people on walking trips.

Hostel is a house of residence for students and is part of an educational institution taking its colour as a commercial consumer. [*Social S.G. of Assisi Sisters* v *K.S.E.B.* (1988)1 Ker LT 727].

**Hostile witness.** A witness who is biased against the examining party or who is unwilling to testify. [Black's *Law Dictionary*, 8th Ed.]. It is also termed adverse witness.

NOTE: A hostile witness may be asked leading questions on direct examination.

If a witness turns hostile, it does not mean that his entire statement is to be discarded. The rule of prudence is that his statement has to be considered with due care and caution. In other words, explicit reliance cannot be placed upon him but if he is duly corroborated by other evidence, his statement can certainly be availed of in favour of the prosecution or in favour of the accused, as the case may be. [*Harpal Singh* v *State of H.P.* 1976 Cr LJ 162].

Permission to cross-examine one's own witness on the footing that he has become hostile should be granted after properly weighing the circumstances. [*Rabindra Dey* v *State of Orissa* AIR 1977 SC 170: 1977 Cr LJ 173].

**Hotel.** A "hotel" is a building held out to the public as a place where all transient persons who come will be received and entertained as guests for compensation and it opens its facilities to the public as a whole rather than limited accessibility to a well-defined private group. [*Ambassador Athletic Club* v *Utah State Tax Commission* 496 P 2d 883].

NOTE: In order to constitute a 'hotel', two elements, *viz.*, (1) access thereto by the public or a section thereof, and (2) supply of articles constituting meals and drinks for a price are necessary. [*Club Mahabaleshwar* v *Municipality of Mahabaleshwar* 61 Bom LR 52].

**House.** The word "house" would in its ordinary sense include any building irrespective of its user. To ascertain the meaning of the word "house", one must understand the subject-matter with respect to which it is used in order to arrive at the sense in which it is employed in a statute. The word "house" is a structure of a permanent character. It is structurally severed from other tenements. It is not necessary that a house if adapted for residential purposes should be actually dwelt in. The idea of the varieties of meanings can be had from the subject-matter of the statute. The word "house" extends to a building which is used for business and should not be restricted to a mere dwelling house. It is not limited to a structure designed for human habitation, and may mean a building or shed intended or used as a habitation or shelter for animals of any kind, a building in the ordinary sense or any building, edifice, or structure enclosed with walls and covered, regardless of the fact of human habitation. Under particular circumstances, the term may be equivalent to and inter-changeable or synonymous with "building", "dwelling house" and sometimes "premises". [*The Tata Engineering and Locomotive Company Ltd.* v *The Gram Panchayat, Pimpri Waghere* AIR 1976 SC 2463: (1976)4 SCC 177: (1977)1 SCR 306].


- **Dwelling house** p. 288.
- **Farm house** p. 347.
- **Gaming house** p. 381.
- **Lodging house** p. 542.
- **Residential house** p. 754.
- **Slaughter-house** p. 800.


**House-breaking.** A person is said to commit "house-breaking" who commits house trespass if he effects his entrance into the house or any part of it in any of the six ways hereinafter described; or if, being in the house or any part of it for the purpose of committing an offence, or, having committed an offence therein, he quits the house or any part of it in any such six ways, that is to say:

*First*—If he enters or quits through a passage made by himself, or by any abettor of the house trespass in order to the committing of the house trespass.

*Secondly*—If he enters or quits through any passage not intended by any person other than himself or an abettor of the offence, for human entrance, or through any passage to which he has obtained access by scaling or climbing over any wall or building.

*Thirdly*—If he enters or quits through any passage which he or any abettor of the house trespass has opened in order to the committing of the house trespass by any means by which that passage was not intended by the occupier of the house to be opened.

*Fourthly*—If he enters or quits by opening any lock in order to the committing of the house trespass, or in order to the quitting of the house after a house trespass.

*Fifthly*—If he effects his entrance or departure by using criminal force or committing an assault or by threatening any person with assault.

*Sixthly*—If he enters or quits by any passage which he knows to have been fastened against such entrance or departure, and to have been unfastened by himself or by an abettor of the house trespass.

*Explanation*—Any out-house or building occupied with a house, and between which and such house there is an immediate internal communication is part of the house within the meaning of this section. [Indian Penal Code 1860, s. 445].

**House of Commons.** The Lower House of Parliament in Great Britain consisting of the representatives of the people, except peers and prelates.

**House of Lords.** The Upper House of Parliament in Great Britain consisting of Lords spiritual and Lords temporal.

**House of the People.** The Lower House of Parliament for the Union of India.

**House trespass.** Whoever commits criminal trespass by entering into or remaining in any building, tent or vessel used as a human dwelling or any building used as a place of worship or as a place for the custody of property is said to commit house trespass. [Indian Penal Code 1860, s. 442].

**However.** This word in a deed or will indicates an alternative intention, a contrast with the previous clause, and a modification of it under certain circumstances.

**Human rights.** The freedoms, immunities, and benefits that, according to modern values (especially at an international level), all human beings should be able to claim as a matter of right in the society in which they live. [Black's *Law Dictionary*, 8th Ed.].

**Hundi.** A bill of exchange.


- **Acceptance of hundi** p. 11.
- **Darshani hundi** p. 224.
- **Shahjog hundi** p. 791.
- **Shahjogi hundi** p. 791.


**Hundi darshani.** A bill of exchange payable at sight.

**Hurt.** Whoever causes bodily pain, disease or infirmity to any person is said to cause hurt. [Indian Penal Code 1860, s. 319].

In such phrases as "to the hurt or annoyance of another", or "hurt, molested, or restrained in his person or estate", this word is not restricted to physical injuries, but includes also mental pain, as well as discomfort or annoyance.


- **Grievous hurt** p. 399.


**Husband.** A married man; one who has a lawful wife living.


- **Ship's husband** p. 795.


**Husband and wife.** In English common law, they were for the most part treated as one person. The property of a wife became with few exceptions, that of the husband. At common law, a husband could not make a conveyance directly to his wife. This could be effected, however, through the medium of a use or trust, or by will. The property distinction between a married woman and an unmarried woman has been almost entirely removed by statute. [Mozley & Whiteley's *Law Dictionary*, 10th Ed.].

NOTE: In India the husband and the wife are treated as separate persons. Husbands and wives under s. 120, Indian Evidence Act are competent witnesses for or against each other in Civil as well as Criminal proceedings. [Ratanlal on *Law of Evidence*, 21st Ed., p. 686].

**Hush-money.** A bribe to hinder the giving of information [Mozley & Whiteley's *Law Dictionary*, 10th Ed.]; a bribe to suppress the dissemination of certain information; a payment to secure silence.

**Hut.** Hut means any building, no material portion of which above the plinth level is constructed of masonry or of squared timber framing or of iron framing. [Cantonments Act 1924, s. 2(*xvi*)].

Under the Bengal Municipal Act 1932, a *hut* means any building which is constructed principally of wood, bamboo, mud, leaves, grass or thatch and includes any temporary structure of whatever size or any small building (not being a masonry building) of whatever material made. [*Burdwan Real Property* v *L.B. Kapuria* AIR 1961 Cal 398].

**Huzur and sarkar.** The words 'sarkar' and 'huzur' do not necessarily mean the government. These words must be understood with reference to the context. These are terms of respect which may be used by a subordinate while addressing his superior. [*Rudreshwari Prasad* v *Rani Probhabati* AIR 1945 Pat 339].

**Hydrogenation.** "Hydrogenation" is a specialised process and is described in *Encyclopaedia Britannica* (1951 Ed., vol. 11, p. 978) as "the treatment of a substance with hydrogen so that this combines directly with the substance treated. The term has, however, developed a more technical and restricted sense. It is now generally used to mean the treatment of an "unsaturated" organic compound with hydrogen, so as to convert it by direct addition to a "saturated" compound. [*State of Maharashtra* v *Hansraj Depar Parle Oil Centre* (1977)2 SCC 216: (1977)3 SCR 78: 1977 Cr LJ 833: 1977 Cr LR (SC) 148: 1977 SCC (Cri) 319].

**Hypothecation.** The pledging of something as security without delivery of title or possession. [Black's *Law Dictionary*, 8th Ed.].

The act of pledging a thing as security for a debt or demand without parting with the possession. [Wharton's *Law Lexicon*].

**Hypothetical question.** A trial device that solicits an expert witness's opinion based on assumptions treated as facts established by evidence. [Black's *Law Dictionary*, 8th Ed.]. It is also termed abstract question.

NOTE: A hypothetical question assumes something for the time being. The facts are assumed for the purpose of the question. The form of question to an expert must be hypothetical. Hypothetical questions should not be put to non-experts.

A hypothetical question is put in this way: "Assuming such and such facts to be true, what is your opinion on the matter?" "Assuming such and such an injury to have been inflicted, what is your opinion as to the nature of the weapon by which it was possibly or probably inflicted?" [*Roghuni* v *R*. 9 C 455, *per* Field, J.].

# Ii

**Ibidem, ibid, id.** In the same place, volume or case.

**Ibraa.** A discharge; remission.

**Ibraanamah.** Deed of acquittance or discharge; a written relinquishment of a claim.

**Icon.** A figure or representation of a thing; an object of particular admiration, especially as a representative symbol of something; a thing which has a characteristic in common with the thing it signifies.

**Iconoclast.** Breaker of images or idols; one who attacks traditional or cherished beliefs.

**Id certum est quod certum reddi potest.** That is certain that can be made certain.

**Iddat.** The time of probation which a divorced Mahomedan woman or widow must wait before she marries again in order to determine whether she is pregnant is called *'iddat'*.

*Iddat* may be described as the period during which it is incumbent upon a woman, whose marriage has been dissolved by divorce or death to remain in seclusion, and to abstain from marrying another husband. [Mulla's *Principles of Mahomedan Law*, 19th Ed., para 257, p. 225].

NOTE: *Iddat* is the period during which it is obligatory for a Mahomedan woman, whose marriage has been dissolved by divorce or death, to remain in seclusion and to abstain from marrying again. This is necessary to ascertain whether she is pregnant, so as to avoid confusion as to parentage. When the marriage is dissolved by divorce, the period of *iddat* is three monthly courses if she is subject to menstruation; otherwise it is three lunar months. If it is found that the woman is pregnant, the period is extended up to delivery of the child. If the marriage is dissolved by death, the period of *iddat* is four months and ten days. But if she is found to be pregnant, the *iddat* lasts for four months and ten days or until delivery of the child, whichever period is longer.

**Idem, ad.** "Of the same mind", that is "agreed". This is a necessary element in a valid contract.

**Idem per idem.** An illustration or proof

**Identifiable constituent.** If a component is capable of identification by a chemical or other test as a component of a finished product, it would be an identifiable constituent. [*State of Madras* v *M.R. Krishnaswamy Naidu* AIR 1970 SC 1027: (1970)26 STC 42: (1971)3 SCC 831].

**Identification.** Proof of identity; the proving that a person, subject, or article before the court is the very same that he or it is alleged, charged, or reputed to be.

**Idgah.** A platform, sometimes screened or enclosed by a brick wall, where Mahomedans assemble for occasional devotions, especially at the season of the *Ids* or festivals. It is usually situated on the outskirts of a town or village. [Wilson's *Glossary*].

**Idiot.** A stupid person; an utter fool; a person of extremely low intelligence; a human being conspicuously deficient in mental powers and in the capacity for self-protection; a person exhibiting the lowest grade of mental development; a foolish fellow; a simpleton.

An idiot is a person afflicted with profound mental retardation. [Black's *Law Dictionary*, 7th Ed.].

An idiot is a person who from birth has no mind. An idiot is known by his perpetual infirmity of nature, for he never has any sense or understanding to contract with any man.

Idiots are defined as "persons so defective in mind from birth or from an early age as to be unable to guard themselves against common physical dangers". [*R.* v *F.* 74 JP 384].

**Idol.** An image of a deity etc. used as an object of worship; a person or thing that is the object of excessive or supreme adulation.

NOTE: A Hindu idol is a juridical person and is capable of holding property and is invested with the power to sue or of being sued. The power is, however, to be exercised through the shebait. [*Tarit Bhusan* v *Sridhar Salagram* AIR 1942 Cal 99: 45 CWN 932].

**If.** In deeds and wills, this word, as a rule, implies a condition precedent, unless it be controlled by other words. [*Hughes* v *John Hancock Mut. Life Ins. Co.* 297 NYS 116, 122].

The word "if" is always expressive of a condition. In legal and ordinary phraseology the word imports a condition. [*Harbans Singh* v *State of Punjab* 1986 Cr LJ 1834, 1837 (FB)].

**Ignorantia facti excusat.** Ignorance of fact excuses.

**Ignorantia judicis est calamitas innocentis.** The ignorance of a judge is the misfortune of the innocent.

**Ignorantia legis neminem excusat.** Ignorance of law excuses nobody.

NOTE: This maxim was originally formulated at a time when the list of crimes, broadly speaking, represented current morality (*mala in se*), but we now have many other crimes that are the results of administrative or social regulation (*mala prohibita*), which are equally governed by the maxim. [Glonville Williams on *Text Book of Criminal Law*, Ed. 1978, p. 405; *State of Maharashtra* v *Mayer Hans George* AIR 1965 SC 722: (1965)1 Cr LJ 641].

The maxim cannot be carried to the extent of saying that every person must be presumed to know that a piece of legislation enacted by a legislature of competent jurisdiction must be held to be invalid in case a differential treatment is prescribed and that he must refuse to submit to it. [*Basheshar Nath* v *Income-tax Commissioner* AIR 1959 SC 149].

There are many cases to be found in which equity, upon a mere mistake of the law without the admixture of other circumstances, has given relief to a party who has dealt with the property under the influence of such mistake. [*Beauchamp* v *Winn* 1873 LR 6 HL 223].

**Ihlal.** Any act or formula by which a transaction illegal at its inception can be made lawful under the Muslim law.

**Ijab.** Under the Muslim law, it means the oral offer by one of the contracting parties in negotiating a marriage, contract, sale etc.

**Ijahar.** A deposition in court; an affidavit; a statement or information to the police.

**Ijanadar.** A person holding an *ijara* which is a lease or farm of land revenue or other proprietary right as distinguished from other kinds of leases of land. [*Padmini Kunwar* v *State of Vindhya Pradesh* AIR 1961 SC 1204: (1961)3 SCR 907].

**Ijara.** A lease or farm of land revenue or other proprietary right as distinguished from *patta* or lease of land for cultivation, though sometimes it is used to indicate just a lease of land of any kind. [*Padmini Kunwar* v *State of Vindhya Pradesh* AIR 1961 SC 1204: (1961)3 SCR 907].

**Ijmali.** Joint, undivided, unpartitioned (as in interest in land).

**Ikhtiar.** An option of divorce granted to a wife by her husband under the Muslim law.

**Ikhtiar-nama.** A power of attorney.

**Ikrar.** Agreement; promise; acknowledgment or assent. The word is often interpreted as agreement. [*Hari Singh* v *Harbans Lal* AIR 1973 All 488].

**Ikrarnama.** A deed of agreement or contract.

**Ilahi.** The era introduced by the Emperor Akbar, beginning with the first year of his reign, A.D. 1556. This era never obtained currency, and is now obsolete.

**Ilaka.** Jurisdiction; the extent of any estate or property.

**Ill health.** Any disorder in health which incapacitates an individual from discharging the duties entrusted to him or affects his work adversely or comes in the way of his normal and effective functioning can be covered by the said phrase. The phrase would include cases of drivers who have developed a defective or sub-normal vision or eye-sight which is bound to interfere with their normal working as drivers. [*Anand Behari* v *Rajasthan State Road Transport Corporation* AIR 1991 SC 1003: (1991)1 SCC 731: 1991 SCC (L&S) 393: 1990 Supp (3) SCR 622: JT 1990(4) SC 794].

**Illatom.** A kind of adoption, whereby a son-in-law is affiliated to a family by custom in Andhra. This custom prevails among the Reddis of the ceded districts. A person who has no son but daughter or daughters, may exercise the right of taking an illatom son-in-law. Regarding succession, the illatom son-in-law stands in the footing of a son and in case of an afterborn natural son takes an equal share. An illatom son-in-law is a boy incorporated into the family with a view to give in a daughter in marriage and is customarily recognised as an heir in the absence of a natural born son. [*P. Lakshmi Reddy* v *L. Lakshmi Reddy* AIR 1957 SC 314: 1957 SCA 197: 1957 SCJ 248: 1957 SCR 195].

It is the affiliation of a son-in-law in consideration of assistance in the management of the family property. A specific agreement to that effect is necessary. But in the case of ancient adoptions, it is permissible to infer such an agreement from long course or conduct and circumstantial evidence. In the ultimate analysis, it is a question of fact whether the factum of adoption is established or not in the circumstances of each case. [*Venkateswaralu* v *China Raghavulu* AIR 1957 AP 604].

**Illegal.** Forbidden by law; unlawful; against or not authorised by law.

▸*Meaning under the Indian Penal Code 1860, s. 43.* The word "illegal" is applicable to everything which is an offence or which is prohibited by law, or which furnishes ground for civil action.

**Illegal contract.** An illegal contract is exceptionally difficult to define. It does not merely mean a contract contrary to the criminal law, although such a contract would indubitably be illegal. But a contract can well be illegal without contravening the criminal law, because there are certain activities which the law does not actually prohibit, but at the same time regards as contrary to the public interest and definitely to be discouraged, for instance, prostitution. While a void contract is not necessarily illegal, an illegal contract is often void. However, the consequences of an illegal contract differ somewhat from those usually produced by a simply void contract, so illegal contracts are usually accorded separate treatment. [P.S. Atiyah: *An Introduction to the Law of Contract*, 3rd Ed., 1981, p. 38].

A contract is illegal, if it involves doing something illegal or contrary to public policy or if the intention of the parties in making the contract is thereby to promote something which is illegal or contrary to public policy. [Sutton and Shannon on *Contracts*, 6th Ed., p. 225].

**Illegal export.** The export of any goods in contravention of the provisions of the Customs Act or any other law for the time being in force. [Customs Act 1962, s. 11H(*a*)].

**Illegal import.** The import of any goods in contravention of the provisions of the Customs Act or any other law for the time being in force. [Customs Act 1962, s. 11A(*a*)].

**Illegal interest.** Exorbitant interest amounting to usury; interest at a higher rate than the law allows.

**Illegality.** That which is contrary to the principles of law, as contradistinguished from mere rules of procedure.

NOTE: *'Illegality' and 'irregularity'—distinction.* An illegality signifies that which is contrary to the principles of law. An irregularity consists in omitting to something which is necessary for the proper conducting of a suit, or doing it in an unreasonable time or improper mode.

**Illegitimate.** In its application to born out of wedlock, it means bastard; base-born; misbegotten, of illicit union; unlawfully begotten; unnatural.

When used as illegal, it means against the law; banned; contrary to law; forbidden; malfeasant; not according to law; prohibited by law; proscribed; unlawful; wrongful; illicit.

**Illegitimate child.** Child who is born at a time when his parents, though alive, are not married to each other. Such child, however, is legitimate if they were married after his conception and before his birth. [*Home of Holy Infancy* v *Kaska* Tex, 397 SW 2d 208].

**Illicit.** Against the law; contrary to law; forbidden by law; censored; illegitimate; immoral; impermissible; improper; out of bounds; outlawed; proscribed; unauthorised; unlawful; without authority.

*Examples:* Illicit cohabitation, illicit relations, illicit trade.

**Illicit cohabitation.** Living together as man and wife of two persons who are not lawfully married, with the implication that they habitually practice fornication. [*Thomas* v *United States* DC Mass, 14 F 2d 228, 229].

**Illicit intercourse.** 'Illicit intercourse' means sexual intercourse between persons not united by marriage or by any union or tie which, though not amounting to a marriage, is recognised by the personal law or custom of the community to which they belong or, where they belong to different communities, of both such communities, as constituting between them a quasi-marital relation. [Indian Penal Code 1860, s. 372, Expl. II].

**Illness.** Sickness, disease or disorder of body or mind.

In Insurance law, a disease or ailment of such a character as to affect the general soundness and healthfulness of the system seriously, and not a mere temporary indisposition which does not tend to undermine or weaken the constitution of the insured. [*Zogg* v *Bankers' Life Co. of Des Moines, Iowa* CCA W Va, 62 F 2d 575, 578].

**Illustration.** That which illustrates, as an example, comparison, anecdote, etc.; that by which a subject or statement is elucidated or explained; the act or art of illustrating.

NOTE: Illustrations to a section are valuable guides in ascertaining the meaning of a section. [*Kumaraswami Chettiar* v *Karuppaswami Moopanar* ILR (1953) Mad 488: AIR 1953 Mad 380].

Illustrations appended to a section cannot modify the language of the section or curtail or expand the ambit of the section. But illustrations form part of the section and are of relevance and value in construing the section. They should not be readily rejected as repugnant to the section. [*Kadorilal* v *Sukhlal Sajan* AIR 1968 MP 4].

**Imam.** A head or chief in religious matters, whether he be the head of all Mahomedans, as the *khalif*, or the priest of a mosque or the leader in the prayers of a congregation. [Wilson's *Glossary*].

**Imambara.** A building in which the festival of the Moharram is celebrated and services in commemoration of the deaths of Ali and his sons Hasan and Husein is performed at that season [Wilson's *Glossary*].

**Imbecile.** Having the mental faculties feeble or defective; feeble minded; characterized by stupidity; one intermediate between an idiot and a maron; a person of abnormally weak, specially an adult with a mental age of about 5; a stupid person.

A person afflicted with severe mental retardation. [Black's *Law Dictionary*, 8th Ed.].

**Imbroglio.** An intricate situation; an embarrassing state of things; a confused or complicated situation.

**Imitation.** Artificial; bogus; counterfeit; faked; pseudo; simulated; spurious;

synthetic; unauthentic; the making of one thing in the similitude or likeness of another.

• **Obvious imitation** p. 618.

**Immediate employer.** 'Immediate employer', in relation to employees employed by or through him, means a person who has undertaken the execution, on the premises of a factory or an establishment to which the Employees' State Insurance Act applies or under the supervision of the principal employer or his agent, of the whole or any part of any work which is ordinarily part of the work of the factory or establishment of the principal employer or is preliminary to the work carried on in, or incidental to the purpose of, any such factory or establishment, and includes a person by whom the services of an employee, who has entered into a contract of service with him, are temporarily lent or let on hire to the principal employer. [Employees' State Insurance Act 1948, s. 2(13)].

**Immediate purpose.** "Immediate purpose" relates to directness rather than speed, although absence of the latter negatives the former. It denotes connection and timely action, but not instant action; yet delayed action is a sign of remoteness of purpose. The expression must be understood as a directly connected and timely purpose, and not a secondary or remote or premature purpose. [*P. Orr and Sons (P) Ltd.* v *Associated Publishers (Madras) Ltd.* (1991)1 SCC 301: JT 1990(4) SC 374: 1990 Supp (2) SCR 615].

**Immediately.** The word 'immediately' should be construed in the light of the facts and circumstances of each case. [*Nitin* v *Executive Engineer* AIR 1986 Guj 141].

The word 'immediately' means without interval of time, without delay, straightway or without any lapse of time. [*Drumbar* v *Jeddo-Highland Coal Co.* 155 Pa Super 57: 37 A 2d 25, 27].

"Immediately" is to be construed as meaning with all reasonable speed, considering the circumstances of the case. [Halsbury's *Laws of England*, 4th Ed., vol. 23, para 1618, p. 1178].

The word 'immediately' is stronger than the expression 'within a reasonable time' and imply prompt, vigorous action, without any delay. [*R.* v *Berkshire JJ.* (1878)4 QBD 469]. It means with all convenient speed. [*Thompson* v *Gibson* 10 LJ Ex 243].

The essence of the expression 'immediately' can be stated thus: In general, it means without interval of time, without delay, straightway or without any lapse of time. It has two meanings: one meaning indicating the relation of cause and effect as direct and proximate, and the other meaning indicating the absence of time between two events. It is not a word or precise signification and does not, in legal proceedings or statutes, necessarily import the exclusion of interval of time or space, but its meaning must be determined by the context in which it is used and the purpose for which the statute using the term was enacted. Depending upon the context, circumstances and events in connection with which it is used, the word has to be sometimes construed liberally, so as to have the effect of the tenor and spirit of the term, so that it could gather its meaning from its application. [*Abdul Majeed* v *State* 1981 LW (Cr) 305 (Mad)].

The word 'immediately' connotes proximity in time to comply. But it has to be noted that the meaning of the word "immediately" has to be determined by the context in which it has been used and the purpose for which the statute using the word was enacted. [*Rao Mahmood Ahmed Khan* v *Ranbir Singh* AIR 1995 SC 2195: JT 1995(2) SC 383].

NOTE: The words "immediately" and "forthwith" have generally the same meaning. They are stronger than the expression "within a reasonable time" and imply prompt, vigorous action without any delay. [*Alsam Holding Co.* v *Consolidated Tax-payers' Mut. Ins. Co.* 4 NYS 2d 498, 505].

**Immemorial.** Existing from before living memory or record; beyond human memory; time out of mind.

**Immemorial usage.** A practice which is being continued from before the time of legal memory; a practice which has existed time out of mind; custom; prescription.

**Immemorial user.** A user when the date of its commencement is not within the memory of man or the date of its commencement is shrouded in the mists of antiquity. [*Patneedi Rudrayya* v *Velugubantla Venkayya* AIR 1961 SC 1821: (1962)1 SCR 836].

**Immobility of labour.** The reluctance or refusal of the displaced labour to move into employment which is available in another area.

**Immoral.** Contrary to good morals; inconsistent with the rules and principles of morality; inimical to public welfare according to the standards of a given community, as expressed in law or otherwise; morally evil; impure; obscene; unprincipled; vicious; or dissolute.

The word "immoral" is a very comprehensive word. Ordinarily it takes in every aspect of personal conduct deviating from the standard norms of life. It may also be said that what is repugnant to good conscience is immoral. Its varying content depends upon time, place and the stage of civilization of a particular society. In short no universal standard can be laid down and any law based on such fluid concept defeats its own purpose. [*Gherulal Parakh* v *Mahadeodas Maiya* AIR 1959 SC 781: 1959 Supp (2) SCR 406].

▸ *Meaning under the Indian Contract Act 1872, s. 23.* The word "immoral" has been given a restricted meaning in the Indian Contract Act. Its juxtaposition with an equally illusive concept, public policy, indicates that it is used in a restricted sense. Decided cases and authoritative textbook writers confined the word "immoral" only to sexual immorality. [*Gherulal Parakh* v *Mahadeodas Maiya* AIR 1959 SC 781: 1959 Supp (2) SCR 406].

**Immoral contract.** A contract that so flagrantly violates societal norms as to be unenforceable. [Black's *Law Dictionary*, 8th Ed.].

**Immoral purpose.** The expression 'immoral purpose' connotes in a wide and general sense all purposes involving conduct which has the property of being wrong rather than right in the judgment of the majority of contemporary fellow citizens. In a narrow sense, the expression may be used implying immoral in respect of sexual conduct. [*Crook* v *Edmondson* (1966)1 All ER 833].

NOTE: Prostitution and living with a man as his mistress will only differ in degree, but the latter is sufficiently immoral. [*Kanchanmala Dassi* v *Lilabati Devi* AIR 1951 Cal 164: 87 CLJ 332].

**Immovable property.** It is property that cannot be moved. It is an object so firmly attached to land that it is regarded as part of the land.

▸ *Meaning under the General Clauses Act 1897, s. 3(26).* "Immovable property" shall include land, benefits to arise out of land, and things attached to the earth, or permanently fastened to anything attached to the earth.

▸ *Meaning under the Registration Act 1908, s. 2(6).* 'Immovable property' includes land, buildings, hereditary allowances, rights to ways, lights, ferries, fisheries or any other benefit to arise out of land, and things attached to the earth or permanently fastened to anything which is attached to the earth, but not standing timber, growing crops nor grass.

▸ *Meaning under the Transfer of Property Act 1882, s. 3.* "Immovable property" shall include land, benefits to arise out of land, and things attached to the earth, or permanently fastened to anything attached to the earth. In this Act, unless there is something repugnant in the subject or context, "immovable property" does not include standing timber, growing crops or grass. [*Board of Revenue* v *A.M. Ansari* AIR 1976 SC 1813: (1976)3 SCR 661: (1976)3 SCC 512: (1976)38 STC 577].

NOTE: Under the Transfer of Property Act, buildings constitute immovable property and machinery if attached to the building for the beneficial enjoyment thereof is also attached to the earth. If the machinery is embedded in the building for the beneficial use thereof, it must be deemed to be a part of the building and the land on which the building is situate. [*Kuppanna Chetty* v *Ambati Ramayya Chetty* AIR 1965 AP 457].

Things rooted in the earth as in the case of trees, and shrubs are immovable property both within the General Clauses Act and the Transfer of Property Act, but in the latter, "standing timber", "growing crop" and "grass" though rooted in earth are not included. [*Mahadeo* v *State of Bombay* AIR 1959 SC 735: 1959 Supp (2) SCR 339].

'Immovable property' does not include standing timber, growing crops or grass. [Transfer of Property Act 1882, s. 3]. The real test for determining whether a tree is movable or immovable property is not the nature of the tree, but the way in which it is intended to be dealt with. If the intention of the parties in respect of a particular transaction is that the tree is to be cut by the purchaser and removed, it will be timber and movable property. But if the intention is that it should after the purchase continue to grow, it may not be timber. [*District Board* v *Churhu Rai* AIR 1956 All 680].

Broadly speaking, the degree, manner, extent and strength of the attachment of the chattel to the earth or building are the main features to be considered. The attachment should be such as to partake of the character of the attachment of the trees or shrubs rooted to the earth or walls or buildings embedded in that sense; the further test is whether such an attachment is for the permanent beneficial enjoyment of the immovable property to which it is attached. An oil engine attached to the earth but removable is not immovable property. [*Perumal Maicker* v *Ramaswami Kone* AIR 1969 Mad 346]. Right to worship in turn is an immovable property; transfer of such right by gift is compulsorily registrable. [*Ram Rattan* v *Bairang Lal* AIR 1978 SC 1393: (1978)3 SCC 236]. Right to collect market dues in respect of a market is an immovable property and any lease of such right is compulsorily registrable. [*Dropadi Devi* v *Ram Das* AIR 1974 All 473].

**Immunity.** Absolution; acquittal; exculpation; exemption; exemption from punishment; freedom from obligation; freedom from prosecution; protection; release from duty; release from charge; safety from prosecution; special privilege; freedom from duty or penalty.

Any exemption from duty, liability, or service of process, specially, such as exemption granted to a public official. [Black's *Law Dictionary*, 7th Ed.].

- **Absolute immunity.** A complete exemption from civil liability, usually afforded to officials while performing particularly important functions, such as a representative enacting legislation and a judge presiding over a lawsuit. [Black's *Law Dictionary*, 8th Ed.].
- **Diplomatic immunity** p. 259.

**Immunity from prosecution.** The definition of the word "immunity" in the context of s. 64 of the Criminal Procedure Code 1973 is: "Freedom or exemptions from penalty, burden or duty". [*Jasbir Singh* v *Vipin Kumar Jaggi* AIR 2001 SC 2734: JT 2001(6) SC 419: (2001)132 ELT 529: (2001)8 SCC 289].

**Immunity of instrumentalities, doctrine of.** This doctrine was enunciated by the Supreme Court of the United States in the case of *McCulloch* v *Maryland* [(1819)4 Wh 316]. According to it, when two Governments as in a Federation are established with a limited jurisdiction, the power of each Government shall be construed as being under an *implied* limitation that it is not to impair the functions of the other. The doctrine has its limited application in India as may be seen in Arts. 285 and 289 of the Constitution of India. [*State of West Bengal* v *Union of India* AIR 1963 SC 1241, 1255].

**Impair.** The word 'impair' cannot be said to have a fixed meaning. It is a relative term affording different meaning in different context and situations. [*Gurbachan Singh* v *Shivalak Rubber Industries* AIR 1996 SC 3057: JT 1996(2) SC 615].

▸*Different meanings.* Adulterate; affect injuriously; contaminate; cripple; crumble; damage; debilitate; devalue; desecrate; harm; hinder; undermine; weaken; decrease in excellence; deprive of power; lessen in power; lessen in value; render feeble.

**Impair materially.** The meaning of the expression 'to impair materially', in common parlance, would mean to diminish in quality, strength or value substantially.

In other words, to make a thing or substance worse and deteriorate. The term "impair materially" is used to mean considerable decrease in quality which may be measured with reference to the antecedent state of things as it existed earlier in point of time as compared to a later stage after the alleged change is made or effected suggesting impairment. [*Gurbachan Singh* v *Shivalak Rubber Industries* AIR 1996 SC 3057: JT 1996(2) SC 615].

**Impartible property.** Impartible property is a property which is invariably held by one person and that it does not devolve on more than one person and that no person has any legal right to demand a partition of it as against the holder thereof.

**Impeach.** Accuse; admonish; bring a charge; bring into discredit; bring to justice; bring up for investigation; cast an imputation upon; cast blame upon; castigate; censure; challenge the credibility of; condemn; denounce; find an indictment against; hold at fault; reprimand.

**Impeachment.** Accusal; accusation; act of discrediting; admonition; denouncement; imputation of dereliction; castigation; censure; condemnation; rebuke; reprimand.

The act by a legislature of calling for the removal from office of a public official, accomplished by presenting a written charge of the official's alleged misconduct.

**Impediment.** Bar; barrier; blockade; blockage; clog; limitation; obstacle; obstruction; disability; drawback; encumbrance; estoppel; fetter; restraint.

Minority, unsoundness of mind, apostasy, etc., are impediments in law. [*Huzrat Syed* v *Commissioner of Wakfs* AIR 1954 Cal 436].

**Impediment to marriage.** Local obstacle to contracting a valid marriage such as relationship of blood within the prohibited degree of consanguinity between the parties.

**Imperative.** Mandatory.

NOTE: A statute is directory when the provisions contain mere matters of direction, and nothing more; but when matters of direction are followed by such words as "that anything done contrary to such provisions shall be null and void to all interest", the statute is imperative.

**Imperceptible.** That cannot be perceived, as by reason of smallness, extreme tenuity or delicacy, distance or gradual progress; inappreciable by the mind or sense; undiscernible. [Webster's *Comprehensive Dictionary*, International Edition].

**Imperfect obligation.** An obligation is said to be imperfect when it is not capable of being enforced by any positive law. Imperfect obligations depend for their fulfilment only upon the will and conscience of those upon whom they rest.

**Implead.** To bring someone into a lawsuit; to bring a new party into the action.

'Implead' means to sue or to prosecute at law or to add as a party in a proceeding, whether civil or criminal. [*Food Inspector, Palghat Municipality* v *Seetharam Rice & Oil Mills* 1974 Ker LT 685 (FB)].

**Implicate.** Accuse; brand; entangle; hold responsible; incriminate; interlace; interwine; involve; make a party to.

To entangle a person in a charge or crime.

**Implication.** Allusion; broad meaning; connotation; hidden meaning; overtone; signification; suggested meaning; tacit inference; indication; insinuation.

**Implied.** This word is used in law in contrast to "express", that is, where the intention in regard to the subject-matter has not manifested by explicit and direct words, but is gathered by implication or necessary deduction from the circumstances, the general language, or the conduct of the parties.

Not directly expressed; recognised by law as existing inferentially. [Black's *Law Dictionary*, 8th Ed.].

**Implied assertion.** Statement which, while not expressed, may be deduced from what is written or spoken.

**Implied contract.** A contract not expressly entered into, but the law infers the existence from acts, circumstances, conduct or relationship.

NOTE: Strictly speaking, the word 'implied' may be more appropriate to contracts implied by law; but it is sometimes used to designate what may be called tacit contracts, that is, contracts where the proposal or acceptance or both are signified, not by words, but by acts or conduct. The conduct must be of such a nature that can only give rise to the inference that there must have been an implied offer and acceptance. [*Umedsingh Hamirasingh* v *Marsden Mills* AIR 1959 Bom 143: 59 Bom LR 985; ss. 9, 68 to 72 of the Indian Contract Act 1872].

Implied contract is of two types—an implied-in-law contract and an implied-in-fact contract.

*Implied-in-law contract* is an obligation imposed by law because of the conduct of the parties, or some special relationship between them, or because one of them would otherwise be unjustly enriched. An implied-in-law contract is not actually a contract, but instead a remedy that allows the plaintiff to recover a benefit conferred on the defendant.

*Implied-in-fact contract* is a contract that the parties presumably intended, either by tacit understanding or by the assumption that it existed.

**Implied easement.** An easement created by law after an owner of two parcels of land uses one parcel to benefit the other to such a degree that, upon the sale of the benefited parcel, the purchaser could reasonably expect the use to be included in the sale. It is also termed easement by implication. [Black's *Law Dictionary*, 8th Ed.].

**Implied power, doctrine of.** A political power that is not enumerated but that nonetheless exists because it is needed to carry out an express power. [Black's *Law Dictionary*, 7th Ed.].

NOTE: The American Supreme Court propounded the doctrine to enable the Congress "to perform the high duties assigned to it". [*McCulloch* v *Maryland* (1819)4 Wh 316]. As a result, the Congress enlarged its jurisdiction by having commerce, defence and internal security powers. But it has no application in India. The Supreme Court is reluctant to apply it: "There can be no reason for giving a broader interpretation to the one power rather than to the other". [*Ramkrishna* v *Municipal Committee* AIR 1950 SC 11, 13].

**Implied prohibition, doctrine of.** This doctrine is the opposite of the doctrine of 'implied powers'. It is based on the maxim: *expressio unius exclusio alterius,* i.e., the express mention of one person or thing is the exclusion of another. It is asserted that the express grant of power on the Congress impliedly prohibits it from interfering with the reserved powers of the States. [*U.S.* v *De Witt* (1869)9 Wall 41, 43].

**Implied repeal.** Repeal effected by irreconcilable conflict between an old law and a new law. It is also termed repeal by implication. [Black's *Law Dictionary*, 8th Ed.].

NOTE: Repeal by implication is only effected when the provisions of a later enactment are so inconsistent with or repugnant to the provisions of an earlier one that the two cannot stand together. [*Ajoy Kumar* v *Union of India* 1981 Lab LJ 368: AIR 1984 SC 1130: 1984 Lab IC 691].

A later statute may repeal an earlier one either expressly or by implication. But repeal by implication is not favoured. [Maxwell on *Interpretation of Statutes*, 12th Ed., p. 191]. The two provisions of the statute have to be read in such a manner that one of them does not necessarily repeal the other. The question of repeal of one provision of a statute by another arises only when two of them are wholly incompatible with each other. [*Bopouli Co-operative Agricultural Society* v *State of Haryana* AIR 1976 Punj 283: 1976 Rev LR 450: 1976 Cur LJ 364].

**Implied term.** A provision not expressly agreed to by the parties but instead read into the contract by a court as being implicit. An implied term should not, in theory, contradict the contract's express terms. [Black's *Law Dictionary*, 7th Ed.].

The phrase 'implied term' can be used to denote a term inherent in the nature of the contract, which the law will imply in every case unless the parties agree to vary or exclude it. [*Sterling Engineering Co.* v *Patchett* (1955)1 All ER 369].

A term or condition, not expressly stipulated, may be implied by court if it is clear that the parties intended such a term or condition. In some cases provisions of law imply certain terms or conditions if not expressly excluded.

**Implied trust.** A trust imposed by law when property is transferred under circumstances suggesting that the transferor did not intend for the transferee to have the beneficial interest in the property.

A trust imposed by a court on equitable grounds against one who has obtained property by wrongdoing, thereby preventing the wrongful holder from being unjustly enriched. Such a trust creates no fiduciary relationship. It is also termed constructive trust; involuntary trust; trust *ex maleficio.* [Black's *Law Dictionary*, 7th Ed.].

**Import.** A product brought into a country from a foreign country where it originated; the process of bringing foreign goods into a country; the meaning; importance; significance; connotation; essence; gravity; purport; substance.

Ordinarily 'import' means to bring something within the municipal limits from a place without its boundaries, irrespective of the consideration as to whether the goods were manufactured within the municipal limits, how long they were outside those limits and for what purpose. [*Manganlal Bhagwandas* v *Ahmedabad Municipality* AIR 1945 Bom 251; *Central India Spinning Weaving and Manufacturing Co. Ltd.* v *Municipal Committee of Wardha* AIR 1958 SC 341: 1958 SCR 1102: 1958 SCJ 604].

▸*Meaning under the Copyright Act 1957, ss. 51 and 53.* The word 'import' means "bringing into India from outside India". It is not limited to importation for commerce only, but includes importation for transit across the country. [*Gramophone Company of India Ltd.* v *Birendra Bahadur Pandey* AIR 1984 SC 667: (1984)2 SCC 534: (1984)2 SCR 664: (1984)1 Comp LJ 362].

▸*Meaning under the Customs Act 1962, s. 2(23).* 'Import', with its grammatical variations and cognate expressions, means bringing into India from a place outside India.


• **Illegal import** p. 427.
• **In the course of import** p. 442.
• **In the course of import or export** p. 442.


**Imported goods.** Any goods brought into India from a place outside India but does not include goods which have been cleared for home consumption. [Customs Act 1962, s. 2(25)].

**Importer.** A person or entity that brings goods into a country from a foreign country and pays customs duties.

▸*Meaning under the Customs Act 1962, s. 2(26).* In relation to any goods at any time between their importation and the time when they are cleared for home consumption, includes any owner or any person holding himself out to be the importer.

**Impose.** To levy or exact a tax or duty.

The word "imposed" means the actual levy of the tax after authority to levy has been acquired by rules duly made and sanctioned, and it is such imposition that is made subject to the general or special orders of the Government. [*Municipality of Anand* v *State of Bombay* AIR 1962 SC 938: (1962)2 SCJ 296].

**Imposition.** The term 'imposition' is generally used for the levy of a tax or duty by legislative provisions indicating the subject-matter of the tax and the rates at which it has to be taxed. [*Assistant Collector of Central Excise, Calcutta Division* v *National Tobacco Co. of India Ltd.* AIR 1972 SC 2563: (1972)2 SCC 560: (1973)1 SCR 822].

**Impossibility.** The fact or condition of not being able to occur, exist, or be done; a fact or circumstance that cannot occur, exist, or be done; in contracts, a fact or circumstance that excuses performance.

NOTE: *'Impracticability' and 'impossibility'—distinction.* 'Impracticability' is a concept different from 'impossibility' for while the latter is absolute, the former introduces at all events some degree or reason and involves some regard for practice. 'Impracticable' presupposes that the action is 'possible' but owing to certain practical difficulties or other reason it is incapable of being performed. [*Major Radha Krishan* v *Union of India* AIR 1996 SC 3091: JT 1996(3) SC 650: (1996)3 SCC 507].

**Impossibilium nulla obligatio est.** There is no obligation to do impossible things. The law does not compel one to do that which one cannot possibly perform. [*Re Presidential Poll* AIR 1975 SC 1682].

**Impossible.** In the language of everyday life a thing is impossible when, according to the ordinary course of human events, no expectation can be entertained that it will happen. [*Shepherd* v *Kottgen* (1877)2 CPD 585].

The word 'impossible' should be construed in a liberal sense, so as to embrace within its purview acts which become impracticable or extremely hazardous and cannot be said to be used in a physical or literal sense. It is sufficient for the act to be impossible, that it becomes impracticable or useless from the view of the object and purpose which the parties had in view. [*Hari Singh* v *Diwani Vidyawatt* AIR 1960 J&K 91].

The word 'impossible' is not to be used in the sense of physical or literal impossibility. The performance of a contract may not only be literally impossible, but it may be impracticable and useless from the point of view of the object and purpose which the parties had in view, and if an untoward event or change of circumstances totally upsets the very foundation upon which the parties rested their bargain, it may very well be said that the promisor finds it impossible to do the act which he promised to do. [*Satyabrata Ghose* v *Mugneeram Bangur & Co.* AIR 1954 SC 44: 1954 SCR 310: 1954 SCJ 1].

NOTE: The plea of impossibility will not be entertained by the court if in spite of supervening events, the object and purpose of the parties is not rendered useless and the contract can be performed substantially though not literally. [*Ganga Singh* v *Santosh Kumar* AIR 1963 All 194].

**Impost.** A tax or duty levied on imports.

It is a custom or tax imposed on articles brought into a country and it is most usually secured before the importer is allowed to exercise his rights of ownership over them because of the evasion of law.

The word "impost" in its broader sense means "any tax or tribute imposed by authority and applies as well to a tax on persons as a tax on merchandise". [*Smith* v *Turner* 7 How (US) 283: 12 L ed 702].

NOTE: An illegal impost must be an unreasonable restriction and will infringe the right of the citizen to carry on his business, trade or occupation under Art. 19(1)(*g*) and this infringement can be made the subject-matter of a challenge under Art. 32 of the Constitution of India. [*Mohammad Yasin* v *Town Area Committee, Jalalabag* 1952 SCR 572, 578].

**Impotence.** A man's inability to achieve an erection and therefore to have sexual intercourse. [Black's *Law Dictionary*, 8th Ed.].

Impotence means a practical impossibility to perform sexual act in a complete and perfect manner. [*P* v *K* (1982)2 DMC 380; *Lata Vasant Gawade* v *Vasant Narayan Gawade* (1985)1 DMC 294].

"'Impotence' in my understanding of the word is physical disability for sexual connection. I have not been referred to nor have I been able to find any judicial definition of the word. The cases seem to have arisen entirely upon the existence of some defect or malformation making carnal intercourse impossible and either proved as a physical fact or inferred from a refusal on the part of the alleged impotent to consummate". [*Hale* v *Hale* (1927)2 DLR 1137, *per* Walsh, J.].

NOTE: Impotence is established if at the time of the marriage either of the spouses was incapable of effecting the consumption either due to structural defect in the organs of generation rendering complete sexual intercourse impracticable or due to some other cause. [*Gudivada Venkateswararao* v *Smt. Gudivada Nagamani* AIR 1962 AP 151].

Impotence also includes frigidity or invincible repugnance on the part of a spouse to physical act. The expression is not confined to physical or structural defect making consummation impossible. Annulment of marriage is grantable even of wife's unwillingness to sexual intercourse. [*D. Padmavathi* v *Kalinai Ravikumar Varma* (1987)1 ALT 355].

**Impotency.** Inability of a man or woman to perform the act of sexual intercourse.

Impotency is 'physical incapacity of accomplishing the sexual act'.

The term 'impotency' has been understood by English judges in matrimonial cases as meaning incapacity to consummate the marriage, that is to say incapacity to have sexual intercourse, which is one of the objects of marriage. [*R. Varghese* v *T.J. Ponnen* AIR 1968 Ker 129; *Jagdish Kumar* v *Sita Devi* AIR 1963 Punj 114].

NOTE: *'Impotency' and 'sterility'—distinction.* 'Impotency' is physical incapacity of accomplishing the sexual act. 'Sterility' means inability for procreation of children.

Impotency is to be distinguished from sterility which may in some cases accompany impotency but is not necessarily associated with it, the two expressions denoting lack of two different powers. [*Jagdish Lal* v *Shyama Mohan* AIR 1966 All 150].

**Impotent.** Destitute of or lacking in power, physical, moral or intellectual; not potent; weak; feeble; destitute of sexual power; lacking in self-control. [Webster's *Comprehensive Dictionary*, International Edition].

A party is impotent if his or her mental or physical condition makes consummation of the marriage a practical impossibility. [*Yuvraj Digvijay Singh* v *Yuvrani Pratap Kumari* AIR 1970 SC 137].

**Impotentia excusat legem.** Inability is an excuse in law.

**Impound.** To place (something, such as a car or other personal property) in the custody of the police or the court, often with the understanding that it will be returned intact at the end of the proceeding; to take and retain possession of (something, such as a forged document to be produced as evidence) in preparation for a criminal prosecution. [Black's *Law Dictionary*, 7th Ed.].

To place a suspected document in the custody of the law, when it is produced at a trial. [Wharton's *Law Lexicon*, 14th Ed.].

The meaning of the word 'impound' includes 'to take legal or formal possession of'. [*Varghese* v *State of Kerala* AIR 1989 Ker 248].

The word 'impound' means 'to confine as in a pound, to restrain within limits, to take legal possession etc. [*Varghese* v *State of Kerala* AIR 1989 Ker 248].

**Impracticable.** Not practicable, incapable of being performed or accomplished by the means employed or at command; not reasonably practicable.

"Impracticable" is defined as incapable of being effected for lack of adequate means; impossible of performance; not feasible. "Impracticable" means impossible or unreasonably difficult of performance, and is a much stronger term than "expedient".

"Impracticable" means 'impossible to carry out' and is normally used for a specific procedure or course of action. [*Union of India* v *Harjeet Singh Sandhu* AIR 2001 SC 1772: JT 2001(4) SC 597: (2001)5 SCC 593].

It is a conception different from that of impossibility; the latter is absolute, the former introduces at all events some degree of reason and involves at all events some regard for practice. [*Jayne* v *National Coal Board* (1963)2 All ER 220].

'Impracticable' means not possible or not feasible. At any rate, it means something very much more than 'not reasonably practicable'. [*Moorcroft* v *Thomas Powles* (1962)3 All ER 741].

NOTE: 'Impracticable' means impracticable from the reasonable point of view and the court should take a common sense view of the matter and must act as a prudent man of business. [*Bengal and Assam Investors* v *J.K. Eastern Industries* AIR 1956 Cal 658: 60 CWN 956].

**Impractical.** It means simply 'unrealistic' or 'not sensible' [*Union of India* v *Harjeet Singh Sandhu* AIR 2001 SC 1772: JT 2001(4) SC 597: (2001)5 SCC 593].

**Impression, first.** See FIRST IMPRESSION p. 356.

**Imprest system.** This is a system of disbursing by means of advances and refunds, *e.g.*, the system of advancing a petty cashier a lump sum, which he accounts periodically, and is refunded with the amount spent. The petty cash account, therefore, remains consequently in debt only for the original amount advanced. The system is often adopted in the case of branches of a business which are advanced a certain amount to pay expenses and are then reimbursed by the head office for the amount expended. [Osborn & Grandage's *Concise Commercial Dictionary*].

**Imprimatur.** A licence to print or publish; official approval.

**Imprisonment.** The act of confining a person, specially in prison; the state of being confined; a period of confinement.

Any total restraint on the liberty of the person, for however short a time, by the use or threat of force or by confinement is an imprisonment. To compel a person to remain in a given place or to go in a given direction against his will is an imprisonment. [Halsbury's *Laws of England*, 3rd Ed., vol. 38, p. 765]. "Imprisonment" includes detention of any description. [Halsbury's *Laws of England*, 4th Ed., vol. 18, para 256, p. 107].

▸ *Meaning under the General Clauses Act 1897, s. 3(27).* Imprisonment shall mean imprisonment of either description as defined in the Indian Penal Code.

• **False imprisonment** p. 341.

**Improper/undue influence.** The improper use of power or trust in a way that deprives a person of free will and substitutes another's objective. [Black's *Law Dictionary*, 7th Ed.].

Improper or undue influence is such dominion which prevents a normal human being from exercising his discretion and free will.

Section 16 of the Indian Contract Act defines undue influence thus: "A contract is said to be induced by 'undue influence' where the relations subsisting between the parties are such that one of the parties is in a position to dominate the will of the other and uses that position to obtain an unfair advantage over the other".

NOTE: Consent to a contract, transaction, relationship, or conduct is voidable if the consent is obtained through undue influence.

Section 19A of the Indian Contract Act 1872, lays down that when consent to an agreement is caused by an undue influence, the agreement is a contract voidable at the option of the party whose consent was so caused.

**Improperly.** Not properly; not in accordance with accepted rules of behaviour.

NOTE: The word 'improperly' can refer only to cases in which, although the forms of law have been observed, there has been a fraud on the Act or an abuse of the powers given by the legislature. [*Jitendra Nath Ghosh* v *Chief Secretary* 36 CWN 1088].

**Improvement.** The act or an instance of improving or being improved; something that improves, specially an addition or alteration that adds to value. [*Concise Oxford Dictionary*, 9th Ed.].

The act or process of improving; betterment; amelioration; something that is better than something previous; a beneficial change or addition; an advance. [Webster's *Comprehensive Dictionary*, International Edition].

An addition to real property, whether permanent or not; especially, one that increases its value or utility or that enhances its appearance. [Black's *Law Dictionary*, 7th Ed.].

**Improvident.** Lacking foresight; incautious; taking no thought for future needs; lacking judgment; lacking prudence; careless; extravagant; happy-go-lucky; imprudent.

**Impugn.** Assail; assail by argument; attack by words; call in question; challenge as false; oppose as false; raise questions.

**In.** The word 'in' is not a word of art. Its true effect and meaning must depend on the context in which it is used. [*Spedding Dinga Singh* v *Punjab State* AIR 1968 Punj 548: ILR (1969)1 Punj 672].

▸ *Various meanings.* Within the bounds of; contained or included within, *e.g.*, six rooms in the house; amidst; occupied with or concerned with; *e.g.*, in search of truth; wearing, decorated with etc.; made out of; under or based on the law of, *e.g.*, to bring an action in contract.

The preposition 'in' does not always mean or is limited to inside of a particular thing. The connotation of the preposition 'in' will depend on the context. The word 'in' may mean 'in respect of or in relation to'. [*Corporation of Calcutta* v *Rajkumar* AIR 1954 Cal 20 (DB)].

**In a manner oppressive.** It means manner which is burdensome, harsh and wrongful. [*Needle Industries (India) Ltd.* v *Needle Industries Newey (India) Holdings Ltd.* AIR 1981 SC 1298: (1981)3 SCR 698: (1981)3 SCC 333: (1982)1 Comp LJ 1].

**In accordance with.** The words 'in accordance' mean 'in conformity' or 'as provided for'. [*Mahesh Chandra* v *Tara Chand Modi* AIR 1958 All 374: ILR (1958)2 All 817].

NOTE: Where a building is to be made in accordance with the plans, it is sufficient if the building is in substantial accordance with the plans. [*R.* v *London County JJ.* (1889)24 QBD 341].

**In accordance with law.** In accordance with the rules and procedure prescribed under the law.

An application for execution would be in accordance with law if it is in accordance with the rules and procedure prescribed therefor, and it does not cease to be such an application even though subsequently the court rejects the prayer made. [*Darogi Mandal* v *Kameshwar Singh* AIR 1957 Pat 299: ILR (1956) Pat 907].

NOTE: Where in an application for execution a prayer was made against the representatives of the judgment-debtor for their arrest, without showing that they were personally liable for the satisfaction of the decree, the application is not in accordance with law. [*Isharchand* v *Rawat* AIR 1957 Raj 341: ILR (1957)7 Raj 260].

**In accordance with the form.** In accordance with the form prescribed.

NOTE: There is no material difference between the expressions 'in the form' or 'in accordance with the form'. Where a statute requires an agreement to be in accordance with the form prescribed by it, then unless the contrary is clearly expressed, it is sufficient compliance with the statute if the agreement is substantially in the form; and inconsequential variation is immaterial. [*Banarsi Das* v *Cane Commissioner* AIR 1956 All 725: ILR (1957)1 All 282].

**In advance of calls.** When a shareholder makes payment prior to call, he is said to pay in advance of call.

**In alieno solo.** In another's land.

**In alio loco.** In another place.

**In arbitrio judicis.** At the discretion of the Judge.

**In arrear.** The words 'in arrear' connote in the strict sense a reference to a sum which has become due and payable and has not been paid. They may, however, be used in a secondary sense to indicate some deficiency which is capable, either certainly or contingently, of being made good. [*Coulson* v *Austin Motor Co. Ltd.* (1927)43 TLR 493].

Behind in the discharge of a debt or other obligation, *e.g.*, the tenants were in arrears with the rent; at the end of a term or period instead of the beginning, *e.g.*, the interests, fees, and costs are payable in arrears. [Black's *Law Dictionary*, 7th Ed.].

**In articulo mortis.** At the point of death.

NOTE: Statements made by a man in *articulo mortis* called a dying declaration, can be given in evidence after his death on the trial of anyone accused of his murder or man-slaughter. [Indian Evidence Act 1872, s. 32].

**In ballast.** A vessel is in ballast when it carries some heavy substance for stability for want of cargo.

**In bond.** Goods are said to be in bond or bonded when duty has been paid on them and they are placed in a store or warehouse approved by the appropriate authority.

**In camera.** In chambers; in private.

A cause is said to be heard 'in camera' either when the hearing is heard before the judge in his private chambers or when all spectators are excluded from the courtroom.

The words 'in camera' mean that except the witnesses under examination and those representing the parties, others are to be excluded. [*Poona Labour Union* v *State of Maharashtra* (1969)2 Lab LJ 291 (Bom)].

NOTE: In every suit or proceeding relating to matters concerning the family the proceedings may be held *in camera* if the court so desires and shall be so held if either party so desires. [Civil Procedure Code 1908, Or. 32A, r. 2].

**In camera proceedings.** Trial or hearing held in a place not open to the public.

**In charge of.** In the care or custody of, or entrusted to the management or direction of.

**In conjunction with.** In association with.

**In connection with.** The expression implies some *nexus* between the two. [*I.T.P. (London) Ltd.* v *Winstanley* (1947)1 All ER 177].

**In consequence of.** The expression implies causation. [*Braby (Frederick) & Co.* v *Bedwell* (1926)1 KB 456].

**In course of transmission by post.** A postal article shall be deemed to be in course of transmission by post from the time of its being delivered to a post office to the time of its being delivered to the addressee or of its being returned to the sender or otherwise disposed of under Chapter VII. [Indian Post Office Act 1898, s. 3(*a*)].

Until an article despatched by post is delivered or can be said to be delivered, it will be deemed to be in course of transmission. [*Radha Kishan* v *State of U.P.* AIR 1963 SC 822: 1963 Supp (1) SCR 408: (1963)1 Cr LJ 809].

**In criminalibus probationers debent esse luce clariores.** In criminal cases the proofs ought to be clearer than light.

**In curia.** In court.

**In due course.** At the appropriate time; in the natural order.

**In due course of law.** A matter may be said to have happened 'in due course of law', if it is the result and operation of the law invoked by the ordinary method of any judicial proceeding—civil or criminal. [*Sheo Saran Lal* v *Lal Mohammad* 12 CWN 70].

▸ *Meaning under the Transfer of Prisoners Act 1950, s. 3(2).* The expression 'in due course of law' in the context in which it appears must be interpreted as meaning 'under some rule or enactment in force'. Detention of a prisoner is governed not only by the relevant rules and regulations in the jail manual of the particular State where he happens to be imprisoned for the time being, but also by all the laws of that State governing all classes of prisoners. [*Sitaram Barelal* v *State of M.P.* AIR 1969 MP 252].

**In esse.** Actually existing; in actual existence; in being. It is distinguished from 'in posse' which means 'that which is not, but may be'. Example—a child before birth is in posse; after birth, in esse. A writ court is concerned only with the rights of the citizens in esse.

**In extenso.** At full length; in extension; from beginning to end, leaving out nothing.

**In extremis.** At the last gasp; in extremity; in the last illness.

**In fictione juris semper acquitas existit.** Equity is the life of a legal fiction.

**In flagrante delicto.** In the very act. Caught in the act of adultery or crime.

**In forma pauperis.** In the character or manner or condition of a pauper; in the manner of an indigent who is permitted to disregard filing fees and court costs.

**In futuro.** In future; at a future time; the opposite of *in praesenti*.

**In good faith.** The expression means with due care and attention. [*Madhavrao Narayanrao* v *Ram Krishna* AIR 1958 SC 767: 1958 SCJ 963: 1959 SCR 564: (1959)1 SCA 145].

**In gross.** In a large quantity or sum; without deduction, division, or particulars; by wholesale.

**In invitum.** Against a person's will.

**In law.** In the intendment, contemplation, or inference of the law; implied or inferred by law; existing in law or by force of law.

**In-law.** A relative by marriage rather than blood, *e.g.*, relationship of parents of wife to husband.

**In lieu of.** Instead of; in place of; in substitution of.

**In limine.** On or at the threshold; at the very beginning; preliminarily; at the outset.

**In loco parentis.** In the place of a parent; instead of a parent; charged, factitiously, with a parent's rights, duties, and responsibilities.

A person in *loco parentis* means a person taking upon himself the duty of a father of a child to make a provision for that child. [*Bennet* v *Bennet* (1879)10 Ch D 474].

**In pais.** Done without legal formalities; legal transaction that has taken place without legal proceedings; out of court.

**In pari delicto, potior est conditio possidentis (or defendentis).** Where both parties are equally at fault, the condition of the possessor (or defendant) is the more favourable. For the applicability of the maxim the parties to the suit should also be the parties to the fraud. [*Raja Ram* v *Daulat Ram* AIR 1980 All 161].

NOTE: The phrase *in pari delicto* suggests two things. First, there should be an act of delinquency, an act repugnant to law, an act illegal act. Secondly both the parties, should be delinquent and that too equally, with the same degree of guilt. The word *'possidentis'* indicates the fact of possession as owner. It excludes those whose possession is precarious, terminable at will by another person, like the possession of a lessee, an agent or a borrower. These kinds of precarious possession would not normally emerge out of illegal transaction between parties. Those who have come into possession of a thing from an illegal transaction would claim to be owners in their own right. [*Mrs. M.M. Roy* v *N.V.P. Pandian* (1985)1 Cur Civ Cas 501 reversing AIR 1979 Mad 42].

Where the circumstances are such that the court will refuse to assist either party, the party in possession will not be disturbed. [*Naman Shriniwas Kini* v *Ratilal* AIR 1959 SC 689: 1959 SCJ 635].

**In pari materia.** Upon the same matter or subject; relating to the same matter.

- **Statutes in pari materia.** "Statutes *in pari materia*" are those relating to the same person or thing or having a common purpose. [*Undercofler* v *L.C. Robinson & Sons, Inc.* 141 SE 2d 847, 849].

NOTE: Statutes *in pari materia* are to be construed together so that inconsistencies in one statute may be resolved by looking at another statute on the same subject.

**In personam.** Against the person.

An action is said to be *in personam* when its object is to determine the rights and interests of the parties themselves in the subject-matter of the action, however the action may arise, and the effect of a judgment in such an action is merely to bind the parties to it. A normal action brought by one person against another for breach of contract is a common example of an action *in personam* [R.H. Graveson: *Conflict of Laws,* p. 98 (7th Ed. 1974)].

NOTE: A judgment *in personam* binds only the parties to the proceedings, as distinguished from one *in rem* which fixes the status of the matter in litigation once for all, and concludes all persons. [Stroud's *Judicial Dictionary*, 5th Ed.].

**In praesenti.** At present; right now. It is used in opposition to *in futuro*.

**In promptu.** At hand; in readiness.

**In pursuance of.** 'Conformable to' or 'in accordance with'. [*Sadaria* v *Rajasthan Board of Revenue* AIR 1954 Raj 224: ILR (1954)3 Raj 861].

**In re.** In the matter of; concerning; regarding.

NOTE: The expression is often used in instituting matters other than actions, in which there is no plaintiff or defendant, as in insolvency, probate proceeding etc.

**In re aliena.** In another's property.

**In regard to.** The words 'in regard to' occurring in a statute should be given the interpretation justified by the context in which they occur. In the context in which they occur in s. 115(5) of the States Reorganization Act 1956, these words mean 'for or for the purpose of'. [*M.A. Jaleel* v *State of Mysore* AIR 1961 Mys 210].

**In relation to.** Having relation to the matter in issue.

▸ *Meaning under the Constitution of India, Art. 227.* The words 'in relation to which' appearing in Art. 227 obviously refer to the word 'territories' and not the words 'courts and tribunals'. [*Waryam Singh* v *Amarnath* AIR 1954 SC 215].

▸ *Meaning under the Criminal Procedure Code, s. 165(1)(b).* The words 'in relation to' do not mean that the offence, must have been committed after the proceeding had started. Even if the offence was committed prior to the proceeding, it can be said to be in relation to the proceeding, if the proceeding is undertaken in pursuance of it. If the proceeding is related to an offence, the offence itself is related to the proceeding. [*Hrishikesh Nag* v *State* AIR 1965 Tripura 13].

▸ *Meaning under the Trade Marks Act 1938 (U.K.).* The words 'in relation to' in the Trade Marks Act would seem to be used in order to cover the case of the use of a mark in an advertisement where there is no impression of the mark on the object, but the mark is used to indicate the origin not of a specific physical object offered for sale but of the goods advertised. [*Bismag Ltd.* v *Amblins (Chemists) Ltd.* (1949)1 Ch 667].

**In rem.** Against a thing; involving or determining the status of a thing, and therefore the rights of persons generally with respect to that thing. [Black's *Law Dictionary*, 7th Ed.].

A technical term used to designate proceedings or actions instituted against the thing, in contradistinction to personal actions, which are said to be *in personam*.

- **Action in rem.** An 'action in rem' is a proceeding that takes no cognizance of owner but determines right in specific property against all the world, equally binding on everyone. [*Flesch* v *Circle City Excavating & Rental Corp.* 210 NE 2d 865, 868].

- **Judgment in rem.** An adjudication pronounced upon the status of some particular thing or subject-matter by a tribunal having competent authority. [*Booth* v *Copley* 140 SW 2d 662, 666].

  A judgment *in rem* is that judgment which is conclusive not only against the party thereto but also against the whole world. It is binding on all persons in so far as their interests in the property are concerned. [*Booth* v *Copley*, supra].

**In respect of.** The words 'in respect of' should be given the widest meaning, viz., 'relating to' or 'with reference to'. [*Tolaram Relumal* v *State of Bombay* AIR 1954 SC 496: 1954 Cr LJ 1333: (1955)1 SCR 158].

The words 'in respect of' could mean more than "consisting of" or "namely". [*Bicbar Ltd.* v *Inland Revenue Commissioners* (1962)3 All ER 294].

▸ *Meaning under tax laws.* Indian tax laws use the expression as synonymous with the expression "on". Thus, the expression "in respect of the goods" as used in r. 5(1)(*i*) of the Madras General Sales Tax (Turnover and Assessment) Rules 1939, was held to mean only "on the goods". [*State of Madras* v *Swastik Tobacco Factory* AIR 1966 SC 1000].

▸ *Meaning under the Indian Railways Act 1890 s. 3(14) [since repealed].* The words 'in respect of' used in s. 3(14) may be taken to mean 'for the provision of' and not 'for the user of'. Therefore, irrespective of the actual user by any particular consignor of the stations, sidings and other things mentioned therein, terminal charges are leviable by reason of the mere fact that these things have been provided by the

Railway Administration. [*Shahdara (Delhi) Saharanpur Light Railway Co. Ltd.* v *Upper Doab Sugar Mills Ltd.* AIR 1960 SC 695: (1960)2 SCR 926].

▸*Meaning under the Code of Criminal Procedure, s. 195(1)(c).* The words 'in respect of a document produced or given in evidence in such proceeding' in s. 195(1)(*c*) are wide enough to include even a document which was prepared before the proceedings started in a court of law but was produced or given in evidence in that proceeding. [*Har Prasad* v *Hans Ram* AIR 1966 All 124: 1966 Cr LJ 244].

**In situ.** In its own place; in its original position.

**In specie.** In kind; in the same or like form.

**In status quo.** In the condition in which it was.

**In terrorem.** In fright or alarm or terror; by way of threat.

A condition in a will or gift which is intended to frighten or intimidate the donee is said to be *in terrorem*.

NOTE: When a contract has been broken if a sum is named in the contract becomes payable for the breach or some penalty, the plaintiff is entitled to reasonable compensation or the penalty stipulated for. The reason is that the sum or the penalty has been inserted *in terrorem.* [Indian Contract Act 1872, s. 74].

**In testimonium.** In testimony or witness whereof.

**In the course of.** The dictionary meaning of the words 'in the course of' is "during (in the course of time, as time goes by), while doing". [*Regional Director, ESI Corpn.* v *Francis De Costa* (1996)6 SCC 1: JT 1996(8) SC 118: (1996)3 SCJ 264: AIR 1997 SC 432].

The word 'course' etymologically denotes movement from one point to another. The expression 'in the course of' not only implies a period of time during which the movement is in progress but postulates also a connected relation. [*State of Travancore-Cochin* v *Shanmugha Vilas Cashew Nut Factory* AIR 1953 SC 333: 1953 SCJ 471: 1954 SCA 1059: 1954 SCR 53].

The expression 'in the course of' in Art. 286 of the Constitution postulates that the transaction of sale must be an integral part of the activity of exporting the goods out of the country. [*Mahadeo Ram Bali Ram* v *State of Bihar* AIR 1959 Pat 30].

**In the course of employment.** The words "in the course of employment" mean in the course of the work which the workman is employed to do and which is incidental to do. [*Mackinnon Mackenzie & Co. Private Ltd.* v *Ibrahim Mohammad Issak* AIR 1970 SC 1906: (1970)1 SCR 869: (1969)2 SCC 607].

**In the course of import.** The course of import of goods starts at a point when the goods cross the Customs barrier of the foreign county and ends at a point after the goods cross the Customs barrier in the importing country. Where the importer pursuant to the earlier contract delivered the shipping documents to the Government against payment when the goods were on the high seas, the sale took place in the course of import into India. [*J.V. Gokal* v *Assistant Collector* (1960)2 SCR 852].

**In the course of import or export.** A sale or purchase in the course of import or export within the meaning of Art. 286(1)(*b*) of the Constitution includes (*a*) a sale or purchase which itself occasions the import or export, (*b*) a sale or purchase which takes place while the goods are on the high seas on their import or export journey, and (*c*) the last purchase by the exporter with a view to export and the first sale by the importer to a dealer after arrival of the imported goods. [*State of Travancore-Cochin* v *Shanmugha Vilas Cashew Nut Factory* AIR 1953 SC 333: 1953 SCJ 471: 1954 SCA 1059: 1954 SCR 53].

**In the course of the same transaction.** See under SAME TRANSACTION p. 773.

**In the interest of general public.** The expression is very wide and embraces public security, public order and public morality. [*Bharatsingh* v *State of Madhya*

*Pradesh* AIR 1964 MP 175: (1964)2 Cr LJ 160].

A legislation meant for the benefit of a well-defined class will be deemed to be in the interest of the general public regardless of the smallness of the number of persons primarily benefited by the legislation. [*Kishori Lal* v *State* AIR 1957 Punj 244: 1957 Cr LJ 1173: ILR (1957) Punj 1388].

• **Interest of the general public** p. 472.

**In the ordinary course of business.** The expression is susceptible of one meaning namely, that there should be a series of transactions as distinguished from one transaction. A stray transaction cannot constitute an ordinary course of business. [*Virayya* v *Subba Rao* AIR 1959 AP 647].

**In the pay of.** In the employment of *Manshanker Prabhashankar* v *State* [AIR 1970 Guj 97: 1970 Cr LJ 679].

**In toto.** Entirely; wholly; in the whole; completely.

**In transit.** See IN TRANSITU.

**In transitu.** In transit; on the way or passage; while passing from one person or place to another; in the course of transportation.

NOTE: Goods are in transit so long as they are on their passage. Goods are deemed to be in course of transit from the time when they are delivered to a carrier or other bailee for the purpose of transmission to the buyer until the buyer or his agent takes delivery of them from such carrier or other bailee. [Sale of Goods Act 1930, s. 5(1)].

**In ventre as mere.** In the mother's womb.

**Inalienable.** Not transferable or assignable; not subject to alienation; not capable of being conveyed; not capable of being sold; not capable of being transferred; unable to be bought; unable to be disposed of; untouchable; the characteristic of those things which cannot be bought or sold or transferred from one person to another, such as rivers and public highways and certain personal rights.

**Inalienable rights.** Rights which are not capable of being surrendered or transferred without the consent of the one possessing such rights. [*Morrison* v *State* Mo App, 252 SW 2d 97, 101].

**Inam.** A grant by the Government, often revenue-free.

The term 'inam' means in its ordinary and accepted sense a grant of freehold interest. Where the deed does not divest the transferor of his ownership in the properties, there can be no inam, however extensive the interest which might be conveyed to the transferee. A lease of property, therefore, cannot be said to be a grant of an inam. [*Govinda Reddi* v *Pattabi Rama Reddi* AIR 1954 Mad 161: (1953)2 MLJ 478].

**Incapacitated person.** Any person who is impaired by reason of mental illness, mental deficiency, physical illness or disability, advanced age; chronic use of drugs, chronic intoxication, or other cause to the extent that he lacks sufficient understanding or capacity to make or communicate responsible decisions concerning his person.

**Incapacity.** Want of capacity; want of power or ability to take or dispose; want of legal ability to act; inefficiency; incompetency; lack of adequate power.

The quality or state of being incapable, want of capacity, lack of physical or intellectual power, or of natural and legal qualification; inability, incapability, disability, incompetence. [*Bole* v *Civil City of Ligonier* 161 NE 2d 189, 194].

**Incerta quantitas vitiat actum.** An uncertain quantity vitiates the act.

**Incest.** The crime of sexual intercourse or cohabitation between a man and woman who are related to each other within the degrees wherein marriage is prohibited by law. [Black's *Law Dictionary*, 5th Ed.].

Sexual relations between family members or close relatives, including children related by adoption. [Black's *Law Dictionary*, 7th Ed.].

**Incestuous adultery.** Adultery between relatives; adultery committed by persons who are closely related.

▸ *Meaning under the Divorce Act 1869, s. 3(6) [since omitted].* Adultery committed by a husband with a woman with whom, if his wife were dead, he could not lawfully contract marriage by reason of her being within prohibited degrees of consanguinity (whether natural or legal) or affinity.

**Inchmaree clause.** This is a special clause inserted in marine insurance policies to cover losses to the hull or machinery of a vessel caused through negligence of the master, engineers, mariners etc., or through explosion, breakages or any latent defect in the machinery or hull. To recover the loss, the shipowners must not be guilty of negligence. The clause is almost universally inserted in policies on steamships. [Osborn & Grandage's *Concise Commercial Dictionary*].

In marine insurance, provision in policy protecting one from perils resulting from negligence of master, or from any latent defect in machinery or hull, charterer, mariners, engineers and pilots. [Black's *Law Dictionary*, 5th Ed.].

In maritime law, an insurance policy provision that protects against risks not caused by nature, such as a sailor's negligence or a latent defect in machinery. [Black's *Law Dictionary*, 8th Ed.].

NOTE: This term is taken from a British ship, the *Inchmaree*, whose sinking in 1884 gave rise to litigation that led to the clause bearing its name.

**Inchoate**. Imperfect; partial; unfinished, begun, but not completed; as a contract not executed by all the parties. [*State ex rel. McCubbin* v *McMillan* Mo App, 349 SW 2d 453, 462].

**Inchoate instrument.** An unrecorded instrument that must, by law, be recorded to serve as effective notice to third parties. [Black's *Law Dictionary*, 7th Ed.].

NOTE: Until the instrument is recorded, it is effective only between the parties to the instrument.

Inchoate instruments are dealt with in s. 20 of the Negotiable Instruments Act 1881. Where a person signs and delivers to another a paper duly stamped and either wholly blank or having written thereon an incomplete negotiable instrument he thereby gives *prima facie* authority to the holder thereof to make or complete a negotiable instrument for the specified amount and not exceeding the amount covered by the stamp.

**Incident.** As adjective, it means dependent upon; subordinate to; arising out of, or otherwise connected with; following upon; in connection with; in relation to; pertaining to; related to; relating to; relative to; subject to; bearing upon; appertaining to.

In its use as noun, it means a discrete occurrence or happening; affair; episode; occurrence; a dependent, subordinate, or consequential part.

**Incidental.** The word 'incidental' has reference to a matter of casual nature only. [*State of Orissa* v *Chakobai Ghelabai & Co.* AIR 1961 SC 284].

The word 'incidental' means happening, or likely to happen as a result of or in connection with something more important, being an incidental, casual, hence secondary or minor, but usually associated. [*Delhi Cloth and General Mills Co. Ltd.* v *The Workmen* AIR 1967 SC 469: (1967)1 SCR 882; *National Textile Corporation* v *State* (1988)2 Raj LR 47].

A thing is incidental to another if it merely pertains to something else as primary. [*Royal Talkies* v *Employees' State Insurance Corporation* (1978)4 SCC 204; *State of Tamil Nadu* v *Binny Ltd., Madras* AIR 1980 SC 2308: 1980 (Supp) SCC 686: (1982)49 STC 17; *Hukum Chand Jute Mills Ltd.* v *L.A. Tribunal* AIR 1958 Cal 68: 63 CWN 141].

The expression "incidental" means necessary in certain contexts which does not mean a matter of casual nature only. [*Shroff & Co.* v *Municipal Corporation of Greater Bombay* 1989 Supp (1) SCC 347: JT 1988(3) SC 406: (1988)38 ELT 243: (1989)72 STC 150: 1988 Supp (2) SCR 406: (1988)3 Comp LJ 146].

**Incidental or consequential order.** Incidental or consequential orders are those which follow as a matter of course, being necessary compliments to the main order passed without which the latter order would be incomplete or ineffective. [*M.A. Mahammed Ali* v *Dr. R. Ramadoss* AIR 1966 Mad 441: (1966)1 MLJ 535].

**Incidental power.** A power that, although not expressly granted, must exist because it is necessary to the accomplishment of an express purpose. [Black's *Law Dictionary*, 7th Ed.].

The incidental power is one that is directly and immediately appropriate to the execution of the specific power created and not one that has a slight or remote relation to it. Furthermore, the want of an express enumeration of powers does not exclude such incidental powers as are reasonably necessary to accomplish the corporate purpose. [*Luxmi Tea Co. Ltd.* v *Pradip Kumar Sarkar* 1989 Supp (2) SCC 656].

**Incidental to a dispute.** It means in connection with the dispute or associated with the dispute. [*National Textile Corporation* v *State* (1988)2 Raj LR 47].

**Incite.** To arouse; urge; provoke; encourage; spur on; goad; stir up; instigate; set in motion; enthuse; excite; foment; prevail upon; exert pressure; stimulate.

In criminal law, it means to provoke or stir up, instigate someone to commit a criminal act or a crime. In this sense, it is nearly synonymous with "abet".

▸ *Meaning under the Industrial Disputes Act 1947, s. 27.* The words 'instigates' and 'incites' signify something deeper than a mere asking of a person to do a particular act. There must be something in the nature of solicitation to constitute instigation or incitement under s. 27. The words seem to convey the meaning 'to goad or urge forward or to provoke or encourage the doing of an act'. What acts would amount to instigation or incitement will depend upon the particular facts of each case. [*State of Bihar* v *Ranen Nath Roy Choudhury* AIR 1958 Pat 259: 1958 Cr LJ 662].

**Include.** To confine within; hold as in an inclosure; take in; attain; shut up; contain; inclose; comprise; comprehend; embrace; involve; to contain as a part of something.

The word 'include' in interpretation clause is used to enlarge the meaning of the word or phrase. The word or phrase must be construed as comprehending not only such thing as it signifies according to its natural import, but also those things which the interpretation clause declares that they shall be included. [*Commissioner of Income Tax* v *Taj Mahal Hotel* AIR 1972 SC 168].

The word 'include' in the statutory definition is generally used to enlarge the meaning of the preceding words and it is used by way of extension, and not with restriction.

The word 'include' is very generally used in interpretation clauses in order to enlarge the meaning of words or phrases occurring in the body of the statute, and when it is so used, these words or phrases must be construed as comprehending not only such things as they signify according to their natural import but also those things which the interpretation clause declares that they shall include. [*C.I.T., Andhra Pradesh* v *Taj Mahal Hotel, Secunderabad* AIR 1972 SC 168: (1972)1 SCR 168: (1971)3 SCC 550; *Regional Director, Employees' State Insurance Corporation* v *High Land Coffee Works of PFX Saldanha & Sons* AIR 1992 SC 129: (1991)3 SCC 617: JT 1991(3) SC 325: (1991)5 SCR 88].

The word 'include' in definition clauses enlarges the meaning of the words and phrases occurring in the body of the statute. [*M.M. Upadhayya* v *State* 1996 Cr LJ 450].

The word 'include', when used in a clause, enlarges the meaning of the expression defined to comprehend not only such things as they signify according to their natural import but also those things which the clause declares that they shall include. [*P. Kasilingam* v *PSG College of Technology* AIR 1995 SC 1395].

**NOTE: When the legislature uses the words 'mean' and 'include', such definition is to be given a wider meaning and is not exhaustive or**

restricted. [*Krishi Utpadan Mandi Samity* v *Shankar Industries* 1993 Supp (3) SCC 361].

There cannot be any inflexible rule that the word 'include' should be read always as a word of extension without reference to the context. The word 'include' may be used in the sense of 'means'. [*S.G.R. Tiles Manufacturers* v *State of Gujarat* AIR 1977 SC 90: (1977)1 SCR 878: (1977)1 SCJ 397: 1977 SCC (Lab) 15: (1976)4 SCC 601].

**Including.** The expression 'including' is very generally used in interpretation clause to enlarge the meaning of words or phrases occurring in the body of the statute; and when it is so used these words or phrases must be construed as comprehending not only such things as they signify according to their natural import, but also those things which the interpretation clause declares they shall include. The word 'including' therefore is a term of extension. It imports addition. It adds to the subject-matter already comprised in the definition. [*S.M. James* v *Abdul Khair* AIR 1961 Pat 242].

**Inclusio unius est exclusio alterius.** The inclusion of one is the exclusion of another.

**Income.** The return in money from one's business, labour, or capital invested; gains, profits.

The money or other form of payment that one receives, usually periodically, from employment, business, investments, royalties, gifts, and the like. [Black's *Law Dictionary*, 7th Ed.].

"Income" connotes a periodical monetary return coming in with some sort of regularity, or expected regularity from definite sources. [*E.D. Sassoon & Co. Ltd.* v *Commissioner of Income Tax, Bombay* AIR 1954 SC 470: 1954 SCJ 771: (1954)26 ITR 27: (1955)1 SCR 313; *A.K.T.K.M. Vishnudatta Andharjanam represented by D.V. Nambudiripad Desamangalam* v *Commissioner of Agricultural Income Tax, Trivandrum* AIR 1970 SC 2055: (1970)2 SCC 165: (1970)78 ITR 58: (1971)1 SCR 535].

The word 'income' ordinarily in normal sense, connotes any earning or profit or gain periodically, regularly or even daily in whatever manner and from whatever source. It is a word of very wide import. [*Universal Radiators* v *CIT* AIR 1993 SC 2254: (1993)2 SCC 629: (1993)2 SCR 775: JT 1993(3) SC 150: (1993)201 ITR 800].

The expression "income" in its normal connotation does not mean mere production or receipt of a commodity which may be converted into money. Income arises when the commodity is disposed of by sale, consumption or use in the manufacture or other processes carried on by an individual *qua* that commodity. [*S.S. Rajalinga Raja* v *State of Madras* AIR 1967 SC 814: (1967)1 SCR 950: (1967)63 ITR 617].

The expression 'income' includes not merely what is received or what comes in by exploiting the use of a property but also what one saves by using it oneself. That which can be converted into income can be reasonably regarded as giving rise to income. [*Bhagwan Dass Jain* v *Union of India* AIR 1981 SC 907: (1981)2 SCR 808: (1981)2 SCC 135: (1981)128 ITR 315].

▸ *Meaning under the Constitution of India.* The expression 'income' in Entry 82, List 1 cannot be subjected, by implication, to any restriction by the way in which that term might have been deployed in a fiscal statute. The expression 'income' in the legislative entry has always been understood in a wide and comprehensive connotation to embrace within it every kind of receipt or gain either of a capital nature or of a revenue nature. [*Elel Hotels and Investments Ltd.* v *Union of India* (1989)3 SCC 698: (1989)74 STC 146: (1989)178 ITR 140: (1989)2 SCR 880: JT 1989 (Supp) SC 195: AIR 1990 SC 1664: (1990)3 Comp LJ 267].


- **Accumulated income** p. 23.
- **Deferred income** p. 242.
- **Earned income** p. 289.
- **National income** p. 598.
- **Net income** p. 606.
- **Unearned income** p. 865.


**Income escaping assessment.** An income escapes assessment when the process of assessment has not been initiated at all, as also in the case where it has resulted in no assessment after completion of the process of assessment. [*Anandji Haridas* v *S.P. Kasturi* AIR 1968 SC 565: (1968)1 SCA 663: (1968)1 SCJ 820: (1968)1 ITJ 586: (1968)21 STC 326].

NOTE: The expression 'escaped assessment' includes that of a turnover which has not been assessed at all, because for one reason or other no assessment proceedings were initiated and therefore no assessment was made in respect thereof. The assessment proceedings must be held to be pending from the time the said proceedings were initiated until they were terminated by a final order of assessment. [*Ghanshyamdas* v *Regional Assistant Commissioner* AIR 1964 SC 766: (1964)1 SCJ 121: (1964)1 ITJ 74: (1964)14 STC 976].

**Income-tax.** A tax on income. It is levied under various Schedules in respect of interest on Government securities and other profits arising from public revenue dividends; professional or trade earnings or profits and from interest and other annual profits or gains; official and other salaries. [Mozley & Whiteley's *Law Dictionary*, 10th Ed.].

It is a tax on income as opposed to capital, though in practice, the dividing line between income receipt and capital receipt is very thin.

NOTE: Realisation of the income-tax in India is regulated by the Income-tax Act 1961 and the charging section is s. 4 of the Act.

**Inconsistent.** Mutually repugnant or contradictory; contrary, the one to the other, so that both cannot stand but the acceptance or establishment of the one implies the abrogation or abandonment of the other. [*Basti Sugar Mills Co. Ltd.* v *State of U.P.* AIR 1979 SC 262: (1979)1 SCR 590: (1979)2 SCC 88].

NOTE: *Provisions of two Acts—when become 'inconsistent'.* If they relate to the same subject-matter, to the same situation and both substantially overlap and are co-extensive and at the same time so contrary and repugnant in their terms and impact that one must perish wholly if the other were to prevail at all, then, only then, are they inconsistent. [*Basti Sugar Mills Co. Ltd.* v *State of U.P.* AIR 1979 SC 262: (1979)1 SCR 590: (1979)2 SCC 88].

**Incorporation.** The formation of a legal body with quality of perpetual existence and succession, except by Charter or Act of Parliament.

The act or process of forming or creating a corporation. [Black's *Law Dictionary*, 5th Ed.].

The formation of a legal or political body, with the quality of perpetual existence and succession, unless limited by the act of incorporation. [*Abbott* v *Limited Mut. Compensation Ins. Co.* 85 P 2d 961, 964].

**Incumbent.** A person who is in present possession of an office; one which is legally authorised to discharge the duties of an office. [*Hilliard* v *Park* 370 SW 2d 829, 839].

**Incumbrance.** Any right to, or interest in, land which may subsist in another to diminution of its value, but consistent with the passing of the fee. [*Knudson* v *Weeks* DC Okl, 394 F Supp 963, 976].

A claim, lien, charge, or liability attached to and binding real property, *e.g.*, a mortgage, judgment lien; lease; accrued and unpaid taxes. [Black's *Law Dictionary*, 5th Ed.].

A claim or liability that is attached to property or some other right and that may lessen its value, such as a lien or mortgage; any property right that is not an ownership interest. [Black's *Law Dictionary*, 8th Ed.].

A claim, lien, or liability attached to property as a mortgage. This is the sense in which it is ordinarily used. It must be a burden or liability that run with the land. [*National Textile Corporation* v *State of Maharashtra* AIR 1977 SC 1566: (1977)3 SCC 4: (1977)3 SCR 525].

"Incumbrance" means a charge upon a claim against and arising out of a private grant or contract. [*Brijnandan Singh* v *Jamuna Prasad* AIR 1958 Pat 589].

It is also spelt as encumbrance.

**Incuriam.** See PER INCURIAM p. 652.

**Indecent.** Offensive to common propriety; offending against modesty or delicacy; grossly vulgar; obscene; lewd; unseemly; unbecoming; indecorous; unfit to be seen or heard; morally offensive.

NOTE: *'Indecent' and 'obscene'—difference.* The word 'indecent' or 'obscene' conveys one idea, namely, offending against the recognised standards of propriety, indecent being at the lower end of the scale and obscene at the upper end of the scale. An indecent article is not necessarily obscene, whereas an obscene article almost certainly must be indecent. [*R.* v *Stanley* (1965)1 All ER 1035].

**Indecent exhibition.** The act of publicly displaying or offering for sale something that is outrageously offensive.

**Indecent exposure.** Exposure to sight of the private parts of the body in a lewd or indecent manner in a public place. The term refers to exhibition of those private parts which instinctive modesty, human decency or self-respect require shall be kept covered in presence of others.

An offensive display of one's body in public, especially of the genitals. [Black's *Law Dictionary*, 8th Ed.].

**Indefeasible.** Incapable of being defeated, revoked, lost, avoided or made void; immutable; imperishable; imprescriptible; ineradicable; inextinguishable; inviolable; irreversible; irrevocable.

**Indemnify.** To restore the victim of a loss, in whole or in part, by payment, repair, or replacement; to save harmless; to secure against loss or damage; to give security for the reimbursement of a person in case of an anticipated loss falling upon him; to make good; to compensate; compensate for injury; make reparation; make restitution; recompense for past loss.

NOTE: A duty to indemnify may arise out of contract or by operation of law. A duty to indemnify may be annexed by operation of law to various particular kinds of contract. For instance, on the sale of shares in a company the transferee is bound to indemnify the transferor against future calls, whether made by the company or by the liquidator. If the lessee, who has assigned his interest, has to pay rent during the period of the assignment, he can recover from the assignee, because law imposes on the assignee the duty to indemnify. [*Wolveridge* v *Steward* (1833)1 Cr&M 644].

**Indemnity.** Act of holding harmless; assurance against loss; compensation; protection against loss; recompense; redemption; reimbursement; restitution; security against damage, loss.

A collateral contract or assurance, by which one person engages to secure another against an anticipated loss or to prevent him from being damnified by the legal consequences of an act or forbearance on the part of one of the parties or of some third person. The term pertains to liability for loss shifted from one person held legally responsible to another person. [*Boyle* v *Burt* Iowa, 179 NW 2d 513, 515].

The term is also used to denote a compensation given to make the person whole from a loss already sustained, as where the government gives indemnity for private property taken by it for public use. It means, also, restitution or reimbursement.

A legislative act, assuring a general dispensation from punishment or exemption from prosecution to persons involved in offences, omissions of official duty, or acts in excess of authority, is called an indemnity. Strictly it is an act of indemnity.

• **Contract of indemnity** p. 191.

**Indenture.** A written agreement under which bonds and debentures are issued, setting forth maturity date, interest rate, and other terms.

A deed to which two or more persons are parties, and in which they enter into reciprocal and corresponding grants or obligations towards each other; a deed or elaborate contract signed by two or more parties.

**Independent contractor.** Generally, one who, in exercise of an independent employment, contracts to do a piece of work according to his own methods and is subject to his employer's control only as to end product or final result of his work. [*Hammes* v *Suk* 190 NW 2d 478, 480, 481].

One who renders service in course of independent employment or occupation, and who follows employer's desires only as to results of work, and not as to means whereby it is to be accomplished. [*Sparks* v *L.D. Folsom Co.* 217 Cal App 2d 279; *Housewright* v *Pacific Far East Line Inc.* 229 Cal App 2d 259; *Dowling* v *Mutual Life Ins. Co. of New York* La App, 168 So 2d 107, 112].

A person who contracts with another to do something for him but who is not controlled by the other nor subject to the other's right to control with respect to his physical conduct in the performance of the undertaking. [Black's *Law Dictionary*, 5th Ed.].

One who is hired to undertake a specific project but who is left free to do the assigned work and to choose the method for accomplishing it. [Black's *Law Dictionary*, 7th Ed.].

One who is entrusted to undertake a specific project but who is left free to do the assigned work and to choose the method for accomplishing it. [Black's *Law Dictionary*, 8th Ed.].

"One who undertakes to produce a given result but so that in the actual execution of the work he is not under the order or control of the person for whom he does it, and may use his own discretion in things not specified beforehand". [*Shivanandan Sharma* v *Punjab National Bank Ltd.* 1955 SCR 1427: 1955 SCJ 407: AIR 1955 SC 404: 1955 SCA 878 quoting Pollock's *Law on Torts*, 15th Ed., pp. 62, 63].

NOTE: *'Independent contractor' and 'servant'—distinction.* An independent contractor is charged with a work, and has to produce a particular result; but the manner in which the result is to be achieved is left to him. A servant, on the other hand, may also be charged with some work and asked to produce a particular result, but is subject to the directions of the master as to the manner in which the result is to be achieved. [*Shankar Balaji* v *State of Maharashtra* AIR 1962 SC 517].

*'Workman' and 'independent contractor'—point of determination.* What determines whether a person is a workman or independent contractor is whether he has agreed to work personally or not. If he has, he is a workman and the fact that he takes assistance from other persons would not affect his status. [*D.C. Works Ltd.* v *State of Saurashtra* 1957 SCR 152].

*'Agent', 'servant' and 'independent contractor'—distinction.* An agent is to be distinguished on the one hand from a servant and on the other from an independent contractor.

A servant acts under the direct control and supervision of his master, and is bound to conform to all reasonable orders given to him in the course of his work; an independent contractor, on the other hand, is entirely independent of any control or interference and merely undertakes to produce a specified result, employing his own means to produce that result. An agent, though bound to exercise his authority in accordance with all lawful instructions which may be given to him from time to time by his principal, is not subject in its exercise to the direct control or supervision of the principal. An agent, as such is not a servant, but a servant is generally for some purpose his master's implied agent, the extent of the agency depending upon the duties or position of the servant. [*Lakshminarayan Ram Gopal and Son Ltd.* v *Government Excess Profits Tax* AIR 1954 SC 364, 367].

**Indian Christian.** A native of India who is, or in good faith, claims to be of unmixed Asiatic descent and who professes any form of Christian religion. [Indian Succession Act 1925, s. 2(*d*)].

▸*Meaning under the Indian Christian Marriage Act 1872, s. 3.* The expression 'Indian Christian' includes the Christian descendants of natives of India converted to Christianity, as well as such converts.

**Indian coin.** See under COIN p. 152.

**Indian company.** A company formed and registered under the Companies Act 1956 (1 of 1956), and includes—(*i*) a company formed and registered under any law relating to companies formerly in force in any part of India (other than the State of Jammu and Kashmir); (*ii*) in the case of Jammu and Kashmir, a company formed and registered under any law for the time being in force in that State: Provided that the registered office of the company in all cases is in India. [Income-tax Act 1961, s. 2(26)].

**Indian Consular Officer.** The Consul-General, Consul, Vice-Consul, Consular agent and Pro-Consul appointed as such by the Central Government, and includes any person authorised by the Central Government to perform the functions of Consul-General, Consul, Vice-Consul, Consular agent or Pro-Consul. [Merchant Shipping Act 1958, s. 3(17)].

**Indian Consulate.** The office of a Consular Officer of the Government of India where a register of births is kept or where there is no such office, such office as may be prescribed. [Citizenship Act 1955, s. 2(*d*)].

**Indian currency.** Currency which is expressed or drawn in Indian rupees, but does not include special bank notes and special one-rupee notes issued under s. 28A of the Reserve Bank of India Act 1934 (2 of 1934). [Foreign Exchange Management Act 1999, s. 2(*q*)].

**Indian customs waters.** Waters extending into the sea to a distance of twelve nautical miles measured from the appropriate base line on the coast of India and includes any bay, gulf, harbour, creek or tidal river. [Customs Act 1962, s. 2(28)].

**Indian naval reserve forces.** The naval reserve forces raised and maintained by the Central Government. [Navy Act 1957, s. 3(9)].

**Indian navy.** The regular naval forces raised and maintained by the Central Government [Navy Act 1957, s. 3(10)].

**Indian ship.** A ship registered as such under the Merchant Shipping Act 1958 and includes any ship registered at any port in India at the commencement of the said Act which is recognized as an Indian ship under the proviso to sub-sec. (2) of s. 22 of the Merchant Shipping Act 1958.

**Indian soldier.** Indian soldier means any person subject to the Army Act 1950 or the Air Force Act 1950 or the Navy Act 1957. [Indian Soldiers (Litigation) Act 1925, s. 2(*b*)].

**Indian standard.** The standard (including any tentative or provisional standard) established and published by the Indian Standards Institution, in relation to any article or process, indicative of the quality and specification of such article or process. [Indian Standards Institution (Certification Marks) Act 1962, s. 2(*c*)].

**Indicia.** Signs; indications; characteristic marks; characteristics; expressions; features; hints; indications; manifestations; means of recognition; circumstances which point to the existence of a given fact as probable, but not certain.

> NOTE: The term is much used in civil law in a sense nearly or entirely synonymous with circumstantial evidence. It denotes facts which give rise to inferences, rather than inferences themselves.

**Indict.** Accuse; bring a formal accusation against; call to account; charge; charge with offence; charge with the commission of a crime.

**Indictment.** Accusal; accusation; allegation; charge; complaint; written accusation.

An indictment is merely a charge which must be proved at trial beyond a reasonable doubt before defendant may be convicted. [*U.S.* v *Zovluck* DC NY, 274 F Supp 385, 390].

An indictment is only an accusation, it is the physical means by which a defendant is brought to trial; its sole purpose is to identify the defendant's alleged offence, and it is not evidence that the offence charged was committed. [*U.S.* v *Glaziou* CA NY, 402 F 2d 8, 15].

An indictment is a written accusation, preferred before the Crown Court, signed by the proper officer of that court and charging one or more persons with the commission of one or of a number of offences. [Halsbury's *Laws of England*, 4th Ed., vol. 11, para 193, p. 118].

> NOTE: Indictment is equivalent to charge under s. 211 of the Code of Criminal Procedure 1973. Chapter XVII of the Code deals with it.

**Indigent person.** A person is an indigent person,—(*a*) if he is not possessed of sufficient means (other than property exempt from attachment in execution of a decree and the subject-matter of the suit) to enable him to pay the fee prescribed by law for the plaint in such suit, or (*b*) where no such fee is prescribed, if he is not entitled to property worth one thousand rupees other than the property exempt from attachment in execution of a decree, and the subject-matter of the suit. [Order 33, r. 1, Code of Civil Procedure 1908 as amended by the Amendment Act 1976].

**Indirect evidence.** Proof of collateral circumstances from which a fact in controversy, not directly attested by witnesses or documents, may be inferred. It is also called circumstantial and presumptive evidence. [Wharton's *Law Lexicon*].

Proof of some other fact or facts from which, taken either singly or collectively, existence of particular fact in question may be inferred as necessary or probable consequence. [*United Textile Workers of America, AFL-CIO, Local Union No. 120* v *Newberry Mills, Inc.* DC SC, 238 F Supp 366, 372].

**Indirect tax.** A tax on a right or privilege, such as an occupation tax or franchise tax; a tax which can be shifted by one person to another.

NOTE: If a tax is levied on a dealer in respect of his total sale, he no doubt pays the tax but he recovers it from his customers. Hence sales-tax is an indirect tax. Tax on commodities is usually an indirect tax. A direct tax like the income-tax cannot be shifted.

**Individual.** As noun, this term denotes a single person as distinguished from a group or class, and also, very commonly, a private or natural person as distinguished from a partnership, corporation, or association; but it is said that this restrictive signification is not necessarily inherent in the word, and that it may, in proper cases, include artificial persons. [Black's *Law Dictionary*, 5th Ed.].

The term includes not only a human being but is wide enough to include a group of persons forming a unit. It includes a corporation created by statute, e.g., a university, a bar council or the trustees of a baronetcy trust incorporated by a Baronetcy Act. It would also include a minor or a person of unsound mind. [*Commissioner of Income Tax* v *Sodra Devi* 1958 SCR 1].

NOTE: A Hindu undivided family is an 'individual'. [*Mommad Keyi* v *Wealth Tax Officer* AIR 1962 Ker 110; *Jain Merchants Cooperative Housing Society Ltd.* v *HUF of Manubhai Kalyanbhai Shah* (1995)1 Guj LR 19].

A Hindu deity falls within the meaning of the word 'individual'. [*Jogendra Nath Naskar* v *Commissioner of Income Tax* AIR 1969 SC 1089: (1969)74 ITR 33: (1969)1 SCC 555: (1969)3 SCR 742; *Commissioner of Wealth Tax* v *Ellis Bridge Gymkhana* AIR 1998 SC 120; *Official Trustee of West Bengal* v *Commissioner of Income Tax* (1974)3 SCC 616].

**Induce.** Actuate; bring about; bring to pass; call forth; exercise influence over; motivate; persuade; precipitate; prevail upon; stimulate; to influence to an act or course of conduct.

The dictionary meaning of the word "induce" is to "prevail on, persuade". [*Kalya Singh* v *Genda Lal* AIR 1975 SC 1634: (1975)3 SCR 783: (1976)1 SCC 304].

NOTE: 'Induce or attempt to induce' does not mean controlling the will. [*Hari Ram* v *Election Tribunal* AIR 1970 All 146].

**Induct.** To put in enjoyment or possession, especially to introduce into possession of an office or benefice, with customary ceremonies; to bring in; initiate; to put formally in possession; appoint; introduce into office.

**Induction.** Act or process of inducting.

**Industrial.** The term 'industrial' means 'of or belonging to industry especially manufacturing, a division of productive or profit-making labour, especially one that employs a large number of personnel and capital, especially in manufacturing'. [*Ram Swarup* v *Janki Das Jai Kumar* AIR 1976 Del 219].

**Industrial concern.** Any concern engaged or to be engaged in the manufacture, preservation or processing of goods or in shipping or in mining or in the hotel industry or in the transport of passengers or goods by road or by water or by air or in the generation or distribution of electricity or any other form of power. [Industrial Development Bank of India Act 1964, s. 2(*c*)].

**Industrial disease.** Physical disorder which is caused by or is incidental to particular occupation [*Lumbermen's Mut. Cas. Co.* v *Rozan* 30 A 2d 474, 475]; a disease gradually produced by being engaged in a particular employment. It is also termed 'occupational disease'.

NOTE: Schedule II to the Workmen's Compensation Act 1923, contains a list of occupational diseases for which workmen are entitled to compensation from the employers. An occupational disease is deemed an injury by accident arising out of and in the course of employment under s. 3 of the Act.

**Industrial dispute.** 'Industrial dispute' means any dispute or difference between employees and employers, or between employers and workmen, or between workmen and workmen, which is connected with the employment or non-employment or the terms of employment or with the conditions of labour of any person. [*Workmen, Hindustan Lever Ltd.* v *Hindustan Liver Ltd.* AIR 1984 SC 1683: (1984)4 SCC 392, referring to Industrial Disputes Act 1947, s. 2(*k*)].

The term "industrial dispute" connotes a real and substantial difference having some element of persistency and continuity till resolved and likely, if not adjusted, to endanger the industrial peace of the undertaking or the community. When parties are at variance and the dispute or difference is connected with the employment, or non-employment, or the terms of employment or with the conditions of labour, there comes into existence an industrial dispute. [*Shambu Nath Goyal* v *Bank of Baroda* AIR 1978 SC 1088: (1978)2 SCR 793: (1978)2 SCC 353].

The words "industrial dispute" convey the meaning to the ordinary mind that the dispute must be such as would affect large groups of workmen and employers ranged on opposite sides on some general questions on which each group is bound together by a commonality of interests, such as wages, bonuses, allowances, pensions, provident fund, number of working hours per week, holidays, and so on. Having regard to the modern conditions of society where capital and labour have organised themselves into groups for the purpose of fighting their disputes and settling them on the basis of the theory that union is strength, and collective bargaining has come to stay, a single employee's case might develop into an industrial dispute, when as it often happens, it is taken up by the trade union of which he is a member, and there is a concerted demand by the employees for redress. [*D.N. Banerji* v *P.R. Mukherjee* AIR 1953 SC 58].

NOTE: The dispute to be an "industrial dispute" must arise in relation to an industry. [*Madras Gymkhana Club* v *Workers of Gymkhana Club* (1967)2 Lab LJ 720].

The definition of "industrial dispute" requires three things, namely, (1) there should be a dispute or difference; (2) the dispute or difference should be between employees and employers, or between employers and workmen, or between workmen and workmen; and (3) the dispute or difference must be connected with the employment or non-employment or the terms of employment or with the conditions of labour of any person. [*The Standard-Vacuum Refining Co. of India* v *Their Workmen* AIR 1960 SC 948: (1960)3 SCR 466: (1961)1 SCJ 84, referring to Industrial Disputes Act 1947, s. 2(*k*)].

Though the applicability of the Industrial Disputes Act to an individual dispute as opposed to a dispute involving a group of workmen is excluded, if the workmen as a body or a considerable section of them make common cause with the individual workman, then such a dispute would be an industrial dispute. [*The Newspapers Ltd.* v *The State Industrial Tribunal, U.P.* AIR 1957 SC 532: 1957 SCR 754: 1957 SCJ 566].

Only collective disputes and not a mere individual dispute will fall within the scope of the Industrial Disputes Act. But even an individual dispute can become an industrial dispute, if it is taken up by a union of workmen or a number of workmen. [*Buckingham and Carnatic* v *B. and C. Mills Staff Union* AIR 1960 Mad 106: (1959)2 Lab LJ 781].

A dispute between an employer and an employee who has been dismissed and who makes a claim for reinstatement and compensation, would be an 'industrial dispute'. [*Central Provinces Transport Services Ltd.* v *Raghunath Gopal Patwardhan* 1956 SCR 956: AIR 1957 SC 104: 1957 SCJ 58].

The term "industrial dispute" is wide enough to justify a dispute about the propriety of the retrenchment as well as the propriety in not giving the retrenched employee an opportunity to be re-employed when an occasion arises. [*Cawnpore Tannery Ltd., Kanpur* v *S. Guha* AIR 1967 SC 667: (1961)2 Lab LJ 110].

**Industrial espionage.** One industrial house's spying on another to steal the other house's trade secrets or other proprietary information.

**Industrial goods.** Goods which are destined and designed to produce other goods as contrasted with consumer goods; goods such as equipment and machinery used for the production of other goods or services. It is also termed capital goods.

**Industrial Tribunal.** Industrial Tribunal means—(*i*) any Industrial Tribunal constituted under the Industrial Disputes Act 1947 (XIV of 1947); or (*ii*) in relation to cases where an appeal lies from any court, wage board or other authority set up in any State under any law relating to adjudication of industrial disputes made, whether before or after the commencement of this Act, by the legislative authority of the State to any other court, board or authority set up in the State under such law, that court or authority exercising appellate jurisdiction within the State; or (*iii*) in relation to other cases, where no appeal lies under any law referred to in sub-clause (*ii*), any court, board or other authority set up in any State under such law. [Industrial Disputes (Appellate Tribunal) Act 1950, s. 2(*c*)].

NOTE: The Industrial Tribunal to which a dispute is referred to under the U.P. Industrial Tribunal Act 1947 is a court within the meaning of s. 10 of the U.P. General Clauses Act 1904. [*Viswamitra Press Karyalaya* v *The Workers of Viswamitra Press* AIR 1953 SC 41: (1953)4 SCR 272: 1953 SCJ 13].

**Industrial undertaking.** Any undertaking pertaining to a scheduled industry carried on in one or more factories by any person or authority including Government. [Industries (Development and Regulation) Act 1951, s. 3(*d*)].

▸*Meaning under the Central Industrial Security Force Act 1968, s. 2(b).* Industrial undertaking means any undertaking pertaining to a scheduled industry and includes an undertaking engaged in any other industry, or in any trade, business or service which may be regulated by Parliament by law.

NOTE: To be an industrial undertaking the work of manufacture or production should be carried on in one or more factories by any person or authority including Government. [*E. Sefton & Co.* v *Textile Mill Mazdoor Union* AIR 1958 All 80].

A business establishment carried out only by 22 workers is not an "industrial undertaking" as defined under s. 3(*d*) of the Industries (Development and Regulation) Act 1951. [*Ramanarayan Satyanarayan Agarwal Distilleries Pvt. Ltd.* v *Associated Alcohols and Breweries Ltd.* AIR 1995 SC 1686].

**Industry.** Diligence in the performance of a task; systematic labour for some useful purpose, especially work in manufacturing or production; a particular form or branch of productive labour; an aggregate of enterprises employing similar production and marketing facilities to produce items having markedly similar characteristics. [Black's *Law Dictionary*, 7th Ed.].

Any department or branch of art, occupation, or business conducted as a means of livelihood or for profit; especially, one which employs much labour and capital and is a distinct branch of trade. [*Dessen* v *Department of Labour and Industries of Washington* 66 P 2d 867, 869].

In the *Shorter Oxford English Dictionary* the word "industry" is defined as "a particular branch of productive labour; a trade or manufacture". According to Webster's *Third New International Dictionary* (1961 Ed.) the word "industry" means "(*a*) systematic labour especially for the creation of value; (*b*) a department or branch of a craft, art, business or manufacture, a division of productive and profit making labour especially one that employs a large personnel and capital especially in manufacturing; (*c*) a group of productive or profit making enterprises or organisations that have a similar technological structure of production and that produce or supply technically substitutable goods, services or sources of income". [*Harakchand Ratanchand Banthia* v *Union of India* (1969)2 SCC 166: AIR 1970 SC 1453: (1970)1 SCR 479].

The expression 'Industry' has many meanings. It means 'skill', 'ingenuity', 'dexterity', 'diligence', 'systematic work of labour', 'habitual employment in the productive arts', 'manufacturing establishment' etc. [*MSCO Pvt. Ltd.* v *Union of India* AIR 1985 SC 76].

▸ *Meaning under the Industrial Disputes Act 1947, s. 2(j).* 'Industry' means any business, trade, undertaking, manufacture or calling of employers and includes any calling, service, employment, handicraft, or industrial occupation or avocation of workmen.

The word 'industry' as defined in s. 2(*j*) is in two parts. The first part says that it means any business, trade, undertaking, manufacture or calling of employers and then it goes on to say in the second part that it includes any calling, service, employment, handicraft or industrial occupation or avocation of workmen. The concept that "industry is ordinarily something which employers create or undertake" is gradually yielding place to the modern concept which regards industry as a joint venture undertaken by employers and workmen—an enterprise which belongs equally to both. An activity can be regarded as an 'industry' within the meaning of s. 2(*j*) only if there is relationship of employer and employees and the former is engaged in business, trade, undertaking manufacture or calling of employers and the latter, in any calling, service, employment, handicraft or industrial occupation or avocation. [*The Workmen of Indian Standards Institution* v *The Management of Indian Standards Institution* AIR 1976 SC 145: (1976)2 SCR 138: (1975)2 SCC 847].

The definition of industry is in two parts, the first from the point of view of employers and the second, from the angle of employees. In its first part it means any trade, business, undertaking, manufacture or calling of employers. This part determines an industry by reference to occupation of employers in respect of those activities specified by the five words and they determine what an "industry" is, and what the cognate expression industrial is intended to convey. But the second part standing alone cannot define industry. [*Secretary, Madras Gymkhana Club Employees' Union* v *Management of the Gymkhana Club* AIR 1968 SC 554: (1968)1 SCR 742].

The word 'industry' as defined in s. 2(*j*) must take its colour from the definition. An industry is to be found when the employers are carrying on any business, trade, undertaking, manufacture or calling of employers. If they are not, there is no industry as such. [*The Management of Safdarjung Hospital, New Delhi* v *Kuldip Singh Sethi* AIR 1970 SC 1407: (1970)1 SCC 735: (1971)1 SCR 177].

'Industry' as defined in s. 2(*j*) has a wide import. Where there is (*i*) systematic activity, (*ii*) organized by co-operation between employer and employee (the direct and substantial element is chimerical), and (*iii*) for the production and/or distribution of goods and services calculated to satisfy human wants and wishes (not spiritual or religious but inclusive of material things or services geared to celestial bliss e.g. making on large scale prasad or food), *prima facie*, there is an industry in that enterprise. [*Bangalore Water Supply & Sewerage Board* v *A. Rajappa* AIR 1978 SC 548: (1978)3 SCR 207: (1978)2 SCC 213].

NOTE: Hospitals would come within the definition of the expression 'industry'. [*Bangalore Water Supply & Sewerage Board* v *A. Rajappa* AIR 1978 SC 548: (1978)3 SCR 207: (1978)2 SCC 213]. A group of hospitals run by a State for giving medical relief to citizens and imparting medical education is an 'industry'. [*State of Bombay* v *Hospital Mazdoor Sabha* AIR 1960 SC 610: 1960 SCJ 679: 1960 SCR 866: (1960)2 SCA 243]. If a hospital, nursing home or dispensary is run as a business in a commercial way, there may be found elements of an industry there. Then the hospital is more than a place where persons can get treated for their ailment. It becomes a business. [*Management of Safdarjung Hospital, New Delhi* v *Kuldip Singh Sethi* AIR 1970 SC 1407: (1970)1 SCC 735].

A municipality or a municipal corporation is an industry. [*Municipal Committee* v *Ram Lal Jain* AIR 1965 Punj 15].

The business of the chartered accountant is not an industry. In the first place, the professional income of the firm is earned solely by the efforts of the partners and other qualified chartered accountants, after the termination of the services of the audit clerks. In the second place, there is no evidence at all that the firm carried on any business other than that of a chartered accountant. [*R.K. Iyer* v *Fifth ITO, West Bengal* AIR 1968 Cal 159]. However, a solicitor's establishment may be an industry. [*Bangalore Water Supply & Sewerage Board* v *A. Rajappa* AIR 1978 SC 969].

When a research laboratory is more an institution discharging government functions and a domestic enterprise than a commercial enterprise, it is not an 'industry' within s. 2(*j*) of the Industrial Disputes Act 1947. [*Physical Research Laboratory* v *K.G. Sharma* (1997)4 SCC 257].


- **Chemical industry** p. 140.
- **Textile industry** p. 840.


**Industry carried on under the authority of the Central Government.** The expression does not mean the same thing as controlled industry. For an industry to be carried on under the authority of the Central Government, it must be an industry belonging to the Central Government, that is to say, its own undertaking. A controlled industry in spite of the sweeping controls exercised upon it by the Central Government is not necessarily an industry carried on by or under the authority of the Central Government. [*Bharat Glass Works* v *State of West Bengal* AIR 1957 Cal 347].

**Inelastic demand.** It is a condition where a considerable rise or fall in the price of a commodity has little effect on the quantity demanded. Demand tends to be inelastic when there are no close substitute for a commodity, or in the case of necessaries of life or when demand is based on habit, or when expenditure on the commodity concerned forms only a small proportion of a person's total expenditure.

**Inelastic supply.** It is a condition where a rise in the price of a commodity on the market fails to call-forth an increase in output.

**Inertia selling.** It is delivering goods to people, who have not ordered them, offering them on approval for a specified period. On the expiry of the period, it is assumed that the receiver has decided to purchase them. This leads to goods being purchased simply because it is too much troublesome to return them to the sender. [J.L. Hanson on *A Dictionary of Economics and Commerce*, 6th Ed.].

**Inevitable.** Incapable of being avoided; fortuitous; transcending the power of human care, foresight, or exertion to avoid or prevent; destined; fated; foreordained; ineluctable; inescapable; predestined; unavoidable; unpreventable.

**Inevitable accident.** Inevitable accident is that which the party charged with the offence could not possibly prevent by the exercise of ordinary care, caution and skill. [*McBride* v *Stitt* (1944) NI 7].

An unavoidable accident; one produced by an irresistible physical cause; an accident which cannot be prevented by human skill or foresight, but results from natural causes, such as lightning or storms, perils of the sea, inundations or earthquakes, or sudden death or illness. [Black's *Law Dictionary*, 5th Ed.].

An accident that cannot be avoided because it is produced by an irresistible physical cause that cannot be prevented by human skill or reasonable foresight. [Black's *Law Dictionary*, 7th Ed.].

NOTE: Also termed as unavoidable accident, it has been considered a means of avoiding both civil and criminal liability.

**Inexpedient.** Not expedient; disadvantageous in the circumstances; unadvisable; impolitic. [*Murlidhar Agarwal* v *State of U.P.* AIR 1974 SC 1924: (1974)2 SCC 472: (1975)1 SCR 575].

**Infamous.** Shameful or disgraceful; possessing notorious reputation; famous or well known in a derogatory sense.

**Infamous conduct.** Shameful or disgraceful conduct.

Infamous conduct on the part of a professional person means no more than serious misconduct, judged according to rules, written or unwritten, governing the profession. [*Nesamoney Daniel* v *State* AIR 1967 Mad 281: ILR (1967)2 Mad 295].

NOTE: The expression has acquired particular meaning in the context of such professional people as a medical practitioner, an advocate or a chartered accountant. In the medical world, the expression has a special meaning. If it is shown that a medical man, in the pursuit of his profession, has done something with regard to it which would be reasonably regarded as disgraceful and dishonourable by his professional brethren of good repute and competency, it is open to the Medical Council to find that he has been 'guilty of infamous conduct in a professional respect'. [*Nesamoney Daniel* v *Government of Madras* AIR 1967 Mad 281].

**Infant.** A child during the earliest period of its life; a baby; a child under seven years of age; a minor; a thing in an early stage of its development.

**Infanticide.** The killing of an infant soon after birth.

NOTE: The fact of the birth distinguishes this act from 'foeticide' which term denotes the destruction of the foetus in the womb.

**Infectious disease.** A disease liable to be transmitted by air, water, etc.; a disease apt to spread quickly affecting others. It is also termed contagious disease.

NOTE: Cholera, leprosy, enteric fever, smallpox, tuberculosis, diphtheria, plague, influenza, venereal disease, are examples of infectious or contagious disease.

**Inferior court.** A court is inferior to another court when an appeal lies from the former to the latter.

Every court of limited jurisdiction, circumscribed by statutory limitations regarding territory, pecuniary limits and subject-matter is a court of inferior jurisdiction. [*Issardas S. Lulla* v *Hari* AIR 1962 Mad 458].

NOTE: The High Court acting in its Original Criminal Jurisdiction is an inferior court within the meaning of s. 435 of the Code of Criminal Procedure to the Appellate Side of the High Court. [*Emperor* v *Krishnaji Vithal* AIR 1949 Bom 29: 49 Cr LJ 593].

**Infest.** The word 'infest' appears to have been derived from the Latin word 'infestate' which meant to assail or molest. According to the *Oxford English Dictionary* (vol. V, p. 259) the word 'infest' means 'to attack, assail, annoy, or trouble (a person or thing) in a persistent manner; to visit persistently or in large number for purposes of destruction or plunder'; 'to swarm in or about, so as to be troublesome'. The word is now used especially for insects which attack plants, grain, etc., in large swarms. [*Municipal Corporation of Delhi* v *Kacheroo Mal* AIR 1976 SC 394: (1976)2 SCR 1: (1976)1 SCC 412: 1976 Cr LJ 336: 1976 SCC (Cri) 30].

Webster's *New International Dictionary*, vol. 1, p. 1247 gives the meaning of the word 'infest' as to trouble greatly by numbers or by frequency of presence; to assail or annoy persistently and in numbers to frequent and molest or harass; as fleas infest dogs and cats. [*Kacheroo Mal* v *State* 1971 Del LT 138: 73 Punj LR (DS) 101].

According to Webster's *New World Dictionary* (1962 Ed.) 'infest' means "to overrun or inhabit in large numbers, usually so as to be harmful or bothersome, swarm in or about."

According to Webster's *Illustrated Contemporary Dictionary* (Encyclopedic Editicn), 'infest' means "to overrun or spread in large numbers so as to be unpleasant or unsafe". [*State (Delhi Administration)* v *Puran Mal* AIR 1985 SC 741: (1985)3 SCR 464: 1985 SCC (Cri) 289: 1985 Cr LJ 921: (1985)2 SCC 589].

**Infidel**. One who denies the existence of God; an unbeliever in any particular religion or belief; one who professes no religion that can bind his conscience to speak the truth.

**Infidelity.** The state of being an infidel; lack of belief; lack of fidelity, specially, violation of the marriage vow by adultery; disloyalty; unfaithfulness to a sexual partner; abandonment of allegiance; bad faith; betrayal of oath; betrayal of trust; lack of faith; lack of loyalty; perfidiousness; unfaithfulness to an obligation.

**Infirm.** Physically weak, especially through age; lacking soundness, resolution, stability, or firmness; not legally secure; voidable.

**Inflammable.** Readily set on fire; capable of being inflamed; susceptible of combustion; combustible; easily excited or roused to passion.

**Inflation.** In its use as decrease in value of currency, it means boost in prices; currency devaluation; decrease in purchasing power; hike in prices; a monetary condition where the quantity of money is increasing more rapidly than output.

> NOTE: Causes of inflation are two: (*a*) heavy Government expenditure not covered by taxation or by borrowing from the people. In such circumstances, the Government will have to cover its expenditure by increasing the quantity of money, always the easiest option when it wishes to avoid unpopularity; (*b*) attempting to maintain full employment by simulating demand by an increase in the money supply, there being a tendency to over stimulating demand, thereby producing over full employment. [J.L. Hanson on *A Dictionary of Economics and Commerce*, 6th Ed.].

**Influence.** As noun means authority; command; control; dominance; hold; importance; leverage; power; predominance; superiority; weight; supremacy.

As verb means actuate; arouse; brainwash; bring pressure to bear; cajole; motivate; prompt; pull strings.

- **Improper influence** p. 437.
- **Undue influence** p. 864.

**Information.** While used as 'charge', it means accusal; accusation; charge; criminal accusation; formal accusation; formal criminal complaint; official criminal charge; presecutorial complaint; written accusation.

In its application to 'facts', it means communique; data; news; notice; notification; specifics; statistics.

While used as 'knowledge', it means acquired facts; acquired knowledge; available facts; communication; communique, compilations; revelation.

'Information' means instruction or knowledge concerning facts and particulars. [*Indian & Eastern Newspapers Society, New Delhi* v *Commissioner of Income Tax, New Delhi* AIR 1979 SC 1960: (1979)4 SCC 248: (1979)119 ITR 996: (1980)1 SCR 442].

The word 'information' is synonymous with knowledge or awareness, in contradistinction to apprehension, suspicion or misgiving. [*Commissioner of Income Tax, Punjab* v *Jagannath* AIR 1957 Punj 226: 59 Punj LR 454].

The term 'information' means the act or process of informing, communication, or reception of knowledge. It may be knowledge acquired directly as by observation from others. [*Commissioner of Income Tax, Punjab* v *Jagannath* AIR 1957 Punj 226: 59 Punj LR 454].

▸ *Meaning under the Right to Information Act 2005, s. 2(f)*. 'Information' means any material in any form, including records, documents, memos, e-mails, opinions, advices, press releases, circulars, orders, logbooks, contracts, reports, papers, samples, models, data material held in any electronic form and information relating to any private body which can be accessed by a public authority under any other law for the time being in force.

NOTE: A statement by a body, not competent to create law, as the internal audit party of the income-tax department, is merely 'opinion' and cannot be regarded as 'information'. [*Indian & Eastern Newspapers Society, New Delhi* v *Commissioner of Income Tax, New Delhi* AIR 1979 SC 1960: (1979)4 SCC 248: (1979)119 ITR 996: (1980)1 SCR 442; *Jai Prakash* v *Radhey Shyam* (1987)2 Crimes 363 (All)].

'Information' includes data, text, images, sound, voice, codes, computer programmes, software and data bases or micro film or computer generated micro fiche. [Information Technology Act 2000, s. 2(*v*)].

- **Definite information** p. 242.
- **First information report** p. 356.
- **Information as to law.** 'Information as to law' contemplates information as to the law created by a formal source, that is, from a competent legislature or from a competent judicial or quasi-judicial authority. [*Indian & Eastern Newspapers Society, New Delhi* v *Commissioner of Income Tax, New Delhi* AIR 1979 SC 1960: (1979)4 SCC 248: (1979)119 ITR 996: (1980)1 SCR 442].

**Infringement.** Abuse of privilege; breach; contravention; disobedience; entrance upon domain of another; repudiation; violation of a privilege; violation of a regulation; wrong doing; violation of a law, contract, or right; a trespass or encroachment upon.

**Infringement of copyright.** Unauthorised use of copyrighted material, *i.e.*, use without permission of copyright holder.

NOTE: Section 51 of the Copyright Act 1957 lays down the circumstances when copyright in a work shall be deemed to be infringed.

**Infringing copy.** It means (*i*) in relation to a literary, dramatic, musical or artistic work, a reproduction thereof otherwise than in the form of a cinematograph film; (*ii*) in relation to a cinematographic film, a copy of the film made on any medium by any means; (*iii*) in relation to a sound recording, any other recording embodying the same sound recording, made by any means; (*iv*) in relation to a programme or performance in which such a broadcast reproduction right or a performer's right subsists under the provisions of this Act, the sound recording or a cinematographic film of such programme or performance, if such reproduction, copy or sound recording is made or imported in contravention of the provisions of this Act. [Copyright Act 1957, s. 2(*m*)].

**Ingress.** The act, or right of, entering; access; entrance.

**Ingress, egress, and regress.** These words express the right to enter, go upon, and return from the lands in question.

**Ingrossing.** The act of making a fair and perfect copy of any document from a rough draft of it, in order that it may be executed or put to its final purpose.

**Inhabitant.** Dweller; householder; occupier; permanent resident; one who resides actually and permanently in a given place, and has his domicile there. [*Ex parte Shaw* 36 L Ed 768].

The word 'inhabitant' cannot be said to have any fixed meaning; the meaning should be given according to the subject-matter or context. [*Abdul Gani* v *Commissioner of Police* AIR 1949 Bom 365: 51 Cr LJ 7].

NOTE: It presupposes natural person not artificial persons. When Municipal Law states that alteration of boundaries can be objected to by inhabitants, Gram Panchayat being artificial person cannot object. [*Gram Panchayat* v *State of H.P.* AIR 1990 Punj 88].

**Inherent power.** An authority possessed without its being derived from another; a right, ability, or faculty of doing a thing, without receiving that right, ability, or faculty from another; a power that necessarily derives from an office, position, or status.

**Inherit.** Acquire from ancestors; be the heir of; come into possession as an heir; receive by bequest; receive by devise; receive by descent; receive by succession; take by descent; take by inheritance; take by succession; to take or receive as heir of the former possessor at his decease, get by legal descent or succession.

"Inherit" means succession by descent. It means to receive property as heir. The word 'inherit' relates to right of succession to the real estate of a person dying intestate. [*Ayi Ammal* v *Subramania Asari* AIR 1966 Mad 369: (1966)1 MLJ 411].

**Inheritance.** Property received from an ancestor under the laws of intestacy; property that a person receives by bequest or devise.

The expression "inheritance" or "succession" as used in the constitutional enactments is not to be understood as confined to cases of 'devolution' in the strict sense of a passing of inheritance in property from the dead to the living but as comprehending also the adjustment of the rights and obligations that subsist between the parties governed by Hindu law. [Hindu Women's Rights to Property Act 1941; *Re Hindu Women's Rights to Property Act 1937* AIR 1941 FC 72: (1941)2 MLJ 12].

NOTE: "Inheritance" is in some sort a legal and fictitious continuation of the personality of the dead man, for the representation is in some sort identified by the law with him who he represents. The rights which the dead man can no longer own or exercise *in propria persona* and the obligations which he can no longer *in propria persona* fulfil, he owns, exercises and fulfils in the person of a living substitute. To this extent, and in this fiction, it may be said that legal personality of a man survives his natural personality; until his obligations being duly performed, and his property duly disposed of, his representation among the living is no longer called for. [*Chiranjilal Shrilal Goenka* v *Jasjit Singh* (1993)2 SCC 507: (1993)2 SCR 454: JT 1993(2) SC 341].

- **Estate of inheritance** p. 320.

**Iniquum est aliquem rei sui esse judicem.** It is unjust for anyone to be judge in his own cause; no one should be a judge in his own cause.

**Initiate.** Begin; break ground; bring into use; commence; introduce; launch; lay the foundation; lead the way; originate; set afoot; set going; take the initiative; take the lead.

To 'initiate' means 'to originate' or 'to take the first step'. [*Artisan Press Ltd.* v *Income Tax Appellate Tribunal* (1958)33 ITR 670].

**Injunction.** Ban; bidding; command to undo wrong; judicial order to refrain from an act; prohibition; proscription; restraining order.

A judicial process operating *in personam*, and requiring a person to whom it is directed to do or refrain from doing a particular thing. [*Gainsburg* v *Dodge* 101 SW 2d 178, 180].

An injunction is a judicial process whereby a party is ordered to refrain from doing or to do a particular act or thing. In the former case it is called a restrictive injunction, and in the latter a mandatory injunction. [Halsbury's *Laws of England*, 4th Ed., vol. 24, para 901, p. 511].

NOTE: In India, the law as to injunction is contained in the Specific Relief Act 1963, and the Code of Civil Procedure 1908.

- **Mandatory injunction.** One which (1) commands the defendant to do some positive act or particular thing; (2) prohibits him from refusing or persisting in a refusal to do or permit some act to which the plaintiff has a legal right; or (3) restrains the defendant from permitting his previous wrongful act to continue operative, thus virtually compelling him to undo it.

When, to prevent the breach of an obligation, it is necessary to compel the performance of certain acts which the court is capable of enforcing, the court may in its discretion grant an injunction to prevent the breach complained of, and also to compel performance of the requisite acts. Such injunction as granted is called mandatory injunction. [Specific Relief Act 1963, s. 39].

NOTE: A mandatory injunction forbids the defendant to permit the continuance of a wrongful state of things that already exists when the injunction is issued. [*State* v *R.D. Singh* AIR 1977 Raj 241].

- **Permanent injunction.** One intended to remain in force until the final termination of the particular suit.
- **Perpetual injunction.** An injunction which finally disposes of the suit, and is indefinite in point of time.

Perpetual injunction is such by which a party is perpetually enjoined from the assertion of a right, or from the commission of an act, which would be contrary to the rights of the other party. [Specific Relief Act 1963, s. 37(2)]

NOTE: It can be granted by the decree made at the hearing and upon the merits of the suit.

- **Preliminary injunction.** An injunction granted at the institution of a suit, to restrain the defendant from doing or continuing some act, the right to which is in dispute, and which may either be discharged or made perpetual, according to the result of the controversy, as soon as the rights of the parties are determined.
- **Prohibitory injunction.** An order of a court in the form of a judgment which directs one not to do a certain thing. It is sometimes called a restraining order.

NOTE: A prohibitory injunction forbids a defendant to do a wrongful act which would be an infringement of some right of the plaintiff, legal or equitable. [*State* v *R.D. Singh* AIR 1972 Raj 241]. Its primary purpose is pressing matters in *status quo*. It never assumes finality to dispose of the rights. [*Irnvaram* v *Padmavathamma* (1978)2 Andh WR 308].

- **Temporary injunction** p. 833.

**Injuria non exusat injurium.** One wrong does not justify another.

**Injuria sine damno.** The maxim means injury without damage. Wherever there is an invasion of a legal right, the person in whom the right is vested is entitled to bring an action and may be awarded damages although he has suffered no actual damage. Thus, the act of trespassing upon another's land is actionable even though it has done the plaintiff not the slightest harm. The law presumes damage owing to the mischievous tendency of the act and therefore prohibits it absolutely. In short, a man is entitled to have his person and property preserved inviolable. This is illustrated by *Ashby* v *White* [(1703)2 Ld Raym 438]. As observed by Lord Holt, CJ.: "Every injury imports a damage, though it does not cost the party one farthing; a damage is not merely pecuniary, but an injury imports a damage, when a man is thereby hindered of his right."

**Injury.** Physical harm or damage; violence; abuse; adversity; harmful act; any wrong, damage, or mischief done or suffered; a wrong or damage done to another; the unlawful infringement or privation of rights; wrongful action or treatment.

The violation of another's legal right, for which the law provides a remedy; a wrong or injustice; harm or damage. [Black's *Law Dictionary*, 8th Ed.].

Injury is wrongful action or treatment, harm or damage. The word has relation to acts which are wrongful and not to lawful acts. [*A. Venkanna* v *R. Venkata Rao* AIR 1957 AP 453].

In legal parlance, 'injury' means any wrong or damage done to another, either in his person, rights, reputation or property. In other words, it means an act which harms, hurts or damages, irrespective of the consideration how the harm, hurt or damage may arise. [*Surendrasingh* v *Lal Sheoraj Bahadursingh* AIR 1975 MP 85: 1975 MPLJ 57].

The word 'injury' is of large import. It cannot be restricted to mean bodily injury but may include injury by which damage or loss has been caused to property. [*Kamal Kusha* v *S. Kripal Singh* 1987 Kash LJ 211].

▸ *Meaning under the Indian Penal Code 1860, s. 44.* The word 'injury' denotes any harm whatever illegally caused to any person, in body, mind, reputation or property.

▸ *Meaning under the Workmen's Compensation Act 1923, s. 3.* The word 'injury' does not mean merely physical injury but may include a strain which causes exposure to draught or causes a chill. [*Indian News Chronicle Ltd.* v *Luis Lazarus* AIR 1951 Punj 102].

NOTE: *"Injury" and "annoyance"—distinction.* 'Injury' means unlawful infringement or privation of a right and 'annoyance' in law means much the same thing as nuisance. [*Municipal Committee* v *State of Madhya Pradesh* AIR 1962 MP 40: 1961 MPLJ 667].

- **Employment injury** p. 305.
- **Irreparable injury** p. 480.
- **Legal injury** p. 526.
- **Personal injury** p. 659.
- **Serious bodily injury** p. 787.

**Injustice.** The withholding or denial of justice; an unjust state of affairs; an unjust act; unfairness.

In law, it almost invariably applies to the act, fault, or omission of a court. Injustice may be done by the negligence, mistake, or omission of the court itself.

**Inland.** Within a country, state or territory; within the interior part of a land mass; the interior part of a country or region, away from the coast or border.

▸ *Meaning under the Indian Post Office Act 1898, s. 2(b).* The expression 'inland', used in relation to a postal article, means (*i*) posted in India and addressed to any place in India or to any place for which a Post Office is established by the Central Government beyond the limits of India; or (*ii*) posted at any Post Office established by the Central Government beyond the limits of India and addressed to any place for which any such Post Office is established or to any place in India.

**Inland instrument.** A promissory note, bill of exchange or cheque drawn or made in India and made payable in, or drawn upon any person resident in India shall be deemed to be an inland instrument. [Negotiable Instruments Act 1881, s. 11].

**Inland trade.** A trade wholly managed at home in one country.

**Inland water.** Inland water means any canal, river, lake or navigable water [Indian Railways Act 1890, s. 3(3) [since repealed]; Indian Steam Vessels Act 1917, s. 2(2)].

**Inland water-way.** Any canal, river, lake or other navigable water in India. [Marking of Heavy Packages Act 1951, s. 2(*b*)].

**Inmate.** Captive; convict; prisoner; dweller; inhabitant; occupant; occupier; resident; roomer.

A person confined in a prison, hospital, or other institution; one who lives with others in a dwelling. [Black's *Law Dictionary*, 7th Ed.].

**Innkeeper.** An innkeeper is one who makes it his business to entertain travellers and passengers, and provide lodging and necessaries for them and their horses and attendants. He publicly professes that he keeps an inn, and will receive therein all travellers who are willing to pay an adequate price, and who come in a situation in which they are fit to be received. A person who receives guests out of mere hospitality is not an innkeeper. A house which supplies only lodging is not an inn.

**Inns of court.** Inns of court are Lincoln's Inn, the Inner Temple, and the Middle Temple and Gray's Inn. They enjoy the exclusive privilege of conferring the rank or degree of barrister, the possession of which constitutes an indispensable qualification for practising as counsel in the superior courts. The Inns of court are governed by officers called "benchers", to whom application is made by students wishing to be called to the Bar. [Mozley & Whiteley's *Law Dictionary*, 10th Ed.].

**Innuendo.** Accusation; aspersion; charge; hint; implied indication; imputation; indirect allusion; inference; insinuation; oblique allusion; overtone; reflection.

An oblique remark or indirect suggestion, usually of a derogatory nature; an explanatory word or passage inserted parenthetically into a legal document. [Black's *Law Dictionary*, 7th Ed.].

In criminal law, an innuendo takes the form of a statement in an indictment showing the application or meaning of matter previously expressed, the meaning of which would not otherwise be clear. [Black's *Law Dictionary*, 7th Ed.].

In the law of defamation, an innuendo is the plaintiff's explanation of a statement's defamatory meaning when the meaning is not apparent from the statement's face. [Black's *Law Dictionary*, 7th Ed.].

**Inofficious will.** A will which is not consonant with the testator's natural affection and moral duties is called an inofficious will. [*Prasannamayi* v *Baikuntha* 49 Cal 132].

NOTE: An inofficious will may throw some light upon the question of the testator's condition of mind. [*Harwood* v *Baker* 3 Moo PC 282]. In an inofficious will the testamentary act is so unlike the product of a healthy and independent mind that the act alone is strongly evidential of the existence of some extrinsic undue influence.

**Input.** What is put in or taken in, or operated on by any process or system; something put into a system or device, as energy into a machine, food into the body, data into a computer, or a signal into an electronic device; a place or point of introduction, as of data into a computer.

NOTE: The tyres, tubes and batteries purchased for fitment in the vehicle, which could not be operative without it, are "inputs". [*Tata Engineering & Locomotive Company Ltd.* v *State of Bihar* (1994)6 SCC 479].

**Inquest.** Determination of damages; investigation; search into facts; legal investigation; a judicial inquiry to ascertain the facts relating to an incident; the inquiry by a coroner or medical examiner into the manner of the death of any one who has been slain, or has died suddenly or by violence or in prison.

NOTE: The inquest is concerned with discovering whether in a given case the death was accidental, suicidal, homicidal or caused by some animal and in what manner or by what weapon or instrument the injuries appearing on the person of the deceased have been caused. [*Mettu Pentayya, in re* AIR 1960 AP 545: 1960 Cr LJ 1402].

The scope of inquest report is limited to the extent of ascertaining whether a person has died under suspicious circumstances or an unnatural death and, if so what is the apparent cause of death. [*Podda Narayan* v *State of A.P.* AIR 1975 SC 1252: 1975 SCC (Cri) 427: (1975)4 SCC 153: 1975 Cr LJ 1062; *Om Prakash* v *State (Delhi Administration)* 1979 Cr LJ (NOC) 141 (Del): ILR (1979)1 Del 735].

**Inquire.** Conduct research; delve into; examine; explore; probe; pry into; search into; seek information; survey; make a formal investigation.

The word 'inquire' means to make investigation, that is, to examine systematically in detail. [*Hirendra Nath* v *Life Insurance Corporation* AIR 1976 Cal 88].

**Inquiry.** Examination into facts or principles; exploration; inquisition; interrogation; investigation; probe; inquest; search for information; analysation; delving into evidence; hearing of evidence; inquisition.

Legal proceedings in which facts are found on the basis of which liability or disliability of a person is judged. It connotes an act of seeking truth, information or knowledge about something. Though synonymous with inquisition, investigation, probe or inquest, it acquires specific meaning by the context in which it is used. [*Jamunabai Motilal* v *State of Maharashtra* AIR 1978 Bom 200].

The meaning of the term 'inquiry' is investigation into facts, causes, effects and relations generally. 'Inquiry is road to the truth', said Gladstone. The Chamber's *Twentieth Century Dictionary* lays down the meaning of the term 'inquiry' as the search for knowledge, investigation, a question. [*Tuneswar Prasad Singh* v *State of Bihar* AIR 1978 Pat 225: 1978 Cr LJ 1080].

▸*Meaning under the Criminal Procedure Code 1973, s. 2(g) [old s. 4(1)(k)].* The section defines 'inquiry' as 'every inquiry other than a trial, conducted under the Code by a magistrate or court'.

An inquiry is something different from trial and that 'inquiry' stops when 'trial' begins. [*Sevaranna* v *State* 1957 Andh WR 123].

The term 'inquiry' does not include a 'trial' but only refers to a judicial inquiry into the matter by a magistrate or other court. [*R.P. Kapoor* v *Pratap Singh Kairon* AIR 1966 All 66: 1966 Cr LJ 115].

An inquiry in an action is not limited to what a man can see with his own eyes; it signifies a judicial inquiry with witnesses. [*Wenlock* v *River Dee Co.* 19 QBD 155].

• **Court of inquiry** p. 293.

• **Due inquiry** p. 285.

• **Further inquiry** p. 379.

**Insanity.** Aberration of mind; abnormality; alienation of mind; delirium; delusion; deranged intellect; disordered intellect; disordered mind; loss of reason; mental abnormality; mental derangement; mental incapacity; mental unsoundness; paranoia.

Any mental disorder characterized by temporary or permanent irrational or violent deviations from normal thinking, feeling or behaviour; any degree of mental unsoundness resulting in inability to distinguish between right and wrong, to control the will, foresee the consequence of an act, make a valid contract, or manage one's own affair; lack of sound sense; extreme folly. [Webster's *Comprehensive Dictionary*, International Edition].

Any mental disorder so severe enough that it prevents a person from having legal capacity and excuses the person from criminal or civil responsibility. [Black's *Law Dictionary*, 7th Ed.].

> NOTE: 'Insanity' implies the existence of either or both of the mental conditions, namely, an incapacity (*i*) to know the nature of the act; and (*ii*) to know that the act is wrong or contrary to law. [*Sankaran* v *State* 1994 Cr LJ 1173 (Ker)].
>
> For the purposes of criminal law, the test of insanity, according to the M'Naghten Rules, is at the time of the commission of an act: was the accused labouring under such a defect of reason from disease of the mind as not to know the nature and quality of the act he was doing; or if he did know it, did he know that it was wrong? This test has been adopted in criminal jurisprudence of India. [*State of Orissa* v *Bagh Syama* 1977 Cr LJ (NOC) 21 (Ori); *Gunadhar Mondal* v *State of W.B.* 1979 Cr LJ 178 (Cal); *Mitu Khadia* v *State of Orissa* 1983 Cr LJ 1385; *Sundar Bairagi* v *State of Orissa* 1984 Cr LJ 124].
>
> M'Naghten Rules do not apply to momentary failure to concentrate. A mere absent-mindedness is not insanity. [*R.* v *Clarke* (1972)56 Cr App R 225 quoted in Archbold on *Pleading, Evidence and Practice in Criminal Cases*, 41st Ed., Art. 17-43].

• **Legal insanity.** It is the insanity which affects not only the cognitive faculties of the mind, which guide our actions, but also our emotions which prompt our actions and the will by which our actions are performed. It is only unsoundness of mind which materially impairs the cognitive faculties of the mind that can form a ground of exemption from criminal responsibility, the nature and the extent of the unsoundness of mind required being such as would make the offender incapable of knowing the nature of the act or that he is doing what is wrong or contrary to law. It is this rule which is the basis of s. 84, IPC. [*Kalicharan* v *Emperor* ILR (1947) Nag 226; *Baswantrao Bajirao* v *Emperor* ILR (1948) Nag 711].

**Insemination.** Implantation; impregnation; introducing semen into a female by natural or artificial means.

• **Artificial insemination** p. 76.

**Insist.** Be obstinate; be resolute; command; demand; emphasize; enforce; exert pressure; force upon; lay stress on; persist; press earnestly; put pressure on; stand firm.

> NOTE: Something short of compelling but what would constitute insistence is a matter for careful investigation and for evidence. [*Rigby* v *Rigby* (1944) P 33].

**Insolvent.** Brankrupt; defaulting; indebted; moneyless; out of funds; penniless.

▸ *Meaning under the Sale of Goods Act 1930, s. 2(8).* A person is said to be "insolvent" who has ceased to pay his debts in the ordinary course of business, or cannot pay his debts as they become due, whether he has committed an act of insolvency or not.

**Inspection.** Appraisal; assessment; careful scrutiny; critical examination; critical viewing; evaluation; inquiry; reconnaissance; study; surveillance; survey; usual examination.

A careful examination of something, such as goods (to determine their fitness for purchase) or items produced in response to a discovery request (to determine their relevance to a lawsuit). [Black's *Law Dictionary*, 7th Ed.].

• **Committee of inspection** p. 158.

**Instalment.** Part payment; partial payment; periodic payment; a periodic partial payment of a debt; different portions of the same debt payable at different successive periods as agreed.

A part or a portion, especially of debts or other pecuniary liability.

**Instance.** Case in point; example; illustration; model; paradigm; representative selection; sample; specimen.

**Instance of.** At the behest of; at the solicitation of; at the urging or suggestion of.

NOTE: Instance does not imply the same degree of obligation to obey as does "command". [*State of Kerala* v *Adimurthy* AIR 1983 SC 822: 1983 Cr LJ 1077: (1983)2 Crimes 228: (1983)2 SCWR 179: 1983 Cr App R (SC) 321].

**Instead of.** The words 'instead of', though naturally imply some, do not necessarily mean, a total substitution. The expression may mean modification of something. [*Wilcock Kay* v *Dewhirst* (1898)1 Ch 95].

**Instigate.** To stimulate or goad to an action, especially a bad action. One of its synonymous is "abet". [*Hughes* v *Van Bruggen* 105 P 2d 494, 499].

The word "instigate" in common parlance would mean to go, to urge forward or to provoke, incite or encourage to do an act. [*State of Bihar* v *Ranen Nath* AIR 1958 Pat 259].

The word "instigate" in the literary sense means to incite, set or urge in, stir up, goad, stimulate, provoke etc. [*Premila Patnaik* v *State of Orissa* 1992 Cr LJ 2385].

**Instigation.** Actuation; agitation; animation; cajolery; coaxing; excitation; exhortation; goading; incitation; incitement; provocation; solicitation; stimulation; urging.

The act by which one incites another to do something, as to commit some crime or to commence a suit.

**Institute.** As noun means academy; association; concern; institution; establishment; guild; organisation; society; union; a legal treatise or commentary, such as Coke's Institutes (published in 1628 in four volumes).

As verb means to inaugurate or commence, as to institute an action [*Post* v *U.S.* 40 L Ed 816]; to set up; to originate; to start; to introduce; to nominate, constitute, or appoint.

NOTE: A criminal case on complaint is said to be instituted in court only when the court takes cognizance of alleged offence. [*Jamuna Singh* v *Bhadai Shah* AIR 1964 SC 1541: (1964)2 Cr LJ 468; *Kunti Lal* v *State of Rajasthan* (1988)1 Raj LR 494].

**Institution.** According to the dictionary meaning, the term 'institution' means 'a body or organisation of an association brought into being for the purpose of achieving some object'. *Oxford English Dictionary* defines an 'institution' as 'an establishment, organisation or association, institution for the promotion of some object especially one of public or general utility, religious, charitable, educational, etc.'. Other dictionaries define the same word as organised society established either by law or the authority of individuals for promoting any object, public or social. [*K.V. Krishna Rao* v *Sub-Collector, Oagole* (1969)1 SCWR 999: (1969)1 SCJ 687: (1969)2 SCA 255: AIR 1969 SC 563].

In the *Oxford Dictionary*, 'institution' is defined as 'an establishment, organisation or association instituted for the promotion of some object especially one of public utility, religious, charitable, educational etc.' [*K.V. Mathew* v *District Manager, Telephones* AIR 1984 Ker 40, 41: 1983 Ker LT 1022].

▸ *Other meanings.* The commencement or inauguration of anything, as the commencement of an action, such as civil or criminal; an established custom, system, organisation; an elementary rule, principle, or practice; an establishment, especially one of public character or one affecting a community.

It is a little difficult to define the meaning of the term 'institution' in the modern acceptation of the word. It means an undertaking formed to promote some defined purpose having in view generally the instruction or education of the public. It is the body (so to speak) called into existence to translate the purpose as conceived in the minds of the founders into a living and active principle. [*Manchester Corporation* v *McAdam* (1896) AC 500].

**Instrument.** Evidential writing; executed and delivered writing; formal writing; solemn writing; writing which gives formal expression to a legal act; a written document.

'Instrument' means a formal legal writing *e.g.* a record, charter, deed of transfer or agreement. [Jowitt's *Dictionary of English Law*].

An 'instrument' is a writing and generally means a writing of a formal nature. Where there is a power to appoint by any deed or instrument or by will, any writing, such as a letter, which refers to the power, is an instrument. [*Vishnu Pratap Sugar Works (P) Ltd.* v *Chief Inspector of Stamps* AIR 1968 SC 102: (1968)1 SCJ 633].

An 'instrument' is a writing and generally means a writing of a formal nature. [*Umaji Keshao Meshram* v *Radhika Bai* AIR 1986 SC 1272: 1986 (Supp) SCC 401: (1986)1 SCR 731].

Ordinarily, the word 'instrument' would refer to documents executed by the parties. [*Purshottam H. Jdye* v *V.B. Pottdar* AIR 1966 SC 856: (1966)7 SCR 353].

▸ *Meaning under the Notaries Act 1952, s. 2(b); Indian Stamp Act 1899, s. 2(14).* Instrument includes every document by which any right or liability is, or purports to be, created, transferred, modified, limited, extended, suspended, extinguished or recorded.

▸ *Meaning under the Transfer of Property Act 1882, s. 3.* "Instrument" means a non-testamentary instrument.

The expression is used to signify a deed *inter partes* or a charter or a record or other writing of a formal nature. But in the context of the General Clauses Act it has to be understood as including reference to a formal legal writing like an order made under a statute or subordinate legislation or any document of a formal character made under constitutional or statutory authority. Instrument includes an order made by the President in the exercise of his constitutional powers. [*Mohan Choudhury* v *Chief Commissioner* AIR 1964 SC 173: (1964)1 SCA 611: (1964)1 Cr LJ 132].

NOTE: 'Instrument' includes awards made by Industrial Courts. [*Purshottam H. Jadye* v *V.B. Potdar* AIR 1966 SC 856: (1966)2 SCR 353].

Instrument includes notifications. [*Vinod Rao* v *State of Gujarat* 1980 Cr LR (Guj) 283].

The expression 'instrument' covers a trust deed. [*Som Prakash Rekhi* v *Union of India* AIR 1981 SC 212: (1981)2 SCR 11: (1981)1 SCC 449].

'Instrument' does not include Acts of Parliament unless there is a statutory definition to that effect in any Act. [*Vishnu Pratap Sugar Works (P) Ltd.* v *Chief Inspector of Stamps* AIR 1968 SC 102: (1968)1 SCJ 633].

A will is an instrument. [*Bishun Shree* v *Suraj Mukhi* AIR 1966 All 563].

The word 'instrument' in s. 1 of the Interest Act is wide enough to cover a decree. [*Savitribai* v *Radhakishan* AIR 1948 Nag 49: ILR (1947) Nag 393].

An instrument is something by which an injury, simple or grievous, could be inflicted. [*Chaurasi Manji* v *State of Bihar* AIR 1970 Pat 322: 1970 Cr LJ 1235].

When used as tool, it means apparatus; appliance; contributing force; equipment; channel; machine; medium; vehicle.


- **Inchoate instrument** p. 444.
- **Inland instrument** p. 461.
- **Negotiable instrument** p. 604.


**Instrument of partition.** Any instrument whereby co-owners of any property divide or agree to divide such property in severalty, and includes also a final order for effecting a partition passed by any revenue authority or any civil court and an award by an arbitrator directing a partition. [Indian Stamps Act 1899, s. 2(15)].

**Instrument of title.** 'Instrument of title' in s. 103 of the Indian Contract Act 1872, means the same thing as 'document of title'.

A railway receipt is an instrument of title. [*Ramdas* v *Amarchand* 43 IA 164: AIR 1916 PC 7].

**Instrument of trust.** The instrument, if any, by which the trust is declared is called the instrument of trust. [Indian Trusts Act 1882, s. 3].

**Instrumentality.** Channel; device; equipment; machinery; instrument; vehicle; intermediary; medium.

A thing used to achieve an end or purpose; a means or agency through which a function of another entity is accomplished, such as a branch of a governing body. [Black's *Law Dictionary*, 8th Ed.].

▸*Instrumentality of State and the Constitution of India.* Article 12 of the Constitution of India provides that unless the context otherwise requires, "the State" includes the Government and Parliament of India and the Government and the Legislature of each of the States and all local or other authorities within the territory of India or under the control of the Government of India. *The other authorities within the territory of India or under the control of the Government of India are called Instrumentality of State.* The tests for being an Instrumentality of State are formulated in the case *R.D. Setty* v *International Airport Authority* [AIR 1979 SC 83: (1979)1 SCR 509: (1979)1 SCC 23]. There are several factors which may have to be considered namely as to whether there is any financial assistance given by the State, and if so, what is the magnitude of such assistance, whether there is any other form of assistance, given by the State, and if so, whether it is of the usual kind or it is extraordinary, whether there is any control of the management and policies of the corporation by the State and what is the nature and extent of such control, whether the corporation enjoys State conferred or State protected monopoly status and whether the functions carried out by the corporation are public functions closely related to governmental functions. This particularisation of relevant factors is however not exhaustive and by its very nature it cannot be, because with increasing assumption of new task, growing complexities of management and administration and the necessity of continuing adjustment in relations between the Corporation and Government calling for flexibility, adaptability and innovative skills, it is not possible to make an exhaustive enumeration of the tests which would invariably and in all cases provided an unfailing answer to the question whether a corporation is governmental instrumentality or agency. Moreover, even amongst these factors described above, no one single factor will yield a satisfactory answer to the question and the court will have to consider the cumulative effect of these various factors and arrive at its decision on the basis of a particularise inquiry into the facts and circumstances of each case. Pursuing the question further the Supreme Court in *Ajay Hasia* v *Khalid Mujib* [AIR 1981 SC 487: (1981)2 SCR 79: (1981)1 SCC 722] laid down the following principle.

The test for determining if an authority falls within the definition of State in Art. 12 is whether it is an instrumentality or agency of the Government. The inquiry has to be not as to how the juristic person is born but why it has been brought into existence. It is, therefore, immaterial whether the corporation is created by a statute or under a statute. The concept of instrumentality or agency of the Government is not limited to a corporation created by a statute but is equally applicable to a company or society and in a given case it would have to be decided, on a consideration of the relevant factors, whether the company or society is an instrumentality or agency of the Government so as to come within the meaning of the expression 'authority' in Art. 12. The tests for determining as to when a corporation can be said to be an instrumentality or agency of Government, given in *International Airport Authority* case (*ibid*) are not conclusive or clinching, but they are merely indicative indicia which have to be used with care and caution, because while stressing the necessity of a wide meaning to be placed on the expression 'other authorities', it must be realised that it should not be stretched so far as to bring in every autonomous body which has some nexus with the Government within the sweep of the expression.

The aforesaid tests were approved in the case *Som Prakash Rekhi* v *Union of India* [AIR 1981 SC 212: (1981)1 SCC 449: (1981)2 SCR 111: (1981)1 SCJ 458: (1981)1 Lab LJ 79].

In another Supreme Court case, it was held: "For the purposes of Art. 12 one must necessarily see through the corporate veil to ascertain whether behind that veil is the face of an instrumentality or agency of the State. The Central Inland Water Transport Corporation squarely falls within these observations and it also satisfies the various tests which have been laid down. Merely because it has so far not the monopoly of Inland Water Transportation is not sufficient to divest it of its character of an instrumentality or agency or the State. It is nothing but the Government operating behind a corporate veil carrying out a governmental activity and governmental function of vital public importance. There can be no doubt that the corporation is the 'State' within the meaning of Art. 12 of the Constitution". [*Central Inland Water Transport* v *Brojo Nath Ganguly* AIR 1986 SC 1571: (1986)3 SCC 156]. Thus, a Regional Rural Bank under deep and pervasive control of Central Government is an Instrumentality of State. [*Prarthana Bank* v *Vijay Kumar Goel* AIR 1989 SC 1977: (1989)3 SCJ 367].

NOTE: *Organisations held to be Instrumentalities of the State.* The following are Instrumentalities of the State and thus have been held to answer the definition of State under Art. 12, Constitution of India. Project & Equipment Corporation. [*A.L. Kalra* v *Project & Equipment Corpn.* AIR 1984 SC 1361]; Indian Council of Agricultural Research [*Ramchandra* v *Union of India* AIR 1984 SC 541: 1984 Lab IC 301]; Statistical Institute registered under the Societies Registration Act and governed by the Statistical Institute Act 1959 [*B.S. Minhas* v *Indian Statistical Institute* AIR 1984 SC 363]; Food Corporation of India [*Workmen of F.C.I.* v *F.C.I.* AIR 1985 SC 670]; Bihar State Electricity Board [*Surya Narayan Yadav* v *B.S.E.B.* AIR 1985 SC 941]; W.B. State Electricity Board [*Panchu Gopal* v *W.B.S.E.B.* (1990)1 CLJ 251]. An aided school receiving substantial grant from Government and subject to Regulation made by Education Department [*Manmohon Singh* v *Commr. U.T., Chandigarh* AIR 1985 SC 354]; Oil and Natural Gas Commission [*K.C. Joshi* v *Union of India* AIR 1985 SC 1046]; every Municipal Corporation, local authority [*Dinesh Kumar* v *Motilal Nehru Medical College, Allahabad* AIR 1985 SC 1415]; Central Inland Water Transport Corpn. [*Central Inland Water Transport Corpn.* v *Brojo Nath Ganguly* AIR 1986 SC 1571]; a bank constituted under the Regional Rural Banks Act 1976 [*M.K. Agarwal* v *Gurgaon Gramin Bank* AIR 1988 SC 286; *Chairman, Prarthana Bank* v *Vijay Kumar* AIR 1989 SC 1977]; Sainik School Society. [*All India Sainik Schools Employees Association* v *Defence Minister-cum-Chairman, B.O.G.* AIR 1989 SC 88].

*Organisations held not to be Instrumentalities of the State.* Institute of Constitutional and Parliamentary studies registered under the Societies Registration Act is not a State within the meaning of Art. 12, Constitution of India. [*Tekraj* v *Union of India* AIR 1988 SC 469]. A Cooperative Central Bank registered under Cooperative Societies Act of the relevant State is not a State within the meaning of Art. 12. [*Konaseema Cooperative Central Bank* v *Seetharama Raju* AIR 1990 AP 171].

**Insubordination.** State of being insubordinate; disobedience to constituted authority; refusal to obey some order which a superior officer is entitled to give and have obeyed; wilful or intentional disregard of the lawful and reasonable instructions of the employer.

**Insufficient grounds.** The words 'insufficient grounds' mean without reasonable and probable cause. [*Jeevanlal* v *Central Bank of India* AIR 1953 MB 90: ILR (1953) MB 29].

**Insult.** Speak to or treat with scornful abuse or indignity; offend the self-respect or modesty of; something so worthless or contemptible as to be offensive.

The word 'insult' in the legal parlance means to treat with offensive disrespect or to offer indignity to a person. [*Baste Subrayalu* v *Robert Mariadassou* 1987 Cr LJ 272 (Mad)].

Any act or speech meant to hurt the feelings or self-respect of another or treat a person with insolence or contempt by words or action would amount to an insult. [*Baste Subrayalu* v *Robert Mariadassou*, supra].

**Insurable interest.** A legal interest in another person's life or health or in the protection of property from injury, loss, destruction, or pecuniary damage. [Black's *Law Dictionary*, 8th Ed.].

An insurable interest in a life policy means that the person effecting the policy must, by the happening of the death of the person insured, be likely to sustain some pecuniary loss or liability. [*Mooris* v *Britannic Assurance Co*. (1931)2 KB 125].

**Insurable value.** Value of property for insurance purposes; the worth of the subject of an insurance contract, usually expressed as a monetary amount.

For fire insurance purpose, it is based on the value of the property less indestructible parts (land). For title insurance purposes, the sales price (market value) is used.

**Insurance.** Assurance against loss; bond against risk; contract against future loss; contract against unknown contingencies; guarantee against loss; indemnity against loss; pledge, promise, protection against loss; security against loss; warranty against loss.

A contract whereby, for a stipulated consideration, one party undertakes to compensate the other for loss on a specified subject by specified perils; a contract whereby one undertakes to indemnify another against loss, damage, or liability arising from an unknown or contingent event and is applicable only to some contingency or act to occur in future.

The act of providing against a possible loss, by entering into a contract with one who is willing to give assurance—that is to bind himself to make good such loss should it occur. In this contract the chances of benefit are equal to the insurer and the insured. The first actually pays a certain sum and the latter undertakes to pay a larger if an accident should happen. The one renders his property secure; the other receives money with the probability that it is a clear gain. The instrument by which the contract is made is called a policy, the stipulated consideration a premium. [Wharton's *Law Lexicon*].

NOTE: A contract of insurance is a *contract uberrimae fidei*, that is, a contract based on utmost good faith. If there is a breach in this good faith by a party, the other may avoid the contract. A contract of insurance is a contract of indemnity except in the case of life insurance. And this is regulated by the Insurance Act 1938 and the Life Insurance Corporation Act 1956.

The business of insurance is divided into two categories, *viz.*, (1) Life Insurance, and (2) General Insurance. The former deals with human life contracts while the latter with insurance against fire, marine risk etc.

The party agreeing to make the compensation is usually called the "insurer" or "underwriter", the other, the "insured" or "assured"; the agreed consideration, the "premium"; the written contract, a "policy"; the events insured against, "risks" or "perils"; and the subject, right, or interest to be protected, the "insurable interest".

- **Accident insurance** p. 15.
- **Cargo insurance.** An agreement to pay for damage to freight damaged in transit.
- **Crop insurance.** Insurance that protects against loss or damage to growing crops from natural perils such as hail and fire.
- **Double insurance** p. 280.
- **E. & O. insurance** p. 289.
- **Fire insurance** p. 354.
- **Guarantee insurance** p. 401.
- **Hazardous insurance** p. 408.
- **Health insurance** p. 409.
- **Life insurance.** A transaction whereby in consideration of a single or periodical payment of premium a sum of money is secured to be

paid on the death of the person whose life is assured. [Mozley & Whiteley's *Law Dictionary*, 10th Ed.].

An agreement between an insurance company and the policyholder to pay a specified amount to a designated beneficiary on the insured's death. [Black's *Law Dictionary*, 7th Ed.].

An insurance on life includes as much an obligation to pay a sum of money if life continues at a date as an obligation to pay a sum of money if life ceases. [*Gould* v *Courts* (1913)3 KB 84].

- **Marine insurance business** p. 562.
- **Policy of insurance** p. 669.
- **Use and occupancy insurance** p. 871.

**Insurance agent.** A person authorised by an insurance company to sell its insurance policies.

▸*Meaning under the Insurance Act 1938, s. 2(10)*. A person licensed under s. 42, who receives or agrees to receive payment by way of commission or other remuneration in consideration of his soliciting or procuring insurance business (including business relating to the continuance, renewal or revival of policies of insurance)

**Insurance company.** A corporation or association that issues insurance policies. [Black's *Law Dictionary,* 7th Ed.].

▸*Meaning under the Companies Act 1956, s. 2(21)*. A company which carries on the business of insurance either solely or in conjunction with any other business or businesses.

▸*Meaning under the Insurance Act 1938, s. 2(8)*. Insurance company means any insurer being a company, association or partnership which may be wound up under the Companies Act 1956, or to which the Indian Partnership Act 1932, applies.

▸*Meaning under the Industrial Disputes Act 1947, s. 2(kk); Industrial Disputes (Banking and Insurance Companies) Act 1949, s. 2*. Insurance company means an insurance company as defined in s. 2 of the Insurance Act 1938 (4 of 1938), having branches or other establishments in more than one State.

**Insurer.** One who agrees, by contract, to assume the risk of another's loss and to compensate for that loss.

▸*Meaning under the Insurance Act 1938, s. 2(9)*. 'Insurer' means—(*a*) any individual or unincorporated body of individuals or body corporate incorporated under the law of any country other than India, carrying on insurance business (not being a person specified in sub-clause (*c*) of this clause) which—(*i*) carries on that business in India, or (*ii*) has his or its principal place of business or is domiciled in India, or (*iii*) with the object of obtaining insurance business, employs a representative, or maintains a place of business in India; (*b*) any body corporate (not being a person specified in sub-clause (*c*) of this clause) carrying on the business of insurance, which is a body corporate incorporated under any law for the time being in force in India; or stands to such body corporate in the relation of a subsidiary company within the meaning of the Indian Companies Act 1913, as defined by sub-sec. (2) of s. 2 of that Act; and (*c*) any person who in India has a standing contract with underwriters who are members of the Society of Lloyd's whereby such person is authorised within the terms of such contract to issue protection notes, cover notes or other documents granting insurance cover to others on behalf of the underwriters, but does not include a principal agent, chief agent, special agent, or an insurance agent or a provident society as defined in Part III.

Though the ordinary meaning to be given to the word 'insurer' is as given in the definition clause in Insurance Act and refers to a person or body corporate etc. carrying on the business of insurance, the word may also refer in the context of certain provision of the Act to any intending insurer or quondam insurer. [*The Vanguard Fire and General Insurance Co. Ltd., Madras* v *M/s. Fraser and Ross* AIR 1960 SC 971, 975].

**Insurgency.** In international law, any uprising against a government of less gravity than a revolution.

NOTE: This is a condition midway between belligerency and piracy and it applies to all revolts and civil wars. The insurgents cannot be recognised as belligerents because of their comparative unimportance or other deficiency in organisation and resources, or their lack of points of contract with the outside world. But since they are carrying on political objects by means known to the laws of war, they cannot be regarded as outlaws by foreign powers. Hence is their position described as *insurgency*. The third States consider the insurgents as the *de facto* authority in the territory under their occupation and maintain with them relations deemed necessary for the protection of their nationals, for securing commercial intercourse and for other purposes connected with the hostilities. When this happens the rebels possess, as against third States, the status of insurgents. [Lawrence's *Principles of International Law*].

**Insurgent.** One who opposes the execution of law by force of arms; a person who, for political purposes, engages in armed hostility against an established government.

**Insurrection.** Anarchy; defiance; disobedience; political upheaval; rebellion; revolution; uprising, an organised resistance to established government; a violent revolt against an oppressive authority.

**Intangible asset.** A non-physical, non-current asset; an asset that is not a physical object. Example: patent, trademark, goodwill.

**Intent.** Aim; design; determination; motive; plan; purpose; scope; resolution.

Design, resolve, or determination with which a person acts. [*Witters* v *United States* 106 F 2d 837, 840].

• **Letter of intent** p. 530.

**Intention.** Aim; design; desire; destination; determination; end in view; end intended; fixed direction; fixed purpose; set purpose; settled determination; target; ultimate purpose; will.

A settled direction of the mind towards the doing of a certain act; that upon which the mind is set or which it wishes to express or achieve; purpose conceived; determination to act in a certain way or to do a certain thing; the willingness to bring about something planned or foreseen.

"Intention is the purpose or design with which an act is done. It is the foreknowledge of the act, coupled with the desire of it, such foreknowledge and desire being the cause of the act, inasmuch as they fulfil themselves through the operation of the will. [John Salmond: *Jurisprudence*, p. 378 (Glanville L. Williams ed., 10th Ed. 1947)].

'Intention' is defined as the fixed direction of the mind to a particular object, or a determination to act in a particular manner. [*S. Raghbir Singh Sandhawalia* v *Commissioner of Income-tax* AIR 1958 Punj 250].

'Intention' connotes a conscious state in which mental faculties are roused into activity and summoned into action for the deliberate purpose of being directed towards a particular and specified end which the human mind conceives and perceives before itself. [*Faqira* v *State* AIR 1955 All 321: 1955 Cr LJ 834 (DB)].

'Intention' is a conscious state in which mental faculties are aroused into activity and summed into action for the purpose of achieving a conceived end. It means shaping of one's conduct so as to bring about a certain event. In the case of 'intention', mental faculties are projected in a set direction. Intention need not necessarily involve premeditation. Whether there is such an intention or not is a question of fact. [*Jai Prakash* v *State (Delhi Admn.)* (1991)2 SCC 32: 1991 SCC (Cri) 299: JT 1991(1) SC 228].

NOTE: 'Intention' requires something more than the mere foresight of the consequences, namely the purposeful doing of a thing to achieve a particular end. [*Jai Prakash* v *State (Delhi Admn.)* (1991)2 SCC 32: 1991 SCC (Cri) 299: JT 1991(1) SC 228].

A man's intention ought to be judged by his acts and not from what may be in his mind. It should be ascertained by taking into consideration the entire transaction. [*S. Raghbir Singh Sandhawalia* v *Commissioner of Income Tax* AIR 1958 Punj 250].

• **Common intention** p. 159.

**Intention of the legislature.** It is a slippery phrase. It may signify anything from intention embodied in positive enactment to speculative opinion as to what the legislature probably would have meant, although there has been an omission to enact it. In a court of law, the intention of the legislature can only be legitimately ascertained from what it has chosen to enact, either in express words or by necessary implication.

**Inter alia.** Among other things.

**Inter-caste.** Between or concerning different castes.

**Inter-connected undertakings.** Two or more undertakings which are inter-connected with each other in any of the following manner, namely: (*i*) if one owns or controls the other, (*ii*) where the undertakings are owned by firms, if such firms have one or more common partners, (*iii*) where the undertakings are owned by bodies corporate,: (*a*) if one body corporate manages the other body corporate or, (*b*) if one body corporate is subsidiary of the other body corporate, or (*c*) if the bodies corporate are under the same management, or (*d*) if one body corporate exercises control over the other body corporate in any other manner, (*iv*) where one undertaking is owned by a body corporate and the other is owned by a firm, if one or more partners of the firm: (*a*) hold, directly or indirectly, not less than 50 per cent of the shares, whether preference or equity, of the body corporate, or (*b*) exercise control, directly or indirectly, whether as director or otherwise, over the body corporate, (*v*) if one is owned by a body corporate and the other is owned by a firm having bodies corporate as its partners, if such bodies corporate are under the same management, (*vi*) if the undertakings are owned or controlled by the same person or by the same group, (*vii*) if one is connected with the other either directly or through any number of undertakings which are inter-connected undertakings within the meaning of one or more of the foregoing sub-clauses. [Monopolies and Restrictive Trade Practices Act 1969, s. 2(*g*). The Act is repealed and replaced by the Competition Act 2002. No such term is defined under the new Act].

**Inter se.** Between or among themselves.

> NOTE: It is used to distinguish rights or duties between two or more persons from their rights or duties to others.

**Inter vivos.** Between living persons.

**Intercourse.** Mutual exchange; commerce; communication; the interchange of ideas; sexual connection; coitus.

> NOTE: There is no intercourse unless the visiting member is enveloped at least partially by the visited organism, for intercourse connotes reciprocity. [*State of Kerala* v *Kundumkara Govindan* ILR (1968)2 Ker 605: 1968 Ker LJ 485: 1969 Cr LJ 818].

• **Illicit intercourse** p. 428.

**Interest.** The word 'interest' is a word of wide connotation.

It ordinarily means concern; curiosity; anxiety; attention to detail; eagerness; enthusiasm; hobby; lively sympathy.

In relation to land or property, it means right, title or legal concern over land; proprietary right or share; right of ownership; a legal share in something; all or part of a legal or equitable claim to or right in property.

> NOTE: A right cannot exist without interest though interest can exist, without a right. Hence, the word 'right' includes 'interest'. [*Azizunnissa* v *Asstt. Custodian of Evacuee Property* AIR 1957 All 561].

In commercial and financial parlance, it means premium for the use of money; profit from money loaned; money paid for use of money lent or for not requiring the repayment of a debt; the compensation fixed by agreement or allowed by law for the use or detention of money. Interest is compensatory in character. [*Pratibha Processors* v *Union of India* AIR 1997 SC 138: (1996)11 SCC 101: JT 1996(9) SC 478: (1996)88 ELT 12]. Interest is a payment to be made by the debtor to the creditor when money was due to the creditor but was not paid or, in other words, was withheld from the creditor by the debtor after the time when the payment should have been made. [*S.R.Y. Sivaram Prasad Bahadur* v *The*

*Commissioner of Income Tax* AIR 1972 SC 260: (1972)1 SCR 320: (1971)3 SCC 726: (1971)82 ITR 527].

Interest, whether statutory or contractual, represents the profit the creditor would have made if he had the use of the money to which he was entitled to. [*S.R.Y. Sivaram Prasad Bahadur* v *The Commissioner of Income Tax* AIR 1972 SC 260: (1972)1 SCR 320: (1971)3 SCC 726: (1971)82 ITR 527]. Strictly speaking, the word 'interest' would apply only to cases where there is a relationship of debtor and creditor. A lender of money who allows the borrower to use certain funds deprives himself of the use of those funds. He does so because he charges interest which may be described as a kind of rent for the use of the funds. [*Ferro Alloys Corporation Ltd.* v *A.P. State Electricity Board* AIR 1993 SC 2005: 1993 Supp (4) SCC 136: (1993)3 SCR 199: JT 1993(3) SC 82].

▸ *Meaning under the Civil Procedure Code 1908.* The word 'interest' in Or. 21, r. 89, has got a very wide import and should be construed very liberally so that any inchoate right which a party may have over a property be sufficient 'interest' to enable him to apply under Or. 21, r. 89. [*Radha Roman Chouduary* v *Gulab Thakur* AIR 1959 Pat 59]. The word 'interest' in Or. 21, r. 89 should not be read in any narrow sense; it is wide enough to cover the interest of the wife of a Hindu governed by the Mitakshara. [*Karimuddin Khan* v *Sachhidananda Jena* 13 Cut LT 25].

The word 'interest' in Or. 22, r. 10 means interest in the property, *i.e.*, the subject-matter of the suit and the interest is the interest of the person who was the party to the suit. [*Shri Rikhu Dev, Chela Bawa Harjug Dass* v *Som Dass (Deceased) through His Chela Shiama Dass* AIR 1975 SC 2159: (1976)1 SCR 487: (1976)1 SCC 103].


- **Compound interest** p. 164.
- **Contingent interest** p. 186.
- **Controlling interest** p. 193.
- **Excessive interest** p. 326.
- **Hereditary interest** p. 412.
- **Illegal interest** p. 427.
- **Insurable interest** p. 468.
- **Leasehold interest** p. 523.
- **Life interest** p. 535.
- **Limited interest** p. 536.
- **Public interest** p. 709.
- **Public interest litigation** p. 709.
- **Same interest** p. 773.
- **Vested interest** p. 879.


**Interest of the general public.** The expression in Art. 19(5) of the Constitution of India does not mean in the interest of the public of the whole of the Republic of India. The expression means nothing more than 'in the public interest' and it may well be that legislation affecting a limited class of persons or a limited area might well be legislation in the public interest, though the public of other parts of India might not be directly affected by such legislation. [*Iswari Prasad Goenka* v *N.R. Sen* AIR 1952 Cal 273: 55 CWN 719].

NOTE: Interests of the general public cannot be deemed to be synonymous with interests of the public of the whole of the country. A legislation meant for the benefit of a well-defined class will be deemed to be in the interest of general public regardless of the smallness of the number of persons primarily benefited by the legislation. [*Kishori Lal* v *State* AIR 1957 Punj 244: ILR (1957) Punj 1388].


- **In the interest of general public** p. 442.


**Interest reipublicae ut sit finis litium.** The public interest requires that disputes should be finally settled.

**Interest upon interest.** The expression does not mean compound interest. It means that interest is payable on interest in arrear. [*Muthu Chettiar* v *Meenakshisundaram Ayyar* AIR 1928 PC 35].

**Interested.** Affected; affiliated; associated; biased; concerned; directly affected by the outcome of a controversy; influenced; involved.

The term "interested" postulates that the person concerned must have some direct interest. [*Dalbir Kaur* v *State of Punjab* (1976)4 SCC 158: 1976 SCC (Cri) 527: AIR 1977 SC 472: (1977)1 SCR 280: 1977 Cr LJ 273].

**Interested person.** A person having a property right in or claim against a thing.

**Interested witness.** A witness who has a direct and private interest in the matter at issue.

NOTE: A close relative who is a very natural witness cannot be regarded as an interested witness. [*Dalbir Kaur* v *State of Punjab* (1976)4 SCC 158: 1976 SCC (Cri) 527: AIR 1977 SC 472: (1977)1 SCR 280: 1977 Cr LJ 273].

**Interfere.** Be an obstacle; clog; encroach; hinder; impede; infringe; inhibit; intercede; interrupt; intervene; intrude; meddle; obstruct; prevent; thwart; work against.

To enter into, or take part in, the concerns of others. [*People ex rel. Benefit Ass'n of Railway Employees* v *Miner* 56 NF 2d 353, 356].

The word 'interfere' means any action which checks or hampers the functioning or hinders or tends to prevent the performance of duty. [*Chandra Shashi* v *Anil Kumar Verma* JT 1994(7) SC 459: (1995)1 SCC 421: 1995 SCC (Cri) 239: (1995)1 SCJ 84: (1995)78 ELT 7].

**Interlineation.** The act of writing between the lines of an instrument; also what is written between lines.

Not only writing something between the lines but also putting something into one of the lines. [*Bagshawe* v *Canning* (1882)32 JP 583].

**Interlocutory.** Interim, intermedial; intermediary; intervening; interventional; non-final; non-permanent; not final; provisional; temporary; tentative; transitory.

Interim or temporary, not constituting a final resolution of the whole controversy. [Black's *Law Dictionary*, 8th Ed.].

**Interlocutory order.** An order which does not deal with the final rights of the parties, but either—(1) is made before judgment and gives no final decision on the matters in dispute, but is merely on a matter of procedure, or (2) is made after judgment, and merely directs how the declarations of right already given in the final judgment are to be worked out, is termed 'interlocutory'. An interlocutory order, even though not conclusive of the main dispute, may be conclusive as to the subordinate matter with which it deals. [Halsbury's *Laws of England*, 4th Ed., vol. 26, para 506, p. 240].

The expression "interlocutory order" denotes an order of purely interim or temporary nature. [*Usmanbha Dawoodbhai Menon* v *State of Gujarat* AIR 1988 SC 922: (1988)2 SCC 271: (1988)3 SCR 225: 1988 Cr LJ 938: 1988 SCC (Cri) 318].

The interlocutory order is one passed during the progress of the proceedings, that is to say, interlocutory order must be an order passed after the initiation of the proceedings and before the final order disposing of the matter. [*Amalendu Ghosh* v *Prem Pathak* 80 CWN 933].

NOTE: Order 39, rr. 6 to 10 of the Code of Civil Procedure 1908, deal with interlocutory orders while Or. 20, rr. 12 to 17 of the Code provide for interlocutory decrees.

▸ *Meaning under the Criminal Procedure Code 1973, s. 397(2).* The term "interlocutory order" in s. 397(2) of the Criminal Procedure Code 1973 has been used in a restricted sense and not in any broad or artistic sense. It merely denotes orders of a purely interim or temporary nature which do not decide or touch the important rights or the liabilities of the parties. Any order which substantially affects rights of the accused, or decides certain rights of the parties cannot be said to be an interlocutory order so as to bar a revision to the High Court against that order, because that would be against the very object which formed the basis for insertion of this particular provision in s. 397 of the Criminal Procedure Code 1973. [*Amar Nath* v *State of Haryana* AIR 1977 SC 2185: (1977)4 SCC 137: 1977 Cr LJ 1891: 1977 SCC (Cri) 585: (1978)1 SCR 222].

NOTE: An interlocutory order though not conclusive of the main dispute, may be conclusive as to the subordinate matter with which it deals. [*Madhu Limaye* v *The State of Maharashtra* AIR 1978 SC 47: (1978)1 SCR 749: 1978 Cr LJ 165: 1978 SCC (Cri) 10: (1977)4 SCC 551].

**Interloper.** A person who interferes or intermeddles into business to which he has no right; one who interferes without justification; one who trades illegally; one who encroaches on rights of others.

**Intermeddle.** To interfere wrongly with property or the conduct of business affairs officiously or without right or title; to interfere with the business of another.

> NOTE: Intermeddler is on the same footing as an *executor de son tort* in English law. He is one who in any way whatsoever dabbles with or comes in touch with the estate of the deceased. [*Sudama Devi* v *Jogendra Choudhury* AIR 1987 Pat 239, 244].
>
> The term "legal representative" includes any person who intermeddles with the estate of the deceased. [Code of Civil Procedure 1908, s. 2(11)].

**Intermediary.** Agent; arbiter; connecting link; connection; emissary; go-between; link; mediary; mediator; medium; middleman; negotiator.

▸*Meaning under the West Bengal Estates Acquisition Act 1954, s. 2(1).* "Intermediary" as defined by the section includes a proprietor, tenure-holder, under tenure-holder, or any other intermediary above a Raiyat. A patni right holder is a proprietor and therefore included within the meaning of intermediary under the Act. [*Union of India* v *Nihar Kanta Sen* AIR 1987 SC 1713: (1987)2 SCR 1108: (1987)3 SCC 465: JT 1987(2) SC 555].

▸*Meaning under the Constitution of India.* Article 31A(2)(*b*) mentions a number of intermediaries as such, like sub-proprietors, under-proprietors, tenure holders but does not give a complete enumeration of all intermediaries that may be existing in estates all over India and therefore uses the words "other intermediary" to bring in all kinds of intermediaries existing in an estate. [*Karimbil Kunhikoman* v *State of Kerala* AIR 1962 SC 723].

**Internal security.** That branch of law and government dealing with measures to protect the country from subversive activities.

> NOTE: 'Internal security' is an expression of width sufficient to comprehend the concept of public order. Internal disturbances can threaten the security of the state and such disturbances may assume grave proportions so as to have a direct impact on public order. [*Abdul Aziz* v *The District Magistrate, Burdwan* (1973)1 SCC 301: AIR 1973 SC 770].

**International agreement.** A treaty or other contract between different countries. Examples: General Agreement on Tariffs and Trade (GATT), North American Free Trade Agreement (NAFTA).

> NOTE: International agreements are also known as treaties, conventions, pacts, accords.

**International arbitration.** Settlement of differences between States by judges of their own choice and on the basis of respect for law.

> NOTE: The outstanding accomplishment of The Hague Conference of 1899 was the creation of the Permanent Court of Arbitration. It was not a permanent tribunal, but a list of judges nominated in advance by the signatory powers to the number of four each. Such Judges were to be available at all times, and were to act, in default of agreement to the contrary, in accordance with fixed rules of procedure. The parties were to choose their arbitrators from the general list. Each party was to appoint two arbitrators. The four arbitrators and the umpire chosen by them constituted the tribunal which was to decide the controversy. [Fenwick's *International Law*].

**International Court of Justice.** The 15-member U.N. tribunal that sits primarily at The Hague, Netherlands, to adjudicate disputes between countries that voluntarily submit cases for decision. Appeal from the court lies only with the U.N. Security Council.

> NOTE: It is the judicial arm of the United Nations. It has jurisdiction to give advisory opinions on matters of law and treaty construction when requested by the General Assembly, Security Council or any other international agency authorized by the General Assembly to petition for such opinion. It has jurisdiction, also, to settle legal disputes between nations when voluntarily submitted to it. Its judgments may be enforced by the

Security Council. Its jurisdiction and powers are defined by statute, to which all member states of the U.N. are parties. Judges of such court are elected by the General Assembly and Security Council of U.N.

**International criminal court.** A court that was established by the U.N. Security Council to adjudicate international crimes such as terrorism. The court was repeatedly proposed and discussed throughout the 20th century, but was established only in 1998. In the absence of any international criminal code, the court applies general principles of international criminal law.

**International criminal police organisation.** An international law-enforcement group founded in 1923 having headquarters in Lyons, France. The organization gathers and shares information on transnational criminals with more than 180 member nations. It is also known as Interpol.

**International economic law.** International law relating to investment, economic relations, economic development, economic institutions, and regional economic integration.

**International law.** The law that regulates the intercourse of nations; the law of nations; the customary law that determines the rights and regulates the intercourse of independent nations in peace and war; the legal principles governing the relationships between nations.

International law may be defined as that body of law which is composed for its greater part of the principles and rules of conduct which States feel themselves bound to observe and, therefore, do commonly observe in their relations with each other, and which includes also—(*a*) the rules of law relating to the functioning of international institutions or organisations, their relations with each other, and their relations with States and individuals; and (*b*) certain rules of law relating to individuals and non-State entities so far as the rights or duties of such individuals and non-State entities are the concern of the international community. [Starke's *International Law*, 10th Ed., p. 3].

**International Monetary Fund.** This is an international monetary authority to which member countries contribute fixed quotas of their currency and gold. Its purpose is to assist countries through temporary difficulties in their balance of payments by allowing borrowing from the fund.

An agency of the United Nations established to stabilise international exchange rates and promote balanced trade.

**International river.** See under RIVER p. 765.

**International voyage.** A voyage from or to a port or place in India to or from a port or place outside India. [Merchant Shipping Act 1958, s. 3(18A)].

**Interpleader.** Interpleader is a form of joinder open to one who does not know to which of several claimants he or she is liable, if liable at all. It permits him or her to bring the claimants into a single action, and to require them to litigate among themselves to determine which, if any, has a valid claim.

**Interpleader suit.** A suit to determine a right to property held by a usually disinterested third party, called a stakeholder, who is in doubt about ownership and who therefore deposits the property with the court to permit interested parties to litigate ownership. [Black's *Law Dictionary*, 7th Ed.].

▸ *Meaning under the Code of Civil Procedure 1908, s. 88.* Where two or more persons claim adversely to one another the same debt, sum of money or other property, movable or immovable, from another person who claims no interest therein other than for charges or costs and who is ready to pay or deliver it to the rightful claimant, such other person may institute a suit interpleader against all the claimants for the purpose of obtaining a decision as to the person to whom the payment or delivery shall be made and of obtaining indemnity for himself.

**Interpol.** See INTERNATIONAL CRIMINAL POLICE ORGANISATION.

**Interpolation.** The act of inserting words into a document to change or clarify the meaning. In a negative sense, interpolation can refer to putting extraneous or false words into a document to change its meaning.

'Interpolation' means insertion after the document has been executed and does not include corrections made before completing the document. [*Surjeet Kaur* v *State of M.P.* 1994 MPLJ 630].

**Interpretation.** The art or process of discovering and ascertaining the meaning of a statute and other written document; the process by which the courts seek to ascertain the meaning of the legislature through the medium of the authoritative forms in which it is expressed.

The very concept of interpretation connotes the introduction of elements which are necessarily extrinsic to the words in the statute. [*Commissioner of Wealth Tax* v *Hashmatunnisa Begum* AIR 1989 SC 1024: (1989)1 SCR 155: 1989 Supp (2) SCC 43: JT 1989(1) SC 92: (1989)40 ELT 239: (1989)176 ITR 98].

NOTE: Interpretation is of two kinds, namely, literal and functional. The former is that which regards exclusively the verbal expression of the law. Functional interpretation, on the other hand, is that which departs from the letter of the law, and seeks elsewhere for some other and more satisfactory evidence of the true intention of the legislature. In other words, it is necessary to determine the relative claims of the letter and the spirit of the enacted law. In all ordinary cases, the courts must be content to accept the letter of the law as the exclusive and conclusive evidence of the spirit of the law. [Salmond on *Jurisprudence*, 12th Ed., p. 132].

**Interpretation clause.** A provision in a statute or a deed which expresses the meaning of certain words occurring in the statute or deed, as the case may be.

**Interpretation of Constitution.** The art or process of discovering and ascertaining the meaning of the provisions of the Constitution keeping in mind the philosophy or the spirit and the sense of the Constitution.

NOTE: The constitutional instrument is *sui generis* and its interpretation cannot always run on the same lines as the interpretation of statutes made in exercise of the powers conferred by it. The Constitution must receive generous interpretation so as to give all its citizens the full measure of justice so proclaimed instead of the austerity of tabulated legalism. So the expositors of a constitutional instrument are to concern themselves not with words and mere words only, but as much with philosophy or the spirit and the sense of the Constitution. [*Akhil Bharatiya Soshit Karmachari Sangha* v *Union of India* AIR 1981 SC 298: (1981)2 SCR 185: (1981)1 Lab LJ 209].

The language of the Constitution should be interpreted as if it were a living organism capable of growth and development. It should be interpreted in a broad and liberal spirit, and not in a narrow and pedantic sense. [*State of Rajasthan* v *Shamlal* AIR 1960 Raj 256: ILR (1960)10 Raj 652].

**Interrogatory.** A written question, usually in a set of questions, submitted to an opposing party in a lawsuit as part of discovery; question in writing exhibited or addressed on behalf of one party to an action to the other before the trial thereof.

NOTE: In any suit the plaintiff or the defendant by leave of the court may deliver interrogatories in writing for the examination of the opposite parties or any one or more of such parties, and such interrogatories when delivered shall have a note at the foot thereof stating which of such interrogatories each of such persons is required to answer: Provided that no party shall deliver more than one set of interrogatories to the same party without an order for that purpose: Provided also that interrogatories which do not relate to any matters in question in the suit shall be deemed irrelevant, notwithstanding that they might be admissible on the oral cross-examination of a witness. [Code of Civil Procedure 1908, Or. 11, r. 1].

**Interruption.** A break in continuity or uniformity. The occurrence of some act or fact, during the period of prescription, which is sufficient to arrest the running of the statute of limitations. It is said to be either "natural" or "civil", the former being caused by the act of the party; the latter by the legal effect or operation of some fact or circumstance. Interruption of the possession is where the right is not enjoyed or exercised continuously; interruption of the right is where the person having or claiming the right ceases the exercise of it in such a manner as to show that he does not claim to be entitled to exercise it. [Black's *Law Dictionary*, 5th Ed.].

NOTE: An easement should be enjoyed without interruption for the requisite period. Explanation added to s. 25 of the Limitation Act 1963, says: "Nothing is an interruption within the meaning of this section unless where there is an actual discontinuance of the possession or enjoyment by reason of an obstruction by the act of some person other than the claimant, and unless such obstruction is submitted to or acquiesced in for one year after the claimant has notice thereof and of the person making or authorising the same to be made."

Explanation II of s. 15 of the Indian Easements Act 1882, says: "Nothing is an interruption within the meaning of this section unless where there is an actual cessation of the enjoyment by reason of an obstruction by the act of some person other than the claimant, and unless such obstruction is submitted to or acquiesced in for one year after the claimant has notice thereof and of the person making or authorising the same to be made". Explanation III provides: "Suspension of enjoyment in pursuance of a contract between the dominant and servient owners is not an interruption within the meaning of this section."

An interruption with a right to destroy an easement, to be effective, must result in actual discontinuance of the enjoyment of the right of the claimant. The more extended interpretation, given by English decisions, is not to be made under the Indian laws. [*Ram Sarup* v *Abdul Haq* 12 Lah 741: AIR 1931 Lah 395].

**Interstate route.** An interstate route is one of which one of the terminals falls in one State and the other in another State. [*Ch. Khazan Singh* v *State of U.P.* AIR 1974 SC 669: (1974)2 SCR 562: (1974)1 SCC 295].

**Interstate sale.** If the movement of goods from one State to another is the result of a covenant or an incident of the contract of sale, then the sale is an interstate sale. [*Union of India* v *M/s. K.G. Khosla & Co. Ltd.* AIR 1979 SC 1160: (1979)3 SCR 453: (1979)2 SCC 242: (1979)43 STC 457].

**Interstate sale or purchase.** A sale or purchase of goods shall be deemed to take place in the course of interstate trade or commerce if the sale or purchase—(*a*) occasions the movement of goods from one State to another; or (*b*) is effected by a transfer of documents of title to the goods during their movement from one State to another. [Central Sales Tax Act 1956, s. 3].

**Interstate trade or commerce.** The expression is not necessarily confined to trade or commerce between the States as such. It is interstate trade where goods sold or purchased under contracts of sale move from one State to another. The movement of goods from one State to another is the insignia of interstate trade, though the trade is very often between individuals, firms, companies and corporations. [*Dhiraj Lal Mehta* v *Commissioner of Commercial Tax* AIR 1963 Cal 442].

If a sale occasions the movement of goods from one State to another, then it can be deemed to have taken place in the course of interstate trade or commerce within the meaning of s. 3(*a*) of the Central Sales Tax Act 1956. It is not necessary that the contract of sale must itself provide for and cause the movement of goods or that the movement of goods must be occasioned specifically in accordance with the terms of the contract of sale. It is immaterial whether the property in the goods passes in one State or another. The question as regards nature of sale, that is whether it is an interstate sale or intrastate, does not depend upon the circumstances as to in which State the property in the goods passes. [*Union of India* v *K.G. Khosla* 1979 SCC (Tax) 101].

**Intervener.** A person, not a party to the suit, who intervenes either on his own behalf or on behalf of the public or a portion thereof; a person who voluntarily interposes in an action or other proceeding with the leave of the court.

**Intestate.** Without making a will.

▸*Meaning under the Hindu Succession Act 1956, s. 3(g).* A person is deemed to die intestate in respect of property of which he or she has not made a testamentary disposition capable of taking effect.

- **Dying intestate** p. 288.

**Intikal.** Removal from one place to another, transfer, alienation or assignment of any interest in immovable property.

**Intimidation.** Unlawful coercion; extortion; duress; putting in fear.

> NOTE: Whoever threatens another with any injury to his person, reputation or property with intent to cause alarm to that person or to cause that person to do an act which he is not legally bound to do, commits criminal intimidation under s. 503 of the Indian Penal Code. It is a punishable offence under s. 506 of the Code.
>
> The essential ingredient of intimidation is the coercive threat to use unlawful means so as to compel a person into doing something that he is unwilling to do, or not doing something that he wishes to do; and the party so threatened must comply with the demand rather than risk the threat being carried into execution. [*Stratford* v *Lindley* (1964)2 All ER 209].

**Intoxication.** A condition produced by excessive use of alcoholic stimulants [*In re Palani Goundan* AIR 1957 Mad 546: 58 Cr LJ 976]; excessive use of intoxicating liquor or drugs.

- **State of intoxication.** State of intoxication means the state of drunkenness, so that the person intoxicated would be incapable of knowing the consequences of his action. [*Narayanan Nair* v *State* AIR 1952 Trav-Co 239: 1952 Cr LJ 1095].

**Intra vires.** Within the scope or power or authority. It is opposite of *ultra vires*.

**Invasion.** Aggression; attack; intrusion; hostile entry; violation; attack on rights; incursion; the incursion of an army for conquest or plunder; encroachment; act of invading.

**Invention.** Invention is the finding out or discovery of something not found out or discovered before. It is not necessary that the invention should be something complicated but the inventor must be the first one to adopt it. The thing discovered must be novel or new. A new invention may consist of a new combination, so as to produce a new or important result. [*Raj Prakash* v *Mangal Ram* AIR 1978 Del 1].

In patent law, it means the act or operation of finding out something new; the process of contriving and producing something not previously known or existing, by the exercise of independent investigation and experiment. It also involves the article or contrivance or composition so invented. [*Smith* v *Nichols* 22 L Ed 566; *Hollister* v *Mfg. Co.* 28 L Ed 901].

▸ *Meaning under the Patents Act 1970, s. 2(j).* Invention means any new and useful—(*i*) art, process, method or manner of manufacture; (*ii*) machine, apparatus or other article; (*iii*) substance produced by manufacture; and includes any new and useful improvement of any of them and an alleged invention.

"Invention" means any manner of new manufacture and includes an improvement and an allied invention. A patentable invention, apart from being a new manufacture, must also be useful because lack of utility is one of the grounds on which a patent can be revoked. [*Bishwanath Prasad Radhey Shyam* v *Hindustan Metal Industries* (1979)2 SCR 757: (1979)2 SCC 511: AIR 1982 SC 1444].

▸ *Meaning under the Patents (Amendment) Act 2002 (w.e.f. 20.5.2003).* "Invention" means a new product or process involving an inventive step and capable of industrial application.

**Inventory.** A detailed list of articles of property; a list or schedule of property, containing a designation or description of each specific article; quantity of goods or materials on hand or in stock; an itemised list of various articles with their estimated or actual value.

> NOTE: An executor or administrator is to exhibit in court an inventory containing a full and true estimate of all the property in possession and all credits and all debts within six months from the grant of probate or letters of administration. [Indian Succession Act 1925, s. 317].

**Invest.** To confer power or authority; to grant someone control or authority over; vest; appoint; authorise; charter; commission; confer power; endow with authority; grant power, authority.

To spend or apply money in order to earn a financial return; to make use of any property for future benefits or advantages; to make an investment; employ capital; infuse funds; provide capital.

To invest is to apply money in the purchase of some property from which interest or profit is expected and which property is purchased in order to be held for the sake of income which it will yield. [*Re Wragg-Wragg* v *Palmer* (1919)2 Ch 58].

**Investigation.** Careful search, study; close inquiry, scrutiny; detailed examination; collection of facts; inquire to ascertain facts; inquiry; exhaustive study; exploration; systematic search.

▸*Meaning under the Code of Criminal Procedure 1898, s. 4(1) and the Code 1973, s. 2(h).* Investigation includes all proceedings under the Code for the collection of evidence conducted by a police officer or by any person (other than a Magistrate) who is authorised by a Magistrate in this behalf.

NOTE: The word 'investigation' cannot be limited only to police investigation but, on the other hand, the said word is of wider connotation and flexible so as to include the investigation carried on by any agency whether he be a police officer or a person not being a police officer under the direction of a Magistrate to make an investigation vested with the power of investigation. [*Directorate of Enforcement* v *Deepak Mahajan* AIR 1994 SC 1775: (1994)3 SCC 440: 1994 Cr LJ 2269: (1994)70 ELT 12: JT 1994(1) SC 290: 1994 SCC (Cri) 785: (1995)82 Comp Cas 103].

The investigation commences as soon as an authority decides to take the first step whether by way of seeking evidence or by way of seeking explanation from the person concerned. It is not necessary that it should commence with the communication of an accusation to the person concerned. Nor is there any rule of justice or fair play which requires the authority to seek the comments of the person concerned before embarking upon an investigation. [*Liberty Oil Mills* v *Union of India* AIR 1984 SC 1271: (1984)3 SCR 676: (1984)3 SCC 465: (1984)2 Comp LJ 124: 1984 Cr LR (SC) 495].

Investigation generally consists of the following steps: (1) proceeding to the spot; (2) ascertainment of the facts and circumstances of the case; (3) discovery and arrest of the suspected offender; (4) collection of evidence relating to the commission of the offence which may consist of (*a*) the examination of various persons (including the accused) and the reduction of their statements into writing if the officer thinks fit, (*b*) the search of places or seizure of things considered necessary for the investigation and to be produced at the time of trial, and (5) formation of the opinion as to whether on the materials collected there is a case to place the accused before a Magistrate for trial and, if so, taking the necessary steps for the same by the filing of a charge-sheet under s. 173. [*Rishbud* v *State of Delhi* AIR 1955 SC 196: (1955)1 SCR 1150: 1955 SCA 258: 1955 SCJ 283: 1955 Cr LJ 526; *State of Madhya Pradesh* v *Mubarak Ali* AIR 1959 SC 707: 1959 SCJ 843: 1959 Cr LJ 920: 1959 Supp (2) SCR 201: (1960)1 SCA 95].

**Investment.** Capital outlay; employment of capital; invested money; invested property; loan at interest; outlay.

Any expenditure to acquire property or other assets in order to produce revenue; the asset so acquired; the placing of capital or laying out of money in a way intended to secure income or profit from its employment. [*Securities & Exchange Commission* v *Wickham* DC Minn, 12 F Supp 245, 247].

'Investment' means in common parlance putting out money on interest, either by way of loan, or by the purchase of income producing property. [*Commissioner of Income-tax, Lucknow* v *U.P. Co-operative Federation Ltd.* AIR 1989 SC 915: JT 1989(1) SC 258: (1989)176 ITR 435: (1989)1 SCR 586: (1989)2 Comp LJ 43].

**Investment company.** A company formed to acquire and manage a portfolio of diverse assets by investing money collected from different sources. [Black's *Law Dictionary*, 7th Ed.].

▸*Meaning under the Insurance Act 1938, s. 2(10A).* A company whose principal business is the acquisition of shares, stocks, debentures or other securities.

▸*Meaning under the Income Tax Act 1961, s. 109(ii), omitted w.e.f. 1.4.1988.* "Investment company" means a company whose business consists wholly or mainly in dealing in or the holding of investments.

**Invitee.** An invitee is a person invited to enter premises of an occupier with his consent on business in which he and the occupier have a common interest, e.g., a customer entering a ship. It is the duty of the occupier to take reasonable care that the invitee will be reasonably safe in using the premises for the purpose for which he is invited. [*Vide:* The English Occupiers' Liability Act 1957].

**Invoice.** A list of goods sent or shipped, usually stating the price and charge therefor; account of merchandise; schedule of items and their respective prices.

A list of goods which have been sold by one person to another, stating the particulars and prices. The invoice is sent by the seller to the buyer, either along with the goods or separately by post. [Mozley & Whiteley's *Law Dictionary*, 10th Ed.].

An itemized list of goods or services furnished by a seller to a buyer, usually specifying the price and terms of sale; a bill of costs. [Black's *Law Dictionary*, 7th Ed.].

- **Consular invoice.** Consular invoice is an invoice used in foreign trade signed by the consul of the country for which the shipment is destined. This facilitates entry in the destination country, the quantity, value etc. of the shipment being pre-verified.

**I.O.U.** Abbreviation for the words 'I owe you'. It is a written acknowledgment of debt.

It is merely an acknowledgment of debt; it is neither a promissory note nor a receipt. [*State* v *Pareswar Ghasi* AIR 1968 Ori 20].

**Ipse dixit.** He himself said it. An assertion made by a person, but without proof or foundation.

**Ipso facto.** By the very nature of the case.

**Ipso jure.** By the law itself.

**Irregularity.** Something irregular, especially, an act or practice that varies from the normal conduct of an action [Black's *Law Dictionary*, 8th Ed.]; violation or non-observance of established rules and practices; the want of adherence to some prescribed rule or mode of proceeding. [*Krishna Lal* v *State of J&K* 1994 SCC (L&S) 885].

Irregularity implies failure to go through all the prescribed formalities. [*M'Ginty* v *Board of Management* 1951 CLT 92].

The word "irregularity" in common English parlance means and implies contrary to rule. There is, however, no reason to restrict the ordinary meaning of the word 'irregularity and confine it to procedural defects only. That word clearly covers any case where a thing has not been done in the manner laid down by the statute, irrespective of what that manner might be. [*Rambhau* v *State of Maharashtra* AIR 2001 SC 2120: JT 2001(5) SC 121: 2001 Cr LJ 2343: (2001)4 SCC 759 drawing reference to *Martin Burn Ltd.* v *Corpn. of Calcutta* AIR 1966 SC 529: (1966)1 SCR 543 and *Corpn. of Calcutta* v *Chandoolal Bhai Chand Modi* AIR 1953 Cal 773: 53 CWN 882].

NOTE: An order is irregular if the procedure followed is in violation of the principles of natural justice and fair play. [*Kesava Rao* v *Subbaraju* AIR 1957 AP 55].

**Irreparable injury.** An injury that cannot be adequately measured or compensated by money and is therefore often considered remediable by injunction. [Black's *Law Dictionary*, 7th Ed.]. It is also termed irreparable harm.

Irreparable injury is that which, if not prevented by injunction, cannot be afterwards compensated by any decree, which the court can pronounce in the result of the cause. [*A-G* v *Hallett* (1847)16 M&W 569].

'Irreparable injury' does not mean that there must be no physical possibility of repairing the injury, but means only that the injury must be a material one, namely one that cannot be adequately compensated by way of damages. [*Dalpatkumar* v *Prahlad Singh* (1992)1 SCC 719].

**Irrevocable.** Incapable of being revoked or altered.

> NOTE: Wills are never irrevocable. It is revocable even where the maker calls it irrevocable. [Indian Succession Act 1925, s. 62]. A gift is ordinarily irrevocable except in certain circumstances. [Transfer of Property Act 1882, s. 126].

**Is.** The word 'is' has application only to the state of affairs existing at the present time. [*Jagir Kaur* v *Jaswant Singh* AIR 1963 SC 1521].

The word "is" although normally referring to the present often has a future meaning. It may also have a past signification as in the sense of "has been". [*F.S. Gandhi by L.Rs.* v *Commr. of Wealth Tax, Allahabad* (1990)3 SCC 624: (1990)184 ITR 34: JT 1990(3) SC 476: (1990)2 SCR 886].

**Ishtihar.** Notice, public notice, proclamation, advertisement.

**Issue.** The meaning of the word "issue" has to be gathered from the context in which it is used. [*Delhi Development Authority* v *H.C. Khurana* AIR 1993 SC 1488: (1993)3 SCC 196: 1993 SCC (L&S) 736: JT 1993(2) SC 695].

As noun, in its application to matter in dispute, it means cause; debatable point; disputed point of law; disputed question; fact put in controversy by the pleadings; field of inquiry; item on the agenda; material point; material point deduced by the pleadings; matter in hand; matter in question; matter of contention; point in question; topic under consideration.

As noun, in its application to shares and securities, it means a class or series of securities that are simultaneously offered for sale.

As noun, in its application to progeny, it means child; children; lineal descendants; offspring. 'Issue' in this sense indicates both males and females. [*Kunju Kesavan* v *M.M. Philip* AIR 1964 SC 164: (1964)3 SCR 634].

As verb, it means to give exit to; to send forth, or allow to pass out; to let out; to give or send out authoritatively or officially; to send forth or deal out formally or publicly; to emit, put into circulation. [*Delhi Development Authority* v *H.C. Khurana* AIR 1993 SC 1488: (1993)3 SCC 196: 1993 SCC (L&S) 736: JT 1993(2) SC 695].

As verb, it also means announce; assert, declare; disclose; distribute; divulge; give public notice of; make a public announcement; make known; notify publicly; proclaim; promulgate; pronounce; publicise; put forward; release; break forth; burst forth; come forward; come out; manifest.

"Issue" is the act of sending out, putting into circulation, deliver with authority or delivery. [*Banarsi Debi* v *Income Tax Officer* AIR 1964 SC 1742: (1964)2 SCJ 258: (1964)53 ITR 100: (1964)7 SCR 539; *M.M. Isaphani* v *Commissioner of Income Tax* AIR 1969 Cal 464].


- **At or before settlement of issues** p. 83.
- **Facts in issue** p. 337.
- **Fiduciary note issue** p. 351.
- **Joinder of issue** p. 486.
- **Leave no issue** p. 523.
- **Matter in issue** p. 569.


**Issue estoppel.** See under ESTOPPEL p. 321.

**Issued.** The expression "issued" and "served" are used in interchangeable terms and in the legislative practice of our country are sometimes used to convey the same idea. [*Commissioner of Wealth Tax, U.P.* v *Kundan Lal Behari Lal* (1975)4 SCC 844: (1975)99 ITR 581: AIR 1976 SC 1150].

The dictionary meaning of the expression 'issued' takes in the entire process of sending notice as well as service thereof. [*Banarsi Debi* v *Income Tax Officer, Calcutta* AIR 1964 SC 1742: (1964)7 SCR 539: (1964)2 SCJ 258: (1964)53 ITR 100; *Commissioner of Wealth Tax, U.P.* v *Kundan Lal Behari Lal* (1975)4 SCC 844: (1975)99 ITR 581: AIR 1976 SC 1150]. Notice issued and notice served convey the same idea. [*Shiv Saran Lal* v *State of M.P.* AIR 1980 MP 93: 1980 MPLJ 218].

**Issues.** Issues arise when a material proposition of fact or law is affirmed by the one party and denied by the other. Material propositions are those propositions of law or fact which a plaintiff must allege in order to show a right to sue or a defendant must allege in order to constitute his defence. Issues are of two kinds—(*a*) issues of fact and (*b*) issues of law. [Code of Civil Procedure 1908, Or. 14, r. 1].

NOTE: Issues to be framed must be confined to material questions of fact (or law), to *facta probanda* and not to *facto probantia*, that is to say, evidence by which material questions of facts are proved or disproved. [*Lekhraj Diddi* v *Sardar Sarwan Singh* AIR 1971 MP 172: 1971 MPLJ 438: 1971 MPWR 425]. The issues are to be framed on proper appreciation of pleadings. [*Vinod Kumar* v *State of H.P.* AIR 1959 SC 223].

It also means the profits or proceeds from any source of revenue, such as lands, houses etc.

**Issues and profits.** As applied to real estate, comprehend every available return therefrom, whether it arise above or below the surface.

**Istafa.** A surrender or relinquishment, as by a tenant to the landlord. A deed of surrender [*Ram Charan* v *Raniganj Coal Co.* ILR 26 Cal 29]; designation.

**Istimrari.** Permanent, perpetual (as a tenure or lease of land or other immovable property). Such a tenure or lease may or may not be heritable. [*Jabeda Khatun* v *Mozaffar Ali* AIR 1926 Cal 322: 30 CWN 807].

- **Mukarrari istimrari** The words 'mukarrari istimrari' do not in their lexicographical sense primarily imply any heritable character in the grant as the term 'mourasi' does, but they simply imply permanency from which in a secondary sense such heritable character might be inferred, it always being doubtful whether they meant permanent during the lifetime of the persons to whom they were granted or permanent as regards hereditary character, and the words do not *per se* convey an estate of inheritance. [*Kamakhaya* v *Ram Raksha* 55 IA 212: AIR 1928 PC 146: 32 CWN 897: 30 Bom LR 1361: 55 MLJ 882].

**It shall be lawful.** The words 'it shall be lawful' are distinctly words of permission only—they are enabling and empowering words. [*Julius* v *Oxford* (1880)5 AC 214].

The expression should be taken to convey the meaning that if the law had not been enacted, there would have been no authority to do the act. [*C.R.M. Ready Money Ltd.* v *State* AIR 1956 Bom 304].

**Ita utere tuo ut alienum non laedas.** Use your own property so as not to injure your neighbour.

**Iwaz.** Exchange, consideration.

**Iwaz-nama.** Deed of exchange.

# Jj

**Jactitation.** In medical parlance, it means the restless tossing of the body in illness; a morbid restlessness, as in acute disease; the twitching of a limb or muscle.

In law, it means a false assertion repeated to the injury of another; a false boasting; a false claim; boasting of something which is challenged by another.

**Jactitation of marriage.** The offence of falsely claiming to be a person's spouse; a false assertion of marriage.

Jactitation of marriage is an action for the false, malicious and inexcusable boast and assertion by a person that someone else is married to him or her.

NOTE: Jactitation of marriage is a cause of action which arises when a person falsely alleges that he or she is married to the petitioner and the remedy sought is a perpetual injunction against the respondent to cease making such allegations. [Gaveson on *Conflict of Laws*, 6th Ed., p. 368].

**Jadid.** It means 'new', 'modern', 'recent'. The word *'jadid'* does not exclude the conception of 'newness' on account of an addition to the amount or an account of the revision or newness of the settlement. *'Jadid'* includes 'new kind' also, but newness denoted by the term is not confined to newness in kind only. It includes newness in amount and settlement as well, whether such revision be under the existing law or under any future law. [*Rabindra* v *Surendra* AIR 1945 Cal 129].

**Jaggery.** "Jaggery" or gur is defined as any product obtained by boiling or processing juice pressed out of sugarcane.

NOTE: According to dictionary meaning *Shakkar* falls within the meaning of "jaggery". [*Mohammed Yamin* v *State of U.P.* AIR 1973 SC 484: (1973)1 SCR 350: (1972)2 SCC 184: 1972 Cr LJ 1198: 1972 SCC (Cri) 655].

**Jagir.** Ordinarily a *'jagir'* is an assignment in land or money for the support of a certain dignity and for the troops annexed thereto. It is either conditional or unconditional. The assignment is for a stated term, and more usually, it is for the lifetime of the holder, lapsing on his death, to the state, although not unusually renewed to his heir, on payment of a *nazarana* or fine. It is sometimes specified to be a hereditary one. [*Umrao Singh Ajit Singhji* v *Bhagwati Singh Balbir Singh* AIR 1956 SC 15].

NOTE: *Jagir* includes all grants conferring right on the grantee in respect of land revenue, but does not include any cash allowance. [*Maharajadhiraj Himmatsinghji* v *State of Rajasthan* JT 1986 SC 851: AIR 1987 SC 82: (1987)1 SCR 209: (1987)1 SCC 52].

The essential features of a *jagir* are that it is held under a grant from the ruler, and that the grant is of the land revenue. It was a life grant and succession to it depended on recognition by the ruler. It was impartible, and inalienable. But in course of time, however, grants came to be made with incidents annexed to them different from those of the *jagirs*. Some of them were heritable, though impartible; as few of them were both heritable and partible. Thus, both in its popular sense and legislative practice, *the word 'jagir' is used as connoting state grants which conferred on the grantees rights 'in respect of land revenue'*. In Art. 31A of the Constitution, *jagir* was meant to cover all grants under which the grantees had only rights in respect of revenue and were not the tillers of the soil. Maintenance grants in favour of persons who were not cultivators such as members of the ruling family would be *jagirs* for purposes of Art. 31A. [*Thakur Amar Singhji* v *State of Rajasthan* AIR 1955 SC 504: (1955)2 SCR 303: 1955 SCJ 523].

**Jagirdar.** One who holds a *jagir. Jagirdar* is a person to whom the land revenue of any land has been assigned in whole or in part by the Government or by an officer of the Government.

**Jaidad.** Assets, funds, resources, property, estate.

Jaidad usually means immovable property, and when it is used for movable, some word as *Mankula* is prefixed. [*Saiyed Mahmud* v *Mohammad Zubair* 31 All 523].

**Jail warrant.** It is an authority given to the jail department intimating the date on which the accused is to be produced by them in court. It can also be termed as production warrant. [*Mohan* v *State of Rajasthan* (1983)2 Crimes 616 (Raj)].

**Jajman.** A person who engages a priest for the performance of religious ceremony; disciple.

**Jalkar.** The term *'jalkar'* is ambiguous. It may mean a grant of a right of fishery or it may mean the grant of a sheet of water together with the subsoil, whether the one or the other must be decided upon the construction of the original grant if available or must be determined with regard to the subsequent history of the property. [*Prankishore Tarafdar* v *Sarada Prosad Pakrashi* AIR 1923 Cal 358: 37 CLJ 580].

The term is a general one signifying 'water rights' and might therefore aptly include the right to drift and stranded timbers as well as the right to fishing or any other interest of a similar kind in the produce of the river. [*Amriteswari Bibi* v *Secretary of State* 24 IA 33, *per* Lord Watson].

NOTE: The mere use of the word *'jalkar'* would not give a right of fishery in a public tidal navigable river. This word may be perfectly satisfied by applying to the right to fish within enclosed water, such as *jheel* in *zamindari*.

A *jalkar* right is an immovable property within the meaning of the General Clauses Act. [*Ram Gopal Byak* v *Nuruddin* ILR 20 Cal 446].

The holder of *jalkar* right is not a non-agricultural tenant. [*Aswini Kumar* v *State of W.B.* 63 CWN 933]. In view of the changed definition of land in s. 2(7), W.B. Land Reforms Act as amended by the W.B.L.R. (Am.) Act 1981 which definition includes within the ambit of land, even tank and tank fishery, fishery it appears holder of *jalkar* now has become a raiyat within the meaning of the term in s. 2(10), W.B. Land Reforms Act.

**Jama.** Total; aggregate; deposit; debit or receipt side of an account. Rent or revenue payable by a *zamindar* or tenant.

The word *'jama'* is well-understood by the people who are all conversant with the language used by the Indian bankers. The word *'jama'* means deposit and nothing more. [*Ram Rekha* v *Har Narain Ram* AIR 1936 Lah 587].

**Jama kharach.** Receipts and disbursements; debits and credits of an account.

**Jamabandi.** The *jamabandi* when referred to in the deed of mortgage means the rent roll and the account of collections kept by the mortgagee in possession. The Patwari's *Jamabandi* cannot be accepted as a substitute for the private accounts of the mortgagee. [*Sheorani Bibi* v *Gauri Shanker* AIR 1926 Oudh 514].

**Jamabandi papers.** They show the quantity of land by each cultivator, its different qualities, the rate of rent for each kind of land, the total rent for all the land of that particular kind in each cultivator's possession and, lastly, the grand total for all the land of every kind held by him. [Field's *Evidence*, 7th Ed., p. 134]. They cannot be treated as independent evidence. [*Chamarni Bibi* v *Ainullah* 9 WR 451].

**Jami.** Land.

**Jami jama.** The word *'jami jama'* indicates land as well as rent or when taken together in the abstract sense means rent-bearing tenanted land. [*Lakshan Chandra* v *Narim Sardar* AIR 1932 Cal 508: 36 CWN 341].

**Janashin.** *'Rasnashin'* and *'janashin'* are Persian words, though they are frequently used in documents written in the Urdu and retain the same meaning as they convey in Persian. The most appropriate equivalents in which they can be rendered for the purpose of the translation are 'successors' and *'locum tenens'*. [*Rameshwar* v *Balraj* AIR 1932 Oudh 327].

**Jangad.** The dictionary meaning of the word *'jangad'* is 'approval'. The word *'jangad'* does mean 'sale or return' wherever the same is found. When the goods are entrusted *jangad*, it cannot be assumed that they are goods to be sold on approval rather than goods given to be shown for approval. [*Amritlal* v *Bhagwandas* AIR 1939 Bom 435].

**Janitor.** A person who has the care of a building.

**Janmam.** The exclusive right to, and hereditary possession of the soil in Malabar is denoted by the term janmam which means birth right and the holder thereof is known Janmi, Janmakaran or mutalalan. "Janmam", thus, may be described as a hereditary proprietorship. It is the freehold interest in the property in Kerala. A Janmam interest may, therefore, be described as proprietary interest of a landlord in lands, and such a Janmam right is described as "estate" in the Constitution. [*Balmadies Plantations Ltd.* v *State of Tamil Nadu* AIR 1972 SC 2240: (1972)2 SCC 133: (1973)1 SCR 258].

**Janmam rights.** Janmam rights in the States of Madras and Kerala are rights of hereditary proprietorship in land. These rights, like the rights created by grant of *jagir* or *inam* relating to land which included agricultural lands or waste lands or forests and hills, are brought within the definition of the word "estate", and are, therefore, liable to be acquired by the State under Art. 31A(1)(*a*) of the Constitution. [*State of Kerala* v *The Gwalior Rayon Silk Manufacturing (Wvg.) Co. Ltd.* AIR 1973 SC 2734: (1973)2 SCC 713: (1974)1 SCR 671].

**Janmi.** Janmi means a person entitled to the absolute proprietorship of land and includes a trustee in respect thereof. [*Balmadies Plantation Ltd.* v *State of Tamil Nadu* AIR 1972 SC 2240: (1972)2 SCC 133].

**Janta.** The English word 'known' is not coextensive with the Urdu word *'janta'*. The latter is very often used not only for what one knows but also for what one believes or even thinks. [*Abdus Subhan* v *Nusrat Ali* AIR 1937 Oudh 170].

**Jawab.** Reply.

**Jaziah.** A capitation tax levied on all who refused to become Muhammadans. It was abolished in India by Akbar, but reimposed by Aurangzeb.

**Jeopardy.** Crisis; danger, endangerment; imperilment; periliousness; precariousness; uncertainty; vulnerability; danger, especially of severe harm or loss; exposure to or danger of death, loss or injury; danger resulting from being on trial for a criminal offence; the peril in which a defendant is put when placed on trial for a crime.

NOTE: The rule against double jeopardy says that no person shall be prosecuted and punished for the same offence more than once. [Constitution of India, Art. 20(2)].

• **Double jeopardy** p. 281.

**Jeroyiti.** It means cultivation. The word *'jeroyiti'*, especially when prefixed to the word *'right'* or *'hakku'* has come to mean 'right of occupancy'. [*D. Tatayya* v *Venkata* AIR 1928 Mad 786].

**Jeroyiti land.** The word "*jeroyiti* land" may mean cultivable or arable land. But it may also mean 'assessable' or 'assessed land' as opposed to *inam* land. It is only the context that must decide what meaning to be given to the word. [*D. Tatayya* v *Venkata* AIR 1928 Mad 786].

**Jestha putra.** The eldest son.

**Jetsam.** Goods which are cast into the sea and thus sink and remain under water. If unclaimed, they are the property of the State. [Cf. *Flotsam*].

**Jettison.** Cast overboard; discard; dispense with; dispose of; eject; eliminate; expel; get rid of; part with; throw away; toss overboard.

The throwing overboard either from a ship or aircraft of goods as a necessity to lighten the vessel or aircraft in a storm, or to prevent capture or for other sufficient cause.

**Jetty.** A pier or breakwater constructed to protect or defend a harbour, coast, etc.; a structure in a body of water serving to control or divert a current, protect a harbour or the like, or as a wharf or pier; a projection of stone or other material serving as a protection against the waves; a kind of pier for loading and unloading cargo from a vessel.

**Jewellery.** The terms 'jewel' and 'jewellery', refer to articles of value used for adornment, especially those made from gold, silver or precious stones. The terms are, therefore, wide enough to cover not merely precious stones or articles of adornment made with the use of precious stones, but also other articles of value made from gold, silver, platinum or precious metals. Ordinarily speaking, when a person talks about jewellery, he includes ornaments which are made of gold, silver or any other precious metal also irrespective of whether these articles have precious stones embedded in them or not. [*CWT* v *Smt. Binapani Chakravarty* AIR 1995 SC 1380: 1995 Supp (2) SCC 262: (1995)214 ITR 721: JT 1995(3) SC 506].

**Jihad.** A war against infidels; a holy war.

**Job.** Assignment; avocation; vocation; business; occupation; calling; employment; trade; profession; function; labour; responsibility; mission.

It may also mean a specific task or piece of work to be done for a set fee or compensation.

**Jobber.** One who buys and sells goods for others; one who buys and sells articles in bulk and resells them to dealers; a wholesaler; a middleman; one who buys and sells on the stock exchange; one who does piecework.

**Joinder.** Bringing together; concatenation; unification; linking; joining or coupling together; uniting two or more constituents or elements in one; concurrence.

In legal parlance, it means the uniting of parties or claims in a single lawsuit.

**Joinder of causes of action.** Joining in one suit several causes of action.

> NOTE: Rules 3, 4 and 5 of Or. 2 of the Code of Civil Procedure 1908, deal with joinder of causes of action.
>
> Where it appears to the court that the joinder of causes of action in one suit may embarrass or delay the trial or is otherwise inconvenient, the court may order separate trials or make such other order as may be expedient in the interests of justice. [Code of Civil Procedure 1908, r. 6, Or. 2].

**Joinder of charges.** Two or more charges joined together in one action; the charging of an accused with two or more crimes as multiple counts in a single indictment or information.

**Joinder of issue.** The submission of an issue jointly for decision; the acceptance or adoption of a disputed point as the basis of argument in a controversy.

**Joinder of parties.** Joining of two or more persons in one action, either as plaintiffs or as defendants, if any common question of law or fact exists.

> NOTE: Rules 1 and 3 of Or. 1 of the Code of Civil Procedure 1908 deal with the joinder of plaintiffs and defendants respectively.

**Joint account.** A bank or brokerage account opened by two or more people, by which each party has a present right to all funds in the account and, upon the death of one party, the survivor/survivors become the owner/owners of the account, with no right of the heirs or devisees of the deceased party to share in it.

An account in two or more names. [*Harbour* v *Harbour* 181 SW 2d 805, 807].

**Joint adventure.** Any association of persons to carry out a single business enterprise for profit, for which purpose they combine their property, money, effects, skill, and knowledge. [*Fulton* v *Fulton* Mo App, 528 SW 2d 146, 155].

NOTE: Where persons enter into an agreement constituting a partnership limited to a joint trading adventure, and goods are purchased, ostensibly by an individual adventurer but really for the purpose of the joint adventure, the adventurers are liable as partners; but there is no such responsibility for goods purchased before the partnership agreement upon the credit of an individual adventurer, though they are afterwards brought into stock as his contribution to the joint adventure. [*Karmali* v *Vora Karimji* (1915)42 IA 48].

**Joint and several bond/note.** A joint and several bond or note is one in which the obligors or makers bind themselves both jointly and individually to the obligee or payee, so that all may be sent together for its enforcement, or the creditor may select one or more as the object of his suit.

**Joint and several liability.** A liability is said to be joint and several when the creditor may sue one or more of the parties to such liability separately, or all of them together at his option.

When two or more persons declare themselves jointly and severally bound, this means that they render themselves liable to a joint action against all, as well as to a separate action against each, in case the conditions of the bond or agreement be not complied with. [Mozley & Whiteley's *Law Dictionary*, 10th Ed.].

NOTE: When two or more persons make a joint promise, the promisee may , in the absence of express agreement to the contrary, compel any one or more of such joint promisors to perform the whole of the promise. [Indian Contract Act 1872, s. 43]. Here, the liability of the joint promisors is joint and several.

**Joint authorship.** As to literary property, such exists where there is a common design to the execution of which several persons contribute. Mere alterations, additions or improvements, whether with or without the sanction of the author, will not entitle the person making them to claim to be a joint author of the work. Joint labour in furtherance of a common design is required to claim joint authorship. [*Edward B. Marks Music Corporation* v *Jerry Vogel Music Co.* DC NY, 140 F 2d 266, 267].

Joint authorship means a work produced by the collaboration of two or more authors in which the contribution of each author is not distinct from that of the other author or authors. [Copyright, Designs and Patents Act 1988 (U.K.), s. 10(1)].

**Joint estate.** Any of the following five types of estate: (1) a joint tenancy; (2) a tenancy in common; (3) an estate in coparcenary; (4) a tenancy by the entirety, or (5) an estate in partnership. [Black's *Law Dictionary*, 7th Ed.].

Joint estate involves unity of interest, unity of title, unity of time, and unity of possession and joint tenants must have the same interest accruing under the same conveyance, commencing at the same time, and held under the same undivided possession. [*Mosser* v *Dolsay* 27 A 2d 155].

**Joint family property.** Properties owned by a joint Hindu family are joint family properties or coparcenary properties. In such properties each of the members of the coparcenary has some interest.

**Joint landlords.** All the co-sharers immediately under whom the tenant holds, whether such co-sharers receive their quota of rent from the tenant jointly or separately.

**Joint-stock company.** An unincorporated association of individuals possessing common capital, the capital being contributed by the members and divided into shares, of which each member possesses a number of shares proportionate to the member's investment; a partnership in which the capital is divided into shares that are transferable without the express consent of the partners. [Black's *Law Dictionary*, 7th Ed.].

▸ *Meaning under the Companies Act 1956, s. 566.* So far as it relates to the registration of companies as companies limited by shares, a joint-stock company means a company having a permanent paid-up or nominal share capital of fixed amount divided into shares, also of fixed amount, or held and transferable as stock, or divided and held partly in the one way and partly in the other, and formed on the principle of having for its members the holders of those shares or that stock, and no other persons.

**Joint tenancy.** Joint tenancy is a form of co-ownership which is distinguished by four unities, namely, unity of possession, unity of interest, unity of title and unity of the time of the commencement of such title. The peculiar feature of joint tenancy is that the right of survivorship prevails among the joint tenants.

NOTE: Joint tenancy is unknown to Hindu law, except in the case of coparcenary between the members of an undivided family. [*Bahu Rani* v *Rajendra* 60 IA 95: AIR 1933 PC 72]. Joint tenancy is also unknown to Mahomedan law. [*Kasim Ali* v *Ratna* AIR 1938 Mad 677].

**Joint tortfeasors.** Two or more tortfeasors who contributed to the claimant's injury and who may be joined as defendants in the same lawsuit. [Black's *Law Dictionary*, 8th Ed.].

They are persons who have committed the same wrongful act, who are jointly and severally responsible for the whole damage, as in the cases of vicarious liability, agency and common action. [Jowitt's *Dictionary of English Law*, 2nd Ed.].

**Joint venture.** A "joint venture" exists where there is a special combination of two or more persons jointly seeking to profit in some specific venture without actual partnership or corporate designation. [*Fulton* v *Fulton* Mo App, 528 SW 2d 146, 155].

A business undertaking by two or more persons engaged in a single defined project. The necessary elements are: (1) an express or implied agreement; (2) a common purpose that the group intends to carry out; (3) shared profits and losses; and (4) each member's equal voice in controlling the project. [Black's *Law Dictionary*, 7th Ed.].

NOTE: The expression "joint venture" is more frequently used in the United States. It connotes a legal entity in the nature of a partnership engaged in the joint undertaking of a particular transaction for mutual profit or an association of persons or companies jointly undertaking some commercial enterprise wherein all contribute assets and share risks. It requires a community of interest in the performance of the subject-matter, a right to direct and govern the policy in connection therewith, and duly, which may be altered by agreement, to share both in profit and losses. [*New Horizons Ltd.* v *Union of India* (1995)1 SCC 478].

**Joint will.** A single will executed by two or more testators, usually disposing of their common property by transferring their separate titles to one devisee. [Black's *Law Dictionary*, 7th Ed.].

A joint will is a will made by two or more testators contained in a single document, duly executed by each testator, disposing either of their separate properties or of their joint properties. It is not, however, recognised in English law as a single will. It operates on the death of each testator as his will disposing of his own separate property, and is in effect two or more wills. [*K. Gobindan* v *T.T. Lakshmi Amma* AIR 1959 SC 71, quoting Halsbury's *Laws of England*, 2nd Ed., vol. 34, p. 17].

**Jote.** The word *'jote'* by itself is an ambiguous word which may mean a tenure or a holding. [*Abdul Latif* v *Khajeh* AIR 1939 Cal 354, 366].

The word *'jote'* does not necessarily mean an occupancy holding, it may mean a *raiyati*, under *raiyati*, or any sort of holding for the purpose of cultivation. [*Upendra Kishore* v *Shaik Khalil Fakir* AIR 1932 Cal 568: 139 IC 544].

The word *'jote'* means that it is a tenure. *'Jote'* simply means a tenancy. [*Sariatualla* v *Joyenuddin* AIR 1935 Cal 462: 39 CWN 454].

*'Jote'* is a perfectly general expression meaning tenancy of any kind. [*Narendra Chandra De* v *Rajendra Chandra Chanda* AIR 1941 Cal 506].

**Journal.** Biographical record; cash book; contemporary account; daily paper; daily register; daybook; logbook; magazine; periodical.

A day-book or diary of transactions used by merchants, mariners, tradesmen, etc., in their business. [Wharton's *Law Lexicon*].

A book or record kept usually daily, as of the proceedings of a legislature or the events of a ship's voyage; in double entry bookkeeping, a book in which original entries are recorded before being transferred to a ledger; a periodical or magazine, especially one published for a scholarly or professional group. [Black's *Law Dictionary*, 7th Ed.].

**Journalist.** A person employed to write for, edit, or report for, a newspaper, journal, or newscast; one who manages, edits, or writes for a journal or newspaper.

- **Working journalist** p. 904.

**J.P.** An abbreviation of the term "Justice of the Peace".

**Judex non potest esse testis in propria causa.** A judge cannot be a witness in his own cause.

**Judge.** As noun means adjudger; adjudicator; administrator of justice; arbiter; one who dispenses justice; a public official appointed or elected to hear and decide legal matters in court [Black's *Law Dictionary*, 7th Ed.]; a public officer who, by virtue of his office, is clothed with judicial authority. [*State ex rel. Mayer* v *City of Cincinnati* 19 NE 2d 902].

▸ *Meaning under the Code of Civil Procedure 1908, s. 2(8)*. 'Judge' means the presiding officer of a civil court, who is invested with authority to determine any cause or question in the court of judicature. [*K. Naidu* v *State of Tamil Nadu* 1977 Cr LJ 1013].

▸ *Meaning under the Indian Penal Code, s. 19.* The word 'Judge' denotes not only every person who is officially designated as a judge, but also every person, who is empowered by law to give in any legal proceeding, civil or criminal, a definitive judgment, or a judgment which, if not appealed against, would be definitive, or a judgment which, if confirmed by some other authority, would be definitive, or who is one of a body of persons, which body of persons is empowered by law to give such a judgment.

As verb it means adjudge; adjudicate; arbitrate; ascertain; assess; decide; draw a conclusion; examine; sit in judgment; value.

- **Activist judge.** An activist judge is he who chooses from a number of lawful possibilities open to him only that possibility that changes the existing law. Sometimes an activist judge is identified as one who seeks to adapt the law to the changing needs of life based on conviction that a widening gap between life and law leads to a state of instability that continues until the law changes. An activist judge in that case is taken as one who believes in stability through motion. [*Penumbra of Natural Justice* by Tapash Gan Choudhury, 2nd Ed., p. 308].

- **Judge de facto.** A judge *de facto*, is one who is not a mere intruder or usurper but one who holds office, under colour of lawful authority, though his appointment is defective and may later be found to be defective. Whatever be the defect of his title to the office, judgments pronounced by him and acts done by him when he was clothed with the powers and functions of the office, *albeit* unlawfully, have the same efficacy as judgments pronounced and acts done by a judge *de jure*. Such is the *de facto* doctrine, born of necessity and public policy to prevent needless confusion and endless mischief. [*Gokaraju Rangaraju* v *State of Andhra Pradesh* AIR 1981 SC 1473: 1981 Cr LR (SC) 294: 1981 Cr LJ 876: 1981 SCC (Cri) 652: 1981(1) SCALE 706: (1981)3 SCC 132].

- **Self-restrained judge.** A self-restrained judge is he who chooses from among a number of lawful possibilities the one that preserves the existing system. A self-restrained judge is identified as one who seeks to maintain stability in the law, seeks certainty, consistency and continuity. [*Penumbra of Natural Justice* by Tapash Gan Choudhury, 2nd Ed., p. 308].

**Judge advocate general.** Senior legal officer and chief legal advisor of the Army, Navy and Air Force.

**Judge-made law.** The law established by judicial precedent and decisions; law having its source in judicial decision as opposed to law having its source in statute or administrative regulation.

The law established by judicial precedent rather than by statute; the law that results when judges construe statutes contrary to legislative intent. [Black's *Law Dictionary*, 8th Ed.].

**Judgment.** Ability to distinguish; acumen; appraisal; assessment; close observation; critical faculty; rational faculty; judiciousness; evaluation; ratiocination; weighing; an opinion or estimate; formation of an opinion or notion concerning something by exercising mind upon it.

In legal parlance the word "judgment" means the sentence or final order of a court in a civil or criminal proceeding; the sentence of the law; the final determination or adjudication of the rights of the parties to an action.

The word "judgment" is a word of general import and normally it means judicial determination or decision of a court. [*Udai Narain* v *State of U.P.* 2000 Cr LJ 544 (All)].

A judgment is the final decision of the court intimated to the parties and to the world at large by formal "pronouncement" or "delivery" in open court. It is a judicial act which must be performed in a judicial way. The decision which is so pronounced or intimated must be a declaration of the mind of the court as it is at the time of pronouncement. [*Surendra Singh* v *State of U.P.* AIR 1954 SC 194: 1954 Cr LJ 475].

A "judgment" is defined as the decision of a court of justice upon the respective rights and claims of the parties to an action in a suit submitted to it for determination [*State of Tamil Nadu* v *S. Thangavel* (1997)2 SCC 349]; the expression of the opinion of the court arrived at after due consideration of the evidence and all the arguments. [*U.J.S. Chopra* v *State of Bombay* AIR 1955 SC 633: (1955)3 SCR 94: 1955 SCA 944: 1955 Cr LJ 1410: 1955 SCJ 603, *per* Bhagwati, J.].

▸ *Meaning in Code of Civil Procedure 1908, s. 2(9).* "Judgment means the statement given by the Judge on the grounds of a decree or order". Judgment is the decision of a court of justice upon the respective rights and claims of the parties to an action in a suit submitted to it for determination. It denotes the reason which the court gives for its decision. [*State of Tamil Nadu* v *Thangavel* (1997)2 SCC 349].

NOTE: An order in a proceeding under Or. 21, r. 90 of CPC is a 'judgment' inasmuch as such a proceeding raises controversy between the parties therein affecting their valuable rights. [*Shri Radhey Shyam* v *Shyam Behari Singh* (1970)2 SCC 405].

▸ *Meaning in interpreting the Letters Patent.* As Letters Patent is a special law which carves out its own sphere, the definition of the word 'judgment' appearing in s. 2(9) of the Code of Civil Procedure 1908, cannot be projected into the Letters Patent. [*Shah Babulal Khimji* v *Jayaben D. Kania* AIR 1981 SC 1786: (1981)4 SCC 8].

The word 'judgment' as used in the Letters Patent has a concept of finality in a broader and not in a narrower sense as defined by the Code of Civil Procedure. [*Shah Babulal Khimji* v *Jayaben D. Kania* AIR 1981 SC 1786: (1981)4 SCC 8].

The essential requisites and the exact meaning of the word 'judgment' as used in the Letters Patent were described by Hidayatullah, J. (as he then was) in *Manohar Damodar Bhoot* v *Baliram Ganpat Bhoot* [AIR 1952 Nag 357 (FB)] thus: "A judgment means a decision in an action whether final, preliminary or interlocutory which decides either wholly or partially, but conclusively in so far as the court is concerned, the controversy which is the subject of the action. It does not include a decision which is on a matter of procedure, nor one which is ancillary to the action even though it may either imperil the ultimate decision or tend to make it effective. The decision need not be immediately executable *'per se'* but if left untouched must result inevitably without anything further, save the determination of consequential details, in a decree or decretal orders, that is to say, an executive document directing something to be done or not to be done in relation to the facts of the controversy. The decision may itself order that thing to be done or not to be done or it may leave that over till after the ascertainment of some details but it must not be interlocutory having for its purpose the ascertainment of some matters or details prior to the determination of the whole or any part of the controversy".

The Supreme Court in *Shah Babulal Khimji* v *Jayaben D. Kania* [AIR 1981 SC 1786: (1981)4 SCC 8] opined that the observations of Hidayatullah, J. as expressed in *Manohar Damodar Bhoot* v *Baliram Ganpat Bhoot* [AIR 1952 Nag 357 (FB)] represented the true scope and import of the word 'judgment' as used in Letters Patent.

▸*Meaning in interpreting the Criminal Procedure Code.* The Criminal Procedure Code, unlike the Civil Procedure Code, does not define "judgment" but it has been held that the "judgment" in the Code meant a judgment of conviction or acquittal. [*Dr. Hori Ram Singh* v *Emperor* AIR 1939 FC 43(Z)].

A judgment is the expression of the opinion of the court arrived at after due consideration of the evidence and all the arguments and would therefore either be a judgment of conviction or acquittal. [*U.J.S. Chopra* v *State of Bombay* AIR 1955 SC 633: (1955)3 SCR 94: 1955 SCA 944: 1955 Cr LJ 1410: 1955 SCJ 603].

NOTE: An order of discharge is not a judgment as "a judgment is intended to indicate the final order in a trial terminating in either the conviction or acquittal of the accused". [*per* Sir Arnold White, C.J., in *Emperor* v *Chinna Kaliappa Gounden* 29 Mad 126 (FB) followed in *Emperor* v *Maheshwara Kondaya* 31 Mad 543].

▸*Meaning in interpreting s. 21 of the Arbitration Act 1940 (since repealed).* Section 21 of the Arbitration Act 1940 reads thus: "Where in any suit all the parties interested agree that any matter in difference between them in the suit shall be referred to arbitration, they may at any time before the judgment is pronounced apply in writing to the court for an order of reference". The word "judgment" as used in s. 21 does not refer to the various interlocutory orders and judgments that may be passed during the hearing of the suit and so the word "judgment" cannot be given the meaning assigned to it by s. 2(9) of the Code of Civil Procedure 1908. It cannot mean in the context the statement given by the Judge of the grounds of a decree or order. It must mean a judgment which finally decides all matters in controversy in the suit (including in appellate proceedings). Thus, it follows that it is open to the parties to apply for a reference at any time before the final judgment is pronounced in the suit including in appellate proceedings. [*Ct. A. Ct. Nachiappa Chettiar* v *Ct. A. Ct. Subramaniam Chettiar* AIR 1960 SC 307].

▸*Meaning in interpreting s. 261 of the Income Tax Act 1961 [old s. 66A(2) of the Income Tax Act 1922].* The word "judgment" as used in the section is the decision of the High Court on question of law referred to it and the grounds on which such decision is based. It is not used in the section in its strict and proper sense. [*The Petlad Turkey Red Dye Works Co. Ltd.* v *Commissioner of Income-tax, Bombay North, Ahmedabad* AIR 1963 SC 1484: (1963)1 SCJ 248].

NOTE: Where the High Court in exercise of its advisory jurisdiction passed an interlocutory order calling upon the tribunal to make a supplemental statement of the case, it cannot be said that it was a judgment against which an appeal was competent. [*Tata Iron and Steel Co. Ltd.* v *Chief Revenue Authority of Bombay* AIR 1923 PC 148: 50 Ind App 212; *Delhi Cloth and General Mills Co. Ltd.* v *Income-tax Commissioner* AIR 1927 PC 242: 54 Ind App 421; *Premchand Satramdas* v *State of Bihar* AIR 1951 SC 14: 1950 SCR 799; *Sardar Syedna Taher Seiffuddin Sahib* v *State of Bombay* AIR 1958 SC 253: 1958 SCR 1007; *Jethanand and Sons* v *State of U.P.* AIR 1961 SC 794: (1961)3 SCR 754].

▸*Meaning in interpreting Art. 133(1) of the Constitution of India.* The expression "judgment" in Art. 133(1) in the context in which it occurs means a final adjudication by the court of the rights of the parties and that an interlocutory judgment even if it decides an issue or issues without finally determining the rights and liabilities is not a judgment, however, cardinal the issue may be. [*Tarapore & Co., Madras* v *V/O, Tractors Export, Moscow* AIR 1970 SC 1168].

- **Agreed judgment.** See CONSENT JUDGMENT.
- **Consent judgment.** A judgment, the provisions and terms of which are settled and agreed to by the parties to the action. [*Hargis* v *Hargis* 66 SW 2d 59; *Mathews* v *Looney* 123 SW 2d 871, 872].
- **Error of judgment** p. 315.
- **Final judgment** p. 353.
- **Foreign judgment** p. 365.
- **Interlocutory judgment.** One which determines some preliminary or subordinate point or plea, or settles some step, question, or default arising in the progress of the cause, but does not adjudicate the ultimate rights of the parties, or finally put the case out of court.

  An "interlocutory judgment" is one which reserves or leaves some further question or direction for future determination. [*State ex rel. Great Am. Ins. Co.* v *Jones* Mo, 396 SW 2d 601, 603].
- **Personal judgment.** Judgments in which court has personal jurisdiction over parties [*State* v *Dreyer* 362 P 2d 55, 57]; a judgment that imposes personal liability on a defendant and that may therefore be satisfied out of any of the defendant's property within judicial reach. [Black's *Law Dictionary*, 7th Ed.]. It is also termed judgment *in personam*.
- **Recall a judgment** p. 732.
- **Reverse a judgment** p. 761.
- **Simulated judgment** p. 799.
- **Voidable judgment** p. 884.

**Judgment by default.** A judgment rendered in consequence of non-appearance of the defendant; one entered upon the failure of a party to appear or plead at the appointed time; one entered under statute or rules of court for want of affidavit of defence, plea, answer, and the like, or for failure to take some required step in the cause.

**Judgment creditor.** One who has obtained a judgment in his favour and becomes entitled to enforce it; one who has obtained a judgment against his debtor, under which he can enforce execution.

**Judgment debtor.** A person against whom judgment has been recovered, and which remains unsatisfied; any person against whom a decree has been passed or an order capable of execution has been made. [Code of Civil Procedure 1908, s. 2(10)].

NOTE: A legal representative of a judgment debtor is not a judgment debtor as defined in s. 2(10) of the Code of Civil Procedure 1908, as it cannot be said that a decree has been passed against him, and for purposes of Or. 21, r. 12, the term 'judgment debtor' does not include a legal representative of the judgment debtor. [*Mohomad Liaq* v *Ramji* 4 DLR 208 (All)].

**Judgment in personam.** See PERSONAL JUDGMENT.

**Judgment in rem.** See under IN REM p. 441.

**Judgment of affirmance.** Judgment of the appellate court affirming the decision of the lower court.

**Judgment of reversal.** Judgment of the appellate court reversing the decision of the lower court.

**Judgment per incuriam.** Judicial decision wrongly decided because the judge was ill-informed about the applicable law.

The expression *per curiam* means and implies that the decision is arrived at by the court consisting of two more judges. But judgment *per incuriam* is generally a decision given on ignorance or forgetfulness of the existence of an earlier decision or statute not brought to the attention of the court. [*Mamleswar* v *Kanhaiya* AIR 1975 SC 907: (1975)2 SCC 232: (1975)1 SCWR 405; *Nishikanta* v *Manmohon* (1975)1 CLJ 404, 410].

Decision rendered in ignorance of statute or rule having the force of law is a decision *per incuriam* and is not binding. [*Sitaram Hari Salunkhe* v *L.R. Dubey* AIR 1980 Bom 55: 1979 Mah LJ 864: 1980 Bom CR 140].

NOTE: "As a general rule the only cases in which decisions should be held to have been given *per incuriam* are those decisions given in ignorance or forgetfulness of some inconsistent statutory provision or of some authority binding on the court concerned, so that in such cases some features of the decision or some step in the reasoning on which it is based is found on that account to be demonstrably wrong. The definition is not necessarily exhaustive, but cases not strictly within it which can properly be held to have been decided *per incuriam*, must in our judgment, consistently with the *stare decisis* rule which is an essential part of our law, be of the rarest occurrence". [Rupert Cross & J.W. Harris: *Precedent in English Law* (4th Ed. 1991), p. 149].

Neither judgment *per incuriam* nor a judgment given *sub silentio*, *i.e.*, assuming a position of law as correct, is binding. [*Mamleswar* v *Kanhaiyalal* AIR 1975 SC 907: (1975)2 SCC 232: (1975)1 SCWR 405; *Yeshbai* v *Ganpat* AIR 1975 Bom 21].

**Judices pedanei.** Judges chosen by the litigants.

**Judicia posteriora sunt in lege fortiora.** The latter decisions are stronger in law.

**Judicial.** Belonging to the office of a judge; relating to or connected with the administration of justice; having the character of judgment or formal legal procedure; proceeding from a court of justice; involving the exercise of judgment or discretion.

Of or pertaining or appropriate to the administration of justice, or courts of justice, or a judge thereof, or the proceedings therein. [*State* v *Freitag* 27 P 2d 68].

The word 'judicial' has two meanings. It may refer to the discharge of duties exercisable by a justice in court, or to the administrative duties which need not be performed in court, but in respect of which it is necessary to bring to bear a judicial mind—that is, a mind to determine what is fair and just in respect of the matters under consideration. [*Royal Aquarium* v *Parkinson* (1892)1 QB 431; *Parduman Singh* v *State of Punjab* AIR 1958 Punj 63].

NOTE: The term 'judicial' embraces even the acts of special tribunals which though administrative in character perform functions resembling those of courts. [*Bhailal Jagadish* v *Additional Deputy Commissioner* AIR 1953 Nag 89: ILR (1952) Nag 839].

The term 'judicial' extends to the acts and orders of a competent authority which has power to impose the liability or to give a decision which determines the rights or property of the affected parties. The term embraces even the acts of special tribunals which though administrative in character perform functions resembling those of courts. [*Bhai Lal* v *Addl. Deputy Commissioner, Akola* AIR 1953 Nag 89 (FB)].


- **Extra-judicial** p. 334.
- **Quasi-judicial** p. 720.


**Judicial act.** The action of a judge in trying a cause and rendering a decision. [*Application of Gleit* 33 NYS 2d 629, 630, 631]; an act which involves exercise of discretion or judgment; an act by member of a judicial department in construing law or applying it to a particular state of facts. [*State ex rel. Tharel* v *Board of Com'rs of Creek County* 107 P 2d 542, 549].

NOTE: A judicial act seems to be an act done by a competent authority upon a consideration of facts and circumstances and imposing liability or affecting the rights of others. The essential ingredients of a judicial act are three in number: It must be that of a person or persons who have legal authority to determine questions affecting the rights of parties and in a judicial manner. [*Srirama Rao* v *Suryanarayanamurthi* AIR 1964 Mad 340].

The expression 'judicial act' includes the exercise of quasi-judicial functions by administrative bodies or other authorities or persons obliged to exercise such functions and is used in contrast with what are purely administrative acts. [*Maijan Tea Estate* v *Presiding Officer, Labour Court* AIR 1963 Assam 108].

The function of the Returning Officer acting under s. 36 of the Representation of the People Act 1951, is judicial in character, but he is not to act judicially in discharging it. [*Virendar Kumar Satyawadi* v *State of Punjab* AIR 1956 SC 153: 1956 SCJ 138: 1956 SCR 410: (1955)2 SCR 1013].

**Judicial activism.** A philosophy of judicial decision-making whereby judges allow their personal views about public policy, among others, to guide their decision.

**Judicial approach.** The expression 'judicial approach' postulates (*a*) that the authority in arriving at the decision or taking action must be bound to act fairly and justly, and (*b*) that it does so on the basis to which the objective test can be applied, limited by the consideration of facts and circumstances of the case and the evidence led by the parties and the application of the law. [*Parduman Singh* v *State of Punjab* AIR 1958 Punj 63: ILR (1957) Punj 1629].

**Judicial authority.** The power and authority appertaining to the office of a judge; the official right to hear and determine questions in controversy.

NOTE: It is not necessary that a judicial authority should be strictly a court. It is enough if it is exercising, after hearing evidence, judicial functions in the sense that it has to decide on evidence between a proposal and an opposition. [*Rex* v *London County Council* (1931)2 KB 215; *Parduman Singh* v *State of Punjab* AIR 1958 Punj 63].

**Judicial decision.** Application by a court or tribunal exercising judicial authority of competent jurisdiction of the law to a state of facts proved, or admitted to be true, and a declaration of the consequences which follow. [*In re Knofler's Estate* 52 NE 2d 667, 668].

NOTE: A true judicial decision presupposes an existing dispute between two or more parties and then involves four requisites:

(1) the presentation (not necessarily orally) of their case by the parties to the dispute;

(2) if the dispute between them is a question of fact, the ascertainment of the fact by means of evidence adduced by the parties to the dispute and often with the assistance of argument, by or on behalf of the parties, on the evidence;

(3) if the dispute between them is a question of law, the submission of legal argument by the parties; and

(4) a decision, which disposes of the whole matter by a finding upon the facts in dispute and application of the law of the land to the facts so found, including, where required, a ruling upon any disputed question of law. [*Cooper* v *Wilson* (1937)2 KB 309 (340); *Bharat Bank Ltd., Delhi* v *Employees of the Bharat Bank Ltd., Delhi* 1950 SCR 459: AIR 1950 SC 188; *Maqbool Hussain* v *State of Bombay* 1953 SCR 730: 1953 SCJ 456: 1953 SCA 641: 1953 Cr LJ 1432: AIR 1953 SC 325].

**Judicial discretion.** The exercise of judgment by a judge or court based on what is fair under the circumstances and guided by the rules and principles of law; a court's power to act or not act when a litigant is not entitled to demand the act as a matter of right. [Black's *Law Dictionary*, 7th Ed.].

Judicial discretion means the power the law gives the judge to choose among several lawful alternatives the one that appeals to him the most. Judicial discretion is neither an emotional nor a mental state. It is a legal condition in which the judge has the freedom to choose among a number of options. The existence of the alternative is determined by its lawfulness and not by its effectiveness. [*Penumbra of Natural Justice* by Tapash Gan Choudhury, 2nd Ed., p. 301].

The judicial discretion is the discretion to know through the law what is just. It must be exercised with vigilance and circumspection according to justice, common sense, and sound judgment. [*Sarpanch Lonand Gram Panchayat* v *Ramgiri Goswami* AIR 1968 SC 222: (1968)2 SCA 475: (1968)1 SCJ 768: (1968)1 SCWR 65].

NOTE: For different dimensions of judicial discretion. See *Penumbra of Natural Justice* by Tapash Gan Choudhury, 2nd Ed., p. 302.

**Judicial experience.** The knowledge or skill gained by a person actually working as a judge in a court of law.

NOTE: Legal experience of members of the Bar cannot be regarded as judicial experience. [*Badridass Kanhaiyalal* v *Appellate Tribunal* AIR 1960 Raj 105: ILR (1959)9 Raj 869].

**Judicial notice.** The cognizance of certain facts which judges may properly take and act upon without proof, because they already know them.

The act by which a court, in conducting a trial, or framing its decision, will, of its own motion, and without the production of evidence, recognize the existence and truth of certain facts, having a bearing on the controversy at bar, which from their nature, are not properly the subject of testimony, or which are universally regarded as established by common notoriety.

NOTE: No fact of which the court will take judicial notice need to be proved. [The Evidence Act 1872, s. 56].

The court shall take judicial notice of the following facts: (1) all laws in force in the territory of India; (2) all public Acts passed or hereafter to be passed by Parliament and all local and personal Acts directed by Parliament to be judicially noticed; (3) articles of war for the Indian Army, Navy or Air Force; (4) the course of proceeding of the Constituent Assembly of India, of Parliament and of the legislatures established under any laws for the time being in force in a Province or in the States; (5) the seals of all the courts in India and of all courts out of India established by the authority of the Central Government, the seals of courts of Admiralty and Maritime Jurisdiction and Notaries Public, and all seals which any person is authorised to use by the Constitution or an Act of Parliament or an Act or Regulation having the force of law in India; (6) the accession to office, names, titles, functions and signatures of the persons filling for the time being any public office in any State, if the fact of their appointment to such office is notified in any Official Gazette; (7) the existence, of every State recognized by the Government of India and the National Flag; (8) the divisions of time, the geographical divisions of the world, and public festivals, fasts and holidays notified in the Official Gazette; (9) the territories under the Dominion of the Government of India; (10) the commencement, continuance and termination of hostilities between the Government of India and any other State or body of persons; (11) the names of the members and officers of the court and of their Deputies and Subordinate Officers and assistants and also of all officers acting in execution of its process, and of all advocates, attorneys, proctors, vakils, pleaders and other persons authorized by law to appear or act before it; (12) the rule of the road on land or at sea.

In all these cases, and also on all matters of public history, literature, science or art, the court may resort for its aid to appropriate books or documents of reference.

If the court is called upon by any person to take judicial notice of any fact, it may refuse to do so, unless and until such person produces any such book or document as it may consider necessary to enable it to do so.

**Judicial office.** Office which relates to the administration of justice and should be exercised by persons of sufficient skill and experience in the duties which appertain to them.

- **Holder of judicial office**. The term, under Art. 217(2)(*a*) of the Constitution of India, means the person who exercises only judicial functions, determines causes *inter partes* and renders decisions in a judicial capacity. [*Kumar Padma Prasad* v *Union of India* AIR 1992 SC 1213: (1992)2 SCC 428: 1992(2) SLR 210: JT 1992(2) SC 247].

**Judicial possession.** See under POSSESSION p. 671.

**Judicial power.** The authority vested in courts and judges to hear and decide cases and to make binding judgments on them; the power to construe law and apply the law when controversies arise over what has been done or not done under it; a power conferred on a public officer involving the exercise of judgment and discretion in deciding questions of right in specific cases affecting personal and proprietary interests. [Black's *Law Dictionary*, 7th Ed.].

The action of judge in trying a cause and rendering a decision. [*Application of Gleit* 33 NYS 2d 629].

'Judicial power' is the power to decide cases and controversies in conformity with law and by the methods established by the usages and principles of law. [Edward S. Corwin on *Constitution what it means today*, 14th Ed., p. 204].

NOTE: *Judicial power and legislative power—distinction.* The distinction between a judicial and a legislative act, duty, function, or power is well defined. The first deals with, or determines, what the law is, and what the rights of the parties are with reference to transactions already had. The second relates to, or prescribes, what the law shall be in future cases arising under it. Wherever an act undertakes to determine a question of right or obligation, or of property, as the foundation on which it proceeds, such is to that extent a judicial one, and not the proper exercise of a legislative function. [*Arcot N. Veeraswami* v *M.G. Ramchandra* AIR 1988 Mad 192, 198].

The legislature in India cannot exercise a power which can be described as essentially judicial and not legislative. However, where the legislature upon a finding that there has been lacuna in creating jurisdiction, supplies it, it acts within the legislative field. But, where the legislature goes further than this and compels the determination of a case and the hands of a court taking it completely out of the reach of the court to make a country decision, the matter is one under judicial and not legislative power. [*Biharilal* v *Ramcharan* 1957 MPLJ 505: 1957 JLJ 681].

**Judicial proceeding.** A judicial proceeding is any proceeding in the course of which evidence is or may be taken, or in which any judgment, sentence, or final order is passed on recorded evidence.

Any proceeding wherein judicial action is invoked and taken [*Manmix* v *Portland Telegram* 23 P 2d 138]; a proceeding in a legally constituted court; a proceeding wherein there are parties, who have opportunity to be heard, and wherein the tribunal proceeds either to a determination of facts upon evidence or of law upon proved or conceded facts.

A proceeding in which judicial functions are performed and a final decision affecting either right or liability of one or the other is given. [*Tanajirao* v *H.J. Chinoy* (1969)71 Bom LR 732].

In order to be judicial, a proceeding must relate in some way to the administration of justice or the ascertainment of any right or liability and that all proceedings of a judge are not necessarily judicial. [*Dhani Ram* v *Sub-Divisional Judge* AIR 1965 HP 25].

NOTE: Judicial proceeding includes any proceeding in the course of which evidence is or may be legally taken on oath. [Code of Criminal Procedure 1973, s. 2(*i*)].

Courts have to discharge both administrative and judicial duties. In order that it may be a judicial proceeding, the judge or the magistrate must act in a judicial capacity, that is, as a court. [*Harcharan* v *R.* 9 CWN 364].

The proceedings before the Income-tax Officer are judicial proceedings and all the incidents of such judicial proceedings have to be observed before the result is arrived at. The assessee has a right to inspect the record and all relevant documents before he is called upon to lead evidence in rebuttal in proceedings. [*Suraj Mall Mohta & Co.* v *A.V. Viswanatha Sastri* (1955)1 SCR 448: AIR 1954 SC 545: 1954 SCJ 611: 1954 SCA 743].

Delivery of possession by Nazir is not a judicial proceeding. [*Harcharan* v *R.* 9 CWN 364]. Proceedings under the Land Acquisition Act until the matter comes before the Land Acquisition Judge are only administrative and not judicial proceedings. [*Best & Co. Ltd.* v *Dy. Collector* 2 MWN 348].

**Judicial review.** A court's power to review the actions of other branches or levels of government, especially the court's power to invalidate legislative and executive actions as being unconstitutional; a court's review of a lower court's or an administrative body's factual or legal findings. [Black's *Law Dictionary*, 8th Ed.].

NOTE: A judicial review is a review of the manner in which decision was made. It is not an appeal from a decision. [*E. Merck (India) Ltd.* v *Union of India* AIR 2001 Del 326].

"Judicial review is a protection and not a weapon". [*Lonrho plc.* v *Secretary of State for Trade and Industry* (1989)2 All ER 609, *per* Lord Keith]. It is only supervisory. [*R.* v *Panel on Jake-overs and Mergers, ex. p. Guinness plc.* (1989)1 All ER 509].

The power of judicial review is implicit in a written constitution and unless expressly excluded by a provision of the Constitution, the power of judicial review is available in respect of exercise of powers under any of the provisions of the Constitution. Justiciability relates to a particular field falling within the purview of the power of judicial review. On account of want of judicially manageable standards, there may be matters which are not susceptible to the judicial process. [*A.K. Kaul* v *Union of India* (1955)4 SCC 73, 83].

**Judicial self-restraint.** A philosophy of judicial decision-making whereby judges avoid indulging their personal views and beliefs about public policy to guide their decision and instead interpret the law as legislated and according to precedent.

**Judicial separation.** A separation of man and wife by decree of court, less complete than an absolute divorce. It may be called a limited divorce.

**Judicial service.** The expression "judicial service" means service consisting exclusively of persons intended to fill the post of District Judge or other civil judicial posts inferior to the post of a district judge. [*State of West Bengal* v *Nripendra Nath Bagchi* AIR 1966 SC 447: (1966)1 SCR 771 referring to Art. 236(*b*) of the Constitution of India].

**Judicial tribunal.** It is a body who has the power and whose duty it is to ascertain and determine the rights and enforce the relative duties of contending parties. [*Words and Phrases*, Permanent Ed., vol. 23, as referred to in *Thomas Dana* v *State of Punjab* AIR 1959 SC 375: 1959 Cr LJ 392].

A 'judicial tribunal' is one that dispenses justice, is concerned with legal rights and liabilities, which means rights and liabilities conferred or imposed by 'law'. These legal rights and liabilities are treated by a judicial tribunal as pre-existing; such a tribunal professes merely to ascertain and give effect to them; it investigates the facts by hearing the evidence (as tested by long-settled rules), and it investigates the law by consulting precedents. A judicial tribunal looks for some law to guide it. [*The Encyclopedia of Words and Phrases—Legal Maxims* by Sanagan and Drynan, as referred to in *Thomas Dana* v *State of Punjab* AIR 1959 SC 375: 1959 Cr LJ 392].

**Judiciary.** Administration of justice; body of judges; explicators of the law; interpreters of the law; judicial branch of government; judicial forum; pertaining or relating to the courts of justice; the branch of government responsible for interpreting the laws and administering justice.

That branch of government which is intended to interpret, construe and apply the law. [*Board of Com'rs of Wyandotte County* v *General Securities Corporation* 138 P 2d 479, 487].

**Judicis est jus dicere, non dare.** It is for the judge to administer, not to make, law.

**Judicium non debet esse illusorium; suum effectum habere debet.** A judgment ought not to be illusory; it ought to have its consequence.

**Jura in personam.** Rights available against specific persons.

**Jura in rem.** Rights available against the world at large.

**Jure nature.** According to the law of nature, that is to say, according to the rules of morality or dictates of reason.

**Jurimetrics.** The scientific investigation of legal problems. And these are—(*a*) the mathematical aspects of decision-making, *e.g.*, the simultaneous equations and Boolean Algebra in the analysis of judicial decisions; (*b*) the methodology with machines in relation to legal research especially retrieval and the relation between the computed work and symbolic logic; (*c*) the ability to predict appellate decisions by factorisation and statical methods related to machine potentialities; and (*d*) the quantitative analysis of judicial process. [A.R. Biswas's *Metrics of Legal Philosophy*, Ed. 1971, p. 42].

**Juris consult.** One who is consulted on matters of law; a learned person who gives counsel on questions of law.

**Jurisdiction.** The authority by which courts and judicial officers take cognizance of and decide cases [*Board of Trustees of Firemen's Relief and Pension Fund of City of Marietta* v *Brooks* 67 P 2d 4, 6]; the legal right by which judges exercise their authority [*Max Ams, Inc.* v *Barker* 170 SW 2d 45, 48]; power and authority of a court to hear and determine a judicial proceeding [*In re De Camillis' Estate* 322 NYS 2d 551, 556]; the right and power of a court to adjudicate concerning the subject-matter in a given case; areas of authority; the geographic area in which a court has power or types of cases it has power to hear and decide.

By jurisdiction is meant the authority on which a court has to decide matters that are litigated before it or to take cognizance of matters presented in a formal way for its decision. [Halsbury's *Laws of England*, 4th Ed., vol. 10, para 715, p. 323].

'Jurisdiction' may be defined to be the power of a court to hear and determine a cause, to adjudicate or exercise any judicial power in relation to it. In other words, by jurisdiction is meant the authority on which a court has to decide matters that are litigated before it or take cognizance of matters presented in a formal way for its decision. [*Kunheema Umma* v *Putholath Balakrishna Nair* AIR 1967 Ker 97: ILR (1966)2 Ker 440].

The expression 'jurisdiction' does not mean the power to do or order the act impugned, but generally the authority of the Judicial Officer to act in the matter. [*Anwar Hussain* v *Ajoy Kumar Mukherjee* AIR 1965 SC 1651].

By "jurisdiction" is meant the extent of the power which is conferred upon the court by its constitution to try a proceeding. [*Raja Soap Factory* v *S.P. Shantharaj* AIR 1965 SC 1449: (1965)2 SCR 800].

Jurisdiction is the authority or power of the court to deal with a matter and make an order carrying binding force in the facts. [*A.R. Antulay* v *R.S. Nayak* AIR 1988 SC 1531: (1988)2 SCC 602: 1988 Supp (1) SCR 1: JT 1988(2) SC 325 & 408: 1988 Cr LJ 1661: 1988 Cr LR (SC) 366: 1988 SCC (Cri) 372].

The word "jurisdiction" is a verbal coat of many colours. Jurisdiction originally means the entitlement "to enter upon the enquiry in question". If there is an entitlement to enter upon an enquiry into the question, then, any subsequent error can only be regarded as an error within the jurisdiction. The question of jurisdiction is determinable at the commencement, not at the conclusion of the enquiry. [*Shri M.L. Sethi* v *Shri R.P. Kapur* AIR 1972 SC 2379: (1972)2 SCC 427: (1973)1 SCR 697].

NOTE: A court may have four kinds of jurisdiction, namely (1) territorial jurisdiction as dealt with in ss. 16 to 20 of the Code of Civil Procedure 1908; (2) pecuniary jurisdiction, as dealt with in s. 15 of the Code; (3) specified jurisdiction of matrimonial or testamentary causes; and (4) jurisdiction over foreign sovereigns and diplomatic officers.

A court may lack jurisdiction to hear and determine a particular action or application because (1) of the composition of the court (for example, the bias of the judge), or (2) the subject-matter of the proceedings (for example, title to foreign land), or (3) parties to the proceedings (for example, diplomatic immunity); or although having jurisdiction to hear and determine the proceedings, it may lack jurisdiction to make the kind of order made. [*Oscroft* v *Benabo* (1967)2 All ER 548].

The jurisdiction of a court may be restricted by a variety of circumstances. The question of jurisdiction has to be considered with reference to the value, place and nature of the subject-matter. The classification into territorial jurisdiction, pecuniary jurisdiction and jurisdiction over subject-matter is obviously of a fundamental character. The general rule is that if the court rendering a judgment suffers from want of jurisdiction in respect of any one of the above matters its judgment is a nullity and may be ignored. [*Kunheema Umma* v *Putholath Balakrishna Nair* AIR 1967 Ker 97: ILR (1966)2 Ker 440].


- **Concurrent jurisdiction** p. 168.
- **Defect of jurisdiction** p. 241.
- **Domestic jurisdiction** p. 278.
- **Foreign jurisdiction** p. 365.
- **Lack of jurisdiction** p. 509.


**Jurisdictional fact.** A fact that must exist for a court to properly exercise its jurisdiction over a case, party or thing. [Black's *Law Dictionary*, 7th Ed.].

A jurisdictional fact is one on existence or non-existence of which depends an assumption or refusal to assume jurisdiction by a court, tribunal or an authority. Error in assumption of jurisdiction should not be confused with mistake, legal or factual, in exercise of jurisdiction. In the former, the order is void whereas in the latter, it is final, unless set aside by higher or competent court or authority. An order which is void can be challenged at any time in any proceeding. [*Shrisht Dhawan* v *Shaw Brothers* (1992)1 SCC 534: AIR 1992 SC 1555].

**Jurisprudence.** The philosophy of law, or the science which treats of the principles of positive law and legal relations; the study of legal systems in general.

In the proper sense of the word, "jurisprudence" is the science of law, namely, that science which has for its function to ascertain the principles on which legal rules are based, so as not only to classify those rules in their proper order, and show the relation in which they stand to one another, but also to settle the manner in which new or doubtful cases should be brought under the appropriate rules. Jurisprudence is more a formal than a material science. It has no direct concern with questions of moral or political policy, for they fall under the province of ethics and legislation; but, when a new or doubtful case arises to which two different rules seem, when taken literally, to be equally applicable, it may be, and often is, the function of jurisprudence to consider the ultimate effect which would be produced if each rule were applied to an indefinite number of similar cases, and to choose that rule which, when so applied, will produce the greatest advantage to the community.

**Jurist.** A person famous for knowledge of the theoretical aspects of law; one who is versed or skilled in law.

**Jury.** Jury signifies a body of persons sworn to enquire into a matter of fact and to declare the truth upon such evidence as is placed before them. [Mozley & Whiteley's *Law Dictionary*, 10th Ed.].

**Jus.** A Latin expression which means "law, right". Law in the abstract; a system of law; a legal right, power, or principle. [Black's *Law Dictionary*, 8th Ed.].

*Jus* is more comprehensive than *lex*, though *lex* is one of its elements. *Jus* is not connected with the verb *jubeo*; it does not mean what is commanded by authority, which is true of *lex*. *Jus* is connected with the Latin word *jungere*; it means primarily a joining or fitting and readily glides into the sense of binding. It conveys the idea of valid custom enforced by a human authority, in other words, *jus* is a body of binding rules which the courts recognise as binding. [Barker's *Principles of Social and Political Theory* (1965)].

**Jus ad rem.** Means an inchoate and imperfect right. It is an abridged expression for *jus ad rem acquirendam*; it denotes a right to the acquisition of a thing. [Mozley & Whiteley's *Law Dictionary*, 10th Ed.].

**Jus ex injuria non aritur.** A right does not arise out of an injury.

**Jus tertii.** The right of a third party. If *A*, who *prima facie* is liable to restore property to *B*, alleges that *C* has a paramount title, *A* is said to set up the *jus tertii*. This may not be done by an agent as against his principal. [Mozley & Whiteley's *Law Dictionary*, 10th Ed.].

**Just.** According to law; affording no undue advantage; dispassionate; even-handed; fair-minded; lawful; principled; reasonable; right; rightful; unbiased; unprejudiced; in accordance with law and justice; upright, fair or proper.

Conforming to or consonant with what is legal or lawful; legally right; lawful; reasonable [*National Surety Corporation* v *Mullins* 90 SW 2d 707, 708]; correct, true, due. [*Wisdom* v *Board of Supr's of Polk County* 19 NW 2d 602, 606].

**Just and convenient.** These words have been construed as meaning that 'it is practicable and the interests of justice require it'. [*Madhulal* v *Ramji Das* AIR 1953 MB 85 (DB)].

**Just and equitable.** The principle of 'just and equitable' clause baffles a precise definition. It must rest with the judicial discretion of the court depending upon the facts and circumstances of each case. These are necessarily equitable considerations and may, in a given case, be superimposed on law. Whether it would be so done in a particular case cannot be put in the straitjacket of an inflexible formula. [*Hind Overseas Private Ltd.* v *Raghunath Prasad Jhunjhunwalla* AIR 1976 SC 565: (1976)2 SCR 226: (1976)3 SCC 259].

NOTE: The 'just and equitable' provision does, as equity always does, enable the court to subject the exercise of legal rights to equitable considerations; consideration that is of a personal character arising between one individual and another, which may make it unjust or inequitable, to insist on legal rights, or to exercise them in a particular way. [*Needle Industries (India) Ltd.* v *Needle Industries Newey (India) Holdings Ltd.* AIR 1981 SC 1298: (1981)3 SCR 698: (1981)3 SCC 333: (1982)1 Comp LJ 1].

**Just cause.** Legitimate cause; such causes as will suffice in law to justify the action taken.

A cause outside legal cause, which must be based on reasonable grounds, and there must be a fair and honest cause or reason, regulated by good faith. [*Dubois* v *Gentry* 184 SW 2d 369, 371].

**Just compensation.** It means a settlement which leaves one no poorer or richer than he was before the property was taken [*U.S. ex rel. Tennessee Valley Authority* v *Indian Creek Marble Co.* DC Tenn, 40 F Supp 811, 818, 819]; full and perfect equivalent of the property taken [*Housing Authority of Shreveport* v *Green* 8 So 2d 295, 298]; value of property taken at the time of taking. [*Danforth* v *U.S.* Mo, 84 L Ed 240].

Just compensation means a full and perfect equivalent for the property taken. The equivalent to be rendered for the property taken shall be real, substantial, full and ample. The noun "compensation" standing by itself carries the idea of an equivalent, so that if the adjective "just" had been omitted and the provision was simply that the property should not be taken without "compensation", the natural import would be that compensation should be equivalent to the property and this is emphasised by the adjective "just". Compensation shall be a just equivalent of what the owner has been deprived of by the acquisition of the property by the State. [*State of West Bengal* v *Mrs. Bela Banerjee* AIR 1954 SC 170; *Vajravelu* v *Sp. Dy. Collector* AIR 1965 SC 1017].

**Justice.** Equitableness; equity; fair-mindedness; fair treatment; fairness; justness; rightfulness; uprighteousness.

'Justice isn't something temporal—it is eternal—and the nearest approach to a definition that I can give is, "Justice, is what the right thinking members of the community believe to be fair". [*Excerpts from 'Constitutional Developments in Britain'* by Lord Denning as referred to in *Penumbra of Natural Justice* by Tapash Gan Choudhury, 2nd Ed., p. 3].

- **Administration of justice** p. 40.
- **Court of Justice** p. 203.
- **Ends of justice** p. 307.
- **Natural justice** p. 599.
- **Obstructing justice** p. 617.
- **Preventive justice** p. 683.
- **Substantial justice.** Justice administered according to rules of substantive law, regardless of any procedural error.

**Justice, equity and good conscience.** The origins of the formula lie in the Romano-Canonical sources and go back to the sixteenth century. The Roman materials supplied the query and the scheme was evolved out of the practice of medieval cities of Italy, France and Germany as well as of "Alciatist" jurists. Aristotle took pains to explain that *"justitia"* needs and presupposes *"acquitas"*. The function of *acquitas* is to adjust the written statute to the particular circumstances of the case. And this is done in two ways: (1) to correct, modify and, if necessary, to amend the statute law; and (2) to supplement and otherwise remove the difficulties of the written sources of law. There is also a third sense of *acquitas*—it is where the judge is to fall back upon his "office" to give a decision *ex bono et acquo*, which means "according to good conscience". These ideas were developed in England and incorporated into her legal system. Thus the preamble to the Act of Succession 1925 contains the words, "equity, reason and good conscience". These denote the sources of law other than English Common and Statute Law, that is, the fundamental laws.

The East India Company carried these concepts to India. Thus, in 1668, the Judges appointed in Bombay under the Company's law were charged with behaving themselves "according to good conscience". The Royal Charter of 5th August 1683, setting up courts at Bombay enjoined on the Judges to act "according to rules of equity and good conscience". Similarly this was reiterated in the Royal Charter of 30th December 1687 while establishing a Mayor's Court at Madras. The phrase "justice, equity and good conscience" was replaced by "Justice and right" in the Royal Charters of 1726 and 1753 in respect of Mayor's Court.

The formula was reborn in Calcutta in s. 60 of the Regulation of 5th July 1781: "That in all cases for which no specific directions are given, the respective judges do act according to justice, equity and good conscience". Edward Otte Ives, the Judge of the Murshidabad City Adalat since 1780, was the originator of the formula. And the formula was a device to escape from English law not to call it in. It is only where positive law, custom and equitable analogies cannot be traced that the formula comes into use. [Derrett—"Justice, Equity and Good Conscience" in *Changing Law in Developing Countries* edited by Anderson, 1963, pp. 114-153].

**Justiciable.** Liable to be examined in a court of justice; matter appropriate for court review.

**Justiciable cause.** It must be some cause which should be considered to be real and serious.

> NOTE: Sentimental incompatibility of the women with the husband has been held to be not a justiciable cause for claiming rights under the Hindu Married Women's Right to Separate Residence and Maintenance Act 1946. [*Sidda Setty* v *Muniamma* AIR 1953 Mad 712].

**Justification.** Just, lawful excuse or reason for an act or failing to act.

Justification means explanation with supporting data. [*American Export-Isbrandsten Lines, Inc.* v *Federal Maritime Commission* 417 F 2d 749, 752].

The Shorter Oxford English Dictionary assigns the meaning for "justification": The showing in court that one had sufficient reason for doing that which he is called to answer; the ground for such a plea. [*Raj Kapoor* v *Laxman* AIR 1980 SC 605: (1980)2 SCR 512: (1980)2 SCC 175: 1980 Cr LJ 436: 1980 SCC (Cri) 383].

**Justified.** That which is proved or shown to be fair or right or according to justice. [*Patel Engineering* v *C.B. Rathi* (1984)2 Guj LR 970].

**Justified by law.** An act is justified by law if it is warranted, validated and made blameless by law. [*Raj Kapoor* v *Laxman* AIR 1980 SC 605: (1980)2 SCR 512: (1980)2 SCC 175: 1980 Cr LJ 436: 1980 SCC (Cri) 383].

**Justitia non est neganda, non differenda.** Justice is neither to be denied nor postponed.

**Juvenile.** A boy who has not attained the age of 16 years or a girl who has not attained the age of 18 years. [Juvenile Justice Act 1986. s. 2(*h*)].

A person who has not reached the age at which one should be treated as an adult by the criminal justice system. [Black's *Law Dictionary*, 7th Ed.].

A term which may be, though not commonly, applied to a person who has not reached his or her legal majority for purposes of contracting, marrying, etc. [Black's *Law Dictionary*, 5th Ed.].

▸ *Meaning under the Juvenile Justice (Care and Protection of Children) Act 2000, s. 2(k).* A person who has not completed eighteenth year of age.

'Juvenile' is a word which is used when referring to young criminal offenders.

**Juvenile offender.** A "youthful offender" is a juvenile offender. He is defined as a boy under the age of fifteen years and convicted of any offence punishable with imprisonment or transportation. [Reformatory Schools Act 1897, s. 4(*a*)]. The court may, instead of sentencing him, send him to one of the Reformatory Schools.

# Kk

**Kabaj.** A receipt; a rent receipt.

**Kabala.** A deed of conveyance or transfer of any interest in property.

Kabala merely means a contract. [*Jamandas* v *Chetandas* AIR 1928 Bom 487: 30 Bom LR 1317].

**Kabin-nama.** A deed of dower in a Mahommedan marriage; a marriage settlement.

**Kabja khali makan ka dia hai.** The expression aforesaid does not mean that actual physical vacant possession had been handed over to the purchaser. In document of this type it can equally mean that the legal right of possession not the actual possession has been handed over to the purchaser. [*Yadhishter* v *Ashok Kumar* AIR 1987 SC 558: (1987)1 SCR 516: JT 1986 SC 1021: (1987)1 SCC 204].

**Kabuliyat.** A rent note executed by tenant in favour of the landlord; a counter-part of a *patta* by the landlord to the tenant.

A *kabuliyat* predicates a *patta*. A *patta* is granted by the *zamindar* as a title deed to the tenant. The *kabuliyat,* as its name implies, is a mere acknowledgment, an engagement by the tenant to carry out the terms of the *patta*. [*Raja Srinath Ray* v *Maharaja Pratap* 82 IC 879 (PC)].

**Kachcha adatia.** A general type of agent as opposed to a *pucca adatia*, a special type of agent pleading his credit, and for certain purposes himself acting as the principal, his English counterpart being *del credere* agent. [*Babulal* v *Jagat Narain* AIR 1952 Vin Pra 51].

**Kaimi.** Permanent right. It does not imply fixity of rent. [*Shyama Charan* v *Fakir Charan* AIR 1927 Cal 546].

The word 'Kaimi jote' is applicable to a *raiyat* or a tenure-holder.

**Kalan.** The word 'kalan' denotes different meanings in different contexts. It ordinarily means encumbrance, but in appropriate context it connotes a dispute. [*Ramamurthi Ayyar* v *Kuppuswami Ayyar* AIR 1950 Mad 621].

**Kalpa taru.** A digest on ancient Hindu Law written by Lakhmidara; it is a book of authority on Hindu Law.

**Kamat.** Private lands of the proprietor. [*Harihar Prasad Singh* v *Deonarain Prasad* 1956 SCR 1: AIR 1956 SC 305: 1956 SCA 316: 1956 SCJ 279].

**Kanam.** Usufructuary mortgage or a lease to the creditor.

"Kanam" means a demise with the incidents specified therein. [*Cochin Devaswom Board, Trichur* v *Vamana Setti* AIR 1966 SC 1980: (1966)3 SCR 724].

**Kanam tenant.** "Kanam tenant" is defined as a person who holds land on Kanam tenure. [*Cochin Devaswom Board, Trichur* v *Vamana Setti* AIR 1966 SC 1980: (1966)3 SCR 724].

**Kanango.** Village and district revenue officers who, under the Muslim Rulers, recorded the value, tenure, extent and transfers of lands, assisted in the measurements and survey of lands and explained local practices and public regulations.

**Kandrika.** The word means a portion of a village granted free of rent or on a favourable lease. [*Satti Suri Reddi* v *Kolachina* AIR 1943 Mad 764: 1943 MWN 769: (1943)2 MLJ 528].

**Kangaroo court.** The term is descriptive of a sham legal proceeding in which a person's rights are totally disregarded and in which the result is a foregone conclusion because of the bias of the court.

**Kanun.** Law, rule, regulation or statute.

**Kar.** Rent, cess or tax.

The word *'kar'* includes cess also. [*Annada Charan* v *Habibulla* AIR 1923 Cal 283].

**Karao.** The practice of marrying a widow to her deceased husband's younger brother. It is common among the Jats, Gujars and Ahirs. This is a form of marriage but is not valid amongst the twice born classes of Hindus, e.g., Brahmin, Khatri and Vaish. Any such spouse of valid marriage contracting a second marriage does not answer the offence of bigamy. [*Amar Singh* v *Monki* 1982 All Cr R 148].

**Karar.** Agreement, promise.

**Karkum.** Manager; one who manages the affairs of another; agent.

**Karnavan and karnavati.** The management of a *tarwad* or *tavazhi* ordinarily rests in the eldest male member of the *tarwad* or *tavazhi*. The male manager is called *karnavan* and the female one *karnavati*. [*Achuthan Nair* v *Chinnammu Amma* AIR 1966 SC 411: (1966)1 SCR 454].

**Karta.** A coparcener who manages the family property either under an express or implied authority of other coparceners is called the karta or manager of the joint family. Under the Hindu law a karta has some special rights over the joint family properties.

The word 'karta' as used in wills and other legal documents in Telugu always means heirs, the persons entitled. [*Venkata Krishnayya* v *Vasireddi Madamma* AIR 1928 Mad 926].

The eldest or other managing member of the family is called karta.

**Kat kobala.** A deed of conditional sale; a mortgage by conditional sale. [Transfer of Property Act 1882, s. 58(*c*)].

**Katra.** The primary meaning of the word *"katra"* is enclosure and the secondary meaning is market. Generally, a *katra* would be business locality though there might be purely residential *katras*. [*Bhau Ram* v *Baij Nath Singh* AIR 1962 SC 1476: 1962 Supp (3) SCR 724].

**Kayemi.** The word "kayemi" is never used in describing *zamindari* interest in land. The word is always used in connection with the description of tenant's rights in land and it means a permanent occupancy holding. [*Nahar Lal Shah* v *Bajnath Shah* AIR 1928 Cal 385, 386].

**Kazi.** A judge under the Mahomedan rule.

Now the term denotes person recognised by government whose duties consist in the preparation and attestation of marriage-deeds or in the performance of legalising marriage among Mahomedans. The *kazi* has also certain functions in Mahomedans religious worship where he is considered as the head.

**Keelage.** The right to demand payment of a toll by a ship entering or anchoring in a harbour; the toll so paid.

**Keep.** To continue; to have or retain in one's power or possession; not to lose or part with; to preserve or retain; to maintain, carry on, conduct, or manage; to maintain, tend, harbour, feed and shelter; to maintain continuously and methodically for the purpose of a record; to main continuously and without stoppage and variation.

The ordinary dictionary meaning of the word "keep" is to retain, to maintain or cause to stay or remain in a place, to detain, to stay or continue in a specified condition, position, etc. [*State of Mysore* v *T.V. Sundaram Iyengar & Sons (P) Ltd.* AIR 1980 SC 148: (1980)2 SCR 1: (1980)1 SCC 60; *Maharaja Tourist Service* v *State of*

*Gujarat* JT 1991(2) SC 423: 1992 Supp (1) SCC 489].

**Keep house.** This is an act of bankruptcy which a person commits when he begins to keep to his house and denies himself to his creditors.

**Keep in good condition.** When used in respect of a house, the expression will have a different meaning according to its nature and age. There appears to be no wide distinction between keeping the house in thorough repairs and keeping it in good condition. [*Lurcott* v *Wakely* (1911)1 KB 905].

**Keep to the left rule.** This is "the rule of the road on land or at sea" of which the courts shall take judicial notice under s. 57 of the Indian Evidence Act 1872. This means that the horses and vehicles of all descriptions should keep to the left side of the road. At sea, ships and steam-boats, on meeting, should post their helms so as to pass on the post of left side of each other.

**Keeper.** A custodian, manager, or superintendent; one who has the care, custody, or management of anything or place; one who has or holds possession of anything.

**Keeping down interest.** Payment of interest periodically as it becomes due.

**Kept woman.** Mistress.

**Key industry.** An industry which affects many others and, therefore, the whole of a country's economy. Examples are power industries.

**Key person.** An important officer or employee; a person primarily responsible for the success of a business.

**Khairat.** Alms, charity; lands given as charitable endowments. The term is more especially applicable to grants or alms given by or to Mohammadans. [Wilson's *Glossary*, p. 274].

*Khairat* is equivalent to charity. [*Mohammad Yusuf* v *Azimuddin* AIR 1941 All 235].

**Khaksar.** A Muslim political organisation demanding an undivided Pakistan extending from Karachi to Calcutta. [*Hazi Mumtaz Khan* v *State of U.P.* AIR 1988 All 28].

**Khamar.** Unoccupied land brought under cultivation by the *zamindar*. Khamar land was regarded as the *zamindar's* own land.

**Khandan.** Ordinarily the word *'khandan'* which corresponds with the English expression 'family' means a group of descendants from one common ancestor. [*Abdul Halim Khan* v *Raja Saadat Ali* AIR 1928 Oudh 155].

*'Khandan'* in a general sense applies to blood relations. [*Kalawati Debi* v *Dharam Prakash* AIR 1933 PC 71: 60 IA 90].

**Khandsari.** 'Khandsari' is nothing but sugar. [*Gulshan Khansari* v *Union of India* AIR 1969 All 432: 1968 All LJ 391].

**Khankah.** A Mohammedan monastery; a place where religious men of Mohammedan community reside or receive instructions or perform religious rites. [*Vidya Varuthi* v *Balusami Ayyar* AIR 1922 PC 123: 48 IA 302].

**Kharach.** Expenditure, disbursement, the debit side of an account paper.

**Kharch-i-pandan.** It is a personal allowance to the wife paid under a custom prevailing among Mahommedan families of rank. The allowance is fixed either before or after the marriage and varies according to the means and position of the parties. When the parties to the marriage are minors, the amount of this money is arranged for by their respective parents or guardians. The husband has scarcely any control over the wife's application of the allowance.

**Kharif crop.** Crops sown at the beginning of the rains and reaped from October to December. Rice, jower, cotton, etc., are instances of kharif crop.

**Kharij.** Excluded or separated from the original.

**Kharij dakhila.** A rent receipt in respect of a separated portion of the tenancy.

**Kharij jama.** The word imports that the owner of the *kharij jama* is an independent proprietor. [*Ramkhelawan Sahu* v *Kuldip Sahay* AIR 1926 Pat 152].

**Kharij-nama.** A deed of partition or separation.

**Khas dakhal.** Actual possession.

**Khas-mahal.** District held in the management of the Government. [Wilson's *Glossary*, p. 282].

**Khas possession.** "Khas possession" is equivalent to 'actual possession' and is understood in contra-distinction to the word 'constructive possession'. [*Ramesh Bejoy Sharma* v *Pashupati Rai* AIR 1979 SC 1769: (1980)1 SCR 6: (1979)4 SCC 27].

**Khasarat.** Damage, loss or injury.

**Khasra.** A daybook; a field book of survey [*Bachan* v *Kankar* AIR 1972 SC 2157: (1973)1 SCR 727: (1972)2 SCC 555]; a draft.

**Khata.** An account book or paper, a daybook. The holding or plot held by a tenant.

**Khatauni.** "Khatauni" is an annual Register prepared under s. 32 of the Land Revenue Act 1901. [*Bachan* v *Kankar* AIR 1972 SC 2157: (1973)1 SCR 727: (1972)2 SCC 555: 1973 UJ (SC) 272].

**Khazana.** Rent, revenue, toll, treasure.

**Khewat.** Proprietary land or the land revenue assessed on that land. [*Daya* v *Budh Ram* AIR 1925 Lah 127].

**Khiraj.** Revenue raised from the land. It means the amount claimed by the State as its share of the profits arising from the cultivation of land. Lakhiraj means land exempted from the payment of *khiraj*.

**Khoola.** A form of divorce under Mahomedan law. If a Muslim husband confers power of dissolving the marriage on the wife in exchange of money or property, it is called *khoola* or *mubarat*.

**Khud-khast.** A resident cultivator who cultivates his own hereditary land.

The word *'khud-khast'* means personal cultivation and that is a natural expression which might include both private lands and *bakasht* lands, that is to say, *raiyati* lands, which had come into the possession of the proprietor by surrender, abandonment or otherwise. [*Harihar Prasad* v *Deonarayan Prasad* AIR 1956 SC 305: 1956 SCA 316: 1956 SCJ 279: 1956 SCR 1].

**Kickback.** Payment back by seller of a portion of the purchase price to buyer or public official to induce purchase or to influence improperly future purchases.

A return of a portion of a monetary sum received, especially as a result of a secret agreement. [Black's *Law Dictionary*, 8th Ed.].

**Kidnap.** Abduct; hold for ransom; put under duress; take by force; unlawfully seize; waylay.

**Kill.** In its application to "defeat", it means abolish; abrogate; cancel; crush; destroy; extinguish; invalidate, nullify, overthrow; overturn; quash; repress; vanquish.

In its application to "murder", it means assassinate; deprive of life; execute; exterminate; put to death; slaughter, slay.

**Kiln.** A structure of a permanent nature within which bricks are burnt.

**Kin.** One's relative; family; a relative by blood, marriage, or adoption.

**Kindred.** Kindred or consanguinity is the connection or relation of persons descended from the same stock or common ancestor. [Indian Succession Act 1925, s. 24].

When applied to Hindus, the word includes relations by marriage. [*Dinesh Chandra* v *Biraj Kamini* 15 CWN 945].

**King's Bench.** The Court of King's or Queen's Bench is the Supreme Court of Common Law in Great Britain.

**King's counsel.** Barristers appointed counsel to the Crown, and called within the Bar. [Wharton's *Law Lexicon*].

**Kiraya.** Rent, hire, fare.

**Kiraya-nama.** A document agreeing to pay certain rent, hire or fee.

**Kishan.** A cultivator.

**Kist.** Instalment or periodical portion. The period fixed for payment of instalment. A portion of rent or revenue payable at a specified time.

**Kite-flying.** Means dealing in accommodation bills to raise money.

**Knock down.** The assigning of a lot to a bidder by a tap of the hammer. Property is knocked down when the auctioner, by the fall of his hammer, signifies to the bidder that his bid has been accepted.

**Knock for knock.** This is an agreement between two insurance companies under which each insurance company pays its own insured what he is entitled to under his policy, and does not insist on his bringing an action against the party insured by the other company.

**Know all men by these presents.** Take note. This is an archaic form of address traditionally used to begin certain legal documents such as bonds and powers of attorney, but in modern drafting style the phrase is generally considered deadwood.

**Know-how.** The information, practical knowledge, skills and techniques required to achieve some practical end, especially in industry or technology.

Know-how indicates the way in which a skilled man does his job and is an expression of his individual skill and experience. [*Stevenson Jordan & Harrison* v *Mac Donald & Evans* (1952)69 RPC 10 (CA)].

NOTE: Know-how is considered intangible property in which rights may be bought and sold.

**Knowingly.** With knowledge of the facts upon which the contravention depends. [*Burton* v *Bevan* (1908)2 Ch 240].

**Knowledge.** An awareness or understanding of a fact or circumstance; a state of mind in which a person has no substantial doubt about the existence of a fact. [Black's *Law Dictionary*, 8th Ed.].

Acquaintance with fact or truth [*People* v *Henry* 72 P 2d 915, 921]; act or state of knowing or understanding. [*People* v *Henry*, supra].

A state of mind entertained by a person with regard to existing facts which he has himself observed or the existence of which has been communicated to him by persons whose veracity he has no reason to doubt. [*Emperor* v *Zamir* AIR 1932 Oudh 28].

NOTE: Knowledge can be inferred from the circumstances of the case. [*Emperor* v *Mathuranath De* AIR 1932 Cal 850: 33 Cr LJ 657].

• **Carnal knowledge** p. 124.

**Knowledge and notice.** Knowledge is not synonymous with notice, but when a person is spoken of as having actual or constructive notice, it means that the man is legally chargeable with knowledge.

**Known sources of income.** The expression must have reference to the sources known to the prosecution on a thorough investigation of the case. The expression does not mean sources known to the accused. [*C.S.D. Swami* v *State* AIR 1960 SC 7: (1960)1 SCR 461: 1960 Cr LJ 131: 1960 SCJ 160; *State of Maharashtra* v *Wasudeo Ramchandra Kaidalwar* AIR 1981 SC 1186: (1981)3 SCR 675: 1981 Cr LJ 884: 1981 SCC (Cri) 690: (1981)3 SCC 199].

**Kořakdar.** An officer of court who attaches or distrains goods and property for debt.

**Korfa.** A sub-lessee, whether of a talukdar or of a raiyat. A korfa tenant is not necessarily an under-tenant of a raiyat. [*Secretary of State* v *Jadu Chandra* 21 CWN 452: 39 IC 409].

**Krishak.** A cultivator, a tiller of soil, a husbandman.

**Krishan.** A cultivator, a tiller of soil, a husbandman.

**Kritima adoption.** A form of adoption of child prevalent in Mithila and the adjoining districts. Either a man or a woman can adopt in this form.

**Kudivaram.** A cultivator's share in the produce of the land held by him, as distinguished from the landlord's share which is known as *malvaram*. The expression sometimes means a right to occupy land permanently. [*Rajayya* v *Laxman* AIR 1945 PC 468].

**Kudiyiruppu.** "Kudiyiruppu" means a holding or part of a holding consisting of the site of any residential building, the sites or site of other buildings appurtenant thereto, such other lands as are necessary for the convenient enjoyment of such residential building and easements attached thereto, but does not include a kudiyiruppu. [*Kuchiyan Govinda Swami* v *Kalliani Amma Lakshmi Amma* AIR 1966 SC 1937: 1966 (Supp) SCR 135].

**Kuhl.** An irrigation channel from a stream. [*Dhani Ram* v *Hamira* AIR 1940 Lah 398].

**Kuzhikanam.** "Kuzhikanam" means and includes a transfer of garden lands or of other lands or of both, with the fruit-bearing trees, if any, standing thereon at the time of the transfer, for the enjoyment of those trees and for the purpose of planting such fruit-bearing trees, thereon but shall not include a usufructuary mortgage as defined in the Transfer of Property Act 1882. [*Kuchiyan Govinda Swami* v *Kalliani Amma Lakshmi Amma* AIR 1966 SC 1937: 1966 (Supp) SCR 135].

# Ll

**La-aulad.** It means issueless or without any sons or daughters. [*Nirmal Bahadur* v *Fatesh Bahadur* AIR 1929 All 963].

The expression means without male issue and not issueless. [*Bibi Umatui* v *Nageshwar Buz* AIR 1927 Pat 386].

**Laan.** In Mahomedan law, it signifies testimony confirmed by oath, on the part of the husband and wife.

**Label.** Used as noun, it means brand; description; docket; emblem; identification tag; mark of identification; slip; superscription; tag; ticket.

Small piece of paper, card, fabric, etc., for attaching to an object and giving information about it, instructions for use, etc.; a short classifying phrase or name applied to a person, a work of art, etc.; the logo, title, or trade mark of specially a fashion house or recording company; the piece of paper in the centre of a gramophone record describing its contents etc.; an adhesive stamp on a parcel etc.; a word placed, before, after, or in the course of a dictionary definition etc. to specify its subject, register, nationality, etc. [*Concise Oxford Dictionary*, 9th Ed.].

A slip, as of paper, affixed to something and bearing an inscription to indicate its character, ownership, etc.; a projecting moulding or dripstone over a wall opening. [Webster's *Comprehensive Dictionary*, International Ed.].

An informative logo, title, or similar marking affixed to a manufactured product; any writing (such as a codicil) attached to a larger writing; a narrow slip of paper or parchment attached to a deed or writ in order to hold a seal. [Black's *Law Dictionary*, 7th & 8th Eds.].

An affixation to or marking on a manufactured article, giving information as to its nature or quality, or the contents of a material, package or container, or the name of the maker, etc. [*Higgins* v *Keuffel* 35 L Ed 470].

Used as verb, it means call by a distinctive title; characterize; classify; define; demarcate; denote; designate; distinguish by a mark; earmark; identify; provide with nomenclature; put a mark; set apart; single out; specify.

**Labour.** Work; toil; physical or mental exertion, particularly for some useful or desired end; the working class collectively; workers, specially manual, considered as a social class or political force; the process of childbirth starting from the uterine contractions to delivery; a particular task, specially of a difficult nature.

The meaning of 'labour', *inter alia*, is: "physical or mental exertion, particularly for some useful or desired end". [*Chandrakant Manilal Shah* v *Commissioner of Income-tax* AIR 1992 SC 66: (1992)1 SCC 76: (1992)193 ITR 1: 1991 Supp (1) SCR 546: JT 1991(4) SC 171].

The term normally refers to work for wages as opposed to work for profits; though the word is sometimes construed to mean service rendered or part played in production of wealth. [*Britt* v *Cotter Butte Mines* 89 P 2d 266, 267].

• **Hard labour** p. 406.

• **Immobility of labour** p. 430.

**Labour force.** Workmen of all category.

The labour force includes not only manual or technical workmen but also those that are necessary or considered auxiliary to the productive labour of other but does not include persons in a managerial capacity. [*Madras Gymkhana Club* v *Gymkhana Club* (1967)2 Lab LJ 720 (SC)].

**Labourer.** The word ordinarily denotes one who subsists by physical labour. [*American Surety Co. of New York* v *Stuart* Tex Civ App, 151 SW 2d 886, 888].

A labour is one who does work with his own hands. A person who is a contractor or a sub-contractor and who engages to get work done, but does not engage in any work himself, is not a workman or labourer. [*Anupchand Deepchand* v *Nimraji Marot Rao* ILR (1949) Nag 578: AIR 1949 Nag 329, Mangalmurti, J.].

According to the dictionary meaning a labourer is a person who is engaged in the performance of unskilled labour. Generally speaking, a person who is called upon to do some work which requires some amount of skill, however little that may be, is not regarded as a labour. [*G. Venkatachalam Pillai* v *Labiur & Co.* AIR 1961 Mad 358: (1961)1 MLJ 374].

• **Daily labourer** p. 216.

**Lac.** A resinous substance secreted as a protective covering by the lac insect, and used to make varnish and shellac; the sap of certain trees or plants used for varnish.

'Lac' includes any form of manufactured or unmanufactured lac other than refuge lac. [Produce Cess Act 1966, s. 2(*e*); Indian Lac Cess Act 1930, s. 2(*c*)].

**Laches.** Delay; undue delay; unreasonable delay; unexplained delay; unconscionable delay; prejudicial delay; inexcusable delay; inexcusable delay in assertion of rights; delay that results in disadvantage; negligence; lack of diligence; dereliction; dereliction of duty; failure to litigate within reasonable period; laxity; laggardness.

A person is guilty of laches when he is negligent in the performance of a legal duty, or when he makes delay in asserting a right, in claiming a privilege and in applying for redress. [*Khub Chand* v *State of Rajasthan* AIR 1967 SC 1074; *G.C. Gupta* v *N.K. Pandey* AIR 1988 SC 654, 661].

NOTE: A court of equity refuses its aid to stale demands, where the plaintiff has slept upon his rights and acquiesced for a great length of time. He is then said to be barred by his laches. The defence of laches, however, is only allowed where there is no statutory bar. [Halsbury's *Laws of England*, 4th Ed., vol. 16, para 1476, p. 998].

**Lack of harmony.** 'Lack of harmony' does not necessarily mean promotion of feelings of enmity and hatred. Lack of harmony *simpliciter* means cessation of feelings of friendship. [*A.J. Faridi* v *Union of India* AIR 1970 All 383].

**Lack of jurisdiction.** The phrase may mean lack of power of a court to act in a particular manner or to give certain kinds of relief. [*In re Rowe's Estate* 66 Cal App 2d 594: 152 P 2d 765, 770]. It may consist in court's total want of power to act at all, or lack of power to act in particular case because conditions essential to exercise of jurisdiction have not been complied with, or may consist of lack of jurisdiction over subject-matter or over person.

NOTE: A tribunal may lack jurisdiction if it is improperly constituted, or if it fails to observe certain essential preliminaries to the inquiry. [*Ujjam Bai* v *State of Uttar Pradesh* AIR 1962 SC 1621].

**Lagan or ligan.** Denotes goods cast into or sunk in the sea, but made fastened to a cork or buoy in order that they may be found again. If unclaimed, they belong to the State.

**Laissez-faire.** Let things be. A state of economy where the individual is free to carry on business and conduct himself with the minimum of State control, as opposed to State planning and restriction; in economics, absolutely uncontrolled industrial and commercial competition; non-interference; indifference.

**Lakhiraj.** Land free from payment of rent or revenue to the landlord; a rent-free tenure or holding; a land or estate given by the State exempting the payment of anything by way of rent.

**Lambardar.** The cultivator who, either on his account or as the representative of other members of the village, pays the Government dues and is registered in the Collector's roll according to his number; as the representative of the rest, he may hold the office by descent or by election. [Wilson's *Glossary*].

**Laminated wood.** It means a wood product prepared by placing layer on layer. [*Collector of Central Excise, Shillong* v *Woodcraft Products Ltd.* JT 1995(3) SC 207: (1995)3 SCC 454].

**Lamination.** The manufacture by placing layer on layer. [*Collector of Central Excise, Shillong* v *Woodcraft Products Ltd.* JT 1995(3) SC 207: (1995)3 SCC 454].

**Land.** An immovable and indestructible three-dimensional area consisting of a portion of the earth's surface, the space above and below the surface, and everything growing on or permanently affixed to it; an estate or interest in real property.

Land includes any ground, soil or earth, such as meadows, pastures, woods, moors, waters, marshes and heath; houses and other buildings upon it; the air space above it and all mines and minerals beneath it. It includes anything fixed to the land; and growing trees and crops, except those which, broadly speaking, are produced in the year by the labour of the year. [Halsbury's *Laws of England*, 3rd Ed., vol. 32, p. 249].

In its more general sense, "land" comprehends any ground, soil, or earth whatsoever; including fields, meadows, pastures, woods, moors, waters, marshes, and rock. [*Reynard* v *City of Caldwell* 42 P 2d 292, 296; *Holmes* v *U.S.* CCA Okl, 53 F 2d 960, 963].

In its more limited sense, "land" denotes the quantity and character of the interest or estate which a person may own on land. [*Holmes* v *U.S.* CCA Okl, 53 F 2d 960, 963].

"Land" may include any estate or interest in lands, either legal or equitable, as well as easements and incorporeal hereditaments. [*Reynard* v *City of Caldwell* 42 P 2d 292, 297; *Jones* v *Magruder* DC Md, 42 F Supp 193, 198].

The word "land" which is *nomen generalissimum*, includes, not only the face of the earth, but everything under it or over it. [*The Anant Mills Co. Ltd.* v *State of Gujarat* AIR 1975 SC 1234: (1975)3 SCR 220: (1975)2 SCC 175].

The expression "land" in its legal sense is a comprehensive expression which is wide enough to include structure, if any, raised thereon. [*P. Rami Reddy* v *State of A.P.* AIR 1988 SC 1626: (1988)3 SCC 433]. But "land" under s. 78A of the Calcutta Improvement Act 1911, does not include structures on it. [*Nandu Kumar Banerjee* v *Board of Trustees* AIR 1957 Cal 578].

"Land" means land which is used or capable of being used for agriculture or horticulture and includes land which is an orchard, kharhur or pasturage or forest land or even land perennially submerged under water or homestead of a landholder. [*K.N. Farms Industries Pvt. Ltd.* v *State of Bihar* AIR 1994 Pat 111]. 'Tank' which is used for agriculture purposes would come within the purview of the definition of land. [*K.N. Farms Industries Pvt. Ltd.* v *State of Bihar* AIR 1994 Pat 111; *Shankar Prasad Sahi* v *State of Bihar* AIR 1994 Pat 120; *Jilubhai* v *State of Gujarat* 1994 AIR SCW 4181].

▸ *Meaning under Land Acquisition Act 1894, s. 3(a).* Land includes benefits to arise out of land, and things attached to the earth or permanently fastened to anything attached to the earth.

▸ *Meaning under Constitution of India.* The word "land" in Entry 49 of List 2 is wide enough to include all lands, whether agricultural or not, and it would be plainly unreasonable to assume that it includes non-agricultural lands but does not include agricultural lands. [*Raja Jagannath Baksh Singh* v *State of U.P.* AIR 1962 SC 1563: (1962)46 ITR 169: 1963 Supp (1) SCR 220].

The word 'land' in Entry 18 is not restricted to agricultural land as are the latter portions of it. It would cover all types of land—rural or urban, agricultural or non-agricultural, vacant fallows or pastures. [*Accountant and Secretarial Services Pvt. Ltd.* v *Union of India* AIR 1988 SC 1708: (1988)4 SCC 324: 1988 Supp (1) SCR 493: JT 1988(3) SC 78].


- **Agricultural land** p. 52.
- **Annexed to the land** p. 63.
- **Arable land** p. 73.
- **Cultivable land** p. 212.
- **Forest land** p. 367.
- **Jeroyiti land** p. 485.
- **Rented land** p. 746.
- **Uncultivated land** p. 862.
- **Waste lands** p. 894.


**Land tax.** Property tax. A tax laid upon the legal or beneficial owner of real property, and apportioned upon the assessed value of his land.

**Landed cost.** The cost of purchasing goods including all charges incurred up to the time of landing them in the country of destination.

**Landholder.** Landholder means a person owning an estate or part thereof and includes every person entitled to collect the rents of the whole or any portion of the estate by virtue of any transfer from the owner of his predecessor-in-title or of any order of a competent court or of any provision of law.

The expression "landholder" who obviously is a possessor of interest in land means a person to whom rent is payable, and by legal fiction it shall include his predecessor in interest as also successor in interest to whom the rent was or is payable. [*Richpal Singh* v *Desh Raj Singh* AIR 1981 SC 1960: (1982)1 SCR 368: (1981)4 SCC 194].

**Landless person.** Those persons whose main source of livelihood is agriculture and who are agriculturists residing in the village where the land is situated and who has no land in their name. [*U.P. Bhoodan Yagna Samiti* v *Braj Kishore* AIR 1988 SC 2239: (1988)4 SCC 274: JT 1988(2) SC 15].

**Landlord.** He of whom lands or tenements are holder. He who, being the owner of an estate in land, or a rental property, has leased it to another person, called the "tenant". [Black's *Law Dictionary*, 5th Ed.].

At common law, the feudal lord who retained the fee of the land; one who leases real property to another. [Black's *Law Dictionary*, 8th Ed.].

NOTE: A landlord may not necessarily be the owner. Any person who is entitled to receive rent in respect of any building on his own account or on behalf, or for the benefit of any other person, is a landlord. [*Pukhraj Jain* v *Padma Kashyap* AIR 1990 SC 1133].

An agent is defined as a landlord; so is a trustee; so is a guardian. The definition being wide and also inclusive, does not exclude a person who at all material times acted as a landlord to the knowledge of all the parties concerned and whose authority to deal with the premises has never been disputed. [*Kasturchand* v *Raman Rajan* AIR 1994 SC 217: 1993 AIR SCW 3662].

Receiver cannot be regarded 'landlord' beyond his receivership. [*Ponnammal* v *N. Muthuswamy Chettiar* (1995)1 LW 445 (SC)].

The word 'landlord' does not mean the lord of the soil, but the person between whom and the tenant the relation of landlord and tenant exists. [*Churchward* v *Ford* (1957)2 H&N 446]. The expression includes a tenant (holding under the owner) who has sub-let to a sub-tenant and stands to that sub-tenant in relation of landlord.

The word landlord includes his legal representatives. [*Pukhraj Jain* v *Padma Kashyap* AIR 1990 SC 1133].

▸*Meaning under Requisitioning and Acquisition of Immovable Property Act 1952, s. 2(c).* Any person who for the time being is receiving or is entitled to receive, the rent of any premises, whether on his own account, or on account or on behalf or for the benefit, of any other person or as a trustee, guardian or receiver for any other person, or who would so receive the rent or be entitled to receive the rent if the premises were let to a tenant.

**Landowner.** One who owns land. [Black's *Law Dictionary*, 8th Ed.]. He is the person for the time being receiving the rent of land, whether on his own account or as a trustee for any other person, or who would so receive it if the land were let at a rent.

**Lapse.** As verb, in respect of an estate or right, it means to pass away or revert to someone else because conditions have not been fulfilled or because a person entitled to possession has failed in some duty; in respect of a devise, grant, etc., it means to become void. It may also mean to glide; to pass slowly, silently, or by degrees; to fall or fail.

As noun, it means the termination of a right or privilege because of a failure to exercise it within some time-limit or because a contingency has occurred or not occurred. In its application to wills and estates, it means the failure of a testamentary gift, especially when the beneficiary dies before the testator dies.

**Larceny.** The unlawful taking and carrying away of property of another with intent to appropriate it, to use it inconsistent with latter's rights. [*U.S.* v *Johnson* 433 F 2d 1160, 1163].

Obtaining possession of property by fraud, trick or device with preconceived design or intent to appropriate, convert or steal is "larceny". [*John* v *United States* 79 F 2d 136; *People* v *Cook* 51 P 2d 169, 170].

NOTE: The essential elements of a "larceny" are an actual or constructive taking away of the goods or property of another without the consent and against the will of the owner and with a felonious intent. [*People* v *Goodchild* 242 NW 2d 465, 468].

"Larceny" in English law contemplated permanent gain or loss. [*K.N. Mehra* v *State of Rajasthan* AIR 1957 SC 369].

**Largesse.** Generosity; beneficence; alms giving; aid, assistance; benefaction; bounty; charity.

**Lascivious.** Corrupt; debauched; depraved; goatish; obscene; immodest; immoral; lecherous; lewd; unblushing; carnal; erotic; fleshly; lustful; sex-ridden; promiscuous; unchaste.

Conduct which is wanton, lewd, and lustful, and tending to produce voluptuous or lewd emotions. [Black's *Law Dictionary*, 5th Ed.].

**Lascivious cohabitation.** The offence committed by two persons not married to each other who live together as husband and wife and engage in sexual intercourse. [Black's *Law Dictionary*, 7th Ed.].

The offence committed by an unmarried man and woman who live together as husband and wife and engage in sexual intercourse. [Black's *Law Dictionary*, 8th Ed.].

**Last-in, first out (LIFO).** An accounting method that assumes that the most recent purchases are sold or used first, matching current costs against current revenues. [Black's *Law Dictionary*, 7th Ed.].

A method of identifying and valuing inventories which assumes that last goods purchased are the first ones sold and therefore the goods left in inventory at the end of the year are assumed to be those first purchased. [*L.S. Ayres & Co.* v *U.S.* CA Ind, 285 F 2d 113, 114].

**Latent.** Hidden; concealed; dormant; absconditus; below the surface; behind the scenes, camouflaged; covert; indiscernible; submerged; unapparent; under the surface; undiscovered; unexposed; unmanifested; unrevealed; veiled.

**Latent ambiguity.** A defect which does not appear on the face of language used or an instrument being considered. It arises when language is clear and intelligible and suggests but a single meaning, but some extrinsic fact or some extraneous evidence creates a necessity for interpretation or a choice between two or more possible meanings. [*Conkle* v *Conkle* 31 Ohio App 2d 44: 285 NE 2d 883, 887].

**Latent defect.** See under DEFECT p. 240.

**Lateral.** Pertaining to, proceeding from, or directed towards the side.

**Lateral road.** One which proceeds from some point of the main trunk between its terminal. It is but another name for a branch road, both being part of the main road.

**Law.** Body of rules; established rule; rule of conduct; canon; charter; statute; enactment; legal code; decree; decree absolute; command; expressed command; dictum.

The regime that orders human activities and relations through systematic application of the force of politically organised society, or through social pressure, backed by force, in such a society; the legal system; the aggregate of legislation, judicial precedents, and accepted legal principles; the body of auhoritative grounds of judicial and administrative action; the set of rules or principles dealing with a specific area of a legal system; the judicial and administrative process; legal action and proceedings; a statute; the legal profession. [Black's *Law Dictionary*, 8th Ed.].

The word may, *inter alia*, mean and embrace; body of principles, standards and rules promulgated by government [*State ex rel. Conway* v *Superior Court within and for Greenlee County* 131 P 2d 983, 986]; command which obliges a person or persons and obliges generally to acts or forbearances of a class; constitution or constitutional provision [*Baston Elevated Ry. Co.* v *Commonwealth* 39 NE 2d 87, 109; *Wickham* v *Grand River Dam Authority* 118 P 2d 640, 643]; general rule of human action, taking cognizance only of external acts, enforced by a determinate authority, which authority is human, and among human authorities is that which is paramount in a political society; grant by legislature [*City of Los Angeles* v *Pacific Land Corporation* 41 Cal App 2d 223]; judicial decisions, judgments or decrees [*West* v *American Telephone & Telegraph Co.* 85 L Ed 139]; long-established local custom which has the force of law [*Dubois* v *Hopburn* 9 L Ed 325]; municipal ordinance; prescribed rules of action or conduct [*U.S. Fidelity & Guaranty Co.* v *Guenther* 74 L Ed 683]; rule of civil conduct commanding what is right and prohibiting what is wrong [*Rich Hill Coal Co.* v *Bashore* 7 A 2d 302, 312]; rules promulgated by government [*State ex rel. Conway* v *Superior Court within and for Greenlee County* 131 P 2d 983, 986]; statute or enactment of legislative body [*Shute* v *Frohmiller* 90 P 2d 998, 1001].

Stated broadly, a law generally is a body of rules which have been laid down for determining legal rights and legal obligations which are recognised by courts. [*Rajkumar Nursingh Pratap Singh Deo* v *State of Orissa* AIR 1964 SC 1793].

"Law" means law enacted by the State. Law must have some firmness. Law means positive State-made law. [*Additional District Magistrate, Jabalpur* v *Shivakant Shukla* AIR 1976 SC 1207: 1976 (Supp) SCR 172: (1976)2 SCC 521: 1976 Cr LJ 945: 1976 Cr LR (SC) 303].

NOTE: The test of law is, whether the act in question embodies the command of the sovereign prescribing a binding rule of conduct determining legal rights and obligations. Law is the emanation of the will of the sovereign which prescribes a binding rule of conduct for observance in future and affecting legal rights and obligations of persons subject to his power. [*Kudi Municipality* v *New Chhotalal Mills Co. Ltd.* AIR 1965 Guj 993].

A law must follow the customary forms of law-making and must be expressed as a binding rule of conduct. There is generally an established method for the enactment of laws and the laws when enacted, have also a distinct form. It is not every indication of the will of the ruler, however expressed, which amounts to law. An indication of the will meant to bind as rule of conduct and enacted with some formality either traditional or specially devised for the occasion, results in a law, but not an agreement to which there are two parties one of which is the ruler. [*Nagpur Cotton Mills Ltd.* v *Board of Revenue, M.P.* AIR 1964 SC 888, referred to in *State of Rajasthan* v *Bundi Electric Supply Co. Ltd.* AIR 1970 Raj 36, 46].

▸*Meaning under Constitution of India, Art. 13(3)(a).* Law includes any ordinance, order, bye-law, rule, regulation, notification, custom or usage having in the territory of India the force of law.

The expression 'law' as used in Art. 13 is law enacted in exercise of the legislative power. [*R.S. Nayak* v *A.R. Antulay* AIR 1984 SC 684: (1984)2 SCR 495: (1984)2

SCC 183: 1984 Cr LJ 613: 1984(1) Crimes 568: 1984 Cr LR (SC) 163: 1984 SCC (Cri) 172: 1984(1) SLR 619].

An amendment to the Constitution is law within the meaning of Art. 13(2) and is therefore subject to Part III of the Constitution. [*L.C. Golak Nath* v *State of Punjab* AIR 1967 SC 1643: (1967)2 SCR 762: 1967 SLR 301].

Law is defined under Art. 13(3)(*a*) to include a notification. [*Madhubhai Amathalal Gandhi* v *Union of India* AIR 1961 SC 21: (1961)1 SCR 191: (1961)1 SCJ 442].

In Art. 21, the word "law" has been used in the sense of State made law and not as an equivalent of law in the abstract or general sense embodying the principles of natural justice. [*A.K. Gopalan* v *State of Madras* AIR 1950 SC 27: 1950 SCR 88].

The word "law" in Art. 21 refers to law made by the State and not to positive law or law in the abstract sense embodying the principles of natural justice, and "procedure established by law" means procedure established by law made by the State, that is to say, by the Union Parliament or the Legislatures of the States. [*Ram Chandra Prasad* v *State of Bihar* AIR 1961 SC 1629: (1961)2 Cr LJ 811: (1962)2 SCR 50: (1962)2 SCJ 13].

The word "law" in the expression 'procedure established by law' in Art. 21 means a law which is right, just and fair and not arbitrary, fanciful or oppressive. [*Sunil Batra* v *Delhi Administration* AIR 1978 SC 1675: (1978)4 SCC 494: 1978 Cr LJ 1741: (1979)1 SCR 392: 1979 SCC (Cri) 155].

NOTE: "Law" in Art. 21 affecting personal liberty must satisfy the test of one or more of the rights under Art. 19 and the test of reasonableness under Art. 14. [*Mrs. Maneka Gandhi* v *Union of India* AIR 1978 SC 597: (1978)1 SCC 248: (1979)2 SCR 621].

Executive or departmental instruction does not come under law under Art. 25(2). [*Bijoe Emmanuel* v *State of Kerala* AIR 1987 SC 748: (1986)3 SCC 615: (1986)3 SCR 518: JT 1986 SC 115].

The expression "law" in Art. 26(*d*) meant a law passed by a competent legislature. [*Tilkayat Shri Govindlalji Maharaj* v *State of Rajasthan* AIR 1963 SC 1638: (1964)1 SCR 561: (1964)2 SCJ 715].

*Ordinance—a law.* Under Art. 13(3)(*a*) of the Constitution of India, unless the context otherwise requires, law includes any ordinance, order, by-law, rule, regulation, notification, custom or usage having in the territory of India the force of law.

The definition of "law" in Art. 13, as including an ordinance is limited for the purpose of that Article. By Art. 366 an existing law is defined to include an ordinance. Quite apart from these definitions on general jurisprudential grounds an ordinance will pass as law. [*Gwalior Rayons Silk Mfg. Co.* v *Government of Kerala* AIR 1979 Ker 56: 1978 Ker LT 552]. An ordinance answers the expression "law" as contemplated in Art. 21, Constitution of India. [*A.K. Roy* v *Union of India* AIR 1982 SC 710: 1982 Cr LJ 340: (1982)2 SCJ 68: 1982 MLJ (Cr) 524: 1982 Cr LR (SC) 176: (1982)2 Chand LR (Cr) 333: 1982 SCC (Cri) 152].

*Law—what is not.* By laws of a co-operative society framed in pursuance of the provisions of a statute cannot be held to be law or to have the force of law. [*Co-operative Central Bank* v *Additional Industrial Tribunal* (1969)2 SCC 43: (1970)1 SCR 205: AIR 1970 SC 245: (1970)1 SCJ 295].

An executive order cannot be regarded as 'existing law' or 'law in force'. [*K.O. John* v *State* AIR 1956 Trav-Co 117].


- **According to law** p. 18.
- **Act of law** p. 30.
- **Adjective law** p. 39.
- **Administrative law** p. 41.
- **Authority of law** p. 88.
- **Bylaw** p. 116.
- **Canon law** p. 121.
- **Civil law** p. 145.
- **Common law** p. 159.
- **Conflict of laws** p. 172.
- **Constitutional law** p. 179.
- **Criminal law** p. 208.
- **Due course of law** p. 285.
- **Due process of law** p. 285.
- **Ecclesiastical law** p. 292.
- **Equal protection of the laws** p. 313.
- **Equality before the law** p. 313.

- **Error of law apparent on the face of record** p. 315.
- **Error of law on the face of award** p. 315.
- **Ex post facto law** p. 325.
- **Existing law** p. 329.
- **Fiction of law** p. 351.
- **Foreign system of law** p. 366.
- **General law** p. 384.
- **Gresham's law** p. 399.
- **Heir at law** p. 411.
- **In accordance with law** p. 438.
- **In due course of law** p. 439.
- **In law** p. 440.
- **Information as to law** p. 458.
- **International economic law** p. 475.
- **International law** p. 475.
- **Judge-made law** p. 489.
- **Justified by law** p. 501.
- **Local law** p. 540.
- **Malice in law** p. 553.
- **Maritime law** p. 562.
- **Martial law** p. 565.
- **Marumakkattayam law** p. 566.
- **Matter of law** p. 570.
- **Military law** p. 578.
- **Mistake of law** p. 588.
- **Municipal law** p. 594.
- **Natural law** p. 600.
- **Naval law** p. 600.
- **Obstructing process under law** p. 617.
- **Presumption of law** p. 682.
- **Private international law** p. 686.
- **Prize law** p. 690.
- **Procedure established by law** p. 691.
- **Public international law** p. 710.
- **Quasi-laws** p. 721.
- **Retrospective law** p. 759.
- **Rule of law** p. 767.
- **Substantial question of law.** See under QUESTION p. 721.
- **Source of law** p. 803.
- **Special law** p. 805.
- **Technical defect in law** p. 832.
- **Written law** p. 906.


**Law-abiding.** According to law; law-revering; unimpeachable; within the law; upstanding; well-principled.

**Law and order problem.** If an act is confined to an individual without directly or indirectly affecting the tempo of the life of the community, it may be a matter of law and order only. [*Padma Sadhu* v *State of Orissa* 1999 Cr LJ 4269].

If the propensity or potentiality remains within a few individuals and does not reach even a segment of the community, there is no difficulty at all to term such an act as a breach of law and order but if the propensity and potentiality of one act would affect the tempo of life of a segment of the community, one can unhesitatingly say that it affects the public order. [*Dr. Ram Manohar Lohia* v *State of Bihar* (1966)1 SCR 709: AIR 1966 SC 740: 1966 Cr LJ 608; *Arun Ghosh* v *State of West Bengal* (1970)1 SCC 98: 1970 SCC (Cri) 67: 1970 Cr LJ 1136; *Ram Ranjan Chatterjee* v *State of West Bengal* (1975)4 SCC 143: 1975 SCC (Cri) 400: 1975 Cr LJ 588; *Ashok Kumar* v *Delhi Administration* (1982)2 SCC 403: 1982 SCC (Cri) 451: 1982 Cr LJ 1191].

If a contravention in its effect is confined only to a few individuals directly involved as distinct from a wide spectrum of public, it could raise the problem of law and order only. It is the length, magnitude and the intensity of the terror wave unleased by a particular eruption of disorder that helps distinguish it as an act affecting 'public order' from that concerning 'law and order'. [*Victoria Fernandes* v *Lalmal Sawma* (1992)2 SCC 97: 1992 Cr LJ 702].

**Law charges.** Costs incurred in court in the prosecution or defence to be paid by the party concerned.

**Law graduate.** A person who has obtained a bachelor's degree in law from any university established by law in India. [Advocates Act 1961, s. 2(*h*)].

**Law Lords.** Members of the House of Lords (of England) qualified to perform its legal work; peers in the British Parliament who have held high judicial office, or have been distinguished in the legal profession, *i.e.*, a puisne judge of the High Court or higher office.

**Law merchant.** The term "law merchant" is an ambiguous one. The relationship which it bears to the common law is particularly difficult to define. It is sometimes spoken of as "ancient" and there is a tendency to attribute to it, in an analogy to an immemorial local custom, the requisite of existence from time immemorial. It is sometime said to form part of the common law. This statement, however, is somewhat misleading, for it veils the fact that the law merchant is merely a collection of usages. It may be defined as a number of usages, each of which exist among merchants and persons engaged in mercantile transactions, not only in one particular country but throughout the civilised world, and each of which has acquired such notoriety, not only amongst those persons, but also in the mercantile world at large, that the courts will take judicial notice of it. A usage of the law merchant has therefore two characteristics—it must in the first place amount to *jus gentium*, that is to say, it must be in vogue beyond the limits of the country and its notoriety must be cosmopolitan rather than national; and in the second place it must be of such a nature that it will receive judicial notice in the courts. "It does not follow, however, that every mercantile usage of which the courts take judicial notice forms part of the law merchant. It is composed of those usages of merchants and traders in the different departments of trade which have been ratified by the decisions of courts of law and adopted as settled law with a view to the interests of trade and the public convenience". [Halsbury's *Laws of England*, 3rd Ed., vol. 11, pp. 189, 190].

"The law merchant is sometimes spoken of as a fixed body of law, forming part of the common law, and as it were coeval with it. But as a matter of legal history, this view is altogether incorrect. The law merchant thus spoken of with reference to bills of exchange and other negotiable securities, though forming part of the general body of the *lex mercatoria*, is of comparatively recent origin. It is neither more nor less than the usages of merchants and traders in the different departments of trade, ratified by the decisions of courts of law, which, upon such usages being proved before them, have adopted them as settled law with a view to the interests of trade and the public convenience, the court proceeding herein on the well-known principle of law that, with reference to transactions in the different departments of trade, courts of law, in giving effect to the contracts and dealings of the parties, will assume that the latter have dealt with one another on the footing of any custom or usage prevailing generally in the particular department. By this process, what before was usage only, unsanctioned by legal decision, has become engrafted upon, or incorporated into, the common law, and may thus be said to form part of it. 'When a general usage has been judicially ascertained and established', says Lord Campbell, in *Brandao* v *Barnett* [(1846)12 Cl & F 787, 805] 'it becomes a part of the law merchant, which courts of justice are bound to know and recognise'." [*Goodwin* v *Robarts* (1875) LR 10 Exch 337, *per cur.*, 346].

**Law municipal.** The law of a State, as opposed to international law; rules of civil conduct prescribed by the supreme power in the State.

That which pertains solely to the citizens and inhabitants of a State, and is thus distinguished from political law, commercial law, and international law. [*City of Louisville* v *Babb* CCA Ind, 75 F 2d 162, 165]. In its more common and narrower connotation however it means those laws which pertain to towns, cities and villages and their local government. [*People ex rel. Ray* v *Martin* 294 NY 61: 60 NE 2d 541, 547, 548].

**Law of nations.** Law of nations or international law is the name for the body of customary and treaty rules which are considered legally binding by States in their intercourse with one another.

NOTE: In order to prove a rule of law of nations, it must be shown either to have received the express sanction of international agreement or it must have grown to be part of law of nations by the frequent practical recognition of States in their dealings with one another.

**Law of the flag.** The law of the nation whose flag is flown by a particular vessel; a shipowner who sends a vessel into a foreign port gives notice by the flag to all potential contracting parties of the owner's intent that law to regulate all contracts made involving the ship or its cargo.

It is the law of the county under whose flag a ship sails in which goods are contracted to be carried.

NOTE: The presumption that the proper law is that of the flag operates in the case of all maritime contracts. The presumption is particularly strong in the case of contracts made during the course of the voyage, such as bottomry bonds. The majority of maritime contracts, however, such as charter-parties and bills of lading, are made on land prior to the sailing of the ship, and in such cases the presumption in favour of the law of the flag could be more easily displaced. [Graveson's *Conflict of Laws*, 6th Ed., p. 439].

**Law reports.** Published volumes containing the decisions and opinions of the higher courts of the country.

NOTE: It is provided in s. 3 of the Indian Law Reports Act 1875 that no court is bound to hear and cite the report of any case decided by a High Court, other than a report published under the authority of the State Government. But the practice is otherwise.

**Lawbreaker.** Arsonist; convict; criminal; delinquent; hoodlum; malefactor; malfeasor; offender; wrongdoer.

**Lawful.** According to fiat; according to law; authorised by law; conformable to law; conformable with the law; in accordance with the law; in conformity to the law; law-abiding; legitimate; permissible; sanctioned by law; prescribed by law; warranted by law; within the law; having the qualifications prescribed by law; not contrary to nor forbidden by the law.

"Lawful" means that which is in conformity with the principle or spirit of the law whether moral or judicial. The term does not connote enjoined by law but the opposite of unlawful. [*Captain D'Souza* v *Pashupati Nath Sarkar* 1968 Cr LJ 405 (Cal)].

"Lawful" is defined as "legal, warranted or authorised by law". "Legal" and "lawful" convey the same sense and are usually interchangeable. What is legal is lawful. [*Krishna Kishore Firm* v *Government of A.P.* AIR 1990 SC 2292: 1990 Supp (2) SCR 8: JT 1990(4) SC 241: (1991)1 SCC 184].

The natural meaning in a statute of the words 'it shall be lawful' is permissive only, but if the words are used to effectuate a legal right, they are compulsory. [Wharton's *Law Lexicon*, 14th Ed.].

"The words 'it shall be lawful' [in a statute] are distinctly words of permission only—they are enabling and empowering words. They confer a legislative right and power on the individual named to do a particular thing, and the true question is not whether they mean something different, but whether, regard being had to the person so enabled—to the subject-matter, to the general objects of the statute, and to the person or class of persons for whose benefit the power may be intended to have been conferred—they do, or do not, create a duty in the person on whom it is conferred, to exercise it". [*Julius* v *Oxford (Bp.)* (1880)5 App Cas 214, 229, 230, *per* Lord Penzance].

NOTE: "The words 'it shall be lawful', in a statute, whether obligatory or not, depends on the subject-matter". [*Castelli* v *Groom* (1852)18 QB 490, 495, *per* Crompton, J.].

*"Lawful" and "legal"—principal distinction.* The principal distinction between the terms "lawful" and "legal" is that the former contemplates the substance of law, the latter the form of law. [*Krishna Kishore Firm* v *Government of A.P.* AIR 1990 SC 2292: 1990 Supp (2) SCR 8: JT 1990(4) SC 241: (1991)1 SCC 184]. To say of an act that it is "lawful" implies that it is authorised, sanctioned, or at any rate not forbidden, by law. To say that it is "legal" implies that it is done or performed in accordance with the forms and usages of law, or in a technical manner. [Black's *Law Dictionary*, 5th Ed.]. Lawful is wider in connotation than legal [*Krishna Kishore Firm* v *Government of A.P.* AIR 1990 SC 2292: 1990 Supp (2) SCR 8: JT 1990(4) SC 241: (1991)1 SCC 184]. 'Lawful' visualises all that is not illegal against law or even permissible, whereas legal is associated with provisions in the Act, rules,

etc. [*Krishna Kishore Firm* v *Government of A.P.*, supra].

**Lawful age.** Legal age; full age; majority; the age, usually defined by statute, at which a person is legally capable of agreeing to a contract, executing a will, maintaining a lawsuit, or the like; the age, usually defined by statute, at which a person attains full legal rights, especially civil and political rights, such as, the right to vote.

**Lawful alienation.** It means alienation made completely in accordance with law. It may not mean necessarily for a family consideration. [*Shripad Gajanan Suthanker* v *Dattaram Kashinath Suthankar* AIR 1974 SC 878: (1974)3 SCR 474: (1974)2 SCC 156].

**Lawful arrest.** The taking of a person into legal custody either under a valid warrant or on probable cause that the person has committed a crime. [Black's *Law Dictionary*, 8th Ed.].

**Lawful authority.** The authority who has the right to exercise public power, to require obedience to its lawful commands, to command or act in the public name.

The words 'lawful authority' mean an authority which is given or recognised by law and which permits the act in question to be done. They do not mean an authority which has not been shown to be unlawful. [*Emperor* v *Abidalli Jaffer Bhoy* 49 Bom LR 336: AIR 1947 Bom 465, *per* Sen and Gagendragadkar, JJ.].

**Lawful cause.** Legitimate reason for acting, based on the law or on the evidence in a particular case as contrasted with acting on a whim or out of prejudice or for a reason not recognised by law.

**Lawful damages.** Such damages as the law fixes and are ascertainable in a court of law. [*Carr* v *U.S.* DC Ky, 28 F Supp 236, 241].

**Lawful excuse.** "Lawful excuse" means that there is a justification for the contravention which is recognised by law. [*State of U.P.* v *Firm Deo Dutt Lakhan Lal* AIR 1966 All 73 (FB)].

NOTE: What is lawful excuse depends upon the facts and circumstances of each case and the law. [*State of U.P.* v *Firm Deo Dutt Lakhan Lal*, supra].

**Lawful guardian.** The words 'lawful guardian' are wider than the expression 'legal guardian'. The words mean that whenever the relationship of a guardian and a ward is established by means which are lawful and legitimate, that relationship is intended to be included. [*State* v *Ramji Vithal* AIR 1958 Bom 381: 1958 Cr LJ 1296].

**Lawful heirs.** The words "lawful heirs" used in a will must be construed in their larger and ordinary sense. Where property is devised for life, with remainder to the testator's "lawful heirs", the words "lawful heirs" refer to those persons who were the lawful heirs of the testator at the time of his death.

**Lawful marriage.** Marriage taking place in accordance with law.

NOTE: The presumption in favour of a lawful marriage would arise where there was prolonged and continued cohabitation as husband and wife and where there was no insurmountable obstacle to such a marriage. [*Mohd. Amin* v *Vakil Ahmed* AIR 1952 SC 358: 1952 SCJ 539: 1952 SCR 1133].

**Lawful possession.** "Lawful possession" means a legal possession which is also rightful or at least excusable.

NOTE: The domain of lawful possession is control with some legal basis. Lawful possession is based on some rule, sanction or excuse. A person in possession *de jure*, actually or constructively, has the right to use, enjoy, or alienate property. [*Krishna Kishore Firm* v *Government of A.P.* AIR 1990 SC 2292: 1990 Supp (2) SCR 8: JT 1990(4) SC 241: (1991)1 SCC 184].

"Lawful possession" is not litigious possession; must have some foundation in a legal right to possess the property which cannot be equated with a temporary right to enforce recovery of the property in case a person is wrongfully or forceably dispossessed from it. [*M.C. Chockalingam* v *V. Manickavasagam* AIR 1974 SC 104: (1974)2 SCR 143: (1974)1 SCC 48].

**Lawfully.** The expression postulates cases in which a person holds a relation as either directly to create or by implication reasonably to justify a reference that by some act done for another person the party doing the act is entitled to look for compensation for it to one for whom it is done. [*Nuli Kanaka* v *Tetail Sriranga Venkata* AIR 1966 AP 297 referring to Indian Contract Act 1872, s. 70].

The word 'lawfully' indicates that after something is delivered or something is done by one person for another and that thing is accepted and enjoyed by the latter, a lawful relationship is born between the two which under the provisions of s. 70 of the Indian Contract Act 1872 gives rise to a claim for compensation. [*State of West Bengal* v *M/s. B.K. Mondal and Sons* AIR 1962 SC 779: 1962 Supp (1) SCR 876].

**Lawless.** Having no laws or enforcement of them; disregarding laws; not subject or obedient to law of any sort; without the sanction or authority of law; unruly; disobedient; unbridled, uncontrolled; anarchic; disorderly; rebellious; recalcitrant; unaccountable; wayward.

**Lawmaker.** A legislator; formulator of laws; legislative draftsman; member of a legislature.

**Laws in force.** Laws passed or made by a legislature or other competent authority and existing at the material time and actually in force.

▸ *Constitution of India: Meaning under various Articles*: ARTICLE 13(3)(A). The definition of the phrase 'laws in force' is an inclusive definition and is intended to include laws passed or made by a legislature or other competent authority before the commencement of the Constitution, irrespective of the fact that the law or any part thereof was not in operation in particular areas or at all. In other words, laws, which were not in operation, though on the statute book, were included in the phrase 'law in force'. But the second definition does not in any way restrict the ambit of the word 'law' in the first clause as extended by the definition of that word. It merely seeks to amplify it by including something which, but for the second definition, would not be included by the first definition. There are compelling reasons why custom and usage having in the territory of India the force of the law must be held to be contemplated by the expression 'all laws in force'. [*Sant Ram* v *Labh Singh* AIR 1965 SC 314, 316; *Panch Gujar* v *Amar Singh* AIR 1954 Raj 100: 1954 Raj LW 204].

ARTICLE 20. The expression 'law in force' means 'law actually in force and not law deemed to be in force by retrospective operation of an amendment'. [*Rama Shankar Tewari* v *State* 1954 AWR (HC) 334: 1954 Cr LJ 1212: AIR 1954 All 562 (DB)].

The phrase 'law in force' must be understood in its natural sense as being the law in fact in existence and in operation at the time of the commission of the offence as distinct from the law deemed to have become operative by virtue of the power of legislature to pass retrospective laws. [*Shiv Bahadur Singh* v *State of VP* 1952 SCJ 563: 1953 Cr LJ 1480: AIR 1953 SC 394].

ARTICLE 372. The words 'law in force' are wide enough to include not merely a legislative enactment but also any regulation or order which has the force of law. But an order must be a legislative and not an executive order before it can come within the definition of law. [*Edward Mills Co. Ltd., Beawar* v *State of Ajmer* AIR 1955 SC 25, 31].

**NOTE: A rule of construction is not a 'law in force' within the meaning of Art. 372. [*Superintendent and Remembrancer of Legal Affairs, West Bengal* v *Corporation of Calcutta* AIR 1967 SC 997, 1007].**

**Laws of a State.** The laws enacted by the Legislature of a State as distinguished from executive orders. [*Sundararamier* v *State of Andhra Pradesh* 1958 SCR 1422:1958 SCJ 459: 1958 SCA 492: AIR 1958 SC 468].

**Lawsuit.** An action or proceeding in a civil court; a process in law instituted by one party to compel another to do him justice. [*Shepherd* v *Standard Motor Co.* 92 SW 2d 337].

**Lawyer.** A person learned in law, as an advocate, pleader etc.; any person who prosecutes or defends causes in courts of record or other judicial tribunals.

**Lay.** As noun, in Maritime Law it means a share of the profits of a fishing or whaling trip, akin to wages, allotted to the officers and seamen.

As adjective, it means non-clerical, non-professional.

As verb, it means to allege or assert.

**Lay days.** Running or consecutive days. It is a term used as to the time of loading and unloading ships. They are the days which are allowed by a charter-party for loading and unloading the ship. If the vessel is detained beyond the period allowed demurrage becomes payable. [Jowitt's *Dictionary of English Law*, 2nd Ed.].

**Lay-off.** "Lay-off" means the termination of employment at the employer's instigation, especially, the termination—either temporary or permanent—of a large number of employees in a short time. [Black's *Law Dictionary*, 8th Ed.].

"Lay-off" means to discontinue work or activity; to dismiss or discharge temporarily. When workers are in employment and they are laid off, that immediately results in their unemployment, howsoever temporarily it may be. [*Priya Laxmi Mills Ltd.* v *Mazdoor Mahajan Mandal, Baroda* AIR 1976 SC 2584: (1977)1 SCR 709: (1977)1 SCC 28].

NOTE: The term "lay-off" implies that the employer is not in a position to offer employment to his employee and, therefore, he terminates his employment temporarily during the emergency. [*Nutun Mills* v *Employees' State Insurance Corporation* AIR 1956 Bom 336: ILR (1956) Bom 575].

▸ *Meaning under Industrial Disputes Act 1947, s. 2(kkk).* Lay-off, (with its grammatical variations and cognate expressions), means the failure, refusal or inability of an employer on account of shortage of coal, power, or raw materials or the accumulation of stocks or the breakdown of machinery or natural calamity or for any other connected reason to give employment to a workman whose name is borne on the muster-rolls of his industrial establishment and who has not been retrenched.

NOTE: Every workman whose name is borne on the muster-rolls of the industrial establishment and who presents himself for work at the establishment at the time appointed for the purpose during normal working hours on any day and is not given employment by the employer within two hours of his so presenting himself shall be deemed to have been laid-off for that day within the meaning of this clause:

If, however, the workman, instead of being given employment at the commencement of any shift for any day is asked to present himself for the purpose during the second half of the shift for the day and is given employment then, he shall be deemed to have been laid-off only for one-half of that day: Provided further that if he is not given any such employment even after so presenting himself, he shall not be deemed to have been laid-off for the second half of the shift for the day and shall be entitled to full basic wages and dearness allowance for that part of the day.

Lay-off means the failure, refusal or inability of the employer on account of contingencies mentioned in cl. (*kkk*) to give employment to a workman whose name is borne on the muster-rolls of his industrial establishment. It is merely a fact of temporary unemployment of the workman in the work of the industrial establishment. [*The Workmen of M/s. Firestone Tyre & Rubber Co. of India (P) Ltd.* v *The Firestone Tyre & Rubber Co.* AIR 1976 SC 1775: (1976)3 SCR 369: (1976)3 SCC 819: 1976 Lab IC 1154: 1976(1) Lab LJ 493].

NOTE: The principles governing the case of lay-off are very akin to those applicable to a suspension case. When lay-off is found justified workmen may not be awarded any wages or compensation. [*The Workmen of M/s. Firestone Tyre & Rubber Co. of India (P) Ltd.* v *The Firestone Tyre & Rubber Co.* AIR 1976 SC 1775: (1976)3 SCR 369: (1976)3 SCC 819: 1976 Lab IC 1154: 1976(1) Lab LJ 493].

**Leading case.** A judicial decision that definitively settled an important legal rule or principle and that has since been often and consistently followed; an important, often the most important, judicial precedent on a particular legal issue; a reported case that is cited as the dispositive authority on an issue being litigated.

**Leading counsel.** The advocate to whom is entrusted the conduct of a legal proceeding; the counsel on either side of a litigated action who is charged with the principal management and direction of the party's case, as distinguished from his juniors or subordinates.

**Leading question.** One which instructs witness how to answer or puts into his mouth words to be echoed back [*People* v *Hamilton, Gen. Sess.* 30 NYS 2d 155, 158]; one which suggests to witness the answer desired. [*Little* v *State* 154 P 2d 772, 777; *State* v *Scott* 149 P 2d 152, 153; *Landers* v *State* 39 SW 2d 43, 44].

▸*Meaning under the Indian Evidence Act 1872, s. 141.* Any question suggesting the answer which the person putting it wishes or expects to receive is called a leading question.

NOTE: Leading questions must not, if objected to by the adverse party, be asked in an examination-in-chief or in a re-examination, except with the permission of the court. The court shall permit leading questions as to matters which are introductory or undisputed, or which have, in its opinion, been already sufficiently proved. [Indian Evidence Act 1872, s. 142]. Leading questions may, however, be asked in cross-examination, s. 143 of the Act.

**Leakage.** The waste of a liquid caused by its leaking from a storage container; an allowance against duties granted by customs to an importer of liquids for losses sustained by this waste; loss in value of a piece of intellectual property because of unauthorised copying. [Black's *Law Dictionary*, 8th Ed.].

Leakage means "any stealthy escape either through a small hole which might be discernible or through the pores of the material of which the cask is composed". [*Phoenix Ins. Co. of Hartford* v *De Monchy* (1929)141 LT 439, *per* Lord Dunedin].

**Learning.** Knowledge obtained by study or from instruction; scholarship; erudition; the act of acquiring knowledge or skill.

The word 'learning' is a word which is susceptible of various meanings. In Archbishop Whateley's work upon logic, it is placed among the equivocal words, *i.e.*, words which have two significations. He says, ' "learning" signifies either the act of acquiring knowledge, or the knowledge itself. *Exempli gratia*, he neglects his learning; Johnson was a man of learning'. [*Whicker* v *Hume* (1858)7 HL Cas 124].

'Learning' means imparting knowledge by instruction or teaching. [*Whicker* v *Hume* (1858)7 HL Cas 124, *per* Lord Chelmsford, L.C.].

▸*Meaning under the Hindu Gains of Learning Act 1930, s. 2.* The definition of the term 'learning' is very wide and almost encompasses within its sweep every acquired capacity which enables the acquirer of the capacity to pursue any trade, industry, profession or avocation in life. [*Chandrakant Monilal Shah* v *CIT* (1992)1 SCC 76: AIR 1992 SC 66].

• **Gains of learning** p. 380.

**Lease.** "An instrument in proper form by which the conditions of a contract of letting are finally ascertained, and which is intended to vest the right of exclusive possession in the lessee, either at once, if the term is to commence immediately, or at a future date, if the term is to commence subsequently, is a lease which takes effect from the date fixed for the commencement of the term without the necessity of actual entry by the lessee". [*Words and Phrases Legally Defined*, 2nd Ed. by John B. Saunders].

An instrument is usually construed as a lease if it contains words of present demise; and although it is called an agreement, and contains a stipulation for the subsequent granting of a formal lease, it is construed as a lease if the essential terms are fixed; especially if possession is to be taken under it, and if the covenants which would be inserted in the lease are to be binding at once. [Halsbury's *Laws of England*, 3rd Ed., vol. 23, pp. 435, 436].

▸ *Meaning under the Transfer of Property Act 1882, s. 105.* A lease of immovable property is a transfer of a right to enjoy such property, made for a certain time, express or implied, or in perpetuity, in consideration of a price or promised, or of money, a share of crops, service or any other thing of value, to be rendered periodically or on specified occasions to the transferor by the transferee who accepts the transfer of such terms.

A lease is a partial transfer, *i.e.*, a transfer of a right of enjoyment for a certain time. When the agreement vests in the lessee a right of possession for a certain time, it operates as a conveyance or a transfer and is a lease. [*Puran Singh Sahni* v *Sundari Bhagwandas Kripalani* (1991)2 SCC 180].

The normal connotation of the term "lease" is the preservation of the demised estate to be in occupation and enjoyment thereof for a specified period or in perpetuities for consideration; the corpus by user thereof does not disappear and at the expiry of the term or on termination the same is handed over to the lessor subject to the terms of the contract, express or implied. [*State of Karnataka* v *Subhash Rukmayya Guttedar* AIR 1993 SC 860: 1993 Supp (3) SCC 290, 294: 1992 AIR SCW 3492].

A 'lease' is a transfer of a right to enjoy the property. [*Tirath Ram Gupta* v *Gurubachan Singh* AIR 1987 SC 770: (1987)1 SCC 712: (1987)2 SCR 190: JT 1987(1) SC 365].

▸ *Meaning under the Indian Stamp Act 1899, s. 2(16).* For the purpose of the Stamp Act 'lease' means a lease of immovable property and includes also: (*a*) a *patta*; (*b*) a *kabuliat* or other undertaking in writing not being a counterpart of a lease, to cultivate, occupy or pay or deliver, rent for immovable property; (*c*) any instrument by which tolls of any description are let; (*d*) any writing on an application for a lease intended to signify that the application is granted.

NOTE: *'Lease' and 'licence'—distinction.* A 'lease' is a transfer of a right to enjoy the premises; whereas a 'licence' is a privilege to do something on the premises which otherwise would be unlawful. Section 105 of the Transfer of Property Act 1882 defines a lease. Section 52 of the Indian Easements Act 1882 defines a licence.

It is the creation of an interest in immovable property or a right to possess it that distinguishes a lease from a licence. A licence does not create an interest in the property to which it relates while a lease does. There is in other words transfer of a right to enjoy the property in case of a lease. As to whether a particular transaction creates a lease or a licence is always a question of intention of the parties which is to be inferred from the circumstances of each case. For the purpose of deciding whether a particular grant amounts to a lease or a licence, it is essential, therefore, to look to the substances and essence of the agreement and not to its form. [*Board of Revenue* v *A.M. Ansari* AIR 1976 SC 1813: (1976)3 SCR 661: (1976)38 STC 577].

To ascertain whether a document creates a licence or lease, the substance of the document must be preferred to the form. The real test is the intention of the parties. If the document creates an interest in the property it is a lease; but if it only permits another to make use of the property on which the legal possession continues with the owner it is a licence. If under the document a party gets exclusive possession of the property, *prima facie* he is considered to be a tenant; but the circumstances may be established which negative the intention to create a lease. [*Associated Hotels of India* v *R.N. Kapoor* AIR 1959 SC 1262: (1960)1 SCR 368: (1960)2 SCA 1: 1960 SCJ 453; *Khalil Ahmed* v *Tufelhussein Samasbhai* AIR 1988 SC 184: (1988)1 Ren CJ 180; *Rajbir Kaur* v *Chokosiri* AIR 1988 SC 1845: (1988)2 Ren CJ 316; *K.M. Abdurahiman* v *A.M. Haji* (1989)1 Ren CJ 5 (Ker); *A.K. Seedharan Erady* v *C. Sreedharan Erady* (1989)1 Ren CJ 61 (Ker)].


- **Mining lease** p. 582.
- **Renewal of a lease** p. 745.


**Leasehold.** An estate in realty held under a lease; a tenancy held on lease; land or other property held on lease; real property subject to a lease.

NOTE: The four principal types of leasehold estates are the estate for years, periodic tenancy, tenancy at will, and tenancy at sufferance.

It is also termed leasehold estate; leasehold interest.

**Leasehold interest.** For purposes of eminent domain, the lessee's interest in the lease itself, measured by the difference between the total remaining rent and the rent the lessee would pay for similar space for the same period; a lessor's or lessee's interest under a lease contract. [Black's *Law Dictionary*, 7th Ed.].

**Leave.** The word "leave" has various shades of meaning depending upon the context or intent with which it is used. [*Superintendence Company of India (P) Ltd.* v *Krishan Murgai* AIR 1980 SC 1717: (1980)3 SCR 1278: (1981)2 SCC 246].

Used as noun, it means permission or authorisation to do something; wilful departure with intent to remain away, and not temporary absence with intention of returning; permission to be absent as from duty; absentation; break; freedom from duty; furlough; retreat; vacation; acquiescence; approval; assent; favour; indulgence; liberty; permittance; sanction; sufferance.

Used as verb, it means desert; abandon; forsake; give up; quit; go away from; depart; relinquish; go away from permanently; abandon; cease; desist from; sail; abscond; get off; discard; renounce; abdicate; abjure; disappear; drop out; pull out; resign; retire; run away; accord; assign; confer; bestow; demise; endow; entrust; give by will; grant; hand down; impart.

According to the plain grammatical meaning the word "leave" in relation to an employee would normally be construed as meaning voluntary leaving of the service by him and would not include a case where he is discharged or dismissed or his services are terminated by his employer. Ordinarily the word "leave" appears to connote voluntary action. [*Superintendence Company of India (P) Ltd.* v *Krishan Murgai* AIR 1980 SC 1717: (1980)3 SCR 1278: (1981)2 SCC 246].

• **Sick leave** p. 797.

**Leave no issue.** To die without a surviving child, children, or descendants [Black's *Law Dictionary*, 8th Ed.]; not survived by a child or children or their descendants. [*In re Vigil's Estate* 34 P 2d 667, 668].

**Leave of absence.** Temporary absence from employment or duty with intention to return during which time remuneration and seniority may or may not be suspended [*State ex rel. McGaughe* v *Grayston* 163 SW 2d 335, 341]; a worker's temporary absence from employment or duty with the intention to return.

**Leave of court.** Judicial permission to follow a non-routine procedure; permission obtained from a court to take some action which, without such permission, would not be allowable.

**Ledger.** A book of accounts in which a merchant records financial transactions in the form of debits and credits.

A "ledger" is the principal book of accounts of a business establishment in which all the transactions of each day are entered under appropriate heads so as to show at a glance the debits and credits of each account. [*Foothill Ditch Co.* v *Wallace Ranch Water Co.* 25 Cal App 2d 555: 78 P 2d 215, 220].

• **General ledger** p. 384.

**Legacies.** See LEGACY.

• **Abatement of legacies** p. 3.

**Legacy.** A disposition of personalty by will; something left by will; a bequest.

Strictly the word 'legacy' applies to gift of personalty, but like any other word it has a flexible meaning: any yields to a sufficient context so as to include a gift of reality. [*Re Previte, Sturges* v *Previte* (1931)1 Ch 447, *per* Luxmoore, J.].

NOTE: Legacies are ordinarily divided into two classes, specific legacies and general legacies, general legacies also being described as legacies of quantity or number. A specific legacy must be of some thing or of some interest, legal or equitable, forming part of the testator's estate; it must be a part as distinguished from the whole of his personal property or from the whole of the general residue of his personal estate; it must be identified by a sufficient description, and separated in favour of the particular legatee from the general mass of the testator's personal estate. The forgiveness of a debt by will is a specific legacy of the debt. [Halsbury's *Laws of England*, 4th Ed., vol. 17, para 1228, p. 631].

*"Legacy" and "devise"—distinction.* In a technical sense and strictly construed, "legacy" is a gift or bequest by will of personal property, whereas a "devise" is a testamentary disposition of real estate, but such distinction will not be permitted to defeat the intent of a testator, and such terms may be construed interchangeably or applied indifferently to either personalty or real estate if the context of the will shows that such was the intention of the testator. [*Festorazzi* v *First Nat. Bank of Mobile* 264 So 2d 496, 505].

"Though the word (legacy) be usually taken for the bequest of a personal thing and on the contrary a gift of land by will be commonly (and more properly) called a devise, yet the word (legacy) may, in an extensive sense, be understood to comprehend any kind of estate, real as well as personal, left by the testator's will to any person". [*Beckley* v *Newland* (1723) 2 P Wms 182, 185, 186, *per* Lord Macclesfield, L.C.].

"It has been said, that the word legacy will include a devise of land as well as a bequest of personal estate; ... And it is indeed true, that the word legacy will include a devise of real estate, as well as a bequest of personal". [*Griffyn* v *Griffyn* (1740) Barn Ch 391, 395, *per* Hardwicke, L.C.].


- **Conditional legacy** p. 169.
- **Contingent legacy** p. 186.
- **Demonstrative legacy** p. 248.
- **General legacy** p. 384.
- **Specific legacy** p. 806.
- **Vesting of legacy** p. 880.


**Legal.** Conforming to the law; according to the law; required or permitted by law; not forbidden or discountenanced by law; good and effectual in law. [*Freeman* v *Fowler Packing Co.* 11 P 2d 276, 277].

Lawful; of or pertaining to law. [*Kinsley* v *Herald & Globe Ass'n* 34 A 2d 99, 101].

Authorized by law; cognizable in courts of law; enforceable in a court of law; established by law; governed by law; prescribed by law; warranted within the law.

**Legal age.** The age at which a person acquires full capacity to make his own contracts and deeds and transact business generally or to enter into some particular contract or relation; age of majority.

**Legal aid.** Free or inexpensive legal services provided to those who cannot afford to pay full price. [Black's *Law Dictionary*, 8th Ed.].

**Legal and lawful.** Legal and lawful, normally, convey same sense and are usually interchangeable. What is legal is lawful. But what is lawful may be so without being formally legal. That which is not *stricto legalo* may yet be lawful. It should not be forbidden by law. In fact, legal is associated with provisions in the Act, rules etc. Whereas lawful visualises all that is not illegal against law or even permissible. Lawful is wider in connotation than legal. [*Krishna Kishore Firm* v *Govt. of A.P.* AIR 1990 SC 2292, 2294].

**Legal character.** 'Legal character' means legal status but does not have same meaning as the expression 'civil nature' under s. 9 of the Civil Procedure Code. [*State of Karnataka* v *T. Srinivas* (1987)1 Kant LJ 387].

Legal character as used in s. 42, Specific Relief Act is equivalent to legal status and legal status is a legal right when it involves a peculiarity of the personality arising from anything unconnected with the nature of the act itself which the person of inherence can enforce against the person of incidence. [*Guntur Tobacco Market Committee* v *Yarabothu Narasaiah* AIR 1965 AP 266].

'Legal character' in s. 42 of the Specific Relief Act 1877 (s. 34 of the Act of 1963) means legal status, and legal status is what embodies a concept attributable to a party by law as distinguished from contract. [*Salil Kumar Mukherjee* v *Dhrubendra Nath Basu* 82 CWN 855].

Any question intermingled with the status of a person must be taken to be directly connected with his legal character, e.g., one's date of birth the decision which results in some legal rights attached to the concerned person. [*State of Orissa* v *Indupali Babaji* (1971)2 Cut WR 596].

**Legal compensation.** Legal compensation in its application to land acquired by the State for a public purpose refers solely to the injury done to the property taken, and not to any collateral damages caused to the owner. Compensation cannot be claimed for collateral damages, such as loss of trade, destruction of credit, failure of business prospects etc.

**Legal cruelty.** Cruelty that will justify granting a divorce to the injured party; specific conduct by one spouse that endangers the life, person, or health of the other spouse, or creates a reasonable apprehension of bodily or mental harm. [Black's *Law Dictionary*, 7th Ed.].

Conduct of such a character as to have caused danger to life, limb or health (bodily or mental) or to give rise to a reasonable apprehension of danger. No hard and fast rules can, however, be laid down; and in determining what constitutes cruelty, regard must be had to the circumstances of each particular case, keeping always in view the physical and mental condition of the parties and their character and social status. [*Russell* v *Russell* (1897) AC 525].

Any conduct of the husband which causes disgrace to the wife or subjects her to a course of annoyance and indignity amounts to legal cruelty. [*Kamla Devi* v *Amar Nath* AIR 1961 J&K 33].

**Legal custody.** The care, control, and maintenance of a child awarded by a court to a relative, usually one of the parents, in a divorce or separation proceeding; the detention of a person by virtue of lawful process or authority.

**Legal disability.** A disability imposed by law to do certain things by certain persons.

NOTE: *Examples.* A minor and a person of unsound mind are not competent to enter into a contract [Indian Contract Act 1872, s. 11]. A minor and a person of unsound mind cannot sue or be sued except through a guardian (next friend or guardian) for the suit. [Code of Civil Procedure 1908, Or. 32].

Legal disability extends the period of limitation for institution of a suit or making of an application for execution. [Limitation Act 1963, ss. 6 to 9].

**Legal duty.** An obligation arising from contract of the parties or the operation of the law, *e.g.*, legal duty of husband to support wife and children [*Ferrell* v *Hass* 220 SE 2d 771, 773]; an obligation the breach of which would be a legal wrong.

**Legal entity.** An entity, other than a natural person, who has sufficient existence in legal contemplation that it can function legally, be sued or sue and make decisions through agents as in the case of corporations.

Only a thing recognised by the law as real in itself and distinct from its qualities and attributes. [*Itiavira Thomas* v *Sankaranarayan Kesavan Nampori* AIR 1964 Ker 144: ILR (1963)2 Ker 238].

NOTE: While every legal person is necessarily a legal entity, the converse is not true. [*Itiavira Thomas* v *Sankaranarayan Kesavan Nampori*, supra].

**Legal fiction.** Legal fiction is assumption of fact made by court as basis for deciding a legal question. Legal fiction is a situation contrived by the law to permit a court to dispose of a matter, though it need not be created improperly; an assumption that something is true even though it may be untrue, made especially in judicial reasoning to alter how a legal rule operates.

NOTE: A legal fiction presupposes the correctness of the state of facts on which it is based, and all the consequences which flow from that state of facts have got to be worked out to their logical extent, but due regard must be had in this behalf to the purpose for which the legal fiction had been created. [*Bengal Immunity Co. Ltd.* v *State of Bihar* AIR 1955 SC 661: (1955)2 SCR 603; *K.K. Kamraj Nadar* v *Kunja Thevar* AIR 1956 SC 687: 1958 SCJ 680: 1959 SCR 583].

As to legal fiction the following extracts from Broom may be apposite: Although it shall never be contradicted so as to defeat the ends for which it was invented, it is never to be used at all, except *ad conciliandam acquitatem cum ratione et subtilitate juris*. [Broom's *Legal Maxims*, 10th Ed., p. 80]. A legal fiction must be limited to the purposes for which it is created and not to be extended beyond its legitimate field. [*Commissioner of Sales Tax, U.P.* v *Modi Sugar Mills* AIR 1961 SC 1047: (1961)2 SCR 189; *CIT, Bombay City* v *Amar Chand N. Shroff* AIR 1963 SC 1443: (1963)48 ITR 59 (SC): (1963)1 SCJ 411: 1964 Supp (1) SCR 699; *CIT, Madras* v *Express Newspapers Ltd., Madras* AIR 1965 SC 33: (1965)1 SCWR 182: (1964)53 ITR 250: (1964)8 SCR 188: (1964)2 SCJ 405: (1964)1 ITJ 221; *Braithwaite & Co.* v *Employees' State Insurance Corpn.* AIR 1968 SC 413, 416; *K.S. Dharmadatan* v *Central Government* AIR 1979 SC 1495: 1979 Cr LJ 1127: (1979)4 SCC 204: 1979 SCC (Cri) 958: 1979 Cr LR (SC) 627].

It must be confined to the limited purpose for which it is created. [*C.S.T.* v *Union Medical* AIR 1981 SC 1: 1981 SCR 870: (1981)1 SCC 51; *Karnataka State Road Transport* v *B.A. Jayarama* AIR 1984 SC 790].

**Legal fraud.** Misrepresentation of a material fact made wilfully to deceive, or recklessly without knowledge and acted on by the opposite party to his damages constitutes "legal fraud". [*Coffey* v *Wininger* 296 NE 2d 154, 160].

Breach of duty which has tendency to deceive others and operates to their injury, even though there be no vicious intent constitutes "legal fraud". [*Charleroi Lumber Co.* v *School Dist. of Borough of Bentleyville* 6 A 2d 88, 91].

NOTE: It is synonymous with "constructive fraud". [*Purcell* v *Robertson* 8 SE 2d 881, 883].

**Legal heirs.** Persons to whom law would give decedent's property if decedent died intestate. [*In re Wagar's Estate* 4 NW 2d 535, 536].

Persons entitled under laws of descent and distribution.

NOTE: It is also termed "heirs at law", "lawful heirs", "legal heirs". [*Corwin* v *Rheims* 61 NE 2d 40, 48; *In re Fahnestock's Estate* 50 NE 2d 733, 736].

**Legal injury.** Violation or invasion of legal right. [*American Indemnity Co.* v *Ernst & Ernst* Tex Civ App, 106 SW 2d 763, 765].

**Legal misconduct.** The expression "legal misconduct" is an ambiguous term. It means and includes some honest though erroneous breach of duty, causing a miscarriage of justice. [*Chhogmal Rewatmal* v *Sankal Chand* 53 CWN 828].

It is difficult to give an exhaustive definition of what amounts to legal misconduct. It may, however, be stated that legal misconduct means misconduct in the judicial sense arising from some honest, though erroneous, breach and neglect of duty and responsibility causing miscarriage of justice. It includes failure to perform the essential duties which are cast on a person deciding a cause. It also includes any irregularity of action which is not consonant with general principles of equity and good conscience. [*Indian Minerals Co.* v *Northern India Lime* AIR 1958 All 692].

**Legal necessity.** 'Legal necessity' means the necessity arising out of the kind of pressure which the law recognises as serious and sufficient. [*Ramasumran* v *Shyam Kumari* AIR 1922 PC 356].

**Legal person.** A 'legal person' is any subject-matter other than a human being to which the law attributes personality. Corporations are one species of legal persons invented by the law and invested with a variety of attributes so as to achieve certain purposes sanctioned by the law. [*Som Prakash Rekhi* v *Union of India* AIR 1981 SC 212: (1981)2 SCR 11: (1981)1 SCC 449].

**Legal possession.** 'Legal possession' means that possession which is recognised and protected as such by law. 'Legal possession' is ordinarily associated with *de facto* possession; but legal possession may exist without *de facto* possession, and *de facto* possession is not always regarded as possession in law. A person who, although having no *de facto* possession, is deemed to have possession in law is sometimes said to have constructive possession. [*B.*

*Gangadhar* v *B.G. Rajalingam* (1996)1 LW 145, 147 (Mad)].

**Legal practitioner.** An advocate, vakil or attorney of any High Court, a pleader, Mukhtar or revenue agent. [Advocates Act 1961, s. 2(*i*)].

▸ *Meaning under the Notaries Act 1951, s. 2(c).* Legal practitioner means an advocate or agent of the Supreme Court or any advocate, vakil or attorney of any High Court or any pleader authorised under any law for the time being in force to practise in any court of law.

**Legal proceedings.** The term "legal proceedings" includes all proceedings authorised or sanctioned by law, and brought or instituted in a court or legal tribunal, for the acquiring of a right or the enforcement of a remedy.

The term 'legal proceedings' is of wide import. It will ordinarily mean any proceeding authorised by law for redress of a legal grievance or for vindication of a legal right. As defined by the Bankers' Books Evidence Act 1891 (Act No. 18 of 1891), it means any proceeding or enquiry in which evidence is or may be given and includes an arbitration. [*Pt. Ram Avtar Sharma* v *Chakradhar Saran Sharma* AIR 1971 All 157].

The word 'legal proceedings' mean any civil or criminal proceedings or enquiry in which evidence is, or may be given; and includes an arbitration. [*K. Pakeeraiah* v *Sri Ranganayakaswamivari Temple Machilipatnam represented by its Executive Officer* (1977)1 APLJ 373: (1977)1 Andh WR 369].

'Legal proceeding' is any proceeding in court of justice by which a party pursues a remedy which the law affords him. The term embraces any of the formal steps or measures employed in the prosecution or defence of a suit. It refers to the use of a judicial process. [*K. Pakeeraiah* v *Sri Ranganayakaswamivari Temple Machilipatnam represented by its Executive Officer* (1977)1 APLJ 373: (1977)1 Andh WR 369].

The word 'legal proceedings' is defined to mean proceeding regulated or prescribed by law in which judicial decision may or must be given. [*K. Pakeeraiah* v *Sri Ranganayakaswamivari Temple Machilipatnam represented by its Executive Officer* (1977)1 APLJ 373: (1977)1 Andh WR 369].

The term 'legal proceedings' demonstrates some proceedings the skin to those set into motion by means of suit or prosecution including arbitration proceedings but does not include disciplinary proceedings. [*Iftikhar Ahmad Siddiqui* v *State of M.P.* (1987)13 All LR 811].

NOTE: A proceeding under s. 46 of the Trade Marks Act is a legal proceeding. [*Pt. Ram Avtar Sharma* v *Chakradhar Saran Sharma* AIR 1971 All 157].

The expression 'legal proceeding' is not synonymous with 'judicial proceeding'. The proceedings may be legal even if they are not judicial proceedings, if they are authorised by law. [*Abdul Aziz Ansari* v *State of Bombay* AIR 1958 Bom 279].

**Legal representative.** The term in its broadcast sense means one who stands in place of, and represents the interests of, another. A person who oversees the legal affairs of another. Examples include the executor or administrator of an estate and a court appointed guardian of a minor or incompetent person.

A "legal representative" ordinarily means a person who in law represents the estate of a deceased person or a person on whom the estate devolves on the death of an individual. A legal representative in a given case need not necessarily be a wife, husband, parent and child. [*Gujarat State Road Transport Corporation* v *Ramanbhai Prabatbhai* AIR 1987 SC 1690: (1987)3 SCR 404: (1987)3 SCC 234: JT 1987(2) SC 384: 1987 SCC (Cri) 482].

▸ *Meaning under the Code of Civil Procedure 1908, s. 2(11).* "Legal representative" means a person who in law represents the estate of a deceased person, and includes any person who intermeddles with the estate of the deceased, and where a party sues or is sued in a representative character, the person on whom the estate devolves on the death of the party so suing or sued.

NOTE: It is true that the term also includes a person on whom has devolved the estate of a person who has sued in a representative capacity. But, in the mere fact that a person who had not sued in a representative capacity would not take away his right to be substituted as 'legal representative'. [*P.S. Kano Anal* v *State of Manipur* (1985)2 Civ LJ 288 (Gau)].

The clause 'a person who in law represents the estate of a deceased person' in s. 2(11), CPC 1908, must include different legatees under the will. There is no justification for holding that the 'Estate' in the context must mean the whole of the estate. [*Andhra Bank Ltd.* v *R. Srinivasan* AIR 1962 SC 232].

The definition of "legal representative" includes heirs as well as person who represents the estate even without title either as executors or administrators in possession of the estate of the deceased. [*Custodian of Branches of BANCO National Ultramarino* v *Nalini Bai Naique* AIR 1989 SC 1589: (1989)2 SCR 810: JT 1989 (Supp) SC 159].

▸ *Meaning under Hindu Adoptions and Maintenance Act 1956, s. 21.* The term 'legal representative' includes illegitimate children of a Hindu father, who are entitled to be maintained during their minority as 'dependants'. [*M.V. Shantakumari* v *Dharujee* (1981)22 Guj LR 650 (DB)].

▸ *Meaning under Motor Vehicles Act 1939, s. 110A (new s. 166 of the M.V. Act 1988).* A legal representative in a given case need not necessarily be a wife, husband, parent and child. Parliament intended that the expression 'legal representative' should be given a wider meaning and it should not be confined to the spouse, parent and children of the deceased. The brother of a person who dies in a motor vehicle accident is entitled to maintain a petition, if he is a legal representative of the deceased. [*Gujarat State Road Transport Corporation* v *Ramanbhai Prabhatbhai* AIR 1987 SC 1690: (1987)3 SCR 404: (1987)3 SCC 234: JT 1987(2) SC 384: 1987 SCC (Cri) 482].

The term "legal representative", which is almost always held to be synonymous with the term "personal representative", means, in accident cases, member of family entitled to benefits under wrongful death statute. [*Unsatisfied Claim and Judgment Fund* v *Hamilton* 259 A 2d 302, 306].

**Legal right.** Natural rights, rights existing as result of contract, and rights created or recognised by law. [*Fine* v *Pratt* Tex Civ App, 150 SW 2d 308, 311].

'Legal right' is a difficult concept. Legal right in its strict sense is one which is an assertable claim enforceable before courts and administrative agencies. In its wider sense, a legal right has to be understood as any advantage or benefit conferred upon a person by a rule of law. There are legal rights which are not enforceable though recognized by law. There are rights recognized by International Courts granted by International Law, but not enforceable. A legal right is a capacity of asserting a secured interest, rather than a claim that could be asserted in courts. [*Daniel Hailey* v *State* AIR 1968 Mad 349: 1968 Cr LJ 1282].

A "legal right" may be defined as an advantage or benefit conferred upon a person by a rule of law. [*Shanti Kumar R. Canji* v *The Home Insurance Co. of New York* AIR 1974 SC 1719: (1974)2 SCC 387: (1975)1 SCR 550].

NOTE: 'Legal right' includes not only rights conferred by statute but also those which may be claimed independently of any statute. [*Anandrao Laxmanrao Mandloi* v *Board of Revenue* AIR 1965 MP 237].

**Legal tender.** A legal and valid offer.

**Legatee.** One to whom a legacy is bequeathed or a devise is given under a will or codicil.

The person to whom a legacy in a will is given. The term may be used to denominate those who take under will without any distinction between realty and personalty. [*Brooker* v *Brooker* Tex Civ App, 76 SW 2d 180, 183].

**Legislation.** In its use as enactments, it means acts; bills; body of laws enacted;

canon(s); laws; provisions of a law; regulations; rulings; statutes.

As lawmaking, it means codification of laws; enacting laws; formulating rules for the future; legislative process; preparation of laws; the power to make laws; the act of legislating; the making of laws via legislation, in contrast to court-made laws.

- **Colourable legislation** p. 155.
- **Conditional legislation** p. 169.
- **Delegated legislation** p. 244.
- **Zoning legislation** p. 909.

**Legislator.** Lawmaker; member of a legislative body; one who formulates laws; one who gives or makes laws; one who helps to pass laws; parliamentarian; congressman; senator.

**Legislature.** Body of persons who formulate laws; lawmaking body; lawmaking branch of government; legislative body; parliament; assembly.

The word "Legislature" is used in different senses in different Articles of the Constitution of India and may be in different senses in different places in the same Article and its meaning has to be ascertained keeping in view the subject or context. [*Bhairebendra Narayan Bhup* v *State of Assam* AIR 1956 SC 503: 1956 SCR 303: 1956 SCA 736: 1956 SCJ 543].

Under the Constitution, the "Legislature" of a State includes the Governor, and that a bill passed by such Legislature cannot become a law until it receives the Governor's assent. The term "Legislature" is not always, however, used in the Constitution as including the Governor, though Art. 168 makes him a component part of the State Legislature. In Art. 173, for instance, the word is clearly used in the sense of the "Houses of Legislature" and excludes the Governor. There are other provisions also where the word is used in contexts which exclude the Governor. [*State of Bihar* v *Sir Kameshwar Singh* AIR 1952 SC 252: 1952 SCR 1056].

The word "Legislature" has been used in Art. 389 of the Constitution in the larger sense, namely, comprising all the units that are concerned in the entire legislative process and includes the Governor. [*Bhairebendra Narayan Bhup* v *State of Assam* AIR 1956 SC 503: 1956 SCR 303: 1956 SCA 736: 1956 SCJ 543].

The word "Legislature" in the first part of Art. 252(1) of the Constitution, in the context in which it appears, cannot mean the three component parts of the State Legislature contemplated by Art. 168, but only the House or Houses of Legislature, as the case may be, *i.e.*, excluding the Governor. The fact that both the expressions "Legislature" as well as 'Houses of Legislature' are used in Art. 252 does not mean that the term 'Legislature' must be understood in the sense in which it is used in Art. 168. The term 'Legislature', in the context in which it appears, can only mean the House or Houses of Legislature, as the case may be. [*Union of India* v *Valluri Basavaiah Chowdhary* AIR 1979 SC 1415: (1979)3 SCR 802: (1979)3 SCC 324].

- **Intention of the legislature** p. 471.

**Legitimate.** As adjective, it means that which is lawful, legal, recognized by law, or according to law; as legitimate children, legitimate authority, legitimate sport or amusement. [*People* v *Commons* 148 P 2d 724, 731]; real, valid, or genuine [*United States* v *Schenck* CCA NY, 126 F 2d 702, 705]; official; licensed; mandated; rightful; sanctioned by custom or law.

As verb, it means to make or declare lawful; to confer legitimacy; validate; legitimatize.

**Legitimation.** The making legitimate or lawful that which was not originally so; especially the statutory procedure of legalizing (legitimating) the status of an illegitimate child. Such is usually necessary to assure inheritance rights to child.

**Lend.** To provide money to another for a period of time, usually with interest charge to be incurred by borrower; to give or put out for hire or compensation; to part with a thing of value to another for a time fixed or indefinite to be used or enjoyed by that other, the thing itself or the equivalent of it to be given back at the time fixed, or when lawfully asked for, with or without compensation for the use as may be agreed upon.

The expression 'lend' means in the ordinary parlance to deliver to another a thing for use on condition that the thing lent shall be returned with or without compensation for the use made of it by the person to whom it was lent. [*Ram Ratan Gupta* v *Director of Enforcement* (1966)1 SCR 651: (1966)1 SCJ 670: AIR 1966 SC 495: (1965)2 SCA 880].

**Lessee.** The person to whom the lease is granted; but it is capable of including as well assignees of the lease. [*King* v *Rymill* (1898)67 LJ PC 107].

One who has been given possession of land which is exclusive even of the landlord, except as the lease permits his entry, and except right to enter to demand rent or to make repairs. [*Seabloom* v *Krier* 18 NW 2d 88, 91].

**Lessor.** The grantor of the lease. The assignee of the lessor stands generally in the position of the lessor. [Transfer of Property Act 1882, s. 109].

**Let.** Allow the use of; convey; demise; grant the occupancy of; make available; hire out; rent out; authorise, endorse; give permission.

'Let' may be used so as only to give a licence, and so as to exclude any interest in land. [*Warr* v *London Co.* 73 LJKB 366].

In legal phraseology, the term 'let' ordinarily implies a tenancy and it is in that sense that the term has been used in s. 127(*a*) of the Calcutta Municipal Act 1923. [*Corporation of Calcutta* v *Anil Prokash Basu* AIR 1958 Cal 423].

In its application to contract, it means the act of awarding the contract to the proposer, after the proposals have been received and considered.

In judicial orders and decrees, the word "let" imports a positive direction or command. Thus, the phrase "let the writ issue as prayed" is equivalent to "it is hereby ordered that the writ issue", etc.

**Letter.** It is a communication by one person to another sent in writing, print or type. [*Inland Commercial* v *Union of India* AIR 1982 Del 393].

A communication inclosed, sealed, stamped, carried and delivered by state postal service. [*Hyney* v *U.S.* CCA Mich, 44 F 2d 134, 136].

A written instrument containing or attesting the grant of some power, authority, or right. The word appears in this generic sense in many compound phrases known to commercial law and jurisprudence, *e.g.*, letter of attorney, letter of credit, letters patent etc.

**Letter of allotment.** This is a letter written by a company, notifying to an applicant for share that his application has been allowed and that shares have been allotted to him. The acceptance contained in a letter of allotment must be unconditional.

**Letter of credit.** A letter of credit is in principle an undertaking by a banker to meet drafts drawn under the credit by the beneficiary of the credit in accordance with the conditions laid down therein. [Halsbury's *Laws of England*, 4th Ed., vol. 3, para 131, p. 99].

A letter of credit is a written instrument, addressed by one person to another, requesting the later to give credit to the person in whose favour it is drawn.

A letter of credit is in the nature of a negotiable instrument, and is a letter whereby a person requests another to advance money or give credit to a third person, and promises to repay the person making advancement.

**Letter of intent.** A letter of intent is customarily employed to reduce to writing a preliminary understanding of parties who intend to enter into contract. [*Garner* v *Boyd* DC Tex, 330 F Supp 22, 25].

**Letter rogatory.** 'Letter rogatory' is a formal communication in writing sent by a court in which action is pending to a foreign court or judge requesting that the testimony of a witness residing within the jurisdiction of the foreign court may be formally taken thereon under its direction and transmitted to the issuing court making such request for use in a pending legal contest or action. [*Union of India* v *W.N. Chadha* AIR 1993 SC 1082: 1993 Supp (4) SCC 260, 284: 1993 SCC (Cri) 1171: 1993 Cr LJ 859].

**Letters of administration.** Formal document issued by probate court appointing one as an administrator of an estate.

**Letters patent.** "Letters patent" mean an instrument issued by the Crown Government. [*Umaji Keshao Meshram* v *Smt. Radhika Bai* AIR 1986 SC 1272: 1986 (Supp) SCC 401: (1986)1 SCR 731].

NOTE: Letters patent granted by the sovereigns establishing the High Courts in the various provinces in India are not Acts, but they are granted by virtue of an Act of Parliament and they should be construed in the same way as Acts of Legislature. [*Benoari Lal* v *Emperor* AIR 1943 Cal 285].

**Levy.** As noun means assessment; collection; exaction; seizure; the obtaining of money by legal process through seizure and sale of property.

As verb means to assess; raise; execute; exact; gather; seize; conscript; demand; garnish; raise; take by force; impose; demand.

To 'levy' is to realise or to collect. [*Mahtab Singh* v *State of U.P.* AIR 1979 SC 1263: 1979 Cr LJ 1077].

The term 'levy' is an expression of wide import. It includes both imposition of a tax as well as its quantification and assessment. [*Ujagar Prints* v *Union of India* JT 1988(4) SC 330: (1988)38 ELT 535: AIR 1989 SC 516: (1989)3 SCC 488: (1989)74 STC 401].

In reference to taxation, the word may mean the legislative function and the declaration of the subject and rate or amount of taxation. [*People* v *Mahoney* 91 P 2d 1029; *City of Richmond* v *Eubank* 18 SE 2d 397, 403].

NOTE: A levy cannot be a fee because there is no provision of service being rendered in respect of it. It would indisputably be a tax. [*Corporation of Calcutta* v *Liberty Cinema* AIR 1965 SC 1107: (1965)1 SCA 657].

**Lewd.** Obscene; lustful; indecent; lascivious; lecherous; immodest; immoral; morally impure; morally unrestrained; lubricious; offensive; pornographic; salacious; scandalous; scurrilous; sexually indecent; unchaste; vulgar.

The term signifies that form of immorality which has relation to moral impurity [*United States* v *Barlow* DC Utah, 56 F Supp 795, 797]; or that which is carried on in a wanton manner. [*Rubhuhn* v *Cahill* DCNY, 31 F Supp 47, 49].

**Lewd and lascivious cohabitation.** Illicit cohabitation; the living together of a man and woman not married to each other as husband and wife.

**Lewd person.** One who is lawless, bad, vicious, unchaste, indecent, obscene, lascivious. [*State* v *Harlowe* 24 P 2d 601].

**Liability.** Accountability; accountableness; answerability; bounden duty; legal obligation; legal responsibility; drawback, hindrance; burden; contract obligation; duty to pay; debt; encumbrance; indebtedness; unliquidated claim.

▸ *Various other definitions.* Every kind of legal obligation, responsibility, or duty [*Mayfield* v *First Nat. Bank of Chattanoega, Tenn*, CCA Tenn, 137 F 2d 1013, 1019]; an obligation one is bound in law or justice to perform [*State ex rel. Diederichs* v *Board of Trustees of Missoula County High School* 7 P 2d 543, 545]; duty to pay money or perform some other service [*Dehne* v *Hillman Inv. Co.* CCA Pa, 110 F 2d 456, 458]; fixed liability [*Vandegrift* v *Riley* Cal Sup, 16 P 2d 734, 736]; all character of debts and obligations. [*Public Market Co. of Portland* v *City of Portland* 130 P 2d 624, 643, 646].

The term 'liability' is of large and comprehensive significance, and when construed in its usual and ordinary sense, it expresses a state of being under obligation in law or in justice. [*First National Bank* v *Sant Lal* AIR 1959 Punj 328: ILR (1958) Punj 2357].

The word 'liability' has a wide connotation. It is a broad term of large and comprehensive significance and means legal responsibility or obligation to do a thing. [*Mohd. Yaqub* v *Union of India* AIR 1971 Del 45 (FB)].


- **Absolute liability** p. 9.
- **Acknowledgement of liability** p. 25.
- **Contingent liability** p. 186.
- **Current liability** p. 213.
- **Demand liabilities** p. 247.
- **Discharged from liability** p. 263.
- **Joint and several liability** p. 487.
- **Limited liability** p. 536.
- **Several liability** p. 790.
- **Vicarious liability** p. 880.


**Liable.** Legally bound; subject to; under an obligation; exposed or opened to something undesirable; answerable; accountable; chargeable; justly responsible; obliged in law; vulnerable.

Exposed or subject to a given contingency, risk, or casualty, which is more or less probable. [*Pacific Fire Ins. Co.* v *Murdoch Cotton Co.* 99 SW 2d 233, 235].

Future possible or probable happening which may not actually occur, and relates to any occurrence within the range of possibility. [*Alabama Great Southern R. Co.* v *Smith* 96 So 239, 240; *Pacific Fire Ins. Co.* v *Murdoch Cotton Co.* 99 SW 2d 233, 235].

The word 'liable' means a future possibility or probability of happening which may or may not actually occur. [*State* v *Amru Tulshi Ram* AIR 1957 Punj 55: ILR (1957)1 Punj 426].

The word 'liable' is normally interpreted to mean exposed to a certain contingency or casualty. It means a future possibility, probability, happening which may or may not actually occur. [*Nago Atmaramji Kohale* v *State of Maharashtra* 1977 Mah LJ 163].

The ordinary meaning of the word 'liable' in a legal context is to denote the fact that a person is responsible at law. [*Litlewood* v *George Wimpey & Co. Ltd.* (1953)2 All ER 915].

The word 'liable' occurring in many statutes has been held as not conveying the sense of an absolute obligation or penalty but merely importing a possibility of attracting such obligation, or penalty, even where this word is used along with the words 'shall be'. [*Supdt. and Remembrancer of Legal Affairs* v *Abani Maity* (1979)4 SCC 85: AIR 1979 SC 1029: (1979)3 SCR 472: 1979 Cr LJ 897: 1979 SCC (Cri) 902].

**Li'an.** Li'an is testimony confirmed by oath and accompanied with imprecation. Under the pure Mohomedan law, if a man charges his wife with adultery, he may be called upon to confirm it by oath coupled with an imprecation saying that the curse of God be upon him if he is a liar. The wife is entitled to sue for a divorce on the ground that her husband has falsely charged her with adultery.

**Libel.** A libel is a false and defamatory statement made or conveyed by written or printed words without lawful justification or excuse.

Any publication which exposes an individual to hatred, contempt or ridicule, being published without lawful excuse, is a libel. [*Wilson* v *Reed* (1860)2 F&F 149].

NOTE: Libel is a criminal offence punishable under s. 500 of the Indian Penal Code. It is also a civil wrong actionable without proof of special damage. [*D'Silva* v *Potenger* ILR (1946)1 Cal 157].

**Liberty.** Absence of foreign rule, absence of restraint; absence of servitude; emancipation; exemption from control; freedom from captivity; freedom of action; power of choice; unconstraint; freedom from all restraints except such as are justly imposed by law.

Liberty means the faculty of willing and power of doing what is willed without influence or interference from other sources. [Leiber cited by Raymond G. Gettel: *Reading of Political Science*, p. 160].

The word "liberty" includes and comprehends all personal rights and their enjoyment. [*Rosenblum* v *Rosenblum* 42 NYS 2d 626, 630].

'Liberty' must be something which results from a permission given to, or something enjoyed under sufferance by, a particular person or body of persons, as distinguished from something enjoyed by sufferance by all and sundry. [*Le Strange* v *Pettefar* (1939)161 LT 300].

• **Civil liberty** p. 145.

• **Personal liberty** p. 659.

**Liberty of the Press.** The right to print and publish the truth, from good motives and for justifiable ends; the right to publish whatever one may please.

> NOTE: Freedom of speech and expression guaranteed by sub-cl. (*a*) of cl. (1) of Art. 19 of the Constitution of India includes liberty of the Press. But reasonable restrictions may be imposed upon the liberty of the Press in the interest of public order, decency or morality, or in relation to contempt of court, defamation or incitement to an offence.

**Liberty of worship.** The right freely to worship in any mode and in accordance with any belief which does not violate the laws of morality or property, nor infringe upon personal right.

> NOTE: Freedom of religion is one of the fundamental rights guaranteed by the Constitution of India, subject *inter alia* to public order, morality and health.

**Licence.** Approval; authority; authorisation; clearance; entitlement; formal permission; leave; written permission; a permit from an authority to own or use something; do something; unrestrained liberty of action; abuse of privilege; disregard of propriety.

The permission by competent authority to do an act which, without such permission would be illegal, a trespass, or a tort [*People* v *Henderson* 218 NW 2d 2, 4]; permission to do a particular thing, to exercise a certain privilege or to carry on a particular business or to pursue a certain occupation [*Blatz Brewing Co.* v *Collins* 160 P 2d 37, 39, 40]; privilege from state or sovereign. [*M. Itzkowtz & Sons* v *Geraghty* 247 NYS 703, 704].

▸ *Application to real property.* Licence with respect to real property is a privilege to go on premises for a certain purpose, but does not operate to confer on, or vest in, licensee any title, interest, or estate in such property. [*Timmons* v *Cropper* 172 A 2d 757, 759].

▸ *Meaning under the Indian Easements Act 1882, s. 52.* Where one person grants to another or to a definite number of other persons a right to do, or continue to do, in or upon the immovable property of the grantor, something which would, in the absence of such right, be unlawful, and such right does not amount to an easement or an interest in the property, the right is called a licence.

> NOTE: A licence is normally created where a person is granted the right to the premises without becoming entitled to exclusive possession of them, or the circumstances and conduct of the parties show that all that was intended was that the grantee should be granted a personal privilege with no interest in land. A mere licence does not create any estate or interest in the property to which it relates; it only makes an act lawful which otherwise it would be unlawful. [Halsbury's *Laws of England*, 4th Ed., vol. 27, paras 8 and 9, p. 16].
>
> A "licence" confers a right to do or continue to do something in or upon immovable property of grantor which but for the grant of the right may be unlawful, but it creates no estate or interest in the immovable property of the grantor. [*Sohan Lal Naraindas* v *Laxmidas Raghunath Gadit* (1971)1 SCC 276: (1971)3 SCR 319].

• **Exclusive licence** p. 327.

• **Renewal of a licence** p. 745.

• **Revocation of a licence** p. 762.

**Licensee.** A licensee is a person who has been permitted to do or continue to do, in or upon the immovable property of the grantor, something which would, in the absence of such permission, be unlawful; the holder of a licence.

A licensee is one who is in occupation under a subsisting agreement for licence. The agreement for licence must be subsisting on the date on which he claims to be a licensee. [*Ludhichem Agencies* v *Ahmed R.V. Peer Mohamed* AIR 1981 SC 1998: (1981)4 SCC 273: (1982)1 SCR 712].

**Lien.** The word "lien" originally means 'binding', from the Latin *ligamen*. Its legal meaning is 'right to retain'. [*Triveni Shankar Saxena* v *State of U.P.* AIR 1992 SC 496: 1992 Supp (1) SCC 524].

"Lien" is defined as a charge or security or encumbrance upon property [*Theatre Realty Co.* v *Aronberg-Fried Co.* CCA Mo, 85 F 2d 383, 388]; a claim or charge on property for payment of some debt, obligation or duty [*Sullins* v *Sullins*, 396 P 2d 886, 888]; security for a debt, duty or other obligation [*Hurley* v *Boston R. Holding Co.* 54 NE 2d 183, 193]; tie that binds properly to a debt or claim for its satisfaction. [*U.S.* v *1364, 76875 Wine Gallons, More or Less, of Spirituous Liquors* DC Mo, 60 F Supp 389, 392].

Lien in its primary or legal sense is a right at Common Law in one man to retain that which is rightfully and continuously in his possession belonging to another until the present and accrued claims of the person in possession are satisfied. In this primary sense it is given by law and not by contract. [Halsbury's *Laws of England*, 4th Ed., vol. 28, para 502, p. 221].

The word "lien" is a generic term and, standing alone, includes liens acquired by contract or by operation of law. [*Egyptian Supply Co.* v *Boyd* CCA Ky, 117 F 2d 608, 612].

NOTE: There is no such thing as a lien on a service as such. A lien is always on a post, so that by saying that the employee had been in the secretariat, it can in no way be implied that he had a general lien entitling him to such promotions as he would have got had he remained in the secretariat. [*Ananthan Pillai* v *State* AIR 1968 Ker 234: (1968)2 Lab LJ 657].

Lien just connotes the right of a civil servant to hold the post substantively to which he is appointed. Generally when a person with a lien against a post is appointed substantively to another post, he acquires a lien against the latter post. Then the lien against his previous post automatically disappears. The principle being that no Government servant can have simultaneously two liens against two posts in two different cadres. [*Ramlal Khurana* v *State of Punjab* AIR 1989 SC 1985, 1987].

A person can be said to acquire a lien on post only when he has been confirmed and made permanent on that post and not earlier. [*Triveni Shankar Saxena* v *State of U.P.* AIR 1992 SC 496: 1992 Supp (1) SCC 524].

*Kinds of lien.* Liens are of two kinds—general and particular. A general lien is the right to retain the property for a general balance of accounts. Bankers, factors, wharfingers, attorneys of a High Court and policy-brokers have general lien. [Indian Contract Act 1872, s. 171]. A particular lien is a right to retain property for charges on account of labour employed or expenses incurred upon the property detained. A bailee has a particular lien. [Indian Contract Act 1872, s. 170].

The word "lien" is now variously described and used under different contexts such as 'contractual lien', 'equitable lien', 'specific lien', 'general lien', 'partner's lien', etc. [*Triveni Shankar Saxena* v *State of U.P.* AIR 1992 SC 496: 1992 Supp (1) SCC 524].


- **Attorney's lien** p. 85.
- **General lien** p. 384.
- **Maritime lien** p. 562.
- **Vendor's lien** p. 877.


**Life.** That state of animals, humans and plants or of an organized being, in which its natural functions and motions are performed, or in which its organs are capable of performing their functions; the interval between birth and death; the sum of the forces by which death is resisted. [Black's *Law Dictionary*, 5th Ed.].

That vital existence, the loss of which means death; the period of animate existence from birth until death, or a part of it; the condition which distinguishes active animals and plants from inorganic matter, including the capacity for growth, functional activity, and continual change preceding death.

'Life' dictionarily means, "state of functional activity and continual charge peculiar to organised matter, and especially to the portion of it constituting an animal or plant before death; animate existence;

being alive". [*Kartar Singh* v *State of Punjab* (1994)3 SCC 569: 1994 SCC (Cri) 899: 1994 Cr LJ 3139: JT 1994(2) SC 423].

- *Meaning under Indian Penal Code 1860.* The word "life" denotes the life of a human being unless the contrary appears from the context (s. 45). Human life begins at conception. [*Roe* v *Wade* 35 L Ed 2d 147].
- *Meaning under Constitution of India, Art. 21.* The expression "life" has a much wider meaning [*Board of Trustees of the Port of Bombay* v *Dilip Kumar Raghavendranath Nadkarni* AIR 1983 SC 109: (1983)1 SCR 828: (1983)1 SCC 124]. The word "life" in Art. 21 means not merely the right to the continuance of a person's animal existence, but a right to the possession of each of his organs, arms, legs, etc. [*Kharak Singh* v *State of U.P.* AIR 1963 SC 1295: (1963)2 Cr LJ 329: (1964)1 SCR 332: (1964)2 SCJ 107]. "Life" includes not merely physical existence but also the use of any faculty or limb as also the right to live with human dignity. [*Bachan Singh* v *State of Punjab* AIR 1982 SC 1325: 1982 SCC (Cri) 535: (1982)3 SCC 24: (1983)1 SCR 145]. Life includes livelihood. [*Olga Tellis* v *Bombay Municipal Corporation* AIR 1986 SC 181].
- *Other meanings.* The duration of a thing's existence or of its ability to function (*e.g.* the engine has a life of five years); the manner of one's existence (*e.g.* start a new life leaving the old); liveliness, energy (*e.g.* full of life); the source or essence of existence.

**Life annuity.** Annual payment during the continuance of the life of a person.

An engagement to pay an income yearly during the life of some person; also the sum thus promised. An annuity, depending on the continuance of an assigned life or lives, is sometimes called a life annuity. [*Bodine* v *Commissioner of Internal Revenue* CCA 3: 103 F 2d 982, 985].

**Life boat.** It is a boat specially made for saving life in a storm or shipwreck or other accidents at sea.

**Life estate.** An estate which is to be enjoyed during the life of any person.

An estate whose duration is limited to the life of the party holding it, or some other person.

**Life imprisonment.** Life imprisonment means imprisonment for life. No doubt many people come out while they are still alive, but when they do come out, it is only on licence, and the sentence of life imprisonment remains on them until they die. [*R.* v *Foy* (1962)2 All ER 246 CCA].

**Life insurance (assurance).** See under INSURANCE p. 468.

**Life interest.** An interest in any property tenable during the life of any person.

A claim or interest in real or personal property, not amounting to ownership, and limited by a term of life, either that of the person in whom the right is vested or that of another. [Black's *Law Dictionary*, 5th Ed.].

An interest in real or personal property measured by the duration of the holder's or another named person's life. [Black's *Law Dictionary*, 7th Ed.].

**Life-jacket.** The expression "life-jacket" includes any appliance capable of being fitted on the body, having the same buoyancy as a life-jacket.

**Light motor vehicle.** A transport vehicle or omnibus, the gross vehicle weight of either of which or a motor-car or tractor or roadroller, the unladen weight of any of which, does not exceed 7,500 kilograms. [Motor Vehicles Act 1988, s. 2(21)].

**Limb.** Any appendage projecting from a main structure; a projecting part of a person's or animal's body such as an arm, leg, or wing.

NOTE: An eye is a limb. [*Lipton India Ltd.* v *Gokul Chand Mondal* 1981 Lab IC 1300 (Cal) (FB)].

**Limitation.** The act or an instance of limiting; the process of being limited; restriction; circumscription; a restrictive condition or stipulation; a legally specified period beyond which an action cannot be brought, or a property right is not to continue; a period of time fixed by law within which certain acts are to be performed to render them valid; the creation by deed or devise of a lesser estate out of a fee simple.

A limitation is a form of words which creates an estate and denotes its extent by designating the event upon which it is to commence and the time for which it is to endure. It marks the utmost time for which the estate can continue. It appears in two forms. A direct limitation marks the time by denoting the size of the estate in familiar terms, *e.g.* by using such expressions as "for life" or "in fee simple"; a determinable limitation gives an interest for one of the times possible in a direct limitation, but also denotes some event that may determine the estate during the continuance of that time. [Cheshire's *Modern Real Property*, 10th Ed., p. 286].

• **Conditional limitation** p. 169.

**Limitation over.** A limitation over includes any interest in the same property to be enjoyed after the prior interest granted expires or is exhausted. Thus, in a gift to *A* for life and the remainder to *B*, the remainder is a limitation over to *B*.

**Limitations, statutes of.** For most actions, periods of limitation are prescribed by statute with the consequence that an action begun after the period of limitation has expired is not maintainable. The statutes which impose periods of limitation for classes of actions are called statutes of limitation.

**Limited company.** A company limited by shares or by guarantee. [Companies Act 1956, s. 2(23)].

**Limited estate.** An estate the enjoyment of which is limited as to time or manner.

**Limited interest.** Interest short of full ownership in immovable property, for example, life interest, Hindu woman's interest.

**Limited liability.** The liability is limited up to a certain extent, as of a shareholder of a company.

**Limited owner.** An owner whose interest in the property is not absolute but qualified.

"Limited owner" commonly means a person with restricted rights as opposed to full owner with absolute rights. In relation to property absolute, complete or full ownership comprises various constituents such as the right to possess, actual or constructive, power to enjoy, that is to determine manner of use extending even to destroying, right to alienate, transfer or dispose of etc. Any restriction or limitation on exercise of these rights may result in limited or qualified ownership. [*Kalawatibai* v *Soiryabai* AIR 1991 SC 1581: (1991)3 SCC 410: (1991)2 SCR 599: JT 1991(2) SC 385].

The words "limited owner" connote a right in the property to which the possession of the female Hindu may be legitimately traced, that which is not a full right of ownership. [*Gulwant Kaur (Smt.)* v *Mohinder Singh* AIR 1987 SC 2251: (1987)3 SCC 674: (1987)3 SCR 576: (1987)3 SCC 674: JT 1987(3) SC 121].

**Lineal consanguinity.** Lineal consanguinity is that which subsists between two persons, one of whom is descended in a direct line from other, as between a man and his father, or as between a man and his son.

**Lineal descendant.** A person in the direct line of descent such as a child or grandchild as contrasted with a collateral descendant, such as a niece.

NOTE: The term 'lineal descendant' is not restricted to male descendants only but is wide enough to include all descendants, male and female. [*Bhimnath* v *Tara* AIR 1929 PC 162].

**Liquid assets.** Readily realisable property, such as coins, notes and other gilt-edged securities; cash, or assets immediately convertible to cash.

**Liquidate.** Finish; conclude; terminate or wind up business affairs; assemble and apportion assets; settle accounts with the debtors and creditors.

To pay and settle [*Farmers State Bank & Trust Co.* v *Brady* 152 SW 2d 729, 732]; to adjust [*State ex rel. Banister* v *Cantley*

52 SW 2d 397, 399]; to assemble and mobilize the assets, settle with the creditors and the debtors and apportion the remaining assets, if any, among the stockholders or owners [*United States* v *Metcalf* CCA Cal, 131 F 2d 677, 679]; to gather in the assets, convert them into cash and distribute them according to the legal rights of the parties interested. [*Fleckner* v *Bank of U.S.* La, 5 L Ed 631].

**Liquidated damages.** See under DAMAGES p. 219.

**Liquidation.** Winding-up or settling with creditors and debtors [*Wilson* v *Superior Court in and for Santa Clara County* 43 P 2d 286, 288]; winding-up of corporation so that assets are distributed to those entitled to receive them; to cease from transacting business and gather in assets, settle debts, and divide surpluses, if any; elimination by killing.

**Liquidator.** An officer appointed to conduct the winding-up of a company.

**Liquidity, international.** The availability of credit or foreign currency requirements to finance international trade. The extent of international liquidity depends partly on the balance of payments and reserves position of trading countries and partly on the policy pursued by the International Monetary Fund.

**Liquor.** Alcoholic beverage made by distillation.

"Liquor" includes spirits of wine, methylated spirits, spirits, wine, toddy, beer, and all liquid consisting of or containing alcohol. [*Southern Pharmaceuticals and Chemicals, Trichur* v *State of Kerala* AIR 1981 SC 1863: (1981)4 SCC 391: (1982)1 SCR 519].

▸ *Meaning under Government of India Act 1935, Entry 31, List II.* The word 'liquor' covers not only those alcoholic liquids which are generally used for beverage purposes and produce intoxication, but also all liquids containing alcohol. It may be that the latter meaning is not the meaning which is attributed to the word 'liquor' in common parlance especially when that word is prefixed by the qualifying word 'intoxicating', but having regard to the numerous statutory definitions of that word, such a meaning could not have been excluded from the scope of the term 'intoxicating liquor' as used in Entry 31 of List II of the Act 1935. [*State of Bombay* v *F.N. Balsara* AIR 1951 SC 318: 1951 SCR 682: 52 Cr LJ 1361: 1951 SCJ 478; *State of U.P.* v *Synthetics and Chemicals Ltd.* (1980)2 SCC 441: AIR 1980 SC 614].

NOTE: Liquor is contrasted with wines which are made by fermentation.

**Lis.** A controversy or dispute; a suit or action at law. The word 'lis' is a stage in the process of arriving at an administrative decision. It commences with the show cause notice and then takes a quasi-judicial character. [*State of Madras* v *Tiruneveli Municipal Council* (1967)1 MLJ 47].

**Lis pendens.** A pending suit; jurisdiction, power, or control which courts acquire over property in suit pending action and until final judgment.

A notice, recorded in the chain of title to real property, required or permitted in some jurisdictions to warn all persons that certain property is the subject-matter of litigation, and that any interests acquired during the pendency of the suit are subject to its outcome. [Black's *Law Dictionary*, 7th Ed.].

**List.** A number of connected items, names, etc., written or printed together usually consecutively to form a record or aid to memory.

A docket or calendar of causes ready for trial or argument, or of motions ready for hearing.


- **Blacklist** p. 106.
- **Cause list** p. 129.
- **Civil list** p. 145.
- **Waiting list** p. 889.


**Listing.** 'Listing' means the admission of the securities of a company to trading privileges on a Stock Exchange. The principal objectives of 'listing' are to provide ready marketability and impart liquidity and free negotiability to stocks and shares; ensure proper supervision and control of dealings therein; and protect the interests of shareholders and of the general investing public. [*Raymond Synthetics Ltd.* v *Union of India* AIR 1992 SC 847: (1992)2 SCC 255: (1992)73 Comp Cas 762: (1992)1 SCR 481: JT 1992(1) SC 463].

**Literary work.** The expression 'literary work' covers work which is expressed in print or writing, irrespective of the question whether the quality or style is high. [*University of London Press Ltd.* v *University Tutorial Press Ltd.* (1916)2 Ch 601].

▸*Meaning under the Copyright Act 1957, s. 2(o).* Literary work includes computer programmes, tables and compilations including computer databases.

• **Original literary work.** 'Original literary work' signifies that the product must originate from the author in the sense that it is the result of a substantial degree of skill, industry or experience employed by him. [*Ladbroke (Football) Ltd.* v *William Hill (Football) Ltd.* (1964)1 All ER 465].

**Litigation.** The expression 'litigation' means a legal action including all proceedings therein, initiated in a court of law with the purpose of enforcing a right or seeking a remedy. [*Janata Dal* v *H.S. Chowdhary* JT 1992(5) SC 213: 1992(3) Crimes 199: (1992)4 SCC 305: AIR 1993 SC 892: 1993 Cr LR (SC) 10: 1993 Cr LJ 600: 1993 SCC (Cri) 36].

**Litigious.** "Litigious" means disputed or disputable or marked by intention to quarrel, inviting controversy, relating to or marked by litigation which is the subject of law suit. [*Krishna Kishore Firm* v *Government of A.P.* AIR 1990 SC 2292: 1990 Supp (2) SCR 8: JT 1990(4) SC 241: (1991)1 SCC 184].

**Litigious possession.** See under POSSESSION p. 672.

**Livestock.** 'Livestock' generally means live animals. In great majority of cases it would include, and would be thought to include, the poultry on the farm. [*Wardhaugh (A.F.) Ltd.* v *Mace* (1952)2 All ER 28].

'Livestock' means animals with life and not the 'dry fish'. [*Smt. Lashmi Dry Fish Traders* v *State* AIR 1986 AP 330].

'Livestock' is defined as domestic animals used or raised on a farm. [*Boland* v *Cecil* 150 P 2d 819, 822].

The term in its generic sense includes all domestic animals. [*Meader* v *Unemployment Compensation Division of Industrial Accident Board* 136 P 2d 984, 987].

It includes fur bearing animals raised in captivity. [*Fromm Bros.* v *U.S.* DC Wis, 35 F Supp 145, 147].

▸*Meaning under the Agricultural Holdings Act 1948, s. 94 (England).* "Livestock" includes any creature kept for the production of food, wool, skins or fur or for the purpose of its use in the farming of land or the carrying on in relation to land of any agricultural activity.

**Living.** Having life; active; livelihood; means of subsistence; functioning; existing; surviving; continuing in operation.

Literally it signifies the pecuniary resources by means of which one exists. [*Leroux* v *Industrial Accident Commission of California* 35 P 2d 624, 626].

NOTE: Living at a given period includes a child *en ventre* at the period and born afterwards. [*Re Salaman De Pass* v *Sonnenthal* (1908)1 Ch 4].

**Living accommodation.** Living accommodation is something in which somebody resides and, therefore, it is the dwelling house and it is something distinct from entertainment, domestic or other services or other benefits or facilities of whatsoever nature and also it is distinct from supplies or services. [*Butter (Inspector of Taxes)* v *Bennett* (1962)2 All ER 204].

**Living in adultery.** A continuous course of adulterous life, as distinguished from one or two lapses from virtue [*Rajani Prabhakar Lokur* v *Prabhakar Raghavendra Lokur* AIR 1958 Bom 264: ILR (1958) Bom 577]; leading a life of continuous immorality. [*Chandra Chittar Lodhi* v *Mst. Nanaee* AIR 1965 MP 268].

The term has now been consistently held to mean an outright adulterous conduct where the wife lives in a quasi-permanent union with the man with whom she is committing adultery. [*Kasturi* v *Ramaswami* 1980 MLJ (Cri) 124 (Mad)].

**Living together as husband and wife.** In ordinary acceptation of words in common understanding, it means maintaining a home and living together in same household or actually cohabiting under conditions which would be regarded as constituting a family relation. [*McPadden* v *Morris* 13 A 2d 679, 680]. It means the dwelling together in same house, eating at same table, the two parties holding themselves out to world and conducting themselves toward each other as husband and wife. [*Lipp* v *Lipp* Mo App, 117 SW 2d 364, 366].

A husband and wife are living together, not only when they are residing together in the same house, but also when they are living in different places, even if they are separated by the high seas, provided the consortium has not been determined. [*R.* v *Creaner* (1919)1 KB 564 CCA].

**Living wage.** Wages sufficient for a workman and his family to live on without privation.

NOTE: The living wage should enable the male earner to provide for himself and his family not merely the bare essentials of food, clothing and shelter but a measure of frugal comfort including education for the children, protection against ill health, requirements of essential social needs, and a measure of insurance against the more important misfortunes including old age. [*Express Newspaper Pvt. Ltd.* v *Union of India* AIR 1958 SC 578].

**Lloyd's.** It is a society of underwriters, insurance brokers, merchants, bankers, shipowners, etc., formerly regulated by a deed of association, of 1811, and now incorporated by a special Act of 1871. The objects of the society are the carrying on of the business of marine insurance by members of the society; the protection of the interests of members of the society in respect of shipping and cargoes and freight; the collection, publication and diffusion of intelligence and information with respect to shipping.

**Loan.** A lending; moneys borrowed; time payment. A 'loan' is defined as delivery by one party to and receipt by another party of sum of money upon agreement, express or implied, to repay it with or without interest [*Isaacson* v *House* 119 SE 2d 113, 116]; anything furnished for temporary use to a person at his request, on condition that it shall be returned, or its equivalent in kind, with or without compensation for its use. [*Liberty Nat. Bank & Trust Co.* v *Travelers Indem. Co.* 295 NYS 2d 983, 986].

The word 'loan' includes not only an actual advance whether of money or in kind but also a transaction on a bond bearing interest executed in respect of a past liability, *i.e.*, an instrument which is in renewal of a past advance of money. [*Jiwanlall Chariya* v *Rameshwarlall Agarwalla* AIR 1967 SC 1118: (1967)1 SCWR 627: (1967)1 SCR 190: (1966)36 Comp Cas 866].

NOTE: A loan necessarily supposes a return of the money loaned. [*CIT* v *Bazpur Co-operative Sugar Factory Ltd.* AIR 1989 SC 1866: 1989 Supp (2) SCC 240].

*'Loan' and 'deposit'—distinction.* The distinction between a loan and a deposit is that in the case of a loan, it is ordinarily the duty of the debtor to seek out the creditor and to pay the money according to the agreement. In the case of a deposit, it is the duty of the depositor to go to the depositee and to make a demand for it. [*Gurcharan Das* v *Rom Rakha* AIR 1937 Lah 81].

The terms "loan and deposit" are not mutually exclusive, and the fact that a deposit is made with the object of inducing the person with whom the deposit is made to have dealing with the depositor and for the specific purpose of being held as security for the due performance by the depositor of his part of the contract, would not prevent a deposit from being really in the nature of a loan. [*K.M.S. Lakshmanier and Sons* v *Commissioner of Income Tax and Excess Profits Tax, Madras* AIR 1953 SC 145: 1953 SCR 1057: 1953 SCJ 222: (1953)23 ITR 202].

• **Accommodation loan** p. 16.
• **Bridging loan** p. 112.

- **Dead loans** p. 227.
- **Secured loan** p. 782.
- **Term loan** p. 836.

**Lobbying.** Seeking to influence the vote of a member of the legislature.

**Local area.** The proper meaning to be attached to the words 'Local Area' in Entry 52 of List II (State List) of the Constitution of India (when the area is a part of the State imposing the law) is an area administered by local body like a municipality, a district board, a local board, a union board, a Panchayat. [*Diamond Sugar Mills Ltd.* v *State of UP* AIR 1961 SC 652; *Shaktikumar M. Sancheti* v *State of Maharashtra* (1995)1 SCC 351].

The term 'local area' is wide enough to include any part of a State and it may cover more than one district. [*State of MP* v *Kailash Chandra Verma* 1978 Jab LJ 842: 1978 Cr LR (MP) 120].

**Local authority.** *Meaning under General Clauses Act 1897, s. 3(31).* The expression "local authority" is defined as meaning "a municipal committee, district board, body of port commissioners or other authority legally entitled to, or entrusted by the Government with, the control or management of a municipal or local fund. [*Patel Premji Jiva by LRs.* v *State of Gujarat* (1971)1 SCC 815; *Union of India* v *R.C. Jain* AIR 1981 SC 951: (1981)2 SCC 308: (1981)2 SCR 854; *R. Sarangapani* v *Port Trust of Madras* AIR 1961 Mad 234].

NOTE: A proper and careful scrutiny of the language of s. 3(31) suggests that an authority, in order to be a 'local authority', must be of like nature and character as a Municipal Committee, District Board or Body of Port Commissioners, possessing, therefore, many, if not all, of the distinctive attributes and characteristics of a Municipal Committee, District Board, or Body of Port Commissioners, but, possessing one essential feature, namely, that it is legally entitled to or entrusted by the Government with, the control and management of a municipal or local fund. [*Union of India* v *R.C. Jain* AIR 1981 SC 951: (1981)2 SCR 854: (1981)2 SCC 308].

The Calcutta Dock Labour Board is a local authority within the meaning of Or. 21, r. 48(1), Code of Civil Procedure 1908, and under s. 3(31) of the General Clauses Act. [*Bhikari Behara* v *Dhanapati Bentia* AIR 1970 Cal 176: 74 CWN 943].

Delhi Development Authority is a 'local authority'. [*Union of India* v *R.C. Jain* AIR 1981 SC 951: (1981)2 SCC 308: (1981)2 SCR 854].

Unless it is shown that the State Transport Corporation is an authority and is legally entitled to and entrusted by the Government with control or management of a local fund it cannot be regarded as a local authority. [*Valjibhai Muljibhai* v *State of Bombay* AIR 1963 SC 1890].

▸ *Meaning under the Cattle Trespass Act 1871, s. 3.* 'Local authority' means any body of persons for the time being invested by law with the control and administration of any matters within a specified local area.

**Local candidate.** A local candidate in service means a temporary Government servant not appointed regularly in accordance with the rules of recruitment to that service. [*Dr. S.T. Venkataiah* v *State of Mysore* AIR 1969 Mys 186].

A 'local candidate' in service means a temporary Government servant not appointed regularly as per rules of recruitment to that service. When the appointment of a local candidate would be regularised it would be in consonance with the rules. [*R.N. Nanjundappa* v *T. Thimmiah* (1972)1 SCC 409: AIR 1972 SC 1767].

**Local fund.** Any fund under the control or management of a local authority.

**Local Government.** The Government of any specified local area within a State or other major political unit; the body of persons constituting such a Government.

**Local improvement.** A public improvement made in a particular locality, by which the real property adjoining or near such locality is specially benefited. [*Floyd* v *Parker Water & Sewer Sub-District* 17 SE 2d 223, 227].

**Local law.** A local law is one which operates over a particular locality instead of over the whole territory of the State [*Ulrich* v *Beatty* 139 Ind App 174]; one whose operation is confined within territorial limits, other than those of the whole State or any properly constituted class or locality therein. [*State* v *Kallas* 94 P 2d 414, 420; *Ravitz* v *Steurele* 77 SW 2d 360, 364].

▸ *Meaning under the Indian Penal Code 1860, s. 42.* A 'local law' is a law applicable only to a particular part of India.

**Local usage.** A practice or method of dealing regularly observed in a particular place and such that it may be considered by the court under certain circumstances in interpreting a document.

**Locality.** It must be understood to mean a compact area smaller than city, town or village but larger than the vicinity of a building. [*Kochhummini Pillai* v *Parukutty Amma* 1986 KLJ 113; *Joseph Thomas* v *Ouseph Joseph* 1986 KLT 398].

A definite region in any part of space; geographical position [*Warnock* v *Kraft* 30 Cal App 2d 1: 85 P 2d 505, 506]. Place; vicinity; neighbourhood; community. [*Conley* v *Valley Motor Transit Co.* CCA Ohio, 139 F 2d 692, 693; *Lukens Steel Co.* v *Perkins* 107 F 2d 627, 631].

**Lock-out.** Cessation of furnishing of work to employees or withholding work from them in effort to get for employer more desirable terms. [*Zura* v *Marblehead Stone Division, Standard Slag Corp.* 224 NE 2d 176].

The word 'lock-out' means refusal on the part of an employer to furnish work to his operatives except on conditions to be accepted by the latter collectively. [*Feroz Din* v *State of West Bengal* AIR 1960 SC 363: (1960)2 SCR 319: 1960 Cr LJ 527: 1960 SCJ 248: (1960)1 Lab LJ 244].

▸ *Meaning under the Industrial Disputes Act 1947, s. 2(l).* 'Lock-out' means the temporary closing of a place of employment, or the suspension of work, or the refusal by an employer to continue to employ any number of persons employed by him.

> NOTE: In the case of a lock-out, the industry as such is not closed down even temporarily; only particular workers are refused work. Closing down a business, even temporarily, is distinct and different from a lock-out. [*Indian Metal* v *Industrial Tribunal* AIR 1953 Mad 98].

**Lockup.** A place of detention in a police station, court or other facility used for persons awaiting trial.

**Loco parentis.** A person in *loco parentis* means a person taking upon himself the duty of father of a child. [*Bennet* v *Bennet* (1897)10 Ch D 474].

**Loco price.** The ex-warehouse price of goods.

**Locum tenens.** One who holds the place of another. One who lawfully executes the office of another.

**Locus standi.** A place of standing; standing in court; a right of appearance in a court of justice, or before a legislative body, on a given question.

The right of a party to an action to appear and be heard on the question before any tribunal. [*S.P. Gupta* v *Union of India* 1981 Supp SCC 87: AIR 1982 SC 149; *People's Union of Democratic Rights* v *Union of India* AIR 1982 SC 1473; *J. Mahapatra* v *State of Orissa* AIR 1984 SC 1572: (1984)2 SCC 103; *K. Sudarshan* v *Commr., Corpn. of Madras* AIR 1984 Mad 292; *Krishna Kanta Jaiswal* v *Vice-Chancellor, B.H.U.* AIR 1984 All 305].

**Lodger.** Boarder; dweller; habitant; indweller; occupant; resider; roomer.

An occupant who has mere use without actual or exclusive possession. [*Roberts* v *Casey* 36 Cal App 2d, Supp 767; *Coggins* v *Gregorio* CCA NM, 97 F 2d 948, 951].

Lodger has been defined as a tenant of part of another's house, one who for time being has his home at his lodging place, one who has leave to inhabit another man's house, one who inhabits portion of a house of which another has general possession and custody, one who lives at board or in a hired room or who has a bed in another's house, one who lives in a hired room or rooms in house of another, one who occupies hired apartments in another's house. The term is also defined as a person who lives and sleeps in a place, a person whose occupancy is a part of a house and subordinate to and in some degree under the control of a landlord or his representative. The term is used to indicate a personal relationship of some one lodging somewhere with somebody. [*Marden* v *Radford* 229 Mo App 789: 84 SW 2d 947, 955, 957, 959].

**Lodging house.** A lodging house is a house for lodging of lodgers on a contract for a definite time.

Houses containing furnished apartments which are let out by the week or by the month, without meals, or with limited meals. [*Marden* v *Radford* 84 SW 2d 947, 955].

"In its plain and ordinary meaning and although in any case there may be various incidental features annexed, 'lodging house' signifies a house containing furnished rooms which are privately let out by the week or month". [*Lord Nelson Hotel Co. Ltd.* v *Halifax* (1956), 1 DLR (2d) 561, *per* Rand, J. (dissenting) at p. 564].

**Log or log-book.** Log or log-book is a book with a permanent record made of all events occurring during a ship's voyage including her rate of progress shown by the ship's log. [Mozley & Whiteley's *Law Dictionary*, 10th Ed.].

**Loss.** Calamity; catastrophe; deprivation; ill fortune; ill luck; waste.

Loss is a generic and relative term. It signifies the act of losing or the thing lost; it is not a word of limited, hard and fast meaning and has been held synonymous with, or equivalent to, "damage", "damages", "deprivation", "detriment", "injury", and "privation". [*Mason* v *City of Albertville* 158 So 2d 924, 927].

"Loss" is a generic term. It signifies some detriment or deprivation or damage. [*Consumer Unity & Trust Society* v *Chairman & Managing Director, Bank of Baroda* (1995)2 SCC 150].

It may mean—

* act of losing, or the thing lost [*Fidelity Union Casualty Co.* v *Wilkinson* Tex Civ App, 94 SW 2d 763, 766];
* bad and uncollectable accounts [*Duke* v *Cregan* 12 P 2d 354, 355];
* a decrease in value of resources or increase in liabilities; depletion or depreciation or destruction of value; deprivation; destruction [*Wells* v *Thomas W. Garland, Inc.* Mo App, 39 SW 2d 409, 411];
* failure to keep that which one has or thinks he has; injury [*United Service Automobile Ass'n* v *Miles* 161 SW 2d 1048; *United States* v *City of Nat. Bank of Duluth* DC Minn, 31 F Supp 530, 534, 535];
* shrinkage in value of estate or property; state or fact of being lost or destroyed [*Logan* v *Johnson* 10 SE 2d 653, 655];
* that which is gone and cannot be recovered or that which is withheld or that of which a party is dispossessed [*Walker* v *Thomas* 75 F 2d 667, 669];
* unintentional parting with something of value [*Providence Journal Co.* v *Broderick* CCA RI, 104 F 2d 614, 616].

The word 'loss' in Railways Act means that the goods have disappeared in the course of transit and neither the railway nor the consignor nor the consignee are or is in a position to trace them. [*Union of India* v *Sha Vastimull Harakchand* AIR 1959 Mys 13: ILR (1958) Mys 481].

The word 'loss' in Art. III of the Indian Carriage of Goods by Sea Act means and includes any loss caused to a shipper or a consignee by reason of the inability of the ship or the carrier to deliver part or whole of the goods, to whatever reason such a failure may be due. [*East and West Steamship Co.* v *S.K. Ramalingam Chettiar* AIR 1960 SC 1058: (1960)2 SCA 544: (1960)3 SCR 820].

• **General average loss** p. 383.

• **Net loss** p. 606.

• **Wrongful loss** p. 907.

**Loss leader.** When an item of goods, or a range of goods, is offered for sale by a retailer at a price which represents a loss to him in order to tempt customers in to buy it and potentially other goods which are on sale at a profit, the item which shows a loss is known as the loss leader. [Osborn & Grandage's *Concise Commercial Dictionary*].

Item sold by a merchant at very low price and sometimes below cost in order to attract people to store with the hope that they will buy additional items on which a profit will be made. [Black's *Law Dictionary*, 5th Ed.].

Goods or commodity sold at a very low price, usually below cost, to attract customers to buy other items. [Black's *Law Dictionary*, 7th Ed.].

**Lost grant.** Presumption of lost grant remains one of the methods by which an easement may be acquired. Twenty years uninterrupted enjoyment of an easement raises a presumption of a lost grant namely that it had been created by a deed of grant which had been lost. The presumption of lost grant is rebuttable only by evidence that making such grant is impossible.

NOTE: The doctrine of lost grant has no application to the case of inhabitants of particular localities seeking to establish rights of user to some piece of land or water. Since the right originated in a grant, its owners, whether original or by devolution, had to be such persons as were capable of being recipients of a grant, and a right exercisable by the inhabitants of a village from time to time is neither attached to any estate in land nor is it such a right as is capable of being made the subject of a grant, there being no admissible grantees. No lost grant in respect of a fishery could be presented in favour of a fluctuating and unascertained body of persons, as the inhabitants of a particular village. [*Braja Sundar Deb* v *Moni Behara* AIR 1951 SC 247: 1951 SCJ 363: 1951 SCR 431].

**Lost or not lost.** A phrase sometimes inserted in policies of marine insurance. It signifies that the contract is meant to relate back to the beginning of a voyage now in progress, or to some other antecedent time, and to be valid and effectual even if, at the moment of executing the policy, the vessel should have already perished by some of the perils insured against, provided that neither party has knowledge of that fact or any advantage over the other in the way of superior means of information. [*Hooper* v *Robinson* 98 US 528: 25 L Ed 219; *Insurance Co.* v *Folsom* 21 L Ed 827].

**Lottery.** A chance for a prize for a price. Essential elements of a lottery are consideration, prize and chance and any scheme or device by which a person for a consideration is permitted to receive a prize or nothing as may be determined predominantly by chance. [*State* v *Wassick* W Va, 191 SE 2d 283, 288].

The lottery has been compendiously defined as a scheme for the distribution of money by chance. It usually, if not always, takes the form of the creation of a fund by the participants in the lottery, who buy tickets or pay subscriptions in consideration of an offer by the promoters to award them a prize on some contingency, the happening whereof depends on chance. [*Barnes* v *Strathern* (1929) SC (J) 41, *per* Lord Clyde].

A "lottery" means a chance for a prize for a price and unless all the three essential elements, namely chance, consideration and prize are present the scheme or the transaction would not amount to a lottery. [*H. Anraj* v *Government of Tamil Nadu* AIR 1986 SC 63: (1986)1 SCC 414: 1985 Supp (3) SCR 342: (1986)61 STC 165].

A lottery is a scheme for the distribution of prizes by lot or chance. [*Emperor* v *Gurbaksh* AIR 1934 Lah 840].

NOTE: A lottery is a weighing contract. [*Darabji Tata* v *Bance* 42 Bom 676]. Whoever keeps an office for drawing lottery, not being a State lottery or a lottery authorised by the State Government, is punishable under s. 293A of the Indian Penal Code.

**Low-water mark.** Line on the shore marking the lowest ebb of the tide.

▸ *Meaning under the Major Ports Trust Act 1963, s. 2(l).* 'Low-water mark', in relation to a port, means a line drawn through the lowest points reached by ordinary spring-tides at any season of the year at that port.

**Lucid interval.** A period of sanity which intervenes between two attacks of insanity. Acts done during such an interval are valid. [Mozley & Whiteley's *Law Dictionary*, 10th Ed.].

Intervals occurring in the mental life of an insane person during which he is completely restored to the use of his reason, or so far restored that he has sufficient intelligence, judgment, and will to enter into contractual relations, or perform other legal acts, without disqualification by reason of his disease. [*Oklahoma Natural Gas Corporation* v *Lay* 175 Okl 75: 51 P 2d 580, 583].

**Luggage.** Suitcases, bags, etc. to hold a traveller's belongings; anything burdensome or heavy to carry; baggage.

• **Personal luggage** p. 660.

**Lunatic.** An idiot or person of unsound mind. [Indian Lunacy Act 1912, s. 3(5), since repealed].

**Luxury.** The connotation of the word "luxury", is something which conduces enjoyment over and above the necessaries of life. It denotes something which is superfluous and not indispensable and to which we take with a view to enjoy, amuse or entertain ourselves. [*A.B. Abdul Kadir* v *State of Kerala* AIR 1976 SC 182: (1976)2 SCR 690: (1976)3 SCC 219].

"Luxury" connotes extravagance or indulgence, as distinguished from the needs and necessities of life. The New Dictionary of Thought has there thoughtful things to say to luxury "on the soft bed of luxury most kingdom have expired", war destroys men, but luxury destroys mankind, at once corrupts the body and the mind. [*Express Hotels Private Ltd.* v *State of Gujarat* AIR 1989 SC 1949: JT 1989(3) SC 72: (1989)74 STC 157: (1989)178 ITR 151: (1989)2 SCR 893: (1989)3 SCC 677: (1990)3 Comp LJ 275].

An expenditure on something which is in excess of what is required for economic and personal well-being would be expenditure on luxury although the expenditure may be of a nature which is incurred by a large number of people, including those not economically well off. [*A.B. Abdul Kadir* v *State of Kerala* AIR 1976 SC 182: (1976)2 SCR 690: (1976)3 SCC 219].

# Mm

**Machine.** Any combination of mechanisms for utilizing, modifying, applying, or transmitting energy whether simple or complex; an apparatus using or applying mechanical power, having several parts each with a definite function and together performing certain kinds of work; an instrument that transmits a force or directs its application.

A device or apparatus consisting of fixed and moving parts that work together to perform some function. [Black's *Law Dictionary*, 7th Ed.].

A machine in its popular sense is a piece of mechanism which, by means of its interrelated parts, serves to utilise or apply power; but does not include anything that is merely a reservoir or conduit, although connected with something which is without doubt a machine. [*Aucland City Corpn.* v *Aucland Gas Co. Ltd.* (1919) NZLR 561 (CA), *per* Sem, J.].

A machine is a device meant to convert a slow motion at some point into a rapid motion at the other desired point or the device to convert rotatory motion into linear motion or the device to step down electricity of higher voltage into a lower voltage. [*Cuttack Municipality* v *Executive Engineer, S.E. Board* ILR (1975) Cut 1365].

'Machine' means a mechanical device consisting of a planned and organized arrangement of various parts, each part having definite functions and as a result of combined functioning some work, which may be impossible or difficult for human physical power to perform or even if it can be done, it cannot be done continuously for a long period or with the speed and with the same uniformity with which the machine does the same work, is performed. [*K.B. Dani* v *State of Karnataka* (1979)1 Kant LJ 286 (DB)].

NOTE: *Machine—what is—examples:*

- An electrical transformer being a device to change voltage and current in the electrical circuit from one voltage to another is a machine. [*Cuttack Municipality* v *Executive Engineer, S.E. Board* ILR (1975) Cut 1365].
- A crane can be described as a machine. [*British Railways Board* v *Liptrot* (1967)2 All ER 1072 (HL)].
- Sewai-ki-machine has been held to be machine. [*Commissioner of Sales Tax, U.P., Lucknow* v *Ramesh Pd. Batuk Pd., Varanasi* (1975)36 STC 367].
- Hair clipper was held to be a machine. [*Commissioner of Sales Tax* v *Chandok Traders* (1973)32 STC 614].

*Machine—what is not—example:*

- Looms which are merely worked by power would hardly fall within the meaning of the word 'machine'. [*Sales Tax Commissioner, U.P.* v *Lodha Singh Mal Singh* AIR 1971 SC 2221: (1971)2 SCC 407].

▸ *Other meanings.* A person who acts mechanically and with apparent lack of emotion; one who acts in a mechanical manner; a robot; the controlling system of an organization, *e.g.*, the party machine.

• **Calculating machine** at p. 118.

**Machinery.** The word 'machinery' has no definite legal meaning. In popular sense, it means primarily a number of machines taken collectively. [*Aucland City Corpn.* v *Aucland Gas Co. Ltd.* (1919) NZLR 561, 586 (CA)].

The word 'machinery' when used in ordinary language *prima facie* means some mechanical contrivances which, by themselves or in combination with one or more other mechanical contrivances by the combined movement and inter-dependent operations of their respective parts, generate power or evoke, modify, apply direct natural forces with the object in each case of effecting a definite and specific result. [*Corporation of Calcutta* v *Cossipore Municipality* AIR 1922 PC 27].

Any mechanical contrivance where energy is transmitted from one point to another is machinery. [*Om Engineering Co. Pvt. Ltd.* v *Commissioner, Sales Tax, U.P.* (1976)38 STC 553: 1976 Tax LR 1429].

The word 'machinery' can be stated to be an instrument designed to transmit and modify the application of power, force and motion. [*Orissa Agro Industries Corporation Ltd.* v *State of Orissa* (1994)19 STJ 95].

Machinery denotes some mechanical contrivance which, by itself or in combination with other mechanical devices generate power or evoke, modify, apply or direct natural forces and effect a definite and a specific result. [*RME Works* v *Commissioner, Sales Tax* 1976 MPLJ 244].

The word 'machinery' must mean more than collection of ordinary tools. [*Commissioner of Income Tax, Madras* v *Mir Mohammad Ali* AIR 1964 SC 1693: (1964)7 SCR 846: (1964)53 ITR 165: (1964)2 SCJ 354: (1965)1 SCWR 247].

▸ *Meaning under the Factories Act 1948, s. 2(j).* Machinery includes prime movers, transmission machinery and all other appliances whereby power is generated, transformed, transmitted or applied.

NOTE: Machinery does not cease to be machinery merely because it has to be used in conjunction with one or more machines. Nor does it cease to be machinery merely because it is, for instance, installed as part of a manufacturing or industrial plant. [*Commissioner of Income Tax, Madras* v *Mir Mohammad Ali* AIR 1964 SC 1693: (1964)7 SCR 846: (1964)53 ITR 165: (1964)2 SCJ 354: (1965)1 SCWR 247].

*'Machinery'—what is—examples:*

- A diesel engine is a machinery. [*Commissioner of Income Tax, Madras* v *Mir Mohammad Ali* AIR 1964 SC 1693: (1964)7 SCR 846: (1964)53 ITR 165: (1964)2 SCJ 354: (1965)1 SCWR 247].
- A hand pump used for lifting water is 'machinery'. [*Om Engineering Co. Pvt. Ltd.* v *Commissioner, Sales Tax, U.P.* (1976)38 STC 553: 1976 Tax LR 1429].
- Water pump was held to fall in the category of machinery. [*Basant Industries, Agra* v *Commissioner of Sales Tax* (1975)36 STC 209].

*'Machinery'—what is not—examples:*

- The seat on which the crane driver sits is not part of the machinery of the crane. [*British Railways Board* v *Liptrot* (1967)2 All ER 1072 (HL)].
- The body of a motor car cannot be described as part of the machinery of a car. [*British Railways Board* v *Liptrot* (1967)2 All ER 1072 (HL)].

• **Dangerous machinery** p. 223.
• **Defect in machinery** p. 241.
• **Textile machinery** p. 841.
• **Transmission machinery** p. 853.

**Magistrate.** The description "Magistrate" is the common denomination under which are included all those who are entrusted, whether by commission or appointment, or by virtue of their office, with the conservation of the peace and the hearing and determination of charges in respect of offences against it. [Halsbury's *Laws of England*, 3rd Ed., vol. 25, p. 103].

The term in its generic sense refers to a person clothed with power as a public civil officer, or a public civil officer invested with executive or judicial power. [*Ex parte Noel* Ky, 338 SW 2d 903, 907].

In a general sense, a "Magistrate" is a public officer, possessing such power, legislative, executive, or judicial, as government appointing him may ordain, although in a narrow sense he is regarded as an inferior judicial officer. [*Shadwick* v *City of Tampa* Fla, 250 So 2d 4, 5].

▸ *Meaning under various Acts.* 'Magistrate' shall include every person exercising all or any of the powers of a Magistrate under the Code of Criminal Procedure for the time being in force. [General Clauses Act 1897, s. 3(32)].

'Magistrate' means a Magistrate of the first class or a Presidency Magistrate. [Extradition Act 1962, s. 2(*g*)].

'Magistrate' means a Presidency Magistrate, District Magistrate, Sub-Divisional Magistrate or a Magistrate of the first class specially empowered by the State Government to perform the functions of a Magistrate. [Indian Lunacy Act 1912, s. 3(6) (since repealed)].

Magistrate means—(1) in relation to a metropolitan area within the meaning of cl. (*k*) of s. 2 of the Code of Criminal Procedure 1973, a Metropolitan Magistrate; (2) in relation to any other area, the Chief Judicial Magistrate. Sub-Divisional Judicial Magistrate or such other Judicial Magistrate of the first class as the State Government may, by notification, empower to perform the functions of a Magistrate under this Act. [The Mental Health Act 1987, s. 2(*h*)].

'Magistrate' does not include the head of a village discharging magisterial functions in the Presidency of Fort St. George or elsewhere, unless such headman is a Magistrate exercising the powers of a Magistrate under the Code of Criminal Procedure 1882. [Indian Evidence Act 1872, s. 26, Explanation].

'Magistrate' shall include all persons within the general police district, exercising all or any of the powers of a Magistrate. [Police Act 1861, s. 1].

'Magistrate' means a person exercising powers under the Code of Criminal Procedure 1973, not less than those of a Magistrate of the second class, and includes in the towns of Calcutta, Madras and Bombay a Presidency Magistrate. [Indian Ports Act 1908, s. 3(1)].

'Magistrate' means any person exercising the full powers of a Magistrate and includes a Magistrate of Police. [Press and Registration of Books Act 1867, s. 1].

'Magistrate' means in the Presidency-towns, a Presidency Magistrate, and elsewhere a Magistrate of the first class or (when specially empowered by the State Government to try cases under this Act) a Magistrate of the second class. [Opium Act 1878, s. 3].

The expression "Magistrate" has been defined to mean a District Magistrate, a Sub-divisional Magistrate, a Presidency Magistrate, or a Magistrate of the first class specially empowered by the State Government by notification in the Official Gazette, to exercise jurisdiction under the Suppression of Immoral Traffic in Women and Girls Act 1956. [*State of U.P.* v *Kaushaliya* AIR 1964 SC 416: (1964)4 SCR 1002: (1964)1 Cr LJ 304].

The expression "Magistrate" in s. 190 of the Criminal Procedure Code 1973 is a compendious term which includes Judicial Magistrate of the second class and the Executive Magistrate. [*A.R. Antulay* v *R.S. Nayak* AIR 1984 SC 718: (1984)2 SCC 500: (1984)2 SCR 914: 1984 Cr LJ 647: 1984 SCC (Cri) 277: 1984(1) SLR 666].

**Magistrate of the District.** The chief officer charged with the executive administration of a district and exercising the powers of a Magistrate, by whatever designation the chief officer charged with such executive administration is styled. [Police Act 1861, s. 1].

**Magna Carta.** The Great Charter originally granted by King John in 1215, and afterwards re-enacted by Parliament more than 30 times. It contained provisions to protect the subject from abuse of the Royal Prerogative in the matter of arbitrary arrest and imprisonment, and from various extortions.

**NOTE:** The barons assembled in the latter part of 1214 and swore to openly rebel unless King John confirmed by a formal Charter the ancient liberties of England. A conference between the King and the armed barons opened on Monday, 15th June 1215, and lasted till 19th June 1215. Articles of agreement were drawn up and sealed and these articles came to be known as the Magna Carta or the Great Charter, which *inter alia* provides as follows: "No freeman shall be taken or imprisoned; ...... nor will we pass upon him nor condemn him, but by lawful judgment of his peers ...... To no man will we sell, to no man deny, to no man delay, justice or right."

For Magna Carta and the battle for independence of judiciary in England. [*Penumbra of Natural Justice* by Tapash Gan Choudhury, 2nd Ed., p. 229].

**Mahajan.** A great man; a merchant; a banker; a moneylender; a creditor.

**Mahal.** A house; an estate; a tract of land.

**Mahant.** The head of a *Matt.*

NOTE: *Mahant* of a *Matt* is not a mere manager or custodian. He has, however, large powers for the benefit of the institution of which he is the head. He can incur expenditure for the institution but not for himself. He is to discharge the duties as a trustee and is answerable as such. [*Sudhindra Thirthaswamiar* v *Commissioner for Hindu Religious and Charitable Endowments, Mysore* AIR 1963 SC 966: (1963)2 SCA 340: 1963 Supp (2) SCR 302].

**Mahimai.** *'Mahimai'* means religious purpose. [*The Commissioner of Income Tax (Central), New Delhi* v *Bijli Cotton Mills (P) Ltd., Hathras, District Aligarh* AIR 1979 SC 346: (1979)2 SCR 241: (1979)1 SCC 496: (1979)116 ITR 60].

A *'Mahimai'* is a donation for charity consisting of a fixed percentage on the sales or profits on commercial transactions done by the 'donor'. [*State of Madras* v *S.S.M. Paripalana Sangam* AIR 1962 Mad 48].

NOTE: *'Mahimai'* cannot be claimed as a trade allowance. It is a deduction made out of the price payable to the seller and is intended to be utilised for purposes of charity. It has nothing to do with the transaction as such and is really a contribution levied at the time of the transaction for a purpose unconnected with it. It cannot, therefore, be properly regarded as a trade allowance. [*P.P. Kutti* v *State of Madras* (1954)1 MLJ 117: AIR 1954 Mad 621 (DB)].

**Mail bag.** The expression 'mail bag' includes a bag, box, parcel or any other envelope or covering in which postal articles in course of transmission by post are conveyed, whether it does or does not contain any such article. [Indian Post Office Act 1898, s. 2(*c*)].

**Mail ship.** A ship employed for carrying mails.

▸ *Meaning under the Indian Post Office Act 1898, s. 2(d).* A ship employed for carrying mails, pursuant to contract or continuing arrangement, by the Central Government or Her Majesty's Government or the Government of any British possession or foreign country.

**Maim.** To deprive of the use of a bodily part; mutilate; disable; cripple; impair.

The deprivation of a member proper for defence in fight, as an arm, leg, finger, eye, or a foretooth; yet not a jaw-tooth, or an ear, or a nose, because they have been supposed to be of no use in fighting. [Wharton's *Law Lexicon*, 14th Ed.].

"Maihem or maim is where by the wrongful act of another any member is hurt or taken away, whereby the party is made unperfect to fight: as if a bone be taken out of the hand ...... But the cutting of an ear or nose, or breaking of the hinder teeth, or such like is no maihem, because it is rather a deformity of body than diminishing of strength ......" [Termes de La Ley 283-84 (1st Am. ed. 1812)].

NOTE: To constitute "maiming" an injury must be permanent. [*R.* v *Feans* (1844)1 Car & Kir 539].

The expression "maiming" refers to injuries permanently by affecting the use of a limb or other member of the body. [*Emperor* v *Juman Sajan* AIR 1947 Sind 66].

The break a man's leg is a sufficiently serious injury to amount to a maiming. [*R.* v *Schultz* (1962)133 Can CC 174, *per* Smith, C.J.A.].

**Main.** Principal; leading; primary; chief; most important in size, extent, rank, importance, strength or utility.

With regard to electricity, "main" means any electric supply line through which energy is or intended to be supplied to the public. [*State of U.P.* v *Hindustan Aluminium Corpn.* AIR 1979 SC 1459: (1979)3 SCR 709: (1979)3 SCC 229].

With regard to supply of water, "main" means a pipe laid for the purpose of giving a general supply of water as distinct from a supply to individual consumers and includes any apparatus used in connection with such a pipe.

**Mainly.** The word 'mainly', according to the ordinary plain meaning, means, substantially, principally, chiefly, as far as practicable or so far as possible. [*Smt. Swaran Lata* v *Union of India* (1979)2 SCR 953: (1979)3 SCC 165].

**Maintain.** The term is variously defined as acts of repairs and other acts to prevent a decline, lapse or cessation from existing state or condition; bear the expense of; carry on; commence; continue; furnish means for subsistence or existence of; hold; hold or keep in an existing state or condition; hold or preserve in any particular state or condition; keep from change; keep from falling, declining, or ceasing; keep in existence or continuance; keep in force; keep in good order; keep in proper condition; keep in repair; keep up; preserve; preserve from lapse, decline, failure, or cessation; provide for, rebuild; repair; replace supply with means of support; supply with what is needed; support; sustain; uphold. Negatively stated, it is defined as not to lose or surrender, not to suffer or fail or decline. [*El Paso County Water Imp. Dist. No. 1* v *City of El Paso* DC Tex, 243 F 2d 927, 931].

"The word 'maintain' when used in relation to the state or condition of things is not always used in the same sense. It may be used to indicate the continuance of a particular state or condition, as when one says of someone that 'he maintains his buildings just as they were'. But on occasion it takes colour from the work of maintenance and is used in reference to the acts done or requisite to be done in the course of maintenance, as when one says of another that 'he maintains his buildings methodically'. This latter use gives the word 'maintained' in relation to machinery rather the meaning of 'serviced' or 'looked after' or 'attended to'." [*Galashiels Gas Co. Ltd.* v *O'Donnell* (1949) AC 275, 286, *per* Lord MacDermott].

The word "maintain" has several meanings in law, including that of keeping in repair. [*A.G.* v *Kavanagh* (1938) IR 368].

To "maintain" an action is to uphold, continue on foot, and keep from collapse a suit already begun, or to prosecute a suit with effect. [*George Moore Ice Cream Co.* v *Ross* Ga., 289 US 373: 53 S Ct 620: 77 L Ed 1265]. To maintain an action or suit may mean to commence or institute it; the term imports the existence of a cause of action. Maintain, however, is applied to actions already brought, but not yet reduced to judgment. [*Smallwood* v *Gallardo* 72 L Ed 152].

NOTE: 'Maintain' may be a word of ambiguous import but ambiguity may disappear in the context in which the word is used. [*Hamilton* v *National Coal Board* (1960) SLT 24 (HL): (1960) AC 633].

**Maintenance.** Act of maintaining, keeping up, supporting; livelihood; means of sustenance. [*Federal Land Bank of St. Louis* v *Miller* 42 SW 2d 564, 566].

The furnishing by one person to another, for his support, of the means of living, or food, clothing, shelter, etc., particularly where the legal relation of the parties is such that one is bound to support the other, as between father and child, or husband and wife. [*State ex rel. Blume* v *State Board of Education of Montana* 34 P 2d 515, 519].

The supplying of the necessaries of life. [*Federal Land Bank of St. Louis* v *Miller* 42 SW 2d 564, 566].

Term 'maintenance' means primarily food, clothing and shelter, but it does include such items as reasonable and necessary transportation or automobile expenses, medical and drug expenses, utilities and household expenses. [*Hughes* v *Hughes* La App, 303 So 2d 766, 769].

'Maintenance' means the act of maintaining, and denotes the regular supply of food, clothing and lodging; the provision of the necessaries and of the conveniences of life. [*Kallin* v *Kallin* (1944) SASR 73, *per* Mayo, J.].

Maintenance is generally intended to mean lodging, boarding, medical attention and other necessaries of life, but not merely necessities of life. In the case of children, the expression would naturally include cost of education also. [*Aliyar* v *Pathu* (1988)2 Ker LT 446, 452 (Ker)].

▸ *Meaning in legal action.* There are many definitions of maintenance, all seeming to express the same idea.

Blackstone calls it 'an officious intermeddling in a suit which no way belongs to one by maintaining or assisting either party with money or otherwise to prosecute or defend it'. [Bl. Com. Book iv. C.10, s. 12].

Lord Coke says 'maintenance' 'signifieth in law a taking in hand, bearing up, or upholding of a quarrel, or side, to the disturbance or hindrance of common right'. [Co. Litt. 368b].

'Maintenance is when any man gives or delivers to another that is plaintiff or defendant in any action any sum of money or other thing to maintain his plea, or takes great pains for him when he hath nothing therewith to do, then the party grieved shall have a writ against him called a writ of maintenance' [Termes de la Ley as quoted in *Bardlaugh* v *Newdegate* (1883)11 QBD 1].

'Maintenance is the officious assistance by money or otherwise, proffered by a third person to either party to a suit, in which he himself has no legal interest, to enable them to prosecute or defend it'. [Story on *Contract*, Ch. vii, s. 578].

▸ *Meaning in matrimonial affairs.* 'Maintenance' is a very wide word, and ...... it should be read as covering everything which a wife may in reason want to do with the income which she enjoys. It includes much more than food, lodging, clothes, travelling, and so on. It includes, for instance, charity and making arrangements for the future, thus incurring various liabilities in her discretion ...... [*Acworth* v *Acworth* (1943) P 21, 22 (CA), *per* Scott, L.J.].

"Maintenance does not only mean the food a wife puts in her mouth. It also means her clothes, the house in which she lives, and the money which she is to have in her pocket, all of which vary according to the means of her husband. Maintenance cannot mean only mere subsistence". [*Re Borthwick, Borthwick* v *Beauvais* (1949)1 All ER 472: (1949) Ch 395, *per* Harman, J.].

"Maintenance", necessarily must encompass a provision for residence. Maintenance is given so that the lady can live in the manner, more or less, to which she was accustomed. The concept of maintenance must, therefore, include provision for food and clothing and the like and take into account the basic need of a roof over the head. [*Mangat Mal* v *Punni Devi* (1995)6 SCC 88: JT 1995(7) SC 506: AIR 1996 SC 172].

NOTE: 'Maintenance' under s. 125, Cr. P.C. 1973, includes expenses for fooding, clothing, residence, medical, educational and other expenses relating to normal pursuit of life. [*Ashwini Kumar Sinha* v *Rashmi Sinha* (1997)1 Pat LJR 295, 297].

▸ *Meaning in property affairs.* "Maintenance" means the upkeep, or preserving the condition of property to be operated.

NOTE: "Maintenance" includes repairs. "'Maintenance' is a vague word. It is not necessarily distinguished from 'repair'. It may in some contexts be the same as 'repair', and it may in some contexts have a wider meaning which includes repairing as well as other operations". [*Day* v *Harland and Wolf, Ltd.* (1953)2 All ER 387, *per* Pearson, J.].

**Maintenance of law and order.** The expression 'maintenance of law and order' means prevention of disorders of comparatively lesser gravity and of local significance. [*B. Sundara Rao* v *State of Orissa* AIR 1972 SC 739: (1972)3 SCC 11: 1972 SCC (Cri) 138].

**Maintenance of public order.** By the expression "maintenance of public order" what is intended is the prevention of grave public disorder. [*B. Sundara Rao* v *State* *of Orissa* AIR 1972 SC 739: (1972)3 SCC 11: 1972 SCC (Cri) 138].

**Majority.** Full age; legal age; the age at which, by law, a person is entitled to the management of his own affairs and to the enjoyment of civic rights.

NOTE: The age of majority is eighteen years in the case of ordinary persons, and, in the case of persons where property is administered by the court of wards or for whose person a guardian is appointed under the Guardians and Wards Act, the age of majority is twenty-one years.

It may also mean the greater number; the number greater than half of any total; bulk; larger part; lion's share; major part; predominant part; preponderance.

• **Absolute majority** p. 9.

**Make.** To cause to exist [*United States* v *Giles* 81 L Ed 493]; to form, fashion, or produce; to do, perform or execute; to do in form of law; to perform with due formalities; to execute in legal form; to support or sustain; accomplish; actualise; carry into effect; carry into execution; effectuate; enforce; give birth to; give origin to; give rise to; manufacture.

**Make allowance.** To allow deduction or abatement. [*Ram Chandra Pal* v *Hiramba Kumar Pal* AIR 1952 Cal 502: 55 CWN 686].

**Making-up price.** The price at which stocks and shares are closed in one stock exchange account and carried over the next account.

**Makkathayam.** "Makkathayam" means gift by the father. [*Kunju Kesavan* v *M.M. Philip* AIR 1964 SC 164: (1964)3 SCR 634].

**Makkathayam property.** Makkathayam property is defined to mean property obtained from the husband or father by the wife or child or both of them, by gift, inheritance or bequest. [*Kunju Kesavan* v *M.M. Philip* AIR 1964 SC 164: (1964)3 SCR 634].

**Mal.** A prefix meaning bad, wrong, fraudulent.

NOTE: *Example*: Maladministration, malpractice, malversation, etc.

It also means 'wealth', 'property', 'revenue', 'rent' derivable from land. It means the full land revenue. In India, it was used for the public revenue from any source whatever, but more especially for that derived from land, to which sense, as fiscal term, it is now restricted, or the revenue claimed by the Government from the produce of cultivated lands. [*Rabindra Chandra Ghose* v *Surendra Chandra Ghose* AIR 1945 Cal 129].

**Mala fide.** As adjective means acting or done in bad faith. As adverb means in bad faith. It is opposite of *bona fide* (good faith).

NOTE: *Mala fide* is not meaningless jargon. It has proper connotation. The expression *mala fide* in the facts of each case can only be appreciated from records. There cannot possibly be any set of guidelines in regard to proof of *mala fides*. *Mala fides* depend upon own facts and circumstances. There must be factual support for the allegation of *mala fides*. Mere use of word *mala fide* would not by itself make a petition entertainable. The court must scan factual aspect and come to its own conclusion. [*Prabodh Sagar* v *Punjab State Electricity Board* AIR 2000 SC 1684: (2000)5 SCC 630: JT 2000(5) SC 378].

**Mala fide exercise of power.** A "*mala fide* exercise of power" does not necessarily imply any moral turpitude and may only mean that the statutory power is exercised for purpose other than those for which the power was intended by law to be exercised. [*Additional District Magistrate, Jabalpur* v *Shivakant Shukla* AIR 1976 SC 1207: 1976 (Supp) SCR 172: (1976)3 SCC 521: 1976 Cr LJ 945: 1976 Cr LR (SC) 303].

**Mala in se.** Acts wrong in themselves; acts morally wrong; offences against conscience.

**Mala prohibita.** Acts prohibited by human laws; prohibited wrongs or offences.

**Maladministration.** The term is used interchangeably with misadministration, and both words mean "wrong administration".

**Male.** Pertaining to the masculine sex.

**Male lineal descendant.** "Male lineal descendant" must mean a male descendant in the male line. [*Oddie* v *Woodford* (1821)3 My & Cr 584, *per* Lord Eldon, L.C.].

'Male lineal' has been construed to mean as though it were one word, signifying 'male in a line of males'. [*Thellusson* v *Rendlesham (Lord)* (1859)7 HL Cas 429, *per* Bramwell, B.].

NOTE: In speaking of a man and his male descendants as a class, no one would conceive the son of a female descendant as included. [*Bernal* v *Bernal* (1838)3 My & Cr 559, *per* Cottenham, L.C.].

This expression includes, however, illegitimate son of sudra born of concubine in continuous and exclusive keeping of father. [*Sai Ram* v *Narain Rao* 1944 AWR (Rev) 136].

**Malfeasance.** Bad conduct; ill conduct; evil doing; deviation from rectitude, illegal action; injurious action; wrongful action; wrongful conduct.

It is a comprehensive term including any wrongful conduct that affects, interrupts or interferes with the performance of official duties. [*State ex rel. Knable* v *Frater* 89 P 2d 1046, 1048].

Malfeasance is a wrongful act which the actor has no legal right to do, or any wrongful conduct which affects, interrupts, or interferes with performance of official duty, or an act for which there is no authority or warrant of law or which a person ought not to do at all, or the unjust performance of some act, which party performing it has no right, or has contracted not, to do. [*Daugherty* v *Ellis* 97 SE 2d 33, 42].

NOTE: The word 'malfeasance' would apply to a case where an act prohibited by law is done by a person. [*Khairul Bashar* v *Thana Lal* AIR 1957 All 553].

**Malguzari.** It means revenue and not rent. [*Chattra Kumari* v *W.W. Broucke* 54 IA 432: AIR 1927 PC 250].

Malguzari means revenue assessment—the payment of land revenue. It is a term also applied to assessed lands or to lands paying revenue to government, also the rent of such lands. But when in the same passage the words *'abwab'* and *'malguzari'* both are used, the *'malguzari'* must be taken as used in contradistinction to the other word *'abwab'* and *'malguzari'* must be taken in its strict appropriate sense of 'land revenue' only. [*Rabindra Chand Ghose* v *Surendra Chandra Ghose* AIR 1945 Cal 129].

**Malice.** The intentional doing of a wrongful act without just cause or excuse, with an intent to inflict an injury or under circumstances that the law will imply an evil intent. A condition of mind which prompts a person to do a wrongful act wilfully, that is, on purpose, to the injury of another, or to do intentionally a wrongful act toward another without justification or excuse. A conscious violation of the law (or the prompting of the mind to commit it) which operates to the prejudice of another person. A condition of the mind showing a heart regardless of social duty and fatally bent on mischief. [*Cockrell* v *State* 135 Tex Cr R 218: 117 SW 2d 1105, 1109, 1110].

Malice in common acceptation means ill will against a person, but in its legal sense it means a wrongful act done intentionally without just cause or excuse. [*Bromage* v *Prosser* (1825)4 B & C 247].

'Malice' is a wish to injure a party, rather than to vindicate the law. It is indicative of an evil mind which is disdainful of duties, social or legal and disregards the duties to others. In common parlance, malice means ill will against person but, in legal acceptance, it means a wrongful act done intentionally without just cause or excuse ... It is a disposition which impels injury to another without cause, from a spirit of revenge, or for personal gratification. It may be implied from a deliberate intention to do a wrong without justification. Malicious act is not one which is done accidentally, thoughtlessly or negligently, but designed wilfully or wantonly. [*Bhupinder Singh* v *State of Haryana* AIR 1968 Punj 406].

'Malice' means the presence of some improper and wrongful motive, that is to say, an intent to use the legal process in question for some other than its legally appointed and appropriate purpose. [*Jogendra Garobadu* v *Lingaraj Patra* AIR 1970 Ori 91].

Malice means improper or indirect motive other than a desire to vindicate public justice or a private right. It need not necessarily be a feeling of enmity, spite or ill will; it may be due to a desire to obtain a collateral advantage. [*S.T. Sahib* v *Hasan Ghani Sahib* AIR 1957 Mad 646].

'Malice' in its legal sense means malice such as may be assumed from the doing of a wrongful act intentionally without just cause or excuse, or for want of reasonable or probable cause. [*Smt. S.R. Venkataraman* v *Union of India* AIR 1979 SC 49: (1979)2 SCR 202: (1979)2 SCC 491].

**Malice in fact.** It "means an actual malicious intention on the part of the person who has done the wrongful act". [*Shearer* v *Shields* (1914) AC 808 (HL), *per* Viscount Haldane].

It is *maltus animus* indicating that the defendant was actuated either by spite or ill will against the plaintiff, or by indirect or improper motives. [*Gaylord Restaurant* v *M. Chambarai* AIR 1975 Mad 108 (110, 112)]. It is also called express or actual malice.

**Malice in law.** Malice in law is not necessarily personal hate or ill will, but it is that state of mind which is reckless of law and of the legal rights of the citizen.

It means the intentional doing of a wrongful act without just cause or excuse. [*Lyons* v *St. Joseph Belt Ry. Co.* 84 SW 2d 933, 934].

Malice in law means the doing of a wrongful act intentionally without just cause or excuse. [*Bromage* v *Prosser* (1825)4 B & C 247].

NOTE: A person who inflicts an injury upon another in contravention of the law is not allowed to say that he did it with an innocent mind. He is taken to know the law, and he must act within the law. He may, therefore, be guilty of malice in law; although so far as the state of mind is concerned, he acts ignorantly, and in that sense innocently. [*Shearer* v *Shields* (1914) AC 808, 813; *Ghulam Rasool Baba* v *State of J&K* 1982 Sri LJ 138, 142].

Acting on a legally extraneous or obviously misconceived ground of action is a case of malice in law. [*Regional Manager* v *Pawan Kumar Dubey* AIR 1976 SC 1766: (1976)3 SCC 334: (1976)3 SCR 540].

The phrase denotes absence of legal excuse. [*N.C. Jute Mills* v *Finance Ministry* AIR 1966 Cal 151: 70 CWN 290: (1965)2 Comp LJ 152].

It is also called implied malice.

**Malicious conduct.** Wilful neglect of duty, with reckless disregard of the consequences.

**Malicious prosecution.** One begun in malice without probable cause to believe the charges can be sustained. [*Beaurline* v *Smith* Tex Civ App, 426 SW 2d 295, 298].

A malicious prosecution is an abuse of the process of the court by wrongfully setting the law in motion on a criminal charge. [Halsbury's *Laws of England*, 3rd Ed., vol. 25, p. 348].

NOTE: The foundation of an action for malicious prosecution lies in abuse of the process of court by wrongfully setting the law in motion and it is designed to discharge the perversion of the machinery of justice for an improper purpose. [*Shri Lakhanlal Misra* v *Kashi Nath Dube* AIR 1960 MP 171: 1960 Cr LJ 829].

In malicious prosecution, the onus of proving that the prosecutor did not act honestly or reasonably lies on the person prosecuted. [*Dallison* v *Caffery* (1964)2 All ER 610 (CA), *per* Diplock, L.J.].

In a suit for damages for malicious prosecution the plaintiff must prove that the defendant acted without reasonable and probable cause and that the defendant was actuated by malice. [*N.P. Sankaran Nair* v *P.V. Rama Ayer* AIR 1960 Ker 131: ILR (1959) Ker 1189].

To be actionable as a tort the process (of the court) must have been without reasonable and probable cause and must have been instituted or carried on maliciously. The plaintiff must prove damage, except where the charge endangers his fame, in which case damage is implied. [Halsbury's *Laws of England*, 3rd Ed., vol. 25, p. 348].

**Malik.** An owner possessed of full proprietary rights including a full right of alienation. [*Sasiman Chaudharin* v *Shib Narain* 49 IA 25: AIR 1922 PC 63].

The word 'malik' imports full proprietary rights unless there is something in the context to indicate an intention to the contrary. [*Saraju Bala Debi* v *Jyotirmoyee Debi* 58 IA 270: AIR 1931 PC 170].

The expression conveys the idea of absolute ownership unless the context or surrounding circumstances indicate otherwise. [*Peary Lal* v *Rameshwar Das* AIR 1963 SC 1703: 1963 Supp (2) SCR 834: (1964)1 SCJ 85].

The term 'malik' when used in a will or other document as descriptive of the position which a devisee or donee is intended to hold, has been held apt to describe an owner possessed of full proprietary rights, including a full right of alienation, unless there is something in the context or in the surrounding circumstances to indicate that such full proprietary rights were not intended to be conferred. [*Navneet Lal* alias *Rangi* v *Gokul* AIR 1976 SC 794: (1976)2 SCR 924: (1976)1 SCC 630].

**Malik kamil.** The word 'malik' is not a term of art implying full proprietary ownership free from any limitation. On the contrary, it is a term which has to be interpreted according to the surrounding circumstances of each case. The addition of the word *'kamil'* does not have any sensible effect, although it is without doubt a slightly stronger term or form of expression to say that someone is *malik kamil* or absolute owner that he is only *malik* which in proper cases would also mean absolute owner. [*Ara Begum* v *Dy. Commissioner, Gonda* AIR 1941 Oudh 529].

The words *malik kamil* (absolute owner) and *nasal bad nasal* (generation after generation) used in a deed or will are descriptive of a heritable and alienable estate in the donee and they connote full proprietary rights unless there is something in the context or in the surrounding circumstances which indicate otherwise. [*Bajrang Bahadur* v *Bakhraj Kuer* 1952 SCJ 655: 1953 SCR 232: AIR 1953 SC 7: 1953 SCA 368].

**Malik kamil dwami.** Absolute estate. [*Parmodh Singh* v *Labh Singh* AIR 1955 Punj 49].

**Malik mustakil.** The words "malik mustakil" in the compromise indicate conferral of absolute ownership to the widow. [*Krishna Beharilal* v *Gulabchand* AIR 1971 SC 1041: 1971 (Supp) SCR 27: (1971)1 SCC 837].

**Malikana.** An allowance for proprietary rights given by the Government to proprietors who decline to engage for the *jamas* proposed to them and whose lands were in consequence let in farm or held *khas* by the Government. [*Rameshwar* v *Secretary of State* ILR 39 Cal 1].

It is a right to receive a portion of the profits of an estate for which the Government has made a settlement with another person when the real proprietor has neglected to pay his revenue or has declined to come in and make a settlement or to accede to the rate at which the lands are assessed. [*Mahendranarayana* v *Abdul Gafur* AIR 1932 Cal 49].

Regulation VIII of 1793 (s. 43) described *malikana* as an allowance to proprietors in consideration of their proprietary rights.

Baden-Powell's *Lands Systems of British India*, Vol. II, p. 717 said that *malikana* in Bengal and places other than the Punjab usually means an allowance to an ex-proprietor by way of solatium for a lost right. [*State of Bihar* v *Maharaja Pratap Singh Bahadur* AIR 1969 SC 164, 166].

**Maliki.** The Malikis are a sub-sect of the Sunni Mahomedans of India. They are puritanical and strict in morals.

**Malversation.** Misbehaviour in an office, employment, or commission as breach of trust, extortion, etc. [Wharton's *Law Lexicon*, 14th Ed., p. 623].

In French law, this word is applied to all grave and punishable faults committed in the exercise of a charge or commission (office), such as corruption, exaction, concussion, larceny.

**Man.** A person of the male sex. A male of the human species above the age of puberty.

In its most extended sense, the term includes not only the adult male sex of the human species, but women and children.

**Manage.** In the context of business, "manage" means "to control, to guide, to administer, to conduct or direct affairs; carry on 'business'. [*R. Dalmia* v *The Commissioner of Income Tax, New Delhi* AIR 1977 SC 988: (1977)2 SCR 654: (1977)2 SCC 467: (1977)106 ITR 895].

**Management.** "Management" includes the act of managing by direction or regulation or administration or control or superintendence. [*R. Dalmia* v *The Commissioner of Income Tax, New Delhi* AIR 1977 SC 988: (1977)2 SCR 654: (1977)2 SCC 467: (1977)106 ITR 895].

NOTE: It is, however, different from mere power of superintendence. Powers of superintendence and control would not amount to management, management being the administration of day-to-day affairs. [*Karnataka State Board of Wakfs* v *Mohd. Azeemuddin* (1982)1 Kant LJ 59].

One meaning of the term 'management' is: 'the Board of Directors' or 'the apex body' or 'Executive Committee at the helm which guides, regulates, supervises, directs and controls the affairs of the Society'. In this sense it may not include the individuals who under the overall control of that governing body or committee, run the day-to-day business of the Society. Another meaning of the term 'management', may be: 'the act or acts of managing or governing by direction, guidance, superintendence, regulation and control, the affairs of a Society'. [*Gujarat State Co-operative Land Development Bank Ltd.* v *P.R. Mankad* AIR 1979 SC 1203: (1979)3 SCC 123: (1979)2 SCR 1023].

**Manager.** The word 'manager' in relation to a company or corporation means one who has charge of corporation and control of its business, or of its branch establishments, divisions, or departments, and who is vested with a certain amount of discretion and independent judgment. [*Braniff* v *McPherren* 58 P 2d 871, 872].

The phrase 'manager of the company', *prima facie*, according to the ordinary meaning of the words, connotes a person holding, whether *de jure* or *de facto*, a post in or with the company of a nature charging him with the duty of managing the affairs of the company for the company's benefit. [*Re Johnson (B.) & Co. (Builders), Ltd.* (1955)2 All ER 775 (CA), *per* Jenkins, L.J.].

Manager is one who has the management of the whole affairs of a company; not an agent (who is to do a particular thing) or a servant who is to obey orders, but a person who is entrusted with power to transact the whole of the affairs of a company. [*Gibson* v *Barton* (1875) LR 10 QB 329, *per* Blackburn, J.].

"Manager" means a person who, subject to the control and direction of the directors, has the management of the whole affairs of a company and includes a director or any other person occupying the position of a manager by whatever name called and whether under a contract of service or not. To satisfy the aforesaid definition a person, which could include a firm, body corporate or an association of persons, apart from being in management of the whole affairs of a company had to be "subject to the control and direction of the directors". This definition has undergone a substantial change under the Companies Act 1956. Under this Act, s. 2(24) defines the expression "manager" thus: "Manager" means an individual (not being the managing agent) who, subject to the superintendence, control and direction of the Board of Directors, has the management of the whole, or substantially the whole, of the affairs of a company, and includes a director or any other person occupying the position of a manager, by whatever name called and whether under a contract of service or not. In this definition three conditions are required to be satisfied: (*a*) the manager must be an individual, which means that a firm or a body corporate or an association is excluded and cannot be manager (a fact which is expressly made clear in s. 384); (*b*) he should have the management of the whole or substantially the whole of the affairs of the company; (*c*) he should be subject to the superintendence, control and directions of the Board of Directors in the matter of managing the affairs of the company. [*Commissioner of Income Tax, Kerala* v *Alagappa Textile (Cochin) Ltd.* AIR 1980 SC 235: (1980)1 SCR 723: (1980)1 SCC 214: (1979)120 ITR 480: (1979)49 CC 947].

The word 'manager' will not apply to a man who acts once or twice, but he must be a delegate having the control of all the affairs of the company. [*Gibson* v *Barton* (1875) LR 10 QB 329, *per* Quain, J.].

The word "manager" in relation to a religious or charitable endowment is not a term of art. The said word denotes the person who is in charge of the administration of the endowment or manages the property or supervises the performance of the charity, and the word is one of very wide and general import. [*State Wakf Board* v *Subramanyam* AIR 1977 Mad 79].

The designation of "manager" implies general power and permits reasonable inferences that the employee so designated is invested with the general conduct and control of his employer's business. [*U.S. Auto Ass'n* v *Alexander Film Co.* DC Mun App, 93 A 2d 770, 771].

**Managing agent.** A person with general power involving the exercise of judgment and discretion, as opposed to an ordinary agent who acts under the direction and control of the principal. [Black's *Law Dictionary*, 7th Ed.].

Any individual, firm or body corporate entitled, subject to the provisions of the Companies Act, to the management of the whole, or substantially the whole, of the affairs of the company by virtue of an agreement with the company, or by virtue of its memorandum or articles of association, and includes any individual, firm or body corporate occupying the position of a managing agent. [Companies Act 1956, s. 2(25) (since omitted w.e.f. 13.12.2000); Factories Act 1948, s. 2(*o*) (since omitted w.e.f. 1.12.1987); Coal Mines Provident Fund and Bonus Scheme Act 1948, s. 2(*ff*)].

'Managing agent' means any person appointed or acting as the representative of another person for the purpose of carrying on such other person's trade or business, but does not include an individual manager subordinate to an employer. [Workmen's Compensation Act 1923, s. 2(*f*); Employees' State Insurance Act 1948, s. 2(14A)].

'Managing agent' means a person, firm or company entitled to the management of the whole affairs of a company by virtue of an agreement with the company and under the control and direction of the directors except to the extent if any, otherwise provided for in the agreement, and includes any person, firm or company occupying such position by whatever name called. [Insurance Act 1938, s. 2(13)].

NOTE: 'Managing agent' includes—(*i*) secretaries and treasurers, (*ii*) where the managing agency is a company, and director of such company, and any member thereof who holds substantial interest in such company, and (*iii*) where the managing agent is a firm, any partner of such firm. [Banking Regulation Act 1949, s. 5(*gg*)].

"Managing agency" is itself business. [*J.K. Trust, Bombay* v *The Commissioner of Income Tax/Excess Profits Tax, Bombay* AIR 1957 SC 846: 1958 SCR 65: 1957 SCJ 845].

**Managing contractor.** With reference to coking coal mine or coke oven plant, managing contractor means the person, or body of persons, who, with the previous consent in writing of the State Government, has entered into an arrangement, contract or understanding with the owner of a coking coal mine or coke oven plant under which the operation of the coking coal mine or coke oven plant is substantially controlled by such person or body of persons. [Coking Coal Mines (Nationalisation) Act 1972, s. 3(*i*); *Industrial Supplies Pvt. Ltd.* v *Union of India* AIR 1980 SC 1858: (1981)1 SCR 375: (1980)4 SCC 341].

**Managing director.** A director who, by virtue of an agreement with the company or of a resolution passed by the company in the general meeting or by its Board of Directors or, by virtue of its memorandum or articles of association, is entrusted with substantial powers of management which would not otherwise be exercisable by him and includes a director occupying the position of a managing director, by whatever name called. [Companies Act 1956, s. 2(26)].

▸ *Meaning under the Central Industrial Security Force Act 1968, s. 2(e).* 'Managing director', in relation to an industrial undertaking, means the person (whether called a managing agent, general manager, manager, chief executive officer or by any other name) who exercises control over the affairs of that undertaking.

▸ *Meaning under the Banking Regulation Act 1949, s. 5(h).* 'Managing director', in relation to a banking company, means a director who, by virtue of an agreement with the banking company or of a resolution passed by the banking company in the general meeting or by its Board of Directors or by virtue of its memorandum or articles of association, is entrusted with the management of the whole or substantially the whole of the affairs of the company and includes a director occupying the position of a managing director, by whatever name called.

**Mandamus.** It is a Latin expression which means 'we command'.

This is the name of a writ issuing from a court of competent jurisdiction, commanding an inferior tribunal, board, corporation, a person to perform a purely ministerial duty imposed by law. [*Nebel* v *Nebel* 85 SE 2d 876, 882].

It is an extraordinary writ which lies to compel performance of ministerial act or mandatory duty where there is a clear legal right in plaintiff, a corresponding duty in defendant, and a want of any other appropriate and adequate remedy. [*Cohen* v *Ford* 339 A 2d 175, 177].

A writ of *mandamus* is a direction, or order, issued to remedy a grave error, or to set right some injustice. It is a common remedy for the enforcement of constitution, ministerial and non-discretionary judicial duties and to test constitutional questions. It is ordinarily issued to compel the discharging of obligations, and ordering that to be done, which a law requires to be done. It is not issued, so as to compel an inferior tribunal, or authority, to exercise its discretion in a particular and specified manner, specially where it is not shown, that all or any of the alternative reliefs have been denied to the applicant. In order that *mandamus* may issue to compel to do something, it must be shown that the statute has imposed a legal duty and the appellant has a legal right under the statute to enforce the performance of that legal right. [*Shivendra* v *Nalanda College* AIR 1962 SC 1210, 1211].

"A writ of *mandamus* is a prerogative writ and not a writ of right, and it is in this sense in the discretion of the court whether it shall be granted or not. The court may refuse to grant the writ not only upon the merits, but upon some delay, or other matter personal to the party applying for it; in this the court exercises a discretion which cannot be questioned ......" [*R.* v *All Saints, Wigan (Churchwardens)* (1876), 1 App Cas 611, 620, *per* Lord Chelmsford].

NOTE: The grant of an order of *mandamus* is, as a general rule, a matter for the discretion of the court. It is not an order granted as of right and it is not issued as a matter of course. Courts will not exercise jurisdiction unless substantial injustice has ensued or is likely to ensue. [*B. Radhakrishnan* v *State of Madras* AIR 1960 Mad 231].

*Mandamus* can be granted only when there is in the applicant a right to compel the performance of some duty cast on the opponent. [*State of Madhya Pradesh* v *Mandawar* AIR 1954 SC 493: 1954 SCJ 503: 1954 SCA 767].

The Supreme Court can, under Art. 32 of the Constitution of India, issue *mandamus* while the power to issue such writ lies upon the High Court under Art. 226.

• **Certiorarified mandamus** p. 134.

**Mandatory.** Compulsory; obligatory; peremptory; imperative; essential; binding; commanding; without choice.

NOTE: The terms "mandatory" and "directory" refer to the method by which the legislature sets about attaining its object. When a statute is passed for the purpose of enabling something to be done and prescribes the formalities which are to attend its performance, those prescribed formalities which are essential to the validity of the thing when done are called *imperative* (or mandatory); but those which are not essential, and may be disregarded without invalidating the thing to be done, are called *directory.* [Craies on *Statute Law*, 6th Ed.]. This distinction consists in that the former must be strictly observed while the latter may be substantially complied with. [*H.V. Kamath* v *A. Ishaque* (1955)1 SCR 1104, 1126: AIR 1955 SC 223].

But in regard to constitutional provisions, Cooley holds them always to be mandatory. A Treatise on the Constitutional Limitations (1972), pp. 78-83: "Constitutions usually do not prescribe rules of proceeding except when such rules are looked upon as essential to the thing to be done; and they must then be regarded in the light of limitations upon the power to be exercised." Thus, in the Indian context cls. (4) and (5) of Art. 22 of the Constitution of India relating to the procedural requirements have been held to be 'mandatory'. [*Jaynarayana* v *State of West Bengal* AIR 1970 SC 675, 679].

When the legislature prescribes the manner or form in which a duty is to be performed or a power exercised, it seldom lays down what will be the legal consequences of failure to observe its prescriptions. The courts formulate their own criteria for determining whether the procedural rule is to be regarded as mandatory. If the procedural rule is regarded as mandatory, disobedience thereof will render void or voidable what has been done. On the other hand, if the procedural rule is regarded as directory, disobedience of it will be treated as an irregularity not affecting the validity of what has been done. Substantial compliance with the statutory provisions may, however, be needed if the deviation is to be excused as a mere irregularity. [*Penumbra of Natural Justice* by Tapash Gan Choudhury, 2nd Ed., p. 137].

In order to determine whether the procedural rule in the matter of performing a duty or exercise of a power is mandatory or directory, the whole scope and purpose of the enactment must be considered, and the importance of the provision that has been disregarded is to be assessed and the relation of that provision to the general object sought to be secured by the Act must also be looked into. [*Penumbra of Natural Justice* by Tapash Gan Choudhury, 2nd Ed., p. 137].

**Mandatory injunction.** See under INJUNCTION p. 459.

**Mandi.** A market; a market for any particular article.

**Mandir.** A temple; a building or room where a deity is kept.

**Manner.** "Manner" means method of procedure. [*Asnew Drums Private Ltd.* v *Maharashtra State Finance Corporation* (1971)3 SCC 602: AIR 1972 SC 801: (1972)1 SCR 351].

**Manu.** A great Hindu sage, who is the author of an important Smriti that bears his name. The Smritis constitute the principal source of Hindu law. There are numerous Smritis ascribed to the authorship of different sages and 20 of these have been enumerated by Yajnavalkya. The first name in the list is that of Manu. According to Brihaspati, the first rank among the law-givers belongs to Manu, as he embodies the true sense of the Vedas in his work; that Smriti which is opposed to the tenor of the law of Manu is not approved. The Code of Manu has always been treated by Hindu sages and commentators, from the earliest times, as being of paramount authority.

**Manufacture.** The word 'manufacture' is derived from Latin words *'menus'* and *'factura'*, literally, put together by hand. Now it means the process of making products by hand or machinery. 'Manufacture' may, therefore, be defined as the making of goods or wares by manual labour or by machinery. [*Modern Candle Works* v *Commissioner of Taxes, Assam, Gauhati* (1988)1 Gau LR 310].

The dictionary meaning of the word 'manufacture' is 'transform or fashion raw materials into a changed form for use. [*D.D. Gopal Krishna* v *State of Punjab* (1969)1 SCJ 19].

The word 'manufacture' according to its dictionary meaning, is the making of articles or material (now on a large scale) by physical labour or mechanical power. [*Shorter Oxford English Dictionary*, vol. I, p. 1203]. According to the Permanent Edition of Words and Phrases, vol. 26, 'manufacture' implies a change but every change is not manufacture and yet every change in an article is the result of treatment, labour and manipulation. But something more is necessary and there must be transformation; a new and different article must emerge having a distinctive name, character or use. [*Allenbury Engineers Pvt. Ltd.* v *Ramkrishna Dalmia* AIR 1973 SC 425: (1973)2 SCR 257: (1973)1 SCC 7].

Webster's *New International Dictionary*, 2nd Ed., Vol. II, gives the following meaning of the word 'manufacture': the process or operation of making wares or any material produced by hand, by machinery or by other agency, often such process or operation carried on systematically with division of labour and with the use of machinery; anything made from raw materials by hand, by machinery or by art; the making of anything by any agency or process. [*Deputy CIT* v *Shree Lalit Fabrics Pvt. Ltd.* (1992)198 ITR 190].

The expression 'manufacture' has, in ordinary acceptation, a wide connotation; it means making of articles, or material, commercially different from the basic components, by physical labour or mechanical process. [*CST, U.P.* v *Dr. Sukhdeo* (1969)1 SCWR 1004: 1969 STC 385: AIR 1969 SC 499: (1969)1 SCA 569].

The word 'manufacture' used as verb is generally understood to mean as bringing into existence of a new substance and does not mean merely to produce some change in a substance however minor in consequence the change may be. [*Union of India* v *Delhi Cloth and General Mills Co. Ltd.* AIR 1963 SC 791: 1963 Supp (1) SCR 586].

'Manufacture' implies a change, but every change is not 'manufacture' and yet every change of an article is the result of treatment, labour and manipulation. But something more was necessary as there must be transformation, a new and different article must emerge having a distinct name, character or use. [*Collector of Central Excise, Madras* v *Kutty Flush Doors and Furniture Co. (P) Ltd.* AIR 1988 SC 1164: (1988)3 SCR 363: JT 1988(2) SC 93: (1988)35 ELT 6: 1988 Cr LR (SC) 329: (1988)70 STC 314: 1988 (Supp) SCC 239].

The word 'manufacture' implies a change but every change in the raw material is not manufacture. There must be such a transformation that a new and different article must emerge having a distinct name, character or use. [*Collector of Central Excise, Baroda* v *Ambalal Sarabhai Enterprises (P) Ltd.* (1989)4 SCC 112: JT 1989(3) SC 341: (1989)43 ELT 214: (1989)3 SCR 784: (1990)185 ITR 87: (1990)77 STC 190: AIR 1990 SC 59].

It is only when the change, or a series of changes take the commodity to the point where commercially it can no longer be regarded as the original commodity but in stead is recognised as a new and distinct article that a manufacture can be said to take place. [*Chowgule & Co. Pvt. Ltd.* v *Union of India* AIR 1981 SC 1014: (1981)2 SCR 271: (1981)1 SCC 653: (1981)47 STC 124].

▸ *Meaning under Excise Law.* 'Manufacture', in excise law, means to bring into existence a new substance and does not mean merely to produce some change in a substance. [*Collector of Central Excise, Bombay II* v *Kiran Spinning Mills* AIR 1988 SC 871: (1988)2 SCC 348: (1988)2 SCR 1006: JT 1988(1) SC 369: (1988)34 ELT 5].

NOTE: It is true that etymological word 'manufacture' properly construed would doubtless cover the transformation but the question is whether that transformation brings about fundamental change, a new substance, is brought into existence or a new different article having distinctive name, character or use results from a particular process or a particular activity. The taxable event under the excise law is 'manufacture'. In this sense, cutting of long length fibre into short length fibre does not amount to 'manufacture' for the purpose of excise duty. [*Collector of Central Excise, Bombay II* v *Kiran Spinning Mills* AIR 1988 SC 871: (1988)2 SCC 348: (1988)2 SCR 1006: JT 1988(1) SC 369: (1988)34 ELT 5].

It is a law now that excise is a duty on manufacture. Manufacture is the process or activity which brings into existence new, identifiable and distinct goods. Anything required to make the goods marketable must form part of the manufacture and any raw material or any materials used for the same would be component part for the end product. Thus 'manufacture' in the sense it is used in the excise law is not complete until and unless wrapping is done. [*Collector of Central Excise* v *Eastend Paper Industries* (1989)4 SCC 244].

▸ *Meaning under the Income Tax Act 1961.* The word "manufacture" has not been defined in the Act. In the absence of a definition of the word "manufacture" it has to be given a meaning as is understood in common parlance. It is to be understood as meaning the production of articles for use from raw or prepared materials by giving such materials new forms, qualities or combinations whether by hand labour or machines. If the change made in the article results in a new and different article then it would amount to a manufacturing activity. [*Aspinwall and Co. Ltd.* v *C.I.T., Ernakulam* (2001)7 SCC 525: JT 2001(7) SC 555: (2001)133 ELT 18].

▸ *Meaning under the Industrial Disputes Act 1947.* Manufacture is a kind of productive industry in which the making of articles or material, often on a large scale, is by physical labour or mechanical power. [*Secretary, Madras Gymkhana Club Employees' Union* v *Management of the Gymkhana Club* AIR 1968 SC 554: (1968)1 SCR 742].

▸ *Meaning under the Patents and Designs Act 1911.* 'Manufacture', according to the definition of the term in s. 2(11) of the Act, includes not only "any art, process or manner of providing, preparing or making an article" but also "any article prepared or produced by the manufacturer". [*M/s. Bishwanath Prasad Radhey Shyam* v *Hindustan Metal Industries* (1979)2 SCR 757: (1979)2 SCC 511: AIR 1982 SC 1444].

▸ *Meaning under the Transfer of Property Act 1882.* The word 'manufacture' in s. 106, must be construed in a popular sense, namely, production of a new or a different article or the process must be such as converts one kind of article into another kind. [*Sati Prasanna Mukherjee* v *Md. Fazal* AIR 1952 Cal 320: 86 CLJ 12].

To manufacture, according to its Dictionary meaning, means "to work up materials into forms suitable for use". The word "material" does not necessarily mean the original raw material, for a finished article may have to go through several manufacturing processes before it is fit and made ready for the market. What is itself a manufactured commodity may constitute a "material" for working it up into a different product. Thus, for example, for the tanner, the material would be the raw hide, but the leather itself a manufactured article would constitute the material for the shoemaker's business, and one cannot say that the shoemakers are not manufacturers because they do not work on raw hides. To constitute "manufacture", it must be proved that a certain commodity was produced. That the process of production must involve either labour or machinery. That the end product which comes into existence after the manufacturing process is complete, should have a different name and should be put to a different use. In other words, the commodity should be so transformed so as to lose its original character. [*Idandas* v *Anant Ramchandra Phadke (dead) by LRs* AIR 1982 SC 127: (1982)1 SCC 27: (1982)1 SCR 1196].

NOTE: *'Manufacture'—what is—examples:* (*i*) The activity of collecting, storing and supplying blood amounts to 'manufacture' for the purposes of s. 18(*c*) of Drugs and Cosmetics Act 1940. [*Subodh S. Shah* v *Director, Food and Drugs, Food and Drugs Control Office, Ahmedabad* AIR 1997 Guj 83].

(*ii*) In market rice is a different commodity from paddy, and therefore, when there is a conversion of paddy into rice through rice mills, there is either production of rice or manufacture of rice from paddy. [*K.C. Pazhanimala* v *State of Kerala* AIR 1969 Ker 154 (FB); *T.P. Sundaralingam* v *State of Madras* AIR 1971 Mad 245; *Municipal Council Domoh* v *Vrajlal Manilal & Co.* AIR 1982 SC 844].

*'Manufacture'—what is not—examples:* (*i*) Collection of sand from the river bed is not 'manufacture'. [*Commissioner of Sales Tax, M.P.* v *Gorelal Dube* (1980)1 WN 193].

(*ii*) Printing on bottles will not amount to 'manufacture' within the meaning of s. 2(*f*) of the Central Excise and Salt Act 1944. [*Union of India* v *JG Glass Industries Ltd.* AIR 1998 SC 839].

**Manufacturer.** A manufacturer is a person by whom or under whose direction and control the articles or materials are made. [*CST, U.P.* v *Dr. Sukhdeo* (1969)1 SCWR 1004: 1969 STC 385: AIR 1969 SC 499: (1969)1 SCA 569].

**Manufacturing process.** A process by which a different entity comes into existence.

NOTE: In order to prove that there was a manufacturing process, it is essential to prove that the article must change its nature and it becomes an altogether different commercial article. [*Mewal Lal* v *Tara Ram* AIR 1973 All 165].

The broad test to determine whether a process is a manufacturing process is to see whether it brings a complete transformation of the old components so as to produce a commercially different article or commodity. [*P.C. Cheriyan* v *Barfi Devi* AIR 1980 SC 86: (1980)2 SCC 461: (1980)1 SCR 961].

Cutting and drying arecanuts and garbling of pepper held to be a manufacturing process. [*State* v *Madhogaria* AIR 1959 Ker 200].

Dying and printing etymologically mean manufacturing processes under s. 2(*f*) of the Central Excises and Salt Act 1944. [*Empire Industries Ltd.* v *Union of India* (1985)2 Comp LJ 260: (1985)20 ELT 179: 1985 Supp (1) SCR 292: (1985)3 SCC 314: AIR 1986 SC 662: (1986)162 ITR 846: (1987)64 STC 42].

The process of manufacture in relation to tobacco includes the preparation of cigarettes etc. and in relation to manufactured tobacco includes the labelling or relabelling of containers or the adoption of any other treatment to render the product marketable to the consumer. [*J&K Cigarettes Ltd.* v *Superintendent of Central Excise* 1988 Sri LJ 393].

**Manuscript.** Handwritten or typewritten composition or document; writing as opposed to print.

Manuscript is the paper or other material on which the writing is made. [*Macmillan* v *Dent* (1906)1 Ch 101: 75 LJ Ch 99].

An author's work product which is submitted to the publisher either in his own hand or typewritten. [Black's *Law Dictionary*, 5th Ed.].

An unpublished writing; an author's typescript or written work product that is proposed for publication. [Black's *Law Dictionary*, 8th Ed.].

**Map.** Measurement of any kind, whether of weight, length or capacity, but especially line measure; a measure; a portion or quantity determined by measure. Also a measure of grain in husk. [Wilson's *Glossary*].

A representation on a plane surface of any region, as of the earth's surface; a chart; figuratively, any exact delineation.

**Marginal note.** A brief notation, in the nature of a subheading, placed in the margin of a printed statute for ease of reference. [Black's *Law Dictionary*, 7th Ed.].

NOTE: The side note, although it forms no part of the section is of some assistance, inasmuch as it shows the drift of the section. [*Bushell* v *Hammond* (1904)2 KB 563: 73 LJKB 1005].

Though the marginal note forms no part of the section, it will be of some assistance in interpreting a section inasmuch as it shows the drift or the trend of the section and elucidates and illustrates its meaning when there is any doubt about the meaning of the words used. [*Rajaraja Varman* v *K.K. Krishnan Nair* AIR 1958 Mad 117: (1956)2 MLJ 46].

Marginal note cannot affect the construction of the language used in the body of the section if it is otherwise clear and unambiguous. [*Western India Theatres Ltd.* v *Municipal Corporation* AIR 1959 SC 586: 1959 Supp (2) SCR 71: 1959 SCJ 300: (1959)2 SCA 145].

**Marine.** Of or relating to the sea; of or relating to the sea navigation or commerce.

**Marine insurance business.** The business of effecting contracts of insurance upon vessels of any description, including cargoes, freights and other interests which may be legally insured, in or in relation to such vessels, cargoes, freights, goods, wares, merchandise and property of whatever description insured for any transit by land or water, or both, and whether or not including warehouse risks or similar risks in addition or as incidental to such transit and includes any other risk customarily included among the risks insured against in marine insurance policies. [Insurance Act 1938, s. 2(13A)].

**Mariner.** A seaman or sailor; one engaged in navigating vessels upon the sea.

**Marital.** Of or relating to, or connected with, the status of marriage.

**Marital rights.** Rights and incidents arising from the marriage; those arising from marriage and constituting its object, and therefore embracing what the parties agree to perform towards each other and to society. Cohabitation right is a marital right.

**Maritime law.** That system of law which particularly relates to marine commerce and navigation, to business transacted at sea or relating to navigation, to ships and shipping, to seaman, to the transportation of persons and property by sea, and to marine affairs generally.

**Maritime lien.** A lien which attaches to the ship, cargo or freight.

A special property right in a ship given to a creditor by law as security for a debt or claim subsisting from the moment the debt arises with right to have the ship sold and debt paid out of proceeds. Such a lien is a proprietary interest or right of property in the vessel itself, and not a cause of action or demand for personal judgment against the owner. The lien is enforced by a direct proceeding against the vessel or other property in which it exists.

**Mark.** A symbol, impression, or feature on something, usually to identify it or distinguish it from something else; the sign, writing or ticket put upon manufactured goods to distinguish them from others; a token, evidence, or proof, as for example, "a mark of fraud"; monetary unit, e.g. German Deutsche mark.

▸ *Meaning under the Trade and Merchandise Marks Act 1958, s. 2(j).* 'Mark' includes a device, brand, heading, label, ticket, name, signature, word, letter or numeral or any combination thereof.

▸ *Meaning under the Trade Marks Act 1999, s. 2(m).* 'Mark' includes a device, brand, heading, label, ticket, name, signature, word, letter or numeral, shape of goods, packaging or combination of colours or any combination thereof.

▸ *Meaning under the Indian Standards Institution (Certification Marks) Act 1952, s. 2(g).* 'Mark' includes a device, brand, heading, label, ticket, pictorial representation, name, signature, word, letter or numeral or any combination thereof.

**Market.** A place of commercial activity in which articles are bought and sold. [*Zemel* v *Commercial Warehouses* 40 A 2d 642, 643].

"A market is a place to which sellers who have not found buyers take their goods in the hope of finding buyers, and to which buyers resort in the hope of finding the goods they want". [*Scottish Co-operative Wholesale Society Ltd.* v *Ulster Farmers' Mart Co. Ltd.* (1959)2 All ER 486, 495 (HL), *per* Lord Somervell of Harrow].

At common law a market is a franchise conferring a right to hold a concourse of buyers and sellers to dispose of the commodities in respect of which the franchise is given. The term is also applied to the like right when conferred by Act of Parliament. Though strictly applicable to the right itself, the term is often applied to the concourse of buyers and sellers, or to the market-place, or to the time of holding the market. A gathering of buyers and sellers, though held at regular intervals in a fixed place, if it is not held by virtue of a franchise or under statutory authority, is not in law a market, and cannot enjoy the privileges of a franchise market or fair. [Halsbury's *Laws of England*, 3rd Ed., vol. 25, p. 381].

An emporium of commerce or place of buying and selling. 'Market' is a place set apart for the meeting of the general public of buyers and sellers freely open to such to assemble together, where any seller may expose his goods for sale and any buyer may purchase. [*Public Prosecutor* v *Cheru Kutty* 87 IC 973: AIR 1925 Mad 1095].

Under the U.P. Municipalities Act 1916 "market" means and includes any place or places for buying or selling, *inter alia* grains where more than four stalls or shops are occupied on any plot of land owned by the same owner or owners, or where wholesale transaction by way of auction or sale of more than twenty maunds is carried on. [*Afzal Ullah* v *State of U.P.* AIR 1964 SC 264: (1964)4 SCR 991: (1964)1 Cr LJ 156].

'Market' ordinarily means a place where business is being transacted. That was probably all that is meant at a time when trade was not developed and when transactions took place at specified place. In modern parlance, the word 'market' has come to mean business as well as the place where business is carried on. Labour market, for example, is not a place where labourers are recruited, but the conditions of the business of labour is carried on. The word 'market' being thus capable of meaning both business and the place where the business is carried on, the question in what sense it is used in a particular statute must be decided on a consideration of the context of that statute. [*Waverly Jute Mills Co. Ltd.* v *Raymon & Company (India) Pvt. Ltd.* AIR 1963 SC 90: (1963)1 SCA 391: (1963)2 SCR 209].

A market connotes freedom of bargain. There may be a market completely circumscribed by price control, but within such control, the area of operation would still be a commercially free area. [*Commissioner of Agricultural Income-tax* v *Manmatha Nath* AIR 1958 Cal 192].

By the term "market" is also understood the demand there is for any particular article; as for example, the car market is depressed.

▸ *Meaning under the Cantonments Act 1924, s. 2(xx).* 'Market' includes any place where person assemble for the purpose of selling meat, fish, fruit, vegetables, livestock or any other article of food.


- **Banging a market** p. 94.
- **Bull market** p. 114.
- **Buyer's market** p. 116.
- **Free and open market** p. 373.
- **Municipal market** p. 594.
- **Open market** p. 626.
- **Pegged market** p. 649.
- **Public market** p. 710.


**Market overt.** An open, legally regulated public market where buyers, with some exceptions, acquire good title to products regardless of any defects in the seller's title. [Black's *Law Dictionary*, 7th Ed.].

The market to be a market overt must be an 'open public and legally constituted one'. [*Lee* v *Bayes* (1856)18 CB 599, *per* Jervis, C.J.].

NOTE: Where goods, other than goods belonging to the Crown, are sold in market overt according to the usage of the market, the buyer acquires a good title to the goods, provided he buys them in good faith and without any notice of any defect or want of title on the part of the seller. The title is liable to be defeated, however, in the case of stolen goods. The rule for the protection of buyer and seller is not thereby protected, and an action for conversion lies against one who wrongfully sells and delivers the goods of another in market overt. If, after a sale in market overt, the seller becomes again the owner of the goods, the title in the original owner revives.

The doctrine of market overt is a principle of English law. Suffice it to say that the Indian legislature did not think it proper to introduce this principle into Indian law as being unsuitable to Indian conditions. [*Rameshwar* v *Tara Singh* AIR 1958 Raj 269].

**Market price.** Market price is synonymous with market value and means the price actually given in current market dealings, or the price at which the supply and demand are equal. [*Public Service Commissioner of State* v *Montana-Dakota Utilities Co., N.D.* 100 NW 2d 140, 146].

**Market value.** Market value means the price of the commodity in the market as between the manufacturer and an ordinary purchaser. [*Orchard* v *Simpson* (1857)2 CBNS 299].

The market value of an article or piece of property is the price which it might be expected to bring if offered for sale in a fair market; not the price which might be obtained on a sale at public auction or a sale forced by the necessities of the owner, but such a price as would be fixed by negotiation and mutual agreement, after ample time to find a purchaser, as between a vendor who is willing (but not compelled) to sell and a purchaser who desires to buy but is not compelled to take the particular article or piece of property. [*U.S.* v *Certain Property in Borough of Manhattan City, County and State of New York* CANY, 403 F 2d 800, 802].

Market value is the price which a willing vendor might reasonably expect to obtain from a willing purchaser. [*Union of India* v *Ram Meher* (1973)1 SCC 109: AIR 1973 SC 305].

"Market value" means the price that a willing purchaser would pay to a willing seller for the property having due regard to its existing condition with all its existing advantages and its potential possibilities when laid out in the most advantageous manner excluding any advantages due to the carrying out of the scheme for which the property is compulsorily acquired. [*Thakur Kanta Prasad Singh (dead) by LRs.* v *State of Bihar* AIR 1976 SC 2219: (1976)3 SCC 772: (1976)3 SCR 585; *Prithvi Raj Taneja (dead) by LRs.* v *State of Madhya Pradesh* AIR 1977 SC 1560: (1977)2 SCR 633: (1977)1 SCC 684].

In so far as the land is concerned, "market value" means what a willing purchaser would pay to willing seller for the property having regard to the advantages available to the land and the development activities which may be going on in the vicinity and the potentiality of the land. This is usually done by finding the market value of similar land. [*Mahabir Prasad Santuka* v *Collector, Cuttack* AIR 1987 SC 720: (1987)1 SCC 587: (1987)2 SCR 289: JT 1987(1) SC 401].

**Marketable.** Saleable; such things as may be sold in the market; merchantable.

'Marketable' means saleable, or suitable for sale. [*Indian Cable Co. Ltd.* v *Collector of Central Excise* AIR 1955 SC 64].

**Marketable security.** A security that the holder can readily sell on a stock exchange or an over-the-counter market. [Black's *Law Dictionary*, 7th Ed.].

A security of such a description as to be capable of being sold in any stock market in India or in the United Kingdom. [Indian Stamp Act 1899, s. 2(16A)]. The words "of such a description" are important, for the test is not whether the security is quoted on the Stock Exchange but whether it is of such a description as to be capable, according to the practice of the Stock Market, of being bought and sold although there may not be a market for the security in question. [*Brown* v *Coms. of Inland Revenue* (1985)2 QB 598].

**Marketable title.** See under TITLE p. 844.

**Marriage.** Legal union of one man and one woman as husband and wife. [*Singer* v *Hara* 522 P 2d 1187, 1193].

NOTE: "Marriage, in its origin, is a contract of natural law; it may exceed between two individuals of different sexes, although no third person existed in the world, as happened in the case of the common ancestors of mankind: It is the parent, not the child, of civil society ... In civil society it becomes a civil contract, regulated and prescribed by law, and endowed with civil consequences. In most civilised countries, acting under a sense of the force of sacred obligations, it has had the sanctions of religion superadded: It then becomes a religious, as well as a natural, and civil contract; for it is a great mistake to suppose that, because it is the one, therefore it may not likewise be the other. Heaven itself is made a party to the contract, and the consent of the individuals, pledged to each other, is ratified and consecrated by a vow to God". [*Dalrymple* v *Dalrymple* (1811)2 Hag Con 54, 61-63, *per* Sir William Scott].

The requisites of a valid marriage according to English law are: (1) that each of the parties should as regards age, mental capacity, and otherwise, be capable of contracting marriage; (2) that they should not be reason of kindred or affinity, be prohibited from marrying one another; (3) that there should not be a valid subsisting marriage of either of the parties with any other person; (4) that the parties, understanding the nature of the contract, should freely consent to marry one another; and (5) that certain forms and ceremonies should be observed. [Halsbury's *Laws of England*, 3rd Ed., vol. 19, p. 775].


- **Brahma form of marriage** p. 110.
- **Child marriage** p. 141.
- **Daiva form of marriage** p. 217.
- **Dissolution of marriage** p. 271.
- **Gandharva marriage** p. 381.
- **Impediment to marriage** p. 432.
- **Jactitation of marriage** p. 483.
- **Lawful marriage** p. 518.
- **Nullity of marriage** p. 613.
- **Prajapatya form of marriage** p. 675.
- **Rakshasa form of marriage** p. 724.
- **Restraint of marriage** p. 756.
- **Voidable marriage** p. 884.


**Marriage brokerage contract.** An agreement to pay something for contriving a marriage. It is void as opposed to public policy. [*Baldeo Das* v *Mohmaya* 15 CWN 447; see s. 23, Indian Contract Act 1872].

It is a contract whereby a person undertakes, for reward, to promote marriage, and is not confined to a contract for bringing about a marriage with a particular individual but comprises all contracts for promoting marriages for reward. [*Hermann* v *Charlesworth* (1905)2 KB 123].

**Marriage settlement.** A deed executed in consideration of a marriage about to take place. [*Foster* v *Fowler* 5 Jur NS 99].

NOTE: It is a settlement not by any instrument under which the parties to the marriage take a beneficial interest, but by ante-nuptial or post-nuptial settlements, that is settlements and settlements only, made either in contemplation of, or during, the marriage of the husband and wife whose marriage is in question. The court has no power to vary a settlement which is made by either spouse in general terms and not after, in contemplation of or identifiable with the marriage before the court, but which merely gives the settlor power to appoint an interest to any future wife or husband. [Halsbury's *Laws of England*, 4th Ed., vol. 13, para 1138, p. 528].

**Martial law.** It exists when military authorities carry on government or exercise various degrees of control over civilians or civilian authorities in domestic territory. [*Ochikubo* v *Bonesteel* DC Cal, 60 F Supp 916, 928, 929, 930].

The law administered by military authorities invoked by a Government in an emergency, when the civilian law enforcement agencies are unable to maintain public order and safety.

NOTE: The expression "martial law" is used in three senses. First, it is used to denote the law administered in courts-martial for maintaining discipline within the army. This law applies to the soldiers only; it is embodied in the Army Act 1950, the Air Force Act 1950 and the Navy Act 1957. Secondly, it is used to denote the suspension of the ordinary law and the substitution for it of discretionary government by the Executive exercised through the military. This is the strict sense of the term and it applies to a state of affairs known on the Continent as a "state of siege". When martial law is declared, the civilians are at the mercy of courts-martial and have no redress in ordinary courts against the arbitrary interference with their rights by the Executive. Thirdly, the term is also used to denote the right and duty to maintain public order by force at the time of invasion, rebellion, riot or insurrection. This applies to every citizen as well as to the Executive.

Article 34 of the Constitution of India deals with martial law. Parliament is empowered to pass a legislation indemnifying any person in respect of any act done by him in connection with the maintenance or restoration of order in any area where martial law was in force.

**Marumakkattayam.** The literal meaning of the word "Marumakkattayam" is inheritance through nephews and nieces. The essential difference between Marumakkattayam and the other schools of Hindu law is that the former is founded on the matriarchate while the later is founded upon the agnatic family. In the Mitakshara joint family the members claim their descent from a common ancestor but in a Marumakkattayam family which is known as the tarwad the descent is from a common ancestress. [*M.K. Balakrishna Menon* v *The Assistant Controller of Estate Duty-cum-Income Tax Officer, Ernakulam* AIR 1971 SC 2392: (1971)2 SCC 909: (1972)1 SCR 961: (1972)83 ITR 162].

**Marumakkattayam law.** Marumakkattayam law applied originally by usage to a section of the Hindus inhabiting the South-western Coastal region in India. Some centuries ago a section of the Hindu inhabitants of North Malabar were converted *en masse* to Islam, but they still continued to remain governed by the Marumakkattayam law especially in matters of property relations among members of the family. The principal incident of Marumakkattayam law is that it is market-chate: members of the family constituting a Marumakkattayam tarwad are descended through a common ancestress in the female line with equal rights in the property of the family. Under the customary Marumakkattayam law no partition of the family estate may be made, but items of the family property may by agreement be separately enjoyed by the members. On death the interest of a member developed by survivorship. Management of the family property remained in the hands of the eldest male member, and in the absence of a male member a female member. A tarwad may consist of two or more branches known as thavazhies: each tavazhi or branch consisting of one of the female members of the tarwad and her children and all her descendants in the female line. Every tarwad consisted of a mother and her children—male and female—living in commensality, with joint rights in property. [*N.V.R. Varma Rajah* v *Union of India* (1969)1 SCC 681, 683: AIR 1969 SC 1094; *Achuthan Nair* v *Chinnammu Amma* AIR 1966 SC 411].

**Marz-ul-maut.** A *marz-ul-maut* is a malady or illness, which induces an apprehension of death in the person suffering from it and which eventually results in his death.

There are three tests laid down to determine whether illness is to be regarded as *marz-ul-maut.* They are: (*i*) proximate danger of death so that there is a preponderance of *khauff* or apprehension that at the given time death must be more probable than life. (*ii*) There must be some degree of subjective apprehension of death in the mind of the sick person. (*iii*) There must be external indicia chief among which would be the inability to attend to ordinary avocations. [*Commissioner of Gift-tax* v *Abdul Karim Mohd.* (1991)3 SCC 520: AIR 1991 SC 1847].

A gift made by a Mahomedan during *marz-ul-maut* cannot take effect beyond one-third of his estate after payment of funeral expenses and debts.

**Masculine.** Having the distinguishing qualities of the male sex, or pertaining to males; being of the male gender; a male person; that which is of the male sex; manly, vigorous; of or characteristic of men. It is opposite to faminine.

**Mask.** A covering for all or part of the face; a respirator used to filter air that is inhaled or to supply gas for inhalation; a likeness of a person's face, esp. one made by taking a mould from the face; a disguise or pretence.

• **Gas mask** p. 383.

**Masonry building.** Any building other than a framed building or a hut and includes any structure a substantial part of which is made of masonry or of steel, iron or other metal. [Bengal Municipal Act 1932, s. 3(31); see also Calcutta Municipal Corporation Act 1980, s. 2(51)].

**Mass production.** The production in large quantities of standardised products with the primary object of reducing cost and expediting production.

**Master.** One having authority; one who rules, directs, instructs, or superintends; a head or chief; an instructor; an employer.

A 'master' is one standing to another in such a relation that he not only controls the results of the work of that other but also may direct the manner in which such work shall be done. [*Matonti* v *Research-Cottrell, Inc.* DC Pa, 202 F Supp 527, 532].

A master is one who not only prescribes to the workman the end of his work, but directs, or at any moment may direct the means also, or, as it has been put 'retains the power of controlling the work', as a servant is a person subject to the command of his master as to the manner in which he shall do his work. [*Shivnandan Sharma* v *Punjab National Bank, Ltd.* 1955 SCR 1427: 1955 SCJ 407: (1955)21 MLJ (SC) 247: 1955 SCA 878: AIR 1955 SC 404].

▸*Meaning under the Major Port Trusts Act 1963, s. 2(n).* 'Master', in relation to any vessel or any aircraft making use of any port, means a person having for the time being the charge or control of such vessel or such aircraft, as the case may be, except a pilot, harbour master, assistant harbour master, dock master or berthing master of the port.

▸*Meaning under the General Clauses Act 1897, s. 3(33).* 'Master', used with reference to a ship, shall mean any person (except a pilot or harbour master) having for the time being control or charge of a ship.

**Master and servant.** The relation of master and servant exists where one-person, for pay or other valuable consideration, enters into the service of another and devotes to him his personal labour, for an agreed period. The relation exists where the employer has the right to select the employee, the power to remove and discharge him and the right to direct both what work shall be done and the manner in which it shall be done. [*Matonti* v *Research-Cottrell, Inc.* DC Pa, 202 F Supp 527, 532]. Such term has generally been replaced by "employer and employee".

NOTE: The right to a fair hearing has no application in a mere relationship of master and servant. In a master-servant relationship, if a mere servant is dismissed, there is no remedy by which he can compel the employer to continue to employ him. As between master and servant, the court will not generally grant an injunction to maintain a servant in office. Even if there has been any irregularity in the manner of a servant's dismissal, the servant's only remedy lies in damages. [*Penumbra of Natural Justice* by Tapash Gan Choudhury, 2nd Ed.].

For detailed discussion on exclusion of *audi alteram partem* rule in master-servant relationship. [*Penumbra of Natural Justice* by Tapash Gan Choudhury, 2nd Ed., pp. 98-99].

**Master of the ship.** The person entrusted with the care and navigation of a ship.

**Material alteration.** A material alteration in any written instrument is one which changes its tenor, or its legal meaning and effect; one which causes it to speak a language different in effect from that which it originally spoke. A material alteration of a deed is one which effects a change in its legal effect. [*Boys* v *Long* Okl., 268 P 2d 890, 893].

Any alteration of an instrument is material if it alters the business effect of the instrument. [*Sdffell* v *Bank of England* (1892)9 QBD 555].

A material alteration is one which varies the rights, liabilities or legal position of the parties ascertained by the deed in its original state or otherwise varies the legal effect of the instrument as originally expressed or reduces to certainty some provision which was originally unascertained and as such void, or may otherwise prejudice the party bound by the deed as originally executed. [*Nathulal* v *Gomti Kuar* AIR 1940 PC 160; *Amirudhan* v *Thomco's Bank* AIR 1963 SC 746; *Loonkaran Sethia* v *Ivan E. John* AIR 1977 SC 336: (1977)1 SCR 853: (1977)1 SCC 379].

'Material alteration' with reference to building in its ordinary meaning would mean important alterations, such as those which materially or substantially change the structure of the premises. [*Manmohon Das* v *Bishnu Das* AIR 1967 SC 643]. It means that the nature and character of change or alteration of the building must be of essential and important nature. An alteration is a material alteration when it has the effect of altering the front and structure of the premises. [*Brijendra Nath* v *Harshwardhan* AIR 1988 SC 293: (1988)1 SCC 454].

NOTE: If a person's signature is obtained prior to filling up the blanks, such filling up amounts to a 'material alteration'. [*Punjab National Bank* v *Mehra Bros.* AIR 1983 Cal 335].

**Material defect.** Vital defect; primary defect.

Material defect of property or of title must be of such a nature that it might be reasonably supposed that if the buyer had been aware of it he might not have entered into the contract at all, for he would be getting something different from what he contracted to buy. [*Flight* v *Booth* (1834) Bing (NC) 370]. See Transfer of Property Act 1882, s. 55(1)(*a*).

**Material facts.** The expression "material facts" refers only to primary facts [*Income-tax Officer, Azamgarh* v *M/s. Mewalal Dwarka Prasad* AIR 1989 SC 1088: JT 1989(1) SC 239: (1989)176 ITR 529: (1989)1 SCR 604: (1989)2 SCC 279], such facts which if established would give the petitioner the relief asked for. [*Hardwari Lal* v *Kanwal Singh* AIR 1972 SC 515: (1972)2 SCR 742: (1972)1 SCC 214].

"Material facts" must be such facts as would afford a basis for the allegation made in the petition and would constitute the cause of action as understood in Civil Procedure Code 1908. [*Hari Shanker Jain* v *Sonia Gandhi* (2001)8 SCC 233: JT 2001(7) SC 629].

All those facts which are essential to clothe the petitioner with a complete cause of action are "material facts" which must be pleaded. [*Shri Udhav Singh* v *Madhav Rao Scindia* AIR 1976 SC 744: (1976)2 SCR 246: (1977)1 SCC 511].

The word 'material' in material facts means facts necessary for the purpose of formulating a complete cause of action; and if any one 'material' fact is omitted, the statement or plaint is bad; it is liable to be struck out. [*Roop Lal Sathi* v *Nachhattar Singh Gill* AIR 1982 SC 1559: (1982)3 SCC 487: (1983)1 SCR 702].

**Material irregularity.** Some error of procedure or breach of some provision of law which affects the ultimate decision of the case. [*Shantilal Chunilal* v *Shantilal Fulchand* AIR 1963 Guj 195].

**Material resources.** 'Material resources' as enshrined in Art. 39(*b*) are wide enough to cover not only natural or physical resources but also movable or immovable properties, such as the vehicles, tools, implements and the workshops etc. The mere fact that the resources are material will make no difference in the concept of the word 'resources'. [Constitution of India, Art. 39(*b*); *State of Tamil Nadu* v *L. Abu Kavur Bai* AIR 1984 SC 326: (1984)1 SCR 725: (1984)1 SCC 515].

The expression 'material resources of the community' is confined to natural resources; it is not confined to resources owned by the public; it means and includes all resources, natural and man-made, public and private-owned. [*Sanjeev Coke Manufacturing Co.* v *Bharat Coking Coal Ltd.* AIR 1983 SC 239: (1983)1 SCR 1000: (1983)1 SCC 147].

**Material witness.** A witness who can testify about matters having some logical connection with the consequential facts, esp. if few others, if any, know about those matters. [Black's *Law Dictionary*, 7th Ed.].

A material witness is a witness essential to the unfolding of the narrative on which the prosecution is based. [*Narain* v *State of Punjab* AIR 1959 SC 484: 1959 Supp (1) SCR 724: 1959 Cr LJ 537].

NOTE: A person who is not a witness of occurrence and would not be able to give evidence of the fact on which the prosecution relies is not a material witness. [*Kedar Nath Singh* v *State* 1995 Cr LJ 4121].

If a material witness is deliberately or unfairly kept back, the validity of the conviction may be open to challenge. [*Narain* v *State of Punjab*

AIR 1959 SC 484: 1959 Supp (1) SCR 724: 1959 SCJ 447: 1959 Cr LJ 537].

**Mate's receipt.** Receipt given by the mate of a ship when goods are brought alongside for loading. The mate is the first office of a vessel under the master.

**Math.** In ordinary language it signifies an abode or residence of ascetics. In legal parlance it connotes a monastic institution presided over by a superior and established for the use and benefit of ascetics belonging to a particular order who generally are disciples or co-disciples of the superior. [*Radha Govinda Swamy* v *State of Orissa* (1984)57 Cut LT 188].

A "math" is an institutional sanctum presided over by a superior who combines in himself the dual office of being the religious or spiritual head of the particular cult or religious fraternity, and of the manager of the secular properties of the institution of the math. [*Shri Krishna Singh* v *Mathura Ahir* AIR 1980 SC 707: (1982)2 SCR 660: (1981)3 SCC 689].

NOTE: An institution comes within the definition of 'math' if it satisfies three conditions: (*i*) that the institution be for the promotion of the Hindu religion, (*ii*) that it be presided over by a person whose duty is to engage himself in spiritual service or who exercises or claims to exercise spiritual headship over a body of disciples, and (*iii*) that the office of such person devolves in accordance with the direction of the founder of the institution or is regulated by usage. [*Mahant Shri Sriniwasa Ramanuj* v *Surajnarayan Dass* AIR 1967 SC 256].

**Mathadhipati.** The spiritual head of any Hindu religious institution; Mahunt.

A "Mathadhipati" is a head of a spiritual fraternity. [*The Commissioner, Hindu Religious Endowments, Madras* v *Shri Lakshmindra Thirtha Swamiar of Shri Shirur Mutt* AIR 1954 SC 282: 1954 SCR 1005].

NOTE: The property of a Math is held by the Mathadhipati solely in trust for the purpose of the institution. A Mathadhipati has wide discretion as to application of the income of the Math so as to promote the objects of the Math. [*Mahant Kesho Das* v *Amar Dasji* AIR 1935 Pat 111]. A Mathadhipati has, in addition to his duties, a personal interest of a beneficial character which is much larger than that of a *Sebait* in *debutter* property. He has a right to reside in the Math and has a right to be maintained out of the income of the Math.

**Matrimonial causes.** Actions between the husband and wife respecting the rights under the marriage, such as divorce, judicial separation, restitution of conjugal rights, etc.

**Matrimonial offence.** An offence against the vows of marriage. The vows of marriage are well known. Desertion is certainly one offence, and cruelty, as defined by the law, is another. [*Richardson* v *Richardson* (1949)2 All ER 330].

**Matter.** A subject under consideration, specially involving a dispute or litigation; something that is to be tried or proved; an allegation forming the basis of a claim or defence; facts material to issue; substance as distinguished from form; cause in court; lawsuit; cause in question; business on hand; concern; field of enquiry; item on the agenda; topic for discussion.

▸ *Meaning under the Industrial Disputes Act 1947, proviso to s. 11A.* The 'matter' in proviso to the section refers to the order of discharge or dismissal that is being considered by the tribunal. [*Workmen* v *Firestone Tyre & Rubber Co.* AIR 1973 SC 1227: (1973)1 SCC 813].

**Matter in issue.** That matter on which the plaintiff proceeds by his action, and which the defendant controverts by his pleadings. [*Mackenzie* v *Union Guardian Trust Co.* 247 NW 914].

NOTE: Matters in issue for the purpose of *res judicata* may be classified as: (1) matters directly and substantially in issue; and (2) matters collaterally or incidentally in issue. A matter is directly and substantially in issue if the court considers the adjudication of the issue to be material and essential for its decision. [*Laxman* v *Sarawathi* AIR 1959 Bom 125].

To constitute a matter *res judicata*, it is necessary that it must be in issue directly and substantially, as distinguished from collaterally or incidentally, in a former suit. It is not necessary to constitute a matter directly and substantially in issue that a distinct issue should have been raised upon it; it is sufficient if the matter was in issue in substance. [*Lilabati* v *Bishun Chobey* (1907)6 CLJ 621].

**Matter of fact.** That which is to be ascertained by the senses, or by the testimony of witnesses describing what they have perceived.

A matter involving a judicial enquiry into the truth of alleged facts. [Black's *Law Dictionary*, 7th Ed.].

**Matter of law.** Whatever is to be ascertained or decided by the application of statutory rules or the principles and determinations of the law, as distinguished from the investigation of particular facts, is called "matter of law". [Black's *Law Dictionary*, 5th Ed.].

A matter involving a judicial enquiry into the applicable law. [Black's *Law Dictionary*, 7th Ed.].

**Matter of record.** A matter that has been entered on a judicial or other public record and therefore can be proved by producing that record. [Black's *Law Dictionary*, 7th Ed.].

**Maturity.** The date at which an obligation, such as the principal of a bond or a note, becomes due.

**Maulana.** A Mahomedan of great learning or respectability or a teacher or doctor of Mahomedan theology.

**Maulavi.** A Mahomedan teacher or learned man.

**Maurusi.** Hereditary; obtained by inheritance.

**Maurusi mokarari.** Heritable tenancy at a fixed rent.

**Mauza.** A village; parcels of land having distinct name in the revenue records.

**Maxim.** An established principle or proposition; principle; statement of general truth; aphoristic expression.

Maxims are but attempted general statements of rules of law and are law only to the extent of application in adjudicated cases. [*Swetland* v *Curtiss Airports Corpn.* DC Ohio, 41 F 2d 929, 936].

**May.** An auxiliary verb qualifying the meaning of another verb by expressing ability, competency, liberty, permission, possibility, probability or contingency. [*U.S.* v *Lexington Mill & E. Co.* 58 L Ed 658].

Normally, the word "may" is used to grant a discretion and not to indicate a mandatory direction. [*Smt. Sahodara Devi* v *Government of India* AIR 1971 SC 1599: (1972)3 SCC 156: 1971 (Supp) SCR 230].

As a general rule, the word "may" will not be treated as a word of command unless there is something in context or subject-matter of act to indicate that it was used in such sense. [*Bloom* v *Texas State Bd. of Examiners of Phychologist* Tex Civ App, 475 SW 2d 374, 377].

The word "may" is generally used in permissive or enabling sense. But it is capable of being construed as a compelling duty, particularly when it refers to a power conferred on a court or other judicial authority. [*Ramji Missir* v *State of Bihar* AIR 1963 SC 1088: (1963)2 SCJ 571: (1964)1 SCA 98].

Normally "may" implies directory provision, but where the provision gives power coupled with the duty to perform public duty, the use of the word "may" in the context would mean "must". [*State (Delhi Administration)* v *I.K. Nangia* AIR 1979 SC 1977: 1980 Cr LJ 834: (1980)1 SCR 1016: (1980)1 SCJ 314: 1980 MLJ (Cr) 343].

No expression can be considered in isolation. The word "may" which *prima facie* indicates a directory provision in the context may mean imperative. [*Supdt. L.R.* v *Abani Maiti* AIR 1979 SC 1029: 1979 Cr LJ 897: (1979)2 SCJ 176: 1979 SCC (Cri) 902: 1979 MLJ (Cri) 557].

The word 'may' is often read as 'shall' or 'must', when there is something in the nature of the thing to be done which makes it the duty of the person on whom the power is conferred to exercise the power. [*Govind Rao* v *State of Madhya Pradesh* AIR 1965 SC 1222: (1965)1 SCR 678].

**Mayukha.** A commentary on Mitakshara by Nilkantha Bhatta.

**Mazkur.** Aforesaid; above-mentioned.

**Means.** That through which, or by the help of which, an end is attained; something tending to an object desired; intermediate agency or measure; necessary condition or co-agent; resources; available property; money or property.

A particular expression is often defined by the Legislature by using the word "means". The use of the word "means" indicates that the definition is a hard and fast definition and no other meaning can be assigned to the expression that is put down in definition. [*P. Kasilingam* v *P.S.G. College of Technology* AIR 1995 SC 1395: 1995 Supp (2) SCC 348: JT 1995(3) SC 193: (1995)2 SCJ 155].

**Means and includes.** Where the legislature uses the words 'means' and 'includes' in defining a particular expression, such definition is to be given a wider meaning and is not exhaustive or restricted to the items contained or included in such a definition. [*Krishi Utpadan Mandi Samiti* v *Shankar Industries* 1993 Supp (3) SCC 361].

The words 'means and includes' indicate an exhaustive explanation of the meaning. [*P. Kasilingam* v *P.S.G. College of Technology* AIR 1995 SC 1395: 1995 Supp (2) SCC 348: JT 1995(3) SC 193: (1995)2 SCJ 155].

Where an interpretation clause defines a word to mean a particular thing, the definition is explanatory and *prima facie* restrictive, and whenever an interpretation clause defines a term to include something, the definition is extensive. [*Central Inland Water Transport Corpn. Ltd.* v *Brojo Nath Ganguly* AIR 1986 SC 1571: (1986)2 SCR 278: (1986)3 Comp LJ 1].

**Means of livelihood.** In ordinary meaning, it means resources of livelihood. [*Mohan Lal* v *Mohun Ram* AIR 1970 SC 1022: (1970)3 SCC 177].

**Measure.** As noun it means act; caveat; edict; enactment; prescription; proposal; proposition; regulation; that by which extent or dimension is ascertained, either of length, breadth, thickness, capacity or amount; the rule by which anything is adjusted or proportioned.

As verb it means admeasure; appraise; ascertain dimensions; ascertain size; assess; determine size; determine value; gauge; evaluate; fathom; survey.

**Measure of damages.** The rule, or rather the system of rules, governing the adjustment or apportionment of damage as a compensation for injuries in actions at law.

**Medhatihi.** He is a writer on ancient Hindu Law. He wrote a commentary on Manu. For a long time Medhatihi's commentary on Manu was considered as a paramount authority, and gave law to the Hindus. Manu was certainly the basis of Medhatihi's law; but the great commentator advanced opinions and laid down rules which would satisfy the requirements of his time. In the name of interpretation he greatly modified the laws of Manu to suit the requirements of his age.

**NOTE:** The exposition of the texts of Manu, given by Medhatihi, is at least authoritative, and the explanation of no other commentator can stand in competition with that given by him.

**Medical.** Pertaining, relating or belonging to the study and practice of medicine, or the science and art of the investigation, prevention, cure, and alleviation of disease.

**Medical jurisprudence.** The science which applies the principles and practice of the different branches of medicine to the elucidation of doubtful questions in a court of justice. It is otherwise called "forensic medicine".

**Medicine.** The science and art dealing with the prevention, cure and alleviation of diseases; in a narrower sense that part of the science and art of restoring and preserving health which is the province of the physician as distinguished from the surgeon and obstetrician. [*Burke* v *Kansas State Osteopathic Ass'n.* CCA Kan, 111 F 2d 250, 253].

• **Forensic medicine** p. 366.

**Meeting.** An assembly of persons, esp. to discuss and act on matters in which they have a common interest. [Black's *Law Dictionary*, 7th Ed.].

A meeting means coming together of persons for the purpose of discussing and acting upon some matter or matters in which they have a common interest. [*Sharp* v *Dawes* (1876)2 QBD 26].

The word 'meeting' *prima facie* connotes coming together of persons for certain purposes. In substance, it is a gathering of persons with a specific object in view. [*D.D. Didolkar* v *Nagpur University* AIR 1976 Bom 276; *Awadhoot* v *State of Maharashtra* AIR 1978 Bom 28].

Meeting implies the coming together of persons for certain purposes for consultation; it is an assembly and is not constituted every time a subject is introduced. The entire assembly, as such, transacting the business before it, is the meeting and the fact the number of members present fluctuates during the meeting does not make any difference to the nature of the meeting itself. [*Ved Prakash Dusaj* v *Municipal Corporation* ILR (1958) AP 17].

A meeting is a gathering or assembly of a number of people for purposes of intercourse, entertainment, discussion, legislation and the like or for the purpose of the discussion of matters of public interest, or for the purpose of the expression of views on such matters. [*Law and Practice of Meetings* by Frank Shackleton].

The word 'meeting', when not defined under the relevant statute, has to be construed only in its popular sense. If a common sense view of the matter is taken, it is quite clear that for a meeting there must be at least two persons, because a man cannot meet himself. [*Awadhoot* v *State of Maharashtra* AIR 1978 Bom 28].

NOTE: A meeting can be said to be a meeting only when it meets for the purpose of discussing and deciding something for which the meeting is called. If that purpose cannot be achieved because of lack of the requisite minimum number of members, then it does not constitute a valid meeting. [*S. Seetha Ramaiah* v *Ongole Co-operative Bank* AIR 1974 AP 49].

The expression 'meeting' is synonymous with the expression 'session'. [*Amin Chand* v *State of Punjab* AIR 1953 Punj 40 (DB): 1953 Cr LJ 373: ILR (1953) Punj 384: 54 Punj LR 493].

• **Public meeting** p. 710.
• **Statutory meeting** p. 811.

**Mehar.** In Muhammadan Law, 'mehar' or 'dower' is defined as a sum of money or other property which the wife is entitled to get from the husband in consideration of marriage.

Mehar is "not the exchange or the consideration given by the man to the woman, but an effect of the contract imposed by law on the husband as a token of respect for its subject: the women". [*The Muslim Law of India* by Dr. Tahir Mahmood, p. 71, quoting Justice Syed Mahmood].

NOTE: "Mehar is an essential incident to the status of marriage. Regarded as a consideration for the marriage it is not in theory payable before consummation; but the law allows its division in two parts, one of which is called 'prompt' payable before the wife can be called upon to enter the conjugal domicile, the other 'deferred' payable on the dissolution of the contract by the death of either of the parties or by divorce. When the Kabinnama does not specify the portion that is prompt and that which is deferred, evidence may be given of the custom or usage of wife's family". [*Fuzlunbi* v *K. Khader Vali* AIR 1980 SC 1730, quoted in Tyabji's *Muslim Law*, 4th Ed.].

The quintessence of mehar whether it is prompt or deferred is clearly not a contemplated quantification of a sum of money in lieu of maintenance upon divorce. Divorce is farthest from the thought of the bride and the bridegroom when mehar is promised. [*Fuzlunbi* v *K. Khader Vali* AIR 1980 SC 1730].

**Melvaram and Kudivaram.** Ancient Hindu law recognised only two beneficial interests in the land, *viz.* (1) that of the sovereign, and

(2) that of the cultivator. The sovereign's right was confined to the collection of a share of the produce of the cultivated lands known as Melvaram. The share of the cultivators was known as Kudivaram.

**Member.** In its application as constituent part it means article, branch, category, component, department, division, element, factor, feature, ingredient, integral part, portion, section, segment, sub-division, subordinate part, unit.

In its application as individuals in a group it means affiliate, associate, card-holder, committee person, comrade, co-partner, co-sharer, fellow, participator, person, patron, registered person, shareholder, stockholder, teammate.

As a medical term it means a part or organ of the body; specially a limb or other separate part. [*California Casualty Indemnity Exchange* v *Industrial Accident Commission* Cal App, 82 P 2d 1115, 1116].

In military law, it means a person assigned to a court-marshal to determine guilt and punishment. [Black's *Law Dictionary*, 7th Ed.].

**Member of Parliament.** One having the right to sit in either house of the British/Indian Parliament.

**Memorandum.** A brief note of a thing or things to be remembered; a statement of goods sent from a consignor to a consignee; an informal letter; an informal written note or record outlining the terms of a transaction or contract; a brief written outline of the terms of a transaction; a party's written statement of its legal arguments presented to the court, usually in the form of a brief.

**Memorandum of association.** A document to be subscribed by a required number of persons associated for a lawful purpose, by subscribing which, and otherwise complying with the requisitions of the statute in respect of registration, they may form themselves into an incorporated company. Such a document contains the company's name, registered office, main objects, objects incidental or ancillary to the attainment of the main objects, the liability of the members and the share capital of the company.

**Mens rea.** A guilty mind; a guilty or wrongful purpose; a criminal intent; guilty knowledge and wilfulness. [*United States* v *Greenbaum* CCA NJ, 138 F 2d 437, 438].

The true translation of the phrase *'mens rea'* is "criminal intention, or an intention to do the act which is made penal by statute or by the common law". [*Allard* v *Selfridge & Co., Ltd.* (1925)1 KB 129, *per* Shearman, J. ].

*"Mens rea"* is a state of mind under criminal law, which is considered as the "guilty intention" and unless it is found that the 'accused' had the guilty intention to commit the 'crime' he cannot be held 'guilty' of committing the crime. [*Director of Enforcement* v *M.C.T.M. Corporation (P) Ltd.* AIR 1996 SC 1100: (1996)2 SCC 471: 1996 SCC (Cri) 344: JT 1996(1) SC 79: (1997)88 Comp Cas 449].

*Mens rea* forms a necessary ingredient of an offence unless by express language or by implication the element of *mens rea* is excluded. [*Hariprasad Rao* v *State* AIR 1951 SC 204: 1951 SCJ 296].

NOTE: The presumption that *mens rea* is an essential ingredient in every offence is liable to be displaced either by express words or by the subject-matter with which it deals. [*State of Maharashtra* v *Mayer Hans George* AIR 1965 SC 722].

**Mental cruelty.** A course of conduct on the part of one spouse toward the other spouse which can endanger the mental and physical health and efficiency of the other spouse to such an extent as to render continuance of the marital relation intolerable. [*Steeie* v *Steeie* Fla App, 177 So 2d 873].

'Mental cruelty' can broadly be defined as that conduct which inflicts upon the other party such mental pain and suffering as would make it not possible for that party to live with the other. In other words, mental cruelty must be of such a nature that the parties cannot reasonably be expected to live together. [*V. Bhagat* v *D.*

*Bhagat* (1994)1 SCC 337: AIR 1994 SC 710: (1994)1 SCJ 62: (1994)1 AIR SCW 45: JT 1993(6) SC 428].

NOTE: What acts will constitute mental cruelty depends upon the facts and circumstances of each case. Several factors will have to be taken into consideration, such as, environment, status in society, education, cultural development, local custom, social convention, physical and mental condition of the parties etc. [*Parul Devi* v *Gopi Mondal* AIR 1963 Pat 93].

In matters relating to marriage, the question of mental cruelty should be answered in the light of the norms of marriage ties of the particular society to which the parties belong, their social values, status of the parties, environment of parties etc. [*Bijoli Chowdhury* v *Sukomol Chowdhury* AIR 1979 Cal 87; *Balbir Kaur* v *Dhirdas* AIR 1979 Punj 162: 81 Punj LR 113].

**Mental disorder.** Mental illness, arrested or incomplete development of mind, psychopathic disorder, and any other disorder or disability of mind. [Halsbury's *Laws of England*, 4th Ed., vol. 30 at p. 563].

**Mercantile agent.** "Mercantile agent" means an agent having in the customary course of his business as such agent authority either to sell goods, or to consign goods for the purpose of sale, or to buy goods, or to raise money on the security of goods.

An agent employed to sell goods or merchandise on behalf of the principal. [Black's *Law Dictionary*, 7th Ed.].

**Merchandise.** Articles of commerce; goods for sale; saleable commodities; capital goods; cargo; chattel; consumer durables; consumer goods; wares.

Goods that are bought and sold in business; commercial wares. [Black's *Law Dictionary*, 8th Ed.].

The term is generally not understood as including real estate, and is rarely applied to provisions such as are purchased day by day for immediate consumption, *e.g.*, food. It may include fish, livestock and animals of all descriptions, and minerals.

**Merchant.** A merchant is one who buys and sells commodities as a business and for profit; who has a place of sale and stock of goods; and is generally a trader in a large way. [*R.* v *Wells* (1911)24 OLR 77, *per* Middleton, J.].

A merchant of or in an article is one who buys and sells it, and not the manufacturer selling. [*Fosselyn* v *Parson* (1872) LR 7 Exch 127, *per* Bramwell, B.].

A merchant is one who trades in goods, that is to say, buys and sells goods. It includes a general manager of a trading company. [*Parmeshwari Das* v *Ram Chand* AIR 1952 Punj 34].

Everyone who buys and sells is not, at this day, called a merchant; only those who traffic in the way of commerce by importation or exportation, or carry on business by way of vendition, barter, permutation or exchange and who make it their living to buy and sell by a continued assiduity or frequent negotiation in the mystery of merchandising are esteemed merchants. Those who buy goods to reduce them by their own art or industry into other forms and then to sell them are artificers, not merchants. Bankers and such as deal by exchange are properly called merchants. [Tomlin's *Law Dictionary*].

NOTE: A wine merchant deals in wine generally, port, sherry, claret, champagne, etc. He need not deal in every wine. But if he sold port only, he should properly call himself a port wine merchant. So of a spirit merchant, he sells gin, brandy, rum, whisky, etc., and if he sold brandy only, should call himself a brandy merchant. A porter merchant, in the same way, sells porter generally, London porter, Dublin porter, Cork porter; but if he sold one sort only, he should describe himself accordingly as a Dublin porter merchant. [*Fosselyn* v *Parson* (1872) LR 7 Exch 127, *per* Bramwell, B.]. Because the term "merchant" relates solely to goods, a supplier of services is not considered a merchant. [Black's *Law Dictionary*, 7th Ed.].

• **Commission merchant** p. 157.

**Merchantable.** Fit for sale in the usual course of trade at the usual selling prices; marketable; saleable. [Black's *Law Dictionary*, 8th Ed.].

"Merchantable can only mean commercially saleable". [*Kendall (Henry)*

*& Sons* v *Lillico (William) & Sons, Ltd.* (1968)2 All ER 444, *per* Lord Reid].

As between manufacturer and merchant, and where there is no express stipulation, goods are 'merchantable' if they are reasonably fit for some of the merchants' purposes, though not for others. [*Jones* v *Padgett* 59 LJQB 261: 21 QBD 650].

**Merchantable quality.** The phrase "merchantable quality" is "used as meaning that the article is of such quality and in such condition that a reasonable man acting reasonably would after a full examination accept it under the circumstances of the case in performance of his offer to buy that article whether be buys for his own use or to sell again". [*Bristol Tramways, etc., 2 Carriage Co., Ltd.* v *Fiat Motors Ltd.* (1910) KB 831 (CA), *per* Farwell, L.J.].

"Merchantable quality" means "that the goods comply with the description in the contract, so that to a purchaser buying goods of that description the goods would be good tender". [*Summer, Permain & Co.* v *Webb & Co.* (1922)1 KB 55 (CA), *per* Scrutton, L.J.; *Sorabji Hormusha* v *V.M. Ismail* AIR 1960 Mad 520].

NOTE: Goods are not of "merchantable quality" if, in the form in which they were tendered, they were of no use for any purpose for which the goods which complied with the description would normally be used. [*Brown* v *Craiks Ltd.* (1970)1 All ER 823].

**Merchantable title.** 'Merchantable title' means particularly in the case of a contract for sale of immovable property title free from reasonable doubt. A merchantable title is one which so far as the defendants are concerned, may at all times and under all circumstances be forced upon an unwilling purchaser. [*Indore Wire Co. Ltd., Bombay* v *Kalyandas* 1989 Jab LJ 493 (MP)].

**Merger.** Absorption; amalgamation; assimilation; consolidation; integration; unification; loss of identity; union; the act or an instance of combining or uniting.

- *Meaning in contracts.* In contracts, it means the substitution of a superior form of contract for an inferior form, as when a written contract supersedes all oral agreements and prior understandings. [Black's *Law Dictionary*, 8th Ed.].

- *Meaning in property matters.* In property matters, it means the extinguishment of a lesser estate, right, or liability in a greater one; the absorption of a lesser estate into a greater estate when both becomes the same person's property.

"Whenever a greater estate and a less coincide and meet in one and the same person without any intermediate estate, the less is immediately annihilated; or in the law phrase, is said to be merged, that is, sunk or drowned in the greater". [*Commentaries on the Laws of England* by Blackstone, 4th Ed., vol. II, p. 151].

In India, the legal position as regards merger may be stated thus: The union of the superior and subordinate interests will not automatically cause a merger. Merger will be held to have taken place if the intention to merge is clear and not otherwise. In the absence of any express indication of intention, the courts will proceed on the basis that the party had no intention to merge if it was to his interest not to merge and also if a duty lay on him to keep the interests separate. In deciding the intention of the party the court will have regard also to his conduct. [*Jyotish Thakur* v *Tarakant Jha* AIR 1963 SC 605, *per* Das Gupta, J.].

- *Meaning in criminal law.* In criminal law, it means the absorption of a lesser included offence into a more serious offence when a person is charged with both crimes, so that the person is not subject to double jeopardy.

- *Meaning in corporate field.* In corporate world, it means the absorption of one company that ceases to exist into another that retains its own name and identity and acquires the assets and liabilities of the former.

NOTE: Corporate mergers must conform to statutory formalities and must be approved by a majority of the shareholders.

**Merit.** Praiseworthy quality; virtue; worth; worthiness; deservedness; the element or ground of a claim or defence; the substantive consideration to be taken into account in deciding a case, as opposed to technical or extraneous point.

In matters of selection for medical course 'merit' consists of a high degree of intelligence coupled with a keen and incisive mind, sound knowledge of the basic subjects and infinite capacity for hard work, but that is not enough; it also calls for a sense of social commitment and dedication to the cause of the poor. Merit cannot be measured in terms of marks alone, but human sympathies are equally important. The heart is as much a factor as the head in assessing the social value of a member of the medical profession. This is also an aspect which may, to the limited extent possible, be borne in mind while determining merit for selection of candidates for admission to medical colleges though concededly it would not be easy to do so, since it is a factor which is extremely difficult to judge and not easily susceptible to evaluation. [*Dr. Pradeep Jain* v *Union of India* (1984)3 SCC 654: AIR 1984 SC 1420].

In service matter, 'merit' is a sum total of various qualities and attributes of an employee and his academic qualifications, his distinction in the University, his character, integrity, devotion to duty and the manner in which he discharges his official duties are taken into consideration in determining the merit. Allied to this may be various other matters, or factors, such as his punctuality in work, the quality and out-turn of work done by him and the manner of his dealings with his superiors and subordinates and the general public, his rank in the service and annual confidential report. All these and other factors may have to be taken into account in assessing the merit. [*Guman Singh* v *State of Rajasthan* (1971)2 SCC 452: 1971 (Supp) SCR 900: (1971)2 SCR 799]. 'Merit' is deemed to include initiative and efficiency. [*Management of Brooke Bond India Pvt. Ltd.* v *Their Workmen* AIR 1966 SC 668].

**Mesne profit.** The profits of an estate received by a tenant in wrongful possession between two dates [Black's *Law Dictionary*, 7th Ed.]; intermediate profits, i.e., profits which have been accruing between two given periods. [*Dumas* v *Ropp* 558 P 2d 632, 633].

▸ *Meaning under the Civil Procedure Code 1908, s. 2(12).* Those profits which a person in wrongful possession of such property actually received or might with ordinary diligence have received therefrom, together with interest on such profits, but shall not include profits due to improvements made by the person in wrongful possession.

NOTE: The definition of *'mesne profits'* in s. 2(12) makes it clear that the *'mesne profits'* can be claimed regarding immovable property and not with regard to a motor lorry, as a motor lorry cannot be deemed to be immovable property. [*Kangaban Bira Singh* v *Manipur Drivers' Association Ltd.* AIR 1957 Manipur 9].

The normal measure of *mesne profits* is the value of the user of the land to the person in wrongful possession. [*Fateh Chand* v *Balkissen Das* AIR 1963 SC 1405; *Kesardeo* v *Nathmal Kisanlal* AIR 1966 Bom 266: ILR (1966) Bom 363: 1965 Mah LJ 688].

**Message.** A written or oral communication, often sent through a messenger or other agent, or electronically, *e.g.*, through e-mail or voice mail [Black's *Law Dictionary*, 7th Ed.]; any important communication embodying a truth, principle, or advice; an inspired or significant communication from a prophet, writer, or preacher.

▸ *Meaning under the Indian Telegraph Act 1885, s. 2(3).* Any communication sent by telegraph or given to a telegraph officer to be sent by telegraph or to be delivered.

**Messuage.** A dwelling house together with the curtilage, including any outbuildings. [Black's *Law Dictionary*, 7th Ed.].

The "term messuage denotes all that is occupied together at one and the same time, and no more". [*Kerslake* v *White* (1819), 2 Stark 508, *per* Abbott, C.J.].

NOTE: A house is, by lawyers generally, called a messuage; and the term 'messuage' was formerly considered as of more extensive import than the word 'house'. But such a distinction is not now to be relied on. Both the terms 'messuage' and 'house' will comprise adjoining outbuildings, the orchard and curtilage, or courtyard and, according to the better opinion, these terms will include the garden also. [Williams and Eastwood on *Real Property*, p. 81].

**Metal.** Any of a class of substances including many chemical elements which are in general lustrous, malleable, fusible, ductile solids and good conductors of heat and electricity, *e.g.*, gold, silver, iron, brass, steel, aluminium ingots.

An element that forms a base by combining with a hydroxyl group or groups. It is usually hard, heavy, lustrous, malleable, ductile, tenacious, and a good conductor of heat and electricity.

A composition of some metallic element; an alloy.

NOTE: 'Metal' is generally used to refer to the metal in its primary sense, i.e., metal in the form in which it is marketable as primary commodity. Subsequent forms envolved from the primary form and constituting distinct commodities marketable as such must be regarded as new commercial commodities. Aluminium ingots and billets are 'metal' in primary form, but when rolled into aluminium rolled products and extrusion products they become new commercial commodity and are not included in 'metal'. [*Hindustan Aluminium Corporation Ltd.* v *State of U.P.* (1981)3 SCC 578: AIR 1981 SC 1649: (1981)48 STC 411: (1982)1 SCR 129: (1983)13 ELT 1656].

**Metallurgical factory.** 'Metallurgical factory' means—(*i*) a factory in which iron or steel is being processed or manufactured; (*ii*) any other factory, being a factory in which iron ore is used for any purpose, which the Central Government may, by notification in the Official Gazette, declare to be a metallurgical factory. [Iron Ore Mines Labour Welfare Cess Act 1961, s. 1A(*c*)].

**Metes and bounds.** The boundary lines of land, with their terminal points and angles; a way of describing land by listing the compass directions and distances of the boundaries.

NOTE: It is often used in connection with the Government Survey System.

Partition by metes and bounds is the division of the subject-matter of partition into demarcated areas to be held in severalty.

**Metric system.** A decimal system of weights and measures based on the metre as a unit length and the kilogram as a unit mass.

**Miaad.** Term, period, limit; imprisonment.

**Miaadi.** Limited; for a term only.

**Miaadi patta or ijara.** A lease for a limited time; a terminable lease or settlement; a deed to that effect.

**Mica works.** 'Mica works' is a general term of widest possible import, and includes all kinds of works in relation to mica including mining. [*N.K. Jain* v *Labour Commissioner* AIR 1957 Raj 35: ILR (1957)7 Raj 74].

**Middleman.** One who merely brings parties together in order to enable them to make their own contracts; one who buys at one price from a manufacturer for resale at a higher price.

He "is an agent between two parties; an intermediary who performs the office of a broker or factor between seller and buyer, producer and consumer, land-owner and tenant, etc."

A middleman is an "intermediary or agent between two parties; esp., a dealer (such as a wholesaler) who buys from producers and sells to retailers or consumers". [Black's *Law Dictionary*, 8th Ed.].

"A 'middleman' is a person intervening between supplier and consumer with an interest independent of both, be it only to secure commission on the formation or carrying out of the contract between them". [*Perth Assessor* v *Shields Motor Car Co., Ltd.* (1956) SC 186, *per* Lord Patrick].

**Midshipman.** In Britain, means a naval officer of rank between naval cadet and sub-lieutenant; in US means a naval cadet.

**Migrate.** The word 'migrate' is capable of both a narrower meaning as well as a wider meaning. In its narrower connotation, it means going from one place to another with the intention of permanently residing in the latter place. In its wider connotation, it simply means going from one place to another whether or not with any intention. [*Kulathil Mammu* v *State of Kerala* AIR 1966 SC 1614: 1966 Cr LJ 1217].

The word "migrate" may have in some contexts the wider meaning "come or remove to a place without an intention to reside permanently" and in some context the narrower meaning "come or remove to a place with the intention of residing there permanently". [*Smt. Shanno Devi* v *Mangal Sain* AIR 1961 SC 58: (1961)1 SCR 576: 1961 SCJ 201].

▸ *Meaning under the Constitution of India, Art. 7.* In the Article the word was used in its wider sense though it did not take in movement which was involuntary or for a specific purpose and for a short and limited period. [*State of Assam* v *Jilkadar Ali* (1972)2 SCC 320: AIR 1972 SC 2166: 1972 Cr LJ 1441: 1972 SCC (Cri) 662: (1973)1 SCR 685].

**Migration.** Migration is changing one's abode, quitting one's place of abode and settling permanently at another place. [*Vimla Bai* v *Hiralal Gupta* (1990)2 SCC 22: JT 1989 (Supp) 448: 1989 Supp (2) SCR 759].

**Military aircraft.** Any aircraft belonging to the Armed Forces and includes any armed aircraft in the service of the Armed Forces and any other aircraft used as a transport or auxiliary or in any other way for the purpose of prosecuting or aiding hostilities. [Naval and Aircraft Prize Act 1971, s. 2(*g*)].

**Military Government.** The control of all or most public functions within a country, or the assumption and exercise of governmental functions, by military forces or individual members of those forces; government exercised by a military commander under the direction of the executive or sovereign, either externally during a foreign war or internally during a civil war. [Black's *Law Dictionary*, 7th Ed.].

**Military law.** The branch of public law governing military discipline and other rules regarding service in the armed forces. [Black's *Law Dictionary*, 7th Ed.].

It is described by Wharton in his *Law Lexicon* (14th Ed., pp. 655-656) thus: "*Military law* as distinguished from *Civil law* is the law relating to and administered by military courts and is concerned with the trial and punishment of offences committed by officers, soldiers and other persons, who are subjected for the time being to the same law as soldiers. But the term *'military law'* is frequently used in a wider sense and as including not only the disciplinary but also the administrative law of the army, as for instance, the law of enlistment and billeting".

NOTE: Article 33 of the Constitution of India deals with the military law. Parliament can modify the fundamental rights in their application to the armed forces or forces charged with the maintenance of public order.

**Military stores.** The expression 'Military Stores' is comprehensive enough to cover articles essential for military use inclusive of trailers/water tankers supplies of which are accumulated in the depot for being drawn upon whenever needed. [*Cantonment Board* v *Mahindra Owen Ltd.* AIR 1986 SC 1114: 1986 (Supp) SCC 301: (1986)1 SCR 961].

**Milk.** In common parlance "milk" means the full cream milk as milched from the cattle. It becomes skimmed milk when cream, *i.e.*, fat is extracted from milk. [*Healthways Dairy Products Co.* v *Union of India* AIR 1976 SC 2221: (1976)2 SCR 93: (1976)2 SCC 887].

The word 'milk' is a generic term. 'Cow's milk', 'buffalo's milk', 'goat's milk', 'camel's milk', 'horse's milk', 'donkey's milk', are all different from each other and are consumed by different sections of people, sometimes for ailment, sometimes for improving health and, in the case of 'horse's milk', for exhilaration and nourishment. [*Kisan Trimbak Kothula* v *State of*

*Maharashtra* AIR 1977 SC 435: (1977)2 SCR 102: 1977 Cr LJ 267: 1977 SCC (Cri) 97: (1977)1 SCC 300].

NOTE: Milk includes condensed milk. [*Indodan Milk Products Ltd.* v *CST, U.P.* 1973 Tax LR 2492].

**Milk product.** Milk product means the product obtained from milk such as cream, malai, curd, skimmed milk curd, chhenna, cheese, processed cheese, ice cream, condensed milk sweetened and unsweetened, condensed skimmed milk sweetened and unsweetened, milk powder, skimmed milk powder, partly skimmed milk powder, khoa, infant milk food, table butter and deshi butter. [*Kishan Chand* v *Delhi Administration* AIR 1979 SC 1128: (1979)3 SCR 313: (1979)4 SCC 709: 1980 SCC (Cri) 165].

Section 42(1) of the Agricultural Marketing Act 1958 of U.K. defines "milk product" thus: Any articles of food or drink wholly or partly manufactured or derived from milk.

**Mill.** A "mill" is a building where goods are subjected to treatment or processing of some sort, and where machinery is used for that purpose. The miller in his corn-mill grinds wheat into flour, or oats into oatmeal. So, too, at a scutching-mill, the miller scutches the flax, to prepare it for spinning. The saw-mill the rolling-mill, the flatting-mill, the puffing-mill and the cotton-mill are all buildings where goods are treated or subjected to some process. [*Ellerker* v *Union Cold Storage Co. Ltd.* (1939)1 All ER 23, *per* Macnaghten, J.].

A "mill" is a building where goods are subjected to treatment or processing of some sort or where machinery is used for that purpose. [*Sales Tax Commissioner, U.P.* v *M/s. Ladha Singh Mal Singh* AIR 1971 SC 2221: 1971 (Supp) SCR 941: (1971)2 SCC 407: (1971)28 STC 325].

NOTE: The essential of a mill is a process, carried on by machinery, by which the material subjected to it is made suitable for further treatment in a factory or another mill or for use. [*Inland Revenue* v *Leith Harbour & Docks, Comrs.* (1942) SC 101].

Cold Stores are very similar to 'mills' in all the essential characteristics of such buildings, since they are equipped with machinery for the purpose of subjecting the various commodities which are brought there to an artificial temperature. [*Ellerker* v *Union Cold Storage Co. Ltd.* (1939)1 All ER 23, *per* Macnaghten, J.].

**Mimansa.** A settlement or compromise of a dispute or difference; arbitration award; judgment; schools of Hindu philosophy, namely, *Purvo Mimansa* by *Jaimini* and *Uttar Mimansa* or *Vedanta* by *Vyas*.

**Mind.** In its legal sense, "mind" means only the ability to will, to direct, to permit, or to ascent. [Black's *Law Dictionary*, 5th Ed.].

The source of thought and intellect; the seat of mental faculties. [Black's *Law Dictionary*, 8th Ed.].

• **Abnormality of mind** p. 6.
• **Absence of mind** p. 8.

**Mine.** An underground excavation used to obtain minerals, ores, or other substances; a mineral deposit; a place containing a mineral deposit. [Black's *Law Dictionary*, 8th Ed.].

The dictionary meaning of the word 'mine' is given an excavation in earth for metal, coal, salt, etc. The said definition shows, *inter alia*, that a 'mine' means any excavation, where any operation for the purpose of or searching for obtaining minerals has been or is being carried on. [*Sirajuddin Co.* v *Workmen* (1963)1 SCA 225: 1962 Supp (3) SCR 934].

The word "mine" is not a definite term, but is one susceptible of limitation or expansion according to the intention with which it is used. The original or primary meaning of the word is an underground excavation made for the purpose of getting minerals.

A further meaning of the word "mining" comprehends not only the mineral deposits but also so much of the adjoining strata, whether superjacent or subjacent, as it may be necessary to remove for the purpose of working the mineral in a proper manner. [Halsbury's *Laws of England*, 3rd Ed., vol. 26, pp. 317, 318].

"Mine" means an excavation or system of excavations made for the purpose of, or in connection with, the getting, wholly or substantially by means involving the employment of persons below ground, of minerals (whether in their natural state or in solution or suspension) or products of minerals. [Halsbury's *Laws of England*, 4th Ed., vol. 20, para 407, p. 189].

▸ *Meaning under different Acts—Mines Act 1952, s. 2(j); Industrial Disputes Act 1947, s. 2(bb); Payment of Gratuity Act 1972, s. 2(j).* 'Mine' means any excavation where any operation for the purpose of searching for or obtaining minerals has been or is being carried on, and includes—(*i*) all borings, bore holes and oil wells; (*ii*) all shafts, in or adjacent to and belonging to a mine, whether in the course of being sunk or not; (*iii*) all levels and inclined planes in the course of being driven; (*iv*) all open cast workings; (*v*) all conveyors or aerial ropeways provided for the bringing into or removal from a mine of minerals or other articles or for the removal of refuse therefrom; (*vi*) all adits, levels, places, machinery, works, railways, tramways and sidings in or adjacent to and belonging to a mine; (*vii*) all workshops situated within the precincts of a mine and under the same management and used solely for the purpose connected with that mine or a number of mines under the same management; (*viii*) all power stations for supplying electricity solely for the purpose of working the mine or a number of mines under the same management; (*ix*) any premises for the time being used for depositing refuse from a mine or in which any operation in connection with such refuse is being carried on, being premises exclusively occupied by the owner of the mine; (*x*) unless exempted by the Central Government by notification in the Official Gazette, any premises or part thereof, in or adjacent to and belonging to a mine on which any process ancillary to the getting, dressing or preparation for sale of minerals or of coke is being carried on.

▸ *Meaning under the Oilfields (Regulation and Development) Act 1948, s. 3(b).* 'Mine' means any excavation for the purpose of searching for or obtaining mineral oils and includes an oil well.

▸ *Meaning under the Coking Coal Mines (Nationalisation) Act 1972, s. 3(j).* 'Mine' means any excavation where any operation for the purpose of searching for or obtaining minerals has been or is being carried on and includes—(*i*) all borings and bore holes; (ii) all shafts adjacent to and belonging to or in a mine, whether in the course of being sunk or not; (*iii*) all levels and inclined planes in the course of being driven; (*iv*) all open cast workings; (*v*) all conveyors or aerial ropeways provided for bringing into or removal from a mine or minerals or other articles or for the removal of refuse therefrom; (*vi*) all lands, buildings, works, adits, levels, planes, machinery and equipment, vehicles, railways, tramways and sidings belonging to or in or about a mine; (*vii*) all workshops belonging to or in a mine including buildings, machinery, instruments, stores, equipment of such workshops and the lands on which such workshops stand; (*viii*) all coal in stock or in transit or under production and other stores, stocks and instruments belonging to or in a mine; (*ix*) all power stations belonging to or in a mine or operated for supplying electricity for the purpose of working the mine or a number of mines; (*x*) all lands, buildings and equipment belonging to or in a mine where the washing of coal or manufacture of coke is carried on; (*xi*) all other fixed assets, movable or immovable, and current assets belonging to a mine, whether within its premises or outside.

This definition is changed by the Coal Mines (Nationalisation) Act 1973, s. 2(*h*). Parliament by an enlarged definition of mine in s. 2(*h*) of Coal Mines (Nationalisaton) Act 1973 has indicated the nature of the properties that vest and the question whether a particular asset is taken within the sweep of s. 2(*h*) depends on whether it answers the description given therein. [*Union of India* v *Union Collieries* (1985)1 Cur Civ Cas 615 (SC)].

NOTE: *'Mine'—what is—examples:*

- Stone quarries constitute 'mines'. [*Bandhua Mukti Morcha* v *Union of India* (1984)3 SCC 161].
- A land having large deposits of sand, which is a minor mineral and is being excavated and removed is comprised in or appertained to a mine. [*Shri Tarkeshwar Sio Thakur Jiu* v *Dar Das Dey and Co.* AIR 1979 SC 1669: (1979)2 SCC 106].

*Mine—what is not—examples:*

- 'Mine' does not include coke oven. [*Bharat Coking Coal Ltd.* v *Shri Parmeshwar Kumar Agarwala* (1979)3 SCC 609].
- 'Mines' cannot be interpreted to include minerals not got by mining. [*Pravesh Chandra* v *Narindra Singh* AIR 1962 Pat 14; *Senthil Enterprises* v *State of Tamil Nadu* (1998)109 STC 473 (Mad)].
- 'Mine' excludes an office of mine. [*Sirajuddin Co.* v *Workmen* (1963)1 SCA 225: 1962 Supp (3) SCR 934: (1962)1 Lab LJ 450].

*Distinction between a "quarry" and a "mine".* There is some distinction between a quarry and a mine; the former is an open air excavation of certain classes of minerals and the latter is essentially an underground excavation. [*Bisra Lime Stone* v *Labour Inspector* AIR 1969 Ori 110].

**Miner.** Miners include all artisans, labourers and other persons, working in and about a mine, except the purser, secretary, agent or manager. [Stroud's *Judicial Dictionary*, 5th Ed.].

**Mineral.** The word is not a definite term and is susceptible of limitations or extensions according to intention with which it is used. Standing alone it might by itself embrace the soil, hence include sand and gravel, or, under a strict definition, it might be limited to metallic substances. [*Puget Mill Co.* v *Duecy* 96 P 2d 571, 573, 574].

The term "mineral" as it is used in the public land laws is more restricted than it is when used in some other respects. Its definition has presented many difficulties. It has been held that for purposes of mining laws, a mineral is whenever is recognized as mineral by the standard authorities on the subject. [*United States* v *Toole* DC Mont, 224 F Supp 440, 444].

Black's *Law Dcitionary* (7th Ed.) defines "mineral" thus: Any natural inorganic matter that has a definite chemical composition and specific physical properties that give it value.

The term "minerals", though more frequently applied to substances containing metals, in its proper sense includes all fossil bodies or matters dug out of mines; and Dr. Johnson says, that 'all metals are minerals, but all minerals are not metals'. [*Rosse (Earl)* v *Wainman* (1845)14 M & W 859, *per* Parke, B.].

▸ *Meaning under the Atomic Energy Act 1962, s. 2(c).* 'Minerals' include all substances obtained or obtainable from the soil (including alluvium or rocks) by underground or surface working.

▸ *Meaning under the Mines Act 1952, s. 2(jj).* 'Minerals' means all substances which can be obtained from the earth by mining, digging, drilling, dredging, hydraulicking, quarrying or by any other operation and includes mineral oils (which in turn include natural gas and petroleum).

NOTE: Mineral is a substance that can be got from within the surface of the earth which possesses a value in use, apart from its mere possession of the bulk and weight which makes it occupy so much of the earth's crust. [*Great Western Ry. Co.* v *Carpalla United China Clay Co. Ltd.* (1901)1 Ch 218].

- **Winning a mineral.** It means getting or extracting a mineral from the mine. [*Bihar Mines Ltd.* v *Union of India* AIR 1967 SC 887].

**Minimum wage.** Minimum wage does not mean wage just sufficient for bare sustenance. At present the conception of a minimum wage is a wage which is somewhat intermediate to a wage which is just sufficient for bare sustenance and a fair wage. That concept includes not only the wage sufficient to meet the bare sustenance of an employee and his family, it also includes expenses necessary for his other primary needs such as medical expenses, expenses to meet some education for his children and in some cases transport charges, etc.

NOTE: The concept of minimum wage is likely to undergo a change with the growth of economy and with the change in the standard of living. It is not a static concept. Its concomitants must necessarily increase with the progress of the society. It is likely to differ from place to place and from industry to industry. [*Chandra Bhavan Board* v *State of Mysore* (1969)3 SCC 84, 91: AIR 1970 SC 2042].

**Mining lease.** 'Mining lease', means a lease granted for the purpose of searching for, winning, working, getting, making merchantable, carrying away or disposing of minerals, or for the purposes connected therewith, and includes an exploring or a prospecting licence. The definition is very comprehensive. [*Gujarat Factory Works Pvt. Ltd.* v *S.P. Sood* 10 Law Rep 260: AIR 1967 SC 964].

**Mining operations.** Any operations undertaken for the purpose of winning any mineral. [Mines and Minerals (Regulation and Development) Act 1957, s. 3(*d*)].

NOTE: The essence of 'mining operations' is that it must be an activity for winning a mineral, whether on the surface or beneath the surface of earth. [*Shri Tarkeshwar Sio Thakur* v *Dar Das Dey and Co.* (1979)3 SCC 106].

**Mining right.** It is a right to enter upon and occupy land for the purpose of working it, to obtain from it the minerals or ores. Mining right is obtained under a mining lease for mining purposes, that is, the searching for, winning, working, getting, making merchantable, carrying away or disposing of mines and minerals, or purposes connected therewith. The term 'mining lease' includes a grant or licence for mining purposes.

**Ministerial.** That which is done under the authority of a superior; that which involves obedience to instructions, but demands no special discretion, judgment, or skill. [*State Tax Commission of Utah* v *Katsis* 62 P 2d 120, 123; *Arrow Exp. Forwarding Co.* v *Iowa State Commerce Commission, Iowa* 103 NW 2d 451, 453].

Of or relating to an act that involves obedience to instructions or laws instead of discretion, judgment, or skill. [Black's *Law Dictionary*, 7th Ed.].

**Ministerial act.** One which a person or board performs in a given state of facts in a prescribed manner in obedience to the mandate of legal authority without regard to or the exercise of his or their own judgment upon the propriety of the act being done. [*State Tax Commission of Utah* v *Katsis* 62 P 2d 120, 123; *Gibson* v *Winterset Community School Dist.* 138 NW 2d 112, 115].

"A ministerial act is to be distinguished from other official acts in that the law prescribes the *duty* to be performed with such certainty as to leave nothing to the exercise of discretion or judgment". An example is the execution of a warrant. [Griffith and Street: *Principles of Administrative Law*, 1963].

NOTE: The classification of administrative functions as ministerial or discretionary is relevant for purposes of judicial review of the ultimate decisions as well as from the viewpoint of *modus operandi*. For example, the question of sub-delegation is intimately connected with the function being ministerial or discretionary.

**Ministerial responsibility.** The responsibility of the Ministers to the Legislature.

NOTE: The Constitution of India provides for a Council of Ministers to the President or Governor "to aid and advise" him. [Articles 74 and 163]. And there is a three-fold responsibility for the Ministers. In the first place, the Council is *collectively* responsible to the Parliament or the State Legislature. [*U.N. Rao* v *Indira Gandhi* (1971)2 SCC 63, 67]. Secondly, Ministers are also *individually* responsible for the administration of their respective departments. And this is their responsibility to the President or the Governor, since they hold their office during his pleasure. [*Sharma* v *Ghose* 72 CWN 368]. Thirdly, there is the ultimate responsibility to the political sovereign, that is, the electorate. The Directive Principles of Part IV of the Constitution lay down the norms for the Ministers, who "will have to answer for them before the electorate at the election time".

**Ministry.** The term "Ministry" is wider than "Cabinet", and includes all the holders of political office who go in and out with the

Government. Thus, the Solicitor-General is always a member of the Ministry, but is never in the Cabinet.

The term is also used with reference to a department of the Government to denote the Minister and his associated subordinates.

**Minjoomle.** The word 'minjoomle' merely means 'among all or from among them'; it does not mean 'including'. [*State of Bihar* v *Radha Krishna Singh* AIR 1983 SC 684: (1983)2 SCR 808: (1983)3 SCC 118].

**Minor.** An infant or person who is under the age of legal competence; a person who has not reached full legal age; a child or juvenile.

▸*Meaning under the Child Marriage Restraint Act 1929, s. 2(d).* A person of either sex who is under 18 years of age.

▸*Meaning under the Indian Christian Marriage Act 1872, s. 3.* 'Minor' means a person who has not completed the age of 21 years and who is not a widower or a widow.

▸*Meaning under the Hindu Minority and Guardianship Act 1956, s. 4(a); Hindu Adoptions and Maintenance Act 1956, s. 3(c).* 'Minor' means a person who has not completed the age of 18 years.

▸*Meaning under the Registration Act 1908, s. 2(8).* 'Minor' means a person, who according to the personal law to which he is subject, has not attained majority.

▸*Meaning under the Workmen's Compensation Act 1923, s. 2(ff); Citizenship Act 1955, s. 2(e).* 'Minor' means a person who has not attained the age of 18 years.

▸*Meaning under the Public Provident Fund Act 1968, s. 2(b).* 'Minor' means a person who is not deemed to have attained majority under the Indian Majority Act 1875.

▸*Meaning under the Indian Succession Act 1925, s. 2(e).* 'Minor' means any person subject to the Indian Majority Act 1875, who has not attained his majority within the meaning of that Act, and any other person who has not completed the age of 18 years.

NOTE: A child in the womb cannot be regarded as a minor member of the family. [*Balakrishna Kurup* v *State* AIR 1977 Ker 13].

**Minority.** The state or condition of being under legal age; a group having fewer than a controlling number of votes; a group that is different in some respect such as race or religion belief from the majority; a member of such a group.

"Minority" under Art. 30 of the Constitution of India must necessarily mean those who form a distinct and identifiable group of citizens of India. [*St. Stephen's College* v *University of Delhi* AIR 1992 SC 1630: 1992 AIR SCW 1792: (1992)1 SCC 554: JT 1991(4) SC 548].

**Minutes.** Memoranda or notes of a transaction or proceeding.

Thus, the record of the proceedings at a meeting of directors or shareholders of a company is called the minutes.

Minutes are a record of resolution and matters ancillary thereto and not a complete transcript of every word used in the course of a meeting.

**Minute(s) book.** A book in which a court clerk enters minutes of court proceedings; a record of the subjects discussed and actions taken at a corporate directors' or shareholders' meeting. [Black's *Law Dictionary*, 7th Ed.].

**Miras.** Inheritance or heritability; property or right obtained by inheritance; ancestral tenure or tenancy.

**Mirasi.** Land or office held by hereditary descent.

**Misapplication.** Improper; illegal use of application of funds, property, etc.

It means wrong or incorrect application, not necessarily a wrongful application. [*Official Liquidator* v *K. Joseph Augustus* AIR 1966 Ker 121].

NOTE: The word by itself involves no *mens rea*. It imports no mental element, such as dishonesty or fraud, not even negligence. [*Official Liquidator* v *K. Joseph Augustus* AIR 1966 Ker 121].

**Misappropriation.** The act of misappropriating or turning to a wrong purpose; wrong appropriation; appropriation for a dishonest and/or wrongful use; fraudulent conversion; wrongful conversion of property; wrongful use; malversation.

It may also embrace the taking and use of another's property for sole purpose of capitalizing unfairly on goodwill and reputation of property owner. [*Pocket Books, Inc.* v *Dell Pub. Co.* 267 NYS 2d 269, 272].

**Misbehaviour.** Ill conduct; improper or unlawful behaviour; wrong conduct or improper conduct. [*C. Ravichandran Iyer* v *Justice A.M. Bhattacherjee* 1995 SCC (Cri) 953: JT 1995(6) SC 339].

The expression 'misbehaviour' is of wide import and includes within its ambit criminal misconduct. [*K. Veeraswami* v *Union of India* (1991)3 SCC 655, 744].

NOTE: The word 'misbehaviour' has to be construed with reference to the subject-matter and the context wherein the term occurs having regard to the scope of the Act or the statute under consideration. [*C. Ravichandran Iyer* v *Justice A.M. Bhattacherjee* 1995 SCC (Cri) 953: JT 1995(6) SC 339; *Krishna Swami* v *Union of India* (1992)4 SCC 605].

*Conduct of a Government servant amounting to "misbehaviour".* Misbehaviour by a Government servant would certainly mean a lapse by him from the proper standard of conduct in the discharge of his functions as a Government servant. Every dishonest act of a Government servant amounts to "misbehaviour". [*R.P. Kapur* v *S. Pratap Singh Kairon* AIR 1964 SC 295: (1964)4 SCR 204: (1964)1 Cr LJ 224].

*Conduct of a judge amounting to "misbehaviour".* Every act or conduct or even error of judgment or negligent act by higher judiciary *per se* does not amount to misbehaviour. Wilful abuse of judicial office, wilful misconduct in the office, corruption, lack of integrity, or any other offence involving moral turpitude would be misbehaviour. [*C. Ravichandran Iyer* v *Justice A.M. Bhattacharjee* 1995 SCC (Cri) 953: JT 1995(6) SC 339].

Persistent failure to perform the judicial duties of the judge or wilful abuse of the office *dolus malus* would be misbehaviour. Misbehaviour would extend to conduct of the judge in or beyond the execution of judicial office. [*C. Ravichandran Iyer* v *Justice A.M. Bhattacharjee*, supra].

The special law envisaged by Art. 124(5) of the Constitution of India for dealing with the misbehaviour of a judge is wide enough to include within its ambit every conduct of a judge amounting to misbehaviour including criminal misconduct and prescribes the procedure for investigation and proof thereof. [*K. Veeraswami* v *Union of India* (1991)3 SCC 655].

**Miscarriage.** Abortion, especially before the 28th week of pregnancy; the failure (of a letter, freight, etc.) to reach its destination; abortive attempt; abortive effort; futile effort; ineffectual attempt; misfire; vain attempt, vain effort.

Miscarriage means the expulsion of the product of conception before the 28th week of conception. [*Mahendra Manilal Nanavati* v *Sushila Mahendra Nanavati* AIR 1965 SC 364].

**Mischief.** Evil conduct; foul play; harmful action; frankishness; wrongdoing; conduct which is troublesome; playful malice; harm or injury caused by a person or thing; a person or thing responsible for harm or annoyance.

Black's *Law Dictionary* [7th Ed.] defines "mischief" thus: (1) A condition in which a person suffers a wrong or is under some hardship, esp. one that a statute seeks to remove or for which equity provides a remedy. (2) Injury or damage caused by a specific person or thing. (3) The act causing such injury or damage.

▸ *Meaning under Indian Penal Code 1860, s. 425.* Whoever, with intent to cause, or knowing that he is likely to cause, wrongful loss or damage to the public or to any person, causes destruction of any property, or any such change in any property or in the situation thereof, as destroys or diminishes its value or utility, or affects it injuriously, commits 'mischief'.

**Misconduct.** Bad conduct; improper conduct; disorderly conduct; infamous conduct; unprofessional conduct; delinquency;

dereliction; deviation from rectitude; guilty act; impropriety; malfeasance; misdemeanour; misfeasance; unlawful or improper behaviour; bad management.

Misconduct means denoting any unbusiness like conduct and including negligence or want of proper care which a bailee is to take under s. 152, Contract Act. [*B.N. Railway Co.* v *Moolji Sicka & Co.* AIR 1930 Cal 815: 129 IC 769].

NOTE: It is arduous to capture the concept of misconduct in the strait-jacket of a definition. [*Joseph Vilangadan* v *FACT* (1998)1 Ker LT 18]. The ambit of 'misconduct' has to be construed with reference to the subject-matter and the context wherein the term occurs, regard being had to the scope of the statute and the public purpose it seeks to serve. [*State of Punjab* v *Ram Singh Ex-Constable* (1992)4 SCC 54: (1992)2 SLJ 160].

Misconduct is a generic term and ordinarily means to conduct amiss, to mismanage, wrong or improper conduct, bad behaviour, unlawful behaviour or conduct. [*Joseph Vilangadan* v *FACT* (1998)1 Ker LT 18; *Bhagwan Parshad* v *Inspector General of Police, Punjab* AIR 1970 P&H 81]. It includes malfeasance, misdemeanour, delinquency and offence. [*Bhagwan Parshad* v *Inspector General of Police, Punjab* AIR 1970 P&H 81].

'Misconduct' literally means wrong or improper conduct, i.e., conduct in violation of a definite rule of action. It ordinarily means failure to be done. An omission to do what is required of a person to do may constitute misconduct, even though the person has not acted wilfully or maliciously. [*Shaik Mohammad* v *Governor-General-in-Council* AIR 1954 Nag 337 (DB)].

The word 'misconduct' though not capable of precise definition, its reflection receives its connotation from the context, the delinquency in its performance and its effect on the discipline and the nature of duty. It may involve moral turpitude; it must be improper or wrong behaviour; unlawful behaviour wilful in character; forbidden act; a transgression of established and definite rule of action or code of conduct but not error of judgment, carelessness or negligence in performance of duty; the act complained of bears forbidden quality or character. [*State of Punjab* v *Ram Singh, Ex-Constable* (1992)4 SCC 24: (1992)2 SLJ 160; *Laxmansingh* v *State* (1994)2 Guj LR 1294].

Misconduct is a specific word with specific connotation. It cannot be mere inefficiency or slackness. It is something far more positive, and certainly deliberate disobedience of any order of a superior authority will be one species of misconduct. [*Management of Presidency Talkies* v *N.S. Natarajan* AIR 1969 Mad 121: (1968)2 MLJ 221: (1968)2 Lab LJ 801].

Misconduct implies actuation of some degree of *mens rea* by the doer. Judicial finding of guilt of grave crime is misconduct. [*C. Ravichandran Iyer* v *Justice A.M. Bhattacharjee* 1995 SCC (Cri) 953: JT 1995(6) SC 339]

NOTE: *"Misconduct"—what constitutes—examples:*

- If a servant conducts himself in a way inconsistent with due and faithful discharge of his duty in services, it is misconduct. [*Pierce* v *Foster* (1886)17 QBD 536: 54 LT 664 followed in *Union of India* v *J. Ahmed* (1979)3 SCR 504: AIR 1979 SC 1022: (1979)2 SCC 286: 1979(1) SLR 840].
- A disregard of an essential condition of the contract of service may constitute misconduct. [*Laws* v *London Chronicle (Indicator Newspapers* (1959)1 WLR 698: (1959)2 WLR 285 followed in *Union of India* v *J. Ahmed*, supra].
- A single act of omission or error of judgment would ordinarily not constitute misconduct, though if such error or omission results in serious or atrocious consequences, it may amount to misconduct. [*P.H. Kalyani* v *Air France, Calcutta* (1962)1 SCJ 566: AIR 1963 SC 1756: (1964)2 SCR 104 followed in *Union of India* v *J. Ahmed*, supra].
- When a person on duty (especially in a disciplined service like police force) resorts to drink or in a drunken state acts in an indisciplined manner, it constitutes gravest misconduct warranting dismissal from service. [*State of Punjab* v *Ram Singh, Ex-Constable* (1992)4 SCC 54: (1992)2 SLJ 160].

- Any act which is improper and contrary to the traditions of the profession would constitute misconduct. [*Re S.G. Manore* 1952 Comp Cas 130].
- Judicial finding of guilt of grave crime is misconduct. [*C. Ravichandran Iyer* v *Justice A.M. Bhattacharjee* 1995 SCC (Cri) 953: JT 1995(6) SC 339].

*"Misconduct"—what is not—examples:*

- Taking to drink by itself may not be a misconduct. Out of office hours one may take drink and remain in the house. [*State of Punjab* v *Ram Singh, Ex-Constable* (1992)4 SCC 54: (1992)2 SLJ 160].
- A single act of omission or error of judgment would ordinarily not constitute misconduct. [*Union of India* v *J. Ahmed* (1979)3 SCR 504: AIR 1979 SC 1022: (1979)2 SCC 286: 1979(1) SLR 840].
- Deficiencies in capacity like inefficiency, lack of qualities of leadership and deficiency in the faculty of decision making would not constitute misconduct. [*Union of India* v *J. Ahmed* (1979)3 SCR 504: AIR 1979 SC 1022: (1979)2 SCC 286: 1979(1) SLR 840].
- Act not amounting to a very grave degree of negligence, or serious failure to carry out instruction would not constitute misconduct. [*Gordhan Das* v *Governor-General-in-Council* AIR 1952 Punj 191]. Thus, not entering the railway mark of consignment in railway receipt due to a mere slip of the pen, committed under pressure of work and which anybody might have made was held not to amount to misconduct. [*Gordhan Das* v *Governor-General-in-Council*, supra].

*'Misconduct' and 'negligence'—different notions.* 'Misconduct' and 'negligence' are different notions. Some kinds of negligence may amount to misconduct, while some other kinds of negligence may not amount to misconduct. Misconduct has to be proved and cannot be inferred. [*Ramkrishna Ramnath* v *Union of India* ILR (1960) Bom 507: AIR 1960 Bom 344: 1960 Bom LR 445].

• **Criminal misconduct** p. 208.
• **Grave misconduct** p. 399.
• **Legal misconduct** p. 526.
• **Professional misconduct** p. 695.
• **Wilful misconduct** p. 899.

**Misdelivery.** Delivery of mail, freight, goods, or the like, to person other than authorised or specified recipient.

NOTE: The railway administration cannot be held responsible for misdelivery if it has delivered the animals or goods in good faith to a person who produces the original railway receipt. [Railways Act 1989, s. 80].

**Misdemeanour.** Act committed in violation of law; act of law-breaking; breach of law; offence against the law; guilty act; criminal offence.

All those crimes and offences for which the law has not provided a particular name and which are punishable, according to the degree of the offence, by fine or imprisonment. [*Pickup* v *United Kingdom Dental Board* (1928)2 KB 459, *per* Shearman, J.].

**Misfeasance.** Unlawful use of power; wrongful performance of a normally legal act; injurious exercise of lawful authority; official misconduct; deviation from rectitude; breach of law.

The word 'misfeasance' would apply to a case where a lawful act is done in an improper manner. [*Khairul Bashar* v *Thannulal* AIR 1957 All 553].

The word 'misfeasance' in its application to company means misfeasance in the nature of a breach of trust, that is to say, it refers to something which an officer of such company has done wrongly by misapplying or retaining in his own hands any moneys of the company, or by which the company's property has been wasted, or by which the company's credit improperly pledged. It must be some act resulting in some actual loss to the company. [*Re Canadian Land Reclaiming & Colonizing Co., Coventry & Dixon's* case (1880)14 Ch D 660 (CA)]. Thus, where the directors and manager of a company lent money to a concern of which they are either the sole proprietors or partners, they are guilty of misfeasance. The plea that they did something *bona fide* and in good faith and in the belief that these loans will ultimately turn out to be for the good of the company cannot avail against the charge of misfeasance and misapplication of company's money. [*Indo Burma Industries Ltd., In the matter of* AIR 1956 Cal 648].

NOTE: *"Misfeasance", "nonfeasance" and "malfeasance"—distinction.* "Misfeasance" is the improper doing of an act which a person may lawfully do. "Nonfeasance" means the omission of an act which a person ought to do. "Malfeasance" is the doing of an act which a person ought not to do at all.

**Misjoinder.** The improper joining together of parties to a suit, as plaintiffs or defendants or of different causes of action.

NOTE: Misjoinder is not a ground for dismissal. The improper party is merely dropped on motion of any party or on court's own motion.

Misjoinder in a criminal prosecution is the charging in separate counts of separate and distinct offences arising out of wholly different transactions having no connection or relation with each other. [*Optner* v *U.S.* CCA Mich, 13 F 2d 11, 13].

**Misrepresentation.** False representation; false statement; incorrect assertion; intentional misstatement; misstatement of fact; untrue statement; deceptive statement; any manifestation by words or other conduct by one person to another that, under the circumstances, amounts to an assertion not in accordance with the facts.

▸ *Meaning under Indian Contract Act 1872, s. 18.* 'Misrepresentation' means and includes—(1) the positive assertion, in a manner not warranted by the information of the person making it, of that which is not true, though he believes it to be true; (2) any breach of duty which, without an intent to deceive, gains an advantage to the person committing it, or any one claiming under him, by misleading another to his prejudice or to the prejudice of any one claiming under him; (3) causing, however innocently, a party to an agreement to make a mistake as to the substance of the thing which is the subject of the agreement.

NOTE: A misrepresentation may be either fraudulent or innocent. A misrepre-sentation is fraudulent when it is an untrue statement of fact which is not believed by the person making it to be true. An innocent misrepresentation is an untrue statement of fact made in the honest belief that it is true. [Sutton & Shannon on *Contracts*, 6th Ed., p. 148].

*Misrepresentation and fraud—distinction.* The principal distinction between fraud and misrepresentation is that in the one case the person making the suggestion does not believe it to be true and in the other he believes it to be true, though in both cases it is a misstatement of fact which misleads the other party. [*Niaz* v *Parsottam* 29 All LJ 153].

**Mistake.** Be in the wrong; be erroneous; commit an error; fall into error; some unintentional act, omission, or error arising from ignorance, surprise, imposition, or misplaced confidence.

A mistake exists when a person, under some erroneous conviction of law or fact, does, or omits to do, some act which, but for the erroneous conviction, he would not have done or omitted. It may arise either from unconsciousness, ignorance, forgetfulness, imposition or misplaced confidence. [*Salazar* v *Steelman* 71 P 2d 79, 82].

**Mistake apparent on the record.** A "mistake apparent on the record" must be an obvious and patent mistake and not something which can be established by a long drawn process of reasoning on points on which there may conceivably be two opinions. A decision on a debatable point of law is not a mistake apparent from the record. [*T.S. Balram, Income Tax Officer, Company Circle IV, Bombay* v *M/s. Volkart Brothers, Bombay* AIR 1971 SC 2204: (1971)82 ITR 50: (1971)2 SCC 526: (1972)1 SCR 30].

**Mistake of fact.** It is a mistake caused not by the neglect of a legal duty on the part of the person making it, but by (*i*) an unconscious ignorance or forgetfulness of a fact, past or present, material to the contract; or (*ii*) belief in the present existence of a thing material to the contract which does not exist, or in the past existence of such a thing which has not existed. It is also termed as error of fact.

NOTE: In civil law, mistake of fact or genuine ignorance of the state of affairs will not afford immunity. He who interferes intentionally with the person, property, reputation or other rights of another does so at his peril. Here neither good faith nor reasonable grounds for interference will be heard. There are some exceptions to this but they confirm the general rule.

In criminal law, absolute criminal responsibility for a mistake of fact is quite exceptional. Thus, where a wife deserted by her husband believed in good faith that her husband was dead and married within seven years of desertion, it was held that she was not guilty of bigamy because of mistake of fact. [*R.* v *Tolson* (1889)23 QBD 166].

Under s. 20 of the Indian Contract Act 1872, where both the parties to an agreement are under a mistake as to a matter of fact essential to the agreement, the agreement is void.

**Mistake of law.** A mistake about the legal effect of a known fact or situation. [Black's *Law Dictionary*, 7th Ed.]. It is also termed error of law.

A mistake of law happens when a party, having full knowledge of the facts comes to an erroneous conclusion as to their legal effect. It is a mistaken opinion or inference, arising from an imperfect or incorrect exercise of the judgment, upon facts. [*Page* v *Provines* 66 P 2d 7, 10].

**Mitakshara.** Mitakshara is a running commentary on the Code of Yajnavalkya and a real digest of *Smriti law*. It was written in the latter part of the eleventh century by Vijnaneshwara. In the Mitakshara, which is more of a digest than a mere commentary on a particular *Smriti*, we find the quintessence of the *Smriti law* and its precepts and injunctions. It is of supreme authority throughout India except in Bengal where the Dayabhaga of Jimutavahana is given paramount importance. According to the Mitakshara law, each son acquires at his birth an equal interest with his father, and on the death of the father the son takes the property, not as his heir, but by survivorship. This Mitakshara is sub-divided into four minor schools, *viz.*, the Benares School, the Mithila School, the Maharashtra School and the Dravida School.

**Mitigate.** Abate in intensity; alleviate; ameliorate; assuage; decrease; diminish; give relief; lessen in force; make less severe; moderate in severity; mollify; palliate; reduce; regulate; relieve.

**Mixed economy.** This term is used of the economy of a country in which State and private ownership and production are both present.

**Modification.** A change; alteration; correction; exception; limitation; variation; adaptation; an alteration or amendment which introduces new elements into the details, or cancels some of them, but leaves the general purpose and effect of the subject-matter intact.

'Modification' means variation and includes extension also, although in ordinary parlance the word signifies restriction only. [*Raj Kishen Jain* v *Tulsi Dass* AIR 1959 Punj 291].

NOTE: There may be modification involving an increase. [*Western India Theatres Ltd.* v *Municipal Corporation of Poona* AIR 1959 SC 586: (1959)2 SCA 145: 1959 Supp (2) SCR 71: 1959 SCJ 390].

▸ *Meaning under the Constitution of India, Art. 370(1).* The word 'modification' in the Article includes an amendment. There is no reason to limit the word only to such modification as does not make any radical transformation. [*Puranlal Lakhanpal* v *President of India* AIR 1961 SC 1510].

In its application to statute, though 'modification' implies an alteration so that the effect of alteration is to narrow or enlarge the provision [*G. Venkata Naidu* v *Bellary Central Cooperative Stores* AIR 1967 Mys 203], it has been held that the word does not involve any material or substantial alteration. It signifies changes of such character as are necessary to make the statute suitable to the local conditions of the province. The executive government is not entitled to change the whole nature or policy underlying any particular Act or to take different portions from different statutes and prepare an amalgamation of several laws. [*In re Art. 143, Constitution of India and Delhi Laws Act 1912 etc.* AIR 1951 SC 332: 1951 SCJ 527: 1951 SCR 747].

**Mohturn.** Land granted for the maintenance of great or revered person.

**Moiety.** Half of anything. It may also mean a part or share as distinguished from half part. [*Morrow* v *M'Conville* 11 LR Ir 252].

**Mokarari.** Lease at a fixed rate of rent. The word does not imply perpetuity.

**Molasses.** The heavy, dark-coloured residual syrup drained away in the final stage of the manufacture of sugar by vacuum pans in sugar factories either from sugarcane or by refining gur, when such syrup has fermentable sugars (expressed as reducing sugars), but does not include the final residual syrup left in the manufacture of sugar by the open-pan process. [Indian Power Alcohol Act 1948, s. 3(*a*)].

**Molest.** Sexually abuse; sexually assault; defile; ravish; assault; abuse; disturb; harass; interfere with; interrupt; irk; irritate; pester; torment; ruffle.

**Molestation.** Abuse; ill treatment; interference; intrusion; interruption; irritation; maltreatment; meddling; persecution; vexation.

The persecution or harassment of someone, as in the molestation of a witness; the act of making unwanted and indecent advances to or on someone, esp. for sexual gratification. [Black's *Law Dictionary*, 7th Ed.].

**Money.** Money is that which passes freely from hand to hand throughout the community, in final discharge of debts and full payment of commodities; being accepted equally without reference to the character or credit of the person who offers it, and without the intention of the person who receives it to consume it or apply it to any other use than in turn to tender it to other in discharge of debts or payments for commodities. [*Moss* v *Hancock* 68 LJQB 660: (1899)2 QB 111].

In usual and ordinary acceptation 'money' means coins and paper currency used as circulating medium of exchange, and does not embrace notes, bonds, evidences of debt, or other personal or real estate. [*Lane* v *Railey* 133 SW 2d 74, 79, 81].

Popularly, money may mean wealth. In economics, the essential features of money are: (*a*) that it should be acceptable as a medium of exchange (which implies liquidity); (*b*) that it should serve as a measure of value; and (*c*) that it should serve as a store of value. Anything that performs these functions is money.

In law, "money" may be variously construed, according to the context and surrounding circumstances, particularly in wills: *e.g.*, as cash in hand or in the bank or as invested. [Osborn Grandage's *Concise Commercial Dictionary*].

In the income tax statute, the word money should not be construed on lines of construction of will in which it is construed in its widest sense. In the income tax statute, the scope of the word is limited, because the taxing statute is a legal document using legal words, and is not the naive and artless product of a legally inexperienced and ignorant testator. [*CIT* v *National Grindlays Bank* AIR 1969 Cal 71: 72 CWN 891: (1969)72 ITR 121].


- **Dear money** p. 229.
- **Earnest money** p. 290.
- **Hush-money** p. 424.
- **Mortgage money** p. 592.
- **Pin money** p. 663.
- **Velocity of circulation of money** p. 877.


**Money bill.** A Bill shall be deemed to be Money Bill if it contains only provisions dealing with all or any of the following matters, namely—(*a*) the imposition, abolition, remission, alteration or regulation of any tax; (*b*) the regulation of the borrowing of money or the giving of any guarantee by the State, or the amendment of the law with regard to any financial obligations undertaken or to be undertaken by the State; (*c*) the custody of the Consolidated Fund or the Contingency

Fund of the State, the payment of moneys into or the withdrawal of moneys from any such Fund; (*d*) appropriation of moneys out of the Consolidated Fund of the State; (*e*) the declaring of any expenditure to be expenditure charged on the Consolidated Fund of the State or the increasing of the amount of any such expenditure; (*f*) the receipt of money on account of the Consolidated Fund of the State or the public account of the State or the custody or issue of such money; or (*g*) any matter incidental to any of the matters specified in sub-clauses (*a*) to (*f*). [Constitution of India, Arts. 110, 199].

**Moneylender.** A person whose business is moneylending; one who is ready and willing to lend to all and sundry, provided that they are, from his point of view, eligible. [*Litchfield* v *Dreyfus* (1960)1 KB 584: 75 LJKB 447].

> NOTE: For a person to be a moneylender, he must in the regular course of business advance a loan. The expression 'moneylender' has been so construed as to exclude isolated transaction or transactions of moneylending. [*Gajanan* v *Seth Brindaban* AIR 1970 SC 2007]. A few disconnected and isolated transactions would not make a person engaged regularly in money lending business. [*Ka Icilda Wallang* v *U. Lokendra Suiam* AIR 1987 SC 2047: JT 1987(1) SC 721].

**Monopoly.** Control or advantage obtained by one supplier or producer over the commercial market within a given region; the market condition existing when only one economic entity produces a particular product or provides a particular service. [Black's *Law Dictionary*, 7th Ed.].

A form of market structure in which one or only a few firms dominate the total sales of a product or service.

**Month.** A month reckoned according to the British calendar. [General Clauses Act 1897, s. 3(35); *Bijoy Bhusan* v *Saranan* (1979)1 CHN 154].

It means British calendar month and not days. [*Tamal Lahiri* v *P.N. Tagore* AIR 1978 SC 1811: (1979)1 SCC 75].

▸ *Meaning under the Mines Act 1952, s. 2(jjj) (since omitted w.e.f. 31.5.1984).* 'Month' means the period from the first day of any month reckoned according to the British calendar to the last day of the same month.

▸ *Meaning under the Police Act 1861, s. 1.* 'Month' shall mean a calendar month.

The word 'month' has been defined by Black's *Law Dictionary* [7th Ed.] thus: (1) One of the twelve periods of time in which the calendar is divided. (2) Any time period approximating 30 days. (3) At common law, a period of 28 days; the period of one revolution of the moon. (4) One-twelfth of a tropical year; the time it takes the sun to pass through one sign of the Zodiac, usu. approximately 30 days.

• **Calendar month** p. 118.

**Monument.** Anything that preserves the memory of a person or an event, a building, pillar, tomb, tablet, statue, etc.; any structure, natural or artificial, considered as an object of beauty or of interest as a relic of the past; a historic document or record (sometimes confused with muniment); a stone, post, river, etc, marking a boundary. [*Ram Sarup* v *State of Haryana* AIR 1993 P&H 204: 1993 Punj LJ 299].

• **Ancient monument** p. 61.

• **Protected monument** p. 704.

**Moral turpitude.** Conduct that is contrary to justice, honesty, or morality. [Black's *Law Dictionary*, 8th Ed.].

"Moral turpitude" is an expression which is used in legal as also societal parlance to describe conduct which is inherently base, vile, depraved or having any connection showing depravity. [*Pawan Kumar* v *State of Haryana* AIR 1996 SC 3300: JT 1996(5) SC 155: (1996)2 SCJ 441: 1996(4) SLR 40: (1996)4 SCC 17: 1996 SCC (Cri) 583].

The term "moral turpitude" is rather a vague one and it may have different meanings in different contexts. The term has generally been taken to mean to be a conduct contrary to justice, honesty, modesty or good morals and contrary to what a man owes to fellowman or to society in general. [*Durga Singh* v *State of Punjab* AIR 1957 Punj 97].

NOTE: The basic indicia of moral turpitude are: (*i*) something contrary to justice, honesty or good morals, involving baseness of mind or attitude; (*ii*) that which shocks the moral conscience of society in general; (*iii*) something which will attach a depravity of character to the person guilty thereof. Crime of murder comes within the ambit of moral turpitude. [*Sarju Prasad Singh* v *State of Bihar* 1987 Pat LJR 285 (Pat)].

In its application to professionals, wherever a conduct proved against is contrary to honesty, or opposed to good morals, or is unethical, it may be held that it involves moral turpitude. [*In the matter of "P" an Advocate* AIR 1963 SC 1313: (1963)2 Cr LJ 341: (1964)1 SCR 697].

**Moratorium.** An authorised postponement, usually a lengthy one, in the deadline for paying a debt or performing an obligation; the period of this delay; the suspension of a specific activity. [Black's *Law Dictionary*, 7th Ed.].

A period of permissive or obligatory delay; specially, a period during which an obligor has a legal right to delay meeting an obligation. [*State ex rel. Jensen Livestock Co.* v *Hyslop* 107 P 2d 1088, 1092].

**More or less.** About so much. [*Jancred, Arrol & Co.* v *Steel Co. of Scotland Ltd.* (1890)15 AC 125].

The words are intended to cover slight or unimportant inaccuracies in quantity. [*Carter* v *Finch* 57 SW 2d 408].

**Mortality tables.** Tables of mortality are an account maintained for a large number of years of the ages at which men and women die. By this means the probable number of years any person of a given age and of ordinary health will live may be ascertained with reasonable certainty. The object of mortality tables is to ascertain the rates of mortality prevailing within the community in order that forecasts may be made for the future. The expectation of Life Tables does not show the years a person will live, but the number of years that the average person may be expected to live.

**Mortgage.** Black's *Law Dictionary* [7th Ed.] defines "mortgage" thus: (1) A conveyance of title to property that is given as security for the payment of a debt or the performance of a duty and that will become void upon payment or performance according to the stipulated terms. (2) A lien against property that is granted to secure an obligation (such as a debt) and that is extinguished upon payment or performance according to stipulated terms. (3) An instrument (such as a deed or contract) specifying the terms of such a transaction. (4) Loosely, the loan on which such a transaction is based. (5) The mortgagee's rights conferred by such a transaction. (6) Loosely, any real-property security transaction, including a deed of trust.

▸ *Meaning under the Transfer of Property Act 1882, s. 58(a).* A mortgage is the transfer of an interest in specific immovable property for the purpose of securing the payment of money advanced or to be advanced by way of loan, an existing or future debt, or the performance of an engagement which may give rise to a pecuniary liability.

NOTE: There are six different forms of mortgage in India—(1) Simple mortgage. (2) Mortgage by conditional sale. (3) Usufructuary mortgage. (4) English mortgage. (5) Mortgage by deposit of title deeds. (6) Anomalous mortgage. [Transfer of Property Act 1882, s. 58].

*"Mortgage" and "charge"—distinction.* The difference between a mortgage and a charge is this: Whereas a charge only gives a right to payment out of a particular fund or particular property without transferring that fund or property, a mortgage is in essence a transfer of an interest in specific immovable property. [*Shiva Prasad* v *Beni Madhab* AIR 1922 Pat 529]. A mortgage is good against subsequent transferees but a charge is only good against subsequent transferees with notice.


- **Anomalous mortgage** p. 64.
- **English mortgage** p. 309.
- **Simple mortgage** p. 798.
- **Usufructuary mortgage** p. 871.

**Mortgage by conditional sale.** Where the mortgagor ostensibly sells the mortgaged property—on condition that on default of payment of the mortgage money on a certain date the sale shall become absolute, or on condition that on such payment being made, the sale shall become void, or on condition that on such payment being made, the buyer shall transfer the property to the seller, the transaction is called mortgage by conditional sale, and the mortgagee a mortgagee by conditional sale. [Transfer of Property Act 1882, s. 58(*c*)].

**Mortgage by deposit of title deeds.** Where a person in any of the following towns, namely, the towns of Calcutta, Madras and Bombay and in any other town which the State Government concerned may, by notification in the Official Gazette specify in this behalf, delivers to a creditor or his agent documents of title to immovable property with intent to create a security thereon, the transaction is called a mortgage by deposit of title deeds. [Transfer of Property Act 1882, s. 58(*f*)].

NOTE: The provisions of sub-sec. (*f*) of s. 58 apply to the towns of Kanpur, Allahabad, Lucknow, Coimbatore, Madurai, Rajahmundri, Eluru, Bellari, Adoni, Mangalore, Bangalore, Mysore, Devangere, Delhi and New Delhi.

**Mortgage deed.** The instrument creating a mortgage.

- *Meaning under the Indian Stamp Act 1899, s. 2(17)*. 'Mortgage deed' includes every instrument whereby, for the purpose of securing money advanced, or to be advanced, by way of loan, or an existing or future debt, or the performance of an engagement, one person transfers, or creates to, or in favour of another, a right over or in respect of specified property.
- *Meaning under the Transfer of Property Act 1882, s. 58*. The instrument by which a mortgage is effected is called a mortgage-deed.

NOTE: A mortgage deed typically must contain (1) the name of the mortgagor, (2) words of grant or conveyance, (3) the name of the mortgagee, (4) a property description sufficient to identify the mortgaged premises, (5) the mortgagor's signature, and (6) an acknowledgment. To be effective and binding, a mortgage deed must also be delivered.

**Mortgage money.** The principal money and the interest of which payment is secured for the time being by the mortgage are called the mortgage-money. [Transfer of Property Act 1882, s. 58].

NOTE: 'Mortgage money' includes interest awarded by way of damages. [Code of Civil Procedure 1908, Or. 34, r. 11].

**Mortgagee.** The transferee under a mortgage.

**Mortgagor.** The person who makes the mortgage. It includes a subsequent transferee of the mortgaged property. [Transfer of Property Act 1882, s. 59A].

**Motion.** An application made to a court or judge for the purpose of obtaining a rule or order directing some act to be done in favour of the applicant. [*State* v *James* Mo, 347 SW 2d 211, 216].

An application made to court or a judge by a party to an action or his counsel to obtain some rule or order of court necessary to the process of the action. [*Umavathi* v *N.A. Nanda Shethy* (1975)1 Kant LJ 74: ILR (1974) Kant 1523].

A written or oral application requesting a court to make a specified ruling or order. [Black's *Law Dictionary*, 7th Ed.].

In parliamentary law, the formal mode in which a member submits a proposed measure or resolve for the consideration and action of the meeting [Black's *Law Dictionary*, 5th Ed.]; a proposal made under formal parliamentary procedure. [Black's *Law Dictionary*, 7th Ed.].

Motion is the generic name given to any proposal submitted to Parliament for normal decision. It may be of two kinds —substantive; non-substantive. A substantive motion is a self-contained proposal submitted for the approval of the House and drafted in a way capable of expressing a decision of the House. They are motions of no-confidence in the Council of Ministers, motion on matters of public interest and the like. Reports of the Public

Service Commission may come under the second type of motions. [Lok Sabha and Rajya Sabha Rules].

**Motive.** "Motive" is that which incites or stimulates a person to do an act [*People* v *Weiss* 300 NYS 249, 255]. It is the moving power which impels to action for a definite result. [*Chandra Prakash Shahi* v *State of U.P.* AIR 2000 SC 1706: (2000)5 SCC 152: JT 2000(5) SC 181].

Motive is mainspring of human action. It is cause or reason [*Saradambal Ammal* v *Natesa Mudaliar* (1972)1 MLJ 244]. It is something which prompts a man to form an intention. [*Basdev* v *State of Pepsu* AIR 1956 SC 488: 1956 Cr LJ 919].

NOTE: The words 'motive', 'object', 'purpose' are in application to practical matters difficult strictly to define or distinguish. Sometimes mere animus, such as spite or ill-will, malevolence or a wanton desire to harm without any view to personal benefit is meant. But motive is often used as meaning purpose, something objective and external, as contrasted with a mere mental state. [*Crofter Hand Woven Harris Jweed Co. Ltd.* v *Veitch* (1942) AC 435, 469].

**Motor conveyance.** Any vehicle, vessel or aircraft for the conveyance of human beings, animals or goods, by land, water or air in which petroleum is used to generate the motive power. [Petroleum Act 1934, s. 2(*g*)].

**Motor cycle.** A two wheeled motor vehicle, inclusive of any detachable side-car having an extra wheel, attached to the motor vehicle. [Motor Vehicles Act 1988, s. 2(27)].

**Motor vehicle.** Any mechanically propelled vehicle adapted for use upon roads whether the power of propulsion is transmitted thereto from an external or internal source and includes a chassis to which a body has not been attached and a trailer; but does not include a vehicle running upon fixed rails or a vehicle of a special type adapted for use only in a factory or in any other enclosed premises or a vehicle having less than four wheels fitted with engine capacity of not exceeding twenty-five cubic centimetres. [Motor Vehicles Act 1988, s. 2(28)].

**Movable property.** Property of every description, except immovable property. [General Clauses Act 1897, s. 3(36)].

NOTE: 'Movable property' includes growing crops. [Code of Civil Procedure 1908, s. 2(13)].

'Movable property' includes standing timber, growing crops and grass, fruit upon and juice in trees, and property of every other description, except immovable property. [Registration Act 1908, s. 2(9)].

'Movable property' includes corporeal property of every description, except land and things attached to the earth or permanently fastened to anything which is attached to the earth. [Indian Penal Code 1860, s. 22].

**Muaafi.** Remitted, exempted from payment of rent or tax.

**Muafidar.** A holder of rent-free land, a grantee.

**Muchalaka.** A written agreement; a bond; a deed; a promise not to do something.

**Muffasal.** The country, or the stations in the country, as opposed to the sadar, or principal station or town.

**Mujra.** An authorised deduction; an allowance.

**Mukarari.** A tenancy at fixed rent. The word by itself does not imply any permanent interest.

**Mukarari istemrari.** The words do not *per se* convey an estate of inheritance. [*Kamakhya Narayan* v *Ram Raksha* AIR 1928 PC 146: 15 IA 212].

**Mukhtar.** Legal practitioner having a limited right to practise in civil and criminal courts. [Legal Practitioners Act 1879, s. 9].

**Mukhtarnama.** A written authority given to an agent; a power of attorney; an authority given to a mukhtar to conduct a case in a court.

**Mulct.** A fine of money or a penalty.

**Mulla.** The word 'mulla' is defined as a learned man. This obviously is the etymological meaning, being the same as moulvi or maula, but it has also got the secondary meaning of a village school master or a person in charge of a mosque. It is not equivalent to 'trustee'. [*Bala Tripura Sundaramma* v *Secretary of State* 106 IC 891].

**Multilateral.** Involving more than two parties.

**Multilateral trade.** Free trade between nations.

> NOTE: The greater the freedom of international trade, the greater will be the tendency for the total amount of such trade to increase.

**Multinational corporation.** A company with operations in two or more countries, generally allowing it to transfer funds and products according to price and demand conditions, subject to risks such as changes in exchange rates or political instability. [Black's *Law Dictionary*, 7th Ed.].

**Multiple shops.** This means a chain of retail shops under common management and in the same trade. The geographical spread of such shops may mean that the chain establishes a national reputation for quality and price, which the consumer will expect to find in all branches.

**Multiplicity of actions/suits.** A phrase descriptive of the situation where several different suits or actions are brought upon the same issue against the same defendant. [*Prospect Park & C.I.R. Co.* v *Morey* 140 NYS 380, 385].

The existence of two or more law-suits litigating the same issue against the same defendant. [Black's *Law Dictionary*, 7th Ed.].

**Multiplier.** In economics, this is the ratio between a given increase in new investment and the ultimate increase in national income resulting from it.

**Municipal.** In narrower, more common sense, it means pertaining to a local governmental unit, commonly, a city or town or other governmental unit. In its broader sense, it means pertaining to the public or governmental affairs of a state or nation or of a people. [*Chadwick* v *City of Crawfordsville* 216 Ind 399: 24 NE 2d 937, 941, 942]. Relating to a state or nation, particularly when considered as an entity independent of other states or nations. [*Hammel* v *Little* 66 App DC 356: 87 F 2d 907, 910].

**Municipal Act.** An Act of the legislature constituting a Municipality and conferring powers on it, *e.g.*, the Calcutta Municipal Corporation Act 1980.

**Municipal action.** Exercise of governmental power by a municipal board, agency, or other body, or by a municipal officer. [*Orme* v *Atlas Gas & Oil Co.* 217 Minn 27: 13 NW 2d 757, 761].

**Municipal affairs.** A term referring to the internal business affairs of a municipality. [*Griffin* v *City of Los Angeles* 134 Cal App 763: 26 P 2d 655]. The term is frequently used in constitutional and statutory provisions concerning the power to legislate as to the concerns of municipalities.

**Municipal law.** That which pertains solely to the citizens and inhabitants of a state, and is thus distinguished from political law, commercial law, and international law. [*City of Louisville* v *Babb* CCA Ind, 75 F 2d 162, 165]. In its more common and narrower connotation however it means those laws which pertain to towns, cities and villages and their local government. [*People ex rel. Ray* v *Martin* 294 NY 61: 60 NE 2d 541, 547, 548].

**Municipal market.** A market belonging to or maintained by the Corporation. [Kolkata Municipal Corporation Act 1980, s. 2(55)].

**Municipality.** A body politic created by the incorporation of the people of a prescribed locality invested with subordinate powers of legislation to assist in the civil government of the state and to regulate and administer local and internal affairs of the community. [*State ex rel. McIntire* v *City Council of City of Libby* 82 P 2d 587, 588].

The municipality means, 'an institution of self-government constituted under Art. 243-Q of the Constitution of India. [*Cantonment Board, Secunderabad* v *G. Venketram Reddy* AIR 1995 SC 1210:

(1995)4 SCC 561]. The definition indicates that a corporation or a municipal council or nagar panchayat is constituted on strength of population and the area or place where it is constituted, namely rural or urban. But all the three are deemed to be municipality. [*Cantonment Board, Secunderabad* v *G. Venketram Reddy* AIR 1995 SC 1210: (1995)4 SCC 561].

**Muniment.** A document evidencing the rights and privileges of a person.

**Muniments of title.** Documentary evidences of title. The instruments of writing and written evidences which the owner of lands, possessions, or inheritances has, by which he is enabled to defend the title of his estate.

**Munitions of war.** 'Munitions of war' includes the whole or any part of any ship, submarine, aircraft, tank or similar engine, arms and ammunition, torpedo or mine intended or adopted for use in war, and any other article, material or device, whether actual or proposed, intended for such use. [Indian Official Secrets Act 1923, s. 2(5)].

**Murder.** The unlawful killing of a human being by another with malice aforethought, either express or implied. [*State* v *Hutter* 18 NW 2d 203, 206].

When the word 'murder' is found in a statute it has the meaning which has always been attached to it throughout the ages, namely, an unlawful killing with malice aforethought. [*R.* v *Page* (1953)2 All ER 1355, 1357, *per* Lord Goddard, C.J.].

"Murder is the taking of human life by a person who either (*a*) has a malicious and wilful intent to kill or do grievous bodily harm, or (*b*) is wickedly reckless as to the consequences of his act upon his victim. For murder there must be an evil intent, that is a criminal intent, although it is not necessary that there should be an intent to kill". [*H.M. Advocate* v *Kidd* (1960) SLT 82, 86, *per* Lord Strachan].

NOTE: Culpable homicide is murder if the act by which the death is caused is done with the intention of causing death, or *Secondly*—If it is done with the intention of causing such bodily injury as the offender knows to be likely to cause the death of the person to whom the harm is caused, or *Thirdly*—If it is done with the intention of causing bodily injury to any person and the bodily injury intended to be inflicted is sufficient in the ordinary course of nature to cause death, or *Fourthly*—If the person committing the act knows that it is so imminently dangerous that it must, in all probability, cause death, or such bodily injury as is likely to cause death, and commits such act without any excuse for incurring the risk of causing death or such injury as aforesaid. [Indian Penal Code 1860, s. 300].

In the scheme of the Penal Code, 'culpable homicide' is genus and 'murder' its specie. All 'murder' is 'culpable homicide' but not *vice versa*. Speaking generally, 'culpable homicide' sans, 'special characteristics of murder', is 'culpable homicide not amounting to murder'. [*State of A.P.* v *Rayavarapu Punnayya* (1976)4 SCC 382: AIR 1977 SC 45: 1977 Cr LJ 1].

**Musammat.** Respectable woman; the title generally prefixed to women and abbreviated as "Mst".

**Mushaa.** An undivided share or part of any property.

**Musical work.** Any combination of melody and harmony or either of them, printed, reduced to writing or otherwise graphically produced or reproduced. [Copyright Act 1957, s. 2(*p*)].

▸*Meaning under the Copyright Act 1957, s. 2(p) (substituted w.e.f. 10.5.1995).* A work consisting of music and includes any graphical notation of such work but does not include any words or any action intended to be sung, spoken or performed with the music.

**Muta.** A temporary marriage under the Mahomedan law.

**Mutation.** The process or an act of change, variation, or alteration; a genetic change which, when transmitted to offspring, gives rise to heritable variations.

**Mutatis mutandis.** With the necessary changes. '*Mutatis mutandis*' refers to applicability with suitable modifications. [*S.M. Higher Secondary School* v *The Joint Director* (1995)1 LW 586 (Mad)].

NOTE: The phrase is often used in legislation in applying or extending legislative provisions to same or similar circumstances or to same or similar subjects. It is nothing but a rule of adaptation. [*Debi Mata* v *State of West Bengal* AIR 1972 Cal 497: 76 CWN 308].

Extension of an earlier Act *mutatis mutandis* to a later Act brings in the idea of adaptation; but so far only as it is necessary for the purpose, making a change without altering the essential nature of the thing changed, subject of course to express provisions made in the later Act. [*Ashok Service Centre* v *State of Orissa* (1983)2 SCC 82, 93; *Mariyappa* v *State of Karnataka* AIR 1998 SC 1334].

**Mutawalli.** The manager of wakf property is called a *mutawalli*.

*Mutawalli* means any person appointed either verbally or under any deed or instrument by which a wakf has been created or by a competent authority to be the *mutawalli* of a wakf and includes any person who is a *mutawalli* of a wakf by virtue of any custom or who is a *naib-mutawalli, khadim, mujawar, sajjadanashin, amin* or other person appointed by a *mutawalli* to perform the duties of a *mutawalli* and, save as otherwise provided by the Wakf Act, any person, committee or corporation for the time being managing or administering any wakf or wakf property. [Wakf Act 1995, s. 3(*i*)].

NOTE: Under the Mahomedan law, as soon as a wakf is created, all rights of property pass out of the wakif (dedicator) and vest in the Almighty. The *mutawalli* has no right in the property belonging to the wakf; the property is not vested in him, and he is not a trustee in the technical sense. He is merely a superintendent or manager. [*Vidya Varuthi* v *Balusami* AIR 1922 PC 123].

The founder of a wakf may appoint himself, or his children and descendants, or any other person, even a female, or a non-Mahomedan, to be *mutawalli* of wakf property. A *mutawalli* has no power, without the permission of the court, to mortgage, sell or exchange wakf property unless he is expressly empowered by the deed of wakf to do so.

**Mutilate.** Amputate; batter; bruise; butcher; cripple; cut; damage; deface; deform; deprive of an important part; disfigure; dismember; knock out of shape; maim; mangle; render a document imperfect.

**Mutt.** See MATH p. 569.

**Mutual.** Coadjutant; collaborative; combined; confederated; general; in common; interdependent; bilateral; commutative; corresponding; done reciprocally; interrelated; parallel; reciprocating; reciprocative; reciprocal; two-sided; two-way.

**Mutual account.** An account showing mutual transactions between parties, as by showing debits and credits on both sides of the account. [Black's *Law Dictionary*, 7th Ed.].

NOTE: The distinguishing characteristics of mutual account are: (1) there should be two sets of independent transactions between the parties in one of which one of the parties should hold the position of a debtor and the other that of a creditor, and in the other the reverse position; (2) the dealings should disclose independent obligations on both sides and not merely obligations on one side, the acts done by the other being merely discharge of such obligations; and (3) each party must be able to say to the other 'I have account against you'. [*Union of India* v *Raghaban* AIR 1959 Ker 240].

# Nn

**Nabira.** The Persian word 'Nabira' originally signified grandson or a son's son; but, in common parlance it has come to mean any issue of a son i.e. a grandchild and is not restricted to a grandson only. [*Syed Shah Manzoor Hasan* v *Shamshul Nahar* AIR 1949 Pat 526].

**Nadi.** The word 'Nadi' is used to designate a natural river or stream. [*Harihar Prashad Singh* v *Janak Dulari Kuer* 21 Pat LT 873].

**Naib.** A deputy; a representative; a deputy collector of rent.

**Nakal.** A copy; a duplicate; artificial; an imitation; a transcript of any document.

**Naked.** Bare; devoid of consideration; elementary; fundamental; laid bare; simple; stark; straight; unadulterated; unembellished; unmasked; unornamented; unvarnished; discernible; distinct; easy to see; explicit; in plain view; made public; manifest; prominent; recognizable; noticeable; unconcealed.

**Naked promise.** A promise without consideration.

NOTE: Such a promise is not ordinarily binding and no action can be founded on it.

**Nala.** 'Nala' means a natural watercourse. [*Harihar Prashad Singh* v *Janak Dulari Kuer* 21 Pat LT 873].

**Nalish.** Complain; a civil or criminal case.

**Nambudiri.** An indigenous Malabar Brahmin.

**Name-lender.** When a person buys property with his own money, but in the name of another person or buys property in his own name, but subsequently transfers it into the name of another party, without any intention in either case to benefit such other person, the transaction is called "benami", and the person in whose name the transaction is effected is called "benamidar" or name-lender.

**Namely.** The word "namely" imports enumeration of what is comprised in the preceding clause. In other words it equates what follows with the clause described before. [*State of Bombay* v *Bombay Education Society* AIR 1954 SC 561: 1954 SCA 784: (1954)2 MLJ 359: 1954 SCJ 678: 1955 SCR 568].

**Narcotic.** As adjective it means anæsthetic; anodynous; assuaging; assuasive; calmant; calmative; depressant; dulling; hypnotic; pain-killing; palliative; sedative; soothing; soporiferous; tranquillizing.

As noun it means alleviative; pain reliever; painkiller; hypnotic; calmative; somnifacient; soother; soporific; stupefacient; tranquilliser.

A generic term for any drug which dulls the senses or induces sleep and which commonly becomes addictive after prolonged use.

An addictive drug, esp. an opiate, that dulls the senses and induces sleep; a drug that is controlled or prohibited by law. [Black's *Law Dictionary*, 7th Ed.].

A substance, other than alcohol, which when swallowed or inhaled by, or injected into, a human being induces drowsiness, sleep, stupefaction or insensibility in the human being.

NOTE: Narcotic is a substance which relieves pain, produces sleep, and in large doses brings on stupor, coma and even death, as opium, hemlock, alcohol, etc. Obviously, therefore, if chloral hydrate is hypnotic and sedative it would be a narcotic. [*Indian Chemical and Pharmaceutical Works, Hyderabad* v *State of A.P.* (1966)1 SCA 332: AIR 1966 SC 713].

**Narcotic drug.** "Narcotic drug" means coca leaf, cannabis (hemp), opium, poppy straw and includes all manufactured drugs. [Narcotic Drugs and Psychotropic Substances Act 1985, s. 2(*xiv*)].

**Nasal bad nasal.** Generation after generation.

NOTE: The words used in a deed or will are descriptive of a heritable and alienable estate in the donee and they connote full proprietary rights unless there is something in the context or in the surrounding circumstances which indicate otherwise. [*Bajrang Bahadur* v *Bakhraj Kuer* 1952 SCJ 655: 1953 SCR 232: AIR 1953 SC 7: 1953 SCA 368].

**Nation.** A people, or aggregation of men, existing in the form of an organized jural society, usually inhabiting a distinct portion of the earth, speaking the same language, using the same customs, possessing historic continuity, and distinguished from other like groups by their racial origin and characteristics, and generally, but not necessarily, living under the same government and sovereignty. [*Montoya* v *U.S.* 180 US 261: 21 S Ct 358: 45 L Ed 521; *Worcester* v *Georgia* 8 L Ed 483].

**National currency.** Money (both notes and coins) approved by a national government and placed in circulation as a medium of exchange. [Black's *Law Dictionary*, 7th Ed.].

**National debt.** The total financial obligation of the federal government, including such instruments as Treasury bills, notes, and bonds, as well as foreign debt. [Black's *Law Dictionary*, 7th Ed.].

Money owed by Government, for which it pays interest out of the taxes realised from the public.

Loans, either to meet war expenses, to carry on great public undertakings, or to meet the current deficits of revenue, constitute national debts. Loan is raised by the Government not only from the citizens but also from foreigners.

**National income.** This is the gross total of income earned in a community during a given period by the owners of the various productive factors, *i.e.*, the sum of wages, profits, rents and interest. It is also equal to the value to the final purchaser or consumer of all goods and services produced by members of the community. Net national income is the value of final production less replacement of capital worn out in the productive processes during the period. [Osborn & Grandage's *Concise Commercial Dictionary*].

**National service.** Any service which is likely to assist the defence of India and civil defence or the efficient conduct of military operations and includes such social service as the Central Government may, if it is of opinion that it is necessary for public purposes so to do, by notification specify in this behalf. [National Service Act 1972, s. 2(*c*)].

**Nationality.** A legal relationship involving allegiance on the part of an individual to a State and protection on the part of the State; membership of a particular nation.

NOTE: The fundamental basis of a man's nationality is his membership of an independent political community. A man's nationality is a continuing relationship between the Sovereign State on the one hand and the citizen on the other. This legal relationship involves rights and corresponding duties upon both—on the part of the citizen no less than on the part of the State. [Starke's *International Law*, 10th Ed., p. 340].

*"Nationality" and "citizenship"—whether inter-changeable term.* 'Nationality' and 'citizenship' are not inter-changeable terms. Nationality has reference to the jural relationship which may arise for consideration under international law. On the other hand, citizenship has reference to the jural relationship under municipal law. In other words, nationality determines the civil rights of a person, natural or artificial, particularly with reference to international law,

whereas citizenship is intimately connected with civic rights under the municipal law. [*State Trading Corporation* v *Commercial Tax Officer* AIR 1963 SC 1811].

**Natural.** 'Natural' means, 'indifferent, unbiased, impartial, not engaged on either side'. Conceptually it is not aligning with either view. [*Lily Thomas, Advocate* v *Speaker, Lok Sabha* (1993)4 SCC 234: JT 1993(4) SC 646].

**Natural affection.** The love which one has for his kindred; such affection as naturally subsists between near relatives, as a father and child, brother and sister, husband and wife.

NOTE: It is held to be good consideration under s. 25 of the Indian Contract Act 1872. Thus an agreement made on account of natural love and affection between parties standing in a near relation to each other is a valid contract.

**Natural guardian.** In the absence of a statute, the father of a legitimate child until the child reaches the age of 21 years. [Black's *Law Dictionary*, 7th Ed.].

▸*Meaning under the Hindu Minority and Guardianship Act 1956, s. 6.* The natural guardians of a Hindu minor, in respect of the minor's person as well as in respect of the minor's property (excluding his or her undivided interest in joint family property), are—(*a*) in the case of a boy or an unmarried girl—the father and after him the mother, provided that the custody of a minor who has not completed the age of five years shall ordinarily be with the mother; (*b*) in the case of an illegitimate boy or an illegitimate unmarried girl—the mother, and after her, the father; (*c*) in the case of a married girl—the husband: Provided that no person shall be entitled to act as the natural guardian of a minor under provisions of this section—(*a*) if he has ceased to be a Hindu, or (*b*) if he has completely and finally renounced the world by becoming a hermit (*vanaprastha*) or an ascetic (*yogi* or *sanyasi*).

**Natural justice.** The word 'nature' literally means the innate tendency or quality of things or objects and the word 'just' means upright, fair or proper. The expression 'natural justice' would, therefore, mean the innate quality of being fair. [*Penumbra of Natural Justice* by Tapash Gan Choudhury, 2nd Ed., p. 1].

Natural justice, which is another name of commonsense justice, is 'the natural sense of what is right and wrong' [*P.M. Kurien* v *P.S. Raghavan* AIR 1970 Ker 142] and is the name of those principles which constitute the minimum requirement of justice and without adherence to which, justice would be a travesty. Natural justice accordingly stands for that fundamental quality of fairness which being adopted, justice may not only be done but also appear to be done. [*Penumbra of Natural Justice* by Tapash Gan Choudhury, 2nd Ed., p. 1].

The soul of natural justice is 'fair play in action'. In one case, it has been defined as "quintessence of the process of justice inspired and guided by 'fair play in action'" [*Maneka Gandhi* v *Union of India* AIR 1978 SC 597: (1978)1 SCC 248, *per* P.N. Bhagwati, J.], while in another it has been described "as a distillate of due process of law". [*Fountaine* v *Chesterton, The Times*, August 20, 1968: (1968)112 Sol J 690, *per* Megarry, J.].

The concept of natural justice cannot be confined to any precise definition. It is not justice in the abstract or moral sense and is not even justice according to natural law. [*Bangladesh Steamer Agents' Association* v *Bangladesh* (1981)33 DLR 177 SC (AD), Bangladesh]. In so far as the term 'natural justice' means that a result or process should be just, it is a harmless though it may be a high sounding expression; in so far as it attempts to reflect the old *jus naturale*, it is a confused and unwarranted transfer into the ethical sphere of a term employed for other distinctions; and, in so far as it is resorted to for other purposes, it is vacuous. [*Local Government Board* v *Arlidge* (1915) AC 120: 84 LJKB 72: 111 LT 905, *per* Lord Shaw of Dunfermline].

Justice as defined in a moral, as opposed to a legal sense. [Black's *Law Dictionary*, 8th Ed.]. Natural justice, which is another name of common sense justice, is 'the natural sense of what is right and wrong' [*P.M. Kurien* v *P.S. Raghavan* AIR 1970 Ker 142] and is the name of those principles which constitute the minimum requirement of justice and without adherence to which, justice would be a travesty. Natural justice accordingly stands for that fundamental quality of fairness which being adopted, justice may not only be done but also appear to be done. [*Penumbra of Natural Justice* by Tapash Gan Choudhury, 2nd Ed., p. 1].

'Natural justice' understandably meant no more than 'justice' without the adjective. [*Green* v *Blake* (1948) IR 242, *per* Black, J.].

NOTE: For detailed discussion on natural justice and its various facets vide *Penumbra of Natural Justice* by Tapash Gan Choudhury, 2nd Ed.

**Natural law.** A physical law of nature, for example, gravitation is a natural law; a philosophical system of legal and moral principles purportedly deriving from a universalized conception of human nature or divine justice rather than from legislative or judicial action; moral law embodied in principles of right and wrong. [Black's *Law Dictionary*, 8th Ed.].

NOTE: This expression, "natural law", or *jus naturale*, was largely used in the philosophical speculations of the Roman jurists of the Antonine age, and was intended to denote a system of rules and principles for the guidance of human conduct which, independently of enacted law or of the systems peculiar to any one people, might be discovered by the rational intelligence of man, and would be found to grow out of and conform to his nature, meaning by that word his whole mental, moral, and physical constitution. The point of departure for this conception was the Stoic doctrine of a life ordered "according to nature", which in its turn rested upon the purely supposititious existence, in primitive times, of a "state of nature", that is, a condition of society in which men universally were governed solely by a rational and consistent obedience to the needs, impulses, and promptings of their true nature, such nature being as yet undefaced by dishonesty, falsehood, or indulgence of the baser passions. In ethics, it consists in practical universal judgments which man himself elicits. These express necessary and obligatory rules of human conduct which have been established by the author of human nature as essential to the divine purposes in the universe and have been promulgated by God solely through human reason. [Black's *Law Dictionary*, 5th Ed.].

It is also termed law of nature; eternal law; divine law.

**Natural persons.** Human beings, as distinguished from artificial persons or corporations recognised by the law, *e.g.*, companies.

**Natural rights.** Those which grow out of nature of man and depend upon his personality and are distinguished from those which are created by positive laws enacted by a duly constituted government to create an orderly civilized society. [*In re Gogabashvele's Estate* 195 Cal App 2d 503].

**Naturalisation.** The granting of citizenship to a foreign-born person under statutory authority. [Black's *Law Dictionary*, 7th Ed.].

NOTE: This is a process by which an alien may acquire Indian nationality. Where an application is made by any person of full age and capacity, who is not a citizen of a Commonwealth country like Canada, Australia, New Zealand, etc., for the grant of a certificate of naturalisation, the Central Government may, if satisfied, grant him the necessary certificate of naturalisation. [Citizenship Act 1955, s. 6].

**Nature.** The word 'nature' has been defined as "the fundamental qualities of a person or thing; identity of essential character; sort; kind ..." [*Most Re V. P.M.A. Metropolitan* v *Moran Mar Marthoma* AIR 1995 SC 2001: 1995 Supp (4) SCC 286: JT 1995(5) SC 1].

**Naval law.** A system of regulations for the control of the Navy.

**Navicerts.** A pass or certificate issued by a belligerent exempting a neutral ship or her cargo from contraband control.

NOTE: Navicerts were first introduced by the Government of Elizabeth I in 1590, but were not used on a large scale uptil 1916 when they were instituted by the Allies. They were again introduced on the outbreak of the Second World War in 1939.

**Navigable river.** Those rivers only are navigable in which the tide ebbed and flowed. [*Murphy* v *Ryan* (1868)16 WR 678].

NOTE: The flowing of the tide is a strong *prima facie* evidence of the existence of a public navigable river, but whether it is one or not depends upon the situation and nature of the channel. Not every ditch or cutting which is reached by the tide forms part of the public navigable river, even though it be large enough to admit of the passage of a boat. The question is one of degree and is one for the jury, having regard to all the facts. [*Sim E. Bak* v *Ang Yong Huat* (1923) AC 429].

A navigable river is a public highway navigable by all His Majesty's subjects in a reasonable way and for a reasonable purpose. The public right of a free passage extends to the whole of the navigable channels, and includes all such rights as with relation to the circumstances of each river are necessary for the convenient passage of ships, such as the right of stopping for a reasonable time to unload and of grounding and anchoring. [*Purnendu Bikash* v *Chairman, District Board* AIR 1963 Cal 74].

**Navigation.** The act or the science or the business of traversing the sea or other navigable waters in ships or vessels. [*The Silvia* 171 US 462].

NOTE: Navigation is the science or art of conducting a ship from one place to another. This includes the supply of necessary implements and skilful mariners. The instruments are useless without the skilful mariners, and conversely; navigation includes two things—the supply of the instruments or organs of the ship, and the living instruments, or seamen. If either of these is wanting by the negligence of the owner or of those for whom he is responsible, there is 'improper navigation'. [*The Warkworth* (1884)9 PD 145; *Carmichael* v *Liverpool Sailing-Ship Association* 19 QBD 242].

**Necessaries.** The word has no hard and fast meaning, but varies with the accustomed manner of living of the parties. [*Smitti* v *Roth Cadillac Co.* 145 Pa Super 292].

Necessaries consist of food, drink, clothing, medical attention, and a suitable place of residence, and they are regarded as necessaries in the absolute sense of the word.

Word includes not only those services which are proper and required to sustain life but also those suitable for the individual involved according to his circumstances and condition in life. [*Trask* v *Davis* Mo App, 297 SW 2d 792].

Articles suitable and proper for an infant's position in life, although not actually necessary to his existence, are recognised as necessaries. [Halsbury's *Laws of England*, 4th Ed., vol. 24, paras 416 & 417, pp. 172-173].

**Necessary.** Choiceless; compelling; fated; foreordained; inevitable; inexorable; irresistible; unavoidable; unpreventable; all-important; basic; binding; crucial; fundamental; imperative; indispensable; obligatory; paramount; substantive; vital; essence; essential; indispensable thing; significant.

Those things are necessary to the doing of a thing which are reasonably required or legally ancillary to its accomplishment. [*A-G* v *Walker* 18 LJ Ex 179].

This word must be considered in the connection in which it is used, as it is a word susceptible of various meanings. It may import absolute physical necessity or inevitability, or it may import that which is only convenient, useful, appropriate, suitable, proper, or conducive to the end sought. It is an adjective expressing degrees, and may express mere convenience or that which is indispensable or an absolute physical necessity. It may mean something which in the accomplishment of a given object cannot be dispensed with, or it may mean something reasonably useful and proper, and of greater or lesser benefit or convenience, and its force and meaning must be determined with relation to the particular object sought. [*Kay County Excise Board* v *Atchison T. & S.F.R. Co.* 185 Okl 327: 91 P 2d 1087, 1088].

**Necessary and proper.** The words "necessary and proper" mean appropriate and adapted to carrying into effect given object. [*Petition of Public Service Coordinated Transport* 247 A 2d 888, 891].

**Necessary implication or inference.** Not natural necessity, but so strong a probability of intention that an intention contrary to that which is imputed cannot be supposed. [*Cork County Council & Burke* v *Public Works Commissioners* 1945 IR 561].

One which is inescapable or unavoidable from the standpoint of reason. [*Taylor* v *Twiner* 9 So 2d 644, 646].

**Necessary party.** A "necessary party" is one whose joinder is required in order to afford the plaintiff the complete relief to which he is entitled against the defendant. [*Orange Associates, Inc.* v *Albright* Tex Civ App, 548 SW 2d 806, 807].

Necessary parties are those who must be included in action either as plaintiffs or defendants, unless there is a valid excuse for their nonjoinder. [*City of Hutchinson for Human Relations Commission of Hutchinson* v *Hutchinsons, Kansas Office of Kansas State Employment Service* 517 P 2d 117, 122].

NOTE: *Necessary party and proper party—distinction.* A necessary party is one without whom no order can be made effectively; a proper party is one in whose absence an effective order can be made, but whose presence is necessary for a complete and final decision on the question involved in the proceeding. [*Udit Narain Singh* v *Board of Revenue* AIR 1963 SC 786].

In respect of every suit there are certain persons who are essential to be impleaded as defendants. Those persons fall in two classes—(1) those against whom relief is sought, and (2) those whom the law requires to be impleaded as defendants, even though no relief is sought against them. [*Shitladin* v *Board of Revenue* ILR (1963)1 All 915: AIR 1963 All 519].

**Necessitas non habet legem.** Necessity has no law.

**Necessity.** Controlling force; irresistable compulsion; a power or impulse so great that it admits no choice of conduct; that which makes the contrary of a thing impossible.

In criminal law, it is a 'justification defense for a person who acts in an emergency that he or she did not create and who commits a harm that is less severe than the harm that would have occurred but for the person's actions'. In torts, it means a 'privilege that may relieve a person from liability for trespass or conversion if that person, having no alternative, harms another's property in an effort to protect life or health'. [Black's *Law Dictionary*, 8th Ed.].

When used in relation to power of eminent domain, it does not mean absolute necessity, but only reasonable necessity.


- **Legal necessity** p. 526.
- **Way of necessity** p. 894.


**Negative covenant.** A negative covenant is a covenant or undertaking not to do something. Such a covenant is also called a restrictive covenant.

A negative covenant is a covenant that requires a party to refrain from doing something; esp., in a real-estate financing transaction, the borrower's promise to the lender not to encumber or transfer the real-estate as long as the loan remains unpaid. [Black's *Law Dictionary*, 7th Ed.].

NOTE: A negative covenant ordinarily runs with the land. If *A* sells a park in front of his house to *B* who covenants not to build upon it, and *B* sells the park to *C* who has notice of *B*'s covenant not to build, *A* can enforce the covenant against *C*, for it is a negative covenant running with the land.

First part of s. 40 of the Transfer of Property Act 1882, contains the law in India relating to negative or restrictive covenants. That section provides that where, for the more beneficial enjoyment of his own immovable property, a third person has, independently of any interest in the immovable property of another or of any easement thereon, a right to restrain the enjoyment in a particular manner of the latter property, such right may be enforced against a transferee with notice thereof or a gratuitous transferee of the property affected thereby, but not against a transferee for consideration and without notice of the right nor against such property in his hands.

**Neglect.** As noun means bungling; careless abandon; carelessness; default; delinquency; dereliction; disregard; failure; heedlessness; indifference; indiligence; laxity; laxness; non-fulfilment; non-observance; omission; procrastination remissness; slackness; thoughtlessness.

As verb means be careless; be inattentive; disregard; forget; gloss over; ignore; lay aside; lose sight of; overlook; pass by; pass over; pay no attention; pay no heed to; pay no regard to; procrastinate; skip; take no note; take no notice.

It may mean to omit, fail, or forbear to do a thing that can be done, or that is required to be done, but it may also import an absence of care or attention in the doing or omission of a given act. And it may mean a designed refusal or unwillingness to perform one's duty. [*In re Perkins* 234 Mo App 716: 117 SW 2d 686, 692].

To neglect to do is the omission to do some duty which the party is able to do. [*King* v *Burnell* 12 A&E 468].

The expression 'neglect' means 'to fail to give due care, attention, or time to. To fail through thoughtlessness or carelessness. To ignore or disregard'. [*Laxmi Kant R. Bhojwani* v *Pratapsingh M. Pardeshi* (1995)6 SCC 576].

The word 'neglect' means 'gross neglect', wilful, intentional, culpable or flagrant disregard of duties. [*Baburao Vishwanath Mathpati* v *State* AIR 1996 Bom 227, 239].

Neglect under s. 125, Cr. P.C. 1973 means a default or omission to maintain, in the absence of a demand. [*Mitanjali Mohanty* v *Fanendra Mohanty* 1992 Cr LJ 4046, 4047 (Ori)].

**Negligence.** Negligence is the failure to use such care as a reasonably prudent and careful person would use under similar circumstances; it is the doing of some act which a person of ordinary prudence would not have done under similar circumstances or failure to do what a person of ordinary prudence would have done under similar circumstances. [*Amoco Chemical Corp.* v *Hill* Del Super, 318 A 2d 614, 617].

It is conduct which falls below the standard established by law for the protection of others against unreasonable risk of harm; it is a departure from the conduct expectable of a reasonably prudent person under like circumstances. [*Pence* v *Ketchum* La., 326 So 2d 831, 836].

"Negligence" is absence of reasonable or prudent care which a reasonable person is expected to observe in a given set of circumstances. [*Consumer Utility & Trust Society* v *Chairman & Managing Director, Bank of Baroda* (1995)2 SCC 150: JT 1995(2) SC 51: (1995)1 SCR 698: (1995)83 Comp Cas 187: (1996)1 SCJ 40].

"Negligence" is the omission to do something which a reasonable man is expected to do or a prudent man is expected to do. [*State of Maharashtra* v *Kanchanmala Vijaysing Shirke* AIR 1995 SC 2499: (1995)5 SCC 659: 1995 SCC (Cri) 1002: JT 1995(6) SC 155: (1996)85 Comp Cas 542].

"Negligence" is an omission to do something which a reasonable man guided upon the considerations which ordinarily regulate conduct of human affairs would do or doing something which a prudent and reasonable man would not do. [*Prafulla Kumar Rout* v *State of Orissa* 1995 Cr LJ 1277 (Ori); *Kamlesh Kumar* v *Prahlad* 1985(1) Civ LJ 529 (Raj); *Raju P.M.* v *State of Karnataka* (1977)1 Kant LJ 260].

**NOTE:** In ordinary case which does not involve any special skill, negligence means some failure to do some act which a reasonable man in the circumstances would do, or doing some act which a reasonable man in the circumstances would not do. But where you get a situation which involves the use of some special skill or competence, then the test is the standard of the ordinary skilled man exercising and professing to have the special skill. [*Bolam* v *Friern Hospital Management Committee* (1957)2 All ER 118].

"Negligence" in common parlance may fall short of negligence at law. At law, negligence and duty go together; one is co-related to the other. If there is no such legal duty, there is no negligence in the legal sense. [*Nrisingha Prasad* v *Commissioner of Bhandeswar Municipality* 73 CWN 88].

Negligence is a term of art, but has distinct meanings in different jurisdiction. In torts, damage is an essential ingredient, but that element is not necessary in the law of master and servant. In criminal law, there are series of offences based on negligence in which loss or injury is not material; it is enough if the act is likely to cause injury or endanger life. Sections 279, 285, 287 and 290 of the IPC are illustrative examples. [*Kedar Nath* v *State* AIR 1965 All 233].


- **Contributory negligence** p. 192.
- **Criminal negligence** p. 209.
- **Gross negligence** p. 400.
- **Professional negligence** p. 695.


**Negotiable instrument.** A negotiable instrument means a promissory note, bill of exchange or cheque payable either to order or to bearer. [Negotiable Instruments Act 1881, s. 13].

**Negotiate.** To confer with another so as to arrive at the settlement of some matter; to deal with; manage; to arrange for or bring about by negotiation; to transfer (as a bill of exchange) to another by delivery or endorsement in return for equal value; to convert into cash or the equivalent value.

To meet with another so as to arrive through discussion at some kind of agreement or compromise about something. [*Al Herd, Inc.* v *Isaac* 271 Cal App 2d 749].

The word 'negotiate' used in connection with business transaction ordinarily means to bargain with another respecting a transaction or to conduct communication or conferences with a view to reaching a settlement or agreement. It is not within the domain to strike a bargain and perform the deal. [*Devkubai* v *Rajesh Builders* AIR 1997 Bom 142].

**Negotiation.** Bargaining; consultation; deliberation; discussion; exchange of views; arbitrament.

Negotiation is process of submission and consideration of offers until acceptable offer is made and accepted. [*Gainey* v *Brotherhood of Ry. and S.S. Clerks, Freight Handlers, Ex p. & Station Emp.* DC Pa, 275 F Supp 292, 300].

**Nemo allegans turpitudinem suam audiendus est.** No one alleging his own turpitude should be heard as a witness. The maxim applies when fraud is committed by the party sought to take advantage of the maxim, not fraud on any third party. [*Raja Ram* v *Daulat Ram* AIR 1980 All 161].

**Nemo cogitationis penam patitur.** No one suffers punishment on account of his thoughts.

**Nemo cogitur rem suam vendere, etiam justo pretio.** No man is compelled to sell his own property even for a just price.

**Nemo commodum copere potest de injuria sua propria.** No one can take advantage from his own injury.

**Nemo contra factum suam venire potest.** No man can contravene or contradict his own deed. The principle of estoppel by deed.

**Nemo damnum facit nisi qui id fecit quod facere jus non habel.** No one is considered as doing damage, unless he who is doing what he has no right to do.

**Nemo dare potest quod non nabet.** No man can give that which he has not.

**Nemo dat quod non habet.** No one gives what he does not possess.

**Nemo de domo sua extrahi potest.** No one can be dragged out of his own house. In other words, every man's house is his castle.

**Nemo debet aliena jactura locuplotari.** No one ought to gain by another's loss.

**Nemo debet bis puniri pro uno delicto.** No man ought to be punished twice for one offence. No man shall be placed in peril of legal penalties more than once upon the same accusation.

**Nemo debet bis vexari pro eadem causa.** No one should be twice harassed for the same cause.

**Nemo debet esse judex in propria causa.** No one should be judge in his own cause. This principle applies not only to judicial proceedings but also to quasi-judicial and administrative proceedings. [*J. Mahapatra* v *State of Orissa* AIR 1984 SC 1572, 1575].

**Nemo debet esse judex in propria sua causa.** No one acting judicially should have, or appear likely to have, a bias in favour of one side or the other. [Tapash Gan Choudhury: *Penumbra of Natural Justice*, 2nd Ed., p. 248].

**Nemo debet immiscere se rei ad se hihil, pertinenti.** No one should intermeddle with a thing that in no respect concerns him.

**Nemo debet in communione invitus teneri.** No one should be retained in a partnership against his will.

**Nemo debet locupietari ex alterius incommode.** No one ought to be made rich out of another's loss.

**Nemo debet rem suam sine facto aut defect suo amittere.** No man ought to lose his property without his own act or default.

**Nemo duobus utatur officlis.** No one should hold two offices, *i.e.* at the same time.

**Nemo est supra leges.** No one is above the law.

**Nemo ex aiterius facto pragravari debet.** No man can be burdened in consequence of another's act.

**Nemo ex consilio obligatur.** No man is bound in consequence of his advice. Mere advice will not create the obligation of a mandate.

**Nemo ex doio suo proprio reievetur aut auxilum capiat.** Let no one be relieved or gain an advantage by his own fraud. A civil law maxim.

**Nemo ex proprio doio consequitur actionem.** No one maintains an action arising out of his own wrong. None can find any title to anything on his own mistake or misrepresentation and, no one obtains a cause of action by his own fraud. [*A. Pillai* v *Kerala Public Service Commission* 1981 Lab IC 1671].

**Nemo inauditus condemnari debet si non sit contumax.** No man ought to be condemned without being heard unless he be contumacious.

**Nemo jus sibi dicere potest.** No one can declare the law for himself. No one is entitled to take the law into his own hands.

**Nemo moriturus praesumitur mentire.** One at the point of death is presumed not to lie.

The principle on which the dying declarations are admitted in evidence, is based upon the legal maxim *nemo moriturus praesumitur mentire* i.e. a man will not meet his maker with a lie in his mouth.

NOTE: It has always to be kept in mind that though a dying declaration is entitled great weight, yet it is worthwhile to note that as the maker of the statement is not subjected to cross-examination, it is essential for the court to insist that the dying declaration should be of such nature as to inspire full confidence of the court in its correctness. The court is obliged to rule out the possibility of the statement being the result of either tutoring, prompting or vindictive or a product of imagination. Before relying upon a dying declaration, the court should be satisfied that the deceased was in a fit state of mind to make the statement. Once the court is satisfied that the dying declaration was true, voluntary and not influenced by any extraneous consideration, it can base its conviction without any further corroboration as a rule requiring corroboration is not a rule of law but only a rule of prudence. [*Uka Ram* v *State of Rajasthan* AIR 2001 SC 1814: JT 2001(4) SC 472: 2001 Cr LJ 1821: (2001)5 SCC 254].

**Nemo potest facere per alium, quod per se non potest.** No one can do through another what he cannot do himself.

**Nemo potest facere per obliquum quod non potest facere per directum.** No man can indirectly do that which he cannot do directly.

**Nemo tenetur seipsum accusare.** No man can be compelled to criminate himself.

NOTE: Clause (3) of Art. 20 of the Constitution of India provides that no person accused of any offence shall be compelled to be a witness against himself.

**Nephew.** A son of one's brother or sister, or of one's brother-in-law or sister-in-law.

- **Half nephew** p. 405.

**Nepotism.** Favour; favouritism; leaning; partiality; partisanism; partisanship; preferential treatment; undetachment; family patronage; bestowal of patronage by public officers in appointing others to positions by reason of blood or marital relationship to appointing authority.

**Net.** Clear; actual; irreducible; remaining; residual; residuary; surplus; surviving; that which remains after allowable deductions are made.

**Net asset value (NAV).** Term used in evaluating stock of investment company and arrived at by deducting total liabilities from total market value of all assets of company.

Net asset value of corporation, for stock appraisal purpose, is share which stock represents in value of net assets of corporation, including every kind of property and value, whether realty or personalty, tangible or intangible, goodwill, and corporation's value as going concern. [*In re Watt & Shand* 304 A 2d 694, 698].

The market value of a share in a mutual fund, computed by deducting any liabilities of the fund from its total assets and dividing the difference by the number of outstanding fund shares. [Black's *Law Dictionary*, 7th Ed.].

**Net assets.** A bookkeeping balance obtained by subtracting liabilities from its gross assets. [*Commonwealth* v *Union Trust Co. of Pittsburgh* 345 Pa 298: 27 A 2d 15, 17].

**Net income.** Total income from all sources minus deductions, exemptions, and other tax reductions. Income tax is computed on net income.

In matrimonial jurisprudence the expression would normally mean total income derived less the cost of collection and other compulsory payments such as income tax etc. It does not mean net income after giving deduction for all the expenses incurred by the husband. Expenses which are to be deducted must have some relation or connection with the source of income. [*D. Thankaraj* v *M.C. Pushpa Rose* AIR 1986 Ker 23].

**Net loss.** The excess of all expenses and losses for a period over all revenues and gains of the period.

Any deficit from operations, plus any shrinkage in value of plant investment. [*Ickes* v *U.S. ex rel. Chestatee Pyrites & Chemical Corporation* DC, 77 L Ed 1352].

**Net proceeds.** The amount received in a transaction minus the cost of the transaction such as expenses and commission.

**Net profits.** Total sales revenue less the cost of the goods sold and all additional expenses.

It is the sum divisible after discharging, or making provision for, every outgoing properly chargeable against the period, whether a year or less, for which the profits are to be calculated. [*Glasier* v *Rolls* 42 Ch D 453; *Bishop* v *Smyrna & Cassaba Railway* (1895)2 Ch 596].

Net profits signify the excess of receipts over current expenses and outgoings of a business; the fund which in any year is capable of being applied to the payment of a dividend or capable of being divided between partners as the fruit of the year's operations. [*Re Condran, Condran* v *Stark* (1917)1 Ch 639, 645].

**Net rent.** 'Net rent' means a rent clear of all deductions to which it would otherwise be liable. [*Bennett* v *Wormack* 6 LJOSKB 175, *per* Tenterden, C.J.].

'Net rent' means "that part of the rent which goes into the landlord's pocket, i.e., the rent paid by the tenant, after deducting taxes and charges of collection. [*R.* v *Tomlinson* 9 B&C 166, 167, *per* Bayley, J.].

**Net worth.** Remainder after deduction of liabilities from assets. [*W.H. Miner, Inc.* v *Peerless Equipment Co.* CCA III, 115 F 2d 650, 655].

Net worth of a corporation may be determined by subtracting liabilities from assets or by adding the capital account and surplus account as reflected in general ledger of corporation. [*Eastern Capital Corp.* v *Freeman* 168 NYS 2d 834, 838].

The concept of "net worth" always denotes the excess of the book value of all assets over liabilities and the market value of assets is never taken into consideration.

[*Commissioner of I.T., Bombay* v *Mahindra and Mahindra* AIR 1984 SC 1182: (1983)54 Comp Cas 651: 1983 Tax LR 1286: (1983)3 SCR 773: (1983)144 ITR 225: (1983)4 SCC 392: (1983)3 Comp LJ 30].

**Neutral.** Indifferent; dispassionate; non-aligned; non-interfering; unbiased; impartial; not engaged on either side; not taking an active part with either of the contending sides; unprejudiced; unswayed.

**Neutrality.** Aloofness; detachment; disinterestedness; dispassionateness; impartiality; indifference; non-interference; non-partisanship.

The term is derived from the Latin "neuter". Neutrality may be defined as the attitude of impartiality adopted by third States towards belligerents and recognised by belligerents, such attitude creating rights and duties between the impartial States and the belligerents. Such States do not take part in a war between other States as neutrals. [Oppenheim's *International Law*, 7th Ed., vol. II, p. 653].

The state of a nation which takes no part between two or more other nations at war. [*U.S.* v *The Three Friends* 41 L Ed 897].

**New trial.** A post-judgment retrial or re-examination of some or all of the issues determined in an earlier judgment. [Black's *Law Dictionary*, 7th Ed.].

**News.** It means tidings, new information of recent events, new occurrences as a subject of report or talk. [*AIR Karmachari Sangha* v *AIR Ltd.* AIR 1988 SC 1325, 1329].

• **False news** p. 341.

**Newspaper.** A publication for general circulation, usually in sheet form, appearing at regular intervals, usually daily or weekly, and containing matters of general public interest, such as current events. [Black's *Law Dictionary*, 7th Ed.].

▸ *Meaning under the Working Journalists and Other Newspaper Employees (Conditions of Service) and Miscellaneous Provisions Act 1955, s. 2(b).* Any printed periodical work containing public news or comments on public news and includes such other class of printed periodical work as may, from time to time, be notified in this behalf by the Central Government in the Official Gazette.

NOTE: The expression "newspaper" as defined in the Working Journalists and Other Newspaper Employees (Conditions of Service) and Miscellaneous Provisions Act 1955, includes not merely public news but also comments on public news. Every law report contains the editorial note at the commencement of the decisions printed therein and also comments on the recent decisions. Law reports answer the definition of "newspaper". [*AIR Karmachari Sangha* v *AIR Ltd.* AIR 1988 SC 1325, 1331].

▸ *Meaning under the Press and Registration of Books Act 1867, s. 1; Press Council Act 1965, s. 2(e); Press (Objectionable Matter) Act 1951, s. 2(e).* 'Newspaper' means any printed periodical work containing public news or comments on public news.

▸ *Meaning under the Newspaper (Price and Page) Act 1956, s. 2(b).* 'Newspaper' means any printed periodical work containing public news or comments on public news appearing at intervals of not more than a week.

NOTE: The essential prerequisite of a periodical in order to make it a newspaper is that it must contain mainly public news or comments on public news. [*P.S.V. Iyer* v *Sales Tax Commissioner* AIR 1960 Ori 221].

Any paper to be classified as newspaper must contain a report of recent events. [*Sales Tax Commr.* v *Express Printers* AIR 1983 Bom 190: (1983)52 STC 290: 1983 Tax LR 2871].

**Next friend.** A person who appears in a lawsuit to act for the benefit of an incompetent or minor plaintiff, but who is not a party to the lawsuit and is not appointed as a guardian. [Black's *Law Dictionary*, 7th Ed.].

One acting for the benefit of infant, married woman, or other person not *sui juris*, without being regularly appointed guardian. [*In re Boulware's Will* 258 NYS 522].

NOTE: A "next friend" is not a party to an action, but is an officer of the court, especially appearing to look after the interests of the minor whom he represents. [*Youngblood* v *Taylor* Fla, 89 So 2d 503, 505].

Where a suit is instituted without next friend, the plaint may be taken off the file. [Code of Civil Procedure 1908, Or. 32].

**Next of kin.** The primary and proper meaning of "next of kin" is the nearest in proximity of blood (whether of the whole or half blood) living at the death of the person whose next of kin are spoken of. [*Withy* v *Mangles* 10 LJ Ch 391; *Bullock* v *Downes* 9 HL Cas 1; *Halton* v *Foster* 3 Ch 505; *Re Rees* 44 Ch D 484].

The words 'next of kin' without more mean the nearest blood relations of the *propositus*. The words 'next of kin in blood' indicate an intention to exclude affinity in favour of consanguinity. [*Halton* v *Foster* (1868)3 Ch App 505].

The term "next of kin" is used with two meanings: (1) nearest blood relations according to law of consanguinity and (2) those entitled to take under statutory distribution of intestate's estates, and term is not necessarily confined to relatives by blood, but may include a relationship existing by reason of marriage, and may well embrace persons, who in natural sense of word, and in contemplation of Roman law, bear no relation of kinship at all. [*In re Kyle's Autopsy* Okl, 309 P 2d 1070, 1073].

NOTE: 'Next of kin' includes a widower or widow of a deceased person, or any other person who by law would be entitled to letters of administration in preference to a creditor or legatee of the deceased. [Administrator-General's Act 1913, s. 2(6)]. Degrees of kindred are given in Schedule I to the Indian Succession Act 1925 read with s. 28 of the Act.

**Nibandha.** A periodical allowance or payment; commentary on Smriti Sastras of the Hindus.

**Nickname.** A short name; one nicked or cut off for the sake of brevity.

**Niece.** The daughter of a person's brother or sister, or of a person's brother-in-law or sister-in-law.

- **Half niece** p. 405.

**Nihil habet forum ex secena.** The court has nothing to do with what is not before it.

**Nihil nequam est praesumeddum.** Nothing wicked is to be presumed.

**Nihil quod est contra rationem est licitum.** Nothing is permitted which is contrary to reason.

**Nij jote.** Lands in direct cultivation by proprietors or tenure-holders.

**Nika.** Marriage; a Muhammadan marriage with a widow.

**Nikas.** Adjustment of accounts; rendering of accounts.

**Nilam.** A public or private auction of any property; a court auction.

**Nirdharita.** Ascertained; fixed; stipulated.

**Nirkh.** Rate; price; rate of rent.

**Nisi (unless).** A Latin word meaning 'unless'. In judicial proceeding, it implies having validity of a court's *ex parte* ruling or grant of relief unless the adversely affected party appears and shows cause why it should be withdrawn.

**Nisi prius.** A trial before a judge with a jury.

**Niskar.** Rent-free tenancy; tenant not in fact paying rent. [*Moslema Khatun* v *Fanindra Lal* AIR 1954 Cal 558].

**Niskar bhogdakhal sutrey.** It means that the tenant is not actually paying rent to anybody. [*Moslema Khatun* v *Fanindra Lal* AIR 1954 Cal 558].

**Niyoga.** Appointment to an office or duty; procreation of son by appointment of a person other than the husband in a case where the husband is either dead or impotent or disordered in mind or incurably diseased.

**Nizamat adalat.** See ADALAT p. 37.

**Noabad taluk.** Permanent tenure but not a fixed rent.

**Nolle prosequi.** A *nolle prosequi* is a formal entry on the record by the prosecuting officer by which he declares that he will not prosecute the case further. [*State* v *Gaskins* 210 SE 2d 590, 592].

NOTE: A *nolle prosequi* (to be unwilling to prosecute) puts an end to the indictment on which the accused person is brought before the court. So, he cannot be proceeded against on the same charges, but the rule does not affect the legality or otherwise of any proceedings taken thereafter by the Government against him. [*In re Jitendranath Bose* (1925)52 Cal 590]. It has not the effect of judgment on the merits; and it is not equivalent to a pardon, nor to an acquittal, for the purpose of a plea of *autrefois acquit*.

**Nominal.** Hardly worth mention; in name only; inconsiderable; insignificant; little; minimum; negligible; symbolic; titular; token; trifling; trivial; unsubstantial.

Connected with the transaction or proceeding in name only, not in interest. [*Park Amusement Co.* v *McCaughn* DC Pa, 14 F 2d 553, 556].

**Nominal damages.** See under DAMAGES p. 220.

**Nominal share capital.** Nominal share capital of a company is the face value of its shares. [*A-G* v *Midland Ry.* (1900)2 QB 353].

**Nominate.** Designate, name; to select or propose for appointment to an office or place; to propose as a candidate for election to office; choose; assign; select.

**Nomination.** Naming, proposing or recommending. [*A. Mohambaram* v *M.A. Jayavelu* AIR 1970 Mad 63: 1970 Cr LJ 241].

**Nomination paper.** A paper or form nominating a certain person or persons as candidates for election in any constituency. [Representation of the People Act 1951, s. 33].

**Nominee.** One designated to act for another as his representative in a rather limited sense. It is used sometimes to signify an agent or trustee. It has no connotation, however, other than that of acting for another, in representation of another, or as the grantee of another. [*Schuh Trading Co.* v *Commissioner of Internal Revenue* CCA III, 95 F 2d 404, 411].

**Non-access.** Absence of opportunities for sexual intercourse between husband and wife; the absence of such intercourse.

The word "non-access" includes futility or incapacity of access on account of impotency, want of virility through immature age or other physical incompetency.

**Non-age.** Lack of requisite legal age; a minor.

**Non-apparent easement.** See under EASEMENT p. 291.

**Non-appearance.** The omission to appear in time; a failure of appearance.

**Non-bailable offence.** An offence other than a bailable offence. [Code of Criminal Procedure 1973, s. 2(*a*)].

**Non-cognizable offence.** An offence for, and non-cognizable case means a case in which a police officer has no authority to arrest without warrant. [Code of Criminal Procedure 1973, s. 2(*l*)].

**Non-compos mentis.** Not of sound mind.

**Non est factum.** It is a plea in defence that the deed is not of the defendant.

**Non est regula quin fallit.** There is no rule without an exception.

**Non est reus nisi mens sit rea.** One is not guilty unless his intention be guilty.

**Non facias malum, ut indc veniat bonum.** You are not to do evil that thence good may arise.

**Non-feasance.** Non-performance of some act which ought to be performed, omission to perform a required duty at all, or total neglect of duty. [*Desmarais* v *Wachusett Regional School Dist.* 276 NE 2d 691, 693].

Non-feasance would apply to a case where a person omits to do some act prescribed by law. [*Khairul Bashar* v *Thanu Lal* AIR 1957 All 553].

**Non-obstante.** Notwithstanding; an overriding clause.

A *non-obstante* clause is a legislative device usually employed to give overriding effect to certain provisions over some contrary provisions that may be found either in the same enactment or some other enactment, that is to say, to avoid the operation and effect of all contrary provisions. [*Union of India* v *G.M. Kokil* AIR 1984 SC 1022: 1984 (Supp) SCC 196].

**Non-sequitur.** It does not follow.

**Noscitur a sociis.** It is known from its associates. The meaning of a word is or may be known from the accompanying words. Under the doctrine of "noscitur a sociis", the meaning of questionable words or phrases in a statute may be ascertained by reference to the meaning of words or phrases associated with it. [*Wong Kam Wo* v *Dulles* CA Hawaii, 236 F 2d 622, 626].

A word is known by its associates. It is a rule laid down by Lord Bacon that the coupling of words together shows that they are to be understood in the same sense. And where the meaning of a particular word is doubtful or obscure, or where a particular expression when taken singly is inoperative, the intention of the party using it may be ascertained by looking at adjoining words or at expressions occurring at other parts of the same instrument, for *quoe non valent singula juncta juvant.* [Broom on *Legal Maxims*, 10th Ed., p. 396].

When two or more words susceptible of analogous meaning are coupled together the words take their colour from each other and the words more general are restricted to a sense less analogous to the less general. The doctrine is broader than the maxim *ejusdem generis.* [*Debendra* v *State of Gujarat* AIR 1969 SC 63: (1969)1 SCJ 252: 1969 Cr LJ 285: (1969)1 SCR 235: (1969)2 Lab LJ 116].

**Not exceeding.** The expression generally connotes a maximum. [*Henry* v *Antrim* (1900)2 IR 547].

**Not guilty.** A plea in criminal proceedings by the accused denying the charge; a judgment of the criminal court holding the accused not guilty of the charge.

**Not less than.** The words signify in the smallest or lowest degree; at the lowest estimate; at least.

The expression 'not less than' given number of days means 'clear days'. [*Re Railway Sleepers Co.* 54 LJ Ch 720].

**Not more.** The expression indicates the maximum.

**Not proved.** A fact is said not to be proved when it is neither proved nor disproved. [Indian Evidence Act 1872, s. 3].

**Notary public.** A person authorised by a state to administer oaths, certify documents, attest to the authenticity of signatures, and perform official acts in commercial matters, such as protesting negotiable instruments. [Black's *Law Dictionary*, 8th Ed.].

**Notice.** 'Notice' is knowledge of facts which would lead a person to make inquiry. Hodson, J., did not, however, regard 'notice' as synonym for the word 'knowledge' and stated in a case: "Notice is a word which involves that knowledge may be imparted by notice, but 'notice' and 'knowledge' are not the same thing, although loosely one sometimes talk as if to act with notice and to act with knowledge were indeed the same". [*Cresta Holdings Ltd.* v *Karlin* (1959)3 All ER 656, 657 (CA)].

In another sense, 'notice' means information, an advice or written warning, in more or less formal shape intended to apprise a person of some proceeding in which his interests are involved, or informing him of some fact which it is his right to know and the duty of the notifying authority to communicate. [*Penumbra of Natural Justice* by Tapash Gan Choudhury, 2nd Ed., p. 120].

'Notice' has been held to be a direct and definite statement of a thing, as distinguished from supplying materials from which the existence of such a thing may be inferred. [*Burgh* v *Legge* 8 LJ Ex 258].

By 'notice', the Supreme Court has meant "communication of materials since no one can meet an unknown ground". [*Mohinder Singh Gill* v *The Chief Election Commissioner* AIR 1978 SC 851: (1978)1 SCC 405].

NOTE: For different kinds of notice, its importance, essential requisites, etc. [see *Penumbra of Natural Justice* by Tapash Gan Choudhury, 2nd Ed., Ch. 3].

'Notice' has got different other meanings too. It may as noun mean advertence, careful attention, caution, vigil, admonition, caveat, ultimatum. As verb, it may mean divulge, forewarn, make known, make public, acknowledge, appreciate, be conscious of, examine closely, examine intently, give heed to, pay attention, take cognizance, take stock of.


- **Bankruptcy notice** p. 95.
- **Constructive notice** p. 179.
- **Judicial notice** p. 494.
- **Reasonable notice** p. 730.
- **Take notice** p. 826.


**Notice to quit.** A "notice to quit" is a notice (which generally speaking may be written or verbal) which on its expiry does, of itself and in accordance with the subsisting contract, put an end to a relationship of landlord and tenant.

"Notice to quit" means to terminate a tenancy (whether a periodical tenancy or a tenancy for a term of years certain) given in accordance with the provisions (whether express or implied) of that tenancy.

It is a notice given by an existing landlord to an existing tenant. A person cannot give a valid notice to quit before he has become a landlord, and the recipient of the notice his tenant, or before legal relations exist between them which otherwise permit such a notice. [*Lower* v *Sorrell* (1962)3 All ER 1074 (CA): (1963)1 QB 959].

▸ *Meaning under the Transfer of Property Act 1882, ss. 106 and 111.* Notice to quit is a notice given by the landlord to his tenant to quit and vacate the premises demised to the latter.

**Notification.** A formal announcement of a legally relevant fact, action, or intent, such as notice of an intent to withdraw from a treaty; notice. [Black's *Law Dictionary*, 8th Ed.].

NOTE: A notification required by law to be published in the Gazette is of no effect unless it is so published. [*Mahendra Lal* v *State of U.P.* AIR 1963 SC 1019: (1963)2 SCA 163].

**Noting.** 'Noting' is a minute made by a notary on a bill of exchange of its dishonour by non-acceptance or non-payment.

An intimation to the drawer of a bill of a charge for "nothing", implies presentment to and non-payment by the acceptor. [*Armstrong* v *Christiani* 17 LJCP 181].

**Notwithstanding.** Despite; in spite of; without prevention by; nevertheless.

"Anything in this Act to the contrary notwithstanding" is equivalent to saying that the Act shall be no impediment to the measure. [*Wooler* v *North Eastern Breweries* (1910)1 KB 247].

The expression "notwithstanding anything contained in any other law" prevents reliance on any other law to the contrary. [*Brij Raj* v *S.K. Shaw* AIR 1951 SC 115: 1951 SCJ 238].

**Novation.** "Novation"—a term derived from the civil law—means that there being a contract in existence, some new contract is substituted for it, either between the same parties (for that might be) or between different parties, the consideration mutually being the discharge of the old contract. [*Scarf* v *Jardine* (1882)7 AC 345, 351, *per* Lord Selborne].

"Novation" takes place when one party to a contract releases the other and a third person undertakes the liability of the party released. To constitute novation there must be—(*i*) release of one party; (*ii*) liability undertaken by a new party in consideration of the release of the original party.

NOTE: Substitution of a new contract is the core of novation. If the new contract suffers from legal flaw, such as want of registration, stamps, etc., on account of which it becomes unenforceable, the original contract will not be extinguished and there would be no novation. [*Vishram Arjun* v *Irukulla Shankariah* AIR 1957 AP 784].

**Novus actus interveniens.** "There are invoked certain well-known formulae, such as that the chain of causation was broken, that there was a *novus actus interveniens*. These somewhat august phrases, sanctified as they are by standing authority, only mean that there was not such a direct relationship between the act of negligence and the injury that the one could be treated as flowing directly from the other". [*Lord* v *Pacific Steam Navigation Co., The Oropesa* (1943)1 All ER 211, 213 (CA), *per* Lord Wright].

NOTE: The maxim is set up as a defence sometimes against liability in tort. And the question is how far the general principles of remoteness of damage are affected by the circumstance that the damage has been brought about by the *novus actus interveniens* of person other than the defendant himself. If the consequence is foreseeable, then the defendant is liable; if not, then the defendant is not liable. As observed by Greer, L.J. in *Haynes* v *Harwood* [(1935)1 KB 146, 156]: "If what is relied upon as *novus actus interveniens* is the very kind of thing which is likely to happen if the want of care which is alleged takes place, the principle embodied in the maxim is no defence. The whole question is whether or not the accident can be said to be 'the natural and probable result' of the breach of duty."

**Noxious.** Adverse; bad; baneful; causing danger; contaminated; damaging; dangerous; deleterious; detrimental; fatal; fraught with danger; harmful; hazardous; hurtful; injurious; lethal; menacing; perilous; pernicious; poisonous; precarious; unhealthy.

▸*Meaning under the Prevention of Food Adulteration Act 1954, s. 2(xv).* The word 'noxious' when used in relation to an article of food means that the article is harmful to health or repugnant to human use.

**Nudum pactum.** A bare agreement or promise. It means an agreement without consideration and upon which no action lies unless it be under seal.

**Nuisance.** Nuisance is that activity which arises from unreasonable, unwarranted or unlawful use by a person of his own property, working obstruction or injury to right of another, or to the public, and producing such material annoyance, inconvenience and discomfort that law will presume resulting damage. [*State ex rel. Herman* v *Cardon* 530 P 2d 1115, 1118].

That which annoys and disturbs one in possession of his property, rendering its ordinary use or occupation physically uncomfortable to him. [*Patton* v *Westwood Country Club Co.* 247 NE 2d 761, 763].

A cause or source of annoyance, especially a continuing or repeated invasion or disturbance of another's right, or anything that works a hurt, inconvenience or damage. [*Renken* v *Harvey Aluminium (Inc.)* DC Or, 226 F Supp 169, 175].

"A nuisance must be something which diminishes the value of the plaintiffs' property or interferes with their use or enjoyment of it. The question is one of difficulty and is necessarily one of degree". [*Smith* v *Jaffray* (1886)2 TLR 480, 482 (DC), *per* Grove, J.].

"Any material interference with the ordinary comfort of existence: that would be a nuisance". [*Tod-Heatly* v *Benham* (1888), 40 Ch D 80, 98 (CA), *per* Bowen, L.J.].

This word is incapable of exact or exhaustive definition. It is derived from French word *nuire* which means to injure, hurt or harm. According to *Shorter Oxford Dictionary*, it means 'anything injurious or obnoxious to the community, or to the individual as a member of it, for which some legal remedy may be found'. Literally anything that causes annoyance or that works hurt or injury, harm or prejudice to an individual or the public or anything wrongfully done or permitted which injures or annoys another in the legitimate enjoyment of his legal rights would constitute nuisance. It may be an interference in the enjoyment of property or interference with one's personal comfort. To put it in short, anything done which unwarrantably affects the rights of others, endangers life or health, gives offence to the senses, violates the law of decency or obstructs the comfortable and reasonable use of property, may amount to nuisance. No precise rule can be laid down as to the degree of inconvenience or discomfort that would be a nuisance, but to constitute nuisance the injury caused must be real and not fanciful or imaginary. It must not be such as results only in trifling inconvenience. [*Niader Mal* v *Ugar Sain Jain* AIR 1966 Punj 509: ILR 2 Punj 609: 1965 Punj LR (Supp) 103, quoted in *Gogal Waman* v *Krishanaji Talyarao* (1979)1 Kant LJ 319].

- **Abatement of nuisance** p. 4.
- **Private nuisance** p. 687.
- **Public nuisance** p. 710.

**Null and void.** Means "of no legal effect".

> NOTE: It is a nullity, *e.g.*, an agreement for an illegal consideration. It cannot be enforced, and, in general, money paid under it cannot be recovered by the power.

**Nulla bona.** It relates to the sheriff's return to the writ of *fi. fa.* of "no goods".

**Nullity.** Non-existence; non-being; invalidity.

"Nullity" is a void act or an act having no legal force or validity. [*Krishan Lal* v *State of J&K* (1994)4 SCC 422: JT 1994(2) SC 619: (1994)2 SLJ 64].

> NOTE: A decree is said to be "nullity" if it is passed by a court having no inherent jurisdiction. Merely because a court erroneously passes a decree or there is an error while passing the decree, the decree cannot be called a nullity. The decree to be called a nullity is to be understood in the sense that it is *ultra vires* the powers of the court passing the decree and not merely voidable decree. [*Haralal Moolchand Doshi* v *Barot Raman Lal Ranchhoddas* AIR 1993 SC 1449: (1993)2 SCC 458].
>
> *"Nullity" and "irregularity"—distinction.* "Irregularity" is want of adherence to some prescribed rule or mode of proceeding; whereas "nullity" is a void act or an act having no legal force or validity. The safest rule of distinction between "irregularity" and a "nullity" is to see whether a party can waive the objection; if he can waive, it amounts to irregularity and if he cannot, it is a nullity. [*Krishan Lal* v *State of J&K* (1994)4 SCC 422: JT 1994(2) SC 619: (1994)2 SLJ 64].

**Nullity of marriage.** A marriage declared by a competent court to be a nullity.

> NOTE: In India there are various statutes regulating marriages. Under each of such statutes provision has been made for declaration of nullity of marriage. [Hindu Marriage Act 1955, s. 11; Divorce Act 1869, ss. 18 and 19; Special Marriage Act 1954, s. 24].
>
> The result of a decree of nullity of marriage is that not only are the parties not now married, but they never were. [*In re Wombwell's Settlement* (1922)2 Ch 298, 305, *per* Russell, J.].

**Nullius filius.** The son of no man.

> NOTE: This expression sometimes is applied to a bastard, that is to say, a child born out of wedlock.

**Nullum simile est idem.** Nothing similar is the same.

**Nuncupative will.** A nuncupative will is a will declared by a testator before a sufficient number of witnesses. Such a will is also called an oral will.

> NOTE: When a man makes a nuncupative will he must name his executor and declare his whole mind before witnesses. There is no scope for this kind of will under the Indian Succession Act 1925; but where the Act does not apply a will can be made orally. [*Kalian Singh* v *Sanwal Singh* 7 All 163]. It is, therefore, not competent for any person governed by the Indian Succession Act 1925, to make a nuncupative or oral will. As the Hindus are governed by this Act, they are not competent to make oral wills. But Muhammedans are still competent to make oral wills as they are outside the purview of the Indian Succession Act 1925.

**Nuptias non concubitus sed consensus facie.** No cohabitation but consent makes the marriage.

**Nursery.** A place where young trees are nurtured for the purpose of being transplanted into orchards, gardens, plantations etc.

A room in a house for the special use of young children.

# Oo

**Oath.** Any form of attestation by which a person signifies that he is bound in conscious to perform an act faithfully and truthfully. [*Vaughn* v *State* 177 SW 2d 59, 60].

Affirmation and declaration in the case of persons by law allowed to affirm or declare instead of swearing. [General Clauses Act 1897, s. 3(37)].

"An oath is a religious asseveration, by which a person renounces the mercy and imprecates the vengeance of Heaven if he do not speak the truth". [*R.* v *White* Leach 430, 431].

NOTE: 'Oath' includes a solemn affirmation substituted by law for an oath, and any declaration required or authorised by law to be made before a public servant or to be used for the purpose of proof, whether in a Court of Justice or not. [Indian Penal Code 1860, s. 51].

The procedure of administering oaths is dealt with in the Oaths Act 1969.

**Obiter dictum.** Something said in passing; words of an opinion entirely unnecessary for the decision of the case [*Noel* v *Olds* 138 F 2d 581, 586].

*Obiter dicta* are what the words literally signify, namely, statements by the way. [*Flower* v *Ebbw Vale Steel, Iron & Coal Co.* (1934)2 KB 132].

An 'obiter dictum' is an observation by a judge which is either not necessary for the decision of the case or does not relate to the material facts in issue. [*Jayarama Iyer* v *State* ILR (1953) Hyd 573: AIR 1954 Hyd 56].

NOTE: If a judge thinks it desirable to give his opinion on some point which is not necessary for the decision of the case, that of course has not the binding weight of the decision of the case, and the reasons for the decision. [*Flower* v *Ebbw Vale Steel, Iron & Coal Co.* (1934)2 KB 132, 154].

**Object.** As noun means aim; design; destination; end; final cause; goal; material product; material substance; purpose; subject; substance; target; ultimate purpose; a person or thing to which thought, feeling, or action is directed; something sought to be attained or accomplished.

As verb means attack; be at variance; call in question; challenge; complain; controvert; criticise; disapprove; find fault; oppose; put forward as an objection; state in opposition.

It is judicially defined to be anything which comes within the cognizance or scrutiny of the senses, especially anything tangible or visible. [*Moore* v *Union Mut. Fire Ins. Co.* 22 A 2d 503, 505].

**Obligation.** It is a generic word, derived from the Latin substantive "obligatio", having many, wide, and varied meanings, according to the context in which it is used.

In application to 'duty', it means burden; charge; commitment; compulsion; duty owed; legal responsibility; moral responsibility; performance owed; responsibility; that which a person owes to another; that which is due from a person.

In application to 'liability', it means accountability; amount due; duty to pay money; outstanding debt; that which is owing; unpaid debt; unliquidated claim.

'Obligation' is that which a person is bound to do or forbear; any duty imposed by law, promise, contract, relations of society, courtesy, kindness, etc. [*Rucks-Brandt Const. Co.* v *Price* 23 P 2d 690; *Helvering* v *British American Tobacco Co.* CCA, 69 F 2d 528, 530].

'Obligation' means a binding duty as per agreement or contract, implied or express. The word, according to Osborn's *Concise Law Dictionary*, 4th Ed., means 'a duty, the bond of legal necessity which binds together two or more determinate individuals. It is limited to legal duties arising out of special personal relationship existing whether by reason of a contract or a tort, or otherwise, between two or more individual persons'. The word 'obligation' implies not a moral duty but a legal duty which can be enforced by law and which is imposed upon a person by an outside agency or a third party in respect of the subject matter [*State* v *Iswar Damodar Jew* AIR 1976 Cal 46, 51].

Obligation includes every duty enforceable by law. [Specific Relief Act 1963, s. 2(*a*)]. It is a legal obligation and not merely a social or moral obligation. [*Hyderabad Stock Exchange Ltd.* v *Ranganath Rathi & Co.* AIR 1958 AP 43: (1957)2 Andh WR 10].

The word 'obligation' in s. 54 of the Specific Relief Act 1877, may be taken to be a tie or bond which constrains a person to do or suffer something. It implies a right in another person to which it is correlated and it restricts the freedom of the obligee with respect to definite acts and forbearances but in order that it may be enforced by a court, it must be a legal obligation, and not merely moral, social or religious. [*Hyderabad Stock Exchange* v *Rangnath Rathi* AIR 1958 AP 43].

• **Imperfect obligation** p. 432.

**Obligee.** The person in whose favour an obligation or bond is entered into; a creditor.

**Obligor.** One who is under any legal obligation; a debtor.

**Obliterate.** To destroy utterly; leave no trace of; abolish; annihilate; blot out; wipe out; snuff out; stamp out; demolish; eliminate; destroy; dissipate; efface; erase; exterminate; nullify; obscure; remove the traces; render illegible; render imperceptible.

**Obliteration.** Destruction; annihilation; dissipation; elimination; extermination; wiping out; erasure or blotting out of written words.

Obliteration is the act of obliterating.

NOTE: Placing of a piece of paper over writing would be an obliteration. [*Flinch* v *Combe* (1894) P 191].

No obliteration made in any unprivileged will after the execution thereof shall have any effect, except so far as the words or meaning of the will have been thereby rendered illegible or undiscernible. [Indian Succession Act 1925, s. 71].

**Obscene.** Bawdy; debauched; foul; immodest; immoral; impure; indecent; lascivious; lecherous; lewd; libidinous; licentious; lubricous; lustful; offensive to decency; offensive to modesty; pornographic; salacious; sexy; tending to excite lustful desires; unchaste; unwholesome; vulgar; something that offends against the recognised standards of propriety.

In its ordinary and literal meaning, the word 'obscene' means repulsive, filthy, loathsome, indecent and lewd. [*Public Prosecutor* v *A.D. Sabapathy* AIR 1958 Mad 210: 1958 Cr LJ 647].

The word 'obscene' is not defined in the Penal Code; but it may be taken as meaning offensive to chastity or modesty, expressing or personating to the mind or view something that delicacy, purity and decency forbid to be expressed. [*Ranjeet* v *State of Maharashtra* (1965)1 SCR 65].

NOTE: Basic guidelines for trier of fact in determining whether a work which depicts or describes sexual conduct is obscene is whether the average person, applying contemporary community standards would find that the work, taken as a whole, appeals to the prurient interest, whether the work depicts or describes, in a patently offensive way, sexual conduct specifically defined by the applicable state law, and whether the work, taken as a whole, lacks serious literary, artistic, political, or scientific value. [*Miller* v *California* 37 L Ed 2d 419].

In order that an article should be obscene, it must have the tendency to corrupt the morals of those in whose hands it may fall. [*Public Prosecutor* v *A.D. Sabapathi* AIR 1958 Mad 210: 1958 Cr LJ 647].

*'Indecent' and 'obscene'—difference.* See under 'INDECENT'.

**Obscenity.** Bawdiness; dirtiness; indecency; lechery; lewdness; lubricity; pornography; salaciousness; scurrility; unchastity; vileness; vulgarity; the character or quality of being obscene; conduct tending to corrupt the public morals by its indecency; or lewdness.

NOTE: The classic definition delivered by Cockburn, C.J., in the Queen's Bench in 1868, in *R.* v *Hicklin* [(1868) LR 3 QB 360] was: "... the test of obscenity (in connection with a publication) is this, whether the tendency of the matter charged as obscenity is to deprave and corrupt those whose minds are open to such immoral influences, and into whose hands a publication of this sort may fall".

This test known as the "Hicklin" test given by Cockburn, C.J., in *R.* v *Hicklin* (supra) has been approved by Supreme Court in *Ranjeet* v *State of Maharashtra* [(1965)1 SCR 65].

*'Vulgarity' and 'obscenity'—distinction.* Vulgarity arouses a feeling of disgust and revulsion and also boredom but does not have the effect of depraving, debasing and corrupting the morals of any reader of the novel, whereas obscenity has the tendency to deprave and corrupt those whose minds are open to such immoral influences. [*Samaresh Bose* v *Amal Mitra* 1985 Supp (3) SCR 17: (1985)4 SCC 289: 1985 SCC (Cri) 523: AIR 1986 SC 967: 1986 Cr LJ 24].

*Obscenity and pornography—distinction.* There is difference between obscenity and pornography. Pornography denotes writings, picture etc. intended to arouse sexual desire. But obscenity includes writings etc. not intended to do so but which have that tendency. Both offend public decency and morals. Pornography is obscenity in a more aggravated form. [*P.K. Somanath* v *State of Kerala* 1990 Cr LJ 542, 545].

**Obsolete.** Abandoned; anachronous; antiquated; bygone; discarded; discontinued; disused; extinct; fallen into desuetude; fallen into disuse; no longer in use; out-of-date; out of use; outdated; outmoded; outworn; timeworn.

That which is no longer used. [*Becker* v *Anhenser-Busch, Inc.* CCA Mo, 120 F 2d 403, 416].

NOTE: A law or practice which has ceased to be enforced or be in use by reason of change of manner and circumstances is said to be obsolete. But however obsolete a statute may be, it does not become legally obsolete by mere non-user, though the fact of non-user may be important when the question is whether there has been a repeal by implication. [Jowitt's *Dictionary of English Law*, 2nd Ed.].

A restrictive covenant may become obsolete if the character of the estate changes so that a time comes when the purpose for which the covenant was imposed for the benefit of the estate can no longer be achieved. [*Re, Truman, Hanbury Buxton & Co's Application* (1956)1 QB 261; Stroud's *Judicial Dictionary*, 5th Ed.].

A machine may become obsolete due to total destruction or supersession by new invention. [*Ratna Singh, in re* AIR 1925 Mad 157].

**Obstruct.** Bar; barricade; block; bring to a standstill; choke; circumscribe; frustrate; hamper; hinder; impede; interfere with; interrupt; intervene; stand in the way; thwart; trammel.

To hinder or prevent from progress, check, stop, also to retard the progress of, make accomplishment of difficult and slow. [*Conley* v *United States* CCA Minn, 59 F 2d 929, 936].

One of the general meanings of the word 'obstruct' is to impede, hinder or retard. [*Nazim* v *State* AIR 1957 All 829].

**Obstructed and unobstructed heritage.** The Mitakshara School of Hindu law divides property into two classes, namely, unobstructed heritage and obstructed heritage. Property in which a person acquires an interest by birth is called unobstructed heritage. It is called unobstructed because the accrual of the right to it is not obstructed by the existence of the owner. Thus, property inherited by a Hindu from his father, father's father, or father's father's father is unobstructed heritage as regards his own male issue, that is, his son, grandson and great grandson. His male issues acquire an interest in it from the moment of their birth. Their right to it arises from the mere fact of their birth in the family, and they become coparceners with their paternal ancestor in such property immediately on their birth.

Property, the right to which accrues not by birth but on the death of the last owner without leaving a male issue, is called obstructed heritage. Thus, the property which devolves on parents, brothers, nephews, uncles, etc., upon the death of the last owner is obstructed heritage. Their right to the property arises for the first time on the death of the owner.

NOTE: Unobstructed heritage devolves by survivorship; obstructed heritage by succession.

According to the Dayabhaga, all heritage is obstructed, for, according to the doctrines of that school, no person, not even a son, takes an interest by birth in the property of another. [Mulla's *Hindu Law*, 15th Ed., p. 287].

**Obstructing justice.** Impeding or obstructing those who seek justice in a court, or those who have duties or powers of administering justice therein.

The term applies also to obstructing the administration of justice in any way—as by hindering witnesses from appearing, assaulting process server, obstructing court orders or criminal investigations.

Any act, conduct intended to play on human frailty and to deflect and deter court from performance of its duty and drive it into compromise with its own unfettered judgment by placing it, through medium of knowingly false assertion, in wrong position before public, constitutes an obstruction to administration of justice. [*Toledo Newspaper Co.* v *U.S.* 247 US 402: 38 S Ct 560: 62 L Ed 1186].

**Obstructing process under law.** It means to commit the punishable offence of intentionally hindering the officers of the law in the execution of their duties. [*Nazim* v *State* AIR 1957 All 829].

**Obstruction.** Bar; barricade; barrier; blockade; blockage; clog; constraint; constriction; curb; difficulty; embargo; hindrance; hurdle; impediment; impedition; interference; interruption; limitation; obstacle; preclusion; prohibition; proscription; restraint; restriction; shackle; snag; trammel.

The word 'obstruction' connotes some overt act in the nature of violence or show of violence. It cannot be said that a man obstructs another if that man runs away from arrest, or if he does not actually submit to the arrest. [*Phudhki* v *State* 1955 Cr LJ 278: AIR 1955 All 104].

▸*Meaning under Employees' State Insurance Act 1948, s. 45A.* The word 'obstruction' has to be construed in its narrow sense so as to confine it to an act of physical obstacle, use of force or threatened use of force, a deliberate hurdle preventing an officer from exercising his functions or discharging his duties, and it would not include mere failure to submit an information or to produce books of account. [*Masco Pvt. Ltd.* v *ESI Corporation* (1975)1 Lab LN 131: 1975 Lab IC 562 (Del)].

▸*Meaning under Customs Act 1962, s. 133.* For the purposes of the section obstruction is not confined to physical obstruction and it includes anything which makes it more difficult for the police or public servant to carry out their duties. [*Collector of Customs & Central Excise* v *Paradip Port Trust* (1990)4 SCC 250: AIR 1990 SC 1897].

**Obstruction to a highway.** Obstruction to a highway means doing something which permanently or temporarily removes the whole or part of the highway from public use altogether. [*Trevett* v *Lee* (1955)1 All ER 406].

**Obtain.** Acquire; be in receipt of; come into possession; enter into possession; gain possession; get hold of by effort; get possession of; secure; take possession; acquire in any way.

Procured with effect. It describes a situation when one procures a thing despite opposition from others. [*Zohra Khatoon* v *Md. Ibrahim* AIR 1981 SC 1243: (1981)2 SCR 910: 1981 Cr LJ 754: (1981)2 SCC 509: 1981 SCC (Cri) 517].

▸ *Meaning under the Prevention of Corruption Act 1947, s. 5(1)(d).* The word 'obtain' does not eliminate the idea of acceptance of what is given or offered to be given, though it connotes also an element of effort on the part of the receiver. [*Ram Krishan* v *State of Delhi* 1956 SCR 182: AIR 1956 SC 476: 1956 SCJ 432: 1956 SCC 247: 1956 Cr LJ 837].

The word obtain contemplates demand and acceptance. [*Darshan Singh* v *State of Punjab* 1989 Cr LJ (NOC) 177 (Punj): (1989)95 Punj LR 71: (1988)2 All Cr LR 1012].

'Obtain' means to secure or gain (something) as the result of request or effort. In case of obtainment the initiative vests in the person who received. [*C.K. Damodaran Nair* v *Govt. of India* AIR 1997 SC 551: (1997)9 SCC 477: 1997 SCC (Cri) 654: 1997 Cr LJ 739: JT 1997(2) SC 494].

▸ *Meaning under the Representation of the People Act 1951, s. 123(7).* The word 'obtain' has been used in the sense and meaning which connotes purpose or effort behind the action of the candidate. It does not mean mere passive receipt of assistance without the candidate being even conscious of the fact that the assistance has been rendered. [*Motilal* v *Mungla Prasad* AIR 1958 All 794; *Biresh Misra* v *Ram Nath* AIR 1959 Assam 139].

**Obvious imitation.** An obvious imitation is something which is very close to the original design, the resemblance to the original design being immediately apparent to the eye looking at the two. [*Dunlop Rubber Co. Ltd.* v *Golf Ball Developments Ltd.* (1931)48 RPC 268, 279].

**Occasion.** As noun means advent; affair; chance; conjuncture; episode; event; happening; incident; occurrence; situation; suitable time; condition of affairs; juncture affording ground or reason for something.

As verb means to cause or bring about by furnishing the condition or opportunity for the action of some other cause. [*Smart* v *Raymond* Mo App, 142 SW 2d 100, 104].

> NOTE: An 'occasion' is not a period of twenty-four hours. If we say that a man took out an assurance policy on the occasion of his marriage, we do not mean 'on the day of his marriage', but rather 'at or about the time of his marriage', with the implication that the coincidence in time was designed and not accidental. [*Ideal Life Assurance Co. Ltd.* v *Hirschfield (H.J.) of Hirschfield (A.H.)* (1943)1 KB 442 (CA)].

**Occupation.** Used as 'vocation', it means activity; avocation; business; calling; career; chosen work; employment; livelihood; mission; profession; pursuit; speciality; trade; venture; that which primarily takes up one's time, thought and energies; whatever one follows as the means of making a livelihood.

'Occupation' means activity in a specific line of endeavour which engages or occupies time and attention of a person and which is carried on with a certain amount of continuity or regularity in the sense that it is not 'momentary'—not an isolated or semi-occasional and temporary adventure. [*Commissioner of Expenditure-Tax, Gujarat I* v *Ambalal Sarabhai* (1969)73 ITR 78 (Guj): AIR 1970 Guj 141; *Mridula A. Sarabhai* v *Commissioner of Expenditure-Tax, Gujarat I* (1969)73 ITR 85 (Guj)].

An employ by which a person earns his living in his occupation. [*Adams* v *Graham* (1864) New Rep 372]. The trade or calling by which one ordinarily seeks to get his livelihood. [*Luckin* v *Hamlyn* (1869)21 LT 366].

The word 'occupation' particularly refers to the vocation, profession, trade or calling in which a person is engaged for hire or for profit, and it has been repeatedly held that a person's principal business and chief means of obtaining livelihood constitutes his occupation. The term expresses an idea of continuity, a continuous series of transactions and implies regularity in a specific line of activity. Furthermore, time is a necessary ingredient, and, although it need not be protracted, it must not be momentary. It does not include an isolated or semi-occasional and temporary adventure in another line of adventure. No universal test can, however, be laid down for determining when an activity amounts to an occupation and when it does not. [*Commissioner of Expenditure-tax* v *Ambalal Sarabhai* AIR 1970 Guj 141].

Used as 'possession', it means control; domination; dominion; tenure; the act or process by which real property is possessed and enjoyed; the act or process of taking possession of a place or area; the holding and control of an area by a foreign military force.

In its comprehensive sense, it means possession, actual or constructive, but, in its strict sense, actual possession and use. [*Sainava Umma* v *Kunhammad* 1957 Ker LT 563].

The word 'occupation' means possession which includes both the actual physical possession and deemed physical possession. [*Ratan Lal Rai* v *Sheo Kumar Kamalia* (1996)1 Pat LJR 217].

Occupation means that the owner is in actual physical enjoyment of the house, property or estate by himself, his agents or servants. Strictly speaking, occupation by the owner cannot include the case of sub-tenants, for the actual occupation is in them. A limited form of occupation is residence which involves the dwelling for some time in the year by the owner or his family or by his domestic servants. [*Martin Estates Co. Ltd.* v *Watt & Hunter* 1925 NI 79, 85].

Occupation means actual holding. It is not necessary that the person claiming to occupy should be living on it or using it as a residence. The owner can occupy a place by making use of it in any manner. [*Ramniklal Pitambardas* v *Indradaman Amratlal* AIR 1964 SC 1676].


- **Actual occupation** p. 35.
- **Gainful occupation** p. 380.
- **Traditional occupation** p. 850.
- **Unauthorised occupation** p. 861.


**Occupational disease.** See INDUSTRIAL DISEASE p. 452.

**Occupied territory.** Any territory of a country which is for the time being in the occupation of another country.

**Occupier.** An occupant; one who is in the enjoyment of a thing.

In common parlance, an 'occupier' is one who 'takes' or (more usually) 'holds' possession. In the legal sense, an occupier is a person in actual occupation. [*Industrial Supplies Pvt. Ltd.* v *Union of India* AIR 1980 SC 1858: (1980)4 SCC 341: (1981)1 SCR 375].

- *Meaning under the Employment of Children Act 1938, s. 2(b).* The person who has ultimate control over the affairs of the workshop.
- *Meaning under the Cotton Ginning and Pressing Factories Act 1925, s. 2(g).* 'Occupier' includes a managing agent or other person authorised to represent the occupier.
- *Meaning under the Indian Cotton Cess Act 1923, s. 2(ee); Produce Cess Act 1966, s. 2(h).* 'Occupier' in relation to a mill means the person who has ultimate control over the affairs of the mill and where the said affairs are entrusted to a managing agent, such agent shall be deemed to be the occupier of the mill.
- *Meaning under the Cantonments Act 1924, s. 2(xxiii).* 'Occupier' includes an owner in occupation of, or otherwise using, his own land or building.
- *Meaning under the Slum Areas (Improvement and Clearance) Act 1956, s. 2(f).* 'Occupier' includes—(*a*) any person who for the time being is paying or is liable to pay to the owner the rent or any portion of the rent of the land or building in respect of which such rent is paid or is payable; (*b*) an owner in occupation of, or otherwise using his land or building; (*c*) a rent-free tenant of any land or building; (*d*) a licensee in occupation of any land or building; and (*e*) any person who is liable to pay to the owner damages for the use and occupation of any land or building.

▸*Meaning under the Factories Act 1948, s. 2(n); Employees' State Insurance Act 1948, s. 2(15); Employees' Provident Funds and Miscellaneous Provisions Act 1952, s. 2(k).* 'Occupier' of a factory means the person who has the ultimate control over the affairs of the factory and where the said affairs are entrusted to a managing agent, such agent shall be deemed to be the occupier of the factory.

'Occupier' plainly means the person who runs the factory or warehouse, who regulates and controls the work that is done there, and who is responsible for the fulfilment of the provisions of the Factories Act within it.

NOTE: An occupier need not have exclusive occupation. It will suffice if he has some degree of control. [*Wheat* v *Lacon (E.) & Co. Ltd.* (1966)1 All ER 582]. A statutory tenant under the Rent Restriction Act is an occupier. [*Brown* v *Ministry of Housing and Local Government* (1953)2 All ER 1385].

The expression 'occupier' is not to be equated with 'owner'. The ultimate control over a factory must necessarily be with an owner unless the owner has completely transferred that control to another person. [*John Donald Mackenzie* v *Chief Inspector of Factories* AIR 1962 SC 1351: (1961)2 Lab LJ 412].

**Octroi.** 'Octroi' is a tax levied on the entry of goods within a particular area. [*Ram Krishna Ram Nath Agarwal* v *Secretary, Municipal Committee, Kamptee* 1950 SCR 15: 1950 SCJ 148: AIR 1950 SC 11].

Octrois are taxes on goods brought into the local area for consumption, use or sale. [*M/s. Hiralal Thakorlal Dalal* v *Broach Municipality* AIR 1976 SC 1446: 1976 (Supp) SCR 82: (1976)3 SCC 398].

NOTE: *'Octrois' and 'terminal taxes'—distinction.* Octrois and terminal taxes are different, though they resemble in one respect, namely, that they are leviable in respect of goods brought into a local area. While terminal taxes are leviable on goods imported or exported from the municipal limits, denoting thereby that they are connected with the traffic of goods, octrois are leviable in respect of goods brought into a municipal area for consumption or use or sale. [*Burmah Shell Oil Storage* v *Belgaum Borough Municipality* AIR 1963 SC 906: (1963)2 SCA 221].

See also TERMINAL TAX p. 837.

**Offence.** Breach of the law; criminal deed; unlawful act; wrongdoing; criminality; delinquency; disobedience; evil behaviour; evil deed; infraction; infringement; illegal act; illegal conduct; illegality; impropriety; malefaction; malfeasance; malversation; misdemeanour; misfeasance; transgression.

'Offence' generally is regarded as an action which offends against some statutory provision or involves some crime or misdemeanour known to the common law. [*Re Derbyshire County Council and Derby Corporation* (1896)2 QB 53].

Offence generally implies infringement of public rights as distinguished from mere private rights punishable under criminal law. [*Depot Manager, A.P. State Road Transport Corporation* v *Mohd. Yousuf Miya* (1997)2 SCC 699: 1997 SCC (L&S) 548].

▸*Meaning under the General Clauses Act 1897, s. 3(38).* Any act or omission made punishable by any law for the time being in force.

▸*Meaning under the Border Security Force Act 1968, s. 2(q).* Any act or omission punishable under the Border Security Force Act and includes a civil offence.

▸*Meaning under the Indian Penal Code 1860, s. 40.* Except the chapters and sections mentioned in cls. (2) and (3) of s. 40 of IPC, the word 'offence' denotes a thing made punishable by this Code. In Chapters IV, VA and in ss. 64, 65, 66, 67, 71, 109, 110, 112, 114, 115, 116, 117, 187, 194, 195, 203, 211, 213, 214, 221, 222, 223, 224, 225, 327, 328, 329, 330, 331, 347, 348, 388, 389 and 445, the word 'offence' denotes a thing punishable under this Code or under any special or local law as hereinafter defined. And in ss. 141, 176, 177, 201, 202, 212, 216 and 441, the word 'offence' has the same meaning when the thing punishable under the special or local law is punishable under such law with imprisonment for a term of six months or upwards, whether with or without fine.

▸*Meaning under the Air Force Act 1950, s. 4(xxii).* Offence means any act or omission punishable under the Air Force Act and includes a civil offence.

▸*Meaning under the Army Act 1950, s. 3(xvii).* Offence means any act or omission punishable under the Army Act and includes a civil offence.

▸*Meaning under the Children Act, s. 2(n).* Offence means any offence punishable under any law for the time being in force.

▸*Meaning under the Code of Criminal Procedure 1973, s. 2(n).* Offence means any act or omission made punishable by any law for the time being in force, and it also includes any act in respect of which a complaint may be made under s. 20 of the Cattle Trespass Act 1871.

Section 3(30) of the Bengal General Clauses Act and s. 4 of the Cr. P.C. define "offence" to mean "any act or omission made punishable by any law for the time being in force. [*Sethia Properties* v *T.R. Bhavanani* AIR 1961 Cal 199].

NOTE: An offence means any act or omission made punishable *by any law for the time being in force*. The words under *italics* mean punishable by an Indian law in force in India. So conviction by a Swiss Court for an offence punishable under the Swiss law cannot put an officer to penalties consequent to a conviction for an offence. [*Sushanta Mukherjee* v *Union of India* 79 CWN 796: 1975 CHN 239].

Breach of Customs laws entailing a monetary penalty or forfeiture of goods concerned would be offences as contemplated by Art. 20(3) of the Constitution of India. [*Collector of Customs* v *Calcutta Motor and Cycle Co.* AIR 1958 Cal 682].

• **Accused of any offence** p. 25.
• **Civil offence** p. 145.
• **Continuing offence** p. 187.
• **Extradition offence** p. 334.
• **Matrimonial offence** p. 569.
• **Non-bailable offence** p. 609.
• **Non-cognizable offence** p. 609.
• **Political offence** p. 669.

**Offender.** A person who has committed a crime.

Commonly used in statutes to indicate person implicated in the commission of a crime and includes person guilty of a misdemeanour or traffic offence. [*State ex rel. Smith* v *Jauceson* 19 NW 2d 505, 508].

• **Absconding offender** p. 8.
• **First offender** p. 356.
• **Juvenile offender** p. 501.

**Offer.** As verb means bring forward; hold forth; hold out; invite; lay before; make a bid; make a proposition; make an overture; put forth for acceptance; produce; tender performance; to make a proposal to.

As noun means a commitment to do or refrain from doing some specified thing in the future; a promise; a proposal to do a thing or pay an amount; usually accompanied by an expected acceptance, counter-offer, return promise or act.

An offer or, as it is sometimes called, a proposal means the signification by one person to another of his willingness to enter into a contract with him on certain terms. It may be express or may be implied from the conduct of the party. A mere statement of a person's intention or declaration of his willingness to enter into negotiation is not an offer, and cannot be accepted so as to form a binding contract. [Halsbury's *Laws of England*, 3rd Ed., vol. 8, p. 69].

▸*Meaning under the Indian Contract Act 1872, s. 2(a).* When one person signifies to another his willingness to do or abstain from doing anything with a view to obtaining the assent of that other to such act or abstinence, he is said to make an offer (proposal).

NOTE: The display of an article with a price on it in a shop window is merely an invitation to treat. It is in no sense an offer for sale the acceptance of which constitutes a contract. [*Fisher* v *Bell* (1960)3 All ER 731].

The word 'offer' in the expression 'offers for sale or hire' in s. 51(1)(*b*) of the Copyright Act 1957, is not synonymous with the word 'proposal' in the Indian Contract Act 1872. [*J.H. Bagga* v *A.I.R. Ltd.* AIR 1969 Bom 302: 71 Bom LR 409].

• **Retract an offer** p. 759.

**Offering.** Things offered.

NOTE: In the absence of any custom or express declaration by the donor to the contrary, the offerings made to an idol established for public worship are to be taken to be intended for the maintenance of the shrine with all its rites, ceremonies and charities, and not to become the personal property of the priests. [*Lokenath* v *Batakrishna* AIR 1963 Ori 115].

**Office.** A right, and corresponding duty, to exercise a public trust; a public charge or employment; an assigned duty or function; a position of (especially public) trust or authority.

An office is "a right to exercise a public or private employment, and to take the fees and employments thereunto belonging". [2 Bl Com 36].

An "office" means a public or private employment with certain duties to be performed. [*Dewan Joynal Abedin* v *Abdul Wazed Mian* JT 1987(4) SC 642: 1988 (Supp) SCC 580: (1988)2 SCR 370].

By 'office' is meant the right and duty to exercise an employment or a position of authority and trust to which certain duties are attached. [*Shrilekha Vidyarthi (Kumari)* v *State of U.P.* 1990 Supp (1) SCR 625: JT 1990(4) SC 211: 1990(6) SLR 1: AIR 1991 SC 537: 1991 SCC (L&S) 74].

Its other meaning is a place for the regular transaction of business or performance of a particular service.

An office necessarily implies that there is some duty to be performed. [*Heartley* v *Banks* 5 CBNS 55].

NOTE: The word 'office' has various meanings depending upon its context. An Advocate appointed as a Special Government Pleader to assist the Government Pleader in a particular case does not hold any office, and as such he cannot incur disqualification under Art. 191 of the Constitution. [*Kanta Kathuria* v *Manak Chand* AIR 1970 SC 694].

Its synonyms are post; appointment; situation; place, position.


- **Hereditary office** p. 412.
- **High political office** p. 414.
- **High public office** p. 414.
- **Holder of judicial office** see under JUDICIAL OFFICE p. 495.
- **Judicial office** p. 495.
- **Personal office** p. 660.
- **Principal office** p. 685.
- **Removal from office** p. 744.
- **Under colour of office** p. 862.


**Office of profit.** If "a profit does accrue to the holder of an office or employment by reason of his office or employment, such office or employment is an office or employment of profit". [*Cowan* v *Seymour* (1920)1 KB 500, 511 (CA), *per* Atkin, L.J.].

Office of profit is an office which carries with it remuneration, as distinct from an honorary office. [*Dale* v *Inland Revenue Commissioners* (1953)2 All ER 671: (1954) AC 11].

NOTE: The expression does not connote that the incumbent actually makes a profit from it; if it might reasonably be expected that a man would make a profit of it, it must be considered an office of profit. [*Delane* v *Hillcoat* 9 B&C 313].

An "office of profit" involves two elements namely that there should be such an office and that it should carry some remunerations. [*Chandrasekhar Raju* v *Vyricherla Pradeep Kumar Devi* AIR 1992 SC 1959: (1992)4 SCC 404: JT 1992(5) SC 417].

**Officer.** A person who holds an office of trust, authority, or command.

The ordinary dictionary meaning of the term "officer" is a person appointed or elected to a position of responsibility or authority in a government, society, etc. [*Mohinder Singh* v *State of Haryana* AIR 1989 SC 1367: JT 1989(2) SC 97: (1989)2 SCR 437: 1989(1) SLR 334: (1989)3 SCC 93].

NOTE: The true test in order to determine whether a person is an "officer" of the Government is: (*i*) whether he is in the service or pay of the Government and (*ii*) whether he is entrusted with the performance of any public duty. The public duty may be either a function of the Government delegated to him or may be a duty immediately auxiliary to that of someone who is an officer of the Government. [*G.A. Monterio* v *The State of Ajmer* AIR 1957 SC 13: 1956 SCR 682: 1956 SCJ 730].

**Official confidence.** In confidence of a person holding a position of office; in confidence of a person invested with the authority of an office.

NOTE: Section 124 of the Indian Evidence Act 1872, provides that no public officer shall be compelled to disclose communications made to him in official confidence when he considers that the public interests would suffer by the disclosure.

In dealing with an objection against the production of a document raised under s. 124 of the Indian Evidence Act, the court would have first to determine under s. 162 of the Indian Evidence Act whether the communication in question has been made in official confidence. If the answer to the said question is in the negative, then the document has to be produced; if the answer is in the affirmative, then it is for the officer concerned to decide whether the document should be produced or not. [*State of Punjab* v *Sodhi Sukdev* AIR 1961 SC 493].

**Official receiver.** A receiver appointed by the Government to take charge of the properties of a debtor pending the proceedings for insolvency under the provisions of the Provincial Insolvency Act 1920. On admitting an insolvency petition or thereafter the court may appoint an interim receiver (who may be official receiver) of the properties of the debtor. On making the order of adjudication the properties of the insolvent shall vest in the court or receiver (who may be official receiver). [Provincial Insolvency Act 1920, ss. 20 and 21].

**Official record.** Official records are those kept in the performance of duty by an officer even if not specifically required by statute. [*State* v *Biscoe* 537 P·2d 968, 969].

**Officiate.** Administer; carry out; conduct; discharge a function; fill an office; hold an office; occupy the chair; regulate; superintend; take the chair; *officio fungi*.

To act or to discharge an office, but it is sometimes used with the meaning of 'to act for', or to discharge an office on behalf of some other person. [*Shiv Dayal* v *State of U.P.* AIR 1953 All 664].

According to its ordinary connotation the word 'officiating' is generally used when a servant having held one post permanently or substantively is appointed to a post in a higher rank, but not permanently or substantively, while still retaining his lien on his substantive post *i.e.* officiating in that post till his confirmation. Such officiating appointment may be made when there is a temporary vacancy in a higher post due to the death or retirement of the incumbent or otherwise. In contrast, the word 'temporary' usually denotes a person appointed in the civil service for the first time and the appointment is not permanent but temporary i.e. for the time being, with no right to the post. [*Arun Kumar* v *S.E. Railway* AIR 1985 SC 482: (1985)2 SCC 451].

**Offspring.** The word 'offspring' is a general word; it may mean children. [*Thompson* v *Beasley* (1854)3 Drew 7, 9, *per* Kindersley, V.C.].

"Offspring" may have two meanings, children or issue. So far as the dictionaries are concerned children is the meaning first given. [*Tabuteau* v *Nixon* (1899)15 TLR 485, *per* Byrne, J.].

"The word 'offspring', like the words 'issue' and 'descendants', may be used in different senses. It may mean children only, or it may include more remote descendants ... In my opinion the term 'offspring', in its proper and natural sense, extends to every degree of lineal descendants, and has the same meaning as the word 'issue'. [*Young* v *Davies* (1863)2 Drew & Sm 167, 171, 172, *per* Kindersley].

**Oilfield.** Any area where any operation for the purpose of obtaining natural gas and petroleum, crude oil, refined oil, partially refined oil and any of the products of petroleum in a liquid or solid state, is to be or is being carried on. [Oilfields (Regulation and Development) Act 1948, s. 3(*e*); Payment of Gratuity Act 1972, s. 2(*l*)].

**O.K.** A conventional symbol of obscure origin much used in commercial practice and occasionally in indorsements on legal documents, signifying "correct", "approved", "accepted", "satisfactory", or "assented to".

The colloquial expression means correct, all right, to approve, and is of such common usage that it immediately conveys to the mind of person to whom it is addressed that a proposition submitted is agreed to. [*Muegler* v *Crosthwait* 179 SW 2d 761, 763].

The letters "O.K." on delivery notes and bills mean that the details in those documents are correctly given. [*Dawsons Bank* v *N.M.K.K. (Jap Trading Co.)* AIR 1935 PC 79].

**Okay.** See O.K. p. 623.

**Om.** The expression 'Om' is respected by the Hindus generally and has a special significance in the Hindu scriptures. It is recited at the commencement of the recitations of Hindu religious works. Macdonell in his '*A Practical Sanskrit Dictionary*' states that 'Om' is the sacred syllable used in invocations, at the commencement of prayers, at the beginning and the end of Vedic recitation, and as a respectful salutation; it is a subject of many mystical speculations. In the *Sanskrit-English Dictionary* by Monier-William, it is said that 'Om' is a sacred exclamation which may be uttered at the beginning and end of a reading of the Vedas or previously to any prayer; it is also regarded as a particle of auspicious salutation. But it is difficult to regard 'Om' which is a preliminary to an incantation or to religious books, as having high spiritual or mystical efficacy; it is used at the commencement of the recitations of religious prayers. [*Jagdev Singh Sidhanti* v *Pratap Singh Daulta* AIR 1965 SC 183, 187].

**Ombudsman.** An official or semi-official office to which people may come with grievances connected with the government. The ombudsman stands between, and represents, the citizen before the government.

NOTE: Its forerunner was the Swedish Justitie Ombudsman, first appointed in 1809. This institution was adopted by Finland in 1919, by Denmark in 1953 and by Norway in 1963. New Zealand opted for it in 1962 and England in 1967. But in England the Ombudsman became the Parliamentary Commissioner under the Parliamentary Commissioner Act 1967.

**Omission.** Default in performance; dereliction; failure to perform; passing over; remissness; slip; the act or an instance of omitting or being omitted; something that has been omitted or overlooked; neglect or failure to do something that can and should be done.

NOTE: An accidental omission occurs when something is left out by accident. [*Sutherland & Co.* v *Hannevig Brothers Ltd.* (1921)1 KB 336].

Omission denotes as well a series of omissions as a single omission. [Indian Penal Code 1860, s. 33].

**Omne principale trahit ad se accessorium.** Every principal thing draws to itself the accessory.

**Omne quod solo inaedficatur solo cedit.** Everything which is built upon the soil belongs to the soil.

**Omne testmentum morte consummatum est.** Every will is completed by death.

**Omnia praesumuntur rite esse acta.** All things are presumed to be correctly done.

**Omnibus.** All-embracing; all-inclusive; broad; collective compendious; composite; comprehensive; encyclopedic; encyclopedial; exhaustive; extensive; limitless; of great scope; pandemic; unrestricted; unqualified; unlimited; widespread; wide-reaching.

Relating to or dealing with numerous objects or items at once; including many things or various purposes. [Black's *Law Dictionary*, 8th Ed.].

▸ *Meaning under the Motor Vehicles Act 1988, s. 2(29).* Any motor vehicle constructed or adapted to carry more than six persons excluding the driver.

**On.** Upon; as soon as; near to; along; along side of; adjacent to; contiguous to; at the time of; following upon; in; during; at or in contact with upper surface of a thing.

The words 'on' or 'upon' may either mean before the act done to which it relates, or simultaneously with the act done, or after the act done, according as reason and good sense require, with reference to the context, and the subject-matter of the enactment. [*R.* v *Humphrey* (1839)10 Ad & El 335].

'On' may mean 'after' [*R.* v *Arkwright* (1848)12 QB 960].

In regard to commencement of tenancies, the words 'on', 'on and from', 'at' and 'from' are equivalent expressions. [*Sidebotham* v *Holland* (1895)1 QB 378: 64 LJQB 204].

**On account.** In part payment; in partial satisfaction of.

NOTE: A payment on account implies an acknowledgment of a liability for a larger sum. [*Friend* v *Young* (1897)2 Ch 421, 433].

**On allotment.** In its ordinary sense, it means "as and when allotted". [*Browne* v *Pickering & Co.* (1888)4 TLR 726 (CA), *per* Lord Esher].

**On behalf of.** The difference between the two expressions 'on behalf of' and 'for the benefit of' is well known and recognized in law. The former refers to the representative of the real owner and the latter the holder of legal ownership. [*Kripa Shankar* v *Commissioner of Wealth Tax* AIR 1966 Pat 371].

**On demand.** When presented or upon request for payment [Black's *Law Dictionary*, 7th Ed.].

As between banker and customer who are dealing on an overdraft account, 'on demand' means what it says. [*Lloyds Bank Ltd.* v *Margolis* (1954)1 All ER 734, 738].

The expression 'on demand' in a promissory note means payable immediately and no actual demand is necessary. [*Muthu Gounder* v *Perumayammal* AIR 1961 Mad 347].

NOTE: There is no legal difference between an obligation payable "when demanded" or "on demand" and once payable "on call" or "at any time called for". In each case the debt is payable on demand. [Black's *Law Dictionary*, 5th Ed.].

Ordinarily if money is payable on demand, it is payable at once without any demand [*Edwards* v *Walters* (1896)2 Ch 157, 166]; and the debtor must find out the creditor within reasonable time and pay him. [*Toms* v *Wilson* (1862)32 LJQB 33].

**On or before.** A stipulation to pay on or before a fixed date means an obligation to pay on the date fixed but there is an option to pay on an earlier date. [*Dagger* v *Shepherd* (1946) QB 215, 223].

The expression 'on or before the expiration of the lease' means 'at any time during the continuance of the lease'. [*Indian Electric Works* v *B.S. Mantosh* AIR 1956 Cal 148].

**On presentment.** In a promissory note or bill of exchange the expression 'on presentment' means 'on demand'. [Negotiable Instruments Act 1881, s. 21].

**Onus.** A burden; a burdensome requirement; a load; a disagreeable responsibility; an obligation; inescapable duty; weary load.

**Onus probandi.** Burden of proof.

NOTE: "Onus probandi" in the sense of burden of adducing evidence rests upon the party who would fail if no evidence at all, or no more evidence, as the case may be, were given on either side—*i.e.*, it rests *before* evidence is gone into, upon the party asserting the affirmative of the issue; and it rests, *after* evidence is gone into, upon the party against whom the tribunal, at the time the question arises, would give judgment if no further evidence were adduced. [Phipson on *Evidence*, 13th Ed., pp. 47-48].

**Open contract.** A contract of which the terms are not all expressly mentioned, as a contract to sell land without mentioning the day for completion of the purchase or without stipulation as to title or otherwise. [Wharton's *Law Lexicon*].

**Open court.** A court which has been formally convened and declared open for the transaction of its proper judicial business, or a court which is freely open to spectators. In an open court, the public have access as a matter of right.

"Open court is what any one would take to be a court, with the usual accompaniments of the jury-box, the witness-box, the Judge's seat, and seats for solicitors and counsel and others-in fact, with all those external signs which people are accustomed to suppose necessary for it to be a court". [*Kenyon* v *Eastwood* (1888)57 LJQB 455, 456, *per* Lord Coleridge].

'Open court' meant a court to which the public has a right of admission [*Scott* v *Scott* (1913) AC 417]; and that seems to be "the plain, natural, and ordinary meaning of the words". [*R.* v *Lewes Prison (Governor), Ex p. Doyle* (1917)2 KB 254, 271, *per* Lord Reading, C.J.].

NOTE: In s. 327 of Cr. P.C. 1973, the language itself indicates that even if a trial is held in a private house or is held inside a jail or anywhere, it becomes a venue of trial of a criminal case, and is deemed to be in law an open place and everyone who wants to go and attend the trial has a right to go and attend the trial except the only restriction contemplated is number of persons which could be contained in the premises where the court sits. As soon as a trial is held, whatever the place be, the provisions of s. 327 are attracted and it will be an open court and every citizen has a right to go. [*Kehar Singh* v *State (Delhi Administration)* (1988)3 SCC 609: AIR 1988 SC 1883].

**Open market.** Where it is open to every person to place orders with suppliers company and obtain the supply on payment of price at the prevailing rate, and the sales by the supplier community are not to a limited class only then such purchases are to be treated as purchasers made from open market. [*Ahura Chemical Products Pvt. Ltd.* v *Union of India* AIR 1981 SC 1782: 1981 Tax LR 2835: (1981)4 SCC 277: (1981)8 ELT 613: (1982)1 SCR 621].

**Open policy.** In the field of insurance, an open policy is one in which the value of the subject insured is not fixed or agreed upon in the policy, but is left to be estimated in case of loss. The sum to be paid as indemnity in the case of loss to be proved by the claimant or to be determined by the parties. This determination is called an 'adjustment of the loss'.

NOTE: An open policy is opposed to a valued policy, in which the value of thing insured is settled by agreement between the parties and inserted in the policy.

**Operational research.** This relates to the systematic examination of a business problem in order to find the best balanced solution for improved performance.

**Operative part.** The operative part of a document, as distinguished from the introductory matter, recitals, etc., refers to that part of the document which is intended to create or transfer rights. Thus, in a conveyance or lease, the operative part consists of the operative words of conveyance or demise and the parcels. Sometimes everything which follows the recitals is called operative part.

**Opinion.** Assumption; conclusion; determination; evaluation; judgment; notion; outlook; perspective; point of view; presumption; thinking; viewpoint; a conclusion or judgment held with confidence, but falling short of positive knowledge; the formal announcement of the conclusions of a court in a case before it; a formal statement of reasons for a judgment given; the conclusion of an attorney touching the merits of a submitted case; a belief or assessment based on grounds short of proof; a view held as probable; a formal statement of professional advice.

'Opinion' means something more than mere retaining of gossip or of hearsay; it means judgment or belief, that is a belief or a conviction resulting from what one thinks on a particular question. [*Dolgobinda Paricha* v *Nimai Charan Misra* 1959 Supp (2) SCR 814: AIR 1959 SC 914: (1960)1 SCA 39].

The word 'opinion' according to the *Concise Oxford English Dictionary* means judgment or belief based on grounds short of proof. [*Lalai Singh Yadav* v *State of U.P.* 1971 Cr LJ 1519].

**Opium.** Drug consisting of inspissated juice of opium poppy which is the plant of the species *papaver somniferum L.*

▸ *Meaning under the Opium Act 1878, s. 3.* 'Opium' means—(*i*) the capsules of the poppy (*papaver somniferum L.*) whether in their original form or cut, crushed or powdered, and whether or not juice has been extracted therefrom; (*ii*) the spontaneously coagulated juice of such capsules which have not been submitted to any manipulations other than those necessary for packing and transport; and (*iii*) any mixture, with or without neutral materials, or any of the above forms of opium, but does not include any preparation containing not more than 0.2 per cent. of morphine or a manufactured drug as defined in s. 2 of the Dangerous Drugs Act 1930.

> NOTE: Morphine is the main and principal alkaloid of opium and if morphine is found in any product above 0.2%, the product has to be treated as 'opium'. [*Satish Kumar* v *State* (1989)2 Crimes 109 (Del)].

- **Prepared opium.** The expression 'prepared opium' means opium prepared for smoking and includes dross or any other residues remaining after opium has been smoked.

**Opportunity.** A good chance; a favourable occasion; a chance or opening offered by circumstances; a fit or convenient time.

- **Reasonable opportunity** p. 730.
- **Reasonable opportunity of being heard** p. 730.
- **Reasonable opportunity to show cause** p. 730.

**Oppressive.** Oppressing; harsh or cruel; difficult to endure.

- **In a manner oppressive** p. 438.

**Optimus interpres rerum usus.** The best interpreter of things is usage.

**Option.** Option in its widest interpretation means simply choice or freedom of choice.

The plain meaning of the word 'option' is 'choice'. [*Gardner* v *Blaxill* (1960)2 All ER 457, 460, *per* Paull, J.].

An option is the privilege of being able within a specified period to call for delivery or to make delivery of a definite amount of a particular security at a specified price, and may be dealt in the same way as a security. [Halsbury's *Laws of England*, 3rd Ed., vol. 36, p. 509].

> NOTE: An obligation in a contract can frequently be performed in a large number of ways and the party under obligation can choose any one of the ways he likes. There is, however, a narrower sense in which the word can be used and that is to confer a right of choice specially granted to the holder of the option and to be used solely for his own benefit. It is in this sense that the word is generally used in the business world. [*Reardon Smith Line Ltd.* v *Ministry of Agriculture, Fisheries and Food* (1963)1 All ER 545, 559, *per* Lord Devlin].

**Option of purchase.** A choice given to purchase any property.

**Or.** Normally 'or' must be given disjunctive meaning and should not be read to give it a conjunctive sense. In certain extraordinary context it can be read as 'and'. [*L.I.C. of India* v *D.J. Bahadur* (1981)1 SCR 1083: (1981)1 Lab LJ 1].

In ordinary usage, 'and' is conjunctive and 'or' is disjunctive. But to carry on the intention of legislature it may be necessary to read 'and' in place of the conjunction 'or', and *vice versa*. [Maxwell on *Interpretation of Statutes*, 12th Ed., pp. 232-233].

The word may sometimes be used in conjunctive sense, meaning 'and'. [*Re Hayden Pask* v *Perry* (1931)2 Ch 333; *Tilkayat Shri Govindhalji Maharaj* v *State of Rajasthan* AIR 1963 SC 1638: (1964)1 SCC 561: (1964)2 SCJ 715].

The word 'or' should not be read as 'and' unless obliged. [*Green* v *Premier Glynrhonwy Slate Co. Ltd.* (1828)1 KB 511].

The word can be used in a conjunctive sense if the context so requires to carry out the legislative intent, which is otherwise obvious. [*Goodyear India Ltd.* v *Executive Officer* ILR (1968)2 Punj 695: AIR 1969 Punj 379].

If the words form an affirmative sentence, then the condition of one of the clauses only need be fulfilled. In such a case "or" really means "either" "or". In the *Shorter Oxford Dictionary* one of the meanings of the word "or" is given as "A particle co-ordinating two (or more) words, phrases or clauses between which there is an alternative". It is also there stated, "The alternative expressed by "or" is emphasised by prefixing the first member or adding after the last, the associated adv. either". So, even without "either", "or" alone creates an alternative. If, therefore, the sentence is an affirmative one, then we get two alternatives, any one of which may be chosen without the other being considered at all. [*M/s. Ranchhoddas Atmaram* v *Union of India* AIR 1961 SC 935: (1961)3 SCR 718: (1961)1 Cr LJ 31: (1961)2 SCJ 529].

If, however, the sentence is a negative one, then the position becomes different. The word "or" between the two clauses would then spread the negative influence over the clause following it. This rule of grammar is not in dispute. In such a case the conditions of both the clauses must be fulfilled. [*M/s. Ranchhoddas Atmaram* v *Union of India*, supra].

**Orchard.** A piece of enclosed land with fruit trees; plantation of trees grown from their products, as fruit, nuts, oils, etc.; also, the enclosure or ground containing them.

> NOTE: For connotation of this word, the existence of cultivated fruit trees on a compact area is essential. The trees as such must have two essential characteristics: (1) it must be perennial and not seasonal; (2) the main stem must be woody and not herbacious or pulpy.
>
> A banana plant lacks both these characteristics and cannot be regarded as fruit tree and banana plantation is not orchard. [*Mir Fakir Mohd.* v *State of West Bengal* (1978)2 SCC 36: AIR 1978 SC 1972: (1978)3 SCR 9].

**Order.** The formal expression of any decision of a civil court which is not a decree. [Code of Civil Procedure 1908, s. 2(14)].

A 'judgment' is a decision obtained in an action, and every other decision is an 'order'. [*Onslow* v *Inland Revenue Commissioners* 25 QBD 556, *per* Esher, M.R.].

'Order' covers commands or directions that something shall be done, discontinued or suffered, but it does not include 'sentence' and 'finding'. [*Mahabir Singh* v *Emperor* AIR 1944 Cal 17: 48 CWN 113].

> NOTE: The notings in a file get culminated into an "order" affecting right of parties only when it reaches the head of the department and is expressed in the name of the Governor, authenticated in the manner provided in Art. 166(2). [*State of Bihar* v *Kripalu Shankar* AIR 1987 SC 1554: (1987)3 SCC 34: (1987)3 SCR 1: JT 1987(3) SC 49: 1987 Cr LJ 1860: 1987 SCC (Cri) 442: (1987)2 SLJ 96].

In commercial sense order means a firm request for supply of definite goods emanating from a buyer, an indent placed by a purchaser. [*Consolidated Coffee Ltd.* v *Coffee Board* (1980)3 SCC 358: 1980 SCC (Tax) 279: (1980)46 STC 164: 1980 Tax LR 1723: AIR 1980 SC 1468].

- **Administrative order.** (1) An order issued by a government agency after an adjudicatory hearing. (2) An agency regulation that interprets or applies a statutory provision. [Black's *Law Dictionary*, 7th and 8th Eds.].
- **Banker's order** p. 95.
- **Consequential order.** See INCIDENTAL ORDER p. 444.
- **Date of order** p. 225.
- **Delivery order** p. 247.
- **Ex parte order.** An order made by the court upon the application of one party to an action without notice to the other. [Black's *Law Dictionary*, 7th and 8th Eds.].
- **Final order** p. 353.
- **Illegal order.** An order is illegal if it is opposed to any enactment or any rule having the force of law. [*Kesava Rao* v *Subbaraju* AIR 1957 AP 55].
- **Incidental order** p. 444.
- **Interlocutory order** p. 473.
- **Irregular order.** An order is irregular if the procedure followed is in violation of the principles of natural justice and fair play. [*Kesava Rao* v *Subbaraju* AIR 1957 AP 55].
- **Maintenance of law and order** p. 550.
- **Palpably wrong order** p. 636.
- **Peremptory order** p. 652.
- **Perverse order** p. 661.
- **Point of order** p. 667.
- **Prohibitory order** p. 697.
- **Public order** p. 711.
- **Standing order** p. 808.

• **Until further orders** p. 869.

• **Vesting order** p. 880.

**Ordinance.** Authoritative rule; canon; charter; command; decree; direction; fiat; imperative law; legal command; legislative decree; legislative edict; local legislation; municipal regulation.

NOTE: In U.S.A., an ordinance is an "authoritative law or decree; esp., a municipal regulation. Municipal governments can pass ordinances on matters that the State Government allows to be regulated at the local level. [Black's *Law Dictionary*, 7th and 8th Eds.].

In India under Art. 123 of the Constitution of India the President can promulgate an ordinance on the advice of the Council of Ministers to meet the requirements of a situation when either House of Parliament is not in session. Similarly under Art. 213 of the Constitution the Governor may issue an ordinance on the advice of his Council of Ministers when the Legislative Assembly or where there are two Houses of the Legislature in a State either of them is not in session. Having regard to the conditions prevailing in India the Constitution makers thought that the Ordinance making power should be given to the President to deal unforeseen or urgent matters. The position under Art. 213 of the Constitution vesting such power on the Governor is also the same. [*T. Venkata Reddy* v *State of Andhra Pradesh* (1985)3 SCR 509].

It is fairly established that an ordinance is a "Law" and should be approached on that basis. [*R.K. Garg* v *Union of India* (1982)1 SCR 947; *A.K. Roy* v *Union of India* AIR 1982 SC 710: 1982 Cr LJ 340: (1982)2 SCR 272; *T. Venkata Reddy* v *State of Andhra Pradesh* (1985)3 SCR 509]. The ordinance promulgated under either of the two Arts. 123 and 213 of the Constitution has the same force and effect as an Act of Parliament or an Act of the State Legislature as the case may be. When the Constitution says that the ordinance making power is legislative power and an ordinance shall have the same force as an Act, an ordinance shall be clothed with all the attributes of an Act of Legislature carrying with it all its incidents, immunities and limitations under the Constitution, it cannot be treated as an executive action or an administrative decision. [*T. Venkata Reddy* v *State of Andhra Pradesh* (1985)3 SCR 509].

**Ordinarily.** Usual, normal, common, according to the established order, not characterised by peculiar or unusual circumstances [*Munna Lal Agarwal* v *Rajasthan High Court* (1992)1 Western Law Case 550 (Raj)]; usually or in a large majority of cases [*Bhagbati Primary Fishermen's Co-operative Society* v *State of Orissa* (1987)64 Cut LT 464 (Ori); *Krishna Dayal* v *General Manager, N. Rly*. AIR 1954 Punj 245]; habitually and not casually; normally and not exceptionally [*Re Putta Ranganayakula* AIR 1956 AP 161 (FB)]; in the majority of cases but not invariably [*Nirmal Chand* v *DM* AIR 1976 MP 95]; without exception generally [*Nirmal Chand* v *DM* AIR 1976 MP 95]; as a matter of regular course, in most cases, usually, commonly, as is normal or usual [*State of Uttar Pradesh* v *Shri Ram Gupta* 1972 All Cr R 415]; usual, common, normal, regular, conforming to general order, common in recurrence, often recurring [*State of Uttar Pradesh* v *Shri Ram Gupta* 1972 All Cr R 415 referring to *Corpus Juris Secundum*, vol. 67]; according to common order [*State of Uttar Pradesh* v *Shri Ram Gupta* 1972 All Cr R 415]; not mainly or regularly, but usually and normally. [*State of Kerala* v *Rajappan Nair* 1977 Ker LT 672].

NOTE: The word 'ordinarily' cannot obviously mean always [*Bhagbati Primary Fishermen's Co-operative Society* v *State of Orissa* (1987)64 Cut LT 464 (Ori)]; does not mean 'permanently' nor does mean 'universally' nor also 'invariably' or 'always'. [*Jurawan Prasad Mitra* v *State of UP* 1995 All LJ 1451].

The antonym of 'ordinarily' is extraordinary, unusual or uncommon. [*State of Uttar Pradesh* v *Shri Ram Gupta* 1972 All Cr R 415].

**Ordinarily resides.** The expression means more than temporary residence; a place where one has settled down for a reasonably long period. [*Sarada Nayar* v *Vayankara Amma* AIR 1957 Ker 158].

In the matter of application under s. 25 of the Guardians and Wards Act 1890, for the custody of the minor child, the words "ordinarily resides" should be construed as the place where the mother resides before the presentation of the petition. [*K.C. Sashidhar* v *Smt. Roopa* AIR 1993 Kant 120]. Mother being legal guardian of minor of tender age, her place of residence is place where 'minor ordinarily resides'.

**Ordinary resolution.** A resolution shall be an ordinary resolution when at a general meeting of which the notice required under the Companies Act 1956, has been duly given, the votes cast (whether on a show of hands or on a poll, as the case may be) in favour of the resolution (including the casting vote, if any, of the chairman) by members who, being entitled to do so, vote in person, or where proxies are allowed, by proxy, exceed the votes, if any cast against the resolution by members so entitled and voting. [Companies Act 1956, s. 189].

**Ore tenus.** By word of mouth.

**Original.** Basic; elemental; elementary; fundamental; germinal; maiden; primal; primitive; first in order; bearing its own authority, and not deriving authority from an outside source.

As applied to documents, the original is the first copy; that from which another instrument is transcribed, copied, or imitated.

The originality which is required in the Copyright Act relates to the expression of thought. But the Act does not require that the expression must be in an original or novel form, but that the work must not be copied from another work—that it should originate from the author. [*University of London Press Ltd.* v *University Tutorial Press Ltd.* (1916)2 Ch 601].

The word 'original' used in the Indian Copyright Act 1957, does not imply any originality of ideas but merely means that the work in question should not be copied from some other work, but should originate in the author. [*Agarwala Publishing House* v *Board of H.S.* AIR 1947 All 91].

"Where there are a great number of persons who produce the same article, 'original' means that the article so called is that made by the first inventor. That is the meaning of the word 'original' which the Court of Chancery has always recognised". [*Cocks* v *Chandler* (1871) LR 11 Eq 446, 449, *per* Lord Romilly, M.R.].

**Originating summons.** An originating summons is a summons by which an action may be commenced otherwise than by writ. [*Re Holloway Ex p. Pallister* (1964)2 QB 163].

It is a summons without writ, returnable in the chambers of a judge of the Chancery Division for the determination of particular questions arising in the administration of an estate or trust, without the administration of the whole estate or trust. [Wharton's *Law Lexicon*].

NOTE: Executors, trustees, creditors, legatees, heirs etc. may take out originating summons, returnable before the Judge sitting in chambers on the Original Side of the High Court at Calcutta for determination of the question set out in Chapter XIII, r. 1 of the Original Side Rules of the High Court.

**Ornament.** A thing, in a finished form, meant for personal adornment or for the adornment of any idol, deity or any other object of religious worship, made of, or manufactured from gold, whether or not set stones or gems (real or artificial) or with pearls (real, cultured or imitation) or with all or any of them, and includes parts, pendants or broken pieces of ornament. [Gold (Control) Act 1968, s. 2(*p*)].

**Ostensible.** Able to be seen; apparent; assumable; avowed; deceptive; pretended; delusional; delusive; delusory; discernible; illusionary; illusive; illusory; indubitable; misleading; obvious; overt; patent; plausible; purported; so-called.

The word 'ostensible' has two meanings—(*a*) that the object bears a certain form or appearance without suggesting that it is or is not that of which it has the superficial appearance, and (*b*) that the object bears a certain appearance but is not really that of which it bears the appearance. [*Debi Singh* v *Jagadish Saran* AIR 1952 All 716].

**Otherwise.** In any other way. [*Packwood* v *Union Castle Mail S.S. Co., Ltd.* (1903)20 TLR 59, 60]; in a different manner.

The word "otherwise" means, in another way or manner, by other causes, in other respects, in other conditions. [*United Receland Ltd.* v *State of Haryana* (1996)3 Punj LR 227; *Krishna Gopal* v *Shri Prakash Chandra* (1974)1 SCC 128; *Dhan Raj* v *Municipal Corporation of Delhi* (1972)74 Punj LR (DS) 157].

NOTE: 'Otherwise' when following an enumeration should receive an *ejusdem generis* interpretation much in the same as 'other'. [*Monek* v *Hilton* 46 LJMC 167].

**Otti.** A pledge, a pawn; a mortgage; a mortgage in usufructuary form.

*Otti and Kuzhikanam* imply a possessory mortgage with recognition of a right to compensation for plantation by the mortgagee on the land mortgaged. [*Narayanam Asari* v *Velayudhan Nair* 1968 Ker LJ 409: 1968 Ker LR 187].

**Ouster.** Deprivation; dislodgement; dispossession; ejection; elimination; eviction; exclusion; permanent exclusion; removal; repudiation.

In its application to title of an immovable property, 'ouster' means, dispossession of one co-owner by another where a hostile title is set up by the latter and where the occupation of the latter is not without ownership. [*Smt. Biro* v *Amar Singh* 1996 Punj LJ 110, 113].

NOTE: 'Ouster' does not mean actual driving out of the co-sharer from the property. It will, however, not be complete unless it is coupled with all other ingredients required to constitute adverse possession. Broadly speaking, three elements are necessary for establishing the plea of ouster and in the case of co-owner. They are: (1) declaration of hostile animus; (2) long and uninterrupted possession of the person pleading ouster; and (3) exercise of right of exclusive ownership openly and to the knowledge of other co-owner. [*Vidya Devi* v *Prem Prakash* (1995)4 SCC 496, 505].

To oust is to put out of possession; but it is not essential to prove physical dispossession in order to establish ouster. [*Chandra Kishore* v *Bisweswar Pal* AIR 1928 Cal 216].

**Outgoings.** "'Outgoings' is a proper word to use in connection with rent, salaries, and expenses of management". [*Yates* v *Yates* (1913)33 NZLR 281, 285, *per* Cooper, J.].

The term outgoings is of very wide import, and includes not merely rates, taxes, repairs, and the ordinary expenses of cultivating or managing ... property, but also expenses, though of a capital nature, of works executed by local authorities under their sanitary and other powers which are recoverable from the owner, and are also, in general, charged on the property. [Halsbury's *Laws of England*, 3rd Ed., vol. 34, p. 260].

**Outhouse.** Building belonging to and adjoining a dwelling house.

An outhouse means a house or building belonging to and adjoining a dwelling house, and used for some subsidiary purpose and includes servant's quarters. [*Punjab Province* v *Dr. Lakhmi Dass* AIR 1944 Lah 149].

The expression 'outhouse' must be understood in the common dictionary meaning in the sense that it must be connected with or near or built against a main house. 'An outhouse' must be considered in contradistinction with and in relation to an in-house. An outhouse may be a separate house from a dwelling house but it cannot be independent of or unconnected with either a dwelling house or a main building. [*Consolidated Tea and Lands Co. (India) Ltd., Calcutta* v *CWT, WB* AIR 1970 Cal 335].

An outhouse is in some respects parcel of a dwelling house. [*R.* v *Haughton* 5 C&P 559].

NOTE: A thatched pigsty in a yard adjoining the house may be an outhouse. [*R.* v *Jones* 2 Moody 308].

**Outstanding.** Remaining undischarged; unpaid; uncollected; in arrears; overdue; unliquidated; unsatisfied.

It may also mean incomplete; irresolved; pending; unadjusted; unascertained; undetermined; unfinished; unsettled.

It may further mean august; celebrated; conspicuous; distinguished; elevated; esteemed; extraordinary; illustrious; impressive; luminous; lustrous; noteworthy; peerless; majestic.

**Outstanding accounts.** Such accounts as are due and unpaid. Such accounts are generally deemed good and realisable.

**Over-capitalised.** A company is said to be over-capitalised, when the current or expected amount of profit is insufficient to yield a normal return on its paid-up share capital.

**Over-trading.** This occurs when a business has expanded its turn-over beyond what can be achieved with its existing resources of fixed and working capital.

**Overdraft.** This relates to the amount a customer of a banker has been permitted by the banker to draw in excess of the money paid in. The term may also refer to the condition which exists when vouchers or purchase orders are drawn in amounts in excess of budgeted or appropriated amount.

**Overdue.** Due and more than due; delayed or unpaid. [*Bliss* v *California Co-op. Producers* Cal App, 156 P 2d 259, 260].

A negotiable instrument or other evidence of debt is overdue when the day of its maturity is past and it remains unpaid.

A vessel is said to be overdue when she has not reached her destination in time.

**Overhead (charges).** Charges on account of office expenses, management, interest on capital, and other needs of a business concern.

General expenditures in financial or industrial enterprise which cannot be attributed to any one department or product, excluding cost of materials, labour, and selling. [*Guillot* v *State Highway Commission of Montana* 56 P 2d 1072, 1075].

**Overrule.** To supersede; annul; reverse; make void; reject by subsequent action or decision; abrogate; invalidate; nullify; refuse to sustain; repudiate; rescind; revoke; rule out; set aside; undo.

NOTE: Overruling may be express or implied. Its effect is retroactive except that it does not unsettle matters which are *res judicata*. [Dias on *Jurisprudence*].

*"Reversal" and "overruling"—distinction between.* The distinction between "reversal" and "overruling" is that the first refers to the action of an appellate court in upsetting the *decision* of the lower court in the same case, while the latter refers to the action of a superior court in upsetting the *principle* laid down by a lower court in some other case. Secondly, reversal *may* involve disapproval of the *principle* as stated by the lower court, except where the decision is reversed on some other point. Overruling *necessarily* involves disapproval of the *principle*, but never affects the previous *decision* to that the parties continue to be bound by the doctrine of *res judicata*.

**Overt act.** An open act which must be proved; an outward act done in pursuance and manifestation of an intent or design.

NOTE: Under s. 121A of the Indian Penal Code 1860, conspiracy itself is a crime and it is not necessary to establish an illegal act or omission as overt acts of the conspiracy. The illegal acts or omissions, if established, support the case of the existence of the conspiracy itself, the offence being complete even though two persons conspiring together go no further than the original agreement. [*Jitendra Nath Gupta's* case AIR 1937 Cal 99].

**Overtime.** This relates to time worked and paid for at premium rates beyond the standard period of work for which the basic wage is paid.

In the context of working hours it means period in excess of prescribed working hours. [*Philips India Ltd.* v *Labour Court, Madras* AIR 1985 SC 1034: 1985 Lab IC 854].

**Owelty.** Owelty is the difference which is paid or agreed to be paid by one co-tenant to another for the purpose of equalising a partition. [*Swaminatha Odayar* v *Official Receiver* AIR 1957 SC 577: 1957 SCR 275].

According to 'owelty' the rights and interests of the parties in the property will be separated, only by allowing one of them to retain the whole of the suit property on payment of just compensation to the other. [*Badri Narain* v *Nil Ratan Sarkar* AIR 1978 SC 845: (1978)3 SCC 30, 35].

**Owner.** The person in whom is vested the ownership, dominion, or title of property; proprietor; he who has dominion of a thing—real or personal; one who has the right to possess, use and convey something.

> NOTE: A co-owner is as much an owner of the entire property as any sole owner of a property is. [*Sri Ram Pasricha* v *Jagannath* (1976)4 SCC 184].
>
> The word "owner" does not include in its ambit a person who is mere beneficial or equitable owner. [*Commissioner of Income-tax, Hyderabad* v *Barkat Ali Khan* 1974 Tax LR 90 (DB) (AP)].

▸ *Meaning under the Cantonments Act 1924, s. 2(xxvi).* 'Owner' includes any person who is receiving or is entitled to receive the rent of any building or land whether on his own account or on behalf of himself and others or as an agent or trustee, or who would so receive the rent or be entitled to receive it if the building or land were let to a tenant.

▸ *Meaning under the Mines Act 1952, s. 2(l); Iron Ore Mines Labour Welfare Cess Act 1961, s. 3(d).* 'Owner' when used in relation to a mine means any person who is the immediate proprietor or lessee or occupier of the mine or of any part thereof, and in the case of a mine the business whereof is being carried on by a liquidator or receiver, such liquidator or receiver; but does not include a person who merely receives a royalty, rent or fine from the mine or is merely the proprietor of the mine subject to any lease, grant of licence for the working whereof, or is merely the owner of the soil and not interested in the minerals of the mine; but any contractor for the working of a mine or any part thereof shall be subject to this Act in like manner as if he were an owner, but not so as to exempt the owner from any liability.

▸ *Meaning under the Industries (Development and Regulation) Act 1951, s. 3(f).* 'Owner', in relation to an industrial undertaking, means the person who, or the authority which, has the ultimate control over the affairs of the undertaking and, where the said affairs are entrusted to a manager, managing director or managing agent, such manager, managing director or managing agent shall be deemed to be the owner of the undertaking.

▸ *Meaning under the Hire-purchase Act 1972, s. 2(f).* 'Owner' means the person who lets or has let, delivers or has delivered possession of goods to a hirer under a hire-purchase agreement and includes a person to whom the owner's property in the goods or any owner's rights or liabilities under the agreement has passed by assignment or by operation of law.

▸ *Meaning under the Coking Coal Mines (Nationalisation) Act 1972, s. 3(n).* 'Owners',—(*i*) when used in relation to a mine has the meaning assigned to it in the Mines Act 1952; (*ii*) when used in relation to a coke oven plant means any person who is the immediate proprietor or lessee or occupier of the coke oven plant or any part thereof or is a contractor for the working of the coke oven plant or any part thereof.

▸ *Meaning under the Marine Products Export Development Authority Act 1972, s. 3(j).* 'Owner' in relation to any fishing vessel or in relation to any processing plant or storage premises for marine products or in relation to any conveyance used for transport of marine products includes—(*i*) any agent of the owner; and (*ii*) a mortgagee, lessee or other person in actual possession of the fishing vessel, processing plant, storage premises or conveyance.

> NOTE: The distinction between real owner and ostensible owner is well known. Ostensible owner of property of which the real owner is someone else is neither the owner of the property nor may indeed be in occupation thereof. [*Jagjitlal* v *Gurjinder Arora* (1977)79 Punj LR 124].


- **Absolute owner** p. 9.
- **Landowner** p. 511.
- **Limited owner** p. 536.
- **Part-owners** p. 641.
- **Riparian owner** p. 764.

**Ownership.** Ownership is a right over a determinate thing indefinite in point of user, unrestricted in point of disposition, and unlimited in point of duration.

Ownership consists of innumerable rights over property, for example, the rights of exclusive enjoyment, of destruction, alteration and alienation, and of maintaining and recovering possession of the property from all other persons. Such rights are conceived not as separately existing, but as merged in one general right of ownership. [Halsbury's *Laws of England*, 3rd Ed., vol. 29, p. 371].

NOTE: As a general rule, title to property may be shown by the exercise of acts of ownership in connection with it. Thus, possession is not only *prima facie* evidence of ownership but is also evidence of the highest title to the property in question; as against mere wrong-doers, in cases of trespass to real property, it has even been said to be conclusive. [Halsbury's *Laws of England*, 4th Ed., vol. 17, para 36, p. 28].


- **Absolute ownership** p. 9.
- **Beneficial ownership** p. 100.
- **Transfer of ownership** p. 852.

# Pp

**Package.** A bundle of things packed; a parcel, box, etc. in which things are packed; that which is packed, as for transportation; something wrapped up or bound together; a packet or parcel; a box, case, crate, or other receptacle in which goods are packed; the act or process of packing.

NOTE: The word 'package' means the singular and not the plural, and it contemplates each individual package. A package or parcel is an entry by itself. The goods may be wrapped up into a single package or parcel, or they may be kept loose, in which case each article with a container thereto, would be different parcel or package. [*Radha Krishna Nalhani* v *Union of India* AIR 1957 Pat 231].

The word "package" must indicate something packed and in a bill of lading cannot include cars put on board a ship without any boxes, crates or coverings. [*Studebaker Distributors* v *Charlton Steam Shipping Co.* (1938)1 KB 459].

▸ *Meaning under the Prevention of Food Adulteration Act 1954, s. 2(x).* 'Package' means a box, bottle, casket, tin, barrel, case, receptacle, sack, bag, wrapper or other thing in which an article of food is placed or packed.

▸ *Meaning under the Insecticides Act 1968, s. 3(l).* 'Package' means a box, bottle, casket, tin, barrel, case, receptacle, sack, bag, wrapper or other thing in which an insecticide is placed or packed.

▸ *Meaning under the Trade Marks Act 1999, s. 2(q).* 'Package' includes any case, box, container, covering, folder, receptacle, vessel, casket, bottle, wrapper, label, band, ticket, reel, frame, capsule, cap, lid, stopper and cork.

• **Heavy package** p. 410.

**Packing.** The act or operation of filling an empty space putting up for transportation, etc.; material used to fill up a space around or in something, especially to protect a fragile article in transit; the substance used in adjusting or protecting an article packed; a greasy or other material for closing a joint.

Packing is the packing of the finished manufactured article, which is done to facilitate or make possible its sale or transport for sale to customers. Such packing is the last operation in manufacturing process. Preliminary packing of the raw materials for delivery to the factory is not intended. [*Sree Gopal Paper Mills* v *Inspector of Factories* AIR 1959 All 547; Factories Act 1948, s. 2(*k*)(*i*)].

**Paddy.** Rice before threshing or in the husk.

NOTE: Paddy does not continue to be paddy after dehusking. Rice and paddy are two different things in ordinary parlance. When paddy is dehusked and rice produced, there is change in the identity of the goods. [*Ganesh Trading Co., Karnal* v *State of Haryana* (1974)3 SCC 620: 1974 SCC (Tax) 100; *Babu Ram Jagdish Kumar & Co.* v *State of Punjab* AIR 1979 SC 1475: (1979)3 SCC 616: (1979)44 STC 159].

**Paid.** Past tense and past participle of 'pay' which means to give to what is due for a debt, purchase, etc., recompense, remunerate.

In the context of dividend, the expression "paid" does not contemplate actual receipt of the dividend by the member in general. Dividend may be said to be paid when the company discharges its liability and makes the amount of dividend unconditionally available to the members entitled thereto. [*J. Dalmia* v

*Commissioner of Income Tax, New Delhi* AIR 1964 SC 1866: (1964)2 SCJ 253: (1964)53 ITR 83; *Banaras State Bank Ltd.* v *Commissioner of Income Tax, U.P.* AIR 1970 SC 281].

In the context of s. 43(2) of the Income Tax Act 1961, "paid" means actually paid or incurred according to the method of accounting upon the basis of which the profits and gains are computed under the head 'profits and gains of business or profession'.

In the context of s. 33(2)(*b*) of the Industrial Disputes Act 1947, the word "paid" includes offer to pay.

> NOTE: When the management has offered to pay but the employee refused to accept, compliance with law was deemed to have been made. [*Presidency Talkies* v *Labour Court* (1968)2 MLJ 318: AIR 1969 Mad 87: (1969)1 Lab LJ 90].

**Paid-up capital.** Paid-up capital is so much of the authorised or shared capital of a company which its shareholders or subscribers have paid-up. [*Municipal Council, Vizagapatnam* v *Tea Districts Labour Association* AIR 1932 Mad 160].

**Paikasht raiyat.** A non-resident cultivator of land.

**Pais.** In pais, *i.e.*, by conduct or representation.

> NOTE: Estoppel in pais is known as estoppel by conduct or representation.

**Pala.** Turn of worship of a deity.

**Palpable.** That can be touched or felt; readily perceived by the senses or mind; clear-cut; crystal clear; definite; discoverable; distinct; indisputable; indubitable; recognisable; visible.

Easily perceptible, plain, obvious, readily visible, noticeable, distinct, manifest. [*People* v *Hughey* 47 NE 2d 77, 80].

**Palpably wrong order.** A 'palpably wrong order' means an error which can be felt by a simple touch of the order and not which could be dug out after a long drawn out process of argumentation or ratiocination. [*Gujarat University* v *Sonai P. Shah* AIR 1982 Guj 58, 62 (FB)].

**Panchas.** 'Panchas' is plural of 'panch' meaning an arbitrator.

In regional languages, the recognised meaning of this term is arbitrators. [*Puttappa Edeppa* v *Hasansab Usmansab* (1975)1 Ker LJ 36: ILR (1975)1 Ker 54].

**Panchayat.** A village council consisting of five men to try all disputes. Now it is applied to any meeting of persons to make an inquest, etc.

> NOTE: The word 'panchayat' is more or less an equivalent to the English word 'committee'. [*Asa Ram* v *District Board* AIR 1959 SC 480: 1959 Cr LJ 533: 1959 SCR 452].

**Panchnama.** A *panchnama* is merely a record of what a *panch* sees. [*Valibhai Omraji* v *State* AIR 1963 Guj 145].

**Panda.** Priest of a temple; one who helps others in entering a temple and worship the deity.

**Panic.** Sudden uncontrollable fear or alarm; infectious apprehension or fright; a sudden, unreasonable, overpowering fear, especially when affecting a large number simultaneously; overpowering fright.

'Panic' is a state of mind or reaction to fearsome or gruesome events or even creating unreasoning or hysterical fear, often spreading quickly. It is the effect, the cause being due to many situations. What creates panic can also create terror depending upon the acts with which a person is confronted. [*Ramesh Roy* v *State of West Bengal* AIR 1972 SC 1678: (1972)3 SCC 829: 1972 Cr LJ 1024: 1973 SCC (Cri) 14].

**Panth.** The word 'Panth' is one of Sanskrit origin and etymologically it means the path or the way. By itself it has now come to indicate the Sikh religion, because it has been used by Sikhs to denote their religion and their denomination as the followers of that Panth. In that context, Panth may mean the Sikh religion. [*Kultar Singh* v *Mukhtiar Singh* 1964 Cr LJ 268: AIR 1965 SC 141].

- **Followers of the Panth.** The followers of the Panth would be the persons who follow the path prescribed by the Sikh Gurus and as such, would signify the Sikh community. [*Kultar Singh* v *Mukhtiar Singh* 1964 Cr LJ 268: AIR 1965 SC 141].

**Panthic.** Panthic is an adjective which means of the Panth or belonging to the Panth. [*Kultar Singh* v *Mukhtiar Singh* 1964 Cr LJ 268: AIR 1965 SC 141].

**Paper.** Any written or printed document or instrument; a negotiable document or instrument evidencing a debt; especially, commercial documents or negotiable instruments considered as a group. [Black's *Law Dictionary*, 7th & 8th Eds.].

"Paper" is a manufactured substance composed of fibres—whether vegetable or animal—adhering together, in form consisting of sheets of various sizes and of different thickness, used for writing or printing or other purposes to which such sheets are applicable. [*A.-G.* v *Barry* 28 LJ Ex 211; *Coles* v *Dickinson* 16 CB NS 604; *Maharaja Book Depot* v *State of Gujarat* 1978 Cr LJ 1859: AIR 1979 SC 180: (1979)2 SCR 138: (1979)1 SCC 295: 1979 SCC (Cri) 275].

The word "paper" which is derived from the name of reedy plant papyrus and grows abundantly along the Nile river in Egypt is explained in the *Shorter Oxford English Dictionary*, Vol. 2, 3rd Ed., as: A substance composed of fibres interlaced into a compact web, made from linen and cotton rags, straw, wood, certain grasses, etc., which are macerated into a pulp, dried, and pressed; it is used for writing, printing, or drawing on, for wrapping, things in, for covering the interior of walls, etc.

In *Encyclopaedia Britannica*, Vol. 13, 15th Ed., 'paper' has been defined as the basic material used for written communication and dissemination of information.

In the Unabridged Edition of *The Random House Dictionary of the English Language*, the word 'paper' has been defined as a substance made from rags, straw, wood, or other fibrous material, usually in thin sheets, used to bear writing and printing or for wrapping things, decorating walls, etc.

In Webster's *New World Dictionary*, 1962 Ed., the meaning of the word "paper" is given as follows: thin flexible material in sheets or leaves, made from rags, wood pulp, or other fibrous decorate, etc.

In popular parlance, the word 'paper' is understood as meaning a substance which is used for bearing writing, or printing, or for packing or for drawing on, or for decorating, or covering the walls. [*State of Uttar Pradesh* v *Kores (India) Ltd.* (1976)4 SCC 477: AIR 1977 SC 132: (1977)1 SCR 837: (1977)39 STC 8].

'Paper' is defined as a substance composed of files interlaced into a compact web, made (usually in the form of a thin flexible sheet, most commonly white) from various fibrous materials, as linen and cotton rags, straw, wood, certain grasses etc. which are macerated into a pulp, dried and pressed and subjected to various other processes, as bleaching, colouring, sizing etc, according to the intended use. It is used in various forms and qualities for writing, printing, drawing on, for wrapping things in, for covering the interior walls and for other purposes. [*Collector of Central Excise, Kanpur* v *Krishna Carbon Paper Co.* AIR 1988 SC 2223: JT 1988(4) SC 762: (1988)37 ELT 480: 1988 Supp (3) SCR 12: (1989)72 STC 280: (1989)1 SCC 150].

NOTE: It becomes material to know that the leaves of plants are not paper, though the term no doubt has been taken from papyrus, which people formerly used to write upon as paper now is used. The skins of animals are not also paper. [*A.-G.* v *Barry* 28 LJ Ex 211].

▸ *Meaning under the Indian Stamp Act 1899, s. 2(18).* 'Paper' includes vellum, parchment or any other material on which an instrument may be written.

▸ *Meaning under the Press and Registration of Books Act 1867, s. 1.* 'Paper' means any document including a newspaper, other than a book.


- **Carbon paper** p. 124.
- **Jamabandi papers** p. 484.
- **Nomination paper** p. 609.
- **Ship papers** p. 795.

**Paper book.** A paper book contains all the important papers, namely, pleadings, depositions, judgment, exhibits etc., required for the disposal of an appeal.

NOTE: The High Courts and the Supreme Court have framed detailed rules regarding the preparation of paper books.

**Paper currency.** Notes circulated by the authority of the Government as money. It is put into compulsory circulation as a substitute for coined money.

NOTE: The rupee coin is a token coin made of nickel. It is also printed on paper.

**Paper tape.** A tape in which data for a computer may be recorded by means of a pattern of holes.

**Par.** Equal footing; equal value; equal worth; equalness; equipollence; evenness; identicalness.

- **Stocks and shares at par.** It is the nominal value of stocks and shares, that is, when they are neither at a premium nor at a discount.

  It is an equality subsisting between the nominal or face value of stocks and shares and its actual selling value. When the values are thus equal, the stocks and shares are said to be "at par". If it can be sold for more than its nominal worth; it is "above par"; if for less, it is "below par".

**Par avion.** By air.

**Paragraph.** A short passage in a written or printed discourse begun on a new and usually indented line; a distinct section of a piece of writing beginning on a new usually indented line; any section or subdivision of writing or chapter which relates to a particular point, whether consisting of one or many sentences; a short article, complete and unified, especially in a newspaper.

**Parallel.** Side by side and having the same distance continuously between them, said of lines or planes; a line extending in the same direction and being equidistant at all points from another line.

Essentially alike; precisely similar; analogous, or corresponding; essential likeness.

**Parcel.** Block; portion; section; segment; a group or lot composed of an indefinite number or quantity; a separated part of anything.

A small package or bundle; anything wrapped up; something enclosed in a wrapper. [*Maguire* v *Porter* (1905)2 IR 147].

"Parcel" as used with reference to land generally means a contiguous quantity of land in possession of, owned by, or recorded as property of the same claimant person [*Adams Tree Service, Inc.* v *Transamerica Title Ins. Co.* 511 P 2d 658, 662]; a contiguous quantity of land in the possession of an owner. [*United States ex rel. and for Use of Tennessee Val. Authority* v *Easements and Rights over Certain Land in Hamilton County* DC Tenn, 259 F Supp 377, 382].

**Parcels.** A description of property, formally set forth in a conveyance, together with the boundaries thereof, for its easy identification. Parcels in a conveyance usually begin with the words 'All that'.

**Pardanashin woman.** A woman of rank who lives in seclusion, shut in the Zenana, having no communication except from behind the *parda* or screen with any male persons save a few near relations. [*Satish Chandra* v *Kali Dasi* AIR 1922 Cal 203].

A *pardanashin* woman is a woman of rank, Hindu or Mahomedan, who lives in seclusion shut in the Zenana and having no communication except from behind the *parda* or screen with any male person save a few privileged relations or dependants. [*Shivmala Tej Singh Ingle* v *Ramcharan Kundanlal* 1980 MPLJ 530].

NOTE: A Division Bench of the Gauhati High Court has, however, observed that a *pardanashin* woman need not necessarily be a woman of rank. If on account of the rules and customs of society, she has to keep herself within the Zenana and to lead a life of seclusion without any contact with the outside world, she is a *pardanashin* woman. [*Jubeda Khatun* v *Sulaiman Khan* (1986)1 Gau LR 147].

*Pardanashin woman—who is not.* A lady who conducts herself as a male member by filing suits, complaints in various courts and prosecute them in a manly manner, meeting petition writers, lawyers coming to her way is not a *pardanashin* lady. [*Ghulam Zuhra* v *Habia Begum* AIR 1985 J&K 22].

A woman is not a *pardanashin* woman who communicates with strangers, collects rents from tenants, is literate with a certain amount of education, who subscribes to newspapers and arranges her affairs. [*Shivmala Tej Singh Ingle* v *Ramcharan Kundanlal* 1980 MPLJ 530].

A heavy onus lies upon him who relies upon a deed by a *pardanashin* woman and it must be proved affirmatively and conclusively that the deed was not only executed by but was explained to and really understood by her. [*Bhikary Ram* v *Hedait Mohammad Sahaji* AIR 1958 Ori 62; *Satyadeo* v *Chanderjit* AIR 1966 Pat 110; *Brundaban* v *Iswar* AIR 1983 Ori 172].

**Pardon.** Absolution; acquittal; clemency; exemption from punishment; exoneration; forgiveness; release from penalty; release from punishment.

An act of grace from governing power which mitigates the punishment the law demands for the offence and restores the rights and privileges forfeited on account of the offence. [*Verneco, Inc.* v *Fidelity & Cas. Co. of New York* 219 So 2d 508, 511].

The act or an instance of officially nullifying punishment or other legal consequences of a crime. [Black's *Law Dictionary*, 8th Ed.].

NOTE: A pardon is usually granted by the Chief Executive of a Government. Articles 72 and 161 of the Constitution of India empower the President and the Governor respectively to grant pardon. "Pardon" is one of many prerogatives which have been recognised since time immemorial as being vested in the sovereign, wherever the sovereignty might lie. It is open to the Governor to grant a full pardon at any time even during the pendency of the case in the Supreme Court in exercise of what is ordinarily called mercy jurisdiction. Such a pardon after the accused-person has been convicted by the court has the effect of completely absolving him from all punishment or disqualification attaching to a conviction for a criminal offence. That power is essentially vested in the head of the Executive because the judiciary has no such mercy jurisdiction. But the Governor cannot exercise his power of the suspension of the sentence for the period when the Supreme Court is in seizure of the case. [*K.M. Nanavati* v *State of Bombay* AIR 1961 SC 112: (1961)1 SCR 497: (1961)1 Cr LJ 173: (1961)2 SCJ 100].

*"Pardon" and "dispensation"—distinction.* Pardon differs from dispensation. While dispensation seeks to make the thing prohibited lawful, pardon frees from punishment due for a thing unlawfully done. Yet freedom from punishment is a consequence of dispensation though not its effect. Pardon makes the convict a new man and gives him new credit and capacity. [*K.M. Nanavati* v *State of Bombay* AIR 1961 SC 112: (1961)1 SCR 497: (1961)1 Cr LJ 173: (1961)2 SCJ 100].

**Parent.** The lawful father or mother of someone. The term commonly includes (1) either the natural father or the natural mother of a child, (2) the adoptive father or adoptive mother of a child, (3) a child's putative blood parent who has expressly acknowledged paternity, and (4) an individual or agency whose status as guardian has been established by judicial decree. [Black's *Law Dictionary*, 8th Ed.].

The ordinary meaning of the word 'parent' is father or mother; but it may mean any lineal ancestor. [*Ross* v *Ross* 20 Bea 645].

In some English statutes the word has been defined to include a guardian of, or a person having the legal custody of or the control over or having direct benefit from the wages of a young person or child.

▸ *Meaning under the Fatal Accidents Act 1855, s. 4.* 'Parent' shall include father and mother.

▸ *Meaning under the Vaccination Act 1880, s, 2(2).* 'Parent' means the father of a legitimate child and the mother of an illegitimate child.

- **Surrogate parent** p. 824.

**Pargana.** A tract of a country comprising many villages; a revenue district.

**Pari delicto potior est conditio possidentis.** Where each party is equally at fault, law favours him who is actually in possession.

If a party comes to court to enforce an illegal contract, two answers may be given to his demand, the one, that he must draw justice from a pure fountain, and the other, that *potior est conditio possidentis*. [Broom's *Legal Maxims*, 10th Ed., p. 489].

The phrase in *pari delicto* suggests two things. First, there should be an act of delinquency, an act repugnant to law, an illegal act. Secondly, both the parties should be delinquent and that too equally with the same degree of guilt. The word "*possidentis*" indicates the fact of possession as owner. It excludes those whose possession is precarious, terminable at will by another person, like the possession of a lessee, an agent or a borrower. Those kinds of precarious possession would not normally emerge out of illegal transaction between the parties. Those who have come into possession of a thing from an illegal transaction would usually claim to be the owners in their own right. [*Mrs. M.M. Roy* v *N.V.P. Pandian* (1985)1 Cur Civ Cas 501 reversing *N.V.P. Pandian* v *M.M. Roy* ILR (1978)3 Mad 389: (1978)1 MLJ 417: AIR 1979 Mad 42].

When both the parties are equally at fault either party may rescind the contract when it is in executory stage and can recover from the other party any money paid thereunder. [*Jahed Shaikh* v *K.C. Das* 62 CWN 377].

**Pari passu.** By an equal progress; equally; ratably; without preference; with equal step; on equal footing or proportionately.

The term is used especially of creditors who, in marshalling assets, are entitled to receive out of the same fund without any precedence over each other.

**Parliament.** The supreme legislative body in a sovereign State.

NOTE: Parliament for the Union of India consists of the President and two Houses known as the Council of States and the House of the People. [Constitution of India, Art. 79].


- **Act of Parliament** p. 30.
- **Contempt of Parliament** p. 185.
- **Dissolution of Parliament** p. 271.
- **Member of Parliament** p. 573.


**Parol.** Oral or verbal; expressed or evidenced by speech only; anything done by word of mouth, as parol agreement, parol evidence.

**Parole.** The release of a prisoner from imprisonment before the full sentence has been served. [Black's *Law Dictionary*, 8th Ed.].

A conditional release of prisoner, generally under supervision of a parole officer, who has served part of the term for which he was sentenced to prison. Such may be revoked if he fails to observe the conditions provided in parole order. [Black's *Law Dictionary*, 5th Ed.].

A promise given by a prisoner of war to return at a time appointed or not to take up arms till exchanged; the practice of releasing prisoner of war on an undertaking. [Jowitt's *Dictionary of English Law*].

Release from jail, prison or other confinement after actually serving part of sentence. [*State* v *Ludwig* 344 P 2d 764, 766].

NOTE: It is a form of conditional release. Release on parole is designed to afford some relief to the prisoner in certain specified exigencies, for instance, illness or death of a member of his family or marriage of prisoner or some of the member of the family. It is tantamount to mere suspension of the sentence for the time being keeping the quantum of sentence in tact, i.e., the period in parole is not considered as his being in prison. [*Charanjitlal* v *State (Delhi)* (1985)28 Del LT 92, 96].

Historically "parole" is a concept known to military law and denotes release of a prisoner of war on promise to return. [*Poonam Lata* v *M.L. Wadhawan* AIR 1987 SC 1383: (1987)3 SCC 347: (1987)2 SCR 1123: JT 1987(2) SC 204: 1987 Cr LJ 1130: 1987 SCC (Cri) 506: (1987)30 ELT 3].

Parole is an act of grace and not a matter of right. It is an executive function based on 'humanitarian consideration'. [*Ramesh* v *State of Rajasthan* (1992)1 Western Law Cases 284 (Raj)].

*Parole and bail—distinction.* In a court of law both 'parole' and 'bail' have different connotations. The legal effect of parole is the release of the applicant from jail, till trial or appeal is finally disposed of unless in the mean time application for cancellation is made and allowed. But the effect of the bail is not to set the accused at liberty but to release him to the custody of the sureties. [*Anis Khan* v *State of U.P.* (1987)2 Crimes 565].

**Parsi.** A fire-worshipper.

NOTE: The Parsis settled chiefly in Western India in the State of Maharashtra. They still observe the ancient religion promulgated by Zoroaster. They are distinguished as enterprising merchants, shipbuilders and traders. Their ancestors fled from Persia to India upon the conquest of Persia by the Mohamedans and settled in India in the eighth century.

**Part.** An integral portion, something essentially belonging to a larger whole; that which together with another or others makes up a whole. [*First-Mechanics Nat. Bank of Trenton* v *Norris* 134 NJ Eq 229: 34 A 2d 746, 749].

**Part-owners.** They are persons who are entitled to property jointly, or in common, or in coparcenary. They have a distinct, or at least an independent, although an undivided interest in the property.

NOTE: *Part-owners and partners—distinction.* Part-owners differ from partners in many respects, the principals of which are: (1) that a partner is the agent of his co-partners within the ordinary scope of the business, so that he has power to bind them towards third persons even against their will, while a part-owner, in the absence of a special agreement, has no such power, and can only deal with his own interest in the property; and (2) that a part-owner can transfer his interest to a stranger, while a partner cannot do so without the consent of his co-partners.

As to ships in particular, it has long been settled that part-owners of a ship are not necessarily partners [*Helme* v *Smith* 33 RR 630, 633]; but if they employ the ship in trade or adventure on their joint account, they are partners as to that employment and the profit thereby made. [*Vanamati Sattiraju* v *Bollapragada Pallamraju* (1918)41 Mad 339].

**Part-payment of purchase price.** Money paid as part of the purchase price.

NOTE: Money paid as earnest or deposit is part of the purchase price, but it is principally a security for the performance of the contract for sale; as such it is liable to forfeiture if the transaction falls through on default of the purchaser. But part-payment of the price, not as earnest or deposit, is not liable to forfeiture on default of the purchaser.

It has to be decided in each case whether or not a payment was made as earnest or part-payment of the price. [*K.C.N. Gowda* v *Molakram* AIR 1958 Mys 10].

**Particeps criminis.** A partner in crime. An accomplice in a crime is *particeps criminis*.

**Participate.** Act in concert; act together; be a party to; be in league with; become involved with; have a part in; have a share of; play a part in; share in; take an active part in; experience in common with others; to have or enjoy a part or share in common with others; to partake of; to share or divide.

**Particular.** "Particular" means peculiar or pertaining to a specified person, thing, time or place—not common or general. The meaning of the word "particular" in relation to law means separate or special, limited or specific. [*J.C. Yadav* v *State of Haryana* (1990)2 SCC 189].

**Particulars.** In its ordinary meaning, the word "particulars" means details of items. "Particulars" with reference to a claim means the details of the claim which are necessary in order to enable the other side to know what case he has to meet. [*B.H. Aswathanaryana Singh* v *State of Mysore* AIR 1965 SC 1848: (1966)1 SCR 87].

NOTE: The use of "particulars" is intended to meet a further and quite separate requirement of pleading, imposed in fairness and justice to the defendant. Their function is to fill in the picture of the plaintiff's cause of action with information sufficiently detailed to put the defendant on his guard as to the case he has to meet and enable him to prepare for trial. [*H.V. Kamath* v *Election Tribunal* AIR 1958 MP 168].

**Partisan.** A strong, especially unreasoning, supporter of a party; relating to or unreasonably devoted to a party or faction; an adherent and upholder of an individual or of a party or cause as opposed to the public interest at large, especially a blind or fanatical adherent or devotee; biased; champion; defender; factionary; sectarian; undetached; undispassionate.

**Partition.** Apportion; break up; compartmentalize; distribute; divide into distinct portions; divide proportionately; sectionalize; split up; subdivide.

'Partition" is really a process by which a joint enjoyment is transformed into an enjoyment in severalty. [*The Controller of Estate Duty, Gujarat* v *Shri Kantilal Trikamlal* AIR 1976 SC 1935: (1976)4 SCC 643: (1976)105 ITR 92: (1977)1 SCR 9].

The legal term "partition" is applied to the division of lands, tenements, and hereditaments belonging to co-owners, and the allotment among them of the parts, so as to put an end to community of ownership between some or all of them. [Halsbury's *Laws of England*, 3rd Ed., vol. 32, p. 343].

"Partition" is defined as the dividing of lands held by joint tenants, coparceners, or tenants in common, into distinct portions, so that they may hold them in severalty. And, in a less technical sense, any division of real or personal property between co-owners, resulting in individual ownership of the interests of each. Division between several persons of property which belongs to them as co-owners; it may be compulsory (judicial) or voluntary. [*O'Brien* v *O'Brien* 89 Misc 2d 433: 391 NYS 2d 502, 503].

"Partition" really means that whereas initially all the coparceners have subsisting title to the totality of the property of the family jointly, that joint title is by partition transformed into separate titles of the individual coparceners in respect of several items of properties allotted to them respectively. [*V.N. Sarin* v *Ajit Kumar Poplai* AIR 1966 SC 432: (1966)1 SCR 349].

NOTE: Partition consists in defining the shares of the coparceners in the joint property—actual division of the property by metes and bounds is not necessary to constitute partition. Once the shares are defined, whether by agreement between the parties or otherwise, the partition is complete. The parties may thereafter choose to divide the property by metes and bounds or may continue to live together and enjoy the property in common, as before. If they live together, the mode of enjoyment alone remains joint but not the tenure of the property. It is from the intention to sever followed by conduct which seeks to effectuate that intention, that partition results, mere specifications of share without evidence of intention to sever does not result in partition. [*Girijanandini Devi* v *Bijendra Narain Chowdhury* AIR 1967 SC 1124].

It is severance of joint status and all that is necessary to constitute partition is a definite and unequivocal indication of intention of a member of joint family to enjoy his share in severalty although such intention is required to be communicated to the other members of the family. [*Fatechand Maheshri* v *State of W.B.* 76 CWN 137].

To constitute partition all that is necessary is a definite and unequivocal indication of intention by a member of joint family to separate himself from the family. The further requirement is that this unequivocal intention to separate must be to the knowledge of the persons affected by such declaration. This intention to separate may be manifested in diverse ways. [*Kalyani* v *Narayan* AIR 1980 SC 1173: 1980 (Supp) SCC 298: (1980)2 SCJ 332].

• **Instrument of partition** p. 465.

**Partners.** Persons who have entered into partnership with one another are called individually partners. [Indian Partnership Act 1932, s. 4].

NOTE: Position of shareholders of a company is not analogous to that of the partners. [*Bacha* v *Commissioner of Income-tax* 1955 SCR 876: AIR 1955 SC 74: 1955 SCA 675: 1955 SCJ 68].

*Co-owners and partners—distinction.* The distinction between co-owners and partners is that in the case of co-ownership, the co-owners do not intend to carry on business. On the other hand, the partners intend to carry on business. [*Abdul Badsha* v *Century Wood Industries* AIR 1954 Mys 33: ILR (1953) Mys 427; *Gopalji* v *Nagarmal* AIR 1956 Pat 441].

• **Dormant partner** p. 280.
• **Sleeping partner** p. 800.
• **Working partner** p. 904.

**Partnership.** Partnership is a voluntary contract between two or more competent persons to place their money, effects, labour, and skill, or some or all of them, in lawful commerce or business, with the understanding that there shall be a proportional sharing of the profits and losses between them. [*Burr* v *Greenland* Tex Civ App, 356 SW 2d 370, 376; *Preston* v *State Industrial Accident Commission* 149 P 2d 957, 961, 962].

"An ordinary partnership is a partnership composed of definite individuals bound together by contract between themselves to continue combined for some joint object, either during pleasure or during a limited time, and is essentially composed of the persons originally entering into the contract with one another." [*Smith* v *Anderson* (1880)15 Ch D 247, 273 (CA), *per* James, L.J.].

Partnership involves a contract between the partners to engage in a business with a view to profit. As a rule, each partner contributes either property, skill, or labour, but this is not essential. A person who contributes property without labour, and has the rights of a partner, is usually termed a sleeping or dormant partner. A sleeping partner may, however, contribute nothing. [Halsbury's *Laws of England*, 3rd Ed., vol. 28, pp. 483, 484].

Partnership is the relation between persons who have agreed to share the profits of a business carried on by all or any of them acting for all. [Indian Partnership Act 1932, s. 4; *Dulichand Laxminarayan* v *Commissioner of Income Tax, Nagpur* AIR 1956 SC 354: 1956 SCR 154: 1956 SCJ 317: (1956)29 ITR 535].

NOTE: Contract of partnership may be expressed or implied. It can arise out of mutual understanding between the parties evidenced by consistent course of conduct. [*Sitaram Kalani* v *Manmal Gattani* AIR 1956 MB 60].

- **Dissolution of partnership** p. 272.

- **Particular partnership.** A person may become a partner with another person in particular adventures or undertakings. [Indian Partnership Act 1932, s. 8]. The practice of establishing particular partnership is much favoured by Indian firms with numerous branches.

NOTE: In a particular partnership, the parties unite to share the profits of a single individual transaction or enterprise. Two persons who buy land for immediate sale, purely as a speculation, on an agreement for a division of the profits, constitute a particular partnership. All the requisites of a partnership must be present before a partnership between two persons limited to a single adventure is held to be a partnership. [*Suganmal* v *Mt. Umraobi* AIR 1938 Nag 550].

**Partnership at will.** Where no provision is made by contract between the partners for the duration of their partnership, or for the determination of their partnership, the partnership is partnership at will. [Indian Partnership Act 1932, s. 7].

A "partnership at will" is that it is open to either partner to dissolve the partnership by giving notice. [*Karumuthu Thiagarajan Chettiar* v *E.M. Muthappa Chettiar* AIR 1961 SC 1225: (1961)3 SCR 998: (1962)1 SCJ 31].

**Party.** A body of persons united for some common purpose; a political organization; a social company or gathering.

"Party" is a technical word having a precise meaning in legal parlance; it refers to those by or against whom a legal suit is brought, whether in law or in equity, the party plaintiff or defendant, whether composed of one or more individuals and whether natural or legal persons; all others who may be affected by the suit, indirectly or consequently, are persons interested but not parties. [*Golatte* v *Mathews* DC Ala, 394 F Supp 1203, 1207].

The term, in general, means one having right to control proceedings, to make defence, to adduce and cross-examine witnesses, and to appeal from judgment. [*City of Chattanooga* v *Swift* 442 SW 2d 257, 258].

A "party" to an action is a person whose name is designated on record as plaintiff or defendant. [*M & A Elec. Power Co-op.* v *True* Mo App, 480 SW 2d 310, 314].

▸ *Meaning under the Code of Criminal Procedure 1899, s. 439(5).* The expression 'party' included not only private parties but also the State if it happened to be the party as in police cases. [*State* v *Lachman Murty* AIR 1958 Ori 204].

**Party aggrieved.** Any person having an interest recognized by law in the subject-matter of the judgment, which interest is injuriously affected by the judgment, is a "party aggrieved" and entitled to be heard on appeal. [*Mize* v *Crail* 29 CA 3d 797: 106 Cal Rptr 34, 38].

NOTE; To be "party aggrieved" by judgment, appellant's interest must be immediate, pecuniary and substantial and not nominal or remote consequence of judgment. [*Leoke* v *San Bernardino County* 249 CA 2d 767].

**Party wall.** A division wall between two adjacent properties belonging to different persons and used for mutual benefit of both parties, but it is not necessary that the wall should stand part upon each of two adjoining lots, and it may stand wholly upon one lot. [*Soma Realty Co.* v *Romeo* 220 NYS 2d 752, 755].

▸ *Meaning under the Cantonments Act 1924, s. 2(xxvii).* A wall forming part of a building and used or constructed to be used for the support or separation of adjoining buildings belonging to different owners, or constructed or adapted to be occupied by different persons.

The wall between the two houses belonging to the plaintiffs on one side and the defendant on the other is a party wall. [*Imambhai Kamrudin* v *Rahimbhai Usamanbhai* AIR 1925 Bom 373; 27 Bom LR 503].

NOTE: The word 'party-wall' is used in four different senses—(1) a wall in which two adjoining owners are tenants in common, (2) a wall divided longitudinally into two strips, one belonging to each of the neighbouring owners, (3) a wall which belongs entirely to one of the adjoining owners, but is subject to an easement or right in the other to have it maintained as a dividing wall between the two tenements, (4) a wall divided longitudinally into two moieties, each moiety being subject to a cross easement in favour of the owner of the other moiety. [*Watson* v *Gray* (1880)14 Ch D 192: 49 LJ Ch 243].

**Parwana.** An order, a command, a warrant by a person in authority; a permission or pass.

**Pass.** In legal parlance, it means to utter or pronounce, as when the court passes sentence upon a prisoner; to examine into anything and then authoritatively determine the disputed questions which it involves.

In the language of conveyancing, it means to move from one person to another; change ownership; transfer ownership; transfer title.

When used in connection with negotiable instrument, the word means to deliver, to circulate, to hand from one person to another. [*State* v *Beaver* 145 SE 2d 330].

When the offence of passing counterfeit money or a forged paper is spoken of, the word means to publish, utter, transfer, circulate, impose fraudulently.

The expression may also mean a licence to go and come; a certificate, emanating from an appropriate authority, wherein it is declared that a designated person is permitted to go beyond certain boundaries which, without such authority, he could not lawfully pass; a ticket issued by a railroad or other transportation company, authorising a designated person to travel free on its lines, between certain points or for a limited time.

▸ *Meaning under the Railways Act 1989, s. 2(28).* It may also mean an authority given by the Central Government or a railway administration to a person allowing him to travel as a passenger.

NOTE: *Pass and duty pass—distinction.* Pass means an authority given either by the Central Government or by a railway administration to a person allowing him to travel as a passenger. A duty pass is issued by the railway under the Rules and it can be used only for journeys on duty and a railway servant is not entitled to travel with the duty pass while he is not on duty. [*Mariayayi* v *Union of India* AIR 1971 Mad 488: 84 MLW 461].

• **Property passing on the death.** The expression denotes some actual change in the title or possession of the property which takes place at the death. The assets of a deceased person pass on his death to his legal personal representative. [Halsbury's *Laws of England*, 3rd Ed., vol. 15, p. 10].

Property which 'passes on the death of any person' means property which changes hands at the death. [*Re Bennett Provincial Treasurer* v *Bennett* (1936)2 DLR 291].

**Pass and repass.** The words "pass" and "repass" mean no more than 'going' and 'returning'. [*Hill* v *Browning* (1870)22 LT 712, *per* Mellor, J.].

**Passage.** That by which a person or thing passes or may pass, way, road, path or channel especially when serving as an entrance or exit; act of passing; transit; transition; a way over water or land or through the air; the carriage of passengers by water; price paid for such carriage.

A right, privilege, or permission to pass over land or water; an easement to travel through another's property. [Black's *Law Dictionary*, 8th Ed.].

'Passage' means something in the nature of a feeder of the street [*Oakley* v *Merthyr Tydfil Corpn*. (1922)1 KB 409, 421, *per* Lord Trevethin, C.J.]; something on which people pass. [*Thornton* v *Fisher & Ludlow, Ltd*. (1968)2 All ER 241 (CA)].

'Passage' in ordinary usage suggests "something narrower, in the same way as the description with which one is quite familiar, narrow passages going through various places or between walls or between other bits of land, as the case may be". [*Thornton* v *Fisher & Ludlow Ltd*. (1968)2 All ER 241, 244, *per* Danckwerts, L.J.].

In legislative context, it means enactment; the act of carrying a bill through a legislative body in accordance with the prescribed forms and requisites.

**Passenger.** In general, a passenger is one who gives compensation for a ride. [*Shapiro* v *Bookspan* 318 P 2d 123, 126].

A 'passenger' is a person whom a common carrier has contracted to carry from one place to another. [*Sundari* v *Union of India* AIR 1984 All 277].

A passenger is a person travelling with a valid pass or ticket. [ Railways Act 1989, s. 2(29)]. Passenger would naturally mean person being carried in the vehicle. [*Branch Manager, National Insurance Co.* v *Kahas Beheram* AIR 1997 Ori 19].

The word 'passenger' has various meanings, depending upon the circumstances under which and the context in which the word is used. Sometimes it is construed in a restricted legal sense as referring to one who is being carried by another for hire; on the other occasions, the word is interpreted as meaning an occupant of a vehicle other than the person operating it. [*American Mercury Ins. Co.* v *Bifulco* 181 A 2d 20, 22].

NOTE: *'Passenger'—who is not.* (1) A driver is clearly not a passenger. [*Digby* v *General Accident Fire & Life Assurance Corpn. Ltd.* (1943) AC 121, 130, *per* Lord Maugham]. (2) A trespasser or person travelling without ticket or pass or authority is not a passenger. [*Sundari* v *Union of India* AIR 1984 All 277].

**Passenger train.** A train by which the company professes or offers to carry for hire in ordinary course such travellers as may take advantage of it on payment of their fares. [*Burnett* v *Great North of Scotland Ry. Co.* (1885)10 App Cas 147].

Passenger train means a train intended solely or mainly for the carriage of passengers and other coaching traffic, and includes a troop train. [*Vide* s. 1(25) of the Rules for the guidance of Railways servants framed under s. 47, Indian Railways Act 1890 by Railways Board Circular No. RT 89-A/5 dated September 8, 1906].

**Passing.** In its application to accounts, it means approval of the method of income and expenses.

In its application to decree of a court, it means the passing of a judgment. [*Balabhadra Prodhan* v *Sundarimani Devi* AIR 1995 Ori 180].

In considering the date of passing of an Act of Parliament, the words mean the time when the Royal Assent is given to a bill which has passed both Houses of

Parliament. [*Ex p. Rashleigh, Re Dalzell* (1875)2 Ch D 9 (CA), *per* James, L.J.].

**Passing off.** Selling goods or carrying on business in a manner calculated to mislead the public into believing that goods, business, etc. are those of another person. [Mozley & Whiteley's *Law Dictionary*, 10th Ed.].

NOTE: A passing off action lies for the use of a name or get up which is calculated to cause confusion with the goods of a particular rival trader.

In action for passing off, proof of actual deception is not necessary. If the two marks bear an overall similarity as would be likely to mislead a person usually dealing with the one to accept the other if offered to him, it is enough. [*The National Match Works* v *S.T. Karuppannan* (1978)2 MLJ 257: AIR 1979 MLJ 157].

**Passive trust.** It is a trust as to which the trustee has no active duty to perform. The prime requisite of a passive trust is that the trustee is made in form, a mere holder of the legal title, the right to possession and profits being in another.

NOTE: Where a special duty is to be performed by the trustee in respect to the estate, such as to collect the rents and profits, to sell the estate, etc., the trust is called active.

**Passport.** Strictly a licence to pass a port or haven, that is, a licence for the safe passage of any man from one place to another. [Mozley & Whiteley's *Law Dictionary*, 10th Ed.].

A passport is evidence of permission from sovereign to its citizen to travel to foreign countries and to return to land of his allegiance, as well as request to foreign powers that such citizen be allowed to pass freely and safely. [*Worthy* v *U.S.* CA Fla, 328 F 2d 386, 391].

NOTE: The modern passport is largely an identity and travel document issued to the State's own nationals. In the normal intercourse of State, a foreign national passport is, as a rule, accepted as *prima facie* evidence of the holder's nationality. A passport, whether in England or in the United States of America serves diverse purposes; it is a 'request for protection', it is a document of identity, it is a *prima facie* evidence of nationality; in modern times, it not only controls exit from the state to which one belongs, but without it, with a few exceptions, it is not possible to enter another State. It has become a condition for free travel. [*Satwant Singh Sawhney* v *D. Ramarathanam, Assistant Passport Officer, New Delhi* AIR 1967 SC 1837].

**Passport authority.** An officer or authority empowered to issue passports or travel documents and includes the Central Government. [Passport Act 1967, s. 2(*c*)].

**Patent.** Used as adjective, it means clear; conspicuous; disclosed; easy to be seen; evident; exposed to view; glaring; manifest; noticeable; ostensible; overt; perceivable; perceptible; plain to be seen; revealed; published; uncamouflaged; unconcealed; undisguised; visible; wide open.

As noun, it means certificate of invention; exclusive licence; exclusive privilege; exclusive right; exclusive title; governmental grant; grant of authority; rights to profits accruing.

A 'patent' is defined as a governmental protection to an inventor, securing to him for a specific time the exclusive right of manufacturing, exploiting, using, and selling an invention. [Webster *Comprehensive Dictionary*, International Ed.].

It is defined as the governmental grant of a right, privilege, or authority; the official document so granting. [Black's *Law Dictionary*, 8th Ed.].

An exclusive right granted to a person who has invented a new and useful article or an improvement of an existing article or a new process of making an article; a monopoly right in respect of an invention. [Narayanan: *Patent Law*, 4th Ed., p. 1].

NOTE: The effect of the grant of patent is *quid pro quo, quid* is the knowledge disclosed to the public and *quo* is the monopoly granted for the term of the patent. Section 12, Patents and Designs Act sets out that a Patent once granted confers upon the patentee the exclusive privilege of making, selling and using the invention throughout India and of authorising others so to do. This is *quo*. The *quid* is compliance with the various provisions resulting in the grant of patent. [*Raj Parkash* v *Mangat Ram Choudhary* ILR (1977)2 Del 412: AIR 1978 Del 1].

• **Letters patent** p. 531.

**Patent defect.** See under DEFECT p. 241.

**Patentee.** The person for the time being entered on the register as the grantee or proprietor of the patent. [Patents Act 1970, s. 2(*p*)].

**Pater familias.** A *sui juris* and head of the family.

**Patni.** A heritable tenure directly under the zamindar.

**Patricide.** The crime of killing one's father; also a person guilty of killing his father.

**Patta.** A deed of lease by the landlord to the tenant.

**Patti.** A share or division of land, village or estate.

**Patwari.** The village registrar and accountant.

**Pauper.** A person so poor that he must be supported at public expense; a suitor who, on account of poverty, is allowed to sue or defend without being chargeable with costs; also an indigent criminal defendant who has a right to assigned defence counsel. [Black's *Law Dictionary*, 5th Ed.].

A very poor person, especially one who receives aid from charity or public funds; an indigent. [Black's *Law Dictionary*, 7th & 8th Eds.].

A person is a pauper if he is not possessed of sufficient means (other than property exempt from attachment in execution of a decree and subject-matter of the suit) to enable him to pay the fee prescribed by law for the plaint in such suit, or where no such fee is prescribed, if he is not entitled to property worth one thousand rupees other than the property exempt from attachment in execution of a decree, and the subject-matter of the suit. [Code of Civil Procedure 1908, Or. 33, r. 1—by C.P.C. (Am.) Act 1976 the expression now is 'indigent'].

**Pawn.** A pawn or pledge is a bailment of personal property as a security for some debt or engagement. [Halsbury's *Laws of England*, 3rd Ed., vol. 29, p. 211].

An item of personal property deposited as security for a debt; a pledge or guarantee; the act of depositing personal property in this manner; the condition of being held on deposit as a pledge. [Black's *Law Dictionary*, 7th & 8th Eds.].

▸ *Meaning under the Indian Contract Act 1872, s. 172.* A pawn or pledge is a bailment of goods as security for payment of a debt or performance of a promise. The bailor is called the pawnor and the bailee is called the pawnee.

A pawn is security, where by contract, a deposit of goods is made as security for a debt. The right to property vests in the pledgee only so far as is necessary to secure the debt. In this sense, a pawn or pledge is an intermediate between a simple lien and mortgage which wholly passes the property in the thing conveyed. [*Holliday* v *Holygate* (1968)3 Ex 299; *Lallan Prasad* v *Rahmat Ali* AIR 1967 SC 1322: (1967)1 SCWR 709].

NOTE: 'Pawn' has reference to movable property only. In pawn, the possession is transferred to the creditor.

**Pawn-broker.** A pawn-broker is one whose business it is to lend money, usually in small sums, upon pawn or pledge, and includes, for statutory purposes, every person who carries on the business of taking goods and chattels in pawn. [Halsbury's *Laws of England*, 3rd Ed., vol. 29, p. 210].

A person whose business is to lend money, usually in small sums, on security of personal property deposited with him or left in pawn. [Black's *Law Dictionary*, 5th Ed.].

One who lends money, usually at a high interest rate, in exchange for personal property that is deposited as security by the borrower. [Black's *Law Dictionary*, 7th & 8th Eds.].

**Pawnee.** A pawnee is one who receives a pawn or pledge; the person to whom goods are delivered by another in pledge.

**Pawner.** A pawner is one who, being liable to an engagement, gives to the person to whom he is liable a thing to be held as a security for the payment of his debt or the fulfilment of his liability.

**Pay.** As noun means compensation; wages; salary; fees; commissions; remuneration; allowance; emolument; monetary return; the act or fact of paying or being paid.

As verb, means to discharge a debt by tender of payment due; to deliver to a creditor the value of a debt, either in money or in goods; bear the cost; compensate; defray; remunerate.

In respect of a government employee, 'pay' means amount drawn monthly by a government servant as the pay which has been sanctioned for a post held by him substantively or in an officiating capacity, or to which he is entitled by reason due to of his position in a cadre. [*Gangadhar Upadhya* v *State of U.P.* (1990)1 UPLBEC 542 (All) (DB)].

NOTE: To pay money is to pay it in respect of a right which some person has to receive it. [*Re, Miller* (1893)1 QB 327: 62 LJQB 324].

**Pay day.** Day on which Stock Exchange settlements are concluded; day on which a firm pays its employees.

**Pay roll.** A book, sheet or list, showing names of employees, particulars of wages or salaries payable, appropriate deductions (*e.g.*, income tax), the net wages or salaries payable and the employers' proportion of the contribution.

**Payable.** The word 'payable' is somewhat indefinite in import and its meaning must be gathered from the context in which it occurs. [*New Delhi Municipal Committee* v *Kalu Ram* AIR 1976 SC 1637: (1976)3 SCC 407: 1976 (Supp) SCR 87].

The word 'payable' is a descriptive word, which ordinarily means "that which must be paid or is due, or may be paid" but its correct meaning can only be determined if the context in which it is used is kept in view. [*J.K. Synthetics Ltd.* v *CTO* AIR 1994 SC 2393: (1994)4 SCC 276: JT 1994(3) SC 671: (1994)94 STC 422].

'Payable' generally means that which should be paid. [*New Delhi Municipal Committee* v *Kalu Ram* AIR 1976 SC 1637: (1976)3 SCC 407: 1976 (Supp) SCR 87]. It may also mean that which is 'legally recoverable'. [*New Delhi. Municipal Committee* v *Kalu Ram*, supra]

The word has been frequently understood to mean that which may, can or should be paid and is held equivalent to 'due'. [*J.K. Synthetics Ltd.* v *CTO* AIR 1994 SC 2393: (1994)4 SCC 276: JT 1994(3) SC 671: (1994)94 STC 422].

It may also signify 'an obligation to pay at a future time' as well as 'an obligation to pay at once'. [*MRF Ltd.* v *Asst. Commissioner* (1995)1 KLT 809 (FB)].

The word 'payable' may signify an obligation to pay at a future time, but when used without qualification, it means payable at once. [*Narayanan Chettiar* v *Annamalai Chettiar* AIR 1961 Mad 313].

**Payable on demand.** Payable at once. [*Aiyappankutty* v *Mathoo Mathai* AIR 1955 Trav-Co 65].

**Payee.** A person to whom payment is made; a person to whom the money is or will become payable; one to whom a bill of exchange or promissory note or cheque is made payable.

**Paying-in-slip.** This is the document handed to a bank when money is paid into customer's account. It gives particulars not only of the amount paid in, but specifies whether it be notes, cheques or coins.

**Payment.** 'Payment' is a delivery of money or its equivalent in either specific property or services by one person from whom it is due to another person to whom it is due. [*Sizemore* v *E.T. Barwick Industries, Inc.* 465 SW 2d 873, 875].

'Payment' is a discharge in money or its equivalent of an obligation or debt owing by one person to another, and is made by debtor's delivery to creditor of money or some other valuable thing, and creditor's receipt thereof, for purpose of extinguishing debt. [*Allmon* v *Allmon* Mo App, 306 SW 2d 651, 655].

'Payment' is a recompense for services rendered. [*Bala Subrahmanya Rajaram* v *B.C. Patil* AIR 1958 SC 518: 1958 SCR 1504: 1958 SCJ 851].

Payment signifies satisfaction of a claim. [*Parmeshr* v *Atti* AIR 1958 Punj 79].


- **Appropriation of payments** p. 71.
- **Balance of payments** p. 93.
- **Down payment** p. 282.


**Payment in due course.** Means payment in accordance with the apparent tenor of the instrument in good faith and without negligence to any person in possession thereof under circumstances which do not afford a reasonable ground for believing that he is not entitled to receive payment of the amount therein mentioned. [Negotiable Instruments Act 1881, s. 10].

**Peace.** A state of public tranquility; freedom from civil disturbance or hostility. [Black's *Law Dictionary*, 8th Ed.].

The term, within law of breach of the peace, means tranquility enjoyed by citizens of the municipality or community where good order reigns among its members. [*State* v *Edwards* 123 SE 2d 247, 249].


- **Breach of peace** p. 111.


**Pecuniary.** Of or relating to money; monetary; consisting of money or that which can be valued in money.

**Pecuniary benefits.** Benefits that can be valued in money. [*Dallas Ry. & Terminal Co.* v *Moore* Tax Civ App, 52 SW 2d 104].

NOTE: Obtaining goods on credit cannot be held to amount obtaining pecuniary benefit or advantage. If there is an agreement between an officer and a trader that the officer is not expected to pay for the goods then there is no doubt that this would amount to obtaining pecuniary benefit or advantage, but if there is no such agreement and the officer does not pay, it cannot be said that he had obtained any pecuniary benefit or advantage. [*Delhi Administration* v *S.N. Khosla* AIR 1971 SC 1480: (1971)3 SCR 315: (1971)1 SCC 872: 1971 Cr LJ 1151: 1971 SCC (Cri) 370].

**Pecuniary damages.** See under DAMAGES p. 221.

**Pecuniary gain.** A gain of money or of something having monetary value.

**Pecuniary liability.** The words 'pecuniary liability' cover any liability which is of a monetary nature and includes a mortgage debt. [*Smt. Rajkumari Kaushalya Devi* v *Bawa Pritam Singh* AIR 1960 SC 1030: (1960)3 SCR 570: (1961)1 SCJ 125].

Liability in terms of money. [*Rajkumari Kaushalya Devi (Smt.)* v *Bawa Pritam Singh* AIR 1960 SC 1030: (1960)3 SCR 570: (1961)1 SCJ 125].

**Pedigree.** The term 'pedigree' embraces not only general questions of descent and relationship but also the particular facts of birth, marriage and death, and the times when, either absolutely or relatively, these events happened, provided such facts are required to be proved for some genealogical purpose. [Taylor on *Evidence*, s. 642].


- **Family pedigree** p. 346.


**Pegged market.** Where the price of shares on the Stock Exchange is kept within defined limits by interested parties giving or withholding support.

**Penalty.** A penalty is a sum of money which the law exacts payment of by way of punishment for doing some act which is prohibited or for not doing some act which is required to be done. [*Hidden Hollow Ranch* v *Collins* 406 P 2d 365, 368].

The expression "penalty" involves an idea of punishment. [*Sova Ray* v *Gostha Gopal Dey* AIR 1988 SC 981: (1988)2 SCC 134: (1988)3 SCR 287: JT 1988(1) SC 583].

The word "penalty" is a word of wide significance. Sometimes it means recovery of an amount as a penal measure even in a civil proceeding. An exaction which is not of compensatory character is also termed as penalty even though it is not being recovered pursuant to an order finding the person concerned guilty of a crime. [*Shiv Dutta Rai Fateh Chand* v *Union of India* (1983)3 SCC 529: (1983)3 SCR 198: 1983 Tax LR 2917: 1983 SCC (Tax) 204: (1983)53 STC 289: (1984)148 ITR 664; *Director of Enforcement* v *M.C.T.M. Corporation (P) Ltd.* AIR 1996

SC 1100: (1996)2 SCC 471: 1996 SCC (Cri) 344: JT 1996(1) SC 79: (1996)2 SCJ 81: (1997)88 Comp Cas 449].

▸ *Use of the expression in Constitution of India, Art. 20(1).* The expression penalty is used therein in the narrow sense as meaning a payment which has to be made or a deprivation of liberty which has to be suffered as a consequence of a finding that the person accused of a crime is guilty of the charge. [*Shiv Dutta Rai Fateh Chand* v *Union of India* (1983)3 SCC 529: (1983)3 SCR 198: 1983 Tax LR 2917: 1983 SCC (Tax) 204: (1983)53 STC 289: (1984)148 ITR 664].

▸ *Treatment of the expression for tax purpose.* Penalty is not merely sanction. It is not merely adjunct to assessment. It is not merely consequential to assessment. It is not merely machinery. Penalty is in addition to tax and is a liability. [*Khemka & Co. (Agencies) Pvt. Ltd.* v *State of Maharashtra* AIR 1975 SC 1549: (1975)3 SCR 753: (1975)2 SCC 22: (1975)35 STC 571].

NOTE: *'Penalty' and 'liquidated damages'—test of determination.* Where there is a stipulation in an agreement to pay a sum of money on default, the question that has to be determined is whether the sum mentioned is obviously larger than any damage that could possibly be sustained by the plaintiff by reason of the breach of the contract. If it is larger than any such damage, then it must be held that the sum is penalty and not liquidated damages; if it is not larger, the sum is liquidated damages and not penalty. [*Imperial Tobacco Co. (of Great Britain & Ireland) Ltd.* v *Parsley* (1936)2 All ER 515].

**Pendente lite nihil innovetur.** During a litigation nothing new should be introduced.

**Pending.** About to happen; at hand; close at hand; impending; on coming; in a state of uncertainty; indefinite; indeterminate; open to discussion; open to question; under consideration; unsettled; unsolved.

Remaining undecided; awaiting decision; under consideration. [Black's *Law Dictionary*, 8th Ed.].

'Pending' means awaiting an occurrence or conclusion of action; period of continuance or indeterminacy. [*Schull Const. Co.* v *Board of Regents of Ed.* 113 NW 2d 663, 665].

The word 'pending' means 'impending', "remaining undecided", "not terminated", "awaiting" etc. [*State of Maharashtra* v *Chandra Sekhar Nilkantha* 1975 Mah LJ 607]. The word "pending" will ordinarily mean that the matter is not concluded and the court which has taken cognisance of it can make an order on the matter in issue. [*Lt. Col. S.K. Kashyap* v *State of Rajasthan* AIR 1971 SC 1120: (1971)3 SCR 881: (1971)2 SCC 126: 1971 Cr LJ 832: 1971 SCC (Cri) 452].

In common English parlance, "pending" means and implies 'not concluded'. [*Virendra Prasad* v *Union of India* 90 CWN 1172].

A cause remains pending even after final judgment until the judgment is fully satisfied. [*Salt* v *Cooper* (1880)16 Ch D 544: 50 LJ Ch 529].

A legal proceeding is "pending", as soon as commenced and until it is concluded, *i.e.*, so long as the court having original cognisance of it can make an order on the matters in issue, or to be dealt with therein. [*Ashagarali Nazarali Singaporwalla* v *State of Bombay* AIR 1957 SC 503: 1957 SCA 783: 1957 SCR 678: 1957 Cr LJ 605: 1957 SCJ 421].

'Litigation pending' means any legal proceeding, suit or action remaining undecided or awaiting decision or settlement. [*Garnham* v *Tessier* (1959)27 WWR 682].

The word 'pending', in regard to suit, or proceedings for ejectment, mean pending before a decree was passed by the trial court. It does not refer to appeal. [*Shrimati Dasi* v *Sihanibala Mitra* ILR (1951)1 Cal 559].

**Pension.** It means retirement benefit paid regularly (normally, monthly), with the amount of such based generally on length of employment and amount of wages or salary of pensioner. It is deferred compensation for services rendered. [*State ex rel. Bolen* v *City of Seattle, Wash.* 377 P 2d 454; *Waite* v *Waite* 492 P 2d 13].

A fixed sum paid regularly to a person (or to the person's beneficiaries), esp. by an employer as a retirement benefit. [Black's *Law Dictionary,* 8th Ed.].

Pension is periodical payment of money for past services. [*Beg Mirza* v *State* AIR 1959 All 769; *Bikram Bahadur* v *Commissioner of Income-tax* AIR 1969 MP 127].

NOTE: "Pension" is not merely a statutory right but it is the fulfilment of a constitutional promise inasmuch as it partakes the character of public assistance in cases of unemployment, old-age, disablement or similar other cases of underserved want. Relevant rules merely make effective the constitutional mandate. Pension is a right not a bounty or gratuitous payment. [*Smt. Poonamal* v *Union of India* AIR 1985 SC 1196: (1985)3 SCR 1042: 1985(2) SLR 537: (1985)3 SCC 345].

"Pension" is neither a bounty nor a matter of grace depending upon the sweet will of the employer, neither an *ex gratia* payment. It is a payment for the past service rendered. It is a social welfare measure rendering socio-economic justice to those who in the heyday of their life ceaselessly toiled for the employer on an assurance that in their old age they would not be left in the lurch. The most practical *raison d'etre* for pension is the inability to provide for oneself, due to old age. [*D.S. Nakara* v *Union of India* AIR 1983 SC 130: 1983(2) SLR 246: (1983)1 SCC 305].

**Pensioner.** A recipient or beneficiary of a pension plan. [Black's *Law Dictionary*, 8th Ed.].

The expression is generally understood in contradistinction to one in service. Those who after rendering service retire on superannuation and are in receipt of pension are pensioners. They constitute a homogeneous class; for the purpose of pension benefit they cannot be discriminated from other pensioners. [*D.S. Nakara* v *Union of India* AIR 1983 SC 130: (1983)1 SCWR 390: 1983 Lab IC 1: (1983)1 Lab LJ 104: (1983)1 SCJ 188].

**People.** The aggregate of human beings living under the same government, speaking the same language, or being of the same blood; ethnologically, a body of human beings belonging to the same linguistic stock and having the same culture; the whole body of persons composing a state or nation, or that part of the population invested with political rights; persons collectively; those who are connected with one as subjects, attendants, kinfolk, etc. [Webster *Comprehensive Dictionary*, International Edition].

The aggregate or mass of the individuals who constitute the State. [*Loi Hoa* v *Nagle* CCA Cal, 13 F 2d 80, 81].

**People in general.** The expression signifies all members of the public irrespective of any class or community or of any place. [*Ram Saran* v *Narayan Chandra* AIR 1954 Cal 125].

**Pepper-corn.** A nominal rent reserved where the land is to be held practically rent free, yet the landlord wishes, if necessary, by demanding the pepper-corn to have the tenancy at any time acknowledged by the tenant. In modern times, building leases sometimes reserve a pepper-corn as rent for the first few years.

Rent of pepper-corn is inapt in the case of a mining lease which is really rather a sale at a price payable by instalments than a demise properly so called. [*Re Aldam* (1902)2 Ch 60].

**Per capita.** For each person; literally, by heads.

A distribution *per capita* (by heads) is when a number of individuals, *e.g.*, a class, even though in different degrees of relationship, take the fund distributable among them in equal shares. Its opposite is *per stirpes* (by stocks). [Stroud's *Judicial Dictionary*, 5th Ed.].

This term, derived from the civil law, is much used in the law of descent and distribution, and denotes that method of dividing an intestate estate by which an equal share is given to each of a number of persons, all of whom stand in equal degree to the descendant, without reference to their stocks or the right of representation. It is the antithesis of *per stirpes* (q.v.) [*Buxton* v *Noble* 73 P 2d 43, 47; *MacGregor* v *Roux* 32 SE 2d 289, 291].

A division *"per capita"* means by a number of individuals equally or share and share alike. [*Gilbert* v *Wenzel* 78 NW 2d 793, 794].

**Per curiam.** By the court as a whole. [Black's *Law Dictionary*, 7th & 8th Eds.].

A phrase used to distinguish an opinion of the whole court from an opinion written by any one judge. Sometimes it denotes an opinion written by the Chief Justice or presiding judge, or to a brief announcement of the disposition of a case by court not accompanied by a written opinion. [Black's *Law Dictionary*, 5th Ed.].

**Per diem.** As noun it means a monetary daily allowance, usually to cover expenses; a daily fee.

As adjective, it means based on or calculated by the day.

As adverb, it means by the day; for each day.

**Per incuriam.** Wrongly decided, usually because the judge was or judges were ill-informed about the applicable law. [Black's *Law Dictionary*, 7th Ed.].

The Latin expression *"per incuriam"* means through inadvertence. A decision can be said generally to be given *per incuriam* when the Supreme Court has acted in ignorance of a previous decision of its own or when a High Court has acted in ignorance of a decision of the Supreme Court. The problem of judgment *per incuriam* when actually arises, should present no difficulty as the Supreme Court can lay down the law afresh, if two or more of its earlier judgments cannot stand together. [*Punjab Land Development & Reclamation Corporation Ltd.* v *Presiding Officer, Labour Court* (1990)3 SCC 682].

A judgment *per incuriam* is generally a decision given in ignorance or forgetfulness of the existence of an earlier decision or statute not brought to the attention of the court. [*Mamleswar* v *Kanhaiya* AIR 1975 SC 907; *Nilkantha* v *Manmohan* (1975)1 CLJ 404].

NOTE: *Per incuriam* decisions are not binding. [*Sitaram Hari* v *L.R. Dubey* AIR 1980 Bom 55].

**Per pro.** By procuration. The words indicate that the person signing has but a limited authority to sign, and signs in a representative capacity.

**Per se.** Of, in, or by itself; standing alone, without reference to additional facts; as a matter of law. [Black's *Law Dictionary*, 7th & 8th Eds.].

**Per stirpes.** It is a Latin expression which means "by roots or stocks".

A distribution of property *per stirpes* means distribution according to the stocks and not according to the number of individuals; proportionate division of property between beneficiaries according to their deceased ancestor's share.

It is opposite to *per capita*.

**Peremptory.** Used as adjective to denote absolute, it means complete; decided; decisive, definite; determinate; incontrovertible; overbearing; total; unequivocal; without limitation; final.

Used as adjective to denote imperative, it means assertive; authoritative; commanding; compulsory; decisive; mandatory; obligatory.

Self-determined; arbitrary; not requiring any cause to be shown. [*Wolfe* v *State* 178 SW 2d 274, 279].

"Peremptory", "signifies a final and dominate act, without hope of renewing or altering". [Stroud's *Judicial Dictionary of Words and Phrases*, 5th Ed. referring to Cowel].

**Peremptory order.** A peremptory order is an order whereby a person is required to do something within a fixed time or suffer the consequences. [Halsbury's *Laws of England*, 3rd Ed., vol. 37, p. 104].

NOTE: A peremptory order is meant to be final, unless some very special and urgent circumstances are brought forward as a reason for altering it. [*Falck* v *Axthelm* (1889)24 QBD 174: 50 LJQB 161].

**Performance.** Used as noun to denote execution, it means accomplished fact; achievement; attainment; completion; consummation; fulfilment; implementation; rendition.

Used as noun to denote workmanship, it means accomplishment; ability; achievement; aptitude; artfulness; attainment; capability; exhibition; play; production; craftsmanship; proficiency; quality of execution; quality of work; show; skill; skilfulness; talent; technique; working ability.

Performance of a contract consists in doing, or causing to be done, that which the promisor has promised shall be done. When the promisor has not done that which he promised, it is no answer that he has conferred on the promisee an equivalent or greater benefit by doing something else. [Sutton and Shannon on *Contracts*, 6th Ed., p. 279].

Performance means the successful completion of a contractual duty, usually resulting in the performer's release from any past or future liability; the equitable doctrine by which acts consistent with an intention to fulfil an obligation are construed to be in fulfilment of that obligation, even if the party was silent on the point; a company's earnings; the ability of a corporation to maintain or increase earnings. [Black's *Law Dictionary*, 8th Ed.].

▸ *Meaning under the Copyright Act 1957, s. 2(q) (w.e.f. 10.5.1995).* 'Performance' in relation to performer's right, means any visual or acoustic presentation made live by one or more performers.

NOTE: 'Performance' includes an actor, singer, musician, dancer, acrobat, juggler, conjurer, snake charmer, a person delivering a lecture or any other person who makes a performance. [Copyright Act 1957, s. 2(*qq*)].

**Performer.** He who makes a performance.

▸ *Meaning under the Copyright Act 1957, s. 2(qq) (w.e.f. 10.5.1995).* 'Performer' includes an actor, singer, musician, dancer, acrobat, juggler, conjurer, snake charmer, a person delivering a lecture or any other person who makes a performance.

**Perils of the sea.** An action of the elements at sea of such force as to overcome the strength of a well-founded ship and the normal precautions of good marine practice. [Black's *Law Dictionary*, 7th & 8th Eds.].

Peril of the sea within a marine policy envisions extraordinary and unusual perils which vessel may not reasonably expect to encounter; circumstances which are ordinarily encountered such as predictable winds, tides, wave actions and conditions of the water do not fall within such classification. [*Vining* v *Security Ins. Co. of New Haven* La App., 252 So 2d 754, 757].

"Perils of the sea" are understood to mean those perils which are peculiar to sea and which are of extraordinary nature or arise from irresistible force or overwhelming power, and which cannot be guarded against by ordinary exertions of human skill and prudence. [*New Rotterdam Ins. Co.* v *S.S. Loppersum* DCNY, 215 F Supp 563, 566, 567].

The term "perils of the seas" refers only to fortuitous accidents or casualties of the seas, and does not include the ordinary action of the winds and waves.

NOTE: *Perils of the sea—what are—examples*: (*i*) Loss by pirates is a peril of the sea. [*Pandorf* v *Hamilton* 55 LJQB 553]. (*ii*) Losses by swell of the tide in a dry river are perils of the sea. [*Fletcher* v *Inglis* 2 B & Ald 315]. (*iii*) Damage caused by the incursion of sea-water through a rat-hole, or a strained rivet-hole, is a peril of the sea. [*Hamilton* v *Pandorf* 55 LJQB 553]. (*iv*) Damage to cargo from the heat of the engines, confined through the ventilators being necessarily closed because of exceptionally bad weather, is an "accident of the sea". [*The Thrunscoe* (1897), p. 301].

*Perils of the sea—what are not—examples*: (*i*) Direct damage done to cargo by rats is not a peril of the sea. [*Laveroni* v *Drury* 8 Ex 166; *Kay* v *Wheeler* LR 2 CP 302]. (*ii*) Loss by unseaworthiness, *e.g.*, through insufficiency of coal, is not a loss by a "peril of the sea". [*Ballantyne* v *Mackinnon* (1896)2 QB 455]. (*iii*) Loss caused by improperly stowed cargo is not a loss by a "peril of the sea" within the terms of a bill of lading incorporating The Hague Rules. [*The Grumant* (1973)2 Lloyd's Rep 531].

**Periodic lease.** Lease for a definite period.

**Perishable goods.** Goods which decay and lose their value, if not consumed soon. Fish, fruit and the like are examples of perishable goods.

**Perjury.** Act of oath-breaking; distortion of the truth; false statement; false swearing; perversion of truth; prevarication; violation of an oath; wilful distortion of the truth; wilful falsehood; wilful telling of a falsehood.

The act or an instance of a person's deliberately making material false or misleading statements while under oath. [Black's *Law Dictionary*, 7th & 8th Eds.].

Perjury is a crime committed when a lawful oath is administered, in some judicial proceeding, to a person who swears wilfully, absolutely, and falsely, in a matter material to the issue or point in question. [*Gatewood* v *State* 290 A 2d 551, 553].

Perjury is an assertion upon an oath duly administered in a judicial proceeding, before a competent court, of the truth of some matter of fact material to the question depending in that proceeding, which assertion the assertor does not believe to be true when he makes it, on which he knows himself to be ignorant. [*R.* v *Baker* (1895)1 QB 797].

**Permanent alimony.** A provision in the maintenance and support of a wife during her life time.

Alimony payable in usually weekly or monthly instalments either indefinitely or until a time specified by court order. This kind of alimony may usually be modified for changed circumstances of either party. [Black's *Law Dictionary*, 7th & 8th Eds.]. It terminates upon the death of either spouse and usually upon the remarriage of the obligee. [Black's *Law Dictionary*, 8th Ed.].

Allowances which husband or wife by court order pays to other spouse for maintenance while they are separated or after they are divorced. [*Marriage & Divorce* by A.N. Saha, 6th Ed., p. 402].

An allowance for the support and maintenance of a spouse during his or her lifetime, and its purpose is to provide nourishment, sustenance and the necessities of life to a former spouse who has neither the resources nor ability to be self-sustaining. [*Cann* v *Cann* Fla App, 334 So 2d 325, 329].

NOTE: Section 25 of the Hindu Marriage Act 1955, s. 37 of the Special Marriage Act 1954, provide for permanent alimony and maintenance. Any court exercising jurisdiction under the Acts may, at the time of passing any decree or at any time subsequent thereto, on application made to it for the purpose by either the wife or the husband, as the case may be, order that the respondent shall pay to the applicant for her or his maintenance and support such gross sum or such monthly or periodical sum for a term not exceeding the life of the applicant as, having regard to the respondent's own income and other property, if any, the income and other property of the applicant and the conduct of the parties and other circumstances of the case, it may seem to the court to be just. If the court is satisfied that there is a change in the circumstances of either party at any time after it has made an order as aforesaid, it may, at the instance of either party, vary, modify or rescind any such order in such manner as the court may deem just.

If the court is satisfied that the party in whose favour an order has been made has remarried or, if such party is the wife, that she has not remained chaste, or, if such party is the husband that he has had sexual intercourse with any woman outside wedlock, it may at the instance of the other party vary, modify or rescind any such order in such manner as the court may deem just.

**Permanent disability.** A disability that will indefinitely prevent a worker from performing some or all of the duties that he or she could do before an accident [Black's *Law Dictionary*, 7th & 8th Eds.] or illness. [Black's *Law Dictionary*, 8th Ed.].

A permanent disability is one which causes impairment of earning capacity, impairment of normal use of member, or competitive handicap in open labour market. [*State Compensation Insurance Fund* v *Industrial Acc. Commission* 377 P 2d 902].

It is the permanent reduction of the injured person's power to earn money resulting from an injury. It is such disability as reduces the earning capacity of a workman in every employment which he was capable of undertaking at the time of the accident resulting in the disablement. Loss of one eye, loss of thumb, loss of index finger, etc., are instances of injuries deemed to result in permanent partial disablement. Permanent total disablement shall be deemed to result from the permanent total loss of the sight of both eyes or from any combination of injuries specified in Schedule I to the Workmen's Compensation Act 1923 where the aggregate percentage of the loss of earning capacity, as specified in that Schedule against those injuries, amounts to one hundred per cent.

**Permanent way.** In the case of railway, 'permanent way' includes not only the railway track itself but also all the equipment for guiding a train on its proper course and on its proper track as well as the metals on which it runs and the ground or structure supporting them. The point lines are part of the permanent way, whereas the point rods which move them and are permanetly fastened to them for that purpose are not. [*London & North Eastern Ry. Co.* v *Berriman* (1946) AC 274].

**Permission.** Approval; assent; authority; authorisation; concurrence; formal consent; leave; license; sanction; visa.

An act of permitting, formal consent, authorization, leave, license or liberty granted, and it has a flexible meaning depending upon the sense in which it is used. [*Winterton* v *Van Zandt* Mo., 351 SW 2d 696, 700].

NOTE: "Permission" is a word of wide import and may even survive the death of the person who permits. [*Manohar Nathusao Samarth* v *Marotrao* AIR 1979 SC 1084: (1979)3 SCR 1078: (1979)4 SCC 93].

The word "permission" is comprehensive enough to include subsequent permission. [*L.I.C. of India* v *Escorts Ltd.* 1985 Supp (3) SCR 909: AIR 1986 SC 1370: (1986)1 SCC 264: (1986)1 Comp LJ 91].

▸*Meaning under the Foreign Exchange Regulation Act 1947 (now Foreign Exchange Management Act, 1999), s. 21.* The word 'permission' is a word of wide import. The word means only leave to do some act which but for the leave would be illegal. [*Gobindram* v *Shamji* AIR 1961 SC 1285].

**Permit.** As noun means affirmation; approbation; approval; authority; authorisation; certificate; confirmation; document granting permission; any document which grants a person the right to do something; a licence or grant of authority to do a thing. [*Matter of Building Permit and Zoning* 225 SE 2d 647, 649].

As verb means accord one's approval; agree to; allow; approve; assent; authorise; be indulgent of; confer a privilege; empower; enable; entitle; give clearance; grant permission; make possible; sanction.

Permit means one of two things, either to give leave for an act which without that leave could not be legally done, or to abstain from taking reasonable steps to prevent the act where it is within a man's power to prevent it. [*Berton* v *Alliance Economic Investment Co.* (1922)1 KB 742 (CA), *per* Atkin, L.J.].

The word 'permit' is to be understood as indicative of a formal consent, grant or authorisation or giving an express licence. [*Ram Singh* v *Chief Commissioner* AIR 1968 Punj 470].

The word "permit" connotes an authorisation by a person who has at least a *de facto* control. [*Broad* v *Parish* 64 CLR 588].

The word 'permit' connotes, on the part of the one whose permission is asked, the right effectively to refuse and on the part of the applicant the necessity to ask for and obtain permission, so as lawfully to undertake his proposed course of action. [*Tophams Ltd.* v *Sefton (Early)* (1966)1 All ER 1039].

**Perquisite.** Benefaction; financial reward; incidental profits.

"Perquisite" is defined as "anything gotten by a man's own industry or purchased with his own money, different from that which descends to him from his father or ancestors". [Stroud's *Judicial Dictionary of Words and Phrases*, 5th Ed., referring to Cowel].

Perquisite means personal advantage. [*Owen* v *Pook* (1970) AC 244].

Perquisite is defined as a "privilege or benefit given in addition to one's salary or regular wages". [Black's *Law Dictionary*, 7th & 8th Eds.].

As used in the Income-tax Act 1961 [s. 17(2)], "perquisite" includes—(*i*) the value of rent-free accommodation provided to the assessee by his employer; (*ii*) the value of any concession in the matter of rent respecting any accommodation provided to the assessee by his employer; (*iii*) the value of any benefit or amenity granted or provided free of cost or at concessional rate in any of the following cases—(*a*) by a company to an employee who is a director thereof; (*b*) by a company to an employee being a person who has a substantial interest in the company; (*c*) by any employer (including a company) to an employee whose income under the head "salaries", exclusive of the value of all benefits or amenities not provided for by way of monetary payment, exceeds fifty thousand rupees; (*iv*) any sum paid by the employer in respect of any obligation which, but for such payment, would have been payable by the assessee; (*v*) any sum payable by the employer, whether directly or through a fund, other than a recognised provident fund or an approved superannuation fund, to effect an assurance on the life of the assessee or to effect a contract for an annuity; and (*vi*) the value of any other fringe benefit or amenity as may be prescribed.

**Person.** Human being; human creature; living being; living soul; member of the human race; mortal body; autonomous being.

A human being; an entity (such as a corporation) that is recognised by law as having the rights and duties of a human being; the living body of a human being. [Black's *Law Dictionary*, 7th Ed.].

The word 'person' may very well include both a natural person (a human being), and an artificial person (a corporation). In an Act of Parliament, unless there be something to the contrary, probably it ought to be held to include both. [*Pharmaceutical Society* v *London & Provincial Supply Association* 5 App Cas 857, *per* Lord Blackburn].

'Person', when used in a legal sense, is an apt word to describe a corporation as well as a natural person. [*Royal Mail Steam Packet Co.* v *Braham* (1877)2 App Cas 381 (PC)].

> NOTE: The expression 'person' includes natural person or artificial person like corporation and a joint stock company; but it does not include a state or government. [*Samatha* v *State of A.P.* (1995)2 ALT 233 (DB); *Ram Saran Das* v *Province of East Punjab* AIR 1954 Punj 49 (DB)].

▸*Meaning under the General Clauses Act 1897, s. 3(42).* 'Person' shall include any company or association or body of individuals, whether incorporated or not. The definition of the term in the General Clauses Act is not exhaustive. It is hardly a definition. It only indicates the intention of legislature to treat artificial person as persons. [*Jabbar* v *State of U.P.* AIR 1966 All 590].

▸*Meaning under the Indian Penal Code, s. 11 and scope of criminal liability.* A person includes within its ambit a company or association or body of persons whether incorporated or not. It may seem *prima facie* that a corporate body or a body of unincorporated persons is punishable as an ordinary individual. But, the clause "unless there is anything repugnant to the subject or context" must always be understood to exist in the context of the definitions given in Penal Code. So a corporate body or a company shall not be indictable for offences which can be committed only by a human individual (*e.g.*, rape, bigamy etc.) or for offences which must be punished by imprisonment (e.g. cheating). [*State of Maharashtra* v *Syndicate Bank* AIR 1964 Bom 95: (1964)2 Cr LJ 276: 1964 Mah LJ 308: ILR (1964) Bom 533].

> NOTE: In general, a corporation is in the same position in relation to criminal liability as a

natural person and may be convicted of common law and statutory offences including those requiring *mens rea*. There are, however, crimes which a corporation is incapable of committing or of which a corporation cannot be found guilty as principal; nor can a corporation be convicted of a crime for which death or imprisonment are the only punishments.

Criminal liability of a corporation arises where an offence is committed in the course of corporation's business by a person in control of its affairs to such a degree that it may fairly be said to think and act through him so that his actions and intent are the actions and intent of the corporation. [Halsbury's *Laws of England*, 4th Ed., vol. 11, para 34, p. 30].

▸ *Meaning under the Carriers Act 1865, s. 2.* 'Person' includes any association or body of persons, whether incorporated or not.

▸ *Meaning under the Gift Tax Act 1958, s. 2(xviii), [since repealed].* 'Person' includes a Hindu undivided family or a company or an association or a body of individuals or persons, whether incorporated or not.

▸ *Meaning under the Income-tax Act 1961, s. 2(31).* 'Person' includes—(*i*) an individual, (*ii*) a Hindu undivided family, (*iii*) a company, (*iv*) a firm, (*v*) an association of persons or a body of individuals, whether incorporated or not, (*vi*) a local authority, and (*vii*) every artificial juridical person, not falling within any of the preceding sub-clauses.

NOTE: The word "person" in the Income-tax Act is most generally used to denote what may be termed an entity of assessment, *i.e.* the possessor or recipient of an income which the Act requires to be separately assessed for tax purposes. [*Income Tax Commissioners* v *Gibbs* (1942) AC 402, 418].

▸ *Meaning under the Code of Civil Procedure 1908, Or. 30, r. 10.* The word 'person' does not include a company, because such a construction will be repugnant to the context. [*Modi Vanaspati Mfg. Co.* v *Khaitan Jute Mills* AIR 1969 Cal 496].

▸ *Meaning under the Factories Act 1948, s. 2(n).* The expression 'person' as used in s. 2(*n*) implies only an individual and does not bear scrutiny when construed in the case of a company, a firm of partners or an association of persons. [*J.K. Industries Ltd.* v *Chief Inspector of Factories and Boilers* 1997 SCC (L&S) 1].

▸ *Meaning under the Indian Partnership Act 1932, s. 4.* The word "person" in s. 4 which has replaced s. 239 of the Indian Contract Act contemplates only natural or artificial, that is, legal persons and therefore a firm is not a person and as such is not entitled into partnership with another firm or Hindu undivided family or individual. [*Dulichand Laxminarayan* v *Commissioner of Income Tax, Nagpur* AIR 1956 SC 354: 1956 SCR 154: 1956 SCJ 317: (1956)29 ITR 535].

▸ *Meaning under the Constitution of India, Art. 226.* The term 'person' as it appears in Art. 226 is not to be construed in the parlance of a private person or authority, but will have to be read in relation to the phrase as it appears in Art. 226 of the Constitution where a reference is to a 'person' or 'authority'. The use of the word 'or' clearly indicates that the term 'person' in sum and substance and in relation to an authority means a person in *ex officio* capacity and not a personal or individual status. [*Radhakrishna* v *Mysore Sugar Co. Ltd., Mandya* (1995)2 Kant LJ 607, 616].


- **Artificial person** p. 76.
- **Dangerous person** p. 223.
- **Displaced person** p. 268.
- **Gainfully occupied person** p. 380.
- **Incapacitated person** p. 443.
- **Indigent person** p. 451.
- **Interested person** p. 473.
- **Landless person** p. 511.
- **Legal person** p. 526.
- **Lewd person** p. 531.
- **Natural persons** p. 600.
- **Young person** p. 908.


**Person aggrieved.** A "person aggrieved" must be a man who has suffered a legal grievance, a man against whom a decision has been pronounced which has wrongfully deprived him of something; or wrongfully refused him something; or wrongfully affected his title to something. [*Thammanna* v *K. Veera Reddy* (1980)4 SCC 62: AIR 1981 SC 116: (1981)1 SCR 73; *Gopapandu Biswal* v *Krishno Chandro* (1998)4 SCC 447].

The words 'person aggrieved', in the context of land acquisition, would mean a person who had suffered legal injury or one who has been unjustly deprived or denied of something, which he would be interested to obtain in the usual course or similar benefits or advantage or results in wrongful affection of his title to compensation. [*Babu Ram* v *State of U.P.* JT 1994(7) SC 377: (1995)1 SCJ 573: (1995)2 SCC 689].

NOTE: The words 'person aggrieved' are of wide import and should not be subjected to a restrictive interpretation. They do not include, of course, a mere busybody who is interfering in things which do not concern him; but they do include a person who had a genuine grievance because an order has been made which prejudicially affects his interest. [*Attorney-General of the Gambia* v *Peirra Serr N' Jie* (1961) AC 617, *per* Lord Denning relied in *Maharaj Singh* v *State of U.P.* AIR 1976 SC 2602: (1977)1 SCR 1072: (1977)1 SCC 155].

The meaning of the words 'person aggrieved' may vary according to the context of the statute and that even stranger may be found to have *locus standi* although he may not have any personal interest of his own, provided he is not a busybody or meddlesome interloper, and although a stranger, he moves the court for a right in common with the general public. [*Seethalakshmi Ammal* v *State* AIR 1993 Mad 1; *Nahar Singh* v *Manohar Kumar* AIR 1993 J&K 69].

The expression 'aggrieved person' denotes an elastic, and, to an extent, an elusive concept. Its scope and meaning depend on diverse variable factors, such as the content and intent of the statute of which contravention is alleged, the specific circumstances of the case, and the nature and extent or the petitioner's interest, and the nature and extent of the prejudice or injury suffered by him. The court has to consider whether any of his rights or interest recognised by the general law has been infringed. If the answer is in the negative, he is not an aggrieved person. [*J.M. Desai* v *Roshan Kumar* AIR 1976 SC 578: (1976)3 SCR 58: (1976)1 SCC 671].

**Persona designata.** *'Persona designata'* is a person selected to act in his private capacity and not in his capacity as a judge.

A *persona designata* is a person who is pointed out or described as an individual as opposed to a person ascertained as a member of a class or as filling a particular character. [*Dharmendra Prasad* v *State of Uttar Pradesh* AIR 1969 All 484: 1969 All LJ 19; *Kalekhan* v *Board of Revenue* 1970 MPLJ 917; *Khandwa Municipality* v *Santosh Kumar* AIR 1975 MP 30; *Vasundhara Traders* v *State of Karnataka* 1977 Cr LJ 1539; *Badrilal Jodhraj* v *Girdharilal* AIR 1988 MP 24; *S. Srinivasa Rao* v *High Court of A.P.* AIR 1989 AP 258]. But this does not mean that a *persona designata* cannot be designated in terms of his office. [*Balarama Iyer* v *Krishnan Kanchandi* ILR (1968)1 Ker 1: AIR 1968 Ker 240].

NOTE: The expression *persona designata* connotes person pointed out by name or other personal description in contradistinction to one whose identity is to be ascertained by the office which he holds. So then, where a person is indicated in statute not by name but by an official designation, a question will arise whether the intention was to single him out as a *persona designata*, that is, as an individual, the designation being merely a further description of him, or it was that he would cease to be the person so indicated on losing his official designation. Surely if he be a judicial officer ... and is intended by the statute to act not otherwise than in a judicial capacity or court of civil jurisdiction, he cannot come within the expression *'persona designata'* so that he may, irrespective of his continuance in office, perform the duty. Whether the intention is one or the other has to be gathered from the words used, the nature of the functions to be performed, and the object and purpose of the statute. [*Ram Chandra Rao* v *State of Madras* AIR 1962 AP 58].

**Persona non grata.** Person not wanted; an undesirable person.

In international law and diplomatic usage, it means a person not acceptable for reasons peculiar to himself, to the government to which it is proposed to accredit him in the character of an ambassador or minister.

**Personal action.** Personal action signifies—(1) an action which can be brought only by the person himself who is injured and not by his representatives, (2) an action which is not an action for the recovery of land. [Mozley & Whiteley's *Law Dictionary*, 10th Ed.].

**Personal contract.** Any contract from which it appears that it is the intention of the parties that the services shall be performed only by the person contracting is a personal contract. *A* promise to marry, the contract of a master to instruct his apprentice, of an author to compose a particular work, of a physician or lawyer to render services, etc., are instances of personal contracts.

A personal contract is a contract involving some personal characteristics. For instance, *A* promises to paint a picture for *B* by a certain day at a certain price *A* has been entrusted with the work by reason of his special skill as a painter. This is a personal contract and the painting must be done by *A* himself. If *A* dies before the appointed day, the contract cannot be enforced either by *A*'s representatives or by *B*.

**Personal covenant.** Any agreement, convention or promise of two or more parties, by deed in writing, signed, sealed and delivered, by which either of the parties pledge himself to the other that something is done or shall be done, or stipulates for the truth of certain facts; he who makes the promise is called the covenantor and he to whom the promise is made is called the covenantee. Covenants are personal obligations.

NOTE: A personal covenant merely gives the right to recover damages for non-performance. A personal covenant may deal with any subject, *e.g.*, the payment of a sum of money, the execution of work and labour, etc., or it may relate to or be connected with land.

Covenants connected with land are divided into those which run with the land and collateral covenants. Thus, if a lessee of buildings covenants to repair them, the covenant runs with the buildings and binds the assignee. Opposed to covenants running with the land are collateral covenants, namely, to do something not touching the land demised or conveyed.

**Personal injury.** In a narrow sense, a hurt or damage done to a man's person, such as a cut or bruise, a broken limb, or the like, as distinguished from an injury to his property or his reputation. The phrase is chiefly used in this connection with actions of tort for negligence and under worker's compensation statutes. But the term is also used (chiefly in statutes) in a much wider sense, and as including any injury which is an invasion of personal rights, and in this signification it may include such injuries to the person as libel or slander, criminal conversation, malicious prosecution, false imprisonment, and mental suffering. [*Gray* v *Wallace* 319 SW 2d 582].

In worker's compensation acts, "personal injury" means any harm or damage to the health of an employee, however caused, whether by accident, disease, or otherwise, which arises in the course of and out of his employment, and incapacitates him in whole or in part. [Black's *Law Dictionary*, 5th Ed.].

**Personal liberty.** One's freedom to do as one pleases, limited only by the government's right to regulate the public health, safety, and welfare. Also termed individual liberty. [Black's *Law Dictionary* 7th & 8th Eds.].

The right or power of locomotion, of changing situation, or moving one's person to whatsoever place one's own inclination may direct, without imprisonment or restraint, unless by due course of law. [*Civil Rights Cases* 109 US 3: 3 S Ct 42: 27 L Ed 835].

▸ *Meaning under the Constitution of India, Art. 21.* The expression 'personal liberty' used in that Article is of the widest amplitude and it covers a variety of rights which go to constitute the personal liberty of a man and it also includes rights which have been raised to the status of Fundamental Rights and given additional protection under Art. 19. [*Francis Coralic Mullin* v *Administrator, Union Territory of Delhi* AIR 1981 SC 746: (1981)2 SCR 516: (1981)1 SCC 608: 1981 SCC (Cri) 212 referring to *Maneka Gandhi* v *Union of India* AIR 1978 SC 597: (1978)1 SCC 248: (1978)2 SCR 621].

The term "personal liberty" is used in the Article as a compendious term to include within itself all the varieties of rights which go to make up the personal liberties of a man other than those dealt within several clauses of Art. 19(1). [*Kharak Singh* v *State of U.P.* AIR 1963 SC 1295: (1963)2 Cr LJ 329: (1964)1 SCR 332: (1964)2 SCJ 107].

**Personal luggage.** Ordinary luggage. [*Hudston* v *Midland Railway* LR 4 QB 366].

NOTE: *Personal luggage—what is—example:* Bedding for a passenger's own use on a journey must be held "personal luggage". [*Macrow* v *Great Western Railway* 40 LJQB 304: LR 6 QB 612].

*Personal luggage—what is not—example:* (*i*) Articles of merchandise cannot be considered as personal luggage. [*Cahill* v *London & North Western Railway* 13 CBNS 818; *Great Northern Railway* v *Shepherd* 8 Ex 30; *Belfast & Ballymena Railway* v *Keys* 9 HL Cas 556]. (*ii*) Samples and accounts are not personal luggage of a commercial traveller. [*Bayley* v *Lancashire & Yorkshire Railway* 18 SJ 301]. (*iii*) Documents carried by a solicitor for use in a cause in which he is professionally engaged. [*Phelps* v *London & North Western Railway* 19 CBNS 321]. (*iv*) A child's rocking-horse is not personal luggage. [*Hudston* v *Midland Railway* LR 4 QB 366]. (*v*) Bedding intended for the passenger's household when permanently settled would not be considered to be personal luggage. [*Macrow* v *Great Western Railway* 40 LJQB 304: LR 6 QB 612]. (*vi*) Theatrical properties and costumes belonging to a comedian travelling by railway were held not to be personal luggage. [*Gilbey* v *Great Northern Railway* 36 TLR 562].

*Controversy about an artist's belongings.* Though an easel of an artist on a sketching tour has been held to be his personal luggage [*Macrow* v *Great Western Railway* 40 LJQB 304: LR 6 QB 612], yet it was held that the sketches of an artist are not such luggage. [*Mytton* v *Midland Railway* 28 LJ Ex 385].

Whatever the passenger takes with him for his personal use or convenience, according to the habits or wants of the particular class to which he belongs, either with reference to the immediate necessities or to the ultimate purpose of the journey, must be considered as personal luggage. [*Macrow* v *Great Western Ry.* 40 LJQB 304: LR 6 QB 612].

**Personal office.** Although ordinarily an office would mean the place where official business is transacted, a personal office in contradistinction to an office simpliciter or a commercial office would be a place where an outsider would not normally be admitted. Commercial transaction would not take place. [*V.S. Talwar* v *Prem Chandra Sharma* AIR 1984 SC 664, 666].

**Personal representative.** This phrase (except when otherwise controlled by a context) is synonymous with legal representative. [Stroud's *Judicial Dictionary*, 5th Ed.].

Personal representative means an executor or administrator, whose duty it is to settle the affairs and dispose of the property of a deceased person. [Mozley & Whiteley's *Law Dictionary*, 10th Ed.].

It is defined as a person who manages the legal affairs of another because of incapacity or death, such as the executor of an estate. [Black's *Law Dictionary*, 7th & 8th Eds.].

The phrase may mean next of kin. [*Alger* v *Parrott* LR 3 Eq 328].

**Personal security.** A security on personal obligation.

An obligation for the repayment of a debt, evidenced by a pledge or note binding a natural person, as distinguished from property; a person's legal right to enjoy life, health, and reputation. [Black's *Law Dictionary*, 7th & 8th Eds.].

NOTE: A power to invest on "personal security" seems to include a security on personal property; but, semble, it also includes the security of somebody's personal obligation. [*Forbes* v *Ross* 2 Bro CC 430; *Pickard* v *Anderson* LR 13 Eq 608].

**Personality.** Attributes; characteristics; individuality; individualism; personal identity; selfhood; singularity; egohood; that which constitutes a person; that which distinguishes and characterizes a person.

**Personally interested.** Interested in personal capacity in something of the nature of an expectation of advantage to be gained or of a loss or some disadvantage to be avoided.

In a judicial proceeding, the words do not imply mere intellectual interest of a judge or the court but something of the nature of an expectation of advantage to be gained or of a loss or some disadvantage to be avoided by the person who was said to be interested in the case. [*Johhan Singh* v *Marjad Koeri* AIR 1972 Pat 208].

▸ *Meaning under the Cr. P.C. 1898, s. 556 now Cr. P.C. 1973, s. 479.* "Personal interest" within the meaning of the section is not limited to private interest, and that it may well include official interest also. [*Rameshwar Bhartia* v *State of Assam* AIR 1952 SC 405: 1952 SCJ 559: 1953 SCR 126: 1953 Cr LJ 163].

**Personalty.** Personal property; personal resources; available means; assets; belongings; chattels; movable property.

**Personam.** See IN PERSONAM p. 440.

**Personate.** To pass one's self off as another having a certain identity. [*Lane* v *U.S.* CCA Ohio, 17 F 2d 923].

To assume the person of another, without his consent or knowledge, in order to deceive others, and, in such feigned character, to fraudulently do some act or gain some advantage, to the prejudice of the person counterfeited.

To "personate" means "to pretend to be a person" [*R.* v *Hague* 33 LJMC 81, *per* Crompton, J.]; but, semble, the definition should be "to pretend to be an existing person". [*Whiteley* v *Chappell* LR 4 QB 147].

NOTE: The offence of personating a voter is complete as soon as a person has, to the proper officer, falsely represented himself as the person entitled to vote, even though he stops short of voting. [*R.* v *Hague* 33 LJMC 81].

**Personation.** Act of pretending to be some other person.

**Pertaining to.** In relation to, whether by nature, appointment, or custom.

The words 'pertaining to' mean 'belonging to' or 'within the sphere of'. [*R.* v *Kelly, Ex p. State of Victoria* (1950)81 CLR 64].

NOTE: It is a broad expression which presupposes another subject-matter. These are words of comprehensiveness which might both have a direct significance as also an indirect significance. [*Doypak System* v *Union of India* AIR 1988 SC 782, 799].

**Peruse.** Read carefully or attentively; analyse; browse; check on; scrutinise; conduct research on; examine; delve into; peer into; scan; turn one's graze upon; 'read thoroughly or carefully', 'read, examine carefully'. [*Balakrishnan* v *Muhammed* 1975 Ker LT 623].

▸ *Meaning under the Code of Criminal Procedure 1973, s. 145.* The proper meaning of the word "peruse" is to go through critically, that is, to read attentively and examine critically in detail one by one. [*Sohan Mushar* v *Kailash Singh* AIR 1962 Pat 249].

**Perverse.** Bad; bad-natured; bumptious; cantankerous; corrupt; crabbed; cranky; debauched; depraved; deviating; evil; evil-minded; ill-behaved; ill-natured; nasty; petulant, obstreperous; persisting in fault, error; pugnacious; uncivil; venomous; wrong; thoughtless.

**Perverse finding.** A finding is perverse if it is altogether against evidence. [*Parry's Employees Union* v *Parry & Co.* AIR 1966 Cal 31]. A finding cannot be said to be perverse, if it is against the weight of evidence. [*Parry's Employees Union* v *Parry & Co.*, supra].

**Perverse order.** An order made in conscious violation of pleadings and law is a perverse order. [*M.S. Narayanagonda* v *Girijamma* AIR 1977 Kant 58].

**Perverse verdict.** A verdict so contrary to the evidence that it justifies the granting of a new trial; a verdict that is not only against the weight of evidence but is altogether against the evidence.

**Peshkar.** A subordinate officer under a judicial or executive or revenue officer.

**Petition.** Used as noun, it means application; formal writing embodying a request; formal written plea; formal written request; written application for relief; a formal written request presented to a court or other official body. [Black's *Law Dictionary*, 7th & 8th Eds.].

Used as verb, it means make a requisition; make written application; pray for; prefer a request to; solemnly request; formally urge.

"Petition" means a written statement of material facts, requesting the court to grant the relief or remedy based on those facts. It is a particular mode of seeking redress recognised by law. [*P. Philip* v *Director of Enforcement, New Delhi* AIR 1976 SC 1185: (1976)3 SCR 532: (1976)2 SCC 174: 1976 Cr LJ 920: 1976 SCC (Cri) 241: 1976 Cr LR (SC) 146].

> NOTE: "Petition" includes a prayer in an answer or a cross-petition put in the same document. [*Russel* v *Russel and Roebuck* (1957) P 375].
>
> Petition and application mean the same thing. [*Nanjappa* v *Vimala* AIR 1957 Mys 44].

• **Election petition** p. 296.

**Phalkar.** Pertaining to the produce or fruit trees of the land.

**Philanthropic.** Benevolent; benign; bounteous; charitable; devoted to others; humane; humanitarian; public-spirited.

An act is philanthropic when it indicates goodwill to mankind at large. The word 'philanthropic' is wide enough to comprise purposes which are not charitable in the technical sense. [*Re Macduff, Macduff* v *Macduff* (1896)2 Ch 451 (CA): 65 LJ Ch 700, *per* Stirling, J.].

> NOTE: *Benevolent act and philanthropic act—distinction.* An act may be benevolent if it indicates goodwill to a particular individual only, whereas an act cannot be said to be philanthropic unless it indicates goodwill to mankind at large. [*Re Macduff, Macduff* v *Macduff* (1896)2 Ch 451 (CA): 65 LJ Ch 700].

**Philanthropic purpose.** A philanthropic purpose must be a purpose which indicates goodwill to mankind in general. [*Re Macduff, Macduff* v *Macduff* (1896)2 Ch 451 (CA): 65 LJ Ch 700, *per* Lindley, L.J.].

> NOTE: The promotion of the happiness of mankind is undoubtedly a philanthropic purpose. [*Re Macduff, Macduff* v *Macduff*, supra, *per* Rigby, L.J.].

**Philanthropy.** Disposition or effort to promote the happiness or social elevation of mankind; desire, effort, or beneficence intended to mitigate social evils and social comfort; love of man.

> NOTE: The word 'philanthropy' may include—not cases of a totally exceptional character, but cases of a very wide class indeed, and numerous cases which would be within the popular meaning of philanthropic, and would have nothing to do with charity. [*Re Macduff, Macduff* v *Macduff* (1896)2 Ch 451 (CA): 65 LJ Ch 700, *per* Rigby, L.J.].

**Phonogram.** A telegraphic message sent to or received from a telegraph office by a subscriber over the telephone.

**Phooka.** *'Phooka'* or *'doom dev'* includes any process of introducing air or any substance into the female organ of a milch animal with the object of drawing off from the animal any secretion of milk. [Prevention of Cruelty to Animals Act 1890, s. 2(3)].

It clearly refers to the use of physical means to draw more milk than would be obtained without these physical means. [*Subal Chandra Koley* v *King* AIR 1949 Cal 90].

**Photograph.** A picture formed by means of the chemical action of light or other radiation on sensitive film; a picture taken by photography.

▸*Meaning under the Copyright Act 1956 (U.K.), s. 48(1).* "Photograph" means any product of photography or of any process akin to photography, other than a part of a cinematography film.

NOTE: 'Photograph' includes photo-lithograph and any work produced by any process analogous to photography but does not include any part of a cinematograph film. [Copyright Act 1957, s. 2(s)].

**Picketing.** "Picketing" means watching and besetting and stationing men outside a place where a strike has taken place, and where the workmen have been called out, to compel persons not to go into that place to work for the owner of it as long as the strike lasts. [*Lyons (F.) & Sons* v *Wilkins* (1896)1 Ch 811, 834: 65 LJ Ch 601, *per* A.L. Smith, L.J.].

Picketing means the marching to and fro before the premises of an establishment involved in a dispute, generally accompanied by the carrying and display of a sign, placard or banner bearing statements in connection with the dispute; sometimes accompanied by a polite request asking persons in the employ of the establishment not to assist in the running of that establishment or customers not to patronize that establishment. [*Damodar Ganesh* v *State* AIR 1951 Bom 459].

The term refers to presence at an employer's business by one or more employees and/or other persons to publicise labour dispute, influence employees or customers to withhold their work or business, respectively, or show union's desire to represent employees; picketing is usually accompanied by patrolling with signs. [*C. Comella, Inc.* v *United Firm Workers' Organizing Committee* 292 NE 2d 647, 655].

**Pilferage.** The act of pilfering, or such acts collectively; goods lost through pilfering; the act or an instance of stealing; the items stolen; stealing of small items, generally of stored goods.

To pillage i.e. to rob, plunder or steal especially in small quantity. [*Union of India* v *Sushil Kumar Ganguly* (1988)1 CLJ 505].

**Pilot.** A Helmsman, specifically, one duly qualified by training and licensed by law to conduct vessels in and out of port; one who controls the operation of an airplane, dirigible, or other aircraft; a person who operates the flying controls of an aircraft; a person qualified to take charge of a ship entering or leaving harbour; an experimental undertaking or test, specially in advance of a larger one; a guide; a leader.

▸ *Meaning under the Indian Ports Act 1908, s. 3(3).* A person for the time being authorised by the Government to pilot vessels.

**Pin money.** An allowance of incidentals; an allowance made by a husband to his wife for her personal expenses.

'Pin money' is an allowance made by a husband to his wife for the purchase of dresses and ornaments, in order that his dignity in society may be maintained. It may be a yearly allowance settled on the wife before marriage, or it may be made subsequently in the shape of gifts from time to time for the purposes mentioned. [Halsbury's *Laws of England*, 3rd Ed., vol. 19, p. 838].

A sum given by the husband to the wife "for pocket money". [*Howard* v *Digby* (1834)8 Bligh NS 224, *per* Lord Lyndhurst, L.C.].

A small allowance set apart by a husband for the personal expenses of his wife, for her dress and pocket money. [Black's *Law Dictionary*, 5th Ed.].

**Piracy.** Robbery, kidnapping, or other criminal violence committed at sea; a similar crime committed aboard a plane or other vehicle; hijacking. [Black's *Law Dictionary*, 7th & 8th Eds.].

'Piracy' is only a sea term for robbery. [*A.G. (Hong Kong)* v *Kwok-a-Sing* LR 5 PC 199].

No authoritative and comprehensive definition exists of piracy *jure gentium*. It has been stated that according to international law piracy consists in sailing the seas for private ends without authorisation from the government of any state with the object of committing depredations upon property or acts of violence against persons. The term piracy correctly includes cases where the crew or passengers of a vessel on the high seas rise against the captain and officers and seek by armed force to seize the ship. [Halsbury's *Laws of England*, 3rd Ed., vol. 10, p. 653].

NOTE: Actual robbery is not an essential element in the crime of piracy *jure gentium*, and that a frustrated attempt to commit piratical robbery is equally piracy *jure gentium*. [*Re Piracy Jure Gentium* (1934) AC 586, 600 (PC)].

Piracy, under the law of nations, is an offence against all nations, and punishable by all. [*ReTivnan* (1864)5 B&S 645, 688, *per* Blackburn, J.].

**Pirate.** One guilty of the crime of piracy.

Primarily the pirate is a man who satisfies his personal greed or his personal vengeances by robbery or murder in a place beyond the jurisdiction of a State. The man who acts with a public object may do like acts to a certain extent, but his moral attitude is different, and the acts themselves will be kept within well-marked bounds. He is not only the enemy of the human race but he is the enemy solely of a particular State. [Hall's *International Law*, 5th Ed., p. 259].

The term "pirates" in the Lloyd's policy includes passengers who mutiny and rioters who attack the ship from the shore. Revolutionaries organising and carrying out an armed expedition against the government, however, are not pirates within the meaning of that term in the policy. [Halsbury's *Laws of England*, 3rd Ed., vol. 22, p. 81].

The word 'pirate' may also mean adopt and pass off as one's own; borrow dishonestly; make use of without permission.

**Pirottar.** A grant of a rent-free tenancy to defray the expenses of a pious Mahomedan or his establishment.

**Pit.** The primary meaning of the word "pit" is a vertical excavation, *i.e.*, a shaft, but it may denote either the shaft or the underground workings with or without the shaft, or a colliery as a whole. [Halsbury's *Laws of England*, 3rd Ed., vol. 26, p. 325].

"Pit" has no precise meaning. In reference to underground workings it can denote not only the shafts but also the underground workings to which they give access. It can also describe workings on the surface, whether the mineral is taken from the bottom or the sides of the workings. [Halsbury's *Laws of England*, 4th Ed., vol. 31, para 14, p. 16].

**Pith and substance.** The essential part; the quintessence.

NOTE: When there is a conflict between two entries in the legislative lists, and legislation by reference to one entry would be competent but not by reference to the other, the doctrine of pith and substance is invoked for the purpose of determining the true nature and character of the legislation in question. [*Atiabari Tea Co.* v *State of Assam* AIR 1961 SC 232].

In a Federal Constitution, conflicts often arise between the Union and State legislatures over their legislative powers. To test whether a particular legislature is exceeding its powers, the courts have evolved what is known as the doctrine of pith and substance. In *Governor-General in Council* v *Province of Madras* [(1945) PC 98], where the validity of certain taxes levied under the Madras General Sales Tax Act 1939, was questioned, the Privy Council observed thus: "It is not the name of the tax but its real nature, its pith and substance, which must determine into what category it falls ..."

**Place.** A particular point or portion of space, especially that part of space occupied by or belonging to a thing under consideration; a definite location; space regarded as abode or quarters; position in relative order; an office, appointment, or employment; the position of a figure in relation to the other figures of a given arithmetical series or a group; a residence; a dwelling; a person's rank or status.

Place has to be a definite area marked out in such way as to be recognised a place in the context of s. 2(45) of the Customs Act 1962. [*Bajaj Plastic Ltd.* v *Collector, Central Excise* 1987 Mah LR 681].

**Place of abode.** A person's residence or domicile. [Black's *Law Dictionary*, 7th & 8th Eds.].

"Place of abode" usually means the place of residence. In "Johnson's *Dictionary* 'abode' is defined to be 'habitation, dwelling, place of residence', and 'residence' is defined to be 'place of abode, dwelling'. A man's residence, where he lives with his family and sleeps at night, is always his place of abode in the full sense of that expression". [*R.* v *Hammond* 17 QB 772, *per* Cambell, C.J.].

**Place of business.** A location at which one carries on a business. [Black's *Law Dictionary*, 7th & 8th Eds.].

▸ *Meaning under the Central Sales Tax Act 1956, s. 2(dd).* 'Place of business' includes—(*i*) in any case where a dealer carries on business through an agent (by whatever name called), the place of business of such agent; (*ii*) a warehouse, godown or other place where a dealer stores his goods; and (*iii*) a place where a dealer keeps his books of account.

**Place of public entertainment.** A place open to members of the public without discrimination who desire to be entertained and where means of entertainment are provided. [*Allen* v *Emmerson* (1944)1 All ER 344 (DC)].

▸ *Meaning under the Untouchability (Offences) Act 1955, s. 2(c).* The expression includes any place to which the public are admitted and in which an entertainment is provided or held.

**Place of public worship.** "Place of public worship" means a place by whatever name known, which is used as a place of public religious worship or which is dedicated generally to, or is used generally by, persons professing any religion or belonging to any religious denomination or any section thereof, for the performance of any religious service, or for offering prayers therein, and includes all lands and subsidiary shrines appurtenant or attached to any such place. [*Shastri Yagnapurushdasji* v *Muldas Bhundardas Vaishya* AIR 1966 SC 1119: (1966)3 SCR 242].

**Place of residence.** The expression "place of residence" connotes a place where a person has his dwelling house which need not necessarily be permanent or exclusive. [*Sukh Lal* v *State Bank of India* AIR 1967 SC 543: (1967)1 SCR 317].

**Plagiarism.** Appropriation of a literary composition; copying; imitation of an original; literary forgery; literary piracy; literary theft; the act or an instance of taking and using the thoughts, writings, inventions, etc. of another person as one's own.

**Plaint.** Agony; anguish; complaint; displeasure; dissatisfaction; expression of discontent, grief, pain; lamentation; outcry.

In law, it means an accusation; a charge; a proceeding in inferior courts by which an action is commenced; a statement of grievance containing allegations and claims of remedy in the civil court.

Even though the dictionary meaning of the word is very wide, it has in legal phraseology come to acquire a more limited meaning and that is a statement in writing of the cause of action in a suit. [*STC of India* v *Ironside Ltd.* AIR 1966 Bom 126 (DB)].

▸ *Meaning under the Code of Civil Procedure 1908, Or. 7.* Plaint is a document of the plaintiff on which proceedings in a court of law commences.

The word is the English equivalent of the Latin "querela".

**Plaintiff.** One who commences a law suit; the complaining party in any litigation.

A person who seeks remedial relief for an injury to rights; it designates a complainant. [*City of Vancouver* v *Jarvis* 455 P 2d 591, 593].

> NOTE: 'Plaintiff' includes—(*i*) any person from or through whom a plaintiff derives his right to sue; and (*ii*) any person whose estate is represented by the plaintiff as executor, administrator or other representative. [Limitation Act 1963, s. 2(*i*)].

**Plan.** A design; a delineation; a draft, form or representation; a scheme; a sketch;

method of putting into effect an intention or proposal.

A method of design or action, procedure, or arrangement for accomplishment of a particular act or object. [*Shainwald* v *City of Portland* 55 P 2d 1151, 1156].

• **Approved plan** p. 72.

**Plant.** 'Plant' includes whatever means is used by a businessman for carrying on his business, not his stock-in-trade which he buys or makes for sale; but all goods and chattels, fixed or movable, live or dead, which he keeps for permanent employment in his business. [*Yarmouth* v *France* (1887)19 QBD 647, *per* Lindley, L.J.].

▸ *Meaning under the Income-tax Act 1961, s. 43(3).* The section defines 'plant' in very wide terms saying "plant includes ships, vehicles, books, scientific apparatus and surgical equipments used for the purposes of the business". The expression 'plant' would include any article or object fixed or movable, live or dead, used by businessman for carrying on his business and it is not necessarily confined to an apparatus which is used for mechanical operations or process or is employed in mechanical or industrial business. In order to qualify as plant the article must have some degree of durability. [*Scientific Engineering House (P) Ltd.* v *Commissioner of Income Tax, Andhra Pradesh* 1985 Supp (3) SCR 701: AIR 1986 SC 338: (1986)1 SCC 11: (1986)157 ITR 86].

▸ *Meaning under the Atomic Energy Act 1962, s. 2(e).* 'Plant' includes machinery, equipment or appliance, whether affixed to land or not.

• **Coke oven plant** p. 152.

**Plantation.** A grove cultivated to provide a certain product; an estate on which cotton, tobacco, etc. is cultivated, specially in former colonies, formerly by slave labour; an area planted with trees etc.

"Plantation" means any land used by a person principally for the cultivation of tea, coffee, cocoa, rubber, cardamom or cinnamon referred to as 'plantation crops'. [*The Kannan Devan Hills Produce Co. Ltd.* v *State of Kerala* AIR 1972 SC 2301: (1972)2 SCC 218: (1973)1 SCR 356].

**Plea.** Answer; defendant's answer to charges; legal defence; statement alleged in defence; statement alleged in justification; statement of defence; statement which answers the charges; statements on behalf of the defence; defendant's reply to the plaint.

• **Abatement, plea in** p. 4.

**Plea in bar.** A plea that seeks to defeat the plaintiff's or prosecutor's action completely and permanently. [Black's *Law Dictionary*, 7th & 8th Eds.].

**Plea of justification.** A plea of justification admits facts alleged by the plaintiff, but in effect denies that the plaintiff had any time a good cause of action, either because the conduct of the defendant is justified under some legal right, or because he is excused from liability in the particular case through some act or conduct of the plaintiff. This is also called an avoidance in law.

In an action for damages for defamation, the defendant may take the plea of justification. This is a plea of truth of the words published by the defendant. Truth is a defence in a civil action because a person in justice cannot be allowed to get a sum of money as damages for an injury to a reputation which he did not or ought not to possess. [*McPherson* v *Daniels* (1829)10 B&C at p. 272]. If the words are true, he escapes liability, however improper his motive may have been.

**Plea of pregnancy.** A plea of a woman convicted of a capital crime to stay her execution until she gives birth. [Black's *Law Dictionary*, 7th & 8th Eds.].

**Plead.** Affirm explicitly; assert formerly; assert positively; bring forward; emphasise; make an assertion; put forth; put forward; set forth; state emphatically.

Argue at the bar; argue a point; bring into court; put one's case; state one's case; defend a case; to argue a case in a court of law; to conduct a case in court.

To address the court as an advocate on behalf of either party. [*Jyoti Prokash* v *H.K. Bose* AIR 1963 Cal 178: 66 CWN 211].

**Pleader.** Any person entitled to appear and plead for another in court, and includes an advocate, a vakil and an attorney of a High Court. [Code of Civil Procedure 1908, s. 2(15); Representation of the People Act 1951, s. 79(*e*)].

▸*Meaning under the Code of Criminal Procedure 1898, s. 4(1)(r)*. 'Pleader' used with reference to any proceeding in any court, means a pleader or a mukhtar authorised under any law for the time being in force to practise in such court and includes (1) an advocate, a vakil and an attorney of a High Court so authorised, and (2) any other person appointed with the permission of the court to act in such proceeding.

▸*Meaning under the Code of Criminal Procedure 1973, s. 2(q)*. 'Pleader' when used with reference to any proceeding in any court, means a person authorised by or under any law for the time being in force, to practise in such court, and includes any other person appointed with the permission of the court to act in such proceeding.

**Pleading.** Plaint or written statement. [Code of Civil Procedure 1908, Or. 6, r. 1]; plaintiff's allegations; written statement of defence.

A formal document in which a party to a legal proceeding (esp. a civil lawsuit) sets forth or response to allegations, claims, denials; or defences. [Black's *Law Dictionary*, 7th & 8th Eds.].

NOTE: The definition of pleading according to Madras High Court Original Side Rules would include affidavits also. [*B.S. Adityan* v *R.K. Adityan* (1983)2 MLJ 32].


• **Scandalous pleading** p. 777.

• **Sham pleading** p. 793.


**Pleasure of appointment.** The assignment of someone to employment that can be taken away at any time, with no requirement for notice or a hearing. [Black's *Law Dictionary*, 7th & 8th Eds.].

NOTE: The tenure of office of an employee of the Union or the State in India is only during the pleasure of the President and/or Governor; and accordingly except as provided in the Constitution, there can be no justiciable cause available to a dismissed government employee for getting relief in a court of law. [*K.P. Shankerlingam* v *Union of India* AIR 1960 Bom 431].

**Pledge.** Act of giving one's word; assurance; commitment; guarantee; promise; solemn declaration; statement on oath; word of honour.

The act of providing something as security for a debt or obligation; a bailment or other deposit of personal property to a creditor as security for a debt or obligation.

A pledge is a promise or agreement by which one binds himself to do or forbear something. [*Elmquist* v *Lock* 194 Cal App 2d 372].

▸*Meaning under the Indian Contract Act 1872, s. 172*. The bailment of goods as security for the payment of a debt or performance of a promise is called pledge. The bailor in this case is called the pawner. The bailee is called the pawnee.

**Plimsoll mark.** This is the load line along a ship's side marking the depth to which her proper cargo causes her to sink. Overloading is punishable as an offence.

**Plumber.** A person who fits and repairs the apparatus of a water supply, heating, etc.; one who makes a business of plumbing.

A plumber is one who fits dwellings and public buildings with tanks, pipes, taps, fittings and fixtures for the conveyance of gas, water and sewage. His work is concerned with public health, and the law generally regulates it by requiring a licence. His work is mostly mechanical, calling for the exercise of deftness of the hands rather than the profession of scientific knowledge.

**Plus valet unus oculatus testis quam auriti decem.** One eye-witness is better than ten ear-witnesses.

**Point of order.** It is the duty of the chair to maintain order in a House of the Legislature to enforce its rules. Every member of the House has a right to call the attention of the chair to a breach of order by putting it before it whether there has in fact been any such breach. [May's

*Parliamentary Practice*, 16th Ed., p. 470]. And this is called a "point of order". It is thus a device for the enforcement of rules of the House. The chair gives decision on a point of order and this is final.

NOTE: A point of order includes an objection raised by a member at a meeting for breaches of the rules or regulations, to some defect in the constitution of the meeting (*e.g.* absence of a quorum), to the use of offensive or abusive language, or to invite the attention of the presiding officer that the motion under discussion is not within the scope of the notice, or to any similar infirmity or irregularity in the proceeding. In addition to breaches of the general or special rules, use of insulting or bad language, gross accusations or insinuation and unseemly or contemptible conduct may be taken exception to in this manner. A point of order is primarily intended to determine the interpretation of the rules and regulations governing the meeting; it does not contemplate any discussion on any event. It cannot, therefore, be in the form of an objection to the competence of a member to stand for election to a committee. [*Surat Singh* v *Kishori Lal* (1969)2 SCC 487, 491].

**Police.** As noun it means arm of law; constabulary; custodian of the law; forces of law and order; law enforcement agents.

As verb it means care for; check; control; exercise authority; exert authority; keep in order; keep guard; keep under control; keep vigil; keep watch; preserve public order; regulate; stand guard; watch diligently.

Branch of the government which is charged with the preservation of public order and tranquillity, the promotion of the public health, safety, and morals, and the prevention, detection, and punishment of crimes. [Black's *Law Dictionary*, 5th Ed.].

The governmental department charged with the preservation of public order, the promotion of public safety, and the prevention and detection of crime; the officers or members of this department. [Black's *Law Dictionary*, 7th & 8th Eds.].

**Police officer.** A peace officer responsible for preserving public order, promoting public safety, and preventing and detecting crime. [Black's *Law Dictionary*, 7th & 8th Eds.].

NOTE: A custom's officer cannot be regarded as police officer. [*Assistant Collector of Customs* v *Tilak Raj* AIR 1969 Del 301: 1969 Cr LJ 1245].

**Police power.** The inherent and plenary power of a sovereign to make all laws necessary and proper to preserve the public security, order, health, morality, and justice. It is a fundamental power essential to government, and it cannot be surrendered by the legislature or irrevocably transferred away from government. [Black's *Law Dictionary*, 7th & 8th Eds.].

On the questions of conflict between national and State authorities and the questions whether the State exceeds its just powers in dealing with property and restraining the actions of individuals, it becomes necessary to know the extent of a power in the States. Such a power is known as the police power in the United States. It embraces the system of internal regulation including the preservation of the public order and the prevention of offences against the State as well as the establishment for the intercourse between citizen and citizen, those rules of good manners and good neighbourhood, which prevent conflict of rights and ensure to each the uninterrupted enjoyment of his own rights. [Cooley's *Treatise on the Constitutional Limitations*].

"The police power of a State extends beyond health, morals and safety and comprehends the duty within constitutional limitations, to protect the well-being and tranquillity of a community." [*Kovacs* v *Cooper* 336 US 77 (1949)].

NOTE: The police power was referred to by the Indian Supreme Court and found to exist in Art. 31(1) of the Constitution of India. [*Chiranjitlal* v *Union of India* AIR 1951 SC 41; *State of West Bengal* v *Subodh Gopal* AIR 1954 SC 92]. But the court was reluctant to import this foreign doctrine. Subba Rao, J. added in *Kochuni* v *State of Madras* AIR 1960 SC 1080: "We cannot agree that Art. 31(1) deals with the police power. It enables the State to discharge its functions in the interest of social and public welfare which the State in America can do in the exercise of police power."

**Policy.** In its application to contract, it means contractual obligation; legal document; mutual agreement; mutual undertaking; insurance contract.

In its application to plan of action, it means course of action; course of conduct; established order; fundamental principles; general guidelines; line of action; governing principle; line of conduct; prescribed form; rule of action; stratagem.

It is defined as the general principles by which a government is guided in its management of public affairs; a document containing a contract of insurance; a type of lottery in which bettors select numbers to bet on and place the bet with a "policy writer". [Black's *Law Dictionary*, 7th & 8th Eds.].


- **Banking policy** p. 95.
- **Endowment policy** p. 307.
- **Open policy** p. 626.
- **Public policy** p. 712.
- **Valued policy** p. 875.


**Policy holder.** One who owns an insurance policy, regardless of whether that person is the insured party. [Black's *Law Dictionary*, 7th & 8th Eds.].

**Policy of insurance.** A contract of insurance; a document detailing such a contract. [Black's *Law Dictionary*, 7th & 8th Eds.].

It is defined as a contract whereby insurer, in return for premiums, engages on happening of designated event, to pay certain sum as provided. [*In re O'Neill's Estate* 255 NYS 767, 771].

A policy of insurance is an instrument of recoupment, or mitigation of loss, effected between the insurer and insured, whereby the insurer agrees to pay money, or make good destruction or damages, or do some other thing, on the happening of some event or events. "It is not, like most contracts, signed by both parties, but only by the insurer, who on that account, it is supposed, is denominated an underwriter". [Stroud's *Judicial Dictionary of Words & Phrases*, 5th Ed., p. 1959].

**Political offence.** A crime directed against the security or governmental system of a nation, such as treason, sedition, or espionage. [Black's *Law Dictionary*, 7th & 8th Eds.].

In order to constitute an offence of a political character, there must be two or more parties in the State, each seeking to impose the Government of its own choice on the other, and that if the offence is committed by one side or the other in pursuance of that object, it is a political offence, otherwise not. [*Re Meunier* (1894)2 QB 415].

A political offence is one committed with the object of changing the Government of a State or inducing it to change its policy. [*Rajender Kumar Jain* v *State through Special Police Establishment* AIR 1980 SC 1510: (1980)3 SCR 982: (1980)3 SCC 435: 1980 Cr LJ 1084: 1980 SCC (Cri) 757].

**Political party.** A number of persons united in opinion and organized in the manner usual to the then existing political parties. [*Swindall* v *State Election Board* 32 P 2d 691, 695].

An unincorporated, voluntary association of persons sponsoring certain ideas of government or maintaining certain political principles or beliefs in public policies of government, not a governmental agency or instrumentality. [*Robinson* v *Holman* 26 SW 2d 66, 68].

NOTE: Political parties are voluntary associations for political purposes. Political parties play an important part in a representative democracy. They are divided on questions of public policy. The primary object of a political party is to run the election and mould public opinion. It propagates its ideas through newspapers and political meetings. If it succeeds in capturing the majority of the seats in the legislature, it forms the Government of the day and tries to fulfil its election pledges. It forms the Opposition when it is in a minority.

The primary object of the opposition is to criticise the Gove rnment and to prevent it from doing anything detrimental to the general interest of the country.

**Political question.** A question that a court will not consider because it involves the exercise of discretionary power by the executive or legislative branch of government. [Black's *Law Dictionary*, 7th & 8th Eds.].

**Poll.** The head; the top or back of the head; the blunt or round end of a hammer; the voting at an election; the votes thus registered; the place where voting takes place; a survey of public opinion on a given subject, usually obtained from a sample group.

• **Deed poll** p. 237.

**Polling.** Counting of voters at an election.

**Polygamy.** The condition of having more than one wife or husband at the same time; the state of having more than one mate.

The state of being simultaneously married to more than one spouse; multiple marriages. [Black's *Law Dictionary*, 7th & 8th Eds.].

**Pon.** Consideration; price; premium.

**Port.** A harbour where ships load and unload cargo; any place where persons and cargo are allowed to enter a country and where customs officials are stationed. [Black's *Law Dictionary*, 7th & 8th Eds.].

A place for the loading and unloading of the cargoes of vessels, and the collection of duties or customs upon imports and exports. [Black's *Law Dictionary*, 5th Ed.].

"Port" means any port, river, estuary, haven, dock, canal or other place so long as a person or body of persons is empowered by or under an Act to make charges (i.e. any charges with the exception of light dues, local light dues and any other charges in respect of lighthouses, buoys or beacons and of charges in respect of pilotage) in respect of ships entering it or using the facilities therein. [Halsbury's *Laws of England*, 4th Ed., vol. 1, para 312, p. 219].

A port is a place intended for loading or unloading goods; hence includes the natural shelter surrounding water, as also sheltered water produced by artificial jetties, etc. [*The Baldhill* CCANY, 42 F 2d 123, 125].

A port is a place where a vessel can lie in a position of more or less shelter from the elements, with a view to the loading or discharge of cargo. [*Hunter* v *Northern Marine Insurance Co. Ltd.* (1888)13 App Cas 717, 726, *per* Lord Herschell].

The word 'port' must be construed in its usual and limited popular or commercial sense as a place where ships are in the habit of coming for the purpose of loading or unloading, embarking or disembarking. [*The Mowe* (1915) P 1, 15, *per* Evans].

• **Call at a port** p. 119.

• **Foreign port** p. 365.

**Port charges.** Such charges as a ship would have to pay before she leaves port.

Pecuniary exactions upon vessels availing themselves of the commercial conveniences and privileges of a port. [*Wilkens* v *Trafikaktiebolaget Grangesberg Okelosund* CCA, 10 F 2d 129, 131; *Christianssand Shipping Co.* v *Marshall* DC Pa, 22 F 2d 192, 194].

**Portion(s).** An allotted part; a share, a parcel; a division in a distribution; a share of an estate or the like, received by gift or inheritance. [*Lecompte* v *Davis' Ex'r* 148 SW 2d 292, 295].

• **Definite portions** p. 242.

**Positive covenant.** A positive covenant is a covenant or undertaking to do something.

**Possession.** That condition of facts under which one can exercise his power over a corporeal thing at his pleasure to the exclusion of all other persons. [Black's *Law Dictionary*, 5th Ed.].

The fact of having or holding property in one's power; the exercise of dominion over property; the right under which one may exercise control over something to the exclusion of all others; the continuing exercise of a claim to the exclusive use of a material object; something that a person owns or controls; a territorial dominion of a state or nation. [Black's *Law Dictionary*, 7th & 8th Eds.]

In civil law, it means the detention or use of a physical thing with the intent to hold it as one's own. [Black's *Law Dictionary*, 8th Ed.].

Possession is the visible possibility of exercising physical control over a thing, coupled with the intention of doing so, either against all the world or against all the world except certain persons. There are, therefore, three requisites of possession. First, there must be actual or potential physical control. Secondly, physical control is not possession, unless accompanied by intention; hence if a thing is put into the hand of a sleeping person, he has not possession of it. Thirdly, the possibility and intention must be visible or evidenced by external signs, for if the thing shows no signs of being under the control of anyone, it is not possessed. [Jowitt's *Dictionary of English Law*, 2nd Ed.].

"Possession" is a word of ambiguous meaning, and its legal senses do not coincide with the popular sense. In English law it is treated not merely as a physical condition protected by ownership, but as right in itself. The word "possession" may mean effective, physical, or manual control, or occupation, evidenced by some outward act, sometimes called *de facto* possession or detention as distinct from a legal right to possession. This is a question of fact rather than of law. [*Words & Phrases Legally Defined*, 2nd Ed. by John B. Saunders as Editor].

Possession is the objective realisation of ownership. It is the *de facto* exercise of a claim to certain property and a *de facto* counterpart of ownership. Possession of a right is the *de facto* relation of continuing exercise and enjoyment as opposed to the *de jure* relation of ownership. Possession is the *de facto* exercise of a claim to certain property. It is the external form in which claims normally manifest themselves. Possession is in fact what ownership is in right enforceable at law to or over the thing. [*B. Gangadhar* v *B.G. Rajalingam* (1995)5 SCC 238: (1995)3 SCJ 380: JT 1995(5) SC 630: AIR 1996 SC 780].

Word 'possession' is not purely a legal concept but a polymorphous term which may have different meanings in different contexts. "Possession", implies a right and a fact; the right to enjoy annexed to the right of property and the fact of the real intention. It involves power of control and intent to control. Therefore, the test for determining "whether a person is in possession of anything is whether he is in general control of it". [*Supt. and Remembrancer of Legal Affairs, West Bengal* v *Anil Kumar Bhunja* (1979)4 SCC 274: 1979 Cr LJ 1390: 1979 Cr LR (SC) 664: 1979 SCC (Cri) 1038: AIR 1980 SC 52: (1980)1 SCR 323].

'Possession' is a word of ambiguous meaning and its legal senses do not always coincide with the popular sense. It may not always be synonymous with manual detention or physical retention of the goods or moneys. [*C.I.T.* v *Tarsem Kumar* AIR 1986 SC 1477: (1986)3 SCC 489: (1986)3 SCR 294: JT 1986 SC 220: (1986)161 ITR 505: (1986)26 ELT 10: 1986(8) ECR 504].

NOTE: Possession is an ambiguous term. The law books divide its concept into two broad categories: (*i*) physical possession or possession in fact; and (*ii*) legal possession which need not coincide with possession in fact. The control over the property has always been regarded as one of the tests of physical or *de facto* possession. In the case of possession through agent, it is true that the legal possession would continue to reside in the owner but the actual physical possession would surely be that of the agent. [*Seksaria Cotton Mills Ltd.* v *State of Bombay* AIR 1953 SC 278, 281: 1953 Cr LJ 1116].

• **Actual possession** p. 35.
• **Adverse possession** p. 45.
• **Constructive possession** p. 180.
• **Delivery of possession** p. 247.
• **Discontinuance of possession** p. 264.
• **Entitled to possession** p. 311.

• **Judicial possession.** "Judicial possession" is possession protected by law against wrongful dispossession but cannot *per se* always be equated with lawful possession. [*M.C. Chockalingam* v *V. Manickavasagam* AIR 1974 SC 104: (1974)2 SCR 143: (1974)1 SCC 48].

- **Lawful possession** p. 518.
- **Legal possession** p. 526.
- **Litigious possession.** "Litigious possession" pertains to dispute in which possession may be coterminous with physical or *de facto* control only. Litigious possession may be uncertain in character and may even be without any basis or interest. [*Krishna Kishore Firm* v *Government of A.P.* AIR 1990 SC 2292: 1990 Supp (2) SCR 8: JT 1990(4) SC 241: (1991)1 SCC 184].
- **Settled possession** p. 789.
- **Take possession** p. 826.
- **Unauthorised possession** p. 861.

**Possessory lien.** A lien on the goods of another held by a person.

**Post.** As noun means appointment; berth; charge; incumbency; means of livelihood; office; place; the position or job [*State of Assam* v *Ranga Muhammad* AIR 1967 SC 903: (1967)1 SCR 454: (1967)2 SCJ 443: 1967 SLR 40: (1968)1 Lab LJ 282]; the place and position in service held by a person. [*P.R. Nayak* v *Union of India* AIR 1972 SC 554: (1972)2 SCR 695: (1972)1 SCC 392: 1972 SLR 2190].

The word 'post' means an appointment, job, office or employment. A position to which a person is appointed. [*R.K. Sabharwal* v *State of Punjab* AIR 1995 SC 1371: (1995)2 SCC 745: 1995 SCC (L&S) 548: (1995)1 SCR 791: JT 1995(2) SC 351: (1995)3 SLJ 227.

NOTE: Post is an employment but every employment is not post. A post may be created before the appointment or simultaneously with it. A post under the State means a post under the administrative control of the State. State may create or abolish the post. [*State of Assam* v *Kanak Chandra Dutta* AIR 1967 SC 884: (1967)1 SCR 679: (1967)1 SCJ 461].

It may also mean after; infra.

▸ *Meaning as verb*. Announce publicly; call public attention to; communicate; convey; deliver; give public notice of; make known; proclaim.

To publicise or announce by affixing a notice in a public place; to transfer (accounting entries) from an original record to a ledger; to place in the mail; to make a payment or deposit; to put up. [Black's *Law Dictionary*, 7th & 8th Eds.].

- **Cadre posts** p. 117.
- **Civil post** p. 145.
- **Ex cadre post** p. 117.
- **In course of transmission by post** p. 439.
- **Tenure post** p. 836.

**Post-dated cheque.** One delivered prior to its date, generally payable at sight or on presentation on or after day of its date. [Black's *Law Dictionary*, 5th Ed.].

"A cheque which is dated subsequent to the actual date on which it is drawn, and which is issued before the date it bears, is called a post-dated cheque". [Thomson's *Dictionary of Banking*, 12th Ed., as referred to in *Ashok Yeshwant Badave* v *Surender Madhavrao Nighojakar* AIR 2001 SC 1315: JT 2001(3) SC 508: (2001)2 SCJ 385: (2001)3 SCC 726].

A "post-dated cheque is the same thing as a bill of exchange at so many days' date as intervene between the day of delivering the cheque and the date marked upon the cheque". The "effect of issuing a post-dated cheque is equivalent to giving a promissory note not payable until the date written on the cheque". [Chalmers & Guest on *Bills of Exchange, Cheques and Promissory Notes*, 15th Ed., p. 74, as referred to in *Ashok Yeshwant Badave* v *Surender Madhavrao Nighojakar,* supra].

**Post-mortem.** After death; pertaining to matters occurring after death; done or occurring after death.

NOTE: It is a term generally applied to an autopsy or examination of a dead body, to ascertain the cause of death, or to the inquisition for that purpose by the coroner.

**Post-obit.** An agreement by which the obligor borrows a certain sum of money and promises to pay a larger sum, exceeding the lawful rate of interest, upon the death of a person from whom he has some expectation, if the obligor be then living.

**Post-obit bond.** A bond given by an expectant, to become due on the death of a person from whom he will have property. A bond or agreement given by a borrower of money, by which he undertakes to pay a larger sum, exceeding the legal rate of interest, on or after the death of a person from whom he has expectations, in case of surviving him. Such are common in England. [Black's *Law Dictionary*, 5th Ed.].

**Post office.** The expression "post office" includes every house, building, room, carriage or place used for the purposes of the post office and every letter box provided by the post office for the reception of postal articles. [Indian Post Office Act 1898, s. 2(*h*)].

**Postage.** The duty chargeable for the transmission by post of postal articles. [Indian Post Office Act 1898, s. 2(*f*)].

Charges for postal service. [Black's *Law Dictionary*, 5th Ed.].

**Postage stamp.** Any stamp provided by the Central Government for denoting postage or other fees or sums payable in respect of postal articles under the Indian Post Office Act, and includes adhesive postage stamps and stamps printed, embossed, impressed or otherwise indicated on any envelope, wrapper, postcard or other article. [Indian Post Office Act 1898, s. 2(*g*)].

**Postal article.** The expression 'postal article' includes a letter, postcard, newspaper, book, pattern or sample packet, parcel and every article or thing transmissible by post. [Indian Post Office Act 1898, s. 2(*i*)].

▸ *Meaning under the Tax on Postal Articles Act 1971, s. 2(c).* 'Postal article' means any letter, letter-card, book, pattern or sample packet, parcel or any other article or thing (not being a postcard or a newspaper transmissible by post as a registered newspaper) which is transmissible by post and for the transmission of which postage is chargeable under the Indian Post Office Act 1898 (6 of 1898) and includes a money order, a phonogram and a telegram.

**Posthumous child.** A child born after the death of the father.

**Potential.** The word 'potential' is very wide. In *Oxford Dictionary* it is defined as capable of coming into being a possibility. In Black's *Law Dictionary*, it is defined as extending in possibility but not in act; naturally and probably expected to come into existence at some future time, though not now existing; for example, the future product of grain or trees already planted, or the successive future instalments or payments on a contract or engagement already made. In other words, service which is not only extended to actual users but those who are capable of using it are covered in the definition. [*Lucknow Development Authority* v *M.K. Gupta* AIR 1994 SC 787, 793: 1994 AIR SCW 92: (1994)1 SCJ 103: (1994)80 Comp Cas 714].

**Pottery.** "Pottery" in a wide sense will take in all objects that are made from clay and hardoned by fire, from crude earthen pots to delicate porcelain. [*The South Gujarat Roofing Tiles Manufacturers Association* v *State of Gujarat* (1976)4 SCC 601: AIR 1977 SC 90: (1977)1 SCR 878].

**Poverty.** Bare subsistence; dearth; deficiency; destitution; difficulty; distress; impoverishment; loss of fortune; paucity; poor circumstances; scantiness; shortage; scarceness; scarcity; slender means; sparseness; starvation; straitened circumstances; subsistence level; the state or condition of being poor.

> NOTE: Poverty does not mean destitution. It is a word of wide and somewhat indefinite import. [*Re Coulthurst's Will Trusts* (1951)1 All ER 774].

**Power.** Authority; command; competence; control; dominance; domination; force; hold; influence; jurisdiction; mastery; potency; primacy; supremacy; weight; the ability to act or not to act; dominance, control or influence over another; the legal right or authorisation to act or not to act; the ability conferred on a person by the law to alter, by an act of will, the rights, duties, liabilities, or other legal relations either of that person or of another; a document granting legal authorisation; an authority to affect an estate in land by—(1) creating some estate independently of any estate that the holder of the authority possesses; (2) imposing a charge on the estate, or (3) revoking an existing estate.

Authority to do any act which the grantor might himself lawfully perform. [*Porter* v *Household Finance Corp. of Columbus* DC Ohio, 385 F Supp 336, 341].

Power may be defined as an authority given by one person called the donor to another person called the donee entitling the latter to deal with or dispose of realty or personalty, either absolutely or partially and either for his own benefit or for the benefit of others, and whether or not he is already beneficially interested in the subject-matter before he exercises the authority. [Cheshire's *Modern Real Property*, 10th Ed., p. 191].

It may also mean any form of energy available for doing work, especially energy developed by mechanical or electrical means. In this sense, under s. 3(*d*) of the Central Silk Board Act 1948, 'power' means any form of energy which is mechanically transmitted and is not generated by human or animal agency, and includes electrical energy. Under s. 2(*g*) of the Factories Act 1948, 'power' means electrical energy, or any other form of energy which is mechanically transmitted and is not generated by human or animal agency.

In its application to mathematics, it means the product of a number multiplied by itself a given number of times.

In physics, it means the time rate at which energy is transferred, or converted into work.


- **General power** p. 385.
- **Horse power** p. 421.
- **Implied power, doctrine of** p. 433.
- **Incidental power** p. 445.
- **Inherent power** p. 458.
- **Judicial power** p. 495.
- **Police power** p. 668.
- **Purchasing power** p. 717.
- **Purchasing power parity theory** p. 717.
- **Separation of powers** p. 786.
- **Total voting power** p. 847.


**Power alcohol.** Ethyl alcohol containing not less than 99.5 per cent by volume of ethanol measured at sixty degrees Fahrenheit corresponding to 77.4 over proof strength. [Indian Power Alcohol Act 1948, s. 3(*e*)].

**Power coupled with an interest.** A right or power to do some act, together with an interest in the subject-matter on which the power is to be exercised. It is distinguished from a naked power, which is a mere authority to act, not accompanied by any interest of the donee in the subject-matter of the power. [*Arcweld Mfg. Co.* v *Burney* 121 P 2d 350, 355].

**Power-of-attorney.** An instrument authorising another to act as one's agent or attorney. [Black's *Law Dictionary*, 5th Ed.].

An instrument granting someone authority to act as agent or attorney-in-fact for the grantor; the authority so granted. [Black's *Law Dictionary*, 7th & 8th Eds.].

▸ *Meaning under the Indian Stamp Act 1899, s. 2(21).* 'Power-of-attorney' includes any instrument (not chargeable with a fee under the law relating to court-fees for the time being in force) empowering a specified person to act for and in the name of the person executing it.

▸ *Meaning under the Code of Civil Procedure 1908, Or. 3, rr. 1 and 2.* Power-of-attorney is a formal document by which authority is given to an agent and the instrument is to be construed strictly. A party to a suit may execute a power-of-attorney in favour of a person, who then can engage a pleader on behalf of the principal.

NOTE: The donee of the power-of-attorney can execute any instrument in and with his name and signature and his own seal under s. 2 of the Power-of-Attorney Act 1882. A document requiring registration must be presented by the executant or claimant or by the agent or such person authorised by the power-of-attorney, executed before and authenticated by the Registrar or Sub-Registrar under s. 32 of the Indian Registration Act 1908.

An ordinary power-of-attorney is revocable and automatically terminates upon the death or incapacity of the principal.

**Practicable.** Achievable; capable of being done; not too difficult; realisable; within reach; within the bounds of possibility; workable; that which may be done, practised, or accomplished, performable, feasible, possible.

**Practice.** In its application to custom, it means behaviour; common course; confirmed habit; conventionality; course of conduct; customary course; established order; fixed ways; line of action; order of the day; usage; settled disposition; usual custom.

In its application to procedure, it means approach; arrangement; conduct; governing plan; manner of proceeding; mode of management; protocol; rules of business; way of doing things.

In its application to professional business, it means avocation; calling; career; chosen profession; life's work; occupation; pursuit; specialty; trade; undertaking; vocation.

The word 'practice' connotes repeated events. [*Hindustan Lever Ltd.* v *Ashok V. Kate* AIR 1996 SC 285; (1995)6 SCC 326].

Practice means the same thing as procedure. [*Harish Chandra Bajpai* v *Triloki Singh* AIR 1957 SC 444: 1957 SCA 616: 1957 SCJ 297: 1957 SCR 370].

Practice means 'exercise of any profession or occupation'. [*Council of the Institute of Chartered Accountants* v *B. Mukherjea* AIR 1958 SC 72: 1958 SCA 1132: 1958 SCJ 312: 1958 SCR 371].

Practice in wider sense denotes the mode of proceeding by which a legal right is enforced, as distinguished from the law which gives or defines the right, and by which means of the proceeding the court is to administer the machinery as distinguished from its product. [*Lever Brothers Ltd.* v *Kneale and Bagnall* (1937)2 KB 87].

Practice in its larger sense like procedure, denotes the mode of proceeding by which a legal right is enforced as distinguished from the law which gives and defines the right. [*State of Seraikella* v *Union of India* AIR 1951 SC 253: 1951 SCR 474: 1951 SCJ 425].

Practice means the form, manner, or order of instituting and conducting an action or other judicial proceeding, through its successive stages to its end, in accordance with the rules and principles laid down by law or by the regulations and precedents of the courts. The term applies as well to the conduct of criminal as to civil actions, to proceedings in equity as well as at law, and to the defence as well as the prosecution of any proceeding. [*Wells Lamont Corp.* v *Bowles* Em App, 149 F 2d 364, 366].

The word "practice" as applied to a legal practitioner includes, in the absence of any limiting or restrictive context, both the functions of acting and pleading. The phrase "entitled as of right to practice" is an emphatic affirmation of a right to plead and to act independently of the will or discretion of any to the persons. [*Aswini Kumar Ghose* v *Arabinda Bose* AIR 1952 SC 369: 1952 SCJ 568: 1953 SCR 1: 1953 SCJ 38].

**Practitioner.** He who is engaged in the exercise or employment of any art or profession as contrasted with one who teaches such.

A person engaged in the practice of a profession, esp. law or medicine. [Black's *Law Dictionary*, 8th Ed.].

• **Legal practitioner** p. 527.

**Praja.** Subject; tenant, progeny, offspring; dependant.

**Praja-bill.** Lands in which tenants have been settled.

**Prajapatya form of marriage.** This form is substantially similar to Brahma form, but in this case bridegroom is suitor and he may not be a bachelor. This form of marriage was prevalent under the indigenous Hindu law.

**Pratistha.** Consecration or setting up of an image or temple; a ceremony performed on the completion of a house before it is inhabited; also purification or reconsecration of an idol, house or temple that has been polluted. [Wilson's *Glossary*; *Kapalavayi Kasi Rama Rao* v *Kotta Venkata Ratnam* AIR 1947 PC 88].

**Preamble.** A clause at the beginning of a constitution or statute explanatory of the reasons for its enactment and the objects sought to be accomplished. [Black's *Law Dictionary*, 5th Ed.].

An introductory statement in a constitution, statute or other document explaining the document's basis and objective; esp., a statutory recital of the inconveniences for which the statute is designed to provide a remedy. [Black's *Law Dictionary*, 7th & 8th Eds.].

Generally, a preamble is a declaration by the legislature of the reasons for the passage of the statute and is helpful in the interpretation of any ambiguities within the statute to which it is prefixed. [*Griffith* v *New Mexico Public Service Comm*. 520 P 2d 269, 271].

'Preamble' has been defined in the *Oxford English Dictionary* to mean "a preliminary statement, in speech or writing; an introductory paragraph, section, or clause; a preface, prologue, introduction". It has further been defined there as "an introductory paragraph or part in a statute, deed, or other document, setting forth the grounds and intention of it". [*Mohd. Yousuf Rather* v *State of Jammu and Kashmir* AIR 1979 SC 1925: (1979)4 SCC 370: 1979 SCC (Cri) 999: (1980)1 SCR 258].

NOTE: A preamble to a statute is a preliminary statement of the reasons which have made the passing of the statute desirable, and its position is immediately after the title and date of Royal assent. A preamble may also be used to introduce a particular section or group of sections. [*Dhananjoy Das* v *District Magistrate, Darrang* AIR 1982 SC 1315: 1982 Cr LJ 1779: 1982 SCC (Cri) 488: (1982)2 SCC 521].

The preamble of a statute "is a key to open the minds of the makers of the Act, and the mischiefs which they intend to remedy by the same". [*Termes de la Ley; West Ham* v *Iles* 8 App Cas 388].

A preamble often consists of a series of clauses introduced by the conjunction *whereas*. Such a preamble is sometimes called the *whereas clauses*. [Black's *Law Dictionary*, 8th Ed.].

It is also used to refer to the introductory para of the grounds of detention served upon a detenu. [*Dhananjoy Das* v *District Magistrate, Darrang* AIR 1982 SC 1315: 1982 Cr LJ 1779: 1982 SCC (Cri) 488: (1982)2 SCC 521].

*An aid to the construction of a statute.* A preamble can only be brought in as aid to the construction of a statute if the language is not clear and admits of a plurality of meanings; but where it is clear and unambiguous, it cannot be used to extend or limit the meaning and scope of a statute. [*Secretary of State* v *Maharaja of Bobbili* 46 IA 302].

The terms of a preamble may be resorted to in two classes of cases. The first is where the text of the statute is susceptible of different constructions; the second is where the legislature intended that some limitation should be put on the statute. And the preamble may be used to indicate to what particular instances the enactment was intended to apply. [*Burrakar Coal Co.* v *Union of India* AIR 1961 SC 154].

Though in an ordinary statute court does not attach any importance to the preamble, all importance has, however, to be attached to the preamble in a constitutional statute. [*His Holiness Kesavananda Bharati Sripadagalvaru* v *State of Kerala* AIR 1973 SC 1461: (1973)4 SCC 225: 1973 (Supp) SCR 1].

**Precatory trust.** The words 'precatory trust' are an abominable phrase. They are used as a roundabout way of saying that the court finds that there is a trust although the trust is not expressed, as such, but by words of prayer or suggestion, or the like. [*Re Sanson* 12 TLR 142, *per* Chitty, J.].

Precatory trust is a trust created by certain words, which are more like words of entreaty and permission than of command or certainty. Examples of such words, which the courts have held sufficient to constitute a trust, are "wish and request", "have fullest confidence", "heartily beseech", and the like'. [Black's *Law Dictionary*, 5th Ed.].

Precatory trust is a trust that the law will recognize to carry out the wishes of the testator or grantor even though the statement in question is in the nature of an entreaty or recommendation rather than a positive command. [Black's *Law Dictionary*, 8th Ed.].

NOTE: At one time, the Court of Chancery was very ready to infer a trust from precatory words. The modern tendency is against construing precatory words as creating a trust [*In re, Adams and the Kensington Vestry* (1884)27 Ch D 394], a testator gave all his property to the absolute use of his wife, her heirs, executors, administrators and assigns, in full confidence that she would do what was right as to the disposal thereof between the testator's children, and it was held that the wife took the property beneficially.

**Precedent.** "In law a precedent is an adjudged case or decision of a court of justice, considered as furnishing a rule or authority for the determination of an identical or similar case afterwards arising, or of a similar question of law. The only theory on which it is possible for one decision to be an authority for another is that the facts are alike, or, if the facts are different, that the principle which governed the first case is applicable to the variant facts." [William M. Lile et al., *Brief Making and the Use of Law Books,* p. 288 (3d ed. 1914)].

"A precedent ... is a judicial decision which contains in itself a principle. The underlying principle which thus forms its authoritative element is often termed the *ratio decidendi*. The concrete decision is binding between the parties to it, but it is the obstruct *ratio decidendi* which alone has the force of law as regards the world at large." [John Salmond, *Jurisprudence*, p. 191 (Glanville L. Williams ed., 10th Ed. 1947)].

Courts attempt to decide cases on the basis of principles established in prior cases. Prior cases which are close in facts or legal principles to the case under consideration are called precedents.

Black's *Law Dictionary* [5th Ed.] defines 'precedent' as a rule of law established for the first time by a court for a particular type of case and thereafter referred to in deciding similar cases.

Black's *Law Dictionary* [7th & 8th Eds.] defines 'precedent' as the making of law by a court in recognizing and applying new rules while administering justice; a decided case that furnishes a basis for determining later cases involving similar facts or issues.

NOTE: When a judge, in deciding a case, follows a precedent, he only regards himself bound by the principle underlying the judgment but not by the facts of that case. [*Tribhuvandas Purshottamdas Thakkar* v *Ratilal Motilal Patel* (1968)2 SCJ 92].

*Precedent—when not binding—examples*:

- When it was rendered in ignorance of a statute or a rule having the force of statute. [*Young* v *Bristol Aeroplane Co. Ltd*. (1944) KB 729 (CA): (1944)2 All ER 293].
- When it is inconsistent with an earlier decision of a higher court or an earlier decision of a larger bench of the same court [*Young* v *Bristol Aeroplane Co. Ltd*. (1944) KB 729 (CA): (1944)2 All ER 293; *R.* v *Northumberland Compensation Appeal Tribunal* (1951)1 KB 711: (1951)1 All ER 268].
- When a precedent is passed *sub silentio*. [*Gerard* v *Worth Peris Ltd*. (1936)2 All ER 905].
- When it is overruled by a higher court.

**Precedent sub silentio.** A legal question that was neither argued nor considered in a judicial decision that is or might be treated as a precedent. [Black's *Law Dictionary*, 7th Ed.].

A legal question that was neither argued nor explicitly discussed in a judicial decision but that seems to have been silently ruled on and might therefore be treated as a precedent. [Black's *Law Dictionary*, 8th Ed.].

A precedent *sub silentio* arises when the particular point of law involved in the decision is not perceived by the court or present to its mind, as where the point was decided without argument, without reference to the crucial words of the rule, and without any citation of authority. [*Gerard* v *Worth Peris Ltd*. (1936)2 All ER 905].

**Precept.** An order, writ, warrant, or process; a rule authoritatively given; a mandate.

An order or direction, emanating from authority, to an officer or body of officers, commanding him or them to do some act within the scope of their powers.

NOTE: Under s. 46 of the Code of Civil Procedure 1908, the court passing the decree may issue, on the application of the decree-holder, a precept to any other court competent to execute it by attaching any property belonging to the judgment-debtor. The object of a precept is to enable a decree-holder to obtain an interim attachment in an emergency.

**Predatory.** Characterized by or undertaken for plundering; addicted to pillaging; constituted for living by preying upon others, as a beast or bird; raptorial; exploitative; rapacious.

The word is applied figuratively in the phrase from anti-trust law, predatory pricing. [*Union of India* v *Hindustan Development Corpn*. (1993)3 SCR 128: JT 1993(3) SC 15: (1993)3 SCC 499: AIR 1994 SC 988].

**Predatory pricing.** Unlawful below-cost pricing intended to eliminate specific competitors and reduce overall competition.

**Predecease.** To die before another.

To predecease a person is to die in his lifetime. [*Taylor's Trustees* v *Barnett* 31 SLR 11].

**Predecessor in title.** The expression "predecessor in title" in relation to a tenant or landlord means any person through whom the tenant or landlord has derived title, whether by assignment, by will, by intestacy, or by operation of law.

"Predecessor in title" includes a person whose business or part of whose business has been acquired by the successor whether by succession, purchase, amalgamation, reconstruction or otherwise.

**Pre-emption.** The right to buy before others; the first buying of a thing; the purchase of something under this right.

The word 'pre-emption' is a well-understood term of law. It is a right of substitution conferred on someone either by statute, custom or contract. The right is to step into the shoes of the vendee preferentially on the terms of sale already settled between the vendor and the vendee. [*Vijayalakshmi* v *B.H. Chetty* (1996)3 Sim LJ 1969 (SC)].

**Preference.** The act of favouring one person or thing over another.

The expression "preference" amongst others means prior right, advantage, precedence etc. It signifies that other things being equal, one will have preference over the others. [*Sher Singh* v *Union of India* (1983)3 Comp LJ 306: AIR 1984 SC 200: (1984)1 SCR 464: (1984)1 SCC 107].

**Preference share.** One giving its holder a preference, either as to receipt of dividends or as to payment in case of winding up, or both. [*In re Schaffer Stores Co.* 229 NYS 735, 739].

▸ *Meaning under the Preference Shares (Regulation of Dividends) Act 1960, s. 2(c).* 'Preference share' means a share which carries as respects dividends a preferential right to be paid a fixed amount or an amount calculated at a fixed rate.

**Preference share capital.** With reference to any company limited by shares, whether formed before or after the commencement of the Companies Act 1956, that part of the share capital of the company which fulfils both the following requirements, namely—(*a*) that as respects dividends, it carries or will carry a preferential right to be paid a fixed amount or an amount calculated at a fixed rate, which may be either free of or subject to income-tax, and (*b*) that as respects capital, it carries or will carry, on a winding up or repayment of capital, a preferential right to be repaid the amount of the capital paid up or deemed to have been paid up, whether or not there is a preferential right to the payment of either or both of the following amounts, namely—(*i*) any money remaining unpaid, in respect of the amounts specified in clause (*a*) up to the date of the winding up or repayment of capital, and (*ii*) any fixed premium or premium on any fixed scale, specified in the memorandum or articles of the company. [Companies Act 1956, s. 85(1)].

**Pregnancy.** Time between conception and child birth when a woman is carrying the unborn child in her womb; condition of being pregnant.

- **Plea of pregnancy** p. 666.

**Prejudice.** In its application to injury, it means damage or detriment to one's legal rights or claims; disadvantage; harm; impairment; irreversible damage; wrong.

In its application to preconception, it means bias; favouritism; forejudgment; leaning; preconceived idea; preconceived notion; predetermination; predilection; predisposition; a leaning towards one side of a cause for some reason other than a conviction of its justice.

- **Without prejudice** p. 901.

**Preliminary decree.** A preliminary decree is an interlocutory decree or a provisional decree, which is not final and does not determine the suit, but directs some further proceedings preparatory to the final decree. It is a decree pronounced for the purpose of ascertaining matter of law or fact preparatory to a final decree. [*Lodge* v *Towell* 34 L Ed 153].

A decree is preliminary when further proceedings have to be taken before the suit can be completely disposed of. [Code of Civil Procedure 1908, s. 2(2)].

**Preliminary point.** The expression "preliminary point" in connection with a suit is not confined to such legal points only as may be pleaded in bar of a suit, but comprehends all points or issues whether of fact or law, the determination of which has precluded the necessity for determining other points or issues which have, therefore, been left undetermined. [*Raman Nayar* v *Krishna* AIR 1922 Mad 505 (FB)].

NOTE: Order 41, r. 23, Code of Civil Procedure 1908, provides for the remand of a case by the Appellate Court where the trial court disposed of the suit on a preliminary point.

**Premises.** 'Premises' is a word which is capable of many meanings. [*Gardiner* v *Sevenoaks R.D.C.* (1950)2 All ER 84]. In its popular sense it means that which is put before; that which precedes; the foregoing statements. The word 'premises' signifies what has gone before. [*Beacon Assurance* v *Gibb* 1 Moo PCNS 73].

In its application to conveyancing, it means that part of a deed which precedes the habendum, in which are set forth the names of the parties with their titles and additions, and in which are recited such deeds, agreements, or matters of fact as are necessary to explain the reasons upon which the transaction intended to be entered into is founded.

In its application to estates and property, it means lands and tenements; an estate, including land and buildings thereon. [*F.F. Proctor Troy Properties Co.* v *Dugan Store* 181 NYS 786, 788]. The word 'premises' is commonly used as comprising land and houses and other matters. [*Doe d. Hemming* v *Willetts* (1849)7 CB 709, 715, *per* Wilde, C.J.]. The word "premises" originally became applied to property "from the habit of conveyancers when they were drawing deeds of conveyance referring to property and speaking of 'parcels'. They set out the parcels in the early part of the deed, and later they would refer to 'the said premises', meaning strictly that which had gone before, and gradually by common acceptance 'premises' became applied, as it generally is now, to houses, land, shops, or whatever it may be, so that the word may come to mean generally real property of one sort or another". [*Gardiner* v *Sevenoaks, R.D.C.* (1950)2 All ER 84, 85, *per* Lord Goddard, C.J.]. The word 'premises' is a generic term meaning open land or land with buildings or buildings alone. [*Ardeshir H. Bhiwandiwala* v *State of Bombay* AIR 1962 SC 29: (1962)3 SCR 592: (1962)1 Cr LJ 99].

- **Commercial premises** p. 156.
- **Public premises** p. 712.
- **Residential premises** p. 755.

**Premium.** Premium has several meanings. Premium ordinarily means increased value [*Barrow* v *Methold* 3 WR 629]; a reward for an act done [*Brown* v *Board of Police Com'rs of City of Los Angeles* 136 P 2d 617, 619]; a sum over and above a regular price paid chiefly as an inducement or incentive.

"Premium" is now frequently used to denote the annual payment for keeping up an insurance; or the money paid on an apprenticeship. [*Walter* v *Everard* (1891)2 QB 369: 60 LJQB 738].

The consideration required of an assured for any form of insurance is a money payment universally referred to as a premium. There may be a single lump sum premium, but more commonly the premium is payable either at specified intervals, as in the case of life insurance, or as consideration for successive renewals of the policy. [Halsbury's *Laws of England*, 4th Ed., vol. 25, para 458, p. 253].

"Premium" also includes any like sum, whether payable to the intermediate or a superior landlord; and any sum (other than rent) paid on or in connection with the granting of a tenancy is presumed to have been paid by way of premium except insofar as other sufficient consideration for the payment is shown to have been given. [Halsbury's *Laws of England*, 4th Ed., vol. 5, para 169, p. 85].

In connection with leases, the word "premium" has a well-known meaning. It represents capitalised rent which in fact is the difference between the actual rent and the rent which might otherwise be obtained by the lessor. The lessee pays such amount to the lessor as he would not otherwise part with the possession of the property for the reason that the rent he is entitled to charge under certain rent restriction legislations is too small. [*Gobond Ram* v *Rajphul Singh* AIR 1973 P&H 94]. Premium merely means a lump sum paid as a consideration for the acquisition of lease. So also, if the premium or lump sum is paid by instalments spread over the term of the lease, it still remains of a capital nature. [*Regent Oil Co. Ltd.* v *Strick* (1965)3 All ER 174].

Where the value of assets transferred exceeds the par value, the difference may appropriately be regarded as 'premium' according to the nomenclature used in India. When shares are issued for consideration other than cash, the value of the assets transferred in excess of the par value of shares issued would be regarded as premium for purposes of Indian system of law. [*Commissioner of Income Tax (Central) Calcutta* v *Standard Vacuum Oil Co.* AIR 1966 SC 1393: (1966)59 ITR 685: (1966)1 SCJ 401: (1966)1 Comp LJ 187: (1966)2 SCR 367].

NOTE: *'Premium' and 'rent'—distinction.* The distinction between premium and rent is that the former is paid in consideration of the conveyance implied in the lease and is quantified in lump, whether paid at once or in instalments. But a rent, while it is also in consideration of a lease, is in lieu of enjoyment which the lessee gets. The further feature of rent is that it is payable as and when it accrues. [*Chief Controlling Revenue Authority* v *S.M. Abdul* AIR 1970 Mad 288: (1970)1 MLJ 417].

**Prerogative.** Advantage; authority; exclusive privilege; exclusive right; preference; prior right; priority; vested right.

An exclusive right, power, privilege, or immunity, usually acquired by virtue of office. [Black's *Law Dictionary*, 7th & 8th Eds.].

**Prerogative writ.** A writ issued by a court exercising unusual or discretionary power. Examples are *certiorari, habeas corpus, mandamus*, and prohibition. [Black's *Law Dictionary*, 8th Ed.].

NOTE: In India, prerogative writs are issued under Art. 32 of the Constitution by the Supreme Court and Art. 226 by the High Courts.

**Prescription.** In its application to custom, it means convention; conventional usage; tradition; precedent; usage; practice.

In its use as directive, it means authority; canon; command; decree; doctrine; edict; measure; ruling; theorem.

In its use in medical field, it means a direction of remedy or remedies for a disease, illness, or injury and the manner of using them. It may also mean a formula for the preparation of a drug or medicine.

In its application to claim of title to real property, it means inalienable right; vested right; vested interest. Prescription is the term usually applied to incorporeal hereditaments. It is the name given to a mode of acquiring title to incorporeal hereditaments by immemorial or long-continued enjoyment. [*Hester* v *Sawyers* 71 P 2d 646, 649].

In international law, it means acquisition of sovereignty over a territory through continuous and undisputed exercise of sovereignty over it during such a period as is necessary to create under the influence of historical development the general conviction that the present condition of things is in conformity with international order. [*State of Arkansas* v *State of Tennessee* 310 US 563: 60 S Ct 1026, 1030: 84 L Ed 1362].

NOTE: *'Prescription' and 'limitation'—distinction.* Prescription differs from limitation. The former is one of the modes of acquiring certain rights while the latter bars a remedy. Secondly, prescription is a part of substantive law, but limitation relates to procedure. A person can acquire easements by prescription under s. 25 of the Limitation Act 1963.

**Presence.** It may have various uses. It may mean a person's appearance or bearing, especially when imposing; a person's force of personality; image; outward show; style.

It may mean the state or condition of being present in a certain place and not elsewhere, or within the sight or call, at hand, or in some place that is being thought of; the existence of a person in a particular place at a given time particularly with reference to some act done then and there.

Close physical proximity coupled with awareness. [Black's *Law Dictionary*, 8th Ed.].

- **In the presence of.** It means 'in the sight of'. Where a deed or will is required to be signed in the presence of witnesses, it means that the witnesses should see and be conscious of the act done.

**Presentation.** The act of presenting or bringing something in the presence of someone.

The word 'presentation' may have many meanings according to the context or as circumstances require, and it may mean either 'showing' or 'delivering over'. [*Bartlett* v *Holmes* 22 LJCP 185].

It may mean the 'delivery of a document to an issuer or named person for the purpose of initiating action under a letter of credit'. [Black's *Law Dictionary*, 8th Ed.].

**Preside.** Be at the head of; be in authority; be in charge; be in the chair; hold sway; take charge; act as chairman; act as president; administer.

To occupy the place of authority as of president, chairman, moderator, etc.; to direct, control or regulate proceedings as chief officer, moderator, etc.; to possess or exercise authority.

To occupy the place of authority, esp. as a judge during a hearing or trial; to exercise management or control. [Black's *Law Dictionary*, 7th & 8th Eds.].

To occupy a position similar to that of a President or Chairman; to exercise guidance, direction or control. [*Oriental Fire & General Insurance* v *Murlidhar* AIR 1985 Cal 301, 307].

**Presidency-town.** The local limits for the time being of the ordinary original civil jurisdiction of the High Court of Judicature at Calcutta, Madras or Bombay, as the case may be. [General Clauses Act 1897, s. 3(44)].

**Presumption.** Assumption; belief; anticipation; hypothesis; inference; predilection; predisposition; presupposition; strong probability; reasonable supposition.

A legal inference or assumption that a fact exists, based on the known or proven existence of some other fact or group of facts. [Black's *Law Dictionary*, 7th & 8th Eds.].

A presumption is a rule of law, statutory or judicial, by which finding of a basic fact gives rise to existence of presumed fact, until presumption is rebutted. [*Van Wart* v *Cook* Okl App., 557 P 2d 1161, 1163].

The term 'presumption' in its largest and most comprehensive signification, may be defined to be an inference, affirmative or disaffirmative of the truth or falsehood of a doubtful fact or proposition drawn by a process of probable reasoning from something proved or taken for granted. [*Izhar Ahmad Khan* v *Union of India* AIR 1962 SC 1052: (1962)2 Cr LJ 215].

• **Rebuttable presumption** p. 732.

**Presumption of death.** A presumption which arises upon the disappearance and continued absence of a person from his customary location or home for an extended period of time, commonly seven years, without any apparent reason for such absence. [*Magers* v *Western & Southern Life Ins. Co.* CA Mo., 335 SW 2d 355].

NOTE: Presumptions of life and of death are governed respectively by s. 107 and s. 108 of the Indian Evidence Act 1872. Under s. 107 if it is shown that a person is alive within thirty years, the onus of proving that he is dead is on the person who affirms it. If a person has not been heard of for seven years by those who would naturally have heard of him if he had been alive, the burden shifts under s. 108 to the person who affirms that he is alive.

**Presumption of law.** A presumption of law is one which, once the basic fact is proved and no evidence to the contrary has been introduced, compels a finding of the existence of the presumed fact. The presumption of law is rebuttable and in most cases the adversary introduces evidence designed to overcome it. [Black's *Law Dictionary*, 5th Ed.].

A legal assumption that a court is required to make if certain facts are established and no contradictory evidence is produced [Black's *Law Dictionary,* 8th Ed.].

NOTE: In case of a 'presumption of law' no discretion has been left to the court, and it is bound to presume the fact as proved until evidence is given by the party interested to rebut or disprove it. Instances of such presumptions are to be found in ss. 79-81, 83, 85, 89 and 105 of the Evidence Act. In case of presumptions of law, in the absence of evidence sufficient to rebut it on a balance of probability, a verdict must be directed. [*Syad Akbar* v *State of Karnataka* AIR 1979 SC 1848: 1979 Cr LJ 1374: (1980)1 SCR 95: (1980)1 SCC 30: 1980 SCC (Cri) 59].

**Presumptions of fact.** Such are presumptions which do not compel a finding of the presumed fact but which warrant one when the basic fact has been proved. [Black's *Law Dictionary*, 5th Ed.].

'Presumptions of fact' are inferences of certain fact patterns drawn from the experience and observation of the common course of nature, the constitution of the human mind, the springs of human action, the usages and habits of society and ordinary course of human affairs. [*Syad Akbar* v *State of Karnataka* AIR 1979 SC 1848: 1979 Cr LJ 1374: (1980)1 SCR 95: (1980)1 SCC 30: 1980 SCC (Cri) 59].

NOTE: Section 114 of the Evidence Act is a general section dealing with presumptions of this kind. It is not obligatory for the court to draw a presumption of fact. In respect of such presumptions, the Act allows the judge a discretion in each case to decide whether the fact which under s. 114 of the Evidence Act may be presumed has been proved by virtue of that presumption. [*Syad Akbar* v *State of Karnataka*, supra].

**Presumptive heir.** Presumptive heir is one who, if the ancestor had died immediately, would have been his heir, but whose right of inheritance might be defeated by the contingency of some nearer heir being born.

**Preventive detention.** Confinement imposed generally on a defendant in criminal case who has threatened to violate the law while awaiting trial or disposition, or of a mentally ill person who may harm himself or others. [Black's *Law Dictionary*, 5th Ed.].

Confinement imposed usually on a criminal defendant who has threatened to escape or has otherwise violated the law while awaiting trial, or on a mentally ill person who may cause harm. [Black's *Law Dictionary*, 7th & 8th Eds.].

This is detention of a person without trial in such circumstances that the evidence in the possession of the authorities is not sufficient to draw up a legal charge or to secure the conviction of the detenu by legal proof; but all the same, it is justified. No offence is proved nor any charge formulated, but the justification is dictated by suspicion. [*A.K. Gopalan* v *State of Madras* AIR 1950 SC 27: 1950 SCR 88: 1950 Cr LJ 1383].

It is an anticipatory measure and does not relate to an offence while criminal proceedings are to punish a person for an offence committed by him. [*Alijan Mia* v *District Magistrate, Dhanbad* AIR 1983 SC 1130: 1983 Cr LJ 1649: (1983)4 SCC 301: 1983 Cr LR (SC) 481: (1983)3 SCR 939: 1983 SCC (Cri) 840].

NOTE: Article 22(5) provides two kinds of safeguards against parliamentary legislation, *viz.*, (1) the detenu should be supplied with the grounds of detention, and (2) he should be given reasonable opportunities to make a representation.

The term may also mean: 'An employee's custody of the employer's property without being considered as having legal possession of it'. [Black's *Law Dictionary*, 7th & 8th Eds.].

**Preventive justice.** The system of measures taken by government with reference to the direct prevention of crime. It generally consists in obliging those persons whom there is probable ground to suspect of future misbehaviour to give full assurance to the public that such offence as is apprehended shall not happen, by requiring pledges or securities to keep the peace, or for their good behaviour (e.g. peace bonds). [Black's *Law Dictionary*, 5th Ed.].

Preventive justice consists in obliging those persons, whom there is probable ground to suspect of future misbehaviour, to stipulate with and to give assurance to the public that such offence as is apprehended shall not happen; by finding pledgers or securities for keeping the peace or for their good behaviour. [*R.* v *Sandbach Ex p. Williams* (1935)2 KB 192, 196, D.C., *per* Avory, J.].

**Preventive relief.** Relief preventive in nature.

NOTE: Preventive relief is granted at the discretion of the court by injunction, temporary or perpetual. [Specific Relief Act 1963, s. 36].

**Previous year.** An accounting year comprised of full twelve months preceding the financial year of assessment. It also means an accounting year previous to the present accounting year maintained by the assessee. [*Dhandhania Kadia* v *Commissioner of Income-tax* AIR 1959 SC 219].

**Price.** Amount; appraisal; charge; cost; disbursement; exaction; exchange value; purchase money; selling price; valuation; value.

Black's *Law Dictionary* [5th Ed.] defines the word thus: Something which one ordinarily accepts voluntarily in exchange for something else. The consideration given for the purchase of a thing. Amount which a prospective seller indicates as the sum for which he is willing to sell; market value. The term may be synonymous with cost, and with value, as well as with consideration, though price is not always identical either with consideration.

Black's *Law Dictionary* [7th & 8th Eds.] defines the word thus: The amount of money or other consideration asked for or given in exchange for something else; the cost at which something is bought or sold.

Price is the sum of money or its equivalent at which a thing is valued. [*Johnston, Fear & Kingham and the Offset Printing Co., Pty., Ltd.* (1943)67 CLR 314, 327, *per* Starke, J.].

'Price' is defined as the money consideration for a sale of goods. [Sale of Goods Act 1930, s. 2(10); *CIT Andhra Pradesh* v *Motors and General Stores Pvt. Ltd.* AIR 1968 SC 200; *Gapala Krishna Pillai* v *K.M. Mani* AIR 1984 SC 216: (1984)2 SCC 83].


- **Factory prices** p. 337.
- **Fair price** p. 339.
- **Fancy price** p. 346.
- **Hire-purchase price** p. 418.
- **Loco price** p. 541.
- **Making-up price** p. 551.
- **Market price** p. 564.
- **Sale price** p. 772.
- **Upset price** p. 869.
- **Wholesale price** p. 897.

**Prima facie.** At first sight; at first glance; at first view; at sight; apparently; on the face of the matter; on the first view; to all appearances; presumably.

The expression *"prima facie"* means at the first sight or on first appearance or on face of it, or so far as it can be judged from the first disclosure. [*General Electric Co.* v *Fifth Industrial Tribunal* 92 CWN 464: (1987)2 CLJ 305].

**Prima facie case.** Such as will prevail until contradicted and overcome by other evidence. [*Pacific Telephone & Telegraph Co.* v *Wallace* 75 P 2d 942, 947].

A case which has proceeded upon sufficient proof to that stage where it will support finding if evidence to contrary is disregarded. [*In re Hoagland's Estate* 253 NW 416; *General Electric Co.* v *Fifth Industrial Tribunal* 92 CWN 464: (1987)2 CLJ 305].

NOTE: Courts use concept of *"prima facie"* case in two senses: (1) in sense of plaintiff producing evidence sufficient to render reasonable a conclusion in favour of allegation he asserts; and (2) courts use *"prima facie"* to mean not only that plaintiff's evidence would reasonably allow conclusion plaintiff seeks, but also that plaintiff's evidence compels such a conclusion if the defendant produces no evidence to rebut it. [*Husbands* v *Com. of Pa.* DC Pa, 395 F Supp 1107, 1139].

While determining whether a *prima facie* case has been made out, the relevant consideration is whether on the evidence laid it was possible to arrive at the conclusion in question. [*National Tobacco Co.* v *Fourth Industrial Tribunal* AIR 1960 Cal 249: 64 CWN 304].

**Primary evidence.** Original or first-hand evidence; that evidence which the nature of the case or question suggests as the proper means of ascertaining the truth; the document itself produced for the inspection of the court. [Evidence Act 1872, s. 62].

NOTE: Generally speaking, documents must be proved by primary evidence. In cases specified in s. 65 of the Act, secondary evidence relating to documents may be given, *e.g.*, where the original is lost or is in the possession of the adverse party. It is not always easy to determine what is the original document so as to constitute primary evidence. Sometimes the same document is primary for one purpose and secondary for another.

**Prime Minister.** The responsible head of a ministry or executive government in India and England.

NOTE: Article 74 of the Constitution of India provides that there shall be a council of Ministers with the Prime Minister at the head to aid and advise the President in the exercise of his functions. The President is the nominal head of the Government while the Prime Minister is its real head. A distinction is thus made between the nominal and real executive. [*Ram Jawaya Kapur* v *State of Punjab* AIR 1955 SC 549].

**Primogeniture.** The exclusive right of the eldest son or nearest male relative to inherit.

The state of being the first-born among several children of the same parents; seniority by birth in the same family; the superior or exclusive right possessed by the eldest son, and particularly his right to succeed to the estate of his ancestor, in right of his seniority by birth, to the exclusion of younger sons. [Black's *Law Dictionary*, 5th Ed.].

The state of being the first-born child among siblings; the common-law right of the first-born son to inherit his ancestor's estate, usually to the exclusion of his younger siblings. [Black's *Law Dictionary*, 7th & 8th Eds.].

Primogeniture means first-born and denotes the preferential rights of the seniormost in age to succeed to the estate, since seniormost in age is entitled to succeed to the estate in preference to his younger brother. [*Annasaheb Bapusaheb Patil* v *Balwant* (1995)2 SCC 543, 550].

**Principal.** Cardinal; chief; controlling; dominant; foremost; leading; most important; paramount; primal; ruling; outstanding; the source of authority or right.

▸*Meaning under the Indian Contract Act 1872, s. 182.* A person who employs an agent to do some act for him.

Capital sum placed at interest, due as a debt, or used as a fund, as distinguished from interest or profit. [*Klitgoard* v *Gaines* Tex Civ App, 479 SW 2d 765, 770].

In law of guaranty and suretyship, it means the person primarily liable, for performance of whose obligation the guarantor or surety becomes bound.

The amount actually lent, whether in cash or otherwise.

**Principal debtor.** The person in respect of whose default the guarantee is given is called the "principal debtor". [Indian Contract Act 1872, s. 126].

**Principal employer.** 'Principal employer' means—(*i*) in relation to any office or department of the Government or local authority, the head of that office or department or such other officer as the Government or the local authority, as the case may be, may specify in this behalf, (*ii*) in a factory, the owner or occupier of the factory and where a person has been named as the manager of the factory under the Factories Act 1948 (63 of 1948), the person so named, (*iii*) in a mine the owner or agent of the mine and where a person has been named as the manager of the mine, the person so named, (*iv*) in any other establishment, any person responsible for the supervision and control of the establishment. [Contract Labour (Regulation and Abolition) Act 1970, s. 2(*g*)].

In a factory, "principal employer" is the owner or occupier of the factory and includes the managing agent of such owner or occupier, the legal representative of a deceased owner or occupier, and where a person has been named as the manager of the factory under the Factories Act 1948, the person so named. [*B.M. Lakshmanamurthy* v *The Employees' State Insurance Corporation, Bangalore* AIR 1974 SC 759: (1974)3 SCR 142: (1974)4 SCC 365].

**Principal in the first degree.** Under the English law criminals are divided into four classes: (1) principal in the first degree; (2) principal in the second degree; (3) accessory before the fact; and (4) accessory after the fact.

One who is the actual perpetrator of the crime is called the principal in the first degree. It is not necessary that he should be actually present when the offence is committed; thus one who lays poison or a trap for another is a principal in the first degree. There is no need that the deed be done by the principal's own hands; for it will suffice if it is done through an innocent agent, as for instance, if one incites a child or a madman to murder.

**Principal office.** The "principal office" of an organisation is the place at which the business of the organisation is managed and controlled as a whole. [*Garton* v *Great Western Railway* 27 LJQB 375; *Palvner* v *Caledonian Railway* (1892)1 QB 823; *Clokey* v *London & North Western Railway* (1905)2 IR 251].

**Principle.** Accepted belief; admitted maxim; article of belief; basic truth; basic rule; basic law; doctrine; dogma; formulated belief; philosophy; professed belief; self-evident proposition; self-evident truth; that which pertains to the theoretical part of a science.

"Principle" means a general law or rule adopted or professed as a guide to action. In order words, as opposed to any specific direction governing any particular or specific instance, transaction or situation a principle would be a guiding rule applicable generally to cases or class of cases. [*Consolidated Coffee Ltd.* v *Coffee Board, Bangalore* AIR 1980 SC 1468: (1980)3 SCR 625: (1980)3 SCC 358: (1980)46 STC 164].

**Prior tempore, potier jure.** He who is first in time is preferred in law.

**Priority.** Advantage; commanding position; essential status; importance; precedence; pre-eminence; preference; legal precedence in exercise of rights over the same subject-matter.

**Prison.** Cell; house of correction; house of detention; house of reform; reformatory; a place for the confinement of persons whether as a punishment imposed by law or otherwise in the course of the administration of justice.

• **Civil prison** p. 145.

**Prisoner.** Captive; confined individual; convict; incarcerated person; jailed person; person under arrest; one who is deprived of his liberty.

- **Prisoner under sentence of death.** The expression "prisoner under sentence of death" can only mean a prisoner whose sentence of death has become final and conclusive and indefeasible which cannot be annulled or voided by any judicial or constitutional procedure. [*Sunil Batra* v *Delhi Administration* AIR 1978 SC 1675: (1978)4 SCC 494: 1978 Cr LJ 1741: (1979)1 SCR 392: 1979 SCC (Cri) 155].

**Privacy.** Confidentiality; confidentialness; seclusion; solitariness; solitude.

> NOTE: "Privacy" primarily concerns the individual. It therefore relates to and overlaps with the concept of liberty. The most serious advocate of privacy must confess that there are serious problems of defining the essence and scope of such right. [*Govind* v *State of Madhya Pradesh* AIR 1975 SC 1378: (1975)3 SCR 946: (1975)2 SCC 148: 1975 Cr LJ 1111: 1975 SCC (Cri) 468].

- **Privacy, right of.** The right to be let alone; the right of a person to be free from unwarranted publicity; the right of an individual to withhold himself and his property from public scrutiny, if he so chooses.

> NOTE: The term "right of privacy" is a generic term encompassing various rights recognised to be inherent in concept of ordered liberty; and such right prevents governmental interference in intimate personal relationships or activities, freedoms of individual to make fundamental choices involving himself, his family, and his relationship with others. [*Industrial Foundation of the South* v *Texas Indus Acc. Bd., Tex.* 540 SW 2d 668, 679].

**Private.** Not official; not clothed with office [*People* v *Powell* 274 NW 372, 373]; affecting or belonging to private individuals as distinct from the public generally.

**Private company.** A company which has a minimum paid-up capital of one lakh rupees or such higher paid-up capital as may be prescribed, and by its articles—(*a*) restricts the right to transfer its shares, if any; (*b*) limits the number of its members to fifty, not including—(*i*) persons who are in the employment of the company, and (*ii*) persons who, having been formerly in the employment of the company, were members of the company while in that employment and have continued to be members after the employment ceased; (*c*) prohibits any invitation to the public to subscribe for any shares in, or debentures of, the company; and (*d*) prohibits any invitation or acceptance of deposits from persons other than its members, directors or their relatives: Provided that where two or more persons hold one or more shares in a company jointly, they shall, for the purposes of this definition, be treated as a single member. [Companies Act 1956, s. 3(1)(*iii*)].

Section 3(1)(*iii*) of the Companies Act 1956, defines a "private company" thus: (*iii*) 'private company' means a company which, by its articles, (*a*) restricts the right to transfer its shares, if any; (*b*) limits the number of its members to fifty; and (*c*) prohibits any invitation to the public to subscribe for any shares in, or debentures of, the company. [*Needle Industries (India) Ltd.* v *Needle Industries Newey (India) Holdings Ltd.* AIR 1981 SC 1298: (1981)3 SCC 333: (1981)3 SCR 698: (1982)1 Comp LJ 1].

**Private documents.** All documents other than public documents are private documents. [Indian Evidence Act 1872, s. 75].

**Private international law.** A name used by some writers to indicate that branch of the law which is now more commonly called "conflict of laws". [Black's *Law Dictionary*, 5th Ed.].

Private international law, sometimes called 'conflict of law', is a branch of the civil law of the state, evolved to do justice between litigating parties in respect of transactions, or personal status involving a foreign element. Common rules have been adopted to adjudicate upon disputes involving a foreign element, and to give effect to judgments of foreign courts in certain matters, or as a result of international conventions. [*Viswanathan* v *Abdul Wajid* AIR 1963 SC 1].

**Private nuisance.** Activity which results in an unreasonable interference with the use and enjoyment of another's property. [*Robie* v *Lillis* 299 A 2d 155, 158; *City of Newport News* v *Hertzler* 221 SE 2d 146, 150].

A nuisance affecting a single individual or definite small number of persons in enjoyment of private rights not common to the public. [*Spur Industries, Inc.* v *Del E. Webb Development Co.* 494 P 2d 700, 705].

Anything that by its continuous use or existence works annoyance, harm, inconvenience or damage to another landowner in the enjoyment of his property. [*Mandell* v *Pasquaretto* 350 NYS 2d 561, 566].

**Private road.** Any street, road, lane, gully, alley, passage or square which is not a public street, and includes any passage securing access to four or more premises, belonging to the same or different owners, but does not include a passage provided in effecting a partition of any masonry building amongst joint owners where such passage is less than two metres and fifty centimetres wide. [Calcutta Municipal Corporation Act 1980, s. 2(68) and Bengal Municipal Act 1932, s. 3(43)].

A private road is one established by a private individual, or by a public authority chiefly for the accommodation of an individual or individuals, and at his or their instance and expense. Private roads are ordinarily used by the people of the neighbourhood.

**Private service vehicle.** A motor vehicle constructed or adapted to carry more than six persons excluding the driver and ordinarily used by or on behalf of the owner of such vehicle for the purpose of carrying persons for, or in connection with, his trade or business otherwise than for hire or reward but does not include a motor vehicle used for public purposes. [Motor Vehicles Act 1988, s. 2(33)].

'Private Service Vehicle' means any omnibus constructed or adapted to carry more than nine persons excluding the driver and ordinarily used by or on behalf of the owner of such vehicle for the purpose of carrying persons for, or in connection with his trade or business, or otherwise than for hire or reward; but does not include a motor vehicle used solely for police purpose. [*Tata Engineering and Locomotive Co. Ltd.* v *The Sales Tax Officer and Regional Transport Officer, Poona* AIR 1979 SC 343: (1979)2 SCR 357: (1979)1 SCC 208].

**Privatio praesupposit habitum.** A deprivation presupposes a possession.

**Privatum commodium publico cedit.** Private good yields to public.

**Privilege.** Advantage; affranchisement; allowance; beneficium; benefit; dispensation; exemption; favour; freedom; franchise; immunity; licence.

A particular and peculiar benefit or advantage enjoyed by a person, company, or class, beyond the common advantages of other citizens; an exceptional or extraordinary power of exemption; a right, power, franchise, or immunity held by a person or class, against or beyond the course of law. [Black's *Law Dictionary*, 5th Ed.].

A special legal right, exemption, or immunity granted to a person or class of persons; an exception to a duty. [Black's *Law Dictionary*, 7th & 8th Eds.].

A privilege grants someone the legal freedom to do or not to do a given act. It immunizes conduct that, under ordinary circumstances, would subject the actor to liability. [Black's *Law Dictionary*, 8th Ed.].

A "privilege" is an advantage conferred "over and above the ordinary law". [*Re Miller* (1893)1 QB 327, *per* Esher M.R.; *Winnipeg* v *Barrett* (1892) AC 445].

A privilege is some advantage to an individual or group of individuals. It is a right enjoyed by a few as opposed to a right enjoyed by all. [*Le Strange* v *Pettefar* 161 LT 300].

A "privilege" is the opposite of a duty, and the correlative of a 'no-right'. [*Isha Valimohamad* v *Haji Gulam Mohamad and Haji Dada Trust* AIR 1974 SC 2061: (1974)2 SCC 484].

A privilege is defined as a particular and peculiar benefit or advantage enjoyed by a person, and a concession as a form of privilege. An option to purchase or re-purchase has been held to be such a privilege or concession. [*Shanmugam Pillai* v *Annalakshmi* AIR 1950 FC 38; *K. Simrathmull* v *Nanjalingiah Gowder* AIR 1963 SC 1182; *V. Peechimuthu* v *Gowrammal* AIR 2001 SC 2446: JT 2001(6) SC 162: (2001)7 SCC 617].

NOTE: Immunity from civil action may be described as a privilege, because the word 'privilege' is sufficiently wide to include an immunity. [*Mohanlal Jain* v *Maharaja Shri Sawai Man Singhji* AIR 1962 SC 73: (1962)1 SCJ 641].

In the context of excise enactments, the expression 'privilege' means the licence or permit granted by the State. A citizen can trade in liquor under the excise enactments under a licence to be granted to it for the consideration specified in that behalf and that the trade therein can be carried on only in accordance with the regulatory provisions prescribed by it in that behalf. It is this grant of licence or permit, which is called or is described sometimes as grant of 'privilege'. [*State of Orissa* v *Narain Prasad* (1996)5 SCC 740].

• **Absolute privilege** p. 9.
• **Breach of privilege** p. 111.
• **Excess of privilege** p. 326.

**Privileged communications.** Those statements made by certain persons within a protected relationship such as husband and wife, attorney-client, priest-penitent and the like which the law protects from forced disclosure on the witness stand at the option of the witness client, penitent, spouse. [Black's *Law Dictionary*, 5th Ed.].

A communication that is protected by law from forced disclosure. [Black's *Law Dictionary*, 7th Ed.].

A communication, that is, protected by law from compelled disclosure in a legal proceeding, or that cannot be used against the person who made it. [Black's *Law Dictionary*, 8th Ed.].

NOTE: *Examples of privileged communications.* An informant's communication to a government agency and statements made in a legislative session by a legislator. [Black's *Law Dictionary*, 8th Ed.].

**Privileged document.** A document relating to affairs of State which documents State is not compelled to produce in court. Minister or head of department must decide if disclosure is justified or not; court is to determine even if plea not taken by the State; privilege cannot be waived by State. [*S.P. Gupta* v *Union of India* AIR 1982 SC 149].

**Privileged publication.** In general he who publishes a defamatory statement is liable if this statement turns out not to be true. This rule is subject to a number of exceptions grouped under the title 'privilege'.

The cases in which privilege exist are those in which there is some just occasion for publishing defamatory matter in the public interest.

Privilege is of two kinds, absolute and qualified. No action lies for a statement which is absolutely privileged. The following are the cases in which statement is absolutely privileged: (1) Any statement made in the course of and with reference to judicial proceedings by any judge, juryman, party, witness or advocate. (2) Fair, accurate and contemporaneous reports of public judicial proceedings published in a newspaper. (3) Any statement made in Parliament by a member. (4) Parliamentary papers published by the direction of Parliament. (5) Any statement made by one officer of State to another in course of his official duty. (6) Communications between husband and wife.

The chief instances of qualified privilege are the following: (1) Statements made in the performance of a duty; (2) statements made in the protection of an interest; (3) reports of Parliamentary, judicial and certain other public proceedings; (4) professional communications between solicitor and client. [Salmond on *Tort*, 19th Ed., pp. 178-179 & 184].

**Privileged will.** A will made in the manner provided in s. 66 of the Indian Succession Act 1925, by any soldier being employed in an expedition or engaged in actual warfare, or an airman so employed or engaged, or any mariner being at sea, if he has completed the age of eighteen years, disposing of his property. [Indian Succession Act 1925, s. 65].

**Privity.** Affiliation; attachment; connecting medium; contractual bond; derivative interest; interconnection; mutual relationship; mutuality of interest; successive relationship.

The connection or relationship between two parties, each having a legally recognized interest in the same subject-matter; mutuality of interest. [Black's *Law Dictionary*, 7th Ed.].

In its broadest sense, "privity" is defined as mutual or successive relationships to the same right of property, or such an identification of interest of one person with another as to represent the same legal right. [*Petersen* v *Fee Intern., Ltd.* DC Okl, 435 F Supp 938, 942].

It may also mean derivative interest founded on, or growing out of, contract, connection, or bond of union between parties; mutuality of interest. [*Hodgson* v *Midwest Oil Co.* CCA Wyo, 17 F 2d 71, 75].

The concept of "privity" pertains to the relationship between a party to a suit and a person who was not a party, but whose interest in the action was such that he will be bound by the final judgment as if he were a party. [*Foltz* v *Pullman, Inc.* Del Super, 319 A 2d 38, 41].

**Prize.** Accolade; award; blue ribbon; bounty; distinction; honour; reward; trophy.

Anything offered as a reward of contest; an award or recompense for some act done; some valuable thing offered by a person for something done by others. [Black's *Law Dictionary*, 5th Ed.]. Something of value awarded in recognition of a person's achievement. [Black's *Law Dictionary*, 7th Ed.].

It may also mean a vessel or cargo captured at sea or seized in port by the forces of a nation at war, and therefore liable to being condemned or appropriated as enemy property. [Black's *Law Dictionary*, 7th Ed.].

**Prize chit.** Unless the context otherwise requires, "prize chit" includes any transaction or arrangement by whatever name called under which a person collects whether as a promoter, foreman, agent or in any other capacity, monies in one lump sum or in instalments by way of contributions or subscriptions or by sale of units, certificates or other instruments or in any other manner or as membership fees or admission fees or service charges to or in respect of any savings, mutual benefit, thrift or any other scheme or arrangement by whatever name called, and utilises the monies so collected or any part thereof or the income accruing from investment or other use of such monies for all or any of the following purposes; namely: (*i*) giving or awarding periodically or otherwise to a specified number of subscribers as determined by lot, draw or in any other manner, prize or gifts in cash or in kind, whether or not the recipient of the prize of gift is under a liability to make any further payment in respect of such scheme or arrangement; (*ii*) refunding to the subscribers or such of them as have not won any prize or gift, the whole or part of the subscriptions, contributions or other monies collected, with or without any bonus, premium, interest or other advantage by whatever name called on the termination of the scheme or arrangement, or on or after the expiry of the period stipulated therein, but does not include a conventional chit. [The Prize Chits and Money Circulation Schemes (Banning) Act 1978, s. 2(*e*)].

NOTE: The Bhabatosh Datta Study Group and the Raj Study Group recognized that 'prize chits' were also variously called benefit/savings scheme and lucky draws and that the basic common feature of the schemes were the giving of a prize and the ultimate refund of the amount of all subscriptions. Since prize chits were called differently, 'prize chits', 'benefit/savings schemes', 'lucky draws', etc., it became necessary for the parliament to resort to an inclusive definition so as to bring in all transactions or arrangements containing these two elements.

In defining the expression 'prize chit', the parliament did not intend to depart from the meaning which the expression had come to acquire in the world of finance, the meaning which the Datta and the Raj Study Groups had given it. [*Reserve Bank of India* v *Peerless General Finance Company Ltd.* AIR 1987 SC 1023: (1987)1 SCC 424: (1987)2 SCR 1: JT 1987(1) SC 246: (1987)1 Comp LJ 162].

**Prize court.** An international tribunal created by a special commission under the Great Seal in the time of war to settle questions of capture, prize and booty. [Mozley & Whiteley's *Law Dictionary*, 10th Ed.].

The determination of the legality of the capture by a belligerent of enemy or neutral merchant vessels and of their liability to confiscation rests with the prize courts of the belligerent State. These courts and domestic tribunals organize and exercise their functions in accordance with the provisions of national legislation. But although the authority and the jurisdiction of prize courts are derived from national law, the rules which they apply to the cases coming before them are rules of international law, except in so far as special national legislation might have prescribed a particular interpretation of these rules. The duty of the prize court is to administer with indifference that justice which the law of nations holds out, without distinction, to independent States, some happening to be neutral and some to be belligerent. [Penwick's *International Law*, 3rd Indian Reprint 1971 p. 739].

A court having jurisdiction to adjudicate the captures made at sea in time of war.

**Prize law.** The system of laws applicable to the capture of prize at sea, dealing with such matters as the rights of captors and the distribution of the proceeds. [Black's *Law Dictionary*, 7th Ed.].

**Pro forma.** A Latin expression meaning as a matter of form; as or being a matter of form.

**Pro forma defendant.** Party who is defended only in form and against whom no relief is claimed or claimable.

**Pro forma invoice.** An invoice sent in advance of goods supplied, to predict results, or secure approval.

**Pro rata.** In proportion.

**Pro tanto.** For so much; to that extent.

**Pro tem.** For the time being.

**Probable.** Apparent; conceivable; conjecturable; feasible; foreseeable; full of promise; indubitable; likely; plausible; practicable; promising reasonable; surmisable; to be expected; credible; having the appearance of truth; appearing to be founded in reason or experience; supported by evidence which inclines the mind to believe, but leaves some room for doubt.

The word is used with various shades of meaning. Sometimes it appears to mean more probable than not, sometimes it appears to include events likely but not very likely to occur, sometimes it has a still wider meaning and refers to events the chance of which is anything more than a bare possibility, and sometimes, when used in conjunction with other adjectives, it appears to serve no purpose beyond rounding off a phrase. [*The Wagon Mound etc.* v *Miller Steamship Co.* (1966)2 All ER 709, 713].

**Probate.** Authentication of a will; judicial validation of a will; validation of a testament; will verification proceeding.

The judicial procedure by which a testamentary document is established to be a valid will; the proving of a will to the satisfaction of the court. [Black's *Law Dictionary*, 7th Ed.].

▸ *Meaning under the Indian Succession Act 1925, s. 2(f).* "Probate" means the copy of a will certified under the seal of a court of competent jurisdiction with a grant of administration to the estate of the testator.

NOTE: A probate granted by a competent court is conclusive of the validity of will until it is revoked and no evidence can be admitted to impeach it except in a proceeding taken for revoking the probate. [*Smt. Rukmani Debi* v *Narendra Lal Gupta* AIR 1984 SC 1866: (1985)1 SCC 144].

**Probate court.** A court with the power to declare wills valid or invalid, to oversee the administration of estates, court invested with the power or authority of granting probate; a court which has granted probate.

▸ *Meaning under the Indian Succession Act 1925, s. 264(1).* The District Judge shall have jurisdiction in granting and revoking probates and letters of administration in all cases within his district.

**Probate duty.** A tax laid by government on every will admitted to probate or on the gross value of the personal property of the deceased testator, and payable out of the decedent's estate. [Black's *Law Dictionary*, 5th Ed.].

A duty assessed by government on either every will admitted to probate, or on the gross value of the decedent's personal property. [Black's *Law Dictionary*, 7th Ed.].

▸ *Meaning under the Court Fees Act 1870, s. 19-I.* A fee payable on the net value of the estate of the deceased at the time of grant of probate.

**Probation.** Period of trial; period of testing; conditional suspension of sentence.

The evidence which proves a thing; the act of proving; proof; trial; test. Used in the latter sense when referring to the initial period of employment a new, transferred, or promoted employee must prove or show that he is capable of performing the required duties of the job or position before he will be considered as permanently employed in such position. As applied to teachers, the term means that teacher is on trial, with his competence and suitability remaining to be finally determined. [*Turner* v *Board of Trustees, Calexico Unified School Dist.* 121 Cal Rptr. 705: 535 P 2d 1171, 1178].

**Probationer.** Apprentice; beginner; novitiate; newcomer.

It may also mean criminal released at large; criminal under suspension of sentence; malefactor under suspension of sentence; offender under suspension of sentence; parolee; a convicted offender who is allowed to go at large, under suspension of sentence, during good behaviour.

**Procedendo.** A higher court's order directing a lower court to determine and enter a judgment in a previously removed case. [Black's *Law Dictionary*, 7th Ed.].

Action wherein court of superior jurisdiction orders court of inferior jurisdiction to proceed to judgment but has no bearing on nature of judgment to be entered. [*State ex rel. Jacobs* v *Municipal Court of Franklin County* 269 NE 2d 629, 631].

Writs of supersedeas and procedendo were formerly issued to return to the inferior court to be dealt with a cause or matter removed into the High Court by *certiorari* or to restore an order of an inferior court where an appeal against *certiorari* to quash was allowed. In the former case an order of the court would be made in the proceedings for *certiorari* and in the latter it seems that the successful appeal automatically effects the restoration of the quashed order. [Halsbury's *Laws of England*, 4th Ed., vol. 11, para 1580, p. 827].

**Procedure.** Course of action; established method; line of action; meaning of proceeding; meaning of working; methodology; mode of operation; mode of use; *modus operandi*; particular course of action; process; way of operation.

The judicial process for enforcing rights and duties recognised by substantive law and for justly administering redress for infraction of them. [*Sims* v *United Pacific Ins. Co.* DC Idaho, 51 F Supp 433, 435].

Procedure is machinery for carrying on suit including pleading, process, evidence and practice, whether in trial court or appellate court. [*Brooks* v *Texas Emp. Ins. Ass'n* Tex Civ App, 358 SW 2d 412, 414].

**Procedure established by law.** The expression must be taken to refer to procedure which has a statutory origin. [*A.K. Gopalan* v *State of Madras* AIR 1950 SC 27: 1950 SCJ 174: 1950 Cr LJ 1383].

"Procedure established by law" are words of deep meaning. Amplified, "procedure" means "fair and reasonable procedure" and not formal procedure and "law" is "reasonable law", and not any enacted law. [*M.H. Hoskot* v *State of Maharashtra* (1978)3 SCC 544: AIR 1978 SC 1548; *Maneka Gandhi* v *Union of India* AIR 1978 SC 597: (1978)1 SCC 248].

**Proceeding(s).** Action; action at law; conduct of a lawsuit; course of an action at law; legal action; legal procedure; litigation; prescribed method of action; steps in the prosecution of an action; suit at law.

The regular and orderly progression of a lawsuit, including all acts and events between the time of commencement and the entry of judgment; any procedural means for seeking redress from a tribunal or agency; any act or step that is part of a larger action; the business conducted by a court or other official body; a hearing. [Black's *Law Dictionary*, 7th & 8th Eds.].

The expression 'proceeding' is not a term of art which has acquired a definite meaning. What its meaning is when it occurs in a particular statute or a provision of a statute will have to be ascertained by looking at the relevant statute. [*Ram Chandra Aggarwal* v *State of U.P.* AIR 1966 SC 1888].

The term 'proceeding' is a very comprehensive term and generally speaking means a prescribed course of action for enforcing a legal right. It is not a technical expression with a definite meaning attached to it, but one, the ambit of whose meaning will be governed by the statute. It includes a prescribed mode in which judicial business is conducted. [*Babu Lal* v *Hazari Lal Kishori Lal* AIR 1982 SC 818: (1982)1 SCC 525: (1982)3 SCR 94].

'Proceeding' is a term of wide amplitude. It means a prescribed course of action for enforcing or protecting a legal right and further embracing the requisite steps to be taken whether procedural or substantive. It also means, forms in which relief is sought before courts of law or before other bodies or authorities determining rights and liabilities and in which actions are brought and defended and the manner of conducting them and the mode of deciding them. [*Workmen of Bali Singh Bhagwan Singh* v *Management* AIR 1969 Punj 147: ILR (1968)2 Punj 371; *K.J. Lingan and A.V. Mahayalam* v *Jt. Commercial Tax Officer* AIR 1968 Mad 76].

'Proceeding' is a prescribed course of action for the enforcement of a legal right. [*Smt. Sircar* v *Bisweswar Lal Sharma* AIR 1980 Cal 328 (DB)].

NOTE: A suit, appeal or second appeal can all be described as proceedings. [*Ratanchand Darbarilal Saina* v *Rajendra Kumar Khubchand* AIR 1970 MP 1 (FB)]. The word 'proceeding' includes application for revision. But it is impermissible to extend the meaning of the word 'proceeding' to include an application for special leave under Art. 136 of the Constitution of India. [*Gyan Chand* v *Kunjbeharilal* AIR 1977 SC 858: (1977)2 SCR 324: (1977)3 SCC 317].


- **Abatement of legal proceedings** p. 4.
- **Abatement of proceedings** p. 4.
- **Civil proceeding** p. 146.
- **Collusive proceeding** p. 154.
- **Criminal proceeding** p. 209.
- **Disciplinary proceeding** p. 263.
- **Judicial proceeding** p. 496.
- **Legal proceedings** p. 527.
- **Stay of proceedings** p. 812.
- **Summary proceedings** p. 821.


**Process.** Conduct; continued movement; line of action; methodology; mode of operation; progressive course; series of measures; ways and means.

A method, operation or series of actions intended to achieve some new and useful end or result by changing a material's chemical or physical characteristics. [Black's *Law Dictionary*, 8th Ed.].

The natural meaning of the word 'process' is a mode of treatment of certain materials in order to produce a good result, a species of activity performed on the subject-matter in order to transform or reduce it to a certain stage. According to *Shorter Oxford English Dictionary*, one of the meanings of the word 'process' is "continuous and regular action or succession of actions taking place or carried on in a definite manner and leading to the accomplishment of some result". The activity contemplated by the definition is perfectly general requiring only the continuous or quick succession. It is not one of the requisites that the activity should involve some operation on some material in order to effect its conversion to some particular stage. There is nothing in the natural meaning of the word 'process' to exclude its application to handling. There may be a process which consists only in handling and there may be a process which involves no handling or not merely handling but use also. Any activity or operation which is the essential requirement and is so related to the further operations for the end result would be a process in or in relation to manufacture. [*C.C.E.* v *Rajasthan State Chemical Works* AIR 1991 SC 2222: (1991)4 SCC 473: 1991 Supp (1) SCR 124: JT 1991(4) SC 6: (1991)55 ELT 444].

It may also mean authoritative citation to appear before a court; authoritative command; legal call; a summons or writ, esp. to appear or respond in court.

• **Abuse of process** p. 10.
• **Manufacturing process** p. 561.

**Processing.** 'Processing' means a sequence of operations of changes undergone. [*Diamond Industries* v *Commissioner of Sales Tax, M.P.* 1994 MPLJ 257].

> NOTE: *'Processing' and 'manufacturing'—distinction.* A mere processing does not ordinarily make the original thing to undergo a change losing its original identity. Under manufacturing the original article loses its identity and a thing or article differently known or recognised in common parlance comes into existence. [*Diamond Industries* v *Commissioner of Sales Tax, M.P.* 1994 MPLJ 257].

**Procession.** A procession may be defined as a formal and organised march of two or more persons, 'formal' implying a kind of solemnity or something spectacular, so as to attract attention and 'organised' implying a common intention or unity of purpose. [*Emperor* v *Nana Shahu* AIR 1943 Bom 209].

> NOTE: Some element of an organised march according to system is necessary in order to constitute a procession. Where, therefore, a meeting was permitted to be held in the village, and it was being lawfully held, if a number of villagers came to the meeting, through shouting slogans and carrying musical instruments, that will not be a circumstance leading to the inference that they came in a procession. [*James Surin* v *State* 1953 Cr LJ 1191: AIR 1953 Pat 195 (DB)].

**Proclamation.** Announcement; declaration; exclamation; fiat; mandate; official publication; pronouncement; public announcement; public notice.

A formal public announcement made by the government. [Black's *Law Dictionary*, 8th Ed.].

**Produce.** The verb 'produce' means to accomplish; achieve; breed; bring about; bring forth; bring into being; bring into existence; bring to pass; conceive; contrive; create; draw up; execute; fabricate; formulate; generate; give birth to; give rise to; procreate; result in; turn out; yield; bring forward; bring into view; bring out; bring to light; bring to the fore; demonstrate; disclose; display; divulge; exhibit; expose; hold up to view; lay bare; lay out; make known; make visible; manifest; put on display; reveal; set out; unmask; unscreen.

The verb 'produce' may mean to bring a thing into existence from its raw materials or elements. [*Deputy Commissioner, Agricultural Income-tax, Central Zone, Ernakulum* v *Palampadam Plantation Ltd., Kottayam* AIR 1969 SC 930: (1969)1 SCC 662: (1969)1 SCWR 435: (1969)25 STC 231].

As noun 'produce' means the product of natural growth, labour or capital; articles produced or grown from or on the soil, or found in the soil.

'Produce' means "anything produced or obtained as a result of some operation or work". [*Collector of Central Excise, Coimbatore* v *Protein Products of India Ltd.* JT 1988(4) SC 517: (1988)38 ELT 749: (1989)74 STC 98 (SC): AIR 1989 SC 627].

The word 'produce' is not necessarily confined to what is grown from the ground. It refers also to a finished article or semi-finished article made from raw material. Thus, mollasses can fairly be called the produce of a sugar mill. [*Nihal Chand* v *Jai Ram* AIR 1930 Oudh 165].

- **Agricultural produce** p. 52.
- **Forest produce** p. 367.

**Product(s).** 'Product' means not only 'a thing produced by nature or a natural process' but also 'that which is produced by any action, operation or work; a production'. [*Nakirikanti Panduranga Rao, Managing Partner of Sri Vijaya Commercial Corporation, Jaggayypet* v *State of AP represented by the Special Tahsildar (Land Acquisition) Bandor* (1976)1 Andh WR 41].

The word 'product' means anything produced or obtained as a result of some operation or work. [*Collector of Central Excise, Coimbatore* v *Protein Products of India Ltd.* JT 1988(4) SC 517: (1988)38 ELT 749: (1989)74 STC 98 (SC): AIR 1989 SC 627].

- **Bona products.** The expression 'bona products' merely means anything produced or obtained from bones. Whether such derivation is by a simple physical process or by a chemical reaction would make no difference to the end product. [*Collector of Central Excise, Coimbatore* v *Protein Products of India Ltd.* JT 1988(4) SC 517: (1988)38 ELT 749: (1989)74 STC 98 (SC): AIR 1989 SC 627].
- **Byproduct** p. 116.
- **End product** p. 306.
- **Milk product** p. 579.

**Profession.** Avocation; business; vocation; calling; career; chosen work; employment; engagement; line of work; occupation; office; position; walk of life.

A vocation requiring advanced education and training; collectively, the members of such a vocation. [Black's *Law Dictionary*, 7th & 8th Eds.]. Traditionally, the learned professions were theology, law and medicine; but some other occupations have climbed, and still others may climb, to the professional plane. [*Commonwealth* v *Brown* 20 NE 2d 478, 481].

A profession ordinarily is an occupation requiring intellectual skill, often coupled with manual skill. Thus, a teacher uses a purely intellectual skill while a painter uses both. [*Management of Safdarjung Hospital, New Delhi* v *Kuldip Singh Sethi* AIR 1970 SC 1407: (1970)1 SCC 735].

'Profession' involves the idea of an occupation requiring either purely intellectual skill, or of manual skill controlled as in painting and sculpture, or surgery by the intellectual skill of the operator. [*Indian Medical Association* v *V.P. Shantha* AIR 1996 SC 550].

'Profession' means an occupation carried on by a person by virtue of his personal and specialised qualifications, training or skill. [*Sodan Singh* v *New Delhi Municipal Committee* AIR 1989 SC 1988: (1989)4 SCC 155].

'Profession' is normally associated with the exercise of intellectual or technical equipment resulting from learning of science. [*Sankarânarayan Pillai* v *Executive Officer* AIR 1966 Mad 262: 1966 Cr LJ 764].

NOTE: *Profession—what is and is not—examples:*

- A chartered accountant is approached by his client for advice and guidance in his problems with regard to trade, business or industry, and it is expected that the chartered accountant, to the best of his ability, would be in a position to help him in his difficulties and not betray the confidence that is placed in him. This is one of the elements which should be sought when considering whether a particular person is practising a profession or is merely doing a business. [*N.E. Merchant* v *State* AIR 1968 Bom 283].
- The business of a stock-broker is not a profession. [*Dena Bank, Ahmednagar* v *Prakash Birbhan Katariya* AIR 1994 Bom 343].
- Agriculture which involves physical labour and toil may not be a profession.

[*Sankaranarayan Pillai* v *Executive Officer* AIR 1966 Mad 262: 1966 Cr LJ 764].

**Professional misconduct.** Transgression of the norms or standards expected of a professional in the discharge of his professional duties is professional misconduct.

Any misdemeanour or misdeed or misbehaviour can become an act of delinquency if it infringes the set norms or standards and it can be regarded as misconduct. [*N.G. Dastane* v *Shrikant* S. *Shivde* AIR 2001 SC 2028: (2001)6 SCC 135]. Thus, if it is shown that an advocate in the pursuit of his profession has done something which would be reasonably regarded as disgraceful or dishonourable by his professional brethren of good repute and competency, then it is open to say that he is guilty of professional misconduct. [*A Solicitor, ex p. Law Society, In re* (1912)1 KB 302: 81 LJKB 245, *per* Darling, J.].

**Professional negligence.** A professional's failure to render professional services with the skill, prudence, and diligence that an ordinary and reasonable professional would use under similar circumstances.

A professional's failure to exercise the degree of care and skill that a person of the same profession would use under similar circumstances.

'Professional negligence' is a mistake by a professional which no reasonably competent and careful practitioner would have committed. [*A.S. Mittal* v *State of U.P.* AIR 1989 SC 1570: (1989)3 SCC 223: (1989)3 SCR 241: JT 1989(2) SC 419: 1989 SCC (Cri) 539].

**Profit.** The word 'profit' must be construed according to its ordinary sense—a sense in which it is understood in trade and industry. [*Management of Central Coal Washery* v *Workmen* AIR 1978 SC 1424: (1978)3 SCR 1023: (1978)3 SCC 332].

It is defined as the excess of revenues over expenditures in a business transaction. [Black's *Law Dictionary*, 7th & 8th Eds.].

The fundamental meaning of the word 'profit' is the amount of gain made by the business during the year. [*E.D. Sassoon and Co. Ltd.* v *Commissioner of Income Tax, Bombay* AIR 1954 SC 470: 1954 SCJ 771: (1954)26 ITR 27: (1955)1 SCR 313].

The word 'profit' connotes the idea of pecuniary gain. [*Shivamurthy Swami Inamdar* v *Agadi Sanganna Andanappa* (1971)3 SCC 870].

Profit consists of a sum arrived at by adding up the receipts of a business and by deducting all the expenses and losses including depreciation and the like, incurred in carrying on the business. [*Rushden Heel Co. Ltd.* v *Keene; Rushden Heel Co. Ltd.* v *Inland Revenue Commissioners* (1946)2 All ER 141].


- **Accumulated profit** p. 23.
- **Activity for profit** p. 34.
- **Deficiency of profits** p. 242.
- **Gross profit** p. 400.
- **Issues and profits** p. 482.
- **Mesne profit** p. 576.
- **Office of profit** p. 622.
- **Secret profit** p. 780.
- **Taxable profits** p. 831.


**Profit a prendre.** A right or privilege to go on another's land and take away something of value from its soil or from the products of its soil (as by mining and logging, or hunting) [Black's *Law Dictionary*, 7th & 8th Eds.].

It is a right to take something off another's land and it is this participation in the produce of the soil or in the soil itself that principally distinguishes a profit from an easement. A right is a profit only if the thing to be taken is something that is capable of ownership. [Cheshire's *Modern Real Property*, 10th Ed., p. 467].

NOTE: The right to *profit a prendre* is an easement under the Indian Easements Act 1882. A right to catch and carry away fish on specific portions of a private tank is a *profit a prendre*, which is regarded as immovable property in India. [*Ananda Behara* v *State of Orissa* AIR 1956 SC 17].

**Profit and loss account.** A summary account of any business showing profit and loss for a particular period.

A transfer account of all income and expenses accounts, closed into the retained earnings of a corporation or capital account of a partnership. [Black's *Law Dictionary*, 7th & 8th Eds.].

A profit and loss account is an account designed to show the amount of net profit earned or net loss incurred during the financial period covered by the account, also the various headings under which the profits had been earned and expenses incurred. [*Leonard Biermans Workers' Union* v *Second Industrial Tribunal* AIR 1962 Cal 375].

**Profiteering.** The taking advantage of unusual or exceptional circumstances to make excessive profits, as in the selling of scarce goods at inflated prices during war. [Black's *Law Dictionary*, 7th & 8th Eds.].

**Prohibit.** Ban; banish; bar; block; circumscribe; counteract; curb; debar; deny; disallow; disqualify; embargo; exclude; forbid; foreclose; make illegal; proscribe; quash; regulate; repress; repudiate; restrain; suppress; revoke; shut out; suspend; thwart; veto; negate.

The term 'prohibit' is defined as to hold back; to forbid; to interdict; to prevent, hinder or debar; to forbid or prevent from doing something. In other words, the term 'prohibit' postulates negative command. [*Sujatha Touring Talkies* v *State* AIR 1986 Kant 21, 51].

**Prohibited arms.** 'Prohibited arms' means—(*i*) firearms so designed or adopted that, if pressure is applied to trigger, missiles continue to be discharged until pressure is removed from the trigger or the magazine containing the missiles is empty, or (*ii*) weapons of any description designed or adopted for the discharge of any noxious liquid, gas or other such thing and includes artillery, anti-aircraft and anti-tank firearms and such other arms as the Central Government may, by notification in the Official Gazette, specify to be prohibited arms. [Arms Act 1959, s. 2(*i*)].

**Prohibited degree.** A degree of relationship so close (as between brother and sister) that marriage between the persons is forbidden by law. [Black's *Law Dictionary*, 7th & 8th Eds.].

▸ *Meaning under the Hindu Marriage Act 1955, s. 3(g)*. Two persons can be said to be within the degrees of prohibited relationship of each other. (*i*) if one is a lineal ascendant of the other; or (*ii*) if one was the wife or husband of a lineal ascendant or descendant of the other; or (*iii*) if one was the wife of the brother or of the father's or mother's brother or of the grandfather's or grandmother's brother of the other; or (*iv*) if the two are brother and sister, uncle and niece, aunt and nephew, or children of brother and sister or of two brothers or of two sisters.

**Prohibited goods.** Any goods the import or export of which is subject to any prohibition under the Customs Act or any other law for the time being in force but does not include any such goods in respect of which the conditions subject to which the goods are permitted to be imported or exported have been complied with. [Customs Act 1962, s. 2(33)].

**Prohibition.** Ban; banishment; bar; barrier; check; circumscription; constraint; debarment; determent; deterrence; disallowance; disqualification; embargo; enforced abstention; forbiddance; injunction; preclusion; proscription; repression; repudiation; suppression; taboo; unlawfulness; veto.

A law or order that forbids a certain action; an extraordinary writ issued by an appellate court to prevent a lower court from exceeding its jurisdiction or to prevent a non-judicial officer or entity from exercising a power. [Black's *Law Dictionary*, 7th & 8th Eds.].

Prohibition is a prerogative writ prohibiting any proceedings or matter. The order of prohibition is directed to an inferior tribunal forbidding that court to continue proceedings therein in excess of its jurisdiction or in contravention of the laws of the land. It is a judicial writ, issued by a superior court to an inferior court, forbidding the latter to continue proceedings therein in excess of its jurisdiction or in contravention of the law. [*E.I. Commercial Co.* v *Collector of Customs* AIR 1962 SC 1893].

NOTE: A particular form of the order of prohibition is available in India. This is the order of prohibition granted *"quousque"*, that is, until the inferior court mends its ways. Where a tribunal refuses hearing or legal evidence a prohibition will be issued restraining the tribunal from further proceeding so long as it does not change its illegal methods. And the writ spends itself as soon as the hearing is given or the evidence is admitted, that is when the illegal order is lifted. This is an adaptation of prohibition to suit local conditions. [*Joneja* v *Das Gupta* AIR 1953 Cal 361].

• **Implied prohibition, doctrine of** p. 433.

**Prohibitory order.** An order restraining a party from doing any act. [*N. Baksi* v *O.K. Ghosh* AIR 1957 Pat 528].

**Promise.** Affirmation; asseveration; assurance; avowal; commitment; pledge; understanding; vow.

The manifestation of an intention to act or refrain from acting in a specified manner, conveyed in such a way that another is justified in understanding that a commitment has been made; a person's assurance that the person will or will not do something; the words in a promissory note expressing the maker's intention to pay a debt. [Black's *Law Dictionary*, 7th & 8th Eds.].

▸ *Meaning under the Indian Contract Act 1872, s. 2(b).* When the person to whom the proposal is made signifies his assent thereto, the proposal is said to be accepted. A proposal, when accepted, becomes a promise.

NOTE: In order to convert a proposal into a promise, the acceptance must—(1) be absolute and unqualified; (2) be expressed in some usual and reasonable manner, unless the proposal prescribes the manner in which it is to be accepted. If the proposal prescribes a manner in which it is to be accepted, and the acceptance is not made in such manner, the proposer may, within a reasonable time after the acceptance is communicated to him, insist that his proposal shall be accepted in the prescribed manner, and not otherwise; but, if he fails to do so, he accepts the acceptance. [Indian Contract Act 1872, s. 7].

In so far as the proposal or acceptance of any promise is made in words, the promise is said to be express. In so far as such proposal or acceptance is made otherwise than in words, the promise is said to be implied. [Indian Contract Act 1872, s. 9].

• **Breach of promise** p. 111.

• **Naked promise** p. 597.

• **Reciprocal promises** p. 734.

**Promisee.** One to whom a promise is made.

**Promisor.** One who makes a promise.

**Promissory estoppel.** The principle that a promise made without consideration may nonetheless be enforced to prevent injustice if the promisor should have reasonably expected the promisee to rely on the promise and if the promisee did actually rely on the promise to his or her detriment. [Black's *Law Dictionary*, 7th Ed.].

NOTE: This doctrine has been variously called 'promissory estoppel', 'equitable estoppel', 'quasi-estoppel' and 'new estoppel'. It is a principle evolved by equity to avoid injustice and though commonly named 'promissory estoppel', it is, neither in the realm of contract nor in the realm of estoppel. The true principle of promissory estoppel, seems to be that where one party has by his words or conduct made to the other a clear and unequivocal promise which is intended to create legal relations or affect a legal relationship to a rise in the future, knowing or intending that it would be acted upon by the other party to whom the promise is made and it is in fact, so acted upon by the other party, the promise would be binding on the party making it and he would not be entitled to go back upon it, if it would be inequitable to allow him to do so having regard to the dealings which have taken place between the parties, and this would be so irrespective of whether there is any pre-existing relationship between the parties or not. [*Motilal Padampat Sugar Mills Co. Ltd.* v *State of U.P.* (1979)2 SCC 409: AIR 1979 SC 621; *Ashok Kumar Maheshwari* v *State of U.P.* (1998)2 SCC 502].

In order to invoke the doctrine of "promissory estoppel" it is enough to show that the promisee has, acting in reliance on the promise, altered his position and it is not necessary for him to further show that he has acted to his detriment. [*Motilal Padampat Sugar Mills Co. Ltd.* v *State of U.P.* AIR 1979 SC 621: (1979)2 SCR 641: (1979)2 SCC 409: (1979)118 ITR 326: (1979)44 STC 42].

**Promissory note.** An unconditional written promise, signed by the maker, to pay absolutely and in any event a certain sum of money either to, or to the order of, the bearer or a designated person. [Black's *Law Dictionary*, 7th Ed.].

▸ *Meaning under the Limitation Act 1963, s. 2(k).* Any instrument whereby the maker engages absolutely to pay a specified sum of money to another at a time therein limited, or on demand, or at sight.

▸ *Meaning under the Negotiable Instruments Act 1881, s. 4.* 'Promissory note' is an instrument in writing (not being a bank-note or a currency-note) containing an unconditional undertaking signed by the maker to pay a certain sum of money only to, or to the order of, a certain person, or to the bearer of the instrument.

▸ *Meaning under the Indian Stamp Act 1899, s. 2(22).* 'Promissory note' means a promissory note as defined by the Negotiable Instruments Act 1881; it also includes a note promising the payment of any sum of money out of a particular fund which may or may not be available or upon any condition or contingency which may or may not be performed or happen.

NOTE: Only the Reserve Bank of India can issue any promissory note under s. 31 of the Reserve Bank of India Act 1934.

**Promoter.** Prime mover; enterpriser; encourager; organiser of business/ commercial enterprises; backer; aider; advocate.

A person who encourages or incites; a founder or organiser of a corporation or business venture; one who takes the entrepreneurial initiative in founding or organising a business or enterprise. [Black's *Law Dictionary*, 7th Ed.].

▸ *Meaning under the Companies Act 1956, s. 62(c).* Promoters of a company are those who set in motion the machinery of law for setting up and starting a company. The promoters of a company are liable to pay compensation to a subscriber for any loss sustained by reason of any untrue statement in the prospectus.

**Promotion.** 'Promotion' means 'advancement or preferment in honour, dignity, rank, or grade'. [*State of Rajasthan* v *Fateh Chand Soni* (1996)1 SCC 562, 567].

Promotion as understood under the service law jurisprudence means advancement in rank, grade or both. Promotion is always a step towards advancement to a higher position, grade or honour. [*Tarsem Singh* v *State of Punjab* (1994)5 SCC 392, 396].

NOTE: Promotion can be either to a higher pay scale or to a higher post. [*Union of India* v *S.S. Ranade* (1995)4 SCC 462, 467-468].

**Proof.** Attestation; clear demonstration; clear indication; conclusiveness; evident demonstration; satisfactory evidence; testimony.

The establishment or refutation of an alleged fact by evidence; the persuasive effect of evidence in the mind of a fact-finder; evidence that determines the judgment of a court; an attested document that constitutes legal evidence. [Black's *Law Dictionary*, 7th Ed.].

NOTE: A fact is said to be proved when, after considering the matters before it, the court either believes it to exist or considers its existence so probable that a prudent man ought under the circumstances of the case, to act upon the supposition that it exists. [Indian Evidence Act 1872, s. 3].

Proof does not mean proof to rigid mathematical demonstration, because that is impossible; it must mean such evidence as would induce a reasonable man to come to a particular conclusion. [*Hawkins* v *Powells Tillery Steam Coal Co. Ltd.* (1911)1 KB 988, *per* Fletcher Moulton, L.J.].

Proof of the fact depends upon the degree of probability of its having existed. The standard required for reaching the supposition is that of a prudent man acting in any important matter concerning him. [*M. Narsinga Rao* v *State of*

*A.P.* JT 2000 Supp (3) SC 559: (2000)1 SCJ 300: 2001 Cr LJ 515: AIR 2001 SC 318: (2001)1 SCC 691].

The word 'proof' may also mean standard strength of spirituous liquids.

- **Burden of proof** p. 114.
- **Conclusive proof** p. 167.

**Proof spirit.** This refers to spirit which at a temperature of 51°F. weighs 12/13 part of an equal measure of distilled water and contains 49.28% of alcohol by weight, or 57.1 per cent by volume at 60°F.

**Proper party.** A person is a proper party only if his presence before the court is necessary to enable it to effectually and completely adjudicate upon and settle all the questions involved in the suit. [*Lakshmamma* v *Someshwar Rao* ILR (1953) Hyd 178: AIR 1953 Hyd 170].

A proper party is one in whose absence an effective order can be made, but whose presence is necessary for a complete and final decision on the question involved in the proceeding. [*Udit Narain Singh* v *Board of Revenue* AIR 1963 SC 786].

**Property.** "In its widest sense, property includes all a person's legal rights, of whatever description. A man's property is all that is his in law. This usage, however, is obsolete at the present day, though it is common enough in the older books ... In a second and narrower sense, property includes not all a person's rights, but only his proprietary as opposed to his personal rights. The former constitute his estate or property, while the latter constitute his status or personal condition. In this sense a man's land, chattels, shares, and the debts due to him are his property; but not his life or liberty or reputation ... In a third application ... the term includes not even all proprietary rights, but only those which are both proprietary and *in rem*. The law of property is the law of proprietary rights *in rem*, the law of proprietary rights *in personam* being distinguished from it as the law of obligations. According to this usage a freehold or leasehold estate in land, or a patent or copyright, is property; but a debt or the benefit of a contract is not ... Finally, in the narrowest use of the term, it includes nothing more than corporeal property—that is to say, the right of ownership in a material object, or that object itself." [John Salmond: *Jurisprudence,* pp. 423-24 (Glanville L. Williams ed., 10th Ed., 1947)].

Property means property of a tangible nature, whether real or personal, including money and including wild creatures which have been tamed or are ordinarily kept in captivity, and any other wild creatures or their carcasses if, but only if, they have been reduced into possession which has not been lost or abandoned or are in the course of being reduced into possession, but not including mushrooms growing wild on any land or flowers, fruit or foliage of a plant growing wild on any land. [Halsbury's *Laws of England*, 4th Ed., vol. 11, para 1309, p. 703].

'Property' is a term of the widest import and subject to any limitation or qualification which the context might require, it signifies every possible interest which a person can acquire, hold and enjoy, unless there is something to the contrary. [*J.K. Trust* v *Commissioner of Income-tax* AIR 1957 SC 846: (1958)1 SCR 65].

'Property' means the highest right a man can have to anything, being that right which one has to lands or tenements, goods or chattels which does not depend on another's courtesy; it includes ownership, estates and interests in corporeal things, and also rights such as trademarks, copyrights, patents and even rights *in personam* capable of transfer or transmission such as debts; and signifies a beneficial right to or a thing considered as having a money value, especially with reference to transfer or succession, and to their capacity of being injured. [*R. Cawasjee Cooper* v *Union of India* AIR 1970 SC 564: (1970)1 SCC 248].

'Property' is a term of wide amplitude and, in fact, is the sum of several interests, rights and obligations that arise because of the relation of persons *inter se* and relation of group of persons with the object or corpus of the property. Property thus in law, is both, corpus and capacity. It is the relation of persons to the property that assumes first and primary importance in the matter of law. Ownership, either limited or full is the entitlement of persons to deal with same, ownership being a specific relation of persons to property. [*Hirabai* v *Babu Manika Ingale* 1980 Bom CR 451 (DB)].

'Property', as a legal concept, is the sum of bundle of rights and in the case of tangible property would include the right of possession, the right to enjoy, the right to destroy, the right to alienate and so on. [*Gurudutta Sharma* v *State of Bihar* (1962)2 SCR 292: (1962)1 SCJ 382: AIR 1961 SC 1684].

The word 'property' as defined in Wharton's *Law Lexicon*, 14th Ed., means 'the highest right a man can have to anything, being used for that right which one has to lands for tenements, goods or chattels, which does not depend on another's courtesy. Property is of three sorts: absolute, qualified and possessory'. [*Fulena Singh* v *State of Bihar* 1979 Bih LJ 34].

▸ *Meaning under the Estate Duty Act 1953, s. 2(15), since repealed.* 'Property' includes any interest in property, movable or immovable, the proceeds of sale thereof and any money or investment for the time being representing the proceeds of sale and also includes any property converted from one species into another by any method.

▸ *Meaning under the Gift Tax Act 1958, s. 2(xxii), since repealed.* 'Property' includes any interest in property, movable or immovable.

▸ *Meaning under the Sale of Goods Act 1930, s. 2(11).* 'Property' means the general property in goods, and not merely a special property. [Sale of Goods Act 1930, s. 2(11)].

▸ *Meaning under the Presidency-Towns Insolvency Act 1909, s. 2(e).* 'Property' includes any property over which or the profits of which any person has a disposing power which he may exercise for his own benefit.

▸ *Meaning under the Police Act 1861, s. 1.* The word 'property' shall include any movable property, money or valuable security.

▸ *Meaning under the Constitution of India, Art. 285.* 'Property' is wide enough to take in all kinds of property. [*New Delhi Municipal Council* v *State of Punjab* (1997)7 SCC 339].

There is no good reason to restrict the meaning of the word 'property' to movable property only when it is used without any qualification in s. 405 or in other sections of the Indian Penal Code. Whether the offence defined in a particular section of the Indian Penal Code can be committed in respect of any particular kind of property will depend not on the interpretation of the word 'property' but on the fact whether the particular kind of property can be subject to the acts covered by that section. It is in this sense that it may be said that the word 'property' in a particular section covers only that type of property with respect to which the offence contemplated in that section can be committed. [*R.K. Dalmia* v *Delhi Administration* AIR 1962 SC 1821].

▸ *Meaning under the Indian Penal Code, s. 420.* The word 'property' occurring in s. 420, does not necessarily mean that the thing of which a delivery is dishonestly desired by the person who cheats, must have a money value or a market value, in the hand of the person cheated. Even if the thing has no money value, in the hand of the person cheated, but becomes a thing of value in the hand of the person, who may get possession of it, as a result of the cheating practised by him, it would still fall within the connotation of the term 'property' in s. 420 of IPC. [*State* v *Nagendra Pal Singh* 1994 Cr LJ 2373, 2375 (Del)].

▸ *Meaning under the Indian Penal Code, s. 425.* 'Property' in s. 425, means tangible property capable of being forcibly destroyed and does not include an easement of customary right. [*Rudraraju Ramaraju* v *Emperor* AIR 1930 Mad 973; *Sumitra* v *Dhannu* AIR 1952 Nag 193(1)].

▸ *Meaning under the Hindu Succession Act 1956, s. 14(1).* In s. 14(1) of the Hindu Succession Act, the expression 'property' includes property acquired by a Hindu female by inheritance or devise, or at a partition, or in lieu of maintenance or arrears of maintenance or by gift from any person, whether a relative or not, before, at or after her marriage, or by her own skill or exertion, or by purchase or by prescription, or in any other manner whatsoever. [*R.B.S.S. Munnalal* v *S.S. Rajkumar* AIR 1962 SC 1493].

NOTE: *Property—what is—examples:*

- An actionable claim against the tenants is undoubtedly a species of 'property' which is assignable. [*State of Bihar* v *Sir Kameshwar Singh* AIR 1952 SC 252].
- A chose in action is a property for the purposes of misappropriation. [*Shivnarayan Laxminarayan Joshi* v *State of Maharashtra* (1980)2 SCC 465: AIR 1980 SC 439].
- The communicated order of assessment, received by an assessee, is property since it is of great importance, to an assessee, as containing a computation, of his total assessable income and, as a determination, of his tax liability. [*Ishwarlal* v *State of Maharashtra* AIR 1969 SC 40: 1969 Cr LJ 271: (1969)1 SCWR 394: (1969)1 SCJ 16].
- The right to get pension is 'property'. [*Deokinandan Prasad* v *State of Bihar* (1971)2 SCC 330: AIR 1971 SC 1409].
- A passport is a property. [*Nrisingha Murari Chakraborty* v *State of West Bengal* (1977)3 SCC 7: AIR 1977 SC 1174].
- Decree, both according to the law of India and of Pakistan, is to be treated as property. [*Associated Hotels of India* v *Jodha Mal Kuthiala* AIR 1950 Punj 201].
- The right of a *mohant* over the property of the *math* is, undoubtedly 'property'. [*Sudhindra Thirtha Swamiar* v *The Commissioner for Hindu Religious and Charitable Endowments, Mysore* AIR 1963 SC 966].
- As a share in a partnership is a profit including asset, that would certainly be property. [*Rangaswami Naidu* v *CIT* 70 MLW 34: (1957)31 ITR 711: (1957)1 MLJ 340].
- 'Property' includes right to realise debt due to dissolved firm from third party. [*Baba Commercial Syndicate* v *Chennamesetti* AIR 1986 AP 378].
- When an employee has done his work, the amount of wages earned by him becomes a debt due to him from the employer, and it is property which could be assigned under the law. [*Bombay Dyeing & Manufacturing Co. Ltd.* v *State of Bombay* AIR 1958 SC 328, 334].
- A ferry-boat is property. [*Rudraraju Ramaraju* v *Emperor* AIR 1930 Mad 973; *Sumitra* v *Dhannu* AIR 1952 Nag 193(1)].
- Shebait is both an office and property. [*Raikisori Dassi* v *Official Trustee* AIR 1960 Cal 235].

*Property—what is not—examples:*

- The right of sole management of a temple carrying no beneficial enjoyment of any property does not amount to property. [*Raja Bira Kishore Deb Hereditary Superintendent, Jagannath Temple, Puri* v *State of Orissa* AIR 1964 SC 1501].
- There is no right to property in the tendu leaves before the leaves are plucked. A contract to pluck the leaves does not amount to property. [*Anwar Khan Mehboob Co.* v *State of Madhya Pradesh* AIR 1966 SC 1637].

The word 'property' may have different other meanings. Used as a distinctive attribute, it may mean aspect; attitude; attribute; character; characteristic; distinction; distinguishing quality; distinguishing trait; earmark; feature; individuality; marked feature; marked quality; particularity.


- **Ancestral property** p. 61.
- **Coparcenary property** p. 195.
- **Enemy property** p. 308.
- **Evacuee property** p. 322.
- **Immovable property** p. 430.
- **Impartible property** p. 432.
- **Joint family property** p. 487.
- **Makkathayam property** p. 551.
- **Movable property** p. 593.
- **Real property** p. 727.
- **Self-acquired property** p. 785.
- **Separate property** p. 786.
- **Specific movable property** p. 806.

- **Stolen property** p. 813.
- **Tangible property** p. 828.
- **Transfer of property** p. 852.
- **Trust property** p. 859.

**Property mark.** A mark used for denoting that movable property belongs to a particular person is called a property mark. [Indian Penal Code 1860, s. 479].

**Proportional representation.** An electoral system that allocates legislative seats to each political group in proportion to its popular voting strength.

The method of proportional representation for constituting the Council of States has been adopted in Art. 80 of the Constitution of India. It is a method of election. What is intended by the system is to give a choice to each elector of as many preferences as there are candidates in the field so that the members of the electoral college can have free and full choice as against majority system which restricts the choice to one of the contesting candidates. [*Surendra Pal* v *Shamim Ahmad* AIR 1985 Del 22, 28].

**Proposal.** In its application to report, it means analysis, appraisal; commentary; critical analysis; examination; in-depth analysis; plan; summary; writing.

Used as suggestion, it means design; draft; exhortation; overture; plan; presentation; proposition; recommendation; scheme; suggestion; thought.

Something offered for consideration or acceptance. [Black's *Law Dictionary*, 7th & 8th Eds.].

▸ *Meaning under the Indian Contract Act 1872, s. 2(a).* When one person signifies to another his willingness to do or to abstain from doing anything, with a view to obtaining the assent of that other to such act or abstinence, he is said to make a proposal.

> NOTE: In so far as a proposal or the acceptance of any promise is made in words, the promise is said to be express. In so far as such proposal or acceptance is made otherwise than in words, the promise is said to be implied. [Indian Contract Act 1872, s. 9].

**Proprietor.** Master; owner; landlord; landowner; householder; an owner, especially one who runs a business; one who has the legal right or exclusive title to anything.

Under the Bengal Tenancy Act 1885, a person owning, whether in trust or for his own benefit, an estate or part of an estate was regarded as a proprietor.

**Proprietor of a new or original design.** Proprietor of a new or original design—(*i*) where the author of the design, for good consideration, executes the work for some other person, means the person for whom the design is so executed; (*ii*) where any person acquires the design or the right to apply the design to any article, either exclusively of any other person or otherwise, means, in the respect and to the extent in and to which the design or right has been so acquired, the person by whom the design or right is so acquired; and (*iii*) in any other case, means the author of the design; and where the property in or the right to apply, the design has devolved from the original proprietor upon any other person, includes that other person. [Designs Act 2000, s. 2(*j*)].

**Proprietorship.** Business, usually unincorporated, owned and controlled exclusively by one person. [Black's *Law Dictionary*, 5th Ed.].

A business in which one person owns all the assets, owes all the liabilities, and operates in his or her personal capacity; ownership of such a business. [Black's *Law Dictionary*, 7th Ed.].

It is also termed as sole proprietorship, individual proprietorship.

**Propriety.** The word 'propriety' is capable of a variety of meanings. In the *Oxford English Dictionary*, Vol. VIII, it has been stated to mean 'fitness, appropriateness, aptitude, suitability, appropriateness to the circumstances or conditions, conformity with the requirement, rule or principle; rightness; correctness; justness; accuracy. [*Raman and Raman Ltd.* v *State of Madras* AIR 1956 SC 463: 1956 SCC 259: 1956 SCA 526: 1956 SCJ 368: 1956 SCR 256].

One of the meanings assigned to the expression 'propriety' is justice. [*Babulal Nagar* v *Shree Synthetics Ltd.* AIR 1984 SC 1164: (1984)3 SCR 772].

**Proprio vigore.** By its own force.

**Prorogation.** The act of putting off to another day, especially, the discontinuance of a legislative session until its next term [Black's *Law Dictionary*, 7th & 8th Eds.]; the extension of a court's or judge's jurisdiction by consent of the parties to a case that it would otherwise be incompetent to hear. [Black's *Law Dictionary*, 8th Ed.].

**Prorogue.** To discontinue a session (as of a legislative assembly) or meeting without dissolving it; to put off or postpone or defer.

**Prosecution.** The commencement and carrying out of any action or scheme; a criminal proceeding in which an accused person is tried; the government attorneys who initiate and maintain a criminal action against an accused defendant. [Black's *Law Dictionary*, 7th & 8th Eds.].

'Prosecution' means a proceeding either by way of indictment or information in the criminal courts in order to put an offender upon his trial. [*Thomas Dana* v *State of Punjab* AIR 1959 SC 375: 1959 Supp (1) SCR 274: 1959 Cr LJ 392].

The word 'prosecution' contemplates a proceeding of a criminal nature either before a court or a judicial tribunal. [*Thomas Dana* v *State of Punjab*, supra].

'Prosecution' has been defined as a criminal action; a proceeding instituted and carried on by due course of law, before a competent tribunal, for the purpose of determining the guilt or innocence of a person charged with crime. [*Jasbir Singh* v *Vipin Kumar Jaggi* AIR 2001 SC 2734: JT 2001(6) SC 419: (2001)8 SCC 289].

The term 'prosecution' will normally mean criminal proceedings in general. But for the purpose of the tort or malicious prosecution, it includes all criminal proceedings to which any oral obloquy is attached. The word 'prosecution' in the phrase 'malicious prosecution' is not to be taken to the restricted sense in which it is used in the Civil Procedure Code. [*S.T. Sahih* v *Hasan Ghani Sahib* AIR 1957 Mad 646].


- **Conducting the prosecution** p. 170.
- **Malicious prosecution** p. 553.
- **Stifling a prosecution** p. 812.


**Prospective.** Looking forward; contemplating the future; conceivable; expectant; impending; looked for; potential; upcoming.

**Prospective damages.** See under DAMAGES p. 221.

**Prospectus.** Analysis; announcement; blueprint; bulletin; catalogue; description; outline; plan; platform; programme; scheme; sketch; statement; summary; synopsis.

A printed document that describes the main features of an enterprise (esp. a corporation's business) and that is distributed to prospective buyers or investors; a written description of a securities offering. [Black's *Law Dictionary*, 7th & 8th Eds.].

A brief sketch describing the main features of some proposed enterprise, as the plan of a literary work, or the proposals of a new business; a descriptive outline of an established organisation, as a college. [*Sanjeeva Dadhwal* v *All India Institute of Medical Sciences* AIR 1995 Del 268, 272].

Prospectus is a document which invites persons to take shares in a company and sets forth the advantages of the company; an advertisement is also a prospectus. [*Paramatha Nath* v *Kali Kumar* 51 Cal 440: AIR 1925 Cal 714].

▸ *Meaning under the Companies Act 1956, s. 2(36).* 'Prospectus' means any document described or issued as a prospectus and includes any notice, circular, advertisement or other document inviting offers from the public for the subscription or purchase of any shares in, or debentures of, a body corporate.

**Prostitute.** 'Prostitute' means a woman who offers her body to indiscriminate sexual intercourse, especially for hire. [*Razia* v *State* AIR 1957 All 340 (DB)].

'Prostitute' means a female who offers her body for promiscuous sexual intercourse for hire, whether in money or in kind. [*State of U.P.* v *Kaushaliya* AIR 1964 SC 416: (1964)4 SCR 1002: (1964)1 Cr LJ 304].

NOTE: 'Prostitute' would answer the description of a public prostitute unless she be kept by some person exclusively in which case she can be said to be kept by that person and to be not available for the purpose of prostitution to others. [*Razia* v *State* AIR 1957 All 340 (DB)].

**Prostitution.** The act or practice of engaging in sexual activity for money or its equivalent; commercialized sex; the act of debasing. [Black's *Law Dictionary*, 7th & 8th Eds.].

The offering by a woman of her body for purposes amounting to common lewdness for payment. [*R.* v *Webb* (1963)3 All ER 177].

▸*Meaning under the Immoral Traffic (Prevention) Act 1956, s. 2(f).* The sexual exploitation or abuse of persons for commercial purposes and the expression prostitute shall be construed accordingly.

NOTE: According to English law, prostitution is not confined to acts of sexual intercourse, but will include any form of lewdness and will include active acts of indecency performed by the woman herself, e.g., masturbation of male clients. [*R.* v *Webb* (ibid)]. But according to Indian law, it means offering of body for promiscuous sexual intercourse for hire. [*Manica Achari, in re* AIR 1970 Mad 491: (1970)2 MLJ 380: 1970 MLW (Cr) 157].

**Protected monument.** An ancient monument which is declared to be of national importance by or under the Ancient Monuments and Archaeological Sites and Remains Act. [Ancient Monuments and Archaeological Sites and Remains Act 1958, s. 2(*j*)].

**Protection.** Aegis; armour; asylum; citadel; coverture; custody; fortification; freedom from danger; guard; hedge; patronage; refuge; safekeeping; sanctuary; shelter; shield; support; tutelage.

The act of protecting; protectionism; coverage. [Black's *Law Dictionary*, 7th & 8th Eds.].

**Protest.** As noun means challenge; clamour; complaint; criticism; declaration of disapproval; declaration of opposition; defiance; hostile; demonstration; outcry; repudiation.

As verb it means challenge; complain; contradict; contravene; denounce; disagree; disapprove; discountenance; exclaim against; express opposition; go contrary to; negate; oppose; remonstrate; repudiate; speak against.

A formal statement or action expressing dissent or disapproval; a notary public's written statement that, upon presentment, a negotiable instrument was neither paid nor accepted; a formal statement, usually in writing, disputing a debt's legality or validity but agreeing to make payment while reserving the right to recover the amount at a later time. [Black's *Law Dictionary*, 7th & 8th Eds.].

In the field of taxation, it means a tax payer's statement to the collecting officer that payment is being made unwillingly because, the tax payer believes the tax to be invalid. [Black's *Law Dictionary*, 8th Ed.].

In international law, it means formal communication from one subject of international law to another objecting to conduct or a claim by the latter as violating international law. [Black's *Law Dictionary*, 7th & 8th Eds.].

▸*Meaning under the Negotiable Instruments Act 1881, s. 100.* When a promissory note or bill of exchange has been dishonoured by non-acceptance or non-payment, the holder may, within a reasonable time, cause such dishonour to be noted and certified by a notary public. Such certificate is called a protest.

• **Acceptor supra protest** p. 12.

• **Under protest** p. 862.

**Protocol.** While used as agreement, it means arrangement; charter; concord; covenant; pact; treaty; understanding.

While used as etiquette, it means behaviour; code; conventional practice; conventionalities; customs; decorum; diplomatic code; formalities.

A summary of a document or treaty; a treaty amending and supplementing another treaty; the formal record of the proceedings of a conference or congress; the minutes of a meeting, usually initiated by all participants after confirming accuracy; the rules of diplomatic etiquette; the practices that nations observe in the course of their contacts with one another. [Black's *Law Dictionary*, 8th Ed.].

**Proved.** A fact is said to be proved when after considering the matters before it, the court either believes it to exist, or considers its existence so probable that a prudent man ought, under the circumstances of the particular case, to act upon the supposition that it exists. [Indian Evidence Act 1872, s. 3].

NOTE: The definition of 'proved' as given in s. 3 of the Evidence Act does not draw any distinction between circumstantial and other evidence [*State of Maharashtra* v *Mohd. Yakub* AIR 1980 SC 1111: (1980)2 SCR 1158: 1980 SCC (Cri) 513: 1980 Cr LJ 793: (1980)3 SCC 57] nor does it draw a distinction between civil and criminal cases. Nor does this definition insist on perfect proof because absolute certainty amounting to demonstration is rarely to be had in the affairs of life. Nevertheless, the standard of measuring proof prescribed by the definition is that of a person of prudence and practical good sense. 'Proof' means the effect of the evidence adduced in the case. [*Ch. Razik Ram* v *Ch. Jaswant Singh Chouhan* AIR 1975 SC 667: (1975)4 SCC 769].

**Provided.** On the condition or understanding (that). [Black's *Law Dictionary*, 7th Ed.].

The words 'provided always' generally refer to and qualify what has preceded. [*Mertelli* v *Holloway* 42 LJ Ch 26: LR 5 HL 532].

**Provident fund.** A fund in which subscriptions or deposits of any class or classes of employees are received and held on their individual accounts, and includes any contributions and any interest or increment accruing on such subscriptions, deposits or contributions under the rules of the fund. [Provident Funds Act 1925, s. 2(*e*)].

**Provisions.** Clauses in a statute, contract, or other legal instrument; stipulations made beforehand.

It may also mean stockpile; stock; store; supply.

• **Directory provisions** p. 261.

**Proviso.** A limitation, condition, or stipulation upon whose compliance a legal or formal document's validity or application may depend. [Black's *Law Dictionary*, 7th & 8th Eds.].

In drafting, it supplies a condition, exception or addition.

A proviso is used to limit, modify or expand the main part of section of statute to which it is appended. [*Saginaw County Tp Officers Ass'n* v *City of Saginaw* 130 NW 2d 30, 32].

The office of a 'proviso' in a statute is to restrict or make clear that which has gone before. [*Allen* v *Burkhart* Okl, 377 P 2d 821, 827].

NOTE: A proviso does cut down the ambit of the main provision but it cannot denude the main provision of any efficacy and cannot reduce it to a paper provision. [*Babul Nagar* v *Shree Synthetics* AIR 1984 SC 1164: 1984 UJ (SC) 755: (1984)2 SLJ 67].

A proviso is added to a principal clause primarily with the object of taking out of the scope of that principal clause what is included in it and what the Legislature desires should be excluded. [*Souri Prasad* v *Jayasree Devi* AIR 1989 Ori 81 (FB)].

A proviso may have three separate functions. Normally, a proviso is meant to be an exception to something within the main enactment or to qualify something enacted therein which but for the proviso would be within the purview of the enactment. In other words, a proviso cannot be torn apart from the main enactment nor can it be used to nullify or set at naught the real object of the main enactment. While interpreting a proviso care must be taken that it is used to remove special cases from the general enactment and provide for them separate. [*S. Sundaram* v *R. Pattaviraman* AIR 1985 SC 582: (1985)1 SCC 591: (1985)1 Ren CJ 267]. In short, generally speaking, a proviso is intended to limit the enacted provision so as to except something which would have otherwise been within it or in some measure to modify the enacting clause. Sometimes a proviso may be embodied in the main provision and becomes an integral part of it so as to amount to a substantive provision. [*S. Sundaram* v *R. Pattaviraman* AIR 1985 SC 582: (1985)1 SCC 591: (1985)1 Ren ÇJ 267 followed in *Revlon* v *Kemco Chemicals* AIR 1987 Cal 285].

**Provocateur.** A person who provokes, or incites to action.

• **Agent provocateur** p. 50.

**Provocation.** Abuse; actuation; annoyance; excitation; excitement; fomentation; impulsion; incitement; inflammation; instigation; motivation; prodding; stimulation; stimulus.

Something (such as words or actions) that arouses anger or animosity in another causing that person to respond in the heat of passion. [Black's *Law Dictionary*, 7th Ed.].

The act of exciting another to do something, esp. to commit a crime; something (such as words or actions) that affects a person's reason and self-control, esp. causing the person to commit a crime impulsively. [Black's *Law Dictionary*, 8th Ed.].

Provocation is some act or series of acts done by a person to the accused which would cause in any reasonable person, and actually causes in the accused, a sudden and temporary loss of self-control, rendering the accused so subject to passion as to make him or her for the moment not master of his mind. [*R.* v *Duffy* (1949)1 All ER 932].

• **Grave and sudden provocation** p. 399.

**Proxy.** Agent; authority to act for another; broker; delegate; deputy; dummy; emissary; substitute; substitution; surrogate; written authorisation.

One who is authorised to act as a substitute for another; incorporate law, a person who is authorised to vote another's stock shares; the grant of authority by which a person is so authorised; the document granting this authority. [Black's *Law Dictionary*, 8th Ed.].

The proxy in the matter of attending and voting at a meeting of the company is merely the agent of the shareholder, and as between himself and his principal is not entitled to act contrary to the instruction of the latter. Every proxy is subject to an implied condition that it should only be used if the shareholder is unable or finds it inconvenient to attend the meeting. [*Cousins* v *International Brick Co. Ltd.* (1931)2 Ch 90, 102].

**Public.** 'Public' is a term of uncertain import; it must be limited in every case by the context in which it is used. [*Tatem Steam Navigation Co. Ltd.* v *Inland Revenue Commissioners* (1941)2 KB 194].

Used as adjective in the sense of 'affecting people', it means civic; civil; collective; common; country-wide; general; government; governmental; municipal; national; nation-wide; state.

Used as adjective in the sense 'known', it means aired; announced; broadcast; circulated; disclosed; disseminated; divulged; overt; proclaimed; published; released; reported; revealed; ventilated; widely known.

Used as adjective in the sense 'open', it means accessible; approachable; available; reachable; unprohibited; unreserved; unrestricted.

While used as noun it means body politic; citizenry; community; general public; nation; populace; population.

As adjective it means relating or belonging to an entire community, state, or nation; open or available for all to use, share, or enjoy; having shares that are available on an open market. As noun it means the people of a nation or community as a whole; a place open or visible to the public. [Black's *Law Dictionary*, 7th & 8th Eds.].

Public includes a section of the public. The word 'public', includes in its ordinary acceptation, any section of the public. [*Sri*

*Venkataraman Devaru* v *State of Mysore* AIR 1958 SC 255: 1958 SCJ 382: 1958 SCR 895].

In any specific context, the words 'public' may mean for practical purposes only the inhabitants of a village or such members of the community as would be interested in any particular matter, professional, political, social, artistic or local. [*Tatem Steam Navigation Co. Ltd.* v *Inland Revenue Commissioners* (1941)2 KB 194].


- **General public** p. 385.
- **Interest of the general public** p. 472.
- **Maintenance of public order** p. 550.
- **Notary public** p. 610.
- **Place of public entertainment** p. 665.
- **Place of public worship** p. 665.


**Public authority.** Governmental power or jurisdiction; a governmental agency or corporation that administers the public enterprise. [Black's *Law Dictionary*, 7th Ed.].

A "public authority" is a body which has public or statutory duties to perform and which performs those duties and carries out its transactions for the benefit of the public and not for private profit. Such an authority is not precluded from making a profit for the public benefit. [*Sukhdev Singh* v *Bhagatram Sardar Singh Raghuvanshi* AIR 1975 SC 1331: (1975)3 SCR 619: (1975)1 SCC 421: 1975(1) SLR 605].

A public authority may be described as a person or administrative body entrusted with functions to perform for the benefit of the public and not for private profit. Not every such person or body is expressly defined as a public authority or body, and the meaning of a public authority or body may vary according to the statutory context. [Halsbury's *Laws of England*, 4th Ed., vol. 1, para 6, pp. 9-10].

**Public carrier.** A carrier that is required by law to transport passengers or freight, without refusal, if the approved fare or charge is paid. It is also termed common carrier. [Black's *Law Dictionary*, 7th Ed.].

An owner of a transport vehicle who transports or undertakes to transport goods or any class of goods for another person at any time and any public place for hire or reward, whether in pursuance of the terms of a contract or agreement or otherwise, and includes any person, body, association or company engaged in the business of carrying the goods of persons associated with that person, body, association or company for the purpose of having their goods transported. [Motor Vehicles Act 1939, s. 2(23). The repealing Motor Vehicles Act 1988 contains no such definition].

**Public company.** Clause (*iv*) of s. 3(1) of the Companies Act 1956, defines a "public company" to mean a company which (*a*) is not a private company (*b*) has a minimum paid-up capital of five lakh rupees or such higher paid-up capital, as may be prescribed; (*c*) is a private company which is a subsidiary of a company which is not a private company.

**Public document.** A document of public interest issued or published by a political body or otherwise connected with public business. [Black's *Law Dictionary*, 7th & 8th Eds.].

NOTE: A public document is made by a public officer for the purpose of the public making use of it and being able to refer to it. A document is no public document unless it is prepared by a public servant in the discharge of his official duty. [*Secretary of State* v *Chimanlal* AIR 1942 Bom 161; *Mahtab Din* v *Kasar Singh* AIR 1928 Lah 640].

The following documents are public documents—(1) documents forming the acts or records of the acts—(*i*) of sovereign authority, (*ii*) of official bodies and tribunals, and (*iii*) of public officers, legislative, judicial and executive, of any part of India or of the Commonwealth or of a foreign country; (2) public records kept in any State of private documents. [Indian Evidence Act 1872, s. 74].

*Public documents—what are—examples*:

- Municipal birth certificates, registers and certified copies thereof are public documents. These are conclusive unless disproved. [*Dalim Kumar Sain* v *Smt. Nandarani Dassi* AIR 1970 Cal 292; *Smt. Vanajakshamma* v *P. Gopala Krishna* AIR 1970 Mys 305].

- Municipal death register is a public document. [AIR 1962 Pat 231].
- Decree and judgment are public documents [*Shakuntala Devi Jain* v *Kuntal* AIR 1969 SC 575: (1969)1 SCR 1006: (1969)1 SCJ 912].
- An order sheet is a public document. [*Nanda Kumar Sinha* v *Emperor* AIR 1937 Pat 534].
- An FIR is a public document. [*Ram Jethmalani* v *Director, CBI* 1987 Cr LJ 570 (Del)].
- Process server's report as to delivery of possession is a public document. [*Sita Ram* v *King Emperor* AIR 1927 All 52].
- Statement of witness recorded by a public officer is a public document. [*Chandreshwar Prasad Narain Singh* v *Bisheshwar Pratab Narain Singh* AIR 1927 Pat 61; *Kantilal Ambalal* v *State of Gujarat* AIR 1968 Guj 100: 1968 Cr LJ 758].
- Statements recorded by police under section 161, Cr PC and documents handed over to police to substantiate the statement forming part and parcel of record are public documents. [*Ram Jethmalani* v *Director, CBI* 1987 Cr LJ 570 (Del)].
- Any document properly on record of an Income-tax case as well as final order of assessment is a public document. [*Katikineni Venkata Gopala Narasimha Rama Rao* v *Chitluri Venkataramayya* AIR 1940 Mad 768 (FB); *A.K. Kaderkutty* v *Agricultural Income Tax Officer* AIR 1961 Ker 32].
- Assessment proceedings are public documents. [*Pukh Raj* v *Mishrimal* 1976 Tax LR 986].
- An Income-tax return as well as a statement filed in support of it is a public document. [*Muniayammal Proprietrix, Sarojini Bus Service, Krishnagiri, Salem* v *Third Addl. Income Tax Officer* AIR 1960 Mad 366; *Somanna* v *Subra Rao* AIR 1958 AP 200; *Naim Singh* v *Tikam Singh* AIR 1955 All 388].
- Assessment order is a public document. [*Hira Lal Chaudhury* v *Rumanand Chaudhury* AIR 1959 Pat 515; *Tulsiram Saganeria* v *Smt. Anni Bai* AIR 1963 Ori 11].
- Assessment order of sales tax officer is a public document. [*Allah Bux* v *Ratan Lal Jain* AIR 1958 All 829].
- Enquiry report prepared by a medical officer of a public hospital is a public document. [1990 Cr LJ 1848 (Ori)].
- Memorandum of association of a company is a public document. [*Binani Properties Pvt. Ltd.* v *M. Gulamali Abdul Hossain & Co.* AIR 1967 Cal 390, 400].
- Permit under the Motor Vehicles Act is a public document. [*In re Sabir Ahmed* AIR 1960 MP 318].
- Certified copy of a sale deed is a public document. [1989 Cr LJ 1724 (Guj)].
- Both plaint and written statement are public documents.

*Public documents—what are not—examples:*

- Inspection of book of lands and buildings or municipality is not a public document. [*Jitendra Nath Joardar* v *Makhan Lal Choudhury* 61 CWN 175].
- A solenama is not a public document. [*Smt. Krishna Subala Bose* v *Dhanapati Dutta* AIR 1957 Cal 59].
- Statement of a witness recorded by the police officer in course of investigation is not a public document. [*Natabar Jana* v *State* AIR 1955 Cal 138: 1955 Cr LJ 441; *Sunil Kumar Dutta* v *State of West Bengal* AIR 1963 Cal 431: (1963)2 Cr LJ 129; *Patel Maganbhai Bapujibhai* v *Patel Ishwarbhai Motibhai* AIR 1984 Guj 69].

**Public ferry.** A public ferry is one which is open to all and for which a regular fare is established. The ferryman is a common carrier, bound to take over all who come; he is bound to keep his ferry in good order.

NOTE: Section 6 of the Bengal Ferries Act 1885, has empowered the State Government to declare, establish, define and discontinue public ferries. The control of all public ferries is vested in the Magistrate of the district subject to the direction of the Commissioner. The immediate superintendence of every public ferry is vested in the Magistrate of the district in which such ferry is situated, or in such other officer as the State Government may appoint. And the Magistrate or officer is required, except when the tolls of such ferry are leased out, make all necessary arrangements for the supply of boats and for the collection of tolls. The tolls of any public ferry may be leased by public auction by the Magistrate with the approval of the Commissioner. [Bengal Ferries Act 1885, ss. 7, 8 and 9].

**Public holiday.** A break from work of the people at large.

NOTE: 'Public holiday' includes Sundays and any other day declared by the Central Government, by notification in the Official Gazette, to be a public holiday. [Negotiable Instruments Act 1881, s. 25].

**Public interest.** The general welfare of the public that warrants recognition and protection; something in which the public as a whole has a stake; an interest that justifies governmental regulation. [Black's *Law Dictionary* 7th & 8th Eds.].

A matter of public or general interest does not mean that which is interesting as gratifying curiosity or a love of information or amusement, but that in which a class of the community has a pecuniary interest or some interest by which their legal rights or liabilities are affected. [*South Hetton Co.* v *North Eastern News Association* (1894)1 QB 133: 63 LJQB 293].

This expression means an act beneficial to the general public. It means action necessarily taken for public purpose. Requirements of public interest vary from case to case. [*Babu Ram Verma* v *State of U.P.* 1971 All LJ 653: 1971 SLR 649: (1971)2 Lab LJ 235].

In the context of Motor Vehicles Act, 'public interest' takes within its fold several factors such as the maximum number of permits that may be issued on a route or in any area having regard to the needs and convenience of the travelling public, the non-availability of sufficient number of stage carriage services in other routes or areas which may be in need of running of additional services, the problems of law and order; availability of fuel, problems arising out of atmospheric pollution caused by a larger number of motor vehicles operating in any route or area, the condition of roads and bridges on the routes; uneconomic running of stage carriage services leading to elimination of small operators and employment of more capital than necessary in any sector leading to starvation of capital investment in other sectors etc. Public interest under the Act does not mean the interest of the operators or of the passengers only. [*Rameshwar Prasad* v *State of U.P.* (1983)2 SCC 195: AIR 1983 SC 383].

The expression "public interest", in the context of premature retirement, has a well settled meaning. It refers to cases where the interests of public administration require the retirement of a government servant who with the passage of years has prematurely ceased to possess the standard of efficiency, competence and utility called for by the government service to which he belongs. No stigma or implication of misbehaviour is intended, and punishment is not the objective. [*Gian Singh Mann* v *High Court of Punjab & Haryana* AIR 1980 SC 1894: (1980)4 SCC 266: (1981)1 SCR 507: (1981)1 SLJ 121].

In relation to compulsory retirement, 'public interest' means retention of honest and efficient employees and weeding of inefficient and dishonest. [*Indira Saxena* v *Municipal Council* 1995 Jab LJ 28, 31].

**Public interest litigation (PIL).** Lexically the expression 'PIL' means a legal action intended in a court of law for the enforcement of public interest or general interest in which the public or a class of the community has pecuniary interest or some interest by which their legal rights or liabilities are affected. [*Janta Dal* v *H.S. Chowdhary* (1991)3 SCR 752: JT 1991(3) SC 497: 1991 SCC (Cri) 933: (1992)4 SCC 305: 1993 SCC (Cri) 36].

NOTE: To counteract the evils of the justice being accessible to only rich and opulent the concept of "public interest litigation" was evolved by the Supreme Court in 1982. Any member of the public can maintain an application for an appropriate direction, order or writ in the High Court under Art. 226 and in the case of breach of any fundamental right of such persons or determinate class of persons in Supreme Court under Art. 32 seeking judicial redress for legal wrong or injury caused to such person or determinate class of persons, where the weaker sections of the community are concerned. The Supreme Court would readily respond even to a letter, addressed by such individual acting *pro bono publico*. As a matter of prudence and not as a rule of law, the Court may confine its strategic exercise of jurisdiction in cases where legal wrong or legal injury is caused to a determinate class or group of persons is violated. [*S.P. Gupta* v *Union of India* AIR 1982 SC 149].

**Public international law.** The legal principles governing the relationships between nations; more modernly, the law of international relations, embracing not only nations but also such participants as international organizations, multinational corporations, non-governmental organizations, and even individuals (such as those who invoke their human rights or commit war crimes). [Black's *Law Dictionary* 7th Ed.].

Body of rules which by custom or treaty civilised nations regard as binding upon themselves in their relation with one another, and whose violation gives the injured party a right to redress. International law is a law of imperfect obligation because there is no recognised common superior to enforce it.

**Public juris.** Of public right.

**Public market.** A market open to both purchasers and sellers. [Black's *Law Dictionary,* 7th & 8th Eds.].

**Public meeting.** A meeting open to anyone interested in that issue or purpose for which the meeting is held.

**Public notice.** Notice given to the public or persons affected, usually by publishing in a newspaper of general circulation. This notice is given in matters of public concern.

**Public nuisance.** An unreasonable interference with a right common to the general public, such as a condition dangerous to health, offensive to community moral standards, or unlawfully obstructing the public in the free use of public property. [Black's *Law Dictionary*, 7th & 8th Eds.].

▸*Meaning under the Indian Penal Code 1860, s. 268.* A person is guilty of a public nuisance who does any act or is guilty of an illegal omission which causes any common injury, danger or annoyance to the public or to the people in general who dwell or occupy property in the vicinity or which must necessarily cause injury, obstruction, danger or annoyance to persons who may have occasion to use any public right.

**Public officer.** A person elected or appointed to carry out some portion of a government's sovereign powers [Black's *Law Dictionary*, 7th Ed.]; one who holds or is invested with a public office.

▸*Meaning under the Code of Civil Procedure 1908, s. 2(17).* 'Public officer' means a person falling under any of the following descriptions, namely—(*a*) every Judge, (*b*) every member of an All-India Service, (*c*) every commissioned or gazetted officer in the military, naval or air forces of the Union while serving under the Government, (*d*) every officer of a Court of Justice whose duty it is, as such officer, to investigate or report on any matter of law or fact, or to make, authenticate or keep any document, or to take charge or dispose of any property, or to execute any judicial process, or to administer any oath, or to interpret, or to preserve order, in the court, and every person specially authorised by a Court of Justice to perform any of such duties, (*e*) every person who holds any office by virtue of which he is empowered to place or keep any person in confinement, (*f*) every officer of the Government whose duty it is, as such officer, to prevent offences, to give information of offences, to bring offenders to justice, or to protect the public health, safety and convenience, (*g*) every officer whose duty it is, as such officer, to take, receive, keep or expend any property on behalf of the Government, or to make any survey, assessment or contract on behalf of the Government or to execute any revenue process, or to investigate, or to report on, any matter affecting the pecuniary interests of the Government, or to make, authenticate or keep any document relating to the pecuniary interests of the Government, or to prevent the infraction of any law for the protection of the pecuniary interest of the Government, and (*h*) every officer in service or pay of the Government, or remunerated by fees or commission for the performance of any public duty.

'Public officer' means a person falling under any of the descriptions in cls. (*a*) to (*h*) of s. 2(17) of the Code of Civil Procedure. [*Coal Mines Provident Fund Commissioner* v *Ramesh Chander Jha* AIR 1990 SC 648: (1990)1 SCC 589: (1990)1 SCR 181: JT 1990(1) SC 115].

NOTE: Coal Mines Provident Fund Commissioner receiving salary out of funds of the Board is a Public Officer. [*Coal Mines Provident Fund Commissioner* v *Ramesh Chander Jha* AIR 1990 SC 648: (1990)1 SCC 589: (1990)1 SCR 181: JT 1990(1) SC 115].

**Public order.** "Public order" is what the French call "order publique" and is something more than ordinary maintenance of law and order. [*Kanu Biswas* v *State of West Bengal* AIR 1972 SC 1656: (1972)3 SCC 831: (1973)1 SCR 546: 1973 SCC (Cri) 16].

"Public order" is an expression of wide connotation and signifies state of tranquillity which prevails among the members of a political society as a result of internal regulations enforced by the Government which they have established. [*Rev. Stainislaus* v *State of Madhya Pradesh* AIR 1977 SC 908: (1977)2 SCR 611: (1977)1 SCC 677: 1977 Cr LJ 551: 1977 SCC (Cri) 147].

Public order is synonymous with public peace, safety and tranquillity. [*The Superintendent, Central Prison Fatehgarh* v *Dr. Ram Manohar Lohia* AIR 1960 SC 633: (1960)2 SCR 821: 1960 Cr LJ 1002: 1960 SCJ 567].

It is the even tempo of the life of the community taking the country as a whole or even a specified locality. Any contravention of law always affects order, but before it could be said to affect "public order" it must affect the community or public at large. [*Dr. Ram Manohar Lohia* v *State of Bihar* AIR 1966 SC 740: 1966 Cr LJ 608; *Arun Ghosh* v *State of West Bengal* AIR 1970 SC 1228: 1970 Cr LJ 1136; *Wasiuddin* v *D.M., Aligarh* AIR 1981 SC 2166: 1981 Cr LJ 1825; *Rajendra Singh* v *State of U.P.* 1982 Cr LJ 1987].

**Public place.** At common law a public place is a place to which the public can, and do, have access. It matters not whether they come to that place at the invitation of the occupier or whether they come to it merely with his permission; also that it matters not whether some payment or, indeed, the performance of some small formality, such as the signing of a visitors' book, is required before they are allowed access. [*R.* v *Kane* (1965)1 All ER 705].

A place to which persons are in the habit of resorting, though without any legal title, but without any hindrance or interference is a public place. [*R.* v *Wallard* 14 QBD 63, 66].

▸*Meaning under the Motor Vehicles Act 1988, s. 2(34).* A road, street, way or other place, whether a thoroughfare or not, to which the public have a right of access, and includes any place or stand at which passengers are picked up or set down by a stage carriage.

The term 'public place' in s. 2(34) of the Motor Vehicles Act 1988, includes any place which members of public use and to which they have a right to access. The right of access may be permissive, limited, restricted or regulated by oral or written permission, by tickets, passes, badges or on payment of a fee. What is necessary is that the place must be accessible to the members of public and be available for their use, enjoyment, avocation or other purposes. [*New India Assurance Co. Ltd.* v *Urmila Devi* (1997)1 Pat LJR 31, 34].

'Public place' means a road, street, way or other place; whether a thoroughfare or not to which the public have a right of access and includes any place or stand at which passengers are picked up or set down by a stage carriage. [*Kannammal* v *A.S. Kasim* (1989)1 LR 90 (Mad)].

The expression 'public place' includes any place or stand at which passengers are picked up or set down by a stage carriage. This would mean that any place where a stage carriage plies for the purpose of picking up and setting down passengers would be a 'public place'. [*Prakash Chemicals Pvt. Ltd.* v *Krishna Singh Sata Singh* AIR 1993 Guj 121].

A public place is one where people go, no matter whether they have a right to go or not. The right is not the question. Many shows are exhibited to the public on private property, yet they are frequented by the public—the public go there. [*Kannammal* v *A.S. Kasim* (1989)1 LR 90, 93 (Mad); *R.* v *Wallard* 14 QBD 63].

Public place must be a place which is either open to the public or is used by the public. [*Munshi* v *State* 1954 Cr LJ 765: AIR 1954 All 356].

The test of a place being a public place is whether it is open to the members or the public or not even though there may be certain conditions attached to the entry or the use thereof. What is required is that such a place must be open for entry by an indeterminate number of members of the public. [*State* v *Dohana Jamnadas* AIR 1961 Guj 182].

**Public policy.** Broadly, principles and standards regarded by the legislature or by the courts as being of fundamental concern to the state and the whole of society. [Black's *Law Dictionary*, 7th & 8th Eds.].

'Public policy' connotes some matter which concerns the public good and the public interest. [*Central Inland Water Transport Corporation Ltd.* v *Broja Nath Ganguly* AIR 1986 SC 1571].

NOTE: Public policy is a principle of judicial legislation or interpretation founded on the current needs of the community. The interest of the whole public must be taken into account. The court must certainly weigh the interest of the whole community as well as the interests of a considerable section of it. In some cases the courts have to strike a balance in express terms between community interest and sectional interests. The categories of heads of public policy are not closed. The courts can apply a variable notion of policy as principle of judicial legislation or interpretation in view of the current needs of the community. Public policy does not remain static. It varies from generation to generation and even in the same generation. It cannot remain in fixed moulds for all time. It is variable and depends upon the welfare of the community. [*Murlidhar* v *State of U.P.* AIR 1974 SC 1924].

'Public policy' has been described as an unruly horse. It is a vague and perhaps an unsatisfactory term. Rules of public policy do not belong to a fixed or customary law; they are capable on proper occasions of expansion and modification. Circumstances may change and make a commercial practice expedient. [*Mafizuddin Khan Choudhury* v *Hobibuddin Sheikh* AIR 1957 Cal 336].

The concept of 'public policy' is illusive, varying and uncertain. It has also been described as 'untrustworthy guide', 'unruly horse' etc. [*P. Rathinam* v *Union of India* AIR 1994 SC 1844: 1994 Cr LJ 1605: 1994 AIR SCW 1764: 1994 SCC (Cri) 740: (1994)3 SCC 394: (1994)2 SCJ 545: JT 1994(4) SC 392].

**Public premises.** State or community owned premises not restricted to any one individual's use or possession.

**Public prosecutor.** The "public prosecutor" is the counsel for the Government for conducting prosecution on behalf of the State Government or the Central Government as the case may be. He is an officer and like every advocate practising before court, he owes an obligation to the court to be fair and just. [*Sheonandan Paswan* v *State of Bihar* JT 1986 SC 1132: AIR 1987 SC 877: (1987)1 SCC 288: (1987)1 SCR 702: 1987 Cr LJ 793: 1987 SCC (Cri) 82].

**Public purpose.** Any purpose which directly benefits the public or a section of the public is a 'public purpose'. [*Smt. Venkatamma* v *City Improvement of Trust Board, Mysore* AIR 1972 SC 2683: (1973)1 SCC 188].

The meaning of the phrase 'public purpose' is predominantly a purpose for the welfare of the general public. [*Rustom Cavasjee Cooper* v *Union of India* AIR 1970 SC 564: (1970)3 SCR 531: (1970)1 SCC 248].

The phrase 'public purpose' includes a purpose that is, an object or aim, in which the general interest of the community, as opposed to the particular interest of individuals is directly and vitally concerned. [*State of Bombay* v *R.S. Nanji* AIR 1956 SC 294: 1956 SCR 18: 1956 SCJ 288; *Smt. Somawanti* v *State of Punjab* AIR 1963 SC 151: (1963)3 SCR 774].

The expression 'public purpose' is not capable of a precise definition and has not a rigid meaning. It can only be defined by a process of judicial inclusion and exclusion. In other words, the definition of the expression is elastic and takes its colour from the statute in which it oocurs, the concept varying with the time and state of society and its needs. Whatever furthers the general interests of the community as opposed to the particular interest of the individual, must be regarded as public purpose. [*State of Bihar* v *Maharajadhiraja Sri Kameshwar Singh of Darbhanga* AIR 1952 SC 252: 1952 SCR 889: 1952 SCJ 354].

NOTE: The welfare of a large section of the community is a 'public purpose'. [*Arnold Rodricks* v *State of Maharashtra* AIR 1966 SC 1788: (1966)3 SCR 885].

*Public purpose—what is—examples*:

- Acquisition of estates for the purpose of preventing the concentration of huge blocks of land in the hands of a few individuals and to do away with intermediaries is for a public purpose. [*State of Bihar* v *Maharajadhiraja Sri Kameshwar Singh of Darbhanga* AIR 1952 SC 252: 1952 SCR 889: 1952 SCJ 354; *Visweshwar Rao* v *State of M.P.* 1952 SCR 1020: 1952 SCJ 427; *Raja Suryapal Singh* v *State of U.P.* 1952 SCR 1056: 1952 SCJ 446].
- To provide for rehabilitation of displaced persons is a public purpose. [*H.R. Khandelwal* v *State of U.P.* AIR 1955 All 12].
- Housing the homeless is a public purpose. [*Banji* v *State of Bombay* AIR 1952 Bom 467].
- Where the members of the community are to be benefited by the construction of the temples, the acquisition of land for the purpose of construction of temples must be held to be a public purpose. [*Sri Raja Vasireddi Hariharprasad* v *Kota Jagannadhan* AIR 1955 AP 184].
- Acquisition of land for connecting two temples by road is considered to be a public purpose. [*Bajirao T. Kote* v *State of Maharashtra* (1995)2 SCC 442].
- Development and utilisation of land as industrial and residential areas is a public purpose. [*Arnold Rodricks* v *State of Maharashtra* AIR 1966 SC 1788].

The declaration as to public purpose by the government is final except where it is colourable exercise of power. [*Valjibhai Muljibhai Soneji* v *State of Bombay* AIR 1963 SC 1890].

**Public revenue.** The public revenues of the kingdom and not the receipts or revenues of a local authority. [*Lush* v *Coles* (1967)2 All ER 585].

**Public safety.** "Public safety" ordinarily means security of the public or their freedom from danger. [*Romesh Thappar* v *State of Madras* AIR 1950 SC 124: 1950 SCR 594: 1950 SCJ 418: 1950 Cr LJ 1514; *State of Punjab* v *Sukhpal Singh* JT 1989(4) SC 95: 1989 Supp (1) SCR 420: AIR 1990 SC 231: 1990 Cr LJ 584: 1990 SCC (Cri) 1: (1990)1 SCC 35].

**Public sector.** The part of the economy or an industry that is controlled by the government. [Black's *Law Dictionary*, 7th & 8th Eds.].

**Public security.** See under SECURITY p. 783.

**Public servant.** A 'public servant' is an authority who must be appointed by Government or a semi-government body and should be in the pay or salary of the same and must discharge his duties in accordance with the rules and regulations made by the Government. [*Ramesh Balkrishna Kulkarni* v *State of Maharashtra* AIR 1985 SC 1655: (1985)3 SCC 606: 1985 Supp (2) SCR 345: 1985 SCC (Cri) 407: 1986 Cr LJ 14].

'Public servant' denotes a person falling under any of the descriptions hereinafter following, namely—(1) Every Commissioned Officer in the Military, Naval or Air Forces of India; (2) Every Judge including any person empowered by law to discharge, whether by himself or as a member of any body of persons, any adjudicatory functions; (3) Every officer of a Court of Justice including a liquidator, receiver or commissioner whose duty it is, as such officer, to investigate or report on any matter of law or fact, or to make, authenticate or keep any document, or take charge or dispose of any property or to execute any judicial process or to administer any oath, or to interpret, or to preserve order in the Court; and every person specially authorized by a Court of Justice to perform any of such duties; (4) Every juryman, assessor or member of a panchayat assisting a Court of Justice or public servant; (5) Every arbitrator or other person to whom any cause or matter has been referred for decision or report by any Court of Justice or by any other competent public authority; (6) Every person who holds any office by virtue of which he is empowered to place or keep any person in confinement; (7) Every officer of the Government whose duty it is, as such officer, to prevent offences, to give information of offences, to bring offenders to justice, or to protect the public health, safety or convenience; (8) Every officer whose duty it is, as such officer, to take, receive, keep or expend any property on behalf of the Government, or to make any survey, assessment or contract on behalf of the Government or to execute any revenue process, or to investigate, or to report on any matter affecting the pecuniary interests of the Government, or to make, authenticate or keep any document relating to the pecuniary interests of the Government, or to prevent the infraction of any law for the protection of the pecuniary interests of the Government; (9) Every officer whose duty it is, as such officer, to take, receive, keep or, expend any property, to make any survey or assessment or to levy any rate or tax for any secular common purpose of any village, town or district, or to make, authenticate or keep any document for the ascertaining of the rights of the people of any village, town or district; (10) Every person who holds any office by virtue of which he is empowered to prepare, publish, maintain or revise an electoral roll or to conduct an election or part of an election; and (11) Every person—(*a*) in the service or pay of the Government or remunerated by fees or commission for the performance of any public duty by the Government; (*b*) in the service or pay of a local authority, a corporation established by or under a Central, Provincial or State Act or a Government company as defined in s. 617 of the Companies Act (1 of 1956). [Indian Penal Code 1860, s. 21; Prevention of Corruption Act 1947, s. 2].

'Public servant' as defined in s. 21 of IPC includes not only the State and Central Government employees but also others like judge, juryman, assessor and arbitrator. It also includes every person in the service or pay of the government or remunerated by fees or commission by the government. Each category is different from the other and there is hardly any relationship of master and servant in some of the categories. A judge of the superior court cannot be excluded from the definition of public servant. [*K. Veeraswami* v *Union of India* (1991)3 SCC 665].

NOTE: *Public servant—who is—examples:*

- The holder of a public office such as the Chief Minister is a 'public servant' in respect of whom the Constitution provides that he will get his salary from the Government Treasury so long he holds his office on account of the public service that he discharges. The salary given to the Chief Minister is co-terminus with his office and is not paid like other constitutional functionaries such as the President and the Speaker. [*M. Karunanidhi* v *Union of India* AIR 1979 SC 898: (1979)3 SCC 431: (1979)3 SCR 254: 1979 Cr LJ 773: 1979 SCC (Cri) 691].
- The Minister is a "public servant". In accordance with the instructions issued by the Government he is to preside over the meetings of the Advisory Committee. He does so as a Minister and in execution and discharge of his duty as such public servant. [*Dattatraya Narayan Patil* v *State of Maharashtra* AIR 1975 SC 1685: 1975 (Supp) SCR 145: 1975 Cr LJ 1490: 1975 SCC (Cri) 733: (1976)1 SCC 11].

- The Chairman of the managing committee of a municipality is a "public servant" within the meaning of s. 2 of Prevention of Corruption Act 1947. [*Maharudrappa Danappa Kesarappanavar* v *State of Mysore* AIR 1961 SC 785: (1961)1 Cr LJ 857: (1962)1 SCR 129: (1962)1 SCJ 454].

*Public servant—who is not—examples*:

- A Municipal Councillor does not owe his appointment to any governmental authority. Such a person is elected by the people and functions undeterred by the commands or edicts of a governmental authority. The mere fact that he gets allowance by way of honorarium does not convert his status into that of a 'public servant'. [*Ramesh Balkrishna Kulkarni* v *State of Maharashtra* AIR 1985 SC 1655: (1985)3 SCC 606: 1985 Supp (2) SCR 345: 1985 SCC (Cri) 407: 1986 Cr LJ 14].
- A member of I.A.S. sent on deputation to a registered government society is not a public servant. [*S.S. Dhanoa* v *Municipal Corporation* AIR 1981 SC 1395: (1981)3 SCR 864: (1981)3 SCC 431: 1981 Cr LJ 871].

**Public service.** A service provided or facilitated by the government for the general public's convenience and benefit; government employment; work performed for and on behalf of the government. [Black's *Law Dictionary*, 7th & 8th Eds.].

**Public service vehicle.** Any motor vehicle used or adapted to be used for the carriage of passengers for hire or reward and includes a maxi-cab, a motor-cab, contract carriage and stage carriage. [Motor Vehicles Act 1988, s. 2(35)].

The word 'public' has got a well-known connotation and means a carriage to which any member of the public can have free access on payment of the usual charges. [*Tata Engineering and Locomotive Co.* v *Sales Tax Officer* AIR 1979 SC 343].

**Public street.** Every street which is common to the public is public street.

**Public utility service.** 'Public utility service' means—(*i*) any railway service or any transport service for the carriage of passengers or goods by air; (*ia*) any service in or in connection with the working of any major port or dock; (*ii*) any section of an industrial establishment, on the working of which the safety of the establishment or the workmen employed therein depends; (*iii*) any postal, telegraph or telephone service; (*iv*) any industry which supplies power, light or water to the public; (*v*) any system of public conservancy or sanitation; and (*vi*) any industry specified in the First Schedule which the appropriate Government may, if satisfied that public emergency or public interests so requires, by notification in the Official Gazette, declare to be a public utility service for such period as may be specified in the notification: Provided that the period so specified shall not, in the first instance, exceed six months but may, by a like notification, be extended from time to time by a period not exceeding six months, at any one time if in the opinion of the appropriate Government public emergency or public interest requires such extension. [Industrial Disputes Act 1947, s. 2(*n*)].

**Publication.** Announcement; broadcast; circulation; communication; dissemination; notification; presentation to the public; proclamation; promulgation; pronouncement; propagation; public announcement; revelation; transmission; written discourse.

To make public; to make known to people in general; to bring before public; to exhibit, display, disclose or reveal. [*Tiffany Productions* v *Dewing* DC Md, 50 F 2d 911, 914].

▸*Meaning under the Copyright Act 1957, s. 3 (w.e.f. 10.5.1995)*. 'Publication' means making a work available to the public by issue of copies or by communicating the work to the public.

• **General publication** p. 385.
• **Harmful publication** p. 406.
• **Privileged publication** p. 688.

**Publisher.** One who publishes; one who makes a business of publishing books or periodicals; one who produces and distributes copies of a book, newspaper, etc. for sale.

A publisher is one who projects, conducts and carries on, or is the proprietor of any encyclopaedia, review, magazine, periodical work or work published in a series of books or parts, or any book whatsoever. [(1960)2 Ch D 550].

The publisher is a person who both arranges with the printer for a book or paper to be produced and causes it to be offered to the public. [*Public Prosecutor* v *T. Amarnath Rao* AIR 1960 AP 176].

A man who causes a book to be printed and offers it to the public for sale is a publisher within the meaning of ss. 3 and 12 of the Press and Registration of Books Act 1867. [*G. Alvanar* v *State* (1957)1 MLJ 136].

NOTE: The word 'publisher' does not include the vendor of the newspaper or books. Section 12 read with s. 3 of the Press and Registration of Books Act 1867, clearly indicates that such persons are not included as 'publishers'. [*G. Alvanar* v *State* (1957)1 MLJ 136].

**Puffer.** An agent of the owner who attends an auction sale and bids for the purpose of exciting the other bidders and raising the price. [Sale of Goods Act 1930, s. 64(6)].

**Puisne.** It is a French word originating from 'puis' meaning 'afterwards' + 'ne' meaning 'born' which together means 'afterwards born'.

It denotes law junior as to rank; younger, inferior.

**Puisne judge.** A junior judge; a judge without distinction or title; a judge of a superior court inferior in rank to chief justices.

**Pujari.** A priest in a temple; a person who conducts worship of the deity in a private or public temple.

NOTE: Even those who assist in the performance of *puja* are *pujaris*. [*Thakur Govind* v *Susalli* AIR 1967 All 278].

**Punish.** Bring to retribution; castigate; chastise; condemn; inflict penalty; penalise; reprimand; sentence; take to task.

The ordinary dictionary meaning of the word 'punish' is 'to cause the offender to suffer for the offence' or 'to inflict penalty on the offender'. The word 'punish' denotes or signifies some offence committed by the person who is punished. [*Lakshmi Devi Sugar Mills Ltd.* v *Pt. Ram Sarup* AIR 1957 SC 82: 1957 SCA 10: 1957 SCJ 46].

**Punishable.** Deserving of, or liable to punishment; capable of being punished by law or right. [*State of Maharashtra* v *Jugmander Lal* AIR 1966 SC 940: (1966)3 SCR 1; *Sube Singh* v *State of Haryana* AIR 1988 SC 2235: JT 1988(3) SC 729: 1989 Cr LJ 297: 1989 SCC (Cri) 101: (1989)1 SCC 235].

NOTE: Opinions differ as to whether the word 'punishable' when used in a statute is mandatory or not. In one case, it is said that the expression 'punishable' means 'liable to punishment'. Liable to punishment only means that a person who has contravened a penal provision will have to be punished. Thus, it does not mean anything different from "shall be punished". Punishment is obligatory in either case. [*State of Maharashtra* v *Jugmander Lal* AIR 1966 SC 940: (1966)3 SCR 1]. In another case, it has, however, been said that the word 'punishable' is ordinarily defined as deserving of or capable of or liable to punishment, capable of being punished by law or right, may be punished, or liable to be punished, and not must be punished. [*Sube Singh* v *State of Haryana* AIR 1988 SC 2235: JT 1988(3) SC 729: 1989 Cr LJ 297: 1989 SCC (Cri) 101: (1989)1 SCC 235].

**Punishing.** Punishing is defined as causing suffering or retribution. [*Mohhammad Shabir Maulamaiya* v *State of Maharashtra* 1977 Mah LJ 338, 341].

**Punishment.** Castigation; censure; chastisement; penal retribution; penalisation; penalty; reprimand retribution.

Penalty for the transgression of law [*Lakshmi Devi Sugar Mills Ltd.* v *Pt. Ram Sarup* AIR 1957 SC 82: 1957 SCA 10: 1957 SCJ 46]; that which is inflicted as a penalty, an act or method of punishing, penalty imposed for an offence [*Mohammad Shabir Maulamaiya* v *State of Maharashtra* 1977 Mah LJ 338]; judicial penalty awarded by a court administering criminal law as distinguished from statutory authority. [*N.P. Bahire* v *State of Maharashtra* 1994 Bom Cr Cas 133 (Bom)].

NOTE: *Punishment—what constitutes—examples*:

- Disqualification would be included in a punishment. [*Mohhammad Shabir Maulamaiya* v *State of Maharashtra* 1977 Mah LJ 338].
- Penalty is punishment inflicted by law for its violation for doing or failing to do something that is the duty of the party to do. The two words 'penalty' and 'punishment' are interchangeable and they convey the same idea. [*Thomas Dana* v *State of Punjab* AIR 1959 SC 375: 1959 Cr LJ 392].

*Punishment—what is not—example*:

- Suspension of a workman cannot be a punishment even though it may be of an indefinite duration. [*Lakshmi Devi Sugar Mills Ltd.* v *Pt. Ram Sarup* AIR 1957 SC 82: 1957 SCA 10: 1957 SCJ 46]. Any action of the employer to the detriment of the workman's interest would not be 'punishment', so long as no offence was found to have been committed by the workman. [*Lakshmi Devi Sugar Mills Ltd.* v *Pt. Ram Sarup*, supra].

• **Capital punishment** p. 123.

**Puranas.** The last source of knowledge and law, according to Yajnavalkya, is the Puranas. The principal Puranas are the following: Brahma, Padma, Vishnu, Siva, Bhagabat, Narada, Markandeya, Bhavishya, Brahmavaivarta, Linga, Baraha, Skanda, Bamana, Kurma, Matsya, Garuda and Brahmanda. These Puranas are mythological poems which purport to give an account of creation, to narrate the genealogy of gods, of ancient dynasties and of sacerdotal families, and to describe the different ages of the world; and in doing so they deal with religious rites and duties. None of the Puranas appear to be very ancient. Some appear to contain recent interpolations and additions.

**Purchase.** Acquire ownership of; assume ownership; buy; pay for; procure title to; secure for a consideration.

The popular meaning of purchase is buying for money; its technical legal meaning is acquisition otherwise than by descent or escheat. [*Bolton (H.L.) (Engineering) Co. Ltd.* v *Graham* (1956)3 All ER 624: (1957)1 QB 159].

The legal meaning of the word 'purchase' is not different from its plain meaning which connotes buying for a price or equivalent of price by payment in kind or adjustment towards an old debt or for other monetary consideration. [*Commissioner of Income Tax, A.P.* v *T.N. Aravinda Reddy* (1979)4 SCC 721: (1979)120 ITR 46: AIR 1980 SC 96: (1980)1 SCR 872].

NOTE: Acquisition of goods, which may in its comprehensive sense take in voluntary as well as involuntary transfers, is an ingredient of purchase. Another ingredient of purchase is cash, deferred payment of any valuable consideration. [*Devi Das Gopal Krishnan* v *State of Punjab* AIR 1967 SC 1895].

• **Hire-purchase** p. 417.
• **Hire-purchase agreement** p. 418.
• **Hire-purchase price** p. 418.
• **Words of purchase** p. 902.

**Purchaser.** The person who has purchased or agreed to purchase; opposite of vendor; vendee.

• **Auction purchaser** p. 86.

**Purchasing power.** Money or claims to money or credit available to the public for the purchase of goods and services.

**Purchasing power parity theory.** This is the theory that a change in the relative price levels of two countries will ultimately be followed by a similar change in the exchange rate between them, or *vice versa*.

**Purdanashin.** A woman who by habit or family usage does not come out in the open to conduct her affairs. [*Shyamlal* v *Ranbir Singh* AIR 1951 All 386].

**Purge.** As verb, in its application 'to purify', it means clean; cleanse; clear; deterge; eradicate; evacuate; excrete; filter; refine; get rid of; sweep out; sanctify.

As verb, in its application 'to wipe out by atonement', it means absolve; acquit;

clear; exculpate; excuse; grant absolution; pardon; reclaim; redeem.

**Purohit.** A family priest; one who conducts religious ceremonies of a family or householder.

**Purport.** As noun, it means the idea or meaning that is conveyed or expressed, esp. by a formal document. As verb, the meaning is to profess or claim falsely; to seem to be, e.g., the document purports to be a will, but it is neither signed nor dated. [Black's *Law Dictionary*, 7th Ed.].

The word 'purport' has many shades of meanings. It means fictitious, what appears on the face of the instrument, the apparent and not the legal import. Purporting is, therefore, indicative of what appears on the face of it or is apparent even though in law it may not be so. [*Azimunnissa* v *The Deputy Custodian, Evacuee Properties, Dist. Deoria* AIR 1961 SC 365: (1961)2 SCR 91: (1962)1 SCJ 324].

The word 'purport' means outward appearance, guise, as conveying an impression, etc. [*Travancore Devaswom Board* v *Krishnan* 1980 Ker LT 787].

**Purpose.** Aim; aspiration; design; desire; desired result; destination; drive; expectation; final cause; goal; guiding principle; hope; mission; motivating idea; motive; object; objective; point; resolve; significance.

The word can be used to designate either the main object which a man wants or hopes to achieve by the contemplated act, or it can be used to designate those objects which he knows will probably be achieved by the act, whether he wants them or not. In the criminal law in general, the ordinary sense is the latter one. In the former sense it cannot in practice be distinguished from motive which is normally irrelevant in criminal law. [*Chandler* v *Director of Public Prosecutions* (1962)3 All ER 142].

NOTE: 'Purpose' and 'object' are synonymous words. [*Shridhar Misra* v *Jaichandra* AIR 1959 All 598].


- **Common purpose** p. 159.
- **Domestic purposes** p. 278.
- **Immediate purpose** p. 429.
- **Immoral purpose** p. 430.
- **Philanthropic purpose** p. 662.
- **Public purpose** p. 712.


**Pursuant to.** In compliance with; in accordance with; as authorised by.

**Put option.** In the market of speculation or hedging, it means payment of a commission which secures the right to sell something at an agreed price within a given period. It is the opposite of a call option. Options are used as a means of hedging or speculating in shares or commodities.

**Putative.** Supposed, reputed, commonly accepted, as a putative father of an illegitimate child.

**Putra.** A son.

**Putra pouthra santhathies.** The words would indicate son, grandson, and descendants. The word 'santhathi' is translated as "issue, progency or descendants". [*G. Appaswami Chettiar* v *R. Sarangapani Chettiar* AIR 1978 SC 1051: (1978)3 SCR 520: (1978)3 SCC 55].

**Putra-pautradi.** See GENERATION TO GENERATION p. 386.

**Putra-pautradikrame.** The expression implies heritable right.

**Pyramiding.** This is a term used in connection with holding companies to describe a device whereby a group of persons can, with a minimum outlay of capital, control through successive tiers of subsidiary companies assets many times in excess of the original outlay. In this type of organisation a company which is subsidiary to a holding company is in turn a holding company for other (subsidiary) companies. Persons outside the group of companies may own part of the share capital of subsidiaries. [Osborn & Grandage's *Concise Commercial Dictionary*].

# Qq

**Qua.** In the character or capacity of; considered as.

**Qua-timet.** The expression would mean an action brought to prevent a wrong that is apprehended. [*Keshab Gagoi* v *Hon'ble Speaker, Assam Legislative Assembly* (1995)1 Gau LR 53, 59].

**Quack.** One who practises as a physician or surgeon without adequate preparation or due qualification.

**Qualified.** As adjective in its use as 'competent', it means able; accomplished; capable; eligible; entitled; experienced; fit; proficient; skilled; trained; well-suited; worthy of choice.

As adjective in its use as 'conditioned', it means circumscribed; circumstanced; conditional; controlled; curbed; subject to term.

**Qualified acceptance.** Circumscribed acceptance; limited acceptance.

> NOTE: This is one which in express terms varies the effect of a bill of exchange as drawn, and may be: (1) Conditional—one which makes payment by the acceptor dependent on the fulfilment of a condition, *e.g.*, "Accepted payable when goods are sold"; (2) Partial—an acceptance to pay part of the amount only for which the bill is drawn; (3) Local—an acceptance to pay only at a specified place; (4) Qualified as to time—a bill drawn for two months accepted payable in three months; and (5) Acceptance by some of the drawees only—a bill drawn on *A*, *B* and *C*, accepted by *A* and *B* only.
>
> The holder may refuse to take a qualified acceptance and if he does not obtain an unqualified acceptance he may treat the bill as dishonoured. [Negotiable Instruments Act 1881, s. 86].

**Quality.** As noun in its use as 'attribute', it means characteristic; feature; particularity; peculiarity; singularity; property.

As noun in its use as 'excellence', it means ability; aptness; caliber; competency; fineness; potency; potentiality; soundness; value; worth.

In respect to an article, 'quality' is descriptive of organic composition of substance expressed in definite quantitative units, and definitive of character, nature and degree of excellence of the article. [*Dean Rubber Mfg. Co.* v *U.S.* CA Mo, 356 F 2d 161, 163].

In respect to persons, this term denotes comparative rank; state or condition in relation to others; social or civil position.

In pleading, it means an attribute or characteristic by which one thing is distinguished from another.

**Quando aliquid prohibetur, prohibetur et omne per quod devenitur ad illud.** When anything is prohibited, everything relating to it is prohibited. Whenever a court discovers an attempt at concealment, it would "brush away the cobweb varnish, and shew the transactions in their true light". [*Collins* v *Blantern* (1967)2 Wils KB 347].

**Quantum meruit.** The expression means "as much as he deserves" and it is an expression that describes the extent of liability on a contract implied by law. [*Nardi & Co., Inc.* v *Allabastro* 314 NE 2d 367, 370].

> NOTE: Where the defendant is obliged to pay the plaintiff, *e.g.*, for work done, but no specific sum is owing, the plaintiff can recover a reasonable sum, *quantum meruit*. Such a claim may arise from a contract or in quasi-contract.

[Sutton and Shannon on *Contracts*, 6th Ed., p. 442].

Where one person has expressly or impliedly requested another to render him a service without specifying any remuneration, but the circumstances of the request imply that the service is to be paid for, there is implied a promise to pay *quantum meruit, i.e.*, so much as the party doing the service deserves. Further, if a person by the terms of a contract is to do a certain piece of work for a lump sum, and he does only part of the work, or something different, he cannot claim under the contract, but he may be able to claim on a *quantum meruits, e.g.*, if completion has been prevented by the act of the other party to the contract. [Osborn & Grandage's *Concise Commercial Dictionary*].

**Quantum valebat.** The expression means as much as they are worth. This relates to an action analogous to *quantum meruit*, but brought in respect of goods supplied.

**Quarantine.** Isolation of person afflicted with contagious disease.

To keep persons, when suspected of having contacted or having been exposed to an infectious disease, out of a community, or to confine them to given place therein, and to prevent intercourse between them and people generally of the community. [*Application of Halco* 246 Cal App 2d 553].

**Quarry.** An open or surface excavation, usually for obtaining stone, limestone, marble, slate etc.

NOTE: *Quarry and mine—distinction.* There is some distinction between a quarry and a mine; the former is an open air excavation of certain classes of minerals and the latter is essentially an underground excavation. [*Bisra Lime Stone* v *Labour Inspector* AIR 1969 Ori 110: (1969)2 Lab LJ 112].

**Quash.** Annul; cancel; declare null and void; invalidate; nullify; make void; overthrow; abate; vacate; set aside.

**Quasi.** It is a Latin expression which means as if; almost as it were; analogous to.

The term is used in legal phraseology to indicate that one subject resembles another, with which it is compared, in certain characteristics, but that there are intrinsic and material differences between them. [*Cannon* v *Miller* 155 P 2d 500, 503, 507].

**Quasi-contract.** An obligation which law creates in absence of agreement; it is invoked by courts where there is unjust enrichment. [*Andrews* v *O'Grady* 252 NYS 2d 814, 817].

Quasi-contract means that a man in certain cases is bound as if he had made a contract, though in fact no contract was made. 'Unjust enrichment' or 'restitution' are suggested as alternative expressions. [*Kamalpur (Assam) Tea Estate Pvt. Ltd., Jorhat* v *Supdt. of Taxes, Jorhat* (1988)1 Gau LR 290].

Quasi-contract is an act or event from which, though not a consensual contract, an obligation arises as if from a contract (*quasi ex contractu*). Thus, for instance, an executor or administrator is bound to satisfy the liabilities of the deceased to the extent of his assets received, *as if* he had contracted to do so. [Mozley & Whiteley's *Law Dictionary*, 10th Ed.].

NOTE: Function of "quasi-contract" is to raise obligation in law where in fact the parties made no promise, and it is based on apparent intention of the parties. [*Fink* v *Goadson-Todman Enterprises, Limited* 9 CA 3d 996].

Sections 68 to 72 of the Indian Contract Act 1872, deal with quasi-contracts.

**Quasi-easements.** See under EASEMENT p. 291.

**Quasi-judicial.** Judicial in some sense or aspect, but not in every sense.

The concept of quasi-judicial act implies that the act is not wholly judicial; it describes only a duty cast on the executive body or authority to conform to norms of judicial procedure in performing some acts in exercise of its executive power. [*Nageswar Rao* v *Andhra Pradesh State Road Transport* AIR 1959 SC 308].

NOTE: A quasi-judicial act requires that a decision is to be given not arbitrarily or at the mere discretion of an authority, but according to the facts and circumstances of the case, as determined upon an enquiry held by the authority after giving an opportunity to the party to be affected of being heard and whenever necessary to produce necessary evidence in support of his contentions. [*Province of Bombay* v *Khushaldas Advani* AIR 1950 SC 222: 1950 SCR 621].

**Quasi-laws.** These are circulars and memoranda issued by Government agencies and have the effect of law, although they are not recognised as such by the courts. The income-tax circulars are an example of this. Advice is given on points of interpretation of the Income Tax Act 1961. These represent "near legislation" and the term "quasi" means this.

**Quay.** A convenient place fitted on the shore for the loading and unloading of vessels. It is commonly called a "wharf".

**Question.** A subject or point of investigation, examination or debate; theme of inquiry; problem; matter to be inquired into.

- **Leading question** p. 521.
- **Substantial question of law.** The term does not mean a question of general importance but a substantial question of law between the parties to the case and the question must be one in respect of which there may be difference of opinion. [*State of Tripura* v *J. Mohini Mohan* AIR 1957 Tripura 22; *Chhail Beharital* v *Municipal Board, Agra* AIR 1948 All 189; *Public Prosecutor* v *A.K. Gopalan* AIR 1953 Mad 66].

**Question of fact.** A question of fact is one capable of being answered by way of demonstration. The past history of a company's business is a matter of fact. [*Gadakh Yashwantrao Kankarrao* v *E.V.* alias *Balasaheb Vikhe Patil* AIR 1994 SC 678, 695].

**Question of opinion.** A question of opinion is one that cannot be answered by way of demonstration. The answer to it is a matter of speculation which cannot be proved by any available evidence to be right or wrong. A company's prospects of successful business in the future is a matter of opinion while its past history is a matter of fact. [*Gadakh Yashwantrao Kankarrao* v *E.V.* alias *Balasaheb Vikhe Patil* AIR 1994 SC 678].

**Qui aliquid statuerit parte inaudita altera acquum licet dixerit haud acquum facerit.** He who shall decide anything without the other side having been heard, although he may have said what is right will not have done what is right, or in other words, as it is now expressed these days justice should not only be done but must manifestly appear to have done. This maxim is correlated with the maxim *audi alteram partem*. [*Suryabali* v *6th A.D.J., Deoria* AIR 1989 All 179: 1989 All LJ 248].

**Qui approbat non reprobat.** He who accepts cannot reject. This principle, though originally borrowed from Scots law, is not firmly established in English law. According to it, a party to an instrument or transaction cannot take advantage of one part of a document or transaction and reject the rest. No party can accept and reject the same instrument or transaction. This principle is different from estoppel or waiver. [*New Bihar Biri Leaves* v *State of Bihar* AIR 1981 SC 679: (1981)1 SCC 537: 1981 Cr LR (SC) 360].

**Qui facit per alium facit per se.** He who acts through another acts himself. A principal acts through an authorised agent.

**Qui prior est tempore potior est jure.** He who is first in time has the strongest claim in law.

**Qui sentit commodum, sentire; debet et onus.** He who receives the advantage must also suffer the burden.

**Quid pro quo.** Something for something. It is used in law for giving one valuable thing for another and nothing more than the mutual consideration which passes between the parties to a contract, and which renders it valid and binding.

The literal meaning of the phrase '*quid pro quo*' is one for another, like, charging fee for the service. [*Kewal Krishan Puri* v *State of Punjab* AIR 1980 SC 1008: (1980)1 SCC 416: (1979)3 SCR 1217].

**Quit.** To leave; abandon; abdicate; abjure; forgo; forsake; give up; remove from; surrender possession of; relinquish; renounce; make an exit; pull out; vacate.

**Quo warranto.** A judicial writ commanding a person to show by what authority he exercises an office or franchise never granted or forfeited by some fault.

A writ of *quo warranto* is a writ which lies against the person, who according to the relator is not entitled to hold an office of public nature and is only an usurper of the office. It is the person, against whom the writ of *quo warranto* is directed, who is required to show by what authority that person is entitled to hold the office. The challenge can be made on various grounds, including on the grounds that the possessor of the office does not fulfil the required qualifications or suffers from any disqualification, which debars the person to hold such office. [*B.R. Kapur* v *State of Tamil Nadu* (2001)7 SCC 231: JT 2001(8) SC 40].

NOTE: Broadly stated, the *quo warranto* proceeding affords a judicial enquiry in which any person holding an independent substantive public office, or franchise or liberty is called upon to show by what right he holds the said office—franchise or liberty. If the inquiry leads to the finding that the holder of the office has no valid title to it, the issue of the writ of *quo warranto* ousts him from that office. In other words, the procedure of *quo warranto* confers jurisdiction and authority on the judiciary to control executive action in the matter of making appointments to public offices against the relevant statutory provisions; it also protects a citizen from being deprived of public office to which he may have a right. Before a citizen can claim a writ of *quo warranto*, he must satisfy the court, *inter alia*, that the office in question is a public office and is held by usurper without legal authority, and that necessarily leads to the enquiry as to whether the appointment of the said alleged usurper has been made in accordance with law or not. [*University of Mysore* v *C.D. Govinda Rao* AIR 1965 SC 494].

No writ or direction can be issued to any person who has not been made a party to the proceedings, and without giving him an opportunity to be heard. [*Sangram Singh* v *Election Tribunal Kotah* AIR 1955 SC 425; Singhal's *Jurisprudence*, pp. 231-232].

**Quorum.** Such a number of members of any deliberative body as is necessary for the legal transaction of business; the fixed minimum number of members that must be present to make the proceedings of an assembly or society valid; legal minimum.

Quorum denotes the minimum number of member of any body of persons whose presence is necessary to enable that body to transact its business validly, so that its act may be lawful. It is generally left to committees themselves to fix the quorum for their meetings. [*Punjab University* v *Vijay Singh* AIR 1976 SC 1441: (1976)3 SCC 344: (1976)1 SCWR 510].

**Quota.** Allocation; allotment; apportionment; proportionate contribution; restriction; a quantity of goods etc. which under official controls must be manufactured, exported, imported, etc.; the number of yearly immigrants allowed to enter a country.

Commercially, quota is a licence for a particular time for a particular quantity. Quota cannot be divided and is a matter of privilege. [*Shadi Lal* v *Nagin Chand* AIR 1973 SC 776: (1973)2 SCR 598: (1973)1 SCC 185].

**Q.V.** It is the abbreviation for "quod-vide", which means see. A reference to another passage or title of a book is made by using the word "Q.V.".

# Rr

**Race.** As noun it means ancestry; birth; breed; class; cultural group; culture; ethnic group; ethnic stock; genealogy; a great division of mankind having in common certain distinguishing physical peculiarities constituting a comprehensive class appearing to be derived from a distinct primitive source.

As verb it means accelerate; chase; compete; dash; engage in a contest of speed; enter a competition; move at an accelerated rate of speed; run a race.

**Rack-rent.** Rent of the full annual value of the tenement on which it is charged, or as near to it as possible. [Mozley & Whiteley's *Law Dictionary*, 10th Ed.].

Rent equal to or nearly equal to the full annual value of the property; excessively or unreasonably high rent. [Black's *Law Dictionary*, 8th Ed.].

**Racket.** Conspiracy; corruption; criminal activity; criminality; dishonesty; illegitimate undertaking; illicit business; illicit scheme; improbity; organised illegal activity; underworld activity.

An organised criminal activity, especially the extortion of money by threat or violence; a dishonest or fraudulent scheme or business. [Black's *Law Dictionary*, 8th Ed.].

**Radd.** Rejection; repeal; abrogation; making null and void. In Mahomedan law, if there is some residue left after claims of sharers are satisfied and where there is no residuary, the residue returns to or is to be distributed among the sharers in proportion to their shares. This return is called *Radd*.

**Radiation.** Gamma rays, X-rays and rays consisting of alpha particles, beta particles, neutrons, protons and other nuclear and sub-atomic particles, but not sound or radio waves, or visible, infra-red or ultra-violet light. [Atomic Energy Act 1962, s. 2(*h*)].

**Rafa.** Settlement or adjustment of a difference or dispute.

**Rafanama.** A deed of compromise or settlement of a dispute or difference.

**Raffle.** A form of lottery in which each participant buys one or more chances to win a prize. [Black's *Law Dictionary*, 8th Ed.].

A kind of lottery in which several persons pay, in shares, the value of something put up as a stake or prize, and then determine by chance (as by casting dice or drawing a number) which one of them shall become the sole possessor of it. [Black's *Law Dictionary*, 5th Ed.].

**Ragging.** It is defined as any "disorderly conduct whether by words spoken or written or by an act which has the effect of teasing, treating or handling with rudeness any other student, indulging in rowdy or indisciplined activities which causes or is likely to cause annoyance, hardship or physiological harm or to raise fear or apprehension thereof in a fresher or a junior student or asking the students to do any act or perform something which such student will not do in the ordinary course and which has the effect of causing or generating a sense of shame or embarrassment so as to adversely affect the physique or psyche of a fresher or a junior student". [*Vishwa Jagriti Mission through President* v *Central Government* *through Cabinet Secretary* AIR 2001 SC 2793: (2001)6 SCC 577].

**Rahn**. Mortgage, pledge, pawn.

**Railway accident.** "Railway accident", as used in a policy of insurance against death or injury in a railway accident, means an accident occurring in the course of travelling and arising out of the fact of the journey. It does not necessarily depend on any accident to the railway or machinery connected with it.

**Railway advice.** Document sent by a railway company to a consignee of goods intimating that goods are awaiting his orders at a special station and that demurrage with be chargeable after a date named.

**Railway receipt.** A "railway receipt" is a document of title of goods, and for all purposes, represents the goods. When the railway receipt is handed over to the consignee on payment, the property in the goods is transferred. [*Commissioner of Income-tax, M.P., Bhopal and Nagpur* v *Bhopal Textiles Ltd*. AIR 1961 SC 426: (1961)2 SCR 9: (1961)2 SCJ 45: (1961)41 ITR 72].

**Railway servant.** Any person employed by the Central Government or by a railway administration in connection with the service of a railway. [Railways Act 1989, s. 2(34)].

**Raison d'etre.** What accounts for a thing's existence.

**Raiyat.** A subject; a tenant; a cultivating tenant; a farmer; a cultivator.

• **Paikasht raiyat** p. 636.

**Rajaswa.** Revenue; cess; rent.

> NOTE: The word 'rajaswa' is wide enough to include cess payable under the Cess Act. [*Bhagwan Das* v *Bhupendra Narayan Singha* AIR 1933 Cal 527: 57 CLJ 120].

**Rakshasa form of marriage.** It was a marriage by capture and allowed only to Kshatriyas or military classes.

**Rank.** A social or official position or standing, as in the armed forces. [Black's *Law Dictionary*, 8th Ed.].

The word "rank" has both a narrower as well as a wider meaning. In its ordinary sense it means grade or status. [*N.C. Dalwadi* v *State of Gujarat* AIR 1987 SC 1933: (1987)3 SCR 640: (1987)3 SCC 611: JT 1987(3) SC 152: 1987(4) SLR 505].

> NOTE: The expression 'rank' has reference to a person's classification and not his particular place in the same cadre in the hierarchy of the service to which he belongs. Losing some places in the seniority list is not tantamount to reduction in rank. [*Divisional Perchuni Officer, Southern Railway, Mysore* v *S. Raghavindrachar* AIR 1966 SC 1529].

**Ransom.** As noun it means cost of reclamation; cost of recovery; price of redemption; price of retaking; price of retrieval.

As noun it further means money or other consideration demanded or paid for the release of a captured person or property; the release of a captured person or property in exchange for payment of a demanded price. [Black's *Law Dictionary*, 8th Ed.].

As verb it means to obtain the release of a captive by paying a demanded price; to release a captive upon receiving such a payment; to hold and demand payment for the release of a captive. [Black's *Law Dictionary*, 8th Ed.].

**Rape.** Defilement; defloration; depredation; forcible violation; plunder; ravage; ravishment; sexual assault; unlawful carnal knowledge of a woman by a man forcibly and against her will.

The act of sexual intercourse committed by a man with a woman not his wife and without her consent, committed when the woman's resistance is overcome by force or fear, or under other prohibitive conditions. [*State* v *Lora* 515 P 2d 1086, 1093].

▸ *Meaning under the Indian Penal Code 1860, s. 375.* A man is said to commit "rape" who except in the case hereinafter excepted, has sexual intercourse with a woman under circumstances falling under any of the six following descriptions— *First*—Against her will. *Secondly*—Without her consent. *Thirdly*—With her consent, when her consent has been obtained by putting her or any person in whom she is interested in fear of death or of hurt. *Fourthly*—With her consent, when the man knows that he is not her husband, and that her consent is given because she believes that he is another man to whom she is or believes herself to be lawfully married. *Fifthly*—With her consent, when at the time of giving such consent, by reason of unsoundness of mind or intoxication or the administration by him personally or through another of any stupefying or unwholesome substance, she is unable to understand the nature and consequences of that to which she gives consent. *Sixthly*—With or without her consent when she is under sixteen years of age.

*Explanation*—Penetration is sufficient to constitute the sexual intercourse necessary to the offence of rape.

*Exception*—Sexual intercourse by a man with his own wife, the wife not being under fifteen years of age, is not rape.

Although the modern usage of the word 'rape' extends also to the forcible sexual intercourse by a woman with a man, the dictionary meaning of the said word as well as the offence of rape as defined in the Indian Penal Code speaks only of forcible sexual intercourse by a man with a woman. The latter meaning of the word is accepted in the context of Indian Divorce Act 1869, also. [*Anil Kumar Mahsi* v *Union of India* (1994)5 SCC 704].

• **Acquaintance rape** p. 25.

**Rash and hazardous speculation.** A speculation which no reasonably careful man would enter into having regard to all the circumstances of the case. [*Re Keays* (1891)9 Morr 18: 36 SJ 111].

**Rasi.** A rope; a distance of about 80 cubits; a heap of grain or other things.

**Rate.** Proportional or relative value; the proportion by which quantity or value is adjusted; an amount paid or charged for a good or service. [Black's *Law Dictionary*, 8th Ed.].

"Rate" means a rate, cess or assessment the proceeds of which are applicable to public local purposes and leviable on the basis of a valuation of property, and includes any sum which, although obtained in the first instance by a precept, certificate or other instrument requiring payment from some authority or officer, is or can be ultimately raised out of a rate. [Halsbury's *Laws of England*, 4th Ed., vol. 32, para 203, p. 97].

NOTE: The history of the use of the word 'rate' for purposes of local taxation in English law clearly shows that the word 'rate' was used with respect to a tax which was levied on the net annual value or rateable value of lands and buildings and not on their capital value. [*Patel Gordhandas Hargovindas* v *The Municipal Commissioner, Ahmedabad* AIR 1963 SC 1742; *Godhara Borough Municipality, Godhara* v *Godhara Electricity Co. Ltd.* AIR 1968 SC 1504].

The word 'rate' must be understood, whatever it might in its technical sense mean, to describe a tax the basis of which can be capital value. [*Patel Gordhandas Hargovindas* v *The Municipal Commissioner, Ahmedabad* AIR 1963 SC 1742; *Godhara Borough Municipality, Godhara* v *Godhara Electricity Co. Ltd.* AIR 1968 SC 1504].

▸ *Meaning under the Railways Act 1989, s. 2(35).* 'Rate' includes any fare, freight or any other charge for the carriage of any passenger or goods.

• **Time rate** p. 843.

**Ratification.** Acceptance; acknowledgment; approval; assent; confirmation; consent; corroboration; endorsement; stamp of approval; validation.

The affirmance by a person of a prior act which did not bind him, but which was done or professedly done on his account, whereby the act, as to some or all persons, is given effect as if originally authorised by him. [*Askew* v *Joachim Memorial Home, N.D.* 234 NW 2d 226, 237].

**Ratio decidendi.** It is a Latin expression which means "the reason for deciding".

It is the rule deducible from the application of law to the facts and circumstances of a case which constitutes its *ratio decidendi* and not some conclusion based upon the facts which may appear to be similar. [*Regional Manager* v *Pawan Kumar Dubey* AIR 1976 SC 1766: (1976)3 SCC 334].

NOTE: It is the principle or rule of law on which a court's decision is founded.

Every decision contains three basic ingredients—(*a*) finding of material facts direct and inferential. An inferential finding of fact is the inference which the Judge draws from the direct or perceptible facts; (*b*) statements of principles of law applicable to the legal problems disclosed by the facts; and (*c*) judgment based on the combined effect of (*a*) & (*b*) above. However, for the purposes of the doctrines of precedents, ingredient no. (*b*) is the vital element in the decision. This indeed is the *ratio decidendi*. It is not everything said by the Judge that constitutes a precedent. The principle upon which a case is decided is alone binding on a party. So the analysis of the decision and isolating from it the *ratio decidendi* is material. [*Dalbir Singh* v *State of Punjab* AIR 1979 SC 1384: 1979 Cr LJ 1058: (1979)2 SCJ 314: 1979 Cr LJ (SC) 705: ILR (1979) HP 103: (1979)3 SCC 745: 1979 SCC (Cri) 848].

**Ratio legis est anima legis.** The reason of law is the soul of law.

**Rationalization.** The act or process of rationalizing; the act of bringing an industry into accord with up-to-date methods of organization and operation; the act of making a business etc. more efficient by reorganizing it to reduce or eliminate waste of labour, time, or materials.

**Rationing.** This relates to the fixing of a periodical allowance, *e.g.*, of food, clothing etc. It may be of two kinds—unit system and point system. Under the unit system, available supplies of goods are in effect divided equally among the population by reference to monetary values or physical quantity. The point system of rationing, on the other hand, involves fixing point values for each item and allowing each consumer to exercise selection among items rationed up to a maximum total of points for a particular period.

**Ravish.** To feel with strong emotion, especially delight; enrapture; feel with delight; carry off a person or thing by force; to commit a rape upon; to seize and carry off by violence.

**Ravishment.** Forcible seizure and carrying off of another person specially a woman; rape. [Black's *Law Dictionary*, 8th Ed.].

**Raw materials.** The materials in the state in which they are acquired, which are subjected to manufacturing processes in order to become part of a finished product; unprocessed material needed and used in manufacturing, as contrasted with finished goods.

The expression 'raw materials' ought to be construed in the sense of those basic materials which are required for the production of finished articles which the manufacturer manufactures and not in the sense of unmanufactured material or materials in their raw state. [*Municipal Committee, Burhanpur* v *Allauddin Aolia Saheb* 1957 MPLJ 279 (Nag)].

According to dictionary, it means 'something which is used for manufacturing or producing the goods'. The ordinary common sense is that it is something from which another new or distinct commodity can be produced. When it is used in a taxing statute, it may have related meaning depending on the context in which it has been used. The word 'raw material' has no fixed meaning. It may vary with the use to which it is put. An item may be raw material for manufacturing goods *A* and the goods so produced may itself be raw material for goods *B*. For instance, batteries, tyres and tubes are by themselves finished products. They on their own cannot be considered to be raw materials. But when they are used for equipment in a vehicle then they become raw material for they are essential and necessary for producing the commodity in which they have been used. No vehicle can operate or work, nor can it be said to have been produced unless tyres, tubes and batteries are fixed to it. Use of these items is integrally connected with the ultimate product. They retain their identity in the end product. But that could not exclude it from being treated as raw materials. [*Tata Engineering & Locomotive Company Ltd.* v *State of Bihar* (1996)6 SCC 479].

NOTE: The ingredients used in the chemical technology of manufacture of any end product might comprise amongst others, of those materials which may retain their dominant individual identity and character throughout the process and also in the end product; those which, as a result of interaction with other chemicals or ingredients, undergo chemical or qualitative changes and in such altered form find themselves in the end product; those which, like catalytic agents, while influencing and accelerating the chemical reactions, however, may themselves remain uninfluenced and unaltered and remain independent of and outside the end products and those, which might be burnt up or consumed in the chemical reactions. The question is whether the ingredients of the last mentioned class qualify themselves as are eligible to be called 'raw material' for the end product. One of the valid tests could be that the ingredient should be so essential for the chemical process culminating in the emergence of the desired end product that having regard to its importance in and indispensability for the process, it could be said that its very consumption on burning up is its quality and value as raw materials. In such a case, the relevant test is not its absence in the end product, but the dependence of the end product for its essential presence at the delivery end of the process. The ingredient goes into the making of the end product in the sense that without its absence the presence of the end product, as such, is rendered impossible. This quality should coalesce within the requirement that its utilisation is in the manufacturing process as distinct from the manufacturing apparatus. [*Collector of Central Excise, New Delhi* v *Ballarpur Industries Ltd.* AIR 1990 SC 196].

'Raw material', as commonly understood, is used in the process of manufacture. Printing machinery will certainly not come under the category of 'raw material' ... [*Re K.I. Kosalram* AIR 1968 Mad 113].

**Re.** In the matter of; relating to; in the case of.

NOTE: It is a term frequently used in designating judicial proceedings, in which there is only one party.

**Re-entry.** The act or an instance of retaking possession of land by someone who formerly held the land and who reserved the right to retake it when the new holder let it go; a landlord's resumption of possession of leased premises upon the tenant's default under the lease. [Black's *Law Dictionary*, 7th & 8th Eds.].

**Re-examination.** The examination of a witness, subsequent to the cross-examination, by the party who called him is called re-examination. [Indian Evidence Act 1872, s. 137].

An examination of a witness after a cross-examination, upon matters arising out of such cross-examination. [Black's *Law Dictionary*, 5th Ed.].

In patents, it is a procedure whereby a party can seek review of a patent on the basis of additional references to prior art not originally considered by the patent office.

**Ready and willing.** The expression 'ready and willing' implies not merely the disposition but also the capacity to do the act. [*De Medina* v *Norman* 11 LJ Ex 322].

NOTE: An averment of readiness and willingness is necessary in an action for specific performance of contract. [Specific Relief Act 1963, s. 16].

**Real action.** In English law, the expression means an action brought for the specific recovery of lands, tenements and hereditaments.

**Real property.** In English law, real property means land or thing attached to land which is inheritable and specifically recoverable in law.

**Reason(s).** As noun means foundation; explanation; consideration; genesis; rationale; ground for action; logic; logicalness; rationality; sagacity. A faculty of the mind that helps distinguishing good from evil, truth from falsehood, and enables the possessor to decide inferences from the facts or from propositions.

As verb means figure out; rationalise; examine; analyse; argue; explain; plead; point out; remonstrate.

- **Discrimination with reasons** p. 266.
- **For any other sufficient reason** p. 362.

**Reason to believe.** A person is said to have 'reason to believe' a thing if he has sufficient cause to believe that thing, but not otherwise. [Indian Penal Code 1860, s. 26].

The words 'reason to believe' suggest that the belief must be that of an honest and reasonable person based upon reasonable grounds. The person making such belief may act on direct or circumstantial evidence but not on mere suspicion, gossip or rumour. [*Sheo Nath Singh* v *Appellate Assistant Commissioner, Income Tax, Calcutta* (1972)3 SCC 234].

NOTE: The expression 'reason to believe' is not synonymous with subjective satisfaction of the person making such belief. The belief must be held in good faith; it cannot merely be a pretence. [*Pratap Singh* v *Director of Enforcement* (1985)3 SCC 72: AIR 1985 SC 989].

The words 'reason to believe' contemplate an objective determination based on intelligent care and deliberation involving judicial review as distinguished from purely subjective considerations. [*Melico Fernandes* v *Shri Mohan Nair* AIR 1966 Goa 23: 1966 Cr LJ 1258].

The words 'reason to believe' mean it must be reasonable or in otherwords, it must be based on reasons which are relevant and material. If there is no rational intelligible nexus between the reasons and the belief, so that, on such reasons, no one properly instructed on facts and law could reasonably entertain the belief, the conclusion would be inescapable that there could not be reason to believe. [*S. Ganga Saran & Sons Pvt. Ltd.* v *I.T.O.* (1981)3 SCC 143].

The court can always examine the question of 'reason to believe' though the declaration or sufficiency of the reasons for the belief cannot be investigated by the court. [*Sheo Nath Singh* v *Appellate Assistant Commissioner, Income Tax, Calcutta* (1972)3 SCC 234].

It is open to the court to examine the question whether the reasons for the belief have a rational connection or a relevant bearing to the formation of the belief and are not extraneous or irrelevant to the purpose of the section of a statute. [*S. Narayanappa* v *CIT, Bangalore* AIR 1967 SC 523: (1967)1 SCJ 161: (1967)65 ITR 219].

**Reasonable.** Dictionary meaning of the word 'reasonable' is that which is agreeable to reason, not absurd, within the limits or reason. The expression 'reasonable' means rational according to the dictates of reason and not excessive or immoderate. [*State of M.P.* v *Ram Sarup* 1977 Jab LJ 408, 411: 1977 MPLJ 451: 1977 Cr LR (MP) 59].

The expression 'reasonable' means 'rational—according to the dictates of reason and not excessive or immoderate'. An act is reasonable when it is conformable or agreeable to reason, having regard to the facts of the particular controversy. [*Raghbir Singh* v *CIT* AIR 1958 Punj 250].

If something is not *per se* preposterous or absurd, it must be held to be reasonable. [*Kelvin Cinema* v *State of Assam* AIR 1996 Gau 103, 108].

Terms like 'reasonable', 'fair', 'just' derive their significance from existing social conditions. That action is called reasonable which an informed, intelligent, just minded, civilised man could rationally favour. The concept of reasonableness does not exclude notions of morality and ethics. In the circumstances of a given case, considerations of morality and ethics may have a bearing on the reasonableness of the law in question. [*R.K. Garg* v *Union of India* 1982 SCC (Tax) 30].

NOTE: It is difficult to give an exact definition of the word 'reasonable'. Reason varies in its conclusions according to the idiosyncrasy of the individual and the times and the circumstances in which he thinks. The word 'reasonable' has in law *prima facie* meaning of reasonable in regard to those circumstances of which the actor, called upon to act reasonably, knows or ought to know. [*Rena Drego* v *Lalchand Soni* (1998)3 SCC 341; *Gujarat Water Supply & Sewerage Board* v *Unique Erectors (Gujarat) Pvt. Ltd.* AIR 1989 SC 973: JT 1989(1) SC 157: (1989)39 ELT 493].

**Reasonable and probable cause.** Such grounds as justify any one in suspecting another of a crime, and placing him in custody thereon. It is a suspicion founded upon circumstances sufficiently strong to warrant reasonable man in belief, charge is true. [*Henry* v *U.S.* 361 US 98: 4 L Ed 2d 134].

'Reasonable and probable cause' means a genuine belief, based on reasonable grounds that the proceedings are justified. [*S.T. Sahib* v *Hassan Ghani Sahib* AIR 1957 Mad 646].

'Reasonable and probable cause' means an honest belief in the guilt of the accused based upon a full conviction founded upon reasonable grounds of the existence of a state of circumstances which, assuming them to be true would reasonably lead to any ordinary prudent and cautious man placed in the position of the accuser to the conclusion that the person charged was probably guilty of the crime imputed. [*Nagendra Kumar* v *Etwari Sahu* AIR 1958 Pat 329].

NOTE: In an action for malicious prosecution, the plaintiff must prove absence of reasonable and probable cause. In order that there may be reasonable and probable cause, there must be, first, an honest belief of the accuser in the guilt of the accused; secondly, such belief must be based on an honest conviction of the existence of the circumstances which led the accused to that conclusion; thirdly, such secondly mentioned belief must be based upon reasonable grounds, *i.e.*, such grounds as would lead any fairly cautious man in the defendant's situation so to believe; fourthly, the circumstances so believed and relied on by the accuser must be such as amount to reasonable ground for belief in the guilt of the accused. [*Hicks* v *Faulkner* (1881)8 QBD 167].

**Reasonable care.** The degree of care that a prudent and competent person engaged in the same line of business or endeavour would exercise under similar circumstances. [Black's *Law Dictionary*, 7th & 8th Eds.].

That degree of care which a person of ordinary prudence would exercise in the same or similar circumstances. [*Pampas* v *Cambridge Mut. Fire Ins. Co.* La App, 169 So 2d 200, 201; *Pierce* v *Horvath* 233 NE 2d 811, 815].

NOTE: It is also termed due care; adequate care; proper care.

**Reasonable cause.** Such state of facts an would lead man of ordinary care and prudence to believe that a person has committed a crime or is guilty of crime.

'Reasonable cause', in the context of submission of wealth tax return under the Wealth Tax Act, obviously means a cause which prevents a reasonable man of an ordinary prudence acting under normal circumstances, without negligence or inaction or want of *bona fide* from furnishing the return in time. [*Commissioner of Wealth Tax, Patna* v *Jagdish Prasad Chaudhary* AIR 1996 Pat 58].

**Reasonable classification.** For the purpose of legislation, it is classification based on intelligible differentia having rational relation with the object of the Act. In order to pass the test of 'reasonable classification', the classification must not be "arbitrary, artificial or evasive" but must be based on some real and substantial distinction bearing a just and reasonable relation to the object sought to be achieved by the legislature. [*In re Special Courts Bill* AIR 1979 SC 478: (1979)2 SCR 476; *R.K. Garg* v *Union of India* AIR 1981 SC 2138: (1981)4 SCC 676: (1982)1 SCR 947: (1982)133 ITR 239: (1982)1 Comp LJ 139].

**Reasonable doubt.** A "reasonable doubt" does not mean some light, airy, insubstantial doubt that may flit through the minds of anybody about almost anything at sometime or other; it does not mean a doubt begotten by sympathy out of reluctance to convict; it means a real doubt, a doubt founded upon reasons. [*K. Gopal Reddy* v *State of Andhra Pradesh* AIR 1979 SC 387: (1979)2 SCR 363: (1979)1 SCC 355: 1979 SCC (Cri) 305: 1980 Cr LJ 812].

Doubts would be called reasonable if they are free from a zest for abstract speculation. To constitute 'reasonable doubt', it must be free from an overmotional response.

A reasonable doubt is not an imaginary, trivial or merely possible doubt, but a fair doubt based upon reason and common senses. [*State of U.P.* v *Krishna Gopal* AIR 1988 SC 2154: (1988)4 SCC 302: JT 1988(3) SC 544: 1988 SCC (Cri) 928: 1988 Supp (2) SCR 391: 1989 Cr LJ 288].

NOTE: The reasonable doubt should be a real and substantial one and a well founded actual doubt arising out of the evidence existing after consideration of all the evidence. A mere whim or a surmise or suspicion furnishes an insufficient foundation upon which to raise a reasonable doubt, and so a vague conjecture, whimsical or vague doubt, a capricious and speculative doubt, an arbitrary, imaginary, fanciful, uncertain, chimerical, trivial, indefinite or a mere possible doubt is not a reasonable doubt. Neither is a desire for more evidence of guilt, a capricious doubt or misgiving suggested by an ingenious counsel or arising from a merciful disposition or kindly feeling towards a prisoner, or from sympathy for him or his family. [*Assistant Collector of Central Excise, Calicut* v *V.P. Sayed Mohammed* AIR 1983 SC 168: (1983)1 SCC 370: (1983)2 SCR 225: (1983)12 ELT 193: 1983 Cr LJ 225: 1983 SCC (Cri) 191].

**Reasonable man.** An ordinary man capable of reasoning, who is responsible and accountable for his actions. [*Director of Public Prosecutions* v *Smith* (1960)3 All ER 161: (1961) AC 290]. The standard of due care is the standard of a reasonable and prudent man, that is, the standard of "reasonable foreseeability". [*Donoghue* v *Stevenson* (1932) AC 562].

A reasonable man acts sensibly, does things without serious delay, and takes proper but not excessive precautions. The reasonable man is presumed to be free from both over-apprehension and overconfidence. "The reasonable man connotes a person whose notions and standards of behaviour and responsibility correspond with those generally obtained among ordinary people in our society at the present time, who seldom allows his emotions to overbear his reason and whose habits are moderate and whose disposition is equable. He is not necessarily the same as the average man—a term which implies an amalgamation of counter-balancing extremes". [R.F.V. Heuston: *Salmond on the Law of Torts*, p. 56 (17th Ed. 1977)].

**Reasonable notice.** In the context of time factor, a notice is reasonable when the period of notice is not obviously so unreasonably brief as to frustrate the right of objection. The time factor is elastic in accordance with the gravity of charges or the size of a defence that may be necessary. [*Penumbra of Natural Justice* by Tapash Gan Choudhury, 2nd Ed., pp. 127, 128].

**Reasonable opportunity.** Opportunity is reasonable when it is an effective one and not a mere pretence.

**Reasonable opportunity of being heard.** A cardinal factor in the administration of justice is that a party likely to be affected by any decision be allowed to state his case to the utmost. This calls for a fair and reasonable opportunity of being heard which means that there must always be substantial opportunity and a proper latitude to meet everything which is likely to be considered against a party. [*Penumbra of Natural Justice* by Tapash Gan Choudhury, 2nd Ed., p. 184].

NOTE: The requirement that a reasonable opportunity of being heard, must be given has two elements. The first is that an opportunity to be heard must be given; the second is that opportunity must be reasonable. Both these matters are justifiable, and it is for the court to decide whether an opportunity has been given and whether that opportunity has been reasonable. [*Fedia Pvt. Ltd.* v *S.N. Bilgrani* AIR 1960 SC 415: 1960 SCJ 285: (1960)2 SCR 408].

**Reasonable opportunity to show cause.** Reasonable opportunity to show cause includes not only an opportunity to submit an explanation but also an opportunity to adduce evidence to disprove the charges on the basis of which the action is proposed to be taken against the party aggrieved. [*Rama Shankar* v *Divisional Superintendent* AIR 1956 All 393].

**Reasonable requirement.** It is a question of fact depending upon circumstances of case, connotes something more than desire but less than absolute necessity. [*Petroleum Workers' Union* v *Mohammad & Co.* AIR 1967 Mad 33: (1966)17 STC 1]. The word 'requirement' merely connotes that there should be an element of need. [*Bega Begum* v *Abdul Ahad Khan* AIR 1979 SC 272: (1979)1 SCC 273].

**Reasonable restriction.** The expression "reasonable restriction" signifies that the limitation imposed on a person in enjoyment of the right should not be arbitrary or of an excessive nature, beyond what is required in the interests of the public. [*Bishamber Dayal Chandra Mohan* v *State of Uttar Pradesh* AIR 1982 SC 33: (1982)1 SCC 39: (1982)1 SCR 1137: 1982 SCC (Cri) 53; *P.P. Enterprises* v *Union of India* (1982)2 SCC 33: AIR 1982 SC 1016: (1982)3 SCR 510].

NOTE: In applying the test of reasonableness, the court has to consider the question in the background of the facts and circumstances under which the order was made, taking into account the nature of the evil that was sought to be remedied by such law, the ratio of the harm caused to individual citizens by the proposed remedy, to the beneficial effect reasonably expected to result to the general public. It will also be necessary to consider in that connection whether the restraint caused by the law is more than was necessary in the interests of the general public. [*Narendra Kumar* v *Union of India* AIR 1960 SC 430].

In deciding whether a particular restriction answers the test of reasonable restrictions the following are relevant, namely, (*a*) the court is to bear in mind the directive principles of state policy; (*b*) the restriction must not be arbitrary or of an excessive nature so as to go beyond the requirement of the interest of the general public; (*c*) it is necessary to examine the nature and extent, the purport and the content of the right, nature of the evil sought to be remedied by the statute; the ratio of the harm caused to the citizen and the benefit to be conferred on the person or the community for whose benefit the legislation is passed, urgency of the evil and necessity to rectify the same; (*d*) there must be a direct and proximate nexus or a reasonable connection between the restriction and the object what is sought to be achieved by the statute. Though the tests formulated above are not exhaustive, they undoubtedly provide sufficient guidelines as to decision of the question what constitute reasonable restriction. [*Pathumma* v *State of Kerala* AIR 1978 SC 771: (1978)2 SCJ 632: (1978)2 SCR 537: (1978)2 SCC 1].

In assessing whether or not restrictions imposed contain the quality of reasonableness, a doctrinaire approach should not be made but the essential facts and realities of life have to be duly considered. Where a restriction is imposed by the legislature in public interest in order to advance a particular purpose or carry out the dominant object, such a restriction is undoubtedly a reasonable restriction within the meaning of cls. (5) and (6) of Art. 19 of the Constitution. If the restrictions are in implementation of the directive principles of the Constitution the same would be upheld as being in public interest because the individual interest must yield to the interest of the community. [*Sri Sri Kalimata Thakurani* v *Union of India* AIR 1981 SC 1030: (1981)2 SCR 950: 1981 UJ (SC) 283].

**Reasonable time.** In contracts, it means the time needed to do what a contract requires to be done, based on subjective circumstances. [Black's *Law Dictionary*, 7th Ed.].

Where contract does not fix a time for performance, the law allows "reasonable time" for performance, defined as such time as is necessary, conveniently, to do what the contract requires to be done, as soon as circumstances will permit. [*Houston County* v *Leo L. Landauer & Associates, Inc.* Tex Civ App, 424 SW 2d 458, 463].

NOTE: What is reasonable time is a question of fact and necessarily depends on the circumstances of each particular case.

Reasonable time depends on the nature of the business and the time of the day in relation to which the work is to be done. [*Lakshmana Rao* v *Special Commercial Tax Officer* ILR (1962) AP 1036].

**Rebate.** A deduction from a sum to be paid; a discount; a partial refund of money in consideration of prompt payment; a deduction from a gross amount; slash; pay back; a deduction or drawback from a stipulated payment, charge, or rate, not taken out in advance of payment, but handed back to the payer after he has paid the full stipulated sum; a deduction from a stipulated premium on a policy of insurance.

The word 'rebate' is an apt word to use in respect of a remission. [*Commissioner of Income Tax* v *Anant Rao B. Kamat* (1964)8 SCR 263: (1964)53 ITR 307: (1964)2 SCJ 505].

**Rebellion.** The act of rebelling; organised resistance to a government or to any lawful authority; open resistance to authority, especially organised armed resistance to an established government; breach of orders; defiance; disobedience; insurgence; insurgency; mutiny.

Deliberate, organised resistance, by force and arms, to the laws or operations of the government, committed by a subject. [*Crashley* v *Press Pub Co*. 77 NYS 711].

**Rebuilding work.** Where the nature of the construction is such that, while partaking of the nature of a new building operation, it does not amount to new building but amounts to reconstruction of certain parts of the old building either by taking down the roof or by changing the foundation or by taking down the walls and reconstructing them or otherwise, the work done is 'rebuilding work'. [*Sharma Electric Engineering Works* v *Radha Devi* AIR 1957 Cal 227: ILR (1957)3 Cal 278].

> NOTE: Where the work proposed to be done is reconstruction of the walls, after taking down the old walls, after introducing a steel frame, it is rebuilding work. [*Sharma Electric Engineering Works* v *Radha Devi*, supra].

**Rebus sic stantibus.** A name given to a tacit condition, said to attach to all treaties, that they shall cease to be obligatory so soon as the state of facts and conditions upon which they were founded has substantially changed.

> NOTE: Treaties may be discharged as a result of the *rebus sic stantibus* doctrine. According to this doctrine, a treaty may become null and void in case there is a fundamental change in the state of facts which existed at the time the treaty was concluded. There is an implied term or clause in the treaty—the *clusula rebus sic stantibus*—to the effect that the treaty obligations subsist so long as the essential circumstances remain unchanged. The *rebus sic stantibus* doctrine is one of the enigmas of International Law. Jurists differ as to the nature of the doctrine. The Permanent Court of International Justice held that a change in the original state of facts terminates the treaty. [Case of the Free Zones of Upper Savoy and Gex. Pub PCIJ (1932) series A/B No. 46].

This is an English principle of valuation. *Rebus sic stantibus* i.e. valuation with reference to the property in its actually existing condition, taking into account neither the past conditions nor the future possibilities. [*Bengal Nagpur Rly. Co*. v *Corporation of Calcutta* ILR (1942)2 Cal 152: AIR 1942 Cal 455].

**Rebuttable presumption.** A species of legal presumption which holds good until evidence contrary to it is introduced. [*Beck* v *Kansas City Public Service Co*. Mo App, 48 SW 2d 213, 215].

> NOTE: The presumptions of fact and law—both, when no evidence to the contrary has been introduced, compels a finding of the existence of the presumed fact. [*Syed Akbar* v *State of Karnataka* AIR 1979 SC 1848: 1979 Cr LJ 1374: (1980)1 SCC 30].

**Rebutting evidence.** That which tends to explain or contradict or disprove evidence offered by the adverse party. [*Layton* v *State* 301 NE 2d 633, 636].

**Recall.** Call back; abrogate; annul; cancel; invalidate; nullify; revoke; summon back; take back; withdraw; be reminded of; call up; commemorate; have memories of; keep in mind; know by heart; look back upon; memorialise; recollect; recover knowledge of; refresh one's memory.

**Recall a judgment or an order.** The expression, "to recall" a judgment as understood would be to revoke, cancel, vacate, or reverse a judgment for matters of fact. When a judgment is annulled by reason of errors of law, it is said to be reversed. [*Girdharilal* v *Pratap Mehta* (1990)1 Crimes 205, 208 (Kant)].

> NOTE: *Recall and restoration—distinction.* There is a difference between 'recall and restoration'. Prayer for recall of an order can be made if the applicant shows that there was a mistake of the court while passing its order. When making a prayer for restoration, the applicant must show the sufficiency of cause of his default and the court may exercise its discretion in accepting that cause. In the former, the court has to invoke the doctrine *actus curiae neminem gravabit* (acts of court prejudices none) whereas in the latter the defaulting party has to show the *bona fides* and failure of justice. [*Ghanshyam Raj* v *Union of India* 1997 JIC (Judicial Interpretation on Crimes) 854 (All)].

**Recant.** To withdraw or repudiate formally and publicly. [*Pradlik* v *State* 41 A 2d 906, 907].

**Receipt.** As noun means acquirement; acquisition; admittance; assumption; acknowledgment of payment; certificate of deposit; proof of delivery; proof of payment; income; acceptance; act of receiving.

The act of receiving something; a written acknowledgment that something has been received. [Black's *Law Dictionary*, 8th Ed.]. A writing which acknowledges taking or receiving either money or goods which have been paid or delivered. [*Manley* v *Nelson* 443 P 2d 155, 158]. That which comes in, in distinction from what is expended, paid out, sent away, and the like. [*State* v *Texas Co.* 116 SW 2d 583, 584].

As verb means to acknowledge in writing the receipt of (something); to give a receipt for (something). [Black's *Law Dictionary*, 8th Ed.].

▸ *Meaning under the Indian Stamp Act 1899, s. 2(23).* Receipt includes any note, memorandum or writing—(*a*) whereby any money, or any bill of exchange, cheque or promissory note is acknowledged to have been received, or (*b*) whereby any other movable property is acknowledged to have been received in satisfaction of a debt, or (*c*) whereby any debt or demand, or any part of a debt or demand is acknowledged to have been satisfied or discharged, or (*d*) which signifies or imports any such acknowledgment, and whether the same is or is not signed with the name of any person.


- **Accountable receipt** p. 22.
- **Mate's receipt** p. 569.
- **Railway receipt** p. 724.
- **Ship receipt** p. 795.
- **Warehouse receipt** p. 892.


**Receivable.** That which is due and owing a person. In book-keeping the name of an account which reflects a debt due.

The words 'receivable' and 'payable' are the same thing. 'Receivable' may also be construed as received.

**Receiver.** Acceptor; assignee; benefactor; collector; consignee; recipient.

A custodian of assets involved in litigation and title to assets remain in owner or owners who are parties in proceedings which lead to appointment of receiver who is managing agent of property for benefit of parties. [*A.S.S. Wrecking Co.* v *Guaranty Bank & Trust Co.* 275 NE 2d 724, 728].

"A receiver means a person who receives rents or other income, paying ascertained outgoings; but he does not manage the property in the sense of buying and selling or anything of that kind. ... The receiver merely takes the income and pays necessary outgoings; the manager carries on the trade or business." [*Re Manchester & Milford Railway* 14 Ch D 652, 653, *per* Jessel, M.R.].

A receiver is a person appointed for the collection or protection of property. He is appointed either by the court or out of court by individuals or corporations. In the former case he is an officer of the court deriving his authority from the court's order. In the latter case he is an agent and has such powers, duties and liabilities as are defined by the instrument or statute under which he is appointed and derive from the general law of agency. [Halsbury's *Laws of England*, 3rd Ed., vol. 32, p. 380].

▸ *Meaning under the Code of Civil Procedure 1908, Or. 40, r. 1.* Receiver is a person appointed by the court for collection of rents and profits of, preservation of and improvement of the property in dispute.


- **Official receiver** p. 623.


**Receptacle.** That in which anything is or may be received or stored. [*Bisheshwar Ram Rajwar* v *State of Bihar* 1976 Pat LJR 60].

**Recess.** As noun means break; cessation; halt; interlude; intermission; interval; intervening period; pause; spell; stoppage.

As verb means to adjourn; interrupt; postpone; prorogue; take time out.

A short interval or period of time during which the court suspends business, but without adjourning; the interval, in legislative practice, occurring in consequence of an adjournment, between the sessions of the same continuous legislative body.

The period between the prorogation of Parliament and its re-assembly in a new session. [May's *Parliamentary Practice*].

**Recession.** A temporary setback or slowdown in the economic growth of a nation. It is less severe than a depression.

**Reciprocal promises.** Mutual promises exchanged between two parties.

Promises which form the consideration or part of the consideration for each other are called reciprocal promises. [Indian Contract Act 1872, s. 2(*f*)].

When a contract consists of reciprocal promises to be simultaneously performed, no promisor need perform his promise unless the promisee is ready and willing to perform his reciprocal promise. [Indian Contract Act 1872, s. 51]. Where the order in which reciprocal promises are to be performed is expressly fixed by the contract, they shall be performed in that order; and, where the order is not expressly fixed by the contract, they shall be performed in that order which the nature of the transaction requires. [Section 52, *ibid*]. When one party to a contract containing reciprocal promises prevents the other from performing his promise, the contract becomes voidable at the option of the party so prevented. [Section 53, *ibid*]. When a contract consists of reciprocal promises, such that one of them cannot be performed till the other has been performed, and the promisor of the promise last mentioned fails to perform it, such promisor cannot claim the performance of the reciprocal promise, and must make compensation to the other party for any loss which such other party may sustain by the non-performance of the contract. [Section 54, *ibid*].

**Reciprocate.** Give in return; give and take; act interchangeably; follow successively; interchange; respond; retaliate.

**Reciprocity.** Concord; co-operation; give and take; interchange; interplay; mutuality.

To constitute a binding contract between the parties, there must be reciprocity of assent between them, that is, there must be an assent on the part of each to the contract.

In the sphere of international law, reciprocity denotes that in war one belligerent in its treatment of the person and property of the enemy is guided by the conduct in the like circumstances of the other belligerent; thus if one belligerent releases, on parole, prisoners of war, the other does the same.

The term also denotes the relation existing between two States when each of them gives the subjects of the other certain privileges, on condition that its own subjects shall enjoy similar privileges at the hands of the other State.

**Recital.** Account; depiction; narration; discourse; description.

The formal setting forth or statement of some matter of fact, in any deed or writing, in order to explain the reasons upon which the transaction is founded.

Recitals in a deed are statements which are introductory to, or which are a narrative of what has led up to the necessity of desirability or executing the deed or document. Usually, they open with the word 'whereas'. [Odgers, *Construction of Deeds and Statutes* (1968), 1996 reprint, p. 149]. In conveyancing, sometimes the recitals may detail a long history of title to land. At other times, a recital may be 'a preliminary statement of what the maker of the deed intended should be the effect and purpose of the whole deed, when made.' [*Mackenzie* v *Duke of Devonshire* (1869) AC 400 (HL)].

NOTE: Recitals are generally divided into narrative recitals which set forth the facts on which the instrument is based, and introductory recitals which explain the motive for the operative part. Where the recitals are clear and the operative part is ambiguous, the recital governs the construction. Normally, a recital is evidence as against the parties to the instrument and those claiming under them and in an action on the instrument itself, the recitals operate as an estoppel, though would not be so on a collateral matter. [*Ram Charan Das* v *Girja Nandini Devi* AIR 1966 SC 323: (1966)1 SCJ 61: (1965)1 SCWR 837].

**Reckless.** Careless; disregardful; heedless; impulsive; inattentive; indiscreet; insensible; irresponsible; mindless; thoughtless; uncircumspect; unheeding; unmindful; wanton; wild; not recking; indifferent to consequences.

Gross carelessness; a high degree of carelessness. [*Shawinigon Ltd.* v *Vokins & Co. Ltd.* (1961)3 All ER 396].

"Reck" is an absolute word meaning "heed", "concern" or "care". [*R.* v *Bates* (1952)2 All ER 842, 845]. Hence "reckless" means "careless without dishonesty", and suggests an indifference to risk.

NOTE: For conduct to be 'reckless', it must be such as to evince disregard of, or indifference to, consequences under circumstances involving danger to life or safety to others, although no harm was intended. [*Duckers* v *Lynch* 465 P 2d 945, 948].

**Reclamation.** In case of unarable land, 'reclamation' means rendering it fit for cultivation by physically changing it, *e.g.*, draining a swamp, irrigating desert.

In case of submerged or overflowed land, 'reclamation' means the rescuing of it from being submerged.

**Recognition.** An acknowledgment that something done by another person in one's name has one's authority; ratification; confirmation; admission; appreciation; approval; cognizance; gratitude; identification; perception.

NOTE: Mere inaction is no recognition. [*T.V.V. Warsimbham* v *State of Orissa* AIR 1963 SC 1227: 1963 SCC 263: 1963 Supp (1) SCR 750].

**Recognizance.** Acknowledgment; assurance; bond; commitment; guaranty; promise; security; warranty; surety.

An obligation entered into before a court or magistrate duly authorized for that purpose whereby the recognizor acknowledges that he will do some act required by law which is specified therein. The act of recognizing is performed by the recognizor's assenting to the words of the magistrate and acknowledging himself to be indebted to a certain party in a specific amount to be paid if he fails to perform the requisite act. [*State* v *Vinal* 325 A 2d 81, 83].

"A recognizance is a writing acknowledged by the party to it before a judge or office having authority for the purpose, and enrolled in a court of record. It usually takes the form of a promise, with penalties for the breach of it, to keep the peace, to be of good behaviour, or to appear at the assizes." [William R. Anson: *Principles of the Law of Contract*, pp. 80-81 (Arthur L. Corbin ed., 3d Am. ed. 1919)].

A bond executed by a person undertaking to perform some act or observe some conditions, e.g., to appear when called on or to keep the peace. [Code of Criminal Procedure 1973, ss. 106 and 360].

**Recognized agent.** Recognized agents of parties by whom appearances, applications and acts may be made or done are—(*a*) persons holding powers of attorney, authorising them to make and do such appearances, applications and acts on behalf of such parties; (*b*) persons carrying on trade or business for and in the names of parties not resident within the local limits of the jurisdiction of the court within which limits the appearance, application or act is made or done, in matters connected with such trade or business only, where no other agent is expressly authorized to make and do such appearances, applications and acts. [Code of Civil Procedure 1908, Or. 3, r. 2].

**Recommend.** Acclaim; advance; applaud; approbate; approve; commend; endorse; exalt; laud; give credit; glorify; lend approval; lend support; praise; prescribe; present as worthy; speak highly of.

To advise or counsel [*Kirby* v *Nolte* 173 SW 2d 391]; to praise or commend [*V.M. Kurian* v *State of Kerala* AIR 2001 SC 1409: JT 2001(4) SC 220: (2001)4 SCC 215].

In the matter of employment, it means "suggest as fit for employment". [*A. Pandurangam Rao* v *State of Andhra*

*Pradesh* AIR 1975 SC 1922: (1976)1 SCR 620: (1975)4 SCC 709: 1975(2) SLR 582].

**Recommendation.** Advocation; approbation; commendation; endorsement; exhortation; laudation; prescription; reference; testimonial.

The act of one person in giving to another a favourable account of the character, responsibility, or skill of a third. [Black's *Law Dictionary*, 5th Ed.].

A statement expressing commendation or a message of this nature. [*V.M. Kurian* v *State of Kerala* AIR 2001 SC 1409: JT 2001(4) SC 220: (2001)4 SCC 215].

NOTE: Recommendation refers to an action which is advisory in nature rather than one having any binding effect. [*People* v *Gates* 41 CA 3d 590].

*"Recommendation" and "prescription" of a text book—distinction.* When a text book is prescribed by an appropriate authority having legal power to do so, it has to be followed by the schools. Prescription of a text book carries with it a binding obligation to follow the text book. There is no such obligation when a text book is merely recommended. Recommendation has merely a persuasive effect, it being open to the schools to accept the recommendation or to reject it as they think fit. [*Naraindas Indurkhya* v *State of Madhya Pradesh* AIR 1974 SC 1232: (1974)4 SCC 788: (1974)3 SCR 624].

**Reconstitute.** 'Reconstitute', according to its plain natural connotation, means nothing else than 'constitute again'. [*G.V. Gunayya Chetty* v *V. Desarathamaiah* AIR 1975 SC 1277: (1975)2 SCC 114: 1975 (Supp) SCR 219].

**Reconversion.** Change over; readjustment; rebirth; regeneration; restoration.

It may also mean the notional or imaginary process by which an earlier constructive conversion is annulled and taken away, and the converted property restored to its original quality/character. [Black's *Law Dictionary*, 7th & 8th Eds.].

NOTE: On "reconversion" to Hinduism, a person can once again become a member of the caste in which he was born and to which he belonged before conversion to another religion, if the members of the caste accept him as a member. [*C.M. Arumugam* v *S. Rajgopal* AIR 1976 SC 939: (1976)3 SCR 82: (1976)1 SCC 863].

**Reconveyance.** The restoration or return of something especially an estate or title to a former owner or holder. [Black's *Law Dictionary*, 7th & 8th Eds.].

A reconveyance is the document which a mortgagor (of an English mortgage) takes from the mortgagee when he pays off the mortgage.

**Record.** As noun means account; archive; documentation; dossier; entry; evidence; file; history; note; memorandum; written material.

As noun also means a documentary account of past events, usually designed to memorialise those events; information that is inscribed on a tangible medium or that, having been stored in an electronic or other medium, is retrievable in perceivable form; the official report of the proceedings in a case, including filed papers, a verbatim transcript of the trial or hearing (if any), and tangible exhibits. [Black's *Law Dictionary*, 8th Ed.].

As noun, it is held to mean a written account of some act, court proceeding, transaction, or instrument, drawn up, under authority of law, by a proper officer, and designed to remain as a memorial or permanent evidence of the matters to which it relates [*People ex rel. Simons* v *Dowling* 146 NYS 919, 920]; a memorandum, public or private, of what has been done, ordinarily applied to public records, in which sense it is a written memorial made by a public officer [*Nogueira* v *State* 59 SW 2d 831]; a formal writing of any act or proceeding, and anything entered in the rolls of a court. [*Superintendent and Remembrancer* v *Sardar Bahadur Singh* AIR 1969 Cal 451].

In a fiscal statute, it refers not only to the order of assessment but comprises all proceedings on which the assessment order is based. [*Maharana Mills (P) Ltd.* v *The I.T.O., Porbandar* AIR 1959 SC 881: 1959 Supp (2) SCR 547: (1959)36 ITR 350].

As verb means to historify; historise; inscribe; jot down; keep accounts; list, log; make a memorandum; make a note; make an entry; put in writing; to write, transcribe, or enter in a book, file, docket, register, computer tape or disc, or the like, for the purpose of preserving authentic evidence of.

As verb it is meant to transcribe a document, or enter the history of an act or series of acts, in an official volume, for the purpose of giving notice of the same, of furnishing authentic evidence, and for preservation. [*Shimmel* v *People* 121 P 2d 491, 493].

The word 'record' may also mean 'any disc, tape, performed roll or other device in which sounds are embodied so as to be capable of being reproduced therefrom, other than a sound track associated with a cinematograph film'. [Copyright Act 1957, s. 2(*w*) (as existing before omission on 10.5.1995)].


- **Court of record** p. 203.
- **Error apparent on the face of the record** p. 315.
- **Error of law apparent on the face of record** p. 315.
- **Estoppel of record** p. 321.
- **Matter of record** p. 570.
- **Mistake apparent on the record** p. 587.
- **Official record** p. 623.


**Recording.** The aggregate of the sounds embodied in and capable of being reproduced by means of a record. [Copyright Act 1957, s. 2(*x*) (as existing before substitution on 10.5.1995)].

**Recourse.** The act of seeking help or advice; enforcement of, or a method for enforcing, a right; the right of a holder of a negotiable instrument to demand payment from the drawer or indorser if the instrument is dishonoured; the right to repayment of a loan from the borrower's personal assets, not just from the collateral that secured the loan. [Black's *Law Dictionary*, 7th & 8th Eds.].

**Recruitment.** 'Recruitment', according to the dictionary, means 'enlist'. It is a comprehensive term and includes any method provided for inducing a person in public service. [*K. Narayanan* v *State of Karnataka* 1993(5) SLR 290: AIR 1994 SC 55: 1994 Supp (1) SCC 44: JT 1995(5) SC 102].

The term 'recruitment' connotes and clearly signifies enlistment, acceptance, selection or approval for appointment. [*Prafulla Kumar Swain* v *Prakash Chandra Misra* 1993 Supp (3) SCC 181: 1993(1) SLR 565: JT 1993(1) SC 360].

The word 'recruitment' is comprehensive enough to embrace the content of all the rules including the fitment of candidates recruited to the service vis-a-vis each other. [*Ashoke Kumar* v *Union of India* (1982)1 SCC 497: AIR 1982 SC 795].

NOTE: *'Recruitment' and 'appointment'—distinction.* The words 'recruitment' and 'appointment' are not synonymous and connote different meanings. Recruitment connotes and signifies enlistment, acceptance, selection or approval for appointment and not actual appointment or posting in service. Appointment means an act of posting a person to a particular office. [*Basant Lal* v *State* AIR 1969 Punj 178: ILR (1969)2 Punj 292].

Recruitment is just the initial process which may eventually lead to an appointment. Recruitment and appointment are, thus, two separate concepts and are not synonymous. [*Gurdev Singh Gill* v *State of Punjab* 1968 SLR 538: ILR (1969)1 Punj 231].

The term 'recruitment' connotes and clearly signifies enlistment, acceptance, selection or approval for appointment. Certainly, this is not actual appointment or posting in service. In contradistinction, the word 'appointment' means an actual act of posting a person to a particular office. [*Prafulla Kumar Swain* v *Prakash Chandra Misra* JT 1993(1) SC 360: 1993(1) SLR 565: 1993 SCC (L&S) 960: 1993 Supp (3) SCC 181].

**Rectification.** The act or process by which something is made right or by which a wrong is adjusted.

'Rectification' implies the correctness of an error or removal of defects or imperfections. It implies prior existence of error, mistake or defect, which after rectification is made right, and corrected by removal of the flaws. [*Benarsi Dass*

*Saraf* v *Dalmia Dadri Cement Ltd.* AIR 1959 Punj 232].

NOTE: The essence of rectification is to bring document which was expressed and intended to be in pursuance of a prior agreement, into harmony with that of a prior agreement. Indeed, it may be regarded as a branch of the doctrine of specific performance. It presupposes a prior contract, and it requires proof that, by common mistake, the final completed instrument as executed fails to give proper effect to the prior contract. [*Lovell & Christmas Ltd.* v *Wall* (1911)104 LT 85].

**Reddendum.** A clause in a lease reserving rent payable and whereby the lessor retains some new thing to himself out of that which is demised. It is generally placed after the habendum and is usually expressed by the opening words 'yielding and paying'.

**Redemption.** Deliverance; indemnification; reclamation; recovery; reparation; restoration; retrieval; return; salvation.

'Redemption' is the act of redeeming, which, in its ordinary meaning is equal to bringing off a charge or obligation by payment. [*Srish Chandra* v *CLT* AIR 1961 SC 487: (1961)1 SCJ 495].

The word 'redemption' is defined as the liberation of an estate from a mortgage. [*Webb* v *Williamson* 152 SW 2d 312, 314].


- **Clog on equity of redemption** p. 148.
- **Equity of redemption** p. 314.


**Redemption yield.** The yield to maturity on a redeemable stock, that is to say, the flat yield from interest, plus the net capital gain on maturity, expressed as a composite annual yield.

**Reductio ad absurdum**. The method of improving an argument by showing that it leads to an absurd conclusion.

**Refer to drawer.** A statement by the bank, 'we are not paying; go back to the drawer and ask why' or else 'go back to the drawer and ask to pay'. [*Plunkett* v *Barclays Bank Ltd.* (1936)2 KB 107].

**Reference.** It means attribution; clue; connotation; hint; implied indication; imputation; incidental mention; indication; inference; innuendo; insinuation; subtle communication.

It may also mean ascription; authority; enumeration; documentation; pointing out; referment; relating; substantiation; source material.

It may further mean affirmation; attestation; attesting declaration; authenticated confirmation; averment; avouchment; commendation; certification; confirmation; endorsement; laudation; letter in support; letter of introduction; letter of recommendation; testification; testimony.

The act of sending or directing to another for information, service, consideration, or decision; specifically the act of sending a case to a master or referee for information or decision. [Black's *Law Dictionary*, 8th Ed.].

**Referendum.** Election; expression of choice; plebiscite; popular choice; popular decision; popular vote; ballot; mandate.

The process of referring a state legislative act, a state constitutional amendment, or an important public issue to the people for final approval by popular vote; a vote taken by this method. [Black's *Law Dictionary*, 8th Ed.].

Reservation by people of state, or local subdivision thereof, of right to have submitted for their approval or rejection, under prescribed conditions, any law or part of law passed by law making body. [*Anne Arundel County* v *McDonough* 354 A 2d 788, 796].

In international law, it means an ambassador's request for instructions on subject matter that the ambassador does not have sufficient power to address. [Black's *Law Dictionary*, 8th Ed.].

**Reflation.** Inflation after deflation.

**Reform.** As noun means alteration; amelioration; amendment; betterment; change; correction; development; elevation; enhancement; enrichment; improvement; progression; reclamation; reconstitution; reconstruction; recreation; rectification; refinement; reformation; regeneration; remaking; renewal; renovation; revision.

As verb it means ameliorate; amend; correct; change; form anew; improve; make better; modify; rearrange; recast; reconstitute; reconstruct; rectify; reshape; refashion; refine; regenerate; remake; remodel; reorganize; revolutionize.

**Refuge.** Asylum; hiding place; place of protection; place of safety; shelter.

**Refugee.** A person who flees or is expelled from a country, especially because of persecution, and seeks haven in another country. [Black's *Law Dictionary*, 8th Ed.].

**Refund.** The money returned to a person who overpaid; to return money in restitution or repayment, to repay or restore.

That which is refunded. [*United States* v *Wurts* 82 L Ed 932].

**Refusal.** The denial or rejection of something offered or demanded; the declination of a request or demand, or the omission to comply with some requirement of law, as the result of a positive intention to disobey.

"Refusal" implies the positive denial of an application or command, or at least a mental determination not to comply. A rejection, a denial of what is asked. [*Board of Public Institution of Palm Beach County, Fla.* v *Cohen* CA Fla, 413 F 2d 1201, 1203].

**Refusal to act.** 'Refusal to act' in legal sense means denial to do something which one is obliged to do under law. [*State of West Bengal* v *National Builders* (1993)3 SCJ 634: JT 1993(5) SC 144: AIR 1994 SC 200: (1994)1 SCC 235].

**Register of members of a company.** It is a register maintained by every company wherein the following particulars are entered: (*a*) the name and address, and the occupation, if any, of each member, (*b*) in the case of a company having a share capital, the shares held by each member, distinguishing each share by its number, except where such shares are held with a depository and the amount paid or agreed to be considered as paid on those shares, (*c*) the date at which each person was entered in the register as a member, and (*d*) the date at which any person ceased to be a member. [Companies Act 1956, s. 150].

**Regular.** Periodic; periodical; rhythmic; symmetrical; systematic; uniform.

"Regular" means a consistent course of conduct without any break or breach. [*Raj Kanta (Mrs.)* v *Financial Commissioner, Punjab* AIR 1980 SC 1464: (1980)3 SCR 1006: (1980)3 SCC 589].

**Regular employees.** The expression "regular employees" normally means *bona fide* employees. [*Deepak Sibal* v *Punjab University* AIR 1989 SC 903: (1989)2 SCC 145: JT 1989 (Supp) SC 2: (1989)1 SCR 689: 1989(3) SLR 717].

**Regular payment of rent.** The words 'regular payment of rent' mean that the rent should be paid punctually without any default or laxity. [*Mrs. Raj Kanta* v *The Financial Commissioner, Punjab* AIR 1980 SC 1464: (1980)3 SCR 1006: (1980)3 SCC 589].

**Regularly.** Affixed at certain intervals; regular in point of time; in accordance with some consistent or periodical rule or practice.

The word "regularly" characterises reasonable punctuality, that is to say, one made at regular times or intervals. [*Mranalini B. Shah* v *Bapalal Mohanlal Shah* AIR 1980 SC 954: (1980)4 SCC 251].

The word "regularly" connotes a consistent course of conduct without any break or breach. [*Mrs. Raj Kanta* v *The Financial Commissioner, Punjab* AIR 1980 SC 1464: (1980)3 SCR 1006: (1980)3 SCC 589].

**Regulate.** Balance; coordinate; make uniform; methodize; modulate; put in order; reduce to method; standardise; restore; equilibrium; to administer, conduct, control, determine; govern; preside over; to fix, establish, or control; to adjust by rule, method, or established mode; to direct by rule or restriction; to subject to governing principles or laws.

The word 'regulate' has different shades of meaning and must take its colour from the context in which it is used having regard to the purpose and object of the relevant provisions. [*Jiyajeerao Cotton Mills Ltd.* v *M.P. Electricity Board* JT

1988(4) SC 737: (1988)3 Comp LJ 197: AIR 1989 SC 788: 1989 Supp (2) SCC 52: 1989 Supp (2) SCR 978].

The word 'regulate' means to control, govern, or direct by rule or regulations, to subject to guidance or restrictions, to adapt to circumstances or surroundings. [*Himat Lal K. Shah* v *Commissioner of Police, Ahmedabad* AIR 1973 SC 87: (1973)2 SCR 266: (1973)1 SCC 227: 1973 Cr LJ 204: 1973 SCC (Cri) 280; *Sujatha Touring Talkies* v *State* AIR 1986 Kant 21].

The dictionary meaning of the word 'regulate' is to adjust, to govern or manage, according to certain standard of law, rules, restrictions or governing principles. [*Alluminium Corporation of India Ltd.* v *Coal Board* (1953)61 CWN 55].

Regulate means to govern or direct according to rule or to bring under control of constituted authority, to limit and prohibit, to arrange in proper order, and to control that which already exists. [*Farmington River Co.* v *Town Plan and Zoning Commission of Town of Farmington* 197 A 2d 653, 660].

NOTE: The element of restriction is implicit in the expression "regulate". The word "regulate" is a word of broad import having wide meaning comprehending all facets not only specifically enumerated in the Acts but also embrace within its fold the power incidental to regulation envisaged in good faith in the interest of general public. [*Sujatha Touring Talkies* v *State of Karnataka* AIR 1986 Kant 21: ILR (1985) Kant 2477 (FB)].

**Regulation.** The act of regulating; a rule or order prescribed for management or government; a regulating principle; rule of order prescribed by superior or competent authority relating to action of those under its control.

Regulation ordinarily means prescription of rules for control of conduct. [*Municipal Commissioner* v *Haji Ismail* ILR (1966)1 Punj 481: AIR 1967 Punj 32].

The word 'regulation' has to be read in the context in which it has been used and not *de hors* the context. In *Corpus Juris Secundum* (Vol. 76, p. 615) the word "regulation" has been defined as a rule or order prescribed for management or governance. [*Saurashtra Cement and Chemical Industries* v *Union of India* JT 2000 Supp (3) SC 160: (2000)7 SLT 612: AIR 2001 SC 8: (2001)1 SCC 91].

Regulation is rule or order having force of law issued by executive authority of government. [*State ex rel. Villines* v *Freeman* Okl, 370 P 2d 307, 309].

NOTE: The word 'regulation' cannot have any inflexible meaning as to exclude 'prohibition'. It has different shades of meaning and must take its colour from the context in which it is used having regard to the purpose and object of the legislation. [*K. Ramanathan* v *State of Tamil Nadu* AIR 1985 SC 660: (1985)2 SCR 1028: 1985 SCC (Cri) 162: (1985)2 SCC 116].

**Rehan.** Mortgage, pledge, pawn.

**Reimburse.** Indemnify; make good; make reparation; make restitution; pay back; recompense; repay.

**Reimbursement.** Indemnification; paying back; giving back; recompense; refund; reparation; repayment; replacement; restitution; restoration.

NOTE: *'Reimbursement' and 'contribution'—distinction.* Reimbursement is out from and in contrast to contribution. Contribution is between persons equally bound to pay, e.g., co-judgment-debtors; while reimbursement is between a person interested in a payment and a person bound to make the payment. [*Nandlal Singh* v *Ram Kirit Singh* AIR 1950 Pat 212].

**Reinstate.** Bring back; place in a former state; put back into service; reshape; rehabilitate; reinstall; restore to office.

To place in the same position as before; to restore to the previous position or state. [*Nirmala Gehlot* v *Director of Pri. & Sec. Education* 1982 Raj LR 745].

Reinstatement involves putting the specified person back, in law and in fact, in the same position as he occupied in the undertaking before the employer terminated his employment. [*Hodge* v *Ultra Electric Ltd.* (1943)1 KB 462].

To reinstate a man is to replace him in the position from which he was dismissed and so to restore *status quo ante* the dismissal. [*William Dixon Ltd.* v *Patterson* 1943 SC (J) 78].

NOTE: Reinstatement can only arise where a man has been dismissed or removed from service or his service is terminated, and he is brought back to service. It does not apply where a person is merely suspended. [*H.K. Bhattacharjee* v *Union of India* AIR 1958 Cal 239].

**Reinsurance.** Reinsurance is a contract whereby one party called the "reinsurer" in consideration of a premium paid to him, agrees to indemnify the other against the risk assumed by the latter by a policy in favour of a third party.

'Reinsurance' is defined as an agreement to indemnify the assured, partially or altogether, against a risk assumed by it in policy issued to third party. [*Great American Ins. Co.* v *Fireman's Fund Ins. Co.* CANY, 481 F 2d 948, 950].

It is defined as a contract that one insurer makes with another to protect the first insurer from a risk he has already assumed. [*McDonough Const. Corp.* v *Pan Am. Sur. Co.* Fla App, 190 So 2d 617, 619].

**Relating to.** Connecting to; in relation to.

The words 'relating to' are words of comprehensiveness which might both have a direct as well as an indirect significance depending on the context. They are not words of restrictive content and ought not to be so construed. [*State Wakf Board* v *Abdul Azeez Sahib* AIR 1968 Mad 79].

**Relation.** A relative or kinsman; a person connected by consanguinity; blood tie; common ancestry; common descent; common lineage; a person connected with another by blood or affinity. [*Liprie* v *Michigan Millers Mut. Ins. Co.* La App, 143 So 2d 597, 600].

• **Fiduciary relation** p. 352.

**Relative.** A kinsman; a person connected with another by blood or affinity.

The word 'relative', when used generically, includes persons connected by ties of affinity as well as consanguinity, and, when used with a restrictive meaning, refers to those only who are connected by blood.

**Relator action.** A relator action is an action brought by the Attorney-General in England at the relation (*i.e.* at the instance) of some other persons. By this device it is possible for a private person to set in motion for his own purposes a form of action which really exists for the benefit of the Crown. It is a procedure leading to other remedies, usually an injunction or a declaration.

NOTE: In India, ss. 91 and 92 of the Code of Civil Procedure 1908 govern public nuisance and public charities in respect of this. The Advocate-General or two or more persons having secured his written consent may institute a suit.

**Release.** Abandonment of claim to party against whom it exists, and is a surrender of a cause of action and may be gratuitous or for consideration. [*Melo* v *National Fuse and Powder Co.* DC Colo, 267 F Supp 611, 612].

Giving up or abandoning of claim or right to person against whom claim exists or against whom right is to be exercised. [*Adder* v *Holman & Moody* Inc, 219 SE 2d 190, 195].

It may also mean liberation; discharge, or setting free from restraint or confinement. The act of releasing, liberating, or freeing from restraint, confinement, or servitude; the state of being released; liberation; to set or make free; to liberate from pain, bondage, obligation, etc. [*Parshottam Soma* v *State of Gujarat* 1972 Guj LR 585].

**Relevant.** Applying to the matter in question; affording something to the purpose; bearing on or having reference to the matter in hand; tending to prove or disprove the matters in issue.

• **Facts relevant to the issue.** Facts relevant to the issue, which are sometimes called evidentiary facts, are facts which render probable the existence or non-existence of a fact in issue or some relevant fact. Evidence is relevant if it is logically probative or disprobative of some matter which requires proof. [*R.* v *Kilbourne* (1973) AC 729, 756].

One fact is said to be relevant to another when one is connected with the other in any of the ways referred to in the provisions of this Act relating to the relevancy of facts. [Indian Evidence Act 1872, s. 3].

**Relief.** The public or private assistance or support, pecuniary or otherwise, granted to indigent persons.

It may have another meaning that is deliverance from oppression, wrong or injustice. In this sense, it is used as a general designation of the assistance, redress, or benefit which a complainant seeks at the hands of a court.


- **Consequential relief** p. 174.
- **Further relief** p. 379.
- **Preventive relief** p. 683.


**Religion.** 'Religion' is defined as man's relation to divinity, to reverence, worship, obedience, and submission to mandates and precepts of supernatural or superior beings. In its broadest sense, religion includes all forms of belief in the existence of superior beings exercising power over human beings by volition, imposing rules of conduct, with future rewards and punishments. [Black's *Law Dictionary*, 5th Ed.].

'Religion is the belief which binds spiritual nature of men to supernatural being'. It includes worship, belief, faith, devotion etc. and extends to rituals. [*Most Rev. P.M.A. Metropolitan* v *Moran Mar Marthoma* AIR 1995 SC 2001: 1995 Supp (4) SCC 286: JT 1995(5) SC 1].

"Religion" is that which binds a man with his Cosmos, his Creator or super force. Essentially, religion is a matter of personal faith and belief of personal relations of an individual with what he regards as Cosmos, his Maker or his Creator which, he believes, regulates the existence of insentient beings and the force of the universe. Religion is not necessarily theistic. [*A.S. Narayana Deekshitulu* v *State of A.P.* AIR 1996 SC 1765: (1996)9 SCC 548].

NOTE: Religion is a matter of faith with individuals or communities and it is not necessarily theistic. There are well-known religions in India, like Buddhism and Jainism, which do not believe in God or in any intelligent first cause. A religion undoubtedly has its basis in a system of beliefs or doctrines which are regarded by those who profess that religion as conducive to their spiritual well-being, but it will not be correct to say that religion is nothing else but a doctrine or belief. A religion may not only lay down a code of ethical rules for its followers to accept, but it might prescribe rituals and observances, ceremonies and modes of worship which are regarded as integral parts of a religion, and these forms and observances might extend even to matters of food and dress. [*Commissioner of Hindu Religious and Charitable Endowments, Madras* v *Sri Lakshmindra Thirtha Swamiar* 1954 SCJ 335: AIR 1954 SC 282; *Ratilal Panachand Gandhi* v *State of Bombay* 1954 SCJ 480: 1954 SCA 538: AIR 1954 SC 388].

'Religion' is more than mere matter of faith. [*Smt. Sarla Mudgal, President, Kalyani* v *Union of India* JT 1995(4) SC 331, 347].

The expression 'religion' includes not only the philosophical side of religion, but also religious practices as laid down in the tenets of any religious sect. [*Ram Chandra Devi* v *State of Orissa* AIR 1959 Ori 5].

The term 'religion', whatever be its best definition, clearly refers to certain characteristic types of data (beliefs, practices, feelings, moods, attitudes, etc.). It primarily involves some immediate consciousness of transcendent realities of supreme personal worth vitally influencing life and thought, expressing themselves in forms which are conditioned by the entire stage of development reached by the individual and his environments and tending to become more explicit and static in mythologies, theologies, philosophies and scientific doctrines. [*Ramanasraman* v *Commissioner for Hindu Religious and Charitable Endowments* AIR 1961 Mad 265].

**Religious denomination.** The words "religious denomination" must take their colour from the word "religion" and if this be so, the expression religious denomination must satisfy three conditions: (1) it must be a collection of individuals who have a system of beliefs or doctrines which they regard as conducive to their spiritual well-being, that is a common faith; (2) common organisation; (3) designation by a distinctive name. [*Jagdishwaranand* v *Police Commissioner, Calcutta* AIR 1984 SC 51: 1983 Cr LJ 1872; *Mahadev Kr. Bannerjee* v *State of W.B.* 88 CWN 564, 581].

'Religious denomination' means a religious sect or body having a common faith and organisation and designated by a distinctive name. [*S.P. Mittal* v *Union of India* AIR 1983 SC 1: (1983)1 SCC 51: (1983)1 SCR 729].

**Religious feeling.** 'Religious feeling' means nothing more or less than feeling associated with a person's religious ideas. [*Kitav Ali, Munshi* v *Santi Ranjan Deb* AIR 1965 Tripura 22].

**Religious right.** 'Religious right' is a right of a person believing in a particular faith to practise it, preach it and profess it, it is civil in nature. [*Most Rev. P.M.A. Metropolitan* v *Moran Mar Marthoma* AIR 1995 SC 2001: 1995 Supp (4) SCC 286: JT 1995(5) SC 1].

**Remainder.** Residual estate; reversionary estate; surplus; balance; left over; residuals; residue.

A future interest arising in third person—that is, someone other than the creator of the estate or the creator's heirs—who is intended to take after the natural termination of the preceding estate. [Black's *Law Dictionary*, 7th Ed.].

A future interest arising in a third person—that is, someone other than the estate's creator; its initial holder, or the heirs of either—who is intended to take after the natural termination of the preceding estate. [Black's *Law Dictionary*, 8th Ed.].

A future interest created in some person other than the grantor or transferor. [*Folden* v *Folden* Ohio App, 188 NE 2d 193, 194].

A remainder is an interest granted to a person in succession to a prior interest granted to another person; as in a grant 'to *A* for life and then to *B*' the estate granted to *B* is a remainder. A remainder may be either vested or contingent.

• **Contingent remainder** p. 186.

**Remainder man.** A person entitled to an estate in remainder. Thus, if land be conveyed to *A* for life, and after his death to *B*, *B* is the remainder man.

**Remand.** Command back; order back; reinstitutionalise; restore; return.

The act or an instance of sending something (such as a case, claim or person) back for further action. [Black's *Law Dictionary*, 8th Ed.].

The sending by the appellate court of the cause back to the same court out of which it came, for purpose of having some further action taken on it there. [*Amalgamated Workers Union of Virgin Islands* v *Hess Oil Virgin Islands Corp.* CA Virgin Islands, 478 F 2d 540, 543].

**Remedial.** Affording a remedy; intended to remedy wrongs, abuses, and defects, abate faults; of or relating to a means of enforcing and existing substantive right.

**Remedial action.** An action which is brought to obtain compensation or indemnity. [*Cummings* v *Board of Education of Oklahoma City* 125 P 2d 989, 994].

**Remedial statute.** A remedial statute is one made from time to time to remove defects in the existing law, arising from the inevitable imperfection of legislation, mistake, or other cause.

NOTE: The words of a remedial statute are to be construed largely and beneficially so as to suppress the mischief sought to be remedied and advance the remedy.

**Remedy.** As noun means alleviation; amelioration; corrective measure; reparative measure; solution; antidote; relief. The means of enforcing a right or preventing or redressing a wrong; legal or equitable relief. [Black's *Law Dictionary*, 8th Ed.]. The means by which a right is enforced or the violation of a right is prevented, redressed, or compensated. [*Long Leaf Lumber, Inc.* v *Svolos* La App, 258 So 2d 121, 124].

As verb means alleviate; cure; make amends; heal; redress; set right; work a cure.

• **Civil remedy** p. 146.

**Remission.** Alleviation; assuagement; diminution; discontinuance; exculpation; exoneration; reduction; forgiveness; relaxation; suspension.

A cancellation or extinguishment of all or part of a financial obligation; a release of a debt or claim; a pardon granted for an offence; relief from a forfeiture or penalty; a diminution or abatement of the symptoms of a disease. [Black's *Law Dictionary*, 8th Ed.].

NOTE: A remission of punishment while assumes the correctness of the conviction, only reduces the punishment in part or in whole. An order of remission does not wipe out the offence, nor does it wipe out the conviction. It has only an effect on the execution of the sentence. And this is not the same thing as the order of an appellate or revisional court reducing the sentence of the trial court and substituting for it the reduced sentence. In law the order of remission merely means that the rest of the sentence need not be undergone, leaving the order of conviction by the court and the sentence passed by it untouched. [*Sarat Chandra* v *Khagendranath* (1961)2 SCR 133].

**Remote damages.** Damages not resulting directly from the breach of contract.

**Removal.** In a broad sense, it means the transfer of a person or thing from one place to another.

The word 'removal' contemplates shifting of a thing from one place to another. In excise law, it contemplates physical movement of goods from one place to another. [*J.K. Cotton Spinning and Weaving Mills Ltd.* v *Union of India* 1987 (Supp) SCC 350: JT 1987(4) SC 421: (1987)32 ELT 234: (1988)68 STC 421: AIR 1988 SC 191: (1988)1 SCR 700].

**Removal from office.** It would mean taking off from the place occupied or getting rid of; to withdraw. [*Ramkrishna Gangaram Rathi* v *Kisan Zingrali Madke* AIR 1971 Bom 305].

NOTE: *'Dismissal' and 'removal' from service—distinction.* Removal and dismissal stand on the same footing except as to future employment. In this sense removal is but a species of dismissal. Dismissal disqualifies from future employment while removal does not. [*Shyamlal* v *State of U.P.* AIR 1954 SC 369].

In ordinary parlance, removal and dismissal appeared to be the equivalent of one another, whereas in future of the consequence that follows when a person is dismissed, a distinction has developed in the legal sense. [*Radhanath Rath* v *Sub-divisional Magistrate, Cuttack* 1977 Cut LR (Cr) 82].

Dismissal from service includes removal. [*Khem Chand* v *Union of India* AIR 1958 SC 300: 1958 SCR 1080: 1958 SCJ 497: 1958 SCA 228].

**Remove.** The dictionary meaning of the word 'remove' means 'to discharge, to get rid of; to dismiss'. [*Radhanath Rath* v *Sub-divisional Magistrate, Cuttack* 1977 Cut LR (Cr) 82].

**Remuneration.** Award; compensation; defrayment; indemnification; pay; payment; recompense; reimbursement; reward.

The word 'remuneration', though it includes 'wages', may mean payment, which, strictly speaking may not be called 'wages'. It is a term of much wider import including 'recompense', 'reward', 'payment' etc. [*Commissioner of Income Tax, West Bengal* v *Calcutta Stock Exchange Association Ltd.* AIR 1959 SC 763, 768].

'Remuneration' is only a mere formal version of payment. [*Bala Subrahmanya Rajaram* v *B.C. Patil* AIR 1958 SC 518: 1958 SCR 1504: 1958 SCJ 851].

▸ *Meaning under the Banking Act.* The word 'remuneration' must be given its meaning with reference to the context in which the word occurs in the statute. In the Banking Act, the word 'remuneration' has been used in the widest sense. In that sense, it undoubtedly includes bonus. [*The Central Bank of India* v *Their Workmen* AIR 1960 SC 12: (1960)1 SCR 200: 1960 SCJ 842].

▸ *Meaning under the Constitution of India, Art. 314 (since repealed).* The expression 'remuneration' in the Article is not used in any limited sense as merely salary.

If a man gives his services, whatever consideration he gets for getting his services is a remuneration for them. Consequently, if a person was not receipt of a payment, or in receipt of a percentage, or any kind of payment which would not pay actual money payment, the amount he would receive annually, in respect of this would be remuneration. [*Accountant-General, Bihar* v *N. Bakshi* AIR 1962 SC 505: (1962)2 SCJ 243: 1962 Supp (1) SCR 505].

**Renew.** To begin again; to repeat; to make again; to substitute new for; to restore, re-establish, set up again; to bring back into use or existence; to take up again or afresh; to bring again; to recommence; to replace by some new or fresh theme of the same kind; to restore by means of substitution or a fresh supply; to grant a new one, especially to grant or give for a fresh period. [*R.M. Mehta* v *H.P. F.M. Co. Ltd*. AIR 1976 Mad 194].

The word 'renew' means to acquire again. [*Jagjivan Hiralal Doshi* v *Registrar of Companies* (1989)2 Comp LJ 315 (Bom)].

**Renewal.** Giving new life to; rejuvenation; reanimation; regeneration; resurrection; revamping; revival of an expiring subject; revivification.

The act of restoring or re-establishing; the consideration of a question already disposed of; the re-creation of a legal relationship or the replacement of an old contract with a new contract, as opposed to the mere extension of a previous relationship or contract. [Black's *Law Dictionary*, 8th Ed.].

NOTE: The object of renewal is to prevent discontinuance or forfeiture. [*Gajraj Singh* v *State Transport Appellate Tribunal* JT 1996(8) SC 356: AIR 1997 SC 412: (1997)1 SCC 650].

**Renewal of a lease.** A renewal of a lease is the grant of a fresh lease. It is called "renewal" simply because it postulates the existence of a prior lease which generally provides for renewals as a right. In all other respects, it is really a fresh lease. [*Delhi Development Authority* v *Durga Chand Kaushish* AIR 1973 SC 2609: (1973)2 SCC 825: (1974)1 SCR 535].

NOTE: There is a distinction between a stipulation in a lease to renew it for an additional period and one to extend it, in that, a stipulation to renew requires the making of a new lease, while a stipulation to extend does not. [*R.M. Mehta* v *H.P. F.M. Co. Ltd*. AIR 1976 Mad 194]. In the case of extension the same lease continues in force during additional period by the performance of the stipulated act. [*Pravash Chandra Dalui* v *Biswanath Banerjee* AIR 1989 SC 1834: (1989)2 SCR 401: JT 1989 (Supp) SC 32: 1989 Supp (1) SCC 487].

**Renewal of a licence.** It means a new licence granted by way of renewal. [*Gajraj Singh* v *State Transport Appellate Tribunal* JT 1996(8) SC 356: AIR 1997 SC 412: (1997)1 SCC 650].

**Renewal of a negotiable bill or note.** The renewal of a negotiable bill or note is regarded simply as a prolongation of the original contract. [*Gajraj Singh* v *State Transport Appellate Tribunal* JT 1996(8) SC 356: AIR 1997 SC 412: (1997)1 SCC 650].

**Rent.** Consideration paid usually periodically for the use or occupancy of property; a compensation or return made periodically by a tenant or occupant for the possession and use of lands and corporeal hereditaments; money, chattels, or services issuing usually annually out of lands and tenements as payment for use; a contract by which one party conveys to another party a tract of land or other immovable property, to be held by the other party as owner and in perpetuity, in exchange for payment of an annual sum of money or quantity of fruits. [Black's *Law Dictionary*, 8th Ed.].

An agreed sum of money or other thing payable by the tenant for use and occupation of some property to the landlord; hire of any movable.

▸ *Meaning under the Public Premises (Eviction of Unauthorised Occupants) Act 1971, s. 2(f)*. 'Rent' in relation to any public premises means the consideration payable periodically for the authorised occupation of the premises and includes—(*i*) any charge for electricity, water or any other services in connection with the occupation of the premises, (*ii*) any tax (by whatever name called) payable in respect of the premises, where such charge or tax is payable by the Central Government or the corporate authority.

▸ *Meaning under the Transfer of Property Act 1882, s. 105.* The money, share, service or other thing to be paid by a lessee is called the rent.

In its wider sense 'rent' means any payment made for the use of land or buildings and thus includes the payment by a licensee in respect of the use and occupation of any land or building. In its narrow sense it means payment made by a tenant to landlord for property demised to him. [*Konohada Ramamurthy* v *Gopinath* AIR 1968 SC 919].

'Rent' means a payment made by the tenant to the landlord for use and occupation of the land [*Amlya Kumar* v *Krishna Singh* 1994 MPLJ 218]; any payment which is agreed to be paid by the tenant as consideration for the occupation of a premises. [*Chatterjee S.K.* v *Residence Ltd., Calcutta* 58 CWN 607 (DB)].

NOTE: The word 'rent' in modern times is not confined to payment received for the use of immovable property only but is used in connection with movables also. [*Pukhraj* v *Mohammad Ali* AIR 1957 Raj 279].

If under agreement of tenancy, the municipal tax is payable by tenant, such payment would also constitute rent. [*Sushi Chandra Palit* v *Dhani Brothers* (1971)37 Cut LR 995].

Rent includes payment for amenities with regard to more beneficial and convenient enjoyment of buildings. [*Isherdas Sahni & Bros.* v *Rajeswara Rao* (1968)2 MLJ 233].

The term 'rent' is comprehensive enough to include all payments agreed by the tenant to be paid to his landlord of the use of and occupation not only of the building and its appurtenances but also of furnishings, electric installations and other amenities agreed between the parties to be provided by and at the cost of the landlord. [*Karanani Properties* v *Miss Augustine* 1957 SCA 114: AIR 1957 SC 309].


- **Abatement of rent** p. 4.
- **Agreed rent** p. 52.
- **Dead rent** p. 227.
- **Fair rent** p. 339.
- **Ground rent** p. 401.
- **Net rent** p. 606.
- **Regular payment of rent** p. 739.
- **Standard rent** p. 808.


**Rented land.** Rented land is a piece of land on which there is no building—residential or non-residential—but which has been let for business or trade, as for keeping a firewood stall. [*Attar Singh* v *Inder Kumar* 1967 Cur LJ 242: AIR 1967 SC 773].

**Rentier.** A person whose source of income derives from ownership of property, particularly stocks and shares.

**Repair.** 'Repair' in the ordinary sense means 'to keep something in its normal state'. Where in the normal course, 'work is done on an article or thing to keep it in sound condition that would be repair'. [*Munnel D'Silva* v *Augustine* 1980 Ker LT 106].

The word 'repair' conveys the idea of replacing worn, broken, or lost parts in a thing or restoring the thing to a good condition. [*Khimchand Parshottam* v *Shah Bhupatray Nathalal* AIR 1971 Guj 81; *Manganlal Shivlal* v *Menon Daubhai Mithabhai* (1969)10 Guj LR 336].

'Repair' means 'the making good of defects, including renewal where that is necessary'. [*Per* Salter, LJ in *Creg* v *Planque* (1936)1 KB 669, quoting Lord Blackburn in *Englis* v *Buttery & Co.* (1878) AC 552].

The primary meaning of the word 'repair' is to restore to sound condition that which has previously been sound, but the word is also properly used in the sense of 'to make good'. Moreover, the word is commonly used to describe the operation of making an article good or sound, irrespective of whether the article had been good or sound before. [*Burns* v *National Coal Board* 1958 SLT 34, 39].

NOTE: The term 'repair' would not include the meaning of creating or making of a new thing.

[*Khimchand Parshottam* v *Shah Bhupatray Nathalal* AIR 1971 Guj 81; *Maganlal Shivlal* v *Menon Daudbhai Mithabhai* (1969)10 Guj LR 336].

Repair does not connote a total 'reconstruction'. The basic idea underlying the concept of repair is restoration of an asset to its original condition. This implies that the old structure is retained and is renovated from the damaged condition to its original sound state. Repair always involves an element of renewal but renewal of the whole and substantially the whole cannot be termed repair proper. An addition, material alteration or anything, which substantially improves a thing in value from the original condition except in so far as it is necessary to carry out such restoration cannot be said to be merely repair of that thing; it will be bringing into existence an altered thing; an improved thing; a new thing for all intents and purposes. [*Doraipandi Konar* v *P. Sundara Pathar* AIR 1970 Mad 291; *Dunichand* v *Kishore Chand* (1998)1 Rent CJ 432 (Raj)]. Whether looked upon as repair, or as improvements—all repairs are improvements, though all improvements are not repairs. [*Md. Mohindeen Rowther* v *N.H. Mohd. Mohidden Rowther* AIR 1960 Mad 24].

Complete renovation of body of motor vehicle by putting in new body on old chasis is a case of repair, with a view to earning revenue. [(1968)2 ITJ 418 (Mad)].

Where a building is completely demolished and a new structure is put instead, it would normally be reconstruction, not repair proper. [*Doraipandi Konar* v *P. Sundara Pathar* AIR 1970 Mad 291; *Dunichand* v *Kishore Chand* (1998)1 Rent CJ 432 (Raj)].

In the case of thatched old shed made of very flimsy materials like bamboo and arecanut, the word 'repairs' implies renewal and replacement of parts that have decayed. [*Augustine* v *Chandy* AIR 1973 Trav-Co 462].

A covenant to keep and deliver up the premises in repair is not substantially different if there are additional words such as 'repair reasonably and properly' or 'keep in good repair' or 'sufficient repair' or 'tenantable repair' or other phrases often used. In all such cases the premises should be kept and delivered up in that state of repair in which they ought to be found, if they had been managed by a reasonable-minded owner having regard to the age of the premises and to the character and ordinary uses or the requirements of the tenants of the class likely to take them at the time of their demise or at the commencement of the term. [*Burns* v *National Coal Board* 1958 SLT 34, 112].

- **Good tenantable repair.** 'Good tenantable repair' is such repair as, having regard to the age, character and locality of the house, would make it reasonably fit for the occupation of a reasonable-minded tenant of the class who would be likely to take it. [*Proudfoot* v *Hart* (1890)25 QBD 42: 50 LJQB 389].
- **Tenantable repair** p. 835.

**Repeal.** Abolish; abrogate; annul; cancel; countermand; declare null and void; delete; eliminate; make void; nullify; officially withdraw; render invalid; rescind.

Abrogation of an existing law by legislative act. [Black's *Law Dictionary*, 8th Ed.].

To revoke, rescind or abrogate, by authority. [*Golconda Lead Mines* v *Neill* 350 P 2d 221, 223].

The word "repeal" connotes abrogation or obliteration of one statute by another, from the statute book as completely "as if it had never been passed". When an Act is repealed, "it must be considered (except as to transactions past and closed) as if it had never existed." [*State of Orissa* v *M.A. Tulloch & Co.* AIR 1964 SC 1284: (1964)4 SCR 561 referring to observation of Tindal, C.J. in *Kay* v *Goodurin* (1830)6 Bing 576, 582 and Lord Tenterdon in *Surtees* v *Ellision* (1829)9 B&C 750, 752; *India Tobacco Co. Ltd.* v *The Commercial Tax Officer, Bhavanipore* (1975)2 SCR 612: (1975)3 SCC 512: AIR 1975 SC 155: (1975)35 STC 95].

NOTE: A 'repeal' ordinarily brings about complete obliteration of the provision as if it had never been enacted. The effect is to destroy all incoherent rights and all causes of action which may have arisen under the repealed provisions. [*Navrangpura Gam Dharmada Milkat Trust* v *Ramtuji Ramaji* AIR 1994 Guj 75].

Repeal is not a matter of mere form but one of substance, depending upon the intention of the legislature. If the intention indicated expressly or by necessary implication in the subsequent statute was to abrogate or wipe off the former enactment, wholly or in part, then it would be a case of total or *pro tanto* repeal. If the intention was merely to modify the former enactment by engrafting an exception, or granting an exemption or by super-adding conditions, or by restricting, intercepting or suspending its operation, such modification would not amount to a repeal. [*India Tobacco Co. Ltd.* v *Commercial Tax Officer* (1975)3 SCC 512: (1975)2 SCR 612: AIR 1975 SC 155: (1975)35 STC 95].

*'Repeal' and 'amendment'—distinction.* 'Repeal' of a law means its complete abrogation by the enactment of a subsequent statute, whereas the 'amendment' of a statute means an alteration in the law already existing, leaving some part of the original still standing. [Black's *Law Dictionary*, 5th Ed.].

When a section is being added to an Act or a provision added to a section, the Legislatures commonly entitle the Act as an amendment. When a provision is withdrawn from a section, the Legislatures call the Act an amendment particularly when a provision is added to replace the one withdrawn. However, when an entire Act or section is abrogated and no new section is added to replace it, Legislatures label the Act accomplishing this result a repeal. [*Bhagat Ram Sharma* v *Union of India* AIR 1988 SC 740].

• **Implied repeal** p. 433.

**Replevin.** Recovery of property; reclamation; retaking; retrieval; salvage.

An action for the repossession of personal property wrongfully taken or detained by the defendant, whereby the plaintiff gives security for and holds the property until the court decides who owns it. [Black's *Law Dictionary*, 8th Ed.].

*Replevin* is designed to permit one having right to possession to recover property in specie from one who has either wrongfully taken or detained property. [*Epps* v *Cortese* DC Pa, 326 F Supp 127, 132].

NOTE: Whenever chattels are taken by one person out of the possession of another, whether by way of distress or otherwise, the latter may by way of proceedings in *replevin* recover immediate and provisional possession of them, pending the result of an action brought by him to determine the rights of the parties. It is thus a summary process by which men out of whose possession goods have been taken may obtain their return until the rights to the goods are determined by a court of law. [Salmond's *Law of Torts*, 19th Ed., p. 128].

**Reply.** Counter; refute; rebut; respond; retort; return; answer; make rejoinder.

An address to the court by one party or his advocate in answer to the address by the other party. [Code of Civil Procedure 1908, Or. 18, r. 2(3)].

**Report.** To give an account of, to relate, to tell, to convey or disseminate information [*State* v *Fenster* 199 A 2d 177, 181]; communicate; deliver information; make an announcement; make known; speak about, specify.

A formal oral or written presentation of facts or a recommendation for action; a written account of a court proceeding and judicial decision; a published volume of judicial decisions; a collection of administrative decisions by one or more administrative agencies. [Black's *Law Dictionary*, 8th Ed.].

• **Confidential report** p. 171.
• **Director's report** p. 261.
• **Fair report** p. 339.
• **First information report** p. 356.

**Representation.** Speaking for another; advocacy; assertion of facts; asseveration; declaration; portrayal.

A representation is a statement made by a representator to a representee and relating by way of affirmation, denial, description or otherwise to a matter of fact. The statement may be oral or in writing or arise by implication from words or conduct. [Halsbury's *Laws of England*, 3rd Ed., vol. 26, p. 820].

"Representation" includes any statement or undertaking, whether constituting a condition or warranty or not. [Halsbury's *Laws of England*, 4th Ed., vol. 22, para 227, p. 186].

Representation is defined as any conduct capable of being turned into a statement of fact. [*Scandrett* v *Greenhouse* 11 NW 2d 510, 512].

NOTE: Mere silence cannot amount to representation, but when there is a duty to disclose, deliberate silence may become significant and amount to a representation. [*Greenwood* v *Martins Bank Ltd.* (1933) AC 51].

**Representative.** Agential; characteristic; adumbrative; denotative; illustrative; symbolic; indicative; exemplar; model; sample; specimen; typical example or instance; agent; broker; counsel; delegate; emissary; go-between; messenger; middle man.

One who stands for or acts on behalf of another; a member of a legislature, especially of the lower house. [Black's *Law Dictionary*, 8th Ed.].

One who represents others or another in a special capacity, as an agent, and the term is interchangeable with "agent". [*Sunset Mill & Grain Co.* v *Anderson* 249 P 2d 24, 27].

One who represents another or others, as an agent or delegate; a successor in interest, as heir, executor, administrator or transferee.

NOTE: 'Representative' in s. 47 of the Code of Civil Procedure 1908, includes not only legal representatives but any representative in interest, *e.g.*, any transferee of the interest of a party. [*Sans Kaur* v *Teja Singh* AIR 1946 Lah 142].

• **Legal representative** p. 527.

• **Personal representative** p. 660.

**Reprieve.** Postponement of penalty; quittance; respite; respite from impending punishment; stay of execution; suspension of execution/punishment; temporary relief.

The term 'reprieve' is derived from *reprendre*, to keep back, and signifies the withdrawing of the sentence for an interval of time, and operates in delay of execution.

NOTE: It may take place—(*a*) *ex mandeto regis*, at the mere pleasure of the sovereign; or (*b*) *ex arbitrio judicis*, either before or after judgment; or (*c*) *ex necessitate legis*, as where a woman is capitally convicted and pleads her pregnancy; or (*d*) if the criminal becomes *non compos*.

Articles 72 and 161 of the Constitution of India empower the President and the Governor to grant reprieves. [Wharton's *Law Lexicon*].

**Reprisal.** Reprisals are methods adopted by States for securing redress from another State by taking retaliatory measures. The term connotes coercive measures adopted by one State against another for the purpose of settling some dispute brought about by the latter's illegal or unjustified conduct. It may take various forms such as a boycott of the goods of a State, an embargo, a naval demonstration, or bombardment. [Starke's *International Law*, 10th Ed., p. 520].

The word 'reprisal' denotes an act of retaliation for some injury or attack, specially in warfare, the infliction of similar or severer punishment to the enemy. Divested from the context and used with reference to an act by the government towards the people, the word would be objectionable inasmuch as it implies ideas of retaliation. Reprisals are admissible for international delinquencies only. [*Re Anandbazar Patrika* AIR 1935 Cal 74].

**Repudiation.** Abjuration; abrogation; annulment; cancellation; negation; nullification; renunciation; rejection.

**Repudiation of a contract.** It means refusal to perform duty or obligation owed to other party. [*Pitcher* v *Lauritzen* 423 P 2d 491, 493; *Draughon's Business College* v *Battles* 50 So 2d 788, 790].

NOTE: Repudiation of contract is in nature of anticipatory breach before performance is due, but does not operate as anticipatory breach unless promisee elects to treat repudiation as breach, and brings suit for damages. Such repudiation is but act or declaration in advance of any actual breach and consists usually of absolute and unequivocal declaration or act amounting to declaration on part of promisor to promisee that he will not make performance on future day at which contract calls for performance. [*Robinson* v *Raquet* 36 P 2d 821, 825].

There may be various ways in which a contract may be repudiated. The defendant may deny that there ever was a contract or that the consent to the contract was vitiated by fraud or duress or mistake or illegality or that because of failure of some condition or infringement of some fundamental duty stipulated in the contract, it has become invalid or that he will not perform the contract. But perhaps the commonest application of the word 'repudiation' is what is often called the anticipatory breach of a contract where the party by words or conduct evinces an intention no longer to be bound and the other party accepts the repudiation and rescinds the contract. [*Heyman* v *Darwins Ltd.* (1942) AC 356].

**Repugnant.** Abhorrent; abominable; detestable; disagreeable; disgustful; displeasing; distasteful; hateful; loathsome;; obnoxious; nauseating; objectionable; repellent; unacceptable; unpalatable.

It also means adverse; alien; at odds; clashing; conflicting; contradictory; disagreeing; discordant; incongruous; inharmonious; inimical; irreconcilable; opposing; uncomfortable.

Repugnant really means inconsistent with, and when they cannot stand together at the same time; any one law is inconsistent with another law, as when the command or power or provision in the one law conflicts indirectly with the command or power or provision in the other. [*Vishnu Bhattahiripad* v *Poulo Poulo* ILR (1952) Trav-Co 670: 1953 Ker LT 238: AIR 1953 TC 327 (DB)].

**Reputation.** The esteem in which a person is held by others [Black's *Law Dictionary*, 8th Ed.]; estimation in which one is held. [Black's *Law Dictionary*, 5th Ed.].

General opinion, good or bad, held of a person by those of the community in which he resides. [*State* v *Kiziah* 8 SE 2d 474, 477; *Citizens Bank of Morehead* v *Hunt* 154 SW 2d 730, 731].

NOTE: *"Character" and "reputation"—distinction.* "Character" is made up of the things an individual actually is and does whereas "reputation" is what people think an individual is and what they say about him. [*McNaulty* v *State* 135 SW 2d 987, 989; *James* v *State ex rel. Loser* 145 SW 2d 1026, 1033].

The two terms "reputation" and "character" are prone to be confused. Character would mean fortitude or moral constitution or strength of a person. It has no relevance with the belief or opinion of others in respect of a person. Character in a person is what a person actually is, while reputation is what neighbours and others say "what he is". [*Narottamdas* v *Maganbhai* 1984 Cr LJ 1790].

**Request.** Appeal; ask for; beckon; beg for; beseech; call for; clamour for; command; demand; desire; petition for; order; plead for; pray.

NOTE: Any "request" of the Government to a subordinate authority is tantamount to a positive direction or order and it would be difficult for the subordinate authority to disregard the same. [*Chinta Palli Agency Jaluk Arrach Sales Co-op. Society* v *Secretary, Govt. of A.P.* AIR 1977 SC 2312: (1977)4 SCC 337].

**Require.** Demand; fill the necessity for; stand in need of; to be in need of.

To direct, order, demand, instruct, command, claim, compel, request, need, exact. [*State ex rel. Frohmiller* v *Hendrix* 124 P 2d 768, 773].

To ask for authoritatively or imperatively. [*State* v *Community Distributors, Inc.* 304 A 2d 213, 217].

**Requisite.** Basic; binding; compulsory; essential; imperative; incumbent on; indispensable; mandatory; necessary; needful; obligatory; pressing; requisitory; wanted.

Something more than required. It means properly required. [*State of Bihar* v *Mohammad Ismail* AIR 1966 Pat 1 (FB)].

The word 'requisite' is a strong word; it may be recorded as meaning something more than the word 'required'. It means 'properly required'. [*National Tobacco Co. Employees' Union* v *Labour Court* AIR 1969 P&H 76; *Santimoy Dev* v *Suriya Properties (Pvt) Ltd.* AIR 1976 Cal 81; *J.N. Surty* v *T.S. Chettyar* AIR 1928 PC 103].

The meaning of the term 'requisite' is 'that which is necessary; something indispensible. [*State* v *Hari Shanker* 1971 All Cr R 488 (FB)].

**Requisition.** A demand in writing, or formal request or requirement; the taking or seizure of property by government.

NOTE: The term 'requisition' is used in the sense of taking possession of property for the purpose of the state and for such purposes as may be specified in the statute authorising to take possession of private property for a specified purpose for a limited period. In requisition, the property dealt with is not acquired by the state but is taken out of the control of the owner for the time being for certain specified purposes. Even for this limited purpose, however, the owner becomes entitled to compensation because requisition of the property amounts at least to a temporary deprivation of the property. [*Mangilal Karwa* v *State of M.P.* AIR 1955 Nag 153 (DB)].

*'Requisition' and 'acquisition'—distinction.* In the case of requisition, ownership remains with the owner and it is only possession that is taken. Acquisition means acquiring the ownership in the property. [*Raman Das* v *State of Uttar Pradesh* AIR 1952 All 703; *Income Tax Commissioner* v *Sham Lal* AIR 1963 Punj 411].

**Requisition on title.** Enquiries and requests regarding title made by the intending purchaser which the vendor is called upon to answer and comply with.

**Res.** A thing; an object.

*'Res'* is everything that may form an object of rights and includes an object, subject-matter or status. [*In re Riggle's Will* 205 NYS 2d 19, 21].

By *"res"*, according to the modern civilians, is meant everything that may form an object or rights, in opposition to *"persona"*, which is regarded as a subject of rights. *"Res"*, therefore, in its general meaning, comprises actions of all kinds; while in its restricted sense it comprehends every object of right, except actions. [Black's *Law Dictionary*, 5th Ed.].

**Res derelicta.** Abandoned property; property thrown away or forsaken by the owner, so as to become open to the acquisition of the first taker or occupant.

**Res gestae.** It is a Latin expression which means "things done". The events at issue, or other events contemporaneous with them.

Items of evidence are sometimes said to be part of the *res gestae*, owing to the nature and strength of their connection with the matters in issue, and as such are admissible. *"Res gestae"* is an expression mainly of utility in the criminal law concerning the contemporaneity of statements to incidents but, insofar as contemporaneous statements are relevant and accompany and explain matters in issue, they will be admissible. [Halsbury's *Laws of England*, 4th Ed., vol. 17, para 6, p. 8].

**Res integra.** The term is applied to those points of law which have not been decided, which are untouched by dictum or decision.

**Res inter alios acta alteri nocere non debet.** One person ought not to be injured by the acts of others to which he is a stranger.

**Res ipsa loquitur.** The thing speaks for itself. This maxim applies in actions for negligence where the circumstances of an accident are such that it is so improbable that it would have occurred without the negligence of the defendant, that it can be presumed that it was so caused, *e.g.*, where a moving motor car collides with a stationary vehicle. The onus is on the defendant to disprove the presumed negligence.

*Res ipsa loquitur* is a rule of evidence whereby negligence of alleged wrongdoer may be inferred from mere fact that accident happened provided character of accident and circumstances attending it lead reasonably to belief that in absence of negligence it would not have occurred and that thing which caused injury is shown to have been under management and control of alleged wrongdoer. [*Hillen* v *Hooker Const. Co.* Tex Civ App, 484 SW 2d 113, 115].

NOTE: *Res ipsa loquitur* is not a principle of substantive law. It is a rule of evidence, an expression which it is convenient to apply to those circumstances in which a plaintiff is deemed to have discharged his task of establishing want of care on the part of the defendant without requiring to prove any specific negligence or omission of the defendant. The general rule is that it is for the plaintiff to prove negligence, and not for the defendant to disprove it. In some cases it causes considerable hardship to the plaintiff because, may be that the true cause of the accident lies only with the defendant. The plaintiff can prove the accident; but he cannot prove how it happened so as to show its origin in the negligence of the defendant. This hardship is avoided to a considerable extent by the principle of *res ipsa loquitur*. When all the facts are known, there is no room for application of the maxim; in such a case the only question for consideration is whether an inference of negligence is practically certain or practically impossible. But when all the facts are now known, the maxim helps the plaintiff to discharge the onus which lies upon him, of proving negligence. If the accident is proved in such a way that *prima facie* it could not have happened without negligence on the part of the defendant, then it is for the defendant to explain how the accident could have happened without negligence. [*Associated Cotton Traders* v *Union of India* (1977)2 MLJ 335: 90 MLW 438].

**Res judicata.** It is a Latin expression which means "a thing adjudicated".

It means an issue that has been definitely settled by judicial decision; an affirmative defence barring the same parties from litigating a second lawsuit on the same claim, or any other claim arising from the same transaction or series of transactions and that could have been—but was not—raised in the first suit. [Black's *Law Dictionary*, 8th Ed.].

NOTE: The sum and substance of the whole rule of *res judicata* is that a matter once judicially decided is finally decided. [*Massie* v *Paul* 92 SW 2d 11, 14].

Under the rule of *res judicata* a final judgment rendered by a court of competent jurisdiction on the merits is conclusive as to the rights of the parties and their privies, and, as to them, constitutes an absolute bar to a subsequent action involving the same claim, demand or cause of action. [*Matchett* v *Rose* 344 NE 2d 770, 779].

The three essential elements of the rule of *res judicata* are: (*i*) an earlier decision on the issue, (*ii*) a final judgment on the merits, and (*iii*) an involvement of the same parties, or parties in privity with the original parties.

No court shall try any suit or issue in which the matter directly and substantially in issue has been directly and substantially in issue in a former suit between the same parties, or between parties, under whom they or any of them claim, litigating under the same title, in a court competent to try such subsequent suit or the suit in which such issue has been subsequently raised and has been heard and finally decided by such court. [Code of Civil Procedure 1908, s. 11].

• **Constructive res judicata** p. 180.

**Res judicata pro veritate accipitur.** A thing adjudicated is received as true.

**Res nullus.** A thing which has no owner.

**Rescission of contract.** Annulling, abrogation or unmaking of contract and the placing of the parties to it in *status quo*. [*Sessions* v *Meadows* 57 P 2d 548, 549].

NOTE: A rescission of contact amounts to the unmaking of a contract, or an undoing of it from the beginning, and not merely a termination, and it may be effected by mutual agreement of parties, or by one of the parties declaring rescission of contract without consent of other if a legally sufficient ground therefor exists, or by applying to courts for a decree of rescission. [*Abdallah, Inc.* v *Martin* 65 NW 2d 641, 644].

**Reservation.** Condition; exception; limitation; provision; proviso; qualification; restriction; stipulation.

It may also mean booking; promised to set aside; registration; retainment; withholding.

A clause in a deed or other instrument of conveyance by which the grantor creates, and reserves to himself some right, interest, or profit in the estate granted, which had no previous existence as such, but is first called into being by the instrument reserving it; such as rent, or an easement. [*Board of County Com'rs of Weld County* v *Anderson* 525 P 2d 478, 482].

In its ordinary meaning, the expression 'reservation' means something specifically kept apart for future use or for a specific occasion. [*CIT* v *Standard Vacuum Oil Co.* AIR 1966 SC 1393: (1966)59 ITR 685: (1966)1 ITJ 327: (1966)1 SCJ 401: (1966)1 Comp LJ 187: (1966)2 SCR 367].

A 'reservation' can only mean profit earned by a company and not distributed as dividends to the shareholders but kept back by the Directors for any purpose to which it may be put in future. [*CIT* v *Standard Vacuum Oil Co.* AIR 1966 SC 1393: (1966)59 ITR 685: (1966)1 ITJ 327: (1966)1 SCJ 401: (1966)1 Comp LJ 187: (1966)2 SCR 367].

NOTE: Reservation may be general or specific and unless there is clear indication of the type of reservation, the amount in question would only be treated as mass of undistributed profits. [*Vazir Sultan Tobacco Co. Ltd.* v *CIT* AIR 1981 SC 2105: (1981)4 SCC 435].

**Reserve.** A fund set apart to provide for contingencies; a fund set aside to cover future expenses, losses, or claims; to keep back, to retain, to keep in store for future or special use, and to retain or hold over of a future time. [*Commissioner of Internal Revenue* v *Strong Mfg. Co.* 124 F 2d 360, 363].

NOTE: Nothing can be reserved unless it has been laid by or stored for use or application in a future contingency which is anticipated as certain or likely. A reserve is, by its very nature, a fund which is created and maintained for the purpose of being drawn upon in future. [*Indian Steel* v *Commissioner of Income-tax* AIR 1958 Cal 664].

• **Capital reserve** p. 123.
• **Gold reserves** p. 389.
• **Without reserve** p. 901.

**Reside.** Live, dwell, abide, sojourn, stay, remain, lodge. [*Western-Knapp Engineering Co.* v *Gilbank* CCA Cal, 129 F 2d 135, 136].

To settle oneself or a thing in a place; to be stationed, to remain or stay, to dwell permanently or continuously; to have a settled abode for a time; to have one's residence or domicile; specifically, to be in residence, to have an abiding place, to be present as an element, to inhere as a quality, to be vested as a right. [*State ex rel. Bowden* v *Jensen* Mo, 359 SW 2d 343, 349].

To reside means to live or to have a dwelling place or an abode. [*Rifacatullah Khan* v *Emperor* AIR 1947 All 4].

It is wrong to treat the word 'reside' as equivalent to something in the nature of having a domicile in a particular place, or having a place, as one's place of origin, or the place where one's family used to live. 'To reside' means to live or to have a dwelling place or abode. [*Rafaqat Ullah Khan* v *Emperor* 1948 All LJ 305].

NOTE: The word 'reside' refers to a place of permanent and not merely temporary abode, even though one individual may have more than one residence at the same time for the purpose of being sued. A mere place of temporary and compulsory detention such as a prison, or a temporary residence such as lodgings occupied by a person who has a permanent residence elsewhere is not sufficient. A person, however, may reside at a lodging which he occupies permanently, and if a person has no permanent abode at all, he may be taken to reside at the place where he is temporarily staying. [Halsbury's *Laws of England*, 4th Ed., vol. 10, para 107, p. 66].

The word 'resides' is by no means free from all ambiguity and is capable of a variety of meanings according to the circumstances to which it is made applicable and the context in which it is found. It is capable of being understood in its ordinary sense of having one's own dwelling permanently, as well as in its extended sense. In its ordinary sense 'residence' is more or less of a permanent character. The expression 'resides' means to make an abode for a considerable time; to dwell permanently or for a length of time; to have a settled abode for a time. It is the place where a person had fixed home or abode. Where there is such fixed home or such abode at one place, the person cannot be said to reside at any other place where he had gone on a casual or temporary visit *e.g.* for health or business or for a change. If a person lives with his wife and children in an established home, his legal and actual place of residence is the same. If a person has no established home and is compelled to live in hotels, boarding houses or houses of others, his actual and physical habitation is the place where he actually or personally resides. [*Jeewanti Pandey* v *Kishan Chandra Pandey* (1981)4 SCC 517: AIR 1982 SC 3: (1981)1 SCR 1003].

The word 'reside' carries with it the idea of permanence, that is for a length of time, as well as continuity. [*Ganga Ram* v *Jairam* AIR 1957 Punj 293].

▸ *Meaning in its application to matrimonial affairs.* Reside refers to the place where the husband and the wife last resided together. The place where they resided together permanently, would include a place where they lived together as man and wife, even without there being an intention on their part to continue to live there in that way for some appreciable length of time. [*S. Saroja* v *P.G. Emmanact* AIR 1965 Mys 12].

Even a place of temporary residence is within the meaning of the word 'resides'. It is true that 'resides' implies something more than a brief or flying visit but where the wife was residing in a village and the husband who was employed outside used to come to the village and the husband and wife lived together as such, that would amount to 'resides' within the meaning of the words as used in s. 488, Cr. P.C. [*Sardari Lal* v *Smt. Kaushalya Devi* 58 Punj LR 562: AIR 1957 Punj 34].

**Residence.** The act or fact of living in a given place for some time; the place where one actually lives, as distinguished from a domicile; a house or other fixed abode; the place where a corporation or other enterprise does business or is registered to do business. [Black's *Law Dictionary*, 8th Ed.].

The place of residence of a person is the place where he eats, drinks and sleeps. [*Stoke-on-Trent Borough Council* v *Cheshire County Council* (1913)3 KB 699, 706].

Residence only connotes that a person eats, drinks and sleeps at that place, and not that he owns it. Residence includes permanent as also temporary residence. [*Ratanlal* v *State Transport* AIR 1969 MP 204; *Jeewanti Pandey* v *Kishan Chandra* (1981)4 SCC 517: (1981)1 SCR 1003: AIR 1982 SC 3].

'Residence' must *prima facie* have an element of continuity or regularity in residence and would not mean an intermittent stay such as during the vacations. [*D.N. Chanchala* v *State of Mysore* AIR 1971 SC 1762: 1971 (Supp) SCR 608: (1971)2 SCC 293].

In its ordinary sense, 'residence' is more or less of a permanent character. If a person lives with his wife and children in an established home, his legal and actual place of residence is the same. [*Jeewanti Pandey* v *Kishan Chandra Pandey* (1981)4 SCC 517: (1981)1 SCR 1003: AIR 1982 SC 3].

'Residence' means the place where the man lives and where he has his home. [*Globe Theatres Ltd.* v *Khan Sahib Abdul Gani* ILR (1956) Mys 71: AIR 1956 Mys 57 (FB)].

The word 'residence' connotes a dwelling house where a person lives in a settled abode. [*Ganga Ram* v *Firm Jai Ram* AIR 1957 Punj 293].

▸ *Meaning under the Constitution of India, Art. 16.* The word 'residence' speaks of a whole state as the venue for residential qualification. [*A.V.S. Narasimha Rao* v *State of A.P.* (1969)1 SCC 839: AIR 1970 SC 422].

NOTE: Three principles are to be kept in view in determining the residence of a person. The first principle is that a man can have two residences. He can have a flat in London and a house in the country. He is resident in both. The second principle is that temporary presence at an address does not make a man resident there. A guest who comes for the week-end is not resident. A short-stay visitor is not resident. The third principle is that temporary absence does not deprive a person of his residence. If he happens to be away for a holiday or away for the week-end or in hospital, he does not lose his residence on that account. [*Fox* v *Stork* (1970)3 All ER 7].


- **Actual residence** p. 35.
- **Place of residence** p. 665.


**Residential accommodation.** A building which reasonably accommodates a residential user is residential accommodation, nothing less, nothing else. [*Busching Schmitz Pvt. Ltd.* v *P.T. Menghani* AIR 1977 SC 1569: (1977)2 SCC 835: (1977)3 SCR 312].

**Residential house.** Residential house is a dwelling house as distinct from a house of business, warehouse, office, shop, etc. Residential house is a building, used as a place of abode in which people reside or dwell in contradistinction to one which is used for commercial or business purposes. [*Ganga Ram* v *Firm Jai Ram* AIR 1957 Punj 293].

**Residential premises.** Whatever is suitable or adaptable for residential use, even by making some changes, can be designated residential premises. [*S.P. Jain* v *Krishna Mohan Gupta* JT 1986 SC 979: (1987)1 SCC 191: AIR 1987 SC 222: (1987)1 SCR 411].

**Resign.** Abandon; abdicate; abjure; demit; depart; desist from; divest oneself of; forego; give up; leave; quit; relinquish; renounce; repudiate; step down.

It is not a term of art. To resign means to relinquish and to give up office and employment and one of the dictionary meanings of the term resignation is 'act of giving up'. [*Mettur Spinning Mills* v *Dy. Commissioner of Labour* (1983)1 MLJ 373, 375].

**Resignation.** Abandonment; abdication; abjuration; abjurement; demission; evacuation; forsaking; giving up; leaving; quitting; renouncement.

The act or an instance of surrendering or relinquishing an office, right, or claim; a formal notification of relinquishing an office or position. [Black's *Law Dictionary*, 8th Ed.].

'Resignation' in the dictionary sense, means the spontaneous relinquishment of one's own right. In relation to an office, it connotes the act of giving up or relinquishing the office. [*Union of India* v *Gopal Chandra Misra* AIR 1978 SC 694: (1978)3 SCR 12: (1978)2 SCC 301].

The word 'resignation' means the spontaneous relinquishment of one's own right and in relation to an office, it connotes the act of giving up or relinquishing the office. In the general juristic sense, in order to constitute a complete and operative resignation there must be the intention to give up or relinquish the office and the concomitant act of its relinquishment. [*Moti Ram* v *Param Dev* AIR 1993 SC 1662: (1993)2 SCC 725: (1993)2 SCR 250: JT 1993(2) SC 251].

**Resolution.** Declaration; formal expression; pronouncement; proposition; statement; written announcement; determination; earnestness; firmness; indefatigability; intention; tenacity; will power.

A formal expression of the opinion or will of an official body or a public assembly, adopted by vote. [Black's *Law Dictionary*, 5th Ed.].

A main motion that formally expresses the sense, will, or action of a deliberative assembly; formal action by a corporate board of directions or other corporate body authorising a particular act, transaction, or appointment; a document containing such expression or authorisation. [Black's *Law Dictionary*, 8th Ed.].

• **Ordinary resolution** p. 630.
• **Special resolution** p. 805.

**Respite.** Abeyance; breathing spell; breathing time; halt; pause; relaxation; stay; suspension; temporary stoppage; acquittal; amnesty; discharge; exemption; immunity; pardon; release; stay of execution.

The temporary suspension of the execution of a sentence; a reprieve; a delay; forbearance or continuation of time. [Black's *Law Dictionary*, 5th Ed.].

In civil law, respite is an act by which a debtor, who is unable to satisfy his debts at the moment, transacts with his creditors, and obtains from them time or delay for the payment of the sums which he owes to them.

**Respondeat superior.** Let the principal answer.

**Respondent.** The party against whom an appeal is taken; appellee; the party against whom a motion or petition is filed; one who answers for another or acts as another's security.

The word respondent in s. 25(1) of the Hindu Marriage Act 1955, means the opposite party to the petition. [*Sachindra Nath* v *Banamala* AIR 1960 Cal 575].

**Responsibility.** Accountableness; answerability; bounden duty; commitment; encumbrance; imperative duty; obligation; claims of conscience; compunction; conscientiousness; ethical judgment; moral consciousness; sense of duty; sense of obligation; sense of right and wrong.

The state of being answerable for an obligation, and includes judgment, skill, ability and capacity. [*McFarland* v *George* Mo App, 316 SW 2d 662, 671].

**Restaurant.** Any premises in which is carried on principally or wholly the business of supplying meals or refreshments to the public or a class of the public for consumption on the premises.

Premises where materials of refreshments may be had; a place where refreshments or materials are provided; a public dining-room.

**Restitutio in integrum.** It is a Latin expression which means restoration or restitution to the previous condition.

**Restitution.** Act of restoring; restoration; restoration of anything to its rightful owner; the act of making good or giving equivalent for any loss; damage or injury; and indemnification. [*State* v *Barnett* 3 A 2d 521, 525, 526].

▸ *Meaning under the Limitation Act 1963, s. 144(1).* The word 'restitution' in the marginal note of s. 144(1) in its etymological sense means restoring to a party on the modification, variation or reversal of a decree what has been lost to him in execution of the decree or in direct consequence of the decree. In such a proceeding, the party seeking restitution is not required to satisfy the court about its title or right to the property save and except showing its deprivation under a decree and the reversal or variation of the decree. [*Zafar Khan* v *Board of Revenue, U.P.* 1984 (Supp) SCC 505: AIR 1985 SC 39: (1985)1 SCR 287].

**Restitution of conjugal rights.** A suit for restitution of conjugal right is a matrimonial suit to have the society of the other spouse.

A remedy aimed at preserving the marriage and not at dissolving it as in the case of divorce or judicial separation. [*B.R. Syal* v *Ram Syal* AIR 1968 Punj 489: ILR (1968)2 Punj 388].

**Restraint of marriage.** A bar or limitation to go through a legal marriage.

> NOTE: Every agreement in the restraint of the marriage of any person, other than a minor, is void. [Indian Contract Act 1872, s. 26].

**Restraint of trade.** Contracts or combinations which tend or are designed to eliminate or stifle competition, effect a monopoly, artificially maintain prices, or otherwise hamper or obstruct the course of trade and commerce as it would be carried on if left to the control of natural economic forces. [*U.S.* v *Reading Co.* 253 US 26: 64 L Ed 760; *U.S.* v *Patten* 226 US 525: 57 L Ed 333].

> NOTE: Contracts to restrain a person's liberty of action in carrying on his trade, business, occupation or profession, and all restrains of trade of themselves, if there is nothing more, are contrary to public policy and, therefore, void. But a contract in restraint of trade is not contrary to public policy and is valid if—(*i*) it is reasonable necessary to protect the interests of the person in whose favour it is imposed; and (*ii*) it is not unreasonable as regards the person restrained; and (*iii*) it is not unreasonably injurious to the public. [Sutton & Shannon on *Contracts*, 6th Ed., p. 255].

**Restraint on alienation.** Restriction on the power of alienation.

A provision in an instrument of conveyance which prohibits the grantee from selling or transferring the property which is the subject of the conveyance.

A "restraint on alienation" is any provision in a trust or other instrument which, either by express terms or by implication, purports to prohibit or penalize the use of the power of alienation; the trusts usually involved are spendthrift, discretionary and support trusts. [*Philp* v *Trainor* Fla App, 100 So 2d 181, 183].

> NOTE: An absolute restraint on alienation upon a transferee is void except in the case of a lease. [Transfer of Property Act 1882, s. 10].

**Restrict.** Bar; bind; bound; chain; circumscribe; confine; debar; delimit; entrammel; fetter; forbid; handicap; hedge in; hem in; keep within limits; put under restraint; prohibit; shut out.

To restrain within bounds; to limit; to confine. [Black's *Law Dictionary*, 5th Ed.].

**Restrictive indorsement.** The indorsement of a negotiable instrument followed by delivery transfers to the indorsee the property therein with the right of further negotiation; but the indorsement may, by express words, restrict or include such right, or may merely constitute the indorsee an agent to indorse the instrument, or to receive its contents for the indorser or for some other specified person. [Negotiable Instruments Act 1881, s. 50].

NOTE: The effect of a restrictive endorsement is generally any out of the following: (*a*) It prohibits further negotiation. For example, when the endorsement is "pay *C* only", *C* cannot endorse it away to somebody else. (*b*) It may merely constitute the endorsee an agent of the endorser for special purpose, such as to receive its contents. (*c*) It may vest the title in the endorsee in trust for some other person, as when the endorsement is "the within must be credited to *D*".

**Restrictive trade practice.** 'Restrictive trade practice' is defined to mean a trade practice which has, or may have, the effect of preventing, distorting or restricting competition in any manner and in particular, (*i*) which tends to obstruct the flow of capital or resources into the stream of production, or (*ii*) which tends to bring about manipulation of prices, or conditions of delivery or to affect the flow of supplies in the market relating to goods or services in such manner as to impose on the consumers unjustified costs or restrictions. [*Mahindra and Mahindra Ltd*. v *Union of India* AIR 1979 SC 798: (1979)2 SCR 1038: (1979)2 SCC 529: (1979)49 CC 419; Monopolies and Restrictive Trade Practices Act 1969, s. 2(*o*)].

NOTE: The decision whether the trade practice is restrictive or not has to be arrived at by applying the rule of reason and not on the doctrine that any restriction as to area or price will *per se* be a restrictive trade practice. Every trade agreement restrains or binds persons or places or prices. The question is whether the restraint is such as regulates and thereby promotes competition or whether it is such as may suppress or even destroy competition. To determine this question three matters are to be considered. First, what facts are peculiar to the business to which the restraint is applied. Second, what was the condition before and after the restraint is imposed. Third, what is the nature of the restraint and what is its actual and probable effect. [*Tata Engineering & Locomotive Co. Ltd., Bombay* v *The Registrar of the Restrictive Trade Agreement, New Delhi* AIR 1977 SC 973: (1977)2 SCR 685: (1977)2 SCC 55].

**Resulting trust.** A resulting trust is a trust arising by operation of law in the following cases, namely—(1) where an intention to put the property into trust is sufficiently expressed or indicated, but the actual trust either is not declared in whole or in part or fails in whole or in part; (2) where property is purchased in the name or placed in the possession of a person ostensibly for his own use, but really in order to effect a particular purpose which fails; and (3) where property is purchased in the name or placed in the possession of a person without any intention that he is to hold it in trust, but the retention of the beneficial interest by the purchaser or disposer is presumed to have been intended. [Halsbury's *Laws of England*, 4th Ed., vol. 48, para 597, p. 331].

A resulting trust is where property is ineffectually or incompletely conveyed or where on a conveyance the beneficial interest in property is not completely disposed of; and accordingly the property or the undisposed of beneficial interest in it reverts to the person making the conveyance. It arises by implication when, *e.g.*, the document purporting to convey the property is legally void or conveys the property in trust property but declares no trust or declares trusts which fall or do not exhaust the property; but in the last mentioned case, it has been said that the ordinary and familiar mode of creating a resulting trust is by saying so on the face of the instrument. [*Smith* v *Cooke* (1891) AC 299: 60 LJ Ch 610].

On the failure of the object of the trust there is what is called a resulting trust in favour of those who had given the property. But equity treats trust for charitable purposes as an exception to this rule of resulting trust. [*Nori Venkata Rama* v *Ravi Venkatappayya* AIR 1960 AP 35].

**Resumption.** The taking back of property previously given up or lost. [Black's *Law Dictionary*, 8th Ed.].

The word connotes taking back what is given—what is resumed is not the property of persons from whom it is taken back by the rightful owner. [*Raja Rajendra Malogirao Shitool* v *State of M.P.* AIR 1953 MB 97 (FB)].

Resumption implies taking back by the person who granted the land without any liability to pay compensation. [*Amar Singh* v *State of Rajasthan* AIR 1954 Raj 291].

> NOTE: *'Resumption' and 'acquisition'—distinction.* Resumption and acquisition connote two different legal concepts. While resumption implies that the person or authority which resumes the property has pre-existing rights over it, acquisition carried no such implication, and, in general, while the effect of resumption is to extinguish the interests of the person whose property is resumed, that of acquisition is to vest that interest in the acquirer. [*Thakur Amar Singhji* v *State of Rajasthan* (1955)2 SCR 303: 1955 SCA 766: 1955 SCJ 523: AIR 1955 SC 504].

**Retailer.** A person or entity engaged in the business of selling personal property to the public or to consumers, as opposed to selling to those who intend to resell the items [Black's *Law Dictionary*, 8th Ed.]; a person engaged in making sales to ultimate consumers.

Retailer in relation to the sale of any goods includes every person, other than the wholesaler, who sells the goods to any other person. [*Monopolies and Restrictive Trade Practices Act 1969, s. 2(p)*. The Act is repealed and replaced by the Competition Act 2002. No such term is defined under the new Act].

> NOTE: *'Retailer' and 'wholesaler'—distinction.* The essential distinction between a 'retailer' and 'wholesaler' is that the person buying from the retailer is the ultimate user or consumer of the article or commodity and does not sell it again whereas the one buying from a wholesaler buys only for the purpose of selling the article again. [*Haynie* v *Hogue Lumber & Supply Co. of Gulfport* 96 F Supp 214, 216].

**Retain.** Cling to; continue to hold; hold in possession; possess; preserve; commission; engage; enlist; keep in pay.

> NOTE: One 'retains' only what one already possesses; the word 'retain' is wholly inappropriate for the purpose of conferring a fresh right. [*Abdul Ahad* v *I.G. of Police* AIR 1965 All 142 (FB)].

**Retention in service.** It means continuance in employment. It is quite different from re-employment of an employee after retirement. [*Basanta Kumar* v *Chief Electrical Engineer* AIR 1958 Cal 657].

**Retirement.** Voluntary termination of one's own employment or career, especially upon reaching a certain age; withdrawal from action or for privacy; withdrawal from circulation. [Black's *Law Dictionary*, 8th Ed.].

▸ *Meaning under Payment of Gratuity Act 1972, s. 2(q).* The expression 'retirement' has been defined to mean 'termination of the service of an employee otherwise than on superannuation'. The definition is framed in the widest terms. Except for superannuation, any termination of service would amount to 'retirement' for the purposes of the Act. [*State of Punjab* v *Labour Court* AIR 1979 SC 1981: (1980)1 SCC 5].

**Retortion.** This is a technical term for retaliation by a State against discourteous or inequitable acts of another State. This takes the form of unfriendly legitimate acts within the competence of the State whose dignity has been affronted. Examples are severance of diplomatic relations, revocation of diplomatic privileges, or withdrawal of fiscal or tariff concessions.

> NOTE: *'Reprisal' and 'retortion'—distinction.* The distinction between reprisal and retortion is that reprisals consist of acts which would generally

otherwise be quite illegal whereas retortion consists of retaliatory conduct to which no legal objection can be taken. [Starke's *International Law*, 10th Ed., p. 520].

**Retract.** To draw back, abjure, cancel, repudiate, renunciate, revoke.

**Retract an offer.** To withdraw an offer before acceptance.

**Retraction.** The act of taking or drawing back; abjuration; cancellation; repudiation; renunciation; recision; revocation.

**Retrenchment.** The termination by the employer of the service of a workman for any reason whatsoever, otherwise than as a punishment inflicted by way of disciplinary action, but does not include—(*a*) voluntary retirement of the workman; or (*b*) retirement of the workman on reaching the age of superannuation if the contract of employment between the employer and the workman concerned contains a stipulation in that behalf; or (*bb*) termination of the service of the workman as a result of the non-renewal of the contract of employment between the employer and the workman concerned on its expiry or of such contract being terminated under a stipulation in that behalf contained therein; or (*c*) termination of the service of a workman on the ground of continued ill-health. [Industrial Disputes Act 1947, s. 2(*oo*)].

'Retrenchment' means the termination by the employer of the service of a workman for any reason whatsoever, otherwise than as a punishment inflicted by way of disciplinary action. [*M. Venugopal* v *Divisional Manager, LIC of India, Machilipatnam* AIR 1994 SC 1343: (1994)2 SCC 323: (1994)2 SCJ 62].

NOTE: Retrenchment connotes that the business is being continued, but that a portion of the staff or the labour force is discharged as surplusage. The termination of the services of all the workmen as a result of the closure of the business cannot, therefore, be properly described as retrenchment. [*Hariprasad Shivshankar Shukla* v *A.D. Divakar* 1957 SCR 121: AIR 1957 SC 121: 1957 SCJ 83; *Pipraich Sugar Mills Ltd.* v *Pipraich Sugar Mills Mazdoor Union* 1956 SCR 372: 1957 SCJ 38: 1957 SCA 28: AIR 1957 SC 95].

Striking off the name of a workman from rolls by the employer amounts to termination of service and such termination is retrenchment. [*H.D. Singh* v *Reserve Bank of India* 1985 Lab IC 1733: AIR 1986 SC 132].

**Retrospective.** Extending in scope or effect to matters that have occurred in the past. It is also termed retroactive.

'Retrospective' means looking backward; contemplating what is past; having reference to a statute or things existing before the act in question. [*Darshan Singh* v *Ram Pal Singh* JT 1990(4) SC 561: AIR 1991 SC 1654: 1992 Supp (1) SCC 191].

NOTE: Declaratory Acts are usually held to be retrospective. A remedial Act, on the contrary, is not necessarily retrospective; it takes effect prospectively unless it has been given retrospective effect by express terms or necessary intendment. [*Central Bank of India* v *Their Workman* (1960)1 SCR 200: AIR 1960 SC 12: (1960)1 SCA 454: 1960 SCJ 842].

A change in the law of procedure operates retrospectively. [*Anant Gopal Sheorey* v *State of Bombay* AIR 1958 SC 915: 1958 SCJ 1231; *Ram Kumar* v *First Addl. District Judge* 1978 All WC 405 (FB): (1978)4 All LR 372: (1978)2 Ren CR 74].

**Retrospective law.** 'Retrospective law' means a law which looks backward or contemplates the past; one which is made to affect acts or facts occurring, or rights occurring, before it came into force. [*Darshan Singh* v *Ram Pal Singh* JT 1990(4) SC 561: AIR 1991 SC 1654: 1992 Supp (1) SCC 191].

**Retrospectively.** "Retrospectively" in relation to statutes etc. means 'operative with regard to past time'. The change effected does not say that it shall be operative with effect from any earlier date. [*Punjab University* v *Subash Chander* AIR 1984 SC 1415: (1984)3 SCR 822: (1984)3 SCC 603].

**Return.** As noun means a schedule of information required by governmental bodies, such as the tax return required by the income-tax department; merchandise which is brought back to the seller for credit or refund; profit on sale, or income from investment; the report made by an appropriate authority charged with the official counting of the votes cast at an election.

As verb means to send back; to place in the custody of; to restore; to redeliver.

• **False return** p. 341.

**Returning officer.** The official who conducts an election in a constituency. [Representation of the People Act 1951, s. 21].

**Reunion.** Reunion in Hindu law means living together after partition of the member of a joint family who were parties to the original partition. [*Balabux* v *Bukhmabai* 30 Cal 725 (PC)]. The well-known text of Vrihaspati on *Reunion* runs thus: "He who being once separated dwells again through affection with his father, brother, or paternal uncle is termed united."

NOTE: The commentators are not unanimous as to who may reunite. According to the Mitakshara, the Dayabhaga and the Smriti Chandrika, a member of a joint family once separated can reunite only with his father, brother or paternal uncle, but not with any other relation, as for instance, paternal uncle's son, though such relation was a party to the original partition. According to Vivada Chintamani and the Mayukha, a person may reunite with any relation who was a party to the original partition. Only males can reunite. [*Nanuram* v *Radhabai* AIR 1940 Nag 241].

The effect of a reunion is to remit the reunited members to their former status as members of a joint Hindu family. [*Pran Kishen* v *Mothooramohun* (1865)10 MIA 403, 406].

To constitute a reunion, there must be an intention of the parties to reunite in estate and interest. [*Bhagwan Dayal* v *Reoti Devi* AIR 1962 SC 287, 296]. The mere fact that the parties who have separated live together or trade together after partition does not amount to reunion. [*Venkata Chanchayya* v *Ramalingam* AIR 1957 AP 744].

**Revenue.** Gross income or receipts; earnings; intake; proceeds; return or yield.

The annual or periodical rents, profits, interests or issues of any species of property, real or personal; income of individual, corporation, government, etc. [*Willoughby* v *Willoughby* 19 A 2d 857, 860].

The word 'revenue' is a word of somewhat indefinite import, but in its ordinary sense in relation to a business undertaking it connotes those incomings of the undertaking which are the products of or are incidental to the normal working of the undertaking. [*London, Midland etc.* v *Anglo-Scottish Railways, etc.* 150 LT 361].

▸ *Meaning under the Code of Civil Procedure 1908, Or. 21, r. 66(2).* The expression 'revenue' comprehends only assessments, quit-rents, ground rents or any other charge upon the land payable to Government. It does not include taxes payable to municipality. [*Ramadasjee Baru* v *Tirupathi Devasthanams* AIR 1965 AP 334].

▸ *Meaning under the Constitution of India, Art. 226(1).* The expression 'revenue' appearing in the Article has not been defined, but there can be no manner of doubt that it means 'the income of the nation derived from its taxes, duties or other sources, for the payment of the nation's expenses'. [*Gopi Pershad* v *State of Punjab* 58 Punj LR 480: AIR 1957 Punj 45 (DB)].

**Revenue account.** The account of a firm or a company showing the result of its operations and what profit or loss it has made. For the purpose of ascertaining profits arising from the business of a company, capital account and revenue account are *prima facie* to be treated as separate accounts. The credit balance of revenue account is applicable for dividend.

NOTE: Where a trader dispenses with the services of a particular agent or servant and makes payment for the cancellation of the agency or service agreement, such a payment is properly chargeable to revenue. [*Anglo-Persian Oil Co.* v *Dale* (1932)1 KB 124, 139, 140].

**Reverse.** To overthrow; vacate; set aside; make void; annul; repeal, or revoke.

'Reverse' evidently means 'to set aside'. [*Emperor* v *Edward William Smither* 26 Madras Jurist 1, 15].

**Reverse a judgment.** To reverse a judgment means to overthrow it by contrary decision, make it void, undo or annul it for error. [*Atlantic Coast Line R. Co.* v *St. Joe Paper Co.* CA Fla, 216 F 2d 832, 833].

**Reversion.** A reversion is an estate that arises by operation of law whenever the owner of an estate carves a smaller estate, called a particular estate, out of it in favour of another. The residue of the estate continues in him that made the particular estate. [Cheshire's *Modern Real Property*, 10th Ed., p. 385].

The term 'reversion' has two meanings, first, as designating the estate left in the grantor during the continuance of a particular estate and also the residue left in grantor or his heirs after termination of particular estate. [*Davidson* v *Davidson* 167 SW 2d 641, 642; *Miller* v *C.I.R.* 147 F 2d 189, 193].

NOTE: *'Reversion' and 'remainder'—distinction.* Reversion arises by act of the law, whereas a remainder is by act of the parties. A reversion, moreover, is the remnant left in the grantor, while a remainder is the remnant of the whole estate disposed of, after a preceding part of the same has been given away.

**Reversioner.** A person who is entitled to an estate in reversion; one who is entitled to any future estate or any property in expectancy.

NOTE: Reversioners are the heirs of the last full owner who would be entitled to succeed to the estate of such owner on the death of a widow or other limited owner. The interest of a reversioner is *spes successionis* or a mere chance of succession within the meaning of s. 6 of the Transfer of Property Act 1882, and is not transferable.

**Review.** To re-examine judicially or administratively; a reconsideration; second view or examination; revision; consideration for purposes of correction.

According to the Chamber's *Twentieth Century Dictionary* the word 'review' is reconsideration and as verb it means to see or examine again. According to the Webster's *Seventh New Collegiate Dictionary*, the word 'review' means renewed study of material previously studied. [*Roshanlal Poddar* v *State* (1975)79 CWN 816: 1975 Cr LJ 1583].

The term 'review' means a judicial re-examination of the case in certain specified and prescribed circumstances. [*Gopinath Deb* v *Budhia Swain* (1982)54 Cut LT 515 (DB)].

NOTE: 'Review' is a creature of a statute and cannot be entertained in the absence of a provision thereof. [*Major Chandra Bhan Singh* v *Latafat Ullah Khan* AIR 1978 SC 1814: (1978)1 SCR 891: (1979)1 SCC 321].

Remedy of review, is of very limited scope and it can be availed only in respect of errors apparent on the face of the record. [*Tarakeshwar Singh* v *State of Bihar* (1992)1 Pat LJR 469].

• **Judicial review** p. 496.

**Revise.** Amend; bring upto date; correct; examine; modify; overhaul; reconsider; reconstruct; rectify; re-examine; revamp; review; rework; rewrite.

The word 'revise' means to re-examine or to review or amend [*Mst. Hasmeer Khatun* v *Revenue Officer* AIR 1971 Cal 105: 74 CWN 1020]; to re-examine, to review, to correct, or to amend the fault. [*Ram Kanai Jamini Ranjan Pal Pvt. Ltd.* v *Member, Board of Revenue, West Bengal* (1976)3 SCC 369].

The word 'revise' in the wide sense covers not only the power to confirm or set aside the order of an authority, but also to issue a fresh permission. [*Ram Sarup* v *Sikhar Chand* AIR 1961 All 221].

**Revision.** Re-examination or careful review for correction or improvement; reconsideration; rectification; removal of errors; updated version.

'Revision' means looking back to what is already done and correct the same on review. [*Gangarani Bera* v *State of West Bengal* 1987 CLJ 36].

In Parliamentary law, it means a general and thorough rewriting of a governing document, in which the entire document is open to amend. [Black's *Law Dictionary*, 8th Ed.].

In Military law, it means the reconvening of a general or special court-martial to revise its action or to correct record because of an improper or inconsistent action concerning the findings or the sentence. [Black's *Law Dictionary*, 8th Ed.].

**Revocation.** An annulment, cancellation, or reversal, usually of an act or power. [Black's *Law Dictionary*, 8th Ed.].

The word 'revocation' means annulling, rescinding, withdrawing. [*Pradip Kumar Das* v *State of West Bengal* AIR 1974 SC 2151: (1974)1 Cr LJ 476: (1975)3 SCC 335].

The word 'revocation' is only apposite when it is intended to repeal, annul or withdraw some order which has already become effective. [*Karnal Distillery Co. Ltd.* v *State of Haryana* (1970)1 SCC 116].

Revocation is a process of recall of what has been done; an act of recalling or calling back; the act by which one having the right annuls something previously done. [*Ibrahim Bachu Bafan* v *State of Gujarat* AIR 1985 SC 697: (1985)2 SCC 24: (1985)2 SCR 891: 1985 Cr LJ 533].

With reference to contracts, revocation means withdrawal of an offer by the offerer before its acceptance.

With reference to wills and estates, it means invalidation of a will by the testator, either by destroying the will or by executing a new one.

• **Dependent relative revocation** p. 251.

**Revocation of a licence.** A "revocation" of a licence means that the licence has not been suspended but cancelled for all times to come entailing civil consequences and complete abolition of right for the exercise of which the licence was granted. [*M/s. Laxmi Khandsari* v *State of U.P.* AIR 1981 SC 873: (1981)2 SCC 600: (1981)3 SCR 92].

**Revoke.** To annul or make void by recalling or taking back; to cancel, rescind, repeal, or reverse.

The word 'revoke' carries with it the idea of cancellation by the same power which originally acted and not to setting aside of an original order by higher forum of power or jurisdiction. [*Ibrahim Bachu Bafan* v *State of Gujarat* AIR 1985 SC 697: (1985)2 SCC 24: (1985)2 SCR 891: 1985 Cr LJ 533].

**Revoke with immediate effect.** To revoke from the date thereof. [*R.P. Kapur* v *Union of India* AIR 1967 Punj 417].

**Rig veda.** The earliest sacred writings of the Hindus are the *Vedas*, containing religious as well as legal precepts. The *Vedas* are four in number. Each of them consists of two parts, the first part is called *Sanhita*, and the second part is called *Brahmana*. Of the four *Vedas*, the *Rig Veda* occupies the most prominent position and appears to be the most ancient. The other three *Vedas*, are the *Sam Veda*, the *Yajur Veda*, and the *Atharva Veda*.

NOTE: The *Vedas* are not of much importance to practical lawyers, as they do not at all deal with positive law, but are confined exclusively to the consideration of religious rites and duties. But they furnish us with materials, though indirect and meagre, from which the state of early society and its usage may be gathered and there are some passages containing an incidental allusion to a rule of law, or giving an instance from which a rule of law or usage may be inferred.

**Right(s).** As noun, and taken in an abstract sense, it means justice, ethical correctness, or consonance with the rules of law or the principles of morals.

As noun, and taken in a concrete sense, it means a power, privilege, faculty, or demand, inherent in one person and incident upon another.

As adjective, the term 'right' means just, morally correct, consonant with ethical principles or rules of positive law. It is the opposite of wrong, unjust, illegal.

In a generic sense, the word 'right' is used to mean an immunity from the legal power of another. [*State of Rajasthan* v *Union of India* AIR 1977 SC 1361: (1977)3 SCC 592: (1978)1 SCR 1].

Rights are defined generally as powers of free action.

A 'right' is a legally protected interest. [*Mithilesh Kumari* v *Prem Behari Khare*

AIR 1989 SC 1247: (1989)2 SCC 95: JT 1989(1) SC 275: (1989)40 ELT 257: (1989)177 ITR 97: (1989)1 SCR 621].

A 'right' is an averment of entitlement arising out of legal rules. [*Shanti Kumar R. Canji* v *The Home Insurance Co. of New York* AIR 1974 SC 1719: (1974)2 SCC 387: 1974(2) SLR 538: (1975)1 SCR 550].

The term 'right' comprehends every right known to the law. It includes both corporeal and incorporeal rights including a right of ownership. [*Jasjit Singh* v *Charanjit Kaur* AIR 1995 P&H 177].

A right is an interest which is recognised and protected by law. As it is recognised by law, a man is entitled to have it. As it can be protected by law, the possessor can enforce it by an appropriate action in a court. [*Maloji Narsingh Rao* v *Shanker Saran* AIR 1958 All 775].


- **Birth right** p. 106.
- **Civil rights** p. 146.
- **Claim of right** p. 147.
- **Conjugal rights** p. 173.
- **Electoral right** p. 296.
- **Enforce any right** p. 308.
- **Extinguishment of right** p. 333.
- **Fundamental rights** p. 378.
- **Human rights** p. 423.
- **Inalienable rights** p. 443.
- **Janmam rights** p. 485.
- **Legal right** p. 528.
- **Marital rights** p. 562.
- **Mining right** p. 582.
- **Natural rights** p. 600.
- **Religious right** p. 743.
- **Restitution of conjugal rights** p. 756.
- **Vested right** p. 879.


**Right of private defence.** It is a right available in face of imminent peril to those who act in good faith and in no case can the right be conceded to a person who stage manages a situation wherein the right can be used as a shield to justify an act of aggression. [*State of U.P.* v *Ram Swarup* AIR 1974 SC 1570: (1974)4 SCC 764: 1974 Cr LJ 1035: (1975)1 SCR 409].

NOTE: This right is basically preventive and not punitive. [*Gottipulla Venkata Siva Subbrayanam* v *State of Andhra Pradesh* AIR 1970 SC 1079: (1970)3 SCR 423: (1970)1 SCC 235: 1970 Cr LJ 1004].

**Right of redemption.** The right to disencumber property or to free it from a claim or lien; the right granted by statute only to free property from the encumbrance of a foreclosure or other judicial cell, or to recover the title passing thereby, by paying what is due, with interest, costs, etc.

▸ *Meaning under the Transfer of Property Act 1882, s. 60.* The right of the mortgagor, on payment or tender at a proper time and place, of the mortgage-money, to require the mortgagee (*a*) to deliver to the mortgagor the mortgage-deed and all documents relating to the mortgaged property which are in the possession or power of the mortgagee; (*b*) where the mortgagee is in possession of the mortgaged property to deliver possession thereof to the mortgagor; and (*c*) at the cost of the mortgagor either to retransfer the mortgaged property to him or to such third person as he may direct or to execute and to have registered an acknowledgment in writing that any right in derogation of his interest transferred to the mortgagee has been extinguished.

**Right of re-entry.** This is the right which the lessor has against the lessee for breach of an express condition which provides that on its breach the lessor may re-enter. A right of re-entry implies an estate of reversion and cannot be transferred apart from the estate to which it belongs. The transfer of the reversion, *i.e.*, of the lessor's interest, carries with it the right of re-entry.

**Right of way.** A right belonging to a party to pass over land of another. [*Bouche* v *Wagner* 293 P 2d 203, 209].

"Right of way" is also used to refer to a preference of one of two vehicles, or as between a vehicle and a pedestrian, asserting right of passage at the same place and time, but it is not an absolute right in the sense that possessor thereof is relieved from duty of exercising due care for his own safety and that of others. [*Cheramie* v *Scott* Tex Civ App, 324 SW 2d 87, 90].

- **Private right of way.** A private right of way may be defined as a right to utilise the servient tenement as a means of access to or egress from the dominant tenement for some purpose connected with the enjoyment of the dominant tenement, according to the nature of that tenement. A right of way can validly be made appurtenant to land with which the way has no physical contiguity, but it must be beneficial in respect of the occupation of that land. [Halsbury's *Laws of England*, 4th Ed., vol. 14, para 144, p. 68].

  A private right of way may be defined as a right to utilise the servient tenement as a means of access to or egress from the dominant tenement.

  NOTE: A right of way may be acquired by prescription. [Limitation Act 1963, s. 25].

**Right to begin.** The privilege of opening a case.

NOTE: The party on whom the burden of proof lies has the right to begin.

The plaintiff has the right to begin unless the defendant admits the facts alleged by the plaintiff and contends that either in point of law or on some additional facts alleged by the defendant the plaintiff is not entitled to any part of the relief which he seeks, in which case the defendant has the right to begin. [Code of Civil Procedure 1908, Or. 18, r. 1].

On the day fixed for the hearing of the suit or on any other day to which the hearing is adjourned, the party having the right to begin shall state his case and produce his evidence in support of the issues which he is bound to prove. [Code of Civil Procedure 1908, Or. 18, r. 2(1)].

**Right to practice.** Right to practice includes not merely to plead but also to act. [*In re Lily Isabel Thomas* AIR 1964 SC 855: (1964)2 SCA 536].

**Right to sue.** It means the right to bring a suit asserting a right to relief available to the plaintiff [*Smt. Phool Rani* v *Sh. Naubat Rai Ahluwalia* AIR 1973 SC 2110: (1973)3 SCR 679: (1973)1 SCC 688]; the right to seek relief upon an infringement of the right asserted in the suit. [*State of Bihar* v *Motilal Chamaria* AIR 1964 Pat 127].

NOTE: The term 'right to sue' must be equated with "cause of action", unless the context indicates otherwise. [*Gurdit Singh* v *Munsha Singh* AIR 1977 SC 640: (1977)2 SCR 250: (1977)1 SCC 791].

**Rin.** Debt; loan.

**Ring.** An exclusive combination of persons for illegitimate or selfish purposes; a combination formed by a group of speculators to obtain control of the market. The term also applies to a combination of politicians acting together for the control of State policy.

**Rini.** A debtor; a borrower.

**Riparian owner.** A riparian owner is one whose land abuts on and in part of the bank of a river or stream, whether it be tidal or non-tidal. [*Lyon* v *Fishmongers Co.* 46 LJ Ch 68: 1 App Cas 662].

One who owns land on bank of river, or one who is owner of land along, bordering upon, bounded by, fronting upon, abutting or adjacent and contiguous to and in contract with river. [*State ex rel. Buckson* v *Pennsylvania R. Co.* Del Super, 228 A 2d 587, 594].

**Risk.** Hazard, danger, peril, exposure to loss, injury, disadvantage or destruction, and comprises all elements of danger. [*Knox Jewelry Co., Inc.* v *Cincinnati Ins. Co.* 203 SE 2d 739, 740].

**Rite.** The word 'rite' is a formal procedure or act in a religious or other solemn observance. [*Mumandi Kone* v *Sri Ramnatha Sethupathi* AIR 1982 Mad 170].

**Riti.** Custom; usage; practice; tradition prevalent.

**Ritual.** The word 'ritual' means 'pertaining or relating to, connected with rites'. [*Mumandi Kone* v *Sri Ramnatha Sethupathi* AIR 1982 Mad 170].

**River.** A natural, flowing body of water that empties into another body of water, such as a lake, sea, or channel. [Black's *Law Dictionary*, 8th Ed.].

A natural stream of water, of greater volume than a creek or rivulet, flowing in a more or less permanent bed or channel, between defined banks or walls, with a current which may either be continuous in one direction or affected by the ebb and flow of the tide.

NOTE: River includes any stream, canal, creek or other channels, natural or artificial. [Indian Forest Act 1927, s. 2(5)].

- **Bed of the river** p. 98.
- **International river.** A river that flows through or between two or more countries. [Black's *Law Dictionary*, 8th Ed.].

Where a river passes through several States, it is regarded as an international river. Where a river lies wholly within the territory of one State, it belongs entirely to that State. In the case of an international river, each State owns that part of the river which runs through its territory; but controversy has centered round the question of the rights of the riparian and other States to navigate along the whole length of the river. Several writers on international law, commencing with Grotius, have been of opinion that there is a general right of navigation for all States along such international rivers, but this view has never been generally accepted in practice.

NOTE: Some measure of freedom of navigation on international rivers, however, became established through treaties. The process began with the Treaty of Paris, 1814, and the Vienna Congress of 1815, and continued with the Peace Treaties of 1919-1920, and the subsequent general conventions concluded under the auspices of the League of Nations. As a result, there was, before the Second World War, a limited freedom of passage on most of the great river systems of Europe. Also international authorities had been set up to administer particular river systems. For instance, under the Treaty of Paris, 1856, the European Commission of the Danube was set up to regulate navigation on the lower Danube.

More recent conventions to unify river law are the Bangkok Convention of July 22, 1956, for facilitating inland navigation between Asian countries. Yet, these treaties have neither singly nor cumulatively established a general right of passage along international rivers.

- **Navigable river** p. 601.
- **Tidal navigable river** p. 843.

**Road.** A highway; an open or public passage; a strip of land appropriated and used for purposes of travel and communication between different places.

- **Lateral road** p. 512.
- **Private road** p. 687.

**Robbery.** The illegal taking of property from the person of another, or in the person's presence, by violence or intimidation; aggravated larceny. [Black's *Law Dictionary*, 8th Ed.].

NOTE: Theft is robbery if, in order to the committing of the theft, or in committing thefts or in carrying away or attempting to carry away property obtained by theft the offender for that end voluntarily causes or attempts to cause to any person death or hurt or wrongful restraint, or fear of instant death or of instant hurt or of instant wrongful restraint.

Extortion is robbery if the offender at the time of committing the extortion is in the presence of the person put in fear and commits the extortion by putting that person in fear of instant death, of instant hurt or of instant wrongful restraint to that person or to some other person and by so putting in fear induces the person so put in fear then and there to deliver up the thing extorted. [Indian Penal Code 1860, s. 390].

**Rogatory letters.** A commission from a judge in one country to a judge in another, requesting him to examine witnesses residing in the latter country in a suit pending in the former. [*Bouvier*].

A commission from one judge to another requesting him to examine a witness.

**Roll.** Record of the proceedings of a court or public office; a register; list of persons belonging to particular group; in taxation, the list or record of taxable persons and property, as compiled by assessors.

**Root of title.** The document with which an abstract of title properly commences.

NOTE: If the abstract of title commences with an instrument of disposition it must be such as will form what is called a good root of title; that is to say, it must, as a rule, be an instrument dealing with the whole estate, legal and equitable, in the property sold, containing a description by which the property can be identified, and containing nothing to cast any doubt on the title of the disposing parties. [Williams & Eastwood on *Real Property*, p. 461].

**Rotational.** The word 'rotational' means regular and recurring succession-in-office or duties. [*P.C. Joshi* v *Director-General, Posts and Telegraphs* AIR 1975 SC 1: (1975)1 SCJ 315: (1975)2 SCR 115].

**Roti.** "Roti" is generally used to connote "meals". [*Shanker* v *State of U.P.* AIR 1975 SC 757: (1975)3 SCC 851: 1975 Cr LJ 634: 1975 SCC (Cri) 270].

**Route.** A way, road; a course taken in travelling from one place to another.

Route is an abstract conception of a line of travel between one terminus and another, and to be something distinct from the highway traversed. [*Kelani Valley etc.* v *Colombo-Ratnapura etc.* (1946) AC 338].

In railroad parlance, 'route' means a designated course over a way or right of way, irrespective of the singleness or multiplicity of operation thereon. [*Regenhardt Const. Co.* v *Southern Ry. in Kentucky* 181 SW 2d 441, 444].

'Route' means a line of travel which specifies the highway which may be traversed by a motor vehicle between one terminus and another. [*Mysore State Road Transport Corporation* v *Mysore State Transport Appellate Tribunal* AIR 1974 SC 1940: (1974)2 SCC 750: (1975)1 SCR 615].

A route may mean not only the notional line of travel between one terminus and another, but also the area of the road over which the motor vehicles ply. [*D. Papiah* v *Mysore State Transport Appellate Tribunal* AIR 1976 SC 1731: (1976)3 SCR 28: (1976)1 SCC 953; *Adarsh Travels Bus Service* v *State of U.P.* 1985 Supp (3) SCR 661: (1985)4 SCC 557: AIR 1986 SC 319].

• **Interstate route** p. 477.

**Routine.** 'Routine' means a regular course of procedure a more or less mechanical or unvarying performance of certain acts or duties; regular, unvarying or mechanical procedure, discharge of duties, etc. of a mechanical or unvaried character, performed by rule. [*Gidda Naga Malliah* v *Kothuri Laxmanayya* AIR 1970 AP 289].

**Routine duties of a receiver.** The 'routine' duties of a receiver must be construed to be such duties which are mechanical, regular and unvarying performed by him. [*Gidda Naga Malliah* v *Kothuri Laxmanayya* AIR 1970 AP 289].

**Royalty.** A payment made to an author or inventor for each copy of a work or article sold under a copyright or patent; a share of the product or profit from real property, reserved by the grantor of a mineral lease, in exchange for the lessee's right to mine or drill on the land. [Black's *Law Dictionary*, 8th Ed.].

Royalty is share of product or profit reserved by owner for permitting another to use the property. In its broadest aspect, it is share of profit reserved by owner for permitting another the use of property. [*Alamo Nat. Bank of San Antonio* v *Hurd* Tex Civ App, 485 SW 2d 335, 338].

The word 'royalty' is meant to be employed to secure for the state something out of what the state conveys. Sometimes the term 'royalty' is used in a loose sense so as to convey liability to make periodic payments to the assignor for the period during which the lease would subsist. [*Inderjeet Singh* v *M/s. Karam Chand Thapar* JT 1995(7) SC 56].

Royalties are payments which the government may demand for the appropriation of minerals, timber or other property belonging to the government. Two important features of royalty have to be noticed; that the payment is made for the privilege of removing the articles in proportion to the quantity removed, and the basis of the payment is an agreement. [*Surajdin* v *State of M.P.* AIR 1960 MP 129; *Mohanlal Bhagwati Prasad* v *State of M.P.* 1980 Jab LJ (SN) 67 (DB)].

'Royalty' means a payment reserved by the grantor of a patent, lease of a mine or similar right, and payable proportionately to the use made of the right by the grantee. [*State of Orissa* v *Titaghur Paper Mills Company Ltd.* AIR 1985 SC 1293: (1985)3 SCR 26: 1985 (Supp) SCC 280: (1985)60 STC 213; *District Council* v *Dwet Singh Rymbani* AIR 1986 SC 1930: (1986)4 SCC 38: (1986)3 SCR 569: JT 1986 SC 146].

Royalty also means a payment which is made to an author or composer by a publisher in respect of each article sold under the patent. [*State of Orissa* v *Titaghur Paper Mills Company Ltd.* AIR 1985 SC 1293: (1985)3 SCR 26: 1985 (Supp) SCC 280: (1985)60 STC 213].

NOTE: It is usually a payment of money, but may be a payment in kind, that is, of part of the produce of the exercise of the right. [*State of Orissa* v *Titaghur Paper Mills Company Ltd.* AIR 1985 SC 1293: (1985)3 SCR 26: 1985 (Supp) SCC 280: (1985)60 STC 213].

**Rule.** As noun, 'rule' means an established standard, guide, or regulation; a principle or regulation set up by authority, prescribing or directing action or forbearance; an order made by a court, at the instance of one of the parties to a suit, commanding a ministerial officer, or the opposite party, to do some act, or to show cause why some act should not be done.

As verb, it means to command or require by a rule of court; to settle or decide a point of law arising upon a trial.

▸ *Meaning under the General Clauses Act 1897, s. 3(51).* 'Rule' means a rule made in exercise of a power conferred by any enactment, and shall include a regulation made as a rule under any enactment. [*Sukdev Singh* v *Bhagatram Sardar Singh Raghuvanshi* AIR 1975 SC 1331: (1975)3 SCR 619: (1975)1 SCC 421: (1975)1 SCR 605].

• **Golden rule** p. 389.
• **Work to rule** p. 903.

**Rule absolute.** Rule confirmed after hearing the party on whom notice was served or a rule not discharged.

**Rule nisi.** A rule which will become fully authoritative and binding on a party, unless, on a notice to show cause why the rule should not be made final, the party comes and satisfies the court.

**Rule of law.** A substantive legal principle; the supremacy of regular as opposed to arbitrary power; the doctrine that every person is subject to the ordinary law within the jurisdiction; the doctrine that general constitutional principles are the result of judicial decisions determining the rights of private individuals in the courts; loosely a legal ruling, a ruling on a point of law. [Black's *Law Dictionary*, 8th Ed.].

The expression 'rule of law' connotes the undisputed supremacy of law and envisages a state of things in which everyone respects the law and where law has to be followed by everyone collectively and individually. This supremacy of law is designed to give security to the rights of individuals who are the citizens of a democratic State. [*Laxminarayan Gupta* v *Collector, District Shivpuri* AIR 1956 MB 163].

The rule of law in contradiction to the rule of man includes within its wide connotation the absence of arbitrary power, submission to the ordinary law of the land and the equal protection of laws. [*Harbans Singh* v *State of Punjab* 1987 Cr LJ 1088: (1987)1 Chand LR (Cr) 387].

The rule of law means that decisions should be made by the application of known principles and rules and in general such decisions should be predictable and the citizen should know where he is. [*Jai Singhani* v *Union of India* AIR 1967 SC 142: (1967)2 SCR 703].

NOTE: The rule of law requires that Government should be conducted within the framework of recognised rules and principle which restricts discretionary powers. The expression 'rule of law" has a number of different meanings and connotations. The primary concept is that everything must be done according to law. [*Patil Exhibitors* v *Bangalore City Corporation* AIR 1986 Kant 194, 197].

**Rupiya.** A silver coin formerly prevalent in India.

# Ss

**Sabotage.** An act of malicious damage; deliberately poor workmanship intended to cause damage, obstruction of plans, aims, etc.; deliberate damage to productive capacity; destroy, spoil; make useless.

The term also refers to wilful and malicious destruction of employer's property during a labour dispute or interference with his normal operations. [*Burns* v *US* 274 US 328: 71 L Ed 1077].

**Sacking.** Sacking is a fabric woven with double wrapped yarn. [*Hoare Miller* v *Union of India* 65 CWN 1206].

**Sacrilege.** Stealing things dedicated to the office of religion.

Breaking into a church, chapel or other place of divine worship and committing an offence therein; or, being in such place, committing an offence therein, and breaking out.

**Sadaqah.** A gift by a Mahomedan made with the object of acquiring religious merit.

**Sadar.** Chief; supreme; highest.

**Sadar-adalat.** Chief Court or High Court; sometimes means District Court.

**Sadar dewani adalat.** High Court of civil jurisdiction.

**Sadar nizamat adalat.** High Court of criminal jurisdiction.

**Sadi.** Marriage; marriage ceremony.

**Sadism.** A form of sexual perversion derived from inflicting harm, pain or suffering on another. It is a type of mental disease and the opposite of masochism.

**Safe.** Free of danger or injury; reliable, certain; not hazardous; not involving risk or loss; not likely to disappoint.

**Safe conduct.** A written permission given by a belligerent Government, or one of its naval or military commanders, enabling an enemy subject to go to a particular place or a particular object; an official document assuring protection on a journey or voyage, as in time of war.

**Safe place to work.** In the law of master and servant, a place in which the master has eliminated all danger which in the exercise of reasonable care the master should remove or guard against.

> NOTE: Master's duty to provide a "safe place" to work includes places to and from which the employee might be required or expected to go. [*High Splint Coal Co.* v *Ramey's Adm'x* 112 SW 2d 1007, 1008].

**Sagai.** A form of marriage prevalent among low caste Hindus. It is an informal ceremony of marriage and is recognised as a valid ceremony in case of remarriage. [*Gopi Krishna* v *Mst. Jaggo* AIR 1936 PC 198: 40 CWN 1007].

**Sagotra.** Belonging to the same gotra or stock of persons professing Hindu religion.

> NOTE: Under the Hindu law, agnates having descended from a common male ancestor in the main line belong to the same gotra. So, they are called sagotras.

**Sailor.** A member of the crew of a ship or boat, especially one below the rank of officer; a seaman; mariner.

A person undergoing training as an artificer apprentice not being an officer and receiving fixed pay regularly after administration of oath is treated as 'sailor'. [*Anuj Kumar Dey* v *Union of India* 1997 SCC (L&S) 153].

**Saivites and Vaishnavites.** The image of Shiva is worshipped by his worshippers who are called Saivites and the image of Vishnu is worshipped by his worshippers who are known as Vaishnavites. [*Seshammal* v *State of Tamil Nadu* AIR 1972 SC 1586: (1972)2 SCC 11].

**Sajjadanashin.** Spiritual superior and head of a *khanka* (Mahomedan religious institution). His status is higher than that of a *mutawalli*.

**Saklong.** It is a customary form of marriage amongst the *ahoms* of Assam. The essential custom consists of exchange of knives within a heap of rice. [*Boloram Baruati* v *Suriya Baruati* AIR 1969 Ass 90].

**Sakshi.** Witness; evidence; deposition.

**Sakulyas.** Agnatic relatives under Hindu Law, connected by offerings of *pinda-lepa*.

**Salami.** 'Salami' is a payment by the tenant as price for parting by the landlord with his rights under one lease-holding. It is a lump sum payment as consideration for what the landlord transfers to the tenant. [*Member for the Board of Agricultural Income-tax, Assam* v *Sindhurani Chaudhurani* (1957)32 ITR 169: 1957 SCR 1019: 1959 SCJ 646].

'Salami' is a single payment made for the acquisition of the right of the lessor by the lessee to enjoy the benefits granted to him by the lease. [*Maharaja Chintamani Saran Nath Sah Deo* v *The C.I.T., Bihar and Orissa* (1971)2 SCC 521: AIR 1972 SC 80: (1972)1 SCR 36].

NOTE: The indicia of salami are—(*i*) its single non-recurring character; and (*ii*) payment prior to the creation of the tenancy. It is the consideration, paid by the tenant for being let into possession, and can be neither rent nor revenue but is a capital receipt in the hands of the landlord. The payment may be made in a single sum, but that is not a conclusive test, for *salami* can be paid in a single payment or by instalments. The real test is whether the said amount paid in a lump sum, or in instalments, is the consideration paid by the tenant for being let into possession. [*CIT, Assam* v *Panbari Tea Co. Ltd.* (1965)2 SCJ 350: AIR 1965 SC 1871: (1965)2 ITJ 242: (1965)57 ITR 1].

The right granted by payment of salami may properly be regarded as a capital asset and the money paid to purchase it may properly be held to be a payment on capital account. [*Maharaja Chintamani Saran Nath Sah Deo* v *The C.I.T., Bihar and Orissa* (1971)2 SCC 521: AIR 1972 SC 80: (1972)1 SCR 36].

**Salary.** A reward or recompense for services performed; a fixed periodical compensation paid for services rendered; a stated compensation paid periodically as by the year, month, or other fixed period, in contrast to wages which are normally based on an hourly rate. [Black's *Law Dictionary*, 5th Ed.].

An agreed compensation for services—especially professional or semi-professional services—usually paid at regular intervals on a yearly basis, as distinct, from an hourly basis. [Black's *Law Dictionary*, 8th Ed.].

The 'salary' is remuneration paid to an employee whose period of engagement is more or less permanent in character, for other than manual or relatively unskilled labour. [*Bahadur Prasad* v *State of Bihar* 1989 Pat LJR 1137 (Pat)].

NOTE: *'Salary' and 'wages'—distinction.* There is no substantial difference between the two, both being a recompense for work done or service rendered. The word 'salary' refers to services of non-manual type while the word 'wages' refers to manual services. Then again, salary refers to the time factor or the job done, the recompense being wholly determined on basis of time spent on services or by the work done or on basis of both the parties. The word 'wages' does not imply that compensation is to be determined solely upon basis of time spent in service, but it may be determined by the work done or it could be estimated in either way. [*Gestetner Duplicators Pvt. Ltd.* v *CIT* AIR 1979 SC 607].

**Sale.** A contract between two parties, called, respectively, the seller or vendor and the buyer or purchaser, by which the former, in consideration of the payment or promise of payment of a certain price in money, transfers to the latter the title and the possession of property; passing of title from seller to buyer for a price; transfer of property for consideration either in money or its equivalent. [*Wade-Corry Co.* v *Moseley* 156 SE 2d 64, 65].

'Sale' means any transfer of property in goods for cash or deferred payment or other valuable consideration, including a transfer of property in goods involved in the execution of a contract, but does not include a mortgage, hypothecation, charge or pledge. [*Vishnu Agencies* v *Commercial Tax Officer* 77 CWN 141].

NOTE: Sale is a transfer of ownership in exchange for a price, paid or promised. Such transfer, in the case of tangible immovable property of the value of one hundred rupees and upwards, or in the case of reversion or other intangible thing can be made only by a registered instrument. In the case of tangible immovable property of a value less than one hundred rupees, such transfer may be made either by a registered instrument or by delivery of the property. Delivery of tangible immovable property takes place when the seller places the buyer, or such person as he directs, in possession of the property. [*Pyare Lal* v *Emperor* ILR (1945) All 207: AIR 1945 All 135].

According to the law both of England and of India, in order to constitute a sale, it is necessary that there should be an agreement between the parties for the purpose of transferring title to goods which, of course, presupposes the capacity to contract that it must be supported by money consideration and that as a result of the transaction property must actually pass in the goods. Unless all these elements are present, there can be no sale. Thus, if merely the title to the goods passes, but not as a result of any contract between the parties express or implied, there is no sale. So also, if the consideration for the transfer was not money but other valuable consideration, it may then be an exchange or barter, but not a sale. And if, under the contract of sale, title to the goods have not passed, then there is an agreement to sell and not a completed sale. [*State of Madras* v *Dunkerley & Co. (Madras) Ltd.* 1959 SCA 379: (1958)9 STC 353: 1958 SCJ 698: 1958 SCA 692: AIR 1958 SC 560, *per* Venkatarama Aiyer, J.].

▸ *Meaning under the Transfer of Property Act 1882, s. 54.* 'Sale' is a transfer of ownership in exchange for a price paid or promised or part-paid and part-promised.

▸ *Meaning under the Prevention of Food Adulteration Act 1954, s. 2(xiii).* 'Sale', with its grammatical variations and cognate expressions, means the sale of any article of food, whether for cash or on credit or by way of exchange and whether by wholesale or retail, for human consumption or use or for the analysis, and includes an agreement for sale, an offer for sale, the exposing for sale or having in possession for sale, of any such article and includes also an attempt to sell any such article.

The definition of 'sale' in Prevention of Food Adulteration Act 1954, is designedly wide, it seems a real sale as well as an 'embryonic' sale (like agreement for sale, offer for sale, exposure for sale, possession for sale, attempt at sale) are sales for the purposes of the Act. The sale may be for cash or credit or by way of exchange. The sale may be by wholesale or retail. Thus, every kind, manner and method of sale are covered. Finally, the sale may be 'for human consumption or use, or for analysis'. [*State of Tamil Nadu* v *Krishnamurthy* (1980)1 SCC 167: AIR 1980 SC 538: 1980 Cr LJ 402; *Bhagwan Das Jagdish Chander* v *Delhi Administration* (1975)1 SCC 866: AIR 1975 SC 1309].

▸ *Meaning under the Central Sales Tax Act 1956, s. 2(g).* 'Sale' with its grammatical variations and cognate expressions, means any transfer of property in goods by one person to another for cash or for deferred payment or for any other valuable consideration, and includes a transfer of goods on the hire-purchase or other system of payment by instalments, but does not include a mortgage or hypothecation of or charge or pledge on goods.

The word 'sale' defined in cl. (*g*) of s. 2 is wide enough to include not only a concluded contract of sale but also a contract or agreement of sale provided the agreement of sale stipulates that there was a transfer of property or movement of goods. [*Balabhagas Hulaschand* v *State of Orissa* AIR 1976 SC 1016: (1976)2 SCR 939: (1976)2 SCC 44: (1976)37 STC 207].

'Sale' means transfer of goods by one person to another for cash or for deferred payment or for any other valuable consideration. It cannot mean agreement for sale. [*Consolidated Coffee Ltd.* v *Coffee Board, Bangalore* AIR 1980 SC 1468: (1980)3 SCR 625: (1980)3 SCC 358: (1980)46 STC 164].

NOTE: *'Sale' and 'agreement to sell'—distinction.* Where under a contract of sale the property in the goods is transferred from the seller to the buyer, the contract is called a sale, but where the transfer of the property in the goods is to take place at a future time or subject to some condition thereafter to be fulfilled, the contract is called an agreement to sell. [Sale of Goods Act 1930, s. 4(3)].

An "agreement to sell" is a contract pure and simple whereas a "sale" is a contract plus a conveyance. [*The Instalment Supply Ltd.* v *STO, Ahmedabad-1* AIR 1974 SC 1105: (1974)4 SCC 739: (1974)34 STC 65: (1975)1 SCR 386].


- **Adapting for sale** p. 37.
- **Approval, sale on** p. 71.
- **Bill of sale** p. 105.
- **Bring-and-buy sale** p. 112.
- **Certificate of sale** p. 132.
- **Conditions of sale** p. 169.
- **Fair sale** p. 339.
- **Forced sale** p. 364.
- **Gross sales** p. 400.
- **Interstate sale** p. 477.
- **Interstate sale or purchase** p. 477.
- **Mortgage by conditional sale** p. 592.
- **Simulated sale** p. 799.


**Sale in the course of export.** 'Sale in the course of export' means sale taking place not only during the activities directed to the end of exportation of the goods out of the country but also as part of or connected with such activities. [*Md. Serajuddin* v *State of Orissa* AIR 1975 SC 1564: (1975)2 SCC 47].

NOTE: A 'sale in the course of export' predicates a connection between the sale and export, the two activities being so integrated that the connection between the two cannot be voluntarily interrupted, without a breach of the contract or the compulsion arising from the nature or the transaction. In this sense to constitute a sale in the course of export it may be said that there must be an intention on the part of both the buyer and the seller to export, there must be an obligation to export, and there must be an actual export. [*Ben Gorm Nilgiri Plantations Co-Conoor Nilgiris etc.* v *Sales Tax Officer, Special Circle, Ernakulam* AIR 1964 SC 1752].

The phrase 'sale in the course of export' comprises in itself three essentials: (*i*) that there must be a sale; (*ii*) that goods must actually be exported; and (*iii*) the sale must be a part and parcel of the export. Therefore, either the sale must take place when the goods are already in the process of being exported which is established by their having already crossed the customs frontiers, or the sale must occasion the export. [*Coffee Board, Bangalore* v *Joint Commercial Tax Officer, Madras* (1969)3 SCC 349: AIR 1971 SC 87].

In the case of sales in the course of export or import, the test laid down was a series of integrated activities commencing from an agreement of sale and ending with the delivery of goods to a common carrier for export by land or by sea. [*State of Travancore Cochin* v *Bombay Co. Ltd.* 1952 SCR 1112: AIR 1952 SC 366].

**Sale in the course of inter-State trade.** A "sale in the course of inter-State trade" includes a sale by a trader in one State to a consumer in another State. The expression is not confined to sales between two traders only. [*State of Bombay* v *United Motors (India) Ltd.* AIR 1953 SC 252: 1953 SCR 1069: 1953 SCJ 373: (1953)4 STC 133].

NOTE: A sale which occasions movement of goods from one State to another is a sale in the course of inter-State trade, no matter in which State the property in the goods passes; it is not necessary that the sale must precede the inter-State movement in order that the sale may be deemed to have occasioned such movement; and it is also not necessary for a sale to be deemed to have taken place in the course of inter-State trade or commerce, that the covenant regarding inter-State movement must be specified in the contract itself. It would be enough if the movement was in pursuance of and incidental to the contract of sale. [*Union of India* v *K.G. Khosla & Co. Ltd.* AIR 1979 SC 1160: (1979)3 SCR 453: (1979)2 SCC 242: (1979)43 STC 457].

**Sale of goods.** The words "sale of goods" have to be construed not in the popular sense but in their legal sense and should be given the same meaning which they carry in the

Sale of Goods Act 1930. The expression "sale of goods" is a *nomen juris*, its essential ingredients being an agreement to sell movables for a price and property passing therein pursuant to that agreement. [*T.V. Sundaram Iyengar & Sons* v *State of Madras* AIR 1974 SC 2309: (1975)2 SCR 372: (1975)3 SCC 424: (1975)35 STC 24].

NOTE: On the true interpretation of the expression "sale of goods" there must be an agreement between the parties for the sale of the very goods in which eventually property passes. [*State of Gujarat (Commissioner of Sales Tax, Ahmedabad)* v *Variety Body Builders* AIR 1976 SC 2108: 1976 (Supp) SCR 131: (1976)3 SCC 500: (1976)38 STC 176].

The expression "sale of goods" must be interpreted when used in Entry 54 of List II of the Seventh Schedule to the Constitution as having the same meaning as in the Sale of Goods Act. Any attempt to give to the expressions 'sale', 'goods' or 'sale of goods' an artificial or enlarged meaning or to bring within their scope what would not be comprehended within it would be *ultra vires* and unconstitutional. [*State of Orissa* v *Titaghur Paper Mills Company Limited* AIR 1985 SC 1293: (1985)3 SCR 26: 1985 (Supp) SCC 280: (1985)60 STC 213].

**Sale or return.** This refers to a contract whereby the buyer has the alternative of selling the goods and paying for them, or of returning the goods to the seller within a reasonable time.

**Sale price.** The amount payable to a dealer as consideration for sale of any goods, less any sum allowed as such discount according to the practice normally prevailing in the trade, but inclusive of any sum charged for anything done by the dealer in respect of the goods at the time of or before the delivery thereof other than the cost of freight or delivery or the cost of installation in cases where such cost is separately charged. [Central Sales Tax Act 1956, s. 2(*h*); *Commissioner of Sales Tax, U.P.* v *Rai Bharat Das & Bros*. JT 1988(4) SC 3: (1988)71 STC 277: (1989)1 SCC 143: AIR 1989 SC 315].

**Sali.** Low land; paddy land; a measure for grain containing 20 *seers*.

**Salis.** An arbitrator; an umpire; a third person who is appointed to decide any dispute.

**Salisnama.** An agreement to refer to arbitration. It is sometimes erroneously referred to as an award. [*Mohammed Farooq* v *Rex* AIR 1950 All 501].

**Salus populi est suprema lex.** The welfare of the people, or of the public, is supreme law. Thus, pulling down a house on fire to prevent its spread to other property does not involve liability. It is only in cases of existing, immediate and overwhelming public necessity that any such right exists. It is made an exception by s. 81 of the Indian Penal Code.

**Salvage.** Conservation; extrication; reclaimed materials; reclamation; recovery; retrieval.

It means the preservation of a vessel which is wrecked, stranded or in distress, or the lives of persons belonging to, or the cargo or apparel of, such a vessel. [Halsbury's *Laws of England*, 4th Ed., vol. 25, para 756, p. 384].

**Sama-Veda.** It is one of the four *Vedas*. The *Sama-Veda* consists of prayers and intended to be chanted at sacrifices. A peculiar degree of holiness is attached to it as it is believed to be efficacious in removing sins.

**Samanodaks.** More distant agnates under Hindu law, connected by offerings of water.

**Same.** Identical; referring to a person or thing just mentioned; the same thing as previously mentioned. It generally refers to the last preceding antecedents; one and the same; not distinct. [*State of Maharashtra* v *Najkat Ali Mubarak Ali* AIR 2001 SC 2255: JT 2001 Supp (1) SC 279: 2001 Cr LJ 2588: (2001)6 SCC 311].

The word 'same' would connote that it is 'identical' though in all cases it may not mean that. It may also mean not different. It frequently means of the kind or species or corresponding to. [*K.V.A.M. Ramanathan Chettiar* v *Commissioner of Income Tax* (1973)88 ITR 167 (SC)].

**Same business.** If one business cannot be conveniently carried on after the closure of the other, there would be a strong indication that the two businesses constituted the same business. [*B.R. Ltd.* v *V.P. Gupta, Commissioner of Income Tax, Bombay* AIR 1978 SC 1320: (1978)3 SCR 877: (1978)3 SCC 70: (1978)113 ITR 647].

NOTE: The test for determining whether two lines of business constitute the same business is whether there is any inter-connection, any inter-lacing, any inter-dependence and unity at all embracing those two businesses. A common management of the two businesses, unity of trading organisation, common employees, common determination, a common fund and a common place of business would answer the test. [*Produce Exchange Corporation* v *Commissioner of Income Tax* (1971)1 SCJ 94: (1971)1 ITJ 50: 77 ITR 739: (1971)1 SCR 382: AIR 1971 SC 2028].

**Same interest.** The expression 'same interest' in Or. 1, r. 8, Civil Procedure Code, cannot be interpreted to mean identical interest in its entirety. It includes interests which are similar, though distinct, of persons having common grievance. [*Bachu Singh* v *Bilaso Kuer* ILR 46 Pat 977].

**Same transaction.** The expression suggests a continuity of action and purpose. Whether several offences are so connected together as to form one transaction depends upon whether they are related together in point of purpose or as cause and effect or as principal and subsidiary acts. [*Madan Gopal* v *State* AIR 1968 Cal 79].

In order that a series of acts be regarded as parts of 'the same transaction', they must be connected together in some way, for instance, by proximity of time, unity of place, unity or continuity of purpose or design, or continuity of action. Proximity of time and unity of place are not essential, though they furnish good evidence of what unites several acts. The main test must really be continuity of action by which it is meant the following up of some initial act, through all its consequences and incidents until the series of acts or group of connected acts come to an end, either by attainment of the object or by being put an end to or abandoned. [*Shapurji Sorabji* v *Emperor* AIR 1936 Bom 154; *Debi Prasad* v *Emperor* 212 IC 135; *Raj Kishore Tewari* v *Rex* AIR 1949 All 139; *Faiz Mohammad* v *Emperor* ILR (1945) Kant 100; *Yunus Khan* v *Emperor* 230 IC 262].

The expression "same transaction" from its very nature is incapable of an exact definition. Commonsense and the ordinary use of language must decide whether on the facts of a particular case, it can be held to be in one transaction. It is not possible to enunciate any comprehensive formula of universal application for the purpose of determining whether two or more acts constitute the same transaction. [*Mohan Baitha* v *State of Bihar* AIR 2001 SC 1490; JT 2001(4) SC 27: 2001 Cr LJ 1738: (2001)2 Crimes 83 (SC): (2001)4 SCC 350].

- **In the course of the same transaction.** The expression 'in the course of the same transaction' means during the period when the first act forming the series was committed and the last act ended. [*State* v *Mangtu Ram* AIR 1962 Raj 155: (1962)1 Cr LJ 763].

**Sample.** Archetype, case in point, example; illustration; instance; model; prototype; representative; a small quantity of a commodity, corresponding to the quantity of the entire commodity; specimen.

**Samskar.** Sacramental ceremonies of Hindu in relation to persons.

**Sanad.** A grant of land, title or office by the Mahomedan Government or other authority; a patent; an authority, in writing from the ruling power to hold a land or an office, or to follow a certain calling or profession.

**Sanction.** Used as noun, it means acceptance; acquiescence; affirmation; assent; authorization; consent; immunity; grant; permission; ratification; stamp of approval; validation; condemnation; denunciation; disciplinary action; penal retribution; penalty; retributive action.

Used as verb, it means acquiesce; agree to; allow; approbate; approve; assent to; authenticate; authorise; charter; confer a privilege; confer a right; consent to; empower; endorse; give approval; give permission; gratify; indulge; license; permit; ratify; stand behind; subscribe to; suffer; support; tolerate; uphold; validate.

Sanction not only means prior approval; generally, it also means ratification. [*Re De La Warr* 50 LJ Ch 383: 16 Ch D 587 followed in *Senior Food Inspector, Ananthapur* v *Ravuru Subbiah* 1992 Cr LJ 2289 (AP)].

- **Economic sanction** p. 293.

**Sanitary fittings.** The term 'sanitary fittings' means fittings which promote cleanliness. [*H & R Johnson (India) Ltd.* v *Ahmedabad Municipal Corporation* (1981)22 Guj LR 10 (DB)].

The expression 'sanitary fittings' in the context of the phrase 'water supply and sanitary fitting' which is one single expression, means such pipes or materials as are meant for use for supply of water to or in lavatories, urinals, or bathrooms of private houses or public buildings, and they do not include heavy pipes which are laid underground as mains for carrying water supply from one area or place to another. [*Dy. Commr. of Sales Tax* v *G.S. Pai* (1980)1 SCR 938, 943].

By sanitary fittings one only understands such pipes or materials as are used in lavatories, urinals or bathrooms of private houses or public buildings. Even where a hume pipe is used for carrying the excreted material from the commode to the septic tank that may be treated as 'sanitary fittings'. [*State of U.P.* v *Indian Hume Pipe Co.* (1977)2 SCC 724: AIR 1977 SC 1132].

NOTE: The expression does not include spun pipes but the expression would include such pipes when used in bathrooms or lavatories. [*Indian Iron and Steel Co. Ltd.* v *STO* 32 STC 95: 1973 Tax LR 1793].

Glazed tiles immediately show even little dirt, and can be kept free from dirt with little effort and are generally conducive to healthy conditions. The essential attribute of glazed tiles is that they ensure sanitary conditions. They are, therefore, covered within the expression 'sanitary fittings'. [*H & R Johnson (India) Ltd.* v *Ahmedabad Municipal Corporation* (1981)22 Guj LR 10 (DB)].

**Sanitation.** The removal or neutralisation of elements injurious to health; the maintenance or improving of sanitary conditions; the disposal of sewage and refuse from houses, etc.

The word 'sanitation' is confined to its ordinary meaning in relation to conservancy and drainage and the necessity of avoiding dirt and disease. [*District Board, Ghazipur* v *Lakshmi Narain Sharma* AIR 1961 SC 356: (1961)2 SCR 81: (1962)1 SCJ 319].

**Sans recourse.** Without recourse.

NOTE: An endorser of a negotiable instrument may, by express words in the endorsement, exclude his own liability thereon. [Negotiable Instruments Act 1881, s. 52].

**Santan.** Offspring; descendants; issues.

The word is wide enough to include natural as well as adopted son. [*Dundoobai* v *Vithalrao* 60 Bom 498: AIR 1936 Bom 182].

The word means 'issue' generally and is not limited to male descendants. [*Kumud Krishna Mandal* v *Jogendra Nath Sarkar* 21 CWN 854].

The word 'santan', no doubt, has a meaning *viz.* issues, i.e. either male or female. But it also means a 'line'. Vijnaneswara himself interprets it as meaning a male line alone. [*Gajadhar Prasad* v *Gauri Shankar* AIR 1932 All 417 (FB)].

**Santhathi.** The etymological meaning of '*Santhathi*' is issue of the body. [*Kotta Pullaya* v *Veeraraghavamma* AIR 1954 AP 2].

*Prima facie* the word means legitimate children, but it would mean illegitimate son if he is an heir. [*Maharaja of Venkatagiri* v *Rajeswara Rao* AIR 1939 Mad 614].

Though *Santhati* according to dictionary meaning connotes all classes of issues, yet in a particular context (namely *Varish*) it may mean only male issue. [*K.M.S.L. Sundaramier* v *K.N. Sarojini* AIR 1984 Mad 227].

NOTE: The word includes an adopted son. [*Sangavarapu Venkatasubbarao* v *Mylavarapu Krishnamurthy* AIR 1958 AP 447].

It is an expression wide enough to include natural as well as adopted children. It also includes males as well as females, in descent. [*Muppidathi Ammal* v *Muthuswami Pillai* AIR 1928 Mad 126].

**Sanyasi.** A person is said to have adopted the life of a sanyasi when it is shown that he has actually relinquished and abandoned all worldly possessions and relinquished all desire for them or that such ceremonies are performed which indicate the severance of his natural family and his secular life. In case of orthodox sanyasis, it must also be shown that necessary ceremonies have been performed, such as *pindadana*, Biraja Homa and Prajapathiyesthi without which the renunciation will not be complete. [*Shri Krishna Singh* v *Mathura Ahir* AIR 1980 SC 707: (1981)3 SCC 689: (1982)2 SCR 660].

**Sapinda.** A generic name applied to a person and his six immediate ancestors in his main and male line as he and all of them are connected by the same cake or the *pinda*. In these agnates, there is a smaller division represented by the offerer of the cake or the *pinda* and his three nearest male ascendants viz. father, grandfather and great-grandfather. These are considered to be receiving the entire *pinda* offered.

Two persons are said to be *sapindas* of each other if one is a lineal ascendant of the other within the limits of *sapinda* relationship, or if they have a common lineal ascendant who is within the limits of *sapinda* relationship with reference to each of them. [Hindu Marriage Act 1955, s. 3(*f*)(*ii*)].

Under the Mitakshara, the *sapinda* relationship arises between two people through their being connected by particles of one body, namely, that of the common ancestor, in other words, from community of blood in contradistinction to the Dayabhaga notion of community in the offering of religious oblations. [*Buddha Singh* v *Laltu Singh* 42 IA 208: 37 All 604].

NOTE: A *sapinda*, connected through a male line, is called *gotraja sapinda*. One connected through a female is called *bhinna gotra sapinda* or *bandhu*.

The expression *sapinda* is peculiar to traditional Hindu law and it would be altogether inapposite in the context of citizens of Muslim or Christian faith. [*Jagat Singh* v *Karan Singh* (1987)2 SCC 349: AIR 1987 SC 1279].

**Sapinda relationship.** *Sapinda* relationship with reference to any person extends as far as the third generation (inclusive) in the line of ascent through the mother, and the fifth (inclusive) in the line of ascent through the father, the line being traced upwards in each case from the person concerned, who is said to be counted as the first generation. [Hindu Marriage Act 1955, s. 3(*f*)(*i*)].

**Sapratibandha Daya.** Obstructed heritage. According to Mitakshara, property, the right to which accrues not by birth but on the death of the last owner without leaving male issue is called obstructed heritage or *Sapratibandha Daya*.

**Saptapadi.** This denotes taking of seven steps (by the bridegroom and bride jointly before the sacred fire). It is an essential ceremony (of a shastric Hindu marriage). [*Joyita Saha* v *Rajesh Kumar Pandey* AIR 2000 Cal 107]. Even in an Arya Samaj marriage, *saptapadi* is necessary. [*Ram Awadhi* v *Krishna Nand Lal* AIR 1981 All 432].

**Sarai.** Any building used for the shelter and accommodation of travellers, and includes, in any case in which only part of a building is used as a sarai, the part so used of such building. It also includes a Purao. [Public Sarais and Puraos Act 22 of 1867, s. 2].

**Sarasari.** The word connotes the idea of a temporary settlement; but along with the word 'bemiadi', it means a permanent lease with variable rent. [*Dinanath Kundu* v *Janaki Nath Roy* AIR 1928 Cal 392: 55 Cal 435].

**Saraswati vilas.** A digest on ancient Hindu law written by Pratap Rudra Deb, King of Orissa. It is a work of great authority in Orissa and Madras. It presents a picture of the actual working of the law and not merely a series of abstract statements of old rules. It has been referred to in decisions of various courts.

**Satisfaction.** As noun, in its application to discharge of debt, it means acquitment; acquittal; acquittance; clearance; defrayment; discharge; release from debt; repayment.

As noun, in its application to fulfilment, it means accomplishment; achievement; appeasement; attainment; consummation; enjoyment; gratification; pleasure; success; contentedness.

Payment or fulfilment of a legal debt or obligation; discharge of a legal obligation. Payment in satisfaction may amount to a release. [*Garnett* v *Inland Revenue* 81 LT 633].

▸*Meaning under the Criminal Procedure Code, s. 145.* In relation to the claims or debts, contracts, mortgages and executions, 'satisfied' means discharged, extinguished, paid, released etc., but the word has not been used in this sense in s. 145, Criminal Procedure Code. It is used there as meaning convinced beyond a reasonable doubt. [*Faquir Chand* v *Bhana Ram* AIR 1957 Punj 303].

• **Accord and satisfaction** p. 17.

**Saudayika.** Gifts and bequests from relations made to a Hindu woman. A species of *Stridhan*.

**Saving(s).** Preservation from danger or loss; economy in outlay; prevention of waste; something laid up or kept from becoming expended or lost; a reservation. [*Oklahoma Tax Commission* v *Sisters of the Sorrowful Mother* 97 P 2d 888, 892].

**Saving clause.** An exception to the general rule in a deed or statute.

**Saw.** An implement usually of steel worked by hand or mechanically and with variously shaped blade or edge having teeth of various forms cut in or attached to it for dividing wood, metal, stone, etc. by reciprocating rotary motion. [*Raghunand Prasad and Company* v *Union of India* (1988)2 Raj LR 165 referring to *Concise Oxford Dictionary*].

A tool or instrument consisting essentially (usually) of a thin flat blade or plate of tempered steel with a continuous series of teeth on the edge, used for cutting wood, metal, bone, etc. [*Raghunand Prasad and Company* v *Union of India* (1988)2 Raj LR 165 referring to Webster's *New International Dictionary*, 2nd Ed., vol. 2, Unabridged].

**Saw mill.** A mill which is engaged in cutting wood, stone, or metal. [*Raghunand Prasad and Company* v *Union of India* (1988)2 Raj LR 165].

**Sayar.** Sayar includes whatever is to be paid or delivered by a lessee or licensee on account of right of gathering produce, forest rights, fisheries and the use of water for irrigation from artificial sources. Therefore, the income derived by the landlord from persons who have been given licences to cut and remove *poola* grass from forest has been held to be sayar. [*Ganga Devi* v *State of U.P.* (1972)3 SCC 126: AIR 1972 SC 931 referring to U.P. Tenancy Act 1939].

**Sayer.** All sorts of imposts or taxes in addition to land revenue, but does not include minerals. [*Rajeshwar* v *Bhupendra* AIR 1927 Cal 956: 55 Cal 35].

Sayer means all sorts of imposts in addition to land revenue and does not include minerals.

That which moves; variable imposts distinct from land, rent, or revenues, consisting of customs, tools, licences, duties on goods; also taxes on houses, shops, bazaars, etc. [Wharton's *Law Lexicon*, 14th Ed., pp. 901-902].

**Scandal.** The heedless or malicious repetition of evil reports; injury to reputation, or general comment causing it; malicious defamation by word of mouth; a thing or a person causing general public outrage or indignation; a public affront, especially an irrelevant abusive statement in court; disgraceful, shameful, or degrading acts or conduct; defamatory reports or rumours.

**Scandalising the court.** 'Scandalising the court' would mean hostile criticism of judges as judges or judiciary. [*Dr. D.C. Saxena* v *Chief Justice of India* (1996)5 SCC 216].

NOTE: 'Scandalising the court' is an attack on individual judges or the court as a whole with or without reference to particular cases casting unwarranted and defamatory aspersions upon the character or ability of the judges. [*Brahma Prakash Sharma* v *State of Uttar Pradesh* AIR 1954 SC 10: 1954 Cr LJ 238].

**Scandalous.** Causing, or tending to cause, scandal; approbious; atrocious; damnatory; defamatory; disgraceful; consisting of evil or malicious reports; tending to injure reputation; shocking to the sense of truth, decency, or propriety; despicable; discreditable; dishonourable; ignominious; offensive; scurrilous; shameful; immodest.

**Scandalous pleading.** A pleading is scandalous which alleges anything unbecoming of the dignity of the court to hear or is contrary to good manners, or which charges a crime immaterial to the issue. But the statement of a scandalous fact that is material to the issue is not a scandalous pleading. [*Millington* v *Loring* 50 LJQB 214].

NOTE: A scandalous pleading may be struck out or amended. [Code of Civil Procedure 1908, Or. 6, r. 16].

**Schedule.** Agenda; check list; timetable; any list of planned events to take place on regular basis; a plan of work; any list, catalogue, form, classification, or tabular statement; a programme; a written or printed statement specifying the details of some matter, and often annexed to statutes, petitions, and other documents.

**Scheduled bank.** A bank included in the Second Schedule. [Reserve Bank of India Act, s. 2(*e*); Banking Companies Act 1949, s. 5(*m*); Industrial Development Bank of India Act 1964, s. 2(*g*)].

**Scheduled castes.** "Scheduled castes" and "scheduled tribes" are not a caste within the ordinary meaning of caste. Scheduled castes and tribes are descriptive of backwardness. Scheduled caste is a caste as notified under Art. 366 of the Constitution of India. [*State of Kerala* v *N.M. Thomas* AIR 1976 SC 490: (1976)1 SCR 906: (1976)2 SCC 310].

NOTE: Scheduled castes become such only if the President specifies any castes, races or tribes for the purpose of the Constitution. So, a group or a section of a group which need not be a caste and may even be a hotchpotch of many castes or tribes or even races, may still be a scheduled caste under Art. 341 of the Constitution of India. A 'scheduled caste' need not be a 'caste' in the conventional sense under Art. 341. [*Akhil Bharatiya Soshit Karmachari Sangh (Railway)* v *Union of India* 1980(3) SLR 645: AIR 1981 SC 298: (1981)2 SCR 185: (1981)1 SCC 246].

**Scheduled journey.** "Scheduled journey" means one of series of journeys which are undertaken between the same two places and which together amount to a systematic service operated in such a manner that the benefits thereof are available to memebrs of the public from time to time seeking to take advantage of it. [Air Corporations Act 1967, s. 33 (England)].

**Scheduled tribes.** See SCHEDULED CASTES.

**Scheme.** A systemic plan; a connected or orderly arrangement; an artful plot or plan, usually to deceive others. [Black's *Law Dictionary*, 8th Ed.].

Arrangement; course of action; design; plan; policy; programme of action; schedule; strategy; tactics.

A design or plan formed to accomplish some purpose; a system. [*Snider* v *Leatherwood* Tex Civ App, 49 SW 2d 1107, 1110].

It means a carefully arranged and systematic programme of action, a systematic plan for attaining some object, a project, a system of correlated things. The systematic programme of action has to be a consensual arrangement between two or more persons. [*State of W.B.* v *Swapan Kr.*

*Guha* AIR 1982 SC 949: 1982 Cr LJ 819: (1982)1 SCC 561: 1982 SCC (Cri) 283].

When used in a bad sense, the term corresponds with "trick" or "fraud".

**Scheme of finance.** A scheme indicating the sources from which, and the terms and conditions on which, finances are proposed to be obtained by an undertaking. [Monopolies and Restrictive Trade Practices Act 1969, s. 2(*q*) (since *omitted*). The Act is repealed and replaced by the Competition Act 2002. No such term is defined under the new Act].

**Schizophrenia.** It is a term that includes those illnesses in all age groups, which are characterised from the outset by fundamental disturbances in personality, thinking, emotional life, behaviour, interests and relationship with other people.

NOTE: It involves a tendency for the person to withdraw from the environment and to show an integral disintegration of thinking, feeling and behaviour, resulting in an incongruity between his emotional state and his thoughts and actions, a tendency to form characteristic associations in thinking and a tendency to morbid projection. The disintegration of mental functions in schizophrenia is 'molecular' and quite different from "molar" disassociation found in hysteria and multiple personality.

The clinical features of schizophrenia are the following: (1) withdrawal; (2) splitting —(*a*) thought disorder; (*b*) emotional disconnection; (c) conduct disconnection; (3) paranoid disposition; (4) abnormalities of perception. [Linford Rees on *A New Short Text Book of Psychiatry*, Ed. 1988, p. 132].

'Schizophrenia' is a serious mental disorder marked by irrational thinking, disturbed emotions and breakdown in communication with others. Out of four types of this illness, namely: (*i*) simple schizophrenia; (*ii*) hebephrenia; (*iii*) katatonia; and (*iv*) paranoid schizophrenia, it is only the third variety in which patient is in a state of wild excitement and is destructive, violent and abusive. [*Rameshwari Gupta* v *Ram Narayan Gupta* 1987 All LJ 483: 1987 All LR 64].

Schizophrenia is a type of mental illness and is a form of psychosis, which is more serious than other types of mental illnesses. [*Rohini Prasad Lal Bihari Ram* v *Union of India* 1995 MPLJ 268, 275].

It is a mental disorder, an illness of slow insidious onset developing over years. There may be report of strange, odd and inappropriate behaviour. There will be progressive deterioration in the level of performance at work and school socially; report, examination results and the employment record provides objective and usually reliable indications of intellectual performance, its maintenance and decline. [*Rita Roy* v *Sitesh* (1981)2 CLJ 462: 86 CWN 167: AIR 1982 Cal 136].

On the ground of schizophrenia, a marriage may be dissolved by a decree of divorce. [Hindu Marriage Act, s. 13(i)(*iii*) and Special Marriage Act, s. 27(1)(e)].

**Scienter.** Knowingly—a word applied especially to the clause in a declaration in certain classes of actions in which the plaintiff alleged that the defendant *knowingly* did or permitted that from which arose the damage of which the plaintiff complained. In an action of deceit, the *scienter* must be averred and proved. [Mozley & Whiteley's *Law Dictionary*, 10th Ed.].

The term is used in pleading to signify an allegation (or that part of the declaration or indictment which contains it) setting out the defendant's previous knowledge of the cause which led to the injury complained of, or rather his previous knowledge of a state of facts which it was his duty to guard against, and his omission to do which has led to the injury complained of. The term is frequently used to signify the defendant's guilty knowledge.

The term "scienter", as applied to conduct necessary to give rise to an action for civil damages refers to a mental state embracing intent to deceive, manipulate or defraud. [*Ernst and Ernst* v *Hochfelder* 47 L Ed 2d 668].

**Scrip.** A document that entitles the holder to receive something of value; money, especially paper money, that is issued for temporary use. [Black's *Law Dictionary*, 8th Ed.].

- **Share scrips.** Share scrips are merely documents of title which shows that the person concerned holds the shares of company. [*Rajbans* v *Janki Devi* AIR 1965 Punj 314].

**Scrip dividend.** This is dividend otherwise than in cash. It may take the form of a dividend or bonus out of capitalised reserves, satisfied by the issue of fully-paid shares, or by the discharge of uncalled liability on partly-paid shares previously issued.

**Script.** An original or principal writing; calligraphy; handwriting; jottings; scrawl; written characters; written matter.

**Scrutiny.** Analysis; careful and critical examination; close investigation; minute attention; probe.

The process of examination of nomination papers to find out if they are valid is known as scrutiny. And this is done by the Returning Officer under s. 36 of the Representation of the People Act 1951.

**Scurrilous.** Abusive; disgusting; disrespectful; foul; indecent; insulting; lascivious; lewd; licentious; offensive; opprobrious; vile; vulgar; foul-mouthed.

**Scuttling.** The intentional casting away of a ship for the sake of the insurance money, or to prevent its falling into enemy hands, etc.

**Seal.** Accredit; approve; attest; authenticate; certify; confirm; endorse; impress with mark; imprint; bar; block off; close up; cover; keep from public view; secure.

This is a solemn mode of expressing comment to a written instrument by attaching to it a device or a wafer with an impression.

• **Common seal** p. 160.

**Seal book.** A book kept by the secretary of a large company in which are recorded each date on which the company's seal is used, the manner in which it is used and by whose authority it is used.

**Seamen.** Sailors; mariners; persons whose business is navigating ships, or who are connected with the ship as such and in some capacity assist in its conduct, maintenance or service. The term commonly excludes the officers of a ship. [*City of Los Angeles* v *United Dredging Co.* CCA Cal, 14 F 2d 364, 366].

One whose duties are maritime in character and are rendered on a vessel in navigable waters. [*Helena Glendale Ferry Co.* v *Walling* CCA Ark, 132 F 2d 616, 619, 620].

Section 742 of Merchant Shipping Act 1894 (of England) defines a 'seaman' thus: "Seaman" includes every person (except masters, pilots and apprentices duly indentured and registered), employed or engaged in any capacity on board any ship.

Section 3(42) of Merchant Shipping Act 1958 defines a 'seaman' as every person (except a master, pilot or apprentice/ employed or engaged as a member of the crew of a ship under this Act, but in relation to sections 178 to 183 of the Merchant Shipping Act 1958 includes a master.

Section 2(1) of Seamen's Provident Fund Act 1966 (of India) defines a "seaman" thus: A person employed or engaged as a member of the crew of a ship under the Merchant Shipping Act, but does not include a master navigating or engineering officer, radio officer, medical officer, welfare officer, purser, electrician, nurse, musician, pilot, apprentice or dock barber.

**Search.** Chase after; closely examine; comb; follow the trail of; hunt; scan; look through.

An examination of a person's body, property, or other area that the person would reasonably be expected to consider as private, conducted by a law-enforcement officer for the purpose of finding evidence of a crime. [Black's *Law Dictionary*, 8th Ed.].

Probing or exploration for something that is concealed or hidden from searcher; an invasion, a quest with some sort of force, either actual or constructive. [*People* v *Carroll* 299 NE 2d 134, 140].

Search implies an exploratory examination or probing into or seeking out something which is hidden, sealed, suspected, and not open, exposed or demonstrated. [*Hiralal Chhaganlal* v *State* AIR 1968 Raj 188].

**Search warrant.** Authority to search; judicial order to search; legal document to search.

A judge's written order authorizing a law-enforcement officer to conduct a search of a specified place and to seize evidence. [Black's *Law Dictionary*, 8th Ed.].

NOTE: An authority given by a competent person to an officer to search the house or any other place mentioned therein for any thing or person. Section 93 of the Code of Criminal Procedure 1973 deals with search warrants. [*Sharma* v *Satish Chandra* 1954 SCR 1077].

**Seashore.** That portion of land adjacent to the sea which is alternately covered and left dry by the ordinary flux and reflux of the tides; seacoast; foreshore; all the ground between the ordinary high-water and low-water marks.

**Seaworthy.** Reasonably fit for voyage; sufficiently strong and staunch enough and equipped for voyage.

**Seaworthy vessel.** It signifies that the vessel is properly constructed, prepared, manned, equipped, and provided for the voyage intended.

Seaworthiness of a vessel means that she shall be in a fit state as to repairs, equipment and crew, and in all other respects to encounter the ordinary perils of the voyage. [*Hedley* v *Pinkney & Sons S.S. Co. Ltd.* (1894) AC 222: 63 LJQB 419].

NOTE: A seaworthy vessel must, in general, be sufficiently strong and staunch and equipped with appropriate appurtenances to allow it to safely engage in trade for which it was intended. [*Texaco* v *Universal Marine, Inc* DC La, 400 F Supp 311, 320].

Test of whether a vessel or its equipment is seaworthy is whether the ship or its appurtenances are reasonably fit for her intended service. [*Melancon* v *I.M.C. Drilling Mud.* LA App, 282 So 2d 532, 536].

**Secondary.** It is generally opposed to "primary". It means of a subsequent, subordinate, or inferior kind or class; auxiliary; ancillary.

**Secondary evidence.** That which is inferior to primary or best evidence. It is that species of evidence which becomes admissible, when the primary or best evidence of the fact in question is lost or becomes inaccessible.

That species of proof which is admitted on the loss of primary evidence. There are no degrees of this evidence; for example, if a letter be lost, it may be as good to recite it from memory as to produce a copy. It is the province of the judge to decide whether a document produced be original or not, and until he decides, it is not; no secondary evidence can be put in (unless made admissible by law). [Wharton's *Law Lexicon*, 14th Ed., p. 908].

Secondary evidence is evidence which may be given in the absence of primary evidence, when a proper explanation of its absence has been given. This however is only approximately true, for the law in some cases requires secondary evidence to be given first, and in others allows the production of primary evidence to be optional. [Phipson on *Law of Evidence*, 13th Ed., para 1-07].

▸ *Meaning under the Indian Evidence Act 1872, s. 63*. 'Secondary evidence' means and includes—(1) certified copies given under the provisions of the Evidence Act; (2) copies made from the original by mechanical processes which in themselves ensure the accuracy of the copy and copies compared with such copies; (3) copies made from or compared with the original; (4) counterparts of documents as against the parties who did not execute them; and (5) oral accounts of contents of documents given by some person who has himself seen it.

NOTE: Cases in which secondary evidence relating to documents may be given are enumerated in s. 65 of the Indian Evidence Act 1872.

**Secret profit.** Any profit made secretly by a person taking advantage of the fiduciary relationship.

NOTE: In all fiduciary relationships, *e.g.*, beneficiary and trustee, company and its directors, master and servant, principal and agent, the fundamental rule is that the person entrusted with, or employed to discharge a duty is not to make a secret profit thereby.

**Secret trust.** Where a testator gives property to a person, on an express or implied promise by the legatee or devisee that he will hold it in trust for another person, this is called a secret trust. [*Re Blackwell* (1929) AC 318].

NOTE: A secret trust is not enforced unless communicated in the testator's lifetime; it must be definite, and not illegal. The rule is that if the secret trust would have been valid as an express trust, it will be enforced against the legatee or devisee, while if it would have been invalid as an express trust, the gift fails altogether, so that neither the devisee or legatee nor the object of the trust takes any benefit by it.

The principle upon which secret trusts are enforced is not confined to wills. It applies also where the owner of property has refrained from disposing of it by will (or has revoked a will already made), relying on the promise of, say, *T* who takes the property on an intestacy to dispose of it in favour of *B*. Here, too, *T* holds on trust for *B*. [*Re Gardner, Huey* v *Cunnington* (1920)2 Ch 523].

**Secretary.** One entrusted with the management of business; one who writes for another; the head of a Government department; an officer of a company, or club, etc.

In reference to a corporation or association, refers to an officer charged with the direction and management of that part of the business of the company which is concerned with keeping the records, the official correspondence, with giving and receiving notices, countersigning documents, etc.

A corporate officer in charge of official correspondence, minutes of board meetings, and records of stock ownership and transfer. [Black's *Law Dictionary*, 8th Ed.].

NOTE: A modern company secretary is not a mere clerk but an officer of the company with extensive duties and responsibilities. Under the Companies Act 1956, the term "secretary" means the person, if any, who is appointed to perform the duties which may be performed by a secretary under the Act and any other ministerial or administrative duties [s. 2(45)]. It is usually the duty of the secretary to prepare the minutes of the proceedings of the general as well as directors' meeting. The secretary is the agent of the company through whom the clerical work is done. He must obey the orders of the directors and give effect to their resolutions. A secretary has no authority to bind the company by contract or to make representation as to the company's affairs so as to induce people to take shares.

In parliamentary law, the word denotes an officer charged with recording a deliberative assembly's proceedings. [Black's *Law Dictionary*, 8th Ed.].

**Section.** Compartment; department; class; category; fraction; fragment; group; grouping; segment; part; sub-division.

It may also mean area; block; locale; neighbourhood; parcel of land; plot of ground; surroundings.

In text-books, codes, statutes, and other juridical writings, the smallest distinct and numbered subdivisions are commonly called "sections", sometimes "articles", and occasionally "paragraphs". [Black's *Law Dictionary*, 5th Ed.].

A distinct part or division of a writing, especially a legal instrument. [Black's *Law Dictionary*, 8th Ed.].

**Secular state.** A 'secular state' means a 'non-religious' and not 'irreligious' state. What follows is that the government should not be wedded or bound to any one religion, but should give equality of treatment to every religion practised in the country. [*Perunchithiranar* v *State of Tamil Nadu* AIR 1986 Mad 83: (1985)2 MLJ 56: (1985)98 MLW 208].

**Secured creditor.** A creditor who holds some special pecuniary assurance of payment of his debt, such as a mortgage, collateral, or lien. [Black's *Law Dictionary*, 5th Ed.].

A creditor who has the right, on the debtor's default, to proceed against collateral and apply it to the payment of the debt. [Black's *Law Dictionary*, 8th Ed.].

▸ *Meaning under the Provincial Insolvency Act 1920, s. 2(e)*. A person holding a mortgage, charge or lien on the property of the debtor or any part thereof as a security for a debt due to him from the debtor.

NOTE: 'Secured creditor' includes a landlord who under any enactment for the time being in force has a charge on land for the rent of that land. [Presidency-Towns Insolvency Act 1909, s. 2(g)].

**Secured debt.** A secured debt is a debt secured by mortgage and includes a debt secured by a charge under s. 100 of the Transfer of Property Act. But if on the date of a suit the debt was not secured it cannot be said that the decree related to a secured debt simply because the decree created a charge for some reason or other. [*Rai Bahadur Choudhary Raghuraj Singh* v *Murari Lal* AIR 1967 SC 1631].

**Secured loan or advance.** A loan or advance for which some form of property has been pledged or mortgaged, as in the case of an automobile loan in which title to the vehicle is held as security by lender.

A loan that is secured by property, or securities [Black's *Law Dictionary*, 8th Ed.]. It is also termed collateral loan.

▸ *Meaning under the Banking Regulation Act 1949, s. 5(n).* A loan or advance made on the security of assets the market value of which is not at any time less than the amount of such loan or advance.

**Securities.** Assets; bonds; capital; evidences of debts; evidences of obligations; holdings; invested property; shares; stocks.

Evidences of debts or of property [*State* v *Alhen* 5 SE 2d 844, 845, 847]; evidences of obligations to pay money or of rights to participate in earnings and distribution of corporate, trust, and other property [*Oklahoma-Texas Trust* v *Securities and Exchange Commission* 100 F 2d 888, 890]; stocks, bonds, notes, convertible debentures, warrants, or other documents that represent a share in a company or a debt owed by a company.

▸ *Meaning under the Forward Contracts (Regulation) Act 1952, s. 2(l).* 'Securities' include shares, scrips, stocks, bonds, debentures, debenture-stocks or other marketable securities of a like nature in or of any incorporated company or other body corporate and also Government securities.

▸ *Meaning under the Securities Contracts (Regulation) Act 1956, s. 2(h).* 'Securities' include—(*i*) shares, scrips, stocks, bonds, debentures, debenture stock or other marketable securities of a like nature in or of any incorporated company or other body corporate; (*ii*) Government securities; and (*iii*) rights or interests in securities.

**Security.** Used as pledge, it means bail; bond; collateral; guarantee; pawn; surety; warranty.

Used as stock, it means assets; bill of exchange; capital; certificate of debt; certificate of indebtedness; invested property; negotiable instrument; secured debenture.

Used as safety, it means anchor; assurance; bastion; dependability; impregnability; sanctuary; shelter; support.

Black's *Law Dictionary* [5th Ed.] defines the word thus: Protection; assurance; indemnification. The term is usually applied to an obligation, pledge, mortgage, deposit, lien, etc., given by a debtor in order to assure the payment or performance of his debt, by furnishing the creditor with a resource to be used in case of failure in the principal obligation. Document that indicates evidence of indebtedness. The name is also sometimes given to one who becomes surety or guarantor for another.

Black's *Law Dictionary* [8th Ed.] defines the word thus: Collateral given or pledged to guarantee the fulfilment of an obligation; especially, the assurance that a creditor will be repaid (usually with interest) any money or credit extended to a debtor. A person who is bound by some type of guaranty; surety. The state of being secure, especially from danger or attack. An instrument that evidences the holder's ownership rights in a firm (*e.g.*, a stock), the holder's creditor relationship with a firm or government (*e.g.*, a bond), or the holder's other rights (*e.g.*, an option).

Speaking generally, security is anything that makes the money more assured in its payment or more readily recoverable as distinguished from *e.g.* a mere IOU which is only evidence of a debt. The word is not confined to a document which gives a charge on specific property but includes personal securities for money. [*Chetumal* v *Noorbhoy* 107 IC 213: AIR 1928 Sind 89].

- **Collateral security** p. 153.
- **Foreign security** p. 365.
- **Gift-edged securities** p. 388.
- **Government security** p. 396.
- **Internal security** p. 474.
- **Marketable security** p. 564.
- **Personal security** p. 660.
- **Public security.** Bonds, notes, certificates of indebtedness, and other negotiable or transferable instruments evidencing the public debt of a state or government.

  A negotiable or transferable security that is evidence of government debt. [Black's *Law Dictionary*, 7th & 8th Eds.].

  'Public securities' mean—(*i*) promissory notes, debentures, stock or other securities of the Central Government or of any State Government: Provided that securities, both the principal whereof and the interest whereon have been fully and unconditionally guaranteed by any such Government, shall be deemed, for the purposes of this clause, to be securities of such Government; (*ii*) the debentures or other securities for money issued by or on behalf of any municipal body, Improvement Trust or Port Trust under the authority of any law for the time being in force in India (including the Port Trust securities). [Major Port Trusts Act 1963, s. 2(*u*)].
- **Valuable security** p. 874.

**Security bond.** 'Security bond' is an instrument executed by way of security for the due execution of an office, or to account for money or other property received by virtue thereof, or executed by a surety to secure the due performance of a contract. [Indian Stamp Act 1899, Art. 57].

**Security council.** The executive body of the United Nations, charged with the duty of preventing or stopping wars by diplomatic, economic or military action.

> NOTE: It is composed of five permanent members, namely China, France, Russia, U.K. and U.S.A. and ten additional members elected at stated intervals. The non-permanent members are elected from each of the world's major regions, based on a distribution formula.

**Security deposit.** Money deposited by tenant with landlord as security for full and faithful performance by tenant of terms of lease, including damages to premises. It is refundable unless the tenant has caused damage or injury to the property or has breached the terms of the tenancy or the laws governing the tenancy.

**Security for costs.** Money, property, or a bond given to a court by a plaintiff or an appellant to secure payment of court costs if that party loses. [Black's *Law Dictionary*, 8th Ed.].

> NOTE: Under Or. 25, r. 1 of Code of Civil Procedure 1908, the court may at any stage of a suit either on its own motion or on the application of any defendant order the plaintiff for reasons to be recorded to give within the time fixed by it security for the payment of all costs incurred and likely to be incurred by the defendant; provided that such an order shall be made in all cases in which it appears to the court that a sole plaintiff is, or (when there are more plaintiffs than one) that all the plaintiffs are residing out of India and that such plaintiff does not possess or that no one of such plaintiffs possesses any sufficient immovable property within India other than the property in suit.
>
> The Supreme Court has also framed rules regarding security of costs for the respondent under Arts. 142(1) and 145(1)(*f*) of the Constitution of India.

**Security for good behaviour.** A bond or recognizance which the Magistrate exacts from a defendant brought before him on a charge of disorderly conduct or threatening violence, conditioned upon his being of good behaviour, or keeping the peace, for a prescribed period, towards all people in general and the complainant in particular.

> NOTE: It is also termed a peace bond.
>
> A Magistrate can demand security for good behaviour from (1) persons disseminating seditious matters, (2) from vagrants and suspected persons, and (3) habitual offenders under ss. 108, 109 and 110 of the Code of Criminal Procedure 1973.

**Sedition.** An agreement, communication, or other preliminary activity aimed at inciting treason or some lesser commotion against public authority; advocacy aimed at inciting or producing—and likely to incite or produce—imminent lawless action. [Black's *Law Dictionary*, 8th Ed.].

An insurrectionary movement tending towards treason, but wanting an overt act; attempts made by meetings or speeches, or by publications, to disturb the tranquillity of the state.

**Seduce.** To lead (a person) astray in conduct or belief; to draw away from the right or intended course of action to or into a wrong one; to tempt or entice or beguile to do something wrong, foolish or unintended. [*Narasappa Ashappa* v *State* 1973 Bom LR 221].

The verb 'seduce' is used in two senses. It is used in its ordinary and narrow sense as inducing a woman to stray from the path of virtue for the first time; it is also used in the wider sense of inducing a woman to submit to illicit intercourse at any time or on any occasion.

**Seduction.** The act of seducing; act of man enticing woman to have unlawful intercourse with him by means of persuasion, solicitation, promises, bribes, or other means without employment of force.

The inducing of a girl or woman to part with her virtue for the first time. [*R.* v *Moon* (1910) KB 818].

▸ *Meaning under Indian Penal Code 1860, ss. 366 and 366A.* 'Seduction' means inducing a woman to submit to illicit intercourse at any time or on any occasion. In the ordinary sense seduction means inducing a woman to stray from the path of virtue for the first time. [*Ramesh Amin* v *State of Maharashtra* AIR 1962 SC 1908: (1963)1 Cr LJ 16].

**Seisin.** Possession of land or chattels by one having title thereto; possession of real property under claim of freehold estate; possession with an intent on the part of him who holds real property to claim a freehold interest; right to immediate possession according to the nature of the estate; ownership.

**Seizure.** The act of taking possession of property, *e.g.* for a violation of law or by virtue of an execution. The term implies a taking or removal of something from the possession, actual or constructive, of another person or persons. [*Molina* v *State* 193 NW 2d 874, 877].

The ordinary and natural meaning of seizure is a forcible taking of possession. [*Johnston* v *Hogg* 52 LJQB 343: 10 QBD 432].

'Seizure' implies doing something over and above holding an article in one's hand. [*Chandraka Sao* v *State* AIR 1967 SC 170].

'Seizure' means taking possession contrary to the wishes of the owner of property. [*Gian Chand* v *State* AIR 1962 SC 496].

NOTE: *'Search' and 'seizure'—distinction.* A "search" is a probing or exploration for something that is concealed or hidden from the searcher, whereas a "seizure" is a forcible or secretive dispossession of something against the will of the possessor or owner. [*U.S.* v *Marti* DC NY, 321 F Supp 59, 63].

**Selami (or pagri).** *Selami* (or *pagri*) or premium is a single payment made for the acquisition by the lessees of the right to enjoy the benefits granted to them by the lease. That general right may properly be regarded as a capital asset and the money paid to purchase it may properly be held to be a payment on capital account. [*Kamakshya Narain Singh* v *C.I.T.* 1943 ITR 513 (PC); *Board of Ag. I.T.* v *Sindhurani* (1957)32 ITR 169 (SC)]. The principle is the same whether the premium is for a simple lease of land [*C.I.T.* v *Visweshwar Singh* 1939 ITR 536] or for a lease of mineral rights. [*Raja Siva Prasad Singh* v *Crown* 1 ITC 384].

NOTE: It is impossible to lay down a hard and fast rule that a *selami* can in no case be revenue. Where the *selami* represents payment of rent in advance, it is income. [*Maharaja Chintamani* v *C.I.T.* (1966)62 ITR 167]. The *selami* or premium, which represents the whole or part of the price of the land or the sale price of the leasehold interest, is not income but capital. [*Board of Agr. I.T.* v *Sindhurani* (1957)32 ITR 169 (SC)]. *Prima facie, selami* is not income. It is for the income-tax authorities to show that there do exist facts which would make the *selami* income. [*Prov. of Bihar* v *Maharaja Pratap Udai Nath* 1941 ITR 313].

**Self-acquired property.** In Hindu law, it is the property acquired or obtained by a person, whether coparcener or not, without any detriment to ancestral property. It belongs to him exclusively.

**Self-defence.** The use of force to protect oneself, one's family, or one's property from a real or threatened attack. [Black's *Law Dictionary*, 8th Ed.].

NOTE: If the act alleged to be an assault is done in self-defence it is justified and no unlawful act is committed provided that no more force is used than is necessary for mere defence; and self-defence is a defence even to a charge of aggravated assault involving wounding or grievous bodily harm. [Halsbury's *Laws of England*, 4th Ed., vol. 11, para 1217, p. 647].

"The law of self-defence, as it is applied by the courts, turns on two requirements; the force must have been necessary, and it must have been reasonable". [Andrew Ashworth: *Principles of Criminal Law*, p. 114 (1991)].

**Self-determination.** There remains some difficulty as to the exact meaning of the expression "self-determination". It connotes freedom of choice to be exercised by a dependent people through a plebiscite or some other method of ascertaining the wishes of the people.

**Self-incrimination.** The act of indicating one's own involvement in a crime or exposing oneself to prosecution, especially by making a statement [Black's *Law Dictionary*, 8th Ed.]; acts or declarations either as testimony at trial or prior to trial by which one implicates himself in a crime. [Black's *Law Dictionary*, 5th Ed.].

**Seller.** Vendor; one who has contracted to sell property; a person who sells or contracts to sell goods; the transferor of property in a contract of sale.

▸ *Meaning under the Sale of Goods Act 1930, s. 2(13).* A person who sells or agrees to sell goods.

NOTE: In a contract for sale of goods, the word 'seller' must obviously refer to the party selling under the contract unless there is anything in the context suggesting otherwise. [*Juggilal Kamlapat* v *Paratapmal Rameshwar* (1978)1 SCC 69: AIR 1978 SC 389].

• **Unpaid seller** p. 868.

**Semble.** It seems; it would appear. Means that a point is not decided directly but may be inferred.

**Seminary.** An educational institution, such as a college, academy, or other school; the building in which the institution performs its function. [Black's *Law Dictionary*, 8th Ed.].

Seminary is an educational institution. [*Social S.G. of Assisi Sisters* v *KSEB* (1988)1 Ker LT 727].

**Semper praesumitur pro matrimonio.** The presumption is always in favour of the validity of the marriage.

**Semper specialia generalibul insunt.** Generalities include specialities.

**Senility.** Mental feebleness or impairment caused by old age; an infirmity resulting from deterioration of mind and body experienced in old age.

**Sensus verborum est anima legis.** The spirit of the law.

**Sentence.** Award of punishment; declaration of penalty; decree of punishment; determined punishment; prescribed punishment.

The judgment that a court formally pronounces after finding a criminal defendant guilty; the punishment imposed upon a criminal wrongdoer. [Black's *Law Dictionary*, 8th Ed.].

Any consequence which flows after conviction can be looked upon as sentence. [*Mohammad Shabir Maulamaiya* v *State of Maharashtra* 1977 Mah LJ 338: 1978 Cr LJ 825].

'Sentence' means a direction by which a punishment is prescribed and meted out to a person who has been convicted of an offence. [*Mahabir Singh* v *Emperor* AIR 1944 Cal 17: 48 CWN 113].

- **Death sentence** p. 230.
- **Deferred sentence** p. 242.

**Separate.** To set or keep apart; not shared with another; individually; independently; distinct; disconnected.

It is generally used in law as opposed to 'joint', though the more usual antithesis of the latter term is 'several'.

**Separate property.** The property over which a person has got an absolute power of alienation. A self-acquired property is a person's separate property; the *stridhan* property of a woman is her separate property.

In Hindu law, 'separate property' means self-acquired property of a coparcener, as opposed to joint family property. [*P.N. Venkatasubramania Aiyer* v *P.N. Easwara Aiyar* AIR 1966 Mad 266].

**Separation.** Severance of status of jointness. In its application to matrimonial matter, it means an arrangement whereby a husband and wife live apart from each other while remaining married, either by mutual consent or by judicial decree.

- **Judicial separation** p. 497.

**Separation of powers.** The division of governmental authority into three branches of government—legislative, executive, and judicial—each with specified duties on which neither of the other branches can encroach. [Black's *Law Dictionary*, 8th Ed.].

NOTE: The doctrine of separation of powers was propounded by the French jurist, Montesquieu, in his book *L'Espirit des lois*, 1748, in these words: "There can be no liberty when the legislative and executive powers are joined in the same person or body of Lords because the monarch or body will make tyrannical laws to be administered in a tyrannical way. Nor is there any liberty if the judicial power is not separated from the legislative and the executive power." [Book XI, Chapter 6].

This doctrine is based on the proposition that a concentration of functions is a temptation to tyranny. Montesquieu did not advocate a distinct separation of powers, although this is the construction that is often placed upon his work. Of course, the best method is where the different organs of Government act as restraints upon each other.

**Sequestration.** Annexation; appropriation; attachment; confiscation; deprivation; displacement; distraint; divestment; garnishment; impoundment; take over.

Black's *Law Dictionary* [8th Ed.] defines the word thus: The process by which property is removed from the possessor pending the outcome of a dispute in which two or more parties contend for it. The setting apart of a decedent's personal property when no one has been willing to act as a personal representative for the estate. The process by which a renounced interest is subjected to judicial management and is distributed as the testator would have wished if he or she had known about the renunciation. A judicial writ commanding the sheriff or other officer to seize the goods of a person named in the writ. The court-ordered seizure of a bankrupt's estate for the benefit of creditors. The seizure by a belligerent power of enemy assets. The freezing of a government agency's funds. Custodial isolation of a trial jury to prevent tampering and exposure to publicity, or of witnesses to prevent them from hearing the testimony of others.

A legal process putting a sheriff or other officer of the court in possession of property or goods until a dispute or claim in respect thereof has been disposed of. The term also may mean the taking possession of property of a bankrupt for the purposes of distributing it among his creditors.

Where, by some judicial or quasi-judicial process, property is temporarily placed in the hands of persons called sequestrators, who manage it and receive the rents and profits, the operation is called sequestration.

In the procedure of the High Court of England, sequestration is a means of enforcing obedience to a judgment or order requiring a person to do an act, *e.g.*, pay money into court, deliver up a chattel, etc.

**Sequi debet potentia justitiam, non praecedere.** Power should follow justice, not precede it.

**Seriatim.** It is a Latin expression which means one by one; separately and in order; severally; individually; in a series; successively.

**Serious bodily injury.** Any injury which involves, or in all probability will involve, the permanent loss of any part or section of a body or the use of any part or section of a body, or the permanent loss of or injury to the sight or hearing or any permanent physical incapacity or the fracture of any bone or one or more joints or bones of any phalanges of hand or foot. [Mines Act 1952, s. 2(*q*)].

**Servant.** One employed to perform service in master's affairs, whose physical conduct in performance of the service is controlled or is subject to right to control by the master. [*Brenner* v *Socony Vacuum Oil Co.* 158 SW 2d 171, 174, 175; *Reiling* v *Missouri Ins. Co.* 153 SW 2d 79].

A person in the employ of another and subject to his control as to what work shall be done and the means by which it shall be accomplished. [*Pantell* v *Shriver Allison Co.* 22 NE 2d 497, 499].

One who is employed to render personal service to another otherwise than in the pursuit of an independent calling, and who, in such service, remains entirely under the control and direction of employer. [*Henley* v *State* 2 SE 2d 139, 142].

A servant, for purposes of doctrine of vicarious liability, is one who is employed to perform services for another; and who is subject to such other's control or right to control as regards his physical conduct in the performance of such services. [*Gifford-Hill & Co.* v *Moore* Tex Civ App, 479 SW 2d 711, 714].

"A servant, strictly speaking, is a person who, by contract or operation of law, is for a limited period subject to the authority or control of another person in a particular trade, business or occupation ...... The word servant, in our legal nomenclature, has a broad significance, and embraces all persons of whatever rank or position who are in the employ, and subject to the direction or control of another in any department of labour or business. Indeed it may, in most cases, be said to be synonymous with employee." [H.G. Wood, *A Treatise on the Law of Master and Servant* § 1, at 2 (2d ed 1886)].

The word 'servant' in s. 25, Merchant Shipping Act 1923 (since repealed) means a servant in the constant employ of the owner. The mere engagement of a person to supply seamen does not make that person a servant within s. 25 (now s. 96 of the Merchant Shipping Act 1958). [*Nossibolla* v *D. Stephens* AIR 1952 Cal 339].

A servant is a person subject to the command of his master as to the manner in which he shall do his work. He is an agent who works under the supervision and direction of his employer; a person engaged to obey his employer's orders from time to time. [*Shivanandan Sharma* v *Punjab National Bank Ltd.* AIR 1995 SC 404].


- **Civil servant** p. 146.
- **Domestic servant** p. 278.
- **Government servant** p. 397.
- **Public servant** p. 713.
- **Railway servant** p. 724.


**Servant of Government.** 'Servant of Government' denotes any officer or servant continued, appointed or employed in India by or under the authority of the Government. [Indian Penal Code 1860, s. 14].

**Service.** Any assistance or benefit afforded to another; a useful result or product of labour which is not a tangible commodity; an intangible commodity in the form of human effort, such as labour, skill, or advice; a system of labour and material aids used to accomplish some regular work or accommodation for the public, *e.g.*, telephone service, postal service, etc.; a division of public employment devoted to a particular function, *e.g.*, a diplomatic service; a public duty or function; a ritual prescribed for a particular ministration or observance, *e.g.*, a burial service; marriage service; installation, maintenance, and repair of an article provided by a seller to a purchaser; the act of doing something useful for a person for a fee; a person whose business is to do useful things for others.

In animal husbandry, it means the copulation or covering of a female. In law, it means the formal delivery of a writ, summons, or other legal process; the formal delivery of some other legal notice such as a pleading; delivery of process; handing over legal papers; notification of legal action.

▸ *Meaning under the Competition Act 2002, s. 2(u).* 'Service' means service of any description which is made available to potential users and includes the provision of services in connection with business of any industrial or commercial matters such as banking, communication, education, financing, insurance, chit funds, real estate, transport, storage, material treatment, processing, supply of electrical or other energy, boarding, lodging, entertainment, amusement, construction, repair, conveying of news or information and advertising.


- **Active service** p. 34.
- **Actual service** p. 35.
- **Affidavit of service** p. 47.
- **All-India service** p. 56.
- **Civil service** p. 146.
- **Conditions of service** p. 169.


- **Contract of service.** Service conditions whereof are guided by a contract.

In its application to employment, a contract of service exists if the following three conditions are fulfilled: (*i*) The servant agrees that in consideration of a wage or other remuneration he will provide his own work and skill in the performance of some service for his master. (*ii*) He agrees, expressly or impliedly, that in the performance of that service he will be subject to the other's control in a sufficient degree to make that other master. (*iii*) The other provisions of the contract are consistent with its being a contract of service. [*Ready Mixed Concrete (South East) Ltd.* v *Minister of Pensions and National Insurance* (1968)1 All ER 433].


- **Essential service** p. 317.
- **Foreign service** p. 366.
- **Judicial service** p. 497.
- **National service** p. 598.
- **Public service** p. 715.
- **Public utility service** p. 715.
- **Termination of service** p. 837.


**Service charge.** A charge assessed for the performing of a service. [Black's *Law Dictionary*, 8th Ed.].

That charge assessed by bank against the expense of maintaining a customer's demand deposit or checking account, and is calculated on basis of a formula whereby bank's cost of maintaining account for customer is determined. [*U.S.* v *First Nat. Bank of Jackson* DC Miss, 301 F Supp 1161, 1207].

**Servient heritage or tenement.** The land on which the easement is imposed is called servient heritage and the owner or occupier thereof the servient owner. [Indian Easements Act 1882, s. 4].

**Servitude.** Enclavement; bonds; burden; captivity; charge; compulsion; fetters; indenture; slavery; subjection; subjugation; subordination; subservience.

In law, it means an encumbrance consisting in a right to the limited use of a piece of land or other immovable property without the possession of it; a charge or burden on an estate for another's benefit. [Black's *Law Dictionary*, 8th Ed.].

Servitudes include easement, irrevocable licences, profits, and real covenants.

**Session.** Assembly; audience; conclave; conference; congregation; congress; convention; hearing; meeting.

A meeting or series of related meetings throughout which a court, legislature, or other deliberative assembly conducts business in a continuing sequence; a period during a court martial when the members (or the judge, if trial is before a military judge) deliberate alone.

- **Biennial session.** A session held every two years.
- **Joint session.** In its application to parliamentary affairs, it means the combined meeting of two legislative bodies such as the Lok Sabha and the Rajya Sabha to pursue a common agenda.
- **Open session.** A session to which parties not directly involved are admitted. It is also termed public session.

- **Plenary session.** A meeting of all the members of a deliberative assembly, not just a committee.
- **Regular session.** A session that takes place at fixed intervals or specified times. [Black's *Law Dictionary*, 8th Ed.].

This relates to the period of time between the meeting of a Parliament, whether after a prorogation or dissolution, and its prorogation. [May's *Parliamentary Practice*].

**Set off.** Counter demand; counter poise; equivalent claim; off set; off setting claim.

A defendant's counter demand against the plaintiff, arising out of a transaction independent of the plaintiff's claim; a debtor's right to reduce the amount of a debt by any sum the creditor owes the debtor; the counterbalancing sum owed by the creditor; the balancing of mutual liabilities with respect to a pledge relationship. [Black's *Law Dictionary*, 8th Ed.].

**Set up.** The words "set up" is equivalent to the words "established". "Setting up" means "to place on foot" or "to establish" and is contradistinction to "commence". [*Commissioner of Wealth Tax, Madras* v *Rama Raju Surgical Cotton Mills Ltd.* AIR 1967 SC 509: (1967)1 SCR 761: (1967)63 ITR 478: (1967)1 ITJ 1: (1967)1 MLJ (SC) 25].

**Set up an alibi.** Where an accused person, in order to show that he could not have committed the offence with which he is charged, sets up as his defence that he was elsewhere at the time when the crime is alleged to have been committed, he is said to set up an *alibi*.

**Settled possession.** There is not special charm or magic in the words "settled possession" nor is it a ritualistic formula which can be confined in a straitjacket but it has been used to mean such clear and effective possession of a person, even if he is a trespasser, who gets the right under the criminal law to defend his property against attack even by the true owner. [*Puran Singh* v *State of Punjab* AIR 1975 SC 1674: 1975 (Supp) SCR 299: (1975)4 SCC 518: 1975 Cr LJ 1479: 1975 SCC (Cri) 608].

**Settlement.** The conveyance of property—or of interests in property—to provide for one or more beneficiaries, usually members of the settlor's family, in a way that differs from what the beneficiaries would receive as heirs under the statutes of descent and distribution; an agreement ending a dispute or lawsuit; payment; satisfaction, or final adjustment; the complete execution of an estate by the executor. [Black's *Law Dictionary*, 8th Ed.].

▸ *Meaning under the Estate Duty Act 1953, s. 2(19) (since repealed).* Any disposition including a dedication or endowment, whereby property is settled.

▸ *Meaning under the Indian Stamp Act 1899, s. 2(24).* 'Settlement' means any non-testamentary disposition, in writing, of movable or immovable property—(*a*) in consideration of marriage; (*b*) for the purpose of distributing property of the settlor among his family or those for whom he desires to provide, or for the purpose of providing for some person dependent on him, or (*c*) for any religious or charitable purpose; and includes an agreement in writing to make such a disposition and where any such disposition has not been made in writing, any instrument recording, whether by way of declaration of trust or otherwise, the terms of any such disposition.

▸ *Meaning under the Industrial Disputes Act 1947, s. 2(p).* 'Settlement' means a settlement arrived at in the course of conciliation proceeding and includes a written agreement between the employer and workmen arrived at otherwise than in the course of conciliation proceeding where such agreement has been signed by the parties thereto in such manner as may be prescribed and a copy thereof has been sent to an officer authorised in this behalf by the appropriate Government and the Conciliation Officer.

**NOTE:** The definition of "settlement" in s. 2(*p*) of the Act states that "settlement" means a settlement arrived at between the employer and the workmen. So, normally in order that a settlement between the employer and the workman may be binding on them, it has to be arrived at by agreement between the employer and the workmen. Where the workmen are represented by a recognised Union, the settlement may be arrived at between the employer and the Union. If there is a recognised Union of the workmen and the constitution of Union provides that any of its office-bearers can enter into a settlement with the Management on behalf of the Union and its members, a settlement may be arrived at between the employer and such office-bearer or bearers. But, where the constitution does not so provide specifically, the office-bearer or bearers who wish to enter into a settlement with the employer should have the necessary authorisation by the executive committee of the Union or by the workmen. [*Brooke Bond India Ltd.* v *The Workmen* AIR 1981 SC 1660: (1981)3 SCC 493: 1981(3) SLR 1: (1982)1 SCR 29].

▸ *Meaning under the Gift Tax Act 1958.* 'Settlement' means settling the property, right or claim, conveyance or disposition of property for the benefit of another. [*The Commissioner of Gift Tax, Madras* v *N.S. Getty Chettiar* AIR 1971 SC 2410: (1971)2 SCC 741: (1971)82 ITR 599: (1972)1 SCR 736].

▸ *Meaning under the Specific Relief Act 1963, s. 2(b).* 'Settlement' means an instrument other than a will or a codicil as defined by the Indian Succession Act 1925, whereby the destination or devolution of successive interests in movable and immovable property is disposed of or is agreed to be disposed of.


- **Act of settlement** p. 30.
- **Marriage settlement** p. 565.


**Several liability.** Liability i.e., separate and distinct from another's liability, so that the plaintiff may bring a separate action against one defendant without joining the other liable parties. [Black's *Law Dictionary*, 8th Ed.].

A liability imposed on two or more persons severally or separately.

NOTE: When two or more persons make a joint promise, the promisee may, in the absence of express agreement to the contrary, compel any one or more of such joint promisors to perform the whole of the promise. [Indian Contract Act 1872, s. 43]. As far as the liability under a contract is concerned, s. 43 of the Indian Contract Act makes all joint contracts joint and several. It allows a promisee to sue such one or more of the several joint promisors as he chooses and it is no defence to such a suit that all the promisors must have been made parties. [*Jainarain* v *Surajmull* AIR 1949 FC 211].

**Sewa.** In addition to; apart from. [*Maharajadhiraj of Darbhanga* v *Commissioner of Income-tax* AIR 1925 Pat 313].

**Sex.** Either of the main divisions, male and female, into which living things are placed with reference to the reproductive functions; the sum of the peculiarities of structure and function that distinguish a male from a female organism; males or females collectively; the activity or phenomena of life concerned with sexual desire or reproduction; sexual intercourse.

**Sex appeal.** A physical quality or charm that attracts sexual interest; the capacity to excite interest or attention to sex; sexual attractiveness.

**Sex change.** An apparent change of sex by surgical means and hormone treatment; surgery and hormonal treatment designed to alter a person's gender.

**Sex hormone.** Hormone affecting sexual development or behaviour.

**Sexism.** Sexual prejudice against women; prejudice or discrimination against women on the ground of sex.

**Sexology.** The study of sexual life or relationships specially in human beings; the study of human sexual behaviour.

**Sexual harassment.** A type of employment discrimination consisting in verbal or physical abuse of a sexual nature.

When a superior officer, had harassed, pestered and subjected his lady subordinate by a conduct which is against moral sanction and which did not withstand the test of decency and modesty and which projected unwelcome sexual advances it amounts to sexual harassment. [*Apparel Export Promotion Council* v *A.K. Chopra* AIR 1999 SC 625: (1999)1 SCC 759].

> NOTE: Repeated e-mailing of pornographic pictures by male coworkers to a female colleague who finds the pictures offensive tantamounts to sexual harassment.

**Sexual predator.** A person who has committed many violent sexual acts or who has a propriety for committing violent sexual acts.

**Sexually transmitted disease.** A disease transmitted only or chiefly by engaging in sexual acts with an infected person. It is also termed venereal disease. Common examples of such disease are syphilis and gonorrhea.

**Shafi.** Under Mahomedan law, *shafi* is the person who has the right of pre-emption.

> NOTE: The following three classes of persons and no others are entitled to claim pre-emption, namely—(1) a co-sharer in property (*shafi-i-sharik*); (2) a participator in immunities and appendages, such as a right of way or a right to discharge water (*shafi-i-khalit*); and (3) owners of adjoining immovable property (*shafi-i-jar*), but not their tenants, nor persons in possession of such property without any lawful title.
>
> The right of pre-emption arises only out of a valid, complete and *bona fide* sale. It does not arise out of gift (*hiba*), *sadaqah*, wakf, inheritance, bequest, or a lease even though in perpetuity. Nor does it arise out of a mortgage even though it may be by way of conditional sale; but the right will accrue if the mortgage is foreclosed.

**Shafi-i-khalit.** In Muslim law, this expression is not concerned with rights and duties. It only denotes those who share in the appendage of property. The dominant tenement-holder is *shafi-i-khalit*. It implies that he shares an appendage with the other person who is a servient tenement-holder. Therefore, both the dominant tenement-holder and the servient-tenement holder are *shafi-i-khalit*. [*Phool Chand* v *Neem Chand* AIR 1978 All 539; *Ladu Ram* v *Kalyan Sahaya* AIR 1963 Raj 195].

**Shah jogi hundi.** Shah jogi hundi is a hundi payable only to a respectable holder (shah). At its inception it is a hundi that passes from hand to hand by delivery and requires no endorsement. The body of the hundi requires that it should be paid to a shah. A shah jogi hundi is similar to some extent to a cheque crossed generally which is payable only to or through some banker. The hundi may pass from hand to hand till it reaches a shah who presents it to the drawee for acceptance or payment; then its negotiability ceases. It will not be paid unless the name of the shah by whom it is presented is endorsed on it and unless inquiry is made to identify him and to find out if he is respectable.

**Shahjog hundi.** A shahjog hundi is technically not a bill of exchange or a negotiable instrument as defined in the Negotiable Instruments Act 1881. A shahjog hundi is made payable to a shah, which means a respectable person. [*Central Bank of India* v *Khub Ram* AIR 1960 Punj 157].

**Shakkar.** Shakkar is a product obtained by boiling or processing juice pressed from and out of sugarcane. [*Mohammed Yamin* v *State of U.P.* (1972)2 SCC 184: 1972 Cr LJ 1198: AIR 1973 SC 484].

**Shall.** As used in statutes, contracts, or the like, this word is generally imperative or mandatory. In common or ordinary parlance, and in its ordinary signification, the term "shall" is a word of command, and one which has always or which must be given a compulsory meaning; as denoting obligation. It has a peremptory meaning, and it is generally imperative or mandatory. It has the invariable significance of excluding the idea of discretion, and has the significance of operating to impose a duty which may be enforced, particularly if public policy is in favour of this meaning, or when addressed to public officials, or where a public interest is involved, or where the public or persons have rights which ought to be exercised or enforced, unless a contrary intent appears. [*People* v *O'Rourke* 124 Cal App 752: 13 P 2d 989, 992].

But it may be construed as merely permissive or directory (as equivalent to "may"), to carry out the legislative intention and in cases where no right or benefit to any one depends on its being taken in the imperative sense, and where no public or private right is impaired by its interpretation in the other sense. [*Wisdom* v *Board of Sup're of Polk County* 19 NW 2d 602, 607, 608].

NOTE: The fact that the statute uses the word "shall" while laying down a duty is not conclusive on the question whether it is a mandatory or directory provision. In order to find out the true character of the legislation, the court has to ascertain the object which the provision of law in question has to subserve and its design and the context in which it is enacted. If the object of a law is to be defeated by non-compliance with it, it has to be regarded as mandatory. But when a provision of law relates to the performance of any public duty and the invalidation of any act done in disregard of that provision causes serious prejudice to those for whose benefit it is enacted and at the same time those entrusted with the performance of the public duty have no control over the performance of the duty, such provisions should be treated as a directory one. [*Sharif-ud-Din* v *Abdul Gani Lone* AIR 1980 SC 303: (1980)1 SCR 1177: (1980)1 SCC 403].

Ordinarily the use of the word "shall" *prima facie* indicates that the provision is imperative in character. However, by a catena of decisions, it is well-established that the court while considering whether the mere use of the word "shall" would make the provision imperative, would ascertain the intendment of the legislator and the consequences flowing from its own construction of the word "shall". [*Ganesh Prasad Sah Kesari* v *Lakshmi Narayan Gupta* AIR 1985 SC 964: (1985)3 SCR 825: (1985)3 SCC 53].

The word "shall" in its ordinary import is obligatory. Nevertheless, the word "shall" need not be given that connotation in each and every case and the provisions can be interpreted as directory instead of mandatory depending upon the purpose which the legislature intended to achieve as disclosed by the object, design, purpose and scope of the statute. [*Rubber House* v *Excellsior Needle Industries (P) Ltd.* AIR 1989 SC 1160: (1989)2 SCC 413: (1989)1 SCR 986: JT 1989(1) SC 488].

**Shall be construed as.** The words "shall be construed as" mean "shall be read as". [*State of Bombay* v *Salat Pragji Karamsi* AIR 1957 SC 517: 1957 SCR 745: 1957 Cr LJ 884: 1957 SCJ 493].

**Shall be deemed.** The expression suggests that something shall be assumed as true for certain purposes though really it is not so. [*A.C. Goel* v *First National Bank* AIR 1960 Punj 476].

**Shall be final.** "Shall be final" means it is final and there is an end [*Commissioner of Sales Tax, U.P.* v *Super Cotton Bowl Refilling Works* AIR 1989 SC 922: (1989)1 SCR 421: (1989)1 SCC 643: JT 1989(1) SC 458: (1989)40 ELT 247: (1989)73 STC 61], it cannot be questioned. [*Kanchanbhai* v *Maneklal* AIR 1966 Guj 19: ILR (1965) Guj 111].

NOTE: The use of the expression "shall be final" will have to be understood in the proper context and keeping in view the purpose for which it is used in a section of a statute. [*Aundal Ammal* v *Sadasivan Pillai* JT 1986 SC 1028: AIR 1987 SC 203: (1987)1 SCR 485: (1987)1 SCC 183].

The word 'final" prohibits an appeal, but not an application for revision. [*A.C. Arumugham* v *Jawahar Mills* AIR 1956 Mad 79].

**Shall be forfeited.** 'Shall be forfeited' means 'liable to be forfeited', depending on the setting and the sense of the statute. [*R.S. Joshi* v *Ajit Mills Ltd.* (1977)4 SCC 98: AIR 1977 SC 2279].

**Shall be punishable.** The expression means that the offender shall not escape the penal consequences. No discretion is conferred on court whether to award punishment or not. [*State* v *Jugmandar Lal* AIR 1966 SC 940: (1966)1 SCA 567: 1966 Cr LJ 707].

**Shall have regard to.** 'Shall take into consideration'. [*Sharma Electric Engineering Works* v *Radha Devi* AIR 1957 Cal 227; *Southern Pharmaceuticals and Chemicals* v *State of Kerala* AIR 1981 SC 1863: 1981 Tax LR 2838: (1981)4 SCC 391: (1982)1 SCR 519].

**Shall have regard to the provisions of this Act.** These words merely mean that where the new Act has slightly modified or clarified the previous provisions, the modifications and clarifications should be applied. [*V.K.*

*Verma* v *Radhey Shyam* AIR 1964 SC 1317; *Karan Singh Sobti* v *Shri Pratap Chand* AIR 1964 SC 1305: (1964)4 SCR 647; *S. Kartar Singh* v *Chamanlal* AIR 1969 SC 1288: (1969)1 SCC 760: (1970)1 SCR 9].

**Shall presume.** Whenever it is directed by the Indian Evidence Act that the court shall presume a fact, it shall regard such fact as proved, unless and until it is disproved. [Indian Evidence Act 1872, s. 4].

The words 'shall be presumed' mean that the court is bound to take the fact as proved, until evidence is adduced to disprove it. [*Public Prosecutor* v *A. Thomas* AIR 1956 Mad 166].

NOTE: Where the expression has been used that the court would presume in that event, no discretion has been left with the court and there is a legislative command to it to raise a presumption and regard such fact as proved unless and until it is disproved. In such an eventuality, the question of calling upon the parties to formally prove a document does not arise. [*Haradhan Mahatha* v *Kuhju Mahatha* AIR 1993 Pat 129: (1993)2 Pat LJR 28].

The words 'shall presume' in s. 4 of the Prevention of Corruption Act 1947, indicate a presumption of law and it is obligatory on the court to raise this presumption in every case brought under s. 4. [*State of Madras* v *A. Vaidyanath Iyer* 1958 SCR 580: AIR 1958 SC 61: 1958 SCJ 335].

NOTE: These words "shall presume" are being used in Indian Judicial lore for over a century to convey that they lay down a rebuttable presumption in respect of matters with reference to which they are used. [*Sodhi Transport Co.* v *State of U.P.* AIR 1986 SC 1099: (1986)2 SCC 486: (1986)1 SCR 939].

**Sham.** Counterfeit; fake; imposter; fraud.

A person who pretends to be something that he or she is not; a faker; something that is not what it seems; a transaction without substance that will be disregarded for tax purposes.

**Sham pleading.** A pleading is "sham" only when it is so clearly false that it does not raise any *bona fide* issue. [*Fontana* v *Town of Hempstead* 219 NYS 2d 383, 384].

Those which are inherently false and must have been known by interposing party to be untrue. [*Pentecostal Holiness Church, Inc.* v *Mauney* Fla App, 270 So 2d 762, 769].

**Shamil.** Appurtenant to something; comprehending; including.

**Shamlat deh.** Proprietary body of the village comprising of proprietors who are entitled to have a share in the *shamlat deh* in proportion to their proprietary holding. [*Saroop Singh* v *Hazara Singh* (1986)2 Cur Civ Cas 604, 605].

**Shampoo.** "Shampoo" is a kind of liquid soap. It has all the ingredients of a soap. It may be that the proportion of the ingredients of the liquid soap differ from those of a soap in the form of a cake but that fact would not alter the basic character of shampoo and take it out of the category of soaps. [*State of Gujarat* v *Prakash Trading Co., Ahmedabad* AIR 1973 SC 960: (1973)1 SCR 918: (1972)2 SCC 689: (1972)30 STC 348].

**Share.** Allocation; allotment; apportioned lot; part; commission; portion; proportion; section; segment; slice; corporate interest; stockholding.

An allotted portion owned by, contributed by, or due to someone; one of the definite number of equal parts into which the capital stock of a corporation or joint stock company is divided. [Black's *Law Dictionary*, 8th Ed.].

'Share' means share in the share capital of a company, and includes stock, except where a distinction between stock and shares is expressed or implied. [Companies Act 1956, s. 2(46)].

A share is not a sum of money, it represents an interest measured by a sum of money and make up of diverse rights contained in the contract, evidenced by the articles of association of the company. [*CIT* v *Standard Vacuum Oil Co.* AIR 1966 SC 1393: (1966)59 ITR 685: (1966)1 SCJ 401: (1966)1 Comp LJ 187: (1966)2 SCR 367].

NOTE: A share is movable property, but it is not movable in the same way in which a bale of cloth or bag of wheat is movable property. A share in a company belongs to a totally different category of property. It is incorporeal in its nature, and it consists merely of a bundle of rights and obligations. Every one of these rights and obligations is created by a statute or under statutory instruments of powers which also define their extent, scope, boundaries and incidents. [*S. Viswanathan* v *East India Distilleries and Sugar Factories Ltd.* AIR 1957 Mad 341].

- **Bonus share** p. 109.
- **Deferred shares** p. 242.
- **Equity share capital** p. 314.
- **Founders' shares** p. 370.
- **Holder of a share.** The expression 'holder of a share' denotes, in so far as a company is concerned, only a person who, as a shareholder, has his name entered on the register of members. The expression 'shareholder' or 'holder of share' denotes no other person except a 'member'. [*Howrah Trading Co. Ltd.* v *Commissioner of Income-tax, Central, Calcutta* AIR 1959 SC 775].
- **Nominal share capital** p. 609.
- **Preference share** p. 678.
- **Undivided share** p. 864.
- **Unlisted shares** p. 867.

**Share certificate.** This is an instrument issued under the seal of the company, certifying that the person therein named is entitled to a certain number of shares. It is not a negotiable instrument. It is *prima facie* evidence of his title to the shares of the company.

**Share premium account.** The account to which must be transferred any premium derived from the issue by a company of shares, whether for cash or otherwise.

**Share-hawking or share-pushing.** Calling from house to house endeavouring to sell shares.

**Sharebroker.** See STOCKBROKER p. 813.

**Shareholder.** Stockholder of record; one who owns or holds a share or shares in a company.

A 'shareholder' means the shareholder registered in the books of the company. [*Commissioner of Income-tax, Bombay City II* v *Shakuntala* AIR 1966 SC 719; *Rameshwar Lal* v *CIT* AIR 1967 Assam & Naga 102: (1965)35 Comp Cas 848: (1965)58 ITR 271].

It is only the person whose name is entered in the register of shareholders of the company as the holder of the shares who can be said to be a shareholder *qua* the company and not the persons beneficially entitled to the shares. It is the former who is a 'shareholder' within the matrix and scheme of the company law and not the latter. [*Rameshwari Lal Sanwarmal* v *CIT* (1980)2 SCC 371: AIR 1980 SC 372: (1980)2 SCR 369: (1980)122 ITR 1].

**Sharik.** A co-sharer; a partner; a joint owner.

**Shebait.** High priest. The person who has the right of performing the service of an idol and receiving the customary emoluments.

NOTE: An idol is a juridical person capable of holding property; but the possession and management of the dedicated property belong to the *shebait*.

Property dedicated to an idol vests in it in an ideal sense only; *ex necessitas*, the possession and management has to be entrusted to some human agent. Such an agent of the idol is known as *"shebait"* in Northern India. The legal character of a *shebait* cannot be defined with precision and exactitude. Broadly described, he is the human ministrant and custodian of the idol, its earthly spokesman, its authorised representative entitled to deal with all its temporal affairs and to manage its property. As regards the administration of the *debutter*, his position is analogous to that of a trustee; yet, he is not precisely in the position of a trustee in the English sense, because under Hindu law, property absolutely dedicated to an idol, vests in the idol, and not in the *shebait*. Although the *debutter* never vests in the *shebait*, yet, peculiarly enough, almost in every case, the *shebait* has a right to a part of the usufruct, the mode of enjoyment, and the amount of the usufruct depending again on usage and custom, if not devised by the founder. [*Profulla Chorone Requitte* v *Satya Chorone Requitte* AIR 1979 SC 1682: (1979)3 SCC 409: (1979)3 SCR 431].

**Shell company.** A company whose original business has ceased or is dormant and whose assets have largely been realised and distributed.

> NOTE: The "shell" company retains its name, formal existence and possibly its Stock Exchange quotation, with the result that it may become a convenient corporate vehicle for a different business.

**Sheriff.** The chief officer under the state in a presidency town who is responsible for the services of all processes and who is present in all criminal sessions of a High Court. He is usually appointed for a year.

**Sheristadar.** Keeper of records; highest ministerial officer of the court.

**Shia wakf.** A wakf governed by Shia law. [Wakf Act 1954, s. 3(*j*)].

**Shiah.** A sect amongst Mahomedans, followers of All, son-in-law of Mohammad.

**Ship.** 'Ship' shall include every description of vessel used in navigation not exclusively propelled by oars. [General Clauses Act 1897, s. 3(55)].

▸*Meaning under the Naval and Aircraft Prize Act 1971, s. 2(i).* 'Ship' includes a vessel and a seat with tackle, furniture and apparel of the ship, vessel or boat.

▸*Meaning under the Marine Insurance Act 1963, s. 2(h).* 'Ship' includes every description of vessel used in navigation.

**Ship-of-war.** Any ship belonging to the Armed Forces and includes any armed ship in the service of the Armed Forces and any other ship used as transport or auxiliary or in any other way for the purpose of prosecuting or aiding hostilities. [Naval and Aircraft Prize Act 1971, s. 2(*j*)].

**Ship papers.** The papers which must be carried by a vessel on a voyage, in order to furnish evidence of her national character, the nature and destination of the cargo, and of compliance with the navigation laws. The ship's papers are of two sorts: Those required by the law of a particular country; such as the certificate of registry, licence, charter-party, bills of lading and of health and the like. Those required by the law of nations to be on board neutral ships, to vindicate their title to that character; these are the passport, sea-brief, or sea-letter, proofs of property, the muster roll or *role d'equipage*, the charter-party, the bills of lading and invoices, the logbook or ship's journal, and the bill of health.

'Ship papers' include all books, passes, sea-briefs, charterparties, bills of lading, customs receipts, manifests, certificates, licences, lists, tickets, notes, letters and other documents and writings delivered up or found on board a ship captured at sea or seized in port. [Naval and Aircraft Prize Act 1971, s. 2(*k*)].

**Ship receipt.** A ship receipt is the written acknowledgment of the mate receiving a cargo, acknowledging the receipt of the goods on board, describing it by the marks on them or the boxes.

**Ship's husband.** The agent of the owners in regard to the management of all affairs of the ship in home port.

**Shipping documents.** Generic term to describe all papers which cover a shipment in foreign or inland trade such as bill of lading, letter of credit, certificate of insurance and the like.

**Shop.** The ordinary meaning of the word 'shop' is that it is a place where goods are stored and sold by retail dealers, and not a stall or an open space. [*Amulya Pal* v *R.N. Roy* 54 CWN 850].

In ordinary parlance a 'shop' is a place where the activities connected with the buying and selling of goods are carried on. It is not actually necessary that the delivery of the goods to the purchaser should take place at the premises in which the business of buying or selling is carried on to constitute the said premises into a 'shop'. If orders are received at a place which ultimately fructify into sales and the resulting trading activity is directed from these that place comes to be known as a shop. [*International Ore and Fertilizers Pvt. Ltd.* v *E.S.I. Corporation* (1987)4 SCC 203: (1987)3 SCR 981: JT 1987(3) SC 354: AIR 1988 SC 79].

▸*Bombay Shops and Establishment Act 1948, s. 2(27).* The word "shop" means any premises where goods are sold, either by retail or wholesale, or where services are rendered to customers, and includes an office, a store room, godown, warehouse, or work place, whether in the same premises or otherwise, mainly used in connection with such trade or business but does not include a factory, a commercial establishment, residential hotel, restaurant, eating house, theatre or other place of public amusement or entertainment. [*Kalidas Dhanjibhai* v *State of Bombay* AIR 1955 SC 62: (1955)1 SCR 887: 1955 Cr LJ 193: 1955 SCJ 150: (1954)2 Lab LJ 694].

▸ *West Bengal Shops and Establishment Act 1963, s. 2(13).* Shop means any premises used wholly or in part for the sale of services to customers or for the wholesale or retail sale of commodities or articles, either for cash or on credit, and includes any offices, storerooms, godowns or warehouses, whether in the same premises or elsewhere, used in connection with such sale or with storage of commodities or articles for the purpose of such sale and also includes such other class or classes of premises as the Government may, after taking into consideration the nature of the work carried on there, by notification, declare to be shops for the purposes of W.B. Shops and Establishment Act, but does not include an establishment.

▸ *Untouchability (Offences) Act 1955, s. 2(e).* 'Shop' means any premises where goods are sold either wholesale or by retail or both wholesale and by retail and includes a laundry, a hair cutting saloon and other places where services are rendered to customers.

▸ *Weekly Holidays Act 1942, s. 2(d).* 'Shop' includes any premises where any retail trade or business is carried on including the business of a barber or hair-dresser, and retail sales by auction, but excluding the sale of programmes, catalogues and other similar sales at theatres.

NOTE: *Whether 'shop' includes a premises where basically intellectual activity takes place.* 'Shop' is a place where services are sold on retail basis. [*Employees' State Insurance Corporation* v *R.K. Swamy* (1994)1 SCC 445: 1994 SCC (L&S) 586: AIR 1994 SC 1154: 1994 AIR SCW 428: (1994)1 Comp LJ 225: (1994)1 Lab LJ 636: (1993)67 Fac LR 1145: JT 1993(6) SC 176; *Hindu Jea Band* v *State of Rajasthan* (1987)2 SCC 101: AIR 1987 SC 1166].

A 'shop' though liberally interpreted would take in any place where the services are rendered, but it will not go to the extent of including the premises where basically and mainly intellectual activity is taking place and things are not sold or purchased, a concept which is peculiar to a shop. The services of advertising agent are more in the nature of supply of an idea rather than the supply of any particular tangible service and predominant part of which is played by the mind. It is a creative tool in the hands of men and what is supplied is the product of such an idea for the effective campaign for sale. The activity will not involve sale or purchase. [*WA & Marketing Pvt. Ltd.* v *Jaison Edwards* 1992 Lab IC 727 (Ker)].

**Shoplifting.** Larceny of merchandise from a store or business establishment. Essential constituents of "shoplifting" are (1) wilfully taking possession of merchandise offered for sale in mercantile establishment, (2) with intention of converting merchandise to taker's own use without paying purchase price thereof. [*Yearwood* v *State* 455 SW 2d 612, 617].

**Should.** The past tense of shall. It ordinarily implies an obligation or duty. Although often interchangeable with the word "would", it does not ordinarily express certainty as "will" sometimes do.

**Show cause.** To produce a satisfactory explanation or excuse, usually in connection with a motion or application to a court. [Black's *Law Dictionary*, 8th Ed.].

▸ *Meaning under the Constitution of India, Art. 311 (since amended).* The expression 'showing cause' as used in Art. 311 does not imply that a mere opportunity of submitting an explanation is enough. It implies that adequate opportunity of leading evidence in support of the contention of the person concerned and controverting the contentions raised against him shall be given; and where necessary, opportunity of cross-examining witnesses of the other side and of addressing arguments shall also be afforded. [*Shyam Lal* v *State of U.P.* AIR 1954 All 235 (DB); *Union of India* v *T.A. Verma* AIR 1957 SC 882].

**Shuffa.** Pre-emption; the right of an owner of immovable property to acquire by purchase another immovable property which has been sold to another person. In Mahomedan law the right belongs first to a cosharer in the property sold, secondly to a participator in its appendages and lastly to adjoining owners. Amongst Hindus the right is recognised in some parts of India by custom. Some statutes have provided for pre-emption.

**Sick leave.** An employment benefit allowing a worker time off for sickness, either with or without pay, but without loss of seniority or other benefits; the time so taken by an employee. [Black's *Law Dictionary*, 8th Ed.].

**Sight draft/bill.** An instrument payable on presentment. A bill of exchange for the immediate collection of money. [*United Ben. Fire Ins. Co.* v *First Nat. Bank of Ariz., Phoenix* 405 P 2d 488, 490].

NOTE: A bill of exchange payable at sight is treated as payable on demand. A bill may also be made payable at a fixed period after sight. It must then be presented for acceptance to the drawee in order that the maturity may be fixed.

**Sign.** The word "sign" means to write one's name on, in acknowledging authorship, authorising action, etc. Signing means writing one's name on some document or paper. [*Hindustan Construction Company Ltd.* v *Union of India* AIR 1967 SC 526: (1967)1 SCR 843].

▸ *Meaning under the General Clauses Act 1897, s. 3(56).* 'Sign' with its grammatical variations and cognate expressions shall, with reference to a person who is unable to write his name, include "mark" with its grammatical variations and cognate expressions.

NOTE: The expression unable to write his name includes not only illiterate person, but also literate or educated person who by reason of some disability or infirmity may not be able to write his name. [*P.N. Vallarasu* v *Election Commissioner of India* AIR 1987 Mad 6: 1985 Writ LR 677].

The essential requirement of signing is affixing either by writing with a pen or pencil or by otherwise impressing on the document one's name or 'signature' so as personally to authenticate the document. [*Goodman* v *Eban (F) Ltd.* (1954)1 All ER 763].

It also includes signing of one's name with his authority by somebody else. [*London County Council* v *Vitamins Ltd.* (1955)2 All ER 229]. There must be physical contact between the person and the signature or the mark on the document. [*Commissioner of Income Tax* v *Kesab* AIR 1950 SC 265: 1950 SCR 435: 1950 SCJ 364: 5 DLR (SC) 98].

Whenever signature is necessary, signing must be in strict accordance with the law or rules. Where a person is unable to write his name, he may put his mark in accordance with any law or rules in force. [*Ram Dayal* v *Brijraj Singh* AIR 1970 SC 110].

A person may sign or put his name by means of types, or, if he uses a facsimile for signing his name, he may use it for signature. [*S.C. Devi* v *Union of India* 67 CWN 759].

**Signature.** A person's name, initial or mark used in signing a letter, document, etc.; the act of putting one's name at the end of an instrument to attest its validity; the act of signing a document.

Speaking generally a signature is the writing or otherwise affixing a person's name or a mark to represent his name, by himself or by his authority with the intention of authenticating a document as being that of or as binding on the person whose name or mark is so written or affixed. The insertion of the name, in any part of the writing in a manner to authenticate the instrument is sufficient. The signature be it in the beginning or middle of the instrument is binding as it is at the foot of it. [*Har Kaur* v *Gura Singh* 1986 Punj LJ 382: (1986)90 Punj LR 30: ILR (1987)1 P&H 93: AIR 1988 Punj 41 relying on *Eziekiel & Co.* v *Annoda Charan Sen* AIR 1923 Cal 35].

NOTE: No precise definition of the word "signature" is given in any law in India. In the General Clauses Act there is no exhaustive definition of the word "signature". It merely says that the word "signature" shall include. It includes the affixing of a mark ......

If a statute requires personal signature of a person, which includes a mark, the signature or the mark must be that of the man himself. [*Commissioner of Agricultural Income Tax, W.B.* v *Keshab Chandra Mandal* AIR 1950 SC 265: 1950 SCR 435: 1950 SCJ 364: (1950)18 ITR 569].

A signature may be written by hand, printed, stamped, typewritten, engraved, photographed, or cut from one instrument and attached to another, and a signature lithographed on an instrument by a party is sufficient for the purpose of signing it; it being immaterial with what kind of instrument a signature is made. [*Maricopa County* v *Osborn* 136 P 2d 270, 274].

**Silence.** Absolute quiet; noiselessness; quiescence; speechlessness; stillness; absence of sound; abstinence from speech or noise; the state of a person who does not speak, or of one who refrains from speaking; the avoidance of mentioning a thing, betraying a secret.

NOTE: In the law of estoppel, "silence" implies knowledge and an opportunity to act upon it. [*Pence* v *Langdon* 25 L Ed 420; *Stewart* v *Wyoming Cattle Ranch Co.* 32 L Ed 439].

**Silk.** In the ordinary sense 'silk' means natural or real silk, or something of which natural or real silk is a component. Without the qualification 'artificial', it would not include rayon, and a draper who sells rayon as silk. [*Travancore Rayons Ltd.* v *Municipal Council Perumbavoor* AIR 1958 Ker 149 (FB)].

**Silver.** A shiny white precious metal used for ornaments.

'Silver' includes silver bullion or ingot, silver sheets and plates which have undergone no process of manufacture subsequent to rolling and uncurrent silver coin which is not legal tender in India or elsewhere and jewellery or articles made wholly or mainly of silver. [Foreign Exchange Regulation Act 1947, s. 2(*l*) (since repealed)].

**Similar.** Analogous; homogeneous; equivalent; corresponding; identical; matching; parallel; uniform; synonymous.

Having a general likeness, although allowing for some degree of difference. [*Gangi* v *Sears Roebuck & Co.* 360 A 2d 907, 908].

Word "similar" is generally interpreted to mean that one thing has a resemblance in many respects, nearly corresponds, is somewhat like, or has a general likeness to some other thing but is not identical in form and substance, although in some cases "similar" may mean identical or exactly alike. It is a word with different meanings depending on context in which it is used. [*Guarantee Mut.. Life Ins. Co.* v *Harrison* Tex Civ App, 358 SW 2d 404, 406].

The expression "similar" is a significant expression. It does not mean identical but it means corresponding to or resembling in many respects, somewhat like, or having a general likeness. [*Nat Steel Equipment Pvt. Ltd.* v *Collector of Central Excise* AIR 1988 SC 631: (1988)1 SCC 605: (1988)2 SCR 732: JT 1988(1) SC 228: (1988)69 STC 58: (1988)34 ELT 8: 1988 Cr LR (SC) 198].

The word "similar" may be said to be a word of ambiguous import in the sense that the mere stipulation in a statute that something should be done similarly is insufficient by itself to signify the degree of stipulation with which that thing must be done. [*The C.I.T., Madras* v *T.V. Sundaram Iyenger & Sons (P) Ltd.* (1975)101 ITR 764: 1975 (Supp) SCR 93: AIR 1976 SC 255: (1976)1 SCC 77].

• **Deceptively similar** p. 234.

**Similarly apportioned.** The expression means simply "similarly split up". [*The CIT, Madras* v *T.V. Sundaram Iyenger & Sons (P) Ltd.* (1975)101 ITR 764: 1975 (Supp) SCR 93: AIR 1976 SC 255: (1976)1 SCC 77].

**Simple mortgage.** Where, without delivering possession of the mortgaged property, the mortgagor binds himself personally to pay the mortgage-money and agrees, expressly or impliedly, that, in the event of his failing to pay according to his contract, the mortgagee shall have a right to cause the mortgaged property to be sold and the proceeds of sale to be applied, so far as may be necessary, in payment of the mortgage-money, the transaction is called a simple mortgage and the mortgagee a simple mortgagee. [Transfer of Property Act 1882, s. 58(*b*)].

**Simple trust.** A simple trust is one in which property is vested in one person on trust for another, the nature of the trust not being prescribed by the settlor but being left to the construction of the law, as where property is transferred to *T* on trust for *B* absolutely. In such a case, *T* must permit *B* to enjoy the trust property, and must obey his instructions as to disposing of it. But if *B* in turn becomes a bare trustee of his equitable interest for *C*, *T* will hold directly in trust for *C*. [*Head* v *Lord Teynham* (1783)1 Cox Eq 57].

**Simpliciter.** It is a Latin expression which means simply; without ceremony; in a summary manner; directly; by itself; by its own force, *per se*.

**Simulated contract.** One which, though clothed in concrete form, has no existence in fact. It may at any time and at the demand of any person in interest be declared a sham and may be ignored by creditors of the apparent vendor.

**Simulated fact.** In the law of evidence, a fabricated fact; an appearance given to things by human device, with a view to deceive and mislead.

**Simulated judgment.** One which is apparently rendered in good faith, upon an actual debt, and intended to be collected by the usual process of law, but which in reality is entered by the fraudulent contrivance of the parties, for the purpose of giving to one of them an advantage to which he is not entitled, or of defrauding or delaying third persons.

**Simulated sale.** One which has all the appearance of an actual sale in good faith, intended to transfer the ownership of property for a consideration, but which in reality covers a collusive design of the parties to put the property beyond the reach of creditors, or proceeds from some other fraudulent purpose.

**Sine anno.** Without date.

**Sine die.** Without day.

- **Adjournment sine die.** See ADJOURN SINE DIE p. 39.

**Sine qua non.** Essential condition; essential matter, part, qualification; indispensable condition; absolute condition; prime ingredient; that without which the thing cannot be.

**Sinking fund.** This is an account created by transferring an amount from profit and loss account or appropriation account by debiting that account and crediting sinking fund account in order to provide for the redemption of a known liability or for the renewal of a wasting asset. The amount that this account represents should be invested outside the business in gilt-edged securities and allowed to accumulate at compound interest, the investment being recorded in a sinking fund investment account.

**Sister.** A woman who has the same father and mother with another, or has one of them only. In the first case, she is called sister, simply; in the second, half-sister. The word is the correlative of 'brother'.

- **Half sister** p. 405.

**Site.** A plot of ground set apart for some specific purpose; a seat or ground plot.

'Site' means a place where anything is constructed or planned; as, the site of the new bank; the scene of an event; as the site of the explosion. [*D.B. Bhalerao* v *State* AIR 1986 Bom 295: 1985 Mah LJ 850].

Site means the general locale upon which the house is built. In so far as a flat or storey is concerned, site is that on which a flat or storey immediately is superimposed or stands. [*Attendrooloo Chetty's Charities* v *Sadhana Aushadhalay* (1968)2 MLJ 406: ILR (1969)1 Mad 184].

*Chamber's Dictionary* defines site as situation, especially of a building; ground occupied or set apart for a building. In Stroud's *Judicial Dictionary*, 4th Ed., vol. 5, it is stated that the term 'site' in relation to a house, building, or other erection shall mean the whole space to be occupied by such house, building, or other erection, between the level of the base of the walls. Accordingly, the expression 'site' is not necessarily confined to a particular vacant land but it may also include an already constructed building on a piece of land. [*Sudhir Kumar Ghosh* v *State* (1976-77)81 CWN 791: 1977 Cr LJ 1824].

**Sitting.** A continuous period of being engaged in an activity; a time during which an assembly is engaged in business; the part of the year in which judicial business is transacted.

**Sitting and voting.** The words 'sitting and voting' in Art. 193 of the Constitution imply the summoning of the House under Art. 174 of the Constitution by the Government to meet at such time and place as it thinks fit and the holding of the meeting of the House pursuant to the said summons or an adjourned meeting. An elected member incurs the penalty for contravening Art. 193 of the Constitution only when he sits and votes at such a meeting of the House. [*Pashupati Nath Sukul* v *Nem Chandra Jain* (1984)2 SCC 404: AIR 1984 SC 399].

**Sketch.** A rough draft or general outline; a rough, merely outlined, or unfinished drawing or painting, often made to assist in making a more finished picture.

▸ *Meaning under the Indian Official Secrets Act 1923, s. 2(9).* 'Sketch' includes any photograph or other mode of representing any place or thing.

**Skip.** The name given to the operation in machine accounting whereby particular columns in a tabulation are passed over by means of the manipulation of a key or a lever; a cage, a bucket, or a net in which men or materials are raised and lowered in mines or quarries or in which goods are placed in unloading a ship.

**Slander.** Abusive language; aspersion; character assassination; damaging report; defamatory words; false report; malicious report; revilement; scandal; smear; vilification.

The speaking of base and defamatory words tending to prejudice another in his reputation, office, trade, business, or means of livelihood [*Little Stores* v *Isenberg* 172 SW 2d 13, 16; *Harbison* v *Chicago, R.I. & P. Ry. Co.* 37 SW 2d 609, 616]; the speaking of false and malicious words concerning another whereby injury results to his reputation. [*Johnston* v *Savings Trust Co. of St. Louis* Mo, 66 SW 2d 113, 114; *Lloyd* v *Commissioner of Internal Revenue* CCA 7, 55 F 2d 842, 844].

**Slander of title/goods.** A false and malicious statement, oral or written, made in disparagement of a person's title to real or personal property, or of some right of his causing him special damage. [*Reliable Mfg. Co.* v *Vaughan Novelty Mfg. Co.* 13 NE 2d 518; *Cawrse* v *Signal Oil Co.* 103 P 2d 729, 730].

False and malicious statements discrediting a person's goods or title to the ownership of property.

**Slaughter-house.** A place ordinarily used for the slaughter of animals for the purpose of selling the flesh thereof for human consumption. [Cantonments Act 1924, s. 2(*xxxiv*)].

**Sleeping partner.** A person who supports a partnership with money and name, but who does not actively engage himself in the management of the partnership business. A sleeping partner, in strictness of language, means a partner who is merely passive in the firm, whether known or unknown, in contradistinction to those who are active and who conduct the business of the firm as principals.

NOTE: Unlike a limited partner, the sleeping partner is fully liable for partnership debts. The sleeping partner is also called a dormant partner.

**Smriti.** The smriti is one of the sources of Hindu law. The smriti means what was remembered and is believed to contain the precepts of God, but not in the language they had been delivered. The language is of human origin, but the rules are divine. The authors do not arrogate to themselves the position of legislators, but profess to compile the traditions handed down to them by those to whom the divine commands had been communicated.

NOTE: The smritis are the principal sources of lawyer's law, but they also contain matters other than positive law. The complete Codes of Manu and Yajnavalkya deal with religious rites, positive law, penance, true knowledge and liberation. There are some that deal with positive law alone, such as the Code of Narada. Many others contain nothing of positive law.

**Smuggled goods.** 'Smuggled goods' may be taken to mean goods which have been imported by avoiding the payment of the customs duty leviable thereon, or by evading any legal order or prohibition or restriction on the import of such goods. [*Sitaram* v *State* AIR 1962 Cal 370].

**Smuggling.** The fraudulent taking into a country, or out of it, merchandise which is lawfully prohibited. [*Dunbar* v *U.S.* 39 L Ed 390].

"Smuggle" has well-understood meaning at common law, signifying bringing on shore, or carrying from shore, of goods, wares, and merchandise for which duty has not been paid, or goods the importation or exportation whereof is prohibited. [*Williamson* v *U.S.* CA Cal, 310 F 2d 192, 195].

The word 'smuggling' must be understood as having the ordinary dictionary meaning, *viz.*, carrying of goods clandestinely into a country. Goods may be carried clandestinely in order to evade the payment of customs duty leviable thereon, or in order to evade any legal order of prohibition or restriction on the import of the particular class of goods. [*Sitaram* v *State* AIR 1962 Cal 370].

'Smuggling', in relation to goods, means any act or omission which will render such goods liable to confiscation under s. 111 or s. 113 of the Customs Act. [Customs Act 1962, s. 2(39)].

**So far as may be.** To the extent possible. [*Dr. Pratap Singh* v *Director of Enforcement, Foreign Exchange Regulation Act* AIR 1985 SC 989: (1985)3 SCC 72: (1985)3 SCR 969: (1985)155 ITR 166: 1985 SCC (Cri) 312].

**Socialism.** Absolute equality in the distribution of the physical means of life and enjoyment. It is applied to any system which requires that the land and the instruments of protection should be the property, not of individuals, but of communities or associations or of the government.

NOTE: The Indian conception of socialism with democracy with human dignity is by creation of opportunities for the development of each individual. It is not for the merging of the individual in the society.

**Society.** An association or company of persons (generally unincorporated) united together by mutual consent, in order to deliberate, determine, and act jointly for some common purpose. In a wider sense, the community or public; the people in general. [*Gilmer* v *Stone* 30 L Ed 734]. An association of persons having common interests, beliefs, objects or profession.

• **Benevolent societies** p. 102.
• **Trade protection society** p. 849.

**Sodomy.** Buggery; unnatural carnal intercourse; unnatural sexual intercourse; a carnal copulation by human beings with each other against nature, or with a beast. [*State* v *Young* 13 P 2d 604, 607].

Sodomy is oral or anal copulation between persons who are not husband and wife or consenting adult members of the opposite sex, or between a person and an animal, or coitus with an animal.

**Soil.** The upper layer of earth in which plants grow, consisting of disintegrated rock usually with an admixture of organic remains; finely divided rock mixed with decayed vegetable or animal matter, constituting that part of the surface of the earth in which plants grow.

The word frequently means the surface of the land only, and does not include minerals [*Wakefield* v *Buccleuch* 36 LJ Ch 179]; but it may mean 'down to the centre of the earth'. [Stroud's *Judicial Dictionary*, 5th Ed.].

As verb, it may also mean make dirty; smear or stain with dirt; tarnish; defile; bring discredit to.

**Sola bill.** A single bill of exchange as distinguished from one in a set.

**Solatium.** A sum paid to a person as compensation or consolation for injured feelings.

**Sold note.** It is the name of an instrument in writing given by a broker to a buyer of merchandise in which it is stated that the goods therein mentioned have been sold to him. It is also called 'confirmation' notice.

**Solemnize.** The word "solemnize" means in connection with a marriage, to celebrate that marriage with proper ceremonies and in due form. It follows that unless the marriage is celebrated or performed with proper ceremonies and due form it cannot be said to be solemnized. [*Bhaurao Shankar Lokhande* v *State of Maharashtra* AIR 1965 SC 1564: (1965)2 SCR 837: (1965)2 Cr LJ 544].

**Solicit.** To appeal for something; to ask earnestly; to entreat, implore, or importune; to plead for; to awake or excite to action, or to invite.

**Solicitor.** A lawyer who acts for the client in some matters and assists advocates. In England there are the Solicitors Act 1957 and the Legal Profession Practice Act 1958 to regulate solicitor's profession. On the property side he investigates title to land, prepares contracts of sale, conveyances and wills, obtains probate of wills and frequently acts as executor and trustee. He interviews clients, advises them generally on their legal profession and writes letters. He pilots company promoters through the legal technicalities of forming companies. On difficult questions he takes the opinion of counsel and he also prepares briefs for counsel in legal proceedings in which counsel is employed. [Williams's *Learning the Law*].

A "Solicitor" is an officer of the Supreme Court of Judicature to conduct legal proceedings for his clients. Originally there was a distinction between "Solicitor" and "Attorney"—the former had not the latter's power to bind his principal; subsequently the distinction was between attorneys as agents in actions at law, and Solicitors in chancery. By the Judicature Act 1873 "Attorneys" came to be called "Solicitors". [*Encyclopaedia Britannica*, Vols. 2 and 20]. The British tradition is continued in India, although there have been modifications to suit local conditions. [The Advocates Act 1961 and the Supreme Court Rules 1966].

**Solicitor-General.** He is one of the law officers of the Central Government. His duties are practically the same as those of the Attorney-General, to whom he is subordinate.

**Solitary confinement.** In a general sense, the separate confinement of a prisoner, with only occasional access of any other person, and that only at the discretion of the jailer. In a stricter sense, the complete isolation of a prisoner from all human society, and his confinement in a cell so arranged that he has no direct intercourse with or sight of any human being, and no employment or instruction. [*Medley, Petitioner* 134 US 160: 10 S Ct 384: 33 L Ed 835 relied on in *Sunil Batra* v *Delhi Administration* AIR 1978 SC 1675: 1978 Cr LJ 1741].

**Solo cedit, quicquid solo plantatur.** What is affixed to the soil belongs to the soil.

**Solvency.** Ability to pay debts as they mature; ability to pay debts in the usual and ordinary course of business [*Jeck* v *O'Meara* 122 SW 2d 897, 903]; present ability of debtor to pay out of his estate all his debts.

**Son.** A person's male child, whether natural or adopted; a male of whom one is the parent; an immediate male descendant. [Black's *Law Dictionary*, 8th Ed.].

"Son" as understood in common parlance means a natural son born to a person after marriage. It is the direct blood relationship which is the essence of the term in which "son" is usually understood, emphasis being on legitimacy. In legal parlance, however "son" has a little wider connotation. It may include not only the natural son but also son's son, namely, the grandchild, and where the personal law permits adoption, it also includes an adopted son. Even illegitimate son may be treated as legitimate, as for example, the "son" referred to in s. 16 of the Hindu Marriage Act, as originally enacted. Thus, the term "son" itself is a flexible term and may not be limited to the direct descendant. Its true meaning will depend upon the context in which it is used. [*K.V. Muthu* v *Angamuthu Ammal* JT 1996(11) SC 246: AIR 1997 SC 628: (1997)2 SCC 53: (1997)1 SCJ 48].

▸ *Meaning under the General Clauses Act 1897, s. 3(57)*. 'Son' in the case of any one whose personal law permits adoption shall include an adopted son.

'Son' means a legitimate male issue. [*Gulraj Singh* v *Mota Singh* AIR 1965 SC 608].

The description 'son' in wills means *prima facie* legitimate son. [*In re Flood's Estate* 21 P 2d 579].

**Sound disposing mind.** The sound disposing mind in wills does not mean perfectly healthy mind. It means in plain language an appreciation of the fact that the man is making a will an appreciation of the contents of the will and an appreciation of the nature of the dispositions that he is making having regard to the claims of affection and family relationship and claims of the society or community to which he belongs. [*A.E.G. Carapiet* v *A.Y. Derderian* AIR 1961 Cal 359; *Kameswara Rao* v *Bendapudi* AIR 1962 AP 178].

NOTE: In order to be of a sound disposing mind, a testator must not only be able to understand that he is by his will giving his property to one or more objects of his regard, but he must also have the capacity to comprehend and to recollect the extent of his property and the nature of the claims of others whom by his will he is excluding from participation in that property. [Halsbury's *Laws of England*, 4th Ed., vol. 17, para 898, p. 472].

**Sound mind.** The ability to make a will, direct, or assent. In its application to wills, it means the ability to recognise the natural objects of one's bounty, the nature and extent of one's estate, and the fact that one is making a plan to dispose of the estate after death.

▸ *Meaning under the Indian Contract Act 1872, s. 12*. A person is said to be of sound mind for the purpose of making a contract if, at the time when he makes it, he is capable of understanding it and of forming a rational judgment as to its effect upon his interests.

**Source of law.** A point of origin for law or legal analysis; something that provides authority for legislation and for judicial decisions.

NOTE: Sources of law can be classified as either legal or historical. The former are those sources which are recognised as such by the law itself. The latter are those sources lacking formal recognition by law.

The legal sources of law are authoritative, the historical are unauthoritative. In general, law proceeds from one or more of the following legal sources: from a written constitution, from legislation, from judicial precedent, from custom and from the writings of experts. English law, however, which is without a written condition, proceeds chiefly from two legal sources, legislation and precedent. Legislation is the making of law by the formal and express declaration of new rules by some authority in the State. A precedent, on the other hand, is the making of law by the recognition and application of new rules by the courts themselves in the administration of justice.

It is necessary to recognise two other legal sources in addition to legislation and precedent. These are custom and agreement, being the sources respectively of customary law and conventional law. Customary law is that which is constituted by those customs which fulfil the requirements laid down by law as the condition of their recognition as obligatory rules of conduct. Conventional law is that which is constituted by agreement having the force of special law *inter partes*, in derogation of, or in addition to, the general law of the land.

Classified, therefore, by reference to their legal sources there are four kinds of law—(*a*) enacted law, having its source in legislation; (*b*) case law, having its source in precedent; (*c*) customary law, having its source in customs; and (*d*) conventional law, having its source in agreement. [Salmond on *Jurisprudence*, 12th Ed., pp. 109-114].

**Sovereign democratic republic.** The expression means that the absolute power vested in the people under the Constitution is to be exercised by them through their duly elected representatives. [*Ram Nandan* v *State* AIR 1959 All 101].

**Sovereignty.** The supreme power in a State or country.

"Sovereignty" means "supremacy in respect of power, domination or rank; supreme domination authority or rule". "Sovereignty" is the right to govern. The term "sovereignty" as applied to States implies "supreme, absolute, uncontrollable power by which any State is governed, and which resides within itself, whether residing in a single individual or a number of individuals or in the whole body of the people". Thus, sovereignty, according to its normal legal connotation, is the supreme power which governs the body politic, or society which constitutes the State, and this power is independent of the particular form of Government, whether monarchial, autocratic or democratic. According to Laski in *A Grammar of Politics* 1957, Reprint Chap. II, p. 50: The legal aspect of sovereignty is best examined by a statement of the form given to it by John Austin. In every legal analysis of the State, he argued, it is first of all necessary to discover in the given society that definite superior to which habitual obedience is rendered by the mass of men. That superior must not itself obey any higher authority. When we discover the authority which gives commands habitually obeyed, itself not receiving them, we have the sovereign power in the State. In an independent political community that sovereign is determinate and absolute. Its will is illimitable because, if it could not be constrained to act, it would cease to be supreme, since it would then be subject to the constraining power. Its will is indivisible because, if power over certain functions or persons is absolutely and irrevocably entrusted to a given body, the sovereign then ceases to enjoy universal supremacy and therefore ceases by definition to be sovereign. [*Sardar Govindrao* v *State of Madhya Pradesh* AIR 1982 SC 1201: (1982)2 SCC 414: (1982)3 SCR 729].

**Spare part.** Any integral part of an article which is carried, held or kept reserve for future use or in emergency or which is additional or extra. It implies that such part must be severable or capable of being replaced or substituted. [*Vithal Chhagan & Sons* v *State of Gujarat* (1966)17 STC 96 (Guj)].

'Spare part' means an extra part of a vehicle or machine kept for use in emergency or replacement. The expression 'spare parts' cannot be equated with parts without regard to the colour lent by the word 'spare'. It does not include a component part. [*Commercial Taxes Officer* v *Punjab Engineering Works* (1997)107 STC 58, 61 (Raj)].

**Speaker.** One who speaks or makes a speech; the presiding officer of a large deliberative assembly.

▸ *Meaning under the Constitution of India, Arts. 93 and 178.* A member of the House of the People or the State Legislative Assembly elected to preside over the deliberations of the House.

**Special agent.** An agent authorised to act as such in some particular business, and not generally.

**Special duty.** A special duty connotes a particular type of duty which is allotted to an officer. A person is appointed on special duty by government when special type of work is to be done for the government not on permanent basis but as result of some special circumstances. [*Balak Ram Vaish* v *Badri Prasad* AIR 1969 All 88].

**Special endorsement.** When the endorsement contains not only the signature of the endorser but also the name of the person in whose favour the endorsement is made, then that endorsement is said to be in full or special. Thus, an endorsement, "Pay J.J. or order" or "pay to J.J." followed in each case by the signature of the endorser, is an endorsement in full or special endorsement. Such an endorsement prevents the bill from being transferred by anybody but the endorsee; and none but the special endorsee can sue upon it.

**Special law.** A 'special law' is a law applicable to a particular subject. [Indian Penal Code 1860, s. 41].

The expression 'special law' means a provision of law which is not applicable generally, but which applies to a particular or specified subject or class of subjects. [*Anjanabai Yeshwantrao* v *Yeshwantrao Daulatrao* AIR 1961 Bom 154 (FB)].

**Special occasions.** "Special occasions", in its application to a statute, cannot be equated with fanciful occasions but such as promote the policy of the statute. [*P.N. Kaushal* v *Union of India* AIR 1978 SC 1457: (1978)3 SCC 558: (1979)1 SCR 122].

**Special resolution.** A resolution shall be a special resolution when—(*a*) the intention to propose the resolution as a special resolution has been duly specified in the notice calling the general meeting or other intimation given to the members of the resolution, (*b*) the notice required under the Companies Act 1956, has been duly given of the general meeting, and (*c*) the votes cast in favour of the resolution (whether on a show of hands or on a poll, as the case may be) by members who, being entitled so to do, vote in person, or where proxies are allowed, by proxy, are not less than three times the number of votes, if any, cast against the resolution by members so entitled to voting. [Companies Act 1956, s. 189(*e*)].

**Special trust.** A trust imposing active duties on the trustee; also called an active trust. A special trust is one where a trustee is appointed for the execution of some purpose particularly mentioned. He is not, as in the case of a simple trust, a mere passive depositary of the estate. He is required to exert himself actively in the execution of the settlor's intention, as where a conveyance is made to the trustee to sell the property for the payment of debts.

**Specially empowered.** It means empowerment "for a particular purpose". The word "specially" connotes that it is the empowerment which is special and not the person. [*State of Gujarat* v *Chaturbhuj Maganlal* AIR 1976 SC 1697: (1976)3 SCR 1076: (1976)3 SCC 54: 1976 Cr LJ 1367: 1976 SCC (Cri) 359].

**Specific.** Clearly defined; distinctly and plainly set forth; of, relating to, or designating a particular or defined thing; of or relating to a particular named thing; explicit; conformable to special requirements.

The word 'specific' is specific enough to avoid being vague and general. What is precise, exact, definite and explicit is specific. Sometimes what is specific may also be special, yet they are distinct in semantics. [*Maru Ram* v *Union of India* 1980 Cr LJ 1440, 1455: AIR 1980 SC 2147: 1981 Cr LR (SC) 1: (1981)1 SCR 1196].

The expression may also denote a customs duty chargeable upon imported merchandise by quantity, weight, or number, without regard to value.

**Specific delivery contract.** A forward contract which provides for the actual delivery of specific qualities or types of goods during a specified future period at a price fixed thereby or to be fixed in the manner thereby agreed and in which the names of both the buyer and the seller are mentioned. [Forward Contracts (Regulation) Act 1952, s. 2(*m*)].

**Specific goods.** Goods identified and agreed upon at the time a contract of sale is made. [Sale of Goods Act 1930, s. 2(14)].

**Specific legacy.** Where a testator bequeaths to any person a specified part of his property, which is distinguished from all other parts of his property, the legacy is said to be specific. [Indian Succession Act 1925, s. 142].

A specific legacy is a bequest of a specific part of the testator's personal estate which is so distinguished. A general legacy is a bequest of some thing or money, not necessarily part of the estate and not distinguished from all others of the same kind. [Williams and Mortimer on *Executors, Administrators and Probate*, p. 796].

**Specific movable property.** The words "specific movable property" can mean only such specific items of movable property in respect of which the plaintiff is entitled to claim immediate possession in specie from the defendant who has either wrongfully taken or is wrongfully withholding them from him. [*Raghunath Das* v *Gokal Chand* AIR 1958 SC 827: 1958 SCJ 1067: 1959 SCR 811; Limitation Act 1908, Art. 49].

**Specific performance.** Specific performance is compelling a person to perform his contract. Latter day common law, however, spurned the idea. Its edict: compensation, not compulsion, when the damages were adequate, *cadit questio*. But there are cases where either there was no standard for assessing the damage or the damages were inadequate; it was here that Equity stepped in and in its bid to do 'complete and more perfect justice' evolved the remedy of specific performance. Nevertheless, it being an equitable remedy, no one can claim it as a matter of right and the grant of relief is in the sole discretion of the court, though the discretion has to be exercised on well-settled principles. The remedy is available to both the parties and either party may file a suit even before the due date of completion. A party also need not wait till the other breaks its promise, for the breach of the contract is not an essential part of the cause of action in equity. [*Hashan* v *Zenab* (1960) AC 316; *Marks* v *Lilley* (1959)2 All ER 647].

NOTE: Specific performance is an equitable relief and he who seeks equity can be put on terms to ensure that equity is done to the opposite party even while granting the relief. The final end of law is justice, and so the means to it too should be informed by equity. That is why he who seeks equity shall do equity. [*K. Kalpana Saraswathi* v *Somasundaram Chettiar* (1980)1 SCC 630: AIR 1980 SC 512].

The law as to specific performance of contract is contained in ss. 9 to 26 of the Specific Relief Act 1963.

**Specilia generalibus derogant.** Special words derogate from general ones.

**Speculation.** Assumption; guesswork; hypothesis; inference; presumption; supposition; surmise; theorisation.

It also means bet; calculated risk; fortuity; gamble; gambling; gaming; wager; buying or selling with expectation of profiting by a rise or fall in price; engaging in hazardous business transactions, or investing in risky securities or commodities with the hope of an usually large profit.

• **Rash and hazardous speculation** p. 725.

**Speculative transaction.** A speculative transaction is "a transaction in which a contract for purchase and sale of any commodity including stocks and shares is periodically or ultimately settled otherwise than by the actual delivery or transfer of the commodity or scrips." In the absence of actual delivery, the transactions attracted Explanation 2 to s. 24(1) and must be regarded as "speculative transactions". [*Nirmal Trading Co.* v *Commissioner of Income Tax (Central), Calcutta* AIR 1980 SC 234: (1980)1 SCR 900: (1980)1 SCC 119: (1980)121 ITR 54; Income Tax Act 1922, Explanation 2 to s. 24(1)].

**Speedy trial.** A trial as soon after indictment as prosecution can with reasonable diligence prepare for it. [*People* v *Molinari* 67 P 2d 767, 770].

NOTE: It is a fundamental right of an accused implicit in Art. 21 of the Constitution of India. [*Hussainara Khatoon* v *State of Bihar* AIR 1980 SC 1360].

**Spes successionis.** The right of a person to succeed as heir on the death of another person. It is a bare chance of succession and is not transferable. [Transfer of Property Act 1882, s. 6(*a*)].

**Splitting cause of action.** Dividing a single or indivisible cause of action into several parts or claims and bringing several actions thereon [*Coniglio* v *Wyoming Valley Fire Ins. Co.* 59 NW 2d 74, 78; *Van Brode Mill Co.* v *Kellog Co.* DC Del, 113 F Supp 845, 852]; commencement of action for only part of the cause of action. [*Wood* v *Baker* 341 P 2d 134, 136]

NOTE: To split a cause of action into parts is forbidden. The idea is to prevent a mutiplicity of suits in respect of the same cause of action. Every suit is to include the whole of the claim. If a portion of the claim is omitted, the plaintiff is not permitted to sue for it. [Code of Civil Procedure, Or. 2, rr. 1 and 2].

**Spouse.** Marital partner; marriage partner; mate. The word "spouse" has been understood to connote a husband or a wife which term itself postulates subsisting marriage. [*Smt. Lila Gupta* v *Laxmi Narain* AIR 1978 SC 1351: (1978)3 SCC 258: (1978)3 SCR 922].

**Spurious.** The meaning of the word 'spurious' as given in Webster's *New Twentieth Century Dictionary* is: 'not genuine, not proceeding from true source, not legitimate'. 'Not proceeding from true source' only means that the thing is not what it pretends to be, which only means that it is not genuine or legitimate. [*Chaitanya Kumar Adatiya* v *Sushila Dixit* AIR 1975 SC 1718: (1976)3 SCC 97].

**Squatter.** A squatter is a person who settles or locates on land, enclosed or unenclosed, with no *bona fide* claim or colour of title and without the consent of the owner of the land. [*Ram Singh Pritam Singh* v *Chief Commissioner, Union Territory, Chandigarh* AIR 1968 Punj 470].

**Sruti.** The Sruti is regarded as one of the sources of Hindu law. The Sruti is believed to contain the very words of God. The name is derived from the Sanskrit root "sru" to hear, and signifies what was heard.

NOTE: The Sruti contains very little of lawyer's law; it consists of hymns dealing with religious rites, true knowledge and liberation. There are, no doubt, a few passages containing an incidental allusion to a rule of law, or giving an instance from which a rule of law may be inferred. The Sruti comprises the four Vedas, the six Vedangas, and the Upanishads. The Upanishads embody the highest principles of Hindu religion.

**Stage carriage.** A motor vehicle constructed or adapted to carry more than six passengers excluding the driver for hire or reward at separate fares paid by or for individual passengers, either for the whole journey or for stages of the journey. [Motor Vehicles Act 1988, s. 2(40)].

**Stakeholder.** Generally, a stakeholder is a third party chosen by two or more persons to keep on deposit property or money the right or possession of which is contested between them, and to be delivered to one who shall establish his right to it; and it is one who is entitled to interplead rival or contesting claimants to property or funds in his hands. [*Cochran* v *Bank of Hancock County* 162 SE 2d 765, 770].

A person with whom money is deposited pending the decision of a bet or wager (q.v.). His function is to receive the sums wagered and hold then against the determining event, whether that event be a horse race or otherwise, and then pay them over to the winner. Also a third person chosen by two or more persons to keep in deposit property the right or possession of which is contested between them, and to be delivered to the one who shall establish his right to it. [*State* v *Dudley* 127 NJL 127: 21 A 2d 209, 210].

**Stamp.** Attestation; authentication; certification; engraving; hallmark; identification; impression; imprint; seal; a small label or strip of paper, printed and sold by the government, and required to be attached to mail-matter, and to certain other documents and articles subject to duty or excise.

**Standard.** A type, model, or combination of elements accepted as correct or perfect; a measure or rule applicable in legal cases.

Stability, general recognition, and conformity to established practice.

[*Standard Accident Ins. Co.* v *Standard Surety & Casualty Co.* DCNY, 53 F 2d 119, 120].

- **Gold standard** p. 389.

**Standard rent.** Rent fixed by any authority under any law in force for the time being.

**Standing order.** Rules or regulations relating to procedure of Parliament; rules framed by any authority under statutory powers; a forward-looking order that applies to all cases pending before a court.

A forward-looking order that applies to all cases pending before a court. [Black's *Law Dictionary*, 7th and 8th Eds.].

**Standing timber.** Trees fit for use for building or repairing houses.

> NOTE: Before a tree can be regarded as "standing timber" it must be in such a state that if cut, it could be used as timber; and when in that state it must be cut reasonably early. [*Joseph* v *Joseph Annamma* AIR 1979 Ker 219: 1979 Ker LT 322: ILR (1979)2 Ker 15].
>
> In order that trees may be considered to be standing timber, they must first be trees whose wood is suitable for use for building house, bridges, ships, etc. [*Shantabai* v *State of Bombay* AIR 1958 SC 532].
>
> In India, neem trees or babul trees or teak trees have been held to be standing timber. [*Kunhikoya* v *Ahmed Kutty* AIR 1952 Mad 39]. A fruit-bearing tree would not be standing timber. [*Alisaheb* v *Mohidin* 13 Bom LR 874]. In areas, however, where mango trees are used for building houses, they may be standing timber. [*Krishnarao* v *Babaji* (1900)24 Bom 31].
>
> Section 3 of the Transfer of Property Act enacts that "immovable property" does not include standing timber.

**Stare decisis.** It is a Latin expression which means to stand by things decided; to abide by, or adhere to, decided cases.

"The rule of adherence to judicial precedents finds its expression in the doctrine of *stare decisis*. This doctrine is simply that, when a point or principle of law has been once officially decided or settled by the ruling of a competent court in a case in which it is directly and necessarily involved, it will no longer be considered as open to examination or to a new ruling by the same tribunal, or by those which are bound to follow its adjudications, unless it be for urgent reasons and in exceptional cases." [William M. Lite et at., *Brief Making and the Use of Law Books*, p. 321 (3d ed. 1914)].

Under the doctrine, when court has laid down a principle of law as applicable to a certain state of facts, it will adhere to that principle, and apply it to all future cases, where facts are substantially the same, regardless of whether the parties and property are the same. [*Horne* v *Moody* Tex Civ App, 146 SW 2d 505, 509, 510].

Under doctrine a deliberate or solemn decision of court made after argument on question of law fairly arising in the case, and necessary to its determination, is an authority, or binding precedent in the same court, or in other courts of equal or lower rank in subsequent cases where the very point is again in controversy. [*State* v *Mellenberger* 95 P 2d 709, 719, 720].

Under the doctrine, when point of law has been settled by decision, it forms precedent which is not afterwards to be departed from, and, while it should ordinarily be strictly adhered to, there are occasions when departure is rendered necessary to vindicate plain, obvious principles of law and remedy continued injustice. The doctrine is a salutary one, and should not ordinarily be departed from where decision is of long-standing and rights have been acquired under it, unless considerations of public policy demand it. [*Colonial Trust Co.* v *Flanagan* 25 A 2d 728, 729].

> NOTE: The rule of *stare decisis* is not so imperative or inflexible as to preclude a departure therefrom in any case, but its application must be determined in each case by the discretion of the court and previous decisions should not be followed to the extent that error may be perpetuated and grievous wrong may result. [*Maktul* v *Mst. Manbhari* AIR 1958 SC 918].
>
> *Stare decisis and res judicata—distinction.* The doctrine of *stare decisis* differs from that of *res*

*judicata* in the following ways: (1) *Res judicata* applies to the decision in the dispute, while *stare decisis* operates as to the rule of law involved. (2) The former binds only the parties and their successors, whereas the latter binds everyone. (3) *Res judicata* applies to all Courts, but *stare decisis* is brought into operation only by the decisions of higher Courts. (4) The former takes effect after the time for appeal is past; the latter operates at once. [Dias on *Jurisprudence*, Ed. 1964].

**State.** A body of people occupying a definite territory and politically organised under one government. [*State ex rel. Maisano* v *Mitchell* 231 A 2d 539, 542].

A people permanently occupying a fixed territory bound together by common-law, habits and custom into one body politic exercising, through the medium of an organised government, independent sovereignty and control over all persons and things within its boundaries, capable of making war and peace and of entering into international relations with other communities of the globe. [*United States* v *Kusche* DC Cal, 56 F Supp 201, 207, 208].

▸*Meaning under the Constitution of India, Art. 12.* Those authorities which are invested with sovereign power, i.e. the power to make rules or regulations and to administer or enforce them to the detriment of citizens and others fall within the definition of 'state' in Art 12; and constitutional or statutory bodies which do not share that sovereign power of the state, are not 'state' within the meaning of Art. 12 of the Constitution. [*Rajasthan State Electricity Board* v *Mohan Lal* AIR 1967 SC 1857].

NOTE: Thus, 'the State' includes its Income Tax Department [*Bidi Supply Co.* v *Union of India* AIR 1956 SC 479]; Air India is a State [*Boring Company* v *R.M. Investment Trading Co. Pvt. Ltd.* AIR 1993 Cal 184: (1993)1 Cal LJ 415]; the Gram Panchayat being a local authority stands included in the term 'State' [*Ajit Singh* v *State of Punjab* AIR 1967 SC 856]; educational institutions receiving aid from the government have the character of "the authorities" and come within the scope of the definition of 'State' [*S. David* v *The Correspondent, St. Gabriels Higher Secondary School, Madras* (1995)2 MLJ 291; *Dr. Amin Prakash* v *State of Gujarat* (1981)22 Guj LR 41 (DB)]; the university will be governed by the expression 'the State' for purposes of Part III of the Constitution. [*Sher Singh* v *Vice-Chancellor, Punjab University* AIR 1969 P&H 391].

*State—whether includes union territories.* The definition of 'state' in s. 3(58) in the General Clauses Act after the adaptation in 1956 applies and includes Union territories in Entry 80 of the Union list. [*Advance Insurance Co.* v *Gurudasmal* (1970)1 SCC 633: AIR 1970 SC 1126; *Ram Kishore Sen* v *Union of India* AIR 1966 SC 644: (1966)1 SCR 430].

Used as verb, it means to express the particulars of a thing in writing or in words; to set down or set forth in details; to aver, allege, or declare; to mention by way of reference or in general terms.


- **Act of State** p. 30.
- **Affairs of State** p. 47.
- **Authority controlled by State** p. 88.
- **Buffer state** p. 113.
- **Foreign state** p. 366.
- **Secular state** p. 781.


**State Act.** An Act passed by the Legislature of a State established or continued by the Constitution. [General Clauses Act 1897, s. 3(59)].

**State transport undertaking.** Any undertaking providing road transport service, where such undertaking is carried on by—(*i*) the Central Government or a State Government; (*ii*) any Road Transport Corporation established under s. 3 of the Road Transport Corporations Act 1950; (*iii*) any municipality or any corporation or company owned or controlled by the Central Government or one or more State Governments, or by the Central Government and one or more State Governments; (*iv*) Zilla Parishad or any other similar local authority. [Motor Vehicles Act 1988, s. 2(42)].

**Statement.** Expression in words; a declaration; narration; a summary of facts; a verbal assertion or non-verbal conduct intended as an assertion; a formal and exact presentation or account of facts.

In law, it means a formal narration of facts filed as the foundation for judicial proceeding; a pleading; an account of a person's knowledge of a crime, taken by the police pursuant to their investigation of the offence.

In financial matter, it means a record of transactions in a bank account; a summary of the assets and liabilities of a bank or firm, showing the balance due; a report sent at regular intervals to a debtor of a business firm.

The primary meaning of the word "statement" to be found in *Shorter Oxford English Dictionary* and *Websters New World Dictionary* is 'something that is stated'. Another meaning that is given in the *Shorter Oxford English Dictionary* is 'written or oral communication'. [*Bhogilal Chunilal Pandya* v *State of Bombay* AIR 1959 SC 356: 1959 Supp (1) SCR 310: 1959 Cr LJ 389].

The dictionary meaning of the word 'statement' is the act of stating, reciting or presenting verbally or on paper. The term 'statement', therefore, includes both oral and written statements. [*Saboo* v *State of U.P.* (1965)2 SCWR 464: (1965)2 SCA 292].

'Statement' in s. 162, Cr. P.C. is the entirety of the facts stated by a witness to a police officer during the investigation. All these facts whenever and whatever stated go to constitute his 'statement'. [*Muninajappa* v *State* AIR 1958 Mys 138].

NOTE: When the word 'statement' is not defined in the Act, the dictionary meaning of the word is to be taken in order to discover what it means. Assistance may also be taken from the use of the word 'statement' in other parts of the Act to discover in what sense it has been used therein. [*Bhogilal Chunilal Pandya* v *State of Bombay* AIR 1959 SC 356: 1959 Supp (1) SCR 310: 1959 Cr LJ 389].


- **Appropriation statement** p. 71.
- **Bank statement** p. 95.
- **Defamatory statement** p. 239.
- **Written statement** p. 906.


**Status.** Caliber; caste; class; dignity; eminence; esteem; footing; grade; importance; notability; prominence; standing; state or condition; social position; the legal relation of individual to rest of the community.

The status of an individual, used as a legal term, means the legal position of the individual in or with regard to the rest of a community. [*Niboyet* v *Niboyet* (1878)4 PD 1].

The status of a person means his personal legal condition only so far as his personal rights and burdens are concerned to the exclusion of his proprietary relation. [*Duggamma* v *Ganeshayya* AIR 1965 Mys 97].

Status is a condition of membership of a group of which powers and duties are exclusively determined by law and not by agreement between the parties concerned. [*Roshan Lal Tandon* v *Union of India* AIR 1967 SC 1889].

NOTE: Status is a condition imposed by law and not by act of parties, though it may be predicated in certain cases on some private act. The status when created by a nomination, cannot be withdrawn or cancelled at the mere will of the parties. The law must determine the condition and circumstances under which it can be terminated. Merely because the status originated from the act of a senior head in making the nomination, it would not follow that the senior head can put an end to it by another act. [*Mahalinga Thambiran* v *Arulnandi Thambiran* (1974)1 SCC 150: AIR 1974 SC 199].

"Status" determines a person's legal condition in community by reference to some legal class or group and cannot normally be voluntarily changed. The imposition of status carries with it attribution of a fixed quota of capacity and incapacities, but it does not directly compel the holder to do or refrain from doing any particular act. [*Sri Mahalinga Thambiran Swamigal* v *His Holiness Sri La Sri Kasivasi Arulnandi Thambiran Swamigal* AIR 1974 SC 199: (1974)2 SCR 74: (1974)1 SCC 150].

**Status quo.** Absence of change; conservation of the same situation; preservation of the same condition; existing state of things at any given date.

According to the ordinary legal connotation, the term *"status quo"* implies the existing state of things at any given point of time. [*Bharat Coking Coal Ltd.* v *State of Bihar* 1987 (Supp) 394: JT 1987(4) SC 403: (1988)1 SCR 869: 1988 Cr LJ 396: AIR 1988 SC 127].

*'Status quo'* means condition or state of affairs as existing at that time should be maintained and the same should not be disturbed. [*Manju Kumari* v *State of Bihar* (1996)1 Pat LJR 363].

**Statute.** An act of the legislature declaring, commanding or prohibiting something; a particular law enacted and established by the will of the legislative department of government, the written will of the legislature, solemnly expressed according to the forms necessary to constitute it the law of the state.

▸ *Meaning under the Constitution of India, Arts. 111 and 200.* Act passed by the legislature and assented to by the President of India or Governor of a State.

NOTE: Statutes are of the following kinds: (1) *declaratory*—when they do not profess to make any alteration in the existing law, but merely to declare or explain what it is; (2) *remedial*—when they confer a new favour; (3) *amending*—when they alter the statute law; (4) *consolidating*—when they amalgamate the provisions of existing statutes relating to the same subject-matter, with only such textual amendments as are necessary; (5) *codifying*—when they reduce to one set of rules the existing statute law with respect to any subject.

- **Enabling statute** p. 305.
- **Fiscal statute** p. 356.
- **Limitations, statutes of** p. 536.
- **Remedial statute** p. 743.

**Statutory.** Relating to a statute; required by a statute; created or defined by a statute; conforming to a statute.

**Statutory body.** A body created by or under a statute and owing its existence to a statute.

NOTE: An institution, though not created by a statute, may adopt certain statutory provisions; such an institution is not a statutory body. [*Vaish Degree College* v *Lakshmi Narain* AIR 1976 SC 888: (1976)2 SCR 1006: (1976)2 SCWR 588: (1976)2 SCC 58].

A company incorporated under the Companies Act is not created by the Companies Act but comes into existence in accordance with the provisions of that Act. It is not a statutory body, because it is not created by the statute. It is body created in accordance with the statute. [*Sukdev Singh* v *Bhagatram Sardar Singh Raghuvanshi* AIR 1975 SC 1331, *per* A.N. Ray, C.J.].

**Statutory corporation.** Corporations created by special statutes, such as Damodar Valley Corporation Act 1948, State Bank of India Act 1955, etc. Special powers are given to each individual corporation. [*M. Verghese* v *Union of India* AIR 1963 Cal 421].

NOTE: Statutory corporations are authorities within the meaning of Art. 12, Constitution of India and *vis-a-vis* their employees they are bound to act according to the rules and regulations framed. [*Sukhdev Singh* v *Bhagatram* AIR 1975 SC 1331: 1975 Lab IC 881: 1975(1) SLR 605; *A.L. Kalra* v *Project Equipment Corpn.* AIR 1984 SC 1361: 1984 Lab IC 961: 1984 UJ (SC) 733: 1984(2) SLJ 82: 1984(2) SLR 446: 1984 Cur Civ LJ (SC) 526; *Workmen, F.C.I.* v *F.C.I.* AIR 1985 SC 670].

**Statutory damages.** See under DAMAGES p. 221.

**Statutory meeting.** Every company limited by shares, and every company limited by guarantee and having a share capital, shall, within a period of not less than one month nor more than six months from the date at which the company is entitled to commence business, hold a general meeting of the members of the company, which shall be called "the statutory meeting". [Companies Act 1956, s. 165(1)].

NOTE: A private company is not required to hold any statutory meeting. [Companies Act 1956, s. 165(10)].

**Statutory tenancy.** A "statutory tenancy" is the right of a tenant to remain in possession despite the determination of contractual tenancy on all the terms of the contractual tenancy which are not inconsistent with the invoking Act. The tenant's possession remains protected until the court makes an order for possession against him.

"Statutory tenancy" is a convenient expression for referring to a tenant whose tenancy has been terminated and who would be liable to be evicted but for the protecting statute. [*Damadilal* v *Parashram* AIR 1976 SC 2229: 1976 (Supp) SCR 645: (1976)4 SCC 855]. A statutory tenancy would come to an end either on the surrender of premises by the tenant or on the passing of a decree of eviction. [*Biswabani Pvt. Ltd.* v *Santosh Kumar Dutta* AIR 1980 SC 226: (1980)1 SCC 185: (1980)1 SCR 650].

**Statutory tenant.** A statutory tenant is a tenant who after expiry of period of tenancy is entitled to continue in possession of the rented premises under the provisions of the statute and remains protected by the statute. [*Bhagwan Singh* v *Central Bank of India* AIR 1989 Punj 9].

A person remaining in occupation of premises let to him after the determination of or expiry of the period of the tenancy is commonly, though in law not accurately, called a "statutory tenant". Statutory tenant being a person who enjoys the status of irremovability would enjoy the protection of the statute until he is evicted from the premises under the enabling provision of the statute. [*Biswabani Pvt. Ltd.* v *Santosh Kumar Dutta* AIR 1980 SC 226: (1980)1 SCC 185: (1980)1 SCR 650].

**Stay of proceedings.** To stop or suspend the procedure of court or execution of any order or process of court; to suspend any action or operation of order until something else happens.

**Step in aid of execution.** The expression connotes such step as is calculated to promote, advance or accelerate the execution of the decree, or removing some obstacle from the way of execution. [*Darogi Mondal* v *Kameshwar Singh* AIR 1957 Pat 299].

**Sterility.** Inability for procreation of children. Sterility may in some cases accompany impotency but is not necessarily associated with it. [*Jagdish Lal* v *Shyama Mohan* AIR 1966 All 150].

**Stevedore.** A person or company that hires longshore and harbour workers to load and unload ships [Black's *Law Dictionary*, 8th Ed.]; one whose business is stowing or unloading the holds of vessels; a person employed in loading and unloading ships.

'Stevedore' is a workman employed either as an overseer or a labourer in the loading and unloading of the cargoes of merchant vessels. [*Provident Fund Inspector, Ernakulam* v *B. Paul Abro* AIR 1965 Ker 239].

Roughly speaking, the work of stevedoring is mainly concerned with stowing any discharge of cargo ... [*Kesablal Banerjee* v *Calcutta D.L. Board* AIR 1960 Cal 166].

**Sthanam.** Some of the aristocratic Hindu families in the west coast had attached to their families office called *sthanam* meaning literally 'status rank or dignity'. The holder of *sthanam* was called a *sthanee* or *sthanamdar*. The rulers granted *sthanams* to their chieftains and important public officers which were usually accompanied by a grant of land for the maintenance of the dignity of the officer. One important feature was that *sthanamdar* ceased to have any interest in the property of his tarwad and the members of his tarwad had in their turn only reversionary rights to the *sthanam* properties. The *sthanamdar* had a limited estate. [*M.K. Balakrishna Menon* v *The Assistant Controller of Estate Duty-cum-Income Tax Officer, Ernakulam* AIR 1971 SC 2392: (1971)2 SCC 909: (1972)1 SCR 961: (1972)83 ITR 162].

**Stifling a prosecution.** Agreeing, in consideration of receiving a pecuniary or other advantage, to abstain from prosecuting a person for an offence not giving rise to a civil remedy.

**Stigma.** "Stigma", according to the dictionary meaning, is something that detracts from the character or reputation of a person, a mark, sign, etc. indicating that something is not considered normal or standard. It is a blemish, defect, disgrace, disrepute, imputation, mark of disgrace or shame and mark or label indicating deviation from a norm. In the context of an order of termination or compulsory retirement of a government servant stigma would mean a statement in the order indicating his misconduct or lack of integrity. [*Allahabad Bank Officers' Assn.* v *Allahabad Bank* AIR 1996 SC 2030: (1996)4 SCC 504: 1996 SCC (L&S) 1037: JT 1996(5) SC 275].

**Stock.** The original progenitor of a family; a person from whom a family is descended; a merchant's goods that are kept for sale or trade; the capital or principal fund raised by a corporation through subscribers' contributions or the sale of shares; a proportional part of a corporation's capital represented by the number of equal units or shares owned, and granting the holder the right to participate in the company's general management and to share in its net profits or earnings. [Black's *Law Dictionary*, 8th Ed.].

The plain meaning of the word 'stock' is 'to keep'. [*Sk. Amir* v *State of Maharashtra* AIR 1974 SC 469: (1974)3 SCR 84: (1974)4 SCC 210: 1974 Cr LJ 459].

NOTE: *'Stock' and 'bonds'—distinction.* "Stock" in a corporation is an equity, and it represents an ownership interest, and it is to be distinguished from obligations such as notes or bonds which are not equities and represent no ownership interest. [*U.S.* v *Evans* CA Or, 375 F 2d 730, 731].


- **Buffer stock** p. 113.
- **Dead stock** p. 227.
- **Debenture stock** p. 231.
- **Watering stock** p. 894.


**Stock exchange.** The place at which shares of stock are bought and sold.

Any body of individuals, whether incorporated or not, constituted for the purpose of assisting, regulating or controlling the business of buying, selling or dealing in securities. [Securities Contracts (Regulation) Act 1956, s. 2(*j*)].

**Stock-in-trade.** The equipment, materials or goods with which a merchant or trader carries on business; articles of commerce; available assets; supply on hand; merchandise.

The inventory carried by a retail business for sale in the ordinary course of business; the tools and equipment owned and used by a person engaged in a trade; the equipment and other items needed to run a business. [Black's *Law Dictionary*, 8th Ed.].

**Stockbroker.** One who buys or sells stocks as an agent of others.

**Stocks and shares at par.** See under PAR p. 638.

**Stolen property.** Property, the possession whereof has been transferred by theft or by extortion or by robbery and property which has been criminally misappropriated or in respect of which criminal breach of trust has been committed is designated as "stolen property", whether the transfer has been made or the misappropriation or breach of trust has been committed, within or without India. But, if such property subsequently comes into the possession of the person legally entitled to the possession thereof, it then it ceases to be stolen property. [Indian Penal Code 1860, s. 410].

NOTE: The words 'stolen property' merely denote the attribute or characteristic of the property. If the property is capable of being described as 'stolen property', that would be sufficient to comply with the requirement of the section. The section does not say by whom it should have been stolen. [*Champaklal Ganeshmal* v *State of Maharashtra* AIR 1975 SC 160: (1975)3 SCR 584: (1975)3 SCC 485: 1975 Cr LJ 256: 1975 SCC (Cri) 77].

**Stoppage in transit.** The right of an unpaid seller, who has parted with the possession of the goods, to resume possession while they are in course of transit till payment of the price. [Sale of Goods Act 1930, s. 50].

**Storage.** Safekeeping of goods in a warehouse or other depository [*Lincoln Sav. Bank of Brooklyn* v *Brown* Em App, 137 F 2d 228, 230, 231]; capacity or space for storing; an amount stored; the act of storing; the action of storing or laying up in reservation; the condition or fact of being stored.

'Storage' does not necessarily mean stocking in a house or at a particular place. Its ordinary dictionary meaning is "placing in a store". [*Balabhada Raja Guru Mohapatra* v *State of Orissa* AIR 1954 Ori 95]. If goods are kept or stocked in warehouse, it can be immediately described as an act of 'storage'. [*Bijaya Kumar Agarwala* v *State of Orissa* AIR 1996 SC 2531: (1996)5 SCC 1: 1996 SCC (Cri) 864: 1996 Cr LJ 1577: JT 1996(7) SC 56].

NOTE: 'Storage' in the common parlance connotes the concept of continued possession. There is an element of continuity of possession spread over some time and the concept is connected with the idea of a regular place of storage. Transhipment in a moving vehicle would not amount to storage. [*Prembahadur* v *State of Orissa* (1977)44 Cut LT 629].

**Store.** As noun, it means business house; emporium; establishment; market place; mart; outlet; shop; stall; accumulation; amassment; conservatory; depository; reservoir; stock; stockpile; any place where goods are deposited and sold by one engaged in buying and selling them.

As verb, it means accumulate; amass; assemble; conserve; hoard; deposit; pile up; stockpile; stowaway, keep goods, etc. in safekeeping for future delivery in an unchanged condition.

NOTE: The dictionary meanings suggest that 'storing' has an element of continuity as the purpose is to keep the commodity in store and reprieve it at some future date, even within a few days. [*Bijaya Kumar Agarwala* v *State of Orissa* AIR 1996 SC 2531: (1996)5 SCC 1: 1996 SCC (Cri) 864: 1996 Cr LJ 1577: JT 1996(7) SC 56].

Carrying goods in a vehicle cannot *per se* be 'storing' although it may be quite possible that a vehicle is used as a store. [*Bijaya Kumar Agarwala* v *State of Orissa,* supra].

**Storey.** Division of a house or building reached by one flight of stairs. A house may consist of several storeys. The storey to which there is an entrance from the outside on or near the level of the ground is generally called the ground storey. The storey of a building which is next above the ground storey is called the first storey. The successive storeys above the first storey are the second storey, the third storey, and so on to the topmost storey.

**Stranger.** Alien; foreign person; outsider; unknown person; stranger person.

A person is said to be a stranger to a transaction when he takes no part in it.

Stranger is to be understood not in terms of blood or marriage relationship with the family but as a person unconnected with it, unknown in character and antecedents. [*Vijayalakshmi* v *B. Himantharaja* AIR 1996 SC 2146: 1996 AIR SCW 2602].

NOTE: Thus a person who is not a party to a deed, contract etc., is said to be a stranger to it. Strangers to a suit are those who are not directly interested in the subject-matter in issue, and who have no right to make defence, control the proceedings, or appeal from the judgment.

**Stream.** A watercourse having a source and terminus, banks, and channel, through which waters flow at least periodically, and it usually empties into other streams, lakes, or the ocean, but it does not lose its character as a watercourse even though it may break up and disappear. [*Mogle* v *Moore* 104 P 2d 785, 789; *Everett* v *Davis* Cal App, 107 P 2d 650, 655; *Southern Pac. Co.* v *Proebstel* 150 P 2d 81, 83].

A body of water having a continuous flow in one direction. It consists of a bed, banks, and watercourse. [*St. Paul Fire & Marine Ins. Co.* v *Carroll* Tex Civ App, 106 SW 2d 757, 758].

'Stream' in its primary and natural sense denotes a body of water having, as such body, a continuous flow in one direction. [*M'Nab* v *Roberton* (1897) AC 129].

**Street.** A thoroughfare in a city, town or village, usually wider than an alley or lane.

An urban way or thoroughfare; a road or public way in a city, town, or village, generally paved, and lined or intended to be lined by houses on each side. It includes all urban ways which can be and are generally used for travel, but does not normally include service entrances or driveways leading off from the street onto adjoining premises. [*Hill & Combs* v *First Nat. Bank of San Angelo, Tex.* CCA Tex, 139 F 2d 740, 743].

"Street" includes any bridge, road, lane, footway, subway, square, court, alley or passage, whether a thoroughfare or not, which is for the time being open to the public; and the doorways and entrances of premises abutting on a street and any ground adjoining and open to a street, are treated as forming part of the street. [Halsbury's *Laws of England*, 4th Ed., vol. 11, para 1071, p. 600].

▸ *Meaning under the Cantonments Act 1924, s. 2(xxxvii).* 'Street' includes any way, road, lane, square, court, alley or passage in a cantonment, whether a thoroughfare or not and whether built upon or not, over which the public have a right of way and also the roadway or footway over any bridge or causeway.

▸ *Meaning under the Prevention of Cruelty to Animals Act 1890, s. 2(2).* 'Street' includes any way, road, lane, square, court, alley, passage or open space, whether a thoroughfare or not, to which the public have access.

"Street" means any road, bridge, footway, lane, square, court, alley or passage which the public or any portion of the public, has right to pass along, and includes, on either side, the drains or gutters and the land up to the defined boundary of any abutting property, notwithstanding the projection over such land of any verandah or other superstructure. [*State of U.P.* v *Ata Mohd.* AIR 1980 SC 1785: (1980)3 SCR 1095: (1980)3 SCC 614].

**Stridhan.** According to Hindu law, *stridhan* means such property of a woman over which she has full and unrestricted ownership. She can spend the whole of it or give it away at her own pleasure by gift or will without any reference to her husband. [*Pratibha Rani* v *Suraj Kumar* AIR 1985 SC 628: (1985)1 Crimes 614 (SC): (1985)2 SCC 370: (1985)3 SCR 190: (1985)155 ITR 190: 1985 SCC (Cri) 180: 1985 Cr LJ 817].

NOTE: Ordinarily, the husband has no right or interest in *stridhan* property. He may, however, in times of extreme distress, as in famine, illness or the like, can utilise it but is morally bound to restore it or its value when he is able to do so. This right is purely personal to the husband and the property so received by him in marriage cannot be proceeded against even in execution of a decree for debt. [*Pratibha Rani* v *Suraj Kumar,* supra].

**Strike.** Boycott; collective or concerted refusal to work; suspension of work.

The act of quitting work by a body of workers for the purpose of coercing their employer to accede to some demand they have made upon him, and which he has refused. [*Jeffery-De Witt Insulator Co.* v *N.L.R.B.* 91 F 2d 134, 138].

A cessation of work as a means of enforcing compliance with some demand upon the employer. [*People* v *Tepel* Mag. Ct., 3 NYS 2d 779, 781].

The word 'strike' is of an artificial character and does not represent any legal definition or description. It is an agreement between persons who are working for a particular employer, not to continue working for him. [*Bankey Lal* v *State of U.P.* AIR 1959 All 614].

The word 'strike' means a simultaneous cessation of work on the part of workmen, a body of persons employed in a trade or industry acting in combination, or a concerted refusal or a refusal under a common understanding of any number of persons who are or who have been so employed, to continue to work or to accept employment. [Halsbury's *Laws of England*, 4th Ed., vol. 4, para 1144, p. 581].

A strike is a general concerted refusal by workmen to work in consequence of an alleged grievance. [*Williams Brothers (Hull) Ltd.* v *Naamlooze etc.* (1915)86 LJKB 334].

▸ *Meaning under the Essential Services Maintenance Act 1968, s. 2(b).* 'Strike' means cessation of work by a body of persons employed in an essential service acting in combination or a concerted refusal or a refusal under a common understanding of any number of persons who are or have been so employed to continue to work or to accept employment and includes—(*i*) refusal to work overtime where such work is necessary for the maintenance of any essential service; (*ii*) any other conduct which is likely to result in, or results in, cessation or substantial retardation of work in any essential service.

▸ *Meaning under the Industrial Disputes Act 1947, s. 2(q).* 'Strike' means a cessation of work by a body of persons employed in any industry acting in combination or concerted refusal, or a refusal under a common understanding, of any number of persons who are or have been so employed to continue to work or to accept employment.

NOTE: Refusal under common understanding to continue to work is a strike. A pen-down strike is a strike. [*Punjab National Bank* v *Their Employees* (1959)2 Lab LJ 666: AIR 1960 SC 160].

• **General strike** p. 385.

**Structure.** Any construction, or any production or piece of work artificially built up or composed of parts joined together in some definite manner; that which is built or constructed; an edifice or building of any kind.

NOTE: 'Structure' is a word which is wide enough to cover every kind of building as well as hoardings and erections of various kinds which could not properly be described as buildings. Nevertheless it has sometimes been used judicially as primarily indicating something less than a permanent building, but judges have hesitated to give a definition of either word. [*Almond (Valuation Officer)* v *Birmingham Royal etc.* (1967)2 All ER 317, 321].

• **Dangerous structure** p. 224.

**Sub-agent.** A 'sub-agent' is a person employed by, and acting under the control of, the original agent in the business of the agency. [Indian Contract Act 1872, s. 191].

A sub-agent is a person employed by an agent to assist him in transacting the affairs of his principal. But a mere servant of an agent is not a 'sub-agent'. [*Gulf Refining Co.* v *Shirley* Tex Civ App, 99 SW 2d 613, 615].

**Sub-contractor.** One who takes portion of a contract from principal contractor or another sub-contractor. [*Hardware Mut. Casualty Co.* v *Hilderbrandt* CCA Okl, 119 F 2d 291, 297, 299].

One who takes from the principal or prime contractor a specific part of the work undertaken by the principal contractor. [*Royal Indemnity Co.* v *Kenny Constr. Co.* CA III, 528 F 2d 184, 191].

**Sub judice.** Under or before a judge or court; under judicial consideration.

**Sub-lease.** A lease by a lessee to a sub-tenant under him; under-lease.

**Sub-lessee.** One who has taken a lease from the lessee.

**Sub-letting.** "Sub-letting" means transfer of an exclusive right to enjoy the property in favour of the third party and the said right must be in lieu of payment of some compensation or rent. [*Delhi Stationers and Printers* v *Rajendra Kumar* AIR 1990 SC 1208: (1990)2 SCC 331: JT 1990(1) SC 372: (1990)1 SCR 491].

**Sub modo.** Under condition or restriction or qualification.

**Sub silentio.** In silence; without any notice being taken; without being expressly mentioned.

A decision passes *sub silentio* when the particular point of law involved in the decision is not perceived by the court or present to its mind. The court may consciously decide in favour of one party because of point *X*, which it considers and pronounces upon. It may be shown, however, that logically the court should not have decided in favour of the particular party unless it also decided upon point *Y* in his favour, but point *Y* was not argued or considered by the court. In such circumstances, although point *Y* was logically involved in the facts and although the case had a specific outcome, the decision is not an authority on point *Y*. Point *Y* is said to pass *sub silentio*.

[Salmond on *Jurisprudence*, 12th Ed., pp. 153-154].

NOTE: Neither a judgment *per incuriam* nor a judgment given *sub silentio* is binding. [*Mamleswar* v *Khanhaiyalal* AIR 1975 SC 907: (1975)1 SCWR 405; *Yesbai* v *Ganpat* AIR 1975 Bom 21].

**Subject-matter.** "Subject-matter" in a civil suit means the bundle of facts which have to be proved in order to entitle the plaintiff to the relief claimed by him. [*Vallabh Das* v *Dr. Madan Lal* AIR 1970 SC 987: (1970)1 SCC 761: (1971)1 SCR 211].

**Subject to.** The words 'subject to', when used in a statute, have reference to effecting the intention of the law and the correct meaning is 'conditional upon'. [*K.R.C.S. Balkrishna Chetty & Sons* v *State of Madras* (1961)2 SCR 736: AIR 1961 SC 1152: (1961)1 SCJ 712: (1961)12 STC 114].

**Subordinate.** Placed in a lower order, class, or rank; occupying a lower position in a regular descending series; inferior in order, nature, dignity, power, importance, or the like; belonging to an inferior order in classification, and having a lower position in a recognized scale; secondary; minor; subservient; auxiliary.

The word 'subordinate' is not a term of art and in its dictionary meaning it connotes several ideas including holding of secondary or subservient position. [*Toesh Kumar* v *State of Bihar* 1985 BLJ 19].

The word 'subordinate' in Art. 311(1) of the Constitution means subordinate in rank and not with reference to the functions exercised. [*Mahadev Prasad* v *S.N. Chatterjee* AIR 1964 Pat 285].

**Subordinate legislation.** See DELEGATED LEGISLATION p. 244.

**Subpoena.** Command/order to appear; order to appear in court; requirement to attend; summons.

A subpoena is a command to appear at a certain time and place to give testimony upon a certain matter.

**Subpoena duces tecum.** A writ used to compel a witness to give evidence and bring with him certain specific documents.

A process by which the court, at the instances of a party, commands a witness who has in his possession or control some document or paper that is pertinent to the issues of a pending controversy, to produce it at the trial.

**Subrogation.** Interchange; replacement; substitution; succession; supplantation; surrogation; transference.

The substitution of one person in the place of another with reference to a lawful claim, demand or right, so that he who is substituted succeeds to the rights of the other in relation to the debt or claim, and its rights, remedies, or securities. [*Home Owners' Loan Corp.* v *Baker* 12 NE 2d 199, 201; *Gerken* v *Davidson Grocery Co.* 69 P 2d 122, 126].

The right of one who has paid an obligation which another should have paid to be indemnified by the other. [*Olin Corp. (Plastics Division)* v *Workmen's Compensation Appeal Bd.* 324 A 2d 813, 816].

A device adopted by equity to compel ultimate discharge of an obligation by him who in good conscience ought to pay it. [*Jenks Hatchery, Inc.* v *Elliott* 252 Or 25: 448 P 2d 370, 373].

**Subscribe.** Advocate; agree; guarantee; patronise; pledge; promise to contribute; acknowledge; affix one's signature; approve; attest; certify; confirm; endorse; ratify; underwrite.

'Subscribe' means to write or sign under something in accordance with prescribed regulations where any such exist. [*A.-G.* v *Bradlaugh* 54 LJ QB 213: 14 QBD 667].

**Subsidiary.** Secondary; subordinate; subservient; supplemental; auxiliary; under control of another.

**Subsidiary company.** One that is run and owned by another company which is called the "parent company"; one in which another company, i.e. parent, owns at least a majority of the shares.

▸ *Meaning under the Companies Act 1956, s. 4.* A company shall be deemed to be a subsidiary of another if, but only if—

(*a*) that other controls the composition of its Board of Directors, or (*b*) that other—(*i*) where the first-mentioned company is an existing company in respect of which the holders of preference shares issued before the commencement of the Companies Act 1956, have the same voting rights in all respects as the holders of equity shares, exercises or controls more than half of the total voting power of such company, (*ii*) where the first-mentioned company is any other company, which holds more than half in nominal value of its equity share capital, or (*c*) the first-mentioned company is a subsidiary of any company which is that other's subsidiary.

**Subsidy.** Pecuniary aid directly granted by government to an individual or private commercial enterprise deemed beneficial to the public; any financial assistance afforded by an individual or government to another.

A grant, usually made by the government, to any enterprise whose promotion is considered to be in the public interest. [Black's *Law Dictionary*, 8th Ed.].

The dictionary meaning of 'subsidy' is grant of money from a government to a private enterprise considered as beneficial to the public. [*Commissioner of Income Tax* v *Grace Paper Industries Pvt. Ltd.* (1990)183 ITR 591 (Guj); *Commissioner of Income Tax, Hyderabad* v *P.J. Chemicals Ltd.* AIR 1994 SC 2727: 1994 AIR SCW 4352: (1994)210 ITR 830: JT 1994(6) SC 330].

▸ *Meaning under the Payment of Bonus Act, Second Schedule, Item 6(q).* The word "subsidy" cannot be confined only to those cases where cash payment is made by Government in order that an industry may survive. Even if assistance is given by way of an incentive it would not cease to be a subsidy provided it is a cash payment given by way of assistance and that certain types of assistance particularly those which are only indirect like rebates etc., should be excluded. [*Shri Ambica Mills No. 1* v *The Textile Labour Association, Ahmedabad* AIR 1973 SC 1081: (1973)3 SCR 123: (1973)3 SCC 787].

**Subsist.** Be nurtured; be supported; be sustained; hold on; remain alive; stand fast; stay alive; to have existence; continue to exist; to continue unchanged; to provide with food and clothing; support.

The dictionary meaning of the word 'subsist' is to remain alive as on food, to continue to exist. [*O.P. Gupta* v *Union of India* AIR 1987 SC 2257: (1987)4 SCC 328: JT 1987(3) SC 532: 1987(5) SLR 288: (1988)1 SCR 27].

**Subsistence.** The act of subsisting; that on which one subsists; sustenance; means of support; livelihood; the state of being subsistent.

Subsistence means—means of supporting life, especially a minimum livelihood. [*O.P. Gupta* v *Union of India* AIR 1987 SC 2257: (1987)4 SCC 328: JT 1987(3) SC 532: 1987(5) SLR 288: (1988)1 SCR 27].

**Subsistence allowance.** Allowance paid as a means of supporting life, especially a minimum livelihood. [*O.P. Gupta* v *Union of India* AIR 1987 SC 2257: (1987)4 SCC 328: JT 1987(3) SC 532: 1987(5) SLR 288: (1988)1 SCR 27].

**Subsoil.** The stratum of earth next beneath the surface soil.

> NOTE: The word, *prima facie*, includes all that is below the actual surface down to the centre of the earth. It is, therefore, a wider term than 'mines' or 'quarries', or even than 'minerals'. [Stroud's *Judicial Dictionary*, 5th Ed.].

**Substitution.** The act of substituting or the state of being substituted; the process by which one person or thing takes the place of another person or thing; the designation of a person to succeed another as beneficiary of an estate, usually involving a *fidei-commissum*.

▸ *Meaning under the Code of Civil Procedure 1908, Or. 22.* Bringing in or making party the heirs or legal representatives of a deceased party, so that the proceedings may go in.

It may also mean an amendment by replacing one or more words with others. 'The word "substitution" does not necessarily or always connote two separate steps, that is to say, one of repeal and another of a fresh enactment. Indeed, the natural meaning of the word "substitution" is to indicate that the process cannot be split up into two pieces. If the process described as substitution fails, it is totally ineffective so as to leave intact what was sought to be displaced'. [*State of Maharashtra* v *The Central Provinces Manganese Ore Co. Ltd.* AIR 1977 SC 879: (1977)1 SCR 1002: (1977)1 SCC 643: (1977)39 STC 340].

**Subtenant.** 'Subtenant", literally or statutorily either in the Rent Control Legislations or agricultural tenancies, normally, is a person in possession holding from the tenant. His right or interest depends on provisions in the statute. [*Lala Raghuraj Swarup* v *Hardwari Lal* AIR 1991 SC 2072: (1991)4 SCC 391: (1991)3 SCR 672: JT 1991(3) SC 486].

A tenant under a tenant; an under-tenant. One who leases all or a part of the rented premises from the original lessee for a term less than that held by the latter. [*Peak* v *Gaddy* 3 P 2d 1042, 1043].

**Subversive act.** Act directed toward the overthrow of the government, including treason, sedition, and sabotage.

'Subversive act' means any act which is intended or is likely,—(*i*) to endanger public safety and tranquillity; (*ii*) to organise, further or help the illegal acquisition, possession or use of—(*a*) arms, ammunition or military stores as defined in the Army Act 1959 (54 of 1959); (*b*) explosive substances as defined in the Explosive Substances Act 1908 (6 of 1908); (*iii*) to commit an offence of looting or raiding or to further or help the commission thereof. [West Bengal Maintenance of Public Order Act 1972, s. 2(*g*)].

**Subversive activity.** Subversive activity is such as amounts to actively pursuing such activities as are calculated to subvert the government established by law. [*V.S. Menon* v *Union of India* AIR 1963 SC 1160: 1963 Supp (2) SCR 404].

NOTE: Taking interest in political activities of the Communist Party would not amount to taking part in subversive activities as long as the party is not banned. [*V.S. Menon* v *Union of India*, supra].

**Succession.** The process by which a person becomes entitled to the interest of a deceased person; the devolution of title to property under the law of descent and distribution; acquisition of rights upon the death of another. [*In re Russell's Estate* 95 Cal Reptr 88, 95]; the fact of the transmission of the rights, obligations and charges of a deceased person to his heir. [*Sambadomurthi Mudaliar* v *State of Madras* (1969)2 SCWR 630].

• **Testamentary succession** p. 839.

**Succession certificate.** A certificate granted by a competent court to collect the debts and securities of the deceased, as also to receive interest or dividends on and to negotiate or transfer securities.

NOTE: Succession certificates are granted under the provisions of Part X of the Indian Succession Act 1925.

**Successor.** One that succeeds or follows; one who takes the place that another has left, and sustains the like part or character; one who takes the place of another by succession. [*Thompson* v *North Texas Nat. Bank* Tex Com App, 37 SW 2d 735, 740; *Wawak Co.* v *Kaiser* CCA III, 90 F 2d 694, 697].

**Such.** Alike; similar; of the like kind; of that kind; being the same as what has been mentioned.

The normal meaning of "such" is similar to what precedes. [*State of Maharashtra* v *Dhanalakxmi* 1981 Lab IC 907, 909].

The word 'such' means 'of the same kind', that is to say, 'of the kind mentioned before'. [*Nemichand Sen* v *Kumud Behari* ILR (1951)1 Cal 404].

The word 'such' means 'of that kind; of the same or like kind', the word 'such' always refers to something else and it generally and naturally refers to its last antecedent. [*Commissioner of Income Tax, Punjab, Himachal Pradesh* v *Jagannath* (1957)32 ITR 418: AIR 1957 Punj 226].

**Sud.** Interest.

**Sue.** Bring a legal action; bring to justice; commence a suit; file a legal claim; initiate a civil action; institute a legal proceeding; ask for relief; take to court.

To sue includes not only to prosecute but also to defend. [*Siba Prosad Bhattacharya* v *Bibhuti Bhusan* 92 CWN 513: (1988)1 CHN 1].

▸ *Meaning under Government of India Act 1935, s. 176.* The word "sue" meant the enforcement of a claim or a civil right by means of legal proceedings and was wide enough to include an application for a writ of *certiorari*. [*Province of Bombay* v *Kusaldas S. Advani* AIR 1950 SC 222: 1950 SCJ 451: 1950 SCR 621].

• **Right to sue** p. 764.

**Suffer.** Accede; accept; allow; authorise; be reconciled; be resigned; bear with; put up with; brook; comply; concede; agonise; be afflicted; be impaired; be injured; be subjected to; bear; endure; experience/incur loss; feel pain; sustain damage.

If without committing a legal wrong, a person is in a position to stop a thing, and does not stop it, he 'suffers' it; but he cannot be said to suffer it if he is not in a position either physically to prevent it or if by law he ought not to prevent it. [*Rochford Rural Council* v *Port of London Authority* (1914)2 KB 916].

The customary use of the word indicates some experience of conscious pain. [*New York Life Ins. Co.* v *Calhoun* CCA Mo, 97 F 2d 896, 898].

**Sufficient.** Of such quality, number, force, or value as to serve a need or purpose. [*Nissen* v *Miller* 105 P 2d 324].

The word 'sufficient' means 'adequate', 'enough', 'as much as may be necessary to answer the purposes intended'. It embraces no more than that which provides a plenitude which, when done, suffices to accomplish the purpose intended in the light of the existing circumstances and when viewed from reasonable standard of practical and cautious men. [*Benarsi Das Saraf* v *Dalmia Dadri Cement Ltd.* AIR 1959 Punj 232].

**Sufficient cause.** A legally sufficient reason; just cause; good cause.

'Sufficient cause', an expression found in various statutes, has been construed liberally in keeping with its ordinary dictionary meaning as adequate and enough, that is any justifiable reason. [*Srinder Singh Sibia* v *Vijay Kumar Sood* AIR 1992 SC 1540: (1992)1 SCC 70].

NOTE: In an appeal, the words 'sufficient cause' must generally receive a liberal construction so as to advance substantial justice when no negligence or inaction or want of *bona fide* is imputable to appellant. [*Sarpanch* v *Ramgiri Gosavi* AIR 1968 SC 222; *Sandhya Sarkar* v *Sudharani* AIR 1978 SC 537: (1978)2 SCR 839: (1978)1 SCJ 446; *Union of India* v *Suresh N. Shetty* (1986)1 Civ LJ 580 (Kant)].

**Suffrage.** The right or privilege of casting a vote at public elections.

NOTE: The right of suffrage may be modified or withdrawn by the authority which conferred it. It is a privilege which may be granted or denied by the Government as general policy may require. There have been limitations upon the right of suffrage even in the most liberal democracies.

**Suggestio falsi.** A false suggestion—misrepresentation.

**Sui generis.** A Latin expression which means of its own kind or class.

**Sui juris.** Of one's own right; independent; of full age and capacity.

**Suicide.** The act or an instance of taking one's own life voluntarily and intentionally; self-killing; the deliberate termination of one's existence. Every act of self-destruction is suicide, provided it be intentional act of a party knowing the probable consequences of what he is doing. [*Re, Davis* (1967)1 All ER 688].

**Suit.** Action at law; action to serve justice; cause in court; legal action.

A generic term, of comprehensive signification, referring to any proceeding by one person or persons against another or others in a court of justice in which the plaintiff pursues, in such court, the remedy which the law affords him for the redress of an injury or the enforcement of a right, whether at law or in equity. [*Kohl* v *U.S.* 91 US 367: 23 L Ed 449; *Weston* v *Charleston* 7 L Ed 481; *Syracuse Plaster Co.* v *Agostini Bros. Bldg. Corporation* 7 NYS 2d 897].

NOTE: *'Suit' and 'Appeal'—difference.* The word "suit" includes an appeal from the judgment in the suit. The only difference between a suit and an appeal is that an appeal "only reviews and corrects the proceedings in a cause already constituted but does not create the cause". [*Smt. Dayawati* v *Inderjit* AIR 1966 SC 1423: (1966)3 SCR 275; *Mithilesh Kumari* v *Prem Behari Khare* AIR 1989 SC 1247: (1989)2 SCC 95: (1989)1 SCR 621: JT 1989(1) SC 275: (1989)40 ELT 257: (1989)177 ITR 97].


- **Account suit** p. 22.
- **Administration suit** p. 41.
- **Former suit** p. 369.
- **Friendly suit** p. 374.
- **Interpleader suit** p. 475.
- **Lawsuit** p. 519.
- **Multiplicity of suits** p. 594.


**Sulka.** Marriage fee; money or property given to the bridegroom or bride at the time of marriage of Hindus.

**Summary.** An abridgment; short and speedy; concise; off-hand; brief; compendium.

**Summary procedure.** It implies a short and quick procedure instead of or, as an alternative to, the more elaborate procedure ordinarily adopted or prescribed for deciding a case. [*Mohan Lal* v *Kartar Singh* 1995 Supp (4) SCC 684: JT 1995(7) SC 573].

**Summary proceedings.** The proceedings before a court, tribunal or an authority are called summary proceedings if it is not required to follow the regular formal procedure but is authorised to follow a short and quick procedure for expeditious disposal. [*Mohan Lal* v *Kartar Singh* 1995 Supp (4) SCC 684: JT 1995(7) SC 573].

**Summons.** Authoritative citation to appear before a court; authoritative command; calling to court; written notification to appear in court.

A process of court asking the opposite party to an action to appear and answer the claim preferred by the party who has brought the action.

Instrument used to commence a civil action or special proceeding and is a means of acquiring jurisdiction over a party. [*In re Dell* 290 NYS 2d 287, 289].


- **Originating summons** p. 630.


**Summons case.** A case relating to an offence, and not being a warrant case. [Code of Criminal Procedure 1973, s. 2(*w*)].

**Sunni.** A sect amongst Mahomedans.

**Sunni wakf.** A wakf governed by Sunni law. [Wakf Act 1954, s. 3(*k*)].

**Superannuation.** 'Superannuation' in relation to an employee means—(*i*) the attainment by the employee of such age as is fixed in the contract or condition of service as the age on the attainment of which the employee shall vacate the employment, and (*ii*) in any other case, the attainment by the employee of the age of fifty-eight years. [Payment of Gratuity Act 1972, s. 2(*r*)].

NOTE: Superannuation takes place automatically on an employee reaching a particular age for which a notice is not required. [*P.K.G. Udyog Sangh* v *Jit Ram* 1975 Lab IC 1484 (Punj)].

**Superintendence.** Direction and management; guiding and controlling supervision.

The word "superintendence" would imply administrative control enabling the authority enjoying such power to give directions to the subordinate to discharge its administrative duties and functions in the manner indicated in the order. [*State of Bihar* v *J.A.C. Saldanna* AIR 1980 SC 326: (1980)2 SCR 16: 1980 Cr LR (SC) 17: 1980 Cr LJ 98: 1980 SCC (Cri) 272: (1980)1 SCC 554].

**Supersede.** Discard; annul; displace; make absolute; make void; override; overrule; put in the place of; set aside; stand in stead of; substitute; take the place of; supplant.

'Supersede' means 'to take the place of by reason of superior right, to make useless by superior power, to replace, to set aside', etc. [*Food Inspector* v *Hameed* 1983 Ker LT 901].

**Supervise.** Superintend, oversee the execution of a task, etc.; oversee the actions or work of a person; to have a general oversight of.

The word "supervise" and its derivatives are not words of precise import and must often be construed in the light of the context, for unless controlled they cover simple oversight and direction of manual work of others. [*All India Reserve Bank Employees' Asscn.* v *Reserve Bank of India* AIR 1966 SC 305: (1966)1 SCR 25].

In the ordinary dictionary sense 'to supervise' means to direct or oversee the performance or operation of an activity and to oversee it, watch over and direct. It is work under eye and gaze of someone who can immediately direct a corrective and tender advice. [*C.E.S.C. Ltd.* v *Subhash Chandra Bose* JT 1991(6) SC 373: AIR 1992 SC 573: (1992)1 SCC 441: 1992(3) SLR 16, *per* Punchhi, J.].

**Supervision.** The act of supervising; superintendence; the authority to direct or supervise.

NOTE: The word "supervision" is not one of precise import and is broad enough to require either supervisor's constant presence during work supervised or his devotion thereto of only time necessary to see that it complies with contract specifications, advise as to details, prepare necessary sketches and drawings, etc. The degree of supervision must entirely depend upon the task, and it cannot mean that there must always be a constant supervision throughout. All depends on the facts of each case. [*C.E.S.C. Ltd.* v *Subhash Chandra Bose* JT 1991(6) SC 373: AIR 1992 SC 573: (1992)1 SCC 441: 1992(3) SLR 16, *per* K. Ramaswamy, J.].

**Supply.** To furnish with what is wanted; available aggregate of things needed or demanded; anything yielded or afforded to meet a want; and the act of furnishing with what is wanted. [*Clayton* v *Bridgeport Mach Co.* Tex Civ App, 33 SW 2d 787, 789].

• **Inelastic supply** p. 455.

**Support.** As noun, it means affirmation; approval; authentication; backing; certification; confirmation; endorsement; justification; ratification; substantiation; validation.

As noun, it may also mean assistance; contribution; helping hand; livelihood; maintenance; patronage; protection; subsistence; subsidium; sustenance; upkeep; a source or means of living.

As verb, it means accommodate; aid; bolster; champion; come to the defence of; come to the help of; contribute; cooperate with; defend; endorse; feed; furnish; funds; lend money to; maintain; nourish; patronise; promote; subsidise; supply the necessities of; take care of; affirm; attest; authenticate; back up; bear out; establish; ratify; strengthen; substantiate; account for; defend; make legitimate; say in defence; stand up for.

When used as means of living, the term includes all such means of living as would enable one to live in the degree of comfort suitable and becoming to his station of life. It is said to include anything requisite to housing, feeding, clothing health, proper recreation, travelling expense, and also proper care, nursing, and medical attendance in sickness.

**Suppressio veri.** Wilful concealment of truth.

**Supreme Court.** The court constituted under Art. 124 of the Constitution of India. This is the apex court in India.

The Supreme Court in U.K. is the High Court of Parliament, consisting of king, lords and commons who are invested with a kind of omnipotency in making new laws, repealing and reviving old ones. [Stroud's *Judicial Dictionary*, 5th Ed.].

In U.S.A. it is an appellate court existing in most of the States. In the Federal Court System, and in most States, it is the highest appellate court and the court of last resort. In New York and other

States it is a court of general original jurisdiction possessing also (in New York) some appellate jurisdiction, but not the court of last resort.

**Surcharge.** Added charge; additional charge; excessive burden; extra charge; overassessment; overcharge; an exaction, impost, or encumbrance beyond what is just and right, or beyond one's authority or power; the imposition of an additional tax, impost, or cost.

Etymologically, *inter alia*, surcharge stands for an additional or extra charge or payment. Surcharge is thus a super added charge, a charge over and above the usual or current dues. [*Bisra Stone Lime Co. Ltd.* v *Orissa State Electricity Board* AIR 1976 SC 127: (1976)2 SCR 307: (1976)2 SCC 167].

'Surcharge' means an additional or extra charge or payment. [*D.C.M.* v *Rajasthan State Electricity Board* (1986)2 SCC 431].

The meaning of the word 'surcharge' as given in the *Webster's New International Dictionary* includes among others 'to charge (one) too much or in addition ......' also 'additional tax'. Thus the meaning of surcharge is to charge in addition or to subject to an additional or extra charge. [*Commissioner of Income Tax* v *K. Srinivasan* AIR 1972 SC 491].

The expression "surcharge" in the context of taxation means an additional imposition which results in enhancement of the tax. [*Sarojini Tea Co. (P) Ltd.* v *Collector of Dibrugarh* AIR 1992 SC 1264: (1992)2 SCC 156: (1992)1 SCR 371: JT 1992(1) SC 327].

A surcharge on land revenue is an enhancement of the land revenue to the extent of the imposition of surcharge. [*Sarojini Tea Co. (P) Ltd.* v *Collector of Dibrugarh,* supra].

**Surety.** One who undertakes to pay money or to do any other act in event that his principal fails therein.

Everyone who incurs a liability in person or estate, for the benefit of another, without sharing in the consideration, stands in the position of a "surety", whatever may be the form of his obligation. [*Howell* v *War Finance Corp*. CCA Ariz, 71 F 2d 237, 243].

**Surplus.** The remainder of a thing; the residue or excess; the excess of receipts over disbursements; a corporation's net work, beyond the par value of capital stock. [Black's *Law Dictionary*, 8th Ed.].

The surplus of a corporation means the net assets of the corporation in excess of all liabilities including capital stock. [*Winkelman* v *General Motors Corp*. DCNY, 44 F Supp 960, 996].

• **Accumulated surplus** p. 23.

**Surplusage.** A superfluity, or addition of something unnecessary, in any legal document.

> NOTE: In construing a statute it is sometimes proper to reject words as surplusage; so also in construing a will. Courts, however, lean against constructions which make words unnecessary in an Act, and unless the construction leads to an absurdity, no portion of the statute should be ignored or treated as meaningless or redundant. [*Brahm Deo* v *Haro Singh* AIR 1935 Pat 237, 240]. One should even prefer to give to the words of a statute an extended meaning rather than interpret their meaning as restricted by the context when such restriction would reduce them to mere surplusage. [*Har Narayan* v *Ramji Das* AIR 1914 All 191].

**Surrender.** Abdicate; abjure; cede; disclaim; disown; forego; forfeit; forsake; handover; part with; relinquish; renounce; concede; capitulate; give in; relent; submit; succumb.

Surrender means the giving up of an estate to the person who has it in reversion or remainder, so as to merge it in the larger estate.

▸ *Meaning under the Transfer of Property Act 1882, s. 111(e) and (f)*. Surrender is the yielding up of a smaller estate by the owner thereof to the person entitled to the larger estate of reversion or remainder; on such surrender the lesser estate merges in the larger estate. Surrender may be express or implied.

> NOTE: Surrender is contractual act and occurs only through consent of both parties. [*Motch's Adm'r* v *Portner* 34 SW 2d 744, 745].
>
> Surrender is to be distinguished from abandonment, the former is indicative of consent to resign in favour of the reversioner or giving up a right or thing to another by free will. Abandonment is not giving up to any particular person. [*Daip Singh* v *Kishno* ILR (1968)1 Punj 755].

**Surrender of demised estate.** 'Surrender of demised estate' means yielding up of the estate to the landlord so that the leasehold interest becomes extinct by mutual agreement between the parties or by operation of law. [*Mubarak Hussain* v *Custodian General* AIR 1957 Punj 197].

**Surrogate.** Acting; alternate; delegated; foster; makeshift; provisional; proxy; pseudo; stand-in; substitute.

**Surrogate child.** In some continental countries woman in lieu of profits or only for charges incidental to child-bearing or delivery allow herself to be impregnated by artificial insemination by the sperm from the husband of a childless couple. The mother is called a surrogate mother and the child a surrogate child who is later adopted by the donor-father. Such adoption is essential when particularly the surrogate mother is under coverture because the law mandatorily presumes such child to be the issue of the husband of its mother.

**Surrogate mother.** Woman for fees or for charges incidental to child-bearing or delivery when is impregnated through artificial insemination from the husband of a childless couple is a surrogate mother.

> NOTE: This system has prevailed (even on a commercial scale) in Europe and America for quite sometime. A committee under the chairpersonship of Lady Warneck was set up in 1984 to report on various legal issues involved in it. The report was published in November 1984.

**Surrogate parent.** A person other than a parent who stands in *loco parentis* to the child by virtue of his or her voluntary assumption of parental rights and responsibilities. [Black on *Law Dictionary*, 5th Ed.].

**Surtax.** A tax on tax; an additional tax on what has already been taxed.

**Survey.** A general consideration of something; appraisal; the measurement of a tract of land and its boundaries and contents; an investigation or examination.

- **Cadastral survey** p. 117.

**Survive.** To remain alive after the death of another; to continue to live or exist after certain time or happening of an event.

In the absence of surrounding circumstances to the contrary the words "survive" or "survivor" mean that the survivor must be in existence at and live after the date of the postulated event. The words cannot include a person who comes into existence subsequently. [*Alsopp, Cardinal* v *Warr* (1967)2 All ER 1056].

**Sus per coll.** Let him be hanged by the neck.

**Suspend.** Break off; bring to a standstill; bring to a stop; cease; defer; discontinue temporarily; hold in abeyance; interfere with; lay aside; postpone; shelve; stall; to interrupt; to cause to cease for a time.

The ordinary meaning of the word 'suspend' is 'to debar, usually for a time, from the exercise of a function, to interdict, to stay'. It means temporarily staying the execution of the order or of a function. [*Sajja* v *Habib Rather* 1979 CLR (J&K) 28].

**Suspense account.** A ledger account recording items in regard to which there is some uncertainty as to their proper destination at the time when the entry is made. An example is a remittance through the post received from a customer who omits to state his name in the envelope containing the remittance. This amount may be credited to a suspense account pending further inquiries.

**Swear.** Affirm; assert as true; aver; bind oneself by oath; declare solemnly; state under oath.

▸ *Meaning under the General Clauses Act 1897, s. 3(62).* 'Swear', with its grammatical variations and cognate expressions, shall include affirming and declaring in the case of persons by law allowed to affirm or declare instead of swearing.

**Sweating system.** It involves a system oppressive to the workman whereby an unconscionable or unjust profit is wrung from the sweat of his brow by paying him insufficient wages for his work. There is, generally, a middleman taking advantage of the circumstances in which the workman is placed and grinding down, for his own profit, below the fair rate the wages of those employed. [*Collard* v *Marshall* (1892)1 Ch 571]. The poor people are made to work at starvation wages under this system.

**Syndicate.** Cartel; association; alliance; combine; consortium; federation; guild; league; pool; union.

An association of individuals, formed for the purpose of conducting and carrying out some particular business transaction, ordinarily of a financial character, in which the members are mutually interested.

**System.** Method; manner; mode; orderly combination or arrangement.


- **Feudal system** p. 350.
- **Foreign system of law** p. 366.
- **Tickler system** p. 843.

# Tt

**Tacking.** The process by which a mortgagee may be taking a further mortgage for a further advance upon the same property. It defeats the equitable claims of a mesne encumbrancer, *i.e.*, a person who has lent money on the property after the first but before the further mortgage. [Wharton's *Law Lexicon*].

NOTE: In India tacking is prohibited except in the case provided for by s. 79 of the Transfer of Property Act. [Transfer of Property Act 1882, s. 93].

**Tahsil.** Collection of rent or revenue.

**Tahsildar.** A collector of rent or revenue.

**Taidad.** Number or area or extent of land; a document describing the boundaries of plots of land; a claim to rent-free holding approved by Government.

A *taidad* is an extract from a public register or other document of authority in confirmation of a claim. [*Tarakeshwar Pal* v *Satish* 126 IC 769: AIR 1930 Cal 411].

**Tainted.** Infected; soiled; poisoned; rotten; spoiled; sullied; adulterated; unclean; defiled; befouled; noxious; debased; depraved; dishonest; vicious.

**Taka.** A rupee; a hundred paise; money in general.

**Takavi.** Advances of money made by the Government to the cultivators for agricultural purposes.

NOTE: Advances are made in bad seasons; advances are also made to enable the cultivators to extend their cultivation.

**Take.** To obtain possession or control, whether legally or illegally; to seize with authority; to confiscate or apprehend; to acquire (property) for public use by eminent domain; to seize or condemn property; to acquire possession by virtue of a grant of title, the use of eminent domain, or other legal means; to claim one's rights under. [Black's *Law Dictionary*, 8th Ed.].

The expression 'take' has several meanings, such as 'seize, grasp, capture, catch, receive into the body, appropriate, secure, get, receive by payment, assume, choose, adopt, consume, obtain, derive from source or by some process, receive, enjoy, accept' etc. Thus, it can be seen that the word 'take' is of wide import. Seizure of an article may amount to 'taking'. [*Food Inspector* v *T.V. Hameed* 1983 Ker LT 901].

The meaning of the word 'take' in the Chamber's *Twentieth Century Dictionary* is 'to lay hold of, to get into one's possession, to seize, to catch, to capture, to captivate', etc. In the *Random House Dictionary of the English Language*, Unabridged Ed., the meaning given for the word is possession, control, etc. by force or artifice, to seize or capture, to catch or get, etc. In the Webster's *Dictionary of English Language*, the word 'take' is said to mean to get into one's hands or into one's possession, power or control by force or stratagem, to seize or capture physically. [*Saidu Mohammad* v *Food Inspector* 1973 Ker LT 678].

**Take notice.** The commencing words in the prescribed form by which one party or his pleader gives notice of a motion or petition to the other party. These words also occur in the various processes issued by the court under the Code of Civil Procedure 1908.

**Take possession.** Taking such possession as the property is susceptible of and not actual physical possession. [*State of West Bengal* v *Subodh Gopal* AIR 1954 SC 92: 1954 SCR 587].

**Takeover.** To assume control or management of.

**Takeover bid.** An attempt by outsiders to wrest control from the incumbent management of a target corporation. [Black's *Law Dictionary*, 8th Ed.].

NOTE: The expression relates to an offer by one company to the shareholders in another company to buy their shares at a stated price, which may be higher than the market price of the shares. The consideration of the proposed purchase will be cash, or cash and securities of the company making the offer. The directors of the company to be taken over will support or oppose the offer.

**Takia.** The seat or the place of abode of a Mahomedan fakir; the graveyard of a Mahomedan fakir.

**Taking cognizance of an offence.** Taking notice of an offence by a court of competent jurisdiction.

▸*Meaning under the Criminal Procedure Code, s. 190.* The expression 'take cognizance of an offence' simply means the taking notice of an offence by a court, competent for the purpose in a judicial capacity with a view to the initiation of judicial proceedings against the accused in respect of that offence applying its mind to the facts constituting the offence. [*Nandram* v *State of Rajasthan* 1979 Cr LR (Raj) 439].

The expression "taking cognizance" merely means judicial application of mind of the Magistrate to the facts mentioned in the complaint with a view to taking further action. [*Tula Ram* v *Kishore Singh* AIR 1977 SC 2401: (1977)4 SCC 459: 1977 SCC (Cri) 621: 1978 Cr LJ 8: (1978)1 SCR 615].

Taking cognizance of any offence means that the Magistrate has applied his mind to the contents of the complaint for the purpose of proceeding in a particular way as indicated in the subsequent sections. Where the Magistrate applies his mind for some other purpose, *e.g.*, ordering investigation under s. 156(3), or for issuing a search warrant, he cannot be said to have taken cognizance of the offence. [*Gopal Das* v *State of Assam* AIR 1961 SC 986].

**Talab.** Salary, pay, wages; demand, request for payment.

NOTE: In Mahomedan law before a person can claim pre-emption he must make (*a*) *immediate* demand or *talab-i-mowasibat*, and (*b*) demand in the presence of the buyer or seller and in the presence of at least two witnesses or *talab-ishhad*.

**Talab-dastak.** A summons; a writ; a demand for the payment of revenue.

**Talabana.** Fee for service of any process or summons. [*Kadu* v *Barimali* 1968 MPLJ 398: AIR 1969 MP 20: 1969 Cr LJ 210].

**Talak.** Divorce; dissolution or annulment of marriage by a Mahomedan husband.

NOTE: There are three modes of *talak* under Mahomedan law—(1) *Talak ahasan, i.e.*, by a single pronouncement of *talak* during *tuhr* or period of menstruation followed by abstinence from sexual intercourse, (2) *Talak hasan i.e.*, by three pronouncements of *talak* during three successive periods of menstruation with no sexual intercourse during the entire period, and (3) *Talak-ul-bidaat* or *talak-i-badai, i.e.*, three pronouncements or a single pronouncement of *talak* during a single course of menstruation.

**Tale.** Literary a number or total; a narrative or story, especially fictitious and imaginatively treated; a report of an alleged fact, often malicious or in breach of confidence.

**Tale quale.** In contracts for the sale of produce, "tale quale" signifies that the goods were as sample when shipped, the risk of loss or damage in transit being borne by the buyer.

**Tally.** As noun, it means a piece of wood on which notches or scores are cut as marks of number; a score or mark; a reckoning; a label.

As verb, it means to reckon; count; estimate; mark or cut corresponding notches in; cause to correspond; agree precisely.

'Tally' is to see that two things agree or correspond and, if it is a checking, it must be with something which is presumed to be correct. ... [*Madras Port Trust* v *Annamala Nadar* AIR 1968 Mad 42].

**Tallymen.** Those who sell clothing on credit from door to door; credit-drapers.

**Talon.** This is a certificate attached to a bond, which enables the holder to get a fresh supply of coupons when those originally attached to the bond have been used.

**Taluk.** A small zamindari; a tenure of land under a zamindar.

**Talukdar.** A person owning a taluk.

**Tamadi.** Limitation for a civil action.

**Tamiliknama.** A document by which *maliki* or ownership rights are conferred. [*Ram Gopal* v *Nand Lal* 1950 SCJ 575: 1950 SCR 766: AIR 1951 SC 139].

The term "tamiliknama" means documents transferring *maliki* or ownership rights. [*V. Ramaswami Aiyengar* v *T.N.V. Kailasa Thevar* AIR 1951 SC 189: 1951 SCR 292: 1951 SCJ 278].

**Tamper.** Alter; change; convert; interfere; intermeddle; manipulate.

'Tamper' means to alter for an improper purpose or in an improper way. [*Kerala Public Service Commission* v *Santhamma* (1987)1 Ker LT 75].

**Tampering.** An interference with a thing to misuse it or pervert it or alter it with some design clandestinely, is tampering. It is the circumstances and the purpose or rather the manner in which the alteration is effected which will make the alteration 'tampering' with the real thing. [*Sadra Prasad* v *Shambhu Narain* 1958 All LJ 491].

NOTE: Every alteration is not tampering. In order that an interference with a writing may amount to tampering with the document, the interference should be one which has been done improperly. [*Sadra Prasad* v *Shambhu Narain*, supra].

**Tamsukh.** A bond or a contract stipulating money liability.

**Tamsukh sarti kebala.** A sale with a condition of repurchase. The expression is consistent with a mortgage as well as with a sale. [*Bhoju Mondal* v *Debnath Bhagat* AIR 1963 SC 1906: (1963)2 SCJ 676].

**Tangible property.** Property which may be touched and is the object of sensation, that is, corporeal property. This property is opposed to intangible rights or incorporeal property such as patents, copyrights and the like.

NOTE: Under s. 54 of the Transfer of Property Act 1882, sale of tangible immovable property worth Rs. 100 and upwards can be made only by a registered instrument.

**Tank.** A tank or a *talao*, strictly speaking, is a piece of land having embankments and used for storage of water. The embankment which keeps the water confined is called *bandh* or *pind*, the ditch from which earth is taken for repair of that embankment of *bandh* or *pind* is called pet, or bed of the tank. All these three together, namely: (1) the underground, or the land underneath on which water is stored; (2) the embankment or the *bandh*, which serves the purpose of keeping the water confined, within its boundary, and (3) the bed or pet of the bank is known as tank. [*Sobharam Mahato* v *Raja Mahton* AIR 1957 Pat 278].

**Tap.** This is a stock exchange term for an open source of supply of a security. Securities which are on tap are available in the market in almost unlimited supply from the issuing authority.

**Taqabzul-badhian.** The expression *'taqabzul-badhian'* or 'exchange of equivalents' means that the registration receipt will be handed over to the vendee after he has paid the consideration money. [*Girish Narayan Singh* v *Akhtar Hussain* AIR 1953 Pat 330].

**Taraf.** A division of a tract of land; a division or share of an estate; a subdivision of a pargana including several villages.

**Tare.** This is an allowance for the weight of the container in which goods are packed which is deducted from the gross weight to ascertain the net weight of contents. It also refers to the weight of a motor or railway truck to determine in a similar manner the weight of load after weighing on a weighbridge.

**Tariff.** A book of rates; a table or catalogue, drawn usually in alphabetic order, containing the names of several kinds of merchandise with the duties of customs to be paid for the same as settled by the authority or authorities that hold commerce together.

A schedule or system of duties imposed by a government on imported or exported goods; a duty on imported or exported goods under such a system; a fee that a public utility or telecommunications company may assess for its services; a schedule listing the rates charged for services provided by a public utility. [Black's *Law Dictionary*, 8th Ed.].

**Tariff value.** 'Tariff value' in relation to any goods means the tariff value fixed in respect thereof under sub-sec. (2) of s. 14. [Customs Act 1962, s. 2(40)].

**Tarwad.** 'Tarwad' is the name given to joint family consisting of males and females who have all descended in the female line from a common ancestress.

Expression "tarwad" in Marumakkattayam law is the name given to the joint family consisting of males and females, all descended in the female line from a common ancestress. [*Kalyani (dead) by Lrs.* v *Narayanan* AIR 1980 SC 1173: (1980)2 SCR 1130: 1980 (Supp) SCC 298].

A family governed by Marumakkattayam law is known as a "tarwad", it consists of a mother and her children, whether male or female, and all their descendants whether male or female in the female line. [*Achuthan Nair* v *Chinnammu Amma* AIR 1966 SC 411: (1966)1 SCR 454].

NOTE: Every member of tarwad has equal rights in the property by reason of his or her birth in the tarwad. One or more members of a tarwad cannot claim partition and separate possession of his or their share of the tarwad property without the consent or concurrence of all the members of the tarwad. [*M.K. Balakrishnan Menon* v *Assistant Controller of Estate Duty* AIR 1971 SC 2392: (1971)2 SCC 909: (1972)1 SCR 961: (1972)83 ITR 162].

**Tasdik.** Verification, attestation of a document.

**Taulitnama.** A deed of religious endowment.

**Tavazi.** The word *'tavazi'* has got a definite connotation in Marumakkattayam law. *Tavazi* is a branch of the tarwad and is a distinct entity. It comprises one of the females of the tarwad and her descendants in the female line. It is capable of owning property and taking gifts of property. [*Bhaskaran Thirumulpad* v *Kavunni Thirumulpad* AIR 1954 Mad 987: (1954)2 MLJ 294].

A *tavazi* is a branch of a tarwad. [*Achuthan Nair* v *Chinnammu Amma* AIR 1966 SC 411: (1966)1 SCR 454].

**Tavern.** A house licensed to sell liquor to be drunk on the spot. A "tavern" under an Act dealing with licensed taverns is not only a place where wine is sold and drinkers are entertained, but is also a place where a provision is made for the lodging of wayfaring people.

**Tax.** A monetary charge imposed by the government on persons, entities, transactions, or property to yield public revenue. More broadly, the term embraces all governmental impositions on the persons, property, privileges, occupations, and enjoyment of the people, and includes duties, imposts, and excises. [Black's *Law Dictionary*, 8th Ed.].

It is defined as a pecuniary burden laid upon individuals or property to support the government and is a payment exacted by legislative authority. [*In re Mytinger* DC Tex, 31 F Supp 977, 978, 979].

In a general sense, 'tax' is defined as any contribution imposed by government upon individuals, for the use and service of the state, whether under the name of toll, tribute, tallage, gabel, impost, duty, custom, excise, subsidy, aid, supply, or other name. [*City of New York* v *Jos Hollander* Inc, 42 A 2d 872, 875].

A tax is a compulsory exaction of money by public authority for public purposes enforceable by law and is not payment for services rendered. [*Matthews* v *Chicory*

*Marketing Board* 60 CLR 263, *per* Latham, CJ; *Commissioner, Hindu Religious Endowments, Madras* v *Sri Lakshmindra Thirtha Swamiar of Sri Shirur Mutt* AIR 1954 SC 282: 1954 SCR 1005: 1954 SCJ 335; *State of Maharashtra* v *The Salvation Army, Western India Territory* AIR 1975 SC 846: (1975)3 SCR 475: (1975)1 SCC 509].

"Tax" is the amount payable as a result of the changing provision. It is a compulsory exaction of money by a public authority for public purposes, the payment of which is enforced by law. [*Pratibha Processors* v *Union of India* JT 1996(9) SC 478: (1996)88 ELT 12: (1996)11 SCC 101: AIR 1997 SC 138].

The word "tax" in its widest sense includes all money raised by taxation. It, therefore, includes taxes levied by the Central and the State legislatures, and those known as "rates", or other charges, levied by local authorities under statutory powers. [*D.G. Gouse and Co.* v *State of Kerala* AIR 1980 SC 271: (1980)1 SCR 804: (1980)2 SCC 410].

NOTE: *Essential characteristics of a tax.* The essence of taxation is compulsion, that is to say, it is imposed under statutory power without the tax-payer's consent and the payment is enforced by law. [*Lower Mainland Diary* v *Crystal Diary Ltd.* (1933) AC 168; *Commissioner, Hindu Religious Endowments, Madras* v *Sri Lakshmindra Thirtha Swamiar of Sri Shirur Mutt* AIR 1954 SC 282: 1954 SCR 1005: 1954 SCJ 335; *Nagar Mahapalika Varanasi* v *Durga Dass Bhattacharya* AIR 1968 SC 1119: (1968)2 SCJ 836].

The second characteristic of taxation is that it is an imposition made for public purpose without reference to any special benefit to be conferred on the payer of the tax. This is expressed by saying that the levy of tax is for the purposes of general revenue, which when collected, forms part of the public revenues of the State. As the object of a tax is not to confer any special benefit upon any particular individual, there is, as it is said, no element of *quid pro quo* between the tax-payer and the public authority. [Finday Shirras on *Science of Public Finance*, vol. 1, p. 203; *Commissioner, Hindu Religious Endowments, Madras* v *Sri Lakshmindra Thirtha Swamiar of Sri Shirur Mutt* AIR 1954 SC 282: 1954 SCR 1005: 1954 SCJ 335; *Nagar Mahapalika Varanasi* v *Durga Dass Bhattacharya* AIR 1968 SC 1119: (1968)2 SCJ 836]. The levy of tax is for the purpose of general revenue which when collected forms part of the public revenues of the State. There is no element of *quid pro quo* between the tax-payer and the public authority. [*The State of Maharashtra* v *The Salvation Army, Western India Territory* AIR 1975 SC 846: (1975)3 SCR 475: (1975)1 SCC 509].

The third characteristic of taxation is that it is a part of the common burden, the quantum of imposition upon the tax-payer depends generally upon his capacity to pay. [*Commissioner, Hindu Religious Endowments, Madras* v *Sri Lakshmindra Thirtha Swamiar of Sri Shirur Mutt* AIR 1954 SC 282: 1954 SCR 1005: 1954 SCJ 335; *Nagar Mahapalika Varanasi* v *Durga Dass Bhattacharya* AIR 1968 SC 1119: (1968)2 SCJ 836].

*'Tax' and 'fee'—distinction.* There is no generic difference between a "tax" and a "fee". Both are compulsory exactions of money by public authorities. [*The Hingir Rampur Coal Co. Ltd.* v *State of Orissa* AIR 1961 SC 459: (1961)2 SCR 537; *Union of India* v *Shri R.C. Jain* AIR 1981 SC 951: (1981)2 SCC 308: (1981)2 SCR 854; *Sreenivash General Traders* v *State of A.P.* AIR 1983 SC 1246]. The distinction between the two lies primarily in the fact that whereas a tax is imposed for public purposes and is not, and need not, be supported by any consideration of service rendered in return, a fee is levied essentially for services rendered and as such there is an element of *quid pro quo* between the person who pays the fee and the public authority which imposes it. [*The Hingir Rampur Coal Co. Ltd.* v *State of Orissa* AIR 1961 SC 459: (1961)2 SCR 537]. A tax is levied as part of common burden, while a fee is for a specific benefit or privilege although the special advantage is secondary to the primary motive of regulation in public interest. If the element of revenue for general purpose of the State predominates, the levy becomes a tax. The power of any legislature to levy a fee is conditioned by the fact that it must be "by and large" a *quid pro quo* for the services rendered. [*Sreenivash General Traders* v *State of A.P.* AIR 1983 SC 1246].

The chief purpose of a "tax" is to raise funds for the support of the Government or for a public purpose, while a "fee" may be charged for the privilege or benefit conferred, or service rendered or to meet the expenses connected therewith. [*Southern Pharmaceuticals & Chemicals, Trichur* v *State of Kerala* AIR 1981 SC 1863: (1981)4 SCC 391: (1982)1 SCR 519].

*"Tax", "interest" and "penalty"—distinction.* "Tax", "interest" and "penalty" are three different concepts. "Tax" becomes payable by an assessee by virtue of the charging provision in a taxing statute. 'Penalty', in final matter, ordinarily becomes payable when it is found that an assessee has wilfully violated any of the provisions of the taxing statute. "Interest" is ordinarily claimed from an assessee who has withheld payment of any tax payable by him and it is always calculated at the prescribed rate on the basis of the actual amount of tax withheld and the extent of delay in paying it. It may not be wrong to say that such interest is compensatory in character and not penal. [*Associated Cement Company Limited* v *Commercial Tax Officer, Kota* AIR 1981 SC 1887: (1981)4 SCC 578: (1981)48 STC 466: 1981 Tax LR 3057: (1982)1 SCR 563].


- **Abatement of taxes** p. 4.
- **Corporation tax** p. 197.
- **Direct tax** p. 260.
- **Income-tax** p. 447.
- **Indirect tax** p. 451.
- **Land tax** p. 511.
- **Terminal tax** p. 837.
- **Toll tax** p. 846.


**Tax avoidance.** Legal minimisation of the tax burden on income of an individual resorted to by that individual.

**Tax evasion.** The wilful attempt to defeat or circumvent the tax law in order to illegally reduce one's tax liability; illegally paying less in taxes than the law permits.

**Tax-free dividend.** It means that the declared percentage of dividend is paid by the company to the shareholders in full without any deduction therefrom on account of tax. [*Barjor Hoshangji Vakil* v *Mettur Chemical* AIR 1964 Mad 83].

**Tax payable.** The expression "tax payable" is the amount for which a demand notice is issued. In determining the tax payable, the tax already paid has to be deducted. [*Commissioner of Income Tax, West Bengal-I, Calcutta* v *Vegetable, Products Ltd.* AIR 1973 SC 927: (1973)1 SCC 442: (1973)3 SCR 448: (1973)88 ITR 192].

**Taxable profits.** The expression "taxable profits" is the amount by which the profits during a chargeable accounting period exceed the abatement in respect of that period. [*C.I.T., Calcutta* v *Standard Vacuum Oil Company* AIR 1966 SC 1393: (1966)2 SCR 367: (1966)59 ITR 685].

**Taxation.** The process of taxing or imposing a tax.

▸ *Meaning under the Constitution of India, Art. 366, cl. (28).* "Taxation" is defined to include "the imposition of any tax or impost, whether general or local or special". [*D.G. Gouse and Co.* v *State of Kerala* AIR 1980 SC 271: (1980)1 SCR 804: (1980)2 SCC 410]. The amplitude of that definition, however, has to be cut down if the context otherwise so requires. [*In re Sea Customs Act 1878* AIR 1963 SC 1760: (1964)3 SCR 787: (1964)2 SCJ 51].


- **Double taxation** p. 281.


**Technical.** Belonging or peculiar to an art or profession; highly specialised; highly specific; occupational; professional; specialised; specific; trained; vocational.

The word "technical" is described in the *Concise Oxford Dictionary* to mean a particular art, science or applied science or vocational training dealing with applied science. It is trite to say that when a word has many etymological meanings attributed to it, the same takes its true colour from the text and context. The dictionary meaning of the word "technical" is also "professional" and is used in contradiction with pure sciences to prepare professionals in applied sciences. [*Dean, Goa Medical College, Bambolim, Goa* v *Dr. Sudhir Kumar Solanki* (2001)7 SCC 645: JT 2001(7) SC 335].

The word in contradistinction to the word "substantial" means formal or procedural. Any breach or contravention which is in form only but not in substance may be regarded as technical. [*Govind Karsan* v *State* (1983)24 Guj LR 145].

**Technical defect in law.** A technical defect in law is one which may come within the four corners of it, but, in fact, it does not affect the merits of the case. It is a mistake which does not go to the core of the matter. [*Gangadhar Dandawate* v *Premchand Kashyap* AIR 1958 MP 182].

**Tehsildar.** An officer having charge of the revenue collection.

**Teji-mandi.** The word "teji" means brightness, the word "mandi" means dullness. Thus, "teji" is used to signify a rise in the market price of goods or stock, and "mandi" to signify a fall.

NOTE: In the "teji-mandi" transactions, one party buys what is known as a double option. For this he pays a certain premium, say, Rs. 20 per Rs. 100. On the settling day the buyer has the right to declare himself either a seller or a buyer. If the market falls he will declare himself a seller. If it rises he will declare himself a buyer, *e.g.*, if it be supposed that by the contract price a bar of silver or a bale of cotton is worth Rs. 100. *A* buys the double option for Rs. 20; if the goods rise to Rs. 150 or fall to Rs. 50 he will declare himself a buyer and a seller respectively and in each case will make a profit of Rs. 30. [*Manubhai* v *Keshavji* AIR 1922 Bom 66]. In the case of a "teji-mandi" transaction, the presumption is that it is not a mere wagering transaction. [*Narandas S. Rathi* v *Ghanashyamdas* AIR 1933 Bom 348].

"Teji-mandi operation" is a form of speculation prevailing in Bombay.

**Telegram.** Written matter intended to be transmitted by telegraph. [Tax on Postal Articles Act 1971, s. 2(*e*)].

▸ *Meaning under the Telegraph Act 1869, s. 3 (England)]*. The term "telegram" shall mean any message or other communication transmitted or intended for transmission by a telegraph.

NOTE: *Telegram—whether an authentic document.* A telegram by itself is not an authentic document. It is like an unsigned/anonymous communication. Unless a telegram is confirmed by a subsequent signed application, representation or an affidavit, the contents of the telegrams have no authenticity at all and the same cannot be taken into consideration for assessing the value of the other authentic documents on the record. [*District Magistrate* v *G. Jothisankar* AIR 1993 SC 2633: 1993 Cr LJ 3677: JT 1993(4) SC 356: (1993)3 SCJ 288].

**Telegraph.** Any appliance, instrument, material or apparatus used or capable of use for transmission or reception of signs, signals, writing, images and sounds or intelligence of any nature by wire, visual or other electro-magnetic emission, radio waves of Hertzian waves, galvanic, electric or magnetic means. [Indian Telegraph Act 1885, s. 2(1); Tax on Postal Articles Act 1971, s. 2(*f*)].

NOTE: A telephone was held to be a telegraph. [*Attorney-General* v *Edison Telephone Co.* (1880)6 QBD 244; *Senior Electric Inspector* v *Laxminarayan* AIR 1962 SC 159: (1962)1 SCA 585: (1962)3 SCR 146].

**Telegraph line.** A wire or wires used for the purpose of a telegraph, with any casting, coating, tube or pipe enclosing the same, and any appliances and apparatus connected therewith for the purpose of fixing or insulating the same. [Indian Telegraph Act 1885, s. 2(4)].

"Telegraph line" means a wire or wires used for the purpose of an appliance or apparatus for receiving telegraphic or other communications by means of electricity. The wires of the aerial as well as of the apparatus are used for the purpose of the apparatus receiving communications. [*Senior Electric Inspector* v *Laxminarayan* AIR 1962 SC 159: (1962)1 SCA 585: (1962)3 SCR 146: (1962)1 SCJ 593].

**Telephone.** The word 'telephone' means an apparatus, system or process for the transmission of sound or speech to a distant point. [*N. Krishna Devaraya* v *Union of India* AIR 1996 Kant 189].

**Telephone connection.** The expression 'telephone connection' would mean in common parlance 'connecting two telephone apparatuses so as to enable the caller to avail the speech transmission facility with a desired person'. [*N. Krishna Devaraya* v *Union of India* AIR 1996 Kant 189].

**Television.** A system for reproducing on a screen visual images transmitted by radio signals. [*Shankar Video* v *State of Maharashtra* AIR 1993 SC 2111: (1993)3 SCC 696: JT 1993(4) SC 207].

**Telex.** A post office service for making speedy communications by the use of teleprinters.

**Temperance.** Of, relating to, practising or promoting total abstinence from intoxicants; the principle and practice of total abstinence from intoxicants; teetotalism; sparing use; self-control; abstemiousness.

**Temple.** "Temple" means a place by whatever name known and to whomsoever belonging, which is used as a place of religious worship by custom, usage or otherwise by the members of the Hindu community or any section thereof and includes all land appurtenant thereto and subsidiary shrines attached to any such place. [*Shastri Yagnapurushdasji* v *Muldas Bhundardas Vaishya* AIR 1966 SC 1119: (1966)3 SCR 242].

'Temple' means a place, by whatever designation known, used as a place of public worship and dedicated to, or for the benefit of, or used as of right by, the Hindu community, or any section thereof, as a place of religious worship. [*The Commissioner for Hindu Religious and Charitable Endowments, Mysore* v *Sri Ratnavarma Heggade (Deceased) by his LRs*. AIR 1977 SC 1848: (1977)1 SCR 889: (1977)1 SCC 525].

NOTE: An institution will be regarded as temple if two conditions are satisfied—(1) it must be a place of public religious worship, and (2) it is dedicated to, or for the benefit of, or is used as of right by, the Hindu community or any section thereof as a place of religious worship. [*Poojari Fakir Sadavarthy* v *Commissioner, Hindu Religious and Charitable Endowments* AIR 1963 SC 510: 1962 Supp (2) SCR 276: 1962 SCD 648].

**Temporary act.** If an act contains a proviso that it is to continue in force only for a certain specified time, it is a temporary act. [*Hansraj Moolji* v *State of Bombay* AIR 1957 SC 497: 1957 SCR 634; *T. Kamchinthang* v *State of Manipur* (1984)2 Gau LR 380].

**Temporary alimony.** Interim alimony ordered by the court pending an action for divorce or separation in which one party has made a claim for permanent alimony. [Black's *Law Dictionary*, 8th Ed.].

NOTE: It is also termed provisional alimony; alimony *pendente lite*. Section 24 of the Hindu Marriage Act 1955, provides for temporary alimony.

**Temporary disablement.** 'Temporary disablement' means a condition resulting from an employment injury which requires medical treatment and renders an employee, as a result of such injury, temporarily incapable of work. [Employees' State Insurance Act 1948, s. 2(21)].

**Temporary injunction.** A preliminary injunction issued before or during trial to prevent an irreparable injury from occurring before the court has a chance to decide the case.

▸ *Meaning under the Specific Relief Act 1963, s. 37.* Temporary injunctions are such as are to continue until a specified time, or until the further order of the court and they may be granted at any stage of a suit, and are regulated by the Code of Civil Procedure.

**Tenancy.** The holding of lands or tenements by any form of title, occupancy; the period of holding or occupying lands, tenements; temporary possession; a habitation or dwelling place held of another; the possession or occupancy of land under a lease; a leasehold interest in real estate.


- **Joint tenancy** p. 488.
- **Statutory tenancy** p. 811.
- **Year of the tenancy** p. 908.


**Tenancy at sufferance.** A tenancy arising when a person who has been in lawful possession of property wrongfully remains as a holdover after his or her interest has expired. [Black's *Law Dictionary*, 8th Ed.].

A person who enters on the land by a lawful title, and after his title has ended continues in possession without statutory authority and without obtaining the consent of the person then entitled, is said to be a tenant at sufferance, as distinct from a tenant at will who is in possession with the consent of the landlord. [Halsbury's *Laws of England*, 4th Ed., vol. 27, para 175, p. 130].

NOTE: A tenancy at sufferance is merely a fiction to avoid continuance of possession operating as a trespass. It does not create the relationship of landlord and tenant.

**Tenancy at will.** Tenancy at will arises by contract binding both landlord and tenant; it is determinable at the will of either landlord or tenant.

**Tenancy for a term.** A tenancy of which the commencement and duration of the period are certain or are capable of being ascertained with certainty. It is merely a permissive occupation without a demise.

**Tenancy from month to month.** A tenancy from month to month arises by express agreement or operation of law (*e.g.* s. 106 of the Transfer of Property Act 1882) and continues from month to month until determined by proper notice expiring with the end of a month of the tenancy.

NOTE: When an instrument of lease offends s. 107, T.P. Act but there is admitted payment and acceptance of rent, a tenancy from month to month comes into being. [*Ram Kumar* v *Jagdish* AIR 1952 SC 23: 1952 SCA 79; *Ram Protap* v *National Petroleum* 54 CWN 58; *Radha Charan* v *Pravabati* 63 CWN 535; *Hitkarini Sabha* v *Jabbalpore Corporation* AIR 1961 MP 325]. But the position of law will be totally different and no tenancy in the eye of law will come into being if the lease is void from the beginning.

**Tenancy from year to year.** A tenancy from year to year arises by express agreement or operation of law (*e.g.* s. 106 of the Transfer of Property Act 1882) and continues for successive period of one year each, until determined at the end of a year of tenancy by a proper notice.

**Tenancy in common.** Tenancy in common is a form of co-ownership in which each tenant in common has an equal right to the possession of every part and parcel of the property. [*Biswanath* v *Rabija* 33 CWN 46]. The shares of each tenant in common may be equal or unequal.

**Tenancy in perpetuity.** A tenancy in perpetuity is created by express grant or by a presumed grant and continues until determined by forfeiture.

**Tenant.** One who holds or possesses lands or tenements by any kind of right or title; a person who occupies or possesses any interest in immovable property under another person in consideration of some money or thing of value, paid or payable in future.

▸*Meaning under the Requisitioning and Acquisition of Immovable Property Act 1952, s. 2(h).* Tenant means any person by whom or on whose account rent is payable for any premises and includes such subtenants and other persons as have derived title under the tenant under any law for the time being in force.

Tenant is a word which standing by itself denotes in law 'one who holds lands by any kind of title, whether for years, or for life, or in fee', and does not necessarily mean a lessee, unless it is used in opposition to landlord. [*Ekambara Ayyar* v *Meenatchi Ammal* ILR 27 Mad 401].

NOTE: The payment of rent is not conclusive on the question of creation of existence of relationship of landlord and tenant, the question primarily depends upon the point whether there was any valid transfer of interest in the property sought to be demised. [*H.R. Rikhy* v *Delhi Municipality* AIR 1962 SC 554: (1962)1 SCJ 612: (1962)3 SCR 604; *Jitendra* v *Baduria Municipality* AIR 1967 Cal 423; *Minarani* v *Dasharathi* AIR 1967 Cal 633].

'Tenant' embraces in itself, the heirs of the deceased called 'statutory tenants' as even after the determination of the tenancy, continues to have an estate on the tenanted premises, which are heritable. The heirs of the deceased-tenant in the absence of any provision contrary to the Act step into the position of deceased tenant with all rights and protections under the Act. [*Kasturi Lal* v *Brim Lal* 1986 SLJ 86].

Any person remaining, after the determination of the lease, in possession, with or without the assent of the landlord is also a tenant. [*Tavangowda Tamangowda Patil* v *Yellappa Krishna Muchandni* AIR 1980 SC 590: (1980)3 SCC 105]. The word "tenant" includes any person continuing in possession after the termination of his tenancy. [*A.C. Estates* v *Serajuddin and Co.* AIR 1966 SC 935: (1966)1 SCR 235].

The word "tenant" shall not include any person against whom any decree or order for eviction has been made by a court of competent jurisdiction. [*A.C. Estates* v *Serajuddin and Co.* AIR 1966 SC 935: (1966)1 SCR 235; *Hasmat Rai* v *Raghunath Prasad* AIR 1981 SC 1711: (1981)3 SCR 605: (1981)3 SCC 103].

*Joint tenants and tenants-in-common—distinction.* The basic distinction is that in case of joint tenants there is unity of title and possession, while in case of tenants-in-common, though there is unity of possession there is no unity of title. [*Budh Sen* v *Sheel Ch. Agarwala* 1977 All WC 553]. The heirs of a deceased tenant are joint tenants. [*Shambhudayal* v *Suleman* (1978)2 Ren CJ 533: (1978)2 Ren CR 202: 1978 MPLJ 541: 1978 Jab LJ 398].

• **Desirable tenant** p. 256.
• **Statutory tenant** p. 812.
• **Thika tenant** p. 842.

**Tenant's fixtures.** All things which the tenant has attached to the earth are tenant's fixture.

NOTE: Clause (*h*) of s. 108 of the Transfer of Property Act 1882, permits the lessee to remove, even after the termination of the lease, at any time whilst he is in possession of the property leased but not afterwards, all things which he has attached to the earth: provided he leaves the property in the state in which he received it. The phrase "attached to the earth" includes trees, shrubs, buildings and machinery.

**Tenantable repair.** A repair that will render premises fit for present habitation. [Black's *Law Dictionary*, 8th Ed.].

Tenantable repair imports such a state of repair that the premises may be used and dwelt in not only with safety, but with reasonable comfort by the class of persons by whom, and for the sort of purposes for which, they were to be occupied. [*Proudfoot* v *Hart* (1890)21 QBD 42].

**Tender.** Something unconditionally offered to satisfy a debt or obligation. [Black's *Law Dictionary*, 8th Ed.].

NOTE: A tender to be effective must be unconditional and of the full amount due. [*Bank of Mysore Ltd.* v *B.D. Naidu* AIR 1954 Mys 168].

It may also mean an offer a bid put forward for acceptance; something that serves as a means of payment, such as coin, banknotes, or other circulating medium; money.

NOTE: A tender of money, used as a means of payment, must be made in the current coin of the realm, which is recognised as legal tender. [*Salik Ram* v *Jai Gopal Singh* AIR 1955 All 350].

• **Legal tender** p. 528.

**Tenement.** In popular language a tenement means a house or part of a house capable of separate occupation; property capable of visible and physical occupation, and does not include incorporeal rights.

Property, especially land, held by freehold; a house or other building used as a residence; an apartment. [Black's *Law Dictionary*, 8th Ed.].

'Tenement' correctly means every kind of hereditament, both corporeal and incorporeal. [*Levermore* v *Jobey* (1956)2 All ER 362].

**Tenor.** Feeling; meaning; import; idea; mood; tendency; tone; trend.

An exact copy of an instrument; the exact words of a legal document; the meaning of a legal document. [Black's *Law Dictionary*, 8th Ed.].

The term is used in three senses. First, the tenor of a document is its purport and effect according to its terms. Secondly, the tenor of a bill of exchange is the period of time after which it is payable. Thirdly, an executor according to the tenor is one whose appointment is implied from the words of the will.

**Tenure.** Duration; holding; occupancy; occupation; period; term.

'Tenure' means a term during which an office is held. [*L.P. Agarwal* v *Union of India* AIR 1992 SC 1872: (1992)3 SCC 526: 1992(4) SLR 583: JT 1992(4) SC 220]. 'Tenure' means a fixed term during which an office is held. [*Yeswant Singh* v *State Bank of Indore* 1993 Jab LJ 211].

"Tenure" means the period for which an incumbent of office holds it. [*Union of India* v *Tulsiram Patel* AIR 1985 SC 1416: (1985)3 SCC 398: (1985)3 Comp LJ 45: 1985 Supp (2) SCR 131: 1985(2) SLR 576].

"Tenure" when followed by words of office means 'term of office'. [*Punjab University* v *Khalsa College, Amritsar* AIR 1971 P&H 479].

NOTE: Once a person is appointed to a tenure post, his appointment to the said office begins when he joins and it comes to an end on the completion of the tenure, unless curtailed on justifiable grounds. Such a person does not superannuate, he only goes out of the office on completion of his tenure. The question of prematurely retiring him does not arise. [*L.P. Agarwal* v *Union of India* (1992)3 SCC 526: AIR 1992 SC 1872: 1992(4) SLR 583: JT 1992(4) SC 220].

It may also mean a right, term, or mode of holding lands or tenements in subordination to a senior [Black's *Law Dictionary*, 8th Ed.]; in interest in land subordinate to the *zamindar* or proprietor but above that of a raiyat. 'Tenure' includes a *ghatwali* tenure. [*Manmohan* v *State of Bihar* AIR 1961 SC 189].


- **Ghatwali tenure** p. 387.
- **Under tenure** p. 862.


**Tenure-holder.** Tenure-holder means a person who has acquired from a proprietor or from other tenure-holder, a right to hold land for the purpose of collecting rents or bringing it under cultivation, but establishing tenants on it, and includes also the successor-in-interest of persons who acquired such a right. [Bengal Tenancy Act 1885].

**Tenure post.** In its application to a government servant, a 'tenure post' means a permanent post which an individual government servant may not hold for more than a limited period. [*P.G. Joshi* v *Director General, Posts and Telegraphs* 1974(2) SLR 809: AIR 1975 SC 1: (1975)4 SCC 584: (1975)2 SCR 115].

**Terji.** An abstract of account kept by the collectors and zamindars or other rent-receivers.

**Term.** Used as duration, it means age; lifetime; period; course; incumbency; session; span; spell; time.

Used as provisions, it means article of agreement; clause; condition; covenant; qualification; stipulation; understanding. Used in this sense, the word 'term' includes part of a term also. [*Madan Mohan Pani* v *State of Orissa* AIR 1971 Ori 283].

Black's *Law Dictionary* [8th Ed.] has defined the word, *inter alia*, thus: an expression that has a fixed meaning in some field; a contractual stipulation; provisions that defines an agreement's scope; conditions or stipulations; a fixed period of time.


- **Implied term** p. 433.


**Term loan.** A loan with a specific due date.

According to Reserve Bank direction, 'terms loan' would mean the loan advanced for commercial purposes and not the loans given to the landlords for construction of the buildings to lease back for use by the bank itself. [*State Bank of Patiala* v *Harbans Singh* (1994)3 SCC 495].

NOTE: Such a loan cannot be repaid before maturity without incurring a penalty. It is also termed as 'time loan'.

**Terminal.** The word "terminal" in connection with transportation means the fixed beginning or ending point of a given run. [*Man Mohan Tuli* v *Municipal Corpn. of Delhi* AIR 1981 SC 991: (1981)2 SCC 467: (1981)2 SCR 894; *Express Mills* v *Municipal Committee* AIR 1958 SC 341: 1958 SCJ 604].

'Terminal' also signifies the termini or jurisdictional limits of the municipal area. [*Express Mills* v *Municipal Committee* 1958 SCR 1102: AIR 1958 SC 341: 1958 SCJ 604; *Central India Spinning and Weaving Mfg. Co. Ltd.* v *Municipal Committee, Wardha* AIR 1958 SC 341].

**Terminal charge.** A charge for the use of goods station and for the various duties which a railway company, as common carriers, perform in connection with the goods consigned to them for carriage.

NOTE: Terminal charges are of two categories: (*i*) charges for services; and (*ii*) charges for accommodation and appliances which facilitate business. The 'service terminals' comprise remuneration for the handling of goods at the terminal station *i.e.* where the railway employees are engaged in weighing, loading, unloading etc. As distinguished from this 'service terminals' there are 'station terminal' which are charges for providing accommodation incidental to the business of a carrier, such as 'working charges, repairs, renewals, insurance of station buildings, sidings, sheds, platforms, warehouses, cranes, hydraulic power, fixed appliances etc.' [*Raichand Amulakh Shah* v *Union of India* AIR 1964 SC 1268].

*'Wharfage' and 'demurrage'—whether terminal charges.* Wharfage and demurrage are charges in respect of goods unloaded from wagons and kept at the station and also in respect of goods kept on platforms of the station. So, the said charges could certainly be described as charges in respect of the station. If so, it follows that the said charges are 'terminals'. [*Raichand Amulakh Shah* v *Union of India* AIR 1964 SC 1268].

**Terminal tax.** Terminal tax is tax leviable on goods either imported or exported from the municipal limits. [*Burmah Shell* v *Belgaum Municipality* AIR 1963 SC 906]. The entry of goods into the area of destination immediately attracts payment of terminal tax irrespective of their user. [*Man Mohan Tuli* v *Municipal Corporation, Delhi* (1981)2 SCC 467].

Terminal tax is a tax collected at the terminal or outskirts of a local area. [*Hindustan Construction* v *State of J&K* 1977 Kash LJ 162].

NOTE: *'Terminal tax' and 'octroi'—distinction.* Terminal tax and octroi are similar kinds of terms which are closely interlinked with: (1) destination of goods; (2) the user in the local area on arrival of the goods. There is a very thin margin of difference between a terminal tax and octroi. In the case of a terminal tax, the goods reach their final destination and their entry into the area of destination immediately attracts payment of terminal tax irrespective of their user. In the case of the octroi, however, the tax is levied on goods for their use and consumption. [*Man Mohan Tuli* v *Municipal Corporation, Delhi* (1981)2 SCC 467].

Octrois and terminal taxes are different, though they resemble in one respect, namely, that they are leviable in respect of goods brought into a local area. Terminal taxes are leviable on goods either imported or exported from the municipal limits. But octrois are leviable in respect of goods brought into a municipal area for consumption, use or sale. [*Burmah Shell* v *Belgaum Municipality* AIR 1963 SC 906].

**Termination.** Conclusion; end; limitation as to time, space, existence or extent; the act of setting bounds or limits; the act of ending or concluding.

**Termination of service.** The act of ending or concluding the employer-employee relationship.

Striking off the name of a workman from the rolls by the employer amounts to "termination of service". [*H.D. Singh* v *Reserve Bank of India* (1985)4 SCC 201: 1985 Supp (2) SCR 482: AIR 1986 SC 132]. "Termination" embraces not merely the act of termination by the employer, but the fact of termination, however, produced. [*The State Bank of India* v *Shri N. Sundara Money* AIR 1976 SC 1111: (1976)3 SCR 160: (1976)1 SCC 822].

NOTE: The essential element of termination is that as soon as the services of a person are terminated, all bonds, rights and liabilities are immediately snapped; there is no continuity of any right or benefit whatsoever after termination, except perhaps such rights and benefits as are expressly provided by the statute. [*Bholanath* v *Union of India* (1992)19 ATC 188 (All)].

*Termination of service—whether amounts to dismissal, removal or reduction in rank.* Every case of termination of service is not dismissal, removal or reduction in rank. A termination of service brought about by the exercise of a contractual right is not *per se* dismissal or removal. If the termination of service is brought about otherwise than by way of punishment, no claim for protection under Art. 311(2) can be made. [*Union of India* v *Jiwan Ram* AIR 1958 SC 905].

**Terminus.** The word "terminus" according to *Oxford Dictionary* means a point situated at or forming the end or extremity of something, situated at the end of a line of railway. In other words, terminus means the point to which main action tends, goal end, finishing point, the point at which something comes to an end. [*Man Mohan Tuli* v *Municipal Corporation, Delhi* AIR 1981 SC 991: (1981)2 SCR 894: (1981)2 SCC 467].

'Terminus' means the point at which motion or action ends; goal; end; finishing point; sometimes that from which it starts; starting point; an end; extremity; the point at which something comes to an end. [*Central India Spinning and Weaving Mfg. Co. Ltd.* v *Municipal Committee, Wardha* AIR 1958 SC 341; *Man Mohan Tuli* v *Municipal Corporation, Delhi* AIR 1981 SC 991: (1981)2 SCR 894: (1981)2 SCC 467].

**Terminus a quo.** The starting point.

**Terminus ad quem.** The terminal point.

**Terms and conditions of employment.** It would ordinarily include not only the contractual terms and conditions but those terms which are understood and applied by the parties in practice or habitually or by common consent without being incorporated in the contract. [*Workmen, Hindusthan Lever* v *Hindusthan Lever* AIR 1984 SC 1683: (1984)2 SLJ 364: 1984 Lab IC 1573: (1984)65 FJR 246].

**Territorial waters.** That portion of the sea or ocean which is adjacent to the shores of a country. The generally recognized limit is three miles.

The waters under a state's or nation's jurisdiction, including both inland waters and surrounding sea (traditionally within three miles of the coastline). [Black's *Law Dictionary*, 8th Ed.].

**Territory.** A geographical area included within a particular government's jurisdiction; the portion of the earth's surface that is in a state's exclusive possession and control. [Black's *Law Dictionary*, 8th Ed.].


- **Acquisition of territory** p. 28.
- **Foreign territory** p. 366.
- **Occupied territory** p. 619.


**Terrorism.** The use or threat of violence to intimidate or cause panic, especially as a means of affecting political conduct. [Black's *Law Dictionary*, 8th Ed.].

The threat or use of violence for political purpose by individuals of groups, whether acting for or in opposition to established governmental authority, when such actions are intended to shake, stun or intimidate a target group wider than the immediate victims.

"Terrorism" means the act of terrorising, unlawful acts of violence committed in an organised attempt to overthrow a government or like purposes. [*State of Punjab* v *Sukhpal Singh* JT 1989(4) SC 95: 1989 Supp (1) SCR 420: AIR 1990 SC 231: (1990)1 SCC 35: 1990 Cr LJ 584: 1990 SCC (Cri) 1].

NOTE: It may be possible to describe "terrorism" as use of violence when its most important result is not merely the physical and mental damage of the victim but the prolonged psychological effect it produces or has the potential of producing on the society as a whole. There may be death, injury or destruction of property or even depravation of individual liberty in the process but the extent and reach of the intended terrorist activity travels beyond the effect of an ordinary crime capable of being punished under the ordinary penal law of the land and its main objective is to overawe the Government or disturb harmony of the society or 'terrorise' people and the society and not only those directly assaulted with a view to disturb even tempo, peace and tranquillity of the society and create a sense of fear and insecurity.

Experience shows that "terrorism" is generally an attempt to acquire or maintain power or control by intimidation and causing fear and helplessness in the minds of the people at large or any section thereof and is a totally abnormal phenomenon. What distinguishes "terrorism" from other forms of violence, therefore, appears to be the deliberate and systematic use of coercive intimidation. [*Hitendra Vishnu Thakur* v *State of Maharashtra* AIR 1994 SC 2623: (1994)4 SCC 602: 1994 SCC (Cri) 1087: JT 1994(4) SC 255: 1995 Cr LJ 517].

**Terrorist.** A person who indulges in criminal acts with manifestly political motive without exhausting legitimate remedies at his disposal for getting redressal of his grievances. It means a person who indulges in wanton killing of persons or in violence or in disruption of services or means of communications essential to the community or in damaging property with a view to—(*i*) putting the public or any section of the public in fear; or (*ii*) affecting adversely the harmony between different religious, racial, language or regional groups or castes or communities; or (*iii*) coercing or overawing the Government established by law; or (*iv*) endangering the sovereignty and integrity of India. [Terrorist Affected Areas (Special Courts) Act 1984, s. 2(*h*)].

"Terrorist" means one who adopts or supports the policy of terrorism. [*State of Punjab* v *Sukhpal Singh* JT 1989(4) SC 95: 1989 Supp (1) SCR 420: AIR 1990 SC 231: (1990)1 SCC 35: 1990 Cr LJ 584: 1990 SCC (Cri) 1].

**Test.** Something by which to ascertain the truth respecting another thing; a criterion, standard or norm.

To bring one to a trial and examination; to ascertain the truth or the quality or fitness of a thing.

- **Breath test** p. 111.

**Testament.** Binding agreement; solemn promise; expression of conviction; testamentary declaration; will.

A will of personal property; a will of land is not called a testament. The word "testament" is now seldom used except in the heading of a formal will, which usually begins—"This is the last will and testament of me, A.B., etc." [Jowitt's *Dictionary of English Law*, 2nd Ed.].

Traditionally, a will disposing of personal property; will. [Black's *Law Dictionary*, 8th Ed.].

**Testamentary.** Relating or appertaining to a will; relating to administration of the estate of a deceased person.

**Testamentary capacity.** Mental capacity of the testator to make the will in question. The nature of the instrument executed, its simplicity or complexity is one ingredient of testamentary capacity.

NOTE: To constitute a good testamentary disposition, the testator must retain a degree of understanding to comprehend what he is doing—to have a volition or power of choice. [*Swinfen* v *Swinfen* (1958)175 Er 862]. It usually refers to the absence some disability which prevents a person from making a valid will; thus infants and mental patients have no testamentary capacity. [Jowitt's *Dictionary of English Law*, 2nd Ed.].

**Testamentary expenses.** Expenses incurred in connection with taking out probate and administration of the estate of the testator.

**Testamentary guardian.** A guardian appointed by a person's will or codicil over his or her minor child. [Indian Succession Act 1925, s. 60; Hindu Minority and Guardianship Act 1956, s. 9(1)].

**Testamentary succession.** Distribution of property on the basis of a will.

**Testator.** A deceased person who has left a valid will or codicil; a person who has made a will; a person who dies leaving a will.

In modern usage, a person who leaves a will is called a testator, regardless of sex.

**Testatrix.** A female testator.

**Testatum.** A clause in a deed or clauses in a deed which witness the operative act to be effectuated by the deed. It generally begins with the words 'Now this indenture witnesseth'.

**Testimonium clause.** A provision at the end of an instrument reciting the date when the instrument was signed, by whom it was signed and in what capacity. The cause traditionally begins with the phrase "In witness whereof".

**Testimony.** Asseveration; averment; avowal; declaration of facts; deposition; disclosure; evidence by a competent witness.

Evidence that a competent witness under oath or affirmation gives at trial or in an affidavit or deposition.

**Text.** The word "text" in its dictionary meaning, means subject or theme. [*Jethanand Betab* v *State of Delhi* AIR 1960 SC 89: (1960)1 SCR 755: 1960 Cr LJ 160: 1960 SCJ 68].

NOTE: In a statute, when an enactment amends the text of another, it amends the subject or theme of it though sometimes it may expunge unnecessary words without altering the subject. The word "text" is comprehensive enough to take in the subject as well as the terminology used in a statute. [*Jethanand Betab* v *State of Delhi,* supra].

**Text book.** The word 'text book' would involve either some original matter contributed and published by the author, or it may even include an intelligent selection of the work of another author or authors for use in schools. It may also include some books which have been copyrighted. If the scheme of the book or books involves a graduated or considered study or training in the particular subject like say, books of drawing, it might be said to be a text book. A copy book cannot, however be strictly a text book in that sense. [*Gopala Chetty* v *Director of Public Instruction, Mysore* ILR (1955) Mys 203: AIR 1955 Mys 81 (DB)].

**Textile.** Fabric or cloth or yarn made, wholly or in part, of cotton or wool or silk or artificial silk or other fibre. [Textile Committee Act 1963, s. 2(*g*)].

The word "textiles" is derived from Latin "texere" which means "to weave" and it means woven fabric. [*Ess Dee Carpet Enterprises* v *Union of India* JT 1989(4) SC 527: 1989 Supp (2) SCR 417: AIR 1990 SC 455: (1990)1 SCC 461].

The meaning of the term "textile" given in the *Oxford Dictionary* is: "a woven fabric; any kind of cloth". It must acquire a body and a texture. [*Delhi Cloth and General Mills Co. Ltd.* v *R.R. Gupta, Commercial Tax Officer, Jaipur* 1976 (Supp) SCR 497: (1976)38 STC 113: (1976)3 SCC 443: AIR 1977 SC 2086].

"Textile" ordinarily means cloth and yarn. [*Shree Meenakshi Mills Ltd.* v *Union of India* AIR 1974 SC 366: (1974)2 SCR 398: (1974)1 SCC 468].

The expression "textiles" includes not only yarn but also man-made fibres or artificial silk. [*Sirsilk Ltd.* v *Textiles Committee* JT 1988(4) SC 592: 1988 Supp (2) SCR 880: AIR 1989 SC 317: 1989 Supp (1) SCC 168].

When yarn, whether cotton, silk, woollen, rayon, nylon or of any other description or made out of any other material is woven into a fabric, what comes into being is a 'textile' and it is known as such. It may be cotton textile, silk textile, woollen textile, rayon textile, nylon textile or any other kind of textile. Whatever be the mode of weaving employed, woven fabric would be 'textiles'. [*Porritts and Spencer (Asia) Ltd.* v *State of Haryana* (1978)42 STC 433: AIR 1979 SC 300: (1979)1 SCR 545: (1979)1 SCC 82].

**Textile factory.** Any premises wherein or within the close or curtilage of which steam, water or other mechanical power is used to move or work any machinery, employed in preparing, manufacturing or finishing or in any process incident to the manufacture of cotton, wool, hair, silk, flax, hemp, jute, tow, china grass, coconut fibre or other material, either separately or mixed together or mixed with any other materials or any fabric made thereof: Provided that the print works, bleaching and dyeing works, lace warehouses, paper mills, flax scutch mills, rope works and hat works shall not be deemed to be textile factories. [*Workers of United Bleachers* v *United Bleachers* AIR 1960 Mad 131].

**Textile industry.** This expression refers to manufacture of textile and not in some isolated processing of pre-existing textile fabrics for their conversion into another article capable of being used for any specified purpose. [*Surgical Dressing Mfg. Co.* v *Punjab State* ILR (1967)1 Punj 747: 1968 Lab IC 722 (Punj)].

**Textile machinery.** The equipment employed directly or indirectly for the processing of textile fibre into yarn and for the manufacture of fabric therefrom by weaving or knitting and includes equipment used either wholly or partly for the finishing, folding or packing of textiles. [Textiles Committee Act 1963, s. 2(*f*)].

**Thak-bust.** A survey showing the boundaries of each *mahal* estate and village.

> NOTE: The thak-bust map is evidence of possession of the property at the time of preparation of the map.

**Thakur.** A deity or idol worshipped by Hindus.

> NOTE: A *thakur* can hold any property but the management is entrusted to the *shebait* or manager.

**Thana.** A police station.

**That is to say.** Ordinarily, the expression "that is to say" is employed to make clear and fix the meaning of what is to be explained or defined. Such words are not used, as a rule, to amplify a meaning while, removing a possible doubt. In usual cases this expression may be followed by illustrative instances. The precise meaning varies with the context. [*State of Tamil Nadu* v *Pyare Lal Malhotra* AIR 1976 SC 800: (1976)3 SCR 168: (1976)1 SCC 834: (1976)37 STC 319; *Shaw Wallace & Co. Ltd.* v *State of Tamil Nadu* (1976)3 SCC 17; *Khajan Singh* v *Commissioner of Sales Tax* (1979)43 STC 173].

> NOTE: Use of expression 'namely', or 'that is to say' followed by description of goods is usually exhaustive unless there are strong indications to the contrary. [*Mahindra Engineering and Chemical Products Ltd.* v *Union of India* (1992)1 SCC 727].
>
> Once the expression 'that is to say' is employed in a taxing notification indicating the article included therein *extenso*, then a general or generic meaning cannot be assigned to the expression which is followed by the words 'that is to say'. [*Commercial Taxes Officer* v *Sitaram Satish Chand and Co.* 1986 Raj LW 369].

**That matter.** The words "that matter" connotes identity of the matter and not their proximity. [*Vijay Kumar Sharma* v *State of Karnataka* AIR 1990 SC 2072: (1990)2 SCC 562: JT 1990(2) SC 448: (1990)1 SCR 614].

**Theatre.** 'Theatre' includes any premises intended principally or wholly for the presentation of moving pictures, dramatic performance or stage entertainments. [Weekly Holidays Act 1942, s. 2(*e*)].

A 'theatre' is 'any edifice used for the performance of dramatic or operatic or other representations, plays or performance'. [*Delite Talkies* v *Jabbalpur Corporation* AIR 1966 MP 298: 1966 MPLJ 687].

**Theatrical performance.** A theatrical performance means not merely dramatic performance, but also operatic or other representations or performances, *e.g.*, cinema. [*Delite Talkies* v *Jabalpur Corporation* AIR 1966 MP 298: 1966 MPLJ 687].

**Theft.** Wrongful taking; stealing; swindling; pilfering fraudulent taking; felonious taking; embezzlement.

Whoever, intending to take dishonestly any movable property out of the possession of any person without that person's consent, moves that property in order to such taking is said to commit theft. [Indian Penal Code 1860, s. 378].

> NOTE: A temporary retention of property by a person wrongfully gaining thereby or a temporary keeping out of property from the person legally entitled thereto, may amount to "theft" under s. 378 of the Indian Penal Code. [*K.N. Mehra* v *State of Rajasthan* AIR 1957 SC 369: 1957 SCR 623: 1957 Cr LJ 552: 1957 SCJ 386].
>
> Illegal seizure of cattle with a view to impounding them is theft. [*Lokenath Sahu* v *Rahas Beura* AIR 1963 Ori 52].

**These presents.** The words 'these presents' in a deed mean not the property but the deed itself. [*Field* v *Hopkins* 59 LJ Ch 174: 44 Ch D 529].

**Thika.** Temporary or non-permanent, as a *thika* tenant or non-permanent tenant.

**Thika tenant.** "Thika tenant" means any person who holds, whether under a written lease or otherwise, land under another person, and is or but for a special contract would be liable to pay rent, at a monthly or at any other periodical rate, for that land to that another person and has erected or acquired by purchase or gift any structure on such land for a residential, manufacturing or business purpose and includes the successors in interest of such person. [*Jnan Ranjan Sen Gupta* v *Arun Kumar Bose* AIR 1975 SC 1994: (1975)2 SCC 526: (1976)1 SCR 105 referring to Calcutta Thika Tenancy Act 1949].

**Third party risks or claims.** Third party claims or risks mean claims by others (except insurer or policyholder) in respect of the negligent use of the car.

NOTE: Section 146 of the Motor Vehicles Act 1988 stipulates no person is permitted to use a motor vehicle in a public place, unless there is in force, in relation to the use of the vehicle, a policy of insurance against third party risk.

The use of the words 'third party' in Ch. XI of the Motor Vehicles Act 1988, clearly refers to the intention of the legislature to point out to a party which is neither the first party nor the second party to a contract of insurance. [*National Insurance Co. Ltd.* v *Faqir Chand* 1996 ACJ 111 (J&K)].

**Thoroughfare.** A frequented way or course, especially, a road or street through which the public have unobstructed passage; highway; any place through which much traffic passes. A thoroughfare is a place which is used as a passage for people to pass through. ... The dictionary meaning of the word indicates that there must be unobstructed transit. That is to say, the place must be used as a passage for the people to pass through. The *Oxford Dictionary* meaning is 'a road; street; lane or path forming a communication between two other roads or streets, or between two places; a public way unobstructed and open at both ends'. A thoroughfare is a wider expression than a 'road' or a 'street', but is narrower than a 'public place'. [*Anatarajani Mohanty* v *State of Orissa* AIR 1951 Ori 51].

NOTE: The essential idea of a thoroughfare is the right of the public to pass and repass over it. A place to which the public are merely entitled to go and over which they have no right of way is not a thoroughfare. There may be thoroughfares across public places, but nevertheless, a thoroughfare is essentially different from a public place. In order to constitute a thoroughfare, it is not however, essential that the public should have a right to ride or drive over it. [*Public Prosecutor* v *K.G. Sivaswamy* (1953)2 MLJ 602: AIR 1954 Mad 249 (DB), *per* Balkrishna Iyer, J.].

The term 'thoroughfare' can include a public place which serves as a passage for the public. But every place of public resort cannot be a thoroughfare. It is only a place which is used by the public for passing from one place to another that will be regarded as a thoroughfare and the expression 'thoroughfare' is not of such wide connotation as to include in its scope every place to which the public have a right to resort. [*Public Prosecutor* v *K.G. Sivaswamy*, supra].

**Threat.** A communicated intent to inflict harm or loss on another or on another's property, especially one that might diminish a person's freedom to act voluntarily or with lawful consent; an indication of an approaching menace; a person or thing that might well cause harm [Black's *Law Dictionary*, 8th Ed.]; an expression of intention to inflict or cause evil, injury, loss or harm; an announcement or omen of impending danger or evil.

NOTE: It is the essence of a threat that it be made for the purpose of intimidating or overcoming the will of the person to whom it is addressed. [*Wood* v *Bowron* 36 LJMC 5: LR 2 QB 21].

**Thug.** A vicious or brutal ruffian.

▸ *Meaning under the Indian Penal Code 1860, s. 310.* A thug is a person who is or shall have been habitually associated with any other or others for the purpose of committing: (*i*) robbery; or (*ii*) child-stealing by means of or accompanied with murder.

**Ticket.** A written or printed piece of paper entitling the holder to enter a place, participate in an event, travel by public transport; a receipt of an item left temporarily for safe keeping; a label attached to a thing and giving its price or other details; a label or tag for attachment or identification; a certificate or license as of a pilot of airplane or the captain of a ship.

A certificate indicating that the person to whom it is issued, or the holder, is entitled to some right or privilege. [Black's *Law Dictionary*, 8th Ed.].

**Tickler system.** A system, usually on cards or in loose leaf books, kept to "tickle" or refresh the memory, *e.g.*, to indicate dates of obligations.

**Tidal navigable river.** Part of the river which under ordinary circumstances is tidal and it is not enough to show that sometimes under unusual circumstances the river at the place in question is affected by the tide. [*Reece* v *Miller* (1882)8 QBD 626: 51 LJMC 64].

**Timber.** 'Timber' includes trees when they have fallen or have been felled, and all wood whether cut up or fashioned or hollowed out for any purpose or not. [Indian Forest Act 1927, s. 2(6)].

Timber implies only such trees as are fit to be used in building and repairing houses. [*Sheikh Ibadullah* v *Lachmi Narain* AIR 1926 All 350; *Rameshwar Singh* v *Basudeva* AIR 1923 Pat 95].

In its popular sense, "timber" is understood to be "imarathi lakri". Legal glossary published by the Ministry of Company Affairs Law and Justice, gives the meaning of "timbers" as wood meant for building or such like use. In the *Chambers 20th Century Dictionary* the meaning of the word "timber" is this: wood suitable for building or carpentry, whether growing or cut, standing trees of oak, ash, elm, or (locally by custom) other kinds etc. Trees less than six inches in diameter have been said not to be timber. [*Mukesh Kumar Aggarwal and Co.* v *State of Madhya Pradesh* AIR 1988 SC 563: 1988 (Supp) SCC 232: (1988)2 SCR 501: JT 1988(1) SC 50: (1988)68 STC 324].

The word "timber" is not confined merely to felled trees in forestry. A log is wood cut up or sawn and is timber. Similarly, a beam is timber shown in a particular way, rafter is timber or log put to a particular use and plank is also timber. [*State of Orissa* v *Titaghur Paper Mills Company Limited* AIR 1985 SC 1293: (1985)3 SCR 26: 1985 (Supp) SCC 280: (1985)60 STC 213].

**Time.** A measure of duration; a point in or period of duration at or during which something is alleged to have occurred. [Black's *Law Dictionary*, 8th Ed.].

• **Dead time** p. 227.

• **Reasonable time** p. 731.

**Time-bar.** A bar to a legal claim arising from the lapse of a defined length of time, especially one contained in a statute of limitations. [Black's *Law Dictionary*, 8th Ed.].

**Time-barred debt.** Debts are called 'time-barred' when they cannot be recovered in courts of law by the statutes of limitations.

**Time immemorial.** A point in time so far back that no living person has knowledge or proof contradicting the right or custom alleged to have existed since then; a point in time beyond which legal memory cannot go.

**Time liabilities.** Liabilities which are not demand liabilities. [Banking Regulation Act 1949, s. 5(*f*)].

**Time policy.** A policy in which the risk undertaken is limited to a specified period of time.

**Time rate.** Wages based on a rate per hour for a standard working week with overtime paid at higher hourly rates. The main alternative system is to base wage payments on results, the piece rate system.

**Tirtha.** A holy place or a place of pilgrimage by Hindus.

**Title.** The name of an Act; the heading of a statute or other legal document. The name of a book or a chapter of a book; the name of a deed or other written, printed or filmed production or musical composition or work of art; an application of honour, dignity or distinction.

The elements constituting legal ownership; a right to possession; interest in any property.

NOTE: The word 'title' in r. 89, Or. 21, Code of Civil Procedure 1908, includes not merely completed title, but a title in process of maturity. [*Rabindra Nath* v *Harendra Kumar* AIR 1956 Cal 462].

- **Abstract of title** p. 10.
- **Bad title** p. 92.
- **Covenant for title.** A covenant for title is an assurance to the transferee that the transferor has the very estate in quality and quantity which he purports to transfer. A covenant for title is broken by the existence of an adverse right, such as an easement of way, or where the transferor has no title to the whole or a part of the property.
- **Deducing the title** p. 236.
- **Defeasible title** p. 240.
- **Defective title** p. 241.
- **Document of title to lands.** The term 'document of title to lands' includes any deed, map, paper or, parchment, written or printed or partly written and partly printed, being or containing evidence of the title, or any part of the title to any real estate or any interest in or out of real estate. [Wharton's *Law Lexicon*].
- **Doubtful title.** Doubtful title means such title as involves a considerable chance of litigation.
- **Good title** p. 391.
- **Instrument of title** p. 465.
- **Marketable title.** A title that a reasonable buyer would accept because it appears to lack any defect and to cover the entire property that the seller has purported to sell. It is also termed merchantable title; clear title; good title. [Black's *Law Dictionary*, 7th Ed.].

  Marketable title in the case of a contract for sale of immovable property means a title free from reasonable doubt. Whether the doubt, under the circumstances of a particular case, is reasonable or not must necessarily depend on the nature of the objections and the facts of the case. A marketable title is one which, so far as its antecedents are concerned, may at all times and under all circumstances be forced upon an unwilling purchaser. [*Oosman* v *Haroon* AIR 1923 Bom 148].
- **Merchantable title** p. 575.
- **Muniments of title** p. 595.
- **Predecessor in title** p. 678.
- **Requisition on title** p. 751.
- **Root of title** p. 765.
- **Slander of title** p. 800.

**Title deeds.** Deeds or other papers which constitute the evidence of a person's legal ownership to any property.

**To be a witness.** "To be a witness" is nothing more than to furnish evidence. A person can be a witness not merely by giving oral evidence but also by producing documents or making intelligible gestures as in the case of a dumb witness. [*M.P. Sharma* v *Satish Chandra, District Magistrate, Delhi* AIR 1954 SC 300: 1954 SCR 1077: 1954 Cr LJ 865: 1954 SCJ 428].

"To be a witness" in its ordinary grammatical sense means giving oral testimony in court. Case law has gone beyond this strict literal interpretation of the expression which may now bear a wider meaning, namely, bearing testimony in court or out of court by a person accused of an offence, orally or in writing. [*State of Bombay* v *Kathi Kalu Oghad* AIR 1961 SC 1808: (1961)2 Cr LJ 856: (1962)3 SCR 10].

**To employ.** "To employ" means use of services of person. [*Central Board of Direct Taxes* v *Aditya V. Birla* JT 1987(4) SC 653: AIR 1988 SC 420: 1988 (Supp) SCC 120: (1988)2 SCR 115: (1988)170 ITR 137].

**To liquidate.** 'To liquidate' means to ascertain and/or apportion. [*Dena Bank* v *K. Motiram Vakil* AIR 1989 Bom 264: (1988)90 Bom LR 275].

**To look after.** 'To look after' means to supervise. [*Nirmal Kumar* v *National Jute Mfg. Corpn. Ltd.* (1987)91 CWN 1].

**To persuade.** 'To persuade' means to induce a person to believe something to lead one to do something. [*Hari Ram Sri Prakash* v *Election Tribunal Mazuffarnagar* AIR 1970 All 146 (FB)].

**To recur.** 'To recur' simply means 'to occur again or to repeat', the word connotes distinct and different repetitions of the same act.

**To serve.** "To serve" means to perform function, do what is required for. [*Coal Mines Provident Fund Commissioner* v *Ramesh Chander Jha* AIR 1990 SC 648: (1990)1 SCC 589: (1990)1 SCR 181: JT 1990(1) SC 115].

**To state.** "To state" is to declare or to set forth, especially in a precise, formal or authoritative manner; to say (something), especially in an emphatic way; to assert. [*State of Uttar Pradesh* v *Lalai Singh Yadav* (1976)4 SCC 213: 1976 SCC (Cri) 556: AIR 1977 SC 202: (1977)1 SCR 616: 1977 Cr LJ 186].

**To supervise.** In the ordinary dictionary sense to supervise is to direct or oversee the performance or operation of an activity and to oversee it, watch over and direct. It is work under eye and gaze of someone who can immediately direct a corrective and tender advice. [*CESC Limited* v *Subhash Chandra Bose* (1992)1 SCC 441].

**To touch.** "To touch" means 'to come in contact with'. [*Sabharwal Brothers* v *Smt. Guna Amrit Thadani of Bombay* AIR 1972 SC 1893: (1973)1 SCR 53: (1973)3 SCC 750].

**Toilet preparation.** 'Toilet preparation' means any preparation which is intended for use in the toilet of the human body or in the perfuming apparel of any description, or any substance intended to cleanse, improve or alter the complexion, skin, hair or teeth, and includes deodorants and perfumes. [Medical and Toilet Preparations (Excise Duties) Act 1955, s. 2(*k*)].

**Toilet requisites.** 'Toilet requisites' is a general expression, and it covers, broadly speaking, three categories of things: (1) toilet preparations; (2) toilet accessories; and (3) toilet instruments. [*Deputy Commissioner* v *Jao Zachariah* ILR (1966) Ker 18: (1965)16 STC 799].

**Tol.** A school or institution for the education of boys in various branches of Sanskrit learning in the orthodox style.

**Toll.** A toll is a payment in respect of some benefit, advantage or service, generally for the use of another's property. [*Mataprasad* v *Election Officer* AIR 1971 MP 136].

A toll is a sum of money, taken in respect of a benefit arising out of the temporary use of land. It implies some consideration moving to the public, either in the form of a liberty, privilege or service. For the valid imposition of a toll, there must be a corresponding benefit. [*State of U.P.* v *Devi Dayal Singh* AIR 2000 SC 961; *Hammerton* v *Earl of Dysare* (1916-18) AC 57, 58; *Hindustan Vanaspati Mfg. Co. Ltd.* v *Municipal Board Pilkhwa* AIR 1962 SC 25; *Mahamed Ibrahim* v *State of U.P.* AIR 1967 SC 14; *Kamaljeet Singh* v *Main Board* AIR 1987 SC 56; *Maheshwar Singh* v *State of Bihar* AIR 1966 Pat 402].

The term 'toll' can properly be applied to any sum of money which is taken in respect of some benefit, the benefit being the temporary use of land. [*Monohar Janardhan* v *Yado Isinath* ILR (1951) Nag 914: AIR 1952 Nag 401].

'Toll' is tribute or custom paid for a privilege, generally for passage over, or for using a bridge, road, ferry or railway. [*Unnikrishnan* v *State of Kerala* (1987)1 Ker LT 774].

Sum of money levied over bridges and roads primarily not for increasing the general revenue but for recouping the expenses incurred in constructing roads and bridges and in maintaining them. [*Maheswari Singh* v *State of Bihar* AIR 1966 Pat 462].

As for *Oxford Dictionary* 'toll' is a charge payable for permission to pass a barrier or use a bridge or road, etc. Toll may not be a fee and the element of *quid pro quo* may not exist. However, toll is not a tax. It can be levied only by way of reimbursement of the amount spent by the state on the construction and repairs of bridges and is levied on the user thereof. Once the cost is recovered, levy of toll must cease. [*Baldeo Chowdhary* v *State of Bihar* (1997)2 Pat LJR 144].

**Toll tax.** A tax imposed in respect of vehicles etc., for the use of roads. A vehicle would be liable to toll tax even if no goods are carried by that vehicle. This term is not synonymous with terminal tax. [*Hindustan Construction* v *State of J&K* 1977 Kash LJ 162].

**Toll traverse.** A toll traverse is connected with the ownership of the soil and is allowed to be charged for the use of the land by the person liable for the tolls. This classification is not applicable to tolls of the other kinds which have no connection with passage. [*Hindustan Vanaspati Mfg. Co. Ltd.* v *Municipal Board, Ghaziabad* AIR 1962 All 25].

**Ton.** 'Ton' is a unit of volume in shipping parlance and is not to be taken as 'weight' as may be commonly understood. [*Great Eastern Shipping* v *Union of India* AIR 1989 Del 289].

**Tools.** Mechanical implements, as carpenter's tools; machine used in making machinery, *e.g.*, lathe; things used in an occupation or pursuit, as tools of one's trade. Utensils used for making sweetmeats are the tools of an artisan. [*Mahabir* v *Raghunandan* AIR 1935 All 848]. "Tools" include sewing machines in a tailor's shop. [*Ahmad Sayeed* v *Kanizak* AIR 1941 All 157].

**Tort.** A civil wrong, which is not exclusively the breach of a contract or the breach of a trust. [Limitation Act 1963, s. 2(*m*)]. It is so called because it is wrested (*tortum*) wrong or crooked. An action for such a wrong is called an *action of tort*. Assault, trespass, *etc*., come under it.

"Tort" dictionarily means 'breach of duty leading to damage'. Same meaning attaches to it in law. In general, torts consist of some act done without just cause or excuse. [*Jay Laxmi Salt Works (P) Ltd.* v *State of Gujarat* (1994)4 SCC 1: JT 1994(3) SC 492].

• **De son tort** p. 226.

**Tort feasor.** One who commits a tort.

**Tortious.** Crooked; wrongful.

**Torture.** The infliction of intense pain to the body or mind to punish, to extract a confession or information, or to obtain sadistic pleasure. [Black's *Law Dictionary*, 8th Ed.].

NOTE: Torture of a human being by another human being is essentially an instrument to impose the will of the 'strong' over the 'weak' by suffering. [*D.K. Basu* v *State of West Bengal* AIR 1997 SC 610: (1997)1 SCC 416: 1997 Cr LJ 743: JT 1997(1) SC 1].

'Torture' is a question of fact—there must be proper effort to prove that aspect of the matter. [*Arvind Singh* v *State of Bihar* JT 2000(5) SC 127: AIR 2001 SC 2124: 2001 Cr LJ 2556: (2001)6 SCC 407].

**Total.** Absolute; whole; not divided; full; complete; entire; unqualified; universal; utter; with no exception.

The words 'total' and 'whole' are synonymous. The dictionary meaning of the word 'whole' is 'total' and *vice versa*. [*Mangala Prasad Jaiswal* v *District Magistrate* AIR 1971 All 77].

**Total disablement.** Such disablement, whether of a temporary or permanent nature, as incapacitates a workman for all work which he was capable of performing at the time of the accident resulting in such disablement. [Workmen's Compensation Act 1923, s. 2(*l*); Employees' State Insurance Act 1948, s. 2(24)].

▸*Meaning under the Personal Injuries (Compensation Insurance) Act 1963, s. 2(h).* "'Total disablement' means such disablement whether of a temporary or permanent nature, as incapacitates a workman for all work which he was capable of performing at the time the injury was sustained: Provided that permanent total disablement shall be deemed to result from every injury, or from any combination of injuries, specified in the Schedule, where the percentage, or the aggregate percentage, of disability as specified in the Schedule against such injury, or combination of injuries, amounts to one hundred per cent or more".

**Total full time earnings.** The expression "total full time earnings" can only mean the earning one earns in a day by working full time on that day; the full time to be in accordance with the period of time given in the notice displayed in the factory for a particular day. [*Shankar Balaji Waje* v *State of Maharashtra* AIR 1962 SC 517: 1962 Supp (1) SCR 249: (1962)1 Cr LJ 497: (1962)2 SCJ 426; drawing reference to Factories Act 1948].

**Total voting power.** 'Total voting power' in regard to any matter relating to a body corporate means the total number of votes which may be cast in regard to that matter on a poll at a meeting of such body if all the members thereof and all other persons, if any, having a right to vote on that matter are present at the meeting, and cast their votes. [Companies Act 1956, s. 2(48)].

**Touching.** 'Touching' means 'concerning'. [*Himangshu Bhusan Chakraborty* v *Nirmal Kumar* AIR 1962 Cal 488].

The word 'touching' means 'in reference or relation to, respecting, regarding or concerning'. [*Gokul Prasad* v *Laxman Singh* AIR 1962 MP 265 (FB)].

NOTE: A dispute touching the business of a cooperative society must necessarily have some concern with the business of the society. [*Gokul Prasad* v *Laxman Singh* AIR 1962 MP 265 (FB)].

The expression 'touching the business of a society' means 'affecting or relating to the business of the society'. [*Farkhundali* v *B. Potdar* AIR 1962 Bom 162].

**Tourist.** A tourist is a person who moves from place to place with a view to see the countryside and to enjoy its surroundings. A person who goes from place *A* to place *B* for meeting his relatives or for a special purpose connected with the service of social obligations even though may be travelling as a passenger cannot be said to be 'tourist'.

**Tout.** To solicit customer persistently; solicit patronage.

▸ *Meaning under the Legal Practitioners Act 1879, s. 2*. In its application to legal profession, 'tout' means a person—(*a*) who procures in consideration of any remuneration moving from any legal practitioner the employment of the legal practitioner in any legal business, or who proposes to any legal practitioner or to any person interested in any legal business to procure, in consideration of any remuneration moving from either of them the employment of the legal practitioner in such business, or (*b*) who for the purpose of such procurement frequents the precincts of civil or criminal courts or of revenue offices, or railway stations, landing stages, lodging places or other places of public resort.

"Tout" means a person who procures, in consideration of any remuneration moving from any Advocate or from any person on his behalf, the employment of such Advocate in any legal business, or who proposes to any Advocate to procure, in consideration of any remuneration moving from such Advocate or from any person on his behalf, the employment of the Advocate in such business, or who for purposes of such procurement frequents the precincts of the court. [*In re Sant Ram* AIR 1960 SC 932: (1960)3 SCR 499: (1961)1 SCJ 98].

**Town.** A center of population that is larger and more fully developed than a village, but that (traditionally speaking) is not incorporated as a city [Black's *Law Dictionary*, 8th Ed.]; a compactly settled area of any size as distinguished from surrounding rural territory; a large densely populated urban area.

The word 'town' in the absence of any definition in the Act has to be understood in the sense in which ordinary people understand it, namely, that it is a place having the main attributes of the existence of houses in close proximity, concentration of a large number of people in a comparatively small area and engagement of the bulk of the population in non-agricultural pursuits. [*Belait Sheikh* v *State of West Bengal* AIR 1952 Cal 753].

'Town' comprises within its sweep even an urban area commonly called a city. [*Beharilal* v *Behari Lal* AIR 1972 J&K 114].

**Toxicology.** The science which treats poisons, their effect, antidotes and recognition of poisons.

**Trade.** A trade is an organised seeking after profits, as a rule with the aid of physical assets. [*Aviation & Shipping Co. Ltd.* v *Murray* (1961)2 All ER 805].

'Trade' indicates a process of buying and selling; it may also mean a calling or industry or class of skilled labour. [*Skinner* v *Jack Breach Ltd.* (1927)2 KB 220].

In ordinary usage it may mean the occupation of a small shopkeeper equally with that of a commercial magnate. It may also mean a skilled craft. It is often used in contrast with a profession. [*National Association etc.* v *Bolton Corporation* (1943) AC 166].

'Trade' in its primary meaning is the exchanging of goods for goods or goods for money; and in a secondary meaning, it is any business carried on with a view to profit, whether manual or mercantile, as distinguished from the literal arts or learned professions and from agriculture. [*National Union* v *M.R. Meher* ILR (1959) Bom 1130: AIR 1960 Bom 22].

The expression 'trade' in its narrow popular sense means "exchange of goods for goods or for money with the object of making profits". In its widest sense, it includes any business carried on with a view to earn profit. The word however takes its meaning from its context. [*State of Gujarat* v *Mahesh Kumar Dhirajlal Thakkar* AIR 1980 SC 1167: (1980)2 SCJ 317: 1980 Cr LJ 919: 1980 MLJ (Cr) 761].

The word "trade" means exchange of goods for goods or goods for money or, any business carried on with a view to profit, whether manual or mercantile as distinguished from the liberal arts or learned professions and from agriculture. [*Secretary Madras Gymkhana Club Employees' Union* v *Management of the Gymkhana Club* AIR 1968 SC 554: (1968)1 SCR 742].

"Trade" in its primary meaning is the exchanging of goods for goods or goods for money, in its secondary meaning for goods it is repeated activity in the nature of business carried on with a profit motive, the activity being manual or mercantile, as distinguished from the liberal arts or learned profession or agriculture. [*State of Punjab* v *Bajaj Electricals Ltd.* AIR 1968 SC 739: (1968)2 SCR 536: (1968)70 ITR 730: (1970)25 STC 82].

▸ *Meaning under the Competition Act 2002, s. 2(x).* 'Trade' means any trade, business, industry, profession or occupation relating to the production, supply, distribution, storage or control of goods and includes the provision of any services.


- **Balance of trade** p. 93.
- **Carry on trade** p. 125.
- **Entrepot trade** p. 311.
- **False trade description** p. 342.
- **Foreign trade** p. 366.
- **Inland trade** p. 461.
- **Interstate trade** p. 477.
- **Multilateral trade** p. 594.
- **Restraint of trade** p. 756.
- **Restrictive trade practice** p. 757.
- **Sale in the course of inter-state trade** p. 771.
- **Stock-in-trade** p. 813.


**Trade association.** A body of persons (whether incorporated or not) which is formed for the purpose of furnishing the trade interests of its members or of persons represented by its members. [Monopolies and Restrictive Trade Practices Act 1969, s. 2(*t*). The Act is repealed and replaced by the Competition Act 2002. No such term is defined under the new Act].

A "trade association" means an association of tradesmen, businessmen or manufacturers for the protection and advancement of their common interest. [*Commissioner of Income Tax, Bombay* v *Royal Western India Turf Club Ltd.* 1953 SCJ 739: (1953)24 ITR 551: AIR 1954 SC 85: 1954 SCR 289].

**Trade cycle.** The alteration of periods of prosperity and depression, of good and bad trade.

NOTE: The principal phases of a trade cycle are—

- *Boom:* Exceptional business activity accompanied by rising prices.

- *Depression:* Large and protected decline in business activity.
- *Recession:* Confidence declines, prices begin to fall, unemployment increases.
- *Recovery:* Confidence revives, investment and employment increase.

**Trade deficit.** See under DEFICIT p. 242.

**Trade discount.** A trade discount is a deduction from the catalogue price of goods allowed by wholesalers to retailers engaged in the trade. The allowance enables the retailer to sell the goods at the catalogue price and yet make a reasonable margin of profit after taking into account his business expenses. [*Dy. Commissioner of Sales Tax (Law), Board of Revenue (Taxes), Ernakulam* v *Advani Coorlikon (P) Ltd:* AIR 1980 SC 609: (1980)1 SCR 931: (1980)1 SCC 360: (1980)45 STC 32: 1980 Tax LR 1601: (1981)8 ELT 801].

A 'trade discount' is a percentage deduction from the regular list or catalogue price or goods. [*A.K. Roy* v *Voltas Limited* 1973 SCC (Tax) 261].

NOTE: A prompt payment discount is a "trade discount" given to the dealers by the company but the "year ending discount" is not a trade discount. [*Asst. Collector of Central Excise* v *Madras Rubber Factory Ltd.* 1986 (Supp) SCC 751: (1987)1 SCR 846: JT 1987(1) SC 41: (1987)27 ELT 553].

**Trade dispute.** Any dispute between employers and workmen or between workmen and workmen, or between employers and employers which is connected with the employment or non-employment, or the terms of employment or the conditions of labour, of any person. [Trade Unions Act 1926, s. 2(*g*)].

**Trade gap.** The margin between the value of visible imports and exports. Together with the margin on invisible trading it makes up the balance of trade.

**Trade practice.** 'Trade practice' means any practice relating to the carrying on of any trade and includes—(*i*) anything done by any person which controls or affects the price charged by, or the method of trading of, any trader or any class of traders, (*ii*) a single or isolated action of any person in relating to any trade. [Monopolies and Restrictive Trade Practices Act 1969, s. 2(*u*) referred to in *Mahindra and Mahindra Ltd.* v *Union of India* AIR 1979 SC 798: (1979)2 SCR 1038: (1979)2 SCC 529].

**Trade protection society.** This is an organisation formed for the protection of and benefit of its members who carry on the trade in question. Members receive confidential reports as to the financial standing of individuals or firms who may be desiring credit, and information as to the deaths or bankruptcy of traders, dissolution of partnerships and winding up of companies, *etc*.

**Trade union.** Any combination, whether temporary or permanent, formed primarily for the purpose of regulating the relations between workmen and employers or between workmen and workmen, or between employers and employers, or for imposing restrictive conditions on the conduct of any trade or business, and includes any federation of two or more trade unions. [Trade Unions Act 1926, s. 2(*h*) referred to in *The Commissioner of Income Tax, West Bengal III, Calcutta* v *Indian Sugar Mills Association* (1974)97 ITR 486: AIR 1975 SC 506: (1975)2 SCR 605: (1975)3 SCC 479].

**Trademark.** A word, phrase, logo, or other graphic symbol used by a manufacturer or seller to distinguish its product or products from those of others. The main purpose of a trademark is to designate the source of goods or services. In effect, the trademark is the commercial substitute for one's signature. [Black's *Law Dictionary*, 8th Ed.].

▸ *Meaning under the Trade Marks Act 1999, s. 2(1)(zb).* A mark capable of being represented graphically and which is capable of distinguishing the goods or services of one person from those of others and may include shape of goods, their packaging and combination of colours.

The term "trademark" means a mark used in relation to goods for the purpose of indicating or so as to indicate a connection in the course of trade between the goods and some person having the right as proprietor to use that mark. The function of a "trademark" is to give an indication to the purchaser or a possible purchaser as to the manufacturer or quality of the goods, to an indication to his eye of the trade source from which the goods come, or the trade hands through which they pass on their way to the market. [*Sumat Prasad Jain* v *Sheojanam Prasad (Dead) by LRs and State of Bihar* AIR 1972 SC 2488: 1972 Cr LJ 1707: (1973)1 SCR 1050: (1973)1 SCC 56: 1973 SCC (Cri) 186].

A trademark is a distinctive mark attached to goods offered for sale in the market so as to distinguish the same from similar goods and to identify them with a particular trader or with his successor as the owner of the particular business. [*M.R. Verma* v *William Hollins* AIR 1947 Lah 29].

NOTE: A trademark includes a registered as well as unregistered trademark. [*State of Orissa* v *Ram Nath* AIR 1972 SC 232: (1972)1 SCC 130].

*"Trademark" and "propertymark"—distinction between.* The distinction between a "trademark" and a "propertymark" is that whereas the former denotes the manufacture or quality of the goods to which it is attached, the latter denotes the ownership in them. In other words, a "trademark" concerns the goods themselves, while a "propertymark" concerns the proprietor. A propertymark attached to the movable property of a person remains even if part of such property goes out of his hands and ceases to be his. [*Sumat Prasad Jain* v *Sheojanam Prasad (Dead) by LRs. and State of Bihar* AIR 1972 SC 2488: 1972 Cr LJ 1707: (1973)1 SCR 1050: (1973)1 SCC 56: 1973 SCC (Cri) 186].

**Tradename.** A name, style, or symbol used to distinguish a company, partnership or business (as opposed to product or service); a name under which a business operates. [Black's *Law Dictionary*, 8th Ed].

A tradename may be, and often is, a trademark, but it has a wider application than that. In its wider sense, it means the name under which a person (or company) carries on, and has habitually carried on, his business, and by which he is known in the trade or business to which his business belongs and which accordingly distinguishes the nature, quality and fame of his goods and dealings. [Stroud's *Judicial Dictionary*, 5th Ed.].

NOTE: A person has a right to restrain anyone else from injuring his business by using his tradename. [*Levy* v *Walkar* 10 Ch D 447: 48 LJ Ch 278].

**Trader.** When a person buys for the purpose of selling or processing or manufacturing that he would become a trader. The term "trader" embraces not just the purchase transaction but the entire transaction of purchase, processing, manufacturing and selling. If a person buys for domestic or personal consumption, then he would not be a trader. [*G. Giridhar Prabhu* v *Agriculture Produce Market Committee* AIR 2001 SC 1363: JT 2001(3) SC 312: (2001)2 SCJ 306: (2001)3 SCC 405].

**Trader's credit.** This is a method of settling a number of debts by making out instructions to a commercial bank to pay the amounts shown to the listed bank accounts of the listed traders. It is a convenient alternative to drawing individual cheques for each debt.

**Tradesman.** A person who carries on trade; one who buys and sells goods for profit.

**Traditional occupation.** "Traditional occupation" means an occupation followed in a family in which it is handed down by an ancestor to his posterity. If there is a section of the population following an occupation of that description that section can be regarded as a class. Such occupations are generally occupations in which some special skills are necessary like those of an artisan or a craftsman. [*Shri Janki Prasad Parimoo* v *State of Jammu and Kashmir* AIR 1973 SC 930: (1973)3 SCR 236: (1973)1 SCC 420: 1973(1) SLR 719].

**Traffic.** Commerce; trade; the sale or exchange of such things as merchandise, bills, and money; the passing or exchange of goods or commodities from one person to another for an equivalent in goods or money; people or things being transported along a route; the passing to and fro of people, animals, vehicles, and vessels along a transportation route. [Black's *Law Dictionary*, 8th Ed.].

> NOTE: Under the Highways Act 1959 (England) s. 295, "traffic" includes pedestrians and animals.
>
> "Traffic" includes rolling-stock of every description, as well as passengers and goods. [Railways Act 1989, s. 2(39)].

**Tramp steamers.** Cargo-carrying ships which "tramp" between the world's ports, their destinations depending on the cargoes they pick up, rather than sailing regularly between the same ports.

**Transaction.** 'A transaction' is a group of acts so connected together as to be referred to by a single legal name as a crime, a contract, a wrong or any other subject of inquiry which may be in issue. [*A.N. Mukerji* v *State* 1969 Cr LJ 1203: AIR 1969 All 489, 497].

The word 'transaction' is from the verb 'transact' which according to dictionary meaning means 'to carry through', accomplish, execute, do or to carry on. It cannot be read narrowly to mean as synonymous to the word 'contract'. In fact, in one contract there may be many business transactions. [*Baldev Kumar* v *Managing Director* AIR 1997 MP 147, 153].

According to its etymological and dictionary meaning, the word 'transaction' means 'carrying through' and suggests not necessarily proximity of time—so much as continuity of action and purpose.

A transaction, in the ordinary sense of the word, is some business or dealing which is carried on or transacted between two or more persons. [*Channoo Mahto* v *Jang Bahadur* AIR 1957 Pat 293].

> NOTE: A transaction entered into by a person should be any act, which is either bilateral or multilateral, and not a mere unilateral action. [*P.K. Subramania* v *Commissioner of Gift Tax* AIR 1968 Ker 190].


- **Benami transaction** p. 100.
- **In the course of the same transaction** p. 442.
- **Same transaction** p. 773.
- **Speculative transaction** p. 806.




**Transfer.** Any method—direct or indirect, absolute or conditional, voluntary or involuntary—of disposing of or parting with an asset or an interest in an asset, including a gift, the payment of money, release, lease, or creation of a lien or other encumbrance.

Earl Jowitt, in 'The Dictionary of English Law' says: In the law of property, a "transfer" is where a right passes from one person to another, either (1) by virtue of an act done by that transferor with that intention, as in the case of a conveyance or assignment by way of sale or gift, etc.; or (2) by operation of law, as in the case of forfeiture, bankruptcy, descent, or intestacy. [*The Mangalore Electrict Supply Co. Ltd.* v *The Commissioner of Income Tax, West Bengal* AIR 1978 SC 1272: (1978)3 SCR 913: (1978)3 SCC 248: (1978)113 ITR 155].

In India, the word "transfer" is defined with reference to the word "convey". The word "transfer" in English law in its narrower and more usual sense refers to the transfer of an estate in land. The word "conveys" in s. 5 of the Transfer of Property Act 1882 is used in the wider sense of conveying ownership. [*Narandas Karsondas* v *S.A. Kamtam* AIR 1977 SC 774: (1977)2 SCR 341: (1977)3 SCC 247].

The word 'transfer' is comprehensive and is regarded generally as comprehending within its scope transfers both of the voluntary and involuntary kinds. Without more, there is no reason for limiting the operation of the word 'transfer' to voluntary acts of transfer so as to exclude compulsory acquisitions of property. [*The Mangalore Electrict Supply Co. Ltd.* v *The Commissioner of Income Tax, West Bengal* AIR 1978 SC 1272: (1978)3 SCR 913: (1978)3 SCC 248: (1978)113 ITR 155].

> NOTE: 'Transfer' is a word of wider import than sale. A transfer may be by means of a lease or mortgage or sale or by any other mode. [*Union of India* v *Maqsood Ahmed* AIR 1963 Bom 110: ILR (1963) Bom 158].
>
> 'Transfer', with its grammatical variations and cognate expressions, includes letting on hire, lending, giving and parting with possession. [Arms Act 1959, s. 2(*k*)].

'Transfer' must necessarily be accompanied by the hand from which and the hand to which something is to be transferred, that is to say, 'transfer' must carry with it 'from' and 'to'. If either of them is wanting, there can be no transfer. [*Deepchand* v *M.P.S.R.T. Corpn.* AIR 1977 MP 42].

Partition effects a transfer so as to convert a joint title of the co-owners into exclusive title of each. [*Shankar Shaw* v *Anukul Chandra* 71 CWN 174].

'Transfer', in relation to a capital asset, includes the sale, exchange or relinquishment of the assets or the extinguishment of any rights therein or the compulsory acquisition thereof under any law. [Income-tax Act 1961, s. 2(47)].

Under the service law, 'transfer' means movement of a government servant from one headquarter station in which he is employed to another such station, to take up the duties of a new post or in consequence of a change of his headquarter. [*Arbind Kumar* v *State of Bihar* (1996)2 Pat LJR 406].

• **Blank transfer** p. 106.
• **Credit transfer** p. 205.

**Transfer of a case.** The removal of a case from the jurisdiction of one court or judge to another by lawful authority.

**Transfer of ownership.** "Transfer of ownership" is a term of wide import and it comprises every mode by which ownership may be transferred from one person to another. The mode of transfer may vary from one kind of property to another; it would depend on the nature of the property to be transferred. [*Madan Mohan Pathak* v *Union of India* AIR 1978 SC 803: (1978)3 SCR 334: (1978)2 SCC 50].

**Transfer of property.** In its general sense, the expression "transfer of property" connotes the passing of rights in the property from one person to another. In one case there may be a passing of the entire bundle of rights from the transferor to the transferee. In another case, the transfer may consist of one of the estates only out of all the estates comprising the totality of rights in the property. In third case, there may be a reduction of the exclusive interest in the totality of rights of the original owner into a joint or shared interest with other persons. An exclusive interest in property is a larger interest than a share in that property. To the extent to which the exclusive interest is reduced to a shared interest it would seem that there is a transfer of interest. [*Sunil Siddharthbhai* v *Commissioner of Income Tax, Ahmedabad, Gujarat* 1985 Supp (3) SCR 102: (1985)156 ITR 509: AIR 1986 SC 368].

▸ *Meaning under the Transfer of Property Act 1882, s. 5.* Section 5 defines "transfer of property" as meaning 'an act by which a living person conveys property, in present or in future, to one or more other living persons, or to himself, or to himself and one or more other living persons'; and "to transfer property", is to perform such act. [*Dattatraya Shanker Mote* v *Anand Chintaman Datar* (1974)2 SCC 799: (1975)2 SCR 224].

NOTE: A deed of release by the husband to wife is held to be a transfer of property within the meaning of the Transfer of Property Act. [*Official Assignee* v *Tehmina Dinshaw* AIR 1972 Mad 187: 1972 MLJ 48].

'Transfer of property' includes a transfer of any interest therein and any charge created thereon. [Presidency Towns Insolvency Act 1909, s. 2(*i*); Provincial Insolvency Act 1920, s. 2(*f*)].

▸ *Meaning under Gift Tax Act 1958, s. 2(xxiv) (since repealed).* Any disposition, conveyance, assignment, settlement, delivery, payment or other alienation of property and, without limiting the generality of the foregoing, includes—(*a*) the creation of a trust in property; (*b*) the grant or creation of any lease, mortgage, charge, easement, licence, power, partnership or interest in property; (*c*) the exercise of a power of appointment of property vested in any person, not the owner of property, to determine its disposition in favour of any person other than the donee of the power; and (*d*) any transaction entered into by any person with intent thereby to diminish directly or indirectly the value of his own property and to increase the value of the property of any other person.

**Transferee.** A person to whom any property or any interest thereof is transferred. Transferee includes a lessee. [*Brij Mohan* v *Chief Administrator* (1980)82 Punj LR 621 (FB)].

**Transferor.** A person who transfers any property or any interest thereof.

**Transhipment.** To transfer from one ship or conveyance to another for further transportation. In common use, this word is equivalent to loading and unloading goods on any vessel, train or lorry for transport. It may also mean the transfer of goods from one ship to another, but not necessarily implying that such goods are transferred direct from ship to ship. It is not correctly used of goods which having been once entered for warehousing are subsequently sold and exported.

**Transmission.** The passing of an inheritance to an heir; the act or an instance of transmitting; that which is transmitted.

The expression 'transmitted by operation of law' in s. 108(1) of the Companies Act 1956, covers those cases where a person or authority acquires an interest in the property by operation of law, without any voluntary act. [*M.K. Sugar Mills* v *I.K. Sugar Mills* AIR 1956 All 135].

The word may also mean a broadcast of radio or television programme; a device that transmits power from the engine of an automobile to the driving wheels and varies the speed ratios between them.

**Transmission machinery.** Any shaft, wheel, drum, pulley, system of pulleys, coupling, clutch, driving belt or other appliance or device by which the motion of the prime mover is transmitted to or received by any machinery or appliance. [Factories Act 1948, s. 2(*i*)].

**Transport.** To carry or convey a thing, person, baggage, etc. from one place to another; consign; deliver dispatch.

Transport is the taking away from place to place by the owner of the property. [*Mahado Prasad* v *Vindhya Pradesh Government* AIR 1952 Vin Pra 86].

'Transport' means transport from the starting point to the ultimate destination and merely passing through a place in the course of journey does not amount to transporting to that place. [*P.K. Natesa Mudali* v *State of Andhra Pradesh* 1971 MLJ (Cr) 573].

NOTE: When a person consigns bags of charcoal to a carrier intending them to be taken from one place to another, he does 'transport' the charcoal. [Re *Appalaswamy* (1949)2 MLJ 389].

It may also mean banish; deport.

**Transport vehicle.** A public service vehicle, a goods carriage, an educational institution bus or a private service vehicle. [Motor Vehicles Act 1988, s. 2(47)].

A 'transport vehicle' means a 'public service vehicle' and a 'public service vehicle', means any motor vehicle either used or adopted to for carrying passengers for hire or reward which determines the category of the motor vehicle whether it is adopted for that purpose or not. It must follow that even if a motor vehicle is occasionally used for carrying passengers for hire or reward, it must be regarded when so used as a public service vehicle and therefore a transport vehicle. [*State of Mysore* v *Syed Ibrahim* (1967)2 SCWR 18: AIR 1967 SC 1424].

**Transportation.** The act of conveying or the process of being conveyed; a system of conveying; vehicles used in transporting; the movement of goods or persons from one place to another by a carrier.

It may further mean the sending away of a convict to a remote place; removal to a penal colony. The expression 'transportation' is now understood in India as referable to life imprisonment. [*State of A.P.* v *Komalla Krishnaiah* 1992 Cr LJ 2446].

NOTE: A person sentenced to transportation for life may be detained in prison for life. [*Sambha Ji Krishan Ji* v *State of Maharashtra* AIR 1974 SC 147: (1974)1 SCC 196].

**Travel.** To go from one place to another; make a journey, especially of some length or abroad. [*New India Assurance Co. Ltd.* v *Annakutty* (1992)2 Ker LT 727: AIR 1993 Ker 299].

**Traveller's cheque.** An instrument that is (*i*) payable on demand, (*ii*) drawn on or payable at or through a bank, (*iii*) designated by the term "traveller's cheque" or by a substantially similar term, and (*iv*) that requires, as a condition to payment, a counter signature by a person whose specimen signature appears on the instrument.

Instrument purchased from bank, or the like, in various denominations, which can be used as cash upon second signature by purchaser. It has the characteristics of a cashier's cheque of the issuer. [*Pines* v *United States* CCA Iowa, 123 F 2d 825, 828].

**Travelling expenses.** Expenses relating to travelling which include meals and lodging and transportation expenses while away from home in the pursuit of a trade or business including that of an employer.

The expression in ordinary acceptance includes the whole cost and inconvenience to which a person is put by being absent from home. [*Ivory* v *Macrae* 35 Sc LR 105].

**Traverse.** 'Traverse' is denial of some facts alleged in pleading by the other side.

NOTE: Where a defendant denies any material allegation of fact in the plaintiff's declaration, he is said to traverse it, and the plea itself is then frequently termed a 'traverse'.

**Treason.** Betrayal of a trust; breach or violation of allegiance; breach of faith; disloyalty; infidelity; insurance; rebellion against the government; sedition; subversion; treachery.

The offence of attempting by overt acts to overthrow the government of the state to which the offender owes allegiance; or of betraying the state into the hands of a foreign power. Treason consists of two elements; adherence to the enemy, and rendering him aid and comfort. [*Cramer* v *U.S.* 65 S Ct 918, 932: 89 L Ed 1441].

• **High treason** p. 414.

**Treasure trove.** Money or coin, gold, silver, plate or bullion found hidden in the earth or other private place, the owner thereof being unknown or unfound, in which case it belongs to the Crown. [Wharton's *Law Lexicon*].

'Treasure trove' means anything of value hidden in the soil or in anything affixed thereto. [Indian Treasure Trove Act 1878, s. 3].

**Treatment.** Treatment would include such steps as would not only tend to effect cure of some disease but also as would prevent further deterioration of the disease. The expression connotes a remedial measure either to cure or to prevent deterioration. [*Himansu Sekhar Nandy* v *D.M., Balasore* (1976)42 Cut LT 1262].

'Treatment' in the *Chamber's Twentieth Century Dictionary* means, way of applying remedies. In *Webster's Dictionary* 'treatment' means manner of applying remedies to cure; mode or course pursued for remedial ends; as, the treatment of a disease; the treatment of a patient. In *Corpus Juris Secundum*, vol. 87, p. 949, the word 'treatment' is said to be also employed to indicate all the steps taken in order to effect a cure of an injury or disease. Cure at the end would include arresting the disease from further worsening as a step towards that end. [*Himansu Sekhar Nandy* v *District Magistrate, Balasore* (1976)42 Cut LT 1262].

**Treaty.** Accord; agreement; agreement between nations; alliance; arrangement; concordance; formal contract; international compact; trace; understanding.

A compact made between two or more independent nations with a view to the public welfare. [*Louis Wolf & Co.* v *United States* Cust & Pat App, 107 F 2d 819, 827; *United States* v *Belmont* NY, 301 US 324: 81 L Ed 1134].

An agreement, league, or contract between two or more nations or sovereigns, formally signed by commissioners properly authorized, and solemnly ratified by the supreme power of each state. [*Edye* v *Robertson* 112 US 580: 28 L Ed 798; *Charlton* v *Kelly* 229 US 447: 57 L Ed 1274].

A treaty is not only a law but also a contract between two nations and must, if possible, be so construed as to give full force and effect to all its parts. [*United States* v *Reid* CCA Or, 73 F 2d 153, 155].

The term "treaty" is wide enough to include an agreement between international organisations *inter se*, or between an international organisation on the one hand and a State or States on the other.

• **Extradition treaty** p. 334.

**Tree.** A perennial woody plant having usually a single self-supporting trunk, with branches and foliage, growing at some distance above the ground, the whole ranging from about 10 feet to as high as 300 feet; any shrub or plant that assumes treelike shape or dimensions; something whose outline resembles that of a tree. [Webster's *Comprehensive Dictionary*, International Ed.].

A 'tree' according to the *Shorter Oxford Dictionary*, is a 'perennial plant' having a self-supporting woody main stem or trunk (which usually) develops wood branches at some distance from the ground and growing to considerable height. [*Mir Fakir Mohd.* v *State of West Bengal* 1978 UJ (SC) 149].

**NOTE: 'Tree' includes palms, bamboos, stumps, brush-wood and canes. [Indian Forest Act 1927, s. 2(7)].**

• **Genealogical tree** p. 383.

**Trespass.** Enter unlawfully; intrude; advance upon; break the law; deviate from rectitude; encroach.

An unlawful act committed against the person or property of another, especially, wrongful entry on another's real property. [Black's *Law Dictionary*, 8th Ed.].

'Trespass' means doing of unlawful act or of lawful act in unlawful manner to injury of another's person or property. [*Waco Cotton Oil Mill of Waco* v *Walker* Tex Civ App, 103 SW 2d 1071, 1072].

'Trespass', in its largest and most extensive sense, signifies any transgression or offence against the law of nature, of society, or the country in which we live; whether it relates to a man's person or his property. Therefore, beating another is a trespass; for which an action of trespass in assault and battery will lie. Taking or detaining a man's goods are respectively trespasses, for which an action of trespass on the case in trover and conversion, is given by the law; so, also, non-performance of promises or undertakings is a trespass, upon which an action of trespass on the case in assumpsit is grounded; and, in general, any misfeasance, or act of one man, whereby another is injuriously affected or damnified, is a transgression, or trespass, in its largest sense; for which an action will lie. [3 Comm. c. 12, Tomlins *Law Dictionary*].

"The term trespass has been used by lawyers and laymen in three senses of varying degrees of generality. (1) In its widest and original signification it includes any wrongful act—any infringement or transgression of the rule of right. This use is common in the Authorised Version of the Bible, and was presumably familiar when that version was first published. But it never obtained recognition in the technical language of the law, and is now archaic even in popular speech. (2) In a second and narrower signification—its true legal sense—the term means any legal wrong for which the appropriate remedy was a writ of trespass—*viz.* any direct and forcible injury to person, land or chattels. (3) The third and narrowest meaning of the term is that in which, in accordance with popular speech, it is limited to one particular kind of trespass in the second sense—*viz.* the tort of trespass to land (trespass *quare clausum fregit*)". [Salmond and Heuston: *Law of Torts*, 20th Ed., pp. 4-5].

The word "trespass" in common English acceptation means and implies unlawful or unwarrantable intrusion upon land. It is a transgression of law or right. [*Kewal Chand Mimani (D) by LRs.* v *S.K. Sen* AIR 2001 SC 2569: JT 2001(6) SC 264: (2001)6 SCC 512].

• **Criminal trespass** p. 209.

• **House trespass** p. 423.

**Trespasser.** One who has committed trespass; one who intentionality and without consent or privilege enters another's property [*Fitzgerald* v *Montogomery County Bd. of Ed.* 336 A 2d 795, 797]; a person who enters on the property of another without any right, lawful authority or an express or implied invitation or license. [*Morris* v *Atchison, T. & S.F. Ry. Co.* 422 P 2d 920, 927].

A 'trespasser' is one who lawfully enters into but unlawfully remains in possession of the property without the consent or acquiescence of the owner. If one goes into possession of the property of another with invitation or permission for instance to a shop or cinema theatre, or marriage hall to celebrate a marriage his initial entry is lawful but if he refuses to leave that place and unlawfully squats on it, he becomes a trespasser of a transient origin with no vestige of right. [*East India Hotels Ltd.* v *Syndicate Bank* JT 1991(6) SC 112: 1992 Supp (2) SCC 29, 44].

A 'trespasser' is a person, entering the premises of another with the knowledge that his entrance is in excess of the permission that has been given to him. [*Kewal Chand Mimani (D) by LRs.* v *S.K. Sen* AIR 2001 SC 2569: JT 2001(6) SC 264: (2001)6 SCC 512].

- **Rank trespasser.** A 'rank trespasser' is one who does not stand in any contractual relationship with the owner of the premises. [*East India Hotels Ltd.* v *Syndicate Bank* 1992 Supp (2) SCC 29, 44: JT 1991(6) SC 112].

**Trespasser ab initio.** Where a person enters land of another with permission but abuses his authority, he becomes a trespasser "from the beginning" *ab initio*.

**Trial.** In its application to experiment, it means analysis; evaluation; examination; in-depth analysis; inspection; probe.

In its application to legal proceeding, it means formal examination by a court of law; formal examination of facts by a court; judicial contest.

In legal parlance, it means a judicial examination and determination of issues between parties to action. [*Gulf, C. & S.F. Ry. Co.* v *Smith* Okl, 270 P 2d 629, 633]; whether they be issues of law or of fact. [*Pulaski* v *State* 126 NW 2d 625, 628].

The word 'trial' has its origin from French 'trier' and Latin 'tris, tria'. In general, when we speak of 'trial', of persons, what are really tried in a civil as well as criminal case are issues. [*Food Inspector, Palghat Municipality* v *Venkatchalam Chettiar* 1979 Ker LT 705 (DB)].

... Broadly speaking, a trial is the examination by a competent court of the facts or law in dispute, or put in issue in a case. It is the judicial examination of issues between the parties, whether they are of law or of fact. [*Sajjan Singh* v *Bhagilal Pandya* AIR 1958 Raj 307].

'Trial' means act of proving or judicial examination or determination of the issues including its own jurisdiction or authority in accordance with law or adjudging guilty or innocence of the accused including all steps necessary thereto. The trial commences with performance of the first act or steps necessary or essential to proceed with trial. [*Union of India* v *Major General Madan Lal Yadav (Retd.)* (1996)2 Crimes 14 (SC): 1996 Cr LR (SC) 390: (1996)4 SCC 127: AIR 1996 SC 1340: 1996 SCC (Cri) 592].

The word 'trial' may be understood in a limited sense, as meaning the final hearing of the petition, consisting of examination of witnesses, filing documents and addressing arguments. It may also connote the entire proceedings before the tribunal from the time that the petition is transferred to it. [*Harish Chandra* v *Triloki Singh* AIR 1957 SC 444: 1957 SCJ 297: 1957 SCR 370; *Indian Bank* v *Maharashtra State Co-operative Marketing Federation Ltd.* (1998)5 SCC 69].

'Trial' means the examination and determination of a cause by a judicial tribunal determination of guilt of innocence of an accused person by a court. According to Webster's *Third New International Dictionary*, vol. 2, 'trial' means the mode of determining a question of fact in a court of law; all proceedings from the time when the parties are called to try their cases.

[*State* v *Haridas Mundhara* (1973-74)78 CWN 929].

In *Dictionary of English Law* by W.H. Byrne, 1923 Ed., the word 'trial' has been defined as 'a step in an action, prosecution or other judicial proceeding by which the questions of fact in issue are decided'.

'Trial' means the entire proceedings before a Tribunal from the reference to the conclusion. [*O.P. Jain* v *Gian Chand* 1959 Supp (2) SCR 516: AIR 1959 SC 837: 1959 SCJ 1030].

NOTE: In criminal matters the inquiry is something different from a trial; inquiry stops when the trial begins. [*Kingam Savaranna* v *State* AIR 1957 AP 472].

Trial commences as soon as the charges are framed. [*Manoj Mozumdar* v *State of W.B.* 1984 Cr LJ 28: 87 CWN 914: (1983)2 CHN 143]. In criminal proceedings the trial continues till the conclusion. [*Asgar Ali* v *State of Bombay* AIR 1957 SC 503].


- **De novo trial** p. 226.
- **Fair trial** p. 339.
- **New trial** p. 607.
- **Speedy trial** p. 806.


**Trial balance.** This relates to a list of ledger account balances taken out at any time, but especially at the end of an accounting period, for the purpose of testing the arithmetical accuracy of the entries in the books of account by ascertaining whether the debit and credit balances of accounts agree in total. The agreement of the trial balance is a necessary preliminary to the preparation of accounts.

**Tribe.** A group of families or communities, linked by social, economic, religious, or blood ties, and usually having a common culture and dialect and a recognised leader.

Tribes are usually composed of a number of local communities, *e.g.*, bands, villages or neighbourhoods, and are often aggregated in clusters of a higher order called nations. The term is seldom applied to societies that have achieved a strictly territorial organisation in large States but is usually confined to groups whose unity is based primarily upon a sense of extended kinship ties. It is no longer used for kin groups in the strict sense, such as clans. [*Kartic Oraon* v *David* AIR 1964 Pat 201].

**Tribunal.** Court of justice; court of law; judgment seat; law court; panel of judges.

The seat of a judge; the place where he administers justice; the whole body of judges who compose a jurisdiction; a judicial court; the jurisdiction which the judges exercise. [Black's *Law Dictionary*, 5th Ed.].

A court or other adjudicatory body; the seat, bench, or place where a judge sits. [Black's *Law Dictionary*, 8th Ed.].

The expression 'tribunal', does not mean the same thing as 'court' but includes, within its ambit, all adjudicating bodies, provided they are constituted by the state and are invested with judicial, as distinguished from purely administrative or executive, functions. [*Durga Shankar Mehta* v *Thakur Raghuraj Singh* (1954)2 MLJ 385: 1954 SCJ 723: AIR 1954 SC 520: (1955)1 SCR 267].

NOTE: The "tribunal" as distinguished from the court, exercises judicial powers and decides matters brought before it judicially or quasi-judicially, but it does not constitute a court in the technical sense. "Tribunal" according to the dictionary meaning is a seat of justice, and in the discharge of its function, it shares some of the characteristics of the court. [*Engineering Mazdoor Sabha* v *Hind Cycles Ltd.* AIR 1963 SC 874: 1963 Supp (1) SCR 625: (1964)1 SCJ 140].

*'Arbitrator'—whether excluded by the term 'tribunal'.* A 'tribunal' literally means a seat of justice. May be, justice is dispensed by a quasi-judicial body, an arbitrator, a commission, a court or other adjudicatory organ created by the State. All these are tribunals and naturally the import of the word "tribunal" embraces an arbitration tribunal. 'Tribunal' *simpliciter* has a sweeping signification and does not exclude 'arbitrator'. The expression 'tribunal' includes, in the statutory setting, an arbitrator. [*Gujarat Steel Tubes Ltd.* v *Gujarat Steel Tubes Mazdoor Sabha* AIR 1980 SC 1896: (1980)2 SCR 146: (1980)2 SCC 593].

- **Administrative tribunal** p. 42.
- **Domestic tribunal** p. 278.
- **Industrial tribunal** p. 453.
- **Judicial tribunal** p. 497.


**Tributary.** A stream which flows into a brook which flows into a river which flows into another river is a tributary of the last river. [*Evans* v *Owen* (1895)1 QB 237: 64 LJMC 59].

NOTE: In ordinary language a tributary is a stream running into another stream. The word has no technical meaning, and its popular meaning is not very indefinite. The question as to what is or is not a tributary must depend upon the peculiar distinguishing circumstances of each case. [*Harbottle* v *Terry* (1882)10 QBD 131, *per* Stephen, J.].

The expression 'tributary' is one of rather indefinite imports and its meaning depends upon the context. [*State of Bombay* v *Laxman* AIR 1960 Bom 490].

**True copy.** A copy that, while not necessarily exact, is sufficiently close to the original that anyone can understand it. [Black's *Law Dictionary*, 8th Ed.].

A true copy is a transcript identical to or substitute to the original but not absolutely exact copy. But nobody can by any possibility, misunderstand it to be not a true copy. The test, is whether any variation from the original is calculated to mislead an ordinary person. [*Dr. Shipra Shantilal and Jhamak Lal* v *Laxminarayan Pande* (1996)5 SCC 181, *per* K. Ramaswamy, J.; *Murarka Radhey Shyam Ram Kumar* v *Roop Singh Rathore* AIR 1964 SC 1545: (1964)3 SCR 573: (1964)1 SCR 688: (1965)1 SCJ 153].

NOTE: A "true copy" means a copy which is wholly and substantially the same as the original. Where, therefore, there are insignificant or minimal mistakes, the court may not take notice thereof. [*Mithilesh Kumar Pandey* v *Baidyanath Yadav* AIR 1984 SC 305: (1984)2 SCC 1: (1985)2 SCR 278].

**Trust.** The right, enforceable solely in equity, to the beneficial enjoyment of property to which another person holds the legal title; a property interest held by one person (the trustee) at the request of another (the settlor) for the benefit of a third party (the beneficiary). [Black's *Law Dictionary*, 8th Ed.].

When a person has property or rights which he holds or is bound to exercise for or on behalf of another or others or for the accomplishment of some particular purpose or particular purposes, he is said to hold the property or rights in trust for that other or those others or for that purpose or those purposes and he is called a trustee. [Halsbury's *Laws of England*, 4th Ed., vol. 48, para 501, p. 272].

▸ *Meaning under the Indian Trusts Act 1882, s. 3.* A trust is an obligation annexed to the ownership of property, and arising out of a confidence reposed in and accepted by the owner, or declared and accepted by him, for the benefit of another, or of another and the owner. The person who reposes or declares the confidence is called the author of the trust; the person who accepts the confidence is called the trustee; the person for whose benefit the confidence is accepted is called the beneficiary; the subject-matter of the trust is called trust-property or trust-money; and the instrument by which the trust is declared is called the instrument of trust.

NOTE: For a trust to be valid, it must involve specific property, reflect the settlor's intent and be created for a lawful purpose. [Black's *Law Dictionary*, 8th Ed.].


- **Author of the trust** p. 87.
- **Breach of trust** p. 111.
- **Cestui que trust** p. 134.
- **Constructive trust** p. 181.
- **Criminal breach of trust** p. 206.
- **Declaration of trust** p. 235.
- **Discretionary trusts** p. 266.
- **Express trust** p. 333.
- **Implied trust** p. 434.
- **Instrument of trust** p. 466.
- **Passive trust** p. 646.
- **Precatory trust** p. 676.
- **Resulting trust** p. 757.
- **Secret trust** p. 780.
- **Simple trust** p. 799.
- **Special trust** p. 805.
- **Unit trust** p. 865.

**Trust property.** The subject-matter of the trust is called trust property or trust money. [Indian Trusts Act 1882, s. 3].

**Trustee.** One who, having legal title to property, holds it in trust for the benefit of another and owes a fiduciary duty to that beneficiary. [Black's *Law Dictionary*, 8th Ed.].

▸ *Meaning under the Specific Relief Act 1963, s. 2(d).* 'Trustee' includes every person holding property in trust.

▸ *Meaning under the Indian Trusts Act 1882, s. 3.* The person who accepts the confidence is called the trustee.

**Turnover.** "Turnover" means the aggregate of the amount of sale prices received or receivable by a dealer in respect of the sale or supply of goods. [*Hindustan Sugar Mills* v *State of Rajasthan* AIR 1978 SC 1496: (1978)4 SCC 271: (1979)43 STC 13: (1979)1 SCR 276].

"Turnover" means the amount of money which is turned over in the business. [*George Cakes (P) Ltd.* v *State of Madras* AIR 1962 SC 1352: (1962)13 STC 98].

▸ *Meaning under the Central Sales Tax Act 1956, s. 2(j).* 'Turnover' used in relation to any dealer liable to tax under the Central Sales Tax Act means the aggregate of the sale prices received and receivable by him in respect of sales of any goods in the course of inter-State trade or commerce made during a prescribed period and determined in the prescribed manner.

The expression "turnover" will include the aggregate of the amounts of sales and purchases and parts of sales and purchases actually made by any dealer during the given period. [*Bhawani Cotton Mills Ltd.* v *State of Punjab* AIR 1967 SC 1616: 20 STC 290].

NOTE: In laws dealing with sales tax, "turnover" includes tax. In calculating the total turnover, there is nothing wrong in treating the tax as part of the turnover. [*George Cakes (P) Ltd.* v *State of Madras* AIR 1962 SC 1352: (1962)13 STC 98].

**Turpitude.** The word 'turpitude' means 'inherent' wickedness. [*Brij Kishore Shukla* v *MPSRT Corporation* 1996(2) SLR 406 (MP)].

'Turpitude' means baseness, deprivity, wickedness. [*Kuldeep Singh* v *State of Punjab* AIR 1994 P&H 242].

# Uu

**Uberrimae fidei.** A Latin expression which means 'of the utmost good faith'.

NOTE: In some contracts law requires *uberrimae fidei* or full disclosure. In contracts of marine, fire and life insurance, the person desiring insurance must set forth all material facts known to him affecting the risk.

A contract of insurance is contract *uberrimae fidei* and there must be utmost good faith on the part of the assured. This imposes a duty and an obligation on the assured to make a full disclosure of all material facts which would affect the mind of the insurer whether to accept the risk or not and on what terms. A false answer or non-disclosure or concealment of a material fact will avoid the policy, even though there is no fraud and the concealment is innocent. [*Rohini Nandan* v *Ocean Accident* AIR 1960 Cal 969].

**Ubi aliquid connceditur, conceditur et id sine quo res ipsa esse non potest.** Where anything is conceded, there is conceded also anything without which the thing itself cannot exist. Every court has by necessary implication the power to do that which is necessary to make its order effective.

NOTE: Under this maxim it was held that Magistrate can grant interim maintenance to wife pending an application under s. 125, Cr.P.C. [*Savitri* v *Govind Singh Rawat* (1985)2 Crimes 872: 1985 BBCJ (SC) 160: (1985)2 DMC 363: AIR 1986 SC 984: 1986 Cr LJ 41: (1986)1 Supreme 31: (1986)1 DMC 1 (SC)].

**Ubi eadem ratio ibi idem lex, et de similibus idem est judicium.** Where the same reason exists, there the same law prevails; and of things similar, the judgment is similar.

**Ubi jus ibi remedium.** Where there is a right, there is a remedy.

**Ubi jus incertum, ibi jus nullum.** Where the law is uncertain, there is no law.

**Ubi supra.** In the place above (mentioned).

**Udasi.** One who is indifferent to worldly things; a religious order among the Sikhs; a mendicant.

**Uhada.** A contract; time fixed for discharge of an obligation or payment of debt or an instalment.

**Ullage.** The quantity required to fill a partly-filled vessel, *e.g.*, a cask consequent upon leakage, or of its having been broached.

**Ultima ratio.** The final argument; the last resort.

**Ultimate.** Last; final; beyond which no other exists; fundamental; primary; maximum.

"Ultimate" and "final" are synonymous. [*Re Wales, Parkinson* v *Woodfull* (1934) VLR 297, 302, *per* Gavan Dufoy, J.].

**Ultimatum.** A final proposal in negotiation in which it is intimated that in case it is not accepted the negotiation must end; anything ultimate; last offer; warning.

**Ultimo.** In the last month.

**Ultra posse non potest esse, et vice versa.** What is beyond possibility cannot exist, and the reverse *i.e.* what cannot exist is not possible.

**Ultra vires.** Beyond the scope, power or authority granted by law; unauthorised.

The term *ultra vires* implies absence of capacity or power of the person to do any act. It is not necessary that an act to be *ultra vires* must be illegal; it may or may not be. [*Anand Prakash* v *Assistant Registrar* AIR 1968 All 22].

An act is said to be *ultra vires* when it is enacted in excess of the legislative power. A rule is *ultra vires* when it is beyond the rule-making power of the authority.

[*P. Janardhana* v *Union of India* AIR 1970 Mys 171].

**Umpire.** An impartial person appointed to make an award or final decision, usually when a matter has been submitted to arbitrators who have failed to agree. [Black's *Law Dictionary*, 8th Ed.].

One who decides differences between arbitrators; a person appointed to arbitrate dispute. [*Re Eyre and Leicester* (1892)1 QB 136: 61 LJQB 438].

NOTE: An umpire only acts when there is a difference between the arbitrators. [*Chouthmal* v *Ramchandra* AIR 1955 Nag 126].

**Unauthorised occupation.** 'Unauthorised occupation', in relation to any public premises, means the occupation by any person of the public premises without authority for such occupation, and includes the continuance in occupation by any person of the public premises after the authority (whether by way of grant or any other mode of transfer) under which he was allowed to occupy the premises has expired or has been determined by any reason whatsoever. [Public Premises (Eviction of Unauthorised Occupants) Act 1971, s. 2(*g*); *Jain Ink Manufacturing Co.* v *Life Insurance Corporation of India* (1980)4 SCC 435: AIR 1981 SC 670: (1981)1 SCR 498].

**Unauthorised possession.** Possession without the authority of law. [*Sanjay Dutt* v *State through CBI, Bombay (II)* (1994)5 SCC 410: 1994 SCC (Cri) 1433: JT 1994(5) SC 540: 1995 Cr LJ 477].

**Unavoidable cause.** A cause that a reasonably prudent person would not anticipate or be expected to avoid.

The expression must be read as something in the nature of an emergency. [*Jenkins* v *Howells* (1949)2 KB 218].

**Uncertain.** Not known; beyond doubt; doubtful; unreliable; erratic.

In ordinary acceptance the word denotes a reasonable element of doubt. [*Hickman* v *Peacey* (1945) AC 304].

**Uncertainty.** The fact or condition of being uncertain.

NOTE: Agreements, the meaning of which is not certain or capable of being made certain, are void under s. 29 of the Indian Contract Act 1872.

A will not expressive of any definite intention is void for uncertainty. [Indian Succession Act 1925, s. 89].

A trust fails if there is any uncertainty as to the intention or the purpose or the beneficiary or the trust property. [Indian Trusts Act 1882, s. 6].

**Unconscionable.** The word 'unconscionable' when used with reference to actions means 'showing no regard for conscience; irreconcilable with that which is right or reasonable'. [*Central Inland Water Transport* v *Brojo Nath Ganguly* AIR 1986 SC 1571: (1986)3 SCC 156].

**Unconscionable bargain.** A transaction or contract which is unreasonable or shockingly unfair or unjust; outrageous in nature. It is one which is irreconcilable with what is right or reasonable. [*Central Inland Water Transport* v *Brojo Nath Ganguly* AIR 1986 SC 1571, 1606: (1986)3 SCC 156, 206].

NOTE: The test of good faith should be the fairness of the bargain. Hard bargaining evidenced by a grossly inadequate consideration is sufficient to make the whole thing suspect in the eye of law and condemn the transaction. [*Sonia Parshini* v *Sheikh Moula Baksha* AIR 1955 Cal 17].

**Unconstitutional.** Contrary to or in conflict with a constitution.

NOTE: An unconstitutional Act is not law; it confers no rights; it imposes no duties; it affords no protection; it creates no office; it is in legal contemplation as inoperative as if it had never been passed. [*Abdul Khader* v *State of Mysore* AIR 1951 Mys 72: 52 Cr LJ 992].

A declaration of unconstitutionality brought about by lack of legislative power does not stand on a different footing from a declaration of unconstitutionality brought about by reason of abridgement of fundamental rights. Both these declarations of unconstitutionality go to the root of the power itself and there is no real distinction between them. They represent but two aspects of want of legislative power. [*Behram Khurshed* v *State of Bombay* 1955 SCR 613: 1955 SCA 1: 1955 SCJ 73: AIR 1955 SC 123: 1955 Cr LJ 215].

**Uncultivated land.** The expression 'uncultivated land' means 'cultivable but not cultivated', i.e. fit for cultivation, but allowed to lie fallow. [*State of Gujarat* v *Gujarat Revenue Tribunal* (1979)4 SCC 40: AIR 1980 SC 91: (1980)1 SCR 233].

NOTE: The grasslands on hilly tracts which are incapable of any cultivation cannot, in law, be treated to be 'uncultivated lands'. [*State of Gujarat* v *Gujarat Revenue Tribunal*, supra].

**Under colour of duty.** When any act is done under a colour which is assumed as a cover or cloak for something which cannot properly be done in performance of the duty or in exercise of the right or office, the act is said to be done under colour of the office or duty or right. [*Virupaxappa Veerappa Kadampur* v *State of Mysore* 1963 Supp (2) SCR 6: AIR 1963 SC 849: (1963)1 Cr LJ 814: (1964)1 SCJ 160].

**Under colour of office.** See UNDER COLOUR OF DUTY.

NOTE: Any rightful act in office is 'by virtue of office' and a wrongful act in office may be 'under colour of office'. [*Aminiya Imammiya* v *Emperor* AIR 1948 Bom 197: 49 Cr LJ 216].

**Under protest.** In its application to payment, the value of the expression 'under protest' is to safeguard the position of the person who makes the payment and to ensure that it may not be said that the payment he made was a voluntary one. [*Bashiam Naidu* v *Corporation of Madras* AIR 1935 Mad 625].

**Under-raiyat.** A tenant under a raiyat or under-raiyat.

**Under tenure.** The term "under tenure" as used in s. 59 of the Landlord and Tenant Procedure Act (VIII of 1869) is not confined to a tenure intermediate between the *zamindar* and the raiyat, but includes any tenure which by title-deeds or by the custom of the country is transferable by sale. [*Krishtendra Roy* v *Aena Bewa* 8 Cal 675].

**Under the authority of.** Pursuant to the authority, such as an agent or servant acts under or pursuant to the authority of his principal or master. [*Heavy Engineering Mazdoor Union* v *State of Bihar* (1969)1 SCC 765: AIR 1970 SC 82].

**Underground.** Under the surface of the earth; being, lying, growing or operating below the surface of the ground or earth.

**Undersell.** Sell cheaper than another person or persons.

**Understanding.** An agreement, especially of an implied or tacit nature; the process of comprehending. [Black's *Law Dictionary*, 8th Ed.].

Something quite different from a binding legal contract; at most the word connotes a gentleman's agreement. [*Milner* v *Percy Bilton* (1966)2 All ER 894].

NOTE: The word is evidence of a legally binding agreement unless the rest of the language used or the surrounding circumstances point to a different conclusion. [*Campbell* v *Inland Revenue Commissioners* (1968)3 All ER 588].

**Undertake.** Accept; assume; carry out; embark upon; endeavour; execute; guarantee; pledge; promise; set in motion; take up; be answerable for; embark upon.

'Undertake' means 'be responsible for'. [*Re F.G. (Films) Ltd.* (1953)1 All ER 615].

Undertake means—to take on oneself; to engage in; to enter upon; to take in hand; set about; attempt; as, to undertake a task or a journey; and, specifically, to take upon oneself solemnly or expressly. To lay oneself under obligation or to enter into stipulation; to perform or to execute; to covenant; to contract. Hence, to guarantee; be surety for; promise; to accept or take over as a charge; to accept responsibility for the care of. To engage to look after or attend to, as to undertake a patient or guest. To endeavour to perform or try; to promise, engage, agree or assume an obligation. [*Kartar Singh Bhadana* v *Hari Singh Nalwa* AIR 2001 SC 1556: JT 2001(4) SC 180: (2001)4 SCC 661].

**Undertaking.** The word "undertaking" is a coat of many colours [*Carew and Company Ltd.* v *Union of India* AIR 1975 SC 2260: (1975)2 SCC 791: (1976)1 SCR 379] and may convey different ideas.

It may mean a promise, pledge, or engagement or a bail bond. [Black's *Law Dictionary*, 8th Ed.].

It also means anything undertaken; any business, work or project which one engages in or attempts; an enterprise. [*The Workmen of Indian Standards Institution* v *The Management of Indian Standards Institution* (1975)2 SCC 847: AIR 1976 SC 145: (1976)2 SCR 138].

The term "undertaking" must be defined as any business or any work or project resulting in material goods or material services and which engages in or attempts as an enterprise analogous to business or trade. [*Secretary, Madras Gymkhana Club Employees' Union* v *Management of the Gymkhana Club* AIR 1968 SC 554: (1968)1 SCR 742].

"Undertaking" means a concern in any industry. [*Gopal* v *Administrative Officer, Madhya Pradesh Khadi and Village Industries Board* 1985 Supp (2) SCR 641: (1985)4 SCC 138: AIR 1986 SC 504].

▸ *Meaning under the Industrial Disputes Act 1947, s. 25FFF.* The word "undertaking" is used in its ordinary sense connoting thereby any work, enterprise, project or business undertaking. [*Workmen of the Straw Board Manufacturing Co. Ltd.* v *Straw Board Manufacturing Co. Ltd.* AIR 1974 SC 1132: (1974)3 SCR 703: (1974)4 SCC 681: 1975 SLJ 115; *Isha Steel Treatment* v *Association of Engg. Workers* AIR 1987 SC 1478: (1987)2 SCC 203: (1987)2 SCR 414: JT 1987(1) SC 548].

▸ *Meaning under the Monopolies and Restrictive Trade Practices Act 1969, 2(v).* The word "undertaking", is a coat of many colours, as it has been used in different sections of the Act to convey different ideas. In some of the sections, the word "undertaking" has been used to denote the enterprise itself while in many other sections it has been used to denote the person who owns it. The definition of the word "undertaking" in s. 2(*v*) of the Act would indicate that 'undertaking' means an enterprise which is engaged in production, supply, distribution or control of goods, etc. [*Carew and Company Ltd.* v *Union of India* AIR 1975 SC 2260: (1975)2 SCC 791: (1976)1 SCR 379].

Undertaking means the entire organisation. A company whether it has a plant or whether it has an organisation is considered as one whole unit, and the entire business of the going concern is embraced within the word 'undertaking'. [*Rustom Cavasjee Cooper* v *Union of India* AIR 1970 SC 564: (1970)1 SCC 248: (1970)2 SCA 37].

• **Dominant undertaking** p. 279.
• **Government undertaking** p. 397.
• **Industrial undertaking** p. 453.

**Undervalue.** To estimate or to put a value less than the real value or price of any property, right or claim.

**Underwrite.** Agree or consent to support; assume a risk; assure; endorse; take responsibility; pledge; promise.

The expression "underwrite" signifies 'accept liability under'. Normally, the expression "underwrite" is used in marine insurance. [*Life Insurance Corporation of India* v *Raja Vasireddy Komalavalli Kamba* AIR 1984 SC 1014: (1984)3 SCR 350: (1984)2 SCC 719].

The word commonly meant 'to agree to take up by way of subscription in a new company or new issue, a certain number of shares if and so far as not applied for by the public'. [*Australian Investment Trusts* v *Strand and Pitt Street Properties Ltd.* AIR 1932 PC 212].

To underwrite as applied to shares means to take and pay for them if the public do not. [Re, *London-Paris Financial Mining Corporation Ltd.* (1897)13 TLR 569].

**Underwriter.** Underwriter is a person who underwrites or subscribes his name to a policy of insurance, thereby undertaking to indemnify the assured against the losses referred to in the policy, to the extent therein mentioned. The word is used especially with reference to marine insurance. [Mozley & Whiteley's *Law Dictionary*, 10th Ed.].

**Underwriting.** The act of assuming a risk by insuring it; the insurance of life or property; the act of agreeing to buy all or part of a new issue of securities to be offered for public sale. [Black's *Law Dictionary*, 8th Ed.].

It is in the nature of an insurance against the possibility of inadequate subscription. The necessity for an underwriting contract arises because a public company cannot proceed to allot shares offered to the public, unless the amount specified in the prospectus as the minimum subscription, is raised by the issue of shares. [*Nani Gopal Lahiri* v *State of U.P.* (1965)35 Comp Cas 30 (SC); *Dena Bank* v *Motiram Vakil* AIR 1989 Bom 264].

'Underwriting' means contracting, with or without condition, to subscribe for the stocks, shares, bonds or debentures of an industrial concern with a view to the resale of the whole or any part thereof. [Industrial Finance Corporation Act 1948, s. 2(*g*); State Financial Corporation Act 1951, s. 2(*g*)].

The word 'underwriting' means that the person named in the underwriting agreement agrees to take up shares specified in the agreement if the public or other persons fail to subscribe for them. The consideration for this contract takes the form of payment of commission, called 'underwriting commission'. [*C.I.T., Kanpur* v *U.P. State Industrial Development Corporation* (1997)4 SCC 701].

**Undivided.** If any meaning is to be given to the word 'undivided', it must be 'not divided and indivisible'. [*Aziz-un-nisa* v *Custodian* AIR 1957 All 561].

**Undivided family.** In ordinary acceptance, a family which has not separated in mess and worship and has undivided property.

NOTE: A Hindu joint family divided in status will be an undivided family *qua* the dwelling house, if there has been no division of the dwelling house by metes and bounds. [*Ramaswami Pillai* v *Subramania Pillai* AIR 1967 Mad 156: ILR (1967)1 Mad 602].

The members of the family may have partitioned all their properties and may have separated in mess and worship, but they would still be an undivided family in relation to the dwelling house, so long as they have not divided it among themselves. [*Botokrishna* v *Akshoy Kumar* AIR 1950 Cal 11].

**Undivided share.** 'Undivided' means 'not divided and indivisible'. If the share of a co-sharer cannot be ascertained and therefore has not been ascertained as in the case of Mitakshara coparcenary property or in the case of interest not derived from title, it would be a case of undivided share. In a tenancy-in-common the share of a co-sharer, though not separated by metes and bounds, is divided, because it has been ascertained. [*Aziz-un-nissa* v *Assistant Custodian* AIR 1957 All 361].

**Undue.** Not yet owed; not currently payable; excessive or unwarranted. [Black's *Law Dictionary*, 8th Ed.].

'Undue' must mean something which is not merited by the conduct of the claimant, or is very much disproportionate to it. [*Sterling General Insurance Co. Ltd.* v *Planters Airways Pvt. Ltd.* AIR 1975 SC 415: (1975)1 SCC 603: (1975)3 SCR 136].

**Undue advantage.** The expression means 'unfair advantage'. [*Mayadhar Paramanik* v *State* 1971 Cut LT 582].

**Undue hardship.** The expression is normally related to economic hardship. [*S. Basudeva* v *State of Karnataka* AIR 1994 SC 923].

**Undue influence.** The improper use of power or trust in a way that deprives a person of free will and substitute another's objective. [Black's *Law Dictionary*, 8th Ed.].

NOTE: Undue influence includes any influence by which the exercise of free and deliberate judgment is excluded. Undue influence is presumed until the contrary is proved when the relation of the parties is such that one is entitled to the confidential advice of the other, as in the case of solicitor and client, of a trustee and his *cestui que trust*, and of a parent contracting with a child who has just come of age. In other cases of confidential relationship, the party seeking to avoid a contract must prove undue influence. [Sutton & Shannon on *Contracts*, 6th Ed., p. 170].

To render influence 'undue' it must be established that the person in a position of

domination has used that position to obtain an unfair advantage for himself and so as to cause injury to the person relying on his authority or aid. It is only when the bargain is with the influencer or brought about by him and is in itself unconscionable that the burden is thrown upon the influence to establish affirmatively that the other party was scrupulously kept separately advised in the independence of a free agent. [*Poosathurai* v *Kannappa* ILR 43 Mad 546; *Niki* v *Kirpa* AIR 1989 HP 51].

Every influence cannot be characterised as undue. A donee can appeal and persuade the donor to make a gift to him. Such appeals and persuasions cannot be characterised as undue influence provided the donor retains the mental capacity. [*Takri Devi* v *Rama Dogra* AIR 1984 HP 11, 15; *Subhas Chandra* v *Gangaprosad* AIR 1967 SC 878; *Afsar Seikh* v *Soleman Bibi* AIR 1976 SC 163].

When the will of the testator is coerced into doing that which he or she does not desire to do, it is undue influence. [*Boudains* v *Richardson* (1906) AC 169].

▸*Meaning under the Indian Contract Act 1872, s. 16.* (1) A contract is said to be induced by undue influence where the relations subsisting between the parties are such that one of the parties is in a position to dominate the will of the other and uses that position to obtain an unfair advantage over the other. (2) In particular and without prejudice to the generality of the foregoing principle, a person is deemed to be in a position to dominate the will of another—(*a*) where he holds a real or apparent authority over the other, or where he stands in a fiduciary relation to the other; or (*b*) where he makes a contract with a person whose mental capacity is temporarily or permanently affected by reason of age, illness, or mental or bodily distress.

▸*Meaning under the Indian Penal Code 1860, s. 171C.* Whoever voluntarily interferes or attempts to interfere with the free exercise of any electoral right commits the offence of undue influence at an election.

▸*Meaning under the Representation of Peoples Act 1951.* The definition of "undue influence" is widely worded and covers all kinds of fraudulent acts or omissions which in any way, directly or indirectly, interfere with the free exercise of any electoral right, and that the definition extends not only to actual interference but even to an attempt to interference. [*Shri Shiv Kirpal Singh* v *Shri V.V. Giri* AIR 1970 SC 2097: (1970)2 SCC 567: (1971)2 SCR 197].

**Unearned income.** Earnings from investments rather than labour; income received but not earned. [Black's *Law Dictionary*, 8th Ed.]. It is also termed 'investment' income.

**Unemployment.** Part of the total labour force which is willing to work but is unable to find employment; the state or condition of being unemployed.

**Unforeseen circumstances.** Circumstances which cannot be foreseen; circumstances which are not expected.

The expression in relation to frustration of the performance of a contract means circumstances for which the contract made no provision. [*Talem Ltd.* v *Gamboa* (1939)1 KB 132].

**Unilateral.** One-sided; a transaction by one party only or by which one party binds himself; not reciprocal.

**Union of India.** The name 'Union of India' has been given to a combination of territories, which together comprises the Union; the Union cannot be said to be located at any place other than where its Government is located for the purposes of issuing or serving any writ issued under Art. 226 of the Constitution. [*Ram Kirpal* v *Union of India* AIR 1955 All 468].

**Unit.** A single thing of any kind. A term sometimes used in the sense of a share.

**Unit trust.** This is a method of investing in shares through the medium of a unit trust investment. The essential principle of a unit trust is the purchase by a management company of a diversified block of stock exchange securities—the "unit", and the transfer of it to a trustee, *e.g.*, a bank, to be held on the trust of a trust deed which divides the unit into sub-units (or "units") to the public at a price which covers the manager's expenses, and also a service charge to provide a profit or remuneration for the managers.

NOTE: Unit trusts may take two forms: "fixed" and "flexible". In a fixed trust, the investments are stated in advance and generally may not be charged; they are fixed or rigid. The managers of a flexible or managed trust are, however, free to select the investments from a wider field and to charge them when advisable.

In India, there is a Unit Trust of India Act 1963. The Unit Trust here is of the "fixed" type and its management vests in a Board of Trustees under s. 9 of the Act.

**University.** An educational institution designed for instruction, examination, or both, of students in many branches of advanced learning, conferring degrees in various faculties, and often embodying colleges and similar institution; an educational institution for higher instruction or for the examination of students already instructed.

Section 2(*f*) of the University Grants Commission Act 1966, defines "university" as meaning one "established or incorporated by or under a Central Act, a Provincial Act, or a State Act" and including "any such institution as may, in consultation with the university concerned, be recognised by the Commission in accordance with the regulations made in this behalf under this Act". The Central Government may also, on the advice of the Commission declare, by notification in the Official Gazette, any institution of higher education other than a university to be a university. Section 3 of the Act.

NOTE: The word "university" is not a word of art. Whether or not an educational institution can claim to be a university depends on the consideration of an ordinary man of good education of university standard. An institution may possess all or most of the essential qualities of a university and yet may not be treated as a university. The onus of proving that the institution is a university must lie on the claimant. [*St. David's College, Lampeter* v *Ministry of Education* (1951)1 All ER 559].

**Unjust enrichment.** Unjust enrichment occurs when a person has retained money or benefits which in justice and equity belong to another. [*Hummel* v *Hummel* 14 NE 2d 923, 927].

NOTE: The three essential elements of unjust enrichment are: (1) enrichment of the defendant; (2) such enrichment is at the expense of the plaintiff; (3) the enrichment is unjust. [*B.P. Exploration Co. (Libya)* v *Hunt (No. 2)* (1982)1 All ER 925 (HL)].

The cause of action in unjust enrichment is independent of contract. [*Woolwich Equitable Building Society* v *Internal Revenue Commission* (1992)3 All ER 737 (HL)].

**Unlawful.** Not authorised by law; illegal; criminally punishable; contrary to law; not enforceable in law; illicit; punishable by law; forbidden by some law.

The word 'unlawful' has practically the same meaning as illegal. [*Chandai* v *Emperor* AIR 1933 All 891].

**Unlawful activity.** Any activity contrary to law. A violation of some prohibitory law and includes all wilful, actionable violations of civil rights, and is not confined to criminal acts. [*State* v *Hailey* 165 SW 2d 422, 427].

▸*Meaning under Unlawful Activities (Prevention) Act 1967, s. 2(f)*. 'Unlawful activity' in relation to an individual or association means any action taken by such individual or association whether by committing an act or by words, either spoken or written, or by signs or by visible representation or otherwise—(*i*) which is intended or supports any claim to bring about, on any ground whatsoever, the cession of a part of the territory of India or the cessation of a part of the territory of India from the Union or which incites any individual or group of individuals to bring about such cession or cessation; (*ii*) which disclaims, questions, disrupts or is intended to disrupt the sovereignty and territorial integrity of India.

**Unlawful assembly.** A meeting held with intent to commit crime by force or execute a common design lawful or unlawful in an unauthorised manner.

▸*Meaning at common law.* An unlawful assembly is a meeting of three or more persons with a common plan in mind which, if carried out, will result in a riot. In other words, it is such a meeting with intent to (*a*) commit a crime by open force, or (*b*) execute a common design lawful or unlawful, in an unauthorised manner likely to cause courageous persons to apprehend a breach of the peace.

▸*Meaning under Indian Penal Code 1860, s. 141.* An assembly of five or more persons is designated an unlawful assembly, if the common object of the persons composing that assembly is—*First*—To overawe by criminal force, or show of criminal force the Central or any State Government or Parliament or the Legislature of any State or any public servant in the exercise of the lawful power of such public servant; or *Second*—To resist the execution of any law, or of any legal process; or *Third*—To commit any mischief or criminal trespass, or other offence; or *Fourth*—By means of criminal force, or show of criminal force, to any person to take or obtain possession of any property, or to deprive any person of the enjoyment of a right of way, or of the use of water or other incorporeal right of which he is in possession or enjoyment, or to enforce any right or supposed right; or *Fifth*—By means of criminal force, or show of criminal force, to compel any person to do what he is not legally bound to do, or to omit to do what he is legally entitled to do.

**Unlawful association.** 'Unlawful association' means any association—(*i*) which has its object any unlawful activity, or which encourages or aids persons to undertake any unlawful activity, or of which the members undertake such activity; or (*ii*) which has its object any activity which is punishable under s. 153A or s. 153B of the Indian Penal Code 1860 (45 of 1860) or which encourages or aids persons to undertake any such activity, or of which the members undertake any such activity: Provided that nothing contained in sub-clause (*ii*) shall apply to the State of Jammu and Kashmir. [Unlawful Activities (Prevention) Act 1967, s. 2(*g*)].

**Unlawful picketing.** Picketing which is not honest or truthful. [*Magill Bros.* v *Building Service Employees' International Union* 127 P 2d 542, 543].

When force or violence is used to persuade or prevent workers from continuing their employment. [*Ex parte Bell* 100 P 2d 339, 343].

**Unless.** Except; but that; except in the circumstance that; if it be not that.

A subordinate conjunction in common usage, connecting a dependent or subordinate clause to the main clause of a sentence. [*Kansas City Structural Steel Co.* v *L.G. Barcus & Sons* Inc, 535 P 2d 419, 423].

**Unless the contrary is proved.** Unless rebutted by cogent evidence. [*C.S.D. Swami* v *State* AIR 1960 SC 7].

**Unlimited company.** Any company not having any limit on the liability of its members is called an unlimited company. Any member can be held responsible for the entire liability of the company to other persons. [Companies Act 1956, s. 12].

**Unliquidated.** Not ascertained in amount; not determined; remaining unassessed or unsettled, as unliquidated damages. [*Davies* v *Turner* 6 SE 2d 356, 358].

A debt is spoken of as "unliquidated", if the amount thereof cannot be ascertained at the trial by a mere computation, based on the terms of the obligation or on some other accepted standard. [*Hettrick Mfg. Co.* v *Barish* 199 NYS 755, 767].

**Unlisted shares.** These are shares which do not appear on the Stock Exchange official list, either for non-compliance with regulations, or because due application has not been made.

**Unmarried.** One who had never been married; one without ever having been married.

The primary meaning of 'unmarried' is 'never having been married' or 'without ever having been married' [*Clarke* v *Colls* 9 HL Ca 601; *Dalrymple* v *Hall* 50 LJ Ch 502: 16 Ch D 715; *Re Sergeant* 54 LJ Ch

159: 26 Ch D 575]; but it is a word of flexible meaning, and 'slight circumstances, no doubt, will be sufficient to give the word its other meaning' of 'not having a husband or wife at the time in question' [*Re Sergeant* (supra)] so as to exclude only the marital right. [Stroud's *Judicial Dictionary*, 5th Ed.].

**Unnatural offence.** The infamous crime against nature, *i.e.*, sodomy or buggery, either with man or beast.

NOTE: Whoever voluntarily has carnal intercourse against the order of nature with any man, woman, or animal shall be punished with imprisonment for life, or with imprisonment of either description for a term which may extend to ten years and shall be liable to fine. *Explanation.* Penetration is sufficient to constitute the carnal intercourse necessary to the offence described in this section. [Indian Penal Code 1860, s. 377].

**Unpaid seller.** The seller of goods is deemed to be an unpaid seller within the meaning of the Sale of Goods Act—(*a*) when the whole of the price has not been paid or tendered; (*b*) when a bill of exchange or other negotiable instrument has been received as conditional payment, and the condition on which it was received has not been fulfilled by reason of the dishonour of the instrument or otherwise. [Sale of Goods Act 1930, s. 45].

**Unreasonable.** Irrational; foolish; unwise; absurd; silly; preposterous; senseless; stupid. [*Southern Kansas State Lines Co.* v *Public Service Commission* 135 Kan 657: 11 P 2d 985, 987]. Not reasonable; immoderate; exorbitant. [*Cass* v *State* 61 SW 2d 500]. Capricious; arbitrary; confiscatory. [*Harris* v *State Corporation Commission* 129 P 2d 323, 328].

NOTE: Unreasonableness is not confined to culpability or callous indifference. It can include, where carried in excess, sentimentality, romanticism, bigotry, wild prejudice, caprice, fatuousness, or excessive lack of common sense. [*Re W. (an infant)* (1971)2 All ER 49].

**Unregistered firm.** A firm not registered under the provisions of Chapter VII of the Indian Partnership Act 1932.

'Unregistered firm' means a firm which is not a registered firm. [Income-tax Act 1961, s. 2(48)].

**Unsound mind.** It refers to one who from infirmity of mind is incapable of managing himself or his affairs. It exists where there is an essential privation of the reasoning faculties, or where a person is incapable of understanding and acting with discretion in the ordinary affairs of life. [*Oklahoma Natural Gas Corporation* v *Lay* 51 P 2d 580, 582].

▸ *Meaning under the Indian Lunacy Act 1912, s. 3(5) (since repealed).* The term "unsound mind" comprehends imbecility, whether congenital or arising from old age, as well as lunacy or mental aberration resulting from disease. It implies some unusual feature of the mind as has tended to make it different from the normal and has in effect impaired the man's capacity to look after his affairs in a manner in which another person without such mental irregularity would be able to do in the matter of his own. The idea suggests some derangement of the mind, whatever be its degree and it is not to be confused with or taken an analogous to a mere mental weakness or lack of intelligence.

NOTE: Nothing is an offence which is done by a person who, at the time of doing it, by reason of unsoundness of mind, is incapable of knowing the nature of the act, or that he is doing what is either wrong or contrary to law. [Indian Penal Code 1860, s. 84].

**Until.** Up to time of. A word of limitation, used ordinarily to restrict that which precedes to what immediately follows it, and its office is to fix some point of time or some event upon the arrival or occurrence of which what precedes will cease to exist. [*Empire Oil and Refining Co.* v *Babson* 77 P 2d 682, 684].

The word 'until' is ambiguous and may be construed either inclusive or exclusive of the day mentioned, according to the subject-matter and the true intent of the document in which it is used. [*Bellhouse* v *Mellor* (1894)3 H&N 116].

No doubt, the expression is equivocal, but there are many cases in which, where the limit is from one day to another, the last day is included. [*Isaacs* v *Royal Insurance Co*. 1870 LR 5 Exch 295, 301].

The word 'until' has both an inclusive and an exclusive meaning according to the context. [*Rajaram* v *R.P. Samarth* AIR 1956 Nag 278].

The word 'until' refers to a condition precedent. [*Krishnan* v *Secretary, Regional Transport Authority* AIR 1956 AP 129].

**Until further orders.** The expression "until further orders" suggest an indefinite period. [*K.C. Joshi* v *Union of India* AIR 1985 SC 1046: (1985)3 SCR 869: 1985(2) SLR 204: (1985)3 SCC 153].

**Unwholesome.** Deleterious to physical or mental health; unsound in quality or condition; diseased or decayed; impaired in health; sickly in appearance; penicious; unhealthy; insalubrious.

The word 'unwholesome' when used in relation to an article of food means that the article is harmful to health or repugnant to human use. [Prevention of Food Adulteration Act 1954, s. 2(*xv*)].

**Unwilling.** Reluctant; averse; not willing.

> NOTE: The word in an agreement for sale enabling a vendor to rescind the contract if he should be unable or unwilling to answer purchaser's requirements should not be construed as giving in arbitrary power to the vendor to annul the contract. He must be reasonably unwilling. [*Woolcott* v *Peggie* 15 App Cas 42: 59 LJPC 44]. Under such a clause the vendor cannot avoid answering reasonable requisitions and exercise the right of rescission. [*Lakhmidas* v *Dorab Tata* 51 Bom 247: AIR 1927 Bom 195].

**Up to.** The words 'up to' may include the last day or may not, and if it is in consonance with justice to interpret it in one of the ways' permissible, there can be no complaint. [*Musharaf Husain* v *Munawar Ali Khan* AIR 1940 Lah 7].

**Upanayana.** The ceremony of investiture of sacred thread to the youths of the twice-born class among the Hindus.

**Upanishad.** The Sruti comprises the four Vedas, the six Vedangas, and the Panishads. The Upanishads embody the highest principles of the Hindu religion. About the Upanishads, the German philosopher Schopenhauer says: "In the whole world, there is no study so beneficial and so elevating as that of the Upanishads. It has been the solace of my life, it will be the solace of my death." The Upanishads deal with theology and the means whereby a person may attain *moksha* or liberation of the soul from the necessity of repeated births and deaths, and its restoration to its original State of Existence, Knowledge and Beatitude.

**Upset price.** The minimum price declared for any property to be sold at auction or public sale; reserved price.

**Urdu.** A dialect prevalent in north-western part of India.

**Urgency.** Urgency according to dictionary means immediate, very important, that which requires immediate attention. Its applicability has to vary. [*Jai Gurudev Dharma Pracharak Sangha* v *State of U.P.* AIR 1985 All 158].

> NOTE: *Urgency and emergency—distinction.* There is not much difference between the words 'urgency' and 'emergency', 'urgency' relates to a situation demanding prompt action, while 'emergency' indicates a situation suddenly arising and demanding prompt action, 'emergency' is a stronger word than 'urgency'. [*Arjan Singh* v *State of Punjab* ILR (1958) Punj 1451: AIR 1959 Punj 538].

**Usage.** Usual or uniform or customary practice or procedure or course of conduct for a long time.

A reasonable and lawful public custom in a locality concerning particular transactions which is either known to the parties, or so well established, general, and uniform that they must be presumed to have acted with reference thereto. Practice in fact. [*Electrical Research Products* v *Gross* CCA Alaska, 120 F 2d 301, 305].

Uniform practice or course of conduct followed in certain lines of business or professions or some procedure or phase thereof. [*Turner* v *Donovan* 39 P 2d 858, 859].

Habitual or customary practice which prevails within geographical or sociological area, and is course of conduct based upon series of actual occurrences, and in order to be controlling upon parties to contract, it must be adopted by them, or be well known to parties or to persons in their circumstances. [*Sam Levitz Furniture Co.* v *Safeway Stores* Inc, 457 P 2d 938, 941].

"Usage" is that which is known as a recurring modern practice in a locality or business; and does not require a prescription, as a custom does. [*Finch's* case 6 Rep 65].

Usage may be broadly defined as a particular course of dealing or line of conduct generally adopted by persons engaged in a particular department of business life, or more fully as a particular course of dealing or line of conduct which has acquired such notoriety, that where persons enter into contractual relationships, in matters respecting the particular branch of business life where the usage is alleged to exist, those persons must be taken to have intended to follow that course of dealing or line of conduct, unless they have expressly or impliedly stipulated to the contrary; that is to say that a rule of conduct amounts to a usage, if so generally known in the particular department of business life in which the case occurs, that, unless expressly or impliedly excluded, it must be considered as forming part of the contract. Usage in this sense must be distinguished from user or enjoyment in relation to incorporeal rights, and from the course of conduct of the persons interested under a particular ancient charter or other ancient document. In this last sense it is limited to the conduct of persons actually affected by the document in question, and may be referred to only for the purpose of showing the meaning of expressions which by reason of their antiquity have become obscure. [Halsbury's *Laws of England*, 3rd Ed., vol. 11, p. 182].

NOTE: "There may be a usage in one place varying from that which prevails in another. Where the usage is general, and prevails to such an extent that a party contracting with a wharfinger must be supposed conusant of it, then he will be bound by the terms of that usage. But then it should be generally known to prevail at that place." [*Holderness* v *Collinson* (1827)7 B & C 212, 216, *per* Bayley, J.].

▸ *Meaning under the Hindu Succession Act 1956, s. 3(d).* 'Usage' signifies any rule which, having been continuously and uniformly observed for a long time, has obtained the force of law among Hindus in any local area, tribe, community, group or family: Provided that the rule is certain and not unreasonable or opposed to public policy; and provided further that in the case of a rule applicable only to a family it has not been discontinued by the family.

NOTE: A usage must be established; that is, it must be known, certain, uniform, reasonable and not contrary to law; but it may be of very recent origin. [*Nallamotu Sivaramabrahman* v *Vanipurapu* AIR 1957 AP 181].


- **General usage** p. 385.
- **Immemorial usage** p. 429.
- **Local usage** p. 541.


**Use.** Act of employing everything, or state of being employed; a purpose, object or end for useful or advantageous nature [*Brown* v *Kennedy* Ohio App, 49 NE 2d 417, 418]; to put or bring into action or service; to employ for or apply to a given purpose [*Beggs* v *Texas Dept. of Mental Health and Mental Retardation* Tex Civ App, 496 SW 2d 252, 254]; to avail oneself of; to put into action or service, especially to attain an end. [*State* v *Howard* 557 P 2d 1280, 1281].

The first meaning assigned to the word 'use' in Johnson's *Dictionary* is 'to employ to any purpose'; it is, therefore, a word of wide signification. [*British Motor Syndicate, Ltd.* v *Taylor & Son* (1900)1 Ch 577, 583, *per* Stirling, J.].

"'Use' is not a word of precise meaning, but in general it conveys the idea of enjoyment derived by the user from the corpus of the object enjoyed." [*Arbuckle Smith & Co., Ltd.* v *Greenock Corpn.* (1960)1 All ER 568, 574 (HL), *per* Lord Radcliffe].

'Use' suggests something done positively. [*State of Uttar Pradesh* v *Ramagya Sharma* (1965)2 SCR 161: AIR 1966 SC 78: (1966)2 SCJ 220].

• **Adapted for use** p. 37.

**Use and occupancy insurance.** This is an insurance providing an indemnity to traders against losses by interruption of business after fires etc.

**User.** Actual mode of enjoyment of right or possession of any property.

In ordinary sense, 'user' means the act of using. [*Nallamotu Sivaramabrahman* v *Vanipurapu* AIR 1967 AP 181].

• **Immemorial user** p. 430.

**Usual covenants.** Covenants which are usually to be found in deeds of similar nature.

> NOTE: The usual covenants by the lessee in a lease are—to pay rent; to pay taxes, except such as are expressly payable by landlord; to keep and deliver up the premises in repair; to allow the lessor to enter and view the state of repair. The usual covenant by the lessor is a qualified covenant for quiet enjoyment. A covenant by the lessee that he would not, without the lessor's consent, 'assign, underlet or part with the possession of the demised premises but such consent not to be withheld to a respectable and responsible tenant' is not a usual covenant. [*Bishop* v *Taylor & Co.* (1891)60 LJQB 556].

**Usufruct.** In the civil law, the right of enjoying a thing, the property of which is vested in another, and to draw from the same all the profit, utility, and advantage which it may produce, provided it be without altering the substance of the thing.

Under Greek Law, a right attached to the person which may not be inherited. [*New England Trust Co.* v *Wood* 93 NE 2d 547, 549].

**Usufructuary mortgage.** Where the mortgagor delivers possession or expressly or by implication binds himself to deliver possession of the mortgaged property to the mortgagee, and authorises him to retain possession until payment of the mortgage-money and to receive the rents and profits accruing from the property or any part of such rents and profits and to appropriate the same in lieu of interest, or in payment of the mortgage-money, or partly in lieu of interest or partly in payment of the mortgage-money, the transaction is called a usufructuary mortgage and the mortgagee an usufructuary mortgagee. [Transfer of Property Act 1882, s. 58(*d*)].

**Usurper.** One who disturbs a man in his right and possession, etc.; one who uses that which is not one's own.

A usurper of franchise is a person who uses a franchise even though he has no right to it.

**Usury.** An unconscionable or exorbitant rate of interest upon money lent or due.

**Ut res magis valeat quam pereat.** It is better for a thing to have effect than to be made void.

**Utbandi.** A tenancy of agricultural land for a short period formerly prevalent in some parts of West Bengal.

**Uterine blood.** Two persons are said to be related to each other by uterine blood when they are descended from a common ancestress but by different husbands. [Hindu Marriage Act 1955, s. 3(*d*); Hindu Succession Act 1956, s, 3(*e*)].

**Utility, marginal.** This is the additional utility which a person enjoys through acquiring one additional unit of any article or service, or according to some economists the utility or importance to the buyer of the least important or marginal part of his current consumption of any commodity.

**Utsarga.** Giving up the ownership of a thing for the benefit of all. [*Commissioner of Income Tax, New Delhi* v *Federation of Indian Chambers of Commerce and Industries, New Delhi* AIR 1981 SC 1408: (1981)3 SCR 489: (1981)130 ITR 186: (1981)3 SCC 156: (1982)2 Comp LJ 451].

**Utter.** To pass off, or to attempt to pass off as genuine a document, die, seal, etc., or counterfeit coin, when it is known to be forged.

A person who knowingly offers counterfeit coin for the purpose of putting it in circulation is guilty of uttering, whether it is accepted or not by the person to whom it is offered. [Halsbury's *Laws of England*, 3rd Ed., vol. 10, p. 647].

# Vv

**Vacancy.** An unoccupied or unfilled post, position, or office; an existing office without an incumbent.

'Vacancy' means an unoccupied post or office. [*R.K. Sabharwal* v *State of Punjab* AIR 1995 SC 1371: (1995)2 SCC 745].

In relation to a post means, *inter alia*, not filled or occupied, devoid of an occupant. In Anderson's *Dictionary of Law*, it is stated thus: 'Vacancy is the state of being empty ... An old office is vacated by death, resignation or renewal. An office newly created is *ipso facto* vacant at creation'. *Shorter Oxford English Dictionary* puts it thus: 'The state or condition of being unoccupied, absence of occupation; unoccupied period or interval; the fact or condition of an office or post being, becoming or falling vacant; a vacant or unoccupied office, post or dignity'. [*Ramchandra Misra* v *Addl. Director of Public Insruction* (1979)47 Cut LT 306 (DB)].

**Vacant.** Bare; blank; empty; not in use; unoccupied; unpossessed; uninhibited; untenanted; unfilled; open; deprived of contents; without inanimate objects; absolutely free. It implies entire abandonment, nonoccupancy for any purpose. [*Foley* v *Sonoma County Farmers' Mut. Fire Ins. Co. of Sonoma* Cal App, 108 P 2d 939, 942].

In landlord-tenant relationship, it means that the tenant should have ceased occupying the accommodation with the intention of not coming back to it again. [*Mahabir Prasad* v *Kewal Krishna* AIR 1953 All 441].

**Vacate.** To annul; to set aside; to cancel or rescind; to render an act void; to put an end to; to move out; to make vacant or empty; to leave; to cease from occupancy.

Vacatc, normally means to go away, to leave. [*Surinder Singh Sibia* v *Vijay Kumar Sood* (1992)1 SCC 70: AIR 1992 SC 1540].

**Vacation.** A recess or leave of absence; a respite or time of respite from active duty or employment; an intermission or rest period during which activity or work is suspended.

It is a period of freedom from duty or work, but not the end of employment. [*In re Dauber* 30 A 2d 214, 216].

**Vacation bench.** A judge or judges of court sitting or holding court during long vacations for disposal of urgent matters.

**Vadium mortuum.** A deed pledge; a mortgage.

**Vagabond.** A vagrant or homeless wanderer without means of honest livelihood. [*Neering* v *Illinois Cent. R. Co.* 50 NE 2d 497, 502].

One who wanders from place to place, having no fixed dwelling, or, if he has one, not abiding in it; a wanderer, especially such who is lazy and generally worthless and without means of honest livelihood.

**Vagrancy.** The act of going about from place to place by a person without visible means of support, who is idle, and who, though able to work for his or her maintenance, refuses to do so, but lives on the charity of others.

"Vagrancy" involves some element of preying upon the public, of maintenance by begging or in some disreputable way. [*R.* v *Heffer* (1969)71 WWR 615].

NOTE: Three ingredients constitute *vagrancy*, namely (1) wandering abroad; (2) lack of means of support; and (3) failure to justify one's presence in the place where found. [*R.* v *Heffer* (1969)71 WWR 615].

**Vagrant.** Wandering or going about from place to place by an idle person who has no lawful or visible means of support and who subsists on charity and does not work, though able to do so [*State* v *Harlowe* 24 P 2d 610]; one who is apt to become a public charge through his own laziness. [*People, on Complaint of McDonough* v *Gesino* Sp Sess, 22 NYS 2d 284, 285].

**Vague.** Imprecise; ambiguous; amorphous; indistinct; uncertain; indefinite, not susceptible of being understood; cloudy; dubious; inexplicit; intangible; perplexing; unclear; undefined.

NOTE: Vagueness is a relative term, and varies according to the circumstances of each case. [*Mohd. Yousuf Rather* v *State of Jammu and Kashmir* AIR 1979 SC 1925: (1979)4 SCC 370: 1979 SCC (Cri) 999: (1980)1 SCR 258].

**Vairagi.** A religious mendicant who has abandoned all worldly pleasures for the worship of Vishnu.

**Vaishnavas.** The followers of Ramanuja are known by the name of Vaishnavas. [*Commissioners, Hindu Religious Endowments, Madras* v *Sri Lashmindra Tirtha Swamiar* 1954 SCR 1005: 1954 SCJ 335: AIR 1954 SC 282].

**Vakalatnama.** An authority in writing by a litigant to his lawyer.

An authority given in writing to a vakil to plead in a particular proceeding ... 'A vakalatnama' may be general. It may specifically confer wide authority upon the lawyer including the authority to compromise and to receive payment. [*Sir Mohammad Yusuf* v *D* AIR 1968 Bom 112].

**Valuable consideration.** Consideration that is adequate to support the bargained for exchange between the parties. [Black's *Law dictionary*, 8th Ed.].

A class of consideration upon which a promise may be founded, which entitles the promisee to enforce his claim against an unwilling promisor.

NOTE: A gain or loss to either party is not essential, it is sufficient if the party in whose favour the contract is made parts with a right which he might otherwise exert. [*Miller Ice Co.* v *Crim* 20 NE 2d 347].

A valuable consideration may be money or money's worth; and in this connection 'valuable' means real, as distinguished from a consideration that is merely illusory or nominal; but it does not mean equivalent. A debt not yet payable may be a valuable consideration. [*Davies* v *Bolton* (1894)3 Ch 678: 63 LJ Ch 743; Stroud's *Judicial Dictionary*, 5th Ed.].

"A valuable consideration in the sense of the law may consist either in some right, interest, profit or benefit accruing to one party, or some forbearance, detriment loss, or responsibility, given, suffered or undertaken by the other". [*Chidambara Iyer* v *P.S. Renga Iyer* AIR 1966 SC 193: (1966)1 SCR 168 quoting *Currie* v *Misa* (1875) LR 10 Ex 162].

The transfer in favour of a charity in discharge of the earlier obligation is a transfer for valuable consideration. Where a charity agreed as a consideration for the transfer of the mortgage interest not to enforce its right to recover that amount from the family and the charity gave up that right in consideration of the mortgage interest acquired by it, the transfer was for a valuable consideration. [*Chidambara Iyer* v *P.S. Renga Iyer* AIR 1966 SC 193: (1966)1 SCR 168].

**Valuable security.** 'Valuable security' denotes a document which is, or purports to be, a document whereby any legal right is created, extended, transferred, restricted, extinguished or released, or whereby any person acknowledges that he lies under legal liability, or has not a certain legal right. [Indian Penal Code 1860, s. 30].

NOTE: An 'order of assessment' is a 'valuable security'. [*Ishwarlal* v *State of Maharashtra* AIR 1969 SC 40: 1969 Cr LJ 271: (1969)1 SCWR 394: (1969)1 SCJ 16]. A certificate found to have been forged to get admission in a college cannot be described as 'valuable security'. [*Bhausaheb Kalu Patil* v *State of Maharashtra* (1980)4 SCC 551: 1980 Cr LJ 1312].

**Valuation.** An estimation or determination of the money value of any property or thing;

the act of ascertaining the worth of a thing; the estimated worth of a thing.

The word 'valuation' in itself and without more, means merely the estimation of a thing's worth, the price set on a thing; it does not connote that the estimation of the worth of the thing or the price set on the thing is necessarily the estimation or setting of some particular person independent of the owner of the thing and its proposed purchaser and ..., it may mean no more than the estimation of the thing's worth in the opinion of reasonable people, the fair value of a thing in the particular circumstances of the case. [*Wenning* v *Robinson* (1964-65) NSWR 614, 624, *per* Asprey, J.].

The expression 'valuation' interpreted in the ordinary meaning of 'appraisement' cannot be said to necessarily include within its ambit the question of category which is a matter of law. The question of determination of valuation or appraisement only arises after it is settled in what class or category it falls. [*Nemi Chand* v *The Edward Mills Co. Ltd.* AIR 1953 SC 28].

**Value.** The estimated or appraised worth of any object or property, calculated in money; the monetary worth or price of something; the amount of goods, services, or money that something will command in an exchange.

To estimate the worth of; to rate at a certain price; to appraise or to place a certain estimate of worth on in a scale of values. [*Hoard* v *Wiley* 147 SE 2d 782, 784].

It may also mean the significance, desirability or utility of something.

• **Annual letting value** p. 63.
• **Annual value** p. 63.
• **Book value** p. 109.
• **Capitalised value** p. 123.
• **Face value** p. 336.
• **For value received** p. 362.
• **Insurable value.** p. 468.
• **Market value** p. 564.
• **Net asset value** p. 606.
• **Tariff value** p. 829.

**Value of assets.** Value of assets in relation to an undertaking means the value of its assets as shown in its books of account after making provision for depreciation or for renewals, or diminution in value. [Monopolies and Restrictive Trade Practices Act 1969, s. 2(*w*) (since *omitted*). The Act is repealed and replaced by the Competition Act 2002. No such term is defined under the new Act].

**Valued policy.** An insurance policy in which the sum to be paid when a loss occurs is fixed by the terms of the contract; one in which the value of the thing is settled by agreement between the parties and inserted in the policy.

**Valuer.** The terms "valuer" and "appraiser" have largely the same meaning, namely a person who sets a price upon, or who estimates the worth or the value, of property. [Halsbury's *Laws of England*, 3rd Ed., vol. 39, pp. 1, 4].

**Variance.** Difference opinion; dispute; disagreement; lack of harmony; dissension; discord; a difference or disparity between two statements or documents that ought to agree.

In criminal procedure, a difference between the allegations in a charging instrument and the proof actually introduced at trial.

**Vastu.** Residential house; site of a dwelling house.

**VAT.** Value added tax. A tax assessed at each step in the production of a commodity, based on the value added at each step by the difference between the commodity's production cost and its selling price.

> NOTE: It is very popular in several European countries and effectively acts as a sales tax on the ultimate consumer. It has been introduced in India since 1st April 2005.

**Veda.** The most authoritative scripture of the Hindus. They are four in number, the *Rigveda*, the *Samaveda*, the *Yajurveda* and the *Atharvaveda*.

The four vedas have four *Mahavakyas*. Those four statements emphasize the one fundamental truth namely that man has the capacity to rise beyond the present position, to surpass himself, to fulfill himself.

Vedas pave the way to God-realisation. [*Kamala* v *Authorised Officer, Land Reforms* AIR 1985 Mad 163].

**Vedanta.** One of the six systems of Hindu philosophy based on Vedas, compiled by Hindu sage Vyasa.

**Vegetable.** From the botanic point of view 'vegetable' may include any plant but in common parlance, it is understood as referring to edible plants or parts of edible plants. [*Saraswati Sugar Mills* v *Haryana State Board* (1992)1 SCC 418: AIR 1992 SC 224].

The word "vegetables", being a word of everyday use must be construed not in any technical sense, not from any botanical point of view, but as understood in common parlance, and must be given its popular sense meaning. So construed, it denotes those classes of vegetables which are grown in a kitchen garden or in a farm and are used for the table. [*State of West Bengal* v *Washi Ahmed* AIR 1977 SC 1638: (1977)3 SCR 149: (1977)2 SCC 246: (1977)39 STC 378; *Mangulu Sahu Ramahari Sahu* v *The Sales Tax Officer, Ganjam* (1972)4 SCC 423: (1973)32 STC 494: AIR 1974 SC 390; *Motipur Zamindari Co.* v *State of Bihar* AIR 1962 SC 660: 1962 Supp (1) SCR 498: (1962)2 SCJ 288: (1962)13 STC 1; *Porritts and Specer (Asia) Ltd.* v *State of Haryana* (1978)42 STC 433; AIR 1979 SC 300: (1979)1 SCR 545: (1979)1 SCC 82; *Ram Bux Chaturbhuj* v *State of Rajasthan* (1961)12 STC 330: AIR 1963 SC 351].

NOTE: *Vegetable—what is not—example*:

- Pan (betel leaves) is not vegetable. [*Ram Bux Chaturbhuj* v *State of Rajasthan* (1961)12 STC 330: AIR 1963 SC 351].
- Sugarcane does not fall within the word 'vegetable'. [*Motipur Zamindary Co.* v *State of Bihar* AIR 1962 SC 660: 1962 Supp (1) SCR 498: (1962)2 SCJ 288: (1962)13 STC 1].

*Vegetable—what is—example*:

- Both chillies and lemons are grown in kitchen gardens or at any rate in farms and they are used for the tables. Hence, they were held to be 'vegetables'. [*Mangulu Sahu Ramahari Sahu* v *The Sales Tax Officer, Ganjam* (1972)4 SCC 423: (1973)32 STC 494: AIR 1974 SC 390].
- Green ginger is a vegetable grown in a kitchen garden or in a farm and is used for the table though not as a principal item of the meal, certainly as a subsidiary item. It is an item which is ordinarily sold by a vegetable vendor and both the vegetable vendor who daily deals in vegetables and the housewife who daily purchases them, would unhesitatingly regard green ginger as a vegetable. [*State of West Bengal* v *Washi Ahmed* AIR 1977 SC 1638: (1977)3 SCR 149: (1977)2 SCC 246: (1977)39 STC 378].

**Vehicle.** Something used as an instrument of conveyance; any conveyance used in transporting passengers or things by land, water or air. [Black's *Law Dictionary*, 8th Ed.].

▸ *Meaning under the Customs Act 1962, s. 2(42).* Conveyance of any kind used on land and includes a railway vehicle.

▸ *Meaning under the Cantonments Act 1924, s. 2(xxxviii).* Vehicle means a wheeled conveyance of any description which is capable of being used on a street, and includes a motor car, motor lorry, motor omnibus, cart, locomotive, tramcar, handcart, truck, motor cycle, bicycle, tricycle and rickshaw.

NOTE: A trailer cannot appropriately be described as a vehicle. [*British Oxygen Co. Ltd.* v *Board of Trade* (1968)2 All ER 177]. A trailer is a vehicle. [*Dixon* v *B.R.S. (Pickfords) Ltd.* (1959)1 All ER 449].

In the absence of any express exclusion, the word "vehicle" can be read to include boat. [*Mohanlal* v *State* AIR 1978 Cal 12].


- **Articulated vehicle** p. 76.
- **Heavy goods vehicle** p. 410.
- **Light motor vehicle** p. 535.
- **Private service vehicle** p. 687.
- **Public service vehicle** p. 715.
- **Transport vehicle** p. 853.


**Vein.** Veins are fissures or cracks in the rocks which are filled with materials of quite a different nature from the rocks in which the fissures occur. In *Encyclopaedia Britannica* 'vein' and 'seam' appear to have the same meanings. 'Seam' is defined in

Webster's *Dictionary* as a thin layer or stratum, *e.g.*, a seam of coal.

**Velocity of circulation of money.** The frequency with which money and credit are transferred from the ownership of one party to another.

**Vendee.** A person to whom anything is sold; a buyer.

**Vendor.** One who sells any property, especially immovable property or interest therein; a seller.

**Vendor's lien.** A seller's lien on land as security for the purchase price.

An equitable security which arises from the fact that a vendee has received from his vendor property for which he has not paid the full consideration, and such lien exists independently of any express agreement. [*Sturdy* v *Smith* Mo App, 132 SW 2d 1033, 1037; *Causer* v *Wilmoth* Mo App, 142 SW 2d 777, 779].

NOTE: This lien may be foreclosed in the same way as a mortgage. The buyer usually has a redemption period within which he is to pay the full purchase price.

An unpaid vendor or seller in possession of the goods is entitled to retain them until payment in three cases—(*i*) where they are sold without stipulation as to credit; (*ii*) where the term of the credit has expired; and (*iii*) where the buyer becomes insolvent. [Sale of Goods Act 1930, s. 48]. The vendor, however, loses his lien where the goods are delivered to a carrier and the buyer obtains possession of them. [Sale of Goods Act, s. 49].

**Veneral disease.** See SEXUALLY TRANSMITTED DISEASE p. 791.

**Venture.** An undertaking that involves risk; risky undertaking; speculation.

• **Joint venture** p. 488.

**Venue.** Loosely, it means the place where a meeting or conference is being held.

In legal parlance, the word is used to denote the proper or a possible place for a lawsuit to proceed, usually because the place has some connection either with the events that gave rise to the lawsuit or with the plaintiff or defendant; the territory over which a trial court has jurisdiction.

NOTE: The Indian law as to the venue of inquiries and trials is to be found in ss. 177 to 189 of the Code of Criminal Procedure 1973. Section 177 provides that every offence shall ordinarily be inquired into and tried by a court within whose local jurisdiction it was committed. Section 177, in fact, adopts the Common Law of England that crimes are local and justiciable only by the local courts within whose jurisdiction they are committed. [*Md. Yusufuddin* v *Queen Empress* 25 Cal 20 PC]. Where a person is accused of the commission of any offence, and of any consequence which has ensued, such offence may be tried by the court within the local limits of whose jurisdiction the act amounting to offence has been done or the consequence of that act has ensued. [Cr. P.C. 1973, s. 179]. Where an offence is committed partly in one local area and partly in another, or where an offence is a continuing one and continues to be committed in more local areas than one, or where the offence consists of several acts done in different local areas, the offence may be tried by a court having jurisdiction over any of such local areas. [*Ibid*, s. 178].

*Venue and jurisdiction—distinction.* Venue does not refer to jurisdiction at all. [*Arganbright* v *Good* 116 P 2d 186]. "Jurisdiction" of the court means the inherent power to decide a case, whereas "venue" designates the particular territory in which a court with jurisdiction may hear and determine the case. [*Stanton Trust and Savings Bank* v *Johnson* 65 P 2d 1188, 1189]. As such, while a defect in venue may be waived by the parties, lack of jurisdiction may not. It has been held that venue has relation to convenience of litigants and may be waived or laid by consent of parties. [*Iselin* v *La Coste* CCA La, 147 F 2d 791, 795].

**Verbatim et literatim.** Word for word and letter for letter.

**Verdict.** Adjudication; answer; conclusion; decision; definitive answer; determination; finding; judgment; opinion; ruling; sentence.

It originates from the Latin "veredictum", which means a true declaration. [*Clark* v *State* 97 SW 2d 644, 646].

In a non-jury trial, it means a judge's resolution of the issues of a case.

In a jury trial, it means the definitive answer given by the jury to the court concerning the matters of fact committed to the jury for their deliberation and determination. [*Ralston* v *Stump* 62 NE 2d 293, 294].

• **Perverse verdict** p. 662.

**Verification.** Confirmation of correctness, truth, or authenticity, by affidavit, oath or deposition.

> NOTE: Object of verification is to assure good faith in averments or statements of party. [*Sheeley* v *City of Santa Clara* 215 Cal App 2d 83].
>
> Save as otherwise provided by any law for the time being in force, every pleading shall be verified at the foot by the party or by one of the parties pleading or by some other person proved to the satisfaction of the court to be acquainted with the facts of the case. The person verifying shall specify, by reference to the numbered paragraphs of the pleading, what he verifies of his own knowledge and what he verifies upon information received and believed to be true. The verification shall be signed by the person making it and shall state the date on which and the place at which it was signed. [Code of Civil Procedure 1908, Or. 6, r. 15].

**Versus.** Against. Abbreviated to v.

**Vertical integration.** Of an industry or a group of companies, it means that specialisation is undertaken at successive stages of production.

**Vessel.** A ship, brig, sloop, or other craft used or capable of being used to navigate on water. [Black's *Law Dictionary*, 8th Ed.].

To qualify as a vessel under the Jones Act, the structure's purpose must to some reasonable degree be to transport passengers, cargo, or equipment from place to place across navigable waters. [Black's *Law Dictionary*, 8th Ed.].

▸ *Meaning under the General Clauses Act 1897, s. 3(63)*. 'Vessel' shall include any ship or boat or any other description of vessel used in navigation.

▸ *Meaning under the Sea Customs Act 1878, s. 3(f); Indian Penal Code 1860, s. 48; Indian Ports Act 1908, s. 3(7)*. 'Vessel' includes anything made for the conveyance by water of human beings or property.

▸ *Meaning under the Major Port Trusts Act 1963, s. 2(z)*. 'Vessel' includes a caisson.

▸ *Meaning under the Merchant Shipping Act 1958, s. 3(55)*. 'Vessel' includes any ship, boat, sailing vessel or other description of vessel used in navigation.

The term "vessel", in admiralty law, is not limited to ships or vessels engaged in commerce. [*St. Hilaire Moye* v *Henderson* CA Ark, 496 F 2d 973, 979]. Many special purpose craft, such as dredges, floating derricks and barges equipped for special purposes or operations are also "vessels". [*Hill* v *Diamond* CA Va, 311 F 2d 789, 791, 792].

Vessel includes boats of every description, both mechanically propelled and those propelled exclusively by oars. [*Panduranga Timbil Industries* v *Union of India* AIR 1992 SC 1194: (1992)2 SCC 635: JT 1992(2) SC 277: 1992 AIR SCW 1158].

> NOTE: Everything, however, that floats is not necessarily a "vessel". For example, a floating dry dock moored by chains and cables to shipyard dock is not a "vessel". [*Keller* v *Dravo Corp*. CA La, 441 F 2d 1239, 1244].

• **Fishing vessel** p. 357.
• **Foreign vessel** p. 366.
• **Seaworthy vessel** p. 780.

**Vest.** Bestow upon; clothe; confer; consign; empower; authorise; endow; entrust; give authority; put in possession; establish.

To give an immediate, fixed right of present or future enjoyment. [*Baldwin* v *Fleck* Tex Civ App, 168 SW 2d 904, 909].

To confer ownership (of property) upon a person; to invest (a person) with the full title to property; to put (a person) into possession of land by the ceremony of investiture. [Black's *Law Dictionary*, 8th Ed.].

> NOTE: By long usage 'vesting' ordinarily means having obtained an absolute and indefeasible right, as contradistinguished from the not having so obtained it. But it cannot be disputed that the word vesting may mean, and often does

mean, that which is its primary etymological signification, namely, vesting in possession. [*Richardson* v *Robertson* (1862)6 LT 75, *per* Lord Granworth].

The word 'vest' has not got a fixed connotation, meaning in all cases that the property is owned by the person or the authority in whom it vests. It may vest in title, or it may vest in possession, or it may vest in a limited sense, as indicated in the context in which it may have been used in a particular piece of legislation. [*Fruit and Vegetable Merchants' Union* v *Delhi Improvement Trust* AIR 1957 SC 344: 1957 SCJ 167: 1957 SCA 373; *Municipal Corporation of Greater Bombay* v *Hindustan Petroleum Corporation* (2001)8 SCC 143: JT 2001(7) SC 370].

The word 'vest' has a variety of meanings. It may mean full ownership or only possession for a particular purpose or clothing the authority with power to deal with the property as agent of another person or authority. [*Fruit and Vegetable Merchants' Union* v *Delhi Improvement Trust* AIR 1957 SC 344: 1957 SCJ 167: 1957 SCA 373: 1957 SCR 1].

**Vested interest.** Indefeasible interest; an interest free from all contingencies.

An interest the right to the enjoyment of which either present or future, is not subject to the happening of a condition precedent. [Black's *Law Dictionary*, 8th Ed.].

One in which there is a present fixed right, either of present enjoyment or of future enjoyment. [*Painter* v *Herschberger* 100 SW 2d 532, 535].

▸ *Meaning under the Transfer of Property Act 1882, s. 19*. Where, on transfer of property, an interest therein is created in favour of a person without specifying the time when it is to take effect, or in terms specifying that it is to take effect forthwith, or on the happening of an event which must happen, such interest is vested, unless a contrary intention appears from the terms of the transfer.

An interest is said to be a vested interest when there is immediate right of present enjoyment or a present right for future enjoyment. A contingent interest becomes a vested interest on the happening of some event or condition. [*Usha Subbarao* v *B.E. Vishveswariah* AIR 1996 SC 2260: (1996)5 SCC 201: JT 1996(6) SC 607].

**Vested remainder.** A remainder that is given to an ascertained person and that is not subject to a condition precedent. [Black's *Law Dictionary*, 8th Ed.].

**Vested right.** A right is vested when the right to enjoyment, present or prospective, has become the property of some particular person or persons as a present interest independent of any contingency. It is a right which cannot be taken away without the consent of the owner. [*Gordhan Das* v *Governor-General* AIR 1952 Punj 103].

Interests which it is proper for state to recognise and protect and of which individual cannot be deprived arbitrarily without injustice. [*American States Water Service Co. of California* v *Johnson* 88 P 2d 770, 774].

A right complete and consummated, and of such character that it cannot be divested without the consent of the person to whom it belongs, and fixed or established, and no longer open to controversy. [*State ex rel. Milligan* v *Ritter's Estate* Ind App, 46 NE 2d 736, 743].

Rights are "vested" when right to enjoyment, present or prospective, has become property of some particular person or persons as present interest. Mere expectancy of future benefits, or contingent interest in property founded on anticipated continuance of existing laws, does not constitute vested rights. [*Bibi Sayeeda* v *State of Bihar* AIR 1996 SC 1936: (1996)9 SCC 516: JT 1996(4) SC 637].

NOTE: There is no vested right which cannot be taken away by a legislature by passing a valid law unless it is specifically prohibited by the constitutional provisions regarding legislative power. Vested right can be taken away both prospectively and retrospective so long as the legislative power is there. [*Maneka Gandhi* v *Indira Gandhi* AIR 1985 Del 114].

None has any vested right in procedure. So alteration of procedural law operates retrospectively. But alteration of law affecting vested right is generally prospective unless contrary is indicated by the statute. [*Mahadeo Prasad Singh* v *Ram Lochan* 1980 All LJ 1019: (1980)6 All LR 548: (1980)4 SCC 354]. No retrospective effect should be given to any statutory provision so as to impair or take away any existing right, unless the statute either expressly or by necessary implication directs that it should have such retrospective effect. [*A.A. Calton* v *Director of Education* AIR 1983 SC 1143, 1145: 1983(1) SLR 785: 1983 UJ (SC) 398: (1983)3 SCC 33].

An unborn person has no vested right under a provision which has been repealed prior to his birth. [*Maneka Gandhi* v *Indira Gandhi* AIR 1985 Del 114].

**Vesting of legacy.** If a legacy is given in general terms, without specifying the time when it is to be paid, the legatee has a vested interest in it from the day of the death of the testator, and, if he dies without having received it, it shall pass to his representatives. [Indian Succession Act 1925, s. 104].

**Vesting order.** An order of a court under which property passes as effectually as it would under a conveyance; a court order passing legal title in lieu of a legal conveyance.

**Vicarious liability.** Indirect legal responsibility.

Liability that a supervisory party (such as an employer) bears for the actionable conduct of a subordinate or associate (such as an employee) based on the relationship between the two parties. [Black's *Law Dictionary*, 8th Ed.].

Liability of the master for the acts of the servant or agent done in the course of his employment.

NOTE: The vicarious liability of the master does not depend on the lawful or unlawful nature of the acts of the servant and the master would be liable for the alleged act of the servant which had taken place in the course of his employment even though the servant may have acted in contravention of some of the provisions of the statute or the rules made thereunder. A master is liable for his servant's fraud perpetrated in the course of master's business, whether the fraud was for the master's benefit or not, if it was committed by the servant in the course of his employment. [*Pirthi Singh* v *Binda Ram* AIR 1987 Punj 56 (FB)].

**Vice.** As noun means a moral failing, blemish or taint; an ethical fault; an immoral habit or trait; immoral conduct, practice or habit; wickedness; corruption; a fault, defect, or imperfection.

As adjective means in the place or stead; substitution for.

**Vice mea.** In my place.

**Vice versa.** Conversely; in inverted order; in reverse manner.

**Vicinity.** Quality or state of being near, or not remote; nearness; propinquity; proximity; a region about, near or adjacent; adjoining space or country. [*Casper* v *City and County of San Francisco* 57 P 2d 920, 922].

'Vicinity' ordinarily means neighbourhood of a place, but different from the place itself. [*Taher Husain* v *State* AIR 1955 Cal 513: 59 CWN 999: 1955 Cr LJ 1336 (DB)].

The word 'vicinity' is a term of relative import and in the absence of the specific statutory significance attaching to it, it must be understood in its dictionary meaning of the neighbourhood of place different from the place itself. [*Taher Husain* v *State* AIR 1955 Cal 513: 59 CWN 999: 1955 Cr LJ 1336 (DB)].

**Victimisation.** The word "victimisation" in the context of industrial disputes is capable of two different interpretations: It connotes a person who became the victim of the employer's wrath by reason of his trade union activities; it also connotes a victim of unfair and arbitrary action. When a word has more than one interpretation, the interpretation which is in favour of the labour should be accepted as they are the poorer section of the people compared to the management. Therefore, the word "victimisation" must be given its normal meaning of being the victim of unfair and arbitrary action. [*Workmen of Williamson Magor & Co. Ltd.* v *Williamson Magor &*

*Co. Ltd.* AIR 1982 SC 78: (1982)1 SCC 117: (1982)2 SCR 42].

**Victimised.** Ordinarily a person is "victimised", if he is made a victim or a scapegoat and is subject to persecution, prosecution or punishment for no real fault or guilt of his own, in the manner, as it were, of a sacrificial victim. [*Bharat Iron Works* v *Bhagubhai Balubhai Patel* AIR 1976 SC 98: (1976)2 SCR 280: (1976)1 SCC 518].

**Vide.** See; refer to.

**Videlicet.** Namely; that is to say. Abbreviated to *viz*.

**Video.** 'Video' is the transmission and reception of a television image. In other words, it is a television image or the electric signals corresponding to it. It pertains to the picture portion of the televised programme. [*Collector of Central Excise* v *Fusebase Eltoto Ltd*. JT 1993(4) SC 280: (1993)67 ELT 30: AIR 1994 SC 1289: 1994 AIR SCW 703].

**Video camera.** A camera for recording images on videotape etc. or for transmitting them to a monitor screen.

**Videoconference.** The use of television sets linked by telephone lines to enable a group of people to communicate with each other in sound and vision.

**Village.** 'Village' should be understood to mean what in vernacular is known as *mauza gaon* or *pind* and includes not only the residential portion but also the lands of the villagers residing in it. Besides the *abadi deh*, a 'village' also includes the *gora deh*, *shamlat deh* and practically all the area owned by the village community. [*State* v *Nand Lal* 1953 Cr LJ 1207: ILR (1952) Patiala 692: AIR 1952 PEPSU 103 (DB)].

The expression "village" connotes ordinarily an area occupied by a body of men mainly dependent upon agriculture or occupations subservient thereto. [*State of U.P.* v *Pradhan Sangh Kshettra Samiti* AIR 1995 SC 1512: 1995 Supp (2) SCC 305: JT 1995(3) SC 252: (1995)2 SCJ 395].

Article 243(*g*) of the Constitution of India defines 'village' to mean a village specified by the governor by public notification to be a village for the purposes of the Part IX and includes a group of villages so specified. It will be apparent from this definition of 'village' that on the one hand, it does not stick to any particular, much less the vintage concept of village *viz*. the anthropologically evolved and sociologically identifiable habitat and on the other, it gives the governor power to specify a village as he may deem fit. [*State of U.P.* v *PSK Samiti* AIR 1995 SC 1512, 1516].

**Village community.** A typical village community consists of members of one family or one clan, holding the village lands in common, and dividing between them the agricultural lands according to the custom of the village.

In a popular sense, it denotes a body of persons bound together by the tie of residence in one and the same village, amenable to village customs and subject to the administrative control of the village officers. [*Rahimuddin* v *Rewal* 30 Cal 635 (PC)].

**Violence.** The use of physical force, usually accompanied by fury, vehemence, or outrage; physical force unlawfully exercised with the intent to harm. [Black's *Law Dictionary*, 8th Ed.].

Unjust or unwarranted exercise of force, usually with the accompaniment of vehemence, outrage or fury. [*People* v *Mcllvain* 130 P 2d 131, 134].

Physical force unlawfully exercised; abuse of force; that force which is employed against common right, against the laws, and against public liberty. [*Anderson-Berney Bldg. Co.* v *Lowry* Tex Civ App, 143 SW 2d 401, 403].

Violence means 'unlawful exercise of physical force, intimidation by exhibition of this'. And violence involves 'great physical force, intense vehement passionate *furious impetus* and *vivid*'. [*Ibrahimkutty* v *State of Kerala* 1984 Ker LT 700].

NOTE: Violence in s. 146 of the Indian Penal Code is not restricted to force used against person only, but extends also to force against inanimate object. [*Sundar Singh* v *State* AIR 1955 All 232].

**Virakt.** A vaishnava inducted into the order of Ramanuja sect. He requires not to perform Shradh for self or Birajahomam to become a virakt. [*Ram Chandra* v *Baradaraj* 1983 All LJ 668: (1983)9 All LR 355].

**Viramitrodaya.** The works which supplement the Mitakshara in Western India are the Vyavahara Mayukha, and the Viramitrodaya. The Viramitrodaya was written by Mitra Misra, and follows the Mitakshara in most points. Its composition may be ascribed to the beginning of the 17th century. It is rather a Benares than a Bombay authority. Mitra Misra, the author of Viramitrodaya, is esteemed in the Benares school. The Viramitrodaya is stated by Colebrooks and others to be a treatise of high authority at Benares; it is properly receivable as an exposition of what may have been left doubtful by the Mitakshara and is declaratory of the law of the Benares School. [*Girdhari Lal* v *Bengal Government* 12 MIA 448, 466].

**Virgin.** A person, especially a woman, who has never had sexual intercourse; a maiden; a chaste young girl or unmarried woman; any female animal before its first occupation; an inexperienced or innocent person; not yet penetrated, used, or tried; undefiled; spotless.

**Virginity.** The state of being unsullied or unused or a virgin; maidenhood.

**Virulent.** "Virulent" is highly poisonous or malignant; venomous; acrimonies. [*Swarajya Lakshmi* v *Dr. G.G. Padma Rao* AIR 1974 SC 165: (1974)2 SCR 97: (1974)1 SCC 58].

The term "virulent" means malignant and infectious. [*Laxmibai* v *Hotchand* (1981)2 MPWN 165].

NOTE: Leprometous leprosy is said to be virulent. It is malignant and contagious. It is also incurable. [*Laxmibai* v *Hotchand* (1981)2 MPWN 165].

'Virulence' as a ground for exclusion from inheritance is treated from an entirely different angle in Hindu religious and legal texts. The general emphasis in those contexts was of the competence of a man to perform his social and religious obligations and no word has been used in these texts which could be referred to as the corresponding Sanskrit word for "virulent". [*Swarajya Lakshmi* v *Dr. G.G. Padma Rao* AIR 1974 SC 165: (1974)2 SCR 97: (1974)1 SCC 58].

**Vis.** Any kind of force, violence, or disturbance relating to a man's person or his property.

**Vis-a-vis.** The relationship of one of two persons or things to the other, when facing or situated opposite each other; face to face; in relation to each other.

**Vis major.** A Latin expression which means a superior force.

A greater or superior force; an irresistible or overwhelming force of nature.

A loss that results immediately from a natural cause without the intervention of man and could not have been prevented by the exercise of prudence, diligence and care. [*National Carbon Co.* v *Bankers Mortg. Co. of Topeka* CCA Kan, 77 F 2d 614, 617].

NOTE: In civil law, the term is sometimes used as synonymous with "vis divina", or the act of God.

*Vis major and force majeure—distinction.* The expression *'force majeure'* is not a mere French version of the Latin expression *'vis major'*. It is a term of wide import.

Difficulties have arisen in the past as to what would legitimately be included in a *force majeure*. Judges have agreed that strikes, breakdown of machinery, which though normally not included in *vis major* are included in *force majeure*. An analysis of rulings on the subject shows that where reference is made to *force majeure*, the intention is to save the performing party from the consequences of anything over which he has no control. [*Dhanrajmal Gobindram* v *Shamji Kalidas & Co.* (1961)3 SCR 1020: (1961)2 SCA 288: AIR 1961 SC 1283].

**Visa.** An endorsement made on a passport by the proper authorities denoting that it has been examined and that the bearer is permitted to proceed; a recognition by the country *ad quem* of the validity of the passport issued by the country *a quo*. [*U.S.* v *Vargas* DCNY, 380 F Supp 1162, 1168].

**Viscount.** A viscount is the fourth in rank of the peers; he ranks above a baron and below an earl; an old title of the sheriff.

**Vishnu.** Hindu God of protector of the universe.

**Vishnuprit.** Land granted rent-free for the worship of Vishnu.

**Viswas bai.** 'Viswas' as per common parlance is love and affection. 'Bai' is an Urdu word. It indicates a sale transaction. In other words, it means a sale as a result of good feelings amongst the parties or because of the trust, reliance or confidence that one reposes in the other. [*Gurubasappa* v *Gurulingappa* AIR 1962 Mys 24].

**Viz.** Namely; that is to say.

**Vocation.** A man's regular calling or business; one's occupation or profession.

The activity on which one spends major portion of his time and out of which he makes his living. [*Employers' Liability Assur. Corporation* v *Accident & Casualty Ins. Co. of Winterthur, Switzerland* CCA Ohio, 134 F 2d 566, 568].

'Vocation' is analogous to 'calling', a word of wide signification, meaning the way in which a man passes his life. Vocation may be lawful or unlawful. [*Partridge* v *Mallandaine* (1886)18 QBD 276: 56 LJQB 251].

**Void.** Void means nugatory, ineffectual or inoperative. [*Hari Sahu* v *Union of India* (1971)37 Cut LT 860].

'Void' in relation to a juristic act, means without legal force, effect or consequence; not binding; invalid; null; worthless; cipher; useless; and ineffectual etc. [*Nutan Kumar* v *2nd Addl. District Judge, Banda* AIR 1994 All 298 (FB)].

NOTE: There is no real difference between 'void' and 'not being valid'. If it is said that a transfer is not valid, the effect would be that it is void. [*Chandrabhan Chunnilal Gour* v *Dr. Shrawan Kumar Khunnolal Gour* AIR 1980 Bom 48].

A thing which is void is *non-est* and it is not necessary to set that aside, though it is sometimes convenient to do so. [*Suresh Chandra* v *State of W.B.* AIR 1976 Cal 110].

'Void agreements' are destitute of all legal effects and force. They are totally ineffectual rather cipher. No legally enforceable relationship, right or liability emanates therefrom. [*Nutan Kumar* v *2nd Addl. District Judge, Banda* AIR 1994 All 298 (FB)].

A contract, which ceases to be enforceable by law, becomes void, when it ceases to be enforceable. [Contract Act 1872, s. 2(*j*)].

▸ *Meaning under the Constitution of India, Art. 13.* It is well settled that the word "void" in Art. 13 means void to the extent of the inconsistency with a fundamental right and the language of the article makes it clear that the entire operation of an inconsistent Act is not wiped out. [*Bhikaji Narain Dhakras* v *State of Madhya Pradesh* AIR 1955 SC 781: (1955)2 SCR 589: 1956 SCJ 48].

**Void contract.** A void contract is one which from the beginning has no legal effect. [Halsbury's *Laws of England*, 3rd Ed., vol. 8, p. 55].

A contract, which ceases to be enforceable by law, becomes void, when it ceases to be enforceable. [Indian Contract Act 1872, s. 2(*j*)].

One which never had any legal existence or effect, and such contract cannot in any manner have life breathed into it. [*National Union Indemnity Co.* v *Bruce Bros.* 38 P 2d 648, 652].

**Voidable.** That which may be avoided or declared void; capable of being adjudged invalid, void, annulled, declared ineffectual.

That which operates to accomplish the thing sought to be accomplished, until the fatal vice in the transaction has been judicially ascertained and declared. [*Slaughter* v *Qualls* 162 SW 2d 671, 674].

The word 'voidable' means that may either be avoided or confirmed.

[*J. Rajeshwarkant Shahdev* v *Neelma Shahdev* (1981)1 MPWN 54].

**Voidable contract.** A voidable contract is one which may be either affirmed or repudiated at the option of one of the parties but not of the other. [Halsbury's *Laws of England*, 3rd Ed., vol. 8, p. 55].

An agreement which is enforceable by law at the option of one or more of the parties thereto, but not at the option of the other or others, is a voidable contract. [Indian Contract Act 1872, s. 2(*i*)].

One which is void as to wrongdoer but not void as to wronged party, unless he elects to so treat it. [*Depner* v *Joseph Zukin Blouses* 13 Cal App 2d 124].

**Voidable judgment.** One apparently valid, but in truth wanting in some material respect. [*Reynolds* v *Volunteer State Life Ins. Co.* Tex Civ App, 80 SW 2d 1087, 1092].

One rendered by a court having jurisdiction but which is irregularly and erroneously rendered. [*Tanton* v *State Nat. Bank of El Paso* Tex Civ App, 43 SW 2d 957, 960; *Gehret* v *Hetkes* Tex Com App, 36 SW 2d 700, 701; *Easterline* v *Bean* 49 SW 2d 427, 429].

**Voidable marriage.** One which is valid when entered into and which remains valid until either party secures lawful court order dissolving the marital relationship. [*Darling* v *Darling* 335 NE 2d 708, 710].

NOTE: Voidable marriage is valid marriage until annulled, though a decree of nullity passed in such a case purports to put the parties retrospectively to the position as if the marriage had been void from its inception. A voidable marriage cannot be impeached after the death of either spouse. [*Sisir Kumar Kundu* v *Sabita Rani Mondal* 75 CWN 932].

A voidable marriage subsists for all purposes till it is avoided. [*Krishna* v *Tulsan Devi* AIR 1972 Punj 305: 1972 Cur LJ 464: 74 Punj LR 561].

**Volenti non fit injuria.** The maxim *"volenti non fit injuria"* means that if one, knowing and comprehending the danger, voluntarily exposes himself to it, though not negligent in so doing, he is deemed to have assumed the risk and is precluded from a recovery for an injury resulting therefrom. [*Munson* v *Bishop Clarkson Memorial Hospital* 186 NW 2d 492, 494].

NOTE: The defence of *volenti non fit injuria* is available to an employer as it is to any other defendant sued in tort, but for the defence to succeed it must be shown not only that the employee fully understood and appreciated the risk and danger of the work, but that in carrying it out he acted as a volunteer in the strictest sense. In practice, therefore, the defence rarely succeeds where the employee is going about his usual work. The principle *volenti non fit injuria* is also a defence to an action for breach of statutory duty provided the employer is not at fault. [Halsbury's *Laws of England*, 4th Ed., vol. 16, para 719, p. 498].

**Voluntarily.** Intentionally; without coercion.

A person is said to cause an effect voluntarily when he causes it by means whereby he intended to cause it, or by means which, at the time of employing those means, he knew or had reason to believe to be likely to cause it. [Indian Penal Code 1860, s. 39]. The word is given a peculiar meaning which is different from the widely understood ordinary meaning of it. [*Abdul Majeed* v *State of Kerala* 1994 Cr LJ 1404 (Ker)].

'Voluntarily' means that the person doing an alleged thing acted of his own volition and knew the nature of his act, and did not act, in performance of a legal duty, not due to coercion, or fraud, or misrepresentation, or mistake. [*Abdul Salam* v *Union of India* AIR 1969 All 223].

Done by design or intention; unconstrained by interference; not impelled by outside influence; without valuable consideration; gratuitous. [Black's *Law Dictionary*, 8th Ed.].

**Voluntary.** Free choice; done with free will; without any compulsion, obligation or valuable consideration. Freely, without compulsion, not under any obligation. [*A-G* v *Ellis* (1895)2 QB 466: 64 LJQB 813].

'Voluntary' is constantly used in two different senses; it is constantly used as the antithesis of something done under compulsion; but it is also used commonly among lawyers—and not uncommonly among other people—as denoting the obtaining or giving of something without anything being obtained in return, *e.g.*, a voluntary conveyance. [*Savoy Overseers* v *Art Union of London* (1896) AC 296].

**Voluntary confession.** A confession given freely, without any benefit or punishment promised, threatened, or expected. [Black's *Law Dictionary*, 8th Ed.].

▸*Meaning under the Indian Evidence Act 1872, ss. 24 and 28.* A confession made by a person accused of an offence, after the impression caused by inducements, threat, or promise has been fully removed.

**Volunteer.** One who takes part in a transaction or does something with which he has no legal concern or interest; one who renders service out of his free will; one who receives a transfer of property without valuable consideration.

**Vote.** An expression of preference or choice; exercise of franchise; expression of opinion as to a contest or election; suffrage.

**Voter.** A person who has a right to vote at an election or contest.

**Voting.** "Voting" is formal expression of will or opinion by the person entitled to exercise the right on the subject or issue in question. In Black's *Law Dictionary* it is explained as, 'the expression of one's will, preference, or choice, formally manifested by a member of a legislative or deliberative body, or of a constituency or a body of qualified electors, in regard to the decision to be made by the body as a whole upon any proposed measure or proceeding or in passing laws, rules or regulations, or the selection of an officer or representative'. [*Lily Thomas Advocate* v *Speaker, Lok Sabha* (1993)4 SCC 234, 236, 237: JT 1993(4) SC 646].

**Voucher.** A document which evidences a transaction, especially a receipt for the payment of money; a written or printed authorisation to disburse money.

**Voyage.** Journey or transit by water; journey through air or space.

Voyage means the contractual voyage from the port of loading to the port of discharge as declared in the appropriate bill of lading. [*The Makedonia, Owners of Cargo Laden on Makedonia* v *Owners of Makedonia* (1962)2 All ER 614].


- **Abandonment of voyage** p. 3.
- **Continuous voyage** p. 188.
- **International voyage** p. 475.


**Voyage charter party.** A contract by charter party, says B.C. Mitra in his *Law of Carriage by Sea* is a contract by which an entire ship or some principal part thereof is let to a merchant who is called the character, for the conveyance of goods on a determined voyage to one or more places, or until the expiration of a specified period; in the former case it is called a "voyage charter party", and in the latter a 'time charterer party'. [*Union of India* v *Gosalia Shipping (Pvt.) Ltd.* AIR 1978 SC 1196: (1978)3 SCR 943: (1978)3 SCC 23: (1978)113 ITR 307].

**Voyeur.** A person who observes something without participating; esp., one who gains pleasure by secretly observing another's genitals or sexual acts.

**Voyeurism.** Gratification derived from observing the genitals or sexual acts of others, usu. secretly.

**Vritti.** Fees and presents to Brahmins for performance of Hindu religious ceremonies.

**Vyabahara Mayuk.** The works which supplement the Mitakshara in Western India are the Vyabahara Mayukh, and the Viramitrodaya. Of these the Mitakshara ranks first and paramount in Maratha Country and in Northern Kanara and Ratnagiri while in Gujarat and apparently also in the island of Bombay, the Mayukh is considered as the overwhelming authority when there is a difference of opinion. [Mayne on *Hindu Law*, 8th Ed., p. 29].

**Vyasa.** The name 'vyasa' belongs to an immortal theologian, the arranger of the

Vedas, the founder of the Vedanta philosophy, the author of the Puranas and the compiler of the Mahabharata. All that is imperishable in Sanskrit literature is comprehended under the name of Vyasa. He is a legendary figure.

There is, however, another Vyasa who is the author of a Code of Hindu law. He is much nearer our time than the author of the Mahabharata. The holy city of Benares was the place where this younger Vyasa delivered his laws to an audience of learned men who were eager to learn from him the nature of the duties and the relations of the different sections of society towards one another. He expounded the rules of conduct which all must obey if they expected freedom from cares in this life and eternal beatitude in the life to come. He concluded his lecture with these words: "He who regulates his conduct according to the laws approved by Vyasa shall never fall." [Sarvadhikari on *Hindu Law of Inheritance*, Tagore Law Lectures 1880, pp. 158-159].

# Ww

**Wa.** It is an Urdu word meaning 'or' and not 'and'. [*Gram Panchayat* v *Tara Chand* (1989)1 Cur Civ Cas 123 (Punj)].

**Wage.** Money payable by an employer to an employee in respect of services daily or at weekly intervals; the part of total production that rewards labour rather than remunerating capital.


- **Basic wage** p. 97.
- **Delayed wages** p. 244.
- **Fair wage** p. 339.
- **Living wage** p. 539.
- **Minimum wage** p. 581.


**Wagering contract.** Wager is something risked on an uncertain event; gambling; stake.

A contract by which two or more parties agree that a certain sum of money or other thing shall be paid or delivered to one of them or that they shall gain or lose on the happening of an uncertain event or upon the ascertainment of a fact in dispute, where the parties have no interest in the event except that arising from the possibility of such gain or loss. The word "wagering" is practically synonymous with the words betting and gambling, and the terms are so used in common parlance and in statutory and constitutional enactments. [*McDonald* v *Bryant* 381 SW 2d 736, 738].

A wagering contract is one by which two persons professing to hold opposite views, touching the issue of a future uncertain event, mutually agree that, dependent upon the determination of that event, one shall win from the other, and that other shall pay or hand over to him a sum of money or other stake; neither of the contracting parties having any other interest in that contract than the sum or stake he will so win or lose, there being no other real consideration for the making of such contract by either of the parties. [*Carlill* v *Carbolic Smoke Ball Co.* (1892)2 QB 484].

NOTE: Agreements by way of wager are void under s. 30 of the Indian Contract Act 1872 and no suit shall be brought for recovering anything alleged to be won on any wager, or entrusted to a person to abide the result of any game or other uncertain event on which any wager is made. However, this section shall not be deemed to render unlawful a subscription or contribution, or agreement to subscribe or contribute, made or entered into for or toward any plate, prize or sum of money, of the value or amount of five hundred rupees or upward to be awarded to the winner or winners of any horse-race.

**Wages.** Payment for labour or services, usually based on time worked or quantity produced; compensation of an employee based on time worked or output of production. [Black's *Law Dictionary*, 8th Ed.].

▸ *Meaning under the Industrial Disputes Act 1947, s. 2(rr).* The definition of the term "wages" reads as follows: "Wages" means all remuneration capable of being expressed in terms of money, which would, if the terms of employment, expressed or implied, were fulfilled, be payable to a workman in respect of his employment, or of work done in such employment, and includes—(*i*) such allowances (including dearness allowance) as the workman is for the time being entitled to; (*ii*) the value of any house accommodation, or of supply of light, water, medical attendance or other amenity or of any service or of any concessional supply of foodgrains or other articles; (*iii*) any travelling concession; (*iv*) any commission payable on the promotion of sales or business or both; but does not include—(*a*) any bonus; (*b*) any contribution paid or payable by the employer to any pension fund or provident fund or for the benefit of the workman under any law for the time being in force; (*c*) any gratuity payable on the termination of his service.

The definition of the word 'wages', as given in cl. (*rr*) of s. 2 is comprehensive enough to include such of the allowances as the workman is for the time being entitled. Yet, despite such comprehension, the inclusive meaning is subject to a meaningful change if there is anything repugnant in the subject or context. [*Bharat Electronic Ltd.* v *Industrial Tribunal, Karnataka, Bangalore* AIR 1990 SC 1080].

NOTE: Under sub-cl. (*iv*) of the above definition, "wage" includes commission payable on promotion of sales or business or both. [*Indian Bank Association* v *Workmen of Syndicate Bank* AIR 2001 SC 946: JT 2001(2) SC 542: (2001)2 SCJ 244: (2001)3 SCC 36].

The term 'wages' ought to include gratuity as well. It may be observed that since 'bonus' payable to a worker under certain circumstances becomes his wages, there is all the greater reason to include gratuity in the category of wages. [*Tirjugi Sitaram* v *Badlu Prasad Bheru Prasad* AIR 1962 MP 361].

▸ *Meaning under the Payment of Wages Act 1936, s. 2(6).* The term "wages" means all remuneration. [*Bala Subrahmanya Rajaram* v *B.C. Patil* AIR 1958 SC 518: 1958 SCR 1504: 1958 SCJ 851].

NOTE: Remuneration payable to an employee under an award or settlement amounts to "wages" within the meaning of the definition. [*Purshottam H. Judye* v *V.B. Potdar* AIR 1966 SC 856: (1966)2 SCR 353].

Section 2(6) defines "wages" to include *inter alia* any remuneration to which the person employed is entitled in respect of any leave period. [*Mangalore Ganesh Beedi Works* v *Union of India* AIR 1974 SC 1832: (1974)3 SCR 221: (1974)4 SCC 43].

▸ *Meaning under the Employees' State Insurance Act 1948, s. 2(22).* 'Wages' means all remuneration paid or payable, in cash to an employee, if the terms of the contract of employment, express or implied, were fulfilled and includes any payment to an employee in respect of any period of authorised leave, lock-out, strike which is not illegal or lay-off and other additional remuneration, if any, paid at intervals not exceeding two months but does not include—(*a*) any contribution paid by the employer to any pension fund or provident fund, or under the Employees' State Insurance Act; (*b*) any travelling allowance or the value of any travelling concession; (*c*) any sum paid to the person employed to defray special expenses entailed on him by the nature of his employment; or (*d*) any gratuity payable on discharge.

NOTE: Bonus in the nature of *ex gratia* payment payable one month after end of each quarter is not includible in "wages" since the bonus in question did not fall under any category or class mentioned in the definition of "wages" as contained in s. 2(22) of the Act. [*Regional Director, Employees' State Insurance Corporation* v *Bata Shoe Co. (P) Ltd.* 1985 Supp (3) SCR 639: (1985)4 SCC 460: AIR 1986 SC 237].

'Inam' paid or to be paid to workmen under the Inam Scheme depending on achievement of minimum target fixed is not 'wages' as defined in the Act. [*Braithwaite Co. (India) Ltd.* v *The Employees' State Insurance Corporation* AIR 1968 SC 413; *Employees' State Insurance Corporation* v *Apex Engineering Pvt. Ltd.* (1998)1 SCC 86].

▸ *Meaning under the Payment of Gratuity Act 1972, s. 2(8).* "Wages" means all emoluments which are earned by an employee while on duty or on leave in accordance with the terms and conditions of his employment and which are paid or are payable to him in cash and includes dearness allowance but does not include any bonus, commission, house rent allowance overtime wages and any other allowance. [*Ticycles of India, Ambattur* v *M.K. Gurumani* (2001)7 SCC 204: JT 2001(7) SC 73].

NOTE: The term 'wages' is not applied to the remuneration of a high or important officer of the State or a company, for instance, but to that of domestic servants, labourers or persons of a similar description. [*Gordon* v *Jennings* (1882)9 QBD 45].

Broadly speaking, wages has been classified into—(1) living wage, (2) fair wage, and (3) minimum wage. A fair wage is the demand and the destination. Its upper limit is the "living wage". The minimum wage is the lower limit of the fair wage. There are two kinds of "minimum wage"—industrial and statutory. An "industrial minimum" is a subsistence wage payable by a unit if it wishes to exist; a "statutory minimum" is something more than a subsistence level wage. Living wage should enable the male earner to provide for himself and his family not merely the bare essentials of food, clothing and shelter, but a measure of frugal comfort including education for the children, protection against ill-health, requirements of essential social needs and a measure of insurance against the more important misfortunes including old age. Fair wage is the mean between the living wage and the minimum wage. [*Express Newspapers* v *Union of India* AIR 1958 SC 578: 1958 SCJ 1113: 1958 SCA 952].

**Waging war.** The expression 'waging war' means waging war in the manner usual in war. [*Mir Hasan Khan* v *State* AIR 1951 Pat 60: 52 Cr LJ 462; Indian Penal Code 1860, s. 121].

NOTE: In order to support a conviction on a charge of waging war, it is not enough to show that the persons charged have contrived to obtain possession of an armoury and have, when called upon to surrender it, used the rifles and ammunition so obtained against the Government troops. It must further be shown that the seizure of the armoury was part and parcel of a planned operation and their intention in resisting the troops of the Government was to overwhelm and defeat the troops and then to go on and crush any further opposition with which they might meet until either the leaders of the movement succeed in obtaining possession of the machinery of the Government or until those in possession of it yielded to the demands of the leaders. [*Mir Hasan Khan* v *State*, supra].

**Waiting list.** A "waiting list" prepared in service matters is a list of eligible and qualified candidates who in order of merit are placed below the last selected candidate. How it should operate and what is its nature may be governed by the rules. [*Gujarat State Dy. Executive Engineers' Assn.* v *State of Gujarat* 1994 Supp (2) SCC 591: 1994 SCC (L&S) 1159: 1994(2) SLR 710: JT 1994(3) SC 559].

**Waive.** In its archaic use as noun, it means a woman who has by her conduct deprived herself of the protection of law; a female outlaw; a woman outlawed.

As verb, it means to abandon, renounce, surrender, or give up (a claim, privilege, right, claim) voluntarily.

**Waiver.** Waiver is an intentional relinquishment of a known right.

NOTE: There can be no waiver unless the person against whom the waiver is claimed had full knowledge of his rights and of facts enabling him to effectual action for the enforcement of such rights. [*Associated Hotels* v *Ranjit Singh* AIR 1968 SC 933].

Waiver means abandonment of a right and it may be either expressed or implied from the conduct, but its basic requirement is that it must be an intentional act with knowledge. [*Motilal Padampat Sugar Mills* v *State of U.P.* AIR 1979 SC 621: (1979)2 SCR 641].

Waiver is the abandonment of a right in such a way that the other party is entitled to plead the abandonment by way of confession and avoidance if the right is thereafter asserted, and is either express or implied from conduct. It may sometimes resemble a form of election, and sometimes be based on ordinary principles of estoppel, although, unlike estoppel, waiver must always be an intentional act with knowledge. [Halsbury's *Laws of England*, 4th Ed., vol. 16, para 1471, p. 992].

NOTE: Waiver is a word which is sometimes used loosely to describe, a number of different legal grounds on which a person may be debarred from asserting a substantive rights which he once possessed or from raising a particular defence to a claim against him which would otherwise be available to him. This arises in a situation where a person is entitled to alternative rights inconsistent with one another. If he has knowledge of the facts which give rise in law to these alternative rights and acts in a manner which is consistent only with his having chosen to rely on one of them, the law holds him to his choice even though he was unaware that this would be the legal consequence of what he did. [*Kammins Ballrooms Co. Ltd.* v *Zenith Investment* (1970)2 All ER 871].

The principle of waiver is simply this, Lord Denning says, if one party, by his conduct, leads another to believe that the strict rights arising under the contract will not be insisted on, intending that the other should act on that behalf, and he does act on it, then the first party will not afterwards be allowed to insist on the strict legal rights when it would be inequitable to do so. There may be no consideration moving from him who benefits by the waiver. There may be no detriment to him by acting on it. There may be nothing on writing. Nevertheless, the one who waives his strict legal rights cannot afterwards insist on them. His strict rights are at any rate suspended so long his waiver lasts. He may on occasion be able to revert to his strict legal rights for the future by giving reasonable notice in that behalf, or otherwise making it plain by his conduct that he will thereafter insist on them. But there are cases where no withdrawal is possible. In that event he is bound by his waiver. He will not be allowed to revert to his strict legal rights. He can only enforce them subject to the waiver. [*W.J. Alan & Co.* v *EL Nasar Export & Import Co.* (1972)2 All ER 127].

The essential element of waiver is that there must be a voluntary and intentional relinquishment of a known right or such conduct as warrants the inference of the relinquishment of such right. It means the forsaking the assertion of a right at the proper opportunity.

*Waiver and estoppel—distinction.* Waiver is distinct from estoppel in that in waiver the essential element is actual intention to abandon or surrender right. While in estoppel such intent is immaterial. The necessary condition is the detriment of the other party by the conduct of the one estopped. An estoppel may result though the party estopped did not intend to lose any existing right. Thus voluntary choice is the essence of waiver for which there must have existed an opportunity for a choice between the relinquishment and the conferment of the right in question. In estoppel such intent is immaterial. [*Pravash Ch. Dolui* v *Biswanath Bannerjee* AIR 1989 SC 1834: JT 1989 (Supp) 92: (1989)2 SCR 401: 1989 Supp (1) SCC 487].

Waiver is contractual and may constitute a cause of action; it is an agreement to release or not to assert a right. [*Satya Narayan* v *Yelloji Rao* AIR 1965 SC 1405: (1965)2 SCJ 678: 1965 SCD 1146].

The doctrine of waiver has no application to fundamental rights enshrined in the Constitution. [*Basheshar Nath* v *Commissioner of Income-tax* 1959 Supp (1) SCR 528: AIR 1959 SC 149]. Nor there cannot be any question of estoppel or ratification in a case where there is contravention of provisions of Art. 299(1), Constitution of India. [*State of Punjab* v *Om Prakash Baldev* AIR 1988 SC 2149: 1988 Rajdhani LR 531].

*Transfer of Property Act 1882—various provisions on waiver.* A forfeiture incurred by a lessee (*a*) for violating a condition, or (*b*) by denying the landlord's title, or (*c*) by being declared an insolvent, is waived by acceptance of rent due since forfeiture. [Section 112]. A notice to quit given by a person may be waived by him by an act showing an intention that the lease subsists. [Section 113]. The buyer of an immovable property may waive requisition under s. 55(1).

*Sale of Goods Act 1930—provisions on waiver.* Where a seller has to fulfil a condition before a contract of sale can be effective, the buyer may waive the condition. [Section 13(*b*)]. But there cannot be any agreement to waive an illegality since it is void on the ground of public policy. [*Dhanukdhari* v *Nathima* 11 CWN 848].

**Wajib-ul-arz.** Village administration papers recording existing rights and customs as also traditions. Statements in Wajib-ul-arz are sufficient proof of custom. [*Balgobind* v *Badri* 50 IA 196: 45 All 413].

**Wakalatnama.** Credentials, letter of authority, power of attorney. [Wilson's *Glossary*, 2nd Ed., p. 554]. A letter appointing a vakil or representative.

**Wakf.** The permanent dedication by a person professing the Mussalman faith of any property for any purpose recognised by the Mussalman law as religious, pious or charitable but does not include any wakf, such as is described in s. 3 of the

Mussalman Wakf Validating Act 1913, under which any benefit is for the time being claimable for himself by the person by whom the wakf was created or by any of his family or descendants. [Mussalman Wakf Act 1923, s. 2(*e*)].

Wakf means the permanent dedication by a person professing Islam of any movable and immovable property for any purpose recognized by the Muslim law as pious, religious or charitable and includes—(*i*) a wakf by user; (*ii*) mushrut-ul-khidmat; and (*iii*) a wakf-alal-aulad to the extent to which the property is dedicated for any purpose recognized by Muslim law as pious, religious or charitable [Wakf Act 1954, s. 3(*l*)]; and 'wakf' means any person making such dedication. [*Board of Muslim Wakfs, Rajasthan* v *Radha Kishan* AIR 1979 SC 289: (1979)2 SCR 148: (1979)2 SCC 468].

▸ *Meaning under the Wakf Act 1995, s. 3(r).* Wakf means the permanent dedication by a person professing Islam, of any movable or immovable property for any purpose recognized by the Muslim law as pious, religious or charitable and includes—(*i*) a wakf by user but such wakf shall not cease to be a wakf by reason only of the user having ceased irrespective of the period of such cesser; (*ii*) 'grants', including mashrut-ul-khidmat for any purpose recognised by the Muslim law as pious, religious or charitable; and (*iii*) a wakf-alal-aulad to the extent to which the property is dedicated for any purpose recognized by Muslim law as pious, religious or charitable.

**Wakf-alal-aulad.** A dedication by a Mahomedan by means of which the property is tied up so that the usufruct might be utilised for the benefit of the members of the family but it must ultimately go for the benefit of the poor. [*Salah* v *Husain* AIR 1955 Hyd 229].

**War.** Hostile contention by means of armed forces, carried on between nations, states, or rulers, or between citizens in the same nation or state. [*Gitlow* v *Kiely* DCNY, 44 F 2d 227, 233].

A contest by force between two or more nations, carried on for any purpose, or armed conflict of sovereign powers or declared and open hostilities, or the state of nations among whom there is an interruption of pacific relations, and a general contention by force, authorized by the sovereign. [*West* v *Palmetto State Life Ins. Co.* 25 SE 2d 475, 477, 478].

What constitutes a state of war is well described in Hall's *International Law*, 4th Ed., p. 63: "When differences between States reach a point at which both parties resort to force, or one of them does acts of violence which the other chooses to look upon as a breach of the peace, the relation of war is set up, in which the combatants may use regulated violence against each other until one of the two has been brought to accept such terms as his enemy is willing to grant". [*Driefontein Mines* v *Janson* (1900)2 QB 343].


- **Act of war** p. 31.
- **Munitions of war** p. 595.
- **Ship-of-war** p. 795.
- **Waging war** p. 889.


**War crimes.** Crimes committed by countries in violation of the international laws governing wars; a violation of the rules of warfare.

> NOTE: Examples of war crimes are the killing of hostages, abuse of civilians in occupied territories, abuse of prisoners of war, and devastation that is not justified by military necessity.

**Ward.** A person usually a minor, who is under a guardian's charge or protection; a territorial division in a city, usually defined for purposes of city government. [Black's *Law Dictionary*, 8th Ed.].

**Ward of court.** A person under the care of a guardian appointed by court; the term has been extended to infants, who are brought under the authority of the court by an application to it on their behalf, though no guardian is appointed by the court. [*Brown* v *Callins* 25 Ch D 60: 53 LJ Ch 370].

**Warehouse.** Structure used for the reception and storage of goods and merchandise.

[*Carter* v *Bauman* CCA Cal, 19 F 2d 855, 856]. The term may include any structure used to hold goods, stores or wares temporarily or for a length of time. [*In re Miller Land & Livestock Co*. DC Mont, 56 F Supp 34, 35].

The word 'warehouse' involves the idea of a place where goods are stored for sale, or at least for some other commercial purpose. But it does not prove that a piece of ground where goods are stored for commercial purposes is necessarily a storehouse in law. [*Buckingham* v *Fulham Corporation* (1905)53 WR 628].

- **Bonded warehouse** p. 108.

**Warehouse book.** A book used by merchants to contain an account of the quantities of goods received, shipped, and remaining in stock.

**Warehouse receipt.** A receipt issued by a warehouseman for goods received by him on storage in his warehouse. It is evidence of title of goods thereby represented. [*Woldson* v *Davenport Mill & Elevator Co.* 13 P 2d 478, 480].

**Warehoused goods.** Goods deposited in a warehouse. [Customs Act 1962, s. 2(44)].

**Warehouseman.** One engaged in business of receiving and storing goods of others for compensation or profit; person who receives goods and merchandise to be stored in his warehouse for hire; one who, as a business and for hire, keeps and stores goods of others. [*State ex rel. and for Use and Benefit of Cawrse* v *American Surety Co. of New York* 35 P 2d 487, 491].

**Waris.** Heir; one having the right of inheritance.

**Warp.** "Warp" means yarn arranged lengthwise on a loom. [*Ess Dee Carpet Enterprises* v *Union of India* 1989 Supp (2) SCR 417: JT 1989(4) SC 527: AIR 1990 SC 455: (1990)1 SCC 461].

**Warrant.** As noun means a writ directing or authorising someone to do an act, especially one directing a law enforcer to make an arrest, a search, or a seizure; a document conferring authority, especially to pay or receive money; an order by which a drawer authorises someone to pay a particular sum of money to another; an instrument granting the holder a long-term option to buy shares at a fixed price. [Black's *Law Dictionary*, 8th Ed.].

As verb means in contracts to promise that a certain facts or state of facts, in relation to the subject-matter, is, or shall be, as it is represented to be; in conveyancing to stipulate by an express covenant that the title of a grantee shall be good, and his possession undisturbed.

- **Arrest warrant.** A written order which is made on behalf of the state and is based upon a complaint issued pursuant to statute and/or court rule and which commands law enforcement officer to arrest a person and bring him before magistrate. [*Pillsbury* v *State* 142 NW 2d 187, 190].
- **Dividend warrant** p. 275.
- **Dock warrant** p. 276.
- **Jail warrant** p. 484.
- **Search warrant** p. 779.

**Warrant-case.** A case relating to an offence punishable with death, imprisonment for life or imprisonment for a term exceeding two years. [Code of Criminal Procedure 1973, s. 2(*x*)].

**Warrant of attorney.** A written authority given to an attorney authorising him to appear in court and prosecute a case or defend a person.

**Warranty.** A promise that a proposition of fact is true; a statement or representation made by seller of goods, contemporaneously with and as a part of contract of sale, though collateral to express object or sale, having reference to character, quality, or title of goods, and by which the seller promises or undertakes to insure that certain facts are or shall be as he then represents them. [*Bell* v *Menzies* 138 SE 2d 731, 732].

▸ *Meaning under the Sale of Goods Act 1930, s. 12(3)*. A warranty is a stipulation collateral to the main purpose of the contract, the breach of which gives rise to a claim for damages but not to a right to reject the goods and treat the contract as repudiated.

NOTE: In the case of some types of contract (e.g. sale, and hire purchase) certain implied terms are classified by statute as conditions or warranties, though the parties are sometimes free to evince a contrary intention. Similarly, common terms in certain types of contracts (e.g. charterparties and contracts of international sale) have, by the process of judicial decision, acquired the status of conditions or warranties and in the absence of clear evidence of a contrary intention will continue to be treated accordingly. In other cases the question whether a term is a condition or a warranty depends upon the intention of the parties as revealed by the construction of the contract, though the fact that a term is called a "condition" or a "warranty" is not necessarily decisive as to its status. [Halsbury's *Laws of England*, 4th Ed., vol. 9, paras 542 and 543, pp. 372-373].

- **General warranty** p. 385.

**Warsha.** The word "warsha" (to be correctly written as 'worsha') means descendants or heirs. [*State of Bihar* v *Radha Krishna Singh* AIR 1983 SC 684: (1983)3 SCC 118: (1983)2 SCR 808].

**Washer.** 'Washer' is understood as 'a flat ring or drilled disc of metal used under the head of a bolt or nut to spread the load when tightened'. In McGraw-Hill's *Encyclopedia of Science and Technology,* it is explained as, 'a flattened, ring-shaped device used to improve the tightness of a screw fastener'. The use of washer in common parlance is explained in the dictionary as 'for placing beneath a nut or at an axle bearing or joint, to serve as a cushion, to relieve friction etc. [*Kirloskar Oil Engines Ltd.* v *Union of India* (1995)2 SCJ 294].

**Wasi.** A testator; an executor or administrator or guardian appointed by will.

**Wasiatnama.** A will or testament.

**Wasilat.** Profits of land; collections of rent or revenue or any other dues.

**Waste.** An abuse or destructive use of property by one in rightful possession.

Spoil or destruction, done or permitted, to lands, houses, gardens, trees, or other corporeal hereditaments, by the tenant thereof, to the prejudice of the heir, or of him in reversion or remainder. [*Camden Trust Co.* v *Handle* 26 A 2d 865, 869].

Unreasonable conduct by owner of possessory estate that results in physical damage to real estate and substantial diminution in value of estates in which others have an interest. [*Pleasure Time, Inc.* v *Kuss* 254 NW 2d 463, 467].

In general waste is such damage to house or land as tends to the permanent and lasting loss of the person entitled to the inheritance. [Cheshire's *Modern Real Property*, 10th Ed., p. 186].

'Waste' is an act or omission by the tenant in possession, occasioning the destruction of, or injury to, "houses, gardens, woods, trees, or in lands, meadows, etc., or in exile of men, to the dishersion of him in the reversion or remainder". [Co. Lit., 53a].

NOTE: There are two kinds of waste—voluntary or actual and permissive. 'Voluntary waste' is a fair divisible into (*a*) meliorating waste and (*b*) equitable waste. The first is that which betters and which is not punishable or restrainable unless substantial damage is proved or some express prohibitive stipulation is broken. [*Doherty* v *Allman* 3 App Cas 709]. And 'equitable waste' is that which a prudent man would not do in the management of his own property. [*Turner* v *Wright* 2 DGF&J 243; Stroud's *Judicial Dictionary*, 5th Ed.].

Waste is either voluntary, *i.e.*, causing waste by doing some act, or permissive, which implies waste caused by an omission.

In cost accounting, waste may be dissected under two headings—(*a*) that which is unavoidable, being part of the process of manufacture, and which may result in a by-product either having a sale value or not; and (*b*) that which is avoidable, being due to faulty methods of manufacture or of records kept. The latter may be sub-divided under—(1) material wastes—due to wrong buying, excess issues of raw material, lack of supervision of manufacture, or spoilage owing to bad workmanship; (2) labour wastes—due to inefficient workers taking longer on the work than the time allowed, training of workmen; and (3) expense wastes—due to lack of proper control over expense incurred, or increase in expenses which cannot be passed on in the sale of the product. [Osborn & Grandage's *Concise Commercial Dictionary*].

In India the mortgagee in possession must not commit waste [Transfer of Property Act 1882, s. 76(*e*)] and the prohibition is enacted in the same words as in the case of a mortgagor in possession under s. 66 and in the case of a lessee under s. 108(*o*).

**Waste lands.** The expression "waste lands" has a well-defined legal connotation. It means lands which are desolate, abandoned, and not fit ordinarily for use for building purposes. Its etymological meaning is land lying desolate or useless, without trees or grass or vegetation, not capable of any use. [*State of Gujarat* v *Gujarat Revenue Tribunal* (1979)4 SCC 40: AIR 1980 SC 91: (1980)1 SCR 233].

The expression "waste land" as contrasted to "arable land", would mean land which is unfit for cultivation and habitation, desolate and barren land with little or no vegetation thereon. [*Rajanand Brahma Shah* v *State of U.P.* AIR 1967 SC 1081: (1967)1 SCR 373; *Ishwarlal Girdharilal Joshi* v *State of Gujarat* AIR 1968 SC 870: (1968)2 SCR 267].

**Wasting assets.** Assets whose value wastes away with use rather than depreciating with time and use.

NOTE: Wasting assets cannot be replaced, *e.g.*, mines and oil wells, and have a useful life limited to the period over which it is economically feasible to extract the substance on which the value of the wasting asset depends.

**Watercourse.** A running stream of water; a natural stream fed from permanent or natural sources, including rivers, creeks, runs, and rivulets. There must be a stream, usually flowing in a particular direction, though it need not flow continuously. It may sometimes be dry. It must flow in a definite channel, having a bed or banks, and usually discharges itself into some other stream or body of water. It must be something more than a mere surface drainage over the entire face of the tract of land, occasioned by unusual freshets or other extraordinary causes. [*Leader* v *Matthews* 95 SW 2d 1138, 1139; *Turner* v *Big Lake Oil Co.* Tex Civ App, 62 SW 2d 491, 493].

Watercourse means a channel which is supplied with water from a canal, but which is not maintained at the cost of the Government, and all subsidiary works belonging to any such channel. [*Beni* v *State* AIR 1966 All 11].

Water flowing underground in a known and well defined channel is not "percolating water", but constitutes a "watercourse". [*Bull* v *Siegrist* 126 P 2d 832, 834].

NOTE: Watercourse is a channel in which water flows, and the grant of a right to make a watercourse may include the right to fill it with water, and use the water flowing in it when made. [*Remfry* v *Surveyor-General of Natal* (1896) AC 558: 65 LJPC 72].

The fact that flood waters make for themselves a temporary channel or follow some natural channel, gully, or depression does not affect their character as "flood waters" or give to the course which they follow the character of a natural "watercourse". [*Mogle* v *Moore* Cal App, 96 P 2d 147, 150, 151; *Everett* v *Davis* Cal App, 107 P 2d 650, 655].

**Watering stock.** Overcapitalisation of a company's share capital due to issuing shares to such an extent that the company is unable to earn profits sufficient to represent a fair commercial return for the shareholders on their capital.

**Way.** A thoroughfare, road or open land for travel or transportation; a thoroughfare or path.

NOTE: All ways are divided into highways and private ways.


- **Carriage way** p. 124.
- **Permanent way** p. 655.
- **Private right of way** p. 764.
- **Right of way** p. 763.


**Way of necessity.** A way of necessity is a right of way which the law implies in favour of a grantee of land over the land of the grantor where there is no other way by which the grantee can get to the land so granted to him or over the land of the grantee where the land retained by the grantor is land-locked. Such a way cannot exist over the land of a stranger. [Halsbury's *Laws of England*, 4th Ed., vol. 14, para 153, pp. 73-74].

**Waybill.** A document acknowledging the receipt of goods by a carrier or by a shipper's agent and the contract for the transportation of those goods. [Black's *Law Dictionary*, 8th Ed.].

Written document made out by carrier listing point of origin and destination, consignor and consignee, and describing goods included in shipment by railroad or motor carrier.

NOTE: Unlike a bill of lading, a waybill is not a document of title and is non-negotiable.

**Weaker section.** "Weaker section" means not every 'backward class' but those dismally depressed categories comparable economically and educationally to scheduled caste and scheduled tribes. [*State of Kerala* v *N.M. Thomas* AIR 1976 SC 490: (1976)1 SCR 906: (1976)2 SCC 310: 1976(1) SLR 805].

**Wealth.** All material objects, capable of satisfying human wants, desires, or tastes, having a value in exchange, and upon which human labour has been expended.

**Wear and tear.** Deterioration caused by ordinary use; the depreciation of property resulting from its reasonable use [Black's *Law Dictionary*, 8th Ed.]; depreciation. [*Macsaga Investment Co. Ltd.* v *Lupton* (1967)2 All ER 930].

The expression is complex in meaning; it implicitly refers to both cause and effect, and in each aspect it covers two classes of disrepair, (*a*) that brought about by the normal or ordinary operation of natural causes, such as wind and weather, in contradistinction to abnormal or extraordinary events in nature such as lightning, hurricane, flood or earthquake; and (*b*) that brought about by the tenant and other persons present in or on the premises with the consent of the tenant, either unintentionally or as a normal incident of a tenant's occupation in the course of the fair or reasonable use of the premises for any of the purposes for which they are let. [*Taylor* v *Webb* (1937)2 KB 283].

It is also termed as fair wear and tear; natural wear and tear.

**Weaving.** Expression "weaving" means to form a fabric by interlacing yarn on a loom. It also means the method or pattern of weaving or the structure of a woven fabric. [*Ess Dee Carpet Enterprises* v *Union of India* 1989 Supp (2) SCR 417: JT 1989(4) SC 527: AIR 1990 SC 455: (1990)1 SCC 461].

**Week.** When an Act does not contain any definition of the word "week", it has to be understood in its ordinary dictionary sense. In the *Shorter Oxford English Dictionary* (3rd Edition), the word "week" has been described as meaning "the cycle of seven days, recognized in the calendar of the Jews and thence adopted in the calendar of Christian, Mohammedan and various other peoples. A space of seven days, irrespective of the time from which it is reckoned. Seven days as a term, for periodical payments (of wages, rent or the like), or as a unit of reckoning for time of work or service." In Webster's *New World Dictionary* (1962 Edition), the meaning of the word "week" is given as "a period of seven days, especially one beginning with Sunday and ending with Saturday; the hours or days of work in a seven-day period". In Stroud's *Judicial Dictionary* (3rd Edition), it is stated that "(1) though a week usually means any consecutive seven days, it will sometimes be interpreted to mean the ordinary notion of a week reckoning from Sunday to Sunday and (2) probably, a week usually means seven clear days". A "week" according to Halsbury's *Laws of England* (3rd Edition), vol. 37 at p. 84 is strictly the time between midnight on Saturday and the same hour on the next succeeding Saturday, but the term is also applied to any period of seven successive days. Bearing in mind the above mentioned dictionary or popular meaning of the term "week" the term has to be taken to signify a cycle of seven days including Sundays. [*B. Shah* v *Presiding Officer, Labour Court, Coimbatore* (1977)4 SCC 384: AIR 1978 SC 12: (1978)1 SCR 701].

▸ *Meaning under the Beedi and Cigar Workers (Conditions of Employment) Act 1966, s. 2(p); Employees' State Insurance*

*Act 1948, s. 2(23); Mines Act 1952, s. 2(r); Weekly Holidays Act 1942, s. 2(f).* A period of seven days beginning at midnight on Saturday.

▸ *Meaning under the Factories Act 1948, s. 2(f).* 'Week' means a period of seven days beginning at midnight on Saturday night or such other night as may be approved in writing for a particular area by the Chief Inspector of Factories.

▸ *Meaning under the Plantations Labour Act 1951, s. 2(j).* 'Week' means a period of seven days beginning at midnight on Saturday night or such other night as may be fixed by the State Government in relation to plantations in any area after such consultation as may be prescribed with reference to the plantations concerned in that area.

▸ *Meaning under the W.B. Shops and Establishment Act 1963, s. 2(16).* 'Week' means a period of seven days (beginning at midnight on Tuesday).

In the context of sub-secs. (1) and (3) of s. 5 of the Maternity Benefit Act 1961, the term "week" signifies a cycle of seven days including Sunday. [*B. Shah* v *Presiding Officer, Labour Court, Coimbatore* (1977)4 SCC 384: 1977 Lab IC 1847: AIR 1978 SC 12: (1978)1 Lab LJ 29].

**Weight.** A measure of heaviness or ponderosity; a measure of the quantity of matter. In a metaphorical sense, it means influence, effectiveness, or power to influence judgment or conduct.

• **Dead weight** p. 227.

**Weights and measures.** Instruments for reducing the quantity and price of merchandise to a certainty that there may be the less room for deceit and imposition.

NOTE: That there should be used in trade only one uniform weight and one uniform measure has been an object with the reformers in all times and countries. Weight is the mode of estimating the heaviness or mass of a substance; a measure is the mode of estimating the length, area or volume.

The standards of weights and lengths were laid down in India in the Standards of Weight Act 1939, and the Measures of Length Act 1899, the standard being the seer, the pound, the yard and their multiples and sub-multiples. These standards, however, were not effectively enforced throughout the country, with the result that different systems of weights and measures prevailed in different parts of the country. Moreover, the same term often represented different units of weight in different areas and in different trades even within the same area. This state of chaos hampered trade and provided opportunity for an exploitation of the masses. The Government felt the necessity for enforcing a uniform system of weights and measures throughout the country and decided to adopt, following the example of nearly 70 countries, a uniform system of weights and measures based on the metric system. Indian Parliament accordingly enacted the Standards of Weights and Measures Act 1956, to establish standards of weights and measures based on the metric system. This Act lays down metre as the primary unit of length and kilogram as the primary unit of mass.

**Welfare.** Well-being, benefit, prosperity, happiness; soundness; affluence.

Welfare simply means benefit. [*Re A (an infant)* (1963)1 All ER 531].

Welfare in connection with custody of a child must be read in its largest possible sense. The court must not only address itself to the child's present comfort and happiness but must also endeavour to look forward and try to consider what is ultimately best in the interest of the child. [*Re B. (an infant)* (1946) NI 1]. The moral and religious welfare of the child must be considered as well as its physical well-being. Nor can the ties of affection be disregarded. [*Re McGrath* (1893)1 Ch 143: 62 LJ Ch 208].

• **General welfare** p. 385.

**Wharf.** A structure on the shores of navigable waters, to which a vessel can be brought for loading or unloading. [Black's *Law Dictionary*, 8th Ed.].

▸ *Meaning under the Major Port Trusts Act 1963, s. 2(za).* 'Wharf' includes any wall or stage and any part of the land or foreshore that may be used for loading or unloading goods, or for embarkation or disembarkation of passengers and any wall enclosing or adjoining the same.

**Wharfage.** Charge for the use of a wharf or a place for receiving or discharging goods to be carried or brought in a ship or railway.

The money paid for landing goods upon, or loading them from, a wharf. [*Manhattan Lighterage Corporation* v *Moore McCormack Line* DCNY, 45 F Supp 271, 273].

Charge for use of wharf by way of rent or compensation. [*Marine Lighterage Corporation* v *Luckenbach S.S. Co.* 248 NYS 71, 72].

▸*Meaning under the Railways Act 1989, s. 2(41).* 'Wharfage' means the charge levied on goods for not removing them from the railway premises after the expiry of the free time allowed for such removal.

**Wharfinger.** The owner or occupier of a wharf; one who for hire receives merchandise on his wharf, either for the purpose of forwarding or for delivery to the consignee on such wharf.

**Whatsoever.** Anything or everything.

The word 'whatsoever' generally excludes any limitation or qualification and implies that the genus to which it relates is to be understood in its utmost generality. [*Duck* v *Bates* 13 QBD 851: 53 LJQB 344].

NOTE: The word repels the implication of the so-called doctrine of *ejusdem generis*. [*Jersey* v *Neath* 22 QBD 565: 58 LJ QB 578].

**Where.** According to dictionary the word 'where' may mean 'place or situation'. In certain context, it may be used in the sense of relation or situation. [*S.G. Glass Works Pvt. Ltd., Chandrapur, Maharashtra* v *Collector of Central Excise and Customs, Nagpur, Maharashtra* AIR 1995 SC 537: (1995)1 SCC 680].

**Whereas.** The word is used in documents to recite a past fact, event or transaction.

It may also mean while by contrast; although; given the fact that; since.

**Whipping.** A form of punishment inflicted on persons found guilty of certain offences.

**White-collar crime.** A nonviolent crime usually involving cheating or dishonesty in commercial matters. Examples include fraud, embezzlements, bribery, and insider trading.

**Whole blood.** Two persons are said to be related to each other by whole or full blood when they are descended from a common ancestor by the same wife and by half-blood when they are descended from a common ancestor, but by different wives. [Hindu Succession Act 1956, s. 3(1)(*e*)(*i*)].

**Wholesale dealer.** One who sells goods in gross to retail dealers rather than selling in smaller quantities directly to consumers. [Black's *Law Dictionary*, 8th Ed.].

One whose business is the selling of goods in gross to retail dealers, and not by the small quantity or parcel to consumers thereof. [*Veazey Drug Co.* v *Bruza* 37 P 2d 294].

▸*Meaning under the Central Excises and Salt Act 1944, s. 2(k).* A person who buys or sells excisable goods wholesale for the purpose of trade or manufacture, and includes a broker or commission agent who, in addition to making contracts for the sale or purchase of excisable goods for others, stocks such goods belonging to others as an agent for the purpose of sale.

**Wholesale price.** That which retailer pays in expectation of obtaining higher price by way of profit from resale to ultimate consumer. [*Guess* v *Montague* DCSC, 51 F Supp 61, 65].

Where a trader sells the whole or a large part of his articles or goods or produce direct at a fixed price to his customers who will be mostly retail dealers, that price can be described as the wholesale price, and if, cash was paid on delivery, the same is described as wholesale cash price. [*Secretary of State* v *Vacuum Oil Co.* 32 Bom LR 1308: AIR 1939 Bom 597].

**Wholesaler.** One who buys in comparatively large quantities, and then resells, usually in smaller quantities, but never to the ultimate consumer. He sells either to a "jobber", a sort of middleman, or to a "retailer", who in turn sells to the consumer. [*Fischbach Brewing Co.* v *City of St. Louis* 95 SW 2d 335, 340].

▶*Meaning under the Monopolies and Restrictive Trade Practices Act 1969, s. 2(x).* 'Wholesaler' in relation to the sale of any goods means a person who sells the goods to any person for the purpose of resale.

NOTE: The Act is now repealed and replaced by the Competition Act 2002 and no such term is defined under the new Act.

**Widow.** A woman whose husband has died and who has not remarried.

The term 'widow' is familiar, well fixed, certain and definite and it is defined, both popularly and legally, to mean a woman who has lost her husband by death and has not taken another; the surviving lawful wife of a decedent; a wife who outlives her husband; one whose husband is dead; a surviving wife; and it has been said that in legal writings 'widow' is an addition given to a woman who is unmarried and whose husband is dead. [*Sushila Devi Somani* v *Kedarnath Gupta* 1987 Jab LJ 450: AIR 1987 MP 65; *Rambai* v *Ramesh Kumar* AIR 1996 MP 144].

**Wife.** A woman who has a husband. The word 'wife' must mean a person who would have been a wife but for the decree of divorce or dissolution passed in the trial court. [*Sivakami Ammal* v *Bangaruswami Reddi* (1954)2 MLJ 396: AIR 1954 Mad 1039].

The term 'wife' appearing in s. 125(1) of the Criminal Procedure Code means only a legally wedded wife. [*Yamunabai* v *Anantrao* 1982 Mah LJ 871: (1982)84 Bom LR 298: 1983 Cr LJ 259 (Bom) (FB): 1983 Hindu LR 229].

The term 'wife' used under s. 125(4), Cr. P.C. would only mean a woman whose marriage relationship is in existence. A divorced woman will not come within the amplitude of s. 125(4) of the Code of Criminal Procedure. [*M. Alavi* v *T.V. Safia* (1992)1 Ker LT 649: (1992)1 Ker LJ 550: AIR 1993 Ker 21].

NOTE: The term 'wife' does not include a woman whose marriage is void. [*Madhab Pradhan* v *Ketaki Pradhan* 1995 Cr LJ 1785, 1787 (Ori)].


- **Battered wife** p. 98.
- **Husband and wife** p. 423.
- **Living together as husband and wife** p. 539.


**Wilful.** Voluntary and intentional, but not necessarily malicious; deliberate; designed; intentional, planned; premeditated; purposed; proceeding from a conscious motion of the will.

Deliberate. [*National Assistance Board* v *Prisk* (1954)1 All ER 400].

'Wilful' means not only intentional but also connotes something which is done without lawful excuse. [*Rice* v *Connolly* (1966)2 All ER 649].

'Wilful' means deliberate or intentional, and not accidental or by inadvertence. [*Kedarnath* v *State* AIR 1965 All 233].

'Wilful' is a word of many meanings, its construction often influenced by its context. [*Screws* v *United States* 89 L Ed 1495]. The word 'wilful' when used in statutes connotes different concepts. In some case it may mean 'wantonly'; in others 'intentionally' or 'deliberately'; in some others 'consciously'. [*Madras State Wakf Board* v *Tajmul Hussain* AIR 1968 Mad 332].

NOTE: 'Wilful' is more commonly used in modern speech of bad conduct or actions than of good, though it does not necessarily connotes blame. [*Wheeler* v *New Merton Board Mills Ltd.* (1933)2 KB 669].

**Wilful default.** 'Wilful default' implies either a consciousness of negligence or breach of duty, or a recklessness in the performance of a duty. [*Re Vickery, Vickery* v *Stephens* (1931)47 TLR 242].

'Wilful default' is indicative of some misconduct in the transaction of business or in the discharge of the duty of omitting to do something either deliberately or by reckless disregard of the fact whether the act or omission was or was not a breach of duty. [*Bhogilal* v *Subramania* AIR 1954 Mad 514].

A default in order to be wilful must be intentional, deliberate, calculated and conscious, with full knowledge of legal consequences flowing therefrom. [*S. Sundaram Pillai* v *V.R. Pattabiraman* (1985)2 SCR 643: AIR 1985 SC 582: (1985)1 SCC 591; *Rakapalli R.R. Gopala* v *N.G.*

*Seharārao* (1989)3 SCJ 493, 495: AIR 1989 SC 2185].

NOTE: A vendor commits a default if he fails to do something which he ought reasonably to do, regard being had to the terms of the contract which he has entered into with the purchaser, and is guilty of wilful default if he so fails when he is a free agent and knows what he is doing and intends to do what he does. An honest mistake, the result of oversight to inadvertence, is not wilful unless persisted in after the attention of the vendor has been called to it. [*Re Postmaster-General* (1906)1 IR 287].

If the default is committed intentionally or deliberately, it is wilful default regardless of the reason why the default was intended. The word 'wilful' must be given full significance. ... It is to be made clear that in order to be wilful, a default need not be habitual or continuous. A single default in the facts and circumstances of a particular case may be wilful. [*Manakarani Hazia* v *Mohinder Singh Jaggi* AIR 1968 Ori 113].

The word 'default' implies not doing something that is reasonable or necessary, something required to be done. When it is coupled with the word 'wilful', the phrase is manifestly intended to signify something more than a mere omission or default. The expression 'wilful default' has been the subject-matter of several decisions in other branches or law. The Merchant Shipping Act in England has used the expression 'wilful default' of the person in charge. In case arising under that Act, the view taken was that it refers to acts arising by the fault of such person, whether intentional or negligent. In the law relating to trustee, wilful default by a trustee is understood as 'the wilfully not doing something which, he ought to do as distinguished form doing something which he ought not to do'. [*Re Vickery* (1931)1 Ch 572].

**Wilful misconduct.** Misconduct committed voluntarily and intentionally. [Black's *Law Dictionary*, 8th Ed.].

An aggravated form of negligence, differing in quality rather than degree from ordinary lack of care. [*Morgan* v *Southern Pac. Transp. Co.* 37 Cal App 3d 1006].

Gross negligence amounts to wilful misconduct. [*Bastable* v *North British Ry. Co.* (1912)49 Sc LR 446].

Wilful misconduct means misconduct to which the will is party as contra-distinguished from accident, and is far beyond any negligence, even gross or culpable negligence, and involves that a person wilfully misconduct himself who knows and appreciates that it is wrong conduct on his part in the existing circumstances to do, or to fail, or omit to do (as the case may be) a particular thing, and yet intentionally does, or fails or omits to do it, or persists in the act, failure or omission, regardless of consequences. [*Sheppard & Son* v *Midland Ry*. (1915)85 LJKB 283].

**Wilful neglect.** Omit to do something intentionally or purposely.

Intentional or reckless failure to carry out a legal duty. [Black's *Law Dictionary*, 8th Ed.].

Wilful neglect suggests intentional, conscious, or known negligence—a knowing or intentional mistake. [*Puget Sound Painters* v *State* 278 P 2d 302, 303].

'Wilful neglect' means that the act was done deliberately and intentionally, and not by accident or inadvertence, so that the mind of the person who does the act goes with it. [*Ardeshir Bhicaji* v *Agent, G.I.P. Ry.* AIR 1928 PC 24].

**Wilfully.** 'Wilfully' presupposes a conscious action, while even by negligence one can allow another to do a thing. [*Om Prakash Gupta* v *State of U.P.* AIR 1957 SC 458: 1957 SCR 423].

"Wilfully" means "intentionally" or "deliberately". [*S. Harnam Singh* v *State* AIR 1976 SC 2140].

**Will.** *Use as noun.* Wish; desire; pleasure; choice; the faculty of conscious, and especially of deliberate action.

A "will" is generally defined as an instrument by which a person makes a disposition of his property, to take effect after his death, and which by its own nature is ambulatory and revocable during his lifetime. [*In re Brown's Estate* Tex Civ App, 507 SW 2d 801, 803].

- *Use as an auxiliary verb.* It is used in mandatory sense of "shall" or "must". It is a word of certainty, while the word "may" is one of speculation and uncertainty.
- *Meaning under the Indian Succession Act 1925, s. 2(h).* 'Will' means the legal declaration of the intention of the testator with respect to his property which he desires to be carried into effect after his death.
- *Meaning under the Indian Penal Code 1860, s. 31.* 'Will' denotes any testamentary document.

It is a testamentary instrument when used in a formed deed. [*Leela Nath* v *Commissioner of Income Tax* 1982 Tax LR 294 (Cal)].

NOTE: 'Will' shall include codicil and every writing making a voluntary posthumous disposition of property. [General Clauses Act, s. 3(64)].


- **Inofficious will** p. 462.
- **Joint will** p. 488.
- **Nuncupative will** p. 613.
- **Privileged will** p. 689.
- **Tenancy will** p. 834.


**Winding-up.** The process of settling accounts and liquidating assets in anticipation of dissolution of a partnership or a corporation.

A process of liquidation of company.

NOTE: A company may be wound up either (*a*) by the tribunal, or (*b*) voluntary. [Companies Act 1956, s. 425].

**Window-dressing.** This is the practice of so arranging the disposition of assets and liabilities as to present a financial picture in a subsequent balance-sheet, which is not representative of the normal financial position of the business.

The deceptive arrangement of something, usually facts or appearances, to make it appear more attractive or favourable. [Black's *Law Dictionary*, 8th Ed.].

**Winning.** According to the *Shorter Oxford Dictionary*, 'to win' has the meaning: (*i*) to get or extract coal or other mineral from the mine, pit or quarry; (*ii*) to sink shaft or make excavation so as to reach a seam of coal or vein of ore ... for working. The expression 'winning' is construed to mean 'getting or extracting minerals from the mines and other incidental purposes'. [*Gujarat Pottery Private Ltd.* v *S.P. Sood* AIR 1967 SC 964: (1967)1 SCA 691: (1967)1 SCR 695: (1968)1 SCJ 307].

'Winning' does not imply a hazardous or perilous activity. The word simply means 'extracting a mineral' and is used generally to indicate any activity by which a mineral is secured. [*Bhagwan Dass* v *State of U.P.* (1976)3 SCC 784: AIR 1976 SC 1393].

The expression in s. 3(*d*), Mines and Minerals (Regulation and Development) Act 1957 means getting the minerals extracted from the mine. [*Bihar Mines Ltd.* v *Union of India* AIR 1967 SC 887].

NOTE: Although in the case of a sand or gravel mine the word winning means collection of sand and gravel from the surface of the earth where there is a natural deposit of sand and gravel, this does not mean that collection of coal, sludge or slurry from a place where they are artificially deposited or dumped will be "winning" within the meaning of the Mines and Minerals (Regulation and Development) Act 1957. [*Industrial Fuel Marketing Co.* v *Union of India* 89 CWN 263, 267].

**Wireless communication.** Any transmission, emission or reception of signs, signals, writing, images and sounds, or intelligence of any nature by means of electricity, magnetism, or radio waves or Hertzian waves, without the use of wires or other continuous electrical conductors between the transmitting and the receiving apparatus. [Indian Wireless Telegraphy Act 1933, s. 2(1)].

**Wireless transmitter.** Any apparatus, appliance, instrument or material used or capable of being used for transmission or emission of wireless communication. [Indian Wireless Telegraphy Act 1933, s. 2(2A)].

**With intent to defraud.** The expression 'intent to defraud' implies conduct coupled with intention to deceive and thereby to injure. [*Vimla* v *Delhi Administration* AIR 1963 SC 1572].

**Within.** When used relative to time it has been defined variously as meaning any time before; at or before; at the end of; before the expiration of; not beyond; not exceeding; not later than. [*Glenn* v *Garrett* Tex Civ App, 84 SW 2d 515, 516].

The word 'within' in relation to a period of time does not usually mean 'during' or 'throughout the whole of'; it is more frequently used to delimit a period 'inside which' certain event may happen. [*Reynolds* v *Reynolds* 1941 VLR 249].

'Within' means on or before. [*Satyavatamma* v *Padmavatamma* AIR 1957 AP 30].

It means "on or before", "not beyond", "nor later than". [*Md. Tajuddin* v *Quamarunissa Begum* 1989 Cr LJ 2285: (1989)2 Andh LT 275: (1989)1 APLJ (HC) 353: (1989)2 Cur Civ Cas 548: 1989 APLJ (Cr) 146].

Where something is to be done within a stated time 'before' a stated date, that means that it is to be done at some time during the course of the stated time, immediately preceding the stated date. [*Thomas* v *Lambert* (1835)4 LJKB 153].

NOTE: An appeal filed on the 30th day is filed within 30 days. [*Thippaswami* v *Mysore Revenue Appellate Tribunal* AIR 1972 Mys 50].

**Without prejudice.** Without loss of any rights; in a way that does not harm or cancel the legal rights or privilege of a party. [Black's *Law Dictionary*, 8th Ed.].

A phrase used in offers, in order to guard against any waiver of right should they be ineffectual and go off. [Wharton's *Law Lexicon*, 14th Ed., p. 1073].

'Without prejudice' means that if the terms are accepted, the dispute shall end. If not, they cannot be used against the writer. [*Tata Oil Mills Co. Ltd.* v *Lokenath Chemical Works* AIR 1987 Cal 13].

In administrative law, the expression "without prejudice" means (*i*) that the matter had not been decided on merits, and (*ii*) that fresh proceedings according to law were not barred. [*Superintendent (Tech. I) Central Excise, I.D.D., Jabalpur* v *Pratap Rai* AIR 1978 SC 1244: (1978)3 SCR 729: (1978)3 SCC 113: 1978 Cr LJ 1266: (1978)114 ITR 231: 1978 ELT (J 613): 1978 SCC (Cri) 371].

NOTE: Where an offer or admission is made "without prejudice", it is meant as a declaration that no rights or privileges of the party concerned are to be considered as thereby waived or lost, except in so far as may be expressly conceded or decided.

**Without recourse.** A phrase used by an endorser of a bill or note, which protects him from liability.

NOTE: When an agent signs or endorses a negotiable instrument, he must signify thereon the capacity in which he does so, otherwise he will make himself personally liable upon the instrument. The best mode for an agent to sign or endorse a bill or note for his principal when he means to make the latter and not himself liable is to sign or endorse the same as *A.B.* (the principal) by his agent *C.D.*, or more shortly, *A.B.*, by *C.D.* These are sufficiently unequivocal to indicate that the agent acts ministerially and not on his own account. [*Jogesh Chandra* v *Mahommad* 57 Cal 695]. The word "sans recourse" or "without recourse to me" are also recommended for excluding liability.

English law in this respect is to be found in s. 16 of the Bills of Exchange Act 1882, which provides *inter alia* that the drawer of a bill, and any endorser, may insert therein an express stipulation negativing or limiting his own liability to the holder.

**Without reserve.** The expression used with reference to auction sale means that there shall be no bidding on the part of the vendor and that whoever bids the highest shall be the purchaser. [*Robinson* v *Wall* (1847)2 Ch 372: 16 LJ Ch 401].

**Witness.** One who sees, knows, or vouches for something, one who gives testimony under oath or affirmation (1) in person, (2) by oral or written deposition, or (3) by affidavit [Black's *Law Dictionary*, 8th Ed.]; one who testifies to what he has seen, heard or otherwise observed [*Wigginton* v *Order of United Commercial Travelers of America* CCA Ind, 126 F 2d 659, 666]; a person attesting genuineness of signature to document by adding his signature. [*In re Gorrell's Estate* 19 A 2d 234, 235].

The word 'witness' must be understood in its natural sense i.e. as referring to a person who furnishes evidence. [*Subedar* v *State* 1953 All LJ 263].


- **Adverse witness** p. 46.
- **Attesting witness** p. 85.
- **Expert witness** p. 331.
- **Hostile witness** p. 422.
- **Interested witness** p. 473.
- **Material witness** p. 568.
- **To be a witness** p. 844.


**Woman.** 'Woman' denotes a female human being of any age. [Indian Penal Code 1860, s. 10].

"Woman" is defined to mean a female who has completed the age of 21 years. [Suppression of Immoral Traffic in Women and Girls Act 1956, s. 2(*j*); *State of U.P.* v *Kaushaliya* AIR 1964 SC 416: (1964)1 Cr LJ 304: (1964)4 SCR 1002].


- **Pardanashin woman** p. 638.


**Wood naptha.** Wood naptha is a distillation of wood and in its crude stage contains only a small percentage of methyl alcohol. From this is prepared methyl alcohol of different strengths. [*Calcutta Chemical Co. Ltd.* v *Assistant Collector of Customs* AIR 1958 Cal 654].

**Wool.** Animal fibres are usually spoken of as hair with the exception of the coat of the sheep which is usually termed 'wool'. Wool has almost invariably been used in the context of sheep hair. [*Madanlal Monoharlal* v *State of Haryana* 1990 STJ 365 (SC)].

**Woolen fabrics.** "Woolen fabrics" means not only woolen garments but also woolen material used as covering or for similar other purposes. [Central Excise and Salt Act 1944, Entry 21; *Union of India* v *Gujarat Woolen Felt Mills* AIR 1977 SC 1548: (1977)3 SCR 472: (1977)2 SCC 870: 1977 ELT (J 24)].

**Woolsack.** The seat of the Lord Chancellor in the House of Lords. It is not strictly within the House, for the Lords may not speak from that part of the Chamber.

**Words of limitation; Words of purchase.** In a conveyance or will, words which have the effect of making the duration of an estate are termed 'words of limitation'. Thus, in a grant to *A* and his heirs, the words "and his heirs" are words of limitation, because they show that *A* is to take an estate in fee simple, and do not give his heirs anything.

'Words of purchase' are words which denote the person who is to take the estate. Thus, if land is granted to *A* for 21 years, and after the determination of that term to *A*'s heirs, the word "heirs" does not denote the duration of *A*'s estate, but the person who is to take the remainder on the expiration of the term, and is therefore called a word of purchase. [Jowitt's *Dictionary of English Law*, 2nd Ed.].

**Work.** *Use as noun.* It means physical and mental exertion to attain an end controlled by and for the benefit of an employer; labour.

In copyright, it means an original expression, in fixed or tangible form (such as paper, audiotape, or computer disk), that may be entitled to common-law or statutory copyright protection.

> NOTE: A work may take different forms, including art, sculpture literature, music, crafts, photography etc.

▸ *Use as verb.* It means to function properly; to produce a desired effect; to perform, either physically or mentally.


- **Equal pay for equal work** p. 312.
- **Literary work** p. 538.
- **Original literary work** p. 538.
- **Musical work** p. 595.
- **Rebuilding work** p. 732.
- **Safe place to work** p. 768.


**Work-charged establishment.** A "work-charged establishment" broadly means an establishment of which the expenses, including the wages and allowances of the staff, are chargeable to "works". [*Jaswant Singh* v *Union of India* (1979)4 SCC 440: 1979(2) SLR 375: AIR 1980 SC 115: (1980)1 SCR 420].

**Work of joint authorship.** 'Work of joint authorship' means a work produced by the collaboration of two or more authors in which the contribution of one author is not distinct from the contribution of the other author or authors. [Copyright Act 1957, s. 2(*z*)].

**Work to rule.** It involves rigid adherence to the rule book governing the work being done, which results in a slowing down of output per man hour.

**Worker.** One who labours to attain an end; a person employed to do work for another; a person who offers to perform services for compensation in the employ of another, whether or not the person is so employed at a given time. [Black's *Law Dictionary*, 8th Ed.].

▸ *Meaning under the Factories Act 1948, s. 2(l).* A person employed directly or through any agency, whether for wages or not, in any manufacturing process, or in cleaning any part of the machinery or premises used for a manufacturing process or in any other kind of work incidental to, or connected with, the manufacturing process, or the subject of the manufacturing process.

A person is a "worker" under s. 2(*l*) of the Factories Act if he is a person employed in the premises or precincts of the factory in any kind of work connected with 'the subject of manufacturing process'. [*Rohtas Industries Ltd.* v *Shri Ramlakhan Singh* AIR 1978 SC 849: (1978)3 SCR 93: (1978)2 SCC 140].

NOTE: The definition of "worker" in the Factories Act does not seem to exclude those employees: who are entrusted solely with clerical duties, if they otherwise fall within the definition of the word "worker". [*The Works Manager, Central Railway Workshop, Jhansi* v *Vishwanath* (1969)3 SCC 95: AIR 1970 SC 488: (1970)2 SCR 726].

Where casual, heterogeneous, miscellaneous and irregular group come at their convenience and do the work at piece-rates and there are no specified hours of work, nor is there any control by the employers over the irregularity and attendance or of the nature, manner or quantum of their work, such employee will not fall under the definition of "worker" under s. 2(*l*) of the Factories Act. [*State of Kerala* v *R.E. D'Souzha* AIR 1971 SC 832: (1971)3 SCR 711: (1971)1 SCC 533: 1971 Cr LJ 689: 1971 SCC (Cri) 241].

▸ *Meaning under the Plantations Labour Act 1951, s. 2(k).* 'Worker' means a person employed in a plantation for hire or reward, whether directly or through any agency, to do any work, skilled, unskilled, manual or clerical, but does not include—(*i*) a medical officer employed in the plantation; (*ii*) any person employed in the plantation (including any member of the medical staff) whose monthly wages exceed rupees three hundred; (*iii*) any person employed in the plantation primarily in a managerial capacity notwithstanding that his monthly wages do not exceed rupees three hundred; or (*iv*) any person temporarily employed in the plantation in any work relating to the construction, development or maintenance of buildings, roads, bridges, drains or canals.

• **Dock worker** p. 276.

**Working capital.** That part of the finances of a business available for its operation; the amount of quick assets which exceed current liabilities.

Current assets (such as cash, inventory, and accounts receivable) less current liabilities. [Black's *Law Dictionary*, 7th Ed.].

It measures liquidity and the ability to discharge short-term obligations.

Cash and other quick assets. [*Crocker* v *Waltham Watch Co.* 53 NE 2d 230, 237]. In accounting, it means the difference between current assets and current liabilities.

**Working conditions.** The general environment, amenities and benefits which people receive at work. As standards of living rise there is pressure for improvement of working conditions, which embrace such things as safety, comfort, and terms of employment.

**Working day.** Days excluding Sundays and holidays. [*Turnbull* v *Cruikshank* (1904)7 F (Ct. of Sess.) 265].

'Working days' means the part of a day during which work is carried on. [*Alvion Steamship* v *Galban Lobo* (1955)1 All ER 457].

**Working funds.** The words "working funds", when used in relation to a banking company, are not to be construed in their ordinary popular sense by reference to a dictionary. They have a history of their own and they have acquired a definite meaning. In the Sastri Award made in 1953 in regard to industrial disputes between certain banking companies and their workmen, the words 'working funds' were defined to mean paid-up capital, reserves and the average of the deposits for 52 weeks of each year for which weekly returns of deposits are submitted to the Reserve Bank of India under the provisions of the Reserve Bank of India Act. [*Workmen of National & Grindlays Bank Ltd.* v *The National & Grindlays Bank Ltd.* AIR 1976 SC 611: (1976)3 SCR 130: (1976)1 SCC 925].

**Working journalist.** "Working journalist" means a person whose principal avocation is that of a journalist and who is employed as such in, or in relation to, any newspaper establishment, and includes an editor, a leader-writer, news editor, sub-editor, feature-writer, copy tester, reporter, correspondent, cartoonist, news-photographers and proof reader. An editor is expressly included in this definition. [*Management of Rashtradoot, Jaipur* v *Rajasthan Working Journalist Union, Jaipur* (1971)3 SCC 96].

**Working partner.** A partner who is required by the terms of the contract of partnership to devote substantially the whole of his time to the business of the firm. [Business Profits Tax Act, s. 2(18)].

**Workman.** 'Workman' means any person (including an apprentice) employed in any industry to do any manual, unskilled, skilled, technical, operational, clerical or supervisory work for hire or reward, whether the terms of employment be express or implied, and for the purposes of any proceeding under this Act in relation to an industrial dispute, includes any such person who has been dismissed, discharged or retrenched in connection with, or as a consequence of, that dispute, or whose dismissal, discharge or retrenchment has led to that dispute, but does not include any such person—(*i*) who is subject to the Air Force Act 1950, or the Army Act 1950, or the Navy Act 1957; or (*ii*) who is employed in the police service or as an officer or other employee of a prison; or (*iii*) who is employed mainly in a managerial or administrative capacity; or (*iv*) who, being employed in a supervisory capacity, draws wages exceeding one thousand six hundred rupees per mensem or exercises, either by the nature of the duties attached to the office or by reason of the powers vested in him, functions mainly of a managerial nature. [Industrial Disputes Act 1947, s. 2(s)].

"Workman" within the terms of s. 2(*s*) is that he should be employed to do the work in an industry and that there should be an employment of his by the employer and that there should be a relationship between the employer and him as between employer and employee or master and servant. [*Workman of the Food Corporation of India* v *The Food Corporation of India* AIR 1985 SC 670: (1985)2 SCR 1065: 1985(1) SLR 625: (1985)2 SCC 136].

NOTE: The definition of workman as given in s. 2(s) is comprehensive and wide enough to include even a part time employee. [*Yashwant Singh Yadav* v *State of Rajasthan* (1989)1 Raj LR 156].

In s. 2(*s*) a timekeeper appointed on *ad hoc* basis posted as LDC and discharging the clerical work falls within the definition of workman. [*Ram Krishna Sharma* v *Samrat Ashok Technical Institute, Vidisha* 1995 MPLJ 53].

An assistant, mainly performing clerical work and incidentally performing some supervisory work, is a workman under the Industrial Disputes Act 1947. [*Arkal Govind Raj Rao* v *Ciba Geigy of India Ltd., Bombay* AIR 1985 SC 985: 1985 Supp (1) SCR 282: (1985)3 SCC 371]. Even if, however, there is some odd technical, clerical or manual work, if the main work is supervisory, an employee cannot be called a workman. [*Burmah Shell Oil Storage and Distributing Company of India Ltd.* v *The Burmah Shell Management Staff Association* AIR 1971 SC 922: (1971)2 SCR 758: (1970)3 SCC 378].

▸ *Meaning under the Employers' Liability Act 1938, s. 2(a).* Any person who has entered into, or works under a contract of, service or apprenticeship with an employer whether by way of manual labour, clerical work or otherwise, and whether the contract is expressed or implied, oral or in writing.

▸ *Meaning under the Trade Unions Act 1926, s. 2(g).* 'Workmen' mean all persons employed in trade or industry whether or not in the employment of the employer with whom the trade dispute arises.

▸ *Meaning under the Workmen's Compensation Act 1923, s. 2(n).* 'Workman' means any person (other than a person whose employment is of a casual nature and who is employed otherwise than for the purposes of the employer's trade or business) who is—(*i*) a railway servant as defined in s. 3 of the Indian Railways Act 1890, not permanently employed in an administrative, district or sub-divisional office of a railway and not employed in any such capacity as is specified in *Schedule II*, (*ii*) employed on monthly wages not exceeding five hundred rupees in any such capacity as is specified in *Schedule II*, whether the contract of employment was made before or after the passing of this Act and whether the contract is expressed or implied, oral or in writing, but does not include any person working in the capacity of a member of the Armed Forces of the Union.

▸ *Meaning under the Contract Labour (Regulation and Abolition) Act 1970, s. 2(1)(i).* 'Workmen' means any person employed in or in connection with the work of any establishment to do any skilled, semi-skilled or unskilled manual, supervisory, technical or clerical work for hire or reward, whether the terms of employment be express or implied, but does not include any such person—(A) who is employed mainly in a managerial or administrative capacity; or (B) who being employed in a supervisory capacity draws wages exceeding five hundred rupees per mensem or exercises either by the nature of the duties attached to the office or by reason of the powers vested in him functions mainly of a managerial nature; or (C) who is an out-worker, that is to say, a person to whom any articles or materials are given out by or on behalf of the principal employer to be made up, cleaned, washed, altered, ornamented, finished, repaired, adapted or otherwise processed for sale for the purpose of the trade or business of the principal employer and the process is to be carried out either in the house of the out-worker or in some other premises, not being premises under the control and management of the principal employer.

▸ *Meaning under the Personal Injuries (Compensation Insurance) Act 1963, s. 2(k).* 'Workman' means any person (other than a person whose employment is of a casual nature and who is employed otherwise than for the purposes of the employer's trade or business) who is employed in any of the employments specified in s. 3.

**Works contract.** Where the main object of work undertaken by the payee of the price is not the transfer of a chattel *qua* chattel, the contract is one for work and labour. [*T.V. Sundaram Iyengar & Sons* v *State of Madras* AIR 1974 SC 2309: (1975)2 SCR 372: (1975)3 SCC 424: (1975)35 STC 24].

NOTE: In a contract for work, there is the person performing work and rendering service. No property in the thing produced may have been his property. [*Commissioner of Sales Tax, M.P.* v *Premji* (1970)2 SCC 287].

**Workshop.** An establishment where manufacture of goods or other materials is carried on; a building or room where any work is carried on; workroom; a seminar or single session for training, discussion, etc.

▸ *Meaning under the Employment of Children Act 1938, s. 2(d).* 'Workshop' means any premises (including the precincts thereof) wherein any industrial process is carried on, but does not include any premises to which the provisions of s. 50 of the Factories Act 1934, for the time being apply.

**Worsha.** See WARSHA p. 893.

**Worship.** Reverence or veneration to a divine being or supernatural power; an expression of reverence by performance of ceremonies; the paying of religious reference, as in prayer, praise, etc.

• **Public religious worship.** By the phrase 'public religious worship' is meant and intended forms or ceremonies of worship distinct from private religious worship. In public worship, the individual worshippers may come from widely different places and may be personally entirely unknown to one another; a congregational as distinct from private and family devotion. [*Church of Jesus Christ* v *Henning* (1963)2 All ER 733].

**Wreck.** In maritime law, it means goods cast ashore from a wrecked vessel and not claimed by the owner within a specified period. [Black's *Law Dictionary*, 8th Ed.].

The word 'wreck', under s. 272 of the Merchant Shipping Act 1923, includes the following when found in the sea or any tidal water or on the shores thereof—(*a*) goods which have been cast into the sea and then sink and remain under water; (*b*) goods which have been cast or fall into the sea and remain floating on the surface; (*c*) goods which are sunk in the sea, but are attached to a floating object in order that they may be found again; (*d*) goods which are thrown away or abandoned; and (*e*) a ship abandoned without hope or intention of recovery.

**Writ.** An order or process issued by a court or judicial officer asking any person to perform or refrain from performing any act.

A court's written order, in the name of a state or other competent legal authority, commanding the addressee to do or refrain from doing some specified act. [Black's *Law Dictionary*, 8th Ed.].

• **Prerogative writ** p. 680.

**Write-down.** To transfer a portion of the cost of an asset to an expense account because the asset's value has decreased. Depreciation and bad debts are examples of assets being written-down to lower values.

**Write-up.** In accounting, this means the recording of an increase in book values without realisation or transfer, presumably to reflect in the accounts an actual or presumed increase in the value of an asset or assets.

It may also mean a publication, such as a newspaper article, about a particular person, thing, or event.

**Written law.** Statutory law; law deriving its force from express legislative enactment.

**Written statement.** The expression "written statement" is a term of specific connotation ordinarily signifying a reply to the plaint filed by the plaintiff. [*Food Corporation of India* v *Yadav Engineer & Contractor* AIR 1982 SC 1302: (1982)2 SCC 499: (1983)1 SCR 95; *Rachappa Guruadappa, Bijapur* v *Gurusiddappa Nuraniappa* JT 1988(4) SC 497: 1988 Supp (3) SCR 884: AIR 1989 SC 635: (1989)3 SCC 245].

**Wrong.** A violation of the legal rights of another, an invasion of right to the damage of the parties who suffer it, especially a tort. [*State ex rel. and to Use of Donelon* v *Deuser* 345 Mo 628: 134 SW 2d 132, 133].

It usually signifies injury to person, property or relative noncontractual rights of another than wrongdoer, with or without force, but, in more extended sense, includes violation of contract. [*Daurizio* v *Merchants' Despatch Transp. Co.* 274 NYS 174].

The word 'wrong' ordinarily means deprivation of right. An act is wrongful if it infringes the legal right of another. [*State of West Bengal* v *Brindaban* AIR 1957 Cal 44].

▸ *Meaning under the Hindu Marriage Act 1955, s. 23(1)(a).* In order to be a "wrong" within the meaning of s. 23(1)(*a*), the conduct alleged has to be something more than a mere disinclination to agree to the offer of reunion and must be misconduct serious enough to justify the denial of the relief to which the spouse is otherwise entitled. [*Dharmendra Kumar* v *Usha*

*Kumar* AIR 1977 SC 2218: (1977)4 SCC 12: (1978)1 SCR 315; *Smt. Saroj Rani* v *Sudarshan Kumar Chadha* AIR 1984 SC 1562: (1984)4 SCC 90: (1985)1 SCR 303].


- **Actionable wrong** p. 33.
- **Continuing wrong** p. 188.
- **Executor of his own wrong** p. 329.


**Wrongful conduct.** Conduct which contravenes some duty which law attaches to relation between parties affected. [*Duncan* v *Lumbermen's Mut. Casualty Co.* 23 A 2d 325, 326].

**Wrongful confinement.** "Wrongful confinement" is a wrongful restraint in such a manner as to prevent that person from proceeding beyond a certain circumscribed limits. [*Shyam Lal Sharma* v *State of Madhya Pradesh* AIR 1972 SC 886: (1972)3 SCR 422: (1972)1 SCC 764: 1972 Cr LJ 638: 1972 SCC (Cri) 470].

**Wrongful dismissal.** An improper dismissal of an employee from service by an employer.

**Wrongful gain.** "Wrongful gain" is gain, by unlawful means of property to which the person gaining is not legally entitled. [Indian Penal Code 1860, s. 23].

Wrongful gain includes wrongful retention of property. [*Krishan Kumar* v *Union of India* AIR 1959 SC 1390].

**Wrongful loss.** "Wrongful loss" is the loss by unlawful means of property to which the person losing it is legally entitled. [Indian Penal Code 1860, s. 23].

**Wrongful restraint.** Whoever voluntarily obstructs any person so as to prevent that person from proceeding in any direction in which that person has a right to proceed, is said wrongfully to restrain that person. [Indian Penal Code 1860, s. 339].

# Yy

**Yajaman vritti.** The office or occupation of a priest.

**Yajamana.** A person who has engaged a priest to perform religious ceremonies, a disciple.

**Yard.** An enclosed space of ground generally attached to a dwelling house; a measure of three feet; a place where articles of merchandise are deposited e.g. a fuel yard.

**Yarn.** According to the *Oxford Dictionary*, "yarn" means any spurn thread specially or kinds prepared by weaving, knitting or rope-making. According to Webster's *New World Dictionary*, it is defined as any fibre, as wool, silk, flax, cotton, nylon etc. spurn into strands for weaving, knitting or making thread. [*Aditya Mills Ltd.* v *Union of India* AIR 1988 SC 2237: (1988)4 SCC 315: JT 1988(4) SC 151: (1988)37 ELT 471: 1988 Supp (2) SCR 668: (1989)73 STC 195].

**Yautaka.** A form of *stridhan* in Hindu law; nuptial gift or presents made to a woman at the time of her marriage.

**Year.** Twelve calendar months beginning January 1 and ending December 31; a consecutive 365-day period beginning at any point; a span of twelve months.

For purposes of law, the term ordinarily means the year reckoned according to the British calendar. It must be considered as 12 calendar and not lunar months. [*Jagdish Ch. Patnaik* v *State of Kerala* (1998)4 SCC 456].

▸ *Meaning under the General Clauses Act 1897, s. 3(66); Indian Penal Code 1860, s. 49.* 'Year' means a year reckoned according to the British calendar.


- **Assessment year** p. 79.
- **Calendar year** p. 118.
- **Financial year** p. 354.
- **Fiscal year** p. 357.
- **Previous year** p. 683.


**Year of the tenancy.** A year or a period of twelve months according to the calendar of the particular tenancy, starting with its date of commencement or any anniversary thereof. [*Indian Iron* v *Baker Ali* AIR 1961 Cal 515].

**Year to year tenancy.** A tenancy which may be determined at the end of first or any subsequent year of the tenancy by a regular notice to quit.

**Yearly.** Annual; extending, occurring, made or done during or upon every year or once a year.

**Yield.** As noun means profit expressed as a percentage of the investment.

As verb means to give up, relinquish or surrender.


- **Redemption yield** p. 738.


**Young person.** A person who is either a child or an adolescent. [Factories Act 1948, s. 2(*d*)]. A child is a person who has not completed his fifteenth year of age and an adolescent is a person who has completed his fifteenth year of age, but has not completed his eighteenth year. [Factories Act 1948, s. 2(*a*) and (*c*)].

▸ *Meaning under the Young Persons (Harmful Publications) Act 1956, s. 2(c).* 'Young person' means a person under the age of twenty years.

▸ *Meaning under the Merchant Shipping Act 1958, s. 3(59).* 'Young person' means a person under eighteen years of age.

# Zz

**Zamindar.** A person who used to hold land under the Government at a fixed revenue; a landlord.

A "zamindar" is presumed to be the owner of underground rights in the tenancies created by him in the absence of evidence that he ever parted with them. [*Sukh Dev Singh* v *Maharaja Bahadur of Gidhaur* AIR 1951 SC 288: 1951 SCR 534: 1951 SCJ 386].

**Zamindari.** The estate held by a zamindar or landlord.

'Zamindari' means a person who is the owner or co-sharer of *mahal* and as such has an interest in the common land of the *mahal* and the management of the *mahal*, has the right to realise rent from tenants and, in the absence of a contract to the contrary, is liable to pay land revenue to the Government. [*Ram Kishore* v *B. Kavindra* AIR 1955 All 59].

**Zaripeshgi.** *Zaripeshgi* leases have been held to be usufructuary mortgages in ordinary circumstances. [*Guljari Lal* v *Ali Ahsan* AIR 1933 All 929].

**Zero.** A mathematical value intermediate between negative and positive values. [*Random House Dictionary of English Language*].

Less than normal; lowest point or degree. [*Shriniwas* v *Keshri Chand* AIR 1984 Raj 14].

**Zone.** A region or area within limits as may be defined for any particular purpose.

• **Buffer zone** p. 113.

**Zoning legislation.** This is a statutory instrument to control and regulate the use of land and the use, height and area of buildings for the purpose of conserving and promoting the health, safety, morals, conveniences and general welfare of the people of the community.

"Zoning" is the name given in the United States to the regulation of building development and uses of property by division into districts having uniform height, use or bulk requirements.

# Words Grouped under Vital Words